PATRICIA HIGHSMITH

HER DIARIES AND NOTEBOOKS

Also by Patricia Highsmith

Nothing That Meets the Eye: The Uncollected Stories of Patricia Highsmith
Small g: A Summer Idyll
The Selected Stories of Patricia Highsmith
Ripley Under Water
The Black House (stories)
Mermaids on the Golf Course (stories)
Found in the Street
Tales of Natural and Unnatural Catastrophes (stories)
People Who Knock on the Door
The Animal-Lover's Guide to Beastly Murder (stories)
Little Tales of Misogyny (stories)
The Boy Who Followed Ripley
Edith's Diary
Slowly, Slowly in the Wind (stories)
Ripley's Game
A Dog's Ransom
Ripley Under Ground
The Snail-Watcher and Other Stories
The Tremor of Forgery
Those Who Walk Away
Plotting and Writing Suspense Fiction (nonfiction)
A Suspension of Mercy
The Glass Cell
The Two Faces of January
The Cry of the Owl
This Sweet Sickness
A Game for the Living
Miranda the Panda Is on the Veranda (children's literature)
Deep Water
The Talented Mr. Ripley
The Blunderer
The Price of Salt (as Clare Morgan)
Strangers on a Train

PATRICIA HIGHSMITH

HER DIARIES AND NOTEBOOKS

1941–1995

EDITED BY
ANNA VON PLANTA

WITH AN AFTERWORD BY
JOAN SCHENKAR

LIVERIGHT PUBLISHING CORPORATION

A Division of W. W. Norton & Company

Independent Publishers Since 1923

For information about permission to reproduce selections from this book, write to
Permissions, Liveright Publishing Corporation, a division of W. W. Norton & Company, Inc.,
500 Fifth Avenue, New York, NY 10110

For information about special discounts for bulk purchases, please contact
W. W. Norton Special Sales at specialsales@wwnorton.com or 800-233-4830

Manufacturing by Lakeside Book Company

Book design by Marysarah Quinn

Production manager: Julia Druskin

ISBN 978-1-324-09099-1

Liveright Publishing Corporation, 500 Fifth Avenue, New York, N.Y. 10110

www.wwnorton.com

W. W. Norton & Company Ltd., 15 Carlisle Street, London W1D 3BS

1 2 3 4 5 6 7 8 9 0

For

GLORIA KATE KINGSLEY SKATTEBOL

and

DANIEL KEEL

Would I were greedy as now forever,
Not for fortune, nor yet knowledge, and not for love—never,
A muscled horse obedient to ruthless master, art,
Exultantly racing till he break his heart.

—NOTEBOOK 12,
June 20, 1945

Writing, of course, is a substitute for the life
I cannot live, am unable to live.

—NOTEBOOK 19,
May 17, 1950

It takes two mirrors for the correct image
of oneself.

—NOTEBOOK 29,
February 23, 1968

CONTENTS

FOREWORD

✒

HOW THIS BOOK CAME TO BE

The last house Patricia Highsmith lived in outwardly looked like a fortress, forbidding and austere, with just two windows facing the street, the openings tiny as arrowslits. In the rare interviews she gave, her one-word answers were dreaded. She refused to authorize a biography during her lifetime. For many years, Patricia Highsmith's writing was the only way to get to know her. It was all the more surprising when, after her death, a long, neatly arranged row of fifty-six thick journals was discovered tucked in the back of her linen closet: eighteen private diaries and thirty-eight notebooks, providing somewhere around eight thousand pages of personal testimonial.

For the very first time, fans and scholars can refer to Patricia Highsmith's personal records to see how she viewed herself. Since Pat started to express herself through writing from a very early age, the emerging portrait spans almost her entire life.

It seems clear that Patricia Highsmith had long planned to have her notebooks published. The uniformity of the Columbia spiral notebooks she used throughout suggests it, even more so the fact that she kept editing them, making comments, cuts, and date changes whenever rereading. Most importantly, there are written instructions. A slip of paper in Notebook 19 shows that Pat's college friend Gloria Kate Kingsley Skattebol had at first been enlisted to publish a selection. Pasted to the April 2, 1950, entry, it reads: "A note after rereading all my notebooks—rather glancing through all of them, for who could possibly read them?—(and Kingsley, have some taste, have at least the taste I have in 1950 in weeding out what is already written, and recently written)." At other times, the author considered burning the notebooks or leaving them to the Lesbian Herstory Archives in Brooklyn. In the end, Pat appointed Daniel Keel the literary executor of her estate, so it fell to him to decide what the author would have wanted to happen with her journals.

The founder of the Swiss publishing house Diogenes had taken over as Pat's German-language publisher in 1967. As a young man, Keel had seen Hitchcock's adaptation of *Strangers on a Train* and stayed seated in the theater until the author's name rolled in the credits. He was determined to publish her books in hardcover because he considered them literature, rather than just genre fiction. After her non-psychological-thriller *Edith's Diary* hit *Der Spiegel*'s Bestseller List in 1978, Pat appointed Keel her worldwide representative. When her longtime American publisher, Harper & Row, rejected two of her books in 1983, the uncertainty of her publishing situation in the United States finally prompted her to transfer the international rights to her complete works to Diogenes.

I first met Pat in 1984, when Daniel Keel placed the manuscript for *Found in the Street* on my desk and informed me that he had arranged a meeting with the author at a nearby hotel for a few days later—and with that, I was her editor. Pat greeted me coolly, disregarding my extended hand. She then ordered a beer and fell silent. It took me half an hour to get a conversation going about the manuscript, which was set in modern-day New York, but struck me as the New York of the 1950s. By the end of our conversation, she even laughed. Back at the office, I told my boss about the initial awkwardness of our encounter. To my amazement, Keel congratulated me effusively on my success, explaining that it had taken him years to coax more than a yes-or-no answer out of her.

When Keel and Highsmith reviewed her papers together before her death, the diaries and notebooks were expressly listed as part of her literary estate alongside her remaining unpublished novels and uncollected short stories. Keel recognized the collection as a literary treasure that should be presented as a unified whole, a task he passed on to me as Patricia Highsmith's longtime editor and later coeditor of her thirty-volume *Collected Works* (Zurich, Diogenes, 2002–2006).

EDITORIAL NOTE

Condensing an estimated eight thousand pages into *one* volume and doing justice to the material was an immense challenge. First, the handwritten pages had to be transcribed, itself the work of years. Gloria Kate Kingsley Skattebol checked the transcripts against the handwritten, often cryptic originals and added some helpful annotations. Then the sheer amount of material necessitated a culling, to carve out the essence of this "behind-the-scenes" work. As the author herself recognized, it would have been a mistake to reproduce the diaries and notebooks word-for-word, riddled as they are with redundancies, chitchat, indiscretions, and gossip; especially in her twenties, her notes from that period being so much more extensive than in later years, when her journaling had developed its cohesive style. Our selection was based on Pat's own focal points.

The book is structured chronologically, broken into five periods based on where Pat was living at the time, from her beginnings in the United States to various locations around Europe in middle age to her final years in Switzerland.

While earlier notebook entries exist, we chose to begin the book with her first diary entry, written in 1941. From this point onward, Pat essentially maintained a double account of her life: whereas she used the diary to detail her intense, at times painful personal experiences, she used the notebook to process these experiences intellectually and muse on her writing. Pat's notebooks were workbooks, and a playground for her imagination. They contain style exercises, insights into art, writing, and painting, and what Pat liked to call *Keime* (a German term meaning "germs"), ideas and whole passages for potential short stories and novels. Her diaries help us better understand the notebooks; they arrange the notebook entries within what seems to be a truthful time frame and personal context. Diary and notebook entries are interwoven and interlocked, the diary entries dated in long form (month, day, year), the notebook entries in numerical form (with slashes), as was Pat's style. While the two formats can be read independently of each other, when read in tandem they help to gain a holistic understanding—in Pat's own words—of an author who concealed the personal sources of her material for her entire life, and whose novels are more likely to distract us from who she was, than lead us to her.

In contrast to the notebooks, which are written almost entirely in English, Pat composed her diary entries through 1952 in up to five languages. There seem to have been various reasons for this. Of course, a language enthusiast and autodidact like Pat would want to acquire new languages, particularly given her aspiration to travel the world and cultivate her more urbane sensibilities. Pat was largely self-taught in French, German, Spanish, and Italian, and described the diaries as "exercise books in languages I do not know." She was an ambitious student, eager to apply and practice what she was learning in her diaries, enjoying the novel means of expression and perspectives on the world each new language offered her. There's much to suggest that the exercise also served to encrypt some of the more intimate details, protecting them against unwelcome prying eyes.

Her French and German entries are the most prominent—curious, flawed, and touchingly literary. We provide several examples of her original entries before translation at the end of the book. Foreign-language passages in the diaries have been translated into English but tagged with superscript lettering to indicate the original language: G/GG for German, F/FF for French, IT/ITIT for Italian, and SP/SPSP for Spanish. Commonplace foreign phrases are left as is.

In editing this collection, we debated whether to indicate omissions. We ultimately decided against it, to avoid bothering the reader with continual ellipses. The reader must, however, bear in mind that what we have printed in this volume represents a mere fraction of Patricia Highsmith's diary and notebook entries. For instance, we have not included ideas Pat began developing for certain pieces that were ultimately discarded. Pat's own omissions and minor oversights have been corrected, while details needed for comprehension have been added in brackets. More extensive explanations, including information on names mentioned, were added in footnotes where available; in those cases where we knew no more about someone than what Pat herself wrote, we refrained from adding footnotes that could do no more than repeat her information. Especially in the 1940s, Pat encounters a multitude of people; those with more of a relevance will soon become familiar to the reader, while others might be mentioned a few times only.

We have reduced all private individuals mentioned in the text to their first names, unless they were already fully named and described in extenso by Highsmith's biographers. And this regardless of the fact that almost all of them, being of Highsmith's age or older, are now deceased. Some important private individuals received pseudonyms by the biographers, such as Pat's longtime English lover in the early 1960s called X by Andrew Wilson and Caroline Besterman by Joan Schenkar; or Camilla Butterfield, a pseudonym used by Schenkar for another 1960s friend. We kept the Schenkar pseudonyms even though both women are deceased. Their families were equally anonymized; in Caroline Besterman's case, her husband is just referred to as "her husband," her son as "her son." We also cut information or refrained from adding it in a footnote when we feared that this might help identify them. Conversely, recognizable public figures Pat introduces, but calls by their initials, are referred to by their full names in brackets, as necessary.

As these are Patricia Highsmith's private diaries and notebooks, her views on people and facts are of course personal and tinted by her personal biases and the biases of the times in which she wrote them. Pat was inconsistent and rough around the edges, and some of her disparaging remarks readers will find offensive, especially when, as is frequently the case, they are addressed toward such perennially marginalized groups as Black Americans and Jews. In the earlier entries, the issue is often one of language, when Pat uses expressions that were common at the time but have since come to be considered derogatory and offensive. The author herself was aware of this, as proven by her request to change the word "negro" to "black" for the 1990 new edition of *Carol*.

Especially in old age, however, it is increasingly not just Pat's language but her views themselves that are offensive, rancorous, and misanthropic. We aim to represent them faithfully. Only in a handful of more extreme instances did we feel it our editorial duty to deny Pat a stage for them, in the same way we did while she was still alive. The sources of her resentment are difficult to pinpoint, notably in the case of her growing anti-Semitism, which grows even more of a mystery embedded as it is in a volume in which we learn about the importance for the author of the many Jews she counts among her close friends, lovers, and favorite artists.

Like most diarists, Pat tended to write more during difficult periods, resulting in a skewed depiction of her life. Other sources confirm that Pat's life was not, in fact, as dark as it might at times appear in these pages. Additionally, as in any self-portrait, the person we encounter in the diaries and notebooks is of course not necessarily the "real" Pat, but instead the person she considered—or wanted—herself to be. The act of remembrance is also one of interpretation, with regard to herself and others. Many people are familiar with the somber, caustic version of Pat, and this volume will be their first encounter with the author as a cheerful young woman with an optimistic, ambitious eye on her future.

The compilation presented here is not meant to be read as an autobiography. Instead, our intention in sharing these entries is to let readers discover, in the author's own words, how Patricia Highsmith became Patricia Highsmith.

Anna von Planta

in close collaboration with Kati Hertzsch,
Marion Hertle, Marie Hesse, and Friederike Kohl

ZURICH, 2021

1921–1940

THE EARLY YEARS

B ORN AN ONLY CHILD in Fort Worth, Texas, in 1921, Mary Patricia
Plangman (known as Pat) grew up as something of a loner. Her parents,
Mary Coates and Jay Bernard Plangman, had divorced before she was born,
and since her mother, an illustrator, was working, Pat spent the first years of
her life in the care of her loving but strictly Calvinist grandmother, who ran
a boardinghouse. In 1924, Mary Coates married photographer and graphic
artist Stanley Highsmith, an intruder in Pat's eyes.

At age three Pat could read, and by age nine her favorite authors included
Dickens, Dostoyevsky, and Conan Doyle. She pored over the illustrated anat-
omy reference her mother used for work and Karl Menninger's *The Human
Mind*, a compendium of popular scientific studies of abnormal human
behavior: "I can't think of anything more apt to set the imagination stirring,
drafting, creating, than the idea—the fact—that anyone you walk past on
the pavement may be a sadist, a compulsive thief, or even a murderer."*

The family of three moved to New York in 1927, but financial, emotional, and marital crises forced Pat to travel back and forth between her
new home and her grandmother's boardinghouse. At one point, she lived
with her grandmother for fifteen months; it was "the saddest year of my
life."† Pat felt abandoned by her mother, something she would never forgive,
especially considering Mary had promised her daughter she would divorce
Stanley. The month Pat spent at a girls' summer camp near West Point, New
York, in 1933 didn't fix things, either. Pat sent daily letters home from camp,
and two years later this correspondence appeared as an article in *Woman's
World* magazine—Pat's first publication, for which she received twenty-five
dollars. This was also the year she met her biological father for the first time;

* Patricia Highsmith in a letter to Karl Menninger on April 8, 1989.
† Patricia Highsmith in a letter to Nini Wells on March 9, 1972.

a graphic artist of German descent, he was one of the reasons she decided to learn German.

Upon returning to New York from Texas, Pat was enrolled at Julia Richman High School, a girls' school with eight thousand students, most of whom were Catholic or Jewish. During this time, new literary preferences began to crystallize: Edgar Allan Poe (with whom she shared a birthday) and Joseph Conrad. With regard to her own writing, Pat felt drawn to the themes of guilt, sin, and transgression. By the time Pat was just fifteen, she was filling thick composition books with literary sketches as well as observations of the people around her. She also penned her first short stories, some of which appeared in her school's literary magazine *Bluebird*. Pat was an intelligent, ambitious, and imaginative teenager, but, saddled with shame because of her secret same-sex inclinations, she came across to others as serious and withdrawn. Patterns of behavior emerged that would prove characteristic of her later romantic life; for instance, she experimented with her first (platonic) love triangle with two other women, including Judy Tuvim, who later rose to fame as the Tony- and Academy Award–winning actress and comedian Judy Holliday.

She also proved herself an incredibly diligent student, and in 1938 was accepted to Barnard College. As an undergraduate, she studied zoology, English, composition, Latin, ancient Greek, German, and logic. During her first semester, Pat began to earnestly dedicate herself to journaling. She started her first notebook, which she called a *"cahier,"* with the words: "A lazy phantom-white figure of a girl dancing to a Tchaikovsky waltz."

Those early entries are a colorful mishmash of observations, comments on the books she was reading, thoughts on what she was learning in college, and ideas about economy in writing. At times she used the notebooks to record homework assignments or write short stories for her English professor Ethel Sturtevant, whom she revered, or try her hand at limericks and even sonnets at various stages of her first few crushes. Almost half of the entries are undated, and we have chosen to omit them in this volume, as they provide readers with little more than passing insight into the life of the young Patricia Highsmith.

1941–1950

EARLY LIFE IN NEW YORK, AND DIFFERENT WAYS OF WRITING

1941

THIS COLLECTION OPENS in 1941, when Patricia Highsmith introduces the first of her diaries—Diary 1a—to be kept in tandem with her notebooks. On April 14, 1941, she writes, "*Je suis fait[e] de deux appétits: l'amour et la pensée* [My appetite is twofold: I hunger for love and for thought]." How much experience is needed, she wonders, in order to write about it? To what extent does one side of this equation feed off the other? The boundaries between Pat's diaries and notebooks are correspondingly porous, and each makes frequent reference to the other. Overall, she fills a total of 450 pages that year, writing in English, French, and German. Pat typically records the day's events late at night or in the early hours of the next morning, before going to bed.

Her workload at Barnard College is demanding, with assignments piling up on top of her own ambitious reading list. She becomes active in the Young Communist League and the American Student Union; when the endless meetings become burdensome to her quicksilver temperament, Pat's political engagement wanes. Much more important to her is her appointment as editor-in-chief of the student literary journal *Barnard Quarterly*, to which she contributes some of her own short stories, including "The Legend of the Convent of St. Fotheringay," a short story that reads like a personal manifesto on religion, gender, and her vocation as a writer. It is about an orphan boy discovered by nuns, who disguise and raise him as a girl. The boy is convinced he's a genius, and at age thirteen blows up the convent in order to live as a man, without religion, and pursue what he believes is his destined path to greatness.

Between her various commitments and her writing, it is not surprising that her grades begin to suffer. By far the primary culprit behind her poor performance, however, is Pat's social life. The Highsmiths live in a one-bedroom apartment—with Pat sleeping on a pull-out couch in the living room— at 48 Grove Street, in the heart of Greenwich Village, and after her school day ends, Pat goes out exploring. Long known as a bohemian hub, the Village is thriving with the arrival of such European émigrés as Claude

Lévi-Strauss, Erich Fromm, and Hannah Arendt. (Illustrious as many of them are, U.S. society is not welcoming its new citizens with open arms. There are strict quotas, and anti-Semitism is widespread, upper-class society being no exception.) It also boasts a vibrant nightlife—and a relatively open gay and lesbian presence, bars and clubs where women in trousers can come and go as they please, free to flaunt their affections. Of course, homosexual love is legally still a crime, and police harassment of gays and raids on the—often Mafia-"protected"—bars are common. But Pat, impressively unfazed for a twenty-year-old, spends whole nights partying up and down MacDougal Street.

There she falls in with an exciting crowd: a tightly knit, closed-off circle of successful, predominantly lesbian artists and journalists.* Having felt guilty and singled out because of her sexual orientation for most of her teenage years, here she is for the first time provided with positive role models, the safe space and encouragement to grow into the person she longs to be. Through Mary Sullivan, who runs the bookshop at the Waldorf Astoria, the twenty-year-old college student gets to hang out with the likes of photographer Berenice Abbott or painter Buffie Johnson, who in turn introduces her to British journalist Rosalind Constable (right-hand woman to magazine magnate Henry Luce, founder of *Time* and *Life* magazines), then lover of artist and art dealer Betty Parsons. Pat is at least ten years younger than her new friends, and the strong influence they supposedly have on her becomes a constant source of conflict between her and her mother, who disapproves strongly of Pat's drinking and rarely going to bed at a sensible hour. Her parents decry her new lifestyle as too extreme and even threaten to stop paying her college tuition if she continues.

"The painfullest feeling is that of your own feebleness; ever as the English Milton says, to be weak is the true misery. And yet of your strength there is and can be no clear feeling, save by what you have prospered in, by what you have done. Between vague wavering capability and indubitable performance, what a difference!"[†]

And here is my diary, containing the body—

---

* For more about this network, see Joan Schenkar's afterword in this book.
† Quote from Thomas Carlyle, *Sartor Resartus* (1835).

JANUARY 6, 1941

[F]First day of school. + Snyder:[*] a play about a woman in which I was a man. Helen[†] was my girlfriend. It was very good. +[‡] Letter from Roger [F.][§] this morning. He says he loves me! A bit young, right?? + Meeting at Elwyn's[¶] tonight. Only 5 girls were present. We will make something of it! + Am now financial secretary of the ASU. I hope to God no one will find out! Mother is very hostile. Particularly because I am not feminine enough.[FF]

1/6/41

One brazen, conceited, decadent, despicable, retrogressive thought for today: I lost myself in a groundless dream, of life in suspension, and third dimension, of my friends and their types—of persons and faces, nameless, only filling spaces—and each one was quite to be expected, where he was—and the picture—which we call "life" or "experience"—was complete—and I saw myself—filling in exactly where I was expected—with no one looking or acting precisely like me. And I liked myself best of all this little group (which was by no means all the world) and I thought how something would be direfully wanting if I were not there.

JANUARY 7, 1941

[F]I read [Stalin's] *Foundations of Leninism*. Very important, including the tactics.[FF]

JANUARY 9, 1941

[F]Read *Taming of the Shrew* last night. Mrs. Bailey[**] very late and very charming. I want to do each lesson in the grammar book so that I can ace the exam. + The "Legend of St. Fotheringay" will be published in the next issue [of *Barnard Quarterly*]. Georgia S.[††] said today that it's the best we've had in years! Sturtevant[‡‡] didn't like my "Movie Date"[§§] story from last year, and she'll be editing the *Quarterly* review this

---

* Another Barnard girl who attended drama class with Pat.
† One of Pat's closest friends at Barnard.
‡ Throughout her first diary, Pat regularly uses the "+" sign as a separator between different topics within one entry, a practice that peters out in her second diary in 1942.
§ One of Pat's admirers.
¶ A fellow communist. Pat was active both in the Young Communist League (YCL) and the American Student Union (ASU).
** Helen Bailey, lecturer in French at Barnard College.
†† Fellow student, also on the *Quarterly* staff.
‡‡ Ethel Sturtevant, assistant professor of English at Barnard and Pat's creative writing instructor.
§§ "Movie Date" was published in the Winter 1940 issue of the *Barnard Quarterly*.

month! + With Arthur* tonight. We will have a Mannerheim Line.†
Mother doesn't even want to set eyes on him! Arthur told me that Keller
read my "House on Morton St."‡ and didn't find it convincing. It's what
I was afraid of. That Keller would know that a college girl had written
it. Isn't it terrible.FF

JANUARY 10, 1941

FViolet here at 9:30. Mother asked her what she thought of Communism—
Violet hesitated: "All the young people are interested in Communism—
it's good—it gives them something to do." (!) Like throw bombs! Right?
+ Too funny! Volley Ball practice. I would like to write a story like the
"Legend" about this. The people are marvelous! + Helped Fanny B. with
logic. She's not very bothered about her work. She wants to get married.
"Ted," who will be a professor. Her mother has no money, and Fanny
won't go to school next year. But she's perfectly happy!FF

JANUARY 11, 1941

FI bought tickets for Lenin's memorial celebration at Madison Square
Garden§ Monday night. Two for Arthur and myself. The Workers' Book-
shop¶ was fun yesterday. Mother Bloor** was there, signing her book
for the regulars. There was a line for Lenin tickets, and everyone was
smiling, as if they were in a propaganda photo. + Bailey at 9. She said
that she liked my story and laughed about Sturtevant's critique. Perhaps
I won't like this story in a year—but right now, I'm not ashamed of it.
+ Va. [Virginia]†† called me at 7:30. I was very happy. Met her at Rocco's‡‡ at 9 with Jack, a gay boy, and Curtis and Jean, two gay girls. Went
to Jumble Shop,§§ etc. Beers and martinis, and now I'm drunk. But Va.

---

* Arthur R., fellow communist and Pat's admirer.
† The "Mannerheim Line" was a defensive fortification line meant to impede the advance of the Red
Army at the start of the Soviet-Finnish war in 1939.
‡ An unpublished story of Pat's.
§ The seventeenth annual Lenin Memorial Meeting was held at Madison Square Garden on January
13, 1941. Earl Russell Browder, then general secretary of the Communist Party USA (CPUSA), gave a
speech, "The Way Out of the Imperialist War."
¶ The Workers' Bookshop of the Communist Party USA on Thirteenth Street near University Place.
** Ella Reeve Bloor (1862–1951), American socialist leader, writer, and trade union organizer.
†† An on-and-off crush Pat has known since high school, usually refered to as Va.
‡‡ Italian restaurant at 181 Thompson Street in Greenwich Village.
§§ The Jumble Shop, a place where women felt comfortable going with other women, was one of Pat's
favorite hangouts. It was originally opened by Frances Russell and Winifred Tucker on Eighth Street
as an antiques shop in 1922, then was turned into a restaurant and expanded to 176 MacDougal Street.
The proprietors hung paintings of their famous and obscure clientele on the walls; some of the patrons
were Ford Madox Ford, Thomas Wolfe, Martha Graham, Arshile Gorky, Willem de Kooning, and
Lee Krasner.

kissed me!! I kissed her two—three—four—five times in the women's restroom at Jumble—and even on the sidewalk!! The sidewalk! Jack is very sweet, and Va. would like to sleep with him—but first she would like to take a trip with me some weekend. She loves me. She will always love me. She told me so, and her actions confirm it.[FF]

JANUARY 12, 1941

[F]Big surprise! Mother and S. [Stanley] persuaded John and Grace[*] to come to the Lenin memorial tomorrow evening! First Stanley didn't even want mother to go, because someone might see her there! Then, when they said they would go, John became curious! + I read *Work of the Seventh Congress*[†] which helped me a lot. Also *Much Ado About Nothing* which is very good. Started [James Joyce's] *Finnegans Wake*.[FF]

JANUARY 13, 1941

[F]Oh—the kisses last night—they were sweet, they were heavenly! Oh, the fine point of seldom pleasure.[‡] Shakespeare, you were right! + A discussion with Latham.[§] She doesn't like my solution to the Spanish situation (in my play): "You had a perfect dramatic situation—and you served up this communist tripe!" (And I only wrote that the revolutionaries conquered the aristocrats!) She advised me to work ("Step on the gas—hard!") and tasked me to write another play. On top of all my work! + Browder very brilliant and convincing tonight. We sang the Internationale.[FF]

JANUARY 14, 1941

[F]Oh—James Joyce is dead. I heard the news yesterday morning. The *Herald Tribune* ran a wonderful obituary! Browder received a 20-minute ovation. 20,000 present etc. David Elwyn says it's because they hate Roosevelt! + Worked on the play. Finished the second draft of the first act. B.B.[¶] likes my play and the stories too, and her opinion's worth more than that of the whole school! + Ludwig Bemelmans[**] has a new book out: *A Donkey Inside*. Brilliant, like all his books. I wonder whether he'll read my story in *Quarterly*.[FF]

---

[*] Patricia Highsmith's uncle and aunt. John Coates was one of Mary Highsmith's brothers; Grace was his wife.
[†] The Seventh Comintern was held in Moscow in 1935.
[‡] Quote from Shakespeare's Sonnet 52.
[§] Professor Minor White Latham, associate professor of English.
[¶] Babs B., high school friend of Pat's and fellow communist.
[**] Ludwig Bemelmans, Austrian-born American writer and illustrator of children's books.

JANUARY 15, 1941

^FI wanted to begin *Anna Karenina*, but a new book, *The Soviet Power* [by Hewlett Johnson], is sitting on my table, nice and neat: how can one read *Anna Karenina* in times like these?!—Oh I'm dreaming! I'd like to travel to Russia with [Babs] B. These days will never come again. I'm exactly like a person in 1917 in America. What should one have read? Nothing except for stuff about the war. Everything else is an escape.^{FF}

JANUARY 16, 1941

^FI am happy—so happy! For many reasons! First of all, Sturtevant liked my story ("Alena").[*] And I finished my play tonight. Mother likes it and says it's less cold than the other plays and stories I've written. + Letter from Jeannot,[†] November 24. He had just received my letter from September 17! He was listening to Artie Shaw[‡] in Boston during the bombing!

+ My grandmother sent me two dollars for my birthday.^{FF}

JANUARY 17, 1941

^FThere will be a party Saturday night when I was supposed to see Ernst![§] Poor Ernst! + [Marijann] K.[¶] seems to like me a lot. As well as the others in her class—to say the least. If only she liked me more! My play is good. I won't be embarrassed to show it to anyone: B. or Judy^{**} or Latham! + The book [*The Soviet Power*] by the Dean of Canterbury. Mostly a compilation of Russian growth statistics. Will be very influential— important. I would like grandmother to see the light before her death. + With John and Grace and parents at the Vanguard^{††} at 10. Judy was there but I didn't bring her to our table, for which mother chastised me severely. I like Judy. (Eddy^{‡‡} is a communist, and also a member of the police!)^{FF}

---

* This story has been lost.

† Jean "Jeannot" David, young French cartoon artist from Marseille and Mary Highsmith's pen pal.

‡ Artie Shaw (1910–2004), American jazz clarinetist and prominent swing band leader in the late 1930s.

§ Ernst Hauser (later Ernest O. Hauser), photojournalist and postwar correspondent for the *Saturday Evening Post*. Author of *Shanghai: City for Sale* and *Italy: A Cultural Guide*. Pat first met him on a boat to Texas after she graduated from high school.

¶ Marijann K. is a fellow student.

** Judy Tuvim, Pat's classmate at Julia Richman High School. She will go on to become the celebrated movie star Judy Holliday.

†† The Village Vanguard is a jazz club at 178 Seventh Avenue South in Greenwich Village. Beyond jazz performances by the likes of Thelonious Monk, Dizzy Gillespie, Miles Davis, and Art Blakey, the venue hosted poetry readings, stand-up routines, and concerts.

‡‡ From Pat's notes, Eddy seems to have been a lover of Judy's.

JANUARY 18, 1941

[F]Mother and I went shopping. Finally a dress for me—very pretty—as well as a jacket and a gray skirt. + I made no progress on my work at all. This morning, John sent me a review of an anticommunist book. By a deserter, like all the deserters the newspapers like to feature. + Hilda's tonight. The regulars were there—but also Mary H. and Ruth. She is charming! A real person. Today was important because I met her. Mary H. told Ruth that I was the most intelligent person of the whole lot and I received many invitations from proper and polite people. I would like to tell mother about it, but I will only tell her about Mary H., and perhaps not everything.[FF]

JANUARY 19, 1941

[F]I'm twenty years old! It's terrific! Presents after breakfast. Just as many as Christmas. A polaroid lamp. And a triangular cushion for studying. + I was supposed to eat with Ernst tonight, but I had to study. Cocktails at the Fifth Ave H.[*] at 5 with John and Grace. Then champagne for Mother and myself. Very good.[FF]

JANUARY 20, 1941

[F]David Jeannot sent me a radiogram yesterday. Happy Birthday![FF] + [G]It occurred to me yesterday that although England doesn't need more men now, if they start fighting in France, then they'll call for the U.S. Army.[GG] [F]Am exhausted by Shakespeare! There's so much I don't know! + Days without any creative work are lost days. An artist, a real artist, would work.[FF]

JANUARY 21, 1941

[F]Sweet are the moments in which I am not thinking of Shakespeare! I am thinking of Mary H., or of evenings in the wonderful future, or of the years ahead of me, of the people I will meet. + [William Saroyan's] *My Name Is Aram* and [Willa Cather's] *Sapphira [and] the Slave Girl*—articles—Shakespeare all day. Now I never want to read Shakespeare again![FF]

JANUARY 23, 1941

[F]A letter from R.R.[†] Haven't read it yet. He bores me. + I thought of the entire plot for an important, but simple short story that I would like to write soon. It's in my body like an unborn child. + Oh my God! The

---

* The Fifth Avenue Hotel, located at 24 Fifth Avenue on the corner of Ninth Street.
† Roger R., a longtime admirer of Pat's.

most important! I have the highest average in my Greek class! Hirst[*]
announced it herself! It's a shame that I'm not writing in my journal
enough. During the summer, I wrote in it every day. When one is at one's
leisure, thoughts flow like beautiful water.[FF]

JANUARY 25, 1941

[F]Catastrophe! Latham gave me a C+! I don't understand. I would honestly have preferred an F to a C+! At least that's a distinction. It's
terrible—worse than standing entirely naked in front of the school! Bad
afternoon because of this grade. Virginia called me. Wanted to spend the
evening with me and told me she loved me. We're going skiing next week.
+ With Peter[†] at Jumble at 7. Three drinks for me. (Three too many.)
Peter is very intelligent. Knows everything about people quickly. And
knows her Shakespeare, dance, etc. But produces nothing. She's four
years older than me. I think I will be as mature as her in four years' time.
More mature, I hope.[FF]

JANUARY 27, 1941

[F]This was the first day I played piano with a certain amount of confidence. It was encouraging. + I wonder whether I would have done better if I hadn't read so much contemporary literature, if I'd read plays for
Latham instead? Two reasons Latham gave me a C: 1. Didn't like a play
that portrayed the South unfavorably. 2. Thinks I'm a communist. 3.
Because I came with high recommendations. Marijann K.—what will
she say?! Oh my God![FF]

JANUARY 29, 1941

[F]French exam this morning. It was difficult and I think I got all the questions I guessed wrong. It's awful! I'm hoping for a B now. I spoke to
Latham, who was very friendly. Told me that my play was very good and
that it will take me a while, that it's precisely because I have written so
many stories that I'm having trouble with the theater. Etc. But I'll keep
going. + With Ernst tonight. Champagne and dinner at the Jumble Shop.
+ Called up M. H. (Ruth). She told me that Mary was observing us last
Saturday, and that she would like to paint us together. We'd make a good
contrast, she thinks. I'd be honored.[FF]

---

[*] Professor Gertrude Hirst, who taught classics at Barnard from 1903 to 1941.
[†] Another girl from her circle of Barnard friends, which also included Helen, Babs P., and Deborah or
Debbie B.

JANUARY 30, 1941

FVery sick. It's the exams, no doubt. I worked very hard, and today is my first day off. Every bone hurts. + My illness—today and yesterday—gave me a bit of that unreal sensation that Proust was so familiar with. I wrote one or two paragraphs just as I liked. It's different—fluid, without any ambition, just for itself. One is happy when one looks at the time and two hours have gone by, as if there is an established time at which one will be in good health again. Did Proust say that already? Probably. But that's how I felt today.FF

1/30/41

From first acquaintance I had never liked my stepfather. I was about four when I met him, and I had already been reading for more than a year. I remember it was a book of fairy tales I had that day. "What's that word?" said my stepfather indicating with a long, crooked, hairy forefinger the most magical phrase I knew.

"Open See-same!" I cried.

"Sess-a-mi!" replied my stepfather with didactic peremptoriness.

"Sess-a-mi," I echoed weakly.

My stepfather smiled indulgently down upon me, his red heavy lips tight together and spread wide below his black moustache. And I knew he was right, and I hated him because he was right like grown-up people always were, always, right, and because he had forever destroyed my enchanting "Open See-same," and because now the new phrase would have no meaning to me, had destroyed my picture, had become strange, unfriendly and unknown.

JANUARY 31, 1941

FMuch better but still sick. I read [George Bernard Shaw's] *Apple Cart*, [Paul Vincent Carroll's] *Shadow and Substance*, and a theater book. I'm diving into theater! I will be good, good, good!!! I will be feared! + I bought *Italian Concerto* with Wanda Landowska.* Mother is waiting to get it. She's somewhat annoyed. No surprises why. She told me that S. sometimes says the most horrible things in an evening. Most of it is just moods, but so strange that she wonders if he isn't an entirely different species to us.FF

---

* A recording of J. S. Bach's *Italian Concerto* by famous Polish harpsichordist and pianist Wanda Landowska (1879–1959).

FEBRUARY 1, 1941

ᶠBought white socks (for men!), which are long enough—at last. Well, below my knees I am now dressed like a man. (It doesn't bother me.) + Grandfather is sick: a kidney disease. They have to get emptied with a tube, sometimes he can't do it by himself. It's difficult.ᶠᶠ

FEBRUARY 2, 1941

ᶠ[Mary] H. at 11. They were still in bed and quickly got up when I rang the doorbell. Mary (I wish she was called something other than "Mary!") is charming to watch. She made a good beginning. In charcoal. Large canvas. We are life size, I with my hands in front of my body, Ruthie reading MSS. [manuscripts] to the left. We are seated. Mary is very intense when she works. She forgets about everything else. We will sit again Saturday or Sunday. Unfortunately, I'm in a jacket and shirt, and my posture is very masculine. What will mother say when she sees it? Something, I'm sure of it!ᶠᶠ

FEBRUARY 3, 1941

ᶠI got an A in French. And there were only two A's in the class. I'm very happy about the beginning of this new semester. Still full of hope for my writing. I have lots of ideas! At 20, I feel a bit guilty. So much time has gone by, and I've done so little.ᶠᶠ

FEBRUARY 5, 1941

ᶠSturtevant for French. Like the picture of a woman in a cookbook. Oh—Mrs. Bailey—! how inspiring she was! But this woman! She's just like my grandmother! *Quarterly* will be a lot of work. Rita R.* is in the infirmary. Georgia S. and I went to see her at 5. I brought her flowers. I like Georgia S. Would like her to invite me over. (She lives alone.) She told me that she writes homosexual stories only to get As from Sturtevant! I read [Eugene O'Neill's] *Emperor Jones*.ᶠᶠ

FEBRUARY 6, 1941

ᶠOh joy of joys! I can move to Mrs. Bailey's class! Miriam G. is in it, but at least we both got A's. I couldn't have sat in the same room as her if I'd gotten less than her! + I finished *Pointed Roofs* by [Dorothy Miller] Richardson. These books can only have been written by women. They

---

* Rita R. was also on the editorial board of the *Barnard Quarterly*.

bore me. They are very "cheery," active, like women when they visit one another. + [Katherine] Mansfield and [Virginia] Woolf are the same.[FF]

FEBRUARY 7, 1941

[F]What a surprise! Brewster gave me a B—in the exam! Marijann K. got a C and bought sodas at Tilson's for all her friends! Logic grades still in the pits. + I saw Helen walking in the rain. "Would you like to play in a love scene with me?" "I'd love to!"—but I wanted to say *for* me. I have often thought of H.M. recently. I wonder if I'm falling in love with her. It could be worse! She's a ravishing woman. I began [Pat Sloan's] *Russia without Illusions* and a biography of Samuel Butler. He was a homosexual, Ruth L. told me.[FF]

FEBRUARY 12, 1941

[F]Bailey published a letter in *Barnard Bulletin* which demands that girls who go to political conventions as delegates without official permission be called "observers." Doris B. probably reported us to the authorities! + I sent "The Heroine"[*] to *Diogenes*,[†] like Ruth suggested.[FF]

2/12/41

When I start buying clothes with generous hems; when I can tell at a glance the defects of a (potential? no) apartment; when I stop eating something I like when I think I've eaten all I should; when I don't fall in love with someone because I don't think they're quite good enough; when I start going to bed at an hour when I can do my best work the next day; when I start saying the anti-liberals have a bit of a side too; when I can think of you without desire, without hope and without longing—then I shall know I am getting old. That I am old.

FEBRUARY 13, 1941

[F]I brought *Quarterly* to the printer's at 4. Marie T. helped me a little. She draws very badly—honestly! I could do better! Perhaps I will draw from now on. + Time is moving too fast for me. There are stories, my sculpture, my friends, my books, my dates, my thoughts, projects—projects! It would be no better if I were a Christian Scientist![‡] I'm sure of it. Otherwise I would be.[FF]

---

[*] "The Heroine" was published by *Harper's Bazaar* in 1945 and included in *O. Henry Prize Stories 1946*.
[†] American literary magazine.
[‡] Christian Science is a set of beliefs originating with founder Mary Baker Eddy (1821–1910), its most popular idea being that praying can cure diseases. Pat's mother was an adherent.

FEBRUARY 14, 1941

^FCoryl's at 8 for League meeting. There was an extraordinary girl: Marcella, whom Babs B. told me about. She is marvelously beautiful when she speaks. I could fall in love with her just by looking at her! + I bought a small bottle of bath foam for mother's valentine.^{FF}

FEBRUARY 15, 1941

^FMary has only painted my hand. But R.'s head was finished on Wednesday, very meager—the whole painting is meager—too much blue in the figures now.^{FF}

FEBRUARY 17, 1941

^FI should be more creative, more original at this age. I tremble to think that I am 20 years old. Nothing! Except for confused emotions. I'm not even in love! I have to finish the ideas I've already had. Then the others will come like a rushing river.^{FF}

2/17/41

I am no longer satisfied with mere "plot" and excitement stories either as I used to be. I've become more thoughtful about what I write, and the result is I'm writing less. Tending more towards the longer thing—the novel—too. I find it hard to see real "worth" in even the best short stories now. Don't know what I'm coming to.

FEBRUARY 19, 1941

^FThings are improving. + Madeleine Bemelmans* spoke to me in class and seemed very friendly. Told me that Ludwig reads his books in bed, laughing loudly! She brought me home (by car). Madeleine told me she thinks her marriage was not the best idea—at least for her. But I think she's told this to a lot of people at school. She talks too much, really. Perhaps she'll invite me to have a drink at their place sometime.^{FF}

FEBRUARY 20, 1941

^FWent to school this evening to help Rita R. with *Quarterly*. Rita R. and I are both brimming with confidence. Rita R. told me that everyone thought I was independent and sure of myself when I was a freshman. It's funny to hear because I wasn't in the slightest. Then I completely changed, she said. Also that I'm the only person who can be editor-in-

---

* Madeleine Freund, Barnard '41 student. Married to Ludwig Bemelmans.

chief next year. + I read a bit of Thomas Wolfe* this morning. It changed my whole day.FF

FEBRUARY 21, 1941

FI saw Mrs. B. for a moment, without speaking to her, from a distance— I could easily fall in love with her, I think. (N.B. Mother said yesterday that Bernard P. [Plangman] once said that he had no need for a woman. I wonder if I'm like that? Time will tell.)FF

FEBRUARY 22, 1941

FMary and Ruth came by to drink daiquiris. Mary looked at the whole apartment. Mother observed her carefully, but she told me that she would never have known she was gay. Mother liked Mary and Ruth. We drank a lot, played records, danced. Ruth is the better dancer. But at dinner, she said, out of the blue: "You don't like me, do you, Pat?" I have the unfortunate habit of letting people know too easily—must eliminate it.FF

2/22/41

I want to set down my choicest item in worldly revelations: The thrill, the unspeakably blissful sensation of being loved. To love unrequited is a privilege. To dream and to hope a joy that heaven could hardly match— but then—to know oneself loved, to hear it from another's lips—this is heaven indeed. (Or if it's not heaven, you say, go take your old heaven and be damned!)

FEBRUARY 24, 1941

FI canceled my date with Ernst. Went to Judy's at 9. Va. called me up beforehand and told me she was a bit sick—it was disappointing. I wanted to see her. Helen, Paula, Ruth, Mary and Ruth, Eddy, Saul B. Everyone a bit drunk. Judy was very attractive. Mary talks too much. We know it. And she's a bit of an old goose. But we love her anyway. + I desire Va. tremendously—there is no one as beautiful as she! I wrote her a short letter. We need to get along better.FF

2/24/41

What each of us mainly wants is flattery, appreciation—or at the very least—quick acceptance. But for whatever else we seek. We should listen

---

* Thomas Clayton Wolfe (1900–1938), American novelist considered one of the greatest voices of his generation. Pat will keep rereading him frequently over the years.

to our own counsel. All we can depend on—all the wonder and value and beauty and love and faith and genius—pleasure and sorrow, hope, passion, understanding—all these are within us, in our own hearts, and minds. And nowhere else.

2/24/41

We must think of ourselves as a fertile land on which to draw. And if we do not, we grow rotten, like an unmilked cow. And if we leave something unexploited it dies within us wasted. But to tax one's powers always at their maximum potentiality—this is the only way to live at all, in the proper sense of the word.

FEBRUARY 25, 1941

[F]Helen received a photograph of Jo Carstairs[*] from Enid F. How these girls beat about the bush! They are both as ripe as apples on a tree ready to be plucked—but not by me! + I spoke to Nina D.[†] about lowering my involvement. I have to do it. Even two nights a week are a big part of my life. + S. Butler's notebooks are charming. And quite stupid, just like mine sometimes.[FF]

2/26/41

The other night at J.'s, when I was very lonely and dull myself too, I was standing by the piano when P. & J. were playing. P. was doping out the base and she turned to me and said, "Is that right?—Is that right, Pat?" It was such a wonderful thing to hear her say my name. To have heard anyone say it at such a time. I cannot express in such short space all that this small thing held in warmth and Menschlichkeit[‡] for me.

FEBRUARY 27, 1941

[F]I heard Elmer Rice[§] speak at the theater. He criticized American theater mercilessly, as well as our spirit. He spoke as if he were at a Communist assembly! It was marvelous! + With Va. tonight. We saw *Philadelphia Story*.[¶] The movies don't amuse me anymore. After that, beers at our favorite café. Now she's going to Caravan[**] on MacDougal St. where

---

* Marion Barbara ("Joe") Carstairs (1900–1993), a wealthy and openly lesbian British heiress and powerboat racer.
† Nina D. is one of the YCL girls.
‡ Humaneness.
§ Elmer Rice (1892–1967), Pulitzer Prize–winning American playwright.
¶ A 1939 play by Philip Barry.
** Bar and nightclub in Greenwich Village.

the best gays go. She's looking for a woman older than me. But she loves me more than any person she meets. I know it, and she told me: we'll go somewhere by accident and discover each other again. Leave it to me!FF

FEBRUARY 28, 1941

FI sold a *Soviet Power* to Frances B. I can only bring them to school when I'm certain someone will buy them.FF

2/28/41

It's important to keep the serious side underlying all our course of life: but it is equally important to temper this with the lighter side. Without it we have sterility and a lack of imagination and progress. On the other hand, completely serious people are so ludicrous that I wonder is not this attitude, in the last analysis, the lightest side. And accordingly, the lightest-minded people—who have a good fundamental intelligence—are the most serious, philosophic and thoughtful. It takes observation and judgment and independence to laugh at things which should be laughed at. However, I shall always keep the heavier side in the more influential position, because basically that is how I am. I do not have to think about it, and it would do me no good if I did. This seems to me important and rather well-observed now. Shall see later. I wonder if ever I shall edit and file all these notes, as Samuel Butler did? And years hence, when I do, refer back to these adolescent contributions.

MARCH 1, 1941

FGood day! A good day! I spent the morning writing and finished the Morton St. story. It's completely different now. They like it at school. + I often think of Madeleine. I wonder whether I can invite her to go riding on Thursday. Dude Ranch on 98 St.

Began *Wolf Solent* by [John Cowper] Powys. The book belongs to Mary H. They have lots of books I'd like to borrow. + Oh, how I would like to go to the country with Madeleine [Bemelmans]! If she doesn't take me home on Monday, I'll be miserable! + Lots of projects in my head!FF

MARCH 2, 1941

FThis was my last day. My part of the painting is done. I don't like the skirt. Ruth came out of the bathroom in her négligée—only her panties!— and wanted to make cocktails, just like that. She got upset at Mary when she suggested putting some clothes on! Quite an interesting discussion alone with Ruth. If one should stay with someone one loves, if he (or she) has had, or is having, an affair with someone else. I would leave. Ruth would stay. A situation like this would destroy my love, I have no doubt. + I have lots of fun ideas—fragmentary ideas, but good ones. I am happy with this. + My play will be performed tomorrow. Oh, my poor heart! I'm full of energy. Would like to do something marvelous—physical or mental. + Good night! Good night, Madeleine! How beautiful you are![FF]

MARCH 3, 1941

[F]A good day. But I received 89 on my Greek exam. That's bad! + Madeleine doesn't talk enough. I wonder what my next move should be. I always feel stronger in the spring—and full of energy, ambition. Love, without doubt, this spring. Who? Someone new. H.M. or—I don't know. Madeleine! Yes. + I wonder how this feeling of energy, hope will be as time passes—as life diminishes. The sensation is so strong and beautiful right now.[FF]

3/3/41

I can think of no great writers or thinkers or inventors who were notorious sots. Poe, of course. But the rosy haze of drunkenness is singularly unproductive—seemingly fertile at first—but put your ideas into concrete practice and they vanish like a soap bubble.

MARCH 4, 1941

[F]The girls in my play didn't want to stay on stage after 11:00. They behaved very badly. I'd like to cut a few throats! I like [Jean Sarment's] *Le pêcheur d'ombres* a lot. + My Morton story is only 6 pages long. It's good. I'm proud of it. + Rose M. asked me to come to the ASU office tonight. I simply don't have the time. + Ernst called me at 10:30. He was opening a bottle of Haig & Haig with Fauge and his girlfriend. I don't understand his love of drink—or at least of scotch. Champagne, yes.[FF]

MARCH 5, 1941

[F]Skipped French to rehearse my play. It was a flop! I don't mind. The soldier was vague. The communist talked too much. I didn't notice any of this when I saw it once in rehearsal. + I acted in a play with Helen. How I could love her! And vice versa, perhaps. I'll try. + Madeleine wasn't there. All the better! + Meeting tonight at Flora's. Coryl criticized me because my report wasn't detailed enough. She's right. She's very militaristic. It's for the best. I was lazy. Will do better next time.[FF]

3/5/41

It has become a platitude that an artist's life should be hard, should be blood and sweat, tears and disappointment, struggle and exhaustion. This fight, I believe, should be in his attitude towards the world: his difficulty lies always in keeping himself apart, intellectually and creatively, maintaining his own identity at the same time he identifies himself with society. But in his own work, there should be none of this pain. He creates a thing because he has mastered it and is familiar with it. He produces it easily, having once taken his idea in his bosom. A great struggle in composition is apparent in his work, and shows it to be an artificial, foreign, and most of all, a feeble and unsure thing. Great work has come easily: I do not mean fluently, but easily, from this sense of mastery, and has been later if necessary polished and changed at leisure, and cheerfully.

3/5/41

I don't know whether I add more items to this notebook when I go out with people or when I stay home alone. Sometimes society is stimulating, sometimes it is stupefying. I'm very happy whenever I have something good on the nights when I've been with people, and I feel rotten on the nights when I've been alone and produce nothing. But I can't say on which nights I feel most fertile.

MARCH 6, 1941

[F]I bumped into Marijann K. while going to school and we sang Alouette* while running to Shakespeare. It's unimportant, but I'm writing it down because it won't happen again in a few years. Even when the proletarian revolution comes. I'm angry when I do nothing important in a day. I could at least sit in a chair and think. + Went to the Finnish Hall[†] tonight. YCL. We played "Mannerheim Line" in the stairwell. Such noise![FF]

MARCH 7, 1941

[F]What a day! First a Greek exam (went well!) in which I laughed a lot about nothing! + At the last minute, I wrote a paper for Le Duc.[‡] They say Mrs. Bailey's husband has gone mad. + I began my short story about

---

* "Alouette" is a French children's song.

† A meeting place for immigrants from Finland at 13 West 126th Street that the YCL sometimes used for their meetings.

‡ Alma LeDuc, assistant professor of French at Barnard College.

the school.* Three judges tonight. Very good! + Then Peter and Helen, very drunk. Helen made a lot of passes at me. We went to Caravan. I danced with Helen and we held hands under the table. Curtis noticed us and made us come to her table. Very impressed with Helen: naturally, she thought she was my girlfriend. Curtis told me that I'm "cute." "It's the company," I said. Curtis will tell Va. That'll be something! Debbie B. very severe, ended the night early. Helen's sleeping there. Oh my God, how she would like to be in my arms tonight. Curtis asked me if I get any studying done at school with Helen there! We'll see if I can.[FF]

MARCH 9, 1941

[F]I'm thinking of Helen. I'm happy. I'm thinking of evenings, sitting at a table—drinking, dancing. All kinds of things. + I finished my wooden head. I cut away too much. It doesn't matter. The wood wasn't good. + The parents and I discussed religion tonight, without coming to any realization, of course. Mother said that this world is a world of dreams, etc. It's impossible to talk with her when she says that I'm a person who hasn't yet carefully thought things through.[FF]

MARCH 10, 1941

[F]My first thought was to go see Helen. When I gave her my well-prepared apology, she said, "Oh, I liked it." "In that case," I said, "let's do it again sometime." + *Quarterly* is here.[FF]

MARCH 12, 1941

[F]Madeleine refused to accept a *Quarterly* yesterday: she doesn't want to see her story.[†] I'd like her to read mine! + Helen is cold. It hurts me. She doesn't call me "darling" anymore, the way she does Peter. I have no one to blame but myself. It will be difficult the next time because she'll be careful. Oh, I'd like to go with Cecilia E. once. An experienced woman. + We held the meeting here last night. Only 7 showed up. We are losing our enthusiasm. There will be a peace conference at Columbia this Saturday where I will speak.[FF]

---

* In reference to Pat's story "Miss Juste and the Green Rompers," published in the *Barnard Quarterly*, Spring 1941; also in *Nothing That Meets the Eye: The Uncollected Stories of Patricia Highsmith* (New York, 2002).
† Madeleine Freund's short story "Genuine Harris Tweed" was also published in the spring 1941 issue of the *Barnard Quarterly*.

MARCH 13, 1941

ᶠI handed out pamphlets from 8:30–9. They called me "Red" to my face! And McGuire* came by (!) She saw me and smiled. Who cares? She'll tell the other professors. + A big piece in the papers (*World Tel.* [*Telegram*]) against the ASU. Red dominated, etc. Lists of our tactics, as if they were illegal! + Very tired tonight—too tired to write, really: smoking on the couch, thinking of a play.— Curtis called me up with an invitation to a party tomorrow night. From a girl called "Mary" who "admired" me at Caravan. I'll invite Helen to go with me tomorrow. I'm thinking about it all the time—I hope she doesn't have a date tomorrow. She can spend the night here!ᶠᶠ

MARCH 14, 1941

ᶠHelen has a date tonight, but otherwise she would have gone with me, and she asked me if I'd receive more invitations! Of course! Well, Peter had a laugh! (I didn't do well on the Greek exam!) + The party was wonderful for two reasons: the hostess (Mary S.)† was very charming— a lot like Bailey. And there was a certain Billie B., much more attractive even than Streng!‡ My God! We sat on the divan together for a while, both drunk. We held hands, etc. Nothing else. She is very grown-up (35?), proper, beautiful—very beautiful, and dresses like Streng. Billie B. whispered that I should call her today. (Home at 5:30.) Oh! As if I wouldn't!ᶠᶠ

MARCH 15, 1941

ᶠI can't think of anything else but Billie B. What a woman! Mary told me yesterday that she told her that she likes me. The two of us and Mary were the best of the bunch. + I slept for three hours. I did a bit of work but didn't go to the peace conference! I called up Billie B. at 1. She wasn't home. And then—!!!!!!! She called me at 4. Called up Mary to ask for my name too! Oh, what a woman, to bother herself for my sake! No, no, that's not the right attitude! Oh, I am so happy I can only think of her!!—I wrote tonight, and then went to the Blue Bowl at 10. Billie was there in a black suit. We drank gin next to the restaurant. She is 30–31. Her husband (!) is a journalist. She lives with a Mary R. I drank too much. I don't know how I decided to go home with her. Perhaps she

---

* Lorna McGuire, associate professor of English and freshman adviser at Barnard College.
† Mary Sullivan ran the bookshop at the Waldorf Astoria Hotel.
‡ Marion Streng, associate professor of physical education at Barnard College.

made the decision. In a taxi. Then I was sick. I got rid of a lot. A bit of coffee and then—bed. Mary's pajamas! My God!^{FF}

MARCH 16, 1941

^F[Billie] didn't do quite right by me. It was incomplete. She is tender, passionate, sweet, and feminine (!) The things one doesn't know until one sleeps with someone! She gave me what seemed like real love. But I've decided she's a bum. Tomorrow I'll tell Peter: "I met a beautiful bum." Home at 12:30. Studied a bit. Billie told me twice that she'll be home tonight at 9. She's expecting me to call her. I won't. I'll make her wait for me! All my excitement has petered out, like the air in a child's balloon: she didn't remain distant enough. Either she truly loves me, or she is easy and shallow—and a bit stupid. She's not as spiritual as I thought. Born in Germany. Height 5'8".^{FF}

MARCH 17, 1941

^FPeter very impressed by my weekend. + Lorna M. told me today that she liked my story*—well-written. But two girls came to her office and wanted to write a letter to the *Bulletin* because my story was against the educational system! + I didn't call Billie at 9, as she suggested. Not until 12. She's still charming. When can she see me? Friday, I said. She doesn't want to go to Caravan. But Curtis called me and told me that we'll go on Friday: Mary, Curtis, etc. Maybe Va. What will she think of Billie?!?!^{FF}

MARCH 18, 1941

^FI'm nervous. Couldn't study today. Helen invited me to have a cigarette—wanted to hear about Billie, etc. When I got home, there was a message from Billie. Mother had taken down her number. "I'm suspicious of your friendship with this woman" (my heart stopped beating) —"She's pursuing us." "Oh, my God, not at all." She simply wanted to know how I got home on Sunday, etc. Then I phoned B. when mother had left. She wanted to do something tonight (but Rita R. will come along). And I told her that she should stop calling me. She tried to remain calm. If only she were more subtle! More intelligent! Anyways— Rita R. came at 8.30. Good evening with my sherry. We danced. She dances very well. Lindy. Then I took her to Barnard. But first, I called

---

* "The Legend of the Convent of St. Fotheringay," which has just been published in the latest *Barnard Quartlery*.

Billie at 12:15. I told her that she's a bum—one of the best. She laughed. Nothing else.[FF]

MARCH 19, 1941

[F]Madeleine brought me home. She's sleeping with Arthur now. (A friend of Ludwig's, perhaps.) Madeleine is strikingly different from my distinguished friends. Ernst received a big piece in a Gramercy newspaper. I told him about Friday night. "Where do you find all these people?"[FF]

MARCH 20, 1941

[F]I studied well. Homer. I smoked cigarettes with Helen and Peter. How they frolic about all day! They would like me to come with them to lunch on Tuesday at the Gold Rail.[*] We drank at lunch. I wore my striped jacket which Va. doesn't like. Helen likes it! She called me "Darling" for the first time since Friday: yes—when I think of Helen, I'm happy. + ASU meeting. Didn't open my mouth. I washed my hair. And I finished the story about gym class![FF]

MARCH 21, 1941

[F]I met mother at L. & T. [Lord & Taylor] where we bought a red corduroy jacket. Marvelous. Mother likes it, which is unusual. I Met Billie at the World's Fair Café.[†] Drank a little. She was very pretty in a gray dress. Then back to her place for coffee. She kept drinking. We sat on the divan for several hours—until 2:30. It was very nice. She invited me—very politely—to stay the night. Mary wasn't there.[FF]

MARCH 23, 1941

[F]I met an insufferable young woman from school on my way to Billie's. She was going to Temple Emanu-El[‡] for a meeting of young gays. What a thing to do on Sunday! My good angel tells me that would be better— but my God! I'll take the devil! Billie very sweet—kisses, etc. She tells me that she likes me a lot. That she wants me. I feel very attracted to her. But I told her I was in love with Helen at school. Billie was very sad—I didn't allow her to touch me—anyways, we decided not to see each other

---

[*] The Gold Rail Bar, located at 2850 Broadway between 110th and 111th on the Upper West Side, was a casual hub for gay patrons.

[†] World's Fair Café was a restaurant and bar at 798 Third Avenue.

[‡] Temple Emanu-El, a Jewish reform synagogue located at 840 Fifth Avenue on the northeast corner of East Sixty-Fifth Street.

for a month. She gave me a little gold chain for my wrist. I won't wear it—and I—I gave her nothing but one cent.[FF]

MARCH 24, 1941

[F]I had a bad evening: in bed. Thinking, writing bad poetry. Accomplished nothing until 1:30 when I had to do my theater homework. I wrote a long letter to Billie. A good letter, but cautious. I'm not in love with her. Oh, if only she were unattainable—how I would love her then![FF]

MARCH 26, 1941

[F]Cecilia phoned me. We had a drink at the Jumble Shop. She told me that I'd changed since the evening when she first met me. That Mickey and she thought of me as "a real lady." Now I seem like I could go to bed with someone: no shame, I suppose. Cecilia told me she liked my poems. Yes, they are good. It's exactly the kind of poetry I need right now. It makes me calm, thoughtful, introspective—sensitive—and tranquility allows me to write good poetry.[FF]

3/26/41

Love goes hurtling.

MARCH 28, 1941

[F]Felt very self-confident: it's filling my days. I don't think it's good. Georgia S. liked "Miss Juste and the Green Rompers." I bought papers for YCL at 3:30. Then I couldn't go to 126 tonight: something else more important came up: Jean was at Jumble at 9. Va. was a bit late, as usual. Curtis and Jack came later. Drinks (enough!) and on to MacDougal Tavern[*] and Caravan. Billie wasn't there. But I saw Frances B., Mary S. with Connie, and John with Mark, etc. Mary S. very charming. Connie told me that Mary has had a crush on me since her party. I'd like Mary to like me. She's clever. Connie said: "Mary likes you because you're intelligent—you have brains, she said." Then at the City Dump.[†] Va. and I went to the Vanguard and then to Judy's where we spent the night: 2:30–6:00 for me. I slept next to Va. naturally. A narrow and cold bed. Judy home at 5. Pretty, warm, charming coming up the stairs! I got home without parents noticing I was out all night.[FF]

---

[*] This may be in reference to Minetta Tavern, located at 113 MacDougal Street, an establishment frequented by E. E. Cummings, Ernest Hemingway, Eugene O'Neill, and Ezra Pound, among others.
[†] NYC City Dump Restaurant, located at 145 Bleecker Street in Greenwich Village, "where Park Avenue meets Bohemia."

3/28/41

Just now the world of experience seems more attractive than the world of books I have just stepped out of. I have not closed the door. I have merely left one room and gone into another. I have found a new confidence in myself. I have become a person at last.

MARCH 30, 1941

^FI feel more relaxed—it's my love—my loves, no doubt. Then Graham R. at 4. Peter's. Daiquiris—don't know how many. Graham began to feel more and more at home—his compliments were lewd—so lewd. Enid F. with a young, sweet boy. Graham was so alive—alive—we danced. Then we kissed: on the divan. Don't know how, but one becomes stupid when drinking. We stayed for the soup. Graham and I left to drink Limericks at his hotel (I waited downstairs for him—it wasn't safe to go up to his room.) Taxi to a Romanian restaurant. I call out to him physically and intellectually, he says. He wanted to go to bed with me—after I told him about my love for a man—who is called Billie.^{FF}

MARCH 31, 1941

^FHelen sweet at school. Something's happening to her, she said. To me too, but I'm not as much of a dreamer. Our grades are going down. Hers the most. She's smoking, not eating, etc. It's me, I think. We very gently touched hands in Latham's class. It's so sweet, and incredibly timid and modest. I was appointed the new editor-in-chief of *Quarterly*. Rita sent me African daisies. Balakian was defeated.^{*FF}

APRIL 2, 1941

^FHelen came and joined me for a cup of coffee. I was writing my editorial statement—that the days of belles lettres are over, etc. Helen told me several interesting things. She's waiting for war because then, everyone will reject the shackles of life, etc. That she wants to have fun any way, with anyone. What the devil! I am having fun.^{FF}

4/2/41

Lately I have been wasting time. I have been doing what I should have regarded with the utmost contempt at the age of sixteen. But it has done this for me: It has shown me that an unbookish life can be very useless. It

---

* Pat defeated Nona Balakian (1918–1991), future literary critic and editor of the *New York Times Sunday Book Review*, who was also on the *Quarterly*'s editorial board, for the top job.

has also shown me how what I have absorbed during my monastic adolescence can be used in a more normal life. And strangely it has made
the books more important in one sense: that they are essential not for
culture—or background—or scholarship—but to enrich the normal life.
These sound like platitudes—at the most, truisms. But it has meant more
to me than that, this discovery. I have seen and lived in the real world for
the first time in my stupid life.

APRIL 4, 1941

^FHome until 11:45. Cralick* and Graham here. Good drinks, Cralick
took a look at my writing. Flexible, developed in spirit but not in
body—! We danced—Cralick and I. I was quite drunk when I left the
house. I read *Best One Acts* of 1940—Percival Wilde (what a name!) on
my way to Billie's. I have to accomplish something of value these days!
Billie in her blue slacks. Generous with her liquor. It bothers me. I drank
too much myself. Billie told me she didn't want me to stay—not when she
was drunk.^{FF}

APRIL 7, 1941

^FAt Flora W.'s for ASU exec. [executive meeting]. They bore me. I won-
der if I would have joined if I'd known? I do no more than sympathize.
Graham came for breakfast yesterday. He stayed all day and this evening, too, working on his book. + A letter from Roger F. Wants me to
come for Easter. We'll see! I have been spending too much money on
drinks. I'd like to buy tickets—or one ticket a week—for the theater.^{FF}

APRIL 9, 1941

^FAlmost got sick because I was so tired. A letter from Dick,[†] who wants
to start up our Thursday night meetings again. Communist reading
circle. + Real hangover. Couldn't think straight today. It's not healthy.
Went home at 9:30 and straight to bed! Slept until 10. Got up and felt
much better. I'd like to write something tomorrow morning. My idea?
I've had it for a while. I hope it's important. I feel as though my life
in the South has given me an inexhaustible reservoir of stories—what
riches!^{FF}

---

* Jeva Cralick, a close friend of Pat's mother's.
† President of the Young Communist League.

APRIL 10, 1941

[F]Good day! First day of break. I began my story about the girl from the South.[*] With the boy D.W.[†] It will be good. + Went to Macy's—on foot—to buy pajamas. Nothing makes me happier than new pajamas![FF]

APRIL 11, 1941

[F]5 pages this morning. + Herbert L.[‡] here at 7:30. Not in uniform. Quite experienced with women now. He's not the same boy anymore. But he still likes Bach. It's a pleasure to see him sitting at the piano. We drank two T. [Tom] Collins with quite some results. He wanted to go to bed together—in some hotel. It bears me down—I don't know—I should have seen Billie tonight. She invited me—but I was with Herb, and I wanted to go to the movies. Billie sent me a little pink rabbit: very cute and small. Herb wants to meet me tomorrow evening at Walgreen's to go to the hotel—I have no desire—otherwise I would do it—I have no scruples. That's not it at all.[FF]

APRIL 12, 1941

[F]Meeting at Coryl's. We accomplished nothing. It's disgusting. I continue to have no enthusiasm. Marcella was there. Gay? Don't know. She doesn't mix business with pleasure. Then I bought a box of cigarettes with a brown and blue hippopotamus on it for mother. And a jar of jelly for Billie. Very pretty but not exciting. + I like [Elmer Rice's] *Flight to the West*. Wonderful. A play that makes you think. Billie will come back to the city from the country just to see me tomorrow.[FF]

4/12/41

I can work like a grub on an idea—on a story—realizing something is of importance in it. Then after a few days dissipating—with the job in the back of my mind, as such jobs always are, I can come home with the truth of it exposed and clear to me. I can sit down to write again with the true meaning finally in my mind. It's inevitable that a young person spend more time living than working. He should. He must. To begin work again is like starting with a new brain, washed clean, yet wiser too.

---

* This story has been lost.
† Possibly a reference to her cousin Dan's son Dan Walton Coates.
‡ Herbert L., an old friend.

4/12/41

I often wonder if it is love I want or the thrill of domination—not thrill exactly but satisfaction. Because this is often more enjoyable than the love itself; though I cannot imagine a domination without love, nor a love without domination. False.*

APRIL 13, 1941

^FI always feel happy when I'm on a walk with my mother. I wrote a bit tonight. Then [at Billie's]. She'd just come from the country. We sat on the couch. Billie was speaking in platitudes, it was like being with my family! She bores me so. I didn't even feel like spending the night! Home at 2:30. And I forgot my key again! I had to wake up Stanley. What a fuss! My mother was angry at 3:00 AM. A rat in bed with them, etc. Made me sweep the living room.^{FF}

APRIL 14, 1941

^FI'm hungry for literature—for books, just the way my body was hungry one or two months ago. My appetite is twofold: I hunger for love and for thought. Together those two can take me anywhere, you know.† I wrote a poem about this.^{FF}

4/14/41

Note on the opposition of body and mind. My mind is now as greedy and as hungry as my body was four months ago—one month ago! It is amazing. They work at cross-purposes. Rather like two buckets on a well rope. One must be filled while the other is emptying!

4/14/41

Having just finished l'affaire B.—, is there any better proof that love disappears when the curiosity and the doubt and the struggle is ended? Mine might have been through forty-eight hours after I met B. I think it was.

APRIL 16, 1941

^FYesterday I met Carter in Wash. Sq Park. He's from Texas. He seemed pensive and told me that a friend had brought him sage—(I thought at

---

* Possibly added retrospectively.

† This entry was written in an imperfect French, leaving some room for interpretation: "*Je suis fait[e] de deux appétits: l'amour et la pensée. Entre ces deux, je suis dans chaque endroit, il faut savoir.*" It is also possible she could have meant to say: "Love and thought, wherever I go, I am always torn between those two," or "I am always looking for one of them."

first that he said "gays")—and this means marijuana: he's tried it perhaps 8 times in a dozen years. + Felicia talked to me regarding my few sales of *Soviet Power*, that I haven't visited their meetings, etc. I am so bored with stuff. Political stuff in particular. + I finished [James Branch] Cabell's *Cream of the Jest*. Full of satire. One must get to know both well-known authors and lesser-known ones: everyone has something.^FF

APRIL 17, 1941

^FCompletely forgot to buy books for the League yesterday afternoon. A Freudian slip. I'd like to get out of it. I'd like some peace and quiet for a while. It's all my fault. I haven't behaved properly recently. But I'd like to get out of the fight until I've done something worth doing.

+ Reading [Pushkin's] *Eugene Onegin*. Bad (doggerel).^FF

APRIL 18, 1941

^FHad dinner with Billie. Fish. I wore my black dress, as she wished. Never-ending nightcaps at Delaney's.* Billie was sad and didn't say much. Difficult, wanted to stay at her place. Had 3–4 drinks I didn't want at Caravan. Then B. and I alone in the diner. 8 St. Billie—"Let's get things straightened out." She told me she's possessive, jealous, wants a lot. Asked me if I still love Va. There's a lot we can't say with words, she told me. Very tired. Sad. Didn't eat her burger. We left at 5. She took my last dollar. Could she have expressed herself more clearly?? I love her because she can't express herself.^FF

APRIL 19, 1941

^FUnfortunately Roger came—and I went out tonight. Fell asleep on the bus—he wanted to drink in nightclubs + I finished the story†—about the boys and the girl in the car. It isn't coherent enough—nor important—? It was written without much inspiration, like a lot of my stories. But I have two ideas that are important (I'm certain of it). One is the nucleus of a novel.^FF

APRIL 20, 1941

^FBillie phoned me at 10:30. Mother answered. Then she said with malice: "Does she want you? Tell her she can have you!" I was cold, because my mother was listening. Watched *Great Dictator* with Arthur. Then

---

* Jack Delaney's was a popular Greenwich Village steak house at 72 Grove Street, near Sheridan Square.
† It is unclear which story she refers to here.

home for pie and cake. My mother still likes him the most of all my male friends. He's a communist too, which pleases me because of my mother. "You're not a communist. You've only got a pink toothbrush," she told me. Full of ambition. I want to read the dictionary, all my books. I'll have to keep a tight schedule until my exams.[FF]

4/21/41

People set such high value upon being loved—even greater—as I've said somewhere before, than the joy of loving—they set such high score by this that they will, without realizing what they are doing, take the greatest pains to make themselves loved, if they see another person interested in them: even if they have no spark of love within them for the interested person. It comes on one—this realization of our desire to be loved, and the realization that one is actually encouraging the lover in every way possible—It comes on one as a shock—of honesty—such honesty—and with it a kind of guilt, a sense of hypocrisy, of shallowness and deception, of decadence and of an unhealthy love of mockery.

APRIL 23, 1941

[F]J. B.[*] sent me a dollar (which will buy a present for Mary S.) but not the slightest comment on "St. Fotheringay." Very tired. Helen was charming in Latham's class. But I haven't touched her since that lovely Monday a month ago. Oh well—I tried to develop an interest in drama but it simply isn't there. Everyone writes plays far more well-rounded than mine. But I don't care. It's not important! I'm thinking about my first novel[†]—about people my age. And about a woman like the one around whom the story will unfold—an intelligent woman forced to turn on them—so she can make a living. That will always be my topic.[FF]

APRIL 24, 1941

[F]We have to decide on our classes for 1942. I'll take Howard:[‡] Advanced Comp. And another semester of Sturtevant. Those two classes will give me a lot of writing practice until I graduate.[FF]

---

* Probably Jay Bernard Plangman, Pat's biological father.
† Pat starts thinking about a novel. She will in fact start writing a "roman d'adolescents," inspired by her college friends, but only in 1943, and with a different story than the one she outlines here—*The Click of the Shutting*, a project she never completes.
‡ Dr. Clare Howard, associate professor of English.

APRIL 25, 1941

[F]Latham asked me why I take so long to write my plays. "You're too fussy," she said. + Called up [Billie]. She wanted to meet Curtis and Jean at Rocco's at 9. Then MacDougal for drinks, where I saw Connie and Mary S., Eddy, and Helen R., Billie and Curtis became more and more drunk at the bar. Then we went to Caravan. Billie sat down, singing along with the music in an effort, I suppose, to appear young and happy. I was disgusted. Then I lost my purse between Jungle Camp and Main Street. Bumped into Dorothy P. Drank 5, spent all my money except for a dollar. My keys, lipsticks and compacts were in the purse—luckily not my wallet. Parents didn't answer the bell. Then back to Main Street and finally home to Dorothy P.'s where I spent the night.[FF]

APRIL 26, 1941

[F]My parents didn't hear the bell. I was worried that they were angry. I didn't tell mother I'd lost my purse. Mother and I saw an exhibition: Rouault and Paul Klee.[*] Went roller skating with Va. tonight: two boys— Lee M. and Frank B. They're in the army. So innocent! Lots of sailors at the rink. Such fresh and young figures compared to last night. I studied well this morning. I feel full of energy, though I know I'm not.[FF]

APRIL 27, 1941

[F]Went to Marjorie Thompson's[†] tonight. Larry M. was there with his mother. Larry is definitely gay. It's amusing how one can put the pieces together! His mother was interpreting what Hitler said. She's confusing the sides—black and white—and believes in Lindbergh[‡] (who resigned today). Larry is more tactful. His mother is from the south and stupid.[FF]

APRIL 28, 1941

[F]At school, I'm told that it's awful I don't come to the meetings anymore (there was one tonight). But for myself, as an individual, my studies are more important.[FF]

---

* Probably "Understanding Modern Art" at the Museum of Modern Art, which also showed works by Picasso, Matisse, Braque, and Cézanne.

† Marjorie Thompson, close friend of Pat's mother's.

‡ Charles Lindbergh Jr. (1902–1974), the first man to cross the Atlantic in a solo flight, was a vigorous opponent of America's entry into World War II. When President Roosevelt decried him as a "defeatist and appeaser," Lindbergh resigned his commission in the Air Force.

4/28/41

Having an automobile is like having your own woman. They're a terrible expense and give you a lot of worry, but once you've had one, you'll
never want to be without one.

APRIL 30, 1941

[F]The plays we are putting on in class are almost professional. Nonetheless, I have to write a better one. Judy at 6. Mother too to see the
apartment. Judy same as ever. Her imagination is at work in everything
she says. Sometimes that's amusing, sometimes boring or disgusting.
But it's needed for her work. When I was there, Va. called. Wanted me
to go with them to a picnic on Saturday. Even if I didn't have a play
to write, I'd have books to read—time flies and I haven't nearly read
enough. Look at [Babs] B.! Does she go on outings every week? Va. was
still angry![FF]

MAY 1, 1941

[F]Finally, I've done my schedule. I've become famous at the registrar's
office for being absentminded. Sturtevant asked me if I was in love with
someone. + I'd like to write my story about the woman who loves the
fake count.* I'll do it well. + Phoned Billie. The days are going by, and
I'm not thinking about her. We'll talk tomorrow, but I have no intention
of spending a lot of money!![FF]

MAY 2, 1941

[F]With Billie tonight at 10. We were supposed to see [the film] *Pépé le
Moko*—but it was already late. In any case, I wanted to talk with her.
She said nothing about her conversation with M. Sullivan but I have no
doubt M.S. told her what I said: that I feel young and stupid around her
friends. So what.[FF]

MAY 3, 1941

[F]Billie invited me to go with her to Mero's tonight.† 10 St. + I could have
done better on yesterday's exam. I knew everything. There's something

---

* Probably in reference to the short story "Silver Horn of Plenty," published in *Barnard Quarterly*
(Winter 1941).
† Gean Harwood and Bruhs Mero organized the Nucleus Club, a small group of lesbian and gay
male friends who regularly partied at their home in Greenwich Village in the late 1930s and early
1940s. They were careful to pull the blinds down and have women and men leave their apartment in
mixed pairs.

that freezes in my brain and prevents me from using my knowledge. It's a bit of defeatism. + We took photographs in the garden. Me in slacks*—my friends will be surprised when I tell them that my mother took the photographs! + I feel beaten down—discouraged from my work. I'm not developing enough, and I often think it's sexual. Don't know. What if these four years are lost! Wasted! I feel incapable of being truly courageous—the way I was when I was 16—14! That was terrific! I wonder whether true love creeps up slowly—subtly—not in a fury! But I love fury!^{FF}

MAY 5, 1941
^FI began studying for my exams. Am happy. I should have gone with [Billie] to the movies tonight. But I had to work on my play. It's getting better (haven't I said so all semester?). I have to study for each subject, and will start when I finish [T. H. White's] *The Sword in the Stone*. Often I look at the books in the library and think about my freshman days—how I wanted to read each book over those four years. I'll do it. And I know that, as soon as I have time, ideas and their realization will fall like rain. With regularity, one produces something. I shouldn't be afraid.^{FF}

MAY 8, 1941
^FThere will be a meeting tomorrow night, so I can't go to Billie's. She wanted me to spend the night. I would have liked to stay a while, then go home. It's difficult to do otherwise as long as I live at home. + Read *Hamlet* tonight! Memorized a few things. Working now. And sleeping enough, which I haven't done since I began university.^{FF}

MAY 9, Friday
^FHow I need peace and quiet. Tonight is the first Friday I've spent at home since the evening with Peter and Helen.^{FF}

MAY 10, 1941
^FA whole day and I haven't opened a book. Looked for slacks this morning. They don't fit me—those for women. + Then quickly to Va. She

---

* Pat often particularly points out wearing pants. To understand why, and its implications, it is crucial to keep in mind that pants for women were still considered innapropriate by many, and cross-dressing a telltale sign of homosexuality. There was a notorious "three-articles-of-clothing" rule—never actually a law, but still widely used by the authorities—that could get anyone arrested who got caught wearing fewer than three articles of gender-appropriate clothing.

actually gave me hers! Went to some place in the north with Frank and Lee. It was amusing, but I'm wasting my time with boys like that. Even Va. wouldn't pay them any mind if they didn't have a car. They're too young, stupid, and ordinary for us.[FF]

MAY 11, 1941—[G]Mother's Day[GG]

[F]My slacks are wonderful! They're a bit short, just as they should be. I have to study a lot now. Also, [Paul] Claudel's play *L'annonce faite à Marie* is very lovely. + Cralick told me in earnest that I could get work at *Vogue* with my drawings. I believe it. I believe everything. Most of all, I believe in myself. I can do anything at all![FF]

MAY 15, 1941

[F]Helen was very pretty today. I brought her books from the library. I like how much it disgusts Va. + I wrote to R. to invite them to spend Decoration Day[*] with Va. and myself. We would like to go north by car—their car. + Good game of tennis with Frances F. Then a shower—both of us naked—makes one feel good.—Then exhaustion. It's a good life. No worries. + I finished my play. "Kiss me Goodbye"—and the heroine is named Helen—of course.[FF]

MAY 16, 1941

[F]I got an A- on a paper for Bailey. + Lee phoned me this evening. I was reading *The Tempest*. Then Va. came by—they were taking a spin in the car. She came to my room alone. I kissed her—caressed her—without the slightest desire or pleasure. I don't know what I'm turning into. + Then [Janet] M. at 10:30. Mary was very (oh very!) sweet to me. Janet is blonde and tall, like Billie. Large apartment. Such opulence! But a bit cheap, just like her. Mary told me that Billie and [Janet] are together now. Janet has a car—and Billie told me last week that she'd sell her soul for a car.[FF]

MAY 17, 1941

[F]Always working. Billie phoned me at 10. She was sorry about last night (but why!). Said that the girls are bitches—it's always the same with Billie—if she's under the impression she needs to handle me with kid gloves, she's wrong. We were never serious. I studied hard. How much

---

* Memorial Day used to be called Decoration Day.

more naïve I was when I lived on Morton St.* I was a cheery, happy child—and confident. Now I've had too many nights drinking.ᶠᶠ

MAY 18, 1941

ᶠNot enough time for studying. Ernst called me yesterday. Wanted to hire me in two weeks.† Probably. + Oh, if only I could feel love like a sixteen-year-old again! I was so happy! Now I'm like an old woman!ᶠᶠ

MAY 19, 1941

ᶠWork! Work! I'm not even reading the papers. A ship sank. 190 Americans.‡ Hitler, perhaps. Everyone is talking about Germany's victory. We've just entered the war.§ + I read *Julius Caesar, Measure for Measure*—etc. It's exciting to study like this: all day! Other men's thoughts.ᶠᶠ

5/19/41

I am drunk now—in a house full of drunks, and everybody is so damned busy expressing himself.

5/19/41

Possible basis for my weltanschauung. That the childishness is never lost, but adulthood put like a veneer over it. We think inside like children, react, and have their desires. The outside manners are an absurd puff of conceit. Ponder this later.

MAY 22, 1941

ᶠI wasted two months on Billie. I don't regret them. But they were wasted, at least in terms of work. I only wrote the one story of "Miss Juste" and two plays. Now I'd like to spread out. Tomorrow we (Virginia and I) will go to Caravan, I think. She's young and sweet, compared to Billie. Oh Billie, you deceived me!! You're nothing but a drunk, nothing but a self-involved lover. A coward—a lazy bum—a passionate woman, but a good-for-nothing.ᶠᶠ

---

* In 1940, Pat took a summer sublet at 35 Morton Street in order to get away from her family—the address will later also feature as a setting in her novel *A Dog's Ransom* (New York, 1972).

† Ernst will employ her for some time to assist him in his writing.

‡ The reference here is not clear: Pat might be referring to the *Robin Moor*, a cargo ship with forty-six people on board, which was intercepted by a German U-boat off the coast of Brazil on May 21, an incident that prompted President Franklin D. Roosevelt to issue a May 27 proclamation that a state of unlimited national emergency exists. This would confirm yet again that Pat often wrote diary entries retrospectively (and backdated them).

§ Not literally: The United States entered the war against Japan on December 8, 1941, one day after the attack on Pearl Harbor.

MAY 23, 1941

[F]I don't care if I don't see V.S. [Virginia] for the next six months. There's lots to do. Each subject once more. + The trouble with Va. and I is that we don't have enough desire. We don't want each other.[FF]

MAY 23, 1941

[F]With Va. tonight, we fought. We won't go together on Decoration Day. I'm letting my feelings lead me, not my spirit. I've depended on it long enough. It's very boring. It's sterile. When I like someone, I'll do what I must without thinking.[FF]

MAY 24, 1941

[F]A good day. The first of my new life. I finished my play *War and the Pettigrews* (now *the P's at War*), 21 pages. + With mother this morning. We strolled, then went to Orbach.* There are times I like being in a crowd. Today I hated it. Sometimes I touch a body and it disgusts me and makes me furious. + Spent the evening at the library. Wonderful books, and I'm still hungry for them. Ernst H. here for tea. Wants to pay me 20.00 a week. I'll do it. + I read *Bury the Dead* (Irwin Shaw) last night. It was good but too obviously communist, I think. It's surprising that he was popular for so long on Broadway. + Va. told me on Friday that Schulberg[†] (or Thomas Wolfe) wrote that a man who is keeping a diary does so because he is afraid of saying what he writes. It's possible. It's true in my case. In any case, I like to follow my progress and regressions.[FF]

5/24/41

That night at the party, when I sat down beside you on the couch and we started talking, you might have been anyone else, any of the other people in the room I talked with that night. I can't say yet what it was exactly that made you suddenly different. But I loved you then, because you were strange. I loved you when you said good night to me. I loved you all the next day, though I couldn't sleep, or eat, or read, or even think coherently about you. Then when I did see you, I felt stupid, or I felt that you would think me stupid because I couldn't take my eyes off you. You were so very offhand and wonderful when I first came. We walked out onto the sidewalk down to a dive of a bar, and sat in a booth. And it was then that something fell away from you like a mantle slipped off the

---

* Orbach's was a department store.

† Budd Schulberg (1914–2009), American writer and TV producer.

shoulders—perhaps I should say like a screen that conceals something not too attractive. I wish I could say what it was. Because if I knew—if it were simple enough to be discovered, I might be able to forget it. I should at least know what to fight, what it is keeping us apart. Perhaps I was shocked because you seemed to give me too much attention. Perhaps I was silly and didn't want anyone, after all, that I really might have. I don't know. But I know that after that wonderful evening before, when you hardly spoke to me, and after that sleepless night and that nerve-shaken day, and the counted hours before I finally saw you again—after all that, the change in you, (or in me) was like the sudden, unwelcome awakening from a glorious dream. An awakening on a Monday morning when, with one's castle and clouds and the silver sea dissolved into a sordid room, one realizes that one has to get up and dress in the cold night in a few minutes and plod through a weary day.

MAY 25, 1941

[F]A disgusting day. Not enough work, not enough pleasure. I spent too much time between the two. I tried to do a pastel drawing. It's difficult. Ink is my true medium. + We had dinner at Jumble Shop at 8 pm tonight. Mary S. came in with two men and a woman. Thankfully, they were straight. One was her husband. I introduced my parents, and she introduced her husband. Her hair didn't look good, but I didn't mind, except that I wanted her to make a good impression on my parents. She is pretty and sweet! Perhaps I could love her. Don't know. And why don't I do it if I can? Because I've become a Hamlet in every way. I'm a good-for-nothing. My heart has stopped beating.[FF]

5/25/41

It's so important that people—especially young people write some poetry during their lives. Even if it is bad poetry. Even if they think they do not like poetry or have no talent for writing it, they should write, and even badly, if it is sincere. And really sincere poetry is seldom bad even if the form is not perfect. But the poetry opens a new vista of the world. It is not so much that we see new things, but that we see old things differently. And this experience is invaluable. It is as soul-shaking as the experience of love. It is more ennobling. It makes philosophers and kings.

5/26/41

Every man and woman, in his or her life, makes decisions, knows emotions comparable to those felt by the characters in the greatest novels and plays. Yet such a small percentage of the world is articulate—the tiny handful of "writers" who, with few exceptions, gain their themes from observation of others, second hand. If we had the pieces in any form, the individual contributions through all the ages, what wouldn't we know now?

MAY 28, 1941

ᶠWrote this morning. Went to N.Y.U. at 12:30. Babs B. was there. There was also a man from the American Writers' Congress.* It's meeting in a week. I'll go. + Latham gave me a B. B in Greek too. C in gym. With Arthur tonight. He almost loves me. Wanted to dive into the world of love, passion, etc. + I saw Katherine Cornell[†] in *Doctor's Dilemma.* Very good. She isn't pretty. Voice slightly high-pitched. A white, clear complexion. The audience, which was largely composed of women, didn't clap when the curtain came down because they were getting dressed: hats and gloves. It was disgusting!ᶠᶠ

5/28/41

We come into the world with a tabula rasa character on which the people about us write their messages. An admired character, we seek to imitate, a detested character, we seek to mold ourselves in the exact opposite. This is a more important factor than heredity or the physical environment.

Miscellania: How to get rid of persistent boy friends. Should I develop a healthy case of dandruff?

MAY 29, 1941

ᶠFirst day of work with Ernst. His dialogue could be better. I said as much as I could. His characters are speaking too formally. Home at 4:45. Not bad.ᶠᶠ

MAY 30, 1941

ᶠDinner with Herb at the Jumble Shop. Sometimes he talks like an ass—especially when he drinks. It's a big flaw. He could easily be a fascist. (They called me yesterday to ask whether I'd come to a communist assembly. Naturally I lied. Another evening with pseudo-pseudo people.) Herb and I tried to have an exciting time in bed. I could have been with

---

* The First American Writers Congress founded the League of American Writers, an association with close ties to the American Communist Party. Writers who joined until the League was disbanded in 1943 include Thomas Mann, Lilian Hellman, John Steinbeck, and Ernest Hemingway.
† Katharine Cornell (1898–1974), actress known as the "First Lady of the [American] Theater."

my grandmother. + Would like to be alone now. Would like to write poetry about my last love—or what have you—[FF]

MAY 31, 1941

[F]The days go by quickly. I get tired in the afternoons—my posterior. No coffee either. Ernst is so comfortable in slacks and a white jacket. No tie. He walks about, smokes a bit, eats his coffee sweets. I've learned a lot from him. I'd like to write like him. I'm almost there: a final draft first, then corrections in pen later. I'd like to write my first long story on long, yellow paper. I don't think that there's a girl Ernst is in love with now. But one never knows with him. The things he does . . . I wonder what [Billie's] doing right now. She's in the country, I think, I hope. She doesn't drink when she's there. Oh, the Saturdays I've spent with her! She kissed me the last time we were together. Unfortunately she doesn't remember. Oh what does it matter! Once, I wrote in my diary that when I become careful—when I am not interested in a person because she is not "good" enough, I will have become old—and now it's happened. I would like to love someone without desiring to be loved.[FF]

JUNE 1, 1941

[F]A ghostly day—no ordinary people on the streets because everyone's out of the city. I wonder what Va.'s doing? + I learned a lot—Don't want to write stories about stupid, useless people. There are so many things crying out to be described. + Graham here 10:00. We talked quietly. The situations and circumstances at the camps are unbelievable.[*] A sentry shot two men obeying his orders! We listened to records. He was wearing my slippers. They look nice on his feet. I'm happy.[FF]

JUNE 2, 1941

[F]Bad day with Ernst. 3½ hours of sleep! Oh well! But he pays me for my work! + Began my story about the girl and the lost purse.[†] Will be good. + S.'s birthday. He's turning 40. Looks 35! + I'm afraid to see my grades. Even if I don't care what I did this semester, I like getting A's. It takes so little to get a B or a C. And then—you're a mediocre student! But next year I'll get excellent grades. I don't regret anything this year. I learned a lot.[FF]

---

[*] The reference to camps here is unclear. Even the earliest rumors about the Holocaust would only begin to emerge later that year. The internment of Japanese Americans did not begin until 1942. She might have meant the United States' own training or "boot camps."
[†] Unidentifiable or lost story.

JUNE 3, 1941

ᶠI got an A in French—and a C in Shakespeare. I don't get it! There were only 5 C's in the class! I hoped for an A! Logic hasn't posted yet. + I wrote 6 good long pages of my *Hangover*. Making progress. I want to read and write for the rest of summer. The past few months—in the past two months, I've done nothing but try to feel things. And didn't succeed, except for cigarettes and liquor.ᶠᶠ

JUNE 6, 1941

ᶠNervous because I'm going to the doctor. Dr. Jennings at 5:15. She's gay—45 years old. Wanted to check me for all kinds of things; examined me for half an hour! I weigh 107 lb. It was hard to endure—vagina, etc. completely normal except for the glands. Have to test my basal metabolism Wednesday. It will cost a lot of money. Probably ¾ of what I'll make this summer. It's too bad, but I can't avoid it. Am constantly disappointed because I'm not in love! One could kill oneself for that. + Saw *Pal Joey*˟ with Arthur tonight. Not as good as I'd hoped for. Songs were excellent. Arthur is falling in love with me, and getting serious. It's tricky. I can't tell him what I feel—because I feel nothing—for or against. How I would like to tell him—even tell myself—that I'm in love with— Helen, Billie, Babs, someone!!!!!!!!!ᶠᶠ

JUNE 7, 1941

ᶠI have no summer clothes. It depresses me to walk through the streets when everyone is wearing light clothes. I am depressed so easily! And happy so easily! + Bought a necklace—pearls. 5 strands. Twisted. Billie will like it. Not a word from her. I'll call her on Monday probably. Commodore tonight.† We heard Millen Brand,‡ Joy Davidman.§ They say Steinbeck these days would no longer be allowed to publish his novel *Grapes of Wrath*. That's how close we are to war. + I'd like to write nonsense-verses—I'll do it.ᶠᶠ

---

* *Pal Joey* is a 1940 musical with music by Richard Rodgers and lyrics by Lorenz Hart. The original Broadway production, directed by George Abbott and starring Vivienne Segal and Gene Kelly, ran for ten months.

† The Commodore was a hotel at Forty-Second Street and Lexington Avenue. It has since been replaced by the Grand Hyatt Hotel.

‡ American poet and novelist Millen Brand (1906–1980) was a member of the League of American Artists. During the McCarthy era, his books were banned from public libraries.

§ Helen Joy Davidman Gresham (1915–1960), American poet and writer who joined the American Communist Party in 1938 and later converted to Christianity. Her best-known work is *Smoke on the Mountain: An Interpretation of the Ten Commandments*.

JUNE 8, 1941

[F]Mother is unhappy at home. Perhaps it's her menopause—don't know—but when it comes, it will be much worse. She cried—said I was heartless. We took a walk at 9 pm tonight, close to the river. "I'm getting old, and there's nothing left for me here." In this house I see my mother and Stanley in a bad way—their work—not good enough—the house doesn't have enough dignity because we don't take enough care of it—my room is the prettiest and cleanest, though I work just as much as they do. Their time is mostly wasted—it all makes me sad—and I have no pity. (I wasn't born like that. A child is never cruel at birth. There it is, stated in brief.) I would like to leave home when I finish school. When my endocrinal glands begin to work, I don't know who I'll be, how I'll feel—who or what I'll love. What I'll want to become. I'll be a new person whom I have to get to know. We'll see. It'll be the most interesting change in my life![FF]

JUNE 9, 1941

[F]My story about grandmother[*] will need to be in the third person in the end. Otherwise there's too much time to cover. I hope that one day I'll re-read all of this—everything in this book [my diary]. My secrets—the secrets that everyone has—are here, in black and white.[FF]

JUNE 10, 1941

[F]Very sad tonight because mother talked to me a lot. I really don't understand her sometimes. After that, Billie found me—could I come to the movies? I was afraid. But mother let me go. We had a drink at Shelton Corner's.[†] Very happy. Home very late, of course. My mother came when I was in the kitchen. Told me I had no respect. That Stanley is noble to do what he does—but Stanley is mostly afraid of getting worked up. That requires more courage than staying calm.[FF]

6/10/41

We love either to dominate or to be bolstered up ourselves. And there is no love without some element of hate in it: in everyone we love, there is some quality we hate intensely.

---

[*] This may be in reference to her third-person short story "Sundays at Grandma's," which Pat brainstormed in Notebook 1 during her pre-college visit to Fort Worth in 1938.

[†] Cocktail lounge and restaurant in Shelton Hotel, Lexington Avenue at Forty-Ninth Street, popular for its "unique Glass Dance Floor."

JUNE 11, 1941

[F]At 15 St. for my metab. test at 8:30. A young woman—very pretty. Don't have the results yet. Then an x-ray, where they almost gave me an enema! I escaped by 2 minutes!! + Mother serious. Almost crying, often. The decision about next year rests with Stanley (school or no school). + Billie sad last night. I told her a bit about my problems—that my glands need adjustment—but nothing else. I told her that I don't trust any of my current emotions. She seemed interested. Naturally.[FF]

JUNE 12, 1941

[F]I told Ernst about what's happening at home. He got angry that I needed to spend all my money on clothes and doctors. He's never much liked mother. But he thinks they'll let me go to school next year anyway. Says my mother is completely childish. + *What Makes Sammy Run* by Budd Schulberg is very original. A lot of *joie de vivre*! It's a young book.[FF]

JUNE 13, 1941

[F]At the doctor's: I have a small pituitary—too small—the anterior node (the first one) is insufficient. Therefore, the thyroid is not strong enough. She gave me a small thyroid injection in the gluteus maximus. Otherwise I'll need to get my head x-rayed to fix it. + Mike Thomas tonight. Penthouse. 15 W. 95. Billie, Rita G, Rose M, Janet M., John M., Billy Livingston (army), Mary S., Curtis, Jean, Venetia (in a green suit—very striking—a bit butchy, but everyone was trying to pick her up). Mary talked to me—seemed to have told the men that I was almost perfect. I was supposed to go to Billie's after the party. But Billie got very drunk and left at 1:30 with Janet. Jean told me I have the most beautiful body she's ever seen. She is, in other words, on the rebound. Bernhard[*] was there too. Not attractive. + I spoke a lot with Mary S. who was flitting about here and there all night. The boys love her! But finally, Mary and I left to get a bite. Childs.[†] We spoke until 4:30. Then she invited me to spend the night. Her apartment's on 58 St. She slept for half an hour on the sofa under two blankets. I was in her bed without proper clothes. Finally, when I suggested that she could sleep next to me, since the bed

---

* German-born American photographer Ruth Bernhard (1905–2006) moved to New York City in 1927 and soon got involved in the lesbian subculture of the artistic community in Manhattan. She became friends with photographer Berenice Abbott and her lover, art critic Elizabeth McCausland, and wrote about her "bisexual escapades" in her memoir. In 1934 Bernhard began photographing women in the nude—soon also photographing Pat.

† The Childs Restaurant near Times Square.

was big enough, she accepted quickly! Very quickly! And then—well, we didn't sleep much, but what does it matter! She's marvelous!^{FF}

JUNE 14, 1941

^FWith Ernst at the Parkside,* two gardenias from Mary S. Ernst was curious, but I kept the card to myself. And lied to him. They are beautiful, fragrant. The card says only: "Mary."^{FF}

JUNE 15, 1941

^FWith Billie last night. She phoned me, very apologetic that she'd left without thinking of me. Rita G. at World's Fair yesterday. Pretty, but not smart. With her Friday night in the bathroom. She kissed me twice. Drunk. I'll see Mary S. Tuesday night. She likes me. I hope I'll be able to like her too. We had breakfast at Schrafft's† at 8 on Saturday. Parents not angry. Why? Ernst nervous because the United States is confiscating money from foreigners: he might make 500.00 less. And he wants me to cure him of his nerves!^{FF}

JUNE 16, 1941

^FGraham was here last night with Walter Marlowe. He's a Jew. Very intelligent. We danced, talked about everything, including Ernst's novel (which he forbade me from doing). + Tired but nervous because of Mary. I wanted a letter. Am still too sensitive! Finally I phoned her: "I'm a bit cross with you, Pat." (I didn't know what to say.) "I called your mother and broke our date Tuesday." I was gutted! Because she didn't hear from me about the flowers! I gave my apologies in my best bad fashion. She told me that she had heard I was with Billie Saturday evening. And not a word of thanks from me about the flowers—well, we said goodbye politely—and no doubt both had a more pleasant evening.^{FF}

JUNE 17, 1941

^FYCL kids here last night. Marcella too. Ann, who works at the Bookshop and who likes Mary Sullivan, didn't give her my message Saturday night. That's why Mary Sullivan was furious—not furious, but skeptical! Ann is jealous of me since last Friday. + Went to see Mary Sullivan at 11:30. She admires me like a painting, she said—she doesn't

---

* Pat and Ernst are working from the Parkside Hotel.
† Schrafft's was a restaurant chain where women could lunch and dine alone. There was one in Greenwich Village on the corner of 13th Street and Fifth Avenue.

want to be Billie's rival: "I don't care to toss my hat in the ring." But most importantly: she would be just as happy if she could admire me but not possess me. She wanted to tell me her terms. She brought me home by taxi.[FF]

JUNE 17, 1941

[F]One is always ready to hear a good word about oneself. Mary S. is intelligent—infinitely more intelligent than Billie! She's come up with a fitting image: that B. wants me to be a pretty child, nice to show to others. That B.B. would be just as happy with a Maxwell Parrish* as a Degas. Billie, I've said for months, doesn't bring out the best in me. But it's different with M. She is the world—she has the whole world—and all the energy in the world within her. And she knows it.[FF']

JUNE 18, 1941

Wrote all morning with great difficulty—and little satisfaction. I am doing the tunnel story of Astoria[†]—with social viewpoint on the playgrounds. + Went to school this P.M. and got the shock of my life: D in Logic. My first D of course. Phi Beta Kappa forever goodbye! It upset me terribly. More than I had believed it would. I just make eligibility for *Quarterly* touching the hurdle-bar as I go over.

JUNE 18, 1941

I shed one lone tear in the subway. Could not read for a while. But I suppose the correct way to look at it is that logic, being math, I could never quite touch it. And by the same token it can never quite touch me. I'm terribly sorry about it, though I can hardly say my social whirling of the past semester is responsible.

JUNE 18, 1941

Cralick here tonight. She fooled around with my hair—putting it up. Says my broad jaw is javanese. That I could get a job modeling or better easily. It's a matter of manner and *savoir vivre*, as I knew when I was fifteen. It requires a leisure that I find impossible to effect while going to school. Perhaps I—I will acquire it after school. My life will be a long

---

* A likely reference to Maxfield Parrish (1870–1966), an American painter best known for his painting *Daybreak*, a popular art print.
† Probably in reference to her (lost) story she'll soon try to publish under the title "Train to Astoria."

one. Everything points to that. I'd like to look very nice Friday night at Abbott's* party.

JUNE 19, 1941

Miserable because I keep thinking of my D in Logic. In the catalogue this comes under "poor"—I wonder if I shall have to make it up in summer school? And if the *Quarterly* eligibility is made from this last semester or the whole year? Because I'm 1/10 short for this semester. What a loss of face that would be! + I felt like being very sad this evening and so I was. Wrote a poem which isn't bad called "Mamma Mia, what is mine on earth?" which came to me de profundis! Yes, the Mary S. affection has a strong element of the maternal. Hers too no doubt. It seems to me that perfectly normal women can take their pleasures so by some quirk in the past which has turned them from men: fear of childbirth, domination, love of independence (rare & generally only in butches). + The parents have, I suppose, stopped my allowance entirely. This makes two weeks now! + (They gave me the 5 bucks this morning.)

JUNE 20, 1941

Nice day at Ernst's, tho he had a stroke of the heat or something at 2:00. Entirely mental I'd say. Then home in all the heat and showered, wrote an hour—seems a pitiful little, but two of my best stories were written that way. Thomas Wolfe's book is making a great stamp in my mind. Mother says he was a colossal egotist & that I resemble him in that respect. Egotist, yes, and genius too. It takes a courage neither she nor Stanley can understand to say "For the first time I realized what a gulf separated the Artist from the Man!"[†]

+ Met Mary S. below Abbott's studio. The party was not too exciting. Mary & I alone in the bathroom. She's quite something. Several people kept interrupting us. Abbott pulled the shades down. And we were the absolute last.

---

* Berenice Abbott (1898–1991), American sculptor and photographer. She is best known for her black-and-white series *Changing New York*, which captured the architecture and shifting social landscape of the city during the Great Depression.

† This exclamation of Pat's was probably inspired by Thomas Wolfe's 1929 novel *Look Homeward, Angel*, the coming-of-age story of an artist who assumed he was naturally superior to the mediocrity of the masses.

6/21/41

We like to say it is love we search our whole life long, or we like to say it is Fame. But it is neither. It is understanding. We seek forever one other human heart we can touch and who can touch ours. We seek indefatigably like a hungry animal. For our heart is forever lonely. Forever alone. And wherever we feel this understanding may be, in a young girl, a young boy, a feeble old man, or a crone of a woman, in a drunkard, in a prostitute, in a madman, in a child, there we will go, and nothing in the world can hold us back.

6/21/41

I have never wanted to write as I do now. I have passed through such a hell of falsehood, tears, mockery, synthetic happiness, dreams, desires and disillusionment, of facades of beauty hiding ugliness, of facades of ugliness hiding beauty, of kisses, and of meretricious embraces, of dope and escape. So I want to write. I must write. Because I am a swimmer struggling in a flood, and by my writing I seek a stone to rest on. And if my feet escape it, I go under.

6/21/41

We don't know where creative ideas arise from. I find they come when the conscious mind is occupied with something else. Knitting, piano playing, reading a book so dull one's mind wanders—these are excellent times. Even when we say we create consciously, is it not from some germ we received by these means? Subconscious, or involuntary thinking, is the only and inevitable means of creation.

JUNE 22, 1941

Russia and Germany at War!!! Extremely depressed & tired. I still get a release from crying. I don't think it's weak if you do it alone. What touches me most now is being loved. This one wants more than Fame and Gold: to be loved, to be understood. And so I cry now, because happiness is so close and so almost—realized.

6/22/41

There are some people we like instantly, before they have even had a chance to flatter us (which is the greatest encouragement to liking a person), because they have that quality of seeing in us what we desire to be, what we are trying to be, and of not seeing that which we are at the moment. We feel that they understand us, we begin to feel that we have attained what we desire ourselves to be, and being made happy by this we inevitably are very fond of the people who can make us feel this way.

JUNE 23, 1941

I feel myself filled with ideas. This summer I must get hold of myself—get acquainted with myself, arrive once more at that perfect equilibrium of discipline and nonsense which is my peculiar norm. I want to read a lot of long stuff like Quixote, Dante, Milton.

6/24/41

In my thesis on Christian Science: start with the origin of religion, its gradual clarification and growing specificness, ritualism: how the conception of God grew in men's own minds, how entirely religion is a product of men's minds. And especially, since man is endowed with the most esteemed of all gifts: intellect; especially how much more worthy he is of his kind if he rationalizes and reasons his own destiny! Like how much nobler for man to depend on man alone!

JUNE 25, 1941

Worked pretty well this A.M. 5 pages done on tunnel story. I keep thinking all day at odd times about "straight" fiction I might do and especially about what medium I should use for my cartoons.

JUNE 26, 1941

Very serious & depressed and feeling that nothing I do is important—or ever will be—I have those moments too. I'm ashamed to say seeing a piece of crap in *The New Yorker* cheered me up—Someday I'll click there. Have a splendid idea I'll do next. [Pierre van Paassen's] *Days of Our Years*—beautiful reading. Mature, slow, and brilliant too. Stanley & I discussing the origins of war at dinner: he believes men's "inherent wickedness" responsible for war, and not the machinations of profiteers—(which is now the accepted fact, and is no longer even decried as Marxism!). + With [Billie] this evening. Saw *Citizen Kane*. Incredible maturity of [Orson] Welles!

JUNE 27, 1941

Had a wonderful evening alone before I went to Billie's. Read, wrote a really good first page to my story then went to see Marjorie Wolf* a moment. She has spent a weekend with Babs B. (who just lost a job at

---

* Marjory Wolf was a high school friend of Pat's and Babs B.'s.

Altman's* because her school record was more political than scholastic).
Marjorie had a lovely girl named Michael with her. How does she get
them?! She paints. Then at B.B.'s at 11:00. S., B., Ruth W. Mary R. came
in later. Very nice indeed. (I always thought so.) And to my surprise,
M.S. was won over to Mary R. and away from her darling Ruth W.—all
because Ruth, for some reason, rather snubbed M.R. on taking leave.
How very petty and female all this is! + Home with Mary in taxi. Mary
had not ironed her pajamas lest something go wrong & I not stay!

JUNE 28, 1941

I need not record what happened last night. I'll never forget it. + And
yet—why must I always stand aside and watch myself and others as
though we were on a stage? I shall never become a part of life. I am not
of it—yet. Flowers came at four this P.M. I assured Ernst he would not
be suspected, because who, with a girl in a hotel room all day, would
bother wooing her with gardenias? Ernst of course thinks Mike Thomas†
sends them—as my parents do too. Mary wrote "That such perfect
moments have a price, I know."

JUNE 29, 1941

Turned over my mystery plot in my head all day. Think I have it air-
tight now. A plot grows from a single meager idea, like a tall flowering
from a scrubby little seed. You can't tell where it comes from, but it
comes inevitably like part of nature's plan for the fertility of the earth:
the brain is fertile too. Smoking a trifle too much: maybe fifteen. Why
should I limit myself? I can at least not inhale. But limiting myself is part
of that lousy system of checks that has made my last six years a form of
imprisonment—that has ruined me really. + I feel very affectionate to
Roger lately. I think we'd get along. + Germans report successes, Russians report successes. The Russians, I think, will hold their own, though
no one seems to think so.

JUNE 30, 1941

Another good day. Wonderful summer ahead—wonderful life ahead.
I'm happy—that old seventh of March confidence returning despite
scholastic setbacks.

---

* B. Altman was a prominent New York City department store located on Fifth Avenue at Thirty-Fourth
Street, no longer in existence.
† Mary is using her friend Mike Thomas's name as a cover when sending flowers so as not to get Pat into
trouble.

JULY 2, 1941

So unbearably hot one loses all initiative. My writing and reading goes sliding by—all I do is shower & dress myself & comb my hair in the best 14 Street cutie manner. (Ernst prefers my hair up!) + I think often of how I'll burn up the town when I get out of school. Blitzkrieg on all sorts of things—cartoons, advertising possibly, & a great many lines of writing.

7/2/41

A novel about the twenty-year-olds. Just out of high school, just in college or just out of it. The bewilderment, the discouragement, the groping, the doubt, the hopes, the uncertainty of any permanence whatever. This could have great significance with respect to the times—economic, politic, the war and the knowledge—latent and unconscious, that we ourselves do not govern ourselves, and therefore are at other people's mercy, if any.

JULY 3, 1941

Cooler day. Came home at 4. Billie called me at 7:30. Would I have a drink. Beverly Bar 8:30–10:30. 3 or 4 there. Talking about nothing important. Mary's house packed, and Mary frigid upon my entree with Billie. But furious. Said [Billie] did it on purpose, etc. That everybody had gasped! When we came in. Girl painter named Buffie Johnson* last night. Rather cute & we got along. Buffie gave me her number. Tired.

JULY 4, 1941

Virginia called up at 6:30. Saw her at Jumble, then Tavern, home, Vanguard. She is a beautiful child, intelligent, smart, and very attractive what's more she loves me. Forever. Went to Judy's at 11:00. The show even better. New staff around. + Called Mary to tell her. Delighted. Also got Buffie out of bed at 1:00 AM. She asked me to cocktails tomorrow.

JULY 5, 1941

Worked with Hauser. And had a dreadful conversation about Eddy's & my conversation last night. He thinks I did him irreparable damage when I said he was sitting on the fence in his writing, while I thought this the most charitable thing I could say under the circumstances. Went

---

* Buffie Johnson (1912–2006), American painter associated with surrealism and abstract expressionism. She studied at Académie Julian in Paris (where she also had private lessons with Camille Pissarro and Francis Picabia and met Natalie Barney, Gertrude Stein, and Alice B. Toklas) and at the Art Students League in New York.

to Buffie's at 5:30. Bijou of a place. 159 E. 46 St. She like a little oriental doll—Persia, I guess. And her work all over the walls. I was pleasantly surprised. Somewhat derivative—the Cézanne, Dalí, Chirico, Laurencin, Renoir School, but some portraits have something too. We sat about drinking Scotch & gin, at least twelve inches between us on the couch (how careful when alone!), and talking art. Buffie'd warned me first off that Bernhard was coming at 7:00. Started to go immediately because of [Mary] S. implications, but decided to make it a test case. Bernhard surprised of course. Said she'd have to tell S. because of her loyalty, etc. But later calmed down & agreed not to mention it. Buffie of course amused. She took my hand on coming in, and I had expected more, asked me soon after would I like to see her Monday night. So I went to the Waldorf [Astoria]. Had dinner with S. & Mike, Dean C., John at Le Moal's.* Back to 98 exhausted. I told Mary I was going away with Virginia next weekend, and we still had a pleasant night. Then about 2:00 Mary lit a cigarette and told me she thought we'd better not see each other again. She mainly resented the fact I didn't want people to know how close we were—the fact is I was protecting her from shame as well as me.

JULY 6, 1941

I simply cannot say, at this time, that I care enough about Mary to say I shall see no one else in the world. She cried a lot tonight. She says it's like when she was a child and couldn't get the pony she wanted. So she cried. But only because she was mad. I hope, in the turmoil of all this Bernhard does not tell Mary I was at Buffie's Friday, that would be the *coup de grâce*. I can't say either that I have degenerated in the last few months. Everybody has his fling. Serious people get hurt in them. And the other person, myself, if they happen to be attractive, gets lots of flattering attentions from the serious (or not-serious people) and has a lot of fun. I've tried to do the things as gently as possible with Mary. She's been more than fair with me. What burns me is that she's ready to go off now with someone else. I should be jealous, yes. Because I want my cake & want to eat it too. I wish desperately that I could find it in myself to settle down, love someone steadily, not be greedy—but I cannot.

JULY 6, 1941

I finally understood Mary better. "Loving you less, I would accept you on those terms. But as it is I can't share you." I don't blame her. I'm not

---

* Le Moal was a French restaurant located at Fifty-Sixth Street and Third Avenue.

in love. But I know in the way of intelligence, fidelity, dependability, and intensity, Mary is superior to Virginia. Perhaps I shall live to regret it—breaking with her. I told Mary what I felt about her. "But it wasn't enough." And it wasn't. I'm still having a thing. When I get ready to pick up the pieces, maybe they won't make one complete person in the world. I'll take that chance. When I got home quite late, letter special delivery from Hauser. He says I needn't show up Monday. Since I've been spreading lies about him, we'd better not meet again. I wrote a nice answer. I must say it didn't faze me. My heart is completely torn up with other things now.

JULY 7, 1941

Spent the morning working. These are the days to fulfill "latent potentialities." + Read Van Paassen's *Time Is Now* today. Favors immediate entree [into war]. I do too. In spite of the communist angle that I've been fooling with. Now that Russia is engaged, we should enter immediately.

To Buffie's at 6:30. We had gin & whiskey. There was a cat. And the Rousseau garden. I told her all my troubles. With Mary and Ernst Hauser. Buffie is charmingly naive—after much delay I finally kissed her—on the couch. She makes love like a Frenchman, whispering passionate things in your ear. How she saw me first at the party. I must say she remembers well. I told her very soon though, that I was in no state of mind for a one-night stand. Buffie was awfully disappointed but she is going to call me afterwards. Going to be in the city indefinitely too! So, very drunk indeed, we went to Tony's for a lobster thermidor. By that time it was very late. Went to Spivy's* for night caps. Buffie, like her decadent fascist nobility, is the tail end of an era. A family in her case. She's merely added this *gaieté* to her list of bizarre accomplishments.

7/8/41

Nothing makes a woman, or a man either, watch her personal appearance so much as having enemies. She never knows when or where she will encounter them, but she must always be in top condition.

---

* Spivy (born Bertha Levine, 1906–1971), noted New York wit, entertainer, and actress, owned a nightclub on East Fifty-Seventh Street, Spivy's Roof, noted for its tolerance of gay performers and patrons. In the early 1940s, aged only twenty-one, Liberace was the club's pianist.

JULY 10, 1941

Buffie should send me a postcard. Hope she does. I keep thinking about
her. I'm at loose ends and I might as well admit it. If I only had one
good recognizably lousy impulse to fight!!! But no—not even that! At
least I might prove myself decent. Was with Arthur tonight. Took a
Staten Island ferry & walked our heads off out there. He says, when I
refused to kiss him, that I'm always psychologically unready but often
physically ready. What an observant lad—if he'd only go a bit further
now!—

JULY 13, 1941

Entirely too beachy and housey to suit me but Virginia likes it. There
was a knocking at our door last night—Virginia nearly hit the ceiling &
clung to me like a wisteria vine. It turned out to be a child. I thought it
would be one of those things—"Why so-an-so's been dead five years!"
Took an enormous hike. Made a sketch or two on a hillside where we
ate lunch. Had a wonderful day. I didn't make any passes at Virginia.
Wouldn't have even with liquor, I think, because, frankly, I can't even
think of anyone but Buffie.

JULY 14, 1941

I'm so happy when I'm alone. I see all sorts of things and get wonderful
ideas. I get to the bottom of myself. Don't know if it's the extra sleep
or Jenning's shots, but I feel full of energy & ideas. Should like to do a
novel. Something brilliant of course. Have two possible ideas that need
expansion & thought. Now [Thomas] Mann's *Death in Venice* is considered brilliant. Anybody can be so with a bizarre idea and a capacity for
smooth writing. The expansion of a novel is appealing to me. But in spite
of my past critical reading, I should think more about plot & action. +
Came home at nine. Looked for want-ad job. Frankly I want the money,
but I'd rather not work this summer, anymore. Could accomplish more
at home. + Virginia thinks I shall be famous. "Would you keep me when
you get famous, Pat?" I said perhaps, if she puts on twenty pounds, and
mends her nasty ways.

JULY 15, 1941

Called Mary S. for date this evening. Ate a lot & finally went home with
her which I wanted to do anyway. I just felt like lying in bed, talking &
doing nothing. But Bernhard, at Mary's gentle hint, came down & gave
us her room. So the whole business. She keeps trying to wean me from

my customary habits. Maddens me in a peculiar way. Says I might be as butch as she and just get pleasure making love. Mary can't stand to be touched herself. We spoke more frankly last night than ever before. Because it was the last time. After all my mind's on Buffie now. And that doesn't mean a great deal to me. I still have not felt the variety. There is still only "me" when it happens.

JULY 16, 1941

Sent "Vacant Lot" and "Train to Astoria"* to *Story* [magazine] also *New Yorker.* + Mary sent flowers. Had a dreadful time at Dr D.'s. He hurt like hell! I can't decide whether I'm in love with Buffie or her painting. I have a boundless admiration for anyone who can do what she does. + Started methodical reading. *War & Peace.* Mont Saint-Michel & Chartres. Survey of English Lit 1700. + Babs B. told me Monday night that Rose M. said she knew about my "women friends." That it seemed to be common knowledge.

JULY 17, 1941

Very happy indeed—and fighting pleasantly against that jag—those delirium tremens that attack me when I have a date on with people like Buffie. Tried to call Mary S. today. I want to tell her I am with Buffie tomorrow so she won't get heart failure as we walk into the Caravan. Also so she won't send flowers. + Saw some excellent exhibits with Mother this PM, Waldo Peirce's *Alzira & Anna*† is splendid! But much like Renoir. Also a good drawing by Picasso which was worth all the rest. I wonder do we always not admire the kind of thing we come nearest doing ourselves?

7/17/41

Why do I always run to morbid subjects!

JULY 18, 1941

This day is momentous for one circumstance: Buffie is off my chest. We sat around till ten thirty. Very pleasant and warm indeed. But why do I lose interest having once got something? And what do I want? Somebody I think younger than I. But definitely someone when I can be respected for my work. I see now how that enters in. It's always present. Otherwise

---

* Neither of those stories has survived.
† Waldo Peirce (1884–1970), painter often called "the American Renoir."

I might just as well be sleeping with a man. I must be head of the partner-ship. I think Buffie is quite serious. She must be about thirty-three. The damned cat stalks about constantly.

JULY 19, 1941

Decided yesterday at 4:30 that I am to go to California with John Coates before the 31st.* + Worked revising this morning. Not too enthusiasti-cally about it tho I do take some pride in "How to write" for the "sleeks." Met Buffie at 1:00 Luncheon at [Hotel] Pierre's. Veddyveddy elegant. Then to Fanny M., girl my age who paints. Drinks. Then to Lola P.'s where I had one of the best evenings, or party evenings, of my life. Very quiet. Only Lola P., Buffie, Rosalind Constable & myself. Haphazard dinner followed by white wine, drunken in boredom at first and later with great enthusiasm. Had delightful conversation with Rosalind. She's on *Vogue* & *Fortune*. Long blond hair & English accent but looks Nor-wegian and she & Lola P. are falling all over themselves to introduce me to Editors, etc. Lola P. is—why describe them?—I shall be seeing them more often, I hope. Got Rosalind's phone number & shall call her before I leave. We got on famously. A lot of bullshit, getting on a magazine. Pull and personality, she says. She got hers on her accent!

JULY 21, 1941

Read some in an unhappy disjointed sort of way. Got slicked up to go to Constable's at 6:30. I called her last night during the party 12:30 AM. She was delighted or seemed so. Lives 667 Madison. Her roommate Natasha [H.] is in New Mexico at Ruth W.'s ranch. We drank & played records. Finally went out to Sammy's.† + Thence to Au Petit Paris.‡ Nice meal & I got very high at one point. Rosalind has a wonderful mouth. Clean, young, and looks like she laughs a lot, which she does. So at 2:00 when I was about to leave, and could easily have done so, she said I should stay because of the hour. She felt like being a cautious mother that night. And indeed she was. She's so wonderfully well-hearted about it all. I slept in her room-mates bed & room. She joined me for a few minutes. We both were kidding around & laughing a lot. Then she left & we slept for a few

---

* That summer, Pat drives across the country to California with her uncle John and aunt Grace.
† The New York institution Sammy's Bowery Follies was a notorious location at 267 Bowery that attracted a mixed and colorful crowd thanks to its cabaret license.
‡ Léon Gerber, a former pastry chef at the Ritz Hotel in Paris, purchased the old Madison Tavern in 1939 and reopened it as Le Petit Paris in 1945.

hours. She has a good portrait of herself by Nelson* in her room. Somewhat like Modigliani.

JULY 22, 1941

We woke at quarter to eight & lay talking the rest of the time. Very very
casual, superior about it all. Thinks I'm surely older, and considers me
probably a somewhat precocious & blatant child. She's got the most
intelligent looking face I've seen outside of Virginia Woolf. Had breakfast & I called Buffie & had an interminable conversation. Walked Rosalind down to Radio City. "You'll be leaving now—I shan't know ever
where to find you again." I gave her reassurance. She's attracted and at
the same time has her tongue in her cheek. I think she's tied up with a
painter who's "coming to live there in September."

JULY 23, 1941

Spent this night with Buffie as I knew I would. Arrived about five—she
gave me a gorgeous pair of cufflinks—gold with a brown stone. Rather
large. Then we picked up Irving D. & Billy Somebody & went to Spivy's
anniversary party. Then home. I'm not in love. Can't even say I wish I
were. Buffie is so damned "bandbox," as Constable so aptly put it.

JULY 24, 1941

Home & restless. Walked a lot. Walter Marlowe came at six. We
couldn't swim where we wanted to. Upstate a ways. Dinner at Fleur de
Lis. His place is really charming. He's done so much with it. A remarkable man. Somewhat of an inferiority complex with women because of
his height & hair. But he's the kind of man I'd marry. + Called Rosalind
at dinner. She thought I'd gone & was pleasantly surprised. She says
it's a good thing I'm leaving because she's too "enthusiastic." I'm sincerely fond of her. Not like I was about Billie. Constable is an admirable
person. And honorable. And intelligent. I wonder if she's the next step
towards a man?

JULY 24, 1941

Enjoyed this last evening with Walter Marlowe so much. He's so wonderfully thoughtful—he makes me feel quite sluggish and careless intellectually. Because his thinking is so rich. It is the most amusing task in

---

* Probably the abstract expressionst painter Leonard Nelson (1912–1993), whose art was exhibited
among others at Betty Parsons's gallery and at Peggy Guggenheim's Art of This Century.

the world—the unraveling of an idea—or the pursuit of an answer. He is what I demand most—an inspiration: because my whole preferences in people are based upon—subconsciously and consciously—a furtherance of my terrific ambitions.

JULY 24, 1941

I should feel so much today that I don't. What will it take & when will it come? I feel a transitory state—because I'm not working regularly & smoking too much. Buffie says she adores me. And I believe her. And how terrible it will be if I suddenly discover my heart is definitely some-place else!? She is so good to me—so thoughtful. And I am absolutely tongue-tied around her. The nice things I think of—that I could say—I can't. I feel shy. Don't know why—perhaps they don't burst out of me. And they really should.

JULY 25, 1941

To Constable's at 5:30. Called for her Reception room on 30th floor. She on the 26. She was very nice to me. We taxied to her place & had two quick drinks. There is so much laughter & so much brains. I believe I'm in love—I didn't need to say believe, but I know it will have to come this way—because now I'm no longer carried off by a stupid pretty face. Kissed me several times. I hate to think of myself as a clever little mon-key showing off for her benefit. There's been too much of that.

JULY 26, 1941

Caught the bus at 10:50 last evening. Graham along to see me off. Hot tiresome trip. I feel blue. Thinking constantly of Rosalind & not at all of Buffie. I am an ungrateful fickle little bastard. It's so much fun to ride along, letting one's mind build things like an Erector Set, and being quite alone as the miles go past, enjoying cigarettes & coffee, and thinking of possible stories, and of Rosalind, and of the busy, active, amusing, and wild life before me—not only next semester, when I shall work like hell, but for all time. I have a great destiny before me—a world of pleasures and accomplishments, beauty and love.

JULY 27, 1941

Saw Chicago this morning. A splendid exhibit at the Chicago Museum of Art. Carl Milles* & International Water Color Show. Still got my mind

---

* Carl Milles, a Swedish sculptor best known for his fountains.

on Rosalind. Buffie is too young for me—not young enough to dominate as I did Virginia, but too giddy and feminine to dominate me. So I lay on my stomach in the park, waiting for the Museum to open, & wrote to Rosalind. Told her I thought I was in love with her, but that I soon blew over, & not to bother. (the hell she won't!) And would she please write to me at Sioux Falls. She'd better!

JULY 28, 1941

We keep stopping at tiny towns—the people all eating heartily. Some sick. And more interesting. After seeing some of the sections I wonder why anyone lives anywhere but N.Y.C. After seeing some of the people, I'm very glad they do.

   In Sioux City for five hours. Went to the library & read Powys' *Meaning of Culture.* Very good & calming. Finally got to Sioux Falls at 3:45, just about at the end of my rope physically. Filthy, dirty. John is preoccupied with his school & Grace is her same stupid self. I'm in a tiny room with one window & no breeze. Temp. nearly 100°. This town is incredibly small. + Don't feel in the least like writing to Buffie. Wonder how I shall go about breaking off—and if she will ever guess it is Rosalind? And if she does, will I lose her friendship entirely? But Rosalind, I gather, is inextricably obligated. I shan't mind—I worship her anyway. God if she only writes me & doesn't worry that my uncle will open them! + S. sent me gardenias the day I left. They were more beautiful than ever.

7/29/41

What I admire most in an individual is a kind of activity—a liveliness either of mind or body or both—which alone can assure the development of the character I prefer. I believe liveliness and animal energy are the sine qua nons.

JULY 30, 1941

Wonderful how reading good prose all day stimulates one's imagination. One even thinks in good English. Had a stupid conversation with Grace on Socialism. She has read nothing, and would not have the mind to assimilate if she had. After a hamburger & a walk returned & found an airmail from Rosalind. I flew up the stairs. One slender page—but what a kiss from her lips. "Darling" but no acknowledgments. A superficial, intellectual style of brilliant writing. Much like her conversation. Plethora of peculiar words. I had written her modestly—4 pages an hour before—and I wrote her again. I think I'm in love, the kind of intellectual, unpassionate love that I shall, I suppose, always give.

7/30/41

The perversity in human nature reaches a peak in the sexual compartments. If one's love affair is running smoothly and a new face appears, which will necessitate an unreasonable amount of trouble and disruption, and delay and unhappiness to attain, one will make for this new face like a man wandering on a desert will make for a distant sign of habitation he has just spied.

JULY 31, 1941

A final pleasant day in the library. No letter from Rosalind though she might have. In my excitement (at leaving tonight) I wrote her again—this time—that I worshipped her—which I do goddamn it. I speculate about what course I might have taken—to be aloof—to have gone without telephoning her, to have disappeared for a summer and to return and find her in love with me. The game would decidedly have been worth the candle. But I, I'm afraid, am not up to the game. I must blurt out all that I feel, with the consolation that, whatever the results, I have been I, and I am that I am. Rosalind, bless her heart, seems to like me as I am. Bought some wonderful blue sneakers this PM. And in those and my gray flannels, we embarked from Sioux Falls.

AUGUST 1, 1941

Tonight at ten thirty-five. A glorious, wild, and fast ride forty miles due west without a turn in the road. Through the blackness, under a half moon. With only the radio playing poor jazz to spoil the romance of it. It was a wonderful experience. Full of promise, expectation, happiness. And—love—to come, ecstasy and success, reward and affection. And my own dreams of no one and nothing except Rosalind.

AUGUST 1, 1941

John and I get up in the mornings, go down and have a good breakfast and then start out. Saw the Rushmore (Borglum) monument* this afternoon. As art it is beyond consideration—as a monument it is an insult to the majesty of the mountains. Stopped rather early at Gillette, Wyoming,

---

* The Mount Rushmore National Memorial in South Dakota was created between 1927 and 1941 by Gutzon Borglum.

and I walked way out in the prairie, only afraid, not of being raped but being robbed, since I had my wallet with me.

AUGUST 2, 1941

Crossed the badlands yesterday, and the Rockies today—ending up at Cody, Wyoming, at 5 o'clock, since there is nothing around the Yellowstone Park. Saw the nightly rodeo here. Local talent—one lad was stomped on in the bareback riding. Rope tricks by Pat Henry, and good showmanship. I spent a lovely hour choosing meticulously one tan cowboy belt I bought from Dave Jones $1.95. The thing, however, came from Ft. Worth Texas. The day was wonderful. Cody is 5,000 feet high. The night cool, I walked into the hills, supper alone at Cowhand café after John & Grace had gone to bed. Cowboys all around. $7.50 shirts and $7.50 Stetsons, and in my happiness I had to write to Rosalind. We shall be in Frisco Tuesday.

AUGUST 3, 1941

Tough day driving. Not enough sleep. Beautiful scenery, canyons and mountains. "Laughing Pig" and "Elephant Head." The more I see of the country, the more faces I see, the more I know there is one home and one face. No home, really, because home is your lover's heart, nowhere on the earth. This evening after a dinner we had a memorable conversation from ten to one when we got to Elko, Nevada. About Socialism first. John doesn't scruple to call Browder an S.O.B., which I should not do to F.D.R. But Grace on one of her tangents told me off about my Communist manners, etc. How I put my foot on the dash, and vote where I want to go, and don't carry out responsibilities about the thermos, etc. I find it hard to argue with them. Each is adamant and unread. And each seems to attack me personally which can make things unpleasant as hell.

AUGUST 4, 1941

Grace last night mentioned that John was giving up business because he didn't want to disappoint me about the trip. Just why this should be so, I don't know because I felt him out most tactfully before deciding. John was quite uncomfortable when that conversation was taking place last night. They were right, of course. I have an arrogance that I shall never lose—that I really don't want to entirely. I should try to be more polite but the hard "knocks" accruing from my native rudeness, I take as the husk around the kernel.

Drove some today; over 100 miles. I don't jerk the wheel as most women do. John was very pleased. Got into Nevada (Reno) in no time at all. Wide-open town. Business booming because of raised prices on cattle and minerals. Everybody's gambling. Got quite merry, on two gin rickeys. I think of Rosalind—I can see her smile in the dark. Lost $1.00 at roulette.

AUGUST 5, 1941

I drove today part way from Reno to Sacramento. Made excellent time and landed in San Francisco at 2:30. The city is all sprawled out & very hilly—the way cities in the west sprawl when they grow instead of growing upward as New York had to—so you have these suburbs practically that take 5 miles and a horse to get to. We established ourselves in Geary St. and I called Rita. I went out on the 6:00 bus. They live in a lovely home 25 rooms. Rented partly. We had dinner & then tramped around. She's a smart kid, with that New York tenseness which is the blessed heritage of the place—that won't let its children rest.

AUGUST 6, 1941

Rita handicapped because of being Jewish in getting a magazine job. Perhaps if I looked like [her] or like Babs B., I should be a martyr to the cause, too. But life is too pleasant now. + All the gay people, it seems, are in L.A.—S.F. is extremely conservative. Must get there. Rita and her sister both expressed their belief that I shall "become a writer." Mainly on account of my "drive."

AUGUST 7, 1941

No letter, no letter, no letter! Is there anything in the world more desolate— Tomorrow surely! What is she thinking about, I wonder. And how often does she think of me, and with what sudden consciousness, I wonder.

8/7/41

Sex, to me, should be a religion. I have no other. I feel no other urge, to devotion, to something, and we all need a devotion to something besides ourselves, besides even our noblest ambitions. I could be content without fulfillment. Perhaps I should be better off in such an arrangement.

8/7/41

A woman is never, or very seldom, hopelessly in love with one man. She can make a calm choice between the man with the money and the man without, the better father and the bad father, who may be handsomer. The woman, because, chiefly because, she has less imagination, has less passion. She brings less, and she takes less.

AUGUST 8, 1941

Decided to go *tout de suite* to Los Angeles as John may be leaving Tuesday for Denver. Was to go tonight but called Rita and there was a letter—from Rosalind of course—and wild horses could not have torn me away without it. Went out, a bit ginny, after dinner. I read it. Non-committal until the last page. "What can I ever give you to keep you in my life? You will go in so many directions. The most I can hope for is that you will come to me when you are tired. Perhaps." And of course, I sat up till two writing to her. What can she give me? Everything. What will she? Everything in one way. Nothing in another. I shan't mind.

AUGUST 9, 1941

Boarded the train at 8:00 AM. Borrowed $15.00 from John. Not such a fast train, but we got to Los Angeles at 5:30. Established myself at the Hotel Bertha & sent a letter to mother immediately saying please don't make me go to Denver, Colorado. I want a verificatory wire by Monday night. I saw the Moon Festival in Chinatown.

AUGUST 10, 1941

Lonely last night. But it's wonderful just to think of Rosalind. Dressed nicely for the Countess. She was glad to see a friend of Constable's, but she was moving. Tomorrow at 6:00 AM. The Countess (Marta) is about 45, blonde-gray, enormous, hard living & drinking. We had a hasty dinner at Brown Derby* which the Countess paid for. Afterwards I wrote Rosalind which is becoming a daily ritual with me. Marta said Rosalind had her first book published when she was sixteen and that she wished she'd find a man to marry because she thinks that's what she wants—(I don't). The Countess asked me point blank if I was in love with Rosalind and treated it with amused tolerance, which I think she really feels. Little interest in the boudoir—well, she's had her day, I suspect. Bought [D. H. Lawrence's] *Lady Chatterley's Lover* .75.

---

* The Brown Derby was a famous Hollywood restaurant with a clientele composed largely of celebrities.

AUGUST 11, 1941

Walked around Chinatown & had some wonderful tortillas & milk (6$!)
+ caught the noon Daylight out of L.A. 40 minutes late. I can think wonderful thoughts while traveling—not concentrating on it, but just as they
emerge from the under-consciousness which is how they must always
come anyway. Arrived at 10:45. Letters from Mother. One surprised no
end that I need money & with $10.00. Wait till they have read my letter
of yesterday morning asking for $30.00! I'm still $5.00 in the hole with
John & broke stony, too. John intends to leave Wed. God if I have to go!

AUGUST 12, 1941

We made a day of it and went to Twin Peaks, where I was the highest
person in San Francisco for a while. Then to a redwood forest and to
San Rafael for an enormous 3 o'clock fish dinner. I didn't want to go to
Denver. I shall have to, because there's no excuse. I'm restless over something.—Would I be more satisfied in N.Y.? I doubt it. I should see Rosalind, but that would only remind me more vividly of what I can't have.
And I should have my all-soothing routine. Yes, I should be happier.

AUGUST 13, 1941

Eureka, Nevada.

   Left S.F. at eight. I wonder under what circumstances I shall next
see it. And with whom. + John let me drive some 70 miles today. Great
fun. Long stretches without towns. All mining around here. The stars
were lovely tonight. What I think of constantly is of making something
of myself—a good job and good living on the side. Something to make
[Rosalind] respect me and take notice of me as something besides an
attractive and precocious child. As a matter of fact, compared to her, I'm
not. Thus women have been, and will always be, the inspiration of all the
best in the world. A man goes to his soul and to the universe, creating
and building, inventing and discovering, only to lay it, or its rewards, at
the feet of some woman.

AUGUST 15, 1941

It's an odd thing, I can't remember Buffie's telephone number, but I can
both of Rosalind's. One up for Herr Freud. Little library where I read
for an hour or so. [Sir James] Jeans, [Irwin] Edman, criticism. Then
back down the lovely mile outside of town.Very, very happy and full of
thwarted ambition—I want to sit down at a typewriter in a room all

alone. I want long days to mull over what I've seen, silent hours to dream out stories that are as delicate, in the first plot germs, as smoke rings. And long evenings, which will be fewer now, I imagine, with Rosalind. Sometimes it's better, however, with a group of people. I've often found it so. We like each other better then. + Played with the animals this morning. Two bouncing dogs with a deer's foot, horses standing in a stream, a black kitten, and two calves. + Wrote Countess Marquiset. A rather conceited letter, saying if she mentioned that about the waitresses in the B. Derby, I'd mail her a time bomb.

AUGUST 16, 1941

Got into Denver, Colorado, at 11. Very pretty town. T.B. cases all over because of the altitude. Read T. S. Eliot this afternoon. He's a splendid poet and a good critic too.

8/16/41

Denver, Colorado.

The few hours I have spent with you—that I have ever spent with you—I can at least amuse myself reliving, over and over again, like a favorite book that one reads a dozen times, each rereading yielding a new emotion, a different thrill. The words of a book are always the same, just as the things we did are always the same. But in the formless, wordless land of imagination, where our short hours are, I can embellish and recolor and project. Outside my window, someplace, they are singing the "Lorelei." *"Ich weiss nicht, was soll es bedeuten, dass ich so traurig bin—"*

AUGUST 17, 1941

A rare day. Breakfasted with John. He's one of those men who govern their womenfolks about when to sit down and when to leave. Bad manners. + Roamed about the city visiting museums, etc. Some good stuff from Mesa Verde. Fossils and mummies and skulls. Read first volume of Stendhal's *Le Rouge et le Noir*. Hearty breakfast, hamburger for lunch and dinner at the Blue Parrot Inn. Apparently, I'm burning it up. Go to bed hungry every night wake up ravenous. I wish it were tomorrow already. I want my mail.

---

* "I don't know what it can mean / that I am so sad . . ." The opening lines of one of Heinrich Heine's most famous poems and which has been set to music by different composers.

AUGUST 18, 1941

Raced down to the post-office before breakfast. But no mail. How alone and neglected it makes one feel! Want to read the *Divine Comedy* while here. However most important is browsing. At the P.O. at 3:30. Letters from mother, with 30 dollars, J. B., Roger, etc. + If it is wonderful to love a woman (the parts of her sweet, irresponsible ways) how much more wonderful to love a woman with a power and will like Rosalind's. How much more challenging she is.

AUGUST 19, 1941

A stinking lousy day. I am up to the neck in scenery! Insupportably boring! Especially when we had to wait 1½ hrs. at the near top of Mt. Evans. A sillier, less pleasant way to ruin a car I can't imagine. How I wished I could have been in the library, finishing [Malcolm Cowley's] *After the Genteel Tradition.*

AUGUST 20, 1941

Somewhat better because we came home early. Saw the Garden of the Gods and such rot. Mushroom rocks the best. Some snaps. Seeing all these peaks and "gorgeous gorges" is a mild form of insanity. John and Grace have to get at least ½ way up every hill they see. The most "gorgeous gorges" are those they do in restaurants.

AUGUST 21, 1941

We shall leave Saturday morning. I'm happy! Chicago—then home! Breakfasted with John & Grace. Library at 10:30. A typical Denver day. Went for mail at one. A letter from Buffie. A dread of opening it and seeing her writing. Whether she still cared. Hoping she did for my ego's sake, for the desire one has always—to be loved—but mainly hoping she did not. Bought Buffie the lucite and gold leaf stone. $5.50. Useless like so many things she likes.

8/21/41

This summer I have climbed, like a struggling Junebug on a fluted lamppost, to a higher ledge. A kind of higher standard, but above all a new hope and confidence. I intend to stay here. Right here and beyond.

8/22/41

It's strange the older I get, the less respect I have for so-called logical thinking. Thinking is creative, and we create subconsciously—in flashes.

When one has a problem to work out—a problem of one's own relations with others, one can seldom arrive at anything by an "assembly of facts." Perhaps after one has dropped the matter—minutes later, there will be a sudden insight, often in a projected imaginary situation which will come or might come—and one will never get closer to the truth than this one flash. We cannot even push the flash further.

AUGUST 23, 1941

Packed this AM. Caught the 1:00 Rocket from Denver. I thought about R. during the train ride and while I was reading [Émile Zola's] *Nana* inattentively. And also about Buffie. Dante had his unrequited love for Beatrice and he had a wife, too. I simply prefer my Beatrice. She is beauty, goodness and intelligence. She is man's striving on the earth. She is a bit of heaven I've been lucky enough to find. How could I ever leave her? And what would I not give up for her! I am leaving the bad for the good. The evil for the pure. And if I ever think this an extravagance, God damn me!

8/23/41

A very small number of people are conscious of their individuality and live always to develop it and to excel. The vast majority try desperately hard to show, in everyway, that they are exactly like everyone else. This gives them a kind of security and self-assurance and contentment.

AUGUST 26, 1941

Very eager to get home. Tired, of course very tired, but happy too. *Wie schön ist die Heimat!** "Und kennst du das Land, wo die Citrönen bluhn? (auf Säulen rüht sein Dach!)"† Sat about talking. I told almost all, I think. Good to see a couple of intelligent faces. Then I called R. around eleven. She was in bed, knitting, having just flown in from Washington. She knew my voice. Her laugh was the same—only so much more wonderful than I could imagine. Shan't tell Buffie I'm in town until after I see R. Should be sober when I speak to B., I suppose. Though it's not the easiest way. + I want to do so much. The one moment of discouragement and doubt comes before all one's things are put away again, when one sees all the old books and thinks that one has read them all and how little one knows anyway, when one sees unfin-

---

* How beautiful is home!
† Excerpts from Goethe's poem "Mignon": "Do you know the land where the lemon-trees bloom . . ."

ished manuscripts and thinks of the labors ahead. I am aiming higher than ever before. God or something give me courage, and power!

AUGUST 27, 1941

R. has been (and is) a wonderful influence on me. I have no desire to mix with [Buffie] or Mary S. or [Billie] the way I was doing. I prefer to stay at home nights. I wonder how long this will last? Yet I am not so cold-blooded as I was. Not since Virginia.

8/27/41

I wish I might write music from twenty to thirty, books from thirty to forty, and paint from fifty to sixty, and perhaps, while I could still wield a mallet, sculpt from forty to fifty.

8/27/41

We live in flashes, like as we think and create in flashes. Possibly the only other times we live is in anticipation. By living here I mean any enjoyment. In my trip to California, I enjoyed very little in the anticipation except the passive excitement. But the moments I shall always treasure were the ride west in the night from Sioux Falls, South Dakota, and the walk in Chamberlain the same night, and hearing Beethoven's Fifth in the middle of the desert in the hours before midnight, and the wonderful letter from Rosalind in South Dakota—reading it, and thinking of it that night as I fell asleep, and the instant when I felt all at once the spirit of the circus in Denver as I watched the percheron horses pulling against their collars (big black heavy leather studded with gold). There was no enjoyment in the keener sense in seeing canyons or mountains too long approached, or seeing the "pièce de resistance," San Francisco from the Twin Peaks. The less happy moments, too, somehow one would not exchange. Whether for curiosity or simple love of emotion, I don't know. There is the deepest sadness in the world in not receiving a letter from someone we love. I felt this. And I have felt, too, the peculiar discomfort and fear when I have received a letter from a person whom one no longer wants. But being in love, unlike all other experiences, visual, physical or mental, is a constant pleasure. Alone or together two people in love are happy. In a sense they are always together, and alone, too. Love is a thing you can have in your pocket.

AUGUST 28, 1941

Worked this AM. Letters from Buffie, against my 31st arrival. My mother likes her handwriting. She is steady. But I simply don't care for her. + Sold some books & went shopping, rather nervously with Mother. + Chez Rosalind's at 7:07, after a drink on myself. Billie A. was there. Gave R. the ice freezers and the record, which she hardly attended because she's tense about her deadline tomorrow night. I wonder shall I grow tired of this arrangement, or have I become so ascetic that I shall find the restraint exhilarating and inspirational? It had better be so. I saw a picture of Betty Parsons,* the painter, who is coming to live with R. Very cute, young, nice forehead. "I chose," says R. She had nothing forced upon her. I didn't kiss her. We lay—or sat—on the couch before driving down to Nino & Nella's for dinner. Then to Jumble Shop. Drove home with R. against her protestations. I merely enjoy breathing the same air for a while. As I say. I can't imagine changing from her. Not her!

AUGUST 29, 1941

Wrote the *Quarterly* booklet. Not bad. And cracky, I hope. It seems everybody is out of town. + Read [Carson McCullers's] *Reflections in a Golden Eye*. Not good at all. + Saw Rogers (Ginger) picture which stank. + Called Rosalind who was out at 11:05 and abed at 11:45. Natasha had to hang up from her room. Rosalind very nice to me. She's giving me a lot of time. Such things as this can be very flattering, I know—and not boring unless one becomes dog-like, which I shall never do. What shall I do? Make myself as amusing as possible, and work like mad to be something.

8/30/41

Sex and alcohol I refute thus: alcohol is not worth its price—as a habitual source of pleasure and inspiration. And sex is a hoax. As big a hoax as a Coney Island sideshow. And as overrated as a trip to Pike's Peak. Marriage is like going back to the same sideshow twice, a moronic thing to do certainly. For women, it is even worse, because they come out on the short end.

---

* Betty Parsons studied painting in Paris, where her circle of friends included Man Ray and Alexander Calder as well as Gertrude Stein and Sylvia Beach. One of her fellow students was Alberto Giacometti. In 1948 she would open her own gallery on Fifty-Seventh Street. She is considered the "mother of abstract expressionism," having represented artists including Jackson Pollock, Mark Rothko, Clyfford Still, Barnett Newman, Hans Hofmann, and Ad Reinhardt.

SEPTEMBER 1, 1941

Sent folder to Comet Press.* A good morning's work rewriting first draft. Three mornings on a 10-page job is not too bad. I thought of my poor Rosalind working perhaps all day. I wonder if her husband is still in love with her. Or if he ever was? Probably not. Damned if he isn't gay. Shall call Buffie tomorrow. I don't like to remember those times when calling her—even the anticipation of it—was a delight. Now I've become so skeptical, I try to choose the faults of anyone I am in love with—with Rosalind it could only be her cynicism. At least this is not a thing like B. [Billie] B.'s stupidity or B. [Buffie]'s fussiness—a thing that could make one wince upon recollection. No I think I have my gimlet eyes open. + Proust is a delight and an inspiration. Perhaps one should reread him every three years.

SEPTEMBER 2, 1941

Rosalind called me Darling today, so there is little more I have to say about this Tuesday. I finished my story, called Buffie (it preyed on my mind horribly) at 10. Called Mary S. and saw her tonight. We had drinks at Rochambeau's.† I told M. how I felt about R. Also that Janet Flanner‡ & Betty P. & the whole bunch are gay, and that they've had their fling and so can now be quite "honorable" because they are tired out physically. If I had more room I'd say it more beautifully.

SEPTEMBER 4, 1941

When mornings begin with rejection slips and end with lectures on four-year-old diets, life begins to be a burden. At least around here. There comes a time, I always say, and all these times seem to come at twenty, when one no longer wants to live at home. Real independence seems attractive. At the same time mother says I never was so young. It's rather confusing. I never was so tense and restless about the house. Now Dr. S.L. is giving new trouble about my Ca [calcium] deficiency. It will necessitate an inlay, which is expensive. + Am working on my gray flannels thing now. Seven pages. Should be fine. I filed all my manuscripts today. What's the trouble with my stuff is no action. My best stories have the most action and are the least labored. Here is my clear lesson.

---

* Comet Press in Brooklyn, where the *Barnard Quarterly* is printed.
† Rochambeau's, a restaurant located at 28 West Eleventh Street.
‡ Janet Flanner, noted freelance writer and journalist based in Paris, who for many years contributed to *The New Yorker* under the pseudonym Genet.

SEPTEMBER 5, 1941

Mother very depressed, and calling me a bastard practically, and contemplating my removal from school. + Date with Virginia & lovely evening. Rode the bus down. Jumble Shop drinks, where I told her in cold sobriety, all about Rosalind, and even showed her the letter, after deliberation. Then to the Caravan. + Then I called Rosalind, my business call about the French men's shop Hermès in Rue de Rivoli, she said. And said she loved my letter & thought the sketch "enchanting" though not flattering, and that she would be seeing a lot more of me, and what about some night next week to meet Betty & Natasha?

SEPTEMBER 6, 1941

Spoke with Dr. S.L. this A.M. with Mother. $15.00 per inlay and 3 of those. Every time I think of [Rosalind] I feel happy. Stanley and mother however tie up my present friends with my past and present extremist conduct. That I have not come down to earth etc. It is a matter of touching something else. Perhaps in their sense I shall never touch earth. This is not I. Nor my genius of person. We are different. + Started the autobiography of Alice B. Toklas [by Gertrude Stein] this eve. Superb writing. I have turned a new leaf in writing. Only stories with real people & plot & action from now on. I thought out a real plot for amusement while out taking a walk. And afterwards even the people looked different on the streets. I felt more of them. Too much of my stuff is cynical and sarcastic.

SEPTEMBER 8, 1941

In a way I do not feel so sad about B. & R. Living with someone you love is so disillusioning. And the element of change—restlessness—in all of us—is on my side at least. + *The New Yorker* would take the slacks story from Hellman.* Wish there were another similar market; but no. Played the piano loud & rather well. + A meeting this evening of the League. I feel uncomfortable with them and useless, because now we are all supposed to be collecting money. I wonder if I should tell them I am a degenerate & be expelled? Called Buffie afterwards at 12:00 sharp. Very short & sweet & would I see her tomorrow? Yes. I shan't tell her, I think, about the other one. But how do I know what I'll say?

---

* Lillian Hellman (1905–1984), American playwright and memoirist.

SEPTEMBER 9, 1941

The Russians & British alternate nights bombing Berlin. The people are going mad, because Göring told them it was impregnable! + Buffie called twice. We arranged a date. Drank three gin rickeys before our rendezvous at [Grand] Ticino's.* (Before that I had been to Dr. S.L.— with Novocaine and read a delightful Bemelmans [book] in the Jumble Shop alone. He's a genius of his own type.) Buffie was late. I was high. She wouldn't eat or drink or smoke at Ticino's. Thence to the Brevoort,† & stinking, expensive dinner, at the end of which I told her. She was quiet, quite unshocked, the way I suppose any properly controlled person would be. No names mentioned, tho I did tell her I was in love. Then in a cab to her house where I put her to bed and filled her hot water bottle. She's doing a silkscreen thing now that I don't like. She was the same as ever. Wants me to call her soon.

SEPTEMBER 10, 1941

A dreadful day because Mother fussing. She is so bitter & so vague— and I am so self-righteous & so vague—she has brought on herself all that I am—I as an individual contribute little. Children's and adolescents' emotions are, I believe, constructive and optimistic. Any deviation is conditioned. + My story is progressing & at Rosalind's at seven. Mrs. Betty Parsons there & another of whom I was terrified until I found her talking of art and saw she knew nothing. Betty is older than Rosalind. Charming, intense, serious & thin. Is managing an art gallery now. Her watercolors are bold and rather good. We danced some and drank a lot. I suppose Rosalind could be very happy with Betty without much trouble. Saw Rosalind Webster's book: "Paddle"‡ clever. Quick. For 1927 I suppose quite daring. But the writing shows great immaturity. British upper class taken off rather wittily.

SEPTEMBER 11, 1941

I can see no one but Rosalind. As I have said before, I shall go with many others, just to keep myself from stagnating—so keep her amused when I am 30 and she 44. But I adore her. And I shall take the rest holding my nose, like a dose of castor oil. Too much reading at once. I should stick to one or two but never do. + Up at Harlem at 7:30. With Richou going

---

* Grand Ticino, a West Village restaurant later used as a setting in the movie *Moonstruck*.
† The Hotel Brevoort, located at Fifth Avenue and Eighth Street, was a fabled gathering spot for years until 1956, when it gave way to an apartment building also named the Brevoort.
‡ Webster was Rosalind Constable's maiden name. The full title of her book is *They Who Paddle*.

door-to-door. The youngest are the most cooperative. F.D.R. spoke
on the sea atrocities. And the need for real shooting all over the place.
Mother won't take coffee with me in the mornings, and won't let me give
her a birthday present. We are in a vicious circle, of which each of us
forms one half. Each the cause and the result. And we can't change our
course. The solutions that occur to me are nothing more than little tangents that fly off and die like sparks.

SEPTEMBER 12, 1941

First day of tranquility in a week. + Looked over that *Vogue* Prix thing.
First entree Nov. 20. 1st quiz.* I think I could write decent articles all
night. I do know things about art, & possibly literature. + Watercolor
this evening. Not like I intended but did a gay thing of Harlem. How
much pleasanter it is to love and not be loved, than to be loved and not
love. Thank God, the delight of giving and the happiness of devotion are
greater than the always momentary pleasure in flattery.

SEPTEMBER 13, 1941

A rather good day. Autumn is definitely creeping into the bones. Letter
from Jeannot with sketches. What a good fellow he is. Guileless and
fun-loving. He is pondering a book, but whether the bitter struggles of
the bewildered Français or the gay café life of Paris, he does not know!
Very very happy, with drinks galore, Jeva & Marjorie tonight. Walter
had business engagement. Managed to get R. in at 12:40. She said I made
a big hit the other night. I felt that I didn't. She said sometimes one does
better when not performing.

SEPTEMBER 14, 1941

Things are coming to a crisis, Stanley says. Mother is nervous, again
talks of removing me from school. I shall be lost. All the jobs I want
require a B.A. She is jealous of my friends. Constantly making comparisons between herself & them and jealous too of my courtesy to Jeva &
Marjorie when they come over. And could I possibly be in love with my
own mother? Perhaps in some incredible way I am. And it is the recal-
citrance in all of us that shows in my ingratitude for my mother's over-
zealous effort to please me, and to do things for me. It is the old story of

---

* The "*Vogue* Prix thing" is likely an initiative for finding new writing talent. Pat works on her submission
well into 1942.

things being too simple—and of our refusal to throw our love to the easiest and most deserving and most logical object.

SEPTEMBER 16, 1941

Finished *Pendennis*. What a moral little thing! How smug, the eternal, complaisant, equanimous, and so intelligent Mr. Thackeray! + Called Rosalind and had a wonderful time. She must have called me darling at least twice. She was suffering a hangover, martinis and benzedrine both in her at 2:30. She said that if she couldn't make it this week she'd hate not seeing me for so long! I couldn't say anything for at least 30 seconds. But painting, when I stood still a moment, whistling the second Brandenburg [concerto by J. S. Bach], I think, I felt an overwhelming love for R., a security of it and a happiness in it. I have waited so long, and this is it.

9/16/41

I thought, eating the last meal of the day, so balanced and attractive, of all the people in the world who'd have given a day's labor, if they had it in them, for a piece of decent meat; and I thought, sending back my butter practically untouched, of all the people in Germany and Italy and occupied France, and in so many places in Europe and Asia that I cannot even begin to name, who have not seen butter or even dirty grease in months. Here I sit in America, sending back my meat unfinished to be dumped into the garbage, brushing the crumbs off my lap, using half my allotted cream measure, declining delicately the cream of mushroom soup in favor of the vegetable vitamin cocktail. What right have I? And what are we to do? How much are we to think, to let ourselves think, to dare to think without losing our minds at the absurdity and inhumanness!

SEPTEMBER 17, 1941

Mother doesn't think I can do the Negro[*] story.[†] Cheery love. + Worked a short morning then went to Jeva's for lunch, with Mother, Marjorie, Nelson, Jeva, (who paid) to Alice Foote's.[‡] Enormous martinis, Jeva looked elegant. Cheveux straight up. Smoking like hell, but I loved her even for that. It was part of her great enthusiasm for the occasion. We told all kinds of jokes.

---

[*] From the eighteenth century to the late 1960s, Negro—much as it is offensive now in both British and U.S. English—was commonly used to describe people of black African origin.
[†] It is unclear which story Pat is referring to.
[‡] Alice Foote MacDougall ran several restaurants named after her, e. g. one in the Hotel Peter Stuyvesant, located at 2 West Eighty-Sixth Street.

SEPTEMBER 18, 1941

With Walter [Marlowe] last night. He says Mother and Stanley are deep conservatives, that I am a strange product & that I should make every effort towards conciliation. I wonder why all the nicest men (Walter & Arthur) are the sexy type? The propositioning type? It is a kind of generosity. An appreciation of pleasures. We almost did it last night.

A lovely day with new books. [Thomas Carlyle's] *Sartor Resartus*, highly recommended by Walter & [Stephen] Spender's *The Destructive Element*.

SEPTEMBER 19, 1941

Friday a rather wonderful day. Paid my bill at school. *Quarterly* bulletin looks nice. Saw Helen. What a tan! What a girl! Made my surrealist thing this afternoon. The writing of course. I think I'll redo "The Heroine" before anything else. But it would be good to have the Fascist thing for the first issue. There is so much to show Rosalind tomorrow! So much reason to be happy! I called her from Barnard—historic Barnard Hall. Shall meet her tomorrow at 6:00!!!! Damn it I've always had what I wanted and shall have it still.

SEPTEMBER 20, 1941

Saturday: Bought *Decision* [by Kay Boyle] yesterday. Very inspirational, poetic. Also the English magazine *Horizon* [by Cyril] Connolly, S. [Stephen] Spender. Worked some and read a bit, but mainly working around preparing for Rosalind like the b. for the b. Had a drink & went up to her office at 6:00. She wasn't there. Waited till 6:30 & phoned. I was supposed to meet her at home! We connected finally at the Shelton & met Mary S. In a dither as usual. Jane doesn't know about her & Helen but is sitting on H.'s doorstep & can't be removed even by the gendarmes. Later to Nino & Nella's. And a good glass of wine that put the finishing touches. We went to the Hotel Albert.* (I kissed her in the ladies' room! and said—I never thought that would happen again.) We met Merino, Floy, Butch from Key West. Went with them to Mrs. Kuniyoshi† & thence to the Vanguard. What fun to go thru the Village streets with Rosalind, holding her hand and feeling very drunk

---

* The Hotel Albert, located at 65 University Place in Greenwich Village, has since been converted into an apartment building.

† Even though the painters Katherine Schmidt and Yasuo Kuniyoshi divorced in 1932, she was still sometimes refered to as Katherine Schmidt Kuniyoshi. So this could be a reference either to her, or to Yasuo Kuniyoshi's second wife, Sara Mazo Kuniyoshi, a dancer, actress, and art curator.

and proud. Before her friends she calls me Baby. "I've got to take Baby home." (In a taxi where I sat on her lap.) Native Gin plus wine is an excellent boilermaker.

SEPTEMBER 21, 1941

Buffie wanted me to brunch with her. But mother & I went to Brooklyn Museum instead. Also called Rosalind. (She says I have telephonitis.) [Ernst] Hauser also called. Dinner date Tuesday. I suppose in a few more years I shan't mind going out 5 times a week either.

SEPTEMBER 23, 1941

Sent "The Heroine" to *Accent** and *New Horizons*† with letters. Went to school to make program changes. Saw Alice G. & Rita R.'s gal with British accent. They think the *Quarterly* folder is just the thing, etc. Had dinner with Hauser at Ticino's. Much white wine. Called Rosalind at 8:30. Betty in the same room, God! There will come a time, but we shall both be drunk when it happens, unfortunately.

SEPTEMBER 25, 1941

Splendid day! Program difficulties all settled. I'm taking American Literature & dropping Howard, etc. + Worked on totem pole which I might give to Marjorie. + This marks the first year that I have tried to think. Perhaps the first half year. Finished [Julien Green's] *The Dreamer.* Very Proustian. An excellent novel. I think Escapism, but it's now becoming the fashion to condone escape.

SEPTEMBER 26, 1941

Met Arthur on the street. He's thinking of getting an apartment so we can carry on our non-existent affair. + At [Emily] Gunning's for Political Council discussion. Painful and short. No special purpose either except collective masturbation of our dormant political consciousness. + Worked on story. Preferred whittling but I must get in a couple of hours writing every day. One is not sufficient anymore. Should like sometime to read thru all my diaries and notebooks. Would take as long as reading the Bible and is more important to me at this moment.

---

* *Accent*, a quarterly of new literature.
† Perhaps in reference to *New Horizons*, a magazine published by Pan American World Airways.

SEPTEMBER 27, 1941

With Ernst from nine to six. Went to Fire Island.* It is wrong to say I am never bored. Beaches bore me beyond words. Travel annoys me, too. Too much time idle, with a person beside you so that you can neither read, nor converse amusingly all the time. We made snapshots. He has a funny little bathing suit with legs. + With Billie B. tonight at Mero's. She drank tea and we danced like a couple of floating sea buoys. Congaed with Bruhs. He and Gean are quite willing I become a member.

SEPTEMBER 28, 1941

Finished my story and Stanley read it, and to my great delight, liked it enormously! Only it needs climax at the end. Too much of the "quiet incident." Still. Such work! And I do want something special for the first issue of *Quarterly*. I felt a peculiar friendliness to Stanley today. His reading my story helped us both. It will be a slow, and painfully self-conscious process for us both. But he didn't think I could write a story like that, probably. So much as has passed, I should like this union feeling with Stanley.

SEPTEMBER 29, 1941

Read [Thomas] More's *Utopia*, first and second books. Worked on little woodman. It takes so little to make me happy. A book, and thou—and not even thou in the flesh, worse luck. I dream of her sometimes, day dreams, when I see her across a restaurant, or in a room with other people, and we look at each other and know, and know that others know, too, that we are ours and nobody else's. That's what I want!

SEPTEMBER 30, 1941

A real wintry day—autumnal and coming. Kingsley, who sent me the phantasia, is the girl with the British accent, raised by English parents. She was in *Quarterly*, Babs P. told me, to see her "comments" and said, "of course they'll print it!" Work—work—work! Mountains of reading! And I'm unhappy because of my hair! I was going to wear it up and I still have that clipped part to contend with. Roger sent me a necklace, rather

---

* Fire Island, just south of Long Island, has been a magnet for gay New Yorkers at least since the 1930s. Legend has it that at Duffy's Hotel in Cherry Grove, Christopher Isherwood and W. H. Auden celebrated gay culture, dressed as Dionysus and Ganymede and carried aloft by a group of singing worshippers. Throughout the years, Pat knew many people who had taken houses there, and she visited regularly.

nice, of tropical fruits. I want to see Rosalind! I want to see Rosalind wherever I turn and wherever I look!

OCTOBER 1, 1941

A good day. Philosophy is with Montague,* but I suppose he's forgotten about the D. Hope so. Read history this afternoon. Reading it like a story and to hell with notes till a later date. Helen damn sweet & asked me for coffee, but I had to study. There'll be plenty of time, if I get started. + Kingsley, when asked by [Minor] Latham what was her stake in life, replied, "Immortality." She interests me because of her self-confidence. Wonder would Rosalind like to meet her? + Finished "Mr. Scott Is Not on Board."† 8,750 words almost. It is graceful! Shall send it to the *Post*‡ for a once-over, then cut it down for something else. Quite an ordeal to type. Should like to do the Fascist kid story of the auto this weekend. Am not writing enough in my notebook. That comes of long slow evenings, reading and musing on my couch.

OCTOBER 3, 1941

I was en route to Chock Full O'Nuts§ for an innocent cup of coffee when Helen dragged me into Tilson's. Peter was there & Tony. Peter: "Your friend Rosalind's name wouldn't be Constable, would it?" Seems she met her at a British Motor unit at 68 St. this summer. We talked quite freely, exchanging friends. Helen: "What is this?" So she went to study & Peter & I got soused at the Gold Rail. I called Rosalind & made a lunch date for the three of us next Friday. "That gives you a whole week of freedom," I said. "Do you think I want freedom from you?"(?) Peter seems very eager to meet R. (Why the hell wouldn't she be?!) Everybody in town, unfortunately is nuts about Rosalind!

OCTOBER 4, 1941

Cut my "Mr. Scott" down some 13 pages. Wonderful! Billie B. [and I] dropped in on Mary S. Mary says Buffie's dull, but God, her antics are same, too. Drinks constantly and the same old exclamations about their

---

* William P. Montague, Johnsonian professor of philosophy at Barnard College. He also taught logic.
† A lost mystery story.
‡ The *Saturday Evening Post,* where Ernst Hauser works. The *Post*'s covers were designed by Norman Rockwell in the 1940s. It reported on political and national news, but also published short stories by young authors such as F. Scott Fitzgerald, John Steinbeck, William Saroyan, and Ray Bradbury.
§ Popular chain of coffee and sandwich counters.

results. All of us are boring if we go out all the time and build no individuality within.

OCTOBER 7, 1941

I wish Helen could stay in the city Friday night and make an evening of it. + Walter phoned. Had been in Washington. Wants a date this weekend—and I don't. + Read some layouts for *Quarterly*. Terribly discouraging. You wonder what sort of introversion and conceit led some of these kids to write!

OCTOBER 11, 1941

Much better day. Even with a hangover. Worked on play this AM. Talked with mother some. There is so little we talk about. Our intellectual conversations reach impasses very soon. She is simply not interested in the abstract, tho there's nothing intrinsically the matter with her brain at all. Read [Edmund Wilson's] *Wound and the Bow*.

OCTOBER 12, 1941

Roger called so I broke the date with Buffie (!) & drove with him upstate. I try to understand the fury in him. What I say to such young people who cannot accept the world that they're in: "What have you done—and what can you do?" and usually it is nothing. Nevertheless, I feel a great affection for Roger. More physical than Arthur—Arthur's is more intellectual.

OCTOBER 13, 1941

Helen M., when asked by Miss Latham to have me as gov't official, said "Miss H. is my hero!" Latham, "Oh is she!" + My clothes depressed me today. Lousy shoes & hair & sweater. Can ruin me physically and mentally. How lucky men are with their very regular clothing! Sent "Mr. Scott" to *This Week*. Mother wrote some housemaid's verse, part one stinks. Second fine.

OCTOBER 14, 1941

Still haven't called Rosalind and I think it's slowly driving me mad. She's never home at night. Does she even think of me? God what a sad life! I think of her when I hear nice music. I think of her every time I have a moment of tranquility, which fortunately for my nerves, is seldom. + I have a psychosis about work. I work till I nearly drop at 9:30—writing my play and then rest 5 minutes & start again. Read [Richard Brinsley Sheridan's] *School for Scandal*.

OCTOBER 15, 1941

Date with Walter. He hums at dinner, and holds my hand when he plays the Brandenburg [concertos] and "Liebestod" [in Richard Wagner's *Tristan and Isolde*] when I had much rather be thinking of Rosalind— that's all I have against him. Also that someday he would like to put the "Liebestod" to the purpose for which it was written! Likes his cake with ice cream, I'd say! To me, it would sacrilege the music—The music was written as an approximation, a synthesis and a sublimation—an artistic condensation of the act. It would be a sensual greed—Ossa on Pelion* and all that. I should merely like to lie with my head in Rosalind's lap— or vice versa.

OCTOBER 16, 1941

Read [C. G. Jung's] *Modern Man [in Search of a Soul]* again. Stanley comes out rather more clearly: toxic condition because of repressed impulses. And he cannot take pleasure in any exterior thing in New York. Even [in] his camera work—an inner private hobby—he is unable to relate to the outside economic world. Lives in movies and books.

OCTOBER 17, 1941

Lunch with Rosalind and Babs. Rosalind had to go at 2:30 but Peter & Helen phoned & came at 2:45. Del Pezzo's.† I had more to drink than was good for me. Helen, too, and I kissed her in the bathroom. She wanted it badly.

OCTOBER 18, 1941

Worked like hell. Six hours at the typewriter. Finished play this AM. Sent Babs P. a note, commending her mariners, etc. I remember in '38 when I used to write to Judy Tuvim. Saw Museum of Modern Art furniture exhibit, and some fine things by George Grosz‡ of Germany. Came home, wrote my editorial and discovered with some dismay that Rita R. said almost the same thing in '40, only less amusingly. Besides I have announced a policy of "less cynicism and more poetry," which absolves me. + Worked very well on "White Monkey"§ this evening. + Letter

---

* In Greek mythology, the giants attempted to reach heaven by piling Mount Olympus and Mount Ossa onto Mount Pelion.
† Del Pezzo Restaurant, frequented by *Life* magazine staff and singers from the Metropolitan Opera, including Enrico Caruso.
‡ George Grosz (1893–1959), German painter who immigrated to the United States in 1933. He later taught at the Art Students League of New York, where Pat will also attend classes.
§ "White Monkey," a (lost) story in progress.

from Babs P. this AM saying Rosalind was worthy of me (!). Unable to contact Buffie. I find the contemplation dreary.

OCTOBER 19, 1941

Graham R. is being shipped to the Philippines. Worked like hell again. Did first act for performance Wednesday & shall do second. Stanley thinks I am "over my head" in my materials, but one can't go writing about school days just because that's what one knows best. I'm quite proud of my editorial. Fun with Graham this evening. He's quite concerned over the scarcity of books where he's going!

OCTOBER 20, 1941

Palma came across with her poems. I want to print the one about love on the bed in the blackness, but she's got cold feet. Babs is considering them tonight. Palma asked me to lunch tomorrow. "I love your profile, frowning," she said—joking of course!

OCTOBER 21, 1941

Rehearsed play 1–2 haphazardly. Helen & I sit together, touching our arms while we watch the drahmah—and finally touching fingers surreptitiously between us. No mention later. No glances—no regrets—only whets the appetite and rattles me, and excites me, I am very nervous and shall be, I suppose, till the magazine is sent off. *Quarterly* is really coming into its own, my summer dreams come true. It depends, as usual, on money.

OCTOBER 23, 1941

Thursday: Rewrote my editorial & met Babs in Time & Life* at 7:00. Rosalind up to her ears in Art & the Everyday Life. Ate at Del Pezzo's. I gave her my editorial to read. Liked it a lot & suggested one little change. Saw the Rodeo afterwards with Babs. Judy called me earlier to check on our date & since R. had to work, went with Babs. The child was rather nervous, inevitably, but Judy nice. Rum drinks, then Eddy arrived, looking like hell. We had more drinks at St. Moritz, where Judy had to have spaghetti too. Home & bed at 5:10!

---

* The Time & Life Building, located at 1271 Avenue of the Americas, headquarters of *Time*, *Life*, and *Fortune* magazines.

OCTOBER 25, 1941

Grand day. Worked on play. Saw the Metropolitan Exhibit of water-colors. I think as I told mother over coffee this afternoon, that the time of social significance (i.e. working class) novel passed with Sinclair's & Norris'* youth. [T. S.] Eliot knows the real tragedy—the spiritual tragedy. The tragedy of the man that has some money and can develop the perversions and contortions of the twentieth century mind. A spiritual wasteland, yes. Furthermore the downfall, or at least the most serious fault of the Communist youth is their stereotyping. They do not allow for spiritual growth (if they have any left) and for emotional changes that only bring maturity.

OCTOBER 26, 1941

Wrote Friday night my poem on the immortality of dental fillings. Might go for *Quarterly*. Worked on play. All but done now. Phoned Babs P. She asked me for a drink at 5:30 & I interrupted studying history and went. We played [Eddy] Duchin records. How nice to sit with Babs and hear good music. Tho I know there could never be anything twixt her & me on my part. Babs said I had a spiritual richness that Peter lacked. That she wished she'd known me sooner, that she had known all along about me.

OCTOBER 28, 1941

Babs asked me yesterday to come for weekend Friday. Shall go. Should be very important. Also says she's not always a decent little girl. Cold as hell. Saw a wonderful suit at A. Constable's† and bought it. $29 reduced from $45! I'll wear it Thursday—for Rosalind—and buy a conga record—for Rosalind—and look my very very best—for Rosalind.

OCTOBER 29, 1941

Ecstatically happy—Walked into a History quiz but must have got a B. Rehearsed Helen, Willey, Roma (swell kid!) and McCormick & Leighton on my play. Went on finally at 3–4 with great success. No applause, but the thing was too shocking. Marijann K. was sitting in. Everybody hanging on their chairs on the third act. Even Latham said it was good professional line. Helen & I can scarcely keep apart at the right times. We hand each other fake guns and our hands cling. Disgraceful! Things

---

* Upton Sinclair (1878–1968) was an American writer known for his socialist views and attention to social and political issues in the United States. Frank Norris (1870–1902) was an American novelist known for his naturalistic depiction of life in the United States.
† Arnold Constable was a department store.

are getting across. Kingsley flunkeying all around for me. She's lived with her mother (that woman!) for 12 years in one room. Hence her dallying around school.

OCTOBER 31, 1941

Met Babs & her father: at Grand Central & rode up—(4.00—Cape Cod. Providence). Babs quite reserved & serious. She's very slow and thoughtful. Long drive with Newt to their house—a gorgeous place—old & well-established—20–15 rooms! Wonderful food + Babs & I ran around, walked, sat by the fire & drank. The night is peculiar—each talking— twin beds. Each claiming to be cold, doing nothing about it but put on sweaters & socks—how much are people shy these days! I told her if she wanted she could share her own bed—I didn't kick & my bed was hers to begin with. But nothing came of that.

NOVEMBER 1, 1941

We played poker this evening where I won like mad. I got high just before the steak fry came on. We made pumpkins and I distinguished myself by tearing a beer can in two with my bare hands. + Babs & I talked from 1:30–4:00 in bed. Babs has almost the same menstrual difficulties. I wonder if it decreases the sexual desire? I still am most attracted physically by someone like Helen—like all the straights I was so violently in love with when I was younger. Babs P. says she is attracted to Helen, too— she wants to get far far away, etc. I'm afraid I want to get closer! + I feel restless & can't stop smoking as I had intended. Now I do not resent the talking chitchat, but only grow weary that it is all a facet of me which is not at all sincere, that I am wasting my time and everybody else's.

NOVEMBER 2, 1941

Read [Alexander Pope's] *Essay on Man*. Babs told me her mother says I was so nice to have around, so attractive! Very nice all right. Drove with Babs from Providence to N.Y. 4–11:30. Hamburgers en route. We talked. She's happy to have someone she can talk to now she says—before she had no one. She says she doesn't like the idea of being physically "unused." I think she'd sooner trust me to have an affair with her than anyone else. She still thinks I'm sincere and very well reputed.

NOVEMBER 3, 1941

I believe my real study days are over. S. [Samuel] Johnson said the same thing. Thank God I was once a grind, a drudge, a thirster after knowledge, and a martinet of myself!!! On that I coast now, and bank forever! + Helen delightful! Winks at me when we meet, and holds my hand in Latham's class, rubs my sleeve surreptitiously with her fingers and generally makes herself very dangerous. + Dined with Mespoulet* (like Voltaire) and Alice K. (like an old mummy) at Nino & Nella's at 7:30. Drank too much. Mespoulet talked exclusively to me, but my conversation was not too brilliant and hers not too entertaining. It is so futile to discuss the war! Really! Everyone has a different opinion—which is just as conclusive as religion! Whether by revolt or by military defeat will Hitler meet his doom, etc.

NOVEMBER 4, 1941

Slept, studied, wrote—resigned from the [Young Communist] League in a well-worded epistle. + Roger sent me 10 bucks to come to Boston. Also pictures of him carrying one Hollywood cutie. + Bought Rosalind a boogie-woogie record—"The Stomp" [by Albert Ammons] and went up there at 8:10. Natasha, Betty, Rosalind eating dinner. My face swollen from my bad eye, etc. and I feel more than ever like a kid! We listened to election votes returns. They are all for La Guardia† of course. Talked of books and men. Very delightful and charming—with Rosalind knitting Del P.‡ a pair of green socks for Xmas—all evening.

NOVEMBER 5, 1941

Fine day. Wore my suit to school with great success. Got A- in History quiz of a week ago. One of very very few, I'm sure. Buffie's [for] tea. Howard, Mrs Hughes,§ Miss Green (awful & I suppose a patron) and Florence Codman, publisher who spoke to B. Parsons last night while I was there. Buffie presented me & heard Codman say "are you the Miss Highsmith Rosalind Constable's been telling me about? I've been wanting, etc." I made a fine impression. + Babs called with the "chance of my life"—tickets to *Macbeth* with Helen Tuesday night! Very nice of her. We did make hash of her play today, too. She's so sweet—never unkind, never impatient. Asked her to come with us Monday night—the Madison Avenue gang.¶

---

* Marguerite Mespoulet, associate professor of French at Barnard College.
† Fiorello La Guardia, mayor of New York City from 1934 to 1945.
‡ Rosalind's friend Lola P.'s husband.
§ Toni Hughes (1907–?), American sculptress whose work was shown several times at the Museum of Modern Art in the 1940s and '50s.
¶ The Madison Avenue gang most likely consisted of Rosalind Constable, Natasha H., and Betty Parsons.

NOVEMBER 6, 1941

Got a card from *Accent* saying they are fighting over my story, etc. We go to press in an alarmingly short time! I phoned Rosalind & got Betty. We talked full quota about the tea yesterday. Unfortunately and very Noël Cowardishly* I'm quite fond of her!

NOVEMBER 7, 1941

Thank God for a little work again. First night at home in over a week. Wrote eleven papers (satire story) of the "Horn of Plenty."[†] Kingsley returned [André Gide's] *The Counterfeiters*,[‡] with the question, why did I lend it her? And she told me she gets violent attachments. Wonder if she knows I'm gay and has a crush on me? + Saw Helen—God, that name is my nemesis. How simple it would be to fall for Helen! And how adolescent. Like preferring a chocolate soda to frogs-legs Provençale!

11/7/41

Kingsley loves my handwriting! Soon she'll be picking up my cigarette butts. She may suspect me and Helen. I wonder if she has a crush on Helen, too?

NOVEMBER 7, 1941

Shall enjoy talking to Babs Monday next. How strange it must seem to her to be presented to a room full of people—all gay—all wonderful—all bewildering, frightening perhaps—and somehow full of foreboding and intimations of the great future. I was thoroughly disgusted last night at Rose M.'s. [She and Billie] are sex machines—as overbalanced as Freud in his theory—God give me people like Rosalind & Betty and Natasha (who would never mention Sylvia at all!). And give me strength to be like them!

NOVEMBER 8, 1941

Slept late & needed it badly. Odds and ends I did this AM. which felt very good, a rare comfortable feeling. What a genius I should be with leisure! + Went to see Wakefield Gallery.[§] Presented my mother to Betty

---

* Noël Coward (1899–1973) was an English playwright, composer, director, actor, and singer. During World War II, he worked for the Secret Service as well as entertaining the troops across Europe, Asia, and Africa.
† "The Silver Horn of Plenty," published in the *Barnard Quarterly*, Winter 1941.
‡ *The Counterfeiters* is a novel by André Gide that prominently features adolescent homosexuality. Pat reads it several times before starting to brainstorm her first novel, *The Click of the Shutting*.
§ The small art gallery in the Wakefield Bookshop at 64 East Fifty-Fifth Street run by Betty Parsons until 1944.

Parsons. Buffie had been in a moment before, she said. I think of Helen & holding her hand, in my odd moments—very odd moments.

NOVEMBER 10, 1941

Helen said she smoked a lot over the weekend too. I wonder if from same reason. She looks at me with an admiring & come-hither eye. Home at 4:30 for the dreadful message that Rosalind has the grippe. Nevertheless met Babs at Buffie's. + Short dinner & to Barnard to see Helen sleeping over. She was delighted so see us. And Babs, ever tactful, left for the John & we fell in each other's arms. I kissed her on the bed. God what goings on! Helen's marvelous!

NOVEMBER 11, 1941

Three hours' sleep & studied this morning early & wrote a fine examination I think. Read *Pride & Prejudice* ½ this PM. & wrote 6 pages final draft on "Silver Horn of Plenty." Kingsley spoke to Babs yesterday. Babs told her she knew of her affection for me—"Is it that obvious? Thinks I'm sincere—the soul of sincerity." I often feel inferior to Babs and Debbie B.'s devotion to ideal. I wonder if I have lost too much in promiscuity? I am ruled too much by physical desire—the moment's prompting. Feel myself more masculine lately, with growing self-confidence. Had a long talk with Muret.* She talked of creative thinkers & career women & the enduring delights of the intellectual life. Asked me to call again.

NOVEMBER 12, 1941

Wrote Helen a note Tuesday that last night was rather nice but Public Opinion would improve if we sat apart in Latham's. Signed verse of experience. She wrote me back (nearly late for 5 o'clock getting it, because I knew she would) To Pat the Prudent. "I think your note was heaven and it really is a shame that we two must be cloven to preserve the Public Name." Oh the delights of the primal stages! I feel gayer every day and must take steps to remedy matters. I suffer from a Puritanical background: it is having the usual effects.

NOVEMBER 14, 1941

Melancholy—never like this—morning. Gym was torture. Kingsley showed up at one, and confessed her fine attachment to me. (Also [Babs]

---

* Dr. Charlotte T. Muret, History Department associate at Barnard College and a renowned expert on modern European history.

P. & Helen.) Then Peter. We had a few, I about 4 martinis. Bought a blue
& red muffler at Lord & Taylor's (drunk) and came home where Jeva &
Mother & I had more drinks. I was high. And not too cheerful. I wanted
a date with Helen & Babs tonight, and as it happened they called at
10:30. If I'd known, I shouldn't have got so drunk. They came by & we
went to the Tavern, Caravan and met Leslie S., unfortunately, who was
with us the rest of the time. More gays at Casino. But Helen was lovely—
wonderful. She looks at me with her heart in her eyes. I'm a lucky son of
a gun. She says I'm cute. Got lipstick all over Helen's collar in the L.R.
[Ladies' Room], but it was worth it—to her I mean. And certainly to me.
We make love all over the place, in fact that's all we do.

NOVEMBER 15, 1941

Slight hangover but gone suddenly at 12. No cigarettes. Read most of
[James Fenimore Cooper's] *Last of the Mohicans*. Went to Brooklyn to
see Comet [Press]. The proofs look good. Shall have to write a couple
of gratis ads to fill spaces [in *Quarterly*]. I keep thinking of Helen—she
keeps intruding. I have a violent physical longing—I don't suppose I've
ever felt such attraction from a straight.

NOVEMBER 16, 1941

Read proofs, wrote ads. Studied English lit. Helen not so seriously on
my mind today—my heart still starts beating but she's just a pleasant
thought—someone to look nice for in school. + Did some work on "Silver Horn of Plenty." Damn it, it should sell somewhere, that's just the
story I should like to sell first—Is great showing even though really my
heart is not in it.

NOVEMBER 17, 1941

Unfortunate day. Rehearsals all the day—*Accent* returned "The Heroine" with marginalia and a long letter: Good but not good enough. A
good yarn—not a document. And send them more. Then Mme Muret
said she liked my stories immensely as she returned my C+ paper on
Machiavelli! Kingsley stalks me around, thinking I go to *Quarterly* when
I get coffee, etc. Pete & Helen amused. Helen looks at me with hungry
eyes. God! What sex appeal that little thing has!

NOVEMBER 19, 1941

Splendid day. My hair up & a white shirt, the button-down Helen loves.
Peculiarly tranquil so I read philosophy "with great delectation." Helen

& Babs were delirious—esp. Babs. Helen has her worried tho. Seems they talked long last night, mainly about how inadvisable things were & how Earl would satisfy her on his heralded return. Evidently Helen agreed with Babs but today found her as magnetic as ever. Boy what a figger she's acquiring, too! She said she'd love it if I came up to the dorms Friday. + My mother said some curious things: that I was like a chameleon with my favorites (girls) while very strong of character in other things. Also that New York social life breeds Lesbians, that I'm always happy when I go out with girls & bored stiff with men. That my girlfriends all live with each other & don't take interest in men, etc. There's the pieces, Bacon,* put them together!

NOVEMBER 21, 1941

Read Shaftesbury tonight. Didn't go to the Caravan but to Helen at Barnard instead at 10:35. No one knows, or shall know. She kisses like a thousand dreams, and her cheek is as soft as nothing I've ever felt. Strangely enough I was *en-bas* most of the time—being quite tired anyway—She's afraid to go further. I think—afraid when I say I might fall in love, because of people involved. Otherwise as far as action is concerned I think she would. I shall never forget this night—It was like some dream when we kissed—when I felt her cheek on mine—so long and hard pressing. I felt no part of my body—it was all sensation—and not in my head, but floating where out in a sea of perfume and white flowers, without time and beyond time.

NOVEMBER 22, 1941

Saturday: Ran into Rosalind & Natasha on 57th. Was with M. & S. & didn't introduce them. Rosalind grinning like mad & both gawking. It would have been disastrous—Natasha!

NOVEMBER 24, 1941

Quarterly's out and looks magnificent! Peter liked the poem & Helen the editorial. Everything elegant! Shall get McGuire to review it. I find it hard—and unpleasant, too—to recall the pinched Freshman years—the pinched belly, the pinched soul, and heart. (And mind.) I've come a long way! I find so much pleasure in the passage of the weeks—idle pleasures but so new to me I am excited—almost contented but not quite and

---

* Francis Bacon (1561–1626), English philosopher, essayist, and statesman, also known for his method of message encoding, Bacon's cipher.

therein lies my salvation. I need to write more & read more. Helen thinks it remarkable that I'm able to keep the friendship of the women I've broken with. I think it's because there is of necessity more an element of Platonism than in the male-female relationship.

NOVEMBER 25, 1941

Went with Helen to lunch at Del Pezzo's. Rosalind & Natasha at 12:50. Was glad N. came. I like her very much. She's least affected of all. Rosalind in wonderful spirits. + Later unwisely had coffee with Helen, and she suffering wounded pride from being left out rather in the presence of Rosalind, told me off about philandering. We saw [Ruth] Bernhard's exhibit at Lord & Taylor's. Helen said she expected something to happen Friday night. That I was the only girl she'd ever been attracted to, & that it's going to be hell the rest of the year. I think she rather enjoys the hell.

NOVEMBER 28, 1941

Pleasant day. So much of the history is fascinating—you want to go on reading biographies & detailed histories—which is what the course is for. Helen absent because of heart flutter. Cigarettes probably. Read [Edmond Rostand's] *Cyrano de Bergerac* 12:00–3:00. Shopped for a blouse & then to Constable's at 6:30. Betty asked me to party Thursday afternoon. I suppose Buffie will be there. Rather exclusive nonetheless. + Rosalind liked my story "Silver Horn of Plenty." "Damned good" she said. Only two phrases on correction. + I am exhausted. It was a week ago this very moment, that I was with Helen—amid the purple lilies at the bottom of the sea—this moment. + There's still no one like Rosalind, however, not even me.

NOVEMBER 30, 1941

This sterile period is indicative really of some progress. Ideas are not bursting on me as they used to—good and bad and mainly bad. Now when I write a story I like to think it will definitely be printed somewhere. It is no longer an exercise in sublimation. It is all the better for it.

DECEMBER 2, 1941

Helen doesn't mention Earl per se anymore. Says anything she does doesn't concern me much. She almost cried. Let's say she did cry. She still would recommence. We attract each other. I see no reason to fool around. No one attracts me beyond reason except Rosalind. Why should I lower myself? It's very flattering the way Helen is about me. The bathroom kisses, miserable as they seemed to me, meant more to her. A kiss is a kiss—a moment made immortal with the rush of wings unseen. Be it in a bathroom or a pastoral arbor. I know that, too. I underestimated her. I thought she was playing. I see in her eyes a devotion that shames me. And yet I don't see that I'm to blame. It was merely a misunderstanding all around. I could take her now—and I could not do it with my soul touched—so I shall not do it at all. I feel a pain at my heart—how many times have I loved unloved.

DECEMBER 3, 1941

Fatigued and slow and sad. Met Gordon [Smith] for lunch—where we discussed morals. He believes in free love—is a pessimist and delighted to find I am, too. I am only a pessimist generally and an optimist specifically. Rehearsed with Helen. Some of those triangles sound like they were written to order. Helen very energetic and impersonal—very fine of her. Nevertheless I miss her horribly. I love her gray skirt. It reminds me of that night in the dorms—warm and fuzzy. Why could I not love her? I would. Only Rosalind stands like a Titan between. Helen is not so high—yet. Wrote her a long letter (5 pages). Read the *Alhambra* of [Washington] Irving.

DECEMBER 4, 1941

All very miserable at school. Gave Helen my note. She looks very tired. And she read it by the river & answered me between 11 & 12. Darling, too, and how she "cries at the oddest moments and always because of you—because I love you so much—" + At Betty's show at 5—thence to Wakefield (Ossorio)* and with her to Midtown. Hope Williams† there, Buffie, Harper, Arden, Hughes, Natasha, Lola, Rosalind (in too tight black suit), but very nice to me. Plenty of drinks. Buffie left right away (6:00) and Lola asked me to cocktails tomorrow. Some fun tomorrow night!

DECEMBER 4, 1941

Had a beer with Helen at 3:50. We both know things are impossible now. She said she'd been wanting something like this to happen to her for a

---

* Alfonso Ossorio, American-Filipino artist best known for his abstract expressionist paintings and unique sculptural *Congregations* series.
† Hope Williams (1897–1990), American actress most noted for her roles in Noël Coward and Oscar Wilde plays.

long while. And she's glad it did happen. Only people don't get mixed up with me & forget it in a hurry. Just as *malheureusement*, I shan't forget it in a hurry.

DECEMBER 5, 1941

Friday: Gloomy day. Short school. Went to Lola's at 6:00. Gillespie, [Toni] Hughes, Buffie (whom I scarcely spoke to), Jimmie Stern & many Frenchmen. Also Melcarth.* Thence to Barnard. Mary S. (also there) said Helen was the cutest thing she'd seen in years. That my taste was in my mouth. I didn't know what she meant. Helen has all the warmth—and she wore her gray suit tight because she knows I love it—and we could not keep our eyes or our hands off each other all evening and it was all very beautiful. She loves me—she said so—in the cold air outdoors. And she means it. Why should I lie? I miss her so when I'm away an hour I can't see straight. The first time I've been in love—the terrific physical appeal plus my love of her—God what a perilous combination!

DECEMBER 6, 1941

Called Helen at 8 at Latham's. She was right there. I hope she had been waiting. We had a terrible time talking. But I managed to tell her that I spent 2 hours reading 20 pages of [Bernard] de Mandeville during which I realized that I should have been the same last night no matter who had been present. "Anybody?" she said. Yes, anybody. Then she said something, but she was crying I know. That's the way it hits you. And she said, "God, I like you!" Which was quite good enough for me in Latham's office. I'm in love with her. I can't imagine what I shall do with myself if she doesn't come through to me. She's wonderful—all the rest seem shams beside her. I love her. But I haven't said the words yet. I practically told her—(I shouldn't have been able to go on, I know) Later—I don't know why I cried—the sweetest tears I've ever known. If I might wash away all my shame!

DECEMBER 6, 1941

This was such a bittersweet day—to use Helen's word. How beautiful her letter was. And how beautifully sad this uncertainty! She can't give me up! I'm sure of that. God help me I'm a lucky bastard. I watched the

---

* Edward Melcarth (1914–1973), American social realist painter whose patrons included Peggy Guggenheim—he designed her iconic bat-shaped sunglasses for her.

moon passing in and out of the black wisps of clouds tonight—a full
moon but very small and high. They were playing the "Good Friday
Music."* And the tears came, tight and exquisite—and I passed in two
minutes from the awfullest possibilities to the best—and back again. Still
I don't know, I don't know. But I believe, I am sure, this is too rare and
too wonderful.

DECEMBER 8, 1941

Japan declares war on United States.†

Miserable at school until I talked with Helen at 1:30. We walked by
the river, then to West End‡ for a beer. I told her then what she meant to
me and God keep me I cried tho I didn't mean her to see it. And she said
"What do you want me to do, Pat?" And that she couldn't send [Earl] off
to war telling him. And I said she must do what she felt she should. That
I loved her for her honesty. She asked me twice "What do you want me
to do, Pat?" God, it was like something terrific shaking me! She said it
was Friday (that Friday) that she realized—that all the melancholia in her
had risen in this last hectic month. I adore her. I don't deserve her. She's
beautiful through & through—and don't I know how rare this is! I spoke
from my heart today. She made me do it—nothing good in me. Good
lord, this is it! this is it!

1800 men killed at Pearl Harbor. Perhaps Graham—

DECEMBER 9, 1941

Rode with Jo P.§ She paid for it. Mausoleum of a house. 5 stories, & two
maids. She rode back to school & had coffee with Helen, Babs, Pete.
They all like her. Lunch with Rosalind. She is *distraite*¶ with the war. She
talked like an adult to me.

DECEMBER 9, 1941

Rosalind talked a long while about parents and about hers. Her mother
is a well-known anti-Semite (Nazi) and the split came over Rosalind's
Jewish friends. Also her mother told her off—while Rosalind stood by

---

* From Richard Wagner's opera *Parsifal*.
† Japan attacked Pearl Harbor on December 7, 1941.
‡ The West End was located at 2911 Broadway. Jack Kerouac was one of the patrons.
§ A new friend of Pat's she has recently met through Va. when the two made plans to go horseriding
together.
¶ Pat most likely means "distraught" (not "distracted").

the window. Then she said "What would you say if I told you it were all true?" And her mother said, "I'd rather see you dead at my feet."

DECEMBER 11, 1941

I gave Helen my letter—my beautiful letter. And she wrote me one back, telling me as she gave it, "You're going to hate me—" And when I read it, it was all might-have-beens and how she must do what she must do, hating it. And how she wants to keep me, and she'll follow along. Contradictions. It was a hasty letter, born of sudden fear. So I cried all afternoon—with Kingsley & then with Helen. And she didn't quite see [that the] overwhelming questions are: What was she struggling with these last weeks? And what did she want with me? (Besides a female joy of conquest—that's all.)

DECEMBER 12, 1941

Coffee with Helen. How perfectly she has recovered, and how well she misunderstands me. I asked her why she had been upset—because she didn't think I cared—What she wanted of me?—for me to love her. Voilà! Such craziness. Yes, I could soon hate her perhaps. She tore through the fine fabric of my sweet life like a meteor. Coquet—with its classic definition. So I lunched with Alice T. & Peter, and afterwards escaped with Pete to New Canaan. Phoned Rosalind from Cortile. "You're in a state." I was crying. And I said "I was being shanghaied & did she want to look in a minute?" I wonder if she gave it ten minutes' thought? Cried with Debbie B. in the kitchen & in general behaved like a cloud of gloom having some bitter fun with Peter by telling her Helen loved her. That accounts for so much, said Peter, swelling with masculine pride. *Cyrano de Bergerac* stuff. Home again at 1:30, mother gone & more gloom. I should be writing now—will I be able to recapture all that I've felt the last few days? One comes to question the value of human emotion: just what is it worth when after exerting the maximum control, something still tears one up?

DECEMBER 13, 1941

Thursday afternoon Kingsley probed all around to find out. Once she asked if it were Rosalind, and then "You haven't fallen in love with Helen, have you?" I think she hates her now, tho of course I covered well about the question. Kingsley told me she's only loved one—me, that if I were a man it would be all she wanted. And Helen said to me at West

End she'd never care for another man (besides Earl). And the juke box played "You Made Me Love You" and it was all very sad.

DECEMBER 14, 1941

All things changed. Read [Henry Fielding's] *Tom Thumb the Great* and *Christ*.* Played the piano and took a walk. This day memorable because I laid out my two plays & can hardly wait to get started on them. This day also memorable for my contrition: I love Rosalind. I have really not been away from her. The last week was like an opium dream—I rather hope to see Helen tomorrow with circles under her eyes. She needs a rest. I associate last week too, with that peculiar phenomenon rare in myself—the menstrual period. God knows women are batty, and God knows why! + Kingsley here at 5:00. Did the proofs together. She told me what a god I am. How all those at school who know me treat me as something out of another world, fearfully—even Babs, Helen & Peter. Did me a lot of good. K. said she hoped I'd never love a man, that she wouldn't like to see me so much in the physical. Sweet child. Billie phoned to drink champagne. No go. Working. Altogether a splendid day. Arthur here—told him gently I loved another—God, the appalling conceit of the man! + How I shall look at Rosalind tomorrow! Like I had never seen her before!

DECEMBER 15, 1941

Lovely evening with Rosalind. Came up in elevator with Betty & Mr. Eastman. Rosalind drunk, and told me she was handicapped "obligated" but too many beautiful dark-haired people around. God, she was lovely to me. Ate at Sammy's. Just what she told me to. She's marvelous—Shall try to get her tickets to *Macbeth*. She said Betty has 89 friends to her 13. That she likes one per year (& I'm it) while Betty picks up six per evening.

DECEMBER 16, 1941

I am smoking too much—pack a day often, but getting the greatest relish out of it. Getting the greatest relish out of everything. Helen & Peter hungover with 13 Scotches apiece yesterday. Look like two pieces of fragile old china. She didn't speak to me today. No doubt she's worse off than ever now—because she was in such close reach—and scored something of a victory and has all my letters to reread—and yet—I'm gone. I feel quite brilliant these days. Home at 1:00. Shopped. Did 8 pages in Philosophy paper. Read D. H. Lawrence's *Assorted Articles* which is lousy.

---

* Possibly Ernest Renan's *The Life of Jesus*.

Phoned Rosalind at 3:10. She was wonderful & stinking from three martinis. I asked her if she felt funny (because I felt funny—like a cloud—
like old china) and she said—"Ye-ss"—always yes—but like a piece of
old cheese. So I asked her to go to *Macbeth* with me Saturday. $3.30
apiece it'll cost—but who else is there glamorous in my life!!!

12/17/41

No man really likes a woman. He is either in love with her or she annoys
him.

12/17/41

God knows love, in this room with us now, is not kisses or embraces or
touches. Not even a glance or a feeling. Love is a monster between us,
each of us caught in a fist.

12/17/41

Passed my first suicide moment this evening. It comes when one stands
confronted with work, empty sheets of paper all about, and inside one's
head, shame and confusion, inside a maelstrom that will not subside,
fragments that will not hang together. Showing essentially how trite and
universal and eternal is every great human emotion. This was a great
human emotion. When I wonder now that I have passed it, if I shall ever
commit suicide, the question is, shall I ever fail myself and others in an
equally important crisis in my life? Life is a matter of self-denial at the
right moments. Looking ahead won't do. We can make out a too rosy
future. Successful living is self-denial without asking why.

DECEMBER 18, 1941

Up early. Wrote Helen last (?) note with the foul word—coquet—and
why I told Peter what I did. Also told Babs about it, and Pete's remark
on being told. Babs might as well know it all. Very interesting from novelist's point of view. December 18, 1941: Our finances are at their nadir;
$100.00 in the bank. Incredible! S. is really worried. Another Maundy
Thursday. Peter scarcely speaking, as Babs informed me Helen & she
had compared notes Monday night during the 13 Scotches. Peter told
Helen I said she was in love with her—So Peter is in a huff—and perma-
nently, if I know Peter. I feel the natural regret at losing a friend. Helen
is icy. If this has severed her it has served its purpose. But she says I still
haven't made her hate me. I should never have said that. Babs main-
tains usual neutrality. I can understand Helen's resentment but Peter's

no. I don't know why yet I said it. I didn't think it would reverberate. I shouldn't put it past [Helen] to have shown Pete my letters. People who meet crises drunk!—I defy her to find one fake word in my letters—I defy her to find one gay gal who would have behaved as well as I did. I defy her.

DECEMBER 19, 1941

A month ago was the night—two weeks ago another night—one week ago another night. Tonight nothing but me. + Up early & studied for History. Think I did well. Muret especially wished me a good Xmas. Babs making it a point to speak. Also Helen said "Hello, Patricia!" God, I couldn't look at her that way now unless she apologized. + Bought Roger sox, mother a fine compact and some garters. Wrote a good poem. "I am too much master of myself." (at 6:00 P.M.) Read Rilke & finished the book. Trivial sometimes, and sometimes wonderfully queer and delicate as in "Girl in Love." Translation sometimes better than the German.

12/19/41

One is never lonely with ideas, but alone or no, how lonely I am without them!

12/20/41

Perhaps I have said this before, but it should be in each notebook: a short story (or a novel-germ) must come from an inspiration which, on first acquaintance, seems better suited for a poem. Action germs are usually successful only when the element of oddity or excitement or queerness is developed. And the writer, like a man in the beginning of his love, should be passive to the inspiration of the world and the earth, who is his seducer. She plays with him, forces herself upon him until he becomes conscious of her. He never seeks deliberately. Inspiration comes many ways at many times, but I like best inspiration with a smile on one's face and a relaxation in the body. Such inspiration is healthy and strong.

DECEMBER 21, 1941

Terribly cold. Hard to walk any distance. Heard [Handel's] *Messiah* at First-Episc. Tonight with Virginia. Little done today except some solid reading. I hate to feel like a sponge, however. Jumble Shop for martinis.

Called R. as usual. Got Natasha in merrie mood—Sylvia M. is here.
Rosalind asked me to pick her up Tuesday at 8 at Crillon's* Party. Eating later also Spivy's thank God. + Virginia quite gorgeous in a beaver
coat—! She propositioned me. My moral code is becoming quite as narrow as my bed. Rosalind or nothing.

12/21/41

The sex act should be done either in a white heat or with the best sense
of humor. Technique is a matter of imagination, and consideration only
of the other person; a talent never found in men.

DECEMBER 22, 1941

Fine day. Finished play. Finished [Thomas Hardy's] *Dynasts*. Finished
staining Marj's figger & delivered that & T. S. Eliot back to Jeva. She
was simply overcome with joy & emotion & bought me two martinis at
the Mansfield.† I asked Jeva was she ever violent, [she] said no.—While
drinking I had the thought women are not hard enough—and are too
ready to speak their weaknesses which a man would keep, more wisely,
to himself. I feel very blunt and slow and honest with Jeva lately. She cau-
tioned me about going entirely with girls—they disappeared finally—you
need some young man to share and in short to foot the bills. Kingsley
here at 6. We did errands & decorated Xmas tree. Got tight & called
Rosalind (who asked me to brunch Xmas day). Read Virginia Woolf's
Between the Acts. Jack Berger of Comet Press asked me to dinner (!).
Knew it was coming.

12/22/41

When this fine maturity comes, what do people like V.W. & J.S.‡ do for
the violence and the unrestraint they must have known in their youth?
Without which the tranquility (afterwards) is nothing but stagnation
(but during which, strangely, nothing comes but shards brittle and
small, fragments and kernels of something great). How do they keep
their production so fine and so powerful, too? What is the secret excitement behind?

---

* Crillon was a restaurant located at 277 Park Avenue.
† The Mansfield Hotel was located at 12 West Forty-Fourth Street.
‡ V.W. could stand for Virginia Woolf, whom she's just read; J.S. possibly for John Steinbeck.

12/22/41

Babs has something fuzzy standing two feet out around her, touching gently in anticipation and warning something warm and comfortable. But I run into people like a steel needle.

12/22/41

Do you remember short days ago we laughed and said how lucky we were that we were the best-looking people we knew, that we were the smartest (almost) and certainly had the best sense of humor. And now that the magic potion that was in our veins has been assimilated, diluted (one might almost say excreted), we see only each other's faults, when we look, and more than that we hate each other because we remember the beautiful bondage and are afraid.

DECEMBER 23, 1941

Another day—generally speaking—delightful. But filled with emotional ups and downs that are becoming common now, they are so much more perceptive when one is alone. Wrote seven pages longhand of "Passing of Alphonse T. Browne."* Will have to be revised no end. Painted a couple of watercolors in which I got something. Someday I shall be good. In everything. Goodness—excellence is my goal. + Jack B. sent me lineotype New Year's Greeting & a babushka. We ate at Ricoto's on Vandam St. He's only 24 & looks 34. Picked up Rosalind at Crillon's at 8. Quite drunk. Fortune party. Went to *Macbeth* where she nodded frequently during first act. After she was too sick to go to Spivy's. Not drunk, just a sore throat. I ministered to her like an angel, she said.

DECEMBER 24, 1941

Worked on story. Wrote Babs & gave family bottle of Crème de Cacao. Delivered it myself. Bought Rosalind Eric Coates' "London Again Suite." Perhaps she can understand English music. I can't think much of it. Buffie called last night about dinner party tonight. I went with her. Drunk & exhausted, phoned Helen secretly after martinis & champagne. She was glad to hear me—I loved her & told her so—and she said to get over it. Buffie knew. At least she knows it isn't Rosalind now.

---

* A (lost) story in progress.

DECEMBER 25, 1941

Most peculiar Xmas. Eyes like golf balls this morning. Breakfast then presents, some eggnog. Got pajamas—Mozart's 23 in A major. K. 488! My dream of three years. To Rosalind's at 2:15. All merry, and presents by the dozen. Del P. very handsome. Lola there, Natasha, Niko,* Betty, Sylvia, Simeon & Guy M. Great success, the whiskey sours & bean soup. Natasha kissed me thrice on entering. Rosalind didn't open my present yet. They all adjourned to Natasha's. Asked me to come, but Stanley was home getting dinner alone so I didn't. Lovely dinner—this barrier between us is too great perhaps. There is now not the desire to break it. I've changed my mind, about money. I once believed it blunted appreciation, but it really heightens it, it lets you get what you need and gives the leisure and security to taste it.

DECEMBER 26, 1941

The seventh morning of work—not bad. + Mary S., Marjorie T. here this evening. Putting her maternal finger on the trouble immediately, Mary [S.] suggests playing along with Rosalind & Helen will come running again. Deception of the most innocent and strategic kind however, is unpleasant. Virginia was to come but she got wind of Mary [S.]. I don't like anyway that she asks me who's coming. Quite rude & childish. She hasn't grown up & I'm not waiting.

DECEMBER 27, 1941

Rosalind called! Very nice & we talked a long while. She wants to see Cocteau's Surrealist film at 5th Avenue. She was on her 5th whiskey sour, & en route to Del's country place. It occurred to me today Betty Parsons is tense & too on the alert. I wonder how confident she is really? And how much Rosalind sees through her? How much she loves her & why?

DECEMBER 28, 1941

Jack B. came at 1:30. Saw *Chapaev*!† Museum of Modern Art. All the Russian things drag finally. Left him there & met Roger who just came in. We drank martinis here. Got a telegram at 7 from mother that

---

* Probably Nicolas Calas (born Nikos Kalamaris), a Greek-American critic and poet who came to New York as one of the first émigré surrealists in 1940.
† *Chapaev*, a Soviet war film, based on a fictionalized biography of a Red Army commander and Russian Civil War hero.

Grampa died this morning. I didn't feel any better for that. Roger polite, but kissed me goodnight, which was distasteful under the circumstances.

DECEMBER 29, 1941

Finished "Passing," but Roger said tonight [that it] doesn't get started soon enough. Too subtle. He wrote a story in the evening, right off, and got an A on it. Well he and I are different. He isn't confident. Tonight he wanted to eat at a French place, so we did (Au Petit Paris) & afterwards to take a horse & buggy thru the park. But he doesn't like T. S. Eliot. I'm at the age where I cease to reform my tastes: I accept what I find— within—without shame. + Phoned Rosalind miserably at 12 and delight-fully at 4! (After doing errands around the house. Stanley doesn't lift a hand.) Del P. asked for me to come to his country place New Year's if they go. Read [Stephen Crane's] *Red Badge of Courage*. Splendid writing + Saw Dumbo with Roger. Not so good, but excellent of its kind. Movies stink. I have been to six this year.

DECEMBER 30, 1941

Sent the "Passing" to *New Yorker, Matrix* & *Accent*. Read *Don Juan*. How much more fun to produce than to absorb sometimes—and some-times the other way. Mary H. phoned, wanted me to come over at 4 so I did. Smaller apt. She's quite depressed, having sold only one sketch at her show. Photographs of our painting: frankly not good. She says she's beginning to feel her age—the lack of spirit to combat difficulties. + No news from mother. I begin to think my letter not lugubrious enough & Stanley didn't like my telegram. We both think, however, flowers out of place for us. Started my story of John and the Jewish Boy.

1942

PATRICIA HIGHSMITH PASSES two major milestones in 1942: she turns twenty-one and graduates college, and although employment proves elusive, Pat is certain she wants to make a living as a writer. She certainly fulfills her desire to write, if only for herself initially. Between the diaries and notebooks, she fills an astounding 750 pages this year with details of her life and ideas for writing, the entries written in a combination of English, Spanish, French, and German.

Pat takes one lover after the next. Very rarely is there someone she is deeply attracted to both physically and emotionally. Her circle of successful older women soon includes exiled German photographer Ruth Bernhard, who introduces her to another German photographer, Rolf Tietgens, and Pat quickly forms an intense bond with both.

The United States joined the Allied Forces in December 1941, but World War II seems to mostly pass Pat by. She does learn first aid, and the Navy recruits her for a course in decoding and plane spotting. Whereas her male lovers and friends are drafted, as a woman Pat is free to quit the service, which she does for lack of patriotism and satisfactory pay.

In May, the Highsmiths finally move to a larger apartment in midtown Manhattan, a step upward on the New York social ladder Pat has long been hoping for—but by that time she is desperate for her own place. Their relationship worsens: Pat's parents despise her so-called snobbish friends. Mary watches in horror as her daughter grows increasingly "masculine" and estranged from her.

Pat receives her B.A. in English in June. Despite letters of recommendation from her friend Rosalind Constable, Pat is not hired by any of the reputable magazines she had hoped, such as *The New Yorker*. Determined to write for a living, she is forced to temp, first at F.F.F. Publications—a house that generates articles on current affairs for the national Jewish press—then as typist for *Modern Baby* magazine, and as a street promoter for a deodorant manufacturer. In mid-December, Pat's luck finally changes when she successfully tries out for a writing job in the comics industry. With a fixed income in sight, the year ends on an optimistic note with Pat's confidence in her talent and potential firmly intact.

❧

PROLOGUE
Look before and look behind,
There's still time to change your mind;
Perfidy no time assuages;
Curst be he that moves these pages
5/2/42

1/1/42

Chestnut for the new Year: our pleasures, preferences, delights, vices, and passions are our vulnerable spots. They are cracks in our dikes, and flaws in our armor, holes in our masks, termites in our wooden legs. And the whole world sad, and all the sadder because the sun is shining, and because the air and the light is the same as at the best, but only man's own sadness oppresses him. It is within him and he makes it around him. Is each of us born with a measured number of tears? Or are they numberless? I wonder often whence comes the sheer energy that keeps us moving? But it would be of no use to ask "why?" We are not able to stop.

JANUARY 1, 1942

First real hangover on New Year's that I can recall. This year I really come of age. Took down the Xmas tree in an orgy of melancholia, and went for a walk (on eggshells) along 8th St. Bumped into a man who said he met me at Billie's last night. Tibor Koeves.* I don't remember a damn thing. He told me about his novel he's starting today. Rosalind phoned at 6:30 PM. I went up. Del, Lola. Betty & Billie there. All solicitous of my health. We had drinks. I feel quite dull, which is mainly [due to] living alone with no routine. This year I shall not only do schoolwork but write in the evenings. I work better and more brilliantly under pressure. Home quite late. Rather low, but prospects in petto. Down but not out—quite.

---

* Tibor Kövès, or Koeves (1903–1953), Hungarian Jewish journalist and author.

JANUARY 2, 1942

Went to Billie A.'s. My clothes there but not my lipstick. Lovely place really. She was just having it cleaned. Cigarette stubs, sandwiches in flowerpots . . . With Walter Marlowe. Dinner at Artist & Writers.* Wonderful talking really. Should put some down.

1/2/42

Why are creative people melancholy? Because they have not the hard frame of behavior all the others wear. They are grass in the wind, to be whipped this way and that, flattened at times on the ground. The creative person would, intellectually, first believe the price too great. Worst of all, the horrible knowledge, that this fighting (the story of it) is invalid for literary purposes.

JANUARY 3, 1942

Mother starts for home tomorrow morning. Her letter said gramps passed very tranquilly, cracking jokes with the boys only the day before. Gramma is living on at the house. They put her to bed with a mild sedative. Will be so unspeakably glad to see mother. Although I can't tell her all my problems she symbolizes all the stability, the femininity, the comfort and warmth of my life. Shall have to take her to the Amen corner† for champagne cocktails and a long talk Friday. + Dinner with Tibor. Told him of family difficulties, and we decided, together, that that restraint was the cause of my emotional knot, which is the cause of this turmoil. He keeps the homosexuality out of it. This thing with H. was the first time I gave my soul—saw my soul or could have given my soul, that is. What I shall want all my life is to give and receive warmth. I suffer from cold physically and psychologically all the time.

JANUARY 4, 1942

Up at terribly late hour: 11:00! Worse than New Years. Finished story— my first which "wrote itself." Perhaps good writing, but needs the climaxes played up. I consistently muff climaxes: literary and factual.

---

* Artist and Writers was a popular hangout for journalists especially from the nearby *Herald Tribune*, but also from *The New Yorker* and the *Times*, who gathered at 215 West Fortieth Street in the afternoon. Women were no longer banned as they had been during the place's speakeasy past, but the atmosphere was rowdy and men dominated the crowd.
† One of the downstairs sitting rooms of the Fifth Avenue Hotel on the northwest corner of Fifth Avenue and Twenty-Third Street.

Read [Walt] Whitman, for whom I have a two-day penchant. Walked in the street and nearly killed myself. What for? Unlike Nietzsche, my best thoughts do not come in the fresh air. More and more I crave change. By God if we don't move in April I shall be sad. We need a couple or three good sized rooms where we can stretch our legs and live with dignity—Shall use my invincible powers of persuasion on mother when she comes.

JANUARY 6, 1942

And the mountain came to Mahomet tonight: Rosalind phoned at 8:20. Reprimanded me for being tight at Billie's. "Rather rude, with people you hardly know—" In general left me uncomfortable the rest of the evening. But she asked when she could see me (for further chastisement) & we have a date for Friday lunch.

JANUARY 7, 1942

Play went over with the greatest success. Latham asked me was it "seemly." She was shocked at first, then laughed loudly, with the rest. Helen still acting dopey. I feel very vague about her. The physical feeling has left like a passing tornado.

JANUARY 8, 1942

Good day. Thornbury* said no novel is great without violent action. Home at 4:30 for tea with mother. She still is in a flurry and I can't talk very much. Says I'm very businesslike to make a date to talk. I was called up by Ladue of math. dept., selected for intelligence work—decoding. Right up my alley. Only 15–20 from seniors chosen. Shall perhaps go to Washington when school is out. I should be good at it.

JANUARY 10, 1942

Marjorie's [Thompson] at seven. I feel the old hostility with mother. It works this way: I'm happy if I can be the boss. Lighting her cigarettes and dominating as I did yesterday. I think I'm disgusted with her conversation—lightheaded, impulsive, trivial and proud, in a crowd—with Marjorie. I don't see myself living with them. Their pettiness begins to annoy me—their triviality—(Perhaps mine in seeing it.)

---

* Ethel M. Thornbury, English professor at Barnard from 1940 to 1943. Pat wrote "Tradition in American Literature" for her course and kept it in her files.

JANUARY 11, 1942

Breakfast with mother. Told her then how I felt about Stanley: that we alone could be amiable together, but his presence is alien. I told her too of the fixation element and that I must try and correct it, not they thru discussion. Purely emotional. I hope she doesn't tell this to Stanley.

JANUARY 12, 1942

Only travelers & lovers live somewhat in the present: there's a possible Thursday night for me & R. & K. this week. And a certain Friday lunch!

1/12/42

I wonder is the measure of emotion budgeted either to be used over a long period of time, or to be shot all at once like a double barrel Winchester?

1/12/42

When I write a novel: D.P. says one can't write a novel about dull people. Even Tolstoi's social significance is shown thru superior-minded people. And Steinbeck won't last, everyone says. No. I should take just my own class, speculate on Texas—New York or New York. And why the desperate heroic themes I often ponder? Why the wild young man, not the person like myself, curious, energetic, seeking, suffering and believing, weeding out and seeking in, finding and losing, failing and succeeding. The bogus people and the few honest people. But irrevocably New York. In fact, perhaps, New York could be the hero, working like a many faceted, powerful, fertile character, upon other worthy characters. (Worthy to be written about.)

JANUARY 13, 1942

All papers back from Thornbury. About 3 A's and four B's. Nice lunch with Babs [P.]. Simply ideal—martinis, omelets, string beans & spinach—and a good talk. She said she hated the secrecy with her family—some day she would have to conceal so much. I asked her what. She said someday, she hoped, she would fall in love with a woman. Spoke with Sturtevant. Said she read my "Silver Horn" twice & thought it was excellent.

1/15/42

I am not interested in people, knowing them. But I am intensely interested in a woman in the dark doorway on Eleventh Street, reading with difficulty the name plates, by the light of a match. Such a scene sets me thinking of all-time, all-place, all–past and present and future happenings. Is this real? Our only reality is in books: the purely fictional distillation from the impurity of reality. This woman in the doorway, I felt, was reality poised for an instant in the impure waters. This scene was perfect as it was. I do not care for humanity in individuals. I do not care to smell their breaths.

JANUARY 20, 1942

Kingsley annoys me. Saw her today & she phoned afterwards, just to tell me how sad I looked. So what? She's so damn unattractive looking! Why the hell doesn't she lose weight? + Rosalind didn't know it was my birthday yesterday—: I didn't expect her to, but it would have been so nice if she had. Perhaps she doesn't give a damn after all.

1/20/42

I love to be in love. It fastens me to the earth, and releases me to play in the clouds. I feel like a tree, taking root with my feet and stretching terribly high with my arms, and bursting all over into little buds.

JANUARY 21, 1942

Up early in the 18th century manner. At school at 9:00. The exam was beautiful and I think I did a good job if I catch Thornbury in a good mood. I should have been very tired, but I was elated over having lunch with Rosalind. Thought about it as much as possible during the exam, and afterwards smiled at everyone and took my leave. + Rosalind hung over, which is getting to be quite a habit. Showed my Naval Dept. paper quiz. She laughed at my answers. Very interested. "No days absent from school." "Physical defects: none." Why don't you put: "I'm perfectly beautiful"? + Then she said out of the blue that Betty's going to be gone over the weekend & she'll be rather free—Odd's Blood and all that!

JANUARY 22, 1942

Read Willa Cather's *Not Under Forty* and [Franz] Boas's *Mind of Primitive Man* & Napoleon's Letters to Marie Louise. + Shall start a story tomorrow I'm quite excited about.+ Did [Renoir's] *La Baigneuse* in water color. Could be better, but rather fits what I wanted it to. I feel wonderful—very confident and happy—about the future. About R. I don't know. Many things are possible. I think she'll not resign a lease with Betty. I shall probably marry Ernst. I like no one better. It will be purely an intellectual decision. I look for no further awakenings. I've

been around, and the sexual world (whether completely explored or not)
I have glimpsed its pearly gates.

1/22/42

Able to think only when I have a background, of music, of voices, of lec-
turing, able to think creatively only in the unconcious, losing the thread
when I realize I am following a thread, much addicted to cigarettes and
alcohol; shy about emotions of any kind and disturbed at their display;
caricaturing my own talents as they lie now, writing facetious (and rather
good) doggerel, sketches and perhaps whole books, specializing in take-
offs and pure whimsy and fantasy; highly critical of people, but with a
circle of friends as wide as the Tropic of Cancer; subsisting mainly on
fruit of citrus nature: rarely going in a church door except to hear Bach
or Händel; fond of 18th century literature and music; dabbling in water
color and stabbing at sculpture; aiming high and believing myself capable of great things. Falling in love more and more easily and "irrevocably." Happier still when most alone.

JANUARY 25, 1942

Mother will doubtless move. She talks about it. While I walked I thought
happily of my story of the executive girl.* It all seemed possible, logical, "true" as Koeves would say. The task is writing it. I must do it.
It's an important thing to me to express. + Heard Bach's B minor mass
with mother. Kyrie Eleison the most beautiful. The rest remains cold
to me except for a few lines, except where I close my eyes. Bach is rich.
+ Mother & I had a beer. I talked of marriage, which is politic as well
as being some concern right now. Mother said she thought of grampa
during the music, that it was almost like having him there.

1/28/42

I believe in inspiration, mad, unreasoned inspiration from the never
never land. I must have the idea, leaping to the surface from the subconscious as a sparkling, cavorting fish leaps an instant above the surface
of the sea. In that instant I must remember; to record and develop is
later duller work perhaps—the only work I will admit. My characters
are purely imaginary, because I seldom am able to go on from one that I
know. I have a strong trend to the evil, like many young people. But not

---

* It is unclear which story she refers to here.

evil hidden behind a mask, and not evil that is oral generally. I hate complicated relations, which really worries me a great deal, (this hate) as a writer because human relations are always, complicated. I am annoyed when real human relations have tangled me, or when even I see them tangling others. And hearing the situations, I forget them easily. Being unintuitive I must meet many people, many kinds of people, worthless people and petty people. Sometimes my friends find it hard to understand.

JANUARY 30, 1942

My notebook grows apace with such stimulation. I keep putting down tripe here. I want to tell Rosalind all about myself—not for impression—but because she is wise, and young at the same time & can understand as I do. Rosalind has a "yes-complex"—a positive, healthy, optimistic complex. She says the word more beautifully than she says any other perhaps, except "darling" which I haven't heard lately. And certainly, she says "yes" more beautifully than anyone else in the world.

FEBRUARY 1, 1942

Pleasant day but not exciting in any way. Too many evenings at home in succession are as bad as too many going out. Mother said [Stanley's] love for her was utterly without inspiration—that he deliberately stifled all creativeness in her. This is partially true, partially alibi—but at any rate what I used two and four years ago on their separation. I wish something would come of it, for mother's sake, soon, even at the risk of changing my own precious plans about an apartment.

FEBRUARY 3, 1942

Kingsley called with wonderful message: She'd been to the Wakefield [Gallery] where B. [Betty] Parsons asked her to sign the register, and asked who'd sent her and said, "Oh Pat! Yes, Rosalind talks about her constantly! About how brilliant she is. In fact I'm rather tired of hearing about her, etc."—(No doubt Betty knew well this conversation would be relayed precisely to me.) Kingsley introduced it thus: "I have it on reliable authority that Rosalind Constable is your slave!"

2/5/42

If people would only leave me to mellow. Like old wine they might trust to age of itself. But they plunge their alien fingers to the bottom. And I am cloudy with the sediment and best left alone.

FEBRUARY 6, 1942

Dinner with Hauser, we cooked, haphazardly, and started from scratch. Plenty of liquor. But no magic—no thrill, no beauty—no imagination, no ecstatic present, now perfect in the lift of a glass or a cigarette as I felt with Rosalind! I merely sit there, thinking of what to say next, stuffing my face and pondering on the personal spiel of certain people. He is all very well. I understand him and really like him—but he is as common to me as my bathmat.

FEBRUARY 9, 1942

Kingsley & I called on Rosalind, bringing her raisins & collecting my books, but she & Natasha were at the Normandie burning* at 49th St. We went over. Didn't see them. The ship's a wreck. Saboteurs. Gave me an idea for a one-acter on the war. *The Saboteurs*—Shall probably even write it, too. Happy evening, once more alive.

2/9/42

If I were a boy now, being in the army, I should be writing action stories probably with new settings—writing with authority I can never acquire through pure imagination. Thus men are thrust into exotic surroundings (foreign) which they are less able to handle than women. While women are left at home, to watch the human relations of long standing, which, while they understand them, and indeed contribute too much to them to understand circumspectly, they are less qualified to handle in the subtleties than their men.

2/9/42

My darling, darling. Darling—no I won't go skiing with you, with a smile of desperate pleasure stretched across my face—because I get so god-damned cold! But yes, my darling, if you'd ask me to swim across the Hudson River in this sub-freezing weather, then I would. Provided of course it's only a whim: if you're certain it's only a whim.

FEBRUARY 10, 1942

The lunch date [with Rosalind] was not wonderful because 1) I was dressed chi-chi, which she doesn't feel comfortable in anymore than I 2) she had work to do & could not drink much 3) we both had colds 4) I'd

---

* The SS *Normandie* was undergoing conversion to a troopship when she caught fire and capsized at a dock in New York City. Although sabotage was suspected, it was never proved.

seen her too recently anyway. She questioned me about working & writing: I said I could do both and needed to do both simultaneously. She said people never do write while working. It remains to be seen. With Buffie at [Fernand] Léger's* madhouse cocktail party. Hughes there first—spoke to her. She'd read my story & liked it ("Silver Horn"). Met Stewart Chaney,† [Arthur] Koestler‡ (very nice). [Buffie] gave me a Valentine rose. Now I feel quite socialized once more. I want to be alone now. Much to read & do. This socialization is necessary like a shot of dope in the arm that hurts going in, but which will make me run a while longer.

2/11/42

Mozart concertos! Aged sixteen in my room at One Bank Street, with the door closed. The piano sings alone, and I lay down my books and close my eyes. One phrase in the slow second movement, with gentle fingertips, touches me like a kiss—I had not noticed the double notes, the dancing phrase in thirds, and it is a revelation—just as a kiss is a revelation from one we have known before, but whose kiss is the new unknown. At sixteen, I lay and asked myself could there be anything ever in the world so wonderfully beautiful, so perfect, as this Mozart concerto? And the answer was, no, not really—only someone might somehow be a concerto.

2/14/42

I had a strong feeling tonight, sitting talking with R. that I was many-faceted like a ball of glass, or like the eye of a fly. One facet is the true one that lets light in without refraction. The others refract and are false. I have to try them all before the proper one is discovered. I have not found the true one yet, which should release my energy in a true stream. I see the right one is in me. It is what people see when they talk to me, when they set me apart for some reason, and say, I have a life ahead. I shall be something. I shall do something. They are all quite sure of that. Surer, sometimes, than I, but not really surer than I. Someday I shall find the facet. It is not so difficult and it will not take forever.

---

* The French painter, sculptor, and film director Joseph Fernand Léger (1881–1955) lived in the United States during World War II before returning to France, where in his later years he developed a style that would greatly influence pop art.
† Stewart Chaney (1910–1969), American stage, set, and costume designer.
‡ Arthur Koestler (1905–1983), Hungarian-born British author, journalist, and political activist. After joining the Communist Party in 1931, he resigned in 1938 after becoming disillusioned with Stalin. In 1940, he wrote the anti-totalitarian novel *Darkness at Noon*, which brought him international fame.

FEBRUARY 17, 1942

I think much about writing. I have written so many beautiful, fresh paragraphs. The problem is synthesis around one idea. As Sturtevant said
years ago, I can write if I had something to write about. Mother fears
a complete blot out of commercial art. Stands to reason—all art-work
except war commodities becomes inessential.

FEBRUARY 18, 1942

Kingsley said first she thought my *cahier* (I brought her yesterday) was
wonderful. [Then] disappointed in the book's lack of originality. (What
the hell did she expect.) And that the cloud of greatness is forever lifted
from me. Tut! Tut! Just as well for both of us. We've heard of another
place 4½ rooms on 57 St. Tomorrow the inspection. Stanley is scared
silly of the rent! Says our income will be taxed beyond belief next year.
Still mother wants a larger living room, I want a decent house. And never
underestimate the power of a woman.

FEBRUARY 19, 1942

Saw our future apartment: 345 E. 57 ST. today with mother. Only drawback is the view: more yards to house backs, ending at level of our ceiling. Not bad. The fireplace isn't real either, but the neighborhood! And
the house! Worked my last afternoon on the crypt course. Latham is
against as a waste of time. I do think the scant chances of remuneration
makes the thing unfair. Patriotic motives are another matter. But I can't
afford the time. I have to prepare for things not yet begun!

FEBRUARY 21, 1942

Roger F. here. Brought me a gardenia. We had martinis, & dinner at
Jumble. He bores me. Said I was too self centered to fall in love. I told
him I was, however, more disgusting double standard talk, and over rat-
ing of sex. A lot he knows about the real Pat!

FEBRUARY 22, 1942

Worked on play. Slow business. But sinking my teeth in more. Kingsley
here & we did the magazine. She made me nervous. Besides I'm never
happy when I see the nakedness of print and my own story there! Naked
in the marketplace, as Hawthorne said.* Were I to write a novel now,

---

* Hawthorne was almost pathologically shy. The quote "The lovers are naked on the market-place
and perform for the benefit of society" is by another of Pat's favorite authors, though: Henry James,
commenting on how George Sand incorporated her affair with Alfred de Musset into her writing.

choosing my deepest sentiment it would be that human beings could make a paradise with their own love if they but knew how—if they but realized what they had. But this theme is of course by my past, too—and present. I don't care to start first on a lesbian novel. There's no need. It comes out well enough in other themes as well. One can't help it. Should like to do something great soon. I feel enough and the expansion, growth and strength emotionally and spiritually. I should write of devotion, and it would be the least cynical, most idealistic piece I'd ever do.

2/23/42

Leviathan! I should like to call my first book. It should be long and deep and wide and high. Thick and rich, too, like America. None of the thinner, twenty-four-hours-in-a-bedroom stuff for me. I should have elaboration with conciseness. Slow reading and fast, fast writing and slow, because a novel needs no standard tempo.

2/23/42

Insincerity: Artists are logically the most insincere people. They must be for a while whatever they work at. A murderer, a poet, a philanderer, a traitor, an explorer, a child, a savant. They are all these in turn, and none of them and nothing themselves. They are their own canvas, a palimpsest of all their creations, and if when not working, they are a dirty smudge of coarse cloth, that is no fault of theirs.

3/2/42

My very first story was "Crime Begins."* I tend to that and do suspense well. The morbid, the cruel, the abnormal fascinates me.

MARCH 3, 1942

The Japanese are making great headway in Java and have really got Rangoon, Burma. Not so good, not so good at lunch. I get depressed in dark clothes, when my hair isn't right. Rosalind looked gorgeous in her gray flannel pinstripe, beige blouse and pearls—just the things for a blonde. We ate at Golden Horn.† How wonderful when Rosalind breaks out in a laugh and says, "I'll have a martini, but I'll go to hell for it!" She said, "My spies tell me your *Vogue* papers are pretty good." But they've found

---

* This story of Pat's has not survived.
† Located on Broadway near Times Square, the Golden Horn was considered the most elegant of Manhattan's Armenian restaurants and attracted theater and sports personalities.

a dream girl. I don't think I advanced myself any. But Rosalind continually says "You're a career woman" or "You're going to be just like us."

MARCH 7, 1942

Pretty nice day—tho still not perfect and it should have been, being entirely in my hands. Where do I fail? A certain discouragement in the morning, starting my one-act *The Saboteurs*—Not bad, but a definite feeling I should have done better. Nevertheless, I have to put something down to start. I can't think very long in the air. Afterwards I'm tolerably willing to revise. Women's uniforms are getting commonplace. I don't see any need for ties.

MARCH 9, 1942

Signed up for Airplane Spotting. A mild young man teaching. Important enough and very interesting.

MARCH 12, 1942

Mother's income is now less than Stanley's. Odd how both are not successes—not failures. One thing—I shall never try to combine work with marriage & a child. One or the other, not both—unless I'm so rich I can take the child & house off my hands. Ran into Berger at Fifth Ave. Playhouse.* ᶠ*Crime et Châtiment*† and *The Brothers Karamazov*. The first is excellent! Harry Baur. Every scene is a masterpiece! A novel like that is a real work of art. A murder—a killing in a novel fascinates me.ᶠᶠ

MARCH 14, 1942

Berger sent flowers, which were here when we came home. Drinks here at six. He's wonderfully outspoken and gets on with the family in an unusually adult fashion—says his mind & that's that. He's getting very fond of me unfortunately. Dined at Cafe Royale,‡ then saw *Café Crown*. Pretty fair. He wants to teach me the Hebrew alphabet since I'm interested. He came home at twelve and never wanted to leave. Nice fellow. And did a swell job on *Quarterly* which I saw Friday. Don't know whether I shall show it to Rosalind or not. Berger mentioned dearth of love stories in my writing. No work of any kind done of course.

---

* Arguably the first art movie house in the United States, it opened on December 16, 1925, and was noted for showing French movies in French.
† A 1935 French film based on the eponymous novel (*Crime and Punishment*) by Fyodor Dostoyevsky.
‡ Restaurant at Second Avenue and Twelfth Street, where the Jewish intellectuals and the stars of the Yiddish theater gathered.

MARCH 17, 1942

Lunch with Rosalind. A gentleman from the Navy called on her about my "applied for job" and questioned especially re the ASU. Rosalind had the British genius of combining honesty with discretion. She's delighted to come to Greek Games*—In fact Betty too and a Mrs. Sikilianos, of Grecian lore from somewhere. Shall get at least four tickets! Rosalind gave me Djuna Barnes' *Nightwood*,† which I shall reserve for some precious day in the Easter holidays.

Read *Democracy at the Crossroads* of [William Pepperell] Montague. Writes better than he speaks. Started [Edward] Gibbon's *Decline & Fall [of the Roman Empire]*. Simply superb! Another great book like [James] Boswell's *J. [The Life of Samuel Johnson]* and I approach it with the same subdued & cautious enthusiasm—an ecstasy of a sort.

3/18/43

The most salient feature of this century is the insignificance of the individual, the consciousness of it in us all, the absence of our rightful dream of greatness, nobility and destiny.

MARCH 19, 1942

MacArthur's‡ in Australia, and got there by motorboat, then flying. The Americans are doing things fast. I'd like to be there! Rosalind & Betty very interested in Jeannot's latest letter. Eight pages about the Grand Prix§ and cartoons. Rosalind said *Life* [magazine] might use it, but I think it's German propaganda. I must get more sleep. I'm dead all the time. One doesn't enjoy things so much. Let this be my motive.

MARCH 21, 1942

Now of course, being twenty-one, I feel a great responsibility to do something good in everything creative. No more reasons for imperfection due to immaturity. Mother in a stew all day about Jack Berger's coming tonight. I wished I hadn't had him to dinner, but I wish more mother'd take things easier. She has a masochistic complex of bearing

---

* Greek Games: Contest at Barnard. In 1942, the fortieth annual Greek Games were held in its gymnasium.
† *Nightwood* (1936) is considered a pioneering work in American lesbian literature and the most important work of writer Djuna Barnes (1892–1982), whom Pat would later also get to know personally.
‡ General Douglas MacArthur, an American five-star general, chief of staff of the United States Army during the 1930s. He played a key role in the Pacific theater in World War II.
§ Possibly the Prix d'Amérique, a harness race, held at the Hippodrome de Vincennes in Paris on the last Sunday of January every year.

an impossible burden which prevents her working at art, she says. I did a little reading, and got her quite tight at dinner. Her opinions on the Negro question,* which we discussed tonight, were vague & unprincipled and emotional. She refuses to think or reason. Berger said he was in love with me. I rather pity him. We all go around chasing each one another's tails and never making it, don't we? He read my play in oddly fifteen minutes, as it should be read. Liked it quite a lot, the dialogue, the idea. The Ghosts. Means more to me than the praise of the whole class!

MARCH 23, 1942

Have discovered this instant why writing this diary is necessary to me. It's been the only time, a few minutes, when I was still today. It makes me quiet a few moments, besides clarifying items that would otherwise drift in my head.

MARCH 24, 1942

Started working again at 9:30 & Rosalind phoned. She asked me was I coming Thurs. night, and what had I been doing? Then out of the blue: "How would you like to be an office girl for Time, Inc.?" I told her yes. Natasha had recommended me to the personnel, and possibly I'd be interviewed. Damn nice of her. Mother says it's ideal. Not too high a salary. Rosalind said they don't keep one on as office girl there very long. The boys are being drafted away, and they're now fooling around with female high school morons.

3/25/42

Probably the most serious handicap to a woman's becoming President is her clothes. Just imagine trying to please every section of the country!

MARCH 26, 1942

Rosalind quite grim. Telling me what not to do—namely not to have my friends up or to make conversational calls on phone—which is equivalent to telling me not to throw cocktail parties in the main foyer! She must think I'm indiscreet! She said she and Natasha think I'm a menace!

---

* We have no information on what exactly Pat's own opinion was at the time on "the Negro question." From later entries we know that she had strong objections to the treatment of Black Americans in her home state of Texas. Certainly, the fact that thousands of Black troops served in World War II while racism and segregation prevailed added fuel to the public debate over equal rights for all.

MARCH 28, 1942

Read [Henry James] *The Ambassadors* this A.M. very happy. Want to work—want to write—express somehow what I feel about the thrilling and wonderful impracticability of being in love with R.

3/28/42

On drinking and the time question. (Forever lost to posterity—forgotten in inebriation.)

MARCH 29, 1942

Fair day. I'm still an old pearl in a new oyster. This house must get mellowed before I can write in it. I feel much better tonight—this minute perhaps—than ever before here. Mother is miserable just now. I'm surprised (pleasantly) to see that Stanley supports me greatly. Mother he says "exaggerates" the situation—that I'm not hopeless. Mother of course says I'm inhuman, I treat her like a dog, I don't do a thing around the house —every whit of which is (a) jealousy (b) inferiority (c) retribution for her not getting sex and consequently looking for guys to go down in the elevator with all night. Met [Florence] Palma at church where we heard the St Matthew Passion. The music did wonders for me. It made me still inside, made me think independently of the two inches before my nose—made me think of myself too however, and sent me home optimistic, having shed a few Xtian tears, but having wandered up and down mentally into the most sordid corners, too. Such is the human mind with no hand on the steering wheel.

MARCH 30, 1942

Mother getting harder to live with. The advertising business will jolly well fold flat if the war goes on. As Berger said last night, many men talk of 5–10 years. Seems to me the art game, unless one strikes the top and stays there, is the most underpaid of all. The war brings at least temporary good wages, so why not avail oneself of them? I see Stanley in a couple of months doing something entirely different, and being a lot happier, too.

MARCH 31, 1942

Berger called, and I'd forgot about Fri. and dated Mary Sullivan. He had tickets. Does him good for a change.

3/31/42

Reading love letters when one is not in love is humiliating. It is being outside looking in.

APRIL 1, 1942

I wonder if I should go out tomorrow? I can't relax, God damn it. I need
a good love affair. All I do is keep myself in perfect shape—for what? For
whom?

APRIL 2, 1942

Slight progress. Worked on story and had lunch with Rosalind—We had
a martini and a half, which she allowed me I suppose because I told her
of the sad situation at home. She's quite eager to meet my mother. With
Hauser tonight. Very very hospitable. We had martinis and ate at Pete's.*
He still wants to get married, wants to meet Rosalind, wants to write a
good non-fiction, and go to China first. Feel like an adult today—like a
more adjusted person—good for writing? Not always.

APRIL 3, 1942

Woolsey Teller† here at one. Free for the day, he was, sadly. But such an
unbearable cliché expert! He got quite nervous and sentimental. Kissed
me on parting. The least I could give him in lieu of time and in return for
Chateaubriand lunching. Walked to 36 St. to give blood. Terribly nice
down there. I damn near fainted however. I feel lonely now. Discouraged
at my progress, and my only joy in life. The only comfortable arms I can
hide in are Rosalind's.

4/3/42

The world needs an injection of naivete. Try to get a job, and you find
this out. The arteries are hard, and people think they know, too well,
what they want. Nothing else will do. Even the escapists, the detective story readers, the movie-goers, have set standards that would put
a Greek aesthete to shame. Variations will not do. The frame must be
there, and within the frame novelty at any cost. The world is too easily
bored by the very things it seeks to escape boredom, because the novelty
which speciously attracts is soon discovered resting in the old frame,

---

* Pete's Tavern, located at 129 East Eighteenth Street, claims to be the oldest operated tavern in New
York, immortalized by O. Henry in his short story "The Lost Blend."
† Woolsey Teller (1890–1954), an openly anti-Semitic and white supremacist writer and editor who
dedicated his career to the promotion of atheism.

without which the novelty never would have gained entry into the great presence: the consuming employing, escaping public.

APRIL 4, 1942

Shall write a Royal Hash of Queerness for *Quarterly*'s next issue. Something out of this world for bizarrity. Phoned Rosalind at 2:10. Called me darling—I always nearly drop the phone.

APRIL 7, 1942

Splendid day. Judy [Tuvim] & I had a fine time. She said I never looked so pretty, etc. that I'd absorbed a lot of glamour in the last few months. I could mention one reason. She's very eager to meet Rosalind.

APRIL 8, 1942

My play (the *Saboteurs*). The audience actually gave a patter of applause. I am the kind of person whose novel (or book) among a dozen others of my classmates, the future alumnae of Barnard would choose to read first. Regardless of actual merit, I should enjoy this privilege.

APRIL 9, 1942

Rosalind agreed with me on the *Daring Young Man* argument* with M &. S. [Mother & Stanley] this AM. Of course, they thought he was not a sensible young man not to work at something else besides writing. The argument was further continued this evening, and elaborated into a harangue by Stanley on all my short-comings. He says I choose friends who'll compliment me. That I behave too dramatically and act a fool all the time. It's the old argument. I could list his vices, too, and his sins of commission and omission. They feel inferior to me. Billie invited me to a cocktail party Saturday afternoon. 5–8. Goodbye Mr. Berger!

4/10/42

A clever brain in sobriety will serve you even better when you are drunk.

APRIL 11, 1942

Berger here at one. I feel uncomfortable with him. Just as, really, I feel uncomfortable and vaguely annoyed when I am with any one person besides Rosalind—or perhaps Helen. I am not yet adjusted—to pure

---

* Likely refers to William Saroyan's story of a young writer dying of starvation, "The Daring Young Man on the Flying Trapeze."

sociability. Even with Judy or Virginia, or Babs, or Wolf I should feel this annoyance. Wrote Helen a letter, still somewhat under the effects of two ½ martinis. Told her I'd split with Kingsley and that I still love her as an eighteen-year-old. I feel distraught. (Berger says I am like the allied army—too thinly deployed on too many fronts.)

APRIL 12, 1942

[Ruth] Bernhard called at 12:30 & we walked on the bridge & Welfare Island.* She's O.K. But we talk (even me!) about nothing in particular. Corregidor† is now getting hell. And I'm smoking too much and life is generally confusing.

APRIL 13, 1942

Bought Ballet Tickets for Rosalind & me Thursday. I was ecstatic she could go! She's coming Thursday quarter to seven, meeting les parents, and having a drink. Highly eventful evening with Bernhard. M. & S. fairly hung around. She was in a gay suit of brown. But so was I and so was Jeva. Otherwise nothing. Bernhard showed some new work and S. was speechless with the thrill of being in the same room with her.

APRIL 14, 1942

Very good day. I think—I think—if it were any one before R. it should be Bernhard. I appreciate her, and I appreciate myself for appreciating her.

APRIL 15, 1942

My feet are killin' me these days, I fancy it hampers my thinking as an otherwise perfect physical specimen. Oh happy tomorrow!

APRIL 16, 1942

Rosalind here at 7:10. Could have been worse on my parents' part, and could have been better on mine. They talked of ballet in that careful way people have of exercising their own voices on first meeting. M. & S. left us soon. Rosalind then said they couldn't have been more friendly. I almost kissed her when we left but not quite—those moments come

---

* Originally Blackwell Island, renamed (in 1921) Welfare Island after the eponymous city hospital there. It hosted a penitentiary (later moved to Rikers Island) and (from 1939) a chronic care hospital. Renamed Roosevelt Island in 1923.
† The Japanese bombarded the Filipino island of Corregidor, which served as U.S. Navy Headquarters in the battle of the Philippines, for five months until finally forcing the surrender of U.S. and Filipino troops in May 1942.

when we are about to put on our coats standing in living-rooms. Taxied there. *Magic Swan** stank, and Shostakovich's choreography little better. We drank Courvoisier between the acts in a vain (rather) attempt to get even with an insolent waiter. Rosalind dropped a great black cloud with the short sentence: "Betty & I are going up to spend a couple of weeks on Papa's estate." Five miles to the house from the gate and all that. Which makes me money crazy all the more. I find shoestring living so distasteful—without even the compensation of artistic satisfaction—that I shall surely remedy my situation.

APRIL 17, 1942

Terrible—simply terrible buying liquor for a party. Bought all kinds of things and answered telephones & read away—strategy of World War one (very interesting)—till Babs came at nine ten. In fact all my guests came—more out of curiosity than because of me I suppose. Babs told me in strictest confidence that my name was on Phi Beta [Kappa] list. Virginia looked wonderful! And I was right proud of her. Fresh as a daisy. In fact it was her birthday. The liquor went like water & food too. Va. & I necked in the hall. I don't bother scrupling about Rosalind. She's enough man of the world to blame me if I don't get a little healthy excitation elsewhere. Eddy & Judy asked me next weekend to their country place. Should like to go but shall be broke and busy.

APRIL 18, 1942

Fine day. Dashed off the 10-page English Literature paper this morning. Went with mother to Matta's† show at the Matisse.‡ Mother was crabby all morning—by God! when a Xtian Scientist is crabby what the hell good is it!? It's proof of failure right there. Pessimism and doubt is supposed to block the channels of love or something. The Matta business is interesting, carefully done, gaudy colors.

APRIL 19, 1942

Very stimulating day though I did little work. Bernhard very glad I phoned & we dressed elaborately in sweaters, went to the tavern &

---

* One-act ballet choreographed by Alexandra Fedorovna after Marius Petipa's third act of *Swan Lake*, composed by Pyotr Ilyich Tchaikovsky.

† Chilean painter and architect Roberto Sebastian Antonio Matta Echaurren (1911–2002).

‡ French art dealer Pierre Matisse opened his own gallery in the Fuller Building at 41 East Fifty-Seventh Street, which existed till his death in 1989 and exhibited Joan Miró, Marc Chagall, Alberto Giacometti, Jean Dubuffet, André Derain, Leonora Carrington, Balthus, and Henri Matisse, whose youngest child he was.

breakfasted. Berenice Abbott there, we didn't speak tho. One over-eager young man fawning over B. She takes her reputation very lightly. Agfa,* for instance overawed by her request for menial job writes that she would please think of a job she might do. Wonderful evening with Walter Marlowe. He does me good, like an outboard motor given a spin with a string. We had much to talk about. Marlowe on me: that I treat my parents as people rather than parents, and they don't like it. And that they (mother) are jealous of me—not being able to stand competition.

APRIL 20, 1942

Latham said in conference I should point up my *Saboteurs* & she'd try and sell it. Terribly absent minded today. Amounts almost to a disease! Lost lipstick & keys. Mother & I got on to more arguments. We approach each other with dissent already in our minds. Things are so bad at home now I'm distracted—I must admit. But the fact is one of us is crazy, and it isn't I.

APRIL 21, 1942

I really hope for some money to do things with. It's been so long since I've had a new something to wear, I shall have to warn my friends when I get something.

APRIL 22, 1942

I should love to see Rosalind, only I've been working so hard I'm not beautiful. These are no days for creative effort. I mean exams not the war.

4/22/42

I know I shall never write—never thoroughly understand—the broader channels, deep mother love, love of soil, family ties. I shall know thoroughly, however, the isolated pleasures of falling in love, of jealousies, of waiting, of watching, of planning, the delirious mad joy of reward, the isolated pleasures of good shoes on a dirt road, of clean socks in the morning, of clean sheets at night, of water going down the parched throat like a metal stream of mercury, the delight of coming into New York from the far West, from the sea, from merely upstate when the lights are strung out across the bridges, twinkling on the river, dotting

---

* For decades, Agfa was one of Europe's major manufacturers of photographic film and equipment, second only to Kodak and Fujifilm.

the shore like a necklace of diamonds, when the beacons play at random on the pylons like wasteful children with a hose, catching an airplane occasionally as a dog catches a ball, and then dropping it, the streams of cars eager to get into the city, each thinking only of himself, coming into New York! With a good band on the radio in the car, and young peoples' voices around me—coming home! What a home!

APRIL 23, 1942

I sigh for the wonderful five days in December. I gave Helen two months, she gave me five days—but at least we both knew living at the crest of the wave, with the inevitable break on the sands we refused to anticipate.

APRIL 24, 1942

A splendid poem of [Judith] Paige's which we'll use—late copy. Wonderful ideas and real power in it. Wish I'd done it. Bernhard here at 4:30. Taxied to Pete's. I don't think she'd think twice about having an affair. We both talked about it, and we are sensitive intelligent people—we should know it was neither a one-night stand, nor the real thing. Went to splendid recital at Weidman's* studio. Shakers the best! Saw Nina D., worse luck. Afterwards hunted up a party. Found something at Fern's (228 W. 13 St.). She's nice—but just misses, the way all of them just miss—a certain spark of mind, a certain discipline and activity of thinking. I made a great hit, as I can sell only one thing in the world: myself, when I want to.

4/24/42

I get stimulation out of even the dullest people. Being amusing for them is like practicing the piano when you are sure no one is listening. You can be freer, attempt bolder things, and often succeed.

APRIL 27, 1942

Phi Beta Kappa ceremony: A wonderful address by Nicholson on noblesse oblige. didn't Babs didn't make it either. Tho she was on the list,

---

* American choreographer and dancer Charles Weidman was considered one of the pioneers of modern dance in America. Together with Doris Humphrey, he started the Humphrey-Weidman Company in 1927. He created the choreography of *Shakers*, about the eighteenth-century American religious group in 1931.

too, I feel that she is one of the intellectual nobility of the school: they don't always hit it right. We both have D's.

APRIL 29, 1942

Very tired. Insomnia last night—probably because I was happy thinking & talking about my paper to Stanley. Mother read it to him in two evenings, in her remarkably uninspired & uninspiring delivery. He thinks it's my best writing. Yes, in the critical way. Should love for Rosalind to read it. Mother never has any disagreement. She yawns, puts it down, goes to bed. She suffers not only now from her habitual lack of interest in any impersonal matter (feminine) but from sheer lack of energy. I see Rosalind Friday. Fifteen days it's been. I have so much to tell her. I shall want to make everything as elegant as possible that day! Wrote a funny little poem about her choice, which she will have to make sometime. The time is coming: whether she wants money, appearance, or the real McCoy. Made sketches. Read Shakespeare. I ponder the Phi Betas lovingly. I should have had it, were there justice in the world. And if there were ever an examination in general knowledge I should top them all. Helen sent me a note saying couldn't I speak to Kingsley because she worries her. I said "Darling—I speak to her twice a day." And Helen held it in her hands the rest of the hour, & the word "darling" was in both our minds. I can't forget her. I won't forget her. She's a slice of heaven walking around on earth. Should like to call Pete & date her Fri. at 11.

APRIL 30, 1942

Lovely day. Letter from Mrs. Fraser (Miss) [of Time, Inc.] saying no in 190 words. Lunched with Rosalind, who kept me waiting pleasantly for an hour & then brought Natasha.

Spoke to Babs today. I looked very nice in hair up & snood, white shirt, gray flannel & red corduroy. Pete turned around & said, "did you call me up last night?" I said, "yes, I did." She was very friendly, & probably is glad as all hell I called, I dare say. Well, I'm glad, too. Very good indeed to be talking again.

5/1/42

Crossing a street is one of the few things one should do by halves in New York. It's no good waiting for the all clear. The safest thing to do, positively, is to charge as soon as you see the white of the center line, providing you can stop yourself when you get there. Standing in this three inch wide margin of safety, all you stand to lose is a couple of great toes or a slice of posterior. Thus people have been known to survive the passing of two streetcars, but this is not advisable for everyone to attempt. When you see two streetcars approaching, jump on the nearest cowcatcher. No faith in human law approaches that of the New Yorker in his center line. Making one, even if it is half a job done, is half a job done. It's a real thrill when you can join the swaying, teetering row of pedestrians on the white line, see their comradely smiles as they all collect themselves for the rest of the charge.

MAY 2, 1942

Wrote 4-page stream of consciousness story à la Sherwood Anderson, in longhand on the young man drunk being kissed at a party, which should get an erection out of Rockefeller. Little else to report except great confidence & happiness, which is odd because:

a) have no money particularly & Rosalind's birthday is three weeks
b) didn't make *Time*
c) didn't make φβκ [Phi Beta Kappa]
d) haven't seen Buffie lately & should, to regain social status if for no other reason.

I'm going to need stimulants (alcoholic, nicotinic or sartorial) in order to work properly. My age or character? I don't care. I don't think I'm intemperate generally speaking. Most people overdo it regularly if they do it at all. I don't. Never have hangovers. Life is much more interesting without them. Mother said Berenice Abbott looked like a "les" (her favorite term) so I said there were men at the party last night.Changed *Vogue* idea. Am doing more difficult but proportionally more interesting article on Art. Chagall, Breton, Miró, [Walter] Quirt, Owens. Ozenfant, Ernst, Tchelitchew, all the ones I like! Went to Marcus Blechman's to see Bernhard. Who should walk in but Judy! She knew him thru the show or something. He looks like he could never dance a step (arthritic) but maybe he can.

MAY 4, 1942

Simple exam in plane spotting. Wonder should we take in Fern's party? The fact is only Buffie, Rosalind, Billie A. are decent gay people—I get so disgusted with these half-baked, dirty, stupid, gay girls, who merely didn't make the normal social grade. This protracted and assiduous reading is excellent right now. An emotional relief from writing, and much more needed background plus ivory towerism, which I know how to take and leave now. Growing into maturity is a matter of knowing how to take one's condiments as needed, resulting in a chef-d'oeuvre, in the kitchen or the study.

MAY 5, 1942

Spoke to Thornbury. Should like much to have a drink with her. She is art to me and has so much of Henry James. Wonderful and strange ideas tonight. I feel myself hastening to maturity. I have unsteady progress—some days like yesterday with inordinate and disturbing physical desire, followed by days of unusual tranquility & satisfaction. It's more than spring. Tonight I read "Tyger Tyger" [William Blake's "The Tyger"] again, the only poem in English perhaps which moves me to tears. It is like all art is in those few lines, all painting, all literature, all poetry, all love and all frustration all fulfilment.

MAY 6, 1942

A drink with Helen & Babs, which led to Pete, which led to two drinks & three, & home & money, & dinner, at Nino's & crazy postcards to people I can't even remember. But the beauty of it all was Helen. God I love her! She told me when Pete was away a moment that she, if she had it all to do again, would be a free woman, meaning the absence of Earl of course. That I was the only woman she'd ever loved before or since. I said did you love me even for a moment? She said she adored me and she still loved me. And we held hands in the car & I wanted to kiss her and it was almost like December! I feel about Helen as I said before and before. She touches something so deep in me that I cannot talk alone with her or look at her without crying. She is the one I could love, eschewing all others, forever and ever.

MAY 7, 1942

Slight hangover. And rainy day. Me despondent, with remorseful thoughts about last night. Only $3.00 but I could have lived on it & had $10 by this week towards the 21st. I rationalize ever thus: that temperance in youth is not a commendable virtue, for it leads to utter constriction in maturity; while intemperance in youth might lead to temperance, tho I shan't be too sorry if it doesn't. Pete & Helen looked very fine in clean clothes and rods. What different worlds they live in—with time and freedom, money and happy homes, food and drink. I'm really sorry to see Babs turning so masculine. She walks every step like a man, wears shirts often, sloppier than ever with her hair, and seems to be getting down on her chin.

[My] teeth look as good as the old days. Great relief.

5/7/42

There may be the girl waiting, the kiss in the dark, the whispered word of promise, the sun in the park on the swans on the lake, the job for me and the job for him and for him, the flag waving bold and free forever, and over and over again the handsome boy meeting lovely girl and all the lovely love pursued and captured. It might all be for the best, God's will might be done to him who helps himself and there might be a friend in need lined with silver standing in a pot of gold but I don't see it that way. I never will. I just don't see it that way.

MAY 8, 1842

Saw [George Bernard Shaw's] *Candida* which I loved with all my heart. What a fine piece of what theater ought to be. Met Mary Sullivan & Henry Streicher (Jesse [Gregg] and Jane O. there too), they were nice, but horrified at the coming of Bernhard. They loathe her for a "bore" and Mary Sullivan says she has done her some nasty tricks. I'm bored, too, with her stories, but there is something true in her which I love, too. We shall never have any kind of an affair for any reason, I know.

MAY 10, 1942

Read some history but terribly restless like all these days: the most restless, undoubtedly of all my life. I am so untried, and now untrying. I cannot loaf and invite my soul. Inside is a maelstrom of love & hate for one person or the other, and my artistic endeavors are either abortive or interrupted, at any rate completely unsatisfactory. Jack called. I envy his peace of mind. Said to M. if she were sick S. might treat her right, but he didn't know about me! I often think my only friend is my little pack of cigarettes.

MAY 11, 1942

Returned to school dressed to the hilt in black. I'd like to do something terrific Friday night. A healthy habit one night a week I call it. Read Blake with pleasure—and thought of D. H. Lawrence in concern with the detachment of sex experience from the flesh—and of course thought of Helen and me. Sex should be the furthest removed from the body, because the essential beauty of sex I knew as we lay there in her room—we both knew. God what work I have ahead. It's such fun to race forward like a steam engine, and see it be crushed before me, leaving a smooth hard packed trail.

MAY 13, 1942

Today—with very little emotion, I had turned it over in words so long—I told Helen to take it for what it was worth, I was in love with her. She said that only made it worse. I said I didn't expect her to give it much credence or credit for enduring, but that I was and that was all. That neither Rosalind nor Va. had I really loved. Maybe she believes me. (She took my *Quarterly* picture lighting the cigarette today. I thought K. had stolen it.) She bitterly, and more bitterly every day regrets committing herself to Earl—I wonder would she stay with me were she to be free?

5/13/42

Yes, maybe sex is my theme in literature—being the most profound influence on me—manifesting itself in repressions and negatives, perhaps, but the most profound influence, because even my failures are results of repressions in body & mind, which are repressions of sex.

MAY 14, 1942

Went to Betty's & Rosalind's tonight, Rosalind getting ready for bed in yellow pajamas at 10! I brought beer, & she was polite enough to take some. Asked me about *Vogue*, etc. Seems to like *Harper's Bazaar* or *Mlle** to get on first. Came home full of love for Helen—and beautiful phrases—not mushy ones—but going deeper perhaps almost touching the right answer. I was born the way I am. I am of good character, I love many things and I am interested in many things. The fact is, however, immediately I am not old enough for Rosalind. Perhaps in six months, perhaps three, if enough happens to me, but now, no. That is all. There is nothing to be ashamed of, and a person of my age & upbringing could hardly have been otherwise.

5/14/42

I am no babbling brook of rebellion,
But a great smooth sea, of varied but honest character

---

* The women's magazine *Mademoiselle* was founded in 1935. It published writing by the likes of Truman Capote and Flannery O'Connor and ran a prestigious internship program, hiring a number of promising college students each summer—referred to as "the Millies"—some of whom, like Joan Didion and Sylvia Plath, went on to become well-known writers themselves.

And if I am green, while other seas are blue,
I was born green and born a sea.

MAY 15, 1942

And I asked her [Rosalind] what she wanted for her birthday—a wallet?
She said no, at first, and started talking about phonograph records—but
I put my foot down. Finally she said the black wallet was an old one of
Betty's & didn't hold money very well, and if I did get one she'd probably use it, which amounted to a green light. I was terribly happy! So
we had a delightful lunch. Afterwards, I looked at Dunhill's & Lord
& Taylor's for wallets, but nothing can compare with an $18.50 job at
Mark Cross which I'm holding. Wonderful ostrich, with ostrich inside,
two compartments (no change section because that looks sissy!). I shall
try & get it before the lunch Thursday—with initials R.C. in gold like
the gold corners. It couldn't be better in all of New York!!! I should
like very much to go on vacation in New Hampshire after school with
Bernhard—but completely with the understanding that nothing happen
between us—I couldn't not for Helen & Constable—or myself. But such
a thing would be all over town. Not a chance! M. & S. think she'd be
wonderful to go away with(!)

MAY 16, 1942

Lunch with Berger very nice. *Tales of Hoffmann** stank! We had loads
of fun giggling like school kids. Later he sent me a dozen poppies, which
are lovely! Intense, nervous, excited, not happy, in spite of my best
intentions.

MAY 17, 1942

It will be twenty-five years from now until I shall have the fortitude to deci-
pher all these pages. We had Bible reading this evening. Then I met Bernhard & Ethel, Fern, Hazel, etc. at Carnegie [Hall] & saw Carmen Amaya!†
She's really passionate—ugly, crude, awful bore, but passionate and that is
all one thinks of. She is very slender, gives all she has in every dance.

---

* *The Tales of Hoffmann* (*Les contes d'Hoffmann*) is an opéra fantastique by French composer Jacques
Offenbach based on three stories by German writer E. T. A. Hoffmann.
† Carmen Amaya (1913–1963), world-famous Spanish Romani flamenco dancer, singer, and actress. She
was the first woman to dance the flamenco in trousers. Fred Astaire admired her talent and President
Roosevelt invited her to perform in the White House.

5/18/42

Creation of the best order comes from the greatest need. Who never has
sat on the edge of his bed weeping through the night, conscious of the
tongueless voice within him, thirsting after the beautiful tone, the exquisite line of verse, the perfect stroke, the flavor in his mouth that would
tell him perfection, does not know what I suffer now, and will never
create. Let me be, says my own voice. Let this first painful child deliver
itself. Then come, if you will, probe and test and kill me, but I shall
never die then. In the air-pockets, in the mountain tops, in the clothes of
all mankind, in the rock of the earth and the cement of the pavements,
in the waters of the seas I shall be then! But I that am heavy laden now,
leave me be. I shall fashion my own tongue out of the dross of the fire, I
shall find it buried in the twisted ashes. It will be there for me, it will be
like no one else's. Then I shall speak not greatness, not life, not growth
perhaps, not family nor brotherly love, but speak the need of others like
me who have not found their tongues, or for whom perhaps there will
never be a tongue but mine. The duty is great and the burden is heavy on
me, but the work will be the deepest joy on earth. Not life shall I create,
not life, but truth above all, as no one has seen it before.

MAY 20, 1942

Happy, happy day! The comprehensive wasn't so hard. I wrote on Shakespeare's audience & the physical stage effects on him. It was so boring I
couldn't even reread it, so it must be quite good. With Bernhard at 9:00
in the Modern Art, Steichen* show. M. & S. left too early. The show was
good American. Later Bernhard & I saw [Berenice] Abbott, Georgia
O'Keeffe,† Carl Sandburg,‡ etc.

MAY 21, 1942

Wonderful wonderful happy day again! Philosophy exam a dreadful bore
at 11:30. Came home & got money & met Rosalind, Betty & Natasha at
Tony's. Del there, and his brother Phil who's nothing like him, but good

---

* Reference to the 1942 exhibit The Road to Victory, co-curated by Luxemburg-born artist Edward
Steichen (1879–1973).
† Georgia Totto O'Keeffe (1887–1986), dubbed the "mother of American modernism," was an American
artist known for her paintings of enlarged flowers, New York skyscrapers, New Mexico landscapes, and
images of animal skulls. During the 1940s, she had two one-woman retrospectives, the first at the Art
Institute of Chicago (1943), her second as the first woman artist to have a retrospective at the Museum
of Modern Art in New York (1946).
‡ Carl August Sandburg (1878–1967) was an American poet and biographer. His biography of President
Lincoln won him a Pulitzer for history in 1940.

Bostonian. Peggy Guggenheim,* Buffie with a Bella, Mrs. Briton, Billie A., etc. We all had a lovely, packed time & moved on together to Chez Paris for dinner. Del P. spoke a long while to Rosalind & me about a job. He thinks *Fortune* is bad if I want to write. Rosalind upholds me embarrassingly well. Chez Paris full of us. Drinking more, etc. and somehow Natasha got perfectly stinking! She was wonderful though. Very passionate about Sylvia. Kissed me, pulled my chair and behaved like a good Russian, said Sylvia was heaven & she'd fight for her till she died! Asked me was I in love with Rosalind & I said no. We had a terrific time— Natasha & I ate at the bar with the men. Rosalind said "where's my present?" at Lola's and she opened it in the bedroom. She seemed very pleased & said she'd surely use it.

MAY 22, 1942

Hangover naturally. I wonder how Rosalind felt and Natasha!? Studied from 10–12. In school late enough & Helen waved at me a moment, and good luck. I was in the same clothes I wore last night, for luck my flannel suit. The exam was dreadfully hard—second & hardest part of Comprehensive. Later discovered thru 2 kids that Latham gave me an A (minus) in playwrighting—one of my prize possessions this year!

5/22/42

Most important facts discovered to date: That if life is a tragedy to those who feel and a comedy to those who think, most people do neither.

MAY 23, 1942

Read [John Millington Synge's] *Riders to the Sea*. Some good speeches—but still a mystery to me how some plays become immortal and others are forgotten. Evening with Berger. Saw *The Strings, My Lord,*† etc. which stank to heaven. Berger says he's in love with me, which is likely true. He says eventually he'll marry me. I feel no less or more attraction to anything male. Kissing them is like kissing the side of a baked flounder, and one mouth might be another. There is something in me independent of mind—pure physical reaction that

---

* Marguerite "Peggy" Guggenheim (1898–1979) was an American heiress known as "the mistress of modern art." A passionate collector and major patron, she amassed one of the most important collections of early and mid–twentieth century, mostly European and American cubism, surrealism and abstract expressionism. In 1938, she opened her first gallery of modern art in London, followed in 1942 by the Art of This Century gallery in New York. After a brief marriage to Max Ernst, she moved to and settled in Venice in 1949, where she lived and exhibited her collection for the rest of her life.
† *The Strings, My Lord, Are False* was a 1942 Broadway play directed by Elia Kazan.

works slowly and sexually as tho under the influence of a regular dose of dope. But I get no great pleasure—and consequently can give not enough in return—from men.

MAY 24, 1942

Another fine day,—tho tired from Berger the night before. He called twice—second time telling me to write in on the male ads for office & editorial work. Good idea. Anyway I'd written to *Mademoiselle*—a good letter—today. Read [Pavel] Biryukov's *Tolstoy* which made great impressions. I flatter myself I resemble him—in temperament, in activities in youth—but do I have the religious pilgrimage to find salvation & happiness? All my life work will be an undedicated monument to a woman. As part of my training now I'm making a plot every night under the shower. Much fun.

MAY 26, 1942

Unfortunately, I got C+ on the Comprehensive. Ignominious enough. I drank too much the night before & was in no way psychologically prepared.

MAY 28, 1942

Sunned on Sutton playground. Very interesting brats there. A nice letter from *Mademoiselle* saying they liked my references & accomplishments. I was in an "active file" and would I come for interview. I should be happy now if I had the A in the comprehensive, if I had a good job with Time, Inc., a promise from Helen and money in my pockets! Utopia! Now I am subdued, depressed, tho still optimistic about getting a job in general. Made sketches, some good, in a furious attempt at self-justification, artistic satisfaction. My energy, fortunately, is irresistible, psychically & mentally. Went to town tonight on my story. A fresh sweep. Pretty good. Also hammered on torso, getting the real meaning out better. The trouble with me is I become absorbed in the manner of presentation rather than the idea. Cashed my 20.00 check from grandma, for graduation, at Jimmy Daniels'.* With it I shall 1) take Rosalind to dinner & shall 2) buy a piece of wood for a figure 3) take Buffie to dinner 4) go out on a binge with Helen & Peter & Babs. Debbie B. I hope. 5) should also do something with mother 6) with Bernhard. Then to

---

* Jimmy Daniels restaurant, located at 114 West 116th Street at Lenox Avenue, owned by the popular café singer of the Harlem Renaissance, James Lesley Daniels.

a Chinese place where I danced with Henry Langston & Sgt. Greene, soldiers—some rough dancing, too. Home awfully late & to bed at 5:30 by daylight.

MAY 29, 1942

Had the pleasure of paying a Constable bill this P.M. to get her electricity turned on again. They were using candles. Wrote in my stride this evening—or at least I know now how to approach the story. Wonderful feeling. Walked with Bernhard & Lucien* this evening late and had coffee & chocolate. Lucien is suppressed, but powerful too. Later Bernhard & I returned & had stuff here. I think she would consider living with me. I should be able to get along with her well.

MAY 30, 1942

I can't fail to think of how it would be with an A. Congratulations, and confirmation of every one's high estimation of me. Which will still survive, however, oddly enough. A depressing day. Mother & Stanley disclosed at dinner that we are in the hole—more money owed than possessed actually. They speculate on going home [to Texas] soon, begging Grandma until the war's over. That's what has knocked us out, of course, the income taxes, the reduced income. I want any kind of job therefore, and fast. These dull, frustrated harassed days are artistically productive: I am so dissatisfied, I must create something, & I work passionately at everything.

MAY 31, 1942

Doubtfully pleasant day. Jack B. here at 9:00 AM but we missed the boat to Rye, & took one around Manhattan instead. Very educational, and nice surroundings. We bummed around in the Syrian markets, in Chinatown from 3 till 8:30. Tea & dinner at Port Arthur,† then a Chinese theater which was quite boring & apparently unsubtle. He constricts me so, however, that I can't even go to the bathroom. I called Bernhard. She came here at 10:30 & met Berger; I got rid of him at 11:00. There comes a time on these excursions when I can't stand to be with anyone—I am miserable with people consistently—for ten or more hours. Talked with Bernhard about this—I can always talk very

---

* Ruth Bernhard's father, Lucian (Lucien) Bernhard (born Emil Kahn, 1883–1972) was a German graphic designer and professor.
† Founded in 1897 by Chu Gan Fai and located at 7–9 Mott Street, the Port Arthur was the first Chinese restaurant in New York to obtain a liquor license.

freely with her. Bernhard thinks I'm very bright, should be a model, or work for *New Yorker*. I wrote a letter in answer to an ad, under Berger's supervision, lying like mad.

JUNE 1, 1942

Sent my *Saboteurs* to Cedar Rapids Play Co., exhausted the last ounce of my patience, fortitude and general energy yesterday. Waking up on a cold gray Monday, sans job, sans everything is not a pleasant thing. I worked with a headache on my Barney story which is growing threadbare from active and constant polishing. At school I discovered to my mild disgust I had only B+ on the Government exam. Raided *Quarterly* bringing home my weight in manila envelopes, stationery, etc. Saw no one, tho today was Sr. picnics & tomorrow graduation!

Read a wacky story of Djuna Barnes in the *Harvard Advocate*, which was certainly written in drunkenness, even if conceived in sobriety. I have appointment with *New Yorker* and [*New York*] *Times* now.

JUNE 2, 1942

Diogenes' [magazine] Arthur Blair sent me "Silver Horn" yesterday with inane comment. I'm launching Blitzkrieg on publications now. Even ideas for sleeks, female stuff! Helen phoned at 1:20. She's going to graduation as Babs and Peter too. I said grad. was like getting married. Helen said she'd surely have drinks before that (yes, seven or eight). The call was depressing & I had to convince myself again I didn't want to go. Caroline Abbott [from *Vogue*] wants to see me at 10 AM. Rosalind also had called, saying not to tell me, lest I get my hopes up. She evidently pushed the interview. I don't think my papers would. I feel optimistic however, and definitely confident I can do what they ask. For Rosalind—for Helen—for me—what incentives do I lack?

JUNE 3, 1942

[Interview with] Mrs. Daves [at *Vogue*],* about ideas I might contribute to the magazine—in which I definitely did not distinguish myself. Rosalind called at 8. Wanted to see me at home at 9:00 P.M, where I was. Showed me her scrapbook of *Vogue* writing, which is horrible and horribly wonderful of its awful, terrifying type—well—nothing I can muster in adjectives can express my complex dislike and mistrust of this hope-

---

* Mrs. Daves may be Jessica Daves, future editor-in-chief of *Vogue*.

less literature. Read part of *Tentation de Saint Antoine* par Flaubert. Wrote Helen a good letter.

6/3/42

I am too familiar to myself—too old—and rather boring. The avenues of varied goals are closing up. And wherever, even, I commence the long pull anew, I shall have with me the same teeth with the same fillings, the same aches on rainy days, the same wrinkles in my forehead. Is this some chance unfortunate combination of elements in me? In my body? In my brain? This scar upon my finger, this birthmark on my arm— should they have been elsewhere, perhaps half an inch? How would another carry them, and how notice them or how forget them? I feel my grave about my shoulders, the light grows dim never to rise again, my breath is feeble and disinterested. Oh, but I shall live so much longer! And there will be moments, whole weeks, whole years when there will be no grave and no mold-smell. But intervals there will be, too, when I, regaining energy meted by the dry crabbed hand of sleep, of food, of intercourse, will see as though my eyes turned inward to reality, the hollow-orbed face of death, the flaking skin like medieval painted saints, and know then that life is one long business of dying.

JUNE 4, 1942

Went shopping. Buffie phoned & I went & sat with her 5–6. She told me she worried about me—sexually, and in a neat catchy presentation like a lawyer's two-edged sword, told me she worried if I had ever had an orgasm. I made no reply. Any being commitment, and nothing being her business, anyway. Lots of nice dates looming around the corner—and loads of details in these many days unwritten.

JUNE 6, 1942

I'm horribly worried about *Vogue*. Rosalind told me not to write. Mad enough today to bite a corkscrew. Bernhard [and I went to see] a wonderful Paul Klee show. His persons, as abstract pattern, are as exciting as Blake somehow. Coffee at the [Central Park] zoo. Rather pleasant, but I feel she is gripping on to me, & I don't like her personally, because she's not my type, & neither would she be good for me, which is worth considering, though I seldom do, correctly.

[Goethe's] *Wilhelm Meisters Lehrjahre* is intolerably dull, even with my patience with classics.

JUNE 8, 1942

Rosalind's heard nothing & neither have I. God I hope so. Read [E. M. Forster's] *Passage to India*. Wonderful feeling today. Painted & sketched. But not very successful. Only mildly so.

JUNE 9, 1942

Jo told me she'd four times been in love, the third with a girl. She's wrestling, she said, with the problem of mores & homosexuality, though she rationalizes herself out of it. Says I overcompensate in hard work, generally implying the truth, and getting nothing out of me to mention.

JUNE 10, 1942

Wonderful, glorious, beautiful, memorable day! Riding with Jo at 7:00 A.M. Very instructive ride, but I wasn't bored with her as expected. Nor last night either. She's an extraordinarily sensitive child—even with horses.

JUNE 11, 1942

Fine day. Worked fairly well on new story—the Sutton Park man.* Mother gives me brief but devastatingly discouraging lecture on how I'm different from other people as a result of behavior in the house, & consequently won't get a job or succeed anyway. I tell her it is sex primarily and my maladjustment to it almost from babyhood as a result of suppressed relations in the family—which is all a child's world for many years. I talked of a psychiatrist, & she talked of M. B. [Mary Baker] Eddy!

Phoned Rosalind at 5 but she'd gone off [for] the weekend (!) *Vogue* had sent me at 4:30 a telegram saying I'd won honorable mention (one of 20) and wishing me luck. Understand they contact me on the interviews promised, however.

JUNE 12, 1942

Worked like a grub this morning. Quite unsatisfied. I should have a theme so great the demands & logical expectations of parents & myself should not intrude. But I haven't. Settling down to some kind of work will really be equivalent to a year's vacation and a private morocco-lined

---

* A story that has not survived.

study. That's how I feel about the New Life to come. I also feel it is just around the corner. Made *New Yorker* appointment again with Shawn.*

JUNE 13, 1942

Worked this morning. I contemplate another stream of consciousness about the independent girl yielding to the ordinary man. Her bitter and pitiful true estimation of him, her flinging his faults, his disgustingness, in his face, and her inevitable yielding, as a purely intellectual yielding, from the desire partially to maintain herself "normal," to win her ration of thrills from youth & from what meager fare N.Y.C. has to offer. Her desire really to maintain Freddie as a friend. Her desire to show herself absent from home for a night, her desire to feel of some importance emotionally in an emotionally starved life. Read Mushroom book in which recondite & eerie subject I delighted! Went with W. Marlowe to see Norma Ringer at 4:30, who was in the middle stages of induced menopause and behaving like a frustrated tabby. Walter is lonely & unappreciated. He thinks I appreciate him, which I do, I might come to sleep with him even.

JUNE 14, 1942

Saw Ernst at 8. We had coffee and a good chat like Goethe & Schiller about affairs of life & the world, politics & society. He's writing to [Edward] Weeks of the *Atlantic Monthly* for me. The drawback is he's in Boston. How nice would an interview summons and a trip there be! Perhaps I should even look up Roger! Pleasant evening. Some good ideas. On mushrooms, on things in general, which makes me feel alive regardless of the other situations & conditions. Oh Rosalind—

JUNE 15, 1942

And this is the day—the *dies irae, dies illa* I said would never come. This day should have a sunrise edged in black and a horizon rimmed in black, and a sunset without sun. It was going to be my lucky day. I worked well in the morning. Met Buffie at seven, after a drink with M. & S, whose wedding anniversary it was. Buffie very free with her liquor & drinking herself. We went to Famous Door† after many drinks at the restaurant. Well the upshot was I lost my wallet. It was not the wallet, not the four

---

* May refer to William Shawn, assistant editor of *The New Yorker*, who oversaw the magazine's coverage of World War II and was later promoted to editor.
† The Famous Door was a jazz and later bebop club in Manhattan made well known by radio bandleaders and musicians like Jimmy Dorsey, Glenn Miller, Billie Holiday, and Count Basie.

dollars. It was Rosalind's letter—the one thing I have, besides memory, that belongs to those wonderful first days, when I was a child of magic (and when I was!) and when Rosalind was heaven with a golden head. It tore something out of me—something I can never possibly recapture! It was that it happened in the cheapest nightclub, when I was disgustingly befuddled, that it happened with Buffie Johnson—I went home with her and the whole damn business happened again. Buffie was ravenous for female companionship and I?—I was at the lowest point of my brief career. But there is little remorse now, and when I decided to study last night I had calculated all the whys & why nots in my head. We woke with mouths & bodies like furnaces & I very soon got up & had a bath. Buffie was affectionate, and I made her lemon juice & fixed coffee & she lent me 4 dollars. No luck at Famous Door.

JUNE 16, 1942

Saw Mr. Shawn of *New Yorker* at 5:00. A wonderfully honest, sincere, modest fellow. Wants to see my stuff, & considering me as "cub reporter" for them now instead of men. Life is interesting, but is like a maze of varying trials and punishments. The one and only reward must lie in the end. Death? Rank symbolism—!

JUNE 17, 1942

Perhaps I should read some poetry. Another black day. They come like the waves I saw on the Pacific—especially shocking, because I trusted so in the Pacific being beautiful and smooth. I phoned Rosalind at seven thirty. She said "you didn't get the job," "I know it," "you could have got that job. [You looked like] just out of bed. The jacket was very nice, but a white blouse that was not too clean, etc." I was mortified, of course, not for myself, but that Rosalind knew me at all, & that the stuff came thru her friend Marcelle. Well, I was stupid in the first place to come without a hat, she said, and stupid not to split a gut, the way she did, to get dressed to the hilt for *Vogue*. Rosalind gave it to me plenty, but said perhaps *Vogue* isn't the place—perhaps—I'd get a job on the *New Yorker* which is infinitely better. But the second prize was anybody's meat & some dame with a neat hair-do got it, that's the bitter truth. It doesn't hurt me that they looked down their lorgnettes, that they said my shirt was dirty when I know it was clean. But only that Rosalind had troubled to recommend me. Well, I did comb my hair first before going in—there are a hundred things I remember, that I'll never forget, but why set them down here. There'll come a time when I shall be bigger than *Vogue* and I can thank my Star I escaped their corrupting influences.

JUNE 18, 1942

Wrote this P.M. & studied Spanish *Si, yo estudio el español y el inglés.* Oh for money in my pocket, for my wallet in my pocket, for Rosalind in my pocket, for a telegram from *Vogue* in my pocket. Jo here for dinner. Made a modest pass at me, which succeeded as well as it could under the domestic circumstances. No ideas. I am depressed, I couldn't, perhaps, sink any lower. The British have lost Tobruk* now, & things look lousy in China. The Japs† are already invading Manchu Siberia, & the papers are playing down our misfortunes.

JUNE 19, 1942

Rosalind couldn't have been nicer to me. We ate shrimps at Crespi's. And in the course of time I told her all about the interview, how frightened I was, how I never should have succeeded at all in the contest if it weren't for her influence, and she told more about her getting on, how some friend was turned down because she was too stylish. I get the impression that R. & Natasha consider *Vogue* a corrupting influence. Life is a series of attacks. On how good one's military strategy is depends one's success. Ernst Hauser here for a very pleasant dinner, which I cooked. Read Havana book. My Spanish doing nicely. I have many ideas. Some bound to pay out. The old habit of getting my brain too much into working gear must still be overcome. Should like to see Madeleine, but really should not like to see anyone until I get a job.

JUNE 20, 1942

Wonder what Jo's next move is? How seriously does she feel about anything, & how much is she afraid of? It wasn't the first time Thursday night, that's the interesting thing. Saw a couple of mediocre exhibits with mother, & on the way home met Buffie & a man(?) coming out of Maison Marie. She deliberately avoided us, which is well enough. Read Santayana's *Life of Reason*, which overall philosophy is full of platitudes but heartening. Jack B. here ᶠwithout a tie. I could have killed him! Oh well—I like him for other reasons.ᶠᶠ He said I should be awarded an

---

* Tobruk is a Libyan port city on the Mediterranean. In 1941 and 1942, it became the scene of several big battles during the African Campaign in World War II.
† While this terminology has since been seen as offensive, it would have been considered quite common wartime rhetoric at the time of Pat's writing.

award for platitudinous remarks! He should know that I'd really rather be alone sometimes, when I must walk beside him, listening to didactic conversation & attempting only occasionally to vary my "hmm-s" with an actual phrase. He should know what goes on in my mind, he would not think it platitudinous! We saw *Iolanthe*,[*] which stank, but was funny because of the lines by the fairy who was a fairy in the play from the waist up, but in reality that and the waist down, too. Went into Grotto,[†] where Berger encountered several remote relatives, very pleased, no doubt, that he was seen with a Shiksa.

JUNE 21, 1942

Worked this morning. Again, unsatisfied with Sutton Place story (the businessman & the girl), which will be, like the Boston story, an exercise in flowery writing. Walked with Bernhard to Blechman's. The pictures of me nude were not exciting, because I did not contribute, mentally, to the subject. Next time I shall know, because I am sure I can do it. So is she. I seem to live on next times, which makes me desperate & furious. Bernhard wants me, but in what capacity I hesitate to think, I am not the excitement she plainly considers a requisite, to love. And yet she paid me the compliment of saying I was the only woman in N.Y.C she felt completely at ease with, with whom she could be all the time. Came home & found flowers (great long gladiolas) from Berger. Cleaned up the old ones badly (I hadn't had time to finish) & mother slapped my face for what she called "back talk" & what I called trite conversation. She was sorry afterwards, & split a gut being nice at the table. Stanley & she talked about difficulties. Stanley has the least intellectual approach, of course, & formulates the most stupid & naïve theories & solutions. Mother sits considering & frowning but does little better. What do they know of my fury, impatience, frustration, ambition, energy, desperation, loves & hates and of my ecstasies!? Nothing! & they never can! Worked well on sculpturing in my anger. Saw Va. tonight. Her home is dirty & sloppy. I have outgrown her, and I find her dull, depressing. Phoned Bernhard at 10:10, saying I had an overwhelming question to ask her. I had intended earlier (in sobriety) asking her if I was in love with her, but wisely postponed this until Friday, at least when she'll meet Rosalind. So we had a most pleasant and unforgettable

---

[*] *Iolanthe* is an 1882 comic opera written by W. S. Gilbert and Arthur Sullivan.
[†] May refer to Grotta Azzurra, a restaurant in Little Italy founded in 1908, frequented by notables such as Enrico Caruso and Frank Sinatra.

hour at Hapsburg House,* which Ludwig [Bemelmans] decorated when he lived there, ate cherries & drank martinis, & talked of the wonderful things that only we can talk of. I need her, & she needs me. There is no one afire for her now, I know. She doubtless will protect herself against future hurting. Hence all this circumspect behavior & conversation from both of us. We are shy. We know each other so well already.

6/21/42

Shower bath at two in the morning. For unadulterated opium dreaming, pipe dreaming, for the most ecstatic time of plans-to-come, creations, ideas, campaigns, rosy futures, or even sheer animal happiness of the present, try the shower bath at 2 AM, before going into the kitchen to absorb the martinis (one or two only) in some good Italian bread and milk.

JUNE 23, 1942

My hair gives me hell. Got some laquer today. [SP]I saw Jo P. and had dinner with her.[SPSP] Again the same thing, Jo very slow & shy, but says kissing me gives her a kind of peace few things can. She said she'd never kissed a girl before. Odd & she does it so well! I read *De Profundis* of [Oscar] Wilde. Studied Spanish.

6/23/42

The remnants of the past, for me, are tattered enough. There is still the charm, however, of the Wednesday afternoon trips to town, when I wore button shoes & walked, holding my Grandmother's hand, over the viaduct which spanned the wonderfully interesting Mexican settlement, with its stray dogs and half clothed children, with the colorful and mysterious activities of the men, who would either be lounging about the shanties, or bringing home (white figures in their clothes) great parcels of groceries, push wagons of vegetables, junk, and newspapers to a grateful family. I remember the movie shows (they were slightly cheaper on Wednesdays) where we saw Clive Brook[†] in Mounted Canadian Police serials and where I could smell the clove my grandmother always laid on her tongue

---

* The original Austrian owners of the Hapsburg House created the restaurant as a private club for their friends. Ludwig Bemelmans became co-owner when they commissioned him with the wall paintings in the dining room. Hapsburg House was used as a location in the Hollywood movie *The Scoundrel* (1935).
† Serials were short ongoing stories often shown before the main movie. There are several that feature the Royal Canadian Mounted Police, the so-called Mounties having long been a popular subject of novels, serials, and movies. Pat connects them in her memory with English actor Clive Brook (1887–1974), a major Hollywood star in her youth.

before going out, to sweeten her breath. She carried her packet full of them, and though I would always be given one, if I wanted it, I never really liked it. I always had a Hershey bar, which I made last throughout the entire show, biting almonds in half and peeling down the tinfoil as the chocolate melted in my hands, licking the scraps of tinfoil before I dropped them on the floor. I remember the colorful visits to the five and ten [store]. (Kresses, a name which to my ears, was the auditory epitome of cheapness—to be used some times in its place, for paper napkins, for safety pins, to be used at others for utter monetary and social contempt.) I remember walking around the backyard in my button shoes, just come from town, when Willie Mae sat in speechless but unenthusiastic admiration of my adventures and pleasures, when I showed her my jumping frog from Kresses that you worked with a pressure of the two handles. I remember Billie Mae in her shapeless denim overalls, the sweat dirt-streaking her freckled forehead, barefooted and dirty toe-nailed, sitting with knees higher than her head in the cement spattered wheelbarrow, and though she envied me the half-finished bag of popcorn, the memory of the serial, the feature and the vaudeville show which would last me until next Wednesday, I envied her more at those times.

This was America—Texas—in 1929.

JUNE 24, 1942

Very pleasant evening ^{SP}at home alone.^{SPSP} Odd news. A Mr. Goldberg* phoned at 11 P.M. asking could I come tomorrow for an interview on the editorial assistant's job for which I wrote long ago. Have an idea I'll get it. He'll probably want to jew me down to eighteen a week, which I shall not take.

JUNE 25, 1942

I guess I got the job. Only 20 per week. I didn't haggle, being poor at haggling. Goldberg seems to be of some repute—somewhere. F.F.F. [Publishers], a Jewish House, giving most of their stuff to Jewish papers. We'll work on a F.D.R. magazine to appear in the newspaper & then possibly in book form (if I'm interested, he said) & I'm to get my royalties, and also to do magazine work if necessary, to make more money. Hours will be hard & irregular. Everyone thinks it's better than I do.

---

* Ben-Zion Goldberg (born in Vilnius named Benjamin Waife, 1895–1972) was an influential—and, because of his pro-Soviet views, controversial—Yiddish journalist and editor. His books include *Sacred Fire: The Story of Sex in Religion* and *The Jewish Problem in the Soviet Union.*

6/25/42

Second reactions: boredom, and wondering, as one walks along the street, what motivates these people who move at top speed, yet with the inevitability of wound-up dolls. And the eternal answer comes: not to keep body & soul together, not primarily to make money, certainly in most cases not from special ambition and desire to create, but from a sense and habit of imitation, from the ties of birth, which are most difficult to break, and perhaps, among the most "thinking" few, to milk the cow of New York while they are young enough to try and catch her flying udders.

JUNE 26, 1942

It's a lousy, journalistic, unscholarly job, and I'm frankly bored & ashamed of it. Why couldn't it be on the scarabs of Tutankhamun? Why not the history of the Dalai lamas? Why not the paleontology of the ancient Cretans? Why not the story of the Philosopher's stone?!

JUNE 27, 1942

SPFirst day of work. I went to the library (42nd Street) at ten thirty. Read magazines all day long. Mr. Goldberg (!) arrived at three, and said I have to write more fully (also more clearly!). He is not wrong.SPSP The work is tedious, slow, & boring, until I see what we are getting on paper. I'm terribly tired. My greatest fear today—this first day, without much sleep the night before—is that I shall not have enough energy to do all I wish. Read Dante tonight. Studied Spanish, worked on a story. I have several worthy ideas to play with. This now is unimportant. Is [this not] really the most frightening sensation of our time, the fear of loss of energy, exhaustion for a machine we care nothing for, the spending of all that is "us"—the consumption of life fluid as though it were gasoline? What is more terrifying than this?—not Purgatory or Hell!

6/29/42

The sensation of failing always, leads to this in the still active person: a desire to be "someone else," the feeling that even with a new and propitious idea, the executor is the same, the executor and artist is "I," bringing inevitably the old train of faults the old plan of stumble-blocks, makes one want a new inside, a whole new inside.

JUNE 29, 1942

Came pretty late to the library. I phoned unavailingly Rosalind & Bernhard, feeling very lost, in spite of myself, and wanting like crazy to have

a lunch date or a date tonight. Went to see R. at 12:10. She had just
made a date. Looked up a file on Goldberg, who was arrested in 41 for
shouting "Scab!" Not a bad record. Came home to eat. Saw Alice T.
when I returned. We had a cigarette. Obviously likes me better than Va.
Well, why not? Va. incidentally has a big picture of me (on the piano) in
her room. Also a sketch. So she still lives with me. Jo sent me a beautiful (rather) alligator billfold, gold tips four. Western Union. With a
card: "A compromise. Jo P." How sweet of her to do that. I thought
of it, & wanted it, but dropped no hints, of course, which I found too
embarrassing.

JUNE 30, 1942
   SPSaw Betty on the way to Del Pezzo's. She didn't see me. Then she and
Rosalind arrived together.SPSP R. finally waved at me. She saw Bernhard
pretty well. I didn't mind in the least, of course, I only hope she didn't
think I was checking up on her. I've written thousands of words today.
Didn't see Goldberg but dropped off my notes. The three other girls
seemed to be loafing. One is gay by the way. Someone made a pass at
Bernhard, which boosted her ego 100%. I don't do that enough to suit
her. Lovely drinking martinis again at lunch.
   With R. tomorrow. Want to buy a suit at Saks. Worked on "Russula,"*
almost done & have real ambitions. Wonderful how one's energy never
wanes. Egypt looks lousy. The British falling back to Alexandria, tho
more allied reinforcements are coming.

JULY 1, 1942
   Rosalind told me I was too vague about what I wanted to do with myself
when I asked for a job. Very likely, only now, with this month's experience, I feel I could do worlds' better. I shall try once more with Fraser
after a few weeks' experience here or elsewhere. Goldberg I find very
boring & he wants me to put the whole article down on paper first! Buffie
phoned for party tomorrow night. Mad costume.

JULY 2, 1942
   Very dull day looking up S.D.R. [Sara Delano Roosevelt], whose sister I
don't know the married name of, and who possessed the dubious distinction of having had an obituary written on her concerning her '62 trip to
China. There is nothing left to find on this trip to China except the knot

---
* Unclear which short story she is referring to here.

speed. Goldberg sent me on a job at 5:30! Louse! Nevertheless, I shall work cheerfully. N.B. We aim to please. Went to Buffie's party later. Buffie was even better than I imagined—better looking in pink corset, tights affair—no sleeves—stopping roughly & abruptly at the crotch. Black net stockings. Also there De la Noux.* Toni Hughes with a fine young man named Keith who knows Ernst Hauser & [Marjorie] Wolf & likes Wolf (!), Julian Levi, Mr. & Mrs. Watts (the husband has beautiful bare feet & knows it) & Teddy & Touche.† Touche is horribly, sickeningly flippant. Teddie I like—tho I never saw such masculine gestures outside of a butch. She was in cream colored tights. Coachman livery or 18th century gallant style, with black boots—may have contributed. Anyway, we talked a long while. Touche puts his beefy arms around every woman eventually, with a flip answer for everything. Said I must come to his place. De la Noux looked lovely as usual. White blouse, prevented from rivaling her teeth by a lavender scarf. Should like to see Teddie & Toni again.

JULY 3, 1942

Easy pleasant day. Went to 25 St. on a job, then back to Goldberg who sat talking with me in the Shanty [restaurant] for an hour about the Venture.‡ It would involve giving all my spare time (even evenings) to reading, if I went into this book. Still Goldberg's methods are sound. I like him, personally, furthermore, & he must like me. I haven't talked salary yet, & I shouldn't write for less than $30. He's looking at my writing this weekend & will probably give me whole chapters to write if he does the outline. That'd be fun.

7/3/42

One's most stubborn addictions, one's deepest loves, such as smoking, drinking, writing—are first unpleasant, almost unnatural things to do. Proving the death instinct at least "present" in the man on the streets, in the ecstatic results of smoking & drinking; proving the arts are born of strangeness, fascination, pain & slow acquaintanceship. Like writing, like painting, like composing music. Still, now, when the writer says, I hate to write, it is the physical effort of the brain which prompts this. He

---

* It is likely this is a misspelling and she means the bisexual writer and designer Eyre de Lanux (1894–1996), also an acquaintance of Rosalind's.
† Cult lyricist and wit La Touche (born John Treville Latouche, 1914–1956) wrote the lyrics for more than twenty musicals, most famously *Cabin in the Sky* with the song "Taking a Chance on Love." He also wrote the "Ballad for Americans" that both Paul Robeson and Bing Crosby performed regularly. He was homosexual, as was probably his wife, Teddie.
‡ "The Venture" refers to one of Goldberg's book projects.

might hate drinking water when he does not want it, but he will for his health, and the inevitable condition of the body prompts it.

JULY 5, 1942

^{SP}A pleasant day because mother was with Marjorie, doing prints. One of my wooden women which I should show to Mr. Crowninshield from *Vogue*.* He buys similar things.

Russia says that the Germans have crossed the lines. The war is going worse for them than before . . . I took a walk with Mother and we had a very serious talk about things at home. She will be more agreeable now, I think. S. is always the same. Didn't speak a word today.^{SPSP}

JULY 7, 1942

I suffer these days not only from diffusion of ideas in writing, but from diffusion of my whole energy. I should love Helen! Perhaps I do. I certainly do whenever I think of her. I certainly found in her & with her what no one else has ever or perhaps can ever give me. Why do I fret about Rosalind? Even about Bernhard?! If Helen is a losing fight what matters that to me! I of the losing fights! I of the ideals in love! ^{SP}Things are better.^{SPSP} Pleasant evening sewing on slipcover, reading Dante. I remember Mrs. Lordner's advice: "If you don't make it these days, you're just dumb." Goldberg asked if I wanted to do the household section of *The Jewish Family Year Book.*† I said yes!

JULY 7, 1942

^{SP}I want to take all my notebooks and read through them for important phrases— use them.^{SPSP} It would be wonderful to do it on a weekend. Alone, in the quiet.

JULY 8, 1942

^FI received my diploma! In real vellum^{FF}—^{SP}it's in Latin, so I couldn't read it! I used a dictionary! But it's beautiful, and I want Grandma to have it. I ate with Rosalind and gave her my magazines from Jeannot. We saw the Malvina Hoffman‡ exhibit. It wasn't good. It occurred to

---

* The cultivated and elegant Francis Welch Crowninshield (1872–1947) was best known for his twenty-one years at the top of *Vanity Fair* during which time he turned it from a mere fashion magazine to one of America's most prominent literary magazines, publishing Aldous Huxley, T. S. Eliot, Gertrude Stein, and Djuna Barnes—all in a single issue. He later also served as an editor for *Vogue*.
† Presumably a reference to *The Jewish Family Almanac 1943*, which was edited by B. Z. Goldberg and Dr. Emil Flesch and published by F.F.F. Publications.
‡ Malvina Hoffman (1885–1966), noted American sculptor.

me that Rosalind might easily get tired of me. I tried to tell her what I thought about my life with—her—with me. That there might not be a reason for me to always stay with her, like—what? Like some nobody!ᔆᴾᔆᴾ

7/8/42

Each person carries around in himself a terrible other world of hell and the unknown. He may rarely see it if he turns his mind to it, but in the course of life he may perhaps see it once or twice, when he is near death or when he is much in love, or when he is deeply stirred by music, by God or by sudden fear. It is an enormous pit reaching below the deepest crater of the earth, or it is the thinnest air far beyond the moon. But it is frightening and essentially "unlike" man as he knows himself familiarly, so we spend all our days living at the other antipodes of ourself.

7/8/42

I'd be very content if I could take a story of two perfectly normal newlyweds, bursting with good health and sexual energy, and make a good story out of it.

JULY 9, 1942

ᔆᴾMr. Goldberg raised my salary, I don't know how much, maybe $23–24. I want to buy a Spanish dictionary. Jack enters the Army on July 29. But he'll be here until August 14. He's serious and sad now.ᔆᴾᔆᴾ Good ideas & pretty happy. Mother cheerful as a cricket!

JULY 12, 1942

Sewed some—very frantically—on the slipcover. Makes me furious because sewing embodies, in a particularly violent and overwhelming form, all the vigors—all the familiar sensations of failure!

JULY 13, 1942

ᔆᴾYesterday was the worst day the Russians have had to date. The Germans have advanced very far into the country. The two armies are almost divided now, N. & S. [North and South], and the Germans are headed for the oilfields. The English have stopped Rommel.

A day full of work. I looked for facts for the article about the budget and I wrote it in the afternoon. A card from Jo P.ᔆᴾᔆᴾ "Your letter was an oasis in a desert of Southern belles, etc." And that she misses me. ᔆᴾAlso, a card from Jeannot. Only *"Espoir"* [hope]. Walter Marlowe here at 7.

Some books. He spoke about how all goes according to the wishes of the rich. Wow! A marvelous meal at the Salle du Bois* and some good conversation. Later we went to Spivy's.[SPSP]

JULY 14, 1942

[SP]Goldberg had a lot of corrections for my article. It's much better now. I did research again for tomorrow's article. Very tired. I told Bernhard that I couldn't do our date tonight. Instead of the theater I read Dante and worked on my story. It's very good, too.[SPSP]

7/14/42

What we call "hell" is an earth-imagined state born of the physical sensations of shame, which are always those of inner "burning."

JULY 16, 1942

[SP]I wanted to see Rosalind the 19th. It's our anniversary. But she won't remember. Never—never—never! *Mademoiselle* called me at eleven. They wanted me to come tomorrow at ten for an interview. There's an opening but they want a stenographer. [SPSP] I should so like to get on *Mademoiselle*—mainly because I would thus redeem myself with Rosalind. If I could only tell her, when I lunch with her Monday that I'm actually working there! I would even go there for less money.

JULY 17, 1942

[SP]I worked the whole day and wasn't able to read or study at all. Paddy Finucane[†] died over the Atlantic in his airplane. The Germans hit his radiator and he wasn't high up enough to get to England. When his plane touched the sea it was probably in pieces! And only twenty-one years old. With Billie B. last night. Drank at the Cape Cod Room. Later we went to her house where I spent the night! Nothing to tell. Billie is bad in bed. I had known about it before. Her bed is also narrow. I woke up early and was at home by eight. The parents will never know.[SPSP]

JULY 18, 1942

[SP]I saw Mr. Goldberg, who told me not to go to *Mlle*. That he is interested in me, which is true. I don't know whether I'll go or stay.[SPSP]

---

* La Salle du Bois at 30 East Sixtieth Street.
† Brendan Eamonn Fergus ("Paddy") Finucane (1920–1942), distinguished Irish fighter pilot.

JULY 19, 1942

SPToday is the day I met Rosalind Constable. I would have been with her tonight. I could have gone deeper or at least drunk a drink to our souls. But she is far away now and never thinks of me. It's also the hottest it has been all year. I worked on my story and will show it to Mr. Goldberg tomorrow. I still want to move, I think that is how I will mature! I read Dante and Heraldry* again with great pleasure. I'd like to write a piece for the theater. Some piece about a soldier—who leaves.SPSP

JULY 20, 1942

SPThe days pass happily, but progress is slow. I worked today with the same tranquility I had in my youth at Morton Street. I wrote a good article about "Trends in Fashion" this morning, and ate lunch with Berger who drank a Tom Collins and read the paper. I felt that he was thinking of me from across the table. He would do anything to please me.

I studied and also wrote two pages of a wonderful story about "Manuel."† It will truly be marvelous! The English are thinking about what might happen if the Germans manage to take Alexandria. Meanwhile the Russians are fighting valiantly. And they're losing. I'm happy—I'm happy and why is that? I don't have anybody. Nobody!SPSP

JULY 22, 1942

SPI wrote this morning, and later Mr. Goldberg asked me for my notebook. I said yes but later decided no. It's not possible to give him anything that isn't good! Bernhard has a studio now with a photographer. She wants me to come with her tomorrow evening to get the room ready but I need to work. I really don't give Mr. Goldberg enough work. I won't receive a larger salary this way! I was thinking too much about myself.SPSP

JULY 23, 1942

SPGoldberg is good. We talked about work, then later about my story. I have to rewrite eight pages. Bernhard called me. But I don't have enough time to play every night.SPSP

---

* Possibly Pat refers to Henry Wall Pereira's book *On Dante's Knowledge of Heraldry* (1898).
† Pat commences a new short story that she will continue to work on for the next few months. This story does not survive.

JULY 24, 1942

B.Z. [Goldberg] in nasty temper ^Fthis evening.^{FF} How much nicer if I worked elsewhere—no wishful thinking allowed, however. I'll spring that place soon enough. Phoned Jack. He was so overjoyed he later sent me a telegram. Studied Spanish—but hereafter my evenings shall commence writing.

7/26/42

Wagner's music—almost any of it good to make love by.
(What horror!—1950)

JULY 27, 1942

^{SP}Mother and I went to Winslow. Excellent dinner. She asked me about Jack and Marlowe. Who do you prefer? Etc. In truth I don't know. She told me Jack adores me. It's true. A bourgeois night for once—we saw *Mrs. Miniver* at [Radio City] Music Hall. Mother ate so much—or drank so much that she kept falling asleep the entire time. The film was marvelous. I phoned Bernhard, and now I regret it because I'll spend the whole night wanting it to be tomorrow.^{SPSP}

JULY 30, 1942

Last night and a year ago, Rosalind wrote me the beautiful letter that made me love her—the letter I got in Sioux Falls, S. Da.—the letter I read till it wore out, the letter I never betrayed, the letter I knew by heart, the letter she believed and I believed in—the letter I would have given a front tooth to keep—the letter I lost. Most of the phrases linger in my mind, I shall hate to see them fade out of memory but it seems silly trying (and failing) to recapture even part of it. ^{SP}Miss Weick* is writing articles now, but none of them are as interesting as mine. Totally without ideas at the moment, but at least writing went well tonight after First Aid class on my story "Manuel." Tonight we looked at the arteries, etc. My girl (the one I'm working with) is pretty, but so big that I couldn't find the vessels. We examined the body, even the toes, the chest, the breast, throat, and back. I want to see Rosalind. I want to go home with her.^{SPSP}

JULY 31, 1942

^{SP}A typical day, smoking far too much, working too much. I went to Fornos Restaurant, where I ordered rice and chicken.^{SPSP} Goldberg said:

---

* A work colleague of Pat's at F.F.F. Publications.

"There's something in your writing that intrigues me—rhythm & an occasional new turn of phrase. But it's inclined to be poetry. Uneven." [SP]I got another raise: $25 per week. Jack told me he spoke with Goldberg. About business. He called me tonight during the blackout.[*] Jack told me that Goldberg paid me a lot of compliments which he will tell me about on Monday.[SPSP]

AUGUST 2, 1942

Sent Rosalind a letter with the "Welcome, soldier!" sex hygiene brochure. I think she's on vacation which is why I haven't seen her in 24 days & 12 hours & 25 minutes.

8/2/42

Why can't I write of apple-blossom faces, of valentines and bedsteads, kitchen fires? Because there's too much wrong with the world, and the old ways are not the way out.

AUGUST 3, 1942

Berger came tonight. Lovely evening. He gave me an unpolished Mexican silver bracelet. Dinner at Proust's which is a sad hashery. I still want time alone tho Jack's fun to be with.

AUGUST 4, 1942

[SP]Met Bernhard near the library. She's still sad—she can't work with Tietgens[†] and d'Arazien[‡] around. Later on I wrote the article about Lasting Peace at the office but Goldberg didn't like the style. He wants to go to Poughkeepsie tomorrow, but by boat, to plan the book about American nationalities.[SPSP]

---

* There was no continuous nightly blackout in wartime New York. But blackout drills were held mostly in the early years of the war, when there were fears that German bombers might appear overhead. In spring 1942, the Army considered that the glow from Manhattan's city lights was silhouetting ships offshore, making them easy targets for Germans that had sunk scores of oil tankers and freighters bound for Britain. So under an Army-ordered dim-out, the neon advertising on Times Square went dark, stores and bars dimmed their exterior lighting, just as streetlights and traffic signals had their wattage reduced, car headlights were hooded, and the Statue of Liberty's torch didn't glow.

† Rolf Tietgens (1911–1984), the "Poet with a Camera," had already published two extraordinary photo books by the time he was forced to leave his native Germany and emigrate to the United States in 1939. He soon succeeded in working for important magazines, getting his photos published in *Popular Photography*, *U.S. Camera*, and in the special issue of *Fortune* for the 1939 New York World's Fair. He also published essays, on topics such as "What Is Surrealism?" In 1941 the Museum of Modern Art acquired two of his pictures for its permanent collection. Pat's book *The Two Faces of January* (1964) is dedicated to him.

‡ Arthur d'Arazien (1914–2004), renowned Turkish-American industrial and commercial photographer.

AUGUST 5, 1942

I miss Rosalind, hundreds—yes, hundreds of people call me up—and I
sigh for one of her chilly yeses. Being with G., telling all day of plot, character, possible plots does make me happy. By the way, Goldberg said he'd
get me a commission from a newspaper (?) to go to USSR after the war!

AUGUST 6, 1942

Worked on this Lasting Peace job this P.M. (I find it difficult and damned
awkward to write on such a pleasant & equivocal matter as "democracy." What can one say that isn't worn out, and isn't too Communis-
tic for the paper?) Turned out something that might just as well have
been titled: "How to Build a Lasting Henhouse." I shall ask Goldberg
to get off Saturday—Bernhard wants to go away. Wrote fairly well after
First Aid. Once more an "excellent," like my partner Margaret Zavada.
(Czecho gal from Peru.) She's very warm, holds my head lovingly and
rests it against her lap as she gropes for my temporal artery.

AUGUST 7, 1942

Berger phoned early, because I wouldn't make a date this weekend. Matter of fact [I have one] with Bernhard. Wrote on Lasting Peace. (Done.)
Hauser must be gone, snatched away, because we had a date tonight &
I didn't hear from him. Perhaps he left on the same clipper tonight as
Queen Wilhelmina,* who went to London. Worked on "Manuel" two
hours tonight—more in fact—and did well. I love it. Hope to make
something rather good. I'm no good at concluding phrases.

8/7/42

Virginia Woolf committed suicide because she could not reconcile art
with human slaughter. Individually (as Virginia Woolf always thought),
one cannot reconcile them, because the individual does not go to war of
his own will. But collectively, wars are an expression of humans just like
murder is. Wars are mass murders, and wars are manifestations of one
facet of human character, a very ancient one. If they are not "inevitable"
long, if the common man may oppose his will to peace, then they have
been heretofore "inevitable" in the sense that intelligent nations have let
themselves be driven into wars by their leaders. If man is anti-war, then
he is merely the corpse in the hands of the murderers, who are perform-

---

* Queen Wilhelmina (1880–1962), queen of the Netherlands from 1890 to 1948. Her radio broadcasts
from London during World War II made her a symbol of Dutch resistance to German occupation.

ing a human action, or one, that is characteristic of humans occasionally, those of us who have the desire of committing murder.

AUGUST 8, 1942

[Bernhard and I] caught the train to Valley Stream. J.J. was swimming, so we bought lunch & ate in the forest, building a minute fire for no reason at all except to smoke up our hair deliciously. J. J. Augustin* is a rather undistinguished German in that indefinite age of 37–38. Two-story house, rather secluded, with Police dog (Silver) and cat (Pussie). He told us of his troubles with the neighbors and FBI. The neighbors are cranks, and accuse him of everything from espionage & homosexuality to wireless operating and procto-phantasm. He made us wonderfully at home, served us Wiener Schnitzel and potato salad, & buzzed about the house like an *echte Hausfrau* [housewife]. But in the afternoon, he told us all about his family in Germany, his mornings, his activities at the house, and of the telephone tapping of the FBI.

His little living room centers about the fireplace, flanked with pho-nograph albums, wood storage, etc. And on the opposite wall is a huge bookcase of German style, one of 5—the only one he was able to get out of Germany. Many first editions, and all expensive editions, particularly those of his own printing or of his father's. They love books on philology and native painting, weaving, etc., and J.J. printed, in conjunction with Gladys Reichard† of Barnard, the only authoritative book on Hopi & Navajo sign painting. He knows about six Indian languages, to read & write. All about are evidences of this Thos. Mannish existence in Ham-burg and München, the days of second breakfasts and long hours with linen-bound volumes of Goethe & Swedenborg. Rolf evidently explained things very well, because he put us into one room, one bed, & probably would have been surprised had we asked for separate ones. The inevita-ble happened, with B. withdrawing (in confusion or impotence or lack of confidence) at the crucial point.

AUGUST 9, 1942

Since I hate beds I am late to them and early from them.

J.J. is an artist. He has done much in his life. It is a pity the line will die with him. There is a French Jewess en route from Cannes, whom

---

* Johannes Jakob Augustin, son of Heinrich Wilhelm Augustin, then owner of the J. J. Augustin printing company in Germany.
† Gladys Reichard, associate professor of anthropology at Barnard College.

he will marry, but she is a Lesbian, & they will not even live together. J.J. is a person I love, like Bernhard, like Rosalind, Betty, Natasha, like Bach and Mozart. Rolf Tietgens arrived around 12:00. We had another lavish dinner, tho J.J. always remarks how low he is in funds, what with lawyers' fees and the American lack of appreciation of his books, he manages to cook with scads of butter, and to have plenty of liquor & cigarettes on hand.

Bernhard & I took a walk in the swampy forests and I was bitten by a police dog in the rear end on the way home. Broke the skin, too. The funniest thing is that Bernhard was trembling and crying as soon as it happened, embraced me all the way home & practically had to be treated for shock. Bernhard very happy all day. Last night was the first time in a year & a half [for] her she said. (A year & a half ago, I was a virgin.) I feel new desire to learn more Bach, & to live as J.J. does, with my books, my tobacco, liquor, music & dogs. I wonder is Bernhard in love with me? Not in the real way I must be, however, & she, too: somewhat madly & unwisely & illogically and definitely suddenly. Unless in all this rest period, her mores erotica have changed. She is so unfortunately feminine inside.

AUGUST 10, 1942

Goldberg asked for me at 10:30 to layout the new book. I made the title: *The People Made America.* And Weick, G. & I compiled the chapters the rest of the day. G. asked me to lunch. Del Pezzo's—all but empty. And really empty without Rosalind or Natasha. Why doesn't she even write me a card? I still feel lonely without her, no matter whom I see, no matter what I do. I feel lonely, very lonely. Jack B. here when I came home. Fried chicken dinner in Mother's finest style. Jack B. & I went up on Empire State, 102 stories. Wrote card to Jeannot. We had Tom Collins & earnest conversation, me being quite reserved, consequently fatigued, bored & boring. I cramp myself so I go to sleep. But one cannot expand in such company. He counsels me against celibacy, etc. Then tonight, horrible bear hugs which I endured as duty, sending a man off to war, etc.

AUGUST 11, 1942

Dropped back on Bernhard at 1:45 but she'd had lunch. Rolf eyes me like a wolf, looking around the studio, always dreaming of something. B. & I went to drugstore where I had a lunch under physical conditions I could hardly bear. Neither can I bear the price of salads, coffee, cigarettes, when I pay all the checks. Bernhard is no check grabber, while I am a check grabber from way back. B. was in a troublesome time of month, and add to that the fact that she is wild that Rolf take me away from her, and you have the unholy spectacle of the female fighting for the young. She wants to tell Rolf he hasn't the chance of a snowball in hell, and wants my sanction to it. She said Rolf thinks it's a terrible thing to do to her, so obviously she has let him think we are together, which is not true by any means. Rolf should know we are not together, then if he wants to do anything about it, he should come to me. However, he wants to talk to B. I warned her against being dependent on me. From my own state of mind this noon, I know she might wonder whether I'm in love with Rolf or not, too. Matter of fact, Rolf I should love easier than anyone I know. I shall someday marry just such a man as he. Though I think his affair with me will go as easily as it came.

Saw Buffie for dinner. Martinis & serious discussion before 8:30 when we went out to Chateaubriand's. C.—that louse, that sheep in clown's clothing—is Lola's lover & has been for over a year. Where Del gets off I can't see. Why does he tolerate it? Has he someone?

Buffie was adorable tonight. Lovely shaped head, lovely hair, and the most exciting perfumes from head to toe. She moves like a strong Indian about the house, amid china closets and lace antimacassars, but her own strength dominates the scene. I love to look at her so. She had me pose for a portrait of someone (Nina Jacobsen) and half naked, too. Meanwhile she kissed me and said her magic words and wanted me to stay. I was tired—too tired—that is all. Otherwise I would have. I find her most attractive physically. Damn, so many people aren't! Buffie would make a night of love of every date I made. Come for tea & stay for breakfast. "It's nice to look at you all evening and then kiss you goodnight," I said. And she called me naughty & laughed at my naiveté. I admire and envy her energy. She doesn't drink or smoke at all now. I must say she looks better for it.

8/11/42

This notebook should see a change, a very important change from all the others. I am no longer fascinated by the decadent, much less captivated by its color, variety and sensational possibilities in literature. And oddly enough, it has been the war that made the change. The war makes a writer, perhaps makes everyone, think of what he loves best. With myself, I had to ask a long while what I loved best, what sort of life I wanted, what rate of speed, what environs, what goal, what amusements and what labors. I like a room of my own, with long evenings in summer, in snowy winter, in the exciting fall and the spring. I like to read my books when the radio is playing Gilbert & Sullivan operettas, or Bach sonatas or Boccherini concertos. Yes and I like the lives of the people I don't know: of the rich old gentleman whose daughter brings his hot chocolate up the stairs to him at four on the dot, when he is finishing his after-lunch pasting in stamp collections. I like the lives of the mechanics of Detroit, who read Dickens on Sunday afternoons because they love him, and because, too, they think they are absorbing culture. I like the farm boys who come to town once a month to see movies and sleep with a girl and buy themselves ten-a-shot drinks. I like the artists, the painters, photographers, window designers, copywriters, playwrights, novelists and short story writers who live with a mildness in their eyes and a calmness in their hands, who do not remember what they had for breakfast, and who do not know what they will have for dinner. I like the poor Jewish family who sits next to me at the Lewisohn Stadium,* the sailor in glasses who reads beside me in the Public Library, the good Chinaman who washes my shirts. I like my Sunday mornings with marmalade from England, the paper at my door, the symphonies in the afternoon, and the toasted marshmallows in the evening. Best of all I like the artists, professed & unprofessed, who of all people, live closest by the belief that man is the most wonderful creation in the world, most wonderful of animals and more wonderful than all creatures of his own brain. That is why I like artists best, because their eyes are open and their brains stirring, because they see and hear and feel suddenly man in new form, and, having captured it, have contributed so much to the great mosaic of wonderful man, which will never be done, and yet never be destroyed. And what do I hate? There is so much to hate, that I cannot tolerate people who say: "I have nothing to say." There is so much to say about the ugliness of line and color, the simple cruelty of leading men to buy what they do not want or need, the sin of publishers who sell inferior literature by advertising campaigns, sell it to those who can afford to buy and who can't afford to buy, who buy it for culture, for escape, for keeping up with the Joneses, to those who buy because someone is having a birthday, and because so-and-so is top of the list, through the purchasing of others like them. I hate the speed, the noise, the absence of prized possessions, the absence of leisure to

---

* For more than fifty years, through 1966, Lewisohn Stadium was a staple of New York City cultural life, drawing hundreds of thousands of spectators to summer symphony concerts.

visit rarely and long, to study long and often, to become familiar with the beautiful lines of one's handmade furniture in one's own home, the failure of machine made shoes to compare with those made by feeling the foot with the hands of a master, the absence of discrimination in art, advertising, printing, ribbons, clothes, and the absence of joy in life due to all of these: haste, economic pressure, fear of want, days without leisure. It is very late. I have said only half the things I love and hate, and said them very badly.

AUGUST 13, 1942

Much better feeling today: mother put my hair up. *Mademoiselle* sent me a letter, would I be interested in being *Charm*'s "feature editor." (i.e. writing captions & goosing refractory writers) Stopped by Bernhard's at 1:30, but she was in Scarsdale. I'd forgotten Rolf was there with my photos. Two of which are good. One very serious I liked. Rolf said: "I knew you'd like that one. Because you look very boyish. You are a boy. You know." Very attentive, & walked me finally up to 57 St. I told him B. & I were not together. Rolf wants to go for a walk Sunday—Van Cortlandt Park but he's afraid Bernhard will be jealous. She shouldn't know. Should like to ask Rolf for dinner Sunday. I know he would find los padres *Spiessbürger* [bourgeois]. Yesterday when I was upset, I could not really think why. The fact was, as I later discovered through intuition alone, that I didn't want B.'s grip on me at all. I want no commitments. I wonder could I be in love with Rolf. Neither of us will admit it can be the opposite sex, and both of us can excuse ourselves by saying it is not, of course, the opposite sex. Buffie showed me photos last night of the "writer" she will probably marry after the war. He's in the army. How lovely she was last night. How nice to be married (both of us) and go on as before, in perfect confidence and harmony.

AUGUST 14, 1942

I guess I feel down. Finished "Manuel" tonight & started another better draft, in the style I know it must be. Went down to S. & S. [Street & Smith] to see some nobody about that feature editor job. A young girl spoke to me, whom I impressed unmercifully. She'll call me later.

Goldberg, however, is very happy about *The People Made America*, the advance folder for which came out today. Should be impossible to leave at such a time, when deadlines must be met. He even wants me to work on the weekend. Finished Dante's *Divine Comedy* this evening,

remembering a few good passages. But the inner life is hard to return
to after a day of trivia. My notebooks go two & three days untouched.
The magic paragraphs don't come without solitude & free quiet hours.
Can't be helped.

AUGUST 15, 1942

Dinner with [Walter] Marlowe. Another gorgeous gardenia. We went to
Café Society Uptown.* The evening uneventful except for revelatory conversation in his room on my sexual reactions. Finally I got around to telling him a) I didn't enjoy attentions of any kind from him or anyone b) I
should not until I had found myself, something to be proud of, something
substantial. He was most sympathetic, but I don't like his joking about
the sexual act, which he considers just as lightly (with his fine adjustment) as ordinary friendship with a girl. "Don't you think sex is here to
stay?" etc. No thanks. Boy, could I show him a thing or two or could I?!
Shall speak to Rolf tomorrow on it—the problem of not trusting rough
trade men, and the problem, too, of mistrusting women's genius & drive.
He should be versed in the subject.

AUGUST 16, 1942

I think this is the strangest day of my life. At any rate I am nearest to
falling in love with—Rolf Tietgens. Met Rolf at 2:00 at Lexington &
59. We rode up to Van Cortlandt Park. He gave me a tiny Mexican
(Indian) doll out of wood, which a little Indian boy made. I told him
first what Walter & I had talked about last night—my inherent dislike
& mistrust of men. So he was downcast. It rained like mad, & we got
soaked. We came home after much delaying and *Pilz* [mushroom] picking, & ate eggs on toast & cake & coffee. He was determined not to
be hungry but ate everything. Then we sat in my room & talked. He
looked over all my books. Especially liking Blake & Donne, whom he
knows thoroughly. We walked down 57th to the river, the only place he
seemed to be happy today. It was actually fun standing there with him,
& very strange because it was fun—the simple reason is, he is the only
man who ever knew all about me. God what a difference between him
and Walter!—and Jack! So we watched the boats & the lights & he told
me all about Hamburg, Lübeck, the marshlands. Then we walked to

---

* Café Society at 1 Sheridan Square in Greenwich Village was the first racially integrated nightclub in the
United States. A second branch, Café Society Uptown, opened in 1940 on Fifty-Eighth Street between
Lexington and Park Avenues.

the cobblestoned street that was deserted & stood there over an hour. He kissed me a few times—rather a mutual thing for a change. It was quite wonderful & perfect, and for several moments I could see happiness and read it in the sky like a strange new word written. He said he was so happy he couldn't eat & sleep for months. And we mustn't tell Bernhard.

So tonight—I am new. I am a new person—and who knows what will come of it? I should like very much to sleep with him. And I know he wants it. So I guess we shall. Where? At his place? At J.J.'s sometime when Bernhard doesn't come? Being with him is like reading a wonderful poem—by Whitman, Wolfe, or the First Voice himself. He reads such things into me, but I am mute beside him. He is quite impracticable & wild. Wants to wipe everyone out by war & start over—but with him wiped out, too. And his brain is tenanted with all the sad Indians he met in the Texas jails. Wild good men, imprisoned on white men's laws.

Would like to go to J.J.'s soon.

AUGUST 17, 1942

^{SP}I worked particularly well this morning. I wrote "Best Movies of the Year," *Mrs. Miniver*, etc^{SPSP} [for Goldberg]. Very amusing to write & read. Took it down to the office at 2:30, stopping by Bernhard's en route: Tietgens there of course. We behaved very well. Bernhard very busy, & studiedly cheerful in spite of fortune's reverses. Rolf came down & walked me to 67th. He told me he'd told J.J. all about it—last night—when he talked with him all this AM. That J.J. was delighted, & said we must come out just the two of us, but that Rolf should be careful with Bernhard. Read Ecclesiastes tonight, & it's splendid. Rolf once shouted it into the desert. My parents think he's an inveterate panhandler—a bum—a vagabond. But they know nothing of things of the spirit. He's as improvident as the wise man in the Bible.

AUGUST 19, 1942

"Statues are building themselves in me, which I should eternalize in monumental paragraphs," I wrote tonight. It centers around Rolf. Bernhard told me tonight, when we had drinks here, that she cannot understand me if I like Rolf (tho I think I assured her I did not love him!) and that were it Rosalind I had succeeded in interesting in me, she could understand & would not mind—Rolf upsets her—tho she says she has no claim on me & told him so. He exaggerates everything either of us says. So it is wisest to say nothing henceforth. We ate at Fleur de Lis,

a rotten place really. Then we saw *Moscow Strikes Back*,* a fine film.
We walked home wonderfully happy, & sat before the river of an hour,
talking magic.

AUGUST 20, 1942

^GYes, I'm happier than ever before. Don't understand it, and besides,
Rolf. I looked out the window at 8:30 and there Rolf came skulking
without a hat, as always, and no jacket. We were so happy to see one
another. Walked along 1st Ave. And drank a beer. (Rolf two.) He was
suffering terribly from the heat. He was crushed to learn I hadn't told
[Bernhard] the truth yet. We stood on our street, the quiet little street
by the river, where grass grows between the stones, green and soft and
waving in the wind, where nearly no one passes, save the occasional
policeman. It was the most wonderful evening. He wants to live with me
and plans to earn money right away to that end. He wants me to come
home with him and talk the whole night through. Yes, and that's what
I want too. But I fear I will become like a regular girl, that a man will
keep me from my work. But on the contrary, he calls me a little boy and
makes me a better writer. What will Rosalind and Natasha & Betty &
Babo, Peter & Helen say? What will the world say?^{GG}

AUGUST 21, 1942

^GRolf sat by the window, and Bernhard wasn't there.^{GG} He was very
happy & said the gods are with us. Yes, he fancies me a boy, and his
homosexuality before came from a Grecian pride in men's superiority
and a mistrust of women's wiles and weaknesses. He likes me because
my body is lean & hard & straight, and because I speak bluntly. He
talked of Germany & his family, while the sun brought out the urine of
the monuments like a yellow rainbow around us. What a city, with no
place to be alone! Berger phoned at 6:30, very disappointed I was "going
away" for the weekend, and in a rage that I am dated all next week.

AUGUST 22, 1942

Woke up sick in the night—ravenously hungry & all food sickening.
Made a stab at working. Got my check, Miss Weick told me to go home.
Very concerned, though she said one true thing: every one who gets
anywhere abuses every law of physical health and 8 hrs. sleep is a myth.

---

* *Moscow Strikes Back* (1942), a feature-length Soviet documentary film that won a 1943 Oscar for Best
Documentary.

[Rolf] came at 7. We sat in my darkened room & talked, shyly at first, because sickness takes all the spirits out of me. He brought me Hamsun's *Mysteries*. He was embarrassed that the lights were out, lest my parents should come home. He has his hair cut short as a convict, still sweats, & wears a denim shirt. The elevator boys look him up & down, but I don't mind.

What a lot has happened in the last seven days! No wonder I became ill.

AUGUST 23, 1942

A pleasant Sunday. A rarity. I finished (wrote an end to) "Manuel" this morning when the family was at church. Reveled in not going out of the house all day except at 6:30 a moment to purchase some C & B marmalade, which was pure whim. I read W. H. Auden's *Double Man*. Rather good. But not so brilliant or concise as [T. S.] Eliot, whom he imitates occasionally. How good to have a day without telephone calls! I read "Manuel" aloud to M. & S. and they liked it—possibly the first time this has happened. I consider them pretty fair critics of a sort. What a pleasant feeling—a story that I'm not ashamed of—one that I'm almost proud of—one that many people would consider better than "Silver Horn of Plenty," though "Manuel"'s not so brilliant. And I am not so pleased with it. But the emotions, etc. were much more difficult to handle, than the simple one of hate, which comes easily to me. I feel gradually very capable of handling complex situations, simple emotions which were heretofore foreign to me. I feel that I'm growing & shall grow, and these growth periods come only on such long, private Sundays.

Tonight I commenced [Franz] Werfel's *Forty Days of Musa Dagh*. The writing is superb! Better than I had dared hope.

8/24/42

Examine any work of art as a scientist would, and it appears a distorted product of a madman. An artist's contribution is the sum of many small madnesses, anomalies, embellished to a beautiful power, trifles which a saner mind would have wisely discarded.

AUGUST 25, 1942

Rosalind phoned me at 9:35 this morning. I was so happy I couldn't talk straight. She told me to come to lunch with her. I spent a hell of a long time choosing my clothes, did about one hour's work this morning.

Lunched for an hour & a half. She looks swell—tan hands & back, and
the old gin flush face, with upper lip slightly peeling from sunburn.

Goldberg read "Manuel." He liked it. Said he'd recognize my writing
in a pile of stories. I feel such a deep happiness now, such a confidence in
my own ability, that Rolf must be a major part of it. Well, say I'm in love
with Rolf & Rosalind, too. That's the simple truth, and what's one to do
about it?

AUGUST 26, 1942

And I live on the knife edge of my emotions these days anyway—much
as Helen did last December. Called for Rolf & we went loping off to
lunch. I was starved. How nice to eat with him when the sunlight falls
on the table, and I feel I can never get enough of him, or the food.
Then we spent an hour getting shoes (F. Simon's 9.00). Red ones, too.
I have decided to go so far as to tell B. She was shortsighted in limiting
me to liking only girls. Really most unbecoming in her—& obviously
self-motivated.

AUGUST 27, 1942

The Duke of Kent was killed Tuesday in a plane crash over England.
Called for Rolf, whom I saw in the window. & made the awful bust of
addressing him before seeing Bernhard there. She was a small piece of ice
thereafter. ᴳSo Rolf whispered to me to tell her everything—and B. and
I went across the street to get drinks.ᴳᴳ One—two—three martinis—
explanations, tears from her—ᴳand everything fell to pieces.ᴳᴳ My class
in First Aid seemed insignificant besides Bernhard there pouring her
heart out. She loves me. She can't take this. We kicked the traces & went
to Hoboken to a clam joint, with sawdust floors and oyster shells. She
says the trouble is that she has exactly to offer what Rolf has—only in
less exciting & intense form. That is true. However, I feel this is the end.
She is wonderful to me, but I love Rolf more. I am not so patient or so
wise that I can choose tenderness over fierceness. Got home after 12:00,
Rolf of course waited for me, & mother said he came over, much disturbed, and alarming them.

AUGUST 29, 1942

I can make no contact with anything but myself—and that with difficulty.
The stricture of the atmosphere stops the beautiful osmosis of the city.
Dulls my brain, clogs my very bowels. The decadence before mine eyes!
As Rolf puts it: this fantastic continent they ruined in a hundred years!

8/30/42

The Wonderful Day in California! The promise—the delight in the half-revealed, half-known. It was a time that can never be reduplicated again—because I was twenty and one half then, and now I am twenty-one and one half—My love was so young that day—two or three encounters old. How can a poem reproduce it adequately? For the words I should use would be, at best, those with the associations of that day, and would, at best, evoke only for me that afternoon. How can I possibly communicate the feeling?

There was rain and I didn't care. I had an awful cold and I didn't care. I was a rocket ready to be touched off, and aimed straight for you.

What does one do with these experiences that shake one's roots? Does one wait?—Then it's hopeless! Moods pass and cannot be revoked either by imagination or deliberate reassembling of circumstances. What remains is not even a particle of the mood, the aura, the intangible emotion, but only the memory of the entire period of time, which even the recalling of whole sentences of dialogue, whole panoramas seen cannot bring back perfectly. Here I write mechanically what I must write to remember what I must remember, inferior, incomplete, impotent compared to the actuality, but nevertheless absorbing me and bewildering me. I loved you so then. I believed so then. I was on top of a mountain breathing thin air. You were all around me, all those two months. I take delight in being impractical about you. An impractical love is the most beautiful and the most fitting. If love should be the deepest touching experience, the most divorced from all other experience, as it surely is, then let it be the most inadvisable. Curse me if I ever spend a moment thinking what I should do, tactics, or what even you would want or expect me to do. Let me be forever that rocket waiting for the match.

AUGUST 31, 1942

This morning mother & I filled the bookcase—rather well, too, even if the spaces are more numerous than I like. Buffie came over at 7:15. Drank a bit of Sherry. She's getting married this week! To some gay soldier named John Latham. After several martinis I took her out to dinner at the Hapsburg House in 55. Charming dinner, but I was so damn tight I ate only ½ of it. Buffie offered to share the bill, but I was feeling much too elegant. We went back to her house, bought beautiful grapes. Two people came over, which annoyed me, because we were listening to

records. I slept at Buffie's house. It might have been great, but I was so
ridiculously tired from the liquor—next time I shan't take the third or
fourth martini.

SEPTEMBER 1, 1942

Mr. Latham called at precisely the wrong moment last night around
one, from California. Buffie has to go there for the wedding, afterwards
coming home, to resume the old life unchanged. She talked very offhand-
edly of it even to my mother. Tried to phone Buffie—one just doesn't say
goodbye after that—she called me, too, when I was out. Called on [Rolf
at] the studio. Looked at his books printed in Germany. He wanted the
shades drawn for no particular reason. So B. passing saw them, called
him down later about "cheap behavior." So neither Rolf nor I want to
or can go there again. Anyway he's taken the 50th St. furnished room
beginning Saturday. Took first aid final orally. Rolf there afterwards.
Lovely walk home & mother fixed coffee while I gave him a few stories.
Including the Subway one* which I think he'll like. I hope so. Wish he
could get money & dress a bit better. Just a bit!

SEPTEMBER 2, 1942

I am almost overwhelmed, crushed, defeated—by all the wonderful
things I have yet to do, make, think, create, plan, taste, love, hate, enjoy,
live. I should never have thought my worst enemy would be fatigue, the
brother of my best virtue, industry. But the fatigue is always physical,
and remediable, never mental or psychic. Lunched wonderfully with
Rosalinds. She's on the wagon to get rid of the gin flush, if it is a gin
flush. Personally I like it. And I don't like R on the wagon. She isn't herself. She has a nice, adequately pleasing veneer. She can display sober,
but it has no mystery. I should like to see her quite drunk—as I have. We
discussed fully the Rolf-Bernhard crisis. She defends me & Rolf. Rosalind said if she goes asking for hard luck, she'll get it. And tho I said B.
had had 6 months of happiness with the right person, Rosalind said she
was lucky to get that, and all our lives we never have the person we want.
I wonder whom she wants? And why can't I—and why can't I? No I am
not ready for Rolf, because I should run to Rosalind's arms the moment
they looked like they were opening to me.

---

* Pat mentions a story about people "writing in the subway" in her diary in July. It's possible that this
is the same one. It could also be the one she will sell to *Home & Food* under the title "Friends" in 1943.

SEPTEMBER 4, 1942

Lunched with Rolf in the automat.* I feel occasionally endangered of my power of detachment that I loved so well before I was working. One must guard it, though I believe undoubtedly it is ever there. It is merely a firm piece of metal to keep polished. There was a terrific explosion in 48 St. at 9:30 this A M. Suicide touched off by the maid's ringing the bell. And Mary Sullivan, says the paper, was blown out of bed!

SEPTEMBER 5, 1942

With Rolf tonight. We walked to Buffie's first. Her mother was there, discouraged the idea of my watering the flowers—and Buffie, who is never to be circumvented, sent Rolf like a flunky out to make a duplicate key. I am the only one in N.Y., besides her mother, who has a key. Very nice of her. ("You too can have a honeymoon—" Buffie whispered.) But the hell with that. I should like much to go there occasionally, look well at all the pictures, browse among her books. She was sending invites to that crazy wedding. At least 500 of them, Cartier Stationery, inside & outside envelopes. And I must send ½ of them on to Mr. John Latham, whose name Buffie has only yesterday learned to spell.

Rolf & I took a walk in the park, where I was compelled to tell him of Helen, and of how we both felt about each other. Men are not magic to me that is all. Perhaps I must have magic instead of bread and meat, as I had rather have a cigarette than a hamburger. Rolf worried lest I run off again with a girl. Let him worry. It will let him down easier if I ever do. But I like Rolf very much, and see no leaving him soon.

SEPTEMBER 6, 1942

GNice day. Got up early to go to J.J.'s with Rolf. Took a long walk along a brook. Rolf is really beautiful. He fell asleep on the sofa by the fire. But eventually came to my room—(he was nervous at first, handling all manner of things in the room). Then he was pleasantly shy, wanted to do everything, but also didn't want it. Am happy he didn't do anything, though, otherwise I'd be disgusted in the morning. He came to me maybe three times. I was shy myself.

Nice breakfast in the kitchen. Rolf tired. He didn't say anything about how I behaved (last night)—as always, I don't know what I want. He really likes me—truly—so gently, so deeply. Rolf wanted to hear

---

* Automats were cafeterias in which individual portions of food were dispensed from small glass-doored compartments.

all my concerns, and I told him about everything I felt for Rosalind—everything. He understands me. He just wants me to be happy and do good work. He wants to help me. Wants to meet Rosalind, too, because "she has such a huge influence on you!" Yes, if I have the money—Friday lunch. We read all sorts of German books, Hölderlin, Goethe, Morgenstern as well as Saroyan, whom it turns out Rolf knows. Love Rolf a lot, but am not yet in love with him.[GG]

SEPTEMBER 7, 1942

Strange day. Worked hard. I wanted to see Rolf, only I was so busy I almost forgot him, then he was walking up & down on 44th St. opposite the studio. He said, if I phoned him in the middle of the night to "go west" he'd pack up & go in 5 minutes. Only his overalls he'd need. Rosalind asked me to come to dinner with her. Betty was not coming until Thursday. She said—letting herself open more to me than almost ever before: "If I were your age, I should find myself dull company." So like her. And my heart bursts with wonderful unspeakable words. She is so strange, unique, wonderful, wunderbar, like nothing on the earth or in heaven, and what do I say? I cannot even say with my eyes—we were both sad. We talked vaguely of the war. I am always vague, because I am neither communist nor reactionary. I had to touch her once & kiss her—in the air—on the right side of her blond hair. She said "Bless you!" & I was gone down the hall, in a burst of tears. Why I don't know.

SEPTEMBER 8, 1942

[G]Rolf came by at 5 to get me. We saw [Frank Wysbar's] *Fährmann Maria*, a very good film from Nazi Germany. Later we walked to his house. Two little garret rooms full of pictures, books. I couldn't settle down, though. I have so much to do. We lay in bed for a minute. Then we came to 57. Very sad. He wanted to lie down in the gutter and die. I felt so sorry I couldn't spend more time with him. Wrote two letters. Had nice thoughts. And read [H. G. Wells's] *World Set Free*, not long, not great, not especially thrilling. But solid.[GG]

SEPTEMBER 10, 1942

I receive wild compliments from the elevator boys—probably duplicated to every girl in the building who isn't a walking mummy. Saw Rolf at 12:20. And again at 5:30. He spends about .20 a day on calls, as he shouldn't. Jo P. came for dinner. She stays unconscionably late. The same thing happened again. I feel sorry for her because she is lonely.

That's all. Afterwards I regretted most bitterly & I see no reason why it should happen again. I am old enough to want to live my own life. I have done experimenting, wasting precious time that is ever running shorter. I should gladly give up—ridiculous phrase—my drinking, dinner going, cocktails, absurdities!

SEPTEMBER 13, 1942

Stalingrad is all but taken. The Russians with incredible courage, have destroyed all retreating bridges & roads, determined to die. Yesterday I sent "These Sad Pillars" to *The New Yorker* care of Mr. Shawn. Even if he doesn't remember me, the thing'll go to the fiction dept. With his note. Also "Manuel" at *Story*. Anxious as ever—as in the rather hopeless days of 1938—because now my powers are coming. I spent several hours turning thru my notebooks, pondering my next thing—certainly no definite story, merely trying to distill the murk of emotions inside me.

9/13/42

The most spiritual and "beautiful" literature has already been written— in the Bible, in the Greek dramas, in their philosophies. What we have to attain is at best the material representation, a poor substitute for the eternities we cannot logically hope to emulate. Spirituality in our day is as difficult to attain as a pair of wings and a halo.

SEPTEMBER 14, 1942

Wrote 3 pages (ᴳvery difficultᴳᴳ) on new story of the virgin mother.* Also pleasant evening because I was alone, those delicate ideas coming, which generally are better literary material (for character) than the physical activities that might occur to one in more disturbing surroundings. Read *Mysterier*.

SEPTEMBER 18, 1942

Saw Rolf tonight after dinner. I should have worked & stayed home, but he was in such good spirits from having money. We went to Buffie's to look at books. We took our clothes off finally & lay a while on the bed. Neither of us feel any physical excitement and neither want nor cause anything to happen. I was terribly restless because of the house, the bed, & memories, and this Rolf couldn't understand. I have decided,

---

* Likely refers to the story titled "Miscellaneous" in her archives, published as "The Hollow Oracle" in *Nothing That Meets the Eye: The Uncollected Stories of Patricia Highsmith* (New York, 2002).

at last, that I have a definite psychosis in being with people. I cannot
bear it very long. Perhaps in all the world there is only Rosalind with
whom I can feel calm for hours on end. With others, I am obsessed by
the sense of time passing, by the [amount] of work that remains for me
to do. Even tonight with Rolf, things were rather bad. We ate later, after
I could stand it no longer. He told me he had never gone to a prostitute,
never slept with a girl.

9/18/42

[Listened to Frederick Delius] "The walk in the Paradise Gardens"—and
I am obsessed by the wonder of what can be done with words, oppressed
by the fear that I can never get at it, never create it with words.

SEPTEMBER 19, 1942

A very fine day. I thought of Rosalind about fifty million times. Worked
this AM. Lerner* said he will put me on seeking advertising (should get
a raise if I'm good!) and that the year-book will have a second edition in
January—in which time I hope to be at Time, Inc. Even if it's pushing a
broom.

Me & mother for lunch at Del Pezzo's very pleasant. Manicotti.
She bought me a blouse ($1 left over) & we saw some exhibits. Oddly
it was [Yves] Tanguy who interested me most. He's a prophet of what
will come, a precursor of decadence. The small tightly-locked objects
in nimbus are mechanico-organic in shapes suggesting frozen power &
movement.

Worked happily on my Christ story.† I have faith in it.

SEPTEMBER 20, 1942

Insufficient reading. I must change my habits or remain a dolt as to
world literature. Rolf came at 2:00. Half sick with la grippe. Fixed him
a hot rum & then we saw the Met's Toulouse-Lautrec‡ exhibit of posters. Really exciting, and depressing when one compares our present
magazine covers and cigarette ads. We went to his place, lay on the bed,
where for a half hour all was fine—perhaps (no doubt) I absorb vicari-
ously some of his sudden tranquility & happiness. Afterwards—well, I
grow self-conscious or else want something physical to happen (a nor-

---

* Another employee at F.F.F.
† Probably again "The Hollow Oracle," the story she refers to as her "story of the virgin mother" above.
‡ Henri Marie de Toulouse-Lautrec-Monfa (1864–1901), French Postimpressionist most famous for his
poster series for the French nightclub Le Moulin Rouge.

mal & purely instinctive half-excitement from proximity) and nothing does happen with Rolf. He is miserable over the fact that he does not grow excited. One could hardly expect him to function as an ordinary man after years of opposite habits. He, however, curses himself, & says he will only make us part unless he can correct it. Really it is unimportant to me, because I love Rosalind, & want nothing else in the physical sense—really I don't want her, because I love her in such a beautiful way. The fact is, I worship her! Home late and dissatisfied. One glimpse of Whitman tonight at Rolf's. Very beautiful.

SEPTEMBER 21, 1942

Wonderful day. I loafed all morning, writing a good letter to Miss Williams of TIME INC. Rolf called at 12:00. I do hope he comes around with his little difficulty. Otherwise he will just say goodbye to me. How dreadful it would be to give up Rosalind because of some imaginary or real physical defect when I love her only in an idealistic way. I think almost all the other times I was in love (perhaps indeed all—except for Helen) it was so physical it depresses me to think of it. All the intensity & vanity of Romeo & Juliet. But Rosalind goes on and on. How nice I chose the right words to tell her last year. "I worship you—" nothing else would have done. Called her this afternoon & tho she was busy she made a date with Rolf & me for tomorrow. Read Colette's *Indulgent Husband* which is the rottenest thing I have seen in years! (Saw K. Kingsley in the library 58 St tonight with her mother. We weren't close enough to speak. She looked the same, hair shorter, all a-fluster, red coat. She would have liked to speak to me I know.)

SEPTEMBER 23, 1942

Worked this A M. at the office & picked up Rolf. Del Pezzo's at 12:25 but Rosalind didn't come until one. How proud I was of her today! She's wonderful to look at, wonderful to hear, to touch! And she was exhilarated with the blood-letting and funny as hell. I think she liked Rolf— tho I wish he'd improve his English. He shall, under my tutelage, & I my German.

Very nicely chilly tonight. And [an] air-raid alarm for unidentified plane. Very disobedient people in N.Y. Disgraceful discipline. Read nothing & suffered the ravages of the world. I work & think much better when I am pure from a day of peace alone. One's brain otherwise grows too fast & superficial.

SEPTEMBER 24, 1942

$30.00 in the bank—all saved since my job began. That means also $30 in defense stamps. The war should mean drastic living changes within a year. Perhaps a better salary will only about lever it to present standards.

The time has come for me to leave Rolf Tietgens. With effort, I might think myself in five minutes into the same positive emotions of a month ago, but of what use is thinking in such things? The truth comes with uncontrollable emotions, which I already feel for someone else. With the frightening sagacity of the "unrelated bystander" Rolf asked me pertinent questions about Rosalind. He said there was "no chance for me" because she's superior in age, attainments, thoughts on Weltanschauung, etc., ᴳall kinds of things that are necessary.ᴳᴳ What do I give her, when she can get more from older women?—nothing but adoration which always flatters older people, Rolf says. I adore her—but how bad she is for my frustration complex! It is more simple to say what living would be without her, perhaps, than to say what it is now in positives.

Bernard* writes that Mr. Plangman is in a sanatorium & Mrs. P. is having a "nervous breakdown."

SEPTEMBER 25, 1942

The Russians, who alone are fighting the war, are holding Stalingrad in the thirty-second day of siege. They fight even for possession of the floors of houses!

I have a dreadful cold & can barely breathe or talk. Rolf's cold. Rolf sold his car to J.J. for $100—He gets $50 & cancellation of 48.00 debt. So we ate royally at lunch at some Hungarian place that served the now phenomenal six-course meal for .50$! Later we saw the *Song of Ceylon* at Museum of M.A. Wonderful memorable stuff. Rolf still wants to see me every day, tho God knows Rosalind should discourage him!

Read almost nothing, because I feel so lousy. Constructive revision of my Christ-story however. By the way the Subway story & "Manuel" bounced today which doesn't discourage me at all. Also Mrs. Williams of Time, Inc. sent me a letter, saying she was interested in what I'd been doing, would like to see me & some research, tho they're not enlarging their training staff at present. Shall ask Rosalind does she mean type-written notes, I suppose so. I feel happy. A long long happiness.

---

* Jay Bernard Plangman, Pat's biological father.

SEPTEMBER 26, 1942

Nice day, after all. Met Rolf at 9:30 at the subway. I read *Mysteries* after we got to J.J.'s, so he thought me very impolite & told me so while we walked. The fact is he is just as difficult as I to get along with & even worse about making concessions to the social graces. We walked in the woods, amazing conversation dealing with *Unterleib* [nether regions]. Nice lunch, & then we tried going to the beach in Rolf's car (now owned by J.J.). The gas ran out in 5 minutes, & after some pushing Dr. Hoffmann brought us home. Rolf & J.J. talked in German in the kitchen, R. told me, & J.J. said what else could you have expected but that she wouldn't love you? It's impossible. So we ate a silent dinner—(Rolf was so isolated he could barely be dragged to the table) & we left in the rain.

9/27/42

Sometimes I feel so much wiser than my body: then I begin to feel wiser than my head, and finally wonder what it is that feels wiser, that is wiser, which brings me once more to the insolvable problem of what am I? I do not believe in happiness or the so-called normalcy as the ideal of human life. People who are "ideally happy" are ideally stupid. Consequently I do not believe in the remedial work of modern psychiatrists. The greatest contribution they could make to the world and to all its posterity would be to leave abnormal people alone to follow their own noses, stars, lodestones, divining rods, phantasies or what have you.

The world is filled with the peas that have rolled down the center of the board into the most full partition. Psychiatrists spend their time trying to push the odd peas over the barrier into the already crowded mean, in order to make mere regular peas to which they sincerely intend to point with pride. I believe that people should be allowed to go the whole hog with their perversions, abnormalities, unhappinesses and construction or destruction. Mad people are the only active people. They have built the world. Mad people, constructive geniuses, should have only enough normal intelligence to enable them to escape the forces that would normalize them.

9/27/42

I have poked so many books into me that I am like an over-stoked oven without a match.

SEPTEMBER 28, 1942

ᴳMy German grandfather died Friday. He was in a sanatorium. Don't know what was wrong. Took a taxi with Rolf to his house with his things. He embraced me, which I don't like one bit. "Is it so repellant?" he asked. Yes, unfortunately!GG

OCTOBER 3, 1942

FA strange day. I worked a lot—not in the morning, but the afternoon! We went to India Shop, where I spotted my next hat—9.75—the price of which mother and I will split. A little hat, like that of a bellboy. Nothing I did today took more than three hours to accomplish. Only Goldberg's poor planning required me to stay at the office.

Rolf phoned me at 5. I didn't want to see him. He got angry at me— was really upset. He called again to tell me that he wanted to see me. At 7. When I got home, tired and sad, I had to lie down for half an hour. Afterwards, he told me what was bothering him: that I've changed, that I've stopped caring about my friends, that nothing will come of this business with R.C. (tho nothing will not come of it!), and that he never wants to see me again if things don't change between us. A long conversation, in which, for some reason, I told him a lot about my physical life, my insecurities and my hopes. He understands. Even though it seems as tho we will never see each other again—at last he understands. I want to accomplish a lot—and though Rolf tells me that I must first become a good person—a great spirit, I want to accomplish a lot, and do so alone, without a man and perhaps without a woman at my side. In the next few years, I will have no need for anyone.FF

OCTOBER 4, 1942

FA good day. But not my day. Went to the office at 2 pm. A large Polish parade this afternoon, but few spectators. Goldberg and I went to the printer's to look at the proofs. I found mistakes that Goldberg hadn't noticed. Then we ate at the Balkan restaurant. Shish kebab. Goldberg knows how to eat! He told me that he wanted me to write a novel—a large *oeuvre*. I also read the Bible. It's a very good book, the greatest, really. My mother has been thinking a lot about my difficulties since I told her last night that I needed to improve my psyche. And my σῶμα [soma, body] too.FF

OCTOBER 5, 1942

FGood day. At the office. So many little things I have to get done. At 6 pm I met Rolf outside the building, bought him a cup of coffee, and we went to Wakefield [Gallery]. Rosalind, Natasha, Nickola, Lola P., Mrs. McKeen, Betty (hair like a broom—exhibition was called "The Ballet in

Art"). Jane O, whose pictures Rolf likes, was there too. I was largely filled with confusion and very anxious, tho I knew most of the crowd. Howard Putzl there too. Irving Prutman. Rolf didn't like the group. Needless to say: a multitude of homosexuals who were looking at each other more than the artworks. It's true. Betty fills me with dread and discomfort. Rosalind pure and pretty, blonde, clean! How I love her! Jo here, ^Gdammit!^{GG} And we couldn't avoid going back to her place, where we listened to records.^{FF}

10/5/42

I walked through a street of brownstones one misty drizzling morning. All the windows black holes except one. There stood a woman, slender, in sweater & belt & skirt, pinning up her short curly hair. I stopped where I was and leaned against a step post. I could not take my eyes from the square of yellow light. I wanted almost uncontrollably to go to her. I wanted to embrace her, feel her heat, smell the fragrance of her body, her hair and her clothing, press the yielding flesh of her arms, I wanted to feel the warm breath of her in my ear and to hear her voice saying affectionate things to me. I could not tear myself away, and to go off to work as I surely had to do, seemed not only painful physically but the most utter insanity. Why? Why must I go? So I stood, and people passed, though very few, and I did not care what they thought of me, I was seized with a paralysis, a nostalgia, a delight, a melancholy, a bewilderment, a fear, a confidence, a certainty, a hope & a despair. I watched her move about the window and I was racked with apprehension lest she go away. And rather than this, to leave me frantic with disappointment and frustration, I turned away my eyes and lifted my feet.

OCTOBER 6, 1942

^FWorked on unpleasant things. Met up with Rolf at 12:30. After a ten-minute lunch at the Automat I wanted to go by the cobbler's briefly and then to the library to read *Brave N.W.* [*Brave New World*]. "Well, goodbye," he said in parting. "I'll see you when you have some time!" Well, even mother told me that I should be tougher on him. I've never been this severe to a man! But I don't care! A good evening. Finished my story of the madwoman*—the first draft. Life alone is so wonderful! Now, at 21, I know what I need. I want to be alone as often as possible.^{FF}

---

* Probably still "The Hollow Oracle" she refers to first as the "story of the virgin mother," then as the "Christ story."

10/6/42

The autobiographical novel is out for me: my childhood & adolescence is a tale told backwards, lighted with will o' the wisps, revealing sporadically decaying corpses and wracked, impassioned faces hurrying through the night on the way to Somewhere which exists only in their own minds. It is what would be called uneventful, but by no means uninteresting psychologically.

OCTOBER 7, 1942

[F]Went to see Mrs. Williams at Time Inc. at 3:30. Shouting at the top of my lungs that I needed to get a job at Time. "Let's stay in touch!" she said, sweeping me out of her office.[FF]

OCTOBER 9, 1942

[F]Happy but so tired I can't think about anything important. I met Rosalind in her office, hair pulled back with a barrette. Very pretty, sweet like a girl, and it makes her look slimmer, too. I wanted to have lunch at the Golden Horn and—yes. Rosalind wore her checked suit, I was glad, we're doing better now. She thinks that the letter from Shawn (which I received this morning) is very good. He invited me to write something for Talk of the Town in October. Mr. Shawn runs *The New Yorker*, Rosalind said. So happy at lunch. I wanted to spend all day, all night with her. All my life! Back at the office, where Goldberg told me that I had to work tomorrow. ("Can you work—") When I told him I wanted more money, he told me that Flesch[*] would give me a raise in two weeks as long as I kept up the work.

Rolf phoned me. Need to kiss him tomorrow. I registered for the primaries at Public School 57. Parents too. Very amusing. I wrote. I worked. But I didn't think one bit.[FF]

10/9/42

You have pressed upon me your standards: spiritual love, sweetness, poetry, beauty, anarchy besides, however, and irresponsibility, bitterness, some mockery, much arrogance & stubbornness, above all contempt for every man who does not see eye to eye with you. You are so painfully right in most cases. It is difficult to deny you. It is difficult not to follow, until one realizes that the following swallows one up like a dust mote in a tornado.

But the fact is, my standards of "love"—(even physical love, yes—

---

[*] Dr. Emil Flesch, also at F.F.F. Publications.

which you of all people, were so quick to incorporate into general love)
my standards of love, beauty and truth are simply not yours. I do not
want the lover who refreshes me with the harmony of his voice, the
tones in his throat as he reads me Blake, nor do I want the lover who
cleaves unto me, whose heart is my heart, whose soul is ever in commu-
nion with mine tho we are apart. Give me rather the lover (or the loved)
who drives me mad with the antithesis of all your peace, who is not
spiritual except in his most ruthlessly physical moods, who never heard
of Blake and doesn't want to—Give me only the beloved with a question and a mystery to solve, who changes faster than I can follow, whose
every gesture, breath, movement is an intense delight to me, who leaves
me no peace when she is gone. And I defy you to tell me that my beloved
is any less spiritual (to me, which is what matters) than yours. And your
Jeremiads I grow tired of, and your eternal masculine conceit. Because
I do not hate the scientific progress, the shameful mess of 1942 and even
the men who now extricate us, you make me feel a compromiser, I am
no compromiser. I am not compromising with you now, as I might.

OCTOBER 10, 1942

Exhausted—after thirteen days (& a few evenings) steady labor. Kingsley accosted me on the street. We had coffee & cigarettes in a drugstore,
she was quite as usual—asked me no embarrassing questions, told me
all about School. Rolf phoned as I came in & after debate (with myself)
decided to meet him at 10. I haven't yet read the letter (delivered) which
he wanted back again. Disgustingly adolescent writing—which I'd kept
to show to Rosalind, and bad would-be Wolfe Lyric (He said he didn't
love me tho every fiber, etc—)

OCTOBER 11, 1942

ᶠWhat a wonderful day! I grew today! A good breakfast. I worked more
calmly than I have in the past three months. I read my story about the
madwoman to M. & S. Mother understands it. But S. said that stories
like this are "beyond him!" Pretty good writing M. thinks. How sweet
life is! I finished Jean Cocteau—*Les Enfants* [*Terribles*]. What a memorable book! Viva!ᶠᶠ

OCTOBER 12, 1942

ᶠA letter from Rolf—that he still wants me, and what would he do without me? He'll yet learn that I don't want to be "owned." An ordinary day

at the office. The world is intruding—and during the night, I lost yesterday's sense of tranquility. Looked for ads in magazines. There are some
for radios, etc. Gave blood at 5:30. Very pleasant. Then read Kafka's *The
Castle* (from Rosalind).[FF] Very good—and imaginative—very tired. The
flesh is weak.

OCTOBER 13, 1942

[F]Never before have I been so enraptured with my life! It's quite an impersonal sensation. It comes when I am alone or with someone, when I am
reading a splendid book, looking at an imaginative image, or listening
to good music. It came today, with fantastic and sustained force, when I
was listening to "Sheep May Safely Graze" by J. S. Bach in a music shop
during my lunch hour. It came on even more strongly when I read a page
in *Mysticism* by [Evelyn] Underhill. It's my faith—it's my life. There is
nothing but art.

Another ordinary day at the office. Miss Weick was moved to the
other office. I'm with Goldberg, around whom I can't smoke as much
as I'd like. I am filled with inexpressible happiness. Yet it is sadness too.
It is much greater than I. I do not concern myself with my own person:
only with my aspirations, my desires, my work. I concern myself with the
things I love.[FF]

OCTOBER 14, 1942

Very happy indeed. Had a hamburger at the old White Tower on Greenwich, & went for a stroll down Eighth Street looking with new ideas
(since Rolf, since my job, since finding out more truths this past month)
& then to the Music Shop. No [Bach cantata] "Wer mir behagt," but
did meet a [F]young Jewish man,[FF] who was very helpful. Offered to
give me his superior record now unobtainable. We saw the Whitney
[exhibit] together. A marvelous painting of Philip Evergood's called
Lily & the Sparrows. Then to gramophone shop with my friend whose
name is Louis Weber, 9 W. 97 St. He wants to bring over records to play
Monday night. Shall ask Marjorie. I love all things—I received happy
thoughts. In some way I am walking with God these days.

OCTOBER 15, 1942

Very tough day. Goldberg talks—anecdotes—so much we never get any
work done & consequently had to work tonight. Herr Goldberg came
home with me—afoot—at 12 midnight, carrying my books.

OCTOBER 16, 1942

^FAn alcoholic day. Alice T. at 1:00. We ate at Castille—very crowded and full, very hot. They are not serving martinis by the carafe yet. She was astounded that I knew so many "important" people who are older than me. Drank two martinis with Valerie Adams at the Hôtel Pierre. She knows Kay Boyle—P. Guggenheim—le Paris. Wanted to bring me with her to the Guggenheims. Also, a matter which disgusts me—Kingsley told her that I was (now) obsessed with a woman—"a woman older than me." It's the most recent mistake—it's the sin which cannot be forgiven, and though there are many things we have forgiven each other for—this is impossible. What can silence her? Do I have to shoot her? With Billie B. at W. Fair tonight. Drank quite a bit. Didn't see a single person, man or woman, who seemed to me intelligent, spiritual, perfect—no one. I have had my fill of drinks and parties for a year.^{FF}

OCTOBER 17, 1942

^FBad day. Worked hard all day, didn't go to see any exhibitions with mother, didn't even manage to brush my teeth because of the booze last night, couldn't do any good work because I'm not being paid what I'm owed—I should have received 1½ for my overtime. I'm angry, furious! But I was a schoolgirl and did nothing—

Jeva phoned me at 8:30. Very sweet—would like to stay with her—no matter where. Bought shoes—which cost all my money—have only $4.00 to get through next week. It torments Flesch so when one asks him for money!

I bought a philodendron—green, tranquil, patient. Unlike me. I'm miserable.^{FF}

OCTOBER 18, 1942

Worked comparatively little on my story but ended second draft. The next I may show to Goldberg. It should be good. Then I'll make over what few things I've done since school, & then perhaps start the novel.

The injustice of my employers oppresses me. I shall leave as soon as possible but first I'll write a letter saying Mr. Flesch had better employ only those unacquainted with the Wagner Act.[*] I should also like to tell Kingsley just what I think of her soon.

There is so much beauty—and I shall see it tomorrow—standing

---

* The National Labor Relations Act of 1935, also known as the Wagner Act, affirmed workers' rights to organize and engage in collective bargaining, or to refrain from such activities.

waiting for a light, reading a snatched page in the library tomorrow—
and today it was so hard to open my work-benighted eyes.

OCTOBER 19, 1942

[F]Very nervous and very awake. Spoke to Goldberg about my assignments. I was so confident and so calm that he couldn't help but
acquiesce—I will receive my overtime instead of a raise.

Saw Rolf Tietgens at 2. Coffee at Caruso's, like the first time. The
idiot told Bernhard that "we are no longer as close as before."

A wonderful evening! Louis Weber came by early, we played his
"Sheep May Safely Graze" which he gave me. Louis asked for some of
my stories. I gave them to him. He particularly liked the "Silver Horn"
which he read here. He observed me closely tonight, saying that I was
very complicated, important—that I've got "the stuff." But he's very
strange. He must live quite alone, of that I'm sure.

P.S. Bernhard phoned me at 9:00. Wants to see me—Thursday night.
I'm very nervous about seeing her again—I was just regaining my sanity.[FF]

OCTOBER 20, 1942

Spoke to Rosalind this A.M. Told her I'm broke for lunch. She said make
it Fri.—she wouldn't be broke. Bad precedent, I say—

My tooth—the one that gave trouble last summer in California—is
hurting again. Consequently I can't receive any communications from
the misty lands or see pictures reflected in the mountain lakes of warm
water. I am here—with my lousy tooth. I wish it were out—I see the
drench of blood and pus, and feel the terrible blessed relief, the bitter
hole in my face, and the relaxation of my brows that have been taut for
weeks.

OCTOBER 21, 1942

[F]With mother at Pete's for dinner—how I dreamed of taking mother out
in the evenings once I had some money. Saw a very good dance performance. Oh—my God! What a woman Jean Erdman is!![*] Tall, slender
(but not too slender!), an intelligent and smiling mouth. What legs, what
a waist! We sat in the first row—only a few feet away. I would have loved
to go backstage and tell her how I felt about her art! It was dangerous
tho, mother might have noticed something.[FF]

---

* Jean Erdman (1916–2020), American modern dancer and choreographer.

OCTOBER 22, 1942

Very late. Read in Library & got caught in first daylight air-raid drill.

Dentist at 3:15—one Ralph Miller, of third rate intelligence, who did "spot-drilling" on this damned upper right & told me the wisdom tooth was pushing the others out of line. $1.00 it still hurts. Worked some this evening, though I go slowly & need much tranquil times. Went to see Bernhard at 9:30 at 155 E. 56—her new address. Rather monkish, one room. She in bed drinking Rock 'n' Rye. Pajamas. She is filled with this "stinko affair" of Rolf's & mine—how we "fled" very indecently—etc. that killed—10–11 o'clock came & still the same subject. So I said if she asked me to come to criticize me she didn't need to because the story had preceded me wherever I've been the last four months. So she grew more friendly. I had shattered her unwise, uncalled for trust, but we might begin from beginning. So—she has a show next Wednesday— and I'm to go—& the evening, too. Not much time in sight & I have a great project in mind.

OCTOBER 23, 1942

^FA wonderful day! Lunch with Rosalind at 12:30. She gave me advice on my hair—I've got to cut it. Yes, it's done now. We discussed art. Then went to Petit Français to see the Surrealist exhibit. It was marvelous! Tanguy, Chagall, Ernst, Berlioz, Lamy, Matta all well-represented. Also a woman, Leonora Carrington,* in whom R. is very interested. Rosalind put a safety pin on one of the nails of Picasso's guitar. We laughed! How I love her! She's always this happy on Fridays because she goes away with Betty on the weekends. It's sad—I suppose. But I'm happy when she is. This is how much I love her.^{FF}

OCTOBER 24, 1942

I am happy. Put 45.00 in bank. Goldberg there, Flesch & Lerner worried at my working, lest I request more money! Saw Rolf. Disgusting behavior, more psychopathic, more neurotic because he has been living alone now. [Dr.] Dobrow's for a filling. He talked more intelligently—I favor the young dentists if they already know enough.

Jack here at 7:45. Rather nice after all. He is so terribly in love with me, and furthermore knows what to do about it, which is more than I can say of Rolf. We saw a Spanish theater vaudeville at 116. Bus ride. Then home for Bach, coffee & cake. He kissed me most passionately—I

---

* Leonora Carrington (1917–2011), British-Mexican surrealist painter and novelist.

shouldn't mind sleeping with him. I might enjoy it—knowing he would so. He's been "rolling around" with all manner of femmes in Manhattan in the last months.

I am filled with confidence & ideas!

10/24/42

And Sunday afternoons I shall go alone and take a golden chariot ride through Central Park. The people will be amorphous subaqueous organisms, suspended in gelatinous depths, or swaying gently upon their pedicles. I shall be able to see their entrails working and pulsing and changing color from red to green to chartreuse. The museums, the zoos will be as castles in a goldfish bowl, and though I do not swim through them, I shall pass through them in my chariot at the same time viewing them from the outside. The park itself will be sunken deep, and only the gray Sunday sky will border its furthest treetops. I shall converse with whom I will, with Phaeton first for courtesy, with the molecules of air I shall exchange pleasantries, with the trees I will hum cantatas, with the rocks of the hillocks I will argue and contest the probability of immortality and the proving of emancipation. I shall make colors, and no colors, sounds and no sounds, at my will, for I shall have the power, being able to imagine these things.

OCTOBER 25, 1942

FRe-read my story of the madwoman. It's very good, but needs another 24h—straight.

With Rolf 2–6:30. He took 12 photographs—several nudes. He gave me books, and we ate at Fish Place—3rd Ave. It's more pleasant now, when he expects nothing of me.FF

OCTOBER 27, 1942

GI'm so tired, so melancholy, so dissatisfied. Saw Rolf at 5:45. The photographs are good. We sat over coffee and looked at the pictures. Later went to the Guggenheim Museum, which beyond doubt houses the city's best pictures. All sorts of Surrealist artists, but especially Paul Klee, Ernst, Miró, de Chirico. Then Jack B. came over, just to pick up a book he'd left behind. (He stayed for several hours, though!) We listened to Bach, Mozart, Beethoven. He leant me *Jesu, der du meine Seele.* But I want to work. Always, and in order to fall asleep tonight, I vowed in writing to go out just once a week now. That alone will hold things together—make me healthy and happy. Otherwise I'm most terribly beat down, oppressed, and neglectful of my own soul. How I need Rosalind! Where in the world do I find beauty but in Rosalind! Whom do I truly and actually love but Rosalind! Who wishes not to see me but Rosalind! I'm a fool not to spend more time with her. She is my heart, my spiritual bread and water—and sometimes, though only in my mind, she is my sin, my escape, but in my soul my one love and lover forever and ever!GG

OCTOBER 28, 1942

GI'm driven quite mad by these nights without rest and solitude upon which the sheep of my soul graze. My heart is so full, it breaks in two, and the pretty jewels and fantasies are like poison in my veins.GG Went to Laboratory Institute at 6:00 & was offered all tea, coffee & whiskey—I took the latter as any man of spirit. When B. came I'd had 2 & had 3 before leaving. Bernhard's pictures looked better than ever. We had a drink—me one too many. So Bernhard said let's go to her place a while. (Why I can't imagine!) And I soon got sick. Had to stay. Bernhard wonderful to me, fetching this & that. She must love me so passionately—well with a certain passion that is not entirely physical, & yet which hasn't let itself go yet either.

OCTOBER 29, 1942

Woke up with slight headache. Should have liked to have breakfast with B. but I scrammed at 8:10. The worst thing is facing the elevator boys, who've learned not to bat an eye. Showered & went to work. I think about the adolescent novel. I am neurotic & young enough to write from memory & autobiography and most of all love! *Liebe! Amor! Amore— amour!* ἀγάπη

Saw Mr. Shawn of the *New Yorker* who very courteously gave me two assignments to prepare for Talk of the Town rewrite man—good stuff—& the secretary took my jobs on the list. Real McCoy. Perhaps no duplicates. Read Sir Thos. Browne—who said tonight: "All things are artificial, for nature is the Art of God."*

OCTOBER 30, 1942

FA good day. Not a lot of work at the office—Goldberg even told me I could work on my stories, but warned me not to read any books, because Flesch noticed that once. Went to see Rosalind in a red shirt, straight hair. She saw Lola P. last night, who's separated from Del.

---

* Quotation from *Religio Medici* (London, 1643).

Mutual agreement. Lola is writing surreal stories now. Rosalind and I discussed stream of consciousness in [Dorothy] Richardson,* whom she doesn't know, Kafka, lots of things. I asked her what she thought about a novel about teenagers—15–18 years old? "Well, it's like saying what about a novel on marriage?—Sure—Sure fire stuff." But then I told her what I want to do with my characters—it will be better than Daly†—of course.[FF] "There should be something said on what the younger generation is thinking—" That's not what I'd write on though & she knows it. I watched her in the bank, where she goes always on Fridays—and she looked very masculine, very gay. Something in the lie of her hair, the squint of her eye. And gosh she can flash a gay smile occasionally! I wonder why she doesn't ask me to their place sometime? I wonder xmas? I wonder my birthday? I wonder ever?

OCTOBER 31, 1942

[F]I am happy, but not very happy—it's as if I'd fallen asleep under an open sky. I am filled with my novel—the teenagers, but there is nothing to write in my notebook—I haven't thought it through yet. It's funny.

   I'd like to have time and more time.

   I'd like to do everything, lots of things both in my head and out of it.

   I'm walking on tiptoes through a world full of traps.[FF]

10/31/42

Sometimes she would see only women friends for weeks at a time. She would say: "I am happy. This is my world," or she would grow disgusted with the recognition of their shortcomings and say: "I have nothing to do with this." Then she would have weeks of masculine company—when she would be the only girl in a house full of homosexual men & boys, each more intelligent, more attractive and beautiful really than the women, and certainly more honest with each other. "This is my world. Here people are square with no vanities," she would say (for indeed the homosexuals she knew were not of the vainer type). But both these conditions palling, switching, palling, she had only to conclude that neither world was "hers" but that hers was a separate world. In short, she could never find her social milieu, and knew even at twenty that she never could. She was quite right, unfortunately.

---

* The English author Dorothy Richardson (1873–1957) is credited with having written one of the first stream-of-consciousness novels.

† Maureen Daly (1921–2006), Irish-born American writer best known for her 1942 novel *Seventeenth Summer*, which she wrote while still in her teens.

11/1/42

Night writing—Certainly all younger writers should write at night, when the conscious brain (the critical faculty) is tired. Then the subconscious has its way and the writing is uninhibited. Even older writers feel some of this—those who either are not good enough to escape self-criticism (of the hyper sort) or who have found no release in their conscious minds, or perhaps those who have pleasant memories of explorative days when they were learning to write.

NOVEMBER 2, 1942

[F]What an excitement! Miss Weick quit today! She couldn't get her typewriter to work, and Lerner was calling her "stupid." Well—she got everything off her chest that had been bothering her for two months—and quit—simply marched out of the office! I addressed envelopes all morning. Goldberg invited me to lunch. I gave him my story about the madwoman, and he told me that I was trying to write in the most difficult fashion—the analytic kind—that the great writers use. That's what interests me; what am I supposed to do about it? This story is really very tricky, because I don't want to write more simply, make it easier. I will move on to other things—as usual.[FF]

NOVEMBER 3, 1942

[F]With [Dr.] Dobrow who was very rude. Because I asked him questions, he accused me of wanting to lecture him about his job! It's ridiculous! I can't go back again. I left, smoking a cigarette. Voted for the first time this morning at 10. Israel Amter made the primary, Flynn, Davis, Poletti, etc. Most are ALP.[*]

I began the story about the hotel to which people who are about to die go.[FF]

NOVEMBER 4, 1942

[F]A good day. I did much more of my own work than that of F.F.F. Went to Brentano's [bookstore] at 10:30. They'll add the *J.F.A.* [*Jewish Family Almanac*] to their stock. If they consider it a periodical. Then back to the office, where I addressed envelopes—but not for too long. No letters. I wrote my piece on undergarments for *The New Yorker*. Not finished yet.[FF]

---

[*] American Labor Party. Both federal and New York State elections were held on November 3, 1942. Israel Amter, Elizabeth Gurley Flynn, and Benjamin Davis Jr. were candidates for the Communist Party.

11/4/42

Preface to *The Book of Pleasant Things*.

I am writing a book of pleasant things because I am so long and so deeply convinced that all things, and by this I mean everything, in the world is not pleasant. If it is pleasant for a time, it is unpleasant eventually by our having to leave it soon, or by invidious comparison which all humans make with something better. Melancholy and pessimism, coupled with a kind and generous heart and a broad mind, are the noblest virtues of man. They let him sink to the depths of himself, no less interesting or splendid than the heights, and they let him taste heavenly delights when he finds their shadows in matters here on earth.

NOVEMBER 5, 1942

FA good day—spent all day thinking of the evening with Rosalind. She came at 7:10. We drank—martinis for me, tomato juice for her, prepared by mother. She was so beautiful. She didn't like the pictures on my walls, or my bathroom. And didn't care for Rolf's photographs.FF She scarcely listened to my Bach, which I had so anticipated—both her not listening, and my listening with her. FI drank too much, which I don't want to do again. We ate at Petit Paris. I paid too much for everything.FF "You shouldn't drink so much. Betty & I both think you drink too much—it's slightly sordid—a good-looking kid like you—" We said good night—and I dared kiss her on the cheek—God knows if she minded. I don't know.

NOVEMBER 7, 1942

Splendid day. Tho I'm going to bed disastrously late, I got fired at 11:25 today. No notice—Flesch never heard of it. I must say I'm glad. Goldberg is sympathetic. Flesch told me no more writing is necessary, etc. Bought Marjorie Thompson a drink at the Mansfield [Hotel], and we saw Bacon's show* with mother. Simply wonderful and with the energy & concentration of a man—some of it. Then tea & the Guggenheim once more, where sat Peggy & the dog, too. Talked to Kiesler.† Very nice.

NOVEMBER 8, 1942

Fine day. I worked hard on *New Yorker* & will be able to show it tomorrow. Saw Rolf at 5. We talked—he says he doesn't love me anymore,

---

* Francis Bacon (1909–1992) would become Pat's favorite painter.
† Frederick John Kiesler (1890–1965), Austrian-American architect, theater and exhibition designer, artist, and sculptor.

would like to kiss me however. I am very cold, and do not trouble sufficiently to analyze him. As always, he said the crucial thing of me—that I
must write what I have experienced, and leave imaginary stories be until
I am strong enough to inject life into them. After indecisions (which are
characteristic of both of us German, stubborn, egocentric and undersexed
people) we went to Petit Paris & had tenderloin steaks, & white wine.

NOVEMBER 9, 1942

Lunched with Bernhard, which she unfortunately couldn't pay for as
scheduled. I have $6.00 & shall have to go into my bank account, which
hurts like I can't say. Also applied for unemployment insurance.

I shall be once more the person I was at fourteen & fifteen & partially sixteen—alive & capable of loving and losing, too. Imaginative
and full of lyricism, the intellect only awakening, & in no danger of
exerting its throttling control. This question of "What do I feel?" is at
the root of all: It affects my writing, my expression, my happiness, and
depends on my food intake, physical habits, etc. I should a) correct menstruation b) think about normal things instead of morbid, even impersonal introspections c) never think of myself except in regard to finding
my emotional responses, and expressing them d) get over the Rosalind
crush, and not regard it as an established course which must be followed
e) say to Bernhard freely all the affection I feel for her so often f) write
only lyrical stuff for a long while g) examine my journals at 14–20 and
see what and why—above all I must believe, as I surely do, that sexual
experience at my age is not absolutely necessary, and that many normal
people, even geniuses, had not had it at my age, that I can come to the
Golden age once more with faith in myself. I carry always this feeling
that some day the cloud will lift, as it does when one studies uncom-
prehendingly mathematics for a long while, and then one day comes
the revelation. So it will—or perhaps already has come to me. Then
Rosalind and Bernhard will take their proper places, dependent on their
characters—both excellent—and not upon me, unless I am truly in love
with one of them.

NOVEMBER 10, 1942

FI worked on my N.Y. [New Yorker] assignment and finally sent it off.
Sent the Jewish Family Almanac to grandmother. Pretty funny. I sang
today while I was walking in the rain—I was singing Bach. And it was as
if I was in love. The rain, wet shoes, the cold, the effort of walking didn't
matter to me at all. Am happy. Have lots of wonderful things to do.FF

NOVEMBER 11, 1942

[F]Rosalind said she'd have lunch with me on Friday. That's good, because I must see her before leaving the city that night. I don't want to sleep with R.B. Naturally, however, they will put us in the same bedroom. Oh! If only Rosalind would take me! If only she would change her mind! How much longer can she stay with someone like Betty? I did nothing much today except write a long story in my notebook about my confused and confusing life for an indifferent posterity. Mr. Shawn received my work today. No one can know how much trepidation I feel—did I say enough, etc.? Mother is worried because she thinks that the letters I write to Gramma are not "warm" enough. Gramma gives me 5.00 a week. I need it badly. It would be good if the *New Yorker* were also to pay me, but it makes no difference. The Germans are marching through France. Marseille has been occupied tonight. The Americans took Africa—without fighting, and the French flotilla coming from Toulon just joined the allies. Everything is all right. Also, the people to whom I wrote the letter on Sunday phoned me to schedule an interview.

I read *Christian Morals* and *Letter to a Friend* by Sir Thos. Browne.[FF]

11/11/42

I feel the multitudinous conceivings of my brain clamoring, from time to time, like molecules of steam under a pot lid. They make a steady din. I do not hope for one so big as to blow the lid off. I must do that myself. I wish I knew the engineering.

NOVEMBER 12, 1942

[F]Lunch with Goldberg at Café Raffier. After I hinted at drinks once or twice, he asked for a martini and an Old Fashioned—then another round halfway through the meal. Not bad! He said my novel is a good idea, it could be sold (!) after or during the war. Am happy. Except that I want to work. I continued working on my story at home. I'll show it to *The New Yorker*. It will be good. My story of the year—my best story since "Heroine" and "Silver Horn." The idea's not so great or different, but it's better written. Tonight at home—I thought in my darkened room about my teenage novel, and I began a notebook especially on this subject.[*]

I've written enough for today. My head keeps working when I am alone here, with nothing "to do" in the world outside.[FF]

---

[*] This specific notebook was lost.

NOVEMBER 14, 1942

[F]Bernhard [and I] left at 11:15. The house in Westport, Conn. belongs to Ms. Beecroft, who lives all alone except for an aunt who may die at any moment. The aunt lives in the room upstairs and lies in bed in a coma. Ms. Beecroft never smiles. We are being fed a lot, and Bernhard's appetite is astounding!

Terribly cold! It's impossible to take a walk on the beach. The water is not far from the house. There is a dog here, Toby, and death, the person upstairs. I am growing sick of Bernhard's egotism. One puts up with it because she is an artist, but after 24 hours it becomes unbearable! I was cold despite myself when we went to bed and I had no desire to kiss her. It's too bad, because she paid for me—and I gave her nothing in return. Anyway, it was really too cold to make love—we slept in all our clothes![FF]

NOVEMBER 15, 1942

[F]I was hungry all day. An egg, toast, and ersatz coffee this morning. One night, then back home. Am very happy, even though I have nothing to do in the city, no means to make a living! I wrote a long letter to R. Constable. Drawings—of the house with the apple tree, of our hostess, of the dying aunt, of our tour on the beach, and ten small scenes of our non-amorous night. I hope they will amuse her.[FF]

NOVEMBER 16, 1942

[F]Woke up very anxious—nothing to do—except find a job. With Rolf 3–6. Several photographs, no clothes, and my face. A letter (note) from M. Clark at *Bow*, to whom I sent my "Silver Horn." Recommended I send it to *Parade*,[*] which I did. She's interested in my work, etc. A ray of sunshine which made me happy—writers work so hard![FF]

NOVEMBER 17, 1942

[F]Still have nothing to do: for money. Called up Shawn—his secretary told me that he'll doubtlessly call me soon. Successfully repaired two mirrors at home. When one has nothing to do, one works like a farmer. Went for a stroll 2–4. I'm not eligible for unemployment—I didn't work long enough. Saw J. Stern[†] on 57 St. around the Ferargil Galleries. Spoke to me. Didn't read enough this week.[FF]

---

* *Parade*, a weekly Sunday supplement to more than seven hundred American newspapers starting in 1941.
† James Stern (1904–1993), Anglo-Irish writer of short stories and nonfiction.

NOVEMBER 18, 1942

[F]Big day! Worked and finished another draft of "Manuel." Then went out for a stroll. Bernhard called me to say that she was let go from [Norman] Bel Geddes.[*FF] Goldberg has a part time job for me. $15 a week, possibly tomorrow. Very nice half evening at home. I read much in Blake, which stimulates me to do wonderful things, generally unrelated to Blake.

11/18/42

The homosexual man seeks his equal or seeks a young man whom he may educate to his equal of intellect and appreciation. This is the ideal, spiritual homosexual. The Lesbian, the classic Lesbian, never seeks her equal. She is Vala,[†] the corporeal understanding, the *soi-disant* male, who does not expect his match in his mate, who would rather use her as the base-on-the-earth which he can never be.

NOVEMBER 19, 1942

Excitement. At 42 St. at 10:45. The office is that overtaxed building, 55 W. on the 7th floor. In room 724 five people hover frantically around one desk, one English typewriter & one Yiddish typewriter. I had to see one Rudko, or Miss Milanov, etc. program for Nov. 29 in Carnegie. Nuts! Anyhow—I couldn't keep the lunch date with R.C. But a Miss Todd of Time, Inc. phoned—Mrs. Williams wants to see me tomorrow at 11:00. A job? Who knows?

Unger, who haunts the office gratuitously, is frantic to have me stay on & do English publicity. I am definitely no longer unemployed.

NOVEMBER 20, 1942

[F]A good day—but very tiring. Time Inc at 11:30. Mrs. Williams doesn't have a job for me—but she and Mrs. Fraser are very interested in the young women who haven't yet come to work at Time, Inc. I told her that I'm also working for the *New Yorker*. Then I phoned Rosalind. She said there was a job at *Harper's Bazaar*. They offered it to her, but she didn't want it. They're looking for two inexperienced girls or a genius—Rosalind.[FF]

---

* Norman Bel Geddes (1893–1958), American stage and industrial designer.
† A term from Germanic mythology for a female shaman and seeress.

11/20/42

Guilty sensations on first drinking alone are easily overcome. The second sensations are those of quiet conviviality—with one's self. All the joys of society, says the introvert, with none of its hideous faces! How can one be happy in New York when all the bad people are merely evil, and all the good people merely compromisers?

NOVEMBER 22, 1942

[F]Good day. Am tired after 5 hours of sleep, but I wrote the best draft of "Manuel" so far. Then I read a bit of *Varouna*. He makes me happy— [Julien] Green writes about things I like, and which make me feel lofty! M. [Marjorie] Wolf came at 3. Went with her to St. Bartholomew's to hear [Bach's] "Brich dem Hungrigen sein Brot," but the words were in English, singers timid & few. An up and down in the service— Episcopalian. We drank 2 martinis at Mario's, then went home for dinner. M. talked civilly with the parents at the table, discussed the Negro question, the people of the South, etc. One listens to her—she has real warmth, a truly human heart, I like her a lot. All alone in the room, we listened, in the shadows, to [two Bach cantatas] "Jesu, der du meine Seele," and "Schafe können sicher [weiden]," holding hands, perhaps desiring to do more. It was very strange! She'd like to live with me— would like to leave her mother—slip out if she doesn't let her. In truth, I imagine she might be a better companion than Bernhard. But I can't do anything else unless we come to an agreement.[FF]

NOVEMBER 24, 1942

[F]I am very happy today because I spoke to Rosalind on the phone. She almost smiled at me. The women from *Harper's* would like to see me— I can use her name. "You don't have to look too fancy. But look your best." She would also like to go to the swing concerts at Town Hall. (I wanted to take her to Cherry Lane* Friday night.) Worked a lot and well this evening, then made a small card for Virginia on the occasion of our anniversary—Thanksgiving—four years! Four years since I laid eyes on her for the first time!

I do not spend enough time thinking when I write. I have a surfeit of ideas and good ideas, but it takes so long to get from them to their actualization. I must change my life.[FF]

---

* Cherry Lane Theatre, located in Greenwich Village, is the longest-running off-Broadway theater.

NOVEMBER 25, 1942

[F]A marvelous time with Bernhard at Del Pezzo, where Christopher Morley[*] was eating a few tables from us. Then we went to see the men who make puppets—marionettes. They are interesting, and like all men who make their livings in New York's nocturnal establishments, they have turned their work into an art par excellence. Now at Sons of Fun[†] and the Rainbow Room. They're both gay, of course.

It's still raining gently, and I walked through the streets after having read a few pages of Kay Boyle in the library. How she writes! So light, but so heavy with meaning! Intelligent and simple people, in old English houses, women who dress like men, who eat eggs while standing in front of the fireplace. Orgies full of sex!

I'd like to write with more lyricism, but I find this quite difficult—the way I find telling my thoughts to Rosalind, or to anyone, difficult. I am constrained. Back at home with Jo P. at 11. We drank coffee and listened to "Schafe können sicher weiden." And "Jesu." She appreciates them, just as I appreciate her records. It's true friendship.[FF]

NOVEMBER 26, 1942

[F]Very anxious. Sometimes I wait all day for those rare moments in which I feel at peace. I'm destroying myself, I know. I'd like to have a corner of my room that's peaceful, where I can write very slowly, and I have one! But whenever I possess something—it loses its value. Office at 10. No one on the streets except for countless British marines, strolling, looking for Times Square, wondering what to do on this peaceful day. Took several letters to the offices in Canal St. in the dirty buildings where the Jewish newspapers have their headquarters. It's disgusting.

Jo P. at 7:45 for dinner with us at the Jumble Shop. Was happy tonight. Gave small presents to the family. Dinner was good. Afterwards, Jo came back home with us. I wanted to kiss her. I am at peace with her, because she makes me live in the moment: neither ahead of time, nor behind. More importantly: lots of notes on my novel after 12.[FF]

NOVEMBER 27, 1942

[F]A sparkling day—a marvelous lunch with Rosalind. We ate at the Golden Horn, both of us starving, and laughed at everything. She's expecting great things of me.—Are you working on your novel? (Yes.)

---

* Christopher Morley (1890–1957), American writer, editor, and cofounder of the *Saturday Review*.
† The musical revue *Sons o' Fun* ran from 1941 to 1943 and starred comedy duo Olsen & Johnson.

The photographs Rolf took of me are good. I was at 8 St with him until 10, because every appointment with Rolf takes the whole evening! Bernhard here at 11:30 when I told her I had photographs by Rolf. She likes them. But she thinks she could do better. I kissed her with pleasure at my door at 1:30. I would have preferred to kiss Rosalind! How I loved Rosalind today![FF]

NOVEMBER 28, 1942

[F]Read a bit more of my journals. I have to read a lot before writing. In any case, I'm almost certain that one must write good stories first. I saw a piece of luggage left behind on the subway platform. I wrote a story about it.[*] Am happy. Bernhard gave me one of her pictures. A less sexual photograph, for my room.[FF]

NOVEMBER 29, 1942

[F]Wrote on my new story about the paralytic and the man who looks like Paley.[†] It will be good—an action-packed story—they find a piece of luggage together—and tonight I wrote half of it by hand, lying on my bed. One must always allow the blood of a story, its muscles, to come naturally into one's mind, without thinking about it. Then it will be good.

The family confronted me about all of my current and former faults, with S. saying that I hadn't improved much since 1935. And "You are not being honest or natural to yourself." Exactly what I told myself three years ago! If only they knew! How different I had to appear from what I wanted! It's no wonder I'm repressed.

I'm smoking too much on Sundays. I'm smoking now. What does it matter? I can't think of one good reason why not.[FF]

11/30/42

Shall I give her the Romantic Symphony for Christmas?—or will she, English like, think it sentimental, hearing an occasional phrase as she lights a cigarette, pours another's drink—shall she miss all that I love, even with her intelligent eyes, her polite ears? I could not stand that. And yet here I sit, listening at this second, and hearing all the deep reds, the rich purples, the autumnal yellows, and burnt oranges, the crisp winds, the warm bricks of the fireplace that we shall never share, that I

---

* She begins work on the short story that will be published as "Uncertain Treasure" in 1943.
† One of her colleagues at F.F.F. who inspired her in the writing of "Uncertain Treasure."

can never give her except in a piece of music, which she may fail really to hear.

DECEMBER 1, 1942

F Strange. Many ideas yesterday. Today: nothing! Went to the library this morning to read *Harper's Bazaar*. It's been around since 1867! Then *Harper's* at 3:30. McFadden made me wait. She's quick, not very chic, but intelligent of course. She'd like to see several of my stories. It makes me happy, because they're the most significant ones—"Heroine," "Mighty Nice Man," "Silver Horn," etc. Mr. Alford at *Modern Baby* offered me work this week (typist stuff) while his daughter is getting married. How much will he pay me? Don't know. At least $20.00, so I could take Rosalind out Friday night. FF

12/2/42

What to do with homosexuality? The transformation of the material is utterly impossible—unless one changes the characters to be abnormally inhibited, so that such things hold all the excitement, the forbidden piquancy of the true first feelings. This makes, generally, a sexual weakling, a schizophrene, an inhibited suppressed person of a vigorous one.

DECEMBER 3, 1942

F Another sleepy day after 8 hours' sleep—for the third day in a row! Don't know what to do! I'm fortified against the wind, can resist the cold, and I'm never hungry. I'm so busy that ideas aren't coming easily, quickly, the way they do when I am calmer during the day, like a true artist. But they're still there. Phoned Rosalind. She laughed when I told her I was working for *Modern Baby*. "It's good training for you?" (Yes, but what isn't?) FF

12/3/42

The effect of sleeping—logginess, mediocrity, absence of excitement & pleasure of hunger, absence of dreams, ideas, greater reality unpleasant. Effects of not sleeping—unreality. Mañana complex, dreams and fancies, hunger, always physical consciousness of some kind pleasant to the ego-centered.

DECEMBER 4, 1942

F Last day at *Modern Baby*, thank God! They only paid me 10.00, which is $3 less than what the union stipulates. Paid my dentist, and I have two dollars left after three days' work. My Christmas present would be a job at *Harper's Bazaar.* I'd like a steady job.

I worked well tonight, which made me happy as usual. Ecstatic! And how!

Big discussion tonight after the parents came home from the movies. They don't like Tietgens' pictures. Janie found one today—and mother was embarrassed—frightfully embarrassed! "It's awful. Neither man nor woman! I don't want them on my walls! Not even on yours!" And that her life is terrible because I'm at home, and that she'd be better off if I were gone. Well, as soon as I find a steady job, I'm gone!ᶠᶠ

DECEMBER 5, 1942

ᶠSaw the Alajalov* exhibition with mother at 5. Greta Garbo† was there, wearing brown suede shoes, with her shopping bags and a big hat to hide her face. But she was still so frightfully beautiful!

I made a big decision tonight: I will buy Rosalind a music box for Christmas. I must give her something that no one else will give her. Buffie came by at 7:30, looking very pretty. Went with her to Nino & Nella, Peter and Helen weren't there. Neither was Bing Crosby, thank God. There were two drunk women, one had lost her son in Africa. Very sad, really. What can I do with this story? On 6th Ave. we browsed through the bookshops, bought books, records, etc! What a music shop! where boys and girls listen to great, exciting swing shift records after midnight. At Tony's 52 St (who sings Italian songs while standing on his head)‡ we saw several of Buffie's friends, the kind who come up to you saying loudly "the last time I saw you was in Paris." It disgusts me. I wasted far too much money frolicking about with her tonight—$5 and I don't have a job right now. And the music box for Rosalind will cost $35.00. Oh, I'll be a miser for the next few weeks!!

Kingsley called me—very calm and quiet. Would like to have lunch

---

* Constantin Alajálov (1900–1987), Armenian-American illustrator and painter best known for designing the covers of publications such as the *Saturday Evening Post, Vanity Fair, Fortune, Life, Harper's Bazaar,* and *Vogue.*

† Pat was a lifelong admirer of Swedish-American actress Greta Garbo (1905–1990). In a tribute published after the actress's death, "My Life with Greta Garbo," published in the *Oldie* on April 3, 1992, Pat remembers stalking Garbo on the streets of Manhattan, once almost colliding with her on a corner. Garbo was part of the Sewing Circle, a clandestine association of lesbian and bisexual women in Hollywood.

‡ Singing Italian songs while doing a headstand was Tony Soma's signature trick. In the 1920s, when Tony's was Dorothy Parker's favorite speakeasy, it was apparently there that she answered a bartender's question of "What are you having?" with her famous line: "Not much fun."

Tues. at 12:30. The traitor! Would like to write Jeannot* but I might endanger him because the Germans are there now and looking for Allied sympathizers.

Quarter to four!FF

DECEMBER 6, 1942

FAte a lot and worked a lot and wrote perhaps the best story of my life. It doesn't have a name yet, but I'll find an excellent one for it. I really must sell this story—even the parents like it. I read it to them tonight after church and mother said it was my best. It's the one about the paralytic. Thinking of Rosalind. I wonder what she was doing today while I was working. W. Marlowe and Jack B. also phoned, but I won't speak with them.FF

12/6/42

You look in a cluttered top drawer and you expect to see either a man or a woman reflected in it, and it is very disturbing when you see neither, or when you see both.

DECEMBER 7, 1942

FHappy, happy (but only because my future is nearing). That's for sure! I want nothing in the world but money! Went to the bank this morning—I have only $63.00—and my ego will force me to buy the $35.00 present for Rosalind. Worked on the good story again this afternoon. Am happy—because the writing is coming along—finally, I am writing like K. Boyle with many adjectives, many strong, sensuous words that one feels in the body.

[Goldberg's] mother-in-law died. Mrs. Sholem Aleichem, the wife of the great writer.†

Read another year of my journal (which I found very boring). Bernhard came over at 8. Then Virginia, then Jo. We had dinner at the Chinese restaurant on Lexington. Virginia very pretty (a glass-blown face, Bernhard said). Then to R.B.'s where she showed us all of her photographs. Jo lay down on the bed, saying nothing, eating nuts, making her observations. Even Virginia found Bernhard charming and "passable."FF

---

* Jeannot lived in Marseille. When the Allied forces landed in North Africa in the fall of 1942, the Germans and Italians retaliated by invading Vichy France.
† Goldberg was married to the daughter of famous Yiddish playwright Sholem Aleichem (1859–1916), one of whose stories was adapted as the musical *Fiddler on the Roof.*

DECEMBER 8, 1942

^FNot so happy because I am tormented by the thought of money—which I do not have. Spoke to Lewis at Amer. Inst. Elec. Engineers at 10 this morning. He would like to hire me but would pay me no more than $25.00 a week. I told him it's hard to live on $25.00 a week. We'll see on Thursday. I would like very much to work for Willard Co. at Paterson, who wants 20,000 women immediately. I definitely need to earn money.

With Kingsley at 12:30. Very pleasant until I brought up Val Adams, and what she had said regarding Rosalind and me. She denied everything, of course. Told me she had only mentioned our names, but she's lying.

Worked well on my story today, which is improving day by day. My prayers have been answered: I will have something to show Rosalind. I wonder whether she'll give me a photograph of herself.^{FF}

DECEMBER 9, 1942

^FWill write my father for money. I've never done that before. Will have work on Monday, thank God! The city was bright and beautiful this morning. I went to Carnegie via 57th St. to buy tickets for Sunday. Snow was falling softly, and though there was a changeable wind, everyone was smiling. Christmas trees are in front of every flower shop, and the snow was dusting them with white flecks, which looked like cotton. I was so happy, not thinking of the past or the future, but only of the present (what a rarity).

Interview with Jacobson at Park Ave. He wants a young girl straight out of college who will edit his new magazine—which is for ordinary women, unlike *Vogue*. Unfortunately, I was dressed like a young girl at *Vogue*, but he may have liked me. I would prefer a job at *Vogue*. Perhaps I'll still get one. Then I saw an excellent exhibition of twentieth century portraits. Buffie was invited to show, but she was in Calif[ornia]. There were lots of photographs by Berenice Abbott—Joyce, Rulin, Laurencin, and also one by Leonora Carrington. What a woman! 25 years old.^{FF}

DECEMBER 10, 1942

^FGood day—a bit of work when I went to *Modern Baby* to do some typing like a slave—form letters. They offered me only 4 dollars—which won't cover my expenses for tomorrow night—if at all! It's absurd, and completely against union regulations! I'm ungrateful, mother says. Bernhard has good nudes of Buffie. I'd like to have one. Miserable walking through the streets this afternoon because I have so little money. Sent

another letter asking for money to father, who has never given me anything, really.

Read a lot of my notebook. 1937. When I began to live a little, with Jones and Peggy, and not with Janet, whom I should have kissed.[FF]

DECEMBER 11, 1942

[F]I wouldn't have thought it possible that a day could be so boring, deadening. One can easily understand how one goes mad doing such work, drinking, smoking, dancing, doing destructive things. Bought a coat. Money is gone, gone, as usual. Have nothing but 13.00 in the bank. But the coat is lovely. Light and warm, soft to the touch.[FF]

12/11/42

Sometimes I have the strange belief that there is a remedy for every sensation of discomfort, physical or mental. When I drink water after long thirst, eat food after hungering, or once every five years take bicarbonate of soda for a digestive ailment (nervous indigestion) and when the pain passes in two or three minutes, the dull ache inside of me lifting and disappearing, keep on at my books with the fathomless ingratitude of a young person who has always been healthy, when such things occur then I think one may always make arrangements to stay comfortable all one's life. And yet this is the very opposite of what I have always believed (since I began believing anything, around the age of fourteen) and what is in my blood to believe. I believe in constant discomfort, varied equally like the ups and downs of a business chart about its line of normalcy, as the natural state of mankind. Therefore these happy, blind, animallike "insights" disturb me.

DECEMBER 12, 1942

This morning I performed the ignominious task of taking three coats to the thrift shop: my polo coat, which has seen so many faire & foul days at Barnard—and Morton Street! My little green Harris Tweed riding jacket, in which I spent the proudest, happiest hours of my life perhaps— and another little blue reefer. I was offered $1.50 for the lot at the first place, and the woman howled with horror when I proposed $4.00 at the second. I came off with $2.00, and bought a bird book and some exquisite doilies at the dime store.

Ended the semi-final draft of Archie, the paralytic. Tonight when mother read it, she found inconsistencies in style, too high a social scale where he lives, etc. And my restless brain jumps even as she speaks, wondering what I shall do next! Oh god the ripeness that is growing in my face, the maturity that is progressing in my heart, my soul, all these are ready to speak. They speak briefly in moments of brief tranquility. Two months earlier, when I had steady work I could have begun the great opus, had the other conditions been present as they are now.

DECEMBER 13, 1942

^FTonight, Carmen Amaya! Who always blows me away! For real! I can [almost] touch her body, taste her on my lips, on my tongue! She fills my blood, burns me! She was terribly, dangerously close to me. I could see her eyes, her lips. Mother was observing me closely, and focused particularly on Bernhard, who was wearing a silk suit and looked like a zombie. Carmen appeared in black stockings in the second act, clapping her hands, directing her sisters, who danced around her, framing her. I wonder how Antonio Triano could restrain himself while dancing with her! Terrific! I wanted to rise up like a balloon, I wanted to embrace her! At B.'s afterwards for sherry. And to look at photographs. Mother was speechless, which pleased me greatly. Perhaps I could truly love Bernhard—when I work hard, when I am calm. Otherwise, women like Carmen Amaya trouble me—and disturb me even more because one can only look at them, but not touch them. It's absurd! When B. and I were alone for a moment, we held hands, kissed on the lips, etc.

It's late. I'm full of sensations and don't want to sleep. Important ideas for my novel tonight—oddly intellectual.^{FF}

DECEMBER 14, 1942

^FArthur told me yesterday that he sold a story to *True Romances*. Or at least the idea. It was written by a woman who writes for the female readers of the magazine, but he made $75.00, which is good. Played piano for a while. It's been wonderful lately, when I'm deeply troubled. Then finished my subway story, though I have to keep working on it. Lou Weber here tonight, who said (and he's right) that I'd put too many insignificant details in it. ("The F. Train" etc.) Was so taken I worked until 3:00 tonight.

With Bernhard at Wakefield [Gallery]. Bemelmans, Gergely, Queenberry show. I can't speak to B. Parsons. She gives me the shivers. I would have liked to tell her how much I liked the show, but her eyes, her lips were observing me!

Bernhard's at 11:00. She asked me what I wanted in a lover. First, I must have the inspiration to work—and then always be happy, full of energy—a vigorous sex life. Bernhard told me that she could live with me forever without a sexual experience, even though she was dying for it! And she kissed me several times. She's afraid that I've suffered too much already because I've been frightened—by Buffie, Mary, Billie. But she knows I'm not like that. I can feel sensations in my head, like last night with C.A., but not in my body.

It's cold. 24°.[FF]

12/14/42

Security on the brink: writing and exulting in a comfortable traditionalism, fatally attracted to the exotic at the same time.

DECEMBER 15, 1942

[F]At Madeleine's [Madeleine Bemelmans's] where I made martinis. She's reading Goethe right now, from the same book we had at school. Ludwig is working with [Mary] MacArthur[*] on a piece based on his old book, *My War with the U.S.* It won't be good. Madeleine spoke about the biological inconvenience of being a woman when she wants to go to greasy spoons, bars, etc. She mentioned once that she seriously considered taking up women, but I told her it wasn't a good idea. After lunch, she stared at me steadily for a minute. Very troubling.

I looked very good today—even though my teeth are tormenting me. It's only in my head: they aren't in bad shape, but I keep getting more and more brown stains, even on the front teeth. Don't know what to do.[FF]

DECEMBER 16, 1942

[F]Went to Michel Publishers[†]—comic monthlies—this morning at 11:30. A man explained the job to me. I'd be a researcher for illustrated stories. Adventure stories in particular. And I'd get to write! I'm happy about it. I was assigned a story on Barney Ross.[‡] I'll finish Friday. Then to Betty Parsons', but only Sylvia was there. We ate and drank at the Winslow. Mother doesn't like it when I come home smelling of gin and having

---

* Drawings of this project survive as part of the actress Helen Hayes's estate—her daughter Mary MacArthur (1930–1949) died of polio at the age of nineteen. Bemelmans's book *My War with the United States* was first published in 1937.
† Michel Publications is the name of an imprint of the American Comics Group founded in 1939.
‡ Barney Ross (1909–1967), boxing champion and war hero.

spent too much money. Bernhard & Buffie called. Bernhard and I will go to see the Amayas Dec. 29!!! What a glorious day!

Goldberg came by at 9. Very agreeable. He spoke to my parents about my writing, that there's something there, etc., that I don't say enough, and that there are still some rough spots in my stories. But he read the story about the paralytic and said, to my great pleasure, that there were no rough spots, that it was perhaps (no, truly!) my best story! Perhaps I'll need an agent to sell them. Work will start next week, or perhaps next month. At 3 F [F.F.F.]. But I would rather slit my throat than go back![FF]

DECEMBER 17, 1942

[F]Oh! Sylvia told me yesterday that Rosalind was not full of "self-chastisement" but that she does exactly what she wants! That's a lie, because Rosalind is English. I had to go to Cooper Union to research Barney Ross. Very interesting, but it took 3 hours. I worked almost 9–10 hours today, without getting much done at all! I wrote the story, but I'll have to reorganize it. I'm still pondering what to get Rosalind. The music box is really too expensive. Am I growing old? I'm working so hard that I can't keep my eyes open at night—but I stay awake at the typewriter. I haven't had any peace and quiet for a week—not even opened a book! In short, one needs work to be happy!

Things are getting worse and worse at home. Mother will be happy to see me go when I find a job. I could be gentle, ask her to let me stay here, but for what? It's not anger or pride: I swallowed them a long time ago—what a luxury. It's my friends—who keep coming. And everyone loves me! (Except those who could give me a job!) But I find it impossible to believe that someone might not like me. She doesn't. But it's not true.

Oh hell! I'd like to have fun, write, love, live, drink, laugh, read, and—worse![FF]

DECEMBER 18, 1942

[F]Good day! Work, work, work! The Barney Ross story is going well. Almost done now, but it's very late. Called up Mr. Sangor,[*] who told me that tomorrow was fine. "I won't be able to tell you anything until the

[*] Entrepreneur and publisher Benjamin William Sangor (1899–1953) founded what would come to be known as the "Sangor Shop," a studio of comic writers and artists at 45 West Forty-Fifth Street producing artwork for different comic imprints, mostly Sangor's son-in-law Ned Pines's Standard Comics with its subsidiaries Better and Nedor Comics; and National Comics, which would eventually evolve into DC Comics. The 1940s are known as the Golden Age of American comic books.

end of next week." (Too bad—nobody hires anyone until after the first!) Then at Carter's (Little Liver Pills) where they need researchers. They want me to ask people on the street about their experience with Little Liver Pills and Arrid.[*] Who cares!

This week maybe the most peculiar of my life—but then I say this almost every week. Mother said she'd like me to "escape" from Bernhard's clutches! But she's been invited on Christmas to drink eggnog and open presents with us![FF]

DECEMBER 19, 1942

[F](Would like to be a child of 12.) Another day in my own inner chaos. And I'm getting a cold!

Mother is becoming worse and worse. It might be her menopause. She's always got "too much to do—not enough time" and I've been given all the privileges without anything left over for the parents! etc. Today she came into my room (at 2:35 AM) and told me "You must love these interviews! You're becoming such a great artist!" In short, I have to get the hell out.

Surprise! Carter's little liver pills wants me Monday 9 AM for their oily work![FF]

DECEMBER 20, 1942

[F]Rolf came here yesterday afternoon, very lively, because mother offered him everything in the house to eat, etc. She treats him like an over-sensitive boy, which he is. I don't feel much. I love him because he is sensitive. Everyone sensitive should love one another. I finished the story which I titled "Uncertain Treasure." It's a true uncertain treasure for me. Buffie [and I] ate out with Simon, where Simon went around kissing everyone (female) and Buffie picked up the bill. She told me the story of her family. Lots of money and hysteria. Then back to hers, where we stayed in bed, read a bit, etc. Then the rest. I did my best. But she did me at least four times. It was sweet; easy and relaxed, luckily.[FF]

DECEMBER 21, 1942

[G]Late to work because Mother didn't wake me till 8:10. On purpose, I'm sure. I had to ask 45 women between the age of 20 and 60: "Do you pre-

---

[*] Her "filler" job at Arrid Deodorant Company is the only post-college job Pat mentions in an article commissioned by the *Oldie* magazine in 1993, omitting her six months as an editorial assistant to Ben-Zion Goldberg at F.F.F. Publications and her seven years in the comic book industry.

fer this or this"—two sentences about Arrid, they're actually both the same. At 12, after we had stood for maybe an hour and a half at Stern's, I phoned Mr. Sangor about my story. He said: "I think you have the makings. I have to look at some others & I'll tell you in 2 days." So I came home at 2, even though I'd surveyed only fifteen women. Last night I felt the scent of Buffie's breath on me for hours. I'm so free with her and wonder what kind of love I feel. Phoned her at 3:00, and she wants to see me Wednesday! Good heavens! Just three days! Arthur here at 8:00. A very nice evening, he told me all his stories, his loves, etc. He has wonderful ideas. He'll be a [Joseph] Conrad someday. Visits! We listened to Schubert's *Die schöne Müllerin*, which is why I'm writing in German. Didn't read anything. Sent my story "Uncertain Treasure" to *Harper's Bazaar*. McFadden sent back my other stories. The letter read: "Thank you for your story. I'm so sorry there isn't any space for it in *Harper's* just now, but we'll keep you in mind." Crap. ^FBut what does it matter. Sangor loves me!^{FF} Seeing Rosalind tomorrow! Want to read Goethe. Want to settle down a little. And don't know where. Made two sketches. One for Buffie that she'll like a lot: an octopus—not I, not she, but—only with fountain pen [*Feder*] and ink [*Tinte*]. *Feder* and *Tinte*, what beautiful words! They remind me of my wonderful first schooldays when I first started learning German, the books with little pictures of children, rucksacks, etc. How wonderful, how peaceful those days were!^{GG}

DECEMBER 22, 1942

^FThings are getting worse and worse: I accosted no one today! My quota was 50, and I pretended to have reached 40 or 41! I parted from the two other girls at Grand Central, took money out of the bank, and went to look for a cup and saucer for Bernhard. I found them: the cup is gray and black—smoked, by the Chinese—they only cost 3.00. Then a martini at Savarin, and then to Del Pezzo to meet Rosalind. I cannot understand the cosmic meaning of this romance: Her eyes never gaze softly upon me, and if they do, only for a second. She wants to see me for Christmas. And she will give me something special for my birthday.

At Raphael Mahler's* for three hours. Typing for him. A charming wife. $2.00. Gramma sent me a dollar. Have $12 now, $20 from the bank today, and still only $30.00 left. Absolutely must find work. Bernhard

---

* Presumably Jewish historian Raphael Mahler (1899–1977). He cofounded the Jewish Young Historians Circle, which later affiliated with the YIVO Institute for Jewish Research, where he was a researcher and editor.

"admitted" tonight that she might be a bad influence on me, when I can "go" to men the way I "went" to Rolf. But she's wrong.

I have to get a new job, because this job will morally corrupt me.[FF]

DECEMBER 23, 1942

[F]Wonderful day but terribly tired. Mr. Sangor called me: I got the job. Will start Monday at 9. 9–5:30 and till one on Saturdays. I'll make at least $30.00 a week. I'm very happy.

Buffie met me downstairs. Very pretty, very perfumed, we went to her place. She treats me like a king or queen or princess. In any case, it pleases me greatly. She told me everything about the terrible treatment Peggy Guggenheim received from Max Ernst.[*] It was somewhat dull, but I wasn't much better. Then we made love. We turned off the lights, and we were together. I was tired, so only once. But oh so sweet! And I spent the night. "I've never had a lover who took so much time," she told me. And that I'll learn to appreciate men one day. It seems impossible. "You're so much nicer than when I met you for the first time." Of course. Buffie's skin is like exquisite liquid, sliding over mine like a piece of satin. We talked about the past like we never have, and I wanted to stay up all night. Buffie would happily have me as her only lover instead of her husband. Perhaps we'll keep our Wednesdays.[FF]

DECEMBER 24, 1942

[F]The girls are very excited about my new job. I'm free on Monday. I almost became hysterical because the music boxes hadn't yet arrived at Brass Town. So, I went to this wonderful boutique where they still sell English hairbrushes. I bought R. one for $12.50—the back is made of golden oak, stiff, slightly yellowish bristles, which are the most expensive kind. I hope she likes it! I will be mortified if she doesn't. I hope that she realizes that it's a pretty good present. I wrapped it carefully, wrote an ordinary card, and brought it to her at 11:00. Also a letter inviting her to the house tomorrow morning, telling her that I have a new job. I'm proud, of course.

Heard a terrible mass at church with [Marjorie] Thompson and the parents—would have made God and his son's hairs stand on end! I have $20.55 in the bank. I should be able to put $10.00 a week into the account

---

* While helping his then-wife Peggy Guggenheim prepare her Exhibition by 31 Women at her newly opened Art of This Century Gallery, Max Ernst fell in love with the painter Dorothea Tanning, whose work was part of the exhibit.

thanks to my job, pay off my coat, buy theater tickets from time to time, etc. I bought dogs made of bronze and iron for mother. Small, discreet, exactly what she wanted. They only cost five dollars. Am happy, and there's so much to think about that I'm not thinking at all.[FF]

DECEMBER 25, 1942

[F]A good day—a Christmas where I felt very grown-up, because I gave just as many presents as I received, perhaps more. I received oil paints from Stanley, a cup and a saucer, etc. Large ashtray. Drinks (brandy) from Marjorie. A bottle of gin. Then Jo P. (she gave me the Fauré Requiem) and M. Wolf here. No Rosalind, of course. We drank egg-nog and ate fruitcake. Bernhard gave photographs to everyone in the family—a small silver pin for me—a lover's knot. She didn't seem pleased with her gift. She thinks of herself all the time, and recently I find myself daydreaming about the sweetest moments with Rosalind and Buffie. Speaking of which, Buffie called me at 10:20 when she was leaving for the country: "Well Sweetie, I wish you a Merry Christmas & success and happiness & a lot of love goes with it—" Goodbye before I could respond. She is sweet, and I thought about her a lot today. Mother kept looking at Bernhard, and sometimes tears came into her eyes. It makes me horribly sad, but I have the right to choose my friends. I have to stop seeing Bernhard this often. That will be one of my New Year's resolutions. Oh! Rosalind phoned me at 7:00. She spent the day brush-ing her hair. I hope it's true. She wanted to see me tonight—also tomor-row night, when we'll have dinner. "It's a beautiful brush!" Exactly what I knew she'd say.

Now, so late, I feel as if I am beginning to live like a human. There is so much to do—and a firm path to follow—like a powerful train on a railroad track.[FF]

DECEMBER 26, 1942

[F]Another holiday—another day of eating. I spent the whole day writing my Barney Ross story. It took so long—so long that I'm embarrassed. Finally—nothing at all, except I phoned Buffie at 5:30. She had guests. But she said: "Call me tomorrow or call me very soon so I can see you!" Mother canceled the 51 dollars I owed her for my coat. That was one of my Christmas gifts, the biggest of them!

Tonight at Rosalind's; a wonderful evening. She was by herself. We spoke about Dalí, Calas, Tanguy, then music. Good intellectual evening.

She gave me *Roman Portraits*, a big book, which Betty recommended. But no photograph of her. It's a shame, though the book is good. We dined at her place—she made bouillabaisse. Afterwards, Scuola di Ballo, Debussy, Petroushka, Sitwell, Penny Candy. And more discussions of music. She wanted to kiss me as I left. She was tired—otherwise I would have tried something. She'd like it. She leaned towards me—and I kissed her on the cheek. It was far too intellectual. Does she prefer me this way? Only in her brain—and yet what does it matter?[FF]

DECEMBER 27, 1942

[F]Bernhard's at 3. She bought presents for the [Amaya] family. For Carmen, a pin, blue with diamonds. Carmen didn't show up for an hour. Then appeared in a white and red jacket, very small, very intense! Bernhard was in a state of the most abject idolization! The house was full of family, friends, neighbors. It was absolutely necessary to speak Spanish, which I had completely forgotten! Bernhard held Carmen's hand for at least ten minutes.

With Buffie tonight. She immediately bowled me over—wanted to make love and nothing else. I was shy—(why the hell?) and couldn't do much. She said some very true things. But she adores me—I drive her crazy, etc. She likes making love to me, etc. I'm full of useless energy—I will accomplish so much this year. I hope that in a year, I will still have this job. Most of all, I'd like something constant and reliable.[FF]

DECEMBER 28, 1942

[F]A good day. Hughes[*] couldn't be nicer. I'm busy right now with the details—then I'll start writing. Met everyone in the office. And I was happy that it rained all day. I had to go home at 12 because even hamburgers cost .15.

No invitations for Dec. 31. Who cares! I want to be home, alone.

With Bernhard at 8:30. We went to the Rainbow Room.[†] When I hear White Xmas I dream about Helen and myself—when we danced together, and she gazed into my eyes, and I into hers. I am absolutely, hopelessly sentimental. Bernhard was crying—because she saw her first love today—whom she never had. It's sad. And she plumbs it to its

---

[*] Richard E. Hughes (born Leo Rosenbaum, 1909–1974), American writer and comic book creator who conceived and scripted stories for Black Terror, Fighting Yank, Pyroman, the Commando Clubs, and Super Mouse. He became an editor at the Sangor Shop in 1943.

[†] Glamorous rooftop bar sixty-five stories above Rockefeller Plaza, one of the highest bars in New York City.

depths. That disgusts me. It's neither German nor Austrian—but simply
Jewish. Arthur came to the R. Room because we had a date! Terrible! I
wanted to give him something, but there are better things to do with my
money.[FF]

DECEMBER 29, 1942

[F]A good day but so tired it felt like an ordeal. R. E. Hughes even nicer. I
clipped stories from periodicals, magazines, and then put together one
frame of "Phyllis the Impregnable Fortress." I have to write it from start
to finish: he wants to teach me slowly. And now, after all the insults,
after this long period of unemployment, there's a job at *Vogue*: Miss
Campbell phoned my mother today, very politely. I'm on their list.
Couldn't yet speak to Rosalind about it. I'm happy—that's important to
note. Would like to start my novel in the new year.[FF]

12/29/42

You and I were born so far beyond the others, in time, in thought, in
pleasures. Where are there two to equal us? There will be never one to
equal us together. What does our genius mean to you, beloved?! What
does this gift mean for you?

12/29/42

And why does she give me Saturday night
And why does she give me Saturday night
And why does she give me Saturday night—
Except to sleep with her!?

DECEMBER 30, 1942

[F]Hughes made me write another four pages. On the SBD[*] in Guadal-
canal. "If it's of any interest to you, I have no doubt you'll be a good
writer." (Who had any doubts?)[FF]

DECEMBER 31, 1942

I was at *Vogue* at 12:00. Miss Campbell says I am "the kind of person
they'd like to have on their staff"(!) tho the $35.00 job she offered is
dull—letters to the editor, etc.

Went to John Mifflin's party with Bernhard at 11:30. The gorgeous

---

* Marine aircraft bomber.

blonde there, at whom I used to stare on Grove St. when she rode her bike. She lives with Cornell, a girl who paints extremely well says Bernhard. The blonde gave me her number etc. She knows Alex Goldfarb.* She is "Texas" something.† Bernhard never looked better. Silver in her hair & very smooth indeed. We later taxied to village with Bill Simmons and Becky & Marjorie. Welcome fun etc.

---

* Alex Goldfarb, alias Josef Peters, notorious communist agitator and spy.
† "The gorgeous blonde" Maggie E., also called "Texas" or "Tex," is lover and roommate to painter Allela Cornell. Cornell studied under Kuniyoshi, Zorach, and Alexander Brook. She was primarily a portraitist, equally skilled in watercolor and oil. She went unrecognized commercially, however, and was forced to do pen-and-ink portraits on the sidewalks of New York for a dollar apiece. Texas, Allela, and Pat will soon form a complicated love triangle.

1943

WORKING FULL-TIME as a comic book scriptwriter at the Sangor Shop certainly does not help Pat in her attempt to reconcile her many passions. For most of the year, she is torn between her desire for independence, her artistic calling, and an energy-sapping social life.

One of very few women in the industry, Pat creates superheroes with alter egos and meets the likes of Stan Lee and Mickey Spillane. Although she earns her keep in comics, her literary ambitions never waver, which might explain why she later keeps mum about this income stream (which ultimately will support her a good six years). For the time being, her day job enables her to secure her own apartment at 356 East Fifty-Sixth Street. Small as the distance to her parents' may be, it's enough to make Pat's heart grow temporarily fonder for her mother.

Pat still paints, draws (with her left hand), and writes (with her right—a reformed left-hander) obsessively. Her burgeoning multilingual diaries and notebooks reach seven hundred pages this year. Prodigious a reader as ever, she has now added Julien Green to her list of favorite authors, alongside Kafka and Freud. Pat also sells her first story to a magazine, "Uncertain Treasure." It features two men in reciprocal pursuit, a hallmark of many Highsmith stories to come.

In April, Pat meets and falls in love with painter Allela Cornell, whom she has to share with another young woman, Maggie E. (aka Tex). More soul mate than flame, Allela seems to fuel Pat's fantasy of having a life partner and moving to a house in the country—a fantasy that wildly contradicts her desire for freedom and unrestrained Manhattan party life. Allela paints a prophetic, somber oil portrait of Pat, which will hang in every one of Pat's future homes.

Pat's swinging nightlife continues to take precedence, and her literary writing suffers as a result. Her impulse is to escape. Toward the end of the year, Pat travels abroad for the first time; she crosses the border to Mexico with Chloe, a blond fashion model from Texas. In the early 1940s, Mexico had replaced Nazi-occupied Paris as the bohemian hot spot of the day, with its promise of long sultry nights and cheap tequila. Pat plans to stay until her savings run dry.

Away from her busy city life, Pat aims to finally make headway on *The Click of the Shutting*, an "adolescent novel" she began in 1942, but that had been germinating in her notebooks for much longer. The book is about a young man who—not unlike her future character Tom Ripley—wonders how it would feel to shed his identity and slip into that of his infinitely more captivating, handsome, and wealthy friend.

JANUARY 1, 1943

ᶠJo stayed after the guests left. We listened to the Fauré, which makes Jo melancholy. Me too, but as Jo and E. A. Poe say, there is sadness in all beauty. Jo very stimulating tonight. When I'm with her, I feel alive, like a writer.ᶠᶠ

1/1/43

Very few people we hate in our life, mostly those with whom we have once been in love. Why? Because we still feel (fear) the vulnerability of our love period.

JANUARY 2, 1943

ᶠWent to Buffie's at 12:30 AM with great difficulty. Parents hadn't a clue. I only went because I was bored—I have enough to do at home, but I'm always in search of pleasure and wisdom. Buffie has both, yet we did nothing but lightly touch on the pleasure of which I was capable—it was not at all sufficient—and did nothing but destroy the somewhat fatal resolutions I made long ago. And in the middle of it all, her husband phoned her from Cal. at 3:00 A.M. and talked for an hour! The whole time I was kissing her and doing what I pleased. What a marriage! I'd love to see Rosalind! I am stupid like that—she doesn't make me happy—but I'll be sad if I don't see her.ᶠᶠ

JANUARY 3, 1943

ᶠVery disturbed, troubled, and can't write anything until I'm out of the house & elsewhere. It's in me, I have no doubt. Rosalind somewhat reserved and sad. She told me that she was also troubled—in a difficult mood, thinking she hasn't done enough for the war. I told her everything about Bernhard, how she doesn't behave the way I'd like. Rosalind said it was a Jewish thing. Then a beer at Jumble Shop. When we were alone for a moment I touched her hand, holding it in mine. And she kissed my hand in leaving.[FF]

JANUARY 4, 1943

[F]I re-read my notebooks. It will take a lot of time to read them all—and I will have to read them before writing the great novel that is growing inside me. ($30.55 in the bank—sad.)[FF]

JANUARY 5, 1943

[F]Good day. All day I wrote short paragraphs which say what we have to get across in our stories—if there is anything at all. Galileo Galilei. Livingstone, Themistocles, Einstein, Cromwell, Newton, etc. Ate a poor man's lunch in Bryant Park and the birds seemed so cold I gave them half. Good evening with Buffie. Instead of the theater, we went to La Conga, where Carmen Amaya was dancing. I wrote her a nice little note (Quien no ha vista Carmen no ha vista nada,[*] etc.), inviting her to drink some *puerto* with us. No answer. Then I went backstage myself, and said I was Bernhard so she'd see me. She was with a sister, dressed in a lace dress, white, frightfully small in the waist. Then back to Buffie's. We slept a bit with great success. Am happy. Buffie is now exhibiting at the "31 women" exhibit at the Guggenheim.[†FF]

JANUARY 6, 1943

[F]Hughes wrote a synopsis for the Rickenbacker story[‡]—a brilliant synopsis, and I'll write the story now. I wrote another story—for Fighting Yank,[§] etc. Now we're playing Bach—"Bist Du bei mir." It's very sweet, tender, and it reminds me of the days in which I studied every night, and when there was always something to write. Now I'm always on the go, and ideas (only) come rarely. I was home alone—reading the last year of my diaries 1935–9. All about Virginia. I wonder why we don't love each other anymore! I wonder what ended this strange love that never began!

---

[*] Whoever hasn't seen Carmen has not seen anything.
[†] The Exhibition by 31 Women was one of the first shows at Peggy Guggenheim's Art of This Century Gallery in New York City. It ran from January 5 through February 6, 1943. Among the the artists exhibited were Buffie Johnson, Djuna Barnes, Frida Kahlo, Leonora Carrington, and Meret Oppenheim.
[‡] Eddie Rickenbacker was a celebrated World War I pilot.
[§] In 1943, alongside *Black Terror*, *Fighting Yank* was the best-known and most important superhero comic produced by Cinema Comics.

Rosalind was sweet over the phone, asked me about work, etc. I'd like to touch her hair now.[FF]

JANUARY 7, 1943

[F]Roosevelt gave a good [State of the Union] address, saying that the Nazis have asked for it—& they are going to get it. And that this congress will have much to do in making of the whole world safe. I retrieved my pullover from La Conga, and for a moment saw Carmen Amaya walking towards me (without seeing me) with her two sisters, like stars in the Pleiades.[FF]

JANUARY 8, 1943

[F]I'm getting more used to the boys at the office. I finished the Rickenbacker story—good work, said Hughes. He's a good writer, and takes his work very seriously. *Harper's Bazaar* sent back my story "Uncertain Treasure" but with a letter from [Mary Louise] Aswell,[*] lit. ed. "Your writing has considerable quality, & while this story is not for us, would you let me see some more of your work?" It's my best story. This job is good for me after all, because it's made me write faster. Lots of action, yet sincerity of a certain fashion—that is necessary. Now I'm ready to write my novel— yes—it's the natural thing to start now. It's at the forefront of my mind. [FF]

JANUARY 9, 1943

[F]A good morning—I still have to write the script for Catherine the Great of Russia.[†] $40.55 in the bank. It's growing slowly. Rosalind's at two. I feel as though we are a bit bored—that we need a big explosion—something![FF]

JANUARY 10, 1943

[F]Read [Julien Green's] *Varouna* and almost finished. Without fail it makes me think of the problem of human identity, the secret of human life. I am at once child and man, girl and woman. Sometimes a grandfather.[FF]

1/10/43

The girl who is about to leave home for the first time—at the age say of twenty or twenty-one. How she feels as she gets a cup of coffee on the

---

[*] Mary Louise Aswell, fiction editor at *Harper's Bazaar*. Under her editorship, *Harper's Bazaar* published early pieces by such writers as Truman Capote, Jean Cocteau, Carson McCullers, and W. H. Auden.
[†] This was another script for *Real Life Comics*.

way home to her parents' house, the night before she is to leave, thinking as she goes out the door of Riker's how depressing would it be if her
meals alone were to be such brief respite, in the days when she will have
only too much time for herself, eating tensely on a stool, without conversation, seeing only her own face opposite her, a bit yellowish in the mirror under the fluorescent lights.

JANUARY 11, 1943

^FAt home, they're always discussing the friends I take out to restaurants,
the theater, etc. Other young ladies go out with young men. And this
costs them nothing, while I spend too much—at least 5.00 every evening.
It's true, but as ever, I prefer putting my own hands up my skirt. At the
office—sent off the Rickenbacker story. "This is really good writing.
Inspirational captions and well hung together." Etc. Most of it is Hughes'
work and I told him so.^{FF}

1/20/43

I have the odd feeling these days that I become more substantial mentally—as far as soundness of character & personality are
concerned—and more insubstantial, more decadent physically. The span
of my rotting and transparent body put against the normal measure
of cosmic hardships is a despair to contemplate. The lineaments of my
face establish themselves in handsome sanity and complacency: inside is
labefaction and imminent death.

1/27/43

I came home one night towards midnight, so drunk with alcohol and
cigarette and sleepiness that I weaved from one side of the pavement
to the other. Out of a Third Avenue bar came a boy and girl about sixteen. "Take care of that cold!" the girl said with all the love, warmth,
sacrificial, miraculous power of women throughout the ages! "You take
care of it for me!" said the boy. "I will!" as they parted. I followed the
girl to her home two blocks away, half trotting over the snow and slush
to keep up with her. I almost spoke to her. I loved the sense of fiction
in the scene. I should not have remembered very well if I had heard this
in soberness. My sodden brain supplied the mood, the style, the atmosphere and the tones unplayed above and below, the multitudinous
sketch lines which a writer might have put in before and after, some of
which he would have left unsaid, like those I imagined I was seeing and
experiencing. Drinking is a fine imitation of the artistic process. The

brain jumps directly to that which it seeks always: truth, and the answer to the question, what are we, and what caverns of thought and passion and sensation can we not attain? There is therefore something of the artist in every drunkard and I say God bless them all. The proportion of men drunks to the smaller number of women drunks is parallel to that of the men artists to the women. And perhaps there is something homosexual about the women drunks too: they care not for their appearance, and they have definitely learned to play.

1/30/43

    Things I wish yet to learn about:

1) Geology—composition past and future of earth
2) Various countries—Poland, Czechoslovakia, Lithuania, Finland, etc. to know the real personality of each—the ur-personality as I come nearest to knowing of England
3) Mathematics—(persistent curiosity, at same time a begrudging of time spent on this branch of knowledge for which I haven't the least aptitude)
4) The Russian language
5) Hebrew language
6) Various scripts of all languages

2/3/43

    Writing—"I want to be"
    Painting—"I want to possess"—all creation is to change oneself psychologically. Not to create for pleasure or art's sake.

2/6/43

It's all but impossible for two artists to be close friends. One will phone demanding to see the other, who may be at the stage where he must be alone. The artists, when together, will be at different rates of speed. In general it is a constant effort to pull each into the other's orbit. They will not merge. It is as simple as two cogged wheels moving at different speeds. They cannot merge.

2/12/43

With you* I am so happy I wish all the world were closed up from us. Near you, I feel such sweet contentment that I would like to whisper to

---

* It is unclear who the "you" is here.

you, this is my journey's end. Let only the stars gaze upon us, let only the sun warm our feet from the other side of the earth, and seal this room and this moment forever!—How sad that I cannot speak such words to you, and that I cannot write them without a pain in the throat like something that wishes to kill me!

2/17/43

Living alone is an experience dominated by small experiences.* One is soon accustomed, logically, to not having an icebox to raid at midnight, to having to do one's own laundry or at least see to it. The real experience of living alone is the water tap always running icy or seething hot, sending prickles of displeasure up one's spine, the running up and down stairs to fetch little pans of water for one's painting, most of all the encountering of strangers in the house to whom one must speak to be civil—whereas in one's own home one could eat, work, live, without disturbing the precarious tide of creative thought in one's subconscious.

The first apparent joy of living alone is the privilege of keeping silent a whole evening when one is in belligerently unsocial spirits.

2/22/43

In my generation (and perhaps for two or three others to come) women are busy attaching themselves to the man's world. Men have been so long attached that they can afford occasional detachment. Therein lies the reason for the woman's characteristic lack of humor in business, characteristic unimaginative, unsympathetic, disciplinary management of her own business and private life, and of the lives of the others who may be under her.

3/5/43

Most people are not what anyone could call passionate. Passion requires one of two factors: complete tranquility as the idle rich Greeks had—or actual suffering and misery, either being endured or remembered vividly with compassion and horror, too.

---

* Thanks to her job, Pat can finally move out. In February she finds a temporary rental, then in early May moves into her first own apartment, a studio at 353 East Fifty-Sixth Street, a stone's throw from her parents' home on East Fifty-Seventh Street. She'll keep returning there and hold on to the lease until the 1950s.

3/20/43

There is a quality, detectable throughout all ages of literature, which can come only when the writer is in love himself. It is the unutterable sweetness Shakespeare wrote into the Romeo and Juliet scenes, the inspiration of the young Jewish poet of our time who wrote simply and literally of the embraces of his sweetheart. It is a masculine quality for it springs from the male desire in love, physical, but mentally sublimated to a fountain of unselfconscious utterance. When one reads such lines unloving, they seem nonsense and sentimentality, certainly indicative of feebleness in the writer. Read them over when we too are in love and each word has its proper, subjective meaning and effect.

MARCH 30, 1943

[F]With Goldberg at Anthony's tonight. The first page is hard, he's right. He's looking for an apartment for me. It's funny. He's truly affectionate.[FF]

MARCH 31, 1943

[F]Very tired at work. I think I should quit this job and find something at *Vogue*. I could write stories at the same time. Sent my two scripts to Fawcett *[FF]

APRIL I, 1943

[F]Bad, uninspired day until I phoned Helen. I'll see her tomorrow. "All right, darling. Goodbye." Oh, I'll remember that "darling"! Sent MSS to Kapeau at Parents' True Comics.[†] I'll have something soon. Am happily thinking of Helen who is doubtlessly in bed at the moment and will look very pretty tomorrow.[FF]

APRIL 2, 1943

[F]Good day but didn't work—had lunch with Helen at the Golden Horn. Drank two vodka martinis. Too much, really. She told me that Kingsley had shown my sketchbook (or some drawing!) to Mespoulet, and Mespoulet said it was vile—horrible and disgusting (!) And that even though my diaries are strangely devoid of sensuality—even when I was obsessed with Rosalind! It makes me sick! Helen wanted to come with

---

* Fawcett Comics is best known for introducing Captain Marvel.
† True Comics was an educational comic book series published by the Parents' Institute from 1941 to 1950.

me tomorrow evening, anywhere, but I don't have a free room for her here. It's a shame!

Work at the office is very boring. I'm jealous of how happy Everett[*] is. His world is full of light—women—meat, sweets, liquor of all kinds! Instead of working, I saw Virginia at the 52nd St. bistro. Later, Kingsley phoned and came by at 11:35. She emphatically denied showing anything to Mespoulet. Someone's lying—or exaggerating.[FF]

APRIL 3, 1943

[F]I wrote five pages before going to Jo P.'s. Stayed late at Jo's, and she invited me to stay the night. I said yes. Two beds, clean and beautiful pajamas. I told Jo that I love her, it's strange, but I love her. She loves when I hold her head in my arms. It's very peaceful with music. But at night—nothing.[FF]

APRIL 4, 1943

[F]Saw Bernhard at 8 o'clock. A drink at Jumble Shop. Then I felt like calling Rosalind. She was with some other women, relaxing a bit, etc. I love Jo P. almost as much as her, perhaps. Not in the same way.[FF]

APRIL 5, 1943

[F]Stanley Kauffmann[†] from Fawcett Pub phoned me this morning and wants to see me. That means work, which means money. The woman from the apartment on 34th St. says I can have it for $40.00 a month with a one-and-a-half-year lease. That's a long time! Almost a twentieth of my life! A tenth! But I think I'll still take it. I'll never be ashamed of this apartment and I can invite all of my friends there. I also asked for a raise and got it! Hughes will talk to Sangor.

Spent tonight at home, where I wrote what may be the beginning of the novel.[‡FF]

APRIL 6, 1943

[F]Nervous last night. I must write lyrically without getting terribly lost. It's so easy to say, but when I write, I write with my whole heart, my

---

* Everett Raymond Kinstler (1926–2019) dropped out of the School of Industrial Art in Manhattan just before his sixteenth birthday to accept a full-time position at Cinema Comics. He later went on to become a renowned portrait artist who painted hundreds of celebrities, including eight U.S. presidents.
† Stanley Kauffmann (1916–2013), American author, editor, and film and theater critic.
‡ Her first novel, *The Click of the Shutting*, which she will abandon later.

entire self, great effort, blood, and lastly, with my head. It will be better to start things differently.

First—Fawcett at 12:30. Kauffmann told me that my stories had excellent dialogue but that my plots were boring! All the same, he gave me two Lance O'Caseys* for which I'll write two episodes.

Worked badly, because I'm always tired lately. Rosalind's at 7:10. We ate dinner at her place. Soup and cheese, coffee—and her—it's heaven, it's paradise! It's all I can ask for, even if it doesn't last. Afterwards, beer and sandwiches at Sammy's. "Comb your hair. You look like Byron with a hangover." She told me many wonderful, private, secretive things— lots of little, unimportant things, but they made me happy. She gives me quick pecks on the cheek, like an old aunt. I want her lips, her intelligent, soft, loving lips! I'll have them one day. Tonight made me certain of it. One can learn so much from the little things.[FF]

APRIL 7, 1943

[F]An ordinary day. Actually, I forgot to call Rosalind—to tell her that last night was wonderful—perhaps the most wonderful night of my life. Hughes only gave me a $4.00 raise. I'll make $36.00. I was a bit sad when he told me. Sy Krim[†] hopped up on benzedrine at 9:40. He disgusts me sometimes. Not his way of living, but his violence. I'm starting to think that Del P. was right: I need a job that doesn't demand any creative effort.[FF]

APRIL 8, 1943

[F]Very, very happy! Worked well tonight. Del Pezzo's at 12:30 with Helen. She told me she wants nothing but good meat, a fullfilled sex-life, a husband who loves everything she loves, books, a job. But she's carefree, she said, not like me—naïve and melancholy. It was almost a perfect day— even found inspiration for a sculpture. But mother's angry at me, and said that I don't listen to the doctor, and that I'll have to pay all my bills in the future myself.[FF]

APRIL 9, 1943

[F]An ordinary day—I didn't sign the lease because they were asking for $50.00 a month including an oven and refrigerator. It's absurd. I'll have to keep looking.[FF]

---

* *Lance O'Casey* was a Fawcett comic book title.

† Seymour Krim (1922–1989), American journalist, author, editor, and educator.

APRIL 10, 1943

[F]For two and a half hours, I was in the dentist's terrible chair. I cried,
I trembled—but he took his time. He's stupid! But cheap. Then I had
a cup of coffee and went to the Perls museum to see the Darrel Austin[*]
exhibit. It was wonderful! Buffie was there and a bit cold towards me. I
have to buy her something and take her out to dinner. My mother—for
whom I bought a pen that doesn't work—gave me milk with egg and
put me to bed.[FF]

APRIL 11, 1943

[F]Parents very cold and unsympathetic. I've got to get out of here immediately. Rosalind's at 9:45. For some reason she was preoccupied, serious.
Cornell's after eating at Grand Ticino. Rosalind has old friends there.
She likes the restaurant. I told her my idea for the story on "Laval" and
the paranoiac.[†] Texas was very agreeable, both of us at her place, beers,
paintings, etc. Texas made a few passes at me. She knows I'm looking for
a woman to live with. Rosalind seems serious sometimes, but she looked
very pretty tonight, almost beautiful. And she likes Cornell, who was
fiercer than ever! We got lost on the subway and walked to Sammy's for
a beer, but Spivy came in, purple suit, big hair, just another boozer. I felt
very ordinary that night, my brain wasn't working any better than that
of the other drunks! Not amusing in the slightest. Home at 2:35 A.M.[FF]

APRIL 13, 1943

[F]Good day. Worked slowly at the office. I haven't been going to bed at a
reasonable hour lately. I imagine that will change when I find an apartment. *Atlantic Monthly* sent "Mountain Treasure" back to me, and I
showed it to Cammarata[‡] who liked it a lot. "Rough spots occasionally."
But I never want to change anything.

I'll take the parents to the circus.

At Mr. Steiner's to deliver books, I noticed that I had left behind
three volumes of personal journals! He must have had a good laugh!
It's awful. Everything—absolutely everything—about Buffie, Rosalind,
Betty, etc. In short, the last three years! I have no doubt that he read all

---

* Darrel Austin (1907–1994), American commercial artist and painter.
† According to Pat's notebook, this lost story is about a man who is persecuted because of his resemblance
to Pierre Laval, a French politician who collaborated with the Germans and was subsequently convicted
of treason.
‡ The artist Alfredo Francesco Cammarata (1905–1993), or "Al Camy'," worked on comics such as
Spectro, *Crime Crushers*, and *Phantom Detective*; he was the first to draw Airboy, an aviator hero who
debuted in 1942.

the notebooks—at least, as much as he wanted to. Texas phoned me at 5:00. I met her at *Vogue*, 46 & Lex. She doesn't want a roommate. But she wants an affair.[FF]

APRIL 14, 1943

[F]A pleasant day but completely disgusted with myself. I have to write for a set time, study for another, eat for another, sleep for another. Right now, I have no discipline whatsoever. I'm halfway satisfied, because I'm doing what I want, but I'm not happy! Ate at 1:30 with Texas at Del Pezzo. She listens and listens to me and tells me that all my ideas are good. She wants it, no doubt, but when? Where? I wonder if I'll do it—for my health. Joseph Hammer phoned. He wants to see me Saturday and Sunday, but it's impossible because I've been hired by a friend of Goldberg's who is writing a dissertation. 200 pages. I should make enough for a gabardine suit.[FF]

APRIL 15, 1943

[F]Feeling very happy, my novel is growing sound. I will write it with lots of people at first—then slower-paced. I must describe the various things that occur in a single day. I wrote a Ghost,[*]

I'm smoking too much now. Bored at lunch. Thought of Texas and decided I'd do it. Called her around 5:00 and saw her at 5:30. I am in great need of strange lips that don't mean anything to me. Am living now in curious excitement.[FF]

APRIL 17, 1943

[F]Am so tired it's a sin! I really am just like my Gregory[†]—full of potential with no clue as to how to begin. Saw Rolf at 1:30. He was almost rude this afternoon, didn't say more than a dozen words, etc. Saw *Skin of Our Teeth* by Thornton Wilder. Bernhard was marvelous, the play too. It's a real piece of theater.

Joseph H. came by at 7:00, laden with gifts—records, books, candy. Stainer's *Crucifixion*, [Franz Schubert's] *Der Tod und das Mädchen*, [Bach's] "Little Fugue in G minor." *Omnibooks of Humor* and *New Yorker* stories. I need books like this. It's funny how one always wants to play their favorite records for friends, and they never listen properly, never understand them. Even [Joseph] H. He was torpedoed between

---

[*] Probably a reference to the comic superhero the Ghost, who first appeared in 1940.
[†] Gregory is a protagonist of her current work-in-progress.

Cuba and Puerto Rico, was on a raft for two days and made $500.00 a month for his pains. He doesn't want to see me again because I'm in love with "Richard"—my pseudonym for Rosalind. It's funny, and sad. Because he loves me, probably—as well as he can.[FF]

4/17/43

Then said the writer to himself in privacy: "I may starve, but I will not work for another man and burn out the oil of my days. How can one be a prostitute in the day and a good lover at night?"

APRIL 18, 1943

[F]A day just like the days I dreamed of when I was fifteen! Slept until 11. Sent proposals off to Fawcett. At 5:30 PM we found my new home—373 E. 56 St., right next to Piet Mondrian,* who uses the same door. Lights, paintings, and for $40.00 a month. One room, kitchen, bath. Small, but it will do until October, when God knows what will happen! I signed a five-month lease. Texas phoned at 6:30. I was so excited, I sang in the streets. Went to Nick's[†] for a drink. I called Rosalind who told me to watch my step with Texas. She's my guardian angel, I told her. Ate at El Charro where we caressed almost the whole night—an excellent dinner, but our hands were always together, lips almost, but not entirely. How lovely Texas is up close! How happy she makes me when she smiles, when she speaks of nothing. How I'd like to see Texas, I told her, in a vast bed, with white sheets, all alone with me. It's so sweet and simple because she wants nothing more than this, and neither do I. At her place, in the hallway, she turned off the lights and kissed me, a long, terribly tender kiss, which she loved just as much as I did. We left one another wanting more. In bed at 5.[FF]

APRIL 20, 1943

[F]While I was working tonight, alone at home, Texas phoned. She told me twice that she loved me, in that joking tone that Southerners have. "Whisper sweet within's—" It's sweet, and I'm light as air when I heard her voice. Today was remarkable. I began to menstruate for the first

---

* The famous Dutch abstract painter Piet Mondrian (1872–1944) moved to Manhattan in 1940 and lived there until his death in 1944.
† Nick's was a tavern and jazz club in Greenwich Village, which had its golden days in the 1940s and 1950s, when musicians such as Bill Saxton, Pee Wee Russell, Muggsy Spanier, Miff Mole, and Joe Grauso performed there.

time in a year and a half—if the little in December 1941 counts. Wrote 5 pages, but I'd like to write the Laval story first. Am very happy.[FF]

APRIL 21, 1943

[F]Good day. Work was easy. Joseph H. came by because he was going to see Ralph Kirkpatrick* and wanted to bring me along. He had a drink with Rosalind yesterday afternoon, during which they talked about me. Joseph said: "She thinks the world of you! She thinks you're a genius." Ralph Kirkpatrick very polite, young (36), lives on 62 & Lex. Two good rooms, lots of books and a harpsichord. He gave us a drink. They wanted to come back here at 9:30, and how can one say no to Ralph Kirkpatrick?[FF]

APRIL 22, 1943

[F]Lunch with Rosalind at Del Pezzo. She's very interested in Joseph H. If he makes a single move on her, I'll slit his throat! She didn't know he was Jewish. He told her I'm a musical genius. (I want to call Allela tomorrow, spend the evening at hers.) My head is always full of music, and I hear each note [G]clear and bright.[GG] My novel—it's a heavy, weighty opus now, and it would be better to leave it for several days so as to retrieve the strong emotions which made me want to write it. I am full of energy, and so they (everyone) think I am a genius. I hear it from all sides.[FF]

APRIL 24, 1943

[F]Good day, but I haven't done anything yet and am becoming more and more disorganized. Started drinking at 2:00 P.M.—saw the excellent Wakefield [exhibition by] Steinberg[†] who is funnier than Bemelmans. Betty Parsons very nice. Then exhibits by Dalí ([G]Horror of horrors![GG]) and Mondrian—which I didn't like. Then Tex and I walked through the streets until we arrived at Stonewall[‡] where I drank two beers. I told Texas frankly that I wanted to sleep with her and nothing else. She swears I'm the only woman she's been with since Cornell. Can I believe her? I called up Rosalind—and Cornell—to whom (Cornell) I said that

* Ralph Leonard Kirkpatrick (1911–1984), world-renowned American harpsichordist who taught at the Mozarteum in Salzburg and at Yale University. Kirkpatrick wrote a biography of Domenico Scarlatti, one of Pat's favorite composers, something she and Tom Ripley—an amateur harpsichordist himself—have in common.
† Saul Steinberg (1914–1999), Romanian-born American cartoonist and illustrator who worked as a freelance artist, primarily for *The New Yorker*.
‡ The Stonewall Inn, located at 57 Christopher Street, in the heart of Greenwich Village, was the scene of New York's first gay rights demonstrations in July 1969. It has since been considered the flash point of the gay liberation movement.

I love Texas simply because she loves me, and I probably won't see her again. Cornell always seems very calm towards me, very light. Perhaps what Texas says isn't true—but she told me that Cornell and she often fight about me. I told Rosalind at 7:10 that I love her very much. "I love you too," Rosalind said. That was the first time she's ever said those words. They make me frightfully nervous. "I'm your guardian angel," she said. Yet tonight, I kissed three girls.

I had a drink at Cornell's. Texas lay down on the bed, and I jumped on her, wrestled, etc. She pulled me down but didn't let me go further. It's funny too. But she's stupid, and just as stupid in bed. I went out at 10:00 to Judy's for Mickey's party. I was the only Christian there. On the balcony I kissed Cecilia, who likes me a lot—and can't wait until I have my apartment where she'll visit me, alone. Danced a lot and with J. Tuvim who was very pretty in black. Home at 5.[FF]

APRIL 26, 1943

[F]Saw Dr. Borak, he'll give me two treatments before my next period in May. I'll finish before Rosalind's birthday. I want a new suit, but I also want to buy something big for her birthday. I don't have to pay rent until June. Months are going by and I'm not working on my novel, but I'm thinking about it, and when I'm alone, it will be like on the tropical ocean. I will write faster, better, and more. Joseph phoned me at 4:00 to tell me that Ralph [Kirkpatrick] is in love with me. I don't believe it. He hasn't even phoned me yet. I'll take Cornell to Bach's St John Passion May 4. Kirkpatrick will be playing harpsichord. I worked on Lance tonight. I need money.[FF]

APRIL 27, 1943

[F]Bumped into Herbert L., now a lieutenant in the Marines, who spent the winter in Russia! He's handsome. Truly handsome, and smokes a pipe. Seemed happy to see me, but he was very shy, probably because of our last date at my place, when we went to bed together.

Phoned Allela—a great conversation in which she was very amusing. She has a great sense of humor and is intelligent enough to display it even when she doesn't feel like it.[FF]

APRIL 28, 1943

[F]Made a call (finally) to Ralph Kirkpatrick at 5:30. He was a bit shy but: "Let's get together & do something some evening." And "Swell"—that I'm coming to St John's Passion Tuesday.

Had a date with Peter and Helen at Jumble Shop at 6:30. They were an hour late and already drunk. A woman at the restaurant read our palms and gave me the best reading, that I won't get married, that I have a big imagination, etc. It made Helen and Peter jealous.

There's so much I want to develop in myself. I spent last night with girls I've already left far behind.[FF]

APRIL 29, 1943

[F]Am thinking with disgust of last night with Helen, who means less and less to me—Peter too. I told a lot to my mother. I want to buy a suit right away and wear my hair up. I phoned up Rosalind tonight to tell her that I will move Saturday afternoon. Wants to see me later this afternoon, and my apartment. I hope she won't think it too small. It's enough, really. Kingsley and Jo came by. Kingsley didn't talk enough for her own liking, so she became boring and intolerable whenever she did! Jo pretended that she had to leave in her car, and K. left too. 11:00. Then at 11:20, Jo came back. "Did you say something about coffee?" I kissed her immediately. We were both in heaven, in paradise. We did almost everything on the sofa—it was our first time, and couldn't have been better if we had planned it. I like her a lot. She seemed to have done all of this before. Finally, she stayed overnight—in the living room. She is sweet, and understands everything, and has all my heart—whatever's left after Rosalind.[FF]

APRIL 30, 1943

[F]Good day, am thinking sweetly of Jo. She came into my room at 8 o'clock, dressed, ready to leave. She spoke to mother over breakfast. She seemed happy, though we didn't mention last night, of course. It was good. But she must have done it before! She couldn't really tell when I came. And she—I don't think she did. Texas came to see me at 5:30—she was smiling, pretty, warm, and wanted to read what I had written. Oh me! Oh Texas! How sweet it is to stroll through the streets with her! We drank beer at the Boar's Head [Tavern], and held hands, and she told me out loud that she wanted to kiss me! Oh paradise! She will sleep with me! Worked on Lance. Almost done.[FF]

MAY 1, 1943

[F]Not a word from Jo P. What's she up to? Perhaps taking a spin in her car somewhere, thinking and wondering whether what happened really happened. I am too. Spent the afternoon settling in here. Now the pictures (paintings) are on the walls, and I'm awaiting the furniture, which will come when the money does.[FF]

MAY 4, 1943

This day might be terribly important. It is now 5:20 A.M. [F]I was very nervous at the office. Met Texas E. and Cornell on 55th St. at 6:45 P.M. Then Cornell and I went to Carnegie Hall, a bit late, where we heard the St John's Passion. Then drinks at the Faisan d'Or. She invited me to come upstairs to her place. Then a glass of milk, then conversation, etc. in which I hope I won her over—I hope so because I adore her, and I told her so already. She said to me: "I could love you very much." She's still on guard. How do I win her? Through modesty, patience, the natural superiority to all her other friends. Finally, I kissed her, and though the first kiss wasn't good, the others—I'll never forget them! I love her, I love her, and I am so happy right now I don't at all care what time it is. I want the morning to come so I can talk to her![FF]

MAY 5, 1943

[G]Last night Cornell made all the first moves, which makes me happy today. I know she loves me, at least a little. Today I couldn't work till I'd called her (at 10:30). All day I felt her lips on mine, and in short, I'm completely in love with her. Nothing like this since Rosalind. Today I also thought that we're too alike and therefore won't love each other long. I won't look at any other "beauties" as long as I've got her.[GG]

[F]Dinner with the parents. Wrote a synopsis for Fawcett's Golden Arrow,* though I didn't get more than three hours of sleep last night. Oh happy day!

Am reading German poetry tonight.[FF]

5/5/43

Compared to the artists, all the rest of us lead very ugly lives. It is only merciful that the overwhelming majority can never be aware of this appalling and depressing discrepancy between the ideal and the merely adequate. So we have the tiny group who are aware of it, melancholy unto death itself, or content to be passive observers, appreciators, sybaritic, hedonistic, infertile save in the spring of their own reflected derivative enthusiasms.

---

* Golden Arrow was a Fawcett comic book series about a western hero.

Enthusiasm. This is the God in the artist which makes him a god. The artist says, *"Fiat lux!"* and there is light.

MAY 6, 1943

[F]Cornell has many work projects outside of the city this summer, perhaps beyond. That would be awful! But she does only have four dollars in the bank and lives on 15.00 a month. Texas E. has no suspicions right now, and it will stay like this. I think of long, tranquil evenings in which we'll work together, read together, lie in bed together listening to music. That's worth more than anything in the world! I adore her. I love her—her soul—and what else? I am certain tonight that I can finish my novel. It's the first time I feel like this in this apartment, and I'm very happy![FF]

MAY 7, 1943

[F]I met Stan,* who told me that they were expecting great things of me at Fawcett. "We have bigger stuff than Lance and Golden Arrow." Perhaps, if I write good scripts, they'll offer me a job. I'd like to earn more money. For my friends. Not for myself.[FF] I think of meeting every other kind of person in the world—in brains and appearance and degrees of human warmth, and I cannot imagine any superior to [Cornell]. She is goodness, godliness, and I compared am a longshoreman who has seen the sights of Singapore and Hong Kong, Nagasaki, and Calcutta. I feel we could be healthy and happy and creative together, finding peace at last—something I've never found. I am lonely, something I thought I never would be—and lonely for Cornell—I was never lonely for Rosalind, because I could not envisage the sort of life we might make together. It was a fantastic dream, of no substance. [Cornell and I] are perfect together! And Tuesday night she kissed me like she meant it.

"Were you drunk?" I asked.

"Yes."

"Do you think I was drunk?"

"Yes. Do you think I was drunk?"

"No. I wasn't."

"Then I wasn't either."

---

* Stan Lee (1922–2018), American comic book author and editor, actor, and film producer. While still a teen, Lee was hired as an assistant at Timely Comics—which would later become Marvel Comics. He was a cocreator of Spider-Man, among many other characters.

"Shall I forget Tuesday night?"
"No."

MAY 9, 1943

[F]Cornell and Texas came to my very clean apartment at 6:45. We drank a pint of gin. Cornell told me that Texas is a bit sad—because she thought I was in love with her; I'll have to be nice and gentle. We went to their place by bus at 9:30. We put Texas to bed and took a walk to get milk. Finally back at her place, downstairs, I dropped the bottle of milk! I cried and cried—I couldn't help myself. She kissed me all over, and I wanted so badly to spend the night there—with her—in the hallway. It was almost impossible to leave! Texas E. and Cornell are good people. They are honest and sweet.[FF]

MAY 10, 1943

[F]Very hungover today until 6:30, when I drank a beer with Sy Krim and Knight—a boy who wants to work in the movies. Cornell phoned me at 10:40 as I was writing a poem, and had just been reading Kafka's *The Castle*. I felt like white, powdery snow—light and clean and thin. She spoke very sweetly, but she knew that I was working. I love her and she loves me; I'm sure of it. But tonight I thought of the problems we'll have with Texas. Texas is sweet and simple like a little girl. I could show her some affection, and it would be safe because she would never do any-thing to hurt Cornell. I've never met two better women. I read over my novel for a bit, and I think it's good. I want to work hard, and I'm afraid of nothing.[FF]

MAY 11, 1943

[F]My darling—Texas—called at 8:40 while I was still asleep! Very sweet. I wonder if she truly loves me—if she loves me enough to tell me so—I'm still vain, after all. Met Cornell at 5:30 at M. [Metropolitan] Museum. 3 martinis (together) at Anthony's. I was shy—she was talking about her friends far from here, and I was jealous, very jealous of these bril-liant men and women she's known for such a long time. I was a chicken tonight, a coward—because I wanted to ask her if she would ever love me. Because I felt as if I couldn't have another hopeless love, like Rosa-lind. But a question like that wouldn't be fair to Cornell. Worked on my novel tonight—a Herculean task. Sometimes I wish I were a painter. But as Rosalind said: "One does what one can."[FF]

5/11/43

I suffer from emotional constipation—even emotional condemnation.
When I am in love, it is a miracle the other person knows it except by my
tortured expression. I think eloquently, and see her across a table and
can say nothing. I dream beautifully. I want to love and be loved with no
shadow of a doubt, I want the two peaks of the mountain breeze blowing
either side of my face and disturbing my hair on top. I want the flux and
outflux and influx free and light, and I want to give it no thought. I want
to live by unconscious thinking. I want only the inspirations, thoughts,
desires, that have come from I know not where. I want the clear face, the
smooth forehead and the tranquil mouth of the Buddha, the Light.

MAY 12, 1943

FA marvelous day! Cornell, Tina, and Marg. were all home. Texas prepared dinner for us all. They were very happy, and Cornell, then Texas,
brought me to the bathroom to embrace and kiss me. It was fantastic. But kissing Cornell was better, and brought me the most pleasure.
Finally, I went to sleep in Cornell's room, in the corner.FF

MAY 13, 1943

FVery important day because I have decided to be an ARTIST instead
of a writer! Slept perhaps 4–5 hours, and saw the sun rise in the white
room—and fall on the painting of a spiritual man. It was a new world—
a world that I understood, that I had understood before, but! Gthat I'd
so far rejected, because I always wanted to write. It is the world beyond
consciousness, the best of all worlds!GG I saw Vaslav Nijinsky*and Ellis†
and Goethe, and then Texas woke up, very happy. Then Cornell—who
kissed me—how sweet she is! To me! She almost loves me, but her life is
so mixed up! She will have to live alone, I'm afraid!

Coffee and rhubarb compote on the bed—the three of us. Then,
when Texas left, Cornell came to my bed and we talked for almost an
hour—I spoke most of the time. Nonetheless, last night her friends
liked me much more than Texas—they liked my face and hands. We lay
down together and listened to Bach Toccata & Adagio in C, Boccherini
Cello Concerto and Mozart Paris Overture. It was unforgettable! Then

---

* Vaslav Nijinsky (1889/1890–1950) was a Polish ballet dancer and choreographer.
† Possibly a reference to Henry Havelock Ellis (1859–1939), an English physician, progressive intellectual,
and social reformer who (co-)wrote the first medical textbook in English on homosexuality in 1879 and
later published on transgender psychology.

I began to menstruate, which disgusted me. She read me a letter from one of her friends and I left. She was looking at me from the window as the bus was leaving. Texas told me that morning that *Vogue* very much likes my ^G"Letter to One's Darling"^{GG}—and that they may run it! It's fantastic.^{FF}

MAY 14, 1943

^FA marvelous day. I spent two hours at lunch! Saw Jack Schiff from Detective Comics* on Lexington Ave. He wants me to give him ideas— not synopses—for any character whatsoever. Met Tex and Cornell for drinks. Met a lot of their friends. Tamiris,† etc. Had dinner at Eddie's Aurora.‡ Very nice. I wanted to kiss Cornell all evening and we tried to hold hands as much as possible. Though Texas tried to stay up, she fell asleep at 11:00. And Cornell was truly troubled. It was sad. The world is beautiful!^{FF}

MAY 15, 1943

^FI've never been as happy as I was today! A quick morning then—with $210 in my pocket ($4.00 now)—went for a beer with Camy—(he pockets money each week which his wife knows nothing about—it disgusts me!) and to buy a pizza for Rosalind who came by at 2:20, while I was on the phone with Cornell. Then we went to Chinatown to get my tattoo. I was a bit ill at ease—but after two bourbons, just fine. It's green—the tattoo§—and almost as small as I wanted. I'm happy about it—not proud but happy. Rosalind enjoyed the afternoon and spoke to several soldiers and sailors. Even went to those bistros where you never usually see a woman.^{FF}

MAY 16, 1943

^FCornell phoned me at 11:30—still very happy too. "God, I love you," I said. And then Texas called a moment later. "Who were you talking to?" I told her Rosalind had called me. "You must be very happy." Phoned

---

* Jack Schiff (1909–1999), American comic book writer and editor, wrote various comics about Detective Comics' (later shortened to DC) best-known superhero, Batman.
† Helen Tamiris (1905–1966), American pioneer of modern dance, choreographer, and teacher. Her works address issues of racism and war. She is best known for her suite of dances called *Negro Spirituals*.
‡ Eddie's Aurora was a small Italian restaurant in Greenwich Village that attracted an "arty" crowd.
§ There is no description of her tattoo in Pat's diary, only that she's considering getting one on her wrist. In 1946, she will mention another visit to a Chinatown tattoo parlor, again with no comment as to the design. According to Kingsley, Pat had a tattoo of her initials in Greek letters on her wrist.

Rosalind. She wanted to see me on the early side, and I went over at 1:30 very happy. Hungover. Rosalind. What a surprise! Texas phoned me again at 5:30, and I phoned Cornell at 4:30. It was a disaster, because Cornell was serious, even sad.[FF] "Take care of your cough," I said, "I don't want you to die." She laughed. "Wish I could say the same." Oh God preserve her. When I die I want my tombstone to say that I was born in 1943—on New Years Day—and on May 4, 1943.

MAY 17, 1943

[F]A good day. Worked hard, but Camy bought me a cup of coffee at 11:00. I showed him my tattoo, and Jeannette too. Texas phoned at 5:20, but I didn't want to go to theirs and then go out with her after dinner to see her friends while Cornell is giving drawing lessons. Phoned Cornell when Tex was leaving. She wanted me to come and draw with them. I said no—but as I was going home, I couldn't resist—I had to go! I was so embarrassed when I entered the room! But I wasn't as uncomfortable as another young lady—a Negro woman who posed very well—and it amused me so I forgot the time. I stayed when the others left. We kissed maybe twice—when we heard Texas coming up the stairs! She came back early—and I didn't want her to know I was there! But nevertheless when Cornell got into bed we kissed wildly—like a dream! She told me that she loves Tex, too. I said, yes, so do I. "But I love you and in a different way." I hope it's sexual![FF]

MAY 18, 1943

[F]Good day—as I was dreaming of Cornell almost all day. Saw [Rolf] at his house for lunch. There's a magazine, *Home & Food*[*] where the editor may like my stories. That would be a miracle. I'm thinking of Cornell, of her tongue in my mouth, of our moist lips—wet—together, of her hands on my body! There's so much to discover and explore that I will die of heat next time we are alone together.

Lots of fun with Rolf. He took nine of my stories—to show them to this woman. Perhaps I will sell one. I feel as though I can do anything at all. I think I will never again write a single word that isn't good. I'll make all the money I want, work in peace, and be very happy with Cornell, who will feel all the things I feel.

I'm full of great confidence![FF]

---

* Rolf Tietgens was *Home & Food*'s art director. The magazine not only bought two of Pat's stories, but also some of her drawings..

5/18/43

The first days of love are sweet, when one must dream long minutes after minutes, when the eyes cloud over like with blindness. (Why is it when one does not concentrate too hard, the sensations of the body are pleasurable and intense in these love dreams? Nature bestows the highest delight, perhaps, upon the more bestial, simple people who do not confuse their lovemaking with intellectual processes, which may be successful in heightening the pleasure, but which generally creates fiasco.) I move around like a glass vial filled to the brim with ecstasy. I am suffused with love, and all my pulses throb when I dream these things. We are gentleness and honesty.

MAY 19, 1943

ᶠWorked all day on Black Terror*—and saved Hughes about $12.00—he would have paid $37.00 for the job—"piece-work." Rolf phoned me to tell me that the editor likes my stories and that they'll buy "Friends"— the one about two people who communicate through the subway doors! I'll make $50.00. Perhaps they'll buy a story a month. It's the day I've been waiting for for six years, and I am so tired right now that it doesn't matter. I'm happy and proud—why—for myself? No! Because Cornell will be proud of me. She will read it, and perhaps she will love me more. I wonder what she's doing right now. Sleeping, I hope. In fact, Texas is in my bed right now. She forgot her keys at home—she says. And she fell asleep—it's already 1:10 A.M. "I don't want Cornell to know," I told her. But Cornell will know, Tex said. There'll be nothing else to say other than she spent the night at my place.

I envy Cornell slightly less today—and I still think that I am emotionally unstable—and perhaps that I won't love her in a week. At the parents' house for dinner. I told them the story about the party at Hoyningen-Huene's and Horst B.† with Rolf. It's astonishing how much I can tell them! The next step is to tell them that Rolf is gay, and that I am too, I suppose.

I'm happy. Am reading *Les pensées* by [Charles] Péguy. Very good.ᶠᶠ

---

* Black Terror was a comic book superhero created by Richard E. Hughes. The character first appeared in January 1941.
† Georg Freiherr von Hoyningen-Huene (1900–1968) and his lover Horst Bohrmann were two of the most noted fashion photographers of their time.

5/19/43

Two hours before the dawn, with the rain speaking in staccato slowly
from the sleeping eaves, the sleepy drip-drip-drip to the moist black
ground, to the wet leaves of the hedges, and the coal dark cement. The
air is not air but a distillate of the night and of what has happened or
might have happened or yet will happen, or of what will be said—by
whom? By the poet with his lover in his heart, pregnant figure soft and
incorporeal as the delicately gray shadows. Man—this is the hour.
Search now whatever you seek vainly in the day and in the night. Search
between the two thin edges of the knives! That together will destroy you!

  Lover, go forth!

MAY 22, 1943

[F]Met mother at Winslow at 1:30 for a drink. I have now realized that she
possesses all the joie de vivre I feel right now. She has always possessed
it. We often discuss homosexuality, and perhaps it won't be long before
I tell her the truth. My love for Cornell seems to me so great, beautiful,
and pure that it should not be kept secret—and yet when I'm with her
and imagine I've already told her, I feel confused, unhappy, and don't
know what to do. I'm so tired that I've almost lost the happiness—
the wild joy—I've had all week. I would be too tired to make love to
Cornell—and that would be a disaster![FF]

5/22/43

Surely there are times when the most ardent and devoted lovers have
no desire —even in the beloved's arms, when the moisture of her lips is
something unpleasant, to be wiped away. Then it seems the kisses and
embraces are the candy one has eaten enough of—and the work one must
do is the bread and meat. This is frightening to experience the first time.
I think it is all the more indicative of the true love, which varies with the
variations of the mind and moods, and is not dependent upon physical
stimulation, but on mental and psychic needs and demands.

MAY 23, 1943

[F]Good day, but I hate Sundays—I never get anything done. I only had
two minutes alone with Cornell. I won't deny it—the desire—the powerful desire is gone. I am not crazy, and I wasn't crazy last week. The kisses
are, as I said, like candy. Now I am in need of bread and meat, and I have
found them within her—solid and plentiful.[FF]

MAY 25, 1943

[F]Had a long talk with Camy over two beers. "If I weren't already hitched, I'd lead you a merry chase!" Cornell's at 8:15. There was a small but shapely young woman there. Like a good Degas. And lots of other people. I drew better than last week. Cornell sat close to me, but I didn't show her my drawing. Afterwards—we were on the sofa—and I told her slowly—everything I've wanted to say for a long time. Texas made a comment about my breasts, and Cornell wanted to know how she knew? And surprisingly enough—Cornell said she thought we were making fun of her—that Texas and I were in love, etc. It's incredible—I don't think she truly believed it. "I think you both want to be nice to me." Cornell prefers to be loved, passive. And she prefers women because she doesn't have to give as much to them as men. But she can love both. I've kissed her a thousand times—but not like Sunday night—I've been smoking too much, and my tongue is bothering me. Peace—we found it for a few moments, when we were together, head to head, lips to lips, fingers running through each other's hair. And we will find it again when we live together.

Bought T. S. Eliot: 4 *Quartets*. $2.00 for 37 pages![FF]

MAY 25, 1943

[F]Fawcett sent me four synopses: they took one Spy Smasher.[*] Three rejected: two Ibis[†] and one S.S. I'm happy. 10 pages means $30.00. Tired at the office—I exerted myself too much last week. Allela came by at 5:30. Incredibly enough, she looked at the pictures with a serious eye, and said it would be fun to be an "inker."[‡] It's awful—![FF]

MAY 27, 1943

[G]Wonderful day, although it would have been better to spend the evening at home. I don't make enough money. Wish I could bring work home to make more.[GG]

MAY 29, 1943

[G]Saw Cornell at 8:15. Bought her 6 bottles of Coke and brought her a frog—which she liked very much. I wanted Texas to go to bed, but she came along to the movies at 42nd Street. Saw *Bucket of Blood*, very

---

[*] Spy Smasher was a superhero who first appeared in *Whiz Comics* #2 (February 1940), published by Fawcett.

[†] Ibis the Invincible was a comic book superhero who first appeared in February 1940.

[‡] In comic book production, an "inker" is an artist who retraces pencil line drawings in ink.

"nice"! I wanted to go home with them after, but have work tomorrow. Love Cornell—her mind, though, because I don't like her body. Her hands, her lips—yes, but not her body.[GG]

MAY 30, 1943

[G]Allela—very loving—called me at 7:00. She wanted to see *Desert Victory*, but not without me. Found her and Tex and Peto on 8th St. Held her hand with such passion during *Desert Victory*, I really am in love! Oh, God! When she pulled my hand—twice—into her lap!—I shot straight up to heaven! Five years ago, such little things (?!) would have aroused me terribly, made me happy. Now I just want more and more, like I always want more money in the bank. They wanted me to spend the night at theirs, but tonight I wanted her too much. It would have been torture. The body wouldn't understand.

I sometimes feel inadequate, compared to Texas. I wonder if Cornell thinks the same? I want to be everything to her. If Bernhard knew, wouldn't she say I was playing the same game as with her and Rolf?[GG]

JUNE 1, 1943

[G]A day of importance—of utmost importance. At 7:30, Tex called. She brought me a glass of brandy. Naturally I drank the entire glass and then we kissed, like lovers, almost like how I kiss Cornell, but without the dreaminess and without the tenderness. And in tears, Tex said how she wanted to make love to me and had even started to, when Cornell phoned. In flagrante delicto—truly, because I couldn't talk straight. She knew everything when she came at ten o'clock. I was completely crushed and couldn't speak. I truly hated Texas. I told them they wanted to make each other jealous. It's true, and that means they still love each other.

"Right now I think you are a bitch," Cornell told me, "I hate this!" And I felt as I did in Dec. 1941, and January. I wanted to jump out a window. Lastly—"I wish I could give you what Texas gives you." "I think you could give me much more." My heart skipped a beat—"Then I won't go jumping out of any windows!" It was wonderful, and her cheeks were as soft as ever. I don't deserve her, but I have her. Everything I've worked for, thought, felt—everything was for her, I know it. It was never for Rosalind, she doesn't understand me any more than I understand her. Cornell wants a lot from me. She already takes a lot from Texas, but "I think you could give me much more." I will never forget that. Our three lives are tightly interwoven. We love each other. What happens now?[GG]

JUNE 3, 1943

ᴳGood day—although it started out sad with Allela. She fought with Texas last night, and Texas threw the clock at the wall. Allela said Tex doesn't want us talking behind her back, etc.

I talked to Camy today, and he said: "If you go out with the other fellow—do it good. His friend doesn't want it any more'n you do." Yes— I could make her so jealous, but that doesn't interest me. I always want to be upright. Can't do it. This all proves that Cornell loved me, I'm sure of it. She wants to hurt herself, torture herself, and may even want me to love Tex for a while so she can feel sorry for herself. It's embarrassing to me, and what a waste of precious time!!!! We won't live forever! (Worked on Bill King.)*ᴳᴳ

JUNE 6, 1943

ᴳSunday—how boring! How useless! I have so much time, I can't settle down enough to work! Looked for milk and cursed the housewives of the Bronx—who had already bought it all up! I hope the useless, unnecessary bottles spoil in their coolers! And they will! Painted a window in the kitchen.† Adam and Eve—Adam hanging from a branch, eating an apple.ᴳᴳ

JUNE 7, 1943

ᴳWent to Eddie's Aurora with Fij and Dolly.ᴳᴳ ᶠLots of coffee. I saw the black-haired woman who lives on Grove St.—the one I fell in love with and who made me feel shy and scared, all when I was 20! She came in with her husband, Crockett Johnson, who writes "Barnaby" for PM.‡ She saw me and smiled at me. Am tired, but happy.ᶠᶠ

JUNE 8, 1943

ᴳFantastic day! Hard work at the office. Dan§ phoned at 12 and we ate together at Del Pezzo. I was terribly bored, though, so I ate like a sailor.

---

* Bill King was an *Exciting Comics* character. The heroic soldier who fought in the Pacific during World War II made his first appearance in April 1940.

† Pat decorates her apartment with trompe l'oeil paintings.

‡ In 1941 Pat had a crush on a beautiful woman she regularly bumped into in her neighborhood. This was Ruth Krauss (1901–1993), an American children's book author who wrote such classic titles as *The Carrot Seed*, still in print today. In 1943, Krauss married Crockett Johnson (1906–1975), an American writer and children's book illustrator who created some of the twentieth century's most beloved comic-strip characters, including Barnaby.

§ Her cousin Dan Coates, who is visiting New York.

Nice to be alone at home this evening. Painted the wall—white fireplace,[*] but didn't finish. Washed up, read ([Freud's] *Moses and Monotheism*).[GG] [F]I was so happy I asked myself whether I should actually go away this summer? I could manage to have fun in the city.[FF]

JUNE 9, 1943

[G]Phoned—110—Cornell phoned me at 8:45, and I phoned her at 12 and 12:30. "Will you miss me?" "A little." "You bitch!" My head is full of work, though, and I'm sure several days will pass before I fully comprehend that she's gone. Worked on Spy Smasher tonight, then Sy Krim stopped by, and later Texas! Pleasant evening, as I finished my work. Feel happy—sold the story about the cripple.[†] That means $100.00, so now I can buy the radio at Lino's.[GG]

JUNE 10, 1943

[G]No letter from Allela, but a card from Bernhard. Mother here to paint my bookcases. And she said I mustn't become like Cornell, crying every night, wanting to be "pretty," but not doing anything about it. She also used the word lesbian. Wrote to Allela, although I was far too tired. Am still happy and full of hope.[GG]

JUNE 11, 1943

[G]What distresses me at the office is the confusion all day long! Worked on Pyroman[‡] synopsis today, and every word was torture! But three stories came back for revisions. Must work more slowly without worrying about how many stories I am able to write. At home, at my parents'. Stanley just got a new job! Industrial Press layout, type orange—art Director. Very nice, and the change will be good for him.

I am full of power, strength, and[GG] I "shall go in so many directions."[§]

JUNE 12, 1943

[G]Met Tex at 2:00, and we went to Leighton's. We found some beautiful silk shirts, marked down from 5.98 to 1.29 (!). We bought five, two striped for me, along with collars and cravats.[GG]

---

[*] Another trompe l'oeil painting, this one of a fireplace.
[†] "Uncertain Treasure."
[‡] Pyroman was a superhero who first appeared in December 1942.
[§] Quote from Rosalind in her letter Pat received in San Francisco on August 8, 1941.

6/13/43

Strange, unearthly perfection of the week after one has fallen in love, when the ringing of a doorbell in one's court seems part of a prearranged and beautiful plan, when the pattern of the people on the street is inevitable and pleasing, when all shadows and substances are distinct, with individual qualities, that one can, with a magic omniscience, understand and feel in detail. What becomes of the evil at such times? We smile at it, if we happen to see it or think of it, and so this proves we are drunken, temporarily, drunken.

JUNE 15, 1943

^GMade the acquaintance of Fenton* at 12:30. Rolf there. Pretty girl. And she wants more writing. At my parents', but I can't stand Dan any longer! Wrote Golden Arrow and sent it to Fawcett. Perhaps the last, because it's time I started living. That means writing, thinking, loving.^{GG}

JUNE 16, 1943

^GGot enough sleep, and work went better. Read Kafka in the sun at 12:30. Now *Home & Food* is using my story about the cripple. Went by Rolf's at 5:45, and he took several photographs. Then we translated a poem by Hölderlin, which sounds very nice. He wanted to eat with me, which is why I didn't do any work. Anyway, how—how could anyone work after discussing ancient Greece and art? We talked about everything beautiful and ugly in the world. We were joined in mind and heart and body. I loved Rolf very much tonight. We paged through *Hellas*, which J.J. [Augustin] made, and he stayed till 2:30 a.m.!^{GG}

6/16/43

The terrifying, bestial ugliness of a scolding voice in the darkness, somewhere. When I lie in bed and hear this, I am seized with fear, shame, and simple pain. Why is it? It is something akin to pity—because we can imagine the same sensations if we watched a murder, when there was no danger of harm to us.

JUNE 18, 1943

^GDan left yesterday—thank God! I am full of love—and desire Allela as I desire endless peace—as I desire answers to all the questions in the world. No letter, and I'm bored talking to myself. Phoned Rolf tonight,

---

* Possibly Fleur Fenton, managing editor at *Home & Food*.

yet I'm still lonely! Took great pleasure in reading the *Encyclopedia Britannica* this morning, since Hughes was out. Egyptology. Then to the dentist at 2:00. The [laughing] gas was sweet, and I wanted it! Hungered for it! Had all kinds of dreams. There were countless circles containing natural phenomena, and I sought with the discovery and bestowal of knowledge that I was God! That I, of all people on earth, lived before the earth's creation, created the earth, and would live to see it end. In short, that I knew the philosophers' secret! Would that it were true!—I wouldn't be happy, in that case, but miserable! Have the tooth.GG

JUNE 20, 1943

GHome at 11:00 and cleaned everything—Mother came, and alone again afterward I painted the fireplace and mantelpiece. And a golden clock, which looks wonderful. Proud of it. But I did absolutely nothing to make money. I painted 4 hours and read Kafka this evening. My dear soul, today was your day!GG

JUNE 21, 1943

GFantastic day. Hot. Worked quickly at the office, wrote a little to A.C. Texas was very attentive this evening and read some of her letter from Allela out loud—that she loved her—loved her very much—and that A.C. wanted her to be with her on vacation. I was so disgusted by Allela's indecision that I soon left the house.GG

JUNE 22, 1943

GI wrote Allela that I have to set out on my own and probably can't see her anymore. That I have no patience for weakness and indecision. And after posting the letter, I wondered why I didn't feel sad and downtrodden about this girl who's become downright indispensable to me and with whom I am inextricably bound. Now—when I recall the many times she said "I love you" to me, I feel neither sad nor hopeless nor ashamed of what I wrote. I don't want to write her again. She'll miss my letters and without a doubt later find some resolve. It—love—is as indispensable to her as she is to me. Got good work done, which surprised me, especially in this heat! I felt good about Cornell—this is the tooth extraction that will "make it all good" again.GG

JUNE 23, 1943

GI had no right to write such things to Allela. It's all true, but I shouldn't have written it. I spent all day thinking about this evening, when I was supposed to call her. Ate at my parents', who seem so common to me—particularly now that I'm in heaven with Allela. At 8 o'clock I called Allela in Wash. D.C. She's coming back Friday, and I'll be at the train station. Her voice sounded beautiful to me, gentle and quiet, and as full of affection and love as she can sometimes make it. Yes, I love her unconditionally. Rewrote S.S. synopsis.GG

JUNE 24, 1943

GO happy, happy day! No letter this morning as I ate peaches and cream, but there was one this evening when I got home. Airmail!!! It was pale red—the stamp—and I laid it on the carpet till I had taken a shower and dusted the house, poured some rum, lit a cigarette—and finally—four yellow pages—all about the cat painting, and on the last page—last line, she wrote: My love Pat really—Allela. And my heart soared once more! I'll keep the letters—(four) of course. Forever.GG

FI cut my hair.FF

JUNE 25, 1943

GToo hot to work or sleep. 96, I think. Cornell comes back today!
Fawcett taking second S.S. and second Lance. That means $54.00. Got good work done, and the longer stories come to me more easily—you can take them further. Read lots of Freud, which brings my heart joy! Psychoanalysis of religion. Wonderfully interesting! Dentist at 1:30. I've recently come to endure all kinds of pain! Nothing is too awful or alien! Home at 6:00 for a shower, then at Penn [Station] at 7:30. Texas E. there too, but I saw Cornell first. Black dress and smiling. We had 2 drinks at Savarin, and there were a few wonderful moments, seeing her—so close to me. She loves us both equally. What will come of it all? What?—I have to hold myself together, without becoming sad or hopeless or hopeful. Must work, because that—working—is the purpose of the life I want to have with Cornell.GG

JUNE 26, 1943

FSaw "Globalism"* at Wildenstein—nothing that Klee, Miró, or Dalí haven't already done. Feininger, etc. and a painter named Sewan (I think) [Schewe]. His work is considered "poetic," and we both were in this hot room, spoke a lot.

---

* The Wildenstein Gallery held its third annual exhibit of work by the Federation of Modern Painters and Sculptors.

Lots to do at home. It's important for me to live alone because I want to plumb all of my moods, and I don't want a woman to come over to me with a mug of hot chocolate! No! In times like these, I consume myself, and I love it. Then, when I wake up, I am still myself, and am happy for it. Energy is a gift of the gods.

Good night! ($280.04 in the bank.)[FF]

JUNE 27, 1943

[F]Not a good day—accomplished nothing of importance. Went to the Metropolitan Museum at 3:30 with mother to see the Bache collection.[*] Magnificent objects, not paintings. The Michelangelo sculptures pleased me greatly, and "*The Young Sophocles*" by (who?).

At home, Krim phoned me. Against my better judgment, went with him to the Hymans'[†] who work for the *New Yorker*. Horrible. But the wife, Shirley Jackson,[‡] was alright. We drank a cup of coffee together (two) and I told her about several of my stories. She writes for all the magazines, and suggested I find an agent. Yes.[FF]

JUNE 29, 1943

[G]Normal day at the office, but too much to do—always too much. The maid didn't come, so I had to clean the entire house for Rosalind. She came over, so I put on my new slip and made a wonderful drink of rum, water, orange, etc. Sugar. "Heaven!—It's heaven!" she said, as she lay on my bed. Rosalind was genuine, laughing, pretty. She drank slowly, looked at my fireplace, which she likes very much. It was raining when she left—but it was a wonderful, rare evening.[GG]

JUNE 30, 1943

[G]Today Mr. Hughes reprimanded me for missing two mistakes in a story. Said that I get to work late, take too long to eat, and that I take the job for granted. "There was a nice spirit when you started—you have to hold on to that, etc." Yes, I was sad, because it was all true and I am so hopelessly bored. Rosalind said: "You shouldn't stay there too long!" Yes, of course. I'm not going away this summer vacation—I don't have the money and there's too much to do here—not in the city, but in my heart and in my soul. I have to look for a new job.

---

* Jules Semon Bache (1861–1944), American banker, art collector, and philanthropist.
† Stanley Edgar Hyman (1919–1970), American literary critic and staff writer for *The New Yorker*.
‡ Shirley Hardie Jackson (1916–1965), American writer of horror and mystery novels (e.g., *The Haunting of Hill House*, *We Have Always Lived in the Castle*) and more than two hundred short stories.

Cornell came at 6:00. We sat a long time, nipping at our drinks, and could finally have a nice conversation. We looked through *Hellas*. And I saw heaven as I kissed her, as I lay with her on the bed, our kisses so wonderful I almost made love to her. But as my hand was about to touch her, the telephone rang—doesn't it just figure?! She almost cried—it would have been so nice. Taxi to hers, and she kissed me for what might be the last time for the next two months! I came home as if on a cloud. Have no money, but no matter—have so much else!GG

JULY 1, 1943

FI feel like the high period—the mania—is here now. 3½ hours of sleep and I feel wonderful! Full of energy! And this morning, I thought of Allela so much I had to go to the bathroom to relieve myself of a large erection. Is that disgusting? Am I a psychopath? Sure—why not? I almost had an orgasm just thinking of her! It can happen! The stories continue to bore me. Two synopses today. Phoned Rosalind at 8:00. Looked at apartments for her. There's a large one above me—that's the apartment Rosalind will probably take. This development gives me a lot to think about. I'm thinking of breakfasts together in the winter when it will be cold, when we will work hard and I will bring her soup, or something else. I love her, and this would suit us better than actually living together.

Camy came from 9:00–10:20. He talks too much about himself. Did nothing.FF

JULY 4, 1943

FBuffie came at 8:30. She likes my apartment—somewhat—my fireplace, yes, but no comment on my drawings. Would like to get a lot done tomorrow. Buffie very stupid tonight. She gave me a pretty red jacket. With the parents—mother and I had another disgusting conversation about Negroes—we haven't done so in two years, and it's just as pointless as mother's remarks on Marjorie Thompson's corpulence. I should stop coming over. She makes me terribly nervous, and that's why I moved out in the first place!FF

JULY 5, 1943

FCornell woke me up with a phone call. She wanted me to come to the train station at 4:00. But I didn't go. Cornell was sad, like a little girl, and mumbled, "Well I want to see you—I want you to see me off." She called me again from the street—(secretly) and—still I said no. She told me that she doesn't think I love her because I'm making her suffer. But she understands that it's because I love her that I can't be content with half-measures. She left very melancholy—and that's what she needs! She must love me passionately or forget me completely. No reading—no writing—a real day off.[FF]

JULY 6, 1943

[F]Spent a miserable day in my heart, in which I experienced all the sadness which I feel now, just like before I met Allela. To give her up would be madness. My body is closed up, my wings are on the ground. And my spirit, my brain, body, and soul revolt against this refusal. Bored at the office. At Fawcett, Magill is going to quit in order to write popular stories for magazines. It's disgusting. All these small minds!

Lola and Rosalind here at 8:20. Rosalind very kind and affectionate tonight. Lola liked my drawings too. I can imagine what R. said about me at dinner—that I have a lot of talent—more than anyone else she knows. Isn't that so? Happy. Headache—but:

1) Cornell will no doubt write me—
2) Rosalind will come live here.
3) Rosalind will come eat here this week.
4) Began the Laval story.
5) A good hour with Péguy.

Yes—my blessings.[FF]

JULY 7, 1943

[F]No letter yet, and I—I asked myself all day whether I should write her—yes or no. But it isn't pride. It's only that I want us to be together. Well—I didn't write and I won't. She's behaving like a woman and waiting for me.[FF]

JULY 8, 1943

[F]Toothache last night, perhaps I'll have to get another one pulled!

At last—a letter from Allela—I opened it with some trepidation! Written in pencil—four pages. She wrote it on the train to Hampton. Her words are so beautiful, her feelings delicate and strong at once! She still loves me, like one spirit loves another, and she will never cease loving me—and though I gain nothing from it—she thinks that love—this love—is worth the suffering and anxiety of waiting. Oh, how true! I know it well! And her letter gave me much hope. I wrote her almost all morning. It's food for my soul!

I may have sold two of my drawings to *Home & Food*. Nitsche* has to see them.

Bored at the office, and desperate for my vacation. Wrote 7 pages of the Laval story. They're good, I think. Had dinner with the parents tonight. When I told them that I'd received an eight-page letter from Cornell, mother said: You're saying that like a lover! What does it matter? I don't care!FF

JULY 10, 1943

FNo one—almost no one—in the office, and even Hughes didn't dare ask me what I was working on! Didn't have a single idea and didn't do a single thing.FF

JULY 11, 1943

FI know I will get a letter tomorrow morning, and so I've gone mad! I've gone as violently mad as I've ever been—when I was 6—12—15—17—20—and now I am mad with greater reason. I am reading good books—the Bible—[Charles] Péguy, [Julien] Green, old books that are the best—and all my love joins with theirs. They are one. In the world, there is one image, one virtue, one work—the truth within man's soul—and I am this man. Only Cornell is compatible with this—the truth of the flesh and the spirit. I felt that this day was full of truths. It is because of days like these that I hope this diary will be re-read one day! I made Virginia pose until one. Not bad, but my drawings could be better. She was ungrateful as usual, but what do I care? I am happy, and rich in the treasures of the spirit!FF

7/11/43

What gentle madness in me. It comes when twilight comes. It is hardly worth mentioning. But it is as strange as the stirring of one leaf on a tree, when there is no wind.

JULY 12, 1943

FMiserable this morning—not like a young girl, but like an old philosopher. I thought quickly and well about lots of things. There was no let-

---

* Possibly Erik Nitsche (1908–1998), Swiss-born graphic designer and artist who contributed to the magazine *Simplicissimus* before moving to New York and working for *Life*, *Vanity Fair*, and *Harper's Bazaar*.

ter from Cornell. I couldn't work at all this morning, and the next few weeks until August and my vacation will be hell! No rest for body or spirit, yet I took a (troubled) walk home at 12:45—and incredibly, still no letter! Oh, I can bear everything except this silence! This solitude! Misery—misery at the office!

Marjorie W. and D. Lawrence tonight. They're a bit strange—the kind of people who don't drink or smoke enough. I made drawings of Marj and D.L. They think I am or will become a good artist.[FF]

7/12/43

The making peace with myself is the hardest, and perhaps will be the greatest accomplishment to my credit when I die.

JULY 13, 1943

[F]I'm ecstatic—a letter arrived—a white, slender letter in the mailbox. I worked well. Now, everything is bearable. Bought two tickets (for R. and myself) for July 15, which is our anniversary, but I won't remind her of this fact. She phoned me. She almost always calls me "darling" now, and I thought tonight that she must love me a lot—because she knows I am faithful—in the only manner she requires—I am always by her side to help. When she moves, for instance! Read Péguy and wrote Cornell a long letter— modest but truthful, in which I told her I'd sold these small drawings—and a message from Péguy—that the body is joined to the soul like two hands in prayer. It's beautiful. Made five new drawings tonight—very pleased—and two are good enough to send to the *New Yorker*.

My love grows and grows for my other soul: Allela Cornell.[FF]

JULY 15, 1943

[F]Texas E. will go to Texas in August—and we'll be left alone together.

Drew tonight, too, without much luck. I have to let go and allow the expressions within my soul to arise.[FF]

JULY 16, 1943

[F]Am largely happy, would very much like to spend some time with R. [Rosalind] C. and speak with her. She has decided against the apartment. (It's an ugly apartment for the money, I think.) Near midnight, I took a short walk around the neighborhood. The moon is big and round, an immense circle in the sky![FF]

7/16/43

To be creative is the only excuse, the only mitigating factor, for being homosexual.

7/16/43

To pass by an open garage, to catch the dynamic aroma of rubber, gasoline and compressed air, to see the rows of shining, black, powerful cars, is physically the most exciting experience I know. It is movement, freedom, leisure, and the absence of all fettering of daily routine.

Yet how selfish to think of such things, when even tonight I read a stirring account of the American landing in Sicily, and for a moment actually saw the body of the young American soldier, his fists clenched, charred to death on a landing barge. How prosaic to relate this experience, these importunate, irrevocable, ineluctable facts!

JULY 18, 1943

ᶠOh God—there's a good life to be had, single, working, making beautiful, lasting things—but I cannot bear this life! It's suicide, it's a sin! I must change it! Made drawings of R., because I would like to make a wooden head,* and I'm getting sick. Being sick is very enticing—tomorrow—mother could take care of me—bring me my letters, my books, and I could write the Laval story, for which I now have a good outline.ᶠᶠ

JULY 19, 1943

ᶠOn this day two years ago, I met R.C. at Lola P.'s. A bad day—a day that should have been so happy! Mostly, it was because of money—which disgusts me, but it's always a problem. Wednesday, I think, I'll go to Sangor and ask for a raise. I deserve at least $125 a week. I'll ask for $75.00(!) Rosalind was late, first at Edward Melcarth's, who will give her a painting for *Fortune*. His figures are beautiful. Rosalind very quiet, almost indifferent towards me. Naturally, she didn't know that today was our anniversary. We are shy together, almost boring and bored, would like to say something to each other—but aren't brave enough to say it.

I'm moving in circles now. Nothing certain except that I must change my life—more money or another job. In any case—talk is cheap! I want

---

* Pat did indeed make this wooden head. Rosalind returned it to her in 1992: "In case you wonder why I am parting with it [. . .], it is because I am putting my house in order. I expect one day soon, if not already, somebody is going to write a life of you, and these evidences of what you do with your left hand might come in handy" (letter from Rosalind, June 30, 1992, Swiss Literary Archives).

to paint. I want to create all sorts of things, and I will. On my walk tonight with Rosalind—I felt once again that we have no one except each other. I believe it.[FF]

JULY 20, 1943

Reading Julien Green today. I thought how foolish of me to go on writing this diary in foreign languages*—and so badly that I don't exercise the speech forms that would come in English—so badly that the words shouldn't appear anywhere but in a grammar notebook—I am so ambitious, that I must telescope 2 separate activities—writing a diary and learning a language.

7/21/43

We can make things alone for pleasure—and the moment they're sold and bring in money, we're ashamed of them! Why? Because too much is expected of the thing that is "sold"? or more likely because we have betrayed this innocent, docile, unsuspecting little living thing.

7/21/43

The ideal life—the activities of a perfect fortnight. Two such fortnights per month, twelve such months per year. Work in the daytime, read and dream and perhaps work at night, thirteen out of the fourteen days. On the fourteenth night, be with a number of congenial people, some with brains and some without. The evening must begin with good conversation, and end in utter drunkenness, carousing, incoherent speech to show the potentialities of the language, incoherent pictures in the eye, to show the miracles of visions and visionaries!

JULY 22, 1943

[F]Still no letter from Allela—and though I'm not miserable, I'm a bit sad. Lately, I can't imagine her face. In a certain sense, I killed that unerring happiness I knew in May! But it will come back when she does. In truth, I don't have enough time to imagine my kisses—as slowly as they should be. Spent some time with mother tonight. I haven't written my grandmother in six months! I didn't even notice! I read some Christian Science, which will do me a lot of good.[FF]

---

* Pat writes this, then promptly reverts to French in her very next diary entry.

JULY 23, 1943

^FI was at the station at 5:45. After having chased down a dozen trains, my eyes almost brimming with tears!—I found Lela, standing all alone, smoking, in front of the big gates of the station! She was wearing her red dress and took my hand. Oh, she looked beautiful! We waited for Texas—then Breevort, where we drank 10 drinks between us. Cornell has obtained an invitation for me to her parents' tomorrow night. Come to dinner! It will be very important. And I'm thrilled about it!^{FF}

7/23/43

At the dentist's—I turn the knob of the door, and with the resistance of the knob—the visit has definitely begun. But I have not composed myself enough. If I had only five more minutes outside the door how much better I could face it! I think about gas. Would Julien Green's and Picasso's gaseous hallucinations not be more interesting than mine? Than other peoples'? But why should they be until their artistic minds have altered them? They would be the same as the next person's until this occurred. Or is there such a thing as an educated subconscious? Is there an intelligent or an artistic subconscious? Especially I reflect that when death comes, I shall be no better prepared. I shall still wish, with all my dwindling strength, for five more minutes in which to formulate some idea of what I am about to experience, two more minutes to make my peace with God, one more minute to kiss her goodbye and to swear that she will join me finally in that realm where there is only perfection.

JULY 24, 1943

^FDid nothing today—except what I wanted. Went to see the parents, saw two exhibitions, then went with mother to the Bowery to buy two shirts, one for me, beige, silk, $2.50. I'd like to get my monogram on the shirt. I read a bit—then to the Cornells' for dinner. Mr. Cornell is tall, somewhat handsome, a bit like Claude Coates. And finally, Allela—the life and blood of the family! She's very brown from the sun. Tex looked very beautiful in her black dress. The grandmother is old, very thin, and smokes and drinks! A bit stiff, dignified, but has a sense of humor. Very good for a grandmother, and knows a bit of German. A weak drink prepared by Mr. Cornell, then a big dinner, very lovely—though I was shy. Cornell very sweet. She took me upstairs, where she kissed me—I kissed her very slowly, very tenderly, both of us standing in her room. How I adore her lips! Oh, we were alone for five minutes! She is still a bit shy, just like me, but she gave me as much as she could! And I did too!^{FF}

JULY 25, 1943

[F]A bad day, the saddest of my life so far. Breakfast at 11:00, too many cigarettes and too much coffee, then drew, none of the drawings any good. Wrote 7½ pages of my story but it was done too fast. At parents' house at 5:30 for Allela and Texas. Then Three Crowns for dinner. I drank too much and my throat hurt—smoked too much—maybe three packs today. In any case I was miserable and sad, because I didn't manage to say any of the things I wanted to. At Nick's together, where we stood at the bar, listening to music. Then at Figi's for a moment, then her apartment on Grove St. My throat hurt badly—and then got worse—I almost wanted to die! And I wrote one or two pages about this when I came home. Tex said that we have Cornell "in common"—she knows about everything, I'm sure. (And at the parents', the conversation was about homosexuality.) And with Allela—when Tex went upstairs—I couldn't speak, so quickly went home. I couldn't kiss her. I touched the most profound depths tonight.[FF]

7/25/43

My own work is unfinished, and I owe a great debt to all those who have fed and clothed me all these years. I owe a different debt to the one I love best. All the tears I should have shed in a long lifetime are coming now and mean nothing to me. There is no life nor truth without the one I love. There is no optimism and no accomplishment. There is no health and no future.

I have wanted long labors, of detail, and perfection, affection and great care, worthy of past artists. Inspiration is a great arc of momentum, and the momentum is love, and love requited. I cannot speak humbly enough of all the humble things I have to speak of. The absence of you has torn my insides out! I am sick with tears, and sick with the stoppage of my love. My love is greater than I, and dammed up has risen and drowned me! What does this night foretell? A quiet house, a peaceful fireplaced room, with a woman in a long brown velvet dress. What does this foretell?—Good work and healthful days? I don't believe it, because God has made this moment too poignant, and actually too perfect of its kind. My mouth is bitter and I don't want to kiss you. No, I am not in command of myself, but love is in command of me, and this love is destructive, though meant to be creative. Never more than at this minute, was I ready to meet the Omnipotent One. Never more fearless, never more proud of myself and never more humbled before this power infinitely greater than I.

JULY 26, 1943

[F]Sick this morning—couldn't speak—but Cornell phoned me at 8:30. Met her at Penn Station at 9:25. We didn't have much to say to each other—just that we had a good time and that there will be more good times to come. Finally, she kissed me on the train. Yes—during these months, I've forgotten to be grateful for her—grateful for the future itself! She is the future—I am the present. I am here, and without her. And now I must work.[FF]

JULY 28, 1943

[F]I've done nothing over the past months except love Allela—but isn't this my entire life? No letter this morning, though I went down to look three times! How sad it is to come home and look at this empty box! If she knew, she'd write, I think. She has to do something without my control. I wrote 6 pages of the Laval story, and I think they're good. I must always stay confident. Was happy and phoned Rolf. He has 16 pages in the next *Coronet*!* Raphael Mahler gave me a call, and will come Sunday night to speak our two languages.[FF]

JULY 29, 1943

[F]I can't work with J. [Jerry] Albert.† It's better in the factory in front of the office. It made me think that I wouldn't want to write if I didn't live in New York! One must have something to fight against before one can produce. Joseph H. phoned me, but I wanted to write tonight—and I wrote six pages. The story is coming along well, I think. Julien Green is giving me a lot of inspiration, and I'd like to write him. He's here now, in the army. (!)‡ Italy is almost defeated. The Germans continue to fight the allies, with more strength than the Italians. I'm hoping for—a letter tomorrow.[FF]

JULY 31, 1943

[G]Pleasant morning and got my money at the bank. $250.00 and $250.00 in bonds, nearly.

Rolf was horrible when I went to visit. He was reading Dalí's autobiography [*The Secret Life of Salvador Dalí*], and as always thinks that no

---

* *Coronet* was a pocket-sized general interest magazine owned by *Esquire* and published from 1936 to 1971.

† Gerald "Jerry" Albert, fellow scriptwriter and also editor at the Sangor Shop.

‡ During the Nazi German occupation of France in World War II, Julien Green supported the French Resistance from the United States.

one understands the stuff but him, and I got the distinct sense he wanted
to fight with me. He's like a woman. When God puts us two together, I'll
be the better man! Tex phoned at 8:15. She said she and Allela decided
to put a bit more money into the house so that they'll be able to spend
their winter evenings more agreeably at home. So sad, so deeply sad,
I've rarely felt like this in my life. When October comes, will I be alone?
Worked hard, though, and finished my Laval story. 25½ pages of yellow
legal pad paper. And I felt better after.^{GG}

AUGUST 2, 1943

^GLetter from Allela. She worked hard last week—and loved it. Nervous
at the office. Short conversation at 6:00 about my requested raise. They're
offering $42.50, which almost made me laugh! We need to speak with
Sangor again. He wanted me, Hughes said, because I was the "healthy
type." I think there are other reasons—little money and no office. (Aren't
I mean!) Painted the cabinet this evening and wrote the necessary letter
to Alice Williams at Time Inc. I want to find another job right away. It
would be nice to say—"if you don't give me $75.00 a week, I'm leaving—"
and then leave! (FEEL VERY ADULT AND REASONABLE!!) Wrote a
good letter to Allela as well. She's coming August 13th! She must come. It
is of cosmic consequence!^{GG}

8/2/43

Almost everybody in the world lives because he believes it is more pleasant than to die. I see for the majority no ambitions and no goals. Love
and work are the two enduring possessions here and hereafter, and how
little do most of us make of them! We make them commonplace, silly
and degraded. And yet all religions teach that to die is to be reborn, that
the afterlife for one who has kept God and love and righteousness intact
is more desirable than this!

AUGUST 3, 1943

^FI can't work in the office any longer! It's completely impossible! Some-
times I think I can't even write another page! And I tell myself that in
three weeks, I'll be gone! Ken [Battlefield] understands, and Marty
Smith does too. But not the others. Met Tex at *Vogue* at 5:30. Also met
Mallison* who liked my drawing of the Hungarian soldier. She said:
"For the love of God, make some other drawings and bring them to

---

* Possibly Clare Mallison, Vogue Studios.

Lieberman at *Vogue*.* You can draw!" Declarations like this make me very sad! Tex and I had drinks at Shelton Corners. I made her dinner. We were happy, we were hungry, and there was love in the kitchen—not physical, but in the air! But my damned tooth ached badly. Couldn't sleep until 4:30.[FF]

AUGUST 4, 1943

[F]Horrible day. My tooth hurt like hell again at 12:30. It has to be pulled. I can't take it any longer! I long for those beautiful days when I worked like a man—at home, for myself, and—

Last night, Tex said that Allela belongs to the whole world. It was very profound! With the parents for a moment by the river. Then at home, mother helped me paint my cabinet. And I'm just as happy now as I was miserable all day long. Wrote Allela of course, but no letter from her since Monday. Tex is leaving for Texas on Friday and I'll have to give her something very nice.[FF]

AUGUST 5, 1943

[F]The office is much better now. I like Everett, as well as everyone else, really. *Partisan Review*[†] arrived, and I'm very proud to have it.[FF]

AUGUST 6, 1943

[G]Nothing at Time, Inc., where I met with Mrs. Williams again. She always looks at me with some kind of sympathy, but shakes her head. She doesn't have a job for me. Am (almost) certain there are no jobs where one can put oneself on display and speak one's mind. Feel so happy about my clean bed, my newspaper, and my milk in the evenings, but am concerned I might be turning bourgeois?[GG]

AUGUST 7, 1943

[G]I couldn't work until I'd asked Mr. Hughes about my raise. Spoke first with Sangor, who's a bigger man than Hughes. A bigger personality. I felt sick by the time they finally called me into the room, and then Sangor said, I'll give you (!) $50.00 a week. And that was that. Drank whiskey with Hughes and he told all sorts of dumb stories and shared a few

---

* Alexander Lieberman, at the time art director at *Vogue*.

† *Partisan Review* was a left-wing political and literary journal founded in 1934 and which, despite the small 1934 edition, had quite some bearing on the literary scene, thanks to the support of authors such as Hannah Arendt, Saul Bellow, James Baldwin, and Susan Sontag, several of whose short stories and essays it first published.

platitudes about Eliot, Wolfe, Steinbeck, etc. And then I went home. My parents are very impressed by my raise, I think. I make $5.00 more than Stanley!GG

AUGUST 10, 1943

FI'm happy beyond all reason! Is it Allela? My new salary? The calm at the office? Whatever the case, I'm happy with work for the moment and will try to remain content for as long as possible, because when I no longer am, I'll quit. Painted the apartment today, movies tonight with mother. We talked about a thousand things, but too quickly and superficially. It will always be like that with mother, and even more so as she grows old. She has never thought seriously or at length about issues that do not involve her. I am full of life, and wonder what will happen this weekend? Will I sleep with—her?FF

AUGUST 11, 1943

GA nice letter from Allela—oh, I knew what it would say! That she's coming on Friday at 5:51, and true enough! We'll be together Saturday evening, and I bought tickets for *Skin of Our Teeth*. And later, Spivy's. Happy at work. Wrote a funny story about Squeak, practically Disney! Went to the dentist, and he drilled my front tooth. Very necessary. Worked with Mother here this evening. The walls are beautiful. Paged through Dickens a little, which made me very happy, as it recalled my childhood.GG

AUGUST 12, 1943

GAm terribly happy but still got good work done. A new hero. The Champion. Who cares?! Looked for clothing fabric with Mother. Mother has known for a long time that I spend most of my money on women, which is why she's encouraging me to spend a bit more on myself. S. and M. here, and the house looks gorgeous! The wall, blue-green, with Bernhard's photograph, is the very best! Oh God—I am happy—and pensive, and should always think of these days! They're the very best!GG

AUGUST 13, 1943

FI felt happy and complete all day, worked well even though I was thinking of Allela—of the moment I'd see her. Well—with 20.00 in my pocket I met her at 6. We were strangely relaxed. There was no one at her apartment. We were like old friends. I lathered her back in the bath, and we sailed the little ship I gave her. It was lovely. Then—in bed together, naked, the light sheets on our two bodies—our soft skin rub-bing together over and over again—she whispered "yes" to me and it was sweeter than anything I've ever known! I fell asleep while she was touching my lips with her marvelously light fingers.—And in the morning, we woke up and discovered each other again. Finally, she touched me first—and I don't know why—but it happened under her fingers. It is paradise to be in bed with her. It's beautiful and complete!FF

AUGUST 14, 1943

FAfter breakfast—I bought her peaches, a banana—she wrote postcards. I am noting down details because this day I'll want to re-read. Went to the Museum of Modern Art. There was an exhibition on Bali. Allela came at 4, an hour late! Rum. It was strange after last night. It was calm, tranquil, and we felt peaceful. I began to think that maybe I don't love her. But it's just that I've never had a woman I've loved. I love her. But tonight, after a walk down Broadway, when we said almost nothing to each other—I was really too tired, too sad, and my new shoes were hurting me. (What kinds of things transpire because of a pair of too-small shoes!) I spoke cruelly to her, told her that she doesn't love me enough. I accused her of being selfish, of taking what she could and giving nothing. At home by 4:45 A.M. very sad, and thinking for the fifth time that I'd given her up.FF

AUGUST 15, 1943

FLast night, I said what should have been said a long time ago—that she doesn't want to change her life. That she lives with Texas because no one better has come along. She didn't deny it. And it made me furious! Can I share her under such circumstances? Today, I think I can. I will be happy and work hard, and derive most of my happiness from work—as I always have.FF

GWe've concluded that we—both—love ourselves better than anyone else, and that therefore, the chain that connects us is stronger than if we were living together. I feel tremendous relief! As does she. I really think we are much closer to one another this way. She called me again at 12:10, after I had worked around the house with pleasure—with great pleasure—and our conversation was full of laughter, full of love, and I am very happy about it. Reading [John William Dunne's] *Experiment With Time.*GG

AUGUST 16, 1943

GYesterday I forgot to say that I've got a woman, or even better, what I've got is an artist. I've got Allela as much as I will ever have any woman, and she's got me the same way. And we've both got as much as we want from each other. We don't want our whole selves taken.[GG]

AUGUST 18, 1943

[F]It's strange what I think of Allela. Will I be searching for something better my entire life? Oh, there's no one better than she! She is the best—the best soul I could find! Dan at the parents', very boring. He lives entirely in the present, and the present is petty and insignificant.[FF]

8/18/43

Looked into a parked car this evening and saw two people kissing, very tenderly, oblivious of the noisy street (57) around them. It was good to see, and I wished then everyone would live at all times as tenderly as they (everyone) surely have been at one moment in their life.

AUGUST 20, 1943

[F]At Rolf's at 1:30. He still loves me a little. But he hates my story (Laval), and he's right. I'll rewrite it.[FF]

AUGUST 21, 1943

[F]Friday—one week ago I was peacefully sleeping next to Allela.[FF] [G]I want to see Allela, kiss her, hug her. Want to live with her. Want to love with her, see the world. Want to work with her. Read [George Frederick Young's] *The Medici* again.[GG]

AUGUST 22, 1943

[G]Rolf came by at 11:45. He loved my fireplace, very impressed, also by my artworks around the house. We went to Central Park and rowed on the lake. Rolf was nice. He went home at 3:00, and I went to see *Forgotten Village* at the museum. Really learned a lot this week. About myself, about work, about Allela.[GG]

AUGUST 23, 1943

[G]No letter from her. One from Rosalind, who got back today. My check from *H. & F.* From her, though—nothing. Am at work with Dan Gordon.[*] Clever artist. Can think of nothing but Allela—she's torturing me.

---

[*] Dan Gordon (1902–1970), an American comic book and storyboard artist and film director. Gordon was one of Famous Studios' first directors, and wrote and directed several Popeye the Sailor and Superman cartoons. Later, at Hanna-Barbera, Gordon worked on several cartoons featuring Yogi Bear, Huckleberry Hound, and others.

Still, I was somehow happy tonight, because I was alone and working. Trying to master an entirely new style. Very, very simple, almost sweet, not like when I used to need so much.[GG]

AUGUST 24, 1943

[G]Oh—fantastic day. The postman woke me at 7:30 with a package from Roger R. (A small glass horse, already broken.) And a letter from Allela! I was so happy—I washed and ran back to bed to read it. "Oh Pat let's try to keep this goodness! I feel that I can with your help." I will always help her.

Gordon drinks. You can tell from his face. He has a strange effect on me: I'm like a sixteen-year-old around Clark Gable. Was being very foolish this afternoon. Bumped into Camy on 56th St. We went to a bar. 3 Tom Collinses, and when I left him alone for a few moments, I think he read my letter to Allela. Doesn't bother me.[GG]

AUGUST 25, 1943

[G]And when I got home, in high-heeled shoes that tortured my feet, tired from working for someone else—I thought how nice it would be to wander the streets in comfortable shoes, the time my own, my work just making beautiful images with words and lines—that would be wonderful and shouldn't be impossible. I shouldn't consider it a dream, but rather something coming soon that requires just a few years or months of work. Tex returns Sunday, and we'll soon be together again, we three. Why? What will happen? What won't?

Preparing the house for Rosalind.[GG]

AUGUST 27, 1943

[G]Am very thin and very happy. Letter from Allela. Went into Dan Gordon's office to see him. When we were alone, he said I should "join him for a walk at Paramount"; it doesn't matter, but—but he has a strange effect on me. Want to drink with him.

24 pages this week. Rosalind had a hangover that sent her to bed at 4! I went over at 7, and we drank and ate. She was tender and nice, but "I smell like old cigarettes" and couldn't kiss her. Saw her to bed with her cat Natashas (Siamese) around her neck. She was dog-tired.

I enjoyed paging through a book on Chirico.[*][GG]

---

[*] Giorgio de Chirico (1888–1978), Italian painter and graphic artist. With Carlo Carrà, he outlined the theoretical tenets of metaphysical painting, one of the most important antecedents to surrealism.

AUGUST 29, 1943

G$285 in the bank. $260 in bonds. Bought all sorts of things this afternoon and felt very independent. My parents came at 9:00 with beer.
They're like good friends. And later, after calling first, Rolf Tietgens
came with a bottle of rum. We almost emptied the bottle, and he spoke
on and on with his wonderful eloquence about the nostalgia we all feel.
He stayed overnight. He was not aroused, of course, but he did feel me
with his hands, and I—yes—it was strange.

The rest is just poetry.GG

AUGUST 29, 1943

GHappy but restless. We ate together at Rosalind's. She said: "You're a
sloppy Joe, I've decided, but I also think you're an artist!" "That's fair,"
I replied. And we drank! After that, went to row on the lake in the park.
Rosalind attracts a lot of attention. Her clothes, etc. We were speaking a
bit slowly, and not very intelligently. Alcohol doesn't improve the mind.
It disgusts me.

Went to my parents'. Mother and I took a walk, where she told me I
should go out more often with young men! That if I looked for men as I
do for women, I could get them. Handsome men, too, who are worthy
of me! And that I should live outside this city at some point. Yes—that is
true. But she knows about the unpleasant experiences I've had with various men, which have been enough to convince me men aren't as good as
women.GG

AUGUST 30, 1943

GDid nothing and did nothing and did nothing, except for painting.
Giorgione—La Venus Masturbataire.* Behind her stand the buildings
of New York. Tired at the office, and now I don't want to sleep. Why? I
want to read and maybe study something. Am an artist and my head is
full of ideas. I want to make a painting every night.

Went to Shelton's at 6:00 with Tex, who had all sorts of experiences in
Texas—and she slept with at least one girl! Tex said she felt "so far from
N.Y.—and that everything was so nice and easy." Yes—but it's not phys-
ically necessary for her, so it is a sin. Right? I couldn't do it. Especially if
Cornell were so clearly mine.GG

---

* Giorgione's *Sleeping Venus*, also known as the Dresden Venus.

AUGUST 31, 1943

[G]Goldberg came over at 8:40. He brought a bottle of champagne (domestic) and we talked for hours. He wants to write a book about the history of Jews throughout the world. I'm to do the research for $30 a week, 8 hours a day. That would get me out of this job, but I'd still be working freelance. A pleasant evening, though, as I return to egotism. I'm going to be a big hit or a big flop. There's no in-between. I am an extraordinary girl. Around Goldberg I felt light, needed, strong, creative, a genius—I am, too![GG]

SEPTEMBER 1, 1943

[G]Happy day. Worked slowly—sad and tired. Saw Posada[*] exhibit at the library. Mexican artist who influenced Orozco[†] and Rivera. Wrote a story for Cinema [Comics] for the first time. Dreadfully moralistic stuff. Jerry says I'm too serious. Boohoo! Cornell says I have what she never will: A creative imagination. I see so many who are much worse than I am! I am good.[GG]

SEPTEMBER 3, 1943

[G]Beautiful, dark day, but how happy I am! Wrote 10 pages at work, despite Jerry's endless interruptions. Met Allela at 53rd and 5th at 5:40. I could see she was sad before I reached her. She's lost her momentum and feels useless as a result. I tried to urge her to leave Tex and live by herself for a while. Cornell: "We could never—never live together! You know that, don't you?" "Sure!" I said, and I meant it![GG]

SEPTEMBER 4, 1943

[G]Allela invited two girls over and wanted to leave them with Tex, but Tex refused to be left alone, so Allela had to stay there. So I drank and wrote like an artist who doesn't need any friends! Natasha called me at 9:30 P.M. to invite me to a social tomorrow evening at Angelica de Monocol's. Rosalind doesn't know about it, but I hope she'll be there tomorrow. Am—what—happy? Yes, I think so.[GG]

SEPTEMBER 5, 1943

[G]Sketched a little. Got ready for the big night at Angelica de Monocol's. Her husband is an artist—and just 24 years old. Made the acquaintance

---

[*] José Guadalupe Posada (1852–1913), Mexican engraver, illustrator, and caricaturist.
[†] José Clemente Orozco (1883–1949), Mexican painter widely considered one of the founding fathers of contemporary Mexican painting alongside Diego Rivera, one of the main representatives of Mexican muralism.

of Chloe—a model for H[attie] Carnegie,* who was very beautiful, and also a lady. All that I remember is that I was sitting with her, my nose in her hair, which was very clean and soft. That I felt her lips with my fingers, and that she said—"I'm really quite straight, but you do something to me." Got home at 4:30! Rosalind very serious and sober, I think.GG

SEPTEMBER 5, 1943

FI was adrift this morning—walked all the way to 72nd and York. I felt dirty and sordid. The first thing I thought of this morning was Chloe's hair, and her innocent lips. She suggested that she come over at 5 this evening. The apartment looked perfect when she came. I had a new bottle of rum out. She looked ravishing, and she knew it. She sat in the chair, looking at me, sipping on her drink and smiling. I made her sit on the bed and finally I just had to embrace her—to which she reacted with sighs. She doesn't know what she wants, she said. That's nothing if not encouragement. Rolf came at 7:00. Dinner with Chianti. GAnd my story, which I will finish tomorrow.GG Chloe gave me her number with pleasure—went to an evening at J. Levy's.† She doesn't know Buffie, but she knows that she's a little phony! Am happy, but it was a lost day—and I have lost doubly if I have lost Cornell FF

SEPTEMBER 6, 1943

FChloe on my mind all day.

Tonight was very serious, finished the Laval story. With Rolf's suggestions. Chloe gave me a ring at 7:30—a lovely conversation. She feigns innocence, but is very amused when I make unseemly suggestions. She came at 0:00—more charming than ever. I was full of thoughts on my work and my books, and showed her my photographs. Finally, I embraced her and kissed her, and it was so sweet—so sweet—I was extremely tender with her because she is like a river—not because she is pretty—no—she is sick too. She was trembling inside. I could feel it when I held her hand. She said that she doesn't want to go to bed with anyone. That she wants a friend who will talk to her and go on long walks. But— finally—after five kisses, after a lot of light touching, we went to the banks of the river and she told me that she had gone on a voyage when

---

* Hattie Carnegie (born Henrietta Kanengeiser, 1886–1956), Austrian-born American fashion designer and entrepreneur.
† Julien Levy (1906–1981), American art dealer whose gallery was located at Fifty-Seventh Street and Madison Avenue and specialized in surrealists, avant-garde artists, and American photography of the 1930s and 1940s.

I'd kissed her. I hope it gave her pleasure, because it was a dream for me. When I wake up tomorrow, I may think it didn't happen. I'm thinking of Allela, of course—will I never manage to be faithful to anyone but myself? Tonight was real life, with which I have nothing to do.[FF]

SEPTEMBER 8, 1943

[G]Thought of nothing but Chloe.[GG] [F]Had lunch with Cornell at 1:00.[FF] [G]Poor child—and great artist[GG]—[F]Someone had cut her hair back to her scalp![FF] [G]She didn't look good enough to take to Del Pezzo.[GG] [F]I told her that nobody is faithful to anyone except themselves. She has no doubt I have another woman on my mind. It's a bit sad—I'm so like a man in that beauty affects me so much. Truly, like the monster I am, Cornell disgusted me today. No stockings—no refinement—and when I read these words again in a year, my heart will weep. Chloe phoned me at 8:30. She speaks slowly, smilingly, and calls me "darling" often. Rosalind phoned me at 9:00. She was surprised, naturally, that I'd seen Chloe. She had "seen" Natica (the 22-year-old girl) and wanted to bring her to the party on Friday, when I'll invite Chloe. I phoned Chloe at 10:00 with the message that "I'm crazy in love with you." Which was true at 10 o'clock, nonetheless.[FF]

SEPTEMBER 10, 1943

[F]I will probably have less money—with the T.S.F.[*] and the parties, I hope—with Chloe—but I'll get used to it. I'm above that, and can do what I want. In every area of my life.[FF] [G]Could barely work at the office. Am so nervous! Prepared myself for Rosalind, who was meant to come first—but it was Chloe who climbed the stairs so lightly. Rosalind—Chloe shone in her eyes, and she had to spend the whole evening at her side. We took a taxi to Sammy's. Rosalind was on the edge of her seat, looking at Chloe all the while, but was jealous of me, because Chloe preferred me. Then Chloe wanted to go to Cerruti's, but Mary S. was there. Ultimately Rosalind shoved Chloe and me into a cab. Chloe wanted to go for a walk, so we got out at 2nd Ave. I spoke quietly to her, "What do you want?" "I want to go home with you," she answered. She pulled off her dress; and was in my bed when I came from the shower. It was wonderful! Terrible! And I lay in bed, and she wanted nothing but that I hold her tight. She's not thin, nearly fat! But how firm her body is! Naturally didn't go to the office Saturday morning. We lay in bed till 1:30

---

[*] TSF (*télégraphie/transmission sans fil*), a wireless radio device Pat wants to buy.

P.M.! Mornings are the most beautiful! But she didn't allow me to touch her. I gave her a ripe black olive. We read what I had written to her—"as Oberon parted the pendant mass of his trees in search of Titania, I will part the melancholy forest of your hair and drink from the secret spring of your mouth"—I wrote that Thursday evening with Goldberg (!) in the room. And she likes it a lot. Went by hers at 6:00 for a drink. Lexy has no character and is not an ideal roommate for Chloe. She wanted me to spend the evening with her, but I had to see Bernhard. When I called Chloe [later], she said she had taken 6 sleeping pills, but Tony was there. Frightened, I went by myself to 56th and 2nd Ave. Drank a beer with a worker who told me a sad story about his girl, then Chloe called back. Tony invited me over. Chloe was on her bed, half asleep. I didn't see her till Tony had gone. Then she asked me incessantly to get into bed with her. At 1:30 I took off my clothes—just as Lexy got back! I was naked! Lexy smiled—she's always smiling, like a fool, and watched over us all night. But there was nothing to see.GG

SEPTEMBER 12, 1943

GWoke in her arms— and she is always so beautiful in bed, so beautiful in the early morning! I said that (and her husband says the same). How nice it was to kiss her when Lexy went to the bathroom. There was a letter from Götz van Eyck* on the bedside table, scribbled in pencil. When I held her close to me, she said: "Don't—you make me want you—so terribly." Naturally I felt like a king—who has spent a second night with a queen! "My God—I've spent almost all weekend with you in bed!" Chloe: "It could be worse!"—

Saw Bernhard at 5:00. Think she likes me as ever. Didn't mention Chloe. Didn't phone Cornell—have no interest in doing so, and I'm disgusted by the thought of kissing her again. Yes, I am fickle when it comes to physical love, but I loved an idea in Cornell—that of art—I still love that in her and will forever and ever—but physically—not anymore!GG

9/12/43

Why this secret fear that I have lost my roots? Because I have given up my love, my physical love, of one who was never more than the embodiment of an idea that I shall always love, and turned it, the physical and

---

* Götz van Eyck (1913–1969), German-born film actor who gained international recognition with leading roles in Henri-Georges Clouzot's *The Wages of Fear* (1953), Fritz Lang's *The Thousand Eyes of Dr. Mabuse* (1960), and Martin Ritt's *The Spy Who Came in from the Cold* (1965).

the imagined (forever imagined!) mental, to one who will surely go away more quickly even than my cigarette smoke. But the remembrance of her never. Will I ever tell her, I wonder, these unpoetic, unbeautiful words—which are the top froth of the too-full vessel. My heart is heavy with confusing emotions, beclouded.

SEPTEMBER 13, 1943

GWonderful day! I don't love Chloe—but she has severed me from Allela. That's no cause for joy, but it had to happen, and not a moment too soon. And when I ultimately leave Chloe (when she ultimately leaves me), I won't shed any tears. She's beautiful, and I visit her as I will someday go to heaven to stay.

Pleasant in the office, and compliments on several stories. Purchased *The Early Chirico* for my mother's birthday and made a down payment for the radio, $75.00, which will arrive this week. Cornell phoned and I found her at the Winslow at 6:00. She's very downcast and looks at me as if she already knows everything. It's a mistake, without a doubt, but I can't look at her, can't take her hand.

Went to my parents' with a box of sweets and my book. We were very happy and content, drank lots of claret, and opened the presents like children. Fell asleep at 10:30—for one hour!—doubtless the wine—and imagined, as I woke, that Cornell had killed herself. It was alien, strange, as if I had taken anesthetics so she could die alone. Read Donne. And sketched.GG

9/13/43

What called me so powerfully and strangely to sleep tonight? I have never slept at such a time before, and this was more frightening than sleep. This was nature's anesthesia. And seeing you today, when nothing more was between us, except the thin and inorganic air, seeing so clearly that you understood, I wonder if as I slept, you died? How? By your own will or God's? Or with the winding down of this outlandish, unproductive machinery? Now at five minutes to midnight, I am afraid to call you. Perhaps I have dreamed, and forgotten, that you died.

SEPTEMBER 14, 1943

GSaw Camy twice, and at 5:30, I was feeling so nervous, we bought a drink at Cocktail's. And I said, "I'm going to see the prettiest woman in New York!" And he started to say something—but stopped. He knows, maybe. I think? Chloe was expecting me. Like every pretty woman, she loves to talk about herself. As we approached 57th, I invited her up for some hot milk. I prepared her milk with love. A little rum found its way in, although she's not drinking this week. And after she finished half the cup, she said "I'm drunk—" and in saying so—or better put, in not saying anything, she pulled me toward her—and it was like heaven itself to feel her hand on my neck! My God, how wonderful! And I kissed her—but deeper than before. Then she went home and I sketched—without much success—but aren't I pretty wealthy?[GG]

SEPTEMBER 15, 1943

[G]Conversation with Leo Isaacs,[*] who really is a poet. Writes lots of poems and hates this ugly world of commercialism. Now, that's a man! Mother was here tonight, and we sketched each other—she made a large gouache of me that didn't turn out too badly. Oh, I am happy—because I have Chloe and because I can now start to work again. Cornell is coming tomorrow evening, something I'm not looking forward to.[GG]

SEPTEMBER 16, 1943

[G]Camy bought two drinks at 6:00. He's considerate, a rare quality in any man. Prepared the house for Cornell. I expected the worst this evening, but I tried, and she tried, and we amused ourselves quite well. Cornell understands how I feel about her. I want nothing more to do with her physically. And that means the end of our love, and she knows that. How smart and understanding nature is, always leading us to the most beautiful! A.C. went home early, and I got to [Chloe and Lexy's] at 11:00. Chloe looked very beautiful and was happy to see me. Without a doubt. Lexy fell asleep. Then we kissed softly, and Chloe whispered my name, which always winds me up. And whenever I tried to leave, she pulled me back. It was heaven. Then I turned out the light and we lay together for a while, our heads alone touching. Our lips barely touched, our teeth barely touched. I kissed her eyes, her lips, her hair, her neck, her breast, her hands. I wanted to kiss her body, her thighs! Came home as happy and high as only a poet could be![GG]

9/16/43

The perfumes of the women will finally drive me mad. My heart beats wild at high noon at the scent of the stenographer with her coffee cup opposite me at the cafeteria table. My head turns reels on the streets and

---

* Leo Isaacs, freelance writer at the Sangor Shop.

a terrible force draws me after the prancing filly, the lumbering dowager, the smooth, straight-limbed Negroes. Anything! Anyone! Let me bury my nose in their clothed bosoms. Perfume! Dream of the nighttime, the promise and the memory of love, proof of the lover and badge of the beloved. Perfume! Sweet and lewd in the bright sunlight, tempter of all the senses.

9/16/43

Idle thought: that the many divorces in America are due to the national ambition. We are always striving, attaining, and not wanting. It is not that we do not know how to dramatize, glorify and romanticize her once we have her, not merely this, but also that we see someone better (physically better, for that is all we take time to explore) just as we see always a job that is better.

SEPTEMBER 17, 1943

ᴳOne week ago Chloe and I first went to bed together! And how wonderful, how godly it was! Could be—certainly am—bored by her mind already, but never by her beauty. She inspires me with wonderful, lively ideas, she excites me with love and life. I'm not in love with her, though, which I told her this evening.ᴳᴳ

SEPTEMBER 17, 1943

ᴳ[Mother and I] visited the Ferargil Galleries to see Constant[*] and Takis[†]—very interesting. Felt lonely and had to go to my parents'. Ate heartily, and they came over to my house to see my radio. It's magnificent! Then as I was writing, the phone rang loudly—and it was Chloe, who said: "I'm at home. I thought maybe you'd like to have a drink with me." She was quite drunk and wanted to stay up all night. It was past 2:30 A.M. when I finally managed to put her to bed. How fine a duty! ᴳᴳ

SEPTEMBER 18, 1943

ᴳChloe busied herself with preparing my breakfast. We had some ham, lots of beautiful fruit, and every time we passed each other, we had to

---

* George Constant (born George Konstantopoulos, 1892–1978), Greek-American modernist painter, etcher, and printmaker.
† Probably Nicholas Takis (1903–1965), an American expressionist painter.

hug and kiss. It was heaven! "Pat, I adore you! I think I'll fall in love with you." Chloe: "Don't you want to get married sometime?" "Yes— sometime." "Why don't you marry me?" "Now you're talking." The Levys—Muriel in particular—have convinced Chloe she should live with them! They live above the galleries on 57th Street—but Chloe wouldn't have enough privacy. I know that our friendship probably won't last long and that our nights together, at least, are already numbered! Chloe is a sprite, a married woman (first of all) whom I must treat like a queen.

Went to Cornell's social at 5:00. Lots of people. Charles Miller, whom I'll see again soon, and Alex Goldfarb, who didn't look so great. More later—it's already 1:30—and I've slept so little.GG

SEPTEMBER 19, 1943

GStrange day. Leo Isaacs confessed that he tried to reach me on the phone from 4–8 yesterday. He was drunk. And had a hangover. We went to Raffier's on 51st St. and had 3 drinks (!) and ate. "You are beautiful," he said. And the first "new person he's met this year." Another drink at Cocktail at 4:00, which made for a very short and drunk afternoon. Jerry and Martin doubtless sensed something, but I don't care. Invited Chloe over for martinis at 6:15. She left too soon—and Leo Isaacs came a short time after. We played the radio. Nothing to say here but that we had a nice evening and drank far too much. He kissed me many times, something I maybe shouldn't have allowed.GG

SEPTEMBER 20, 1943

GNice day—but rather conscious of Leo Isaacs. When I went for coffee at 3:00, he came out of the elevator, and we went down together. Without a doubt, in these two days the entire office already knows about our after- noon. And Marty and Jerry, the two old women, want to know if we spent the evening together. Leo's fallen in love with me (or so I believe, without pride—but with a certain happiness). He won't clean his shoes, because I left a little scuff on them! [He's behaving] like a child—just like I do when I'm in love with a girl, and I like that a lot. "God you're gorgeous!" he said as we drank our coffee. And with that, it's like a nice secret, a private state of being when we're together, even if the whole world is standing around looking at us.

Thought a lot about Chloe, but decided not to call her today. Roger came over at 7:00. We drank, ate at Café Society (the bill was 11.50!), and now he's lying on my bed, snoring. What will happen, I don't know, but

I won't have anything to do with him. I belong to Chloe, and no one else. Leo gave me all of his poems and published writing. I want just one evening to myself!^GG

SEPTEMBER 22, 1943

^GNice day, but got little work done and walked around the city at midday, since I figured Dan and Leo would be drinking. When Chloe turned up with a white necklet under her black suit, when she said my martinis were better than the ones Muriel Levy makes, my heart soared. Went to my parents' for dinner at 8:00, only Mother noticed I had the mark of a woman's lips on my cheek! "Whose been kissing you?" and smiled, as if I were a boy.^GG

9/24/43

Sexual love is the only emotion which has ever really touched me. Hatred, jealousy, even abstract devotion, never—except devotion to myself. But love touched me willy-nilly.

SEPTEMBER 25, 1943

^GViewed several exhibits with Mother after a nice martini at the Winslow Bar. She always looks so pretty. And Chloe didn't phone. I lay restless in bed. Ultimately—I called her at the Levys' at 6:00. And she had broken her appointment with Gifford Pinchot*—had already had several drinks and wanted to eat at my place. I was immediately charmed! I ran and jumped in the air, sang along to the radio—and bought lots of things to eat, far more than we'd be able to. I got ready like a husband, and phoned Rosalind at 7:00, my first martini in hand. Regarding Chloe, she said: "This must be the first time you've been involved with someone who isn't very sensible." And that Chloe could be good for me, because she's so well-dressed. And so Chloe came at 7:50 with a hug and a kiss for me. We drank—and listened to records, and then I prepared this great dinner, which Chloe loved—corn, two lamb chops. And cheese and fruit. How nice, how warm, how lovely to watch Chloe gnaw on the bones! By 1:00 she was already tired. I easily convinced her to stay over. Then she took off her dress, and it was done! Chloe in my bed again. Have known Chloe twenty days and slept with her four times. Went further with her tonight than ever before, but not far enough.^GG

---

* Gifford Pinchot (1865–1946), early American advocate for environmental conservation and twice governor of Pennsylvania.

SEPTEMBER 26, 1943

^GWhat a nice day to finish this book!* In bed with Chloe. I got up at 8:30 to go to the bakery and pick up some brioche and croissants. How patient I was with the French customers in line, who took so long. I ran home to jump back in bed!^{GG}

SEPTEMBER 26, 1943

^GAt 6:20—Chloe invited me to the Levys' for a drink. I don't like them. Julien is like a snake, Muriel like a piglet. And her paintings are even worse. I felt very nervous, very dumb. Hurried home to find Leo. Drank martinis, and he was practically violent in his pronouncements of love. My days are wonderfully rapturous, wonderfully colored, after these nights with Chloe. Went to Nick's, where I saw Charley Miller. And went to Cornell's. Cornell was friendly—at least to me—though I'm not the same as I used to be. How could I be, when my body still smells of Chloe? Got home around 2:00–3:00, where I made coffee for Leo, because he wanted to stay all night. And I was happy as I went to bed at 4:45.^{GG}

SEPTEMBER 27, 1943

^GSad letter from Cornell. She said she doesn't want to see me again, that I might be giving someone else what I once gave her. Leo very curious about my friends. 3½ hours of sleep yesterday, but feel just fine. Most ordinary evening I've had in a long time. Made good progress on a gouache. Went to my parents', too, who love me more and more as a person.^{GG}

SEPTEMBER 28, 1943

^GGave my story "The Barber Raoul" and five spots to *Home & Food*. This morning Mother completely surprised me: she would like to see me go to Mexico, but with Leo! (I'm reminded of the weekends with Ernst Hauser!) I phoned Chloe later—nothing special—but this evening, when I said I might go to Mexico, she said—"Are you going? I'll come with you!" Fun at the dentist at 6:00 with Mother, who also had a tooth pulled. I had the same terrible, wonderful dream that I was God, that everything began in me and would end in me, that I alone understand the mysterious plan. "Book—book—book!" said the running, punching figure circling the cosmos.^{GG}

---

* "This book" refers to "this diary." Pat ends Diary 4b by listing her income and expenses, e.g. "Outgoing: 40.00 rent" or "Incoming 21—Bill King, 27—Spy Smasher."

9/29/43

Basically, the reason I don't like male homosexuals is because we basically disagree. Women, not men, are the most exciting and wonderful creations on the earth—and masculine homosexuals are mistaken and wrong!

OCTOBER 1, 1943

^GI had nervous indigestion all day and felt uncontrollably verbose. That means it's time to begin a long, ongoing project. My book. Yes.

Charley Miller didn't phone, which makes me very happy. He's nice, but I have too many.^GG

OCTOBER 2, 1943

^GCocktails with Mother at my place following a few exhibitions, with Camy, Cornell, and finally Leo Isaacs. Camy and Mother amused themselves well, and Cornell too, but she grew serious when we were alone and had to kiss me. I'm not happy about it. Leo stayed, drinking my Calvert's, which was likely the very reason he came. But I can't spend much time with him without feeling bored and like I'm wasting my time. Want to see Rolf tomorrow.^GG

OCTOBER 3, 1943

^GToday was miserable. Chloe didn't call all day. Short walk with [Marjorie] W., who's in love with David Randolph.* Oh, how wonderful to be straight.—Yes? No! Finally, at 4 o'clock—four o'clock on the dot, Ann T.† came over, who had been riding with Ellen B. We had some tea with baba au rhum. Finally had to call [Chloe]. Did she want to see me again?— "Whatever's best for you," she said, suggesting that it didn't matter to her one way or the other. I was just sick over it. Wanted to get drunk, and we went to Sutton [restaurant]. 3½ martinis. Could barely stand up straight and called Chloe. And I said she wasn't my type, etc. and was just nasty! Don't remember much of the conversation. Ann and I ate a little something, listening to music around midnight. Don't know how it started, but we finally ended up in bed, and Ann said that Virginia asked: "You know what I think of Pat?—You know how long it would take for me to fall for her? Approximately five mintues." "Highsmith, you're terrific!" She stayed till 5:30 AM, and it was very gentle and nice. We both needed it.^GG

---

* David Randolph (1914–2010), American choral conductor (the Cecilia Chorus of New York) and music educator.
† A twenty-five-year-old Pat has recently met, who works at Scribner's.

OCTOBER 4, 1943

ᴳTwo hours of sleep and a good idea for a story.* Chloe promised to call
me. She doubtless wants an apology from me. I'm happy to give it to her.
Don't regret what happened last night, but these love affairs move so
fast! Phoned Ann and she had written a poem about me. She has a brain,
which is very refreshing. Reading Wolfe and want to write a good story.
It's such a good feeling—and so strong, I could barely sleep from 6 to 8
[this morning].ᴳᴳ

10/4/43

A novel about a man who believes himself to be God. What a theme,
and what presumption, because the writer would have to believe himself
God, too, as I, in fact do. Yes, more than the extent to which God is in
me and in all of us.

10/4/43

Your lips have drunk from all my glasses,
Tumblers, beermugs and demi-tasses.
And I can imagine in every chair
The bland impress of your derrière.
We have christened every sheet
With lipstick, love and smudgy feet.
And you have used in this short while
Every telephone number on my dial.
Your green toothbrush in the cabinet
I know will never more be wet.
My tomato juice in the morning, dear,
Will now be drunk without Worcestershire.
Forget all this, and me, if you will.
But I'll remember (and with lover's a thrill)
When others have come, when others have gone,
How beautiful, always, you were at dawn.

OCTOBER 5, 1943

ᴳThought of Chloe from the moment I got up. And had to call her. "Oh,
I'm so torn up! I'm drinking day and night, etc." Chloe wants to see me
again, and finding her in this state, I wanted to help her again. "Let's go to
Mexico!" "Yes, let's," Chloe said. Lunch appointment with Ann T., who

---

* Pat will work on this (lost) story she will later call "The Three" for the following two weeks.

was waiting for me in dark glasses at Scribner. At Del Pezzo's, which I loved, because first Maria turned up, then Natasha H., and finally Bachu. But not Rosalind. We spoke a little too loudly about various love affairs. Ann said, "When can I see you again?" as though I were some grande dame. She was briefly involved with Buffie's friend Peter, and I don't at all like that she's discussing such short affairs. I'm next in line. Did great work this evening. On my story, the theme of which is worthy of Julien Green. Mystical and symbolic, I hope, of the soul itself. Happy—but mostly because Chloe's not upset with me. Yes—I don't like Ann enough.[GG]

OCTOBER 6, 1943

[G]Worked well at the office, which is extraordinary right now. But I am using up too many nerves there. Went to Chloe's. She made strong martinis and we discussed her men. She doesn't want to write Chandler S.* anymore! She doesn't want a divorce! But she also wants to marry Götz [van Eyck]! For God's sake, what does she want? Told her about Sunday night. "You betrayed me!" she said. "You never were mine to betray," I said. "Now we can be good friends." "Yes," she answered. My God! She's a beautiful woman, but I can see right through her because I'm just a bit smarter. Came home at 8:30 and phoned Ann T. She read out four lines from her poem about me, and they were wonderful. "What are you doing Saturday night?"—I want to ask Chloe what she's doing. Finished my story about the boy on the street—myself—I think there's something to it—something I haven't written before.[GG]

10/7/43

How delicate is the scale in which an artist weighs his worth. It must be delicate. There must be no overconfidence in the sustaining of his creative period: there must be confidence only in his honesty, and in nothing else. The reprimand of some slight fault, the polishing of a piece of work, in an evening, instead of the satisfying act of creation, is easily enough to destroy all that gives him joy, courage, pleasure and reward. A wastebasket out of place can do it. A cut in the finger can do it. And only the making of new life can reconstruct the shambles.

OCTOBER 8, 1943

[G]Got sick today, which is the pits, because I want to sleep with Chloe tomorrow. Two Manhattans with Leo. He's going to Guatemala in three

---

* Chandler S., Chloe's husband.

months. Ann called me. Ellen B. threw a whiskey sour in her face when Ann told her she'd slept with a girl! "You whore!" Ellen B. said! Ann can never see her again and had to take the elevator all wet! Didn't get much work done.[GG]

OCTOBER 9, 1943

[G]Happy, happy day. Worked, then met my parents and Claude [Coates]* at Del Pezzo. Hurried home. And then finally, she came. She was so very beautiful—black suit, little black hat, and furs. We listened to the music she likes, "The Last Time I Saw Paris," "Why Do I Love You," and "Make Believe." Later we took a taxi to 8th St. and 5th Ave. And she held my arm and looked so beautiful and smelled so wonderful! I felt too much—and against my wishes—like a man—in a suit, etc. We went to Nick's at 11:30, where I finally found Leo, introduced him to Chloe, and we drank for a few minutes. Chloe was very tired, though, and Leo was asking me all sorts of questions. Chloe eventually said she was going home and left alone. I hurried after her, though, very worried, because she and I were both so drunk. Took a taxi—first to 353 E. 56th, where Chloe—and I—had warm milk with rum. And I took her clothes off. The night was nice . . . more later.[GG]

10/9/43

You can never touch me, my dearest, my beloved. Never.

OCTOBER 10, 1943

[G]We got up at 11:15. Unfortunately, Chloe then called Julien, who demanded she come home and prepare his breakfast. "Pat, I'm so sorry—" she said. I was terribly despondent and hated Julien Levy for twenty minutes, going so far as to call and tell him how angry I was with him. And he hung up on me. It would have been an insult, if he were a stronger character. And I had gotten rolls from the French pâtisserie for Chloe and me! Oh, I was disappointed as a child!

Read *Confessions* of St. Augustine and felt more like a—what?—a man—without sexuality. Phoned Leo at Nick's. He came over, pretty drunk, asking all sorts of questions! He had a big epiphany last night. I had to explain things slowly and carefully. Eventually Chloe called. She was drunk, and I said I was bored of hearing about hangovers. "If you're bored, you know what you can do," she replied. "Goodbye!" Leo told me not to call

---

* One of Pat's maternal uncles.

her back. Of course, he would say that—and throughout the entire conversation, he kept trying to kiss me, etc. And I allowed him. It has to stop. Didn't go to bed till 3:30.^{GG}

OCTOBER 11, 1943

^GI wrote a good poem for [Chloe] and posted it. Got good work done on my story. And read Green. Today I was a poet. And that makes the whole world beautiful.^{GG}

OCTOBER 12, 1943

^GWent to my parents' for dinner at 6:00, but we had to wait for Dan, and having to wait for an hour and a quarter disgusted me terribly. Hurried home, washed my hair, and Ann T. called. She came over in a cold sweat, nervous. Gave her rum. Then Chloe called. She was in the neighborhood and asked first if I was alone. "Yes," I said, not knowing she wanted to come over. But as Ann was reading my poem about Chloe, she entered the room. Walked several blocks with [her], thinking she had something to say, but nothing. Nothing about Ann, about my poem, or about Leo. Nothing—! Ruined my whole evening because I did nothing but entertain my friends. Now I can work.^{GG}

OCTOBER 13, 1943

^GTerrible day. The type of day I always have to fight against. Monday was the only day this week that I was really living and creating. Camy drunk, and we had two at 4 o'clock, one at 6:00, before I found Dan. Funny, how a couple of cowboys in a bar can turn the whole place western! They're all so nice and pure. Especially one "Slugger" Sloan. The rodeo was very fine. Roy Rogers[*]—oh God!

Chloe is moving to Kay French's tomorrow. (N.B. Leo had to make the announcement that "A Chloe called." It made me smile, but he showed no outward emotion.) I told Chloe that I can't express my love out loud—only in poetry. And she—responded that the poem gets better each time she reads it. It makes me happy that she won't throw away these poems for many years—maybe ever. Ann, who received my poem today, said it was wonderful. But she's probably biased.^{GG}

---

* Roy Rogers (1911–1998), popular American country singer and actor, known as the "Singing Cowboy" in numerous western movies from 1938 to 1953.

OCTOBER 14, 1943

^GGot very good work done, even though my hair was flat and the day
was gloomy and strange. Cornell came over at 5—and that bothered
me a little. First I told the story about Saturday evening. About Leo too,
and my parents. ("They know, without a doubt," Cornell said.) Cornell
has seven paintings at the Pinacotheca* and is going to the country on
Wednesday. Camy bought me an eggnog at 3:00. Then he came over here
at 7:00 to bring me a book of Chinese love stories. He talked too much,
but there's less and less I have to say about him. Worked on my story,
which is coming along, but slowly. What will happen Saturday? I want to
spend it with Chloe. And if not, I won't see anyone.^{GG}

OCTOBER 15, 1943

^GExcellent day. Went to the Wakefield at 12:45 to see the Theater in Art
exhibit. Mother was nervous and strange. Said I don't have any time for
my relatives, but plenty of time for that bitch Chloe! If she hadn't been
so ridiculous about it, I'd have left immediately. I will mention it again
at some point and tell her that this kind of behavior is not appropriate.
Of course it's always the same—with Va., with Rosalind, and probably,
don't remember, with Cornell.

Ann T. called at 8:15. Told her all about Chloe. Then she asked me—
which really threw me for a loop—if I'm fickle? Maybe it's true. I've
loved three since New Year's Day: Rosalind, Cornell, Chloe. But Rosalind lasted a good two years. Cornell was an idea, and I still love them
both, love them for the same things I first loved in them. And Chloe—it's
all nice and physical, but physical like a schoolchild, admiring, pure, fair
and beautiful, and precocious, far beyond its years!

Got good work done on my story, which is almost ready to type up.
Am as proud of it as I was of my "Uncertain Treasure." In this story I
show some of my own ignorance and some of the knowledge of being.^{GG}

OCTOBER 16, 1943

^GToday should have been such a nice day. Drank with Leo—too much—
before visiting the van Gogh exhibit. Phoned Chloe twice, and somehow Kay French ended up inviting herself along. They got here at 7:30.
At 11:30, when we were alone [for a moment], Chloe said softly to me:
"I want to stay here. I want you to undress me." My heart leapt, but for

* The Pinacotheca, also known as the Rose Fried Gallery and located at 40 East Sixty-Eighth Street, is
now part of the Tate Gallery.

what? Kay took her home at 11:30. I was terribly disappointed, because if Chloe loved me, if she had any character, she'd have spent the night here. Leo called at 12:00. He's coming over, he said. So depressed—and thought, these are the times that prove men's souls. I wanted to call Ann—all those who truly love me. Was still crying when Leo got here. We took a walk till 3:00. Went to bed, decided not to drink so much next week. Certain I'll never get any sort of satisfaction from Chloe. I want a quiet life, don't need this level of excitement, need to work like a man. I need a woman—but one who loves me deeply and quietly.[GG]

10/16/43

Every artist possesses a core—and this core remains forever untouched. Untouched by the lover and the beloved. However much you may love a woman, she can never enter.

OCTOBER 17, 1943

[G]I finished the story: "The Three." Wrote well. Ann came over at 9:00 and she loved it. She can probably sell it somewhere. Yes, I am strong. Don't need anyone. Certainly not Chloe. I have my art, and my art alone is true.[GG]

OCTOBER 18, 1943

[G]A nice, strange day. Ran into Rosalind and Angelica when I went to 52nd St. to pick up my [phonograph] records. They had hangovers and invited me for a drink. Went to Billy The Oysterman.[*] I was terribly serious. Told them a lot about Chloe. I ultimately recited a few lines of the poem I wrote for Chloe. "So, you're doing great, then," she said. "What better use can you make of a person?" I had just said I didn't need anyone at all.

Couldn't get any work done this afternoon. I wanted to visit [Chloe]. Went to see her at 4 o'clock. God, yes! I remember the days when the chance touch of a girl's hand was heaven to me! And there she lay this afternoon on her bed, and allowed me to kiss her long and hard! And she finally opened her mouth and moved under me and caressed my cheeks! My God, how wonderful!

Swung by *Home & Food*, who want me to illustrate a story. And they've bought my last five spots. Very happy. Just this evening I typed

---

* Billy the Oysterman was one of the best-known seafood restaurants in New York in the 1930s and 1940s.

up my story, "The Three." *Harper's Bazaar* first, I think. Ann called
to tell me I'm a genius. She's read "Silver Horn of Plenty" five hundred
times. And Tex—jubilant about a six-pound beefsteak she had. And
finally—Chloe, the loveliest, at 12:30. She had spent the evening at Betty
Parsons' and ate with her. First she bumped into Rosalind at the Wakefield, because there was an opening. And of course R. invited Chloe for a
drink! At Giovanni [restaurant]. How envious would she be to learn that
I—I—have slept with Chloe six times![GG]

OCTOBER 19, 1943

[G]Yet another strange day. Becoming increasingly serious and increasingly happy without becoming overly self-satisfied. Getting older too. I
simply must write something good soon, and although it's all just words,
the ideas, the intentions are more than that. Work proceeded as usual,
i.e. not very well. Chloe wanted to see me, and I found her at Tony's at
5:40. She had three daiquiris with me. We talked about Rosalind, how I
loved—and love—her, and how I have never felt closer to her than I do
now, but that I am no longer in love with her. That's all true, but when
Chloe said R. bores her, and that she's a big phony (!), I was outraged.
Today I thought that the day will soon come when R. and I are together,
because I am always waiting, really, for her virtues, her mind, and her
wisdom—as these values of mine remain undiminished. Have much to
learn, but I'm a fast learner.[GG]

OCTOBER 20, 1943

[F]I gave Chloe a call. I'd like to see her Saturday night, but if it doesn't
happen, I won't eat my heart out. I'm thinking about my illustrations and
my story, and my days are full of work. Phoned Rosalind at 8:30. I told
her what Chloe said about her when she was drunk, and Rosalind said:
"A magnificent shell! But she bores me terribly. Chloe doesn't understand that the two people she loves—you and Betty—are my two closest
friends." I shouldn't be so nervous.[FF]

OCTOBER 21, 1943

[F]Tired at the office, and when I'm tired everything seems hopeless. Coffee
with Leo, and Chloe called at 5:30. Saturday night?—We'll see! she said.
4½ martinis with Leo, though I wanted to work. I don't know why I want
to drink but—anyway—I was very happy because Chloe phoned me. With
Rosalind—who wanted to see me—at 9:40—although Leo wanted to
make an evening of it. He understands everything, but what does it mat-

ter? "Is Chloe in love with you?" Rosalind asked. "Not at all," I answered.
"That's absurd." And so on and so forth. I really loved tonight a lot.[FF]

OCTOBER 22, 1943

[G]Very good, productive day, because I got nearly enough sleep. Wrote 7
pages this morning. It rained all day. And Chloe has influenza. Two martinis with Leo at 6:00 and dinner at Raffier's. Cleaned the whole house
because Chloe is probably coming over tomorrow evening. She had a
home visit from the doctor and is feeling a little better.[GG]

10/22/43

There will come a time, oh Methuselah, when you will want to declare
your independence of drink and of women. And be alone.

OCTOBER 23, 1943

[G]Terribly depressed to find out Chloe couldn't spend the night. She's
feeling worse. So instead—a drink with Leo—two—and lunch at Hamburger Mary. I've been talking about Rosalind so much (lately) that
he's completely forgotten about Chloe. Didn't get anything done in the
afternoon—this drinking really has got to stop! Two martinis with R.C.
at the Winslow. Had my notebook with me, and she paged through,
commenting on several passages written to Chloe, about Chloe—about
sleeping with women. She eventually said: "Is this your diary?" "No—it's
just literary." Very drunk later and disgusted with myself. Swear I won't
drink next week! I swear it![GG]

OCTOBER 24, 1943

[G]Sad, restless day. Felt hopeless at one o'clock—and went to Cocktail with Leo. Two martinis. Hamburger, and I confessed to him that I
don't want to go to Mexico because he thinks he's in love with me. He
threatened to break the neck of whomever else I might go with. Two
martinis—one brandy, and I felt like a character out of Kay Boyle's *Monday Night*. I have to do a lot of thinking about my life. There's a lot I
have to find myself and give myself. And what that ultimately means is—
writing. Went to my parents', who neither influence nor inspire me. Leo
brought me a magnificent big pumpkin. And only stayed a minute, like
a gentleman. Chloe called at 11:00 and my heart soared! My God, must
I always drink so much that I make a fool of myself? Smoking too much.
Chloe wants to meet Rolf. Probably Tuesday evening. And she wants to
[carve] the pumpkin with me some night.[GG]

OCTOBER 25, 1943

^GGramma arriving at 8:30 AM Thursday. Would go to the station, but prefer to see her first at Mother's house. That will be a happy moment! Chloe came over at 11:20 and stayed till 2:00, during which time we had the longest, most wonderful, most unbelievable kisses! Afterward she said she was crazy, that we were crazy, and that she worshipped me. Made plans to see Rosalind. She said "Yes" and called me "Patsy." They loved my illustrations (at *H & F*) and will probably give me a Christmas story to illustrate.^{GG}

OCTOBER 27, 1943

^GHappy day, but still very tired. Must run an experiment: 1) to get enough sleep 2) to find enough inner peace to dream 3) to write a book 4) to see the world as it truly is for the first time. Does that sound simple? ridiculous? childish? The greatest artists are always childish. I will start the experiment immediately. First and foremost is quieting my soul. Lunch with Rosalind. Told her what Chloe wants and doesn't want, etc. Finally admitted I'm governed by a perverse force, namely that I will stop loving a girl if she starts to love me more than I love her. "We all experience that," she responded sadly. Interesting. Wayne Lonergan, Patricia Lonergan's husband who probably killed her, is gay.* That's what Mother said this morning. Very interesting legal case, because they're both wealthy, etc. Maria and Angelica knew Patricia. Rosalind knows of many "boys" [and] "men" who are very scared, because they don't want their names to be made public.^{GG}

OCTOBER 28, 1943

^GGood day. Got good work done, because something like Gramma's arrival doesn't throw me off at all. Spoke at length with Jerry [Albert], whom I like more and more. Grandmother doesn't look as weak as I'd feared. She showed us lots of family photographs—which will finally be passed on to me. The prettiest one: that of my mother at age thirteen or fourteen. She was an angel! Goldberg called. He'll be in Mexico in January and is working on two books. Called me "Pat" (!) and I, awkward (as an ass), called him B.Z. for the first time. Joseph H. here. He's being court-martialed for disobeying some command or other at sea. Not at all

---

* New York socialite and heiress Patricia Burton Lonergan was found strangled in her bed on October 24, 1943. The murder trial, which ended with the conviction of her husband, Wayne Lonergan, galvanized the press and public. Interestingly, Dominick Dunne compares Lonergan to Patricia Highsmith's Tom Ripley in his article "The Talented Mr. Lonergan" for *Vanity Fair* in July 2000.

interested in seeing him. Texas said Wayne Lonergan (who just confessed to the murder) was at Mifflin's 1942–43 social. That means I met him, but I don't remember it.[GG]

OCTOBER 29, 1943

[G]Spoke with Hughes about Mexico. He doesn't want to let me go, because he says when a writer leaves the company, he never comes back. Too big a time difference between N.Y. and Mexico, etc. Today he dropped all sorts of hints to Camy and Leo, which means: if I go to Mexico, he'll fire me. Talked about it for too long (with Leo) and broke my nice weekly average. My thoughts always return to Chloe. I called her at 10:30 and was invited to spend the night. Of course I went, quick as a thunderbolt. First touched her as she pretended to be asleep, but did not try to arouse her. She was completely dry—really, while I was like a spring. Is that why she's barren? Frostie? Who knows. Götz called from [California] at 3:00 AM, and [they] talked for an hour while I sat in the other room. When I came back in, she kissed me as warmly as ever, but was all scattered.[GG]

OCTOBER 31, 1943

[G]Chloe called me at 1:30—she wanted to see me right away: [she was expecting] a telegram—from Götz, and she couldn't open it. She claimed to have left him at 5:00 AM. Didn't know if I should believe her. Broke my engagements with [Raphael] Mahler, Mother and Ann T.—and went to bed with her. The telegram interrupted us—"Donnie was right and I will never not feel it. And maybe we'll live again I do not know. I have struggled with my arcangel and I have lost. I'll write you one more let-ter." Götz. She showed no emotion—for ten minutes. Then she began to shake, and drank whatever was in the house. She wanted more to drink, and finally, after we put together an answer, we went (she in a skirt with nothing on underneath) to Longchamps. 1½ martinis. Then we came back and went to bed. I made love to her—her first time with a woman—and the earth didn't shake—but I did it well enough—and nothing mat-ters but that I made her happy for a minute. My God, when all of her was on my lips, I knew I would find no peace if I could not express what I had to—love. So I did. Have so much to think about. But one thing is certain: [the time has come to] write something important. Something neces-sary. Something big. A major dream of my being, from deep within. The poems will come later. My heart, though, is full—far too full tonight. It won't allow itself to be poured out.[GG]

NOVEMBER 1, 1943

^GI was swimming in confusion all day: how long will Chloe last? What should I do now, since I never finished my last story? And what about Mexico—up until this evening, I thought I had to know happiness and peace (yes, peace). Otherwise there's no making art or writing. Got good work done. It feels strange, after yesterday, to see my mouth as always, my fingers at work as always, my eyes as always. And I made a woman happy! Today or yesterday evening Chandler suffered through an appendectomy. Chloe is of course very concerned, and I'm happy about that. Reading [Julien Green's] *Closed Garden* with great pleasure.^{GG}

NOVEMBER 2, 1943

^GUneasy all day, and smoked [a lot], despite getting good work done. Spoke to Chloe at 2:30; Chandler's condition is worsening, and Chloe's leaving for California right away. "You'll be happier if I go." "My God! What kind of perversion do you think I have?" I screamed, almost in tears. How sad. How sick and how hopeless! Had the strange and rare pleasure of drinking my own rum by myself. Like a gentleman, like a wise man, and went by Chloe's with a nice, small salad. Kissed her masterfully as she lay on her bed. "You drive me crazy!" she kept whispering. Quiet—heavy—her kisses are heaven!^{GG}

NOVEMBER 3, 1943

^GHappy day—because Mexico is set! Spoke to Hughes about it, and although he can't guarantee my pay, I think he'll try. I.e., I can send stories back to him. News received quietly at my parents', [they're] convinced I'll achieve success in Mexico. Goldberg at 8:30. He gives me so much! Encouragement, etc. and always convinces me I'm a writer. I have got to write a novel in Mexico. Chloe or no Chloe—I'm going!^{GG}

NOVEMBER 4, 1943

^GTold Chloe that I want to leave for Mexico as soon as possible. "Then I'll come with you," she responded. My heart soared! Chloe has an engagement tomorrow evening with Kiki Preston*—a decadent, depraved woman she met a long time ago. Had to go to the theater drunk,

<hr />

* Kiki Preston, née Alice Gwynne (1898–1946), American socialite, distantly related to the Vanderbilt and Whitney families, and a member of the hedonistic Happy Valley set in Kenya. Known for her beauty, her drug addiction, and her many lovers, she allegedly had an illegitimate child with Prince George, Duke of Kent, son of King George V.

Petrouchka. Impatient. Then went straight to Rosalind's. Cutty Sark with Rosalind till two.[GG]

11/6/43

Necessary to be alone to realize how sad one is. And just as necessary to be alone to realize how happy. The last sensation is the rarer and more amazing. But for the happy one the blessings are without end.

11/6/43

An artist cannot live with himself and with a woman, too. How this has ever been arranged I cannot understand.

NOVEMBER 7, 1943

[G]Chloe brought me a bouquet—one rose—several chrysanthemums—which I will keep for the rest of my life. She wants to spend "one month—maybe three" in Palm Springs. And doesn't want to see her husband now. Kiki invited her to stay with her. That's the latest. And it's plenty.[GG]

NOVEMBER 8, 1943

[G]Almost sick all day. Didn't hear from Chloe. She's doubtless shifted her plans again. She shifts faster than the Russian front. Learning Spanish—studying hard.[GG]

NOVEMBER 8, 1943

[G]Nice day. Wore moccasins to work with great success. Stopped by Missouri Pacific [Railroad]. 190.00 roundtrip, and I could have left the 28th. After a conversation with my parents, though, I've decided not to leave before the tenth of December. Worked hard and felt very excited, satisfied, and happy.—But I still want to leave this city. Chloe is staying in Palm Springs for a week. Reading poems.[GG]

11/10/43

Sentiment comes suddenly, in the juice of love, sympathy, sexual emotion desire. It turns on at the turn of your companion's phrase, as a faucet turns. And consciousness can shut it off as soon.

NOVEMBER 11, 1943

[G]Happy day. I'm entering a manic period where I need little sleep or food. Chloe moved to Kiki Preston's this afternoon. For nine days—

officially. Keep getting thinner, although I'm eating a lot. Gramma and Mother very curious about my feelings for Chloe, "Why?" and "What does she have [to offer]?" and "I'd like to learn what strange power this girl has!"GG

NOVEMBER 12, 1943

GCan't get a seat on the train before December 12. That's fine. A secret was revealed at home: We don't like Grandma. She's jealous, talks too much, wants to spend lots of money, and doesn't show any thoughtfulness [toward] Mother. It concerns me to see Mother still trying to understand Grandma, change her, show her where she's wrong. And that Mother's always searching for something that was never there.

A letter tonight from Allela—it was very nice, saying she still loves me, etc. I had to respond right away. Tonight, without the least effort, I began to dream up my novel. That's healthy. The work comes much later.GG

11/12/43

More than most writers realize, or admit, inspiration, whole story places, come from visual objects. a house, a suitcase, a glove in a gutter. Why say indirectly? If indirectly, it is so simple to trace the development, that it becomes directly responsible.

NOVEMBER 13, 1943

G2 martinis with Leo. We're growing apart and awkward and are not happy together. He's living fast, doing lots of little things, but probably lacks the virtue for any bigger dream. That's the dream that makes a great artist.

Went to the Martin Beck Theatre* at 2:45 with Mother and Grandma. K. Dunham† very thrilling, but not like Carmen Amaya. Hurried home. Needed lots of things, which cost me a lot. More gin. It's always the alcohol that makes me poor. Chloe came over at 6:30. I wanted to get her drunk this evening, but without success. She had to go to Kiki's, who's very sick. Chloe said that if she were to fall in love with a woman, it

---

* The Martin Beck Theatre in midtown Manhattan opened on November 11, 1924, and was renamed the Al Hirschfeld Theater in 2003.

† Katherine Dunham (1909–2006), American dancer, choreographer, anthropologist, and activist. In 1937, she founded the all-Black Negro Dance Group, using their performances to protest against segregation. She was one of the first African American choreographers at the Metropolitan Opera in New York. Her dance students included James Dean and Marlon Brando.

would be me. But that she prefers men. It's wonderful—how much drive one has when one's woman leaves in the night. That's how I feel this minute. It was extremely maddening, because I wanted her badly.

Want to get so much done before I leave. And thinking about my book.[GG]

NOVEMBER 14, 1943

[G]Wasted so much time again, but that's how every Sunday goes. Breakfast at my parents', because I'm so lonely when I don't have Chloe. That probably makes me a coward. Then I had to take a walk with Mother, and we hurried to the nearest bar. We [spoke] frankly about my grandmother. Something must be done, because she has the intention of coming here every summer. Mother will grow old, because she drives us all to drinking.

Chloe called. She's worried she could ruin me if we spend time together. I have the strength, the ability, the power, or the indifference to shrug that off. Happy, and unhappy, definitely very busy.[GG]

NOVEMBER 15, 1943

[G]Ordered two seats on the train. Dec. 11 and 12. Chloe is coming with me, I say, because she doesn't have any big plans for herself. I, at least, am decisive, and she's coming with me, if only as a result of my orneriness. Called her at 2:00, told her what I'd done, and she replied: "Good!" Went to the Wakefield Gallery—no Bernhard, but Rosalind, Natasha, and the Calkins, all very friendly toward me. Feel happy.

Jerry is doubtless going to war November 26.

$340.26 in the bank.[GG]

NOVEMBER 18, 1943

[G]Rosalind and Betty came over at 9:30. They were very formal at first, but eventually Chloe called: she and Kiki wanted to stop by for a visit. Kiki is slim,[GG] an old bag from way back. [G]Chloe very drunk when she arrived. Rosalind enjoyed herself immensely. Cheese and Scotch, and long pauses, full of meaning. Kiki was determined not to leave without Chloe, but Betty Parsons somehow managed to throw her out of the house. Betty likes my sketches and paintings. And she wants to include several of them in her next show! Betty liked me very much this evening, and I liked her. Happy about nothing—but especially about my work and my wonderful life! I want to do lots of things. I want to be a giant![GG]

NOVEMBER 19, 1943

^GI'm tremendously happy that Chloe has finally decided to come with me. We spoke for a long time today. She has an income of 81.50 per month. She'll be rich in Mexico, but has little cash at the moment. I'll buy her one-way ticket. Not concerned about it, except maybe about not being concerned.^{GG}

NOVEMBER 20, 1943

^FHappy but terribly nervous. In this instant, after an evening with Chloe, I am completely free of her. Now—with 7 hours of sleep in 48 hours, I want to write, read, do all of the calm and spiritual things which have always occupied me. I am full of strength. Worked with great difficulty of course. I have only $165 in the bank, and after I bought Chloe's ticket, $64.00. A brandy with Camy, who is dearer and dearer to me. The Chagall exhibition—marvelous! He's my old favorite. Also Tamayo*—not good. Camy here at 6:45 to get my table, and no doubt to meet Chloe. He was extremely attentive, cleaned my kitchen, etc. and gave me a massage because I was completely spent. Then Chloe at 7:30. A bit drunk, but she likes Camy and he likes her. Finally alone at 9:00. Chloe very sweet, told me that Kiki tried to give her dope. Kiki rushed into the bathroom on Thursday night, Betty said, to take five big pills. Chloe still wants to go to Mexico. But Kiki, who's worried about Chloe leaving, will do anything to keep her here. And Chloe?—It would hardly make any difference if she didn't come.^{FF}

NOVEMBER 21, 1943

^FGood day—slept until 11:30 when I went to have lunch with my parents. I told them all about Chloe. My mother didn't say much, but was certainly interested. Chloe spoke seriously of our trip for the first time. I gave her instructions on how to obtain her visa. The little darling—she should have a man to do all of this, and I'll do it with pleasure. My parents will probably give me $100. And as a Christmas gift, I'll accept it. At the Museum of Modern Art. Very inspiring. Romantic painting. Oh, I want to paint in Mexico! And made some progress on this long road which will return me to myself. Tranquility is of the essence. But it's difficult—when Kiki could be, at this very moment, in Chloe's bed, giv-

---

* Rufino Tamayo (1899–1991), Mexican painter who painted figurative abstraction with surrealist influences.

ing her dope pills. It deeply troubles me. But in three weeks—less than three weeks—she can't form a habit.[FF]

NOVEMBER 22, 1943

[G]Lunch with Parsons at Del Pezzo. Of course Betty and I spoke mostly about Chloe. She told the sad story of her divorce from her husband.[*] Chloe called me at 3:15. Very despondent and sad. Wanted to leave for Mexico tonight.

Sketched very poorly in class, and don't know why. I have to write to rediscover my self-esteem. God give Chloe the strength to endure these two and a half weeks![GG]

NOVEMBER 24, 1943

[F]Arrived at the office at 11:30 because I had to get some sleep this morning. My tooth hurt so much I couldn't fall asleep until 6:00 AM. Hughes very cold when I came into the office. Jerry said that Hughes always comes into my office when I'm not there. He thinks I spend a lot of time out of the office. At the dentist's at 2:30. The tooth has an abscess and I'll have to get two pulled. The wisdom tooth too. Chloe phoned me at 1:00. Very serious, and not at all drunk. "I'll lose my reputation, but what's the good of a reputation anyway?" I didn't know what to say. "And for whose sake if not yours, my love?" I'll lose mine too—no—but what a great, beautiful loss![FF]

NOVEMBER 25, 1943

[G]Chloe very sweet. I feel more warmly toward her, but still feel shy kissing her. For instance, when I do make the first move, she reponds to me as a lover would. She's concerned I'll fall in love with a Mexican girl. "And where will that leave me?" she asked sadly, smiling.[GG]

NOVEMBER 26, 1943

[F]I'm happy when I think about our departure. We will be together at my parents' house, and it will likely be the closest experience to a honeymoon I will ever know. And the parents will know. The day will come when Chloe, upon waking, will look at me pensively and ask herself, "Who are you?" And I will know then that she is cured and no longer needs me. I will try not to be sad. Leo continues to make outrageous

---

[*] In 1919, Betty married Schuyler Livingston Parsons, a New York socialite ten years her senior, who her family hoped would inspire her to embrace a more conventional lifestyle. They divorced in 1922.

remarks about Chloe, and if I had more respect for my Chloe, I'd punch him!^{FF}

NOVEMBER 27, 1943

^FA miserable day. I haven't done any work in three months, and I'm not lying. I can't seem to collect myself. But my desire to work grows every day. And right now, I am incomplete. I brought all my records to Rosalind in a suitcase. Rum at her place at 4:15, then the Berman* exhibition at J. Levy. Julien not very friendly, but Muriel smiling, very sweet. Then Wakefield, where R., Betty and I were like old friends. 2 martinis, while I was thinking of Chloe. Dinner with Camy, and I was rather drunk. He likely knows everything there is to know about Chloe and myself.^{FF}

NOVEMBER 28, 1943

^GWorked hard and feel happier. Mother had the audacity to call at 9:15 AM, while I was still sleeping. Yes, I want to live like a professor—my quiet hours, my tea, my books, different projects, different studies. The only tumult should be internal. Life is tumultuous as is, but inner tumult is the only kind compatible with work.

Cocktails at my parents' with Bernhard. She looked at my grand mother's photographs. I love Bernhard very much. Nervous dinner with the family. I'm not talking much to Gramma, and although she notices, there's not much I can do to help. Menstruating—a week early. Am very aroused, though, and want Chloe like a husband wants his wife.

Thinking about my novel.^{GG}

NOVEMBER 29, 1943

^GMy grandmother leaves by train tomorrow. Oh! How happy, how excited I was when she arrived. But the terrible feeling grew stronger and stronger—I don't love her. I can't love her. I want these remaining ten days to be quiet. We'll see. I want it with all my heart. I want it more than I want a woman. Thinking about my novel.^{GG}

NOVEMBER 30, 1943

^GHardest, most furious day of my life. Had tooth pulled from 7–8. Perlman gave me 3 Scotches. Hadn't gone under when he pulled the tooth. The same horrific dreams in which Chloe was the only woman in the world, in the entire cosmos, and I knew everything about every-

* Eugene Berman (1899–1972), Russian-born American neoromantic-turned-surrealist painter.

thing, and that the whole world, and history, was a performance for my pleasure! Yes—I felt guilty and weak by comparison—but I was utterly dependent.[GG]

DECEMBER 2, 1943

[G]Terrible day. Saw Dr. B. at 1:00. Vaccine against typhus. Very quick. About a half teaspoon. Afterward I went to Lechay's[*] exhibit. Good watercolors. Big, fine-tasting cup of coffee at Hamburger Heaven. Maybe that's why I got sick so quickly. Nauseous and faint, and I thought without a doubt I'd die. Am certain the doctor gave me a bad vaccine and I could have died. A small child can endure all manner of vaccines, because he doesn't know what he's enduring. But I—with an all too active imagination for bodily pain—cannot endure it. Fever and headache. Typhus.[GG]

DECEMBER 3, 1943

[G]Got my "PASE" to México. Very easy at the consulate-general. I want to plan my entire life. I want the peace of "Come, sweet death!" Quiet days, and a woman?—there I'm not so sure.[GG]

DECEMBER 4, 1943

[G]Doctor Mahler stopped by with three gifts for the Rosenbergs. Two pairs of nylons, [Pearl S. Buck's novel] *Dragon Seed*, and a box of almonds for me. And an oil painting—luckily small. Met Rosalind at 5:00. She paid me the highest compliment, that she only counts Natasha, Betty, and me as friends. That it will be a lonely Christmas, because I won't be here. Went to Chloe's at 8:00. Fever of 103.4. Tony Werner said that the Spanish influenza was highly contagious and an epidemic. I took no precautions against it. Odd—that I want Chloe and don't want her, that I'm convinced I can do everything I want to do with or without her. Restless again. Have much to do, and wasted most of the day.[GG]

12/4/43

God showed a ribald sense of humor when he created the physical body. When I die, I'll think of the sweating, the shivering, the headaches, the unsuccessful love making, the effort of getting up in the morning, and

---

[*] James Lechay (1907–2001), American painter, leader of the Artists Union (an organization of artists employed by the Works Progress Administration), organizer of exhibits of works by Milton Avery, Max Weber, and other WPA artists. In both 1942 and 1943 he was exhibited at the Ferargil Galleries.

laugh so hard that I'll split my sides, if I have any. Then I will live in the realm of pure thought and artistic perception and perfection. But I shall not be so surprised as most, because I expected it all along. Nevertheless, I shall be among the most grateful.

DECEMBER 5, 1943

GChloe's getting better. Her fever is gone and she took a bath. Wanted to go out! Prepared all sorts of books, boxes, etc. (with Mother). Have nothing more to do. I'm taking very few books. Thinking a lot about Rosalind—who made me so happy yesterday. Surely I must truly love her—now that the fire has gone—now that love remains. Now—but first I must make something of myself.GG

12/5/43

I met you by accident. I loved you by accident, and immediately. My love grows more beautiful each year as a good piano grows more rich. As in the first days when my dreams were all future with you, now my thoughts are of us together, the future being much sooner. Now I am solid, without the drunkenness and the unreal excitement and the uncertainty of the trials and tests of each new encounter in each evening. Surely what exists now is love, and surely I have never known it before.

DECEMBER 7, 1943

GSpoke to Ann T. Ellen B. killed herself three weeks ago in Westport. Suicide, with a pistol. It really all goes back to the night when Chloe didn't call me. It's why I got drunk the next night—and Ann stayed [over] and told Ellen all of it, and she wasn't the same after that. Chloe—you really are Helen III of Troy! Spoke to Rosalind, who will always be dear to me. My parents are very concerned because I mentioned I might live with Rosalind someday. "I'd much rather see you with a husband and family," Mother said. Naturally, but I'm not exactly one with nature. Got ready. For my destiny.GG

DECEMBER 8, 1943

GTerribly nervous. I don't know if I can do anything to improve my nerves, or if they'll grow perpetually worse till I'm dead and buried. Met Perlman at 6:00. Ate at Palm Restaurant, 49th St. Fantastic steaks, $3.00 apiece. I didn't want to eat much, though. I want to think, live slowly, compare and taste everything—as one must always live. Radio City— where the movies were so boring I had to get up and call Chloe. Bored to tears is an everyday condition of mine. Perlman guilty of various devilries—he kissed me, to my utter disgust!^{GG}

DECEMBER 9, 1943

^GWorked as always. Mother came by at 12:30 and met Jerry—he thinks I'm "prettier" than my mother. Something dumb as that must mean he's fallen in love with me. Bought shoes, bags, and gifts for the Plangmans. And best of all—Chloe got her visa. The men in the office were of course very polite! Why wouldn't they be? Has Mexico ever seen such a woman?

Jerry gave me Burns Mantle's [*Best*] *Plays*[*] —with an inscription— very kind. I love him very much—and what a strange start (nothing physical until only two weeks ago!).^{GG}

DECEMBER 11, 1943

^GYOU FAITHFULLY SEEK THE ILL AND ERRING AND WE HASTEN WITH WEAK YET EAGER STEPS—TO YOU—TO YOU[†]—We are sick—but together, thank God—^{GG}

DECEMBER 14, 1943

^GSan Antonio at 7:00 AM. Had to find a dentist immediately and saw one at 9:00. Later—finally, peace. Eons later.^{GG}

DECEMBER 14, 1943

^GStill quiet. Still scared. Tooth is worse. Breakfast next door to our terrible, bleak hotel, and later looked for a dentist. Doctor Durbeck, who was supposed to X-ray me. "Abscess, no doubt," he said. A big incision, lots of blood. My fears remain, but I am fighting them with all my might. Finally together with Chloe—who had a headache, who can think of nothing else, we came back to our hotel, still pretty quiet. Chloe thinks I've abandoned her, that I'm a Jekyll-Hyde person.

On the train at 7:30. Much happier, because I thought my suffering was over, my tooth better. In Laredo tonight. We rode [past] the Grand Canyon very late, 1:30 in the morning. Covered wagons, the people quiet, looking at each other meaningfully. Presented our visas. Mexican officers. The censor read our letters, all from G. v. E. [Götz van Eyck]

---

* Robert Burns Mantle (1873–1948) was an American theater critic who founded the annual publication *Best Plays*.
† Fragments from Johann Sebastian Bach's cantata *Jesu, der du meine Seele*.

to Chloe. And he wouldn't let mine in, because there were too many. I should have stayed overnight in Laredo, but C. was afraid of arriving in Mexico alone. She was also afraid of spending the night with me in Laredo. Had to send my luggage back to N.Y., and Ch. promised to pay. She was almost hysterically happy tonight.

But in the morning—[GG]

DECEMBER 15, 1943

[G]—in the morning always so much worse. And the doctors can't do a thing. Read X Science all day, although it doesn't work with Chloe. She isn't happy with anything—I keep leaving her alone, and it's always my fault.[GG]

DECEMBER 16, 1943

[G]The long journey through Mexico, Laredo to Mexico—D.F.[*] Poor children, poor women selling all sorts of things in the villages. They beg and are very clever. C. wants to give away her money, and I must control her. I prefer to learn the language and customs.[GG]

DECEMBER 17, 1943

[G]Reached the Hotel Montejo. Chloe found it. Very charming. Very cheap for gringos. $20.00 a day. I can't write here, the way I want to—this city is wonderful—and not very alien. Chloe very sad, and I keep saying that I'm really quite sick, and that's all. I'm scared, and I can't be myself. Visited the Rosenbergs. Very nice. Rosenberg sold two tickets for a conert at the Palacio de Bellas Artes this evening. It's very inconvenient not to have any of my clothes. If I'd done that to C., she'd never have forgiven me! The books and sketch paper too.[GG]

DECEMBER 18, 1943

[G]For the first time—I heard C. really cuss me out! Two tequila cocktails at 6:00. She said she's better than me, that I'm neurotic, that she wants to leave for Cal. [California] immediately. That I'm a liar. "Why did you invite me to come to Mexico?" Yes—that was tough—![GG]

12/20/43

It is difficult. Yes, yes, it is difficult. So difficult—all the way to the grave.

---

* De Efe/Distrito Federal, or Mexico City.

DECEMBER 21, 1943

[G]Terrible evening with Gene Rossi and his friend Lew Miller, who picked us up as we sat drinking at the restaurant. 2 daiquiris here, plenty, but then another at Tony's. Then Ciro's,[*] a wonderfully sleek nightclub run by Blumenthal,[†] Peggy Fears's[‡] husband. Very very nice, and Chloe very, very pretty. I was wearing my gray suit, which always depresses me. But what does it matter, when Chloe is so beautiful? Lew very serious, because he recently returned from war. Went to Casanova's later. Chloe drank much too much. A certain "Teddy Stauffer"[§] runs the Casanova. Chloe ran into several friends from California and Hollywood. But I didn't drink a thing and was almost bored to tears.[GG]

DECEMBER 22, 1943

[G]Want to buy Chloe a chihuahua for Christmas. It will be like having a child. I'll be very happy once we leave this city. But I'm well aware that it's the best part of the trip for Chloe. Or maybe not. I can't know that for certain. But this city disgusts me, and it's not even Mexico! Saw a wonderful market. They sell all types of figures, animals, people and birds for Christmas decorations. Gene came over, very persistent, very rude, but I have to say, Chloe encourages him. He wants to take her to the horse races Thursday. And to a social Christmas Eve. The twenty-fourth. Lots of Chloe's friends will be there, and I expect she'll go. But not me.[GG]

DECEMBER 23, 1943

[F]Our days are becoming more and more disorganized. We don't get up early, of course, but 9—10—11—whenever. I went to the hospital, where Barrera was. He's about forty, very friendly, and devoted to Betty Parsons. He doesn't like socializing. He suggested we take a house—one week in San Miguel Allende, perhaps. The town Tamayo works in.

---

* Ciro's was a flashy cabaret in the Hotel Reforma decorated with murals by Diego Rivera. Until it closed in 1948, it was one of Mexico City's most luxurious venues, attracting a crowd of rich expats, royals, diplomats, and artists.

† Theatrical promoter Alfred Cleveland Blumenthal (1885–1957) made his fortune in real estate before he left the United States for Mexico to escape the U.S. tax authorities. Ciro's presented him with a useful front in his next business venture, drug trafficking.

‡ Peggy Fears (1903–1994), a former Ziegfeld Follies showgirl, appeared in Broadway musical comedies before becoming a Broadway producer with her husband, Alfred Blumenthal. They were responsible for productions such as the 1932–1933 show *Music in the Air*.

§ Teddy Stauffer (1909–1991), Swiss jazz musician, swing band leader, and hotel and club owner, helped transform Acapulco from a small fishing village into a vacation destination for Hollywood film stars such as Hedy Lamarr, whom he would later marry.

Watched Chloe as she dressed herself for an hour and a half. For Teddy Stauffer. She changed her mind again and again—but I was having fun, and she left very happy. Thought of my novel all evening. Work is going well—even though I'm here. And yet I'm happy. It's past midnight, and Chloe's not back yet. I'm reading Blake and Donne with great pleasure.[FF]

DECEMBER 24, 1943

[F]Last night Chloe got home at 5:35 AM. Naturally we didn't get up before 11. We took a five-hour walk, until I was exhausted! Branches for a manger. I made it myself from 6–8, it's splendid. Jesus is larger than his mother and father. I also made a white, innocent sheep, and an angel, who watches the scene in supplication. Green, with lots of flowers I bought at the market. It made me very happy.

Chloe was supposed to come home to have dinner with me, but she was with Gene Rossi. She doesn't like him, but he creates an interesting situation in which Teddy is jealous of Gene, and vice versa. Teddy Stauffer sent an orchid. It all provides me with innocent amusement, because I always want Chloe to do what she wants. It's 2:00 A.M. now. She said she'd be home early! I ate alone, thinking of the good music that they are playing now in New York, thinking of my family, of Rosalind, to whom I wrote 8 pages tonight—telling her all about my teeth, my troubles, etc. I am filled with satisfaction—thanks to God. The manger is standing by my bed. The angels will fly all night. Their wings will caress me. God bless Chloe tonight, and give her peace. Show her that the truth is within and not without, that the joys of the spirit are the only joys. Teach her selflessness, and the meaning of love. And send her a shining new year.[FF]

DECEMBER 25, 1943

[G]The saddest, most wonderful day. It wasn't Christmas. Like any other depressing day, we slept till 11 o'clock. Big breakfast ($8.00), which I paid, but no presents—I just gave Chloe a nice, big bar of chocolate. She didn't give me anything. At 4:30 we took a walk to Chapultepec Bosque,* where the museum was closed, but where I met a group of friendly soldiers. One talked to me for nearly two hours. It was cold and damp, and we laughed to keep warm. It was the one thing that felt most like Christmas. Teddy invited me over with Chloe. We three had nothing to say.

---

* Bosque de Chapultepec is a large park in central Mexico City.

Chloe never has anything to say—she just drinks. Finally dinner came, but Chloe didn't like it: everything could have been so much nicer. Everything. But it's utterly impossible, as is always impossible with Chloe.

Chloe got into a taxi with Teddy for several minutes. I didn't know if she would spend the night with him, but it was unlikely. She encourages the men, but doesn't give them anything, just like she's never given me anything. But I was in tears as I wrote her a letter [about] how she never would, or could, share anything with me, how I wanted nothing from her but soil for my searching roots. She got back at 3:00. Read my letter—as I blushed in shame. But where to?—Where to—and why? We are done—there's nothing left. I fell asleep with a piece of the chocolate I had given her in my mouth.GG

DECEMBER 26, 1943

GChloe and I went to Chapultepec Bosque, but we got there at 2:30 and the museum was closed. And Chloe, exhausted through and through, had to take a taxi back to the hotel. That's right! God! I shouldn't record such trifles! I should be occupying myself with work! Why do I still mention Chloe? It's ridiculous, and the sooner I'm free of her, the better for me and for everything I hope to accomplish!GG

DECEMBER 27, 1943

GTried to find my luggage from N.Y. Had to go to the Palacio Nacional, etc., and ultimately—it hasn't arrived. I went for a walk at midnight. A man, Hernando Camacho, followed me, and I went with him and his friend to Casanova, where Chloe was with Teddy. I like Camacho very much—although Del P. is the only man I love. We danced (!)—me in huaraches and a black shirt, and we drank tequilas. He kissed me when we got home. He has a brain, and it isn't bad. Regarding Chloe, he said—"Beautiful, but phrenologically speaking nonentity." Wants to ride horses with me tomorrow. Yes—like him very much!GG

DECEMBER 28, 1943

GBarrera is—as Chloe says—without a doubt homosexual. I—yes, I would have sensed it now too. All Proust, *Well of Loneliness,** in his books; and *su amigo* Augusto was at his house again. Decided what I'm

---

* *Well of Loneliness*, a lesbian romance by British author Radclyffe Hall, portrays homosexuality as a natural, God-given state and makes an explicit plea: "Give us also the right to our existence."

going to give Allela for her birthday: a silver bracelet with her name on it. I'll buy one for myself too. And I so hope she'll love it.^{GG}

DECEMBER 29, 1943

^GMy novel needs so much work, and I've been thinking about it, of course, all day. Although much of the story remains to be constructed, I think I can get good work done with my notebooks. Yes—God—what a terrible life Chloe creates for herself! It's sad that she can never forget it, and that she'll be bored and alone in some small town, in real life. Spent the evening with my friends Camacho and España again. Went to a Mexican cinema. I am rich in spirit—and I want to move on. Am happiest when imagining my new life on my own. We moved into a smaller room. Chloe only has about ten pesos left till January 4th. I can't always pay two bills.^{GG}

DECEMBER 30, 1943

^GWent to El Horreo,* but there was no letter. Feel sad about it, and glum. Talked to Barrera, who kindly invited me over tomorrow evening. Mass at church followed by a buffet. I'm very happy about it—I'd love nothing better.^{GG}

12/30/43

Mexico, D.F.—it is so beautiful and the Americans have made it so stinking.

DECEMBER 31, 1943

^GJalapa—Jalapa—Jalapa—I love your name! What have you got for me? Two weeks here already! Spent so much money that I'd be concerned, were it not for the knowledge that I can soon leave for the village. Bernhard said I should be very industrious—and that's why—and for the benefit of my soul—I want to start working now! Rode the second-class omnibus today. Lots of fun, and the people are good and friendly. It's simple, and I like that. I know what disgusts me about this city. It's that I'm not spending enough time by myself. I can't work—i.e., dream without being alone, no more than one can sleep and dream together.

Didn't eat enough today, and one tequila with Chloe at 9:30 nearly wrecked me. Chloe and Teddy left at 10:45. I went to the tavern, where

---

* Unclear, possibly the name of a restaurant Pat had her mail delivered to.

I found España. Another tequila. Then finally Barrera and Augusto. We went to a church—San Filipe—for midnight. Afterward—in the street, we embraced and wished each other a *feliz año nuevo*. Barrera's house—my God, how beautiful! A big table—*ponche caliente con rhum—queso y jamón—tambien caliente—sopa de jitomate—vino*. Barrera couldn't have been more lovely and kind. Barrera and Augusto were wearing ties and shirts with the same pattern, but different colors. After coffee we drove to Chapultepec Heights in Augusto's car—till 4 in the morning. This was the best New Year's Eve I've ever had! Yes—a home! A house—a house for living in! That's what I want! Chloe got back at 4:15. She was drunk, ugly, and dog-tired.[GG]

12/31/43

I hope I sometime pass a new year when my heart is not somewhere where I am not.

1944

PATRICIA HIGHSMITH'S FIRST trip abroad is so important to her that she dedicates a separate diary to it—the aptly named "Mexico Diary," composed in German, French, and rudimentary Spanish. After the tumultuous beginning of her journey, and hoping to finally find the peace and quiet she feels she needs to write, Pat is soon ready to leave not only Mexico City, but also Chloe behind.

Continuing on her travels solo, Pat moves on to Taxco, a picturesque colonial town famed for its silver mining and jewelry production. She spends most of her time there in the highlands, where she withdraws into the cottage she's rented—Casa Chiquita—to work on *The Click of the Shutting*. The novel centers around Gregory, an artistically talented teenager who cannot yet stand on his own two feet. Prone to feelings of inferiority and bouts of infatuation with other boys, he ultimately weasels his way into the life of a rich, spoiled young man—much like Tom Ripley will later insinuate himself into Dickie Greenleaf's. Indeed, Pat herself later comes to see Gregory as a prototype for Tom Ripley; this earlier character is her first literary foray into the great wide world of alter egos, which have otherwise been relegated to her comic book scripts.

Pat remains torn between becoming a painter or writer and imposes a strict work regimen on herself: she paints in the morning, before the light grows harsh, and writes in the evening. She pens yearning missives to her mother and friends back in New York, hundreds of pages of diary and notebook entries, and pointed character descriptions, which she will later transpose into tragic short stories about expats who succumb to alcohol and the exotic in Mexico.

In early May, Pat sets out for home, destitute and exhausted from the Mexican heat, the countless benders, and the futile search for a female lover who really inspires her. On the way back, however, she stops off in Fort Worth to visit her grandmother Willie Mae. She does not write in her diary from May 12 through November 14, a lapse she attributes to her days simply being too full and happy for journaling.

Back in New York, Pat worries again that her work in comics—a more lucrative endeavor, now that she is pursuing it freelance—could be detrimental to her writing. Still, by the end of the year, she manages to secure the help of a literary agent named Jacques Chambrun to sell her stories and her novel-in-progress.

During this time, Pat dates various women concurrently, as is her wont. By late September, though, her relationship with a wealthy heiress from Philadelphia named Natica Waterbury emerges as the most important and lasting thus far. Pat is taken with Natica's daredevil feats (she flies planes) and literary interests (she was Sylvia Beach's assistant at Shakespeare & Company in Paris), but is forced to share her with another well-heeled scion from Philadelphia: Virginia Kent Catherwood, daughter of inventor and manufacturer Arthur Atwater Kent. Both women will profoundly inspire her in life and work for years to come.

❧

JANUARY 1, 1944

SPBoarded the bus at six. Chloe kissed me several times. Jalapa at 12:30. Walked through the town all morning. Very pretty.SPSP

JANUARY 3, 1944

FA marvelous day—some of the streets of this town make me feel almost sick with happiness. It makes something break in my heart—that these people live as God intends them to. For example, at eleven o'clock I heard music coming from a house—Mozart—and when I stopped close to the window to listen, an old man observed me, smiling. Finally, he stopped too, and wished me a happy new year—"*Feliz año, señorita!*"

But my room is cold.FF

1/4/44

Languages—are like games, trying on the brain, competitive between yourself and the native. You and he play by the same rules, as everyone else in the country, and your successes are mildly exhilarating, like points won in sports.

JANUARY 4, 1944

FA horrible day in a horrible room. Sent Chloe two telegrams. The first to ask if she'll come, the second to tell her that I'll come—will leave here tomorrow night. "Vamos a Acapulco," I wrote. She'll be happy, and so will I—it's hot there.[FF]

JANUARY 6, 1944

[F]Rather cold en route. Chloe wasn't there. I took our old room. Hungry, freezing in the morning. Rang Teddy S. who knew her whereabouts. An apartment in Tabasco 130. Joined her at 1:00. She didn't ask me to move in with her.[FF] "You must admit that we didn't really get along great." [F]No letter from New York. Why, with people who truly understand me—why am I always so reserved? Tonight I love Cornell—I have always loved her soul, but tonight I love her—and not because I have finally separated from Chloe, or because I am alone. It's because I am now beginning to see the truth, and beginning to live—and because I am beginning to write out of love for writing.[FF]

1/6/44

A new year's wish—to live with as much dignity as the servant, Pedro, whom I met in Jalapa. He is an a man of fifty or sixty, with grizzled hair close-cut on a round head. He stands upright with a sturdy chest bulging under his shirt, and he smiles easily. He loves to talk, small talk, friendly talk, lit with a personal imagination. His hands are rough and knobby with work, but he says proudly as he greets you, "I bring in my hand the warmth of my master's hand."

JANUARY 7, 1944

[F]Made a new friend, "Larry" H. I think we'll grow very fond of each other in Taxco. Exciting to get there. The road winding up through mountainous landscape, and the stretch before the town is breathtak-ing. Thought of Chloe—with no tenderness in my heart. Felt the urge of writing her that I don't want to see her when she comes to Taxco. That she's never been my friend. Arrived at destination at 1:00. Very lonely, but don't care. I want to be alone.[FF]

JANUARY 8, 1944

[G]Finally—a room, terrace, laundry, and maid (cook) for $45.00 US a month—it's not great—you could live off $5.00 US a week in México, but it's good for Taxco. This evening I started to think and feel. And write, in [my] notebook. The maid prepared my bath. One must make a fire to heat the water. It makes me uncomfortable, uneasy, ordering a girl around. Bought a bottle of wine to bless my future and my arrival.

Bought slacks, stockings, and *cinturón* at the market—$11 pesos—not bad. There's always music in this city. At night, in the morning, in the afternoon. And in some mysterious way, one ends up spending a lot of money.GG

JANUARY 9, 1944

GA good day—but no mail—am used to it by now. There's too much to eat here, and I'll get fat if I don't stop. Impatiently awaiting my typewriter.* Am happy—and ready to work. But I want a fire at night. After all that's happened, I finally want a house to myself. That would be heaven. At least you can wear slacks here—something you can't do in just any little Mexican city.†GG

JANUARY 10, 1944

I have many fleas, Gand crimson blotches on my legs. I'm miserable!GG

JANUARY 11, 1944

GHave found and rented the most beautiful house in Taxco—and written three pages of notes for the novel. Wash basin made of blue stones, lots of sunlight, interesting windows, etc. Everything so pretty and bright and pure! Going up the stars, you can smell the flowers. Am happy—I can have whatever I wish. Even a maid. And peace and quiet—without Chloe whom I don't even like anymore.GG

JANUARY 14, 1944

GAnd when the rain fell last night, I started working on my novel. Nothing good—I started over this evening. I am so happy. I plan to paint and sketch in the morning when there's light. In the evening, when it's dark, I plan to write. I have to write for at least five hours a day. Drink seven cups of coffee a day. I can work—but only when I'm alone—then the ideas rise like water from the ground! Like gold from the ground. Like oil from the ground.GG

1/15/44

How can painters work here in so much light? The light is difficult to work with. Light is not particularly beautiful or interesting. It reveals

---

* Because of the problems with her luggage at the border, Pat is still without her typewriter.
† The expat community was substantial enough in Taxco that Mexican locals were accustomed to seeing women in pants.

too much and makes a painting thin. It is the end, while painting should show the means. The particular specialty of this country is color. The colors should be clear and exaggerated. One cannot do this with an excess of light.

JANUARY 17, 1944

ᴳWhat a strange way to spend my winter! I can easily imagine spending my life here—if I became "famous"—and had enough money and were happy—but—I would always have the feeling that this country is foreign. That's inescapable. Two letters! One from Roger F., the other from Leo Isaacs—a beautiful, "wise" letter. So happy that I had to buy a bottle of wine.ᴳᴳ

JANUARY 20, 1944

ᴳWrote a long letter yesterday to Leo Isaacs, air mail. It is curious—or maybe not so—that I wish he were here. And this letter shall bring him here, especially since he wants it himself. He doesn't know yet that I'm in Taxco, without Chloe, and alone. He'll come. I'll get a telegram soon that he's on his way. Good day. Wrote for a long time: an "introduction" to the novel. Wrote quickly, but it's better I write that way. Otherwise I'm lost in a number of details! Expected Larry* this evening, but she didn't come. Her husband probably arrived. Hoping for a letter from Mother. Why not? Why?ᴳᴳ

JANUARY 21, 1944

ᴳLetter from my mother! And from G. Albert. Sat in a corner at Paco's, drinking 2 tequilas *con limas*, reading and studying the delightful letters. The one from my mother was terribly preachy, but there were also nice words in it—*my darling*, and *darling*—that I would never hear in New York. Can't always sleep well, but the coffee is worth it!ᴳᴳ

JANUARY 25, 1944

ᴳToday at 5—seven letters! Strange—that my mother's letters bother me so much—bothered me to the point that I couldn't work this evening. She preaches to me, because she knows so much—that I drink too much, that I need to clean my house before I can start living in it, that my life is founded on alcohol and duplicity. All lies!

(3 tequilas—and no mirth!)ᴳᴳ

---

* Larry, an occasional lover of Pat's.

1/26/44

The size of paper one writes a letter or a book on is vitally important. The length of the page, the width, even the space between the lines, influences the rhythm of the sentences. Today spent thirty minutes choosing a *cuaderno* into which I would copy my book. Having got a block from the ᔆᴾprinters,ˢᴾˢᴾ I went back and asked to see a longer, larger book. He had one—one like Proust might have written *Remembrance of Things Past* in. Still I debated whether the dialogue would not be influenced by the 10-inch-long lines? Whereas the prose would be to my liking—long and rolling and detailed. I am still debating, although I came off with the smaller notebook.

1/26/44

I never before saw a Mexican village where the natives drank—until I saw Taxco. Strange to think, during the weekdays, that these faces and figures one sees on the streets, working, doing commonplace things, hold also that virus of city life, that hidden cancer that drives one to alcohol! Strange that their uncomplex minds would crave alcohol. On Sundays the streets are full of reeling men, old men, too, cracking their brittle knees on Taxco's cobblestones.

JANUARY 26, 1944

ᴳMy luggage arrived at 4. Quickly wrote an 8 page story.ᴳᴳ

JANUARY 27, 1944

ᴳQuickly wrote another 8 pages till 3:30. 16 pages in 24 hours! Fervently hope—no I'm certain that Hughes will buy them. They're two of the best concepts.ᴳᴳ

2/2/44

Mexico! It has to be seen from a bus window going at maximum speed, just so the luggage on top doesn't pull the bus over. You have to feel the clean wind in your face as you coast down from Mexico, down, down, and the road markers saying, three miles, too late, "*camino sinuoso*."* Sometimes the hills look like the backs of stampeding elephants, sometimes like deep napped rugs thrown carelessly in a heap. They are always

---

* Winding road.

so tremendous that the imagination cannot match them. The road is cut into the sides of hills, and as the crow flies would be four-fifths shorter. Far away two Mexicans in white pants, their shirts and sombreros covered with loads of corn-shucks, walk together far below the road. The petty, noisy, overpopulated peninsula of twentieth century Europe is vulgar and insane compared to this. These two are so wise that they do not know their wisdom, wise enough to be so proud of themselves that they are humble in the landscape and count their lives as two lives in millions. In the air from some house above the road now comes guitar music and soft voices, these musicians who seldom drink or smoke because they can make poetry in the thin daylight. Mexico with her feet in the earth and her crown in the sky.

FEBRUARY 5, 1944

GWrote a tricky scene this afternoon, had a mind filled with difficulties and lively ideas, yet I [search for] answers with Larry. My God! Why am I going with her? I can't bear it any longer! No poetry—no thoughts—no soul! And I really hate drinking, particularly if I fail to get drunk!GG

FEBRUARY 7, 1944

GLetter from Chloe today. She was here, but "circumstances" prevented her from coming to see me. Circumstances in pants!GG

2/10/44

Julien Green was right: one can have but one language for one's every day clothes and one's best hours. There are words, blunt seeming when written, and grating on the ear, which appeal to the emotions and make, unbeknownst to the author, good literature.

2/10/44

A person with an imaginative, complex, and complicating mind needs often the effects of alcohol to let him see the truth, the simplicity, and the primitive emotions once more.

FEBRUARY 12, 1944

GWorked slowly. And seriously. But I don't know if I'm telling my story as well as I could. With Larry—*biftec*, beer—and we saw three kittens at the Chino's. I can take one of them tomorrow! Am very happy!

One—two tequilas at Paco's, where we saw Bill Spratling* drinking with several other gays. What a man! Interesting chin, and highly sensible.GG

FEBRUARY 15, 1944

GWonderful day because I received a letter from Cornell. And two from Mother. I sat in the square, reading. Cornell spent a sad vacation (Christmas Day) with Texas. How wonderful to read her words! "My love— Pat—truly—my love is forever yours—" etc. My heart was full of hope (for what, I don't know) and I responded as soon as I got home.GG

2/17/44

It takes a hell of a lot of time to be in love.

FEBRUARY 18, 1944

GTelegram from B.Z.G. He's in Mexico and will call me tomorrow.GG

FEBRUARY 23, 1944

[Mexico City.] GSaw many buildings around the city. Lots of Orozcos at the preparatory school that were far better than Rivera. Orozco shows people, Rivera [shows] nothing but things. And B.Z.G. [Ben-Zion Goldberg] (who's been holding my hand for days) finally told me he only came to Mexico to see me, etc. I was utterly disgusted. Phoned Chloe— tried to see her later—but by 1:30 AM she wasn't home (although we'd made plans). Goldberg has found great success (he said), but he has not achieved what he came here for: namely, to grow closer. He said that I am impersonal through and through, that I am asexual—but also, that that kind of person doesn't exist.GG

2/27/44

Man without a god is worth nothing at all. The god may be a woman, an inspiration, an ambition, a fetish, an indulgence tempered with ceremony and self-denial, but unless he lives by something which he serves as being greater, consciously, or unconsciously to him, than himself, he is less noble than his own dog.

---

* William Spratling, an American architect, produced jewelry inspired by pre-Columbian designs in his silver workshop in Taxco. He is still known as the "Father of Mexican Silver." His friends included William Faulkner and Diego Rivera.

MARCH 2, 1944

ᴳPrepared myself. And worked. And how unfortunate—that I have an inferiority complex! I don't know why, as it's an accumulation of my falling out
with Rosalind, misfortune with Cornell, misfortune with Buffie, Chloe,
etc. And I'm ashamed of my teeth, a shame I must dispel, and will.ᴳᴳ

MARCH 5, 1944

ᴳWrote to mother. Lately, her letters have been very agreeable, full of
love, says she misses me.ᴳᴳ

MARCH 7, 1944

ᴳLeft tonight, Goldberg and me. The journey was long. Goldberg
observed me all night with concern, and—I hated that. "Should we have
our honeymoon in Acapulco?" But I was utterly disgusted. Especially by
the hubris of these fifty-year-old men.ᴳᴳ

MARCH 8, 1944

ᴳGot to Acapulco at 5:30 A.M.ᴳᴳ

MARCH 9, 1944

ᴳSwam twice. Impossible for me to work by the sea. Have to be alone
first, at least in my own room. Goldberg writes columns, and that's much
different. Wrote to Chloe. Have to write an article about Acapulco.ᴳᴳ

3/9/44

What a desolate, despairing, exquisite thought, that one cannot live
without loving someone. What a more desperate thought, that one cannot create anything without this inspiration!

3/10/44

In whatever milieu the artist first felt himself to be an artist, he should
live and do his work. The desires of an artist, should they be freedom of
scene, social behavior, or the imagined confines of his own mind, should
never be attained in reality, but only in imagination through his work.

MARCH 11, 1944

ˢᴾI worked very hard this morning and afternoon, and at night spoke
about my novel. Goldberg says I'm incapable of loving, that I am in love
with myself. It's not true. Writing this novel is really what troubles me,

which means I have to free myself from the ties holding me back. The food here is always the same. Fish, beans. Pastries at two. Chicken. If only I had a carrot, a banana, a piece of celery without salt! I'd be content! I'm really enjoying reading *History of Mexico*.[SPSP]

MARCH 13, 1944

[SP]I think about Allela all the time, no doubt there's a letter from her waiting for me in Taxco. Goldberg pretends to be very lonely and comes to visit every evening around 11 or 12. Tonight he stayed for two hours. We spoke about my story—about the love between Gregory and Margaret, which could be very potent. In fact, I could be in love with Margaret myself, even before writing her. I find his conversation inspiring, and he is very patient in trying to make me fall in love with him, but it's impossible. Was very happy and relaxed, because I made progress on the novel.[SPSP]

MARCH 18, 1944

[SP]I was really tired tonight and wasn't able to work much. B.Z.G. either. I wish I had more of my novel for him to read before he leaves, but it's not possible. I have the sense that I'll never finish it because there will always be a chapter I want to rewrite.

I have some six freckles![SPSP]

MARCH 22, 1944

[Taxco.] [SP]Letter from B.Z.G., more about our friendship. Got ready to take the bus to El Naranjo[*] this morning, very happy there. [Before,] met Paul Cook[†] in a bar—with no money. Then with a certain "Carlos" to Minas Viejas, where they are mining coal. Later met Paul again in the door of a bar—with money. Two tequilas and then dinner together at the Victoria. Very agreeable. Oh, if only I could live with Paul, I really like him. How annoying, that "the public" assumes—always assumes—that a woman and a man must then also spend the night together.[SPSP]

3/25/44

Night-time! Six o'clock, the hour for forgetting. Seven o'clock, the hour of the phantasy-at-the-bar. Eight o'clock, the hour for the aerial

---

[*] A small village twenty miles from Taxco.

[†] A character inspired by the painter and writer Paul Cook will later resurface in Pat's short story "In the Plaza," published posthumously in *Nothing That Meets the Eye: The Uncollected Stories of Patrriciua Highsmith* (New York, 2002).

romance with the lady in the dark corner who seems to be thinking the same thing, but is she? Nine o'clock, ten o'clock, twelve midnight. The moon is like a tired wheel of chance rolling across the sky, and I am to be found in a bar. Hours and hours I sit watching the business man from Chicago paw a lady who is not his wife, listening to the jaded maria-chis grinding out "Jalisco," absorbing greedily a thousand monotonous details that I have seen a thousand times before, absorbing alcohol to feel things I have felt a thousand times before. This morning, this after-noon, I was complete, replete, and my work was bread in the mouth and why am I incomplete now? Why forever incomplete? The answer means nothing. The question is a vacuum, the answer is less than a vacuum. The vital question, the only question, is why do I guard so vigilantly my incompleteness?

MARCH 29, 1944

[SP]I wrote letters to Allela and my mother. Both are very beautiful, but maybe they weren't worth spending the entire morning on. I'm very sad. But I always am, even when I work well. I think about Allela. I think about Rosalind, and I want them both! It's terrible! I don't have anybody, except my cat.[SPSP]

MARCH 30, 1944

[SP]It's very pleasant to think that I'm turning a new page in my life. There is no end to the pages. I have fleas again. I worked very hard, I wrote a lot. I have to make up for last night, I drank too much and wrote a very sad letter to Rosalind. Working late into the the night, I felt absolutely desperate. I'm constantly sad and hopeless: I think about my life and work, and the thought occurs that I will never accomplish anything. There's no remedy. There are no miracles—neither in my head, nor from the mouth of God.[SPSP]

3/30/44

I want to write the saddest story ever written, a story that compresses the heart and brings tears to the eyes of every man from the lowest peas-ant to the highest genius. I will write it weeping such tears as were never wept at Troy or Carthage or at the Wailing Wall. The sadness will be a purge of my brain and heart, a hot iron to level and clean me, salt of my tears to purify my blood. My body will wring itself and writhe in pity. What story? Maybe mine.

APRIL 1, 1944

I worked this morning until I went to Mrs. Luzi's by appointment. She wasn't ready, & we didn't get off to the Victoria until after two, during which time she had overturned an ink bottle and a quart of milk on her sarape* in pursuit of an imaginary scorpion. The mail man beckoned in the post office & gave me a letter from Ann T.—"Why I love you Patricia Highsmith, will forever remain a Freudian enigma." The rest is probably witty, but seems full of non-sequiturs. She amuses me. She flatters me. She has intelligence of high and rare quality, but can she ever put it to use? I don't know. I wrote her a grateful letter—and late tonight a Purple Paragraph, because for ten minutes, at least I was in love with her. In general, if I had some of her and she some of me, we should both be better writers.

4/2/44

I am lonely in the evenings, when the dusk invades my room, so politely, so subtly inviting me to do the things one cannot do alone. Sometimes the desire is in my arms only, and they are hungry like the stomach is hungry, for the solid embrace. Sometimes the desire is in my lips only and I bite it out of them. Sometimes the desire is a ghostly counter part of me, and stands beside me sadly. In the nights I lie and watch the moon on [its] hopeless quest, and learn anew the inexorable equation, my loneliness of one is the loneliness of one plus one and one times one and two.

APRIL 3, 1944

"April the saddest month—"† T. S. Eliot, where are you? And why the hell don't these goddamn Mexican censors spend a little more time at their jobs and a little less at their meals? I want my books. I can't live without them.

4/3/44

I am lonely for a thousand things. Mainly certain people and certain conversation. Today, this morning, I struggled up almost perpendicular hills, carrying for the tenth time my three valises containing typewriting paper, notebooks, books, behind me an old Mexican carrying the heaviest valise by a strap on his forehead. I don't like the house. I sit in the lit-

---

* Traditional Mexican cloth, usually worn as a cape.
† Correctly cited, the opening line of T. S. Eliot's poem "The Waste Land" (1922) would have to be "April is the cruellest month."

tered room, and ask myself, why am I here after all? Oh drinking is the logical thing, the normal thing, the only thing in this particular night. The other nights will be work, but not this one. I want talk with people, who understand how one can work, and not work and drink, and work again. I want to see Paul Cook, my artist friend, in the Victoria Hotel. I come home to wash and dress for him. Oh we will sit hours in a corner of the hotel bar and perhaps, he will drink tequila with me, though he is not supposed to be drinking now. And the world will be right again, because two minds in the corner of a bar are very strong. But while dressing I suddenly feel tired, and stop with my blouse on and skirt off. I put out my cigarette. I will not go. (The audience applauds.) Besides there is no water to get clean with. I throw down a dinner I do not want, and much coffee. I start to work with "Smiles" on my neighbor's radio. I work until long after midnight, until I am too exhausted to feel lonely, or desirous, or melancholy.

APRIL 4, 1944

Paid my rent, unfortunately, and the turkeys are right outside my window. They are as close as they can possibly be to my ear, without being in my room—all of which prompted me to write a fictitious story of it this afternoon. Terminating in blood revenge. Worked very hard all today, making also what I call the "commercial gesture"—the story— which I should do in the form of writing or drawing each day now, if I expect to exist. Don't know when to expect reimbursements from Chloe. After all this time I consider her behavior skunky. Invited Margot C. for a drink at Paco's; ran into Paul Cook, who crashed with Margot immediately. Then Tony, exuding warmth and friendliness, came over + wanted to contract Paul to do a portrait of Margot. Paul asks 200 dollars. Presently, M.C., Paul & I joined the Peter M.'s, later going to supper at the Victoria. Pleasant, smart people they are. Paul walked me home, stopped at Paco's, met the Newtons, thence ensemble to Chachalaca—a typical Tasqueñan night. Was boosted over this 10 ft. wall at 1:30 by Paul Cook.

APRIL 6, 1944

A typical Tasqueñan day. Something had to be wrong, because the water was flowing and had to go in to the Chino's for café. Coming back met José Barrego, who invited me to lunch. We had a beer at Paco's first. Worked this afternoon on my book. It is terribly slow, and often I am faced with such questions: how am I going to end the story, have I anything to say, and is it worth the trouble? But at the same time, fortunately, I do not believe I could stop now and leave Gregory's story untold. It is a heightening and romanticizing of my own aspirations, found-delights, and material disillusionment coupled with, I believe sincerely, a spiritual awakening.

4/6/44

If I had been born into the home of musicians, I should have died of happiness at the age of four.

APRIL 8, 1944

The rats are playing tag in my roof. Yesterday they ate a tile through and dropped it on the bathroom floor. Today a most melancholy feeling that I am exhausted and that Mexico has done it, and will continue to do it. It will take something more than willpower to keep me here another five months—something approaching the passions of a flagellant.

APRIL 9, 1944

Another day of escapism—very slight drinking, much sociability. Productive of one thing: I am leaving Taxco for San Miguel [de] Allende come May. I dare not—I do not hope for the great renaissance of 1943 there—but at least I'll be away from the drinkers here—getting to be too many, from the corrupt atmosphere, from the hostile natives (somewhat) and from this war of attrition (imagined or real) of Taxco versus the human will. Shall, I fear, have to ask Chloe for some money, & if she does not come across, shall have to go home. Shame! But my own fault for putting it up.

APRIL 10, 1944

Letter from Mother. Ernst pays visits, claims he is still in love with me, as though he ever was; that he thinks Goldberg is in love with me [too]. Unfortunately all leave me cold. I must work out my own mess for myself. Always Paul puts his finger on the trouble. "An artist is licked, when he sets limitations for himself," says Paul, of my saying I can't think of love at the moment. He is right. The excellent critique of short story of mine of Mexican rooster. Not enough emotion. Not enough passion. What have I? Something. Something as honest as the world has ever seen, but whether I can combine this with the all-essential passion or not I don't know. At the same time, I have no doubt but that I have felt equal to the most impassioned of our writers.

APRIL 11, 1944

After eating at Chino's, Paul & I came home ere, & he read my MS—
liking it very much, I'm happy to say. In fact almost raving. Then after
rums it was much too late for him to go home, so he slept here, first on
the porch, then with me—I didn't like the idea, but he kept his side of the
bed and seemed to want to sleep in the same bed just for camaraderie,
which might sound corny to anyone else but not to someone who knows
Paul.

APRIL 12, 1944

Got a $50.00 check from my parents for Easter. What a nice present!
And I felt rather ashamed I did not send them even a card. I get frequent
letters from B.Z.G. and mother now, asking me would I like canned
food, would I like more money, a maid, a pension? And would I want
to come home and work in New Hampshire, from my mother. Stay on
from B.Z.G. Lonely, and homesick, and beginning to hate & fear Mexico. Don't know if I want to stay much longer. I wrote Chloe for money.
Would feel much better with that. Everyone here seems so substantially
placed, tho no more content than I am. Met Mrs. Luzi in the Plaza. She
and her husband have had an amusing quarrel, that I've written up in
my notebook,* and may put into a second book I have in mind doing,
about Taxco—what happens when Americans go to pot—and why they
do. Came home at 12:30 to find my house invaded, my kitten up a tree
yowling, and Paul in my bed! I was so mad I felt like kicking him out, but
made my bed on the porch instead.

APRIL 14, 1944

There is something evil in me that leads me to believe all I touch will be
corrupted or be a failure—I mean all in the creative field. No production
ever is smooth, with sufficient joy. I mean to correct this by "playing" as
much as I can with the work itself. Sketching foolish things helps mostly.
Didn't see Paul all day. Rather unusual. Went to El Naranjo at 1:30.
Got my book box, went to Iguala and came back to Taxco via the most
wretched, foul, disgusting Flecha Roja [bus] that ever crept along the
road. My right foot was on somebody else's, my left foot out a window,

---

* The anecdote about the Luzis finds its way into Highsmith's short story "The Car," first published
in English in *Nothing That Meets the Eye: The Uncollected Short Stories of Patricia Highsmith* (New
York, 2002). While the story ends tragically, in reality Marguerite and her Swiss husband continued to
live in Mexico.

and my rear end dipping into a vat of greasy lamb stew at every rift in the road. 1 hour-and-a-half for a 20 minute trip. Also got my typewriter. My books fill me with joy! La! La! Tonight, so happy I chose Hölderlin to read. There is also Proust! Fragments of my first book, too, some of it excellent writing which will have to be interpolated. I have my work cut out, and will do no dissipating the rest of this month.

4/14/44

Paul Cook—who talks better than he writes or paints. He knows the dramatic and artistic essentials of a creative work. He was a football player, married at thirty-two, to a Texas woman of good and wealthy family. Divorced last year after 14 years because of jealousy on her part, demands, criticism of his drinking. He has always drunk quite a little and now in Taxco drinks quite a lot. Wanted to commit suicide last year and dove a plane into the Atlantic, being rescued immediately. He is the son of a Welsh doctor and an Italian woman. He is 6'3", lanky, blue eyed, and distinguished looking no matter what he does or how he dresses. A good and interesting set of false teeth he has had since twenty-seven, because of some brain or nervous disease. The cantina proprietors adore him, for sincere reasons. He is paid $150 dollars per month by the U.S. Government to catch dope peddlers. Sometimes he makes a catch. Ostensibly, he is the washed-up American painter going to hell in Taxco. He has done what no other American I know had done, made the Mexicans like him, I mean inspired their friendship. Despite his height, despite his blue eyes, they love him.

4/16/44

In Taxco people do not drink to fill social intervals, or as a ritual between four and six, and do not drink for a mild lift, but for total oblivion. In Taxco one has not had a satisfactory drink until one staggers, until one doesn't care that tomorrow is *mañana*, and the whole future is *mañana*, and when that comes—*mañana*. And the present is already just past.

APRIL 17, 1944

Paul has been preaching asexuality, and impersonality, is the most sentimental person, next to myself, whom I know. He is also sub-sexed, as I am. Left him in quite a temper, and it'll be just as well if I don't see him again—for a long, long while.

APRIL 18, 1944

Worked 8 hours today. The first chapter's style is easy and good reading if a certain momentum is kept. Something like Carson McCullers. I
heard from the Selas, Paul Cook was in awfully drunk at 5, and about
to start a fight. He was placed in a taxi by Dr. Newton this PM, but
was not at the hotel at eight. I wonder if he's in jail already? The Selas
said he was trying to send me a note, but couldn't write well enough to
do it. He is sentimental and lonely, disastrous combination. Fleas, ants,
cats, dogs, the Mexicans—all prey upon me. Some want money, some
food, some flesh, but all want something, and as this is their country
they get it.

Reading Oriental Philosophy—very pleasant.

APRIL 22, 1944

We'll leave Monday. I know too many people in Mexico—in Taxco—
and for all one's good intentions—even willpower, it is impossible to
maintain one's independence, and one's stability—while seeing them,
drinking with them—the social system being as vague & informal as it
is. I am running away—yes, but not from myself—from the Tasqueños.

APRIL 23, 1944

I decided not to leave now. It costs less, & things are about to break here.
The Duchess (Mrs. Nina Engelhardt), over many beers, invited me to
stay 3 days at the Sierra Madre next week. She has sacks of money.

APRIL 24, 1944

Much thinking about my book & little writing—& just as well. Paul
thinks it drops after the very first section after Gregory's walking to the
house. I'll never get it published, I think, or want it published, unless
all of it is up to the standard of the first section. Therefore a complete
rewriting is necessary. Spoke long with Paul—my God, what a brilliant,
understanding fellow, & how much he has helped me on my work! My
problem now is not liquor, not homesickness, not laziness certainly, but
strictly physical living conditions. Saw *Casablanca* tonight with Tom G.,
whom I let kiss me at 1:00 AM—why I don't know.

Paul gave me the most charming earrings.

APRIL 25, 1944

Moved into the Sierra Madre at 11:30, & found the Duchess and Del
Gato drinking beer. Life is one long beer & cigarette, not good for the

nerves, the conscience, or that organ producing human happiness, wherever it lies.

APRIL 26, 1944

Shall be glad to see Grandma—very much, and I want to leave. The end of the month. The reason is that due to over-drinking, lack of a house, I have lost myself, with whom I am never bored or lonely.

APRIL 27, 1944

Wrote my mother that I should start home the 4 of May. Conversation gets duller, on everyone else's part and certainly on mine. Americans cruise like hungry sharks over the town, seeking for few moments' companionship with anyone.

Once they spot you, it is impossible, even a little cruel, to shake them off. Paco's is the habitat of the corpses. My cat is the liveliest, most normal creature in Taxco.

APRIL 28, 1944

Dreadfully tight, the tightest, came home & Paul arrived at 2—AM—until 3:30. Said he loved me more than anything else in the world, wanted to stay of course, but absolutely impossible. I wrote 11 beginnings to Rosalind & wrote the 12th letter passably. I love her more than anything else in the world, so help me God! I wonder—I wish—I wonder—I should write more, somehow. I should express myself more & better. I should write stories perhaps instead of a novel. But were I writing stories, I should say I should write a novel!

4/29/44

Art is a stone-faced mountain that we attack again and again, always to be thrown back. We sit long minutes on a rock and look at the mountain with chin in hand, rally ourselves, and attack once more. We break first our noses, then our heads and then our hearts, but our way is in this direction and we cannot turn back. Finally we lie below, prostrate on the ground, and the mountain gives no shade for the flesh or the bones in the hot sun of exposure. And if we are worthy at the last, posterity points to the dents.

MAY 1, 1944

The Duchess, under the effects of three potent drinks, invited me once more! We leave for Mexico Saturday, after Cinco de Mayo, which is another damned thing.

MAY 5, 1944

FLASH! Fragonard catches her first mouse! Am so eager to be off! But my wallet is certainly getting flatter since I met the Duchess, & hers no doubt since she met me.

MAY 6, 1944

Drinks were flowing like tequila (not like water because there is none).

5/8/44

The Monte Carlo Hotel in Mexico City is a stamp of authenticity. Because the place holds them all—those with a sense of humor, those with the individuality and the courage of it. In the Monte Carlo, there is always the feeling that something is about to happen. That it never does, does not matter. Every corner, every wall, every floor, holds a history we do not question out of sheer respect for it, as we do not question a venerable fighter, be he ever so disreputable and feeble, on his own history, out of respect for him.

MAY 11, 1944

Nina had turkey sandwiches for me, & with Tom & Paul, invited, we all got into one taxi & drove to the station. "The stars set in heaven when you go away, Pat," Nina said, almost crying, as she kissed me goodbye. I suspect she did cry, for when the bus pulled out, they were all gone. Oh the wonderful night rides on the bus, when I think, I believe, I know, all things are possible, when the mind, untrammeled, unanchored, moves like a primeval, omniscient, omnipotent thing, from abstraction to concretion, to fantasy to fact, and strings them all together in a wondrous necklace. Then, I believe, I saw my book as different from Joyce's *Portrait*, in no way derivative, in no way, really, necessarily, secondary. I ate a turkey sandwich and smoked some of the Camel cigarettes and for a few hours was in heaven, at least mentally.

MAY 12, 1944

[Monterrey.] A lot of facts written tonight—but there is more in my heart—poetry, hopes, sadness, loneliness, love, inspiration, frustration, and no fear—

5/12/44

I touched the horns of a young buck today, felt the moss-like fuzz on its short horns, slid my palm down its soft neck while it gazed calmly into space. Free, free, it was. Severe in mind and unquestionably, unquestioningly true in heart. But man, and Patricia Highsmith, were born to trouble, as the sparks fly upward.

6/7/44

Weeping, weeping, weeping tonight inexplicably. Inexplicably, except, perhaps, for the possible futility of life. Tonight I am, I hope, Santayana's[*] young man, who will not be a savage because he has wept. Perhaps some day I shall be his old man who is not a fool because he can laugh. But I do not think so. Long before I am old in a physical sense, I shall have killed myself, and left behind me this note: "I am sick to death of compromise in all its hideous guises."

6/10/44

[Texas.] The couple who discover someone has written a foul 4-letter word on their new cement sidewalk, directly in front of the house. The husband is for leaving it to mellow out of its conspicuousness, but the wife first insists it must be filled in, then when it is, and spread wider, and cracked deeply, almost dies of anguish. The husband's indifference hides a certain satisfaction: his wife who has been indifferent to his own desires, indifferent to this his own shocking, hideous, foul, exciting command in Anglo-Saxon is beside herself when she sees it written by an anonymous hand.

6/18/44

Note here: Happy days lead to stagnation of the mind. Happy days even in my opinion, reading, writing, drawing. Nothing has come in the way of ideas in the last two happy days. I used to think such days produced ideas. Now I wonder if frequent disturbance isn't necessary.

6/22/44

Raging mad this afternoon when a small cousin refused to sit properly for a portrait on which I had spent many hours already and had come near losing. I was too nervous to eat dinner, & walked west, west, west, until I found myself suddenly at the edge of town, viewing a broad sweep of the low horizon, bomber plants, oil fields, farms, distant houses, each of which held many souls. And the voice from the clouds said, "Behold

---

* George Santayana (1863–1952), Spanish writer, literary critic, and philosopher.

all this greater-than-you. And think how small is that ruined picture!"
But, alas, the panorama with all the souls was not greater than this
one picture. This is the fact of it. This is what will make me happy or
miserable.

(At such raging times, "suicide" flashes to my mind, as inevitably as
lightning produces thunder.)

7/3/44

Love is no stranger here. He is in the slouch of the soldier on the counter-
stool, in the rolling eye and the gum-chewing jaw of the waitress, in the
flies that copulate on the rims of greasy plates, in the unsubtle music of
the jukebox brought by loudspeakers into every booth, in the baggy back
of the cattleman leaning against the slot machine as he drinks his luke-
warm Jax beer and talks to a blond hussy in slacks. Love is there, too,
warm and red and smiling. Love is only a stranger though in the formal
eating places of big cities, where two people face each other like brick
walls across a table, and Love grows in one only, like a tender shy vine
between two bricks.

7/6/44

Sexual intercourse, while the most perfect thing, is not ever quite perfect.
There is always some one-sided amusement about your or the other person's limitations, and a terrible sadness like defeat in the last ditch. (This
note taken in drunkenness, Ft. Worth, Texas, mid-afternoon.)

7/15/44

[New York.] You have to enjoy the weather always. Walking home from
Sixty-First Street on Second Avenue, eleven beautiful black blocks. (The
moon is not, the lights are, you are, your feet with the spring in them,
this is youth, now!) You inhale the soft cool night, you gaze on the
lighted bar doorways fondly. Your shoes, for once, are comfortable. Your
head is filled with a number of things, among which undoubtedly are the
remnants of your last words with her, the problem of whether one can
be in love with two or three, with the youth's grudging appreciation of
the splendid night, and with the consciousness of health, future, potency.
Breathe deep! Your lungs are still functioning perfectly, your thighs do
not shake too much, your calves are resilient, your toes eager. Every mus-
cle is obedient (taut for an instant, then couchantly relaxed), every dream
will come true.

7/29/44

The aftersmell of summer rain, through a city window, up from lightly moistened tar, cement and red brick, is dusty, dry, organic, containing the sickeningly organic smell of beheaded chickens, their feathers dark-bloody and drying.

8/5/44

What can match in dismalness and melancholy the aria of *Madame Butterfly* drifting from a brownstone window across the street on a Sunday afternoon in summer?

8/6/44

What is so accursed about this century that an artist can do his best work only when his lungs are stabbed with tobacco smoke, when his brain is frenzied with coffee, liquor or benzedrine? A shameful fact, as this is a shameful age!

9/11/44

"Of course I work late at night," the writer said gloweringly. "I have to keep body & soul apart, don't I?"

9/13/44

The day we say goodbye forever to each other,* let us go to some quiet café for a stirrup cup and a Strauss waltz. (Strauss waltzes are so much nicer than you think, darling.) Not that a Strauss waltz is in any way like either of us, but for some strange reason I always think of meeting you, of having met you, to one. And I was so horribly drunk that evening it may have been so. I shall summon the waiter with my grandest flourish and call for a double brandy for myself, and probably a stinger for you, and, oh yes, would you have the string quartet (it will probably be a tired Viennese ensemble) play the Emperor Waltz, or if they do not feel up to it then the An Artist's Life, and after a quarter of an hour please, the halting, but so determined Motor Waltz, which will be our finale. Its halting but so determined phrases are fitting now. We can dream about the straight spines, the rigid arms, the adoring looks we would impale each other with, as we whirled about the ballroom amid the envious company, the couples and couples, who would gyrate in lesser orbits about us like the host of minor planets about Saturn. (Are

---

* It is unclear what woman inspired this and the following entry.

you saturnine, darling?) So I should leave you, with the money for the check, of course, perhaps before the last strains died away, so on the final chord, you could look across the table and see no one, except that ideal you might imagine, that you always did imagine so easily, and with your next stinger coming up, you might drink the one you hold to the dregs, yes, all the powdered ice, and still, still before the evening is over, before you drink half the next stinger, that chair across from you may be filled with someone more charming by far than I, for you, who could never be alone.

10/20/44

Tonight the rain comes down slimily and eternally on my court, making a high-pitched spanking sound with occasional drops, a too sharp sound that plays on the nerves, and when one walks in the rain makes one grimace and shrink as though from a repulsive, chill thing. Tonight I have nothing to do with the rain. Tonight I am in love, for the sixteenth, seventeenth or eighteenth time in my life (I never can remember, nor remember which times should be eliminated) and I have promised it will last until Sunday morning (tonight is Friday), and have been promised it will last until then. Tonight I am as happy, and with as much reason, as an egg in a refrigerator of a big household, rejoicing that so much has happened and still its shell is not cracked. After tonight, after tomorrow night—what? Isn't it a beautiful life? Isn't it beautiful?

10/31/44

Jews—why do I consistently find some fault in them? I dislike them for their mere consciousness of being Jews (none can possibly be without this consciousness), and dislike all the multitudinous, multitudinous, contradictory manifestations of this consciousness. The Christians have made them conscious of being Jews. Therefore, in a sense, being a Christian, I must hate myself.

11/1/44

The first days of being in love—there is no use in struggling against daydreaming. Daydream we must, for every object, everything around us, inside us, is new. All the things we took for granted and were familiar with are no longer familiar. The chair, the wastebasket, the desk, one's own fountainpen, the music we knew and (and thought we knew) and loved are no longer familiar, but quite new things to be re-observed and judged. It is a new world, and we view it like children.

11/6/44

Homosexuals—what is the specific virus that results in the eternal impermanence? Some say it is the ego of the active partner, who after six months must make one more new conquest. This implies, doubtless, that she has tired of the other. Why? Because homosexuals are not often enough romantic. The cart before the horse, this is leading to, though I do not know which is cart and which is horse. Some prescience of imper-manence must poison the mind (the heart) from the outset, and result in a holding back in order to escape the affair with as little pain as possible.

As for myself, I prefer to be romantic. I want the strand of hair, the desperately opened, desperately guarded letter, the scuff on my shoes I will not shine off, the telephone call that means life or death, the sweet pain that comes when the one you love has done you the simplest kind of favor. Two people dancing together, knowing someone will come up soon, within moments, within a minute, within three seconds, tap you on the shoulder and take her away forever. I want the summit to be so high in the clouds my nose bleeds, my ears crackle, my lungs cry for oxygen. I want the end to be a fall deeper than from Mount Everest so that it will terrify me, as I watch the whole world fall with me, that will land me, a heap of rubble, on some lifeless desert, on some unnamed, uncharted planet.

11/13/44

Love, and the expression of it, acts like oil on the machinery of one's whole life.

NOVEMBER 14, 1944

ᴳN.* called at 4:30 AM—lots of questions—and came over at 4:45. These early mornings with her . . . We cooked potatoes (fried, the only way I know) the way she loves them—fried! And later, after several dif-ficulties, which I was probably imagining—it was morning by the time we went to sleep. And then—calls—Mary H., Rosalind (who banged on about buying me a cat for Christmas in order to find out if Natica was here and what happened overnight). Natica [here] till—6! Another day wasted—but Rosalind says there's no such thing as a waste of time! It's just so sweet being with her, and we're just—sad when we have to

---

* Natica Waterbury, Pat's new lover. Natica was, however, already involved with another woman, Virginia Kent Catherwood, like her a product of Philadelphia high society. The two had presumably been acquainted—at the very latest—since their respective debutante balls, events so significant as to receive coverage in the New York Times.

say goodbye. The old line by Shakespeare—"Parting is such—" finally has meaning. Terribly tired, as we usually are, after one night and one day!—two days and one night, or two nights and one day! But wanted to see Bernhard and Cornell for dinner at Romany's.* Natica is moody, doesn't want to say much, but that interests me. She needs something to do, but this is heaven for my starved heart: that she has nothing to do but kiss me again and again. Walked her home at 12:00 midnight. I want to find an unfurnished apartment for her. Then she'll be happy. I'm happy now, but this day was crazy![GG]

11/14/44

Shall I say I can work when I am most unhappy? Perhaps this is the only way I can dupe myself, the only way that will let me produce any work. Anything, you know, to get one's mind off oneself.

NOVEMBER 15, 1944

[G]Natica didn't call me all day. And this evening took the train to Philadelphia. I had the biggest news to tell her—I sold "The Heroine" to *Harper's Bazaar*—and would have been so happy if she were the first to know. But tomorrow at the social, I'll tell Rosalind and Natica with great pride. Am convinced that *Harper's* has a better reputation with regard to literature than any other magazine in the country. How can I express how much Natica means to me?! She's my succor, life itself, and joy. God!—do not forsake me—that she might stay with me! Happy—so happy I can only see my beautiful world, the way I am ascending—as I am doing now, as I have been for three weeks! Tomorrow—makes it three weeks! Natica—it feels much longer. She's counting the weeks too.[GG]

NOVEMBER 19, 1944

[G]Worked alone all day—10 pages of comics. And N. still hasn't called! Her landlady said she spent the night elsewhere, with a friend (as long as it's only a friend!). I was very nervous today, delivered her typewriter to her house, and went for a walk (a cold walk) by myself, trying to believe

---

* Marie Marchand (1885–1961) was a key figure of Greenwich Village bohemia. Whenever her restaurant moved to yet another of many locations, a crowd of devotees was sure to follow. Romany Marie's, as it was invariably called, was especially popular with artists—not least because those who needed it could always get a free meal. Marchand's portrait by Romany regular John Sloan is today housed in the Whitney Museum of American Art.

that I'm very happy, very trusting, that I will always be with her, and always be happy.^{GG}

NOVEMBER 20, 1944

^GAnother day without her! No word! I'm still living with the strength she gave me, but I have to see her—have her—again soon! What does she want? Is she thinking of me? I believe so.^{GG}

NOVEMBER 21, 1944

^GConversation with Mrs. Aswell at *Harper's*, who was very surprised to learn that I haven't studied psychology. Wants to read more of my stories. Very content with the conversation, happy upon coming home to wait for Natica. But she didn't call—until 6:00! Wanted to meet me at a friend's. Went there. Her name is Virginia Catherwood, "an old friend from school." Spoke at length with her in her room. I felt that she knew everything about N. and myself and didn't object, as she likes me. When we joined the others, Natica was jealous—Ginnie mentioned it first. I smiled, it was so unnecessary. Ginnie made me some coffee once the others had left, asked me to stay, but I wanted to see N.! Ginnie called at 2:00—just when Natica came in. Maybe she heard it, but I don't know.^{GG}

NOVEMBER 22, 1944

^GShe came at 12 midnight, brought me this book, and even better, herself. She stayed, and thus passed the most wonderful night we have known! Everything was wonderful—she slept in my arms, and whispered in her sleep, "How can two people have so much?" I was so happy, proud, content, and satisfied, though, that I couldn't fall asleep. Peace, quiet, and the two of us together! This day—Thanksgiving.* I have a lot this year.^{GG}

11/24/44

Perils of a first novel: Every character is one's self, resulting in an oversoft or overhard treatment, neither of which results in the objective, which is essentially what has made good so much of the writing one has done before.

11/26/44

Thank God for work—the only balm in this world. Work, blessed murderer of the monster Time. Work makes the night come, makes hunger,

---

* Thanksgiving is on November 23, and Pat is as usual writing well past midnight.

fatigue, and sleep come. And when Time is dying, even makes the telephone ring. Work balms the flayed nerves, washes the eyes so one may see, mends the heart so one may love. Do you wish on me, beloved, the hell of this morning? Do you know what this morning was like? I hope you do not, and I will spare you a description. I wish only happiness for you, and all joy and good I can give you.

11/26/44

What shall I cry for, mercy or the moon? I do not know which is easier attained.

NOVEMBER 27, 1944

GRained all day. No letter in the letter box, no calls. Had to call Rosalind at 5:10, couldn't stay alone tonight. We read the dictionary, but Kirk was there, so I couldn't stay. At home, worked—had to.GG

NOVEMBER 28, 1944

GCatherwood is in love with Natica. Says Rosalind, and it must be true. At 4:15—as I finally—for the first time in three days, was lying happily, peacefully in bed with a fountain pen, wanting to work, Natica called! Later, nice dinner at the pizzeria. And—bed. It's getting better, nicer, more enjoyable. I am so happy with her, and she with me. But she denied having received my letters. I don't know. Only that I love her, that she is nothing but destruction for me, but that I love her nonetheless.GG

DECEMBER 1, 1944

GOh—thank God it isn't this month one year ago! Excellent day—but without having done much work. Only I read for nearly two hours, a luxury I rarely allow myself. Went to Macy's with Mother for Christmas gifts etc. As usual, the day isn't interesting until I get to Natica. She called at 1:30 AM. Went to the psychiatrist, told him that all her friends are homosexual. "That isn't the cause of your homosexuality," he responded. Of course not, but what else? Looking forward to her coming tomorrow evening.GG

12/1/44

Pulps versus fine writing: One simply cannot concern oneself eight or even five hours a day with nonsense-taken-seriously and not be corrupted by it. The corruption lies in the very habits of thought rather than the habits of expression: the latter could be overcome, but the former concerns the individual's self or soul. I have read recently of "the young men who write movie scenarios and comic strips. They are generally college graduates, people who read the classics in their spare time." Men who know what they are doing, in other words. Perhaps they do. But after a few years, it will be of no use to have dreamed of afternoons browsing in Brentano's Bookshop, to have snatched an hour before bedtime to read a bit of Sir Thomas Browne, to have congratulated oneself on the immunizing power of a college background. The habits of thought, the power to dream without critical influence, the functioning of an artist, will have been riddled as though by termites—and must collapse!

DECEMBER 2, 1944

GToo much satisfaction—that's my fear as I write this Sunday evening. Two months ago it was the opposite. Natica taught me to relax. Now I'm afraid. Natica at 8:00. She was full of things her psychologist had said. He'll see her again Wednesday, [but] she hasn't made any "decision." What kind of decision? She doesn't know, as one never knows, if he's "good" or "bad." At Jane Bowles's at 8:30. Dinner. Too much whiskey and too little coffee. Betty friendly, but N. and I bored. Bowles steadily better the more drunk she gets. Depressing conversation about the war. Bowles explaining she can no longer write etc. Finally, at 3:00, N. and I left. It was freezing, and my house was closer. Only fell asleep at 8:50. But the nights keep getting better, and we're growing in our understanding. When I'm with her, I have something that neither time nor money can buy. Love. Happiness. Don't know how long it will last, but now that I have it, I feel proud, happy, high as a king.GG

DECEMBER 3, 1944

GI'm saying too little about these hours with Natica, hours as I've never had them before! They are Elysium! Heaven! Another human! A woman! My God! The conversations as we lie in bed. The windows, the cigarettes, the glasses of milk or water, the apples, the figs! And the indescribable pleasures, in particular, that we can give each other!GG

DECEMBER 6, 1944

GFriday. I don't know why I recently haven't been writing my diary. These days are (as I am well aware) the best of my life. Yes, for even if I should find something even better, I am young now—and those days won't last. At times they are most happy, at times most sad, but always important, even if they are neither happy nor sad. Am often with Natica, here. And too many hours go by.^{GG}

DECEMBER 12, 1944

^GWorked on the book, and brought what I have to Chambrun* at 4:30. He was very pleased. Loved the synopsis, etc. "I wouldn't be surprised if we sold this book," he said. He likes the title—"The Click of the Shutting"—too.^{GG}

DECEMBER 13, 1944

^GAt 3:30—I was downright sick with cramps worse than I've had in 7 years. Couldn't sleep, and had to call my parents at 5:30 AM. They came over but were useless, helpless, till the doctor came at 8:00 AM. I almost died in the meantime. Totally exhausted with terrible pain in my belly! It was the kind of sickness that makes a person consider his last will and testament. I thought of my own and realized I am prepared to give Rosalind all of my diaries, letters, and notebooks. Natica came over at 3:30. She was an angel! Kissed me many times, although I looked like a potato. Felt better immediately!^{GG}

DECEMBER 16, 1944

^GHappy all day—so often happy these days that I wish there were another word.^{GG}

DECEMBER 18, 1944

^GI wish to write all of Natica's comments, but they're so personal, so soft, so sweet, so memorable, incomparable. One thing: she can't bear leaving me in order to go to Burma or Paris with the Red Cross. I'm clumsy and always say the wrong things. It's difficult and uncomfortable and dangerous to be a woman.^{GG}

DECEMBER 20, 1944

^GBought a beautiful chain for Stanley's pocket watch—pure gold! $30. From mother and myself. He doesn't expect it at all, and it will be so lovely when he sees it. An old French chain.^{GG}

---

* Probably Jacques Chambrun (1906–1976), whom Pat will mention repeatedly in 1945 and who seems to have been her agent for a while. Other clients of his included Mavis Gallant, Stefan Zweig, Franz Werfel, Alma Mahler, Lion Feuchtwanger, and W. Somerset Maugham.

DECEMBER 21, 1944

^GComics till N. called [to say] she was coming over this afternoon, but she didn't show up. Ate with Mother—we're growing closer, and there's no doubt she knows all about my life, loves me, and understands me. Bought a Christmas tree that's rather too big for my little crowns. (Made lots of crowns this afternoon, along with stars, icicles out of scrap paper from Hughes's office last year!) Snowflakes out of white napkins (paper). Natica called just as I was getting home, came over, helped me with the Christmas tree. But after three days of not seeing each other, we first had to embrace, as if it had been weeks.^{GG}

DECEMBER 23, 1944

^GHung stockings on my mantel with Natica's and Rosalind's gifts. Busy all day, especially this evening, when Rosalind came for dinner. Bought a doll's head for Natica that looks a lot like Rosalind's ex-husband. The house was ready when R. arrived—The gifts looked magnificent around the fireplace. Natica didn't arrive till 10:00 o'clock—and the first thing I saw as she entered was the shiny gold bracelet that [Virginia Kent] C. had given her. Next I saw the cat she held in her skirt. A real Siamese cat that's mostly brown. I couldn't love it more!^{GG}

DECEMBER 25, 1944

^GA year ago I was miserable. This morning I got up to the "Hallelujah Choral" and went over to my parents' with my cat, Mrs. Cathay. Everything lovely, breakfast, eggnogg, presents. But N. didn't call from Phil. Forgot the number? Probably.^{GG}

DECEMBER 26, 1944

^GA normal person would say that this time is just what one hopes for, and that I now lead a happy, normal life. But I know better. I'm replete with a bliss that will seldom return. No, this remaining life of mine will scarcely be as pleasant! Slow and steady with the book. I always feel artistically excited, happy in December and January. [It's when] I write and sketch best. Why? The weather or my horoscope?^{GG}

DECEMBER 28, 1944

^GWhen I work (write), I must have the very best—the best cigarettes, a clean shirt, because I'm like a soldier in battle, but in this case the enemy is terrible and brave, and I sometimes fail to prevail.^{GG}

DECEMBER 29, 1944

^GWhy do I start every night with "am happy" or "unhappy"? So far, happiness hasn't been my goal, or even a particular pleasure. Natica called at 2:00. She's back—but at Ginnie C.'s? Promised to maybe come by, but didn't. I didn't mind. Worked. What—what if she spends New Year's Eve with C.? That would be a blow from which I shouldn't recover.^{GG}

DECEMBER 30, 1944

^GWork. And this morning I phoned Rosalind several times, because she had invited Natica and me to dinner. She said that [Virginia Kent] Catherwood would doubtless drive me crazy, that N. has to choose, etc. And I thought [about it] later, writing a page to Natica, in which I broke everything off. Thanked her for everything, too. I knew she spent last night with C., that she prefers other things to seeing me. Figure it's pride, but I can't stand it any longer. The game is not worth the candle. I held onto the letter, though, till this evening.^{GG}

DECEMBER 31, 1944

^GThis day requires more time to describe than I presently have. When I awoke with Natica beside me, I regretted inviting her last night. Today was pleasant enough—things like breakfast, sketching after breakfast, etc. But she was ultimately very cold, she has no intention of breaking things off with Catherwood. So, between two and four this afternoon, I said every horrible thing to her I wanted. That she's only seeing C. because of her money, that she doesn't have the guts to make a real decision. She finally left the house with me at 4:30, saying that she would spend tonight, midnight, alone. The strange thing is, I'm not sad. Even though I naturally wanted to spend this evening with N. She knew that, but she was depressed and couldn't give me anything. At Lola's and Niko's with flowers at 7:30. Rosalind there, too. Later at Marya Mannes', a polite gathering of straight people, who bore me terribly. Not always, but most of the time.^{GG}

1945

ON HER TWENTY-FOURTH BIRTHDAY, Pat takes stock of *The Click of the Shutting* and decides to abandon the 300-page manuscript. Increasingly, Pat turns to drawing to express herself creatively. In the summer, she enrolls in the renowned Art Students League of New York.

Even when not working on a novel, Pat writes tirelessly. She continues to make a living as a comic book scriptwriter, even as many contracts dry up after the war. Over the course of 1945, she also writes more than a dozen psychological short stories that she tries to sell with the help of her agent, but that remain unpublished for many years.

It is not uncommon during this time for Pat to compose long notebook entries and journal twice daily, a practice resulting in diaries upwards of three hundred pages long, largely written in German. Whereas the notebooks contain thoughts on literature, religion, history, sexuality, politics, and current writing projects, Pat attempts to keep up with her complicated (love) life in her diaries. By now the initial thrill of her affair with Natica Waterbury has subsided, and their trysts grow increasingly brief and sporadic. Pat tries to find comfort in other little affairs, though without much success. Allela Cornell, her former lover, attempts suicide toward the end of the year. Pat feels responsible, despite Allela's insistence that Pat had nothing to do with it.

This emotional free-for-all is understandably damaging to Pat's psychological state. She's gripped by depression, weltschmerz, and frequently overcome with curious fears. The stress causes her to lose her period for months on end, which leads to a further fear of pregnancy, as she does sleep with men occasionally. In her double work life, she also pushes herself to the point of physical and mental exhaustion.

As is so often the case, literature provides Pat a way out. In mid-December, while strolling along the Hudson with her mother and stepfather in upstate New York, where the couple has recently moved, Pat comes up with the idea for a story about "two soulmates" who swap murders. She thus begins crafting the plot for her first (finished and published) novel, the international bestseller *Strangers on a Train*.

✍

JANUARY 2, 1945

^GStill alive, working, and happy. I do not know whether I am free from [Natica] already. I am not too proud, I don't know if I am courageous or proud enough. This experience is very fruitful for my notebook, a fact which would greatly disgust N. What do I feel?—Great peace, and no desire to destroy the things that belong or belonged to her. No, I don't feel bitter. I feel free—and am not waiting for a phone call.^{GG}

1/2/45

[Mozart's] Jupiter Symphony, which one associates with one's seventeenth autumn, and the beginning of carnal love. To hear it now, after a dozen loves, after the end of the best, and to find it the same as ever. Yes, seventeen again, with the added pleasure of experience [and] wisdom, with the added pleasure in the fact that seventeen was never so far away as it is at this moment. And still how good is this music! To know that there will come twenty-seven, thirty-seven, and fifty-seven, perhaps, and there will always be the Jupiter.

JANUARY 3, 1945

^GNervous all day. I can't always know whether I'll be working well. Today it was the fact that B. Parsons would be coming for dinner. B. very serious when she arrived. And later our conversation grew so pleasant I didn't even want to eat. On reading my notebooks: "You really are a lonely person, aren't you, Pat? And you have learned this early on, that one is lonely all one's life."^{GG}

JANUARY 4, 1945

^GNothing from Natica. Each day brings more thoughts of her, more understanding, but not forgiveness. I don't like the cat. Her personality—she's inconsiderate towards me, jealous, always whining.^{GG}

JANUARY 8, 1945

^GCornell called, talked long, herself on the edge of suicide. God, what a sad world. Worked hard and rather well. I love her, and it will take time, time, time. And I'll always love her and honor her, because I had more with her than with any other person in my life.^{GG}

1/8/45

To live one's life in the best way possible, one must live and move always with a sense of unreality, of drama in the smallest things, as though one lived a poem or a novel, attaching the greatest importance to the route one takes to a favorite restaurant, believing oneself while browsing in a bookshop, capable of being unmade or made, destroyed or reborn, by the choice of literature one makes. In one's room alone, one should be Dante, Robinson Crusoe, Luther, Jesus Christ, Baudelaire, and in short should be a poet at all times, regarding oneself objectively and the outer world subjectively, compared to which state of mind the reality of the sorrow of a lost love is destructively real and brutal.

JANUARY 9, 1945

^GI truly don't know where the day went. Got up rather early—but for no reason. I couldn't write, think, read, and felt quite discouraged. In what was perhaps a moment of weakness, I phoned N.'s house to say that I wanted her to call me. Now it is 2:00 A.M. and *silentium* in my chamber.^{GG}

1/12/45

I wonder if any moment surpasses that of the second martini at lunch, when the waiters are attentive, when all life, the future, the world seems good and gilded (it matters not at all whom one is with, male or female, yes or no).

1/15/45

Hangovers—Intimations of the tomb. Charming, and so much more interesting physically and mentally than the evenings before them. To be drunk and with the clarity of mind of tomorrow! That is the ideal.

1/16/45

Biographical note—11:50 A.M. I have done hardly any work since breakfast at 10:50. A.M. Why? Because it is snowing in big slow flakes outside my windows, and it has made a white-bearded magic of a discarded but upright Christmas tree that sits in a corner of the little lawn in my court. The chiaroscuro of its branches half covered with snow suggest the pen lines of an artist. The tree stands and seems to think by itself, awaiting something, but also being complete in itself. I am drunk on three cups of coffee. I have a candle on my coffee table, candles are so beautiful at midday, with the snow's gray glare and the gloom of the room on the side away from the windows. Henry James sits on a shelf, inviting me to forget my brief and unimportant day and stay with him in a slow moving, rarified world which I know will leave me clean, belonging finally to no time and no place. The radio plays bassoon sonatas. The potential pleasure of this morning, this day, which I feel only in anticipation, is more intoxicating than any substance or any physical sight. Merely to exist is an ecstatic pleasure. How inadequate are all these words, when the physical sensation now makes me taut, wanting to shout, laugh, leap around my room, and at the same time be quiet and learn and feel all I can!

JANUARY 18, 1945
^GChambrun phoned: Lindley from [D.] Appleton [publishers] likes several chapters, dislikes others, and thinks the book will be too long. That's easy to see, he's right. Tonight, I am more determined than ever that the book shall never be published. Who knows or cares that G.B.S. [George Bernard Shaw] wrote three novels before his first play? One must never count the hours, the work, or the blood and sweat! I must finish this book without love, without courage, without   my love. Today at 3:30 P.M., N. called. Nothing out of the ordinary, but she said she tried to call me once. Yes, I can believe once, but what about the other days? But now it doesn't matter, and though I am trying to make myself believe I still love her, I know that under such conditions I can love no one. My friends tomorrow—God—it occurred to me today that of the eight, I've slept with six. My closest friends.^{GG}

1/18/45
The specter of worthlessness, inferiority, inadequacy, haunts, and this is death in guise. Because when he beckons—I will go. But miserable most, not to love unloved, but to die not having drawn upon one's forces.

JANUARY 19, 1945
^GBIG—DECISION!!!
    Made a big decision on my birthday—I won't finish the book. It's simple—it's not good, has no magic to it—it isn't me. Later more on this—now only the statement that if I felt it a duty (ending the book), I would end it. But this is not so. Today I will begin a new life, happier and more confident. Yes, with my new cup Natica gave to me.^{GG}

JANUARY 21, 1945

ᴳThinking of Cornell. But don't have time for it (i.e. no strong enough inclination) and really not even time for N. But as long as I love N., I will love her truly—there's no happiness otherwise. N. only calls rarely, but when she calls, she stays over. Have to renew my acquaintance with myself. I love Fétiche, and she loves me. At least—a cat!ᴳᴳ

JANUARY 22, 1945

ᴳHappy just as I was at nineteen. My brain is a tabula rasa—and life excites me.ᴳᴳ

JANUARY 24, 1945

ᴳChambrun is trying *The New Yorker* for "Mighty Nice Man."* Now or never.ᴳᴳ

1/24/45

In lieu of a vacation: go someplace in the city by yourself, preferably a place where one has never been before. The Metropolitan Opera House will do. Ballets, after three martinis, dinner, with a friend or two, is not the same. Go alone and stand in the side aisle. Flirt with the young man who turns out, under the light, to be homosexual, or with the young woman with the pixielike hair, who encouraged by your attention, laughs too heartily to herself at Papageno's antics with the silver bells, and so spoils everything. Look at the golden brim of the orchestra's cup, holding thousands of fascinating heads—most of them gray or bald, however—and imagine yourself in Vienna, Paris, London, with no attachments, tabula rasa. The world and its martinis are mine! Incredibly enough, the sensation lasts even when one arrives home and goes happily to bed.

JANUARY 26, 1945

ᴳI would like something more in my life—to love someone, of course. N. doesn't want that, that's clear, that's all. What should I say tomorrow? "Why didn't you call me?" "Why didn't you write me?"—I don't want to ask these questions, but if I pretend not to care, she will also be displeased. Read a lot this week—as one should always do, but I haven't in

---

* "A Mighty Nice Man," written in 1940, is about a young girl who catches the eye of an older man, while her otherwise watchful mother remains oblivious to his intentions. It was originally published in the *Barnard Quarterly* (Spring 1940) and reprinted posthumously in *Nothing That Meets the Eye: The Uncollected Short Stories of Patricia Highsmith* (New York, 2002).

four years. Reading is a habit, said B. Z. [Goldberg], who knows everything.^{GG}

1/26/45
Drawing—opens the heart, when too closely guarded and guided by writing, makes the soul free and once more permits the all essential freedom of association.

JANUARY 27, 1945
^GOne thing only—R. said that I am her best friend. This means a lot, because I have earned it the hard way.^{GG}

JANUARY 28, 1945
^GWork today—only work. Worked on everything, probably too much. What I have lost in my art is confidence in myself. It is hard to combine the two—confidence and a kind of humility and modesty (an affectation, no doubt!) without which everything goes badly. Worked on comics, wood cut.^{GG}

1/28/45
The long, indefinitely long period following a love affair that logically, probably is ended, when the mind believes in the end and the heart still refuses, this is the most difficult to bear because of its dominating sense of futility. Some bestial instinct of self-preservation leads one to seek another object. Then the heart is sickened, remembering how it was once, meeting and loving, without forethought and without warning. Oh, one must never be conscious of love in the mind!

JANUARY 30, 1945
^GNothing but work and duties. Nothing—until 9:45 P.M. when Natica called. (Now she wants to try parachuting!)^{GG}

1/31/45
Nota bene: I must never write about myself or my attitudes toward anything, in a piece of prose. Poetry is another matter. Inspiration is another matter. But I mean as a policy of work, an overall policy.

FEBRUARY 4, 1945
^GNot enough sleep yet. And no word from Natica. Didn't I once say that this book [this diary] shall be written about her alone? Yes, but this

means I can only write that I have had "no word from N." Worked—
much harder when I write comics. Worked for hours without the slightest
satisfaction! But my life is attaining a form of dignity. Reading [Henry]
James with great pleasure. Yes, another book N. gave me.[GG]

FEBRUARY 8, 1945

[G]One of those days when I made dinner. And I will say here and now:
it's not worth the trouble. Worked on my story (three hours) and was
extremely happy at 2:30 PM. But from 2:30 PM until 2:30 AM I was busy
with Cornell. We had a lot to drink, a too rich dinner, and didn't sufficiently discuss the things we had to say to each other.[GG]

2/8/45

It is so simple why people drink—for the confirmation of the fact that
they are the most important individuals in the world. It invests one with
the light, clean fantasy of the novel, the isolation of the poem. It is all,
that the individual captivated, wants. (Drunkenness)

FEBRUARY 12, 1945

[G]Ernst came (at 5) and seems just like three years ago. He stays here for
a month. The life of a war reporter does not seem attractive to me at all.
He wants me to come back with him, or to go to Europe after the war.
He kissed me long—and I don't know why I let him.[GG]

FEBRUARY 25, 1945

[G]A happy day—yes, I can call it "happy," a word I ordinarily only use
for lovers. Robin[*] came at 8 o'clock. Conversing with her is a delight. She
almost wants what I want—a real home, a house filled with familiar furniture, large desks, etc. We need money, and I probably need England—
and she America or France, but we want the same things. I am very
dissatisfied with my social life. It is hard—I love the gay crowd but I do
not like bourgeois society, it bores me. Which to choose?[GG]

FEBRUARY 28, 1945

[G]I must confess that it pains me to read this diary—the pages on Natica! How short the time was in which I knew her! How sweet! How
carefree!—and now she is like a wild animal, far away from me, but

---

* Pat notes in December 1944 that her friend Ann had changed her name to Robin. It is unclear, however,
which Ann she means.

gazing at me as I look at her!!!—Why? And why not? Very agitated—
and working nervously, but quickly. Am too tired—and a bit manic-
depressive.^{GG}

MARCH 3, 1945
^GLast night I ended my second reading of the dictionary. I only think—
that I found Natica during the J's. Made Catherwood's acquaintance
during the P's—that the S's seemed almost unbearable and infinite when
Natica and I broke up.^{GG}

3/4/45
Do you think I want sex? Do you think I am an animal, that I must have
sex every month, every week? I want love, and if it is sex you want, don't
come to me, woman. Sex I can have with any whore in any nightclub!
Sex!—I flee it like I flee the devil! The curve of a head in a photograph is
more fertile than a love experience. The same love as that of the painter
for his brushstroke or the writer for his phrase, the composer for his mel-
ody. Love surrounds, embraces and permeates all things.

MARCH 5, 1945
^GFinished my story for Chambrun. Soon I will know what the world
thinks of it. Tonight alone—quite lost, because I had finished my work
and wanted to do nothing.^{GG}

3/5/45
It is the strangest feeling I have ever known, because the most unlike me
as I know myself: I simply do not want to do anything. I have just finished correcting a story on which I have worked for six weeks, the evening is before me (by now, however, half over) and there are three other
stories I have in mind to do eventually. There are a dozen chores around
the house I might do. I might begin another story of the mechanical kind
that earns my living. I simply cannot summon the urge that for the past
ten years of my life has been present almost constantly—yes! even when
with friends, when it should not have been present!

MARCH 7, 1945
^GVirginia's at 7 o'clock. I love her very much, and she loves me. This is
friendship. But she could, I think, go further. I don't know. I realized
today that without love, without a girl, I am quite lost, half asleep. That's
what I thought until 11 o'clock tonight—! And then I began to think that

I lack only the right kind of work! I want to make a lot of money—but—more importantly, I want to write good stories.ᴳᴳ

MARCH 9, 1945

ᴳBreakfast at the parents', where they read my story, "They," which Chambrun had just returned to me. He wants to send it out immediately—to *L.H.J.* [*Ladies' Home Journal*] and *G.H.* [*Good Housekeeping*]—expecting rejections, but convinced that the story will do something good for me, that he will finally sell it to *H.B.* [*Harper's Bazaar*] or *Charm* [*Magazine*]. Parents like it a lot—said I've improved. Tonight, I worked on a new story, which I don't yet have an ending for. It's about the Luzis of Taxco. I want to write stories like H. James. He is my God!ᴳᴳ

MARCH 10, 1945

ᴳNatica called around 2 in the morning—very drunk. She lectured me on how I should live my life. If I don't come down from my "ivory tower," I won't write about anything real. She screamed delightful words! "I'm calling all my fucking friends—"ᴳᴳ

3/10/45

I love every day in the week, but with a different kind of love for each. Sundays I love and fear. They can be heaven or hell. Mondays are exciting with promise. Wednesdays, though I am generally exhausted by Wednesday and have to declare this some sort of half-Sunday, are pleasant because they are the middle of the week which means Sunday comes soon, Sunday having vague childhood associations, more imagined than ever actual, of casual events and playing with anything that the mind hits on. Saturdays are one martini at lunch and art exhibits, and a nap from exhaustion at 5:30 P.M.

MARCH 12, 1945

ᴳA wonderful evening at Jo P.'s. Food and drink, a fireplace, a Chesterfield, Bach's Chorale #140—what more could one want? I need nothing else. Discussed the question of "ivory towers." "Now you're worth something," she said. "Don't believe you're in an ivory tower." Advised me to get a job with the Red Cross for two months so I can observe all kinds of people and their problems. I love Jo very much. She is a rare treasure.ᴳᴳ

3/16/45

When I feel best physically and mentally, and feel unusually optimistic and forward-searching, there is also present the feeling I may
in an instant become deathly ill, and quickly die. Why this constant
tug-of-war? I believe it is the old game of self-preservation versus
self-destruction.

MARCH 20, 1945

GVery discouraged—as is normal when two people at once throw my
work back in my face! First Mr. Schiff from *Detective* [*Comics*], who said
my stories were an "old hat." Next the sketches for *Seventeen* [maga-
zine], which weren't very good, to be honest.

Rosalind and I discussed Natica—"devilishly attractive and
hopeless!"—R.C.

Germany is almost defeated.GG

MARCH 21, 1945

GBach's birthday two hundred and sixty years ago. More work to do,
but I'm tired. Read "Quiet Night"*—it's very good, I think I can sell
it. How lovely my writing was six years ago! At least I could write
economically—short! Now I always fear that I've included too many
details. I often think I don't have enough to do with the world.GG

3/26/45

To the twenty-three-year-old New Zealander I met tonight in a Sixth
Avenue Penny Arcade. He walked me home and talked of American
education. He did not ask to come upstairs. He kissed me with a clean
mouth in the shadows of my court, and when I said he was an angel, he
insisted that he had bad habits like all the rest. Tomorrow night he leaves
for England. His last night tonight, and I did not invite him upstairs, for
a cup of coffee, a long talk. Why not?—Remembering soldiers who were
not like him, remembering my work tomorrow which is insignificant
compared to war. When I am old and have seen almost everything, then
I'll be sorry I did not ask him up his last night in America.

---

* Presumably written in 1938–1939 in New York, "Quiet Night" tells the story of two sisters trapped in
a love-hate relationship with one another. It first appeared in *Barnard Quarterly* (Fall 1939). A longer,
revised version renamed "The Cries of Love," was published in *Women's Home Companion* (January
1968) and in *The Snail-Watcher and Other Stories*, Highsmith's first collection of short stories (New
York, 1970).

3/28/45

No joy on earth can compare with the artist's after he has done good work. No satisfaction or contentment can compare with it. God visits the artist personally, but people he merely watches.

4/11/45

"A woman is a sometime thing."[*]

APRIL 12, 1945

[G]The President is dead! I heard the first brief announcement on the radio at 5:40 P.M. Couldn't believe it at first—like all the others. He died of a brain aneurism suddenly, in Warm Springs, Ga. The whole world is astonished, and great preparations are being made for his memorial ceremony. The radio is playing only religious music tonight (which I like very much). Bach on four stations at the same time! God, if only Wallace were president now instead of Truman! Work is going quite well. But naturally—with F.D.R. dead, the world is quite different.[GG]

4/15/45

At first glance, war would seem to be a machine greater than the individual who is caught up in it to behave as his character guides him. War is not like the overwhelming emotions of revenge, desire, hatred. War has nothing to do with the human soul, of individuals working upon individuals. It is in the most worldly sense unreal. It is the most artificial of any of man's creations, because it has least to do with the individual. Have this moment read in the letters of Richard Spruce,[†] a suggestion that war-riddled corpses be displayed in formaldehyde in museums, to keep down wars. I think it's a fine idea.

4/16/45

Someday there may be a community of nations, a world communal system, Japan producing artists and gadgets, Germany the scientists and doctors, America the entertainment and corn, France the liquor and the poetry, England the men's clothing and the literature. Seriously, it is one of the happiest of hopes to imagine suspicions forgot, the communal idea reborn in all nations, to imagine the utilization of the remarkable skills of some nations for the good of all the rest. An interdependence with no

---

[*] A song from George Gershwin's opera *Porgy & Bess*.
[†] Richard Spruce (1817–1893), an English botanist and explorer.

fear of starvation of a certain product through the suspicion or hatred of another. Distances have been abolished, language difficulties are next. Then racial pride and prejudice.

4/19/45

Conscience, dear conscience, I dedicate these lines to you. To you, who spoil everything from breakfast in bed, to sex—even in the head. From gorging myself on the most churchly music, to standing thirty seconds longer under a hot shower on a cold night. And should I have an evening free, by some quirk, you can conjure up some work. Dear conscience, you of the long and muscle-bound arms, why was I born with you? Why do I love you so?

4/21/45

Bach's heroic little piano concerto #5 in F Major was interrupted by a special news bulletin from France, that the Russian and Allied armies have met in the district of Dresden.* Germany is split! The greatest fighting armies of the world have broken through to each other and are embracing in the streets of Dresden! And immediately afterward, Bach's second movement continued, with perfect grace and with a terrible beauty! The tears burst from my eyes, and I do not exactly know why. The emotion was like a spasm, its intensity gone before I could explain it . . . Bach walked the streets of Dresden in knee breeches and rather shabby shoes. He was greater, though, than Germany, as Germany was less than God.

APRIL 28, 1945

GAfter an evening of false reports, the news just came that Germany has capitulated. Through Himmler. I have nothing to say—perhaps later. Sketched tonight, and am happy and free as I only am when I paint or sketch. Would like to be an artist.GG

APRIL 29, 1945

GQuite suddenly, I want, perhaps more than any other of my heart's desires, to enjoy my life. I want to be like the Europeans—freed from the dreadful struggle for money! That, in this country, is the mistake of this century!GG

---

* In fact, Torgau in Saxony is considered the place where American and Soviet troops met, on April 25, 1945, the so-called Elbe Day. Dresden itself was not captured by the Red Army until May 8, 1945, while Eisenach, Bach's birthplace, was taken by the U.S. Army at the beginning of April.

MAY 1, 1945

^GHappy day in which I did too little, with not enough motivation. Hitler is dead, but no one knows how he died.^{GG}

MAY 2, 1945

^GWork is much better since last night. Very happy and why—my God, why?! Because I am thinking of Allela—yes, I almost believe that we could still have one another! But these are foolish dreams, I know. She can't believe me. But this love gives me what I need so badly—security and hope, the belief that my life still lies before, rather than behind me, in misfortune. Saw films of the German atrocities with the parents. It is truly dreadful. The audience was silent, the images of the living and the dead terrible.^{GG}

MAY 3, 1945

^GHitler is dead—and did not die a hero's death, as was thought. He took his own life. With Goering. Mussolini died this week too,—the three— F.D.R., Mussolini, and Hitler—dead in two weeks! What does Cornell think about my letter? Is she too busy to call me? Read about the atrocities in Germany—(at Rosalind's). The country is flooded with German horrors! Photographs too!^{GG}

MAY 7, 1945

^GGood day: First Mrs. St. Cyr who talks way too much, hates the Jews, loves the Republicans (everything that disgusts me!). Finally free of her, I went with the parents to see the house in Hastings. And I think we found the house in which I (and they) will create so many wonderful things— but die there? I won't go so far.^{GG}

MAY 8, 1945

^GToday was "VE Day" but half of the city celebrated yesterday. It was a terrible mistake on Ed Kennedy's behalf, who thought he was doing "nothing wrong" by relaying the news.* He endangered the negotiations between Russia and America! (Or Russia and England and Germany.)^{GG}

---

* The American journalist Edward L. Kennedy (1905–1963) was the first Allied journalist to report on the German surrender despite a news embargo.

MAY 10, 1945

^GTried without success to break into S. & S. [Simon & Schuster]. One leafs quickly through my writing there, says: "We don't buy anything—at present—." Visited Timely. Dorothy Roubichek*—Jewish, very friendly, but dear God, how severe with the stories! Finally at mine—terrible evening. Mickey bored me, Alice T. disgusted me! Terrible. Saw *Kiss Them for Me*† from too close up, and still had to pay $3.00 for it. Judy probably good, but the fact I know her changes everything.^{GG}

MAY 11, 1945

^GCarefully prepared myself for lunch at the Colony‡ with Jacques [Chambrun] and Mr. Hall. Both of them very gracious. No news on the stories. They wanted to know, naturally, what I had in petto. "A play," I said, "but no specifics yet." They didn't seem very excited. (Three martinis—the first with mother. The bill must have been much higher than his commission for the story he sold!) We mostly discussed art. With Rolf Tietgens tonight, one of our strange and wonderful evenings. We talked about everything under the sun. More later.^{GG}

5/11/45

It does not matter what happened, but what you think of it.

MAY 12, 1945

^GNot so happy. Rosalind came by at 3:00, she doesn't like my story. Lately, I am depressed by my worthlessness: haven't written anything (good) in three years.

— Haven't been faithful to anyone. That hurts!!!
— Am not worthy of anything.

(Now I am listening to [Bach's] "Bist Du bei mir." It penetrates my heart. But there it finds too much space!)^{GG}

MAY 17, 1945

^GThe comics are becoming harder to think up. And the cat—sometimes I wish it wasn't mine! Just now, late tonight, I began writing a story and have great hopes. No title.^{GG}

---

* Dorothy Roubichek, an editor at Timely, was one of very few women in those days to reach the upper echelons of the comic book industry.
† Judy Holliday's 1945 Broadway debut, which won her that year's Clarence Derwent Award for Most Promising Female.
‡ Colony was an elegant private club in New York.

5/17/45

The beautiful wonderful sensations of working again, after chaotic idleness that is anything but restful. To hell with the ship-getting-its-keel-back theory! This is literally being on top of the world. By dealing with three characters in a story, one somehow gets atop the entire world, understands all humanity (not in a moment, but in time) and above, beneath, through all, one has regained a momentum like that of the whirling earth and all the solar system, one has acquired a heartbeat.

MAY 20, 1945

GA terrible argument—unpleasantness, really, between me and David (tonight). He wanted to kiss me when we sat around a table in a bar, seven of us. Teased me—said, I needed to get "—"—the most horrible language I've ever heard in mixed company. Bob and I left as soon as possible.GG

5/22/45

Thank God for animals! They never think themselves into jams. They are always right. They are an inspiration.

5/26/45

The month of May is manic with sunshine, greenness and Mozart divertimentos. Young greenness sits like jewels in the gray stone foil of the city. Now too sedate, I once fell in love in May. Too early then, now too late to start. The month of May is strangely sexless. Busy with building the inner man, and frames and bookshelves, puttering about the house, forgetting the bread and meat work. The month of May is mad energy spewed into a hundred channels, each proclaiming its beauty and success with a tiny candle-flame at its most extreme end, so that I am a coruscating pinwheel of delight. I want to burn myself out, never counting costs and losses. In June I must rest for the first time, Fatigue, having hovered just above me all this while.

MAY 30, 1945

GCornell is not a quick talker, but when I mention a problem she's great. For example tonight, our old question: Man or no man, cook or no cook? The meals are the hardest, even though it seems strange. We need a man to govern our lives so we don't have to do anything outside our work, can have dinner with friends and then repair to our rooms. Where is this to be found?GG

MAY 31, 1945

ᴳHappy—still happy. Strolled through the city with mother, looking at furniture. We discussed the matter of marriage for a long time. She said (quite rightly) that Cornell and I are wasting a lot of time and energy by trying to have a friendship of some kind (instead of finding a man). Wrote tonight. I like the story.ᴳᴳ

JUNE 2, 1945

ᴳMet AC [Allela Cornell] at GC [Grand Central] at 8:35. The trip was long, but there were some beautiful moments. I wonder whether I will forget this trip like so many others. I have known AC for three years, and we have lived through so much together.ᴳᴳ

JUNE 4, 1945

ᴳIt rained all day. We read and sketched at home; I was very lazy! Tonight, when I tucked her into bed, I felt very close to her. I wanted to sleep with her, I felt as if I almost wanted her. And we tried in the end — but it was quite impossible for me! Decided to go to the A.S.L. [Art Students League] in New York (this summer). It is my true calling, and yet—it is only my insane power over myself which holds me back.ᴳᴳ

JUNE 6, 1945

ᴳLong talk about my tension. Whether it is physical, sexual, or mental. It is likely sexual, of course, and Cornell advised me to have sex with some-one, since love and sex are two different things. I know this in theory, but I can't take my broken body to a girl as if it were a broken watch. An impossible situation. I can't say anything to Cornell, though I think every day that she is the only one I could ever truly love.ᴳᴳ

JUNE 8, 1945

ᴳTonight, after dinner, we took a walk through the fields, and as we lay in the grass, we kissed—finally. Fate had never granted us one this good before.ᴳᴳ

6/8/45

I hate arguments and really refuse to argue, because arguing implies a fixed opinion of something. My most extreme arguments are the silent kind one has with some books. Even these are evoked only when the author's position is insufferable, untenable. The only fixed principles to have, the only truly beneficial, advisable ones, are in the form of a recipe for happiness. If one loses one's formula for happiness or a working amount of optimism, then one is indeed lost.

JUNE 9, 1945

^GMary drove us to the train station, and we took the 10:15 from Bath, looked out the window, and were very silent and somewhat sad, each occupied with her own thoughts. These train trips are pleasant, boring, happy and sad at the same time.^{GG}

JUNE 12, 1945

^GSchool at 9 o'clock [Art Students League]. The class isn't that great. The paintings I have seen seem to me dreadfully academic—though I know it is necessary, it still disgusts me.^{GG}

JUNE 16, 1945

^GRosalind said: "I'm much more excited about your drawings than about your writing, don't you agree?" Something like that—and asked me whether I might want to change careers. It's true. I want to be an artist but not become too serious, too mad about my art—that would be my downfall. I am so low (in my personal relationships) that I cannot write freely. It nonetheless seems that I can draw unreservedly. I know that I am less unhappy and tense when I paint or draw.^{GG}

JUNE 19, 1945

^GSo needed—yesterday, Joe Samstag* liked my painting very much. "Swell—exactly what I wanted—congratulations"—he said. And I was over the moon with happiness! Making progress in the class. I'm so happy I (sometimes) feel like a fool.^{GG}

6/20/45

T.S. said drunkenly tonight: "Never love an artist. When it comes time for them to work, they'll look at you as though they didn't know you, and kick you out in the cold."

6/20/45

Would I were greedy as now forever,
Not for fortune, nor yet knowledge, and for love—never,

---

* Gordon "Joe" Samstag, painter, muralist, and teacher.

A muscled horse obedient to ruthless master, art,
Exultantly racing till he break his heart.

JUNE 22, 1945
^GFinally exhausted after these two weeks of insane strength and energy.
Am happy enough when I write (without much order or discipline) but
when I draw, I feel as I have never felt before: happy like a girl who simply lives and learns and loves, who has never known a dark thought,
who has never thought about her health or mental development. Am I in
love? I don't know. I love AC but I'm not in love with her. A situation that
would no doubt appeal to her if she knew.^{GG}

7/1/45
For future reference: In case of doldrums of mind or body or both, sterility, depression, inertia, frustration, or the overwhelming sense of time
passing and time past, read true detective stories, take suburban train
rides, stand a while in Grand Central—do anything that may give a
sweeping view of individuals' lives, the ceaseless activity, the daedal ramifications, the incredible knots of circumstance, the twists and turns in
all their lives, which no writer is gifted enough to conceive, sitting in the
closeness of his quiet room.

JULY 3, 1945
^GWent to see Rolf this evening. It's a great pleasure to see his house. It
changes from visit to visit, like a museum. And Bobby[*] also makes small
pictures, paintings and things—very pleasant. Rolf advised me to do only
crazy things in my painting and drawing. "Do what no one else does."^{GG}

7/8/45
The actual time spent in creative work each day need be only very little.
The important thing is that all the rest of the day contribute to this stren-
uous time.

7/18/45
Put all your fears into words, paint pictures of your enemies, prose
poems of all apprehensions, doubts, hatreds, uneasinesses, to defeat them
and stand upon them.

---

* Rolf's lover, the art dealer Robert (Bobby) Isaacson. Bobby would later date James Ingram Merrill,
winner of the 1977 Pulitzer Prize for Poetry.

7/25/45

Write as a painter paints, with renewed awareness of the work of choosing and rejecting. Remember (and realize) that a sentence may be set into
the middle of a previously written paragraph, without interfering with
rhythm, that this sentence can be the iron bolt, or the germ cell, or the
life itself, all added later, as the fleck of white at the end of a nose may
quicken the entire portrait. Apply sentences like strokes of color. Survey the work as a whole from time to time and experience it as though
it were a painting. This shift in itself provides a measure of poetry, the
necessary untruth of art. Scenes are necessarily separate pictures, but the
experience of the whole should be orgasmic, productive of the wordless
joy and satisfaction one feels looking at van Gogh's *Night Café* or at
Marsden Hartley's workman's shoes.

AUGUST 7, 1945

GVery happy. *Harper's Bazaar* arrived. My story ["The Heroine"] has
no illustrations, and a stupid paragraph on P.H. at the end which should
have been left out. Mailed it to grandma right away. Mother called. Very
proud, she said, but hadn't seen the story yet. I wanted to say here that
I felt nothing until I saw the magazine in the hands of a stranger this
afternoon—I thought that he might read my story tonight—and then I
felt something.GG

8/10/45

I here highly resolve to spend one hour per day in study, preferably
eleven to midnight, devoting two months to each subject. At this time, I
have been at it a week. God permitting, I shall study at least this amount
the rest of my life.

AUGUST 11, 1945

GBusy—as always. Got the OK for a synopsis from Famous,* my latest
company. Saw girls in uniform in the museum at 3:00. Very nice. Excellent, and left much to the imagination. Possible homosexuality, without
a doubt—and if the two will keep seeing other girls later, that's the question. Terrible soiree at Ann T.'s. A bluestocking, an overaged Bea Lillie†—

---

* Famous Studios, the animation division of Paramount Pictures, had moved to New York City in 1943
and produced the Popeye the Sailor and Superman cartoons.
† A grand dame of the stage, Beatrice Gladys "Bea" Lillie (1894–1989) debuted on Broadway in 1924.
During the war years, the Canadian actress went on tour to support the troops, traveling to the
Caribbean, even Africa and the Middle East. Despite several long-term relationships with men, there
were consistent rumors that Lillie was a lesbian.

abound a dark, roofed-over table. That forced us close together. Everyone siting around, trying to be amusing. I drank way too much gin, was rather sick and left at 1:00 A.M. to go to Allela.[GG]

AUGUST 12, 1945

[G]Allela came at 11:30. Argued bitterly about the war. They are expecting peace with Japan, and A. is angry because I am not worked up. It is not enough for me that millions of men and women are waiting for freedom. It's not enough. Do you understand?[GG]

AUGUST 14, 1945

[G]She is haranguing me because I don't share her feelings on the war! Nervous today and could barely work. Herb L. came at 6:30. Very handsome, out of his uniform for two months now. As bad luck would have it, the declaration of peace came at 7:00 PM! Of course (?) phone calls from Allela. Herb invited us out to dinner. Hotel Pierre, two bottles of champagne—and Allela, who takes everything and gives nothing, wanted to propose a toast to F.D.R., etc. It disgusted me so. Later I slept with Herb, just as I wanted, and immensely enjoyed it! Allela tried to call several times and come up to the room, but we cut the doorbell wires.[GG]

AUGUST 20, 1945

[G]Arrived punctually at 12 at *Harper's Bazaar.* Saw C. Snow (whose temperature never rises above 30°) and accepted work, eight hours per day (!) $45 a week. Wasn't satisfied. I'll start Thursday or Monday. Lots to do. My small cabinet for records arrived, and I spent (sinfully!) 6 hours putting it together. But now my small collection is housed in it, and I am very happy.[GG]

8/21/45

The moral frame of reference. In five words the goal of all my past life & perhaps all my future! Where shall I ever find it? In England, in the Roman Catholic church, in a convent, within myself!? Oh, yes, to make one's own rigid code of laws in regard to society! Perhaps this is the only and final answer. Meanwhile, until our feet find this ladder, until our butterfly wings are fixed with pins and glue upon our labeled panel, then we flounder, drink, vaguely ponder, and flounder eternally some more.

8/21/45

An interview with my agents. It is three in the afternoon in a hot and half-sleeping New York, the month of August. One is in shirtsleeves, collar open, shiny with sweat, and lazily nervous and alert, as after a hangover. The other's impeccable dress is scarcely altered except that he wears no jacket. Both their pairs of hands are sleek, shiny, well cared for, with tiny points of knucklebones showing at the bend.

"If you could put a happy ending on this, Miss Highsmith, I think we could sell it. Just the ghost of a happy ending. That little concession to commercialism shouldn't ruin it. Just the merest touch."

"Like being a little bit pregnant," drawls the other agent.

Polite laughter. What can one say?

"Too bad you write like that, Miss Highsmith. It's sad to write and not be published."

It is not the least sad to write and not be published, but how can I explain this? I do not even begin it. I only sit there, alternately trying to smile, trying to control the leaping words in me.

We do not speak the same language, I think as I go out into the sunshine.

AUGUST 22, 1945

GEveryone is advising me to write a novel. I want to! I want to—!!!GG

AUGUST 24, 1945

GPhoned *Harper's Bazaar* to tell Ms. Snow I don't want the job. My excuse was the money. I don't like changing my mind about things, but it would be nonsense to have less time to work.GG

AUGUST 27, 1945

GAt war with *Harper's Bazaar*. Wish it had been a Blitzkrieg. There at 12 after a nervous morning. Couldn't wait for [Betty Parsons's] call because I had to take my tooth to the laboratory. I can clearly see that everything will go badly this week because I am too rushed. Ms. Snow kept me waiting for an hour. Sent me to various women. Finally, she offered me $75 a week, but it's still not enough. R. Portugal gave me an article to write on P. Mondrian. I don't know how much it will pay.GG

AUGUST 31, 1945

GVery frightened, brought my Mondrian article to *H. Bazaar* and—when Wheelock* was still there, R. Portugal pulled the poor thing out and read

---

* Dorothy Wheelock Edson, features editor at *Harper's Bazaar*.

the first page. "Excellent beginning!" she said, and I breathed for the first time in five days.^{GG}

SEPTEMBER 3, 1945

^GThe last lovely day. I am suddenly wondering whether mother might not, in her despair, try to find happiness alone? Things are truly impossible with S. I think they haven't had sex—in months. It's quite easy to see.

My story—several hours of work. Made mother read the introduction to a book by H. Melville. She read the 50 pages but chastised Melville for neglecting his family.—There is something she will never truly understand: the life of an artist. No more than I can understand the life of a wife, a mother.^{GG}

SEPTEMBER 5, 1945

^GHard work—too hard to be happy—(one needs time for happiness when one is happy enough already—time to play with one's cat, leaf through one's books. But I have no such thing).^{GG}

9/8/45

Should like to determine the reason or the host of reasons why I avoid meeting people, encountering them on my walks, why I avoid greeting even the most pleasant acquaintances by crossing the street when I see them far ahead of me on the sidewalk. Perhaps it is, basically, the eternal hypocrisy in me, of which I've been aware since about thirteen. I may feel, therefore, that I am never quite myself with others, and hating deceit, constitutionally hating it, avoid its necessity. Then, too, I am sure I feel most contacts insignificant, because the polite phrases—there are layers and layers of polite, semi-polite, not quite natural phrases, which must be stripped away, used up, before one reaches the real person. And how rarely this happens! What troubles me somewhat is the superimposed problem of being in touch with humanity. Flatly, I do not want it.

SEPTEMBER 11, 1945

^GThe [prime minister of] Japan, Tojo, shot himself yesterday. Attempted suicide, but he's still alive, thanks to the blood of an American soldier. There will be a tribunal. In Germany too, for various war crimes. Worked hard until I was dog tired. This can't go on. First of all, the price is too high. But right now I have so many expenses—my tooth (which is still not finished!—now—once again—I look like a witch!)—my taxes, and, as always, the rent.^{GG}

SEPTEMBER 12, 1945

^GTake heed, future readers! This diary should be simultaneously compared to my notebooks, so that one will not have the impression I write only of worldly affairs! Worked. Prepared all kinds of things for my mother's birthday. Don't have enough presents. But I have a bottle of Champagne.^{GG}

SEPTEMBER 13, 1945

^GSometimes I feel as though I can't keep up with my work and social life. In ten years, perhaps, I will read this and laugh.^{GG}

9/16/45

Insane note with blushing face. Horror stories I adore, and I haven't even tried to write one since early college days, when I turned out one every six months at least. But I realized then that horror stories were my meat, that horror was, in a sense, my milieu, my *métier*. Should I not allow myself to try to write one horror story? (Chorus of yeses from the unseen, clamoring audience.) Suspense I adore, am excellent at creating because I don't worry about it at all. The accuracy of vision, the confidence unrealized as confidence, these are the sine qua non. Well then, a horror story. Tonight, in the country, the fluttering of a moth at my window screen is enough!

SEPTEMBER 18, 1945

^GInteresting—tried to buy something to "bring on menstruation" and was told that if he had such a thing, he would not be allowed to sell it, because it would be "against the law"! Imagine—against the law! My God! What a country! What a nation! If only I were in France or Russia! So—I called Doctor Borak, and will see him tomorrow. I don't know whether I'm pregnant—what an ugly word! And as I write this, I feel as though I am not pregnant in the least! For months, my period has come two weeks late—and the last time very little—so perhaps it is starting to vanish again.^{GG}

9/20/45

Again and again, for years now, in the most comfortable and happy moments of my life, I remember myself before the age of six, sitting in my beloved overalls before a gas stove in Gramma's living room, reading the evening *Press* or the morning *Star-Telegram*, reading the serials in them, now and again holding the paper close to my nose for it would be still fragrant, almost warm, from the inky press. I recall the sound of the thin old door, wainscoted at the bottom, as my cousin Dan entered, chafing his hands. The house, though plain and ramshackle, showing a hint of poverty even here and there, could always make room for one more, could always provide food for one more mouth, and generously, and love for one more heart.

SEPTEMBER 21, 1945

ᴳTony Pastor's* almost incredibly boring, until I saw a girl—blond hair with a gray band, rather Russian. Really wanted to meet her. She's called Joan. She didn't tell me, but—we have a date, Sunday afternoon at 5 at the 1st Avenue Mayfair [Restaurant].ᴳᴳ

SEPTEMBER 23, 1945

ᴳWas at the Mayfair at 5—she at 5:05. Very quiet—in everything! "But it's really rather fabulous we're having this date, right?" I had to smile. Over two drinks she admitted she's had "an experience" with a guy and a girl. She goes to Tony Pastor's too much, I think. She's really childlike, cute (German). And she makes me laugh of happiness. Ate at Luigi's—Rocco. And to Tony Pastor's for a moment. "I want a commission!," cried May B., who introduced us. Later a Champagne Cocktail at that quiet bar. A typical first night. In Wash. Park   I really just had to embrace and kiss her—when six guys showed up—started to hug us—especially Joan, who was shouting my name. What could I do? I don't want my nose broken! Highly embarrassing. Home late—not in love, but happy.ᴳᴳ

9/27/45

So little motivation, strength of purpose, is needed apparently to turn a woman or a girl from her regular bourgeois world into the road to homosexuality. Why do they choose this? I must discover.

10/10/45

There is the unremitting instinct to find a focus for one's ideas, all one's ideas. There is a need to find someone to please, to make happy, simply to make understand. There is a need for a person (or a thing) to criticize one or to praise. There is a need, in brief, for another ego, much like one's

---

* Tony Pastor's Downtown, a club popular with lesbians at 130 West Third Street, was raided in 1944 on moral charges but survived—apparently backed by the mob.

own, or with only interesting variations. Therefore one falls in love. Yet if a substitute thing might be found for this, the destructive process of love, loving and being disappointed in the person need not be suffered. Therefore, the quest for the substitute. Conceivably it might be God. Conceivably, given the willingness, the necessary devotion and spirituality, it might be a dead hero, a dead friend. Once, however, this alter ego erects itself in whatever fetish of the individual, then the need for love is precluded.

10/11/45

Loneliness is an emotion more interesting than love. And one who is true to his loneliness is more faithful than any lover.

10/15/45

R.v.H.* told me tonight a most interesting situation. His two daughters, aged nine and fourteen are not, he says, developing into people. They read comic books avidly, and have not known the torture of crushes, the agony of self-consciousness and of imagined inferiority (the heroic sense, the desperate, world-ending sense of "I am not like the others"—mine), which to his European mind go on to make the character. How personally it affected me, for I agree with him absolutely! I felt sorry for him, for what he wishes is hopeless. He wishes to make unusual people out of two perfectly ordinary people. He wishes to expand consciousnesses that know better than to be expanded. All that remains for him is to take comfort in the knowledge that his daughters will never suffer as he has done, as I have done. Being European, he blamed this on America.

10/23/45

It is not conscience that prompts me to write, because I am a writer it is only dissatisfaction with this world.

OCTOBER 26, 1945

ᴳLunch with Raimund von Hofmannsthal at Voisin.† He is the most suave, most charming man! Conversing with him is like taking a trip to Europe!

---

* Raimund von Hofmannsthal (1906–1974), son of playwright and poet Hugo von Hofmannsthal. He married Ava Alice Muriel Astor in 1933, the only daughter of American tycoon John Jacob "Jack" Astor IV. In 1939, Raimund married his second wife, Lady Elizabeth Paget, an English aristocrat.
† French restaurant (1912–ca. 1969) and a New York city landmark. It is cited in both Ian Fleming's *Diamonds Are Forever* as well as in F. Scott Fitzgerald's short story "The Lost Decade" (published by *Esquire* in 1939).

He takes an interest in all of his friends' problems—especially Rosalind's and mine. Said he'd been anticipating this date for days, etc.—but no flattery. We discussed culture in America, my work, love, Rosalind.[GG]

10/26/45

Decision: never, never to expect a tranquil emotional life, above all never to count this a requisite for writing. Consequently, to hold emotional life apart from my writing, therefore from my life itself. "Emotional life"—the brick in the road that never can be laid smooth!

10/29/45

Fatigue + coffee = intoxication and elation.
Love + coffee = intoxication and ecstasy.

OCTOBER 30, 1945

[G]Thank God I'm not like B.Z.G.—dead when I am not in love. No, there are the pleasures of the mind. The difficulty is that one cannot enjoy them day in, day out—not all alone. I am leading an erratic life. It will be interesting to see how long I can keep it up.[GG]

10/30/45

Be content, be content, be content, be content.
Be continent. Be continental. And yet insular.

10/31/45

I am three months short of being twenty-five. Life presses upon me like a needle's point. I see things as though they were extremes of what they are. I feel too acutely a slightly pleasant or a slightly unpleasant happening. And all around me, melancholy amounting to real sadness becomes an atmosphere. The slightest tasks are done with great effort, and all life is without joy. Is this epic? Is this sensitivity? No, only the result of a distorted lens.

10/31/45

Whether to write a book about the unhealthy civilization of New York, and thereby rid myself of it; whether to jump clear of it all. At any rate, one must escape from it.

11/5/45

The process of culture—Suffering first of all, generally through love at the age of eighteen or seventeen or sixteen, but such humble and profound misery that one craves the richest medicaments. Therefore, one turns to poetry, music, books. Of course, some sensitivity is prerequisite. And perhaps the process begins long before, with this sensitivity which is present for always. So where has this analysis advanced me?

NOVEMBER 11, 1945

ᴳI feel—no, I know—that when I am in love, and am loved, or at least feel hopeful of it, I can speak with others, say all the right things. And now, if only a desert or a wasteland were before me, I would say everything I do not want to say, be miserable and smoke.ᴳᴳ

11/15/45

Depression—Weltschmerz seizes one like a paralysis, in my case in attacks of two to three hours, generally in the broadest part of the day—between one and six in the afternoon. One cannot move, much less think of work. One cannot think even conclusively on one's own Weltschmerz, for to do this would be to reach some kind of goal, and against the reaching of goals, the entire mind is set.

   Having come through the most ghastly war in history, the nations are again at one another's throats across the peace conference tables, while the governed classes nervously read their newspapers at home, realizing as thousands of generations have realized it after thousands of wars through the ages, that one more war has been fought in vain. Moreover, they have lost a son, a brother, a husband. Moreover, great Europe is broken and poor.

11/21/45

What's the matter with the world? Love is dying like flies.

NOVEMBER 25, 1945

ᴳRaimund came here at midnight, and left me alone with the most troubling conclusions of our conversation: the difficulties and the drawbacks of being gay. That I feel more at ease when I wear men's clothing, that this is not an advantage, etc. It seems I cannot write down here how this conversation impressed me. But I will not forget it.ᴳᴳ

DECEMBER 4, 1945

ᴳBad news—from *H.B.* [*Harper's Bazaar*], a letter from Mrs. Aswell with my story which she couldn't buy. "Your protagonist needs more charisma," she said. And that the topic is played-out. It's so much better than the story they published! But they want the story smooth. Learned from D.D. [David Diamond] that Cornell has been in the hospital for a week. Something with her stomach—and in critical condition for five days! God, and now she has so little will to live![GG]

DECEMBER 5, 1945

[G]Am frightfully hungry for life—to see and learn, so decided to take a trip in January. I'll go alone, take the bus—perhaps to New Orleans, or Kentucky, Virginia, Tennessee. This hunger is the only—most natural and healthy feeling I've had in seven years! Thank God I'm dissatisfied with my small circle of gay friends! Phoned David Diamond for news on Allela. Yes, she attempted suicide—the Sunday after Thanksgiving. Nitric acid—half a bottle, quickly, on the roof, drunk at 6:30 AM after a fight with Annie, who was in her room then. Annie wanted to stay up and drink, Allela wanted to go to bed. And she is not allowed to see any of her loved ones. Later she'll be sent to her parents. How sad, and how unnecessary![GG]

DECEMBER 6, 1945

[G]Tired—but worked hard until 7 o'clock, when Natica arrived punctually. Always glad to have her at my house! Her face is beautiful, her hair even smoother, like fine gold. And tonight we didn't get drunk—didn't need it—but I discovered something I have known for a long time: I have loved no one else since Natica. She is the only woman who I have ever felt physical attraction for. Later lying on the bed, listening to music. We laughed a lot—this is new to me, perhaps because I'm so fat now—and our kisses were so lovely that she stayed in the end. Only once did I almost cry. No, I will never again cry over her.[GG]

12/9/45

The place is here, the time is now. These are the two principles of truth which the intellectual, who of all people professes to be aware of them, never puts into practice. Henry James based his life work on them, and awakened personally too late to them.

12/9/45

A satire—could be of indefinite length—on this twentieth century, which grows ever more like Huxley's *Brave New World*. Yet this would be more affecting because of its reality and instance: the half hour telephone calls to arrange finally a time when two people can see each other for five minutes, the article, in the biggest newspaper of the nation, on the subject of Washington officials' having insufficient time to think, the books in Brentano's and Scribner's entitled, *"How to Think about World Peace," "How to Read a Page,"* all the Durant condensations, the classic abridgements, and et cetera too numerous to mention. Also, and not least, the practice of buying inferior goods with a view to discarding them when they wear out, in order to buy more with one's presumably then increased income. The fact that assistant professors' assistants are offered fifty cents an hour, sub-scrubwoman wages, that the young student when praised by his French teacher, told that he should teach, replies, "Is that all I'm fitted for?" In a word, the reverse of things as they should be. The Black Ages masquerading as the Age of Enlightenment, Racial Equality, Universal Democracy as the Universal Ideal, the Age of the Atom, which is also the age of such Anti-christianity that no man trusts his cousin in possession of it.

King Greed's Reign! No need to shout, "Long live!"

DECEMBER 10, 1945

GAm happy like a fool. Life is opening up before me—and I am an adventurer, a knight, a hero, a—Don Quixote, perhaps. All because I saw N. today—only for a few minutes, but those minutes were worth more than five nights. God, how beautiful life is when it is illuminated by a woman!GG

DECEMBER 11, 1945

GWorked—until I went to see Allela at 4:30 at St. Vincent's. She is lying with a tube up her nose through which she must "eat." She seems dark, thin, lifeless. Her mother was there at first, but she left soon, as if we were lovers. I brought her my best and newest book—Dostoyevsky's short stories. But she has a fever, and can read little. God, how sad that so many people are worried about her, that she must rest for such a long time! She was surprised that her friends are so caring. "Perhaps one learns," she said, "who one's friends are." She didn't know that I knew about the suicide attempt. "It doesn't matter what you do, Pat—I'll always love you." And she asked whether we could go to Minot this winter. "How is your life? How is your love life?" I told her that I had myself all to myself.GG

DECEMBER 15, 1945

ᴳHave almost finished the fifth or sixth draft of my "Aaron" story.* Shorter, but not short enough. Read a book on writing short stories, one of those books I usually hate, but I have decided I must no longer write only for myself.ᴳᴳ

DECEMBER 20, 1945

ᴳI can't deny it, I am lonely because I have heard nothing from Natica! God, I must learn to live without hope, without goals, without love (of the ordinary kind) for Natica. Natica, the secret, the mystery, the fate, the happiness, the sadness of my life.ᴳᴳ

DECEMBER 22, 1945

ᴳOnce more I am typing up my "Aaron" story, which I must finish before beginning—or finishing—something new. Thinking of a novel based on my idea of two soul mates.† How is it possible that Natica can let Christmas go by without saying a word?ᴳᴳ

DECEMBER 28, 1945

⌐Rolf same as ever—my wonderful friend! He talks and talks and talks, until it's one thirty all of a sudden! About the country's economy, the difficulties of writing. We have some differences—he likes [William] Saroyan and finds Proust boring. Says that Geo. Davis found my stories immature. And also—that I have wonderful ideas but don't plumb them. They want magic—a little idea, brought to life with magic. Unfortunately, that's the style in which publishers think. And lately I want to tell stories, describe people, write at length. I love Rolf very much. He has become more relaxed. Also very fat, and worried about it. We promised to see each other more often.ᴳᴳ

12/28/45

For future pondering (no time now): Why does a person take inordinate pride in his appearance, in being dressed fresh and dapper? It affects sometimes the clever and the stupid, the rich and the poor.

---

* The story of Aaron Bentley, a newcomer in a small city who is rumored to have a taboo relationship with a ten-year-old social outcast named Freya, was published posthumously as "The Mightiest Mornings" in *Nothing That Meets the Eye: The Uncollected Stories of Patricia Highsmith* (New York, 2002).
† This will become her future novel *Strangers on a Train*.

*Lovers Chart, which Patricia Highsmith drew up
in 1945 to rank and compare her lovers.
The initials of the women have been removed to
protect their privacy.*

1946

LIFE GETS EVEN MORE hectic for Patricia Highsmith in 1946, both professionally and personally. She has a new agent, Margot Johnson, with whose help she gets two of her latest short stories, "Doorbell for Louisa" and "The World's Champion Ball Bouncer," published in the magazine *Woman's Home Companion*. Rather than develop the idea for *Strangers on a Train*, Pat spends her summer in Kennebunkport, Maine, working on a novel she'll later abandon called *The Dove Descending*.

The influential Catherwood family have a summerhouse in Kennebunkport; daughter Virginia, who goes by Ginnie, is Natica Waterbury's lover—that is, until Pat wins her over in June, thus ending Pat's relationship with Natica once and for all. Before Ginnie becomes Pat's new true love, however, Pat grapples with her feelings for Joan S., as the two visit New Orleans together. Joan is grounded and good, the embodiment of purity and stability—if a little boring. Amid the strife she will later encounter with Ginnie, Pat always wishes she could be satisfied by her "simple" love of Joan.

While Ginnie recovers from her latest jag at the family home, she and Pat discover a new hobby: collecting and breeding snails. The wealthy heiress from Philadelphia, who was denied custody of her child following her divorce, will become (yet another) notoriously unfaithful, obsessive lover for the next year and a half. As in earlier relationships, Pat's life with Ginnie is marked by Pat's central conflict between writing (which requires retreat) and having a love life (which requires the opposite). Pat not only dedicates several short stories to Ginnie, she uses her as inspiration for various female figures, from Carol in *The Price of Salt* to Lotte in *The Tremor of Forgery*.

In October, Joan S. is hospitalized following a failed suicide attempt. A few days later, Allela Cornell dies as a result of her suicide attempt the year before. Given the dramatic end to these recent love affairs, Pat considers therapy for the first time. There's also talk of her marrying Rolf Tietgens, to help him secure citizenship, and to start a family together. But in the end, her other loves prevail—the one she feels for Ginnie, and, not least, her love of freedom and independence.

❦

JANUARY 1, 1946

ᴳA happy day, like all my New Year days. Alive in body and spirit. Natica called me. I told her we were opening a bottle of champagne. So she arrived at 9 o'clock. Ate—then later a conversation with Rosalind, in which I was not much involved. She kissed Rosalind—and I didn't mind. I made a lot of sketches of them on the bed! N. and I left very early to get tattoos in Chinatown. Coffee at Rikers (after a lovely kiss on the steps of the L train!) and back home, where we drank, danced, kissed, and swore our undying love to each other. She wants to have a life with me "in the country." I think it would be better to move to a small city. The old problem—I don't know any. We're thinking of New Orleans, too. Am happy. Wish she'd stayed. She has her reasons. God—so many kisses tonight I'm still drunk!ᴳᴳ

JANUARY 2, 1946

ᴳWorked hard until 11:30 PM. Dog tired. Wrote another new opening for "The Magic Casements"*—simpler, sweeter. He needs the tender kisses of the woman he loves. He cannot deny it. The world (then) seems true— i. e. one sees it as it is.ᴳᴳ

JANUARY 3, 1946

ᴳ[Ernst] Hauser is here—we had dinner. He brought me three leather-bound books from Paris—one in Latin, the others French. And a few Gold Flake cigarettes, which I like a lot. If only Americans preferred milder cigarettes! Hauser's the same as ever. Disappointed I don't read his articles—but it doesn't matter. He's very loving. What will come of it, I wonder? I would have much rather seen Natica tonight! But she didn't call.ᴳᴳ

---

* "Magic Casements" (working title: "The Feary Lands Forlorn") tells the story of a sad, solitary man who encounters a captivating woman at his regular bar one night. They agree to meet at a museum during the day, but the woman fails to keep their appointment, leaving the man all alone. The story was published posthumously in *Nothing That Meets the Eye: The Uncollected Stories of Patricia Highsmith* (New York, 2002).

JANUARY 7, 1946

^GWorked alone—(already) have a title for the story: "The Mightiest Mountains."* And paid a visit to Rolf tonight. God, how I love him! His room is so German, manly, clean! Robert Isaacson, Bobby's father, who looks very young, showed up at the same time. He's getting married in a week to a woman who's only twenty-four years old. Interesting to hear this practical, very ordinary Kansan speaking with Rolf. He doesn't worry much about his son; he joked with Rolf and me, and borrowed $10 before leaving.^{GG}

1/8/46

People unhappy in love never seem to remember others have known the same pain. The desolation one knows when so overcome with grief one cannot even fashion beauty of it and is thus deprived of this last consolation, has been experienced by serious, inconsolable young men since the beginning of time. Thus Schubert's *Die Winterreise*—the first verse being, "Frozen tears! How can my tears be so cold when they come from a heart so warm it could melt all winter's ice." The picture of the melancholy, energy-flagellated young man, roving the countryside, makes one's heart weep in sympathy.

JANUARY 9, 1946

^GWrote too little of the story until midnight. Then Natica phoned at 12:30 AM. She came over and we talked, kissed, drank tea until quarter to five! Time for love is not easily found, and shouldn't be taken lightly. We swore our love to each other once again—what does it count with such a neurotic? But I want to make it count as much as possible! I've promised myself! Saw Margot Johnson,† to whom I gave "The Mightiest Mornings."^{GG}

JANUARY 11, 1946

^G[Allela] Cornell's birthday. Went to see her at 1. She looks worse, though she said she was getting stronger. She weighs only 106, and has to have a tube put down her throat every week. It hurts terribly, she said. Surprised and curious that I'm seeing Natica again. No one knows when she will be discharged from the hospital. In about two months, perhaps. I loved [Natica] tonight as I have never loved before! I

---

* The story she refers to as "the Aaron story" in 1945, later renamed "The Mightiest Mornings."
† Margot Johnson, Pat's new agent.

am enchanted with her! If I can't spend every night of my life with her, I don't want to live! I think (in these moments) that if she or I were to leave, my happiness and my reason to live would be over. And when she finally reciprocates my love (as she did tonight), I am almost sick with happiness and gratefulness.[GG]

JANUARY 15, 1946

[G]Woke up and almost cried because I'd slept until 2:30 PM instead of 8:30 AM! Too much work. Dinner with Natica, whom I met at Chop Suey on Lexington Ave. She had just seen [Virginia] Catherwood and was worried that she was following her. But no. Natica has never looked as beautiful as she did tonight! As I was sitting next to her in the movies, I had difficulty restraining myself. When she uses dirty words, she excites me![GG]

JANUARY 19, 1946

[G]Busy all day with the party so I only had half an hour to myself before the first guest arrived! Finally, only M. & A. & Natica remained, and Natica, who was blind drunk, tried in every way to devastate me: stubbing her cigarettes out on the floor, blocking the sink, necking with Maria until I was practically sick. I stayed with A. in the kitchen, and heard everything taking place on my bed. I was trembling like a dying man, and asked A., "What are they doing?," as if we were in a bad play. Finally Natica stormed out at 4:30, and I ran after her, not wanting us to part on such bad terms (though she had kissed me upstairs and said sweet things to me). "I love you and I'll call you tomorrow!" she said when she got into the cab. She went, I hope, to Catherwood, because she was completely drunk, almost sick. Cleaned the house, more depressed than I've ever been on my birthday.[GG]

JANUARY 21, 1946

[G]Why am I still in love with N.? She's just the same as last year: doesn't call me, hurts me and herself. And—it's raining. Rolf at 7:00—the best hours of my day. Why can't I have such a life for myself? He's grown so much! He's an angel. No wonder Bobby worships him![GG]

JANUARY 22, 1946

[G]Rosalind invited me to a cocktail party at her place on Saturday night, but I can't bear to go; it's hell to see Natica kissing Maria. My small, sour presence will not be missed.[GG]

1/30/46

And in childhood—the scenes we knew then, the specific moments we remember, are preserved in some alcohol of memory, which to the individual's senses possesses a particular flavor and aroma as incommunicable to another fellow being as the description of a color to a blind man. Perhaps it is this, the sealed envelope of childhood each of us carries within him, which contributes to the sense of aloneness that is with us as long as we live.

FEBRUARY 4, 1946

^GWrote 5½ pages, my first children's book.* About Gracey. Am excited, calm, happy after my conversation with my most loyal friend, Rosalind, who is a constant source of support for me.^{GG}

FEBRUARY 6, 1946

^GWent to see Cornell, who's looking much better. Now she seems as if she wants to live! But only weighs around 99 pounds. Her hands look like a bird's. She wants to know about everything—so I told her funny stories about my party, that I had a suit made. "Oh, Pat, I hate to see you with them! You deserve so much better!" I loved her before I left.^{GG}

2/6/46

What does it matter if the months with you were few, the days of happiness so few they would hardly make a week? You made me happier than I had ever been before, so happy that more happiness might have been fatal. And now, reliving those moments with the precious instrument of memory, I recreate you, I recreate myself, and knowing I have attained such godly bliss, I am made finer, greater, humbled, prouder. A part of me will always live in that past, for better or for worse. A part of me will always worship you. (Alas, no. 4/27/50)

FEBRUARY 9, 1946

^GYesterday, I decided to buy a ticket for Natica, and give it to her for Valentine's day. We'll fly together on March 10.^{GG}

---

* Highsmith's first children's book is unfortunately not included in her literary estate.

FEBRUARY 11, 1946

ᴳNow is the time—God, when was it not the time?—in which I need understanding from N. She is not cool towards me, but shows no interest at all. Of course, I want her as much as ever. I give her the biggest presents I can—and only regret that they likely make her even more indifferent towards me.ᴳᴳ

FEBRUARY 12, 1946

ᴳThe city is shut down. Worker's strike—towboat workers. No heat at home, etc. Restaurants and theaters are closed. At Rosalind's for lunch. Very pleasant. She obviously understood that I didn't want to see her friends (that evening). So, I had her the way I like—alone.ᴳᴳ

FEBRUARY 14, 1946

ᴳ1:45 A.M. Just spoke with N. She didn't mention the valentine. But I know she received it. What kind of a girl is she? I wonder what she thinks of the plane ticket? Neither of us wanted to mention it! What a situation!ᴳᴳ

FEBRUARY 16, 1946

ᴳYesterday, she said, "I got your valentine. It's the sweetest thing I've ever seen," etc. Thank God she gave me so much! Will she come or not—? She will come. Went to see Marj. W. (at 9:15), one of my closest four friends: Rolf, [Ruth] Bernhard, Rosalind. How she soothes me when I am troubled! And even when I can tell her so little!ᴳᴳ

FEBRUARY 27, 1946

ᴳHow lovely are days full of work. Lunch with S.W., who seems almost charming to me now. He has written a 244-page novel. The topic seemed somewhat nebulous to me, but perhaps it's only that I am not very interested in other people's work. I'm sorry for it, but I can't change it.ᴳᴳ

MARCH 2, 1946

ᴳCalled N. at 10:45 A.M. In bed. Asked about the article—"Yes, it's finished!" she shouted angrily. "And my skirt? Do you have it?" "You'll get it back! Today!" she shouted, and hung up. God, these impolite hang-ups are quite normal for her. Now I'm angry with her in earnest and am delighted that I will doubtlessly be in New Orleans alone.ᴳᴳ

MARCH 4, 1946

^GAm planning my novel.[*] I have the plot. It's so simple I can hardly dare call it a plot. Am reading [Evelyn Waugh's] *Brideshead Revisited* with great pleasure. A serious novel written with humor. Waiting until tomorrow to call Natica.^{GG}

MARCH 5, 1946

^GVery happy as I was getting dressed to go see Joan [S.] We drank martinis in her room at the Barbizon[†] and played records. I wanted to embrace her and tell her of my troubles. She is so sweet and simple and honest. I invited her to come to New Orleans. "I'll have to think about it," she said. Until Thursday.^{GG}

MARCH 9, 1946

^GRelaxed—just after I told the news to [Richard E.] Hughes: that I'll write fewer comics from now on. "I've heard this so many times before I don't care," he answered. Joan called at four o'clock sharp—(what a delight to know a punctual girl!) and came at 6:30: martinis. I enjoyed introducing Joan to my mother. Of course, mother liked her a lot. When she'd left, mother said, "I like her more than any of the other girls you've gone out with."^{GG}

3/11/46

One plus one is two's a measure
Just for arithmetic, not for pleasure.

3/12/46

New Orleans, the Vieux Carré—It is raining when we come out of Broussard's. It seems part of the fabulous scene, this rain that slides down gray cracked walls and makes the narrow streets glisten red and blue and yellow-orange with the reflections of neon bar signs. Com-

---

* Pat begins her second attempt at a novel, *The Dove Descending*, a title she borrows from her favorite poet, T. S. Eliot. The manuscript, which she abandons after seventy-eight pages, follows a young orphan who travels to Mexico with her despotic aunt in search of a man they both secretly love, a sculptor as handsome as he is afflicted with alcoholism. Aunt and niece alike hope to save him and start a new life together, but he perishes in a storm off the coast of Acapulco.

† New York once had over a hundred residential hotels, but few were as glamorous as the Barbizon Hotel for Women on East Sixty-Third, named after the eponymous nineteenth century school of painters near Fontainebleau, France. It was geared toward a creative clientele, provided music rooms, a swimming pool, and free afternoon tea, and men were not allowed on the residential floors. Its famous onetime residents include Grace Kelly, Liza Minnelli, Sylvia Plath, and Nancy Reagan.

ing out of the restaurant onto such a scene, one cannot speak for an instant—during which silence my escort says in sonorous monotone, "There's absolutely nothing to do. If it's raining—"

MARCH 16, 1946

GJoan's plane was two hours late! Naturally, I was as nervous as if I were waiting for a child to be born! Drank two cups of coffee, with cigarettes, and imagined how beautiful it would be to see the plane—small and delicate—emerge under the full moon against the clouds of the night sky.GG

MARCH 19, 1946

GA wonderful day. I love Joan more and more—she grows more and more beautiful—and it was a day which heralded the night. Took a boat trip down the Mississippi, sketching, laughing, and perhaps falling deeper in love. We didn't talk about it.GG

MARCH 22, 1946

GPerhaps I am lazy, but I feel like a king. There is nothing better in life than traveling the world with one's lover.GG

MARCH 26, 1946

GLast night was the eleventh in a row that we have spent together. And Joan keeps saying, "God, how will I bear it tomorrow night when you're no longer here?" What sweet words to hear! Whether we can kiss one another at the airport—that was the problem!GG

APRIL 5, 1946

GWe visited Cornell, who was in a somewhat better mood, but who is in grave danger. Four nurses. And her stomach, one said, is not even the size of an egg. If she gets a bad cough, she could die, the nurse said. "And it would be better if she could go quickly." God, how those words frighten me! It hadn't occurred to me that Allela might die. It's impossible.GG

APRIL 9, 1946

GJoan's new feelings, which she tries to describe, are very precious to me. Almost every day she says, "Pat, I can't tell you how I feel—" Tonight, when we were in the kitchen, she said, "It's a shame you don't have a room I could sleep in while you work." It was the closest thing to saying that she'd like us to live together. I'd like that very much. We are so in love that one day without seeing one another is maddening—torture. God preserve it.GG

4/10/46

Painting is always so far ahead of writing. The images modern in literature are trite in painting. Goya foreshadowed Zola, Manet, Dos Passos, and de Chirico the loneliness and aloneness of Camus. What does Picasso foreshadow? Bombshells and bombast, masses without organization, a sterile anarchy of mind and heart.

APRIL 11, 1946

GIt occurs to me that we will have difficulties if we are suddenly discovered. Her family's opinion, I think, could separate us like death itself! And the thought that something might separate us is unbearable to me. Tonight, we are both dreaming of tomorrow and the day after tomorrow.GG

APRIL 13, 1946

GThis is heaven—working in my parents' house, sitting with them at the dinner table, and embracing Joan in my room! Tonight—my God, will we never sleep again? We see the sunrise every night!GG

APRIL 14, 1946

GDog tired at 7:15 A.M., when mother came into the bedroom with coffee and fruit juice. My—our—pajamas were in wild disarray, on the bed and the floor, and we were snuggled together in bed. "I don't mean to bother you, you look so cozy," mother said. "It got very hot last night," I remarked. "Yes, I bet," said mother.GG

4/21/46

A story about the tragedy of all my relationships with men (ships, and the *ineluctable* reef I strike!); the happy beginnings, the rapport of the likes & dislikes, the growing, glowing conversations, the good dinners he will (ominously) not let me pay for, the feeling of good will, power, brotherliness and Beethoven's "Ninth Symphony" (the negation of Rilke & Schopenhauer) and finally the impasse, the pass, made maudlin and tedious with liquor, until frustration, boredom makes one squirm in the car seat one has been in too long already. I am almost ready to cry with boredom, regret, the loss forever, the resurge of that deadly sense of impossibility! The tragedy of it!

4/23/46

Cities—none in the world—approaches New York, which is almost the site of the universal womb, or the simulacrum of the Wonderful Bed (physical comfort) from which the recluse, the cosmopolitan, the man of intellect, may stretch forth his hand to obtain whatever thing it be that he desires—food, art, or a character.

APRIL 24, 1946

^GWe signed up for the sculpture class at the Jefferson School. $14.00 for two months. And visited Cornell. The meeting between Joan and Cornell touched me in a strange way. Joan was relaxed, laughing as usual, which made Cornell laugh too. I think A.C. likes her.^{GG}

APRIL 27, 1946

^GA month ago, how Joan feared N.—perhaps I did, too. But now, she is only what she is, a highly attractive, intelligent, dangerous woman. I can never feel towards Joan the way I feel towards her. And vice versa. There is a big difference, and this difference is entirely favorable to Joan.^{GG}

APRIL 28, 1946

^GWorked—and went to see Rolf Tietgens at 7. Every hour spent with him is like—a glimpse of the future? I don't know. I'm afraid to write down that I might have such a life with Joan. I'm afraid because I believe that I have no right, no power, to bind a person as free as her so tightly to me!^{GG}

MAY 10, 1946

^GIf someone were to ask me what the single most important thing in my life is right now, I'd answer, "Time to dream." It's only that relationships with others (Joan) bring to light so many of my inner foibles. Whether I should ignore the fact that Joan counts her pennies, has no cigarettes, doesn't bring enough money home—these are all trifles compared to her worthiness. But these things also disgust me! And I've been alone too long, alone for years. One can't change quickly, but I'm making great progress.^{GG}

5/10/46

Melancholy is directionlessness.

MAY 14, 1946

GLong conversation (until 5!) with Joan about the circumstances of our love affair: firstly, that it doesn't "give her enough." It's too new, too unfamiliar for her, and I don't know whether she can endure it. Her strange, cruel philosophy (the philosophy of a butcher!) is that when something becomes too uncomfortable, too embarrassing, one must cut it off! So she might decide to cut me out of her life completely! It's dreadful! I want her—I need her, but I also need enough time for my work, which is my first great love. In this case, I am making great efforts and sacrifices to hold on to her!GG

MAY 22, 1946

GAlone after all—but only until 11 o'clock, when I went to see Joan at the Barbizon, dressed in Levis, which Joan liked a lot. "You look terrific (in Levis)!" she said, sounding like a schoolgirl with a new crush. But I like it a lot—her excitement! Of all the women I've known, only Joan completes me so perfectly! I need her as I've never needed anyone before.

Later—at 1:00 A.M.—I went to see Catherwood, where N. was, of course. They seemed very funny after J. Especially Ginnie, who made me laugh. Her stories! "Back to the point, Jeanie!," Natica screamed again and again. And Ginnie so polite and attentive, that one must like her despite oneself. They drove me home. "I want to see your room," Ginnie said. And we went upstairs. Very nice too, but didn't go to bed until 4:30 A.M.GG

5/24/46

Let the artist surround himself with the bourgeois. (Thomas Mann was so right, this hankering for the bourgeois.) The artist is forever indelible, ineradicable in him. The artist needs all the bourgeois he can get.

6/1/46

To be alone is nearest that other heaven on earth, to love and be loved.

JUNE 7, 1946

GJoan cried as we lay in bed, heavy and tired. "I'd like to die now!," J. whispered in tears. And I thought of a strange suspicion that I had two or three months ago: that one day—I don't know when—when we are in a small boat, on blue water, she will suddenly jump overboard without a word. Just because she's so happy.GG

JUNE 10, 1946

ᴳI am still occupied with various things, but my life is somehow heavy. And, strangely enough, I am getting tired of Joan.ᴳᴳ

JUNE 13, 1946

ᴳAt Virginia Catherwood's tonight with Joan and Natica. Ginnie was polite as always. I like her, if only because she's on a clear path. I don't think they like Joan very much. Joan is slow, calm, and not fun enough.ᴳᴳ

JUNE 14, 1946

ᴳIt hurts—that N. is so fake (towards Ginnie). "I don't like people like that," Ginnie said. "I like people like you."ᴳᴳ

JUNE 19, 1946

ᴳRead [Joseph] Conrad's "Youth." It warms the heart. He's a philosopher and poet, a true author! If only I could write with such gravity without employing quite so much blood and thunder! I have a stronger grip on my life than I've ever had before. The house is clean, everything is in order. I'm writing and making enough—just enough—money. I have friends, and—to top it off—a woman!ᴳᴳ

JUNE 20, 1946

ᴳDay of hellfire. Evening with Ginnie and Joan. A big salad, which nobody ate much of, and I was quite drunk, which always happens when I mix my own martinis and follow them with red wine, and soon it was midnight. Joan left. Ginnie pretended to leave but stayed—for about ten hours. The other person always has to make the first move for me. Then the kisses, wonderfully sweet, the embrace, dangerous, lovely, because one can feel the other body, the great pleasure and attraction that comes with something new. I've thought it over and realized that I can always reconcile such ugly deeds with my curiosity and "morality." And yet I'm quite ashamed of myself.ᴳᴳ

JUNE 25, 1946

ᴳWhat do I feel? Sometimes I believe that I feel nothing. I love both of them in different ways. When I'm with Joan, I feel as though everything is all right. With Ginnie—it's only physical.ᴳᴳ

JUNE 27, 1946

ᴳCould have spent tonight alone, but saw Ginnie. Last night, as I was falling asleep, J. said, "You don't seem to like sex all that much. You don't enjoy it." God, how can I deny it? Her body no longer entices me.ᴳᴳ

6/28/46

A sad aspect of one's growth—the gradual realization that the ways of the world are those even one's own mind and body are best fitted for. Orange marmalade, bitter in childhood, becomes the most palatable condiment at breakfast. Eight hours' sleep ensure the least concern with sleep—the morning hours prove themselves, despite our will, to be most profitable for production. Ideals wear away, and a mistress apart from home making wife becomes the most pleasant, salubrious, invigorating arrangement. The admission that one is no more different or idealistic than the next one is the beginning of mature wisdom.

(9/14/47 Alas, the above is false, from marmalade to mistress. And the higher wisdom always admits there is no higher than the spiritual. This paragraph was the threshold of a useless year.)

JUNE 29, 1946

ᴳ[Joan] stayed at my place. After a week of Ginnie, I was almost dead of exhaustion. Couldn't fall asleep before 3:00. How sweet Joan is—she always helps me, is always kind and tender. I am the devil, unworthy and impossible.ᴳᴳ

JUNE 30, 1946

ᴳWe both wanted to explain everything, Joan to end it all or at least understand it. It was hard. I didn't know what to say. One can't say that one is bored, that one wants to spend more time alone (to do what?). Finally, she walked down the street alone. And it was the saddest sight I've ever seen.ᴳᴳ

7/1/46

The paramecia and I
Have this in common, that we ply
Our seas in search of friend or foe
Who'll kiss us once and let us go.
(Both of us but stipulate

That the kiss rejuvenate.)
What do we care if kisses please ya?
We are footloose paramecia!
We navigate by pseudopod
And give each passing form a nod,
Houseslipper-like steal up and thrill ya,
But linger on? What could be cilia!
(Both of us but stipulate
That the kiss rejuvenate.)
We figure, what's the use of fission
When a hump completes our mission?
Love is no saner or sweeter than this,
The unique first and final kiss.
(Both of us but stipulate
That the kiss rejuvenate.)
"Goodbye!" we shout, with mutual joy.
And skate on towards the next ahoy.
And who can say we are not clever?
Paramecia live forever.

JULY 9, 1946

GThe story about the Texans is getting worse and worse. There's a mood that isn't right. I'll be happy when it's done! Today at 12:30 P.M. a visit from Natica, who said that Ginnie is still consistently drinking too much. About 12–15 drinks a day. She said Ginnie shakes in the morning before she has a drink. "G. is a sick woman," Natica said. "No one realizes it." I felt love for Natica. Sometimes she can be an angel, or at least a normal person who has all the virtues of a kind, understanding friend. And then all of a sudden, she's useless and horrible again!GG

7/15/46

The sense of life is simply consciousness. There is no other thing. The rest is mere excitement.

JULY 18, 1946

GG. drank a little every hour: watered-down Cutty Sark from a bottle of Listerine. Kissed her on a tree-lined path. God, I don't know why. Maybe I pity her. I wonder whether it will ruin everything with Joan. I think I need both of them.GG

JULY 23, 1946

ᴳWhen Ginnie called me for the fortieth time to say goodbye, I said, "I'd like to see Boston." In half an hour, everything was set: at 4 o'clock I went with Ginnie to Boston, then to her house.ᴳᴳ

JULY 25, 1946

[Kennebunkport, Maine.] ᴳHow pleased G. and her mother are that someone is working in their house, making a living! God, it's hilarious! Her mother praises me to high heavens because I'm "forging my own path." Her children have nothing to do and do little. Ginnie is very proud of me. Every day, we love each other more.ᴳᴳ

7/25/46

The constant need to retire into oneself—daily, if only for half an hour. It is only because reality bores one finally, becomes tragically, depressingly unsatisfying. To have thought of something fantastic in the midst of reality is not enough. It must be set down. And this is not vanity only. One fears that unless the nodes of growth are fixed, one will not grow higher in the next leap of growth.

JULY 26, 1946

ᴳSecond attempt on the opening of the book [*The Dove Descending*]. This one, I think, will work. I'm writing in a little room next to mine and Ginnie's. I write in the morning, before she wakes up, and at night between 11—12—1 o'clock. Ginnie needs nine hours of sleep.ᴳᴳ

JULY 28, 1946

ᴳI am so happy now that life itself is a church, a religion. I ride the bike into Kennebunkport and come back to take a bath and write, and when Ginnie wakes up, I drink a cup of coffee with her. We collect snails and rocks at the beach and compare them to our geological books from the library. In short, we are living like kings.ᴳᴳ

AUGUST 2, 1946

ᴳJoan came by yesterday evening. "Did you go to Maine with Ginnie?" she asked, looking straight into my eyes. "No, Ginnie took the car." Easy response. No, she doesn't suspect anything, I think. But if she did know that I love another woman—I can say "love," because that's how I feel— then everything would be over. It will have to happen, but I can't bear it.ᴳᴳ

8/3/46

At the moment all things in the world are a delight to me—exhilarating to the senses, making the brain so happily drunk that it cannot form phrases. Not that I care now, about anything but loving. I wish only I could imprison this happiness forever in a dozen words, or a half dozen, or one which I might have to invent myself.

8/6/46

Homosexuals: their sexual emotion is their sorest, most vulnerable spot. The least difficulty—and they translate it into insecurity, Weltschmerz, inferiority, congenital bad luck—each of which may be devastating to their own personalities. Thus by yielding until they appear weak, whether they are or not, they defeat their main sexual purpose—to have and to hold. Since a partner, a potential partner, is not attracted by uncertainty or self-pity. Whatever their strength, they never can be strong.

AUGUST 7, 1946

GVery peaceful, very happy. Am writing in the morning and evenings, working in the afternoons. But Joan S. came by unexpectedly at 7 o'clock. She was very cheerful at first and said that she had a lot to tell me. She said she was working "on her own initiative" to make money for the trip, and I finally had to confess that I didn't want to go away with her in the fall. It hurt, of course. And she cried.

This year, I have found a means of making a living. I am thoroughly changed, and why is it unlikely that my love should change too? Yes, these pages should be framed in gold. Have never been so happy. I am playing—playing—for days on end, playing what I want! Playing piano, writing, reading, thinking! I live, and God willing, I love!GG

8/7/46

Love: strangely enough, it's always you who say goodbye to the ones you love the most.

8/11/46

Man has no more soul than a garden snail. The point is, the garden snail has a soul, too.

8/15/46

To be strong and soft at the same time is the wisdom of saints.

AUGUST 16, 1946

ᴳYesterday evening when G. called—I began writing a new story: "The Man Who Got Off the Earth." I'm glad to have an escape, but for me it isn't an escape, it's a boon, a blessing. There is no other time in which I feel so alive. I'd like to tell [Ginnie] that if she doesn't start to drink less, I'll leave her. Yes, I'll tell her soon.ᴳᴳ

AUGUST 31, 1946

ᴳIt takes a long time to describe Ginnie. She is so gentle, so soft, so sweet—and my God, how she loves me! "You have everything—you are everything I love," she always says. "And I am nothing."ᴳᴳ

9/1/46

The gray, sooty white curtains at the window, looped around the heavier drape, the ends waving now and again, in the breeze. This is the color for ghosts. Gray, lived in, organic, not white. Soiled and unwashable.

SEPTEMBER 3, 1946

ᴳAt 5:45 P.M. news from Margot J. that I sold "Doorbell for Louisa"* to *Woman's Home Companion* for $800. M. excited, me too. God, news like this does wonders for my confidence.ᴳᴳ

9/4/46

The tragic desperation the first drink represents—not the social drink but the one taken at three in the afternoon. For one seeks peace of mind, and this drink is not the first resort, but the last. There is before it all the long chain of effort for silence, tranquility, love, faith that has some-how failed.

SEPTEMBER 6, 1946

ᴳWent to see Cornell, who will die very soon, it seems. God, a new face full of fear, which had never been there before. Ginnie almost fainted before we said goodbye. Tonight I cried—I said she was two people. I'm jealous of the bottle. So, without saying it, I made it clear—it's the bottle or me. What does she want?ᴳᴳ

---

* "Doorbell for Louisa," about a middle-aged woman whose job is her whole life, is not a story of frustration and disillusionment, but instead ends with the protagonist's employer inviting her to the Plaza Hotel. The story—according to Pat's records—appeared in *Woman's Home Companion* in 1948. It was also published in *Nothing That Meets the Eye: The Uncollected Stories of Patricia Highsmith* (New York, 2002).

SEPTEMBER 15, 1946

GAt 9:15 P.M. J. called. She said: "You love her more than me, don't you?" And I had to explain in words alone that I had stronger physical feelings for G. I knew that J. was crying, and before she hung up, someone knocked on her door.GG

SEPTEMBER 16, 1946

GAt 6:30 P.M. Ann T. arrived, and later Ginnie. martinis. At 7 o'clock, a call from Sheila: "What does Joan S. mean to you?" "I can't answer that easily—" "She's at Payne Whitney hospital. I think she may have tried to kill herself."GG

SEPTEMBER 17, 1946

GWent to see Joan. Didn't know what to expect. She's unhurt except for a few small razor cuts on her right wrist. (Audrey said there was blood on a pair of pajamas in a corner of Joan's room.) Brought her white flowers. She asked me again if I wanted to leave. "I don't know why they're keeping me prisoner here. I haven't done anything." She was very nervous, downcast, thin. Later I discovered that I only got to see Joan by accident. The doctor doesn't want me to write nor visit her.GG

SEPTEMBER 18, 1946

GEvery night I eat and sleep at Ginnie's. Went to Garden City to have lunch with Joan's mother. "Joan is in love with you, I don't know whether you know. That's what she told the doctor," Mrs. S. said. "Do you have influence over her?" she asked me. Once I almost had to cry. Everything was so hopeless. "Joan would like for you two to remain friends. But I'm afraid that won't be possible."GG

SEPTEMBER 22, 1946

GI don't look back. I'm working on the book, getting up every day at 8:15. And getting letters from publishers who want to publish my "novel."GG

SEPTEMBER 28, 1946

GCollecting snails. Have eleven (now).GG

OCTOBER 3, 1946

GWalked to Ginnie's. She spent the whole day with Natica. Terribly drunk. And when we were lying in bed, she told me that she had something to say to me—I knew: she had gone to bed with N. And I was right. "Only because she was nervous," Ginnie explained. Yes, I understand: there are no clear boundaries with Ginnie. It hurts. I cried a little. I didn't want to touch her.[GG]

OCTOBER 4, 1946

[G]Alone. Spent the night alone, thank God. Worked hard and was very tired at eleven. And at eleven o'clock, Allela died. These words—I am so sad. Could I have imagined such words three years ago? My dearest friend, what a hole you will leave behind. I cried for a few minutes, drank some Schnapps—and worked. I didn't know that this feeling of loss would only grow stronger later.[GG]

OCTOBER 6, 1946

[G]Sick, sad when going to bed. And it seemed as if Allela gently stepped into the room, smiling, in a white dress, and spread her arms—to show me that she was no longer suffering.[GG]

10/6/46

The farmer and the poet, providers of our physical and spiritual nourishment, are the least rewarded members of our society. At times it seems writing has only an amusement value. So be it, good enough. Then one is brought, by the death of a friend, at a funeral service, to the realization that these phrases of God's provision and refuge are not for rare occasions, as we hear them, but for all times and places.

10/6/46

Man has two enemies against which there is no weapon, from which there is no recourse: death and the bottle. Nothing, no person I have ever known has roused my jealousy except these immortal and mortal enemies. Yes, I am jealous of death, he takes my friends from me. I am jealous of alcohol, it takes my loves.

OCTOBER 13, 1946

[G]Every night harder because I remember everything about AC. I have to reread all her letters. I must know what went wrong (with us), I must discover all I can. She threw out most of my letters. There are only the early ones, those from Mexico. I have about 25 from her.

Alone tonight.[GG]

10/14/46

What a void you leave, nothingness desiring nothingness. Having read all your letters I had strength for tonight, comparing them with my diary of the same dates, I see the impossibility then. We thought ourselves older and wiser than we were. We were not wise enough to cast off desires— and desire to you and me was always work, time, aloneness, the proper conditions for thinking and dreaming. Oh God, were any two people ever so alike! We clung to privacy and the cantankerous stove of art, that warmed us well when it chose to light. And I accused you of not loving enough, of loving yourself and your work more. And you accused me of nothing, though these were my own failings I flung in your face. And it was I who was least worthy. And I was jealous of everything, stupidly jealous, being not great enough to understand that you could love many, and that those you had loved you always loved. What pained me tonight was to read "There is so much time really, Pat—"

OCTOBER 20, 1946

ᴳI can't remember clearly. Only that I am working on my book, making no money, and spending almost every night with Ginnie.ᴳᴳ

10/23/46

Alone, one can feel as much after a glass and a half of wine as two martinis with friends. And one can see much more.

OCTOBER 25, 1946

ᴳThis afternoon, J. called, and I told her what the doctor had insisted, that my feelings towards her had changed. Joan was somewhat disappointed, I think. Yes, I wrote her too many letters in which I hoped for something, promised her something. Now I fear her sentiments, and perhaps even more the weakness of my passion.ᴳᴳ

OCTOBER 26, 1946

ᴳIt's hard to say how I feel about Joan. I love her—she's very attractive and physically desirable, just not like Ginnie. But Joan is "better" for me. With her, I feel healthy, alive, honest, strong. But it's not enough—I know that.ᴳᴳ

NOVEMBER 2, 1946

ᴳ[Her] Dr. warned me that Joan was "still the same girl," that I had to make a decision (soon). Joan is dreamy, and wants only to look at me

and kiss me. Yes, I had to kiss her to discover how things were. And they
were the same as ever, just as exciting. And then. "I love you so, Pat"—I
brought her back at 10.

Suddenly alone, half drunk, more surprised, I walked home slowly.[GG]

NOVEMBER 4, 1946

[G]Oh—something interesting: saw Rolf for dinner last week, and we
discussed the possibility of getting married. I have no strong reason
for doing so, but he would receive citizenship and be able to bring his
mother over. (They have no shoes in Germany, for example!) And sometimes, I do want to have a child. But Ginnie said that I have no right to
create a life if I don't want to feed it. Rolf and I are very shy together
and laugh.[GG]

11/4/46

I can never be moderate in anything—not sleeping, eating, working, loving. Who realizes this understands me (who wants to?) but still does not
predict me.

11/4/46

In the midst of working, the thought of having to earn money, more
money, arises—incongruous with life and love, paralyzing. One must not
think of it. There is the steady and untarnished, untarnishable goal of
what one should do.

11/5/46

To J.S. that broke the crooked glass within myself.
Earth has no flower finer than your love,
Which is but you yourself.
These lines I write in tears, before tomorrow
Brings me to you for the last time, our last goodbye.

11/5/46

When I visited Mrs. C. a month after A's [Allela's] death, she said she
often felt A. "has just packed up and gone off on a trip to California.
Then I have to wake up suddenly with a jolt. But so often I packed up her
things for her after she'd gone . . ." Up until the coma, the last two days,
A. thought that she would get well. And for ten days the doctors entered
her room, came out marveling, shaking their heads, not knowing what
kept her alive. "I want you to pose for me, and I'll never have to look for

a model again," A. told one of the doctors two weeks before she died. "I'm going to be out of here in a month or so." When the doctor told her mother, he put his face in his hands and said, "I want to cry, Mrs. C."

11/5/46

The room with V.C. [Ginnie] and Virginia S. inside it. There is no whimsy here, neither is there reality. With a dazed and exhausted and tensely earnest expression, V.S. faces the mechanics of living, the lifting, smoothing, and setting down, V.C. prances about as though replacing a pair of worn pajamas in a closet were the most important function of her day.

Is the air too thin up there? For they have learned nothing, are able to do nothing. They have never heard of Virginia Woolf (I discovered when I told V.S. she resembled her). Nor have they read *Moby Dick*. Proudly they say their children will be financially independent, not realizing they will tie their hands, and worse tie their brains, and model them after their own empty selves.

V.C., I cannot tell you how sweet you are, and how inadequate. There are feelings which know more than the brain, are wiser than the intellect. All that lives really seeks the rightness.

NOVEMBER 6, 1946

^GVisited Joan's doctor, who counseled me to break everything off or ensure Joan's happiness for the next five years. I have decided that we must part. So tomorrow I will go on this sad errand. Suddenly, everything seems pointless, sad, unreal, faded. Cornell, the difficult work on the novel, trouble with Ginnie—nothing serious, only nerves—Joan's unhappiness, the pain I've caused her—and now, breaking up with Joan for no reason. There comes a time when one must grasp one's love like a stick and break it.^{GG}

NOVEMBER 7, 1946

^GSaw Joan—at two o'clock. Everything is unfair. But—I told her. We stood in someone's room, embracing; kissing, kissing for the last time, and it didn't matter that someone was looking at us from across the courtyard. "I hope I can bear it, Pat—I love you so much!" She didn't understand at first, and I had to explain to her that we can't phone or write letters. We were both crying when we parted. God, why? Why?! The only girl you've given me! Why? I want answers. And will go see a psychiatrist soon.^{GG}

NOVEMBER 8, 1946

ᴳThe saddest of days. Brought the "Chas. Samuel" mug to Joan at two. Didn't see her, of course. I put a card in the mug thanking her for everything, that she is sealed within me so that I will never lose her. At 3:30 heard from Margot J. that I'd sold "World's Champion Ball Bouncer"* to *Companion* for $800. I had to tell Joan about it in my last letter, as well as how happy I was with her when I wrote that story.ᴳᴳ

NOVEMBER 9, 1946

ᴳWent to Rolf's last night for his birthday. Excellent dinner, apartment very festive. Rolf cares for me very much, I think, because he went for a walk with me (later) to Ginnie's and spoke very quickly. "If you marry me, I won't permit such things," he said. And I feel hesitant: I want my freedom. I was awfully tired, but made love to Ginnie—God, sometimes I think that even if I were on death's door, I'd have to live just one more hour for her. Visited Rosalind and received Lola C. who came by at 5 o'clock. Briefly discussed some of the problems on my mind:

    1) I have wanted to torture myself for twelve years now.

    2) I don't want someone once I have her.

She'll make an appointment with a psychiatrist for me.†ᴳᴳ

NOVEMBER 11, 1946

ᴳI'm half sick with the dreariness of the world, with the sadness, the deep sadness in myself. When I am alone (in the evenings, at night) I am strong. But after two martinis, at midnight, I'm a crying fool.ᴳᴳ

11/11/46

Pain sends one wandering into the dusk, the dusk of New York. It is all at once all sadness, all beauty, the soft blue gray of the air (and the gray will win), the yellow white red green lights that hang on the blue grayness like ornaments upon a Christmas tree. For it is near Christmas. Christmas, and the one we love! But she will not be with us. She has never been with us for Christmas and will never be. She is gone, she is dead, and all you have of her are the memories bound up in yourself that you carry on and on through the dusk. All at once this terrible sad-

---

* "The World's Champion Ball Bouncer" tells the story of a young Southern family that goes to New York in search of fame and fortune, but whose expectations are checked by a sobering first day in the city. The story is published in the April 1947 issue of *Woman's Home Companion*.

† Pat will try psychoanalysis briefly for the first time in March 1947, then again for longer from November 1948 onward.

ness, inarticulate in the terrible beauty of dusk! Sadness so strange and beautiful and perfectly pure itself, it almost produces a kind of happiness. Where shall I not wander in the years to come? Through so many more dusks, beloved!

NOVEMBER 15, 1946

GNow I have two new holes with snail eggs! And thirty-three snails! Gave Ginnie 7. And [Babs] B. wants a pair! The striped African ones.GG

NOVEMBER 16, 1946

GAsked Ms. S. what she thought of me. Sturtevant: "I think you're pretty good." And she praised me, because I have been forcing myself to write for an hour a day for years. And that I don't need a psychiatrist, that I'm just an artist. She's right. W. S. Maugham said the same: an artist, a poet can never really fall in love, and women are quick to notice.GG

DECEMBER 3, 1946

GAn evening spent reading with Ginnie. Naturally, we had a long, delicious dinner, so we didn't begin our reading until 9:30. The snails are (almost) our greatest delight. From morning to night, we watch Bouncer and Mike, who can usually be found on the leaves of the plant. The little ones eat all day and grow, and we could spend all evening watching them.GG

12/6/46

Dissatisfied with my day's work. Though actually eight pages typewritten, first draft material, is not bad production. And it reads well enough. What is it, underlying all, that creates dissatisfaction? The young person's fear that he is (basically) not on the right track, his own track, that all may have to be scrapped, the way retraced. Added to this as yet unsolvable problem (only time, age, will solve it) is the growing dissatisfaction, like the misery of a lover who has not satisfied his mistress, that inconsolable misery. My mistress, art, I love thee.

DECEMBER 7, 1946

GSomething strange: I feel so little physical attraction for Ginnie, but great tenderness. And this troubles me.GG

12/7/46

The Railroad Trip—the rhythmically swaying diner, the Romanesque women with fascinating though already crows-feet-marked eyes. Lesbians? Lesbians? The balding, pinched and wrinkled though well-fed men who enter, scouting places to sit. Journalists, newspapermen, writers of short stories of the *Saturday Evening Post* variety, hard bitten with the passion (whiskey and soda and cigarettes) of their craft.

12/8/46

10:30 A.M. in the artist's chambers. He sips at a half cup of tepid coffee, bites at a triangle of toast and marmalade, his second breakfast, brought up after the first. He stands on one leg, the foot of the other turned almost at right angles, to the one and catching a glimpse of his face in the mirror, he sees an expression he thinks first is of apprehension, sees finally is only the alertness of composition, imagination, self-abandonment, the very opposite of apprehension so far as personal danger is concerned. (If a lion should enter the room, he might stroke it, like St. Jerome. If an intruder knocks, however, it is another matter.) The air within the cube of his room is motionless and silent, a trifle smoky, almost stale, but he likes it: it is the increase of himself.

And why record these precious sentiments? Precisely because the artist of these times is so divorced from the people whom he creates from, who take a vain pride in not understanding, as though there were any thing to understand, only what they have forgotten since the age of five, plus a discipline a hundred times their own. So stood Mozart, Shakespeare, Henry James, Picasso, Thomas Mann. So will stand artists to the end of time alone in their rooms at 10:30 in the morning.

12/18/46

Sometimes writing is like being seen crying at a friend's funeral.

12/19/46

The rat-race: whether the speed of one's creative development (and production) can match the speed with which one's money and energy must be poured out into New York.

DECEMBER 23, 1946

GGinnie didn't buy any presents at all this morning. Everything in the afternoon over the phone. How will she get in the Christmas spirit?GG

DECEMBER 24, 1946

GBusy. It takes so much time to write a story! Four or five weeks, unless it's a "Doorbell for Louisa." Waited for Ginnie, really, from 2–4, while getting ready for Hastings.* Typical of her not to show in the end. I had to drink several brandies and told her that unless her behavior improved next year, I couldn't continue to love her.[GG]

DECEMBER 25, 1946

[G]Finally, I've grown up: Christmas is too much trouble for me. Mother is helping me wonderfully with my new story. She is truly my best critic.[GG]

DECEMBER 26, 1946

[G]I would like to reread the affair between myself, Joan and Ginnie again. I haven't done so yet, not a single page. I'm somewhat afraid to. And I would also like to write how my love has grown and changed. Now, as I said, I feel as though I'm married. And yet I haven't the slightest desire to physically enjoy her. But in fact, these past two weeks have been the best so far! These gentle feelings are extremely necessary as I grow to know her better and learn that I truly love her. Tonight, when I came to her, it was as though a veil separating us had been lifted: I felt her lips as never before and could barely control myself in bed. I love her madly.[GG]

12/27/46

The Essence of manliness is gentleness; of womanliness, courage.

DECEMBER 31, 1946

[G]Ginnie and I never declare our love as vehemently as when we say good-bye to each other. At 3:00 P.M., when she left, we promised to think of one another, and kiss each other at midnight in our thoughts. I love her very much.[GG]

---

* Hastings-on-Hudson, a suburb of New York where Pat's parents had lived since late 1945.

1947

PATRICIA HIGHSMITH reads voraciously this year and dives headlong into social life, her calendar so full she can no longer keep up with double-entry bookkeeping. Many of her diary entries, still primarily written in clumsy German, are recorded after the fact. There are times she can't even remember what she did the day before.

Virginia (Ginnie) Kent Catherwood serves as both the gas pedal and the brakes for this life in the fast lane. Pat continues to throw herself into the relationship, despite Ginnie's severe alcoholism and inexorable decline. She provides loving care after each of Ginnie's benders and subsequent emotional breakdowns, but the relationship peaks, and, just as Pat was always forced to share Ginnie, she now embarks on affairs of her own.

Pat's days are never long enough, and she even feels her creative development is lagging. The comic book contracts—which she aptly describes in her faulty German as "*Lebensmittel*," which translates literally as the "means of living," but is actually the word for "groceries"—soon fall away entirely. Of the short stories she writes this year, only "The Still Point of the Turning World" sells, and the buyer isn't one of the literary magazines Pat would prefer.

When Pat finally begins drafting *Strangers on a Train*, her literary agent Margot Johnson offers the unfinished manuscript to Dodd, Mead & Co. The publisher enthusiastically accepts the book, but wants to pare down the text and pay Pat less than requested, citing the challenges facing the publishing industry after the war. On the second-to-last day of 1947, Pat completes the key scene of her novel.

JANUARY 1, 1947

ᴳPhoned Ginnie while I was drinking my first martini. And prepared something to eat at home. Ginnie in her gray trousers, the ones with the two green stripes, very happy, confident, looking comfortable as she walked about in the room talking about the big Dupont party. We called Rosalind, were invited over, and went by at 11. I was reminded of the evening when I brought Joan S. to her. I was drunk then too, and very excited for R. to meet my lover. Childish nonsense.^{GG}

JANUARY 2, 1947

^GPrepared a huge dinner for Chloe and Ginnie—a beefsteak from Gristedes—but Chloe didn't show. Ginnie and I quite content alone together. Jo P. and her friend Ellen Hill,* who ate half of my grand-mother's fruitcake. Pigs! I like introducing Ginnie to my friends. Not for my sake, but for hers.^{GG}

JANUARY 6, 1947

^GStrange how it (alcohol) slowly creeps into the brain. Also nervous and troubled because I haven't had a quiet evening in a whole week! I have something like a hangover every morning. And though I'm losing sleep, I feel so much better when I've made love! Then I have the strength of angels!^{GG}

JANUARY 8, 1947

^GReading Kierkegaard. And Hannah Arendt on Existentialism. She suits my personality, I think. Want to study more Kierkegaard.^{GG}

JANUARY 12, 1947

^GYesterday, I sent flowers (white) to the Cornells because it was Allela's birthday, with a card that said: "Sincerely, Pat."

Very excited these days, but I am so in love with Ginnie. I truly love her. What does love need? Time to get to know each other. Now I feel very lonely when I spend a night home alone! This means I probably lose three hours (of time or sleep, and thus work and thought) every day. But she's worth it.

I revised the story, began to type it up. A walk at 7, visited R. for a few minutes. I like to pop in on her, chat with her briefly, discuss a story. R. is like a man, at least more of one than Ginnie!! But when I returned, she was worried; forty minutes! And she'd almost finished cooking dinner! What a dove. Ginnie my love is a dove!

Rosalind said that "Never Seek to Tell Thy Love" is an excellent story,

---

* Pat's first encounter with her future lover Ellen Hill.

that my writing has suddenly improved. I'm very happy about this, because I've been doubting myself with Ginnie. I thought it went better with Joan.[GG]

JANUARY 13, 1947

[G]Got up early and worked hard all morning. Days at Ginnie's are like an enchanted life in heaven, or a castle. The world cannot intrude, and the walls are thick.[GG]

JANUARY 19, 1947

[G]Ginnie was the first one here tonight at 7:30, with flowers. For the first two hours, she kept telling me which guests seemed lonely. Sheila and Audrey, Jo P., Ellen H., Tex, Jan, Mel, Maria and Annette (who I finally kissed without much enthusiasm), Ann K., and Kirk and Rosalind (I was very happy to see them together. Thought they had reconciled, because they kissed for a very long time in the bathroom, but apparently not) and B.B. The house was very clean, with lots to eat, olives, cheese, potato chips, shallots. I only had three drinks all evening. And because I was surprised by Ginnie (kissing Sheila, etc.), I first kissed Audrey (very sweet!) and Annette, who was very curious, which I enjoyed learning. Ginnie and everyone else amused themselves greatly, I think. And I made a huge roast. Rosalind was very sick after two of Ginnie's Cutty Sarks. (Ginnie kept losing her drinks.)[GG]

JANUARY 23, 1947

[G]Rushing, rushing, Ginnie left at 2:35 P.M. So nervous I had to have a Cutty Sark. Quick lunch at Le Valois which we couldn't eat. At the station, Louise was waiting for us with the luggage. Ginnie had a compartment, and we kissed as though we might never see each other again! I gave her a letter, and that was it. God, her sweet, serious face through the window as the train was leaving. From Newark to Margot J. where I learned that *Companion* rejected the N.O. [New Orleans] story. M.J. sent it to *Good Housekeeping*. Rolf Tietgens for dinner, a surprise, very pleasant. I told him without reservation how much I love Ginnie. Now he knows that marriage is out of the question.[GG]

1/27/47

In cynicism, in constructive criticism, in a more vigorous ignoring—how is the sterility of this age to be treated? The prophet may become a poet, but none will follow. Jesus would be crushed in the press of humanity, on Forty-Second Street, any New Year's Eve in the Forties. This is the age of uncertainty, of the artist who vacillates between the devotion to art and the desire for money, well upholstered furniture, the Dunhill lighter. He vacillates in his heart, though he determinedly writes for the *New Masses* and the *Partisan Review*. It is betrayed in his hectic, hit-or-miss style, hitting the one time in ten, stimulated by benzedrine, brandy, cigarettes, by his own exacerbated nerves on the eleventh floor of the hotel in the east fifties, where he tries to write, out of which he will eventually jump.

JANUARY 27, 1947

ᴳThese days, which I am describing so fleetingly—were never more happy, more secure. My writing is so much better, my love is so much stronger; I see everything in the world with much greater passion, and owe this to Ginnie.ᴳᴳ

JANUARY 28, 1947

ᴳReady to work and suddenly mother came over—11—1:30, so I couldn't get anything done today. And I was feeling so creative! To annoy me further, she complained that I was impolite, etc. Had to have a drink. And then we both felt better. For the first time ever, I have no holes in my teeth. I am entering, the doctor said, a time in my life in which my teeth will not rot. Thank God!ᴳᴳ

JANUARY 29, 1947

ᴳWorked. Began to write "Flow Gently, Mrs. Afton."* I already feel rushed, so I won't find any leisure. Am trying to see many people while Ginnie is not in town. And who did I see? Can't remember. Am reading Dostoyevsky. He helps me a great deal—with his exclamation marks, his confusions! He makes me say what I want.ᴳᴳ

1/30/47

A probably healthy tendency in myself: to prefer reading science to fiction when writing a rather unusual story. And this increases, the more unusual the story is, and I take delight in observing plants and animals, the fat curve of a female goldfish's belly, for instance, her delicate armor

---

* Like many of Pat's stories, "Mrs. Afton, Among Thy Green Braes," in which a Southern sophisticate hoodwinks her male psychiatrist, is only published in *Ellery Queen's Mystery Magazine* in the 1960s after she has already become a world-famous novelist. It later also appeared in her short story collection *The Snail-Watcher and Other Stories* (New York, 1970).

gleaming like precious and hardly earthly metal, enclosing the little receptacle of her eggs, the most precious things in the world to her. When I feel like this, then I know the tempo of my life is adjusted to my own inner and constant tempo, and I am willy-nilly, regardless of anything else, happy.

JANUARY 31, 1947

ᴳCocktails with Margot J. When I talk to her, I feel as though I can make a living on fiction. Ginnie calls me every day. And I told the family all about my New York "social life." And I think they are quite jealous. It doesn't please me to write down this secret. And something else: I feel contempt for Stanley for not making more money. This contempt is quite separate from my true respect and love: but I know it is there. Wrote the ending to my story about Ms. Afton. Even after mother complained about me, she listened carefully to my story. And she gave me good advice. "Your writing is improving marvelously," she said, "but despite your life, not because of it."ᴳᴳ

1/31/47

A writer should not think himself a different kind of person from any other, since this is the way to the promontory. He has developed a certain part of himself which is contained in every man: the seeing, the setting down. Only in the realization of this humble and heroic fact can he become what he must be, a medium, a pane of glass between God on the one side and man on the other.

FEBRUARY 6, 1947

ᴳWork. Got up early to go to White Plains. Everything was easy. Now I am legally Mary Patricia Highsmith, and somehow feel stronger for it! Mother took me out to lunch. Discussed things I perhaps shouldn't have—the situation between us, the fact that she hasn't given me back my hundred. "She wants to keep you under her thumb," Rolf said, who thinks I'm in a dangerous spot. Dreadful to think mother may not be a friend after all! And hard to believe. But I know that they would be happy if I had to live with them, that is, if I were unfortunate enough to run out of money.ᴳᴳ

FEBRUARY 12, 1947

ᴳLast night a visit from Jean C., who wanted to try out the typewriter; she's starting a job with a typewriter soon. Did lots of things around the house. How I enjoy having a woman in the house! How happy and satisfied I am! And she looked at me often: so serious and devoted and wanting me so much! A (small) surprise around midnight, after we had leafed through some art books. "What would you do if I kissed you?" And I pulled her towards me. It was very sweet. And I feel a bit guilty.^{GG}

FEBRUARY 18, 1947

^GWent with Jean C. to the movies to see *Well Digger's Daughter* after dinner. She provides me with a kind of reality I find very attractive. I have something quite different with Jean than I do with Ginnie. Jean told me the story of her life during the war. An unpleasant phone call with Ginnie, who was quite drunk, and told me how different we were because she preferred lighter fare and that I disdained her because she was not "intellectual" enough. After 45 minutes I was so disgusted—though I know that I encouraged the feeling so that it would seem quite right for J.C. to spend the night.^{GG}

2/19/47

Your mistake that you did not ring my bell tonight at one fifteen in the morning. Years will come, but not these hours again. Your mistake, I say. My mistake, you are saying in your own apartment, for I was invited by you also. So tonight we lie apart, whereas together we should have postponed the eight hours or so [of] that terrible aloneness that surrounds and saturates us beyond the saturating power of our own milieux: For those who wish to be artists, for those artists who wish to contribute, saturation is necessary, be it good or evil, saturation from an environment. But the *faiblesse* of mind and spirit would ever seek to postpone this horror: a saturation with New York in 1947 is horror indeed.

The clock ticks, taxis draw up and slam their doors, footsteps sound in the courtyard, but they are not yours. Farewell, farewell! But I am denied even the beauty of watching you vanish upon a horizon. And because there is no horizon for your advent either, because your ring would startle me like a pistol shot, I never quite give up the possibility of your coming. Until at last, suffused with a beauty of my own creation, I decide that you give me as much away from me as with me. I settle myself in the last trench of the intellectual slave, a muddy, dark and unhealthily dampish trench. Here grows ringworm and eczema, body lice and cancer, here have human lips never felt a kiss.

2/22/47

A thought-conversation with Marjorie W. tonight. That there is no tragedy only pathos, in this age, because we have no fixed principles, as did
the Greeks. Oedipus so knew he should be punished, he punished himself without hesitation. We have laws. Nothing in crime startles us. And
even pathos can be questioned, is the recipient worthy? The closest to the
Greek system of morals is the individual's private code. A subtle outrage
to inner decency can produce Grecian reaction.

FEBRUARY 24, 1947

ᴳI went to Rosalind's tonight to give her my story. Later I went to Jean
C.'s and, finally, I stayed for the night. I don't like this at all, I love Ginnie, but I do it (did it, and won't do it again) because I must see for myself
how I feel after. I don't feel guilty, and strangely enough I am not sad
that the affair with Ginnie is no longer as pure as it once was.ᴳᴳ

FEBRUARY 25, 1947

ᴳAm writing Real Life Synopses for Standard.* At Angelica's at 7:30.
Remarks made about Jean C. and me. It's not worth it to me, that is to
say, Jean C. doesn't mean enough to me. So I decided I shouldn't see her
anymore.ᴳᴳ

MARCH 1, 1947

ᴳAm working on the story "The End Is Not in Sight." Mother read it by
the fire yesterday—without stopping, which is a good sign. "It's interesting," she said. And later: "Do you think you'll always write about such
strange situations?" I assured her that yes, this has been my path for the
past two years.ᴳᴳ

3/6/47

A momentous year of my life, this twenty-seventh, I know it. (Isn't every
year more momentous after the crucial one of twenty-five? Until the greatest one of thirty—in suffering, not necessarily in action.) A greater happiness is mine, a greater ability to feel, and with it for the first time a greater
concern with the problem of earning my living. The climax approaches.
I see these two lives like those of a slowly narrowing V—the destiny line,
with all the joys of creativity and its certainty, the line of the world, the
Pandora misery of money, its earning, its keeping, its spending.

* One of the comic book publishers the Sangor Shop provides with artwork.

3/8/47

It is endurance that counts, in making love, in the writing of a story or a novel. Every theme must be made love to. This is the great secret of the universe!

MARCH 14, 1947

ᴳGave the Rollo story to M. [Margot] Johnson. "Why don't you go write a story for me that I can be sure to sell?" Was very sad coming back, felt out of touch. The New Orleans story, which always reminds me of Joan S.—I have to make it better. Went to bed very late, with Dostoyevsky on my mind.ᴳᴳ

MARCH 16, 1947

ᴳBreakfast in a diner close by (our cheapest restaurant) and a long discussion about the wealthy, about Jews and their customs with respect to current social mores. B. [Babs] B. is annoyed and angered by the rich. I am not. Or perhaps I simply do not admit it? I am happy—quite proud—that I have so many Jewish friends. It means that my affection for them has nothing fake about it.ᴳᴳ

3/17/47

At twenty-six, I still am not sure of the ingredients for happiness. Nearly ten years ago I realized that one goes to understanding "as an iron filing to a magnet." Now, to confuse one, there is the realization that different people understand one differently, and which is the true understanding? The truest? One is drawn both to the charitable and the brutally honest. Worse, one cannot decide between two loving people who are brutally honest in different ways. And what is the longing for an understanding? Not primarily for leniency, but for a perfection of self. There is that consolation. But there is no—no—no—decision, when the unreasonable heart refuses (unreasonably or reasonably?) to decide.

MARCH 19, 1947

ᴳHow nice (right now) it is to work for someone else! One sits at the typewriter without having to endure the torture of the damned! [Ernst] Hauser dictated an article about Europe's "Iron Curtain" to me in groups of three words. Against the U.S.S.R. of course, how Europe wants a planned economy and not democracy. We ate lots of chocolate, tea, etc. and finished at 3.ᴳᴳ

MARCH 20, 1947

^GMore work with Hauser. Working very hard at night too to finish the New Orleans story before Ginnie's return. And I am exhausted. Only three, four hours sleep. But as always, I enjoy the rush. I need it.^GG

MARCH 25, 1947

^GLots of little things. Today Ginnie was supposed to arrive—but she put it off again! After I almost killed myself with work! I was cursing her today!^GG

3/25/47

Love is a gentle, fluid, silvery thing, like the spring rain tonight, that makes a fantasia of my head, my room, my environs, my world. How I jump at the creak of furniture chilled by the open window! I think of Job in my foundering, grasping quest for solace. I think of everything in the world, perhaps, but my mother. Tonight I would turn all my eloquence to the cursing of myself. Whither have I strayed, God, from the path of happiness? Is it my desire? Is it my material desire and my greed? Shall I live yet more precariously and school myself to care not? Shall I take less thought of food and drink and raiment? Lord, lord, how I would believe! Then my heart would be swept clean, and the veils, the dusty glass before my eyes would break and I should not only see but participate with joyous clarity.

But tonight at twenty-six, alone and lonely and afraid in my room, I chew my nails and listen to my quickened heartbeat. Where is my love, I say? Where are my loves? How have I become so impure?

MARCH 28, 1947

^GStill rewriting the Rollo story—which now has a hero, "Bernard." This story, which three, four people have criticized! I'm changing the whole thing and—I don't know. It might be better, yes, shorter, but all the philosophy, the ideas which made it relevant—thrown away!^GG

MARCH 31, 1947

^GWork. Chauncey Chirp.* Took care of the snails last night. They really do need daily care. I like giving them to Ginnie to hold. Ginnie will arrive on Tuesday at 12:55 P.M. And—we will delight one another, won't

---

* Reference to a Jingle Jangle comic strip featuring the bird Chauncey Chirp.

we? Yes—we won't leave the bed for three days! "Listen—bring every-thing from your house, you understand? I don't want you to have to go back!"GG

APRIL 1, 1947

GI practiced piano before going to Penn Station. Ginnie arrived at 2:15. "How are you, sweetie?" I kissed her cheek, I think. But could (barely) speak to her. A big kiss when we got to her room. I'd brought a few things for the icebox but was frustrated that I hadn't bought flowers! The only ones at Penn Station cost $7.50 for a dozen. Tonight, she sud-denly wanted to see people—I was quite hurt—so we called R.C. and Jean C. Jean C. had nothing to say to me. I suspect that I should feel uncomfortable or nervous around her and Ginnie, but the affair was so quick and simply so meaningless—and I don't think Ginnie will ever find out. One of these days, I'd like to tell her about it. Tonight—when we finally threw Jean out of the house, it was wonderful, and in her embraces, I finally felt myself relax for the first time in months. I truly love her.GG

APRIL 6, 1947

GUp early, worked until Ginnie came in at 11:30. Lunch with Prentiss Kent*—we are very friendly and comfortable with each other now—at Valois, where G. often goes. Champagne, asparagus with hollandaise—we ate well.GG

APRIL 8, 1947

GEven when I am exhausted at night, I must make love to Ginnie. Often more passionately because I'm so tired. Played piano. Am getting better at changing fingers. And—worked—on my new story about Vera Strat-ton, the angry woman of New York—which is already too long. Went to the movies.GG

APRIL 12, 1947

GReading Dostoyevsky's letters. Wonderful. Too bad I can't interest G. in them. I give her so much to read—and nothing comes of it. Tonight, she wanted to see "people." So after dinner at the restaurant, we took the car to see Texas E. Very pleasant time. Later we two went to Soho (a Bistro Night Club) where I was frightfully bored. And when we got home at

---

* Jonathan Prentiss Kent, Ginnie's brother.

11:15, I cried. Suddenly it seemed like everything was impossible. The old story: I want to stay home and read, and she wants to go out. I want her to find someone else for her evenings. Ginnie said that these differences are always canceled out by men and women: that they somehow always go on being happy, etc. And though I can't recall her words exactly, I knew then that she was right. I am the serious fool. Read *P*. [*Paris*] *Review* until 12:30—about Kafka and people like me, until I felt strong and happy again.GG

APRIL 12, 1947

GWorked. And went for a walk with Ginnie in the park. She doesn't let me go to the park in trousers or in a raincoat. So I wore moccasins and my gray suit. I felt so stiff, but it was a nice day, and we watched the boats on the lake. Ate all sorts of things. Finished my story (about Mildred Stratton—no title, but G. suggested "New York, New York").GG

APRIL 16, 1947

GWorked and met mother at the library at 1 o'clock sharp. Talked and talked over lunch with martinis at Cortile. And bought black shoes, just like Ginnie's, I think. Tried to fix Ginnie's hallway door: Natica hit it with a chair! Used drywall. Somewhat symbolic: I repair what N. destroys. That's what I hope for Ginnie. Her room was beautiful and yellow with the windows open. Shining like a summer palace.GG

4/17/47

Perhaps any sort of human association is stimulating to me. If the person is a bore, the mind is released like a sprung clay pigeon the instant it finds itself secluded from the bore. More and better thoughts come then than would have come, I think, during the combined time alone under so-called "ideal" conditions of solitude and quiet.

4/17/47

The essence of unreality in the modern world: (is not nightclubs, but) to look for work in the late afternoon, by appointment even, after having worked at one's own work all day. Now I know how A.C. [Allela Cornell] felt after a morning's painting when she called at a comics' outfit. The oppressive tedium and fatigue about it all—making one's effort at interest, readiness, simple alertness sour in the mouth. Beware these tireless slaves! How do they do it themselves? (Do you *really* want to know?) Where are their moments of reality—at the breakfast table, in bed with their wives? Gardening? Washing their cars? Or are they another species of animal that does not need reality?

APRIL 18, 1947

[G]Work. Saw a few Picassos, which I like more and more now. Why didn't I four years ago? His sketches are astounding! God—if an artist is so good that every movement, almost every breath is pure beauty—he must feel closer to God despite himself.[GG]

APRIL 21, 1947

[G]A perm at Ginnie's beauty salon, Park Ave. $17.50. "I'll pay for it," Ginnie said, but she forgot. It doesn't matter, this little I have! And at least I must look more presentable, I presume, which must please G. I am so very much in love with her—something so new to me—that whatever pleases her must please me. "You don't know," she said, "how often I think of you every day. You make me so happy—simply that you're true, that I can depend on you."[GG]

APRIL 22, 1947

[G]What a pleasure to wake up Ginnie! She has a pair of white pajamas that are just as soft as her skin! To embrace her in them! She smells so warm and sweet lying in bed in the morning! Finished the story for Margot "The Roaring Fire."[*] Tomorrow will be two weeks since I started it. Had lunch with B. Parsons, Strelsa Leeds,[†] Natasha H. and Sylvia—and Jane Bowles,[‡] who was very impressed with my *O. Henry* story[§] and really wanted me to call her after. I will. Margot joined us, too—and looked at me strangely during those ten minutes. Yes, she knows Natasha, etc. God, doesn't Margot know for certain that I'm gay?[GG]

APRIL 23, 1947

[G]My day off. What is it about a day off that makes one so sensitive! I made love to Ginnie passionately—we could barely restrain ourselves at lunch! We ate at Sea Fare (under my apartment) at 2:30—that's how long we took to get ready. We held hands under the table. Waitress was very

---

[*] This story has not survived.

[†] An actress and Broadway performer.

[‡] Jane Bowles (1917–1973) and her husband, Paul (1910–1999), were the epitome of bohemianism. Both writers, they shared a passion for alcohol, travel, and extramarital affairs—bisexual in both cases. For a while in the early forties, the couple lived at 7 Middagh Street under one roof with the likes of W. H. Auden, Carson McCullers, Richard Wright, Benjamin Britten, and Gypsy Rose Lee.

[§] Pat's story "The Heroine," in 1946 one of the *O. Henry Prize Stories*.

understanding. We ate steamed clams, which G. loves. Finally went to see my family, where G. immediately suggested martinis. We changed (kissed) and took the car to a quiet road, where we—but we kept worrying that someone would come. Back home, we made love—between 7–7:45!—and went down calmly afterwards for a cocktail. Ginnie says so often how much she loves me, how happy I make her, how everyone says that she is a different person since last spring—and that it's thanks to me. I like hearing this the most. Drank a lot, but it didn't show, thank God. Tonight, I truly felt at one with Ginnie.^{GG}

APRIL 27, 1947

^GJoan S. at 2:00, we took a walk and sketched in the park. God, when she is lying so close to me—asleep or awake—I can't help myself! I will always remember that night in Hastings when she was lying on the sofa, when I was writing "W.C. Ball-Bouncer." Something peaceful, something exciting, something good flows from her—God. And when I feel it, I don't know what to do—to stay with her or G. What a confession!^{GG}

(The most tragic error of my life—as Henry James might say. Joan was unique—in my world—October 27, 1947)

^GJoan drank her beer slowly and looked at me tenderly. She understands me in a different way than G. I can do more with this understanding than G.'s. In short, it's nothing more than the physical that makes a difference to me. Ginnie is older, yes, and I can learn more from her, but—sometimes, like now and over the next five days, I felt almost nothing for G. and so much for Joan. We ate at a Chinese restaurant. And in her room at the Barbizon she wanted me to kiss her goodbye. It counts more the second time. I love her in an uncertain way, and feel no guilt whatsoever when I kiss her. "I wish you could hold me close forever," she whispered. This is why the day seemed long, and very sad. G. was home when I came back with a piece of caramel cake the next day. "Hold me," she said—in the same hour that J.S. had said it.^{GG}

APRIL 30, 1947

^GWas invited by the editor of *The Writer* magazine to write an article about "writing for a living." I laughed. What do I know about making a living? But I'm very flattered, and would like to write something for him.* ^{GG}

---

* Twenty years later, Pat will write an insightful nonfiction work, *Plotting and Writing Suspense Fiction*, at the invitation of *The Writer*.

5/11/47

That an individual's faults are never quite without pardon, unforgivable—this is perhaps the only adult entry I have ever made in these bloody fifteen *cahiers*.

MAY 20, 1947

ᴳDinner with Jane Bowles. About 5 martinis—her idea—before dinner, which made me sick. I behaved stupidly—and will say no more about it. Both of us were too drunk. Good conversation only before the meal. "Ginnie is dreadful and dreadfully attractive," she said.ᴳᴳ

MAY 22, 1947

ᴳWashed the windows so the summer sun could shine in. And—after two of Ginnie's APAC pills, with a swimming brain—worked with clarity on "Mrs. Afton." My hellish story! So—read, slept for 15 minutes, everything was wonderful! Met Ginnie at the bistro. She was very downcast, silent, complaining. And when we finally began discussing our relationship, I said (although we were both angry) that it was the first time we were actually discussing something. How can one understand women? And to ruin the evening, Sheila, Audrey, and Rolf showed up. Finally we left together for Ginnie's, Ginnie walking the whole way, generously buying Cutty Sark and bourbon. She marched through the streets like a majordomo, hitting the Spivy sign with her newspaper, etc. And at home, the dog, the radio, drinks. At 12:00 the house became suddenly quiet, when we were alone, and she turned to me slowly, somewhat sad.ᴳᴳ

MAY 23, 1947

ᴳReady to leave and work when Ginnie came into the living room at 9:30 AM. She was nervous. After two drinks, she went to bed, where she couldn't stay calm. And suddenly—at 10 AM—she cried out for a doctor! "My nerves!" she cried over and over. I gave her a phenobarbital pill. I didn't really know what was wrong with her. "My fingers are cramping up!" she cried, breathing heavily with fear. She wandered through the apartment completely naked, and I went after her with her bathrobe, shivering myself. "My speech!" And suddenly she couldn't speak anymore! Her lips were sunken in, her face fat and uncomprehending. It was awful and unforgettable. I gave her one more drink (she had to have it, wanted it). And during the whole affair, I called up Jacobson, Ellis, Terwilliger—the almighty doctors who couldn't help in the end. I quickly realized I would not only have to stay the day, but for days. "I'll buy you a new blouse," she whispered, glued to me. God! Later, she sat for several minutes on a chair in the bedroom, half-naked, realizing that she could move her fingers again and speak. Thank God, I said.

And during it all, I hoped that she was truly frightened, and that she won't forget today. It was 2 o'clock before the doctor came. "Alcoholic neurotic." We discussed it together, what she should do if she didn't want to die. And we came up with an excuse for her mother as to why she couldn't come to Philadelphia today. I hurried home to get my typewriter from 4–5. Mrs. Kent called me. I couldn't tell her about the fingers, but she certainly knew that this nerve sickness was caused by Cutty. And Mrs. K. was very happy that I was with her. Now Ginnie must sleep, have orange juice and milk and vegetables. And she is very serious about her new regimen.GG

MAY 28, 1947

GThinking of my novel.* J. Bowles said: "Don't plan. It's always better first to write, then rework it." I just want a strong, clear idea. Was busy all day, started a new story, had to clean our room and finally went to see R.C. to retrieve "Mrs. Afton." Talked too much with Ginnie when we were lying in our two beds. Said that I felt unsure of her, that I didn't have enough in common with her. (Not to mention that I don't have enough of a sex life. Until she's healthy and lively again!) I had to say these things, had to learn if she truly loved me or if I was a mere comfort. I knew that I was tired, nervous, had too much to drink (good for work). And suddenly Ginnie was angry, hit me with her fists, and when I tried to protect myself and sat up in bed so she couldn't fight anymore, she called me a coward, of course.GG

MAY 31, 1947

GDrinking too much (lately). No more schnapps at home. Yesterday evening I spoke with Ginnie for a long time. I told her that I regretted my words. This was our worst fight because Ginnie has the strength of her sickness, the assurance of her mother's love and care and that of others. I promised I would come with her to Phil[adelphia] on Wednesday.GG

---

* Pat begins to work in earnest on what will become her first published novel, *Strangers on a Train* (New York, 1950).

JUNE 2, 1947

ᴳParents. Stanley's birthday was yesterday or today. We bought him a
jacket. If only I had gotten something that nice. Margot Johnson told
me that *Today's Woman* may reprint "The Heroine." "Blue Ribbon
Reprints." With Ms. [Marion] Chamberlain from Dodd, Mead Publishers. She talks too much—but is very nice, I think. It was an evening in
which I felt myself to be all kinds of things—vain, for instance. Should I
be more tender? But mostly it was interesting to observe her. Very satisfied, drunk when I got home at 11:30.ᴳᴳ

6/3/47

Telephone calls. I especially hate long distance calls, even when I don't
have to pay for them. Distance is so exiting, so mysterious, so bounded
by the size of the earth, after all, and by the limitation of aeronautics. I
don't want it banished, for nothing, by a human voice.

JUNE 7, 1947

ᴳ[Philadelphia.] Ginnie sleeps about 11 hours a day, her blood pressure
is at 69 and that's why she believes she has no strength. She is still in the
corner room, and every evening at 11:30, she comes into my room to
look at me silently and ask: "How long will you still be reading?" And
later I go to her room. But sex? God no. And yet I'm with a woman who
arouses me intensely!ᴳᴳ

6/7/47

Again & again I am fooled by the egocentric pseudo-bliss of aloneness
into thinking it makes me perfectly happy. I have to be blasted out of it. I
should never be alone. It is a happiness without love or a woman, which
(to my thinking, for me, now) can never constitute a real happiness. My
intellect may be happy, it is. But I don't even function properly physically.
Isn't this enough proof? Yet for ten years or more, my schizophrenic personality has tricked me. I revel in aloneness again and again, before I
realize, again & again. The real trouble of course, as always with me, is
in trying to find absolute and permanent values & advantages in experiences which are & should be only transitory.

6/7/47

The most important statement in this *cahier*: My life to date has been
conditioned by strife, violence, bitter desperate effort and the absence of

tranquility. It is impossible for me to produce now or in the near future a perfect work of art. All I produce (unless extremely short, produced in blissful madness) must be hectic, unsatisfied & therefore unsatisfying, unless to the desperate few like myself who will read it. I long for tranquility, my worldly & spiritual goal since my fourteenth year, but consciously. Shall I provide my own insuperabilities when I effect it materially? The dearth of it, the great draught, has become so much a part of my psychological make-up.

JUNE 18, 1947

ᴳChanged the ending of "Mrs. Afton" a bit. The story must sell. Finished the two sketches (paintings) of Stanley and mother for the art room. I'll see Ginnie again Friday evening: our first anniversary together, and my first ever. God! It really is wonderful! I will bring her flowers and—we will drink champagne.ᴳᴳ

JUNE 23, 1947

ᴳBegan my novel. Difficult to start. I want a short first part, in which the two boys and the possibility of murder are introduced. After this prologue, the story will start slowly, pleasantly. Ginnie increasingly downcast.ᴳᴳ

7/1/47

Dinner with P.K. [Prentiss Kent] *et famille*—it may be phony but at least it has lightness. The house. At first barren. Then one invests it with one's own personality. This is attained only after three weeks or so. At first it is sad and barren, opulent and stark at once. The Louis Quinze chairs and the gilt frames, the Aubusson rugs contrasting with the sterile white bookless, eternally bookless walls and corners. The bathroom itself, incongruously modern with white cabinets and strip drawer pulls, three weeks later one goes into the same bathroom, and the white modern cabinets are invested with a familiarity. The veneer of self (ME!) over everything.) Self-assertion which is too aggressive, indicative of insecurity & inferiority, I realize. Yet tonight really it is tempered with love.

JULY 7, 1947

ᴳNot yet alone again. But—I am writing more now, I think, than if I were in N.Y. Here everything is so beautiful, and I can kiss my love all day long.ᴳᴳ

JULY 17, 1947

G[New York.] All alone. Ginnie calls every day. And I have learned from Rolf T. that Sheila is with her. What are they doing? I really don't know. "This stinks of an affair," R.C. said.GG

7/17/47

Mortal terror, the terror of the mortal mind: I shall go through life never finding for certain more than one-third the ingredients in that special formula of my own happiness. Solitude, tranquility of mind, excitement of the senses, people, loneliness, success, failure, advantage and handicap, gluttony and abstinence, memory and daydream, transfiguration and reality, love requited and unrequited, the faithful lover and the faithless, fidelity and experiment, curiosity and resignation, all these flow from my pen in less time by far than it takes to write them. But when and by how much of each shall I live? And what have I missed, what included that I do not need? Man must struggle according to his own tortured nature. At twenty-six I say perish the psychiatrists who would remold me. What I am blind to, that I shall remain blind to. Its vision would deprive me of that which I see.

7/19/47

Miraculous, coruscating conversation with R.T. [Rolf Tietgens], in which we concluded, it is the best of all possible worlds for artists. (Question at 3:15 A.M. Would not any conceivable world be the best of all possible worlds for artists? Would not the born artist find his irritating sand grain of unhappiness around which to form his pearl?)

JULY 22, 1947

GRevised 93 pages. Excellent, first part—already done. I will be so happy to see it on white paper. Mother came very early—always when I begin to work. But she helped me a lot around the house. And finally we talked—she loves Ginnie very much—and drank many martinis. At 10:30 PM I went to Ginnie's, was cheerful and very happy to see N. [Natica] and her. Both were in trousers, tired after the trip back from Phil., and looking pretty. Later, alone (N. went home!), Ginnie was very cold and ugly to me: "No, you won't sleep with me!" I lay in bed for a few minutes, then quickly got dressed and left, when Ginnie called down the stairs! Why should I tolerate her coldness? Is this what being grown up means? No kiss, no embrace! I don't understand it, but there's nothing to understand. We should separate, that's all. And in many ways, this is very sad.GG

JULY 25, 1947

ᴳAt parents'. Very busy, free, (thin!). Went with great expectations for the weekend. A few long gins. Very pleasant. I'm excited to show the parents my novel.ᴳᴳ

JULY 26, 1947

ᴳI was just drinking martinis when Ginnie called. Can't deny it, was very happy to hear her voice. "Do you love me?" "Yes, I do," I replied. These days are so strange. I love Ginnie. But I can't bear the thought, can't forget that ever since I left, she's stayed in West Hills with Sheila. If only Sheila had been good enough to leave before I did—but no—she stays, and stays, and stays. Does Ginnie even need me then? Why?ᴳᴳ

AUGUST 3, 1947

ᴳWork was good. Am so happy whenever Bruno appears in the novel! I love him!ᴳᴳ

AUGUST 11, 1947

At 5 o'clock Owen Dodson arrived.* He is very agreeable, just came from Yaddo with lots of news that pleased me. We would have talked longer, but it wasn't possible.

8/20/47

Take nothing seriously and refuse to be sad.

8/25/47

Eat heartily, drink heartily, except of martini cocktails, and open an advertising circular with passion, fling yourself into bed at night, exhausted, and with passion, and alone.

AUGUST 27, 1947

ᴳYesterday Margot J. said that she likes the novel very much. "Both of the mothers are strong characters." (I doubt that.) And said I should show it immediately to [Marion] Chamberlain.

I'm still working on my story. No, only comics today. How capable I am now that I am alone! I washed the walls, cleaned this and that, did everything I had pushed off for so long. And I am not lonely

---

* Owen Dodson, American poet and novelist, was a Yaddo resident in 1947. Yaddo had started admitting Black artists a few years before, beginning with Langston Hughes in 1942.

at all. Walked to 84th St. and back, hungry and thirsty for life on the street! People, children, houses, shops, newspapers! God! I can feel my strength—if only I can maintain my good mood, my sense! Later a visit from Rolf, who was very boring for once. He doesn't want to go to New Mexico without Bobby. Still in love with him. Restless and lonely.[GG]

8/28/47

How I write these days: (or is anybody interested?) I do everything possible to avoid a sense of discipline. I write on my bed (bed made up, myself fully but not decently clothed), having once surrounded myself with ashtray, cigarettes, matches, a hot or warm cup of coffee, a stale part of a doughnut and saucer with sugar to dip it in after dunking. My position is as near the fetal as possible, still permitting writing. A womb of my own.

8/30/47

There is a way.

8/30/47

Wait for inspiration: mine come with the frequency of rodent orgasms.

SEPTEMBER 3, 1947

[G]Spent the whole day typing the story. It's very good! Should I call the novel "Small Rain"? Called up Eleanor Stierham from *Today's Woman*. Burton Rascoe's stories begin in 1948, and mine will be in the first issue.[*] She wants to invite me for a drink next week. All alone. Too hot again. Yes, I miss Ginnie. Especially when I go to bed. And when I sometimes want to talk to her on the phone.[GG]

9/3/47

Advice to a young writer: approach the typewriter with respect and formality. (Is my hair combed? My lipstick on straight? Above all are my cuffs clean and properly shot?) The typewriter is quick to detect any nuance of irreverence and can retaliate in kind, in double measure, and effortlessly. The typewriter is above all alert, sensitive as you are, far

---

* Probably *Today's Woman* has asked the editor and critic Arthur Burton Rascoe (1892–1957) to curate a selection of short stories. In any case, Pat's story "The Heroine" will appear in the *Today's Woman* March 1948 issue.

more efficient in its tasks. After all, it slept better than you did last night, and just a little longer.

9/4/47

The first novel: rather the big messy thing than the little gem of art, an exercise to be reserved for crabbed old age.

SEPTEMBER 4, 1947

^GAlone. Worked. Sleeping less and less—about 3–4 hours. When I begin to fall asleep, I feel a kind of sudden excitation, awakening in my brain, or I think, probably, mostly, of Sheila with my Ginnie, and my heart is filled with murderous thoughts until I can no longer sleep.^GG

9/7/47

This lump of Angst in my throat. The phlegm of twentieth century New York, the uncoughuppable.

9/14/47

First nembutal*—I feel like I have taken strychnine as the capsule slides down. Ten minutes later, tingling in the nerves of the legs. I open my eyes. Do I feel "heaviness"? Not so trite. The legs. Socrates drank the hemlock. It rose from legs to heart. I am terribly alert. The ears begin to tingle. Tiredness tears at the rocks of me, a sea of lassitude tears at the rocks of me. And ebbs away, I turn over. I am awake, blinking brightly. Has it passed? Have I survived it? This is depressing. I could never take the second now, though I've been told it would not matter. The sea rises again. Second onslaught. Now I am afraid. The pill is relentless. It will have me. It has power to fight until it does, more power than I have. It will fight until it has me. Socrates drank the hemlock. What have I taken? What the hell do I know about nembutal? My ears tingle. Is the clock fainter? It is not. The sea rises, goes over my head, but it is not unpleasant, neither am I asleep. A sense of not caring wars with curiosity and fear, as when I am busy drinking the one excessive martini. I give up. I am lost. Socrates drank hemlock . . . Six hours later I awaken. I fancy I am fuzzier than usual, but it soon passes.

---

* Pentobarbital, sold under the trademarked name Nembutal, was prescribed for many years to treat insomnia. It was eventually discontinued as a sleep aid, following widespread abuse and the emergence of new treatments.

9/17/47

Why so like death? Why do the worms crawl? They crawl because I am two, three days dead. Man is all love, man can never die, he is reborn in each new love, he is alive always in the Love of God, his eternal spouse, but in the death of an earthly love each man dies too, and in two or three days, the worms have at him. O, do not think to bury yourself deep enough to escape them! There is no escape. I walk the streets and feel anointed. I walk the streets like the walking dead. I feel on the brink of physical death. I do not wish to die, by stoppage of heart or by being hit by a truck. I am with death, he knows I do not fear him. But I am not ready for him yet. I have work to do: I am the anointed.

9/20/47

Am I pledged to ill health? Pray God, no! I want to live a long while. Sometimes I feel I cannot. Something drives me to the destructive, which is a necessity for my seeing.

SEPTEMBER 21, 1947

ᴳWork. Very happy—the novel is going better. It lives in my heart, at least. And it is the only thing that can make me happy these days. I should say that this day should be written in red ink, because Rosalind asked me if I would like to live with her in a house in the country. It's an idea. We are both dissatisfied with our lives in New York, where one is either lonely or exhausted, it's impossible. What will happen? How much money will I have in a year? Where will I be? With whom? And yet Rosalind (Tex too) said, when I told her of my troubles, "Oh, in two months you'll have someone new to get lost in." We'll see.ᴳᴳ

9/29/47

People say of artists that they live within themselves, but actually they live more outside themselves than ordinary people. It is the same world to which the artist goes when he is inspired or when he works, but the actual actual world is different for him each time he returns to it. (Thank God, or it would be boring to him beyond endurance!) The artist only wonders that ordinary men can tolerate what he knows to them is a constant and same world.

9/30/47

Do always, or almost always unless it interferes with a specific desire to work, do always what you want to do.

10/3/47

Never fret over a character, it has to do with the mysteries of birth. From the minutest beginning, a character is either alive or not. And yet, as in real life, the sickly, fair-haired baby can become a dark brute, filled with vigor or the robust infant the object of its parent's hypochondriacal obsessions.

10/4/47

Dedication: to several women, without whom this (whatever it is) book could not have been written. God! (Not God save women!) I adore them! Without them I would and could do nothing! Every move I make on earth is in some way for women. I adore them! I need them as I need music, as I need drawings. I would give up anything visible to the eye for them, but this is not saying much. I would give up music for them: that is saying much.

OCTOBER 6, 1947

^GDon't feel very well. Am drinking rye now—more than ever. Mother at 10. Lunch. Dentist. I have no time. The curse! It's all too fast! I'm searching for adventure. Dinner with Babs B., who was quite drunk on bourbon, at Tomaldo's.* Beethoven there, the whole place very gay. Drank too much red wine to work. And at 12:45, when I was alone and in bed, the phone rang: Maria and Peggy,† who invited me out for a drink. I went over quickly, evening trousers and everything. Peggy had taken two sleeping pills, but we talked a lot. Four drunk women. What would mother have said! It was very strange!—And then the compliments they paid me, my trousers, etc. "They say you have a brain too, Pat."^{GG}

OCTOBER 10, 1947

^GMy week was disrupted by the dentist. Had little time. Every visit about 1½ hours. And saw Lil [Picard]‡—to learn that she could have dinner with me. She kissed me goodbye last night—I'm a bit in love with you, I think, she said. Lots happening, but no word from Margot

---

* Italian Restaurant at 812 Third Avenue, between Forty-Ninth and Fiftieth Streets.

† Presumably Peggy Fears.

‡ Lil Picard (1899–1994), a German-born, Jewish avant-garde artist more than twenty years Pat's senior, had already made a name for herself as a painter, sculptor, art critic, and photographer. She later served as Andy Warhol's muse and came to bear such honorifics as "the Gertrude Stein of the New York art scene" and "grandmother of the hippies." She was married to banker Hans Felix Jüdell.

on the book. Where is [Marion] Chamberlain? And what does Dodd, Mead think?[GG]

10/13/47

Do not forget patience. Because I have it in such abundance, I am inclined to take it for granted, yet in me it is not always present.

10/15/47

On rereading a few of my notebooks: they are a mirror of a rather bad mind floundering with incredible perseverance, indefatigable curiosity, in all directions at once, never pursuing one direction long enough to think any one subject through.

OCTOBER 17, 1947

[G]Work. Writing more slowly. 270 pages, roughly. And Ginnie called several times—saying that I still love her, and that she cares for me. "But don't you prefer Sheila?" Brought her flowers, cleaned her shoes, and she was very impolite, didn't listen when I spoke, etc., played records that she and Sheila had listened to together, and couldn't bear it when I asked her, "Why are you torturing yourself?" So—at 9:30 I went home to work. (Ginnie is so sick, so weak, it was hell to take her out for a walk.)[GG]

OCTOBER 22, 1947

[G]Busy. And cocktails with Ms. Chamberlain at Michel. She said that Dodd, Mead is not satisfied with the novel as it stands. The 100 pages must be cut down to 60. So—I must cut. Margot came later—but at first Chamberlain and I were alone, and she impressed upon me how the publishing industry must be very careful now, etc. Margot was angry, because D.M. [Dodd, Mead] has a lot of money. Am disappointed only because I need the money, but it will be a better book once I've made the cuts.[GG]

10/23/47

4:00 A.M. I cannot live alone in health. In the night, alone, awake after sleep, I am insane. I read Gertrude Stein. I eat like a Cyclopian giant, only my wine and my whiskey do not make me sleep. I do not desire anyone vaguely or specifically: I merely say, if I had so-and-so, I should not be insane now. I am without discretion, judgment, moral code. There is nothing I would not do, murder, destruction, vile sexual practices. I would also, however, read my Bible. My being is rent with frustration like the curtain before the false temple. Yes, I long to meet a beautiful woman at a tiny black table somewhere, and kiss her hand, and talk of things that would delight her. I long to pare myself as I long to pare my art of the extraneous that corrupts it. It must come first in my work. I drink whiskey to stupefy myself, and regret what it does to my body—fat cells, deterioration of the brain, above all indulgence in a dependence upon materiality when what keeps me awake is a spiritual intangible.

10/29/47

Life chose to play with you like a rubber ball, a soft rubber ball on a gravel field. You bear its scratches, its scars, but none can be said to be yours willingly. You were passive in the game. Your face is lined with life few poets have known, though they would. Your age has grown knowing with life that life painted in it stroke after painstaking stroke, but it is a flat eye on what was once a blank canvas. You pace your apartment alone in pajamas with your wise tortured face, like a bewildered captive of life, and even the alcohol that beclouds your brain is not you, is artificial, is one more cruel stroke of this life you yourself with your petty headstrong will deny, and the intoxication is the last insult to you. Even I, writing these lines at five thirty in the morning, sleepless, haunted by semi dream, semi nightmare, semi hallucination, know that I am touched by the same life, because I am insanely in love with you, yet I sought you and was not passive. When you die, you will die into its grasping hands that are already closing about you. You will die with the same plucked, confused expression on your small face grown wise to overflowing with the life that was too much for your pusillanimity to bear.

(*To V.K.C. [Virginia Kent Catherwood] at 3:30 A.M. sleepless*)

OCTOBER 29, 1947

[G]Haven't heard anything from Ginnie. Why? God, how my life would have been different, better, more beautiful, and more exceptional if I had always worn white collared shirts, gone to church every Sunday, and lived with my parents. Lately, I am not as orderly as usual, and it troubles my soul.[GG]

NOVEMBER 4, 1947

^GLast night was very nice—with Lil at Parsons Gallery Hedda Sterne* exhibit. Wore my turtleneck sweater under my suit, and felt so beautiful (with one of the roses that Joan sent me), that I could have spoken to everyone.^GG

NOVEMBER 4, 1947

^GDisgusting evening with H.S.† Everything was lovely at first—dressing myself after work, making a martini—and later—his boring words: "I don't understand you. Don't you love me? Aren't you at all attracted to me?" God! Finally I told him that I was in love with someone who didn't love me back. And then I called mother in tears. Decided to go to Hastings. Am too distressed and troubled here. And I'll bring along Lil. She needs it too.^GG

11/4/47

Today life is so much concerned with unrealities, things done unwillingly, things done for no apparent purpose, without joy, without satisfaction, a little liquor is necessary to enable one to rediscover one's self. The self is a constructive and real being. The modern world is not.

NOVEMBER 12, 1947

^GWork. But I'm not working fast enough. Why:
  a) Rewriting scenes which I wrote so happily the first time around!
  b) Regretting the time, since I wanted to be in Texas now.
  c) Very disappointed in Ginnie.
  d) Need money—first for the book—and yet I have to give so much of my time to Timely [Comics], who are getting harder and harder to please.
Also—I'm reading [André Gide's] *The Counterfeiters*.^GG

11/13/47

I am troubled by a sense of being several people (nobody you know). Should not be at all surprised if I become a dangerous schizophrene in

---

* Hedda Sterne (née Hedwig Lindenberg, 1910–2011) was an artist of Romanian-Jewish descent. She was also part of Guggenheim's Exhibition by 31 Women and later gained some notoriety for being the only woman in a photograph of the group the Irascible Eighteen. She worked closely with Betty Parsons, who also gave her the exhibition Pat mentions here at Wakefield Gallery, her first solo exhibition in the United States.
† A man she met on a trip to Charleston the year before.

my middle years. I write this very seriously. There is an ever more acute difference—and an intolerableness—between my inner self which I know is the real me, and various faces of the outside world.

NOVEMBER 15, 1947

ᴳStayed at Lil's last night. Discussed things until 3:00 AM as we lay in bed (two beds!). More later. She said I'm the most interesting person she's met in years. Worked on "Still Point of the Turning World"* this afternoon, and went with Lil to the Museum of M. Art to see "Potemkin." I very much enjoy being with Lil: she knows everything about me, but is not emotionally dependent. What is so unbearable? That I have so little money after so much work! Lately, I've often thought (too often) that if I weren't especially strong (or mad), I'd have lost my mind months ago.ᴳᴳ

NOVEMBER 17, 1947

ᴳWorked on "Still Point T.W." and finished it! They wanted "smoother transitions"! Exactly what I didn't want! Burned leaves in the courtyard, which I enjoyed.ᴳᴳ

NOVEMBER 26, 1947

ᴳBrought these 50 pages to Margot—up to page 183, for her flight to Boston today. Very happy to celebrate tonight after five straight days of work! Tonight Peggy, Lil (Rosalind?) for cocktails, and then Jeanne for dinner. Would like her to spend the night. Why not? We don't know each other. But it would do us good. So—why not? And soon after dinner when I was playing records, J. said: "I want to stay over . . . Why don't you invite me?" She's very passionate, and I like this about her. After Ginnie, who was so incredibly difficult, J. is a gift from heaven!! (Five times for her, she said.) And different interesting things: That Tex rarely went down on her. J. feels a bit selfconscious then. Naturally. "I never got such a bang out of it before," she said. Shortly my ego is 100 percent bigger! Breakfast, and then by car to see the family in Hastings. I felt delighted, and she too, as we drove up along the Hudson. Old fashioneds. And a wonderful turkey. I drank quite a lot and spoke like a fool. And came back from Jeanne (when she left at 6 o'clock) with lipstick on my chin. What did the parents think? They like Jeanne.ᴳᴳ

---

* Published in *Nothing That Meets the Eye: The Uncollected Stories of Patricia Highsmith* (Norton: New York, 2002).

11/26/47

Wisdom is to be gained in drunkenness and in the nightmares of the depths of tortured sleep, which are both contrary to God and to happiness, but not to nature. In the night I am myself, both self and a machine, an intuitively accurate one. In the night, I can work purely, by intuition. The night is no man's time but mine. In the night no one calls me. In the silence, I hear my own voices.

12/3/47

The impulse to drink is the same impulse that tends one (male or female, but especially female) to immerse oneself in the one person loved, to be lost, and relieved of identity.

DECEMBER 3, 1947

ᴳNot a great day, since I had to write a synopsis. This ugly business of having to make a living! One day I will be free of it! Completely free! That I have Jeanne—and what "have" means, I do not know—saves me now. Yes, it saves me. We need each other terribly. I told her: "Don't try to love me." Lil is very interested in me and Jeanne. "But aren't you bored?" "No," I answered. Girls with whom I sleep are women to me, and I don't want an intellectual woman. I value warmth much more, I value true love much more. I value a smile full of love much more. Strange—that with Jeanne and Lil, with the drawing class, I have completely changed my circle of friends! And I like it. Most of all, I like seeing Jeanne happier. Every day she is happier, and shows it. She lost 8 pounds after Tex. Tonight she invited me up (for a glass of milk) and it was—right, lovely. It was an evening I would have enjoyed had I been a boy who wanted to marry her. And she was what I wanted—a lady, a real aristocrat.ᴳᴳ

DECEMBER 5, 1947

ᴳMaking slower progress on the book. This week has been typical: Mon. and Tues. alone = 20 pages. Wednesday, Jeanne = 4 pages. Thursday, mother = 5 pages. Friday—disgust—and no pages—but today at 5 o'clock I began writing a short story, one about a girl and a chauffeur. I like the beginning a lot; like T. Capote, I need to rebuild my ego. Drawing class. Lots of men. My work is improving, and it's the greatest source of pleasure in my week. Sometimes I imagine what my life would be like if I were a painter. And yet—yesterday at the Dalí exhibit, I realized that painting is not developed or refined or clear enough (for me). Writing can do everything. Money is increasingly harder to make, I have no news on the novel or the story, and something in me doesn't want to end the book. I know this evil spirit within me already. I have waited for it. And it is here. I am fighting it. Alone. I don't want to bring Jeanne into it. I am so sick of soul that I cannot take in the happiness of a new, sweet love. And Jeanne likely—possibly—loves me. I could love her. She is a person like Joan S., who is good to me, someone for whom one can write poetry. (Strange, but one cannot write poetry about Ginnie or Natica. Mark my words if it isn't true!)[GG]

12/5/47

What do I feel with so much passion as my own angst? Do I feel love so? I pace my one room with fingers in my hair, shouting eloquently, and the one I love lies on my bed and listens—like a handkerchief for all my flying tears. Bitter years of my youth, and one does not live forever, and one is young even a much shorter time. What is it? That I have not yet made myself good enough to earn a comfortable living, to earn enough to be free. I have no angst for the possible constipation of my work either in writing or painting or whatever. I have no angst as to the limitations of my possibilities.

On the contrary it is mere frustration that my days are not long enough, that art is so long to learn, that I must give precious days to a game I do not care to play—the gamble of one's efforts for money. I am a coward, perhaps and perhaps not, not to chuck everything (which means friends, lovers, a home I like, entertainment which is recreation, alcohol and clothes, books and concerts) and work for myself so long as my money lasts. But I am so habituated that I cannot deprive myself of these things and be happy. Only in the arms of someone I love, who loves me, can I find temporary solace. These months, I believe, are the hardest of my life. From July until now. Much more I cannot stand. It is all emotional perhaps, not financial insecurity at all. A change must come swiftly. Or else. (But never suicide.)

DECEMBER 11, 1947

[G]All the news came today: sold "The Still Point of the Turning World" to *Today's Woman* for $800.[*] But Little, Brown doesn't want the novel

---

[*] The story, retitled "The Envious One," about a dissatisfied housewife and mother observing another, happy mother with her lover on a bench in a New York playground, will appear in *Today's Woman*, but not until March 1949.

right now. The novel has no conviction and no atmosphere, Lil said. She's right. And I'm constantly asking myself: Why not? The synopsis did, and the first chapter did. Back then I had Ginnie and a love. In the days immediately following, I wrote quickly, but it would have been better had I written everything out again slowly, by hand. I want to regain the warmth and the atmosphere of the first chapter, that feeling of comfort.^{GG}

DECEMBER 12, 1947

^GJeanne was with me until noon. Even though I've sold a story and written a sellable story, I'm nervous! Very nervous—so I smoke too many cigarettes and want a drink! And I remember the words of my mother: "When you are very successful, you will have no happiness without love." Yes, and sexual, passionate love too. Made the great mistake of writing Ginnie a letter, in which I told her about my "Still Point" (whose kiss is hers).^{GG}

DECEMBER 17, 1947

^GI wanted to write today, but how, when? Saw *Mourning Becomes Electra*—the best movie I've seen in America. Three hours of unrelenting tragedy, but one sees life, albeit in murders and suicides. That's what I want in my book.^{GG}

DECEMBER 19, 1947

Worked alone. Alone tonight too. And happy. And satisfied. I am writing by hand again—and why did I believe that the typewriter would be "faster and clearer"? It's not true. Tucker* is moving quickly—towards murder.

12/25/47

In a novel, let mood motivate each paragraph, start each chapter. I think one is inclined to be oppressed by a sense of narration only—

DECEMBER 26, 1947

^GIt's snowing. 24 inches. The city seems like a different place. Nothing is stirring. But at 9 o'clock, a call from Joan S.! Was alone, writing, and so happy to hear from her. I made a drawing for her of my fireplace with baby Jesus and her stocking. And the face in the fireplace that she loves

---

* Tucker will later be renamed Guy Haines.

so much. Did a lot around the house. Very happy and satisfied. With friends and people like Jeanne, I feel strong and full!^{GG}

DECEMBER 28, 1947

ᴳI'm alone. Writing again in the notebook in which Ginnie wrote on the first page "I love my love!" Five, six double pages a day. Tucker will commit murder tomorrow.^{GG}

12/28/47

Note after writing my first insincere story:* it eats at my brain when I turn from it to write my book. I feel my thoughts are soiled and unclear. God forgive me for turning my talents to ugliness and to lies. God forgive me. I shall not do it again. Only this vow permits me to work any longer tonight at all. Best if I were punished by the story's being a complete fiasco. *Miserere mihi. Dirige me, Domine, sempiterne.*

DECEMBER 30, 1947

ᴳBig day today: wrote the murder, the raison d'être of the novel. Tucker fired his two shots. And Mr. Bruno is dead! I feel as though something has changed today. I am older, quite grown up. Tucker's murder was a big, necessary job, a great step. I can almost see the wrinkles of age on my body. I returned home alone, quite pleased, quite content. I don't want to marry. I have my good friends (most of them European Jews) and girls?—I always have enough of them, have what I want, I think. Also—Valerie Adams, Kingsley, Lil, Jeanne, Joan, these people have shown me that I have already achieved some success in my work. This makes me feel concerned and careful.^{GG}

12/31/47

2:30 A.M. My New Year's Toast: to all the devils, lusts, passions, greeds, envys, loves, hates, strange desires, enemies ghostly and real, the army of memories, with which I do battle—may they never give me peace.

---

* When Pat wrote her story "Where to, Madame?" about a girl and her chauffeur, she did so with the intention of making it "sellable." However, it still took some time until it was published by *Woman's Home Companion* in 1951.

1948

PAT'S ACQUAINTANCE with author Jane Bowles and her associates brings her further into the fold of the New York arts scene. Composer Aaron Copland, choreographer Jerome Robbins, and actor John Gielgud are now in Pat's orbit, and over time she will become acquainted with Carson McCullers, Arthur Koestler, and W. H. Auden. Pat is part of the literati. Mid-January, she meets Truman Capote at one of Leo Lerman's Sunday evening salons. They're instantly intrigued by each other and begin spending time together.

When Pat expresses the need for peace and quiet to work, and relief from her acute pecuniary concerns, it is Capote who recommends for her to apply for a residency at the Yaddo artist colony. Thanks to letters of recommendation from Capote (who wrote his first novel, *Other Voices, Other Rooms* there the year before), her friend Rosalind Constable, and *Harper's Bazaar* fiction editor Mary Louise Aswell, Pat is invited for a two-month stay in May and June of 1948.

Founded in Saratoga Springs in 1900 by financier and industrialist Spencer Trask and his wife, Katrina, the artist colony boasts such twentieth-century creative titans as Leonard Bernstein, Hannah Arendt, Milton Avery, Sylvia Plath, Jonathan Franzen, and David Foster Wallace. Pat will later name Yaddo the beneficiary of her estate and recipient of all future royalties.

Although her writing proceeds apace in the seclusion upstate, and despite Yaddo's strict work hours and lights-out policy, Pat cannot escape her old social habits: she drinks a lot, flirts a lot, and even sneaks off site to meet a girlfriend in the area. However, the discipline of the retreat does leave its mark on her: her bilingual (English and German) diary entries grow more concise, and within just six weeks, she finishes the first draft of *Strangers on a Train*.

Pat's fellow residents at Yaddo include crime novelist Chester Himes, Southern Gothic writer Flannery O'Connor, and English author Marc Brandel. Despite Pat's continued lesbian relationships (and an affair with another man), Marc becomes her on-again, off-again fiancé. In September, he rents a cottage in Provincetown, on Cape Cod, in the hopes that he and Pat might both finish their novels there (and get to know each other better). But the question of marriage for Pat constitutes a constant source of despair. In those years, she seems far more distraught about her sexuality than in her early twenties. While this might partly be due to her age, her personal development also mirrors that of society as a whole: The end of the war for the gay community has constituted a step backward compared to the relative freedom of the war years. Society's vigorous effort to return to "normalcy" will culminate in the persecution of homosexuals—the so-called Lavender Scare—in the McCarthy era, beginning in the late 1940s, and being suspected of being a homosexual is just as serious as being suspected of being a communist.

In a futile attempt to "cure" her homosexuality, she undergoes psychoanalysis. Ironically, it is this therapy that will indirectly lead to her writing a lesbian romance. To help finance her treatment, Pat finds seasonal work before Christmas in the toy department at Bloomingdale's, where she sells a doll to Mrs. E. R. Senn, the wife of a wealthy businessman from New Jersey. Pat is immediately smitten with the elegant blond woman in mink. She returns home that evening and, in a fever signaling a chickenpox infection, Pat begins to write . . .

⁂

JANUARY 1, 1948
ᴳMiserable, but why? I got up too late to enjoy much of the day. Why do I go out so much, when my family has a house in the country? I'm desperate and unhappy. Jeanne didn't make love to me. I don't even want to, but body and nerves are not the same.ᴳᴳ

JANUARY 2, 1948
ᴳWork. Comics. Alone. Dinner at Sturtevant's. She hates women, admires men. She's not so wise.ᴳᴳ

JANUARY 6, 1948
ᴳWatched *Crime and Punishment* with Jeanne. Really good: if only my murders occurred as early in my stories! Dostoyevsky!! My master! Saw Herb L. at 6 o'clock. Same as always—a little nicer, I thought. He writes

six hours a day. Herb was quite drunk by 10:30. His own bottle, what could I do? Had half a mind to sleep with him, but he was utterly out of commission. Disgusted, I called Jeanne at 12:30 AM, and she politely invited me over. Wonderful to run there, find the door open, and stand by her bedside. I made love to her till 4:00 AM.^{GG}

JANUARY 7, 1948

^GAnd Herb still here at 9:30, rather confused when I returned. What a bore! And he'd written, "Where is Pat?—I love you" all over the house! A moron, and I never want to see him again.

JANUARY 8, 1948

^GMaking progress. Drafted extensive notes on paper before starting to write. Jeanne likes Bruno's murder, but not the rest, I think. Alone in drawing class, and I'm reading [Jean-Paul] Sartre's *What Is Literature?* with great pleasure—wonderful—Sartre. I occasionally feel as though I hold art itself in my hands!^{GG}

JANUARY 9, 1948

^GMother at 2:00 and no work done. I drink liquor because I'm so miserable! Jeanne spent the night with me. We're growing happier and happier. It's wonderful but dangerous. I don't want to hurt her. Sent Joan S.. photographs of Lil, Jeanne, and Peggy.^{GG}

JANUARY 12, 1948

^GJeanne's very quiet. Visited her Monday evening as well—10–11—and she gives me so much strength—somehow—that I can write till 2 in the morning afterwards! Anyway—she thinks she needs to find a new circle of friends, and either work or get married. Yes, she needs someone— always. That's the difference. So—I'm her last girl.^{GG}

JANUARY 14, 1948

^GSaw Rolf last night—although I would have preferred to work. I get up late so I need to work late. But Rolf—I like him, and know that woman's sense of obligation to appeal to a man. Strange? But true. So to a beerhall. Very pleasant. I read him Bruno's murder, which he liked a lot. We always discuss our dream homes in New Mexico and New Orleans and the unknown life of the future.^{GG}

JANUARY 18, 1948

^GWent to see Leo Lerman* with Rolf, Irv, and Jeanne. Rather shy, with those three, but Leo was very polite. Spoke with Ruth Yorck,† Schaffner (from *G[ood] Housekeeping* last year), and Leo, who said "Send (your first chapter) to Mrs. Aswell this week." Capote's book *Other Voices, Other Rooms* reviewed in the *Times* and *H[erald] Tribune* today. *Times* wasn't so good, but the *Tribune* was delightful! "Will become the greatest writer of our time!" Williams praised him. He's only 23. Pure poetry, I find.^GG

JANUARY 19, 1948

^GMy birthday. Went to Hastings. Very nice with Old Fashioneds, and lots of little gifts, but not what I wanted: a camera or pajamas. And fantastic food. Cutting the first chapter of the book so Jeanne can work tomorrow. She wants to type for me. Beloved girl. Mother wants to talk and talk. I always go to bed at 4 o'clock in Hastings and get up at 8 o'clock. Stanley works like a dog. Late into the night. My sketches in the living room look very good.^GG

JANUARY 20, 1948

^GVisited the Fearses, both of whom are sick. House of the dead! Today a long letter came from Dodd, Mead, saying they prefer Bruno to Tucker, and that I need to make it Bruno's novel. That I'm "not ready" for a contract. Rita was reading it to me when Jeanne arrived—and kissed me on the head—a disappointment but—something to think about. Anyway— more work.^GG

JANUARY 21, 1948

^GMargot not at all discouraged, as usual—said that Pat C. at Viking [Press] is interested in this kind of novel. So on Thursday, I'll show her

---

* Openly gay writer, critic, and editor Leo Lerman (1914–1994) wrote for the *New York Herald Tribune, Harper's Bazaar, Dance* magazine, and *Vogue.* He was a fixture in New York society who counted Marlene Dietrich, Maria Callas, and Truman Capote among his close acquaintances, and his parties were legendary.

† Ruth Landshoff Yorck, née Levy (1904–1966) was a well-known figure in the Weimar Republic *bohème* before emigrating to the United States. Her Berlin friends included Bertolt Brecht, Thomas Mann, and Albert Einstein; the publisher Samuel Fischer was her uncle and Oskar Kokoschka painted her portrait. She appeared in the silent film *Nosferatu* (1922), but once in New York she gave up acting and turned to writing instead, penning novels, poems, and magazine columns.

again. Have a lot to do. Thinking about Tucker a lot and have been discussing him constantly with Lil. What else today? I don't remember. Memory! One gets old.^{GG}

JANUARY 23, 1948

^GMother. We went to Lil's for dinner. It was so cold, I spent the night at Lil's. In such desperate need for a getaway that sleeping over at hers was a great pleasure. Feel like a different person, a European, when I sleep at Lil's. And am renewed by it.^{GG}

JANUARY 25, 1948

^GWent to Leo's—very pleasant. T. Capote.* Rainer.† And made the acquaintance of Lewis Howard, a writer I liked. Really—dreamed about what it would be like if we were married. Lil enjoyed herself. She compared the evening to those she experienced in Berlin before Hitler: the intellectuals, free thinkers, etc. And said we'd be the first to disappear. She's right. I'm reading [Louis] Adamic on fascism in America.^{GG}

JANUARY 29, 1948

^GThe trash can is full of white pages—everything thrown out. And yet—is Tucker strong enough yet? What will Viking say? I'll soon hear. Happy—back among people! Celebrating this evening! Saw Wolfgang Heider and R[osalind] Constable with two dogs that probably belong to Sylvia. Everyone cheery. Lil drank martinis. And we discussed Truman Capote. R.C. says he has nothing to say, that he's a whim created by Leo L[erman] and *Harper's Bazaar* and *Vogue*, etc. Jeanne stayed over. I love her more and more, but it's not enough for me. She loves me, she said. "Do you want me to love you?" "No," I responded. "Do you love me?" "You know I do," she said.^{GG}

JANUARY 31, 1948

^GIt's terribly cold. About 10°. Vomiting, of course. Got up at 11:30 AM. (It was four by the time we fell asleep.) Called Margot—and visited her to see the editor of [*Woman's Home*] *Companion*. They want my last

---

* Truman Capote, former resident at Yaddo, wrote one of the five necessary letters of recommendation for Pat. In a personal letter to the director of Yaddo, he stated: "She is really enormously gifted, one story of hers shows a talent as fine as any I know. Moreover, she is a charming, thoroughly civilized person, someone I'm quite certain you would like." While Pat was at Yaddo, Capote used her apartment to finish his short story collection *Tree of Night and Other Stories*.

† Luise Rainer (1910–2014), a German-born film actress who won two Academy Awards for her roles in *The Great Ziegfeld* (1936) and in *The Good Earth* (1937).

story, "Where to, Madam?," about the Rolls-Royce driver. But with changes, which I think I can make. And they're paying a thousand dollars. Then on to see Mr. Davis*—the strange man of 31 Rockefeller Plaza, editor of comic books and *Ballet Theatre* publications. He asked if I wanted work. My lucky day! And tonight with Kingsley. She told me what I already know about Tucker: he's weak, and the reader doesn't care what happens to him.ᴳᴳ

FEBRUARY 1, 1948

ᴳI'm doing nothing. And feeling very happy. Took an impromptu trip to Hastings at 3 o'clock—how wonderful it is to have such a home!ᴳᴳ

FEBRUARY 2, 1948

ᴳMy first truly free day in months! If only I had given myself more! I would have written much better!ᴳᴳ

FEBRUARY 5, 1948

ᴳSaw *A Streetcar Named Desire*† with Jeanne yesterday, the best play of my life. I could have cried at the end, it was so accomplished. Jeanne said, "One should only see it with someone he loves." Later— went home, so happy and content, thinking of Jeanne. And wrote her a long, quick letter, in which I attempted to give her some self-confidence. Said that if I were a man (so many of my fantasies begin that way: If I were a man—), I would venture to marry her. ("But you—never marry a writer!")ᴳᴳ

2/9/48

The East River in mid-winter. One comes upon it and stops with a sense of space, of broad and unstoppable, unstopping power that is a strange and frightening sensation to a man who has been imprisoned in the city for weeks and months. The fragments of filthy ice-floes that dot its surface seem the coldest, most miserable, most cruel, most destroyed objects to be found in New York. Some are so weighted with smut, so exhausted and honey-combed by the river, they float quite beneath the surface, and these are the most miserable and hideous of all. One's face must harden a little to look farther across the river. Seagulls that have found a perch-

---

* Blevins Davis (1903–1971), American theatrical producer and a close personal friend of Harry S. Truman and his family. By 1949, he was president of the Ballet Theater of New York (now American Ballet Theater).
† Tennessee Williams's play opened on Broadway on December 3, 1947, directed by Elia Kazan with Marlon Brando in the lead role.

ing place on a flat piece of ice yawp happily from the center of its surface triumphantly in mid-stream—strange and ghostly the sound from afar on the insubstantial river! The scene is gray. Concatenations of floes drift backward here & there confusedly in a divided current. Waste! Waste! And the heart does not dare raise a happier image, a private image, now that the physical eye beholds this physical statement.

My love, where are you now? You who were with me a block ago! In absolute silence a tug boat matted with soot-covered ice as thickly as with rope and truck tires, burrows through ice and water, thrusting on ahead a coal barge, or two, or three. The tiny girl in zippered leggings, who stands near me with her colored nurse, screams with sudden nervous delight at the passing tug. She holds a large doll up to see it! The doll has only empty black ovals for eyes. Beloved, where are you now, where a year hence, then, if you shall be with me again in a moment, when I turn away? A year hence you will not be in my bed—though we love each other now, though we have served each other and made sacrifices for each other, though I and you have given you and me gifts made with our own hands—you will not be with me, but the river, it will be here, if I come again.

And out the window near my desk, snow has found its bed between the close-set backs of apartment buildings. Not for a day was this snow permitted to lie in the white beauty that is its own nature. In its fifteen feet wide defile that extends the length of the block, it has been trampled and mauled by the feet of janitors, children and dogs in quest of food. Above this snow the clotheslines of a hundred Irish families crisscross and tangle. Even the beauty of its sweep extent is prevented by the choppings of fences, dividing one house's yard from the next. Between two slim cables of some sort, a handball is jammed for all time, by an incredible accident. The telegraph poles that support the clotheslines lean powerfully this way and that. Only the buildings are geometrically true. And their confused projecting mess of fire escapes. I must have a picture of this alley out my window. Like New York in minuscule, it works with the space above the ground, the ground being dilapidated cement merely.

2/13/48

The prevalence of "good" and "evil" characters in Dostoyevsky. This interests me, egocentrically, because of my similar tendency. Every true novel inspiration of mine has had these elements. Charles and Bernard in the first book.* Now Tucker and Bruno. I don't care about technicalities. Good and evil are present in a single individual in life, hence my themes, which are self-projections.

FEBRUARY 13, 1948

ᴳI'm seeing more of Lewis Howard. Am inclined to see either Lil or Rosalind. Or, really, Jeanne, in rare moments of weakness. I'm reading Kafka—[Max] Brod and [Paul] Goodman.† I have this persistent suspicion that Lewis will become my husband.ᴳᴳ

FEBRUARY 14, 1948

ᴳI spoke to my mother about my ignorance of birth control. (I feel very feminine tonight.) Mother said she had been afraid, because she'd tried to hurt me as a child!‡ "It's better you learned from the world, etc." Lewis strikes me as very young. "You should have our child!" he said.ᴳᴳ

2/15/48

The sympathetic pain (or sensation) centers of the body. Relieving the over-taxed bladder produces a pain itch sensation in the teeth. It slightly intoxicated (as is often the case when the bladder is overtaxed) the connection seems demonical: the urination which centers about the genitals reacts in the teeth, that seat of earth bound infernal pain and inhuman torture, birth and death, ecstasy and agony, the base and treble of man's apperceptions. The body itself, to me, takes on a transcendent and metaphysical meaning: surely this corporeal machine was devised for something beyond its physical functions, for something beyond and more perverse than beauty, something less pure in intent than a reflection of God, or an exemplar of Nature's most intelligent animal life. Then the sprawled hand becomes a wonderful, frightening and curious part, the hair an astounding phenomenon, the speech magical, the power to love the most blessed, most abstruse, most magnificent faculty of all, and in its beauty surpassing the brightest wing of the rarest butterfly, the pristine majesty of the farthest and highest mountain.

And I feel myself convinced as much as I can be convinced of anything

---

* Her abandoned manuscript *The Click of the Shutting*.
† *Kafka's Prayer* by Paul Goodman (New York, 1947).
‡ Presumably Pat's mother is referring to the fact that she (as she informed her daughter in an undated letter) had tried to abort Pat with turpentine at the beginning of her pregnancy.

that the body has a significance beyond any as yet ascribed to it, that as a house for man's spirit while he is on earth, it is an enigmatic structure to be surveyed insofar as we are able, as an entirely different structure in a foreign land might be surveyed by an industrious visiting architect. Then it seems, too, that the union of male and female, while so complex, is almost universally accomplished in the most primitive way, that we therefore realize but five percent of our complexity, and the proportion known to ourselves is therefore even less than the proportion of an iceberg seen above the surface.

FEBRUARY 17, 1948

ᴳHeard from Margot that Viking didn't like the premise of my novel enough. And the chaos creeps into me, widespread fear, the next war, and in me, downfall, failure—the situation with Jeanne is particularly bad, that we know we have to break things off soon.ᴳᴳ

2/17/48

Already the great dichotomy between the person I am at night, the person I am by day, even doing my own writing. The nocturnal person is far advanced in thought and imagination. The daytime person still lives and works too much with the world which is not mine. I must get them together, and toward the night.

FEBRUARY 18, 1948

ᴳMiserable. Don't want to see anyone. [*Woman's Home*] *Companion* wants more work (on the story ["Where to, Madam?"]), and they're right.ᴳᴳ

FEBRUARY 20, 1948

ᴳTook a walk with Lewis on Wednesday, had a coffee soda at Schrafft's. He makes me much cheerier, the sympathy of a man. And he's both strong and sweet. Something rare.ᴳᴳ

FEBRUARY 21, 1948

ᴳHastings with Dell* and Lil. Miserable, despondent, depressed, because I want to work, because I don't really want Jeanne, because Lewis was bothering me. I want to change my sex. Is that possible? And then, Lewis is a Jew, which makes me feel all the more that I can't give myself to him.

---

* Lil's husband.

But we have so much in common. Drank too many Old Fashioneds and cried this evening.^{GG}

FEBRUARY 22, 1948

^GStill not happy. Reading Kafka and feeling afraid, because I'm so similar to him. And I'm afraid, because Kafka, wonderful as he was, never rose to the level of a great artist!* [Thomas] Mann is greater, because he could project his ideas!^{GG}

FEBRUARY 23, 1948

^GStayed in Hastings until I was finally feeling better. Telling myself I'm not at all disappointed with the book. But I want to have an idea of the whole rounded out in my mind before I start again. Margot said she wants a new synopsis for the novel before I leave for N[ew] O[rleans]. Further uncertainty—Jeanne—^{GG}

FEBRUARY 24, 1948

^G—is not going to N.O., I learned today. And there was reason to believe that we three—my mother, Jeanne and I—would drive there together. Joan called me Monday night. She married Chas. on Sunday (22). Am very happy to hear it!^{GG}

2/24/48

I am concerned at the moment with the biggest problems I have ever been concerned with. My foundations stir under me like huge slabs of stone. Unless they are steady, I can take no pleasure in the small achievements and satisfactions of every day existence—from which I and every normal human being derive greatest happiness.

2/24/48

Comfort, my heart! With gentle comfort, soft as a woman's breast, I should be clothed as in armor!

2/25/48

Work at the bone. Which is to say, at the core of existence (life) after the rest is pared away. My difficulty is, what sort of person am I? Emo-

---

* Only a few of Kafka's works were published in his lifetime. The earliest work to appear was *The Castle*, published posthumously in Germany in 1926 and in English translation in the UK and United States in 1930. A 1941 English edition with a homage by Thomas Mann spurred a surge in Kafka's popularity in English-speaking countries.

tional, violent—these seem closer to my real nature than the refinements of Woolf and James, for instance! Perhaps the refinements I notice are merely part of my screen from life.

FEBRUARY 26, 1948

ᴳCrazier days than any I've ever known. And in the meantime—tried twice to sleep with Lewis. Only when I was so disgusted with myself for asking "So, do you want to go to bed?," and tired and bored, masochism set in. And of course I failed. Lewis, I must say, is an angel of patience. And I like him very much.ᴳᴳ

FEBRUARY 28, 1948

ᴳStarted the snail story.* I like it. But I'm tired. X-rays twice a week at J. Borak's.ᴳᴳ

2/29/48

The most discerning remark I can make about myself at this moment: that my emotions for the past six months (and before that, in endless succession!) have been so thwarted at every point, I can no longer even grasp tiny scenes in my writing with dramatic passion, can barely even express them! This at the psychic nadir of my twenty-seven years—February 29, 1948. Before today, I at least had a target for my centrifugal angst, at least an objective before me! Now I am incapable of the smallest decisions, and cannot even envisage my future life, since I am undecided whether I can be happy alone, or whether I must spend it with someone—in which latter case I shall have to make radical adjustments, either to male or female.

A quandary? Hell.

FEBRUARY 29, 1948

ᴳWhat? Social at Lewis's, so formal—and at Leo's, where I found Truman Capote. Held my hand, apparently very devoted. Wants to see my room.ᴳᴳ

---

* "The Snail-Watcher," a short story that Margot Johnson tried in vain to offer the periodicals, who reacted with rejection and disgust. It was only in 1964 that the story was purchased by Pat's friend Jack Matcha, then editor of the California-based magazine *Gamma*, which went bankrupt immediately after its publication.

MARCH 1, 1948

ᴳTruman at 6. Likes the room. Ate at Louise [Aswell's]. I like him a lot. Jeanne *au lit* though when we returned, which made me mad.ᴳᴳ

MARCH 3, 1948

ᴳHurried—for Hastings. Worked two days on the new synopsis (of my novel), and this evening I'm bringing Kingsley with me (to Hastings) to page through it.ᴳᴳ

MARCH 6, 1948

ᴳVisited Dr. Rudolf Löwenstein, psychoanalyst, last week—Monday. For the first time, I told a stranger that "I am homosexual." And he listened to the story of my life. And said that my case will take about two years. A bit discouraging, but I felt better, just because I had told someone. Truman jokes: "When I was 14 years old, I told my parents that everyone was interested in girls, but that I, T.C., was interested in boys!" And they let him be. Don't want to go back to Löwenstein.ᴳᴳ

MARCH 8, 1948

ᴳBack to N.Y.

Lil loves the snail story. I overflow with joy whenever someone loves something of mine! Trifles! My God! I think of Joan often, of her husband, who now knows and loves the same things in her that I loved and love and that captivated me. But Joan doesn't love him. Her letters make that clear.ᴳᴳ

MARCH 9, 1948

ᴳWent for a walk with Lewis. And we ate (finally) and came back here. I worked for about two hours, while he slept. These past two days, I've written down the first chapter of the book with the new Tucker, Guy Haines. It seems appropriate that not a single line I wrote with Ginnie can remain! God—a sad thing, love. But working with Lewis—while he was here, the world was suddenly better. And he stayed a while—a little better in bed (the second time), but I don't want it, other than out of necessity, not for pleasure. I'm not even curious anymore.ᴳᴳ

MARCH 11, 1948

ᴳPrepared dinner for Truman. Rolf and Mother here when he arrived. We had drinks, and Mother likes him a lot. "So quiet, unlike most N.Y. youngsters." And she praised his novel. Dinner was nice—but nothing remarkable for that gourmet, I don't think. Felt I should make the effort, though. Truman paid $180 to stay here [at my apartment] for two months. M[ary] L[ouise] Aswell, M[arguerite] Young,* etc. Very nice, and wore my dress pants, at Truman's insistence. Stayed out late—and later went for a drink at T. Trouville's. I like going out with little Truman: he is so considerate, and so famous! And so sweet.GG

MARCH 12, 1948

GSent the letters [of recommendation] to Yaddo. Trying to apply for May-June. Mrs. Aswell, Young, and Truman recommending me. And Rosalind. Quite sick. I'm so depressed, my stomach isn't working. I'm still in love with [Jeanne]. That's the truth. I don't regret it, but it makes me sad. Worked a little while Lewis slept, and I suddenly felt so much better, I had the courage to try sleeping with him again. I find it so terribly boring! No pleasure at all! God—how strange! The thing parents around the world forbid their children from doing, as ugly! I tried—really, until I was exhausted. It seems I am so small, and the man is so big. Meaning I have no interest in doing it.GG

MARCH 13, 1948

GNevertheless, happier today. Prepared all day for Carl Hazelwood† who arrived at 6:30. Carl very nice, we talked about him—he told me more, he said, than he ever told his wife or mother. And also said men are dirty. Carl has never enjoyed sexual intercourse. God! I play with the thought—that I could so easily marry Carl, that I prefer him to Lewis, that he would barely alter my life. I could "love" him, because he needs love so badly. And it would be an escape.GG

MARCH 14, 1948

GWork. Rosalind at 5:30. Martinis. She has a wonderful job now: just reading new books, seeing new actors, paintings, etc. and reporting on them.‡ Exactly what she would be doing if she didn't need to work. Visited Jeanne, because I was so drunk. And had no interest in staying the night, although I'd have been invited to. Hope that was the last time.GG

---

* The novelist Marguerite Young, like Mary Louise Aswell, wrote a letter of recommendation for Pat's Yaddo residency.
† Carl Hazelwood is a young man Pat has recently met.
‡ According to Daniel Bell, publishing magnate Henry Luce named Rosalind Constable editor of an in-house newsletter—*Rosie's Bugle*—which informed all Luce editors of the cultural topics they should cover.

MARCH 15, 1948

ᴳIf only I'd known how to write a book before I started!ᴳᴳ

MARCH 16, 1948

ᴳSketched the scene out the window, as I once sketched my house in
Taxco before leaving forever. Have the feeling I won't come back here.
Sent Bruno's murder to Yaddo, and a story.ᴳᴳ

MARCH 26, 1948

My mother alarmed me by telling me she may give up the house, come
down here to live. What causes all this upset? Only a shortage of money.
And she says I do not give her the encouragement I should. Behind this
are many factors: 1) resentment of S. [Stanley] who should be providing her more 2) stubborn attitude, that since she stayed with him when
I fought for a divorce, she should take what he gives 3) childish attitude
of the freelance artist, that if he is not supported, he should at least not
be compelled to pay for the people who are steady salary earners 4) the
conviction that my parents' house is their bank, a bigger one by far than
my own, which my mother continually reminds me of, saying I am "well
off" 5) resentment at having lent her money without interest when it was
inconvenient for me to lend it, that I am eternally left holding the bag by
creditors 6) resentment that my mother says "You pay now. We'll settle
later" and never does.

3/29/48

In Houston: even in a cheap beer saloon, frequented by fairies, generally
lower middle-class, clerks, knowing little of the arts, for instance, there
is still that terrifying glance of knowledge exchanged across the room,
from them by me, still that overwhelming sense of fraternity, bridging
place, personality, interests. One realizes then that the sex life motivates
& controls all. (I am myself entirely a mass of tributaries from this great
river in me.)

MARCH 30, 1948

[Fort Worth.] Grandma & I leave at 4:15 P.M. I forgot my Proust on
the front porch, reading instead *The Atlantic*, which is most stimulating. The train ride is pleasant, and I feel well dressed in my gray suit,
gray turtle neck, crown belt. I am attracted to the quiet, intellectual girl
across the aisle, who gets off in Dallas. With clothes, with personal security, desire rises again. Tonight in Ft. Worth, a letter from Margot, with

"Where to, Madam," rejected by the *Companion*. Momentary chaos, despair, quickly disappearing. Here in this sloppy house, incredibly more dilapidated than before, somewhere are those myriad hair-like roots which nourish my main root, formed in air and water.

MARCH 31, 1948

The days go by and I call no one.

APRIL 3, 1948

Have rented a typewriter, and begun, in good mood, another ending on the *Comp.* story. It flows. Yet each day that goes by—where is the writing I wish to do? I feel it in me. Shall I be like those people without number who feel a destiny to write magnificent works one day? Yet looking at them I know I am different, and I put my trust in my intensity—my enormous need—which I do not see at all in them. The fortune-teller's remark to my mother in N.O. haunts me: "You have one child—a son. No, a daughter. It should have been a boy, but it's a girl." All around me, the happy, light-hearted, happily living couples of the south. Courtship is so easy, the attainment so easy, their bodies so fortunate.

4/4/48

Venturing into the world again, among people, when a trip with two other people (are they people like me?) to a store becomes an adventure worthy of a hero, a voyage testing the skill and courage of a sea captain. The clay of myself, molded to a certain idiosyncratic shape by my hundred days of solitude, is pushed, poked, stabbed, smashed at a score of points at once, hammered into the mold of everyone else, beaten into a proportion just according to the laws of the world. My own work then is seen in proportion. And this is the precious gain: that works in progress are seen not to be the all of myself even, as I had thought, but microcosms in the universe of myself, in which float nebulously (I feel it now), thousands of other microcosms, scores of solar systems. Can a man express his all in a single work?

4/5/48

In the night, things exist naked; I am in perfect communication with them. (In the night, the concrete and the abstract are naked; one can make love to them.)

APRIL 10, 1948

My mother awakened me at 9 with a call that I have been admitted to Yaddo. I am thrilled and delighted. Such a relief, like a soldier, to have one's life planned for the next 10–12 weeks! My mother pleased too, and grandma impressed. Grandma read all about Yaddo in the pamphlet. How wide in range are her interests—how much grander a person is she than all her offspring. Constantly I think how the family since her children's generation has steadily married downward, with the exception of Claude. I read F. B. Simkins *The South Old & New, a History 1820–1947* with great enthusiasm every night until late. Am retyping my Mexican story. It is so good, so far as facts go. Maybe Margot can do something. What for a title?

4/24/48

[New Orleans.] Chicory coffee and over fatigue—How perfect these nightmarish moments—On awakening to close the green transom. Get a drink for medical purposes, there is that last brilliant cannon shot on the battleground of myself—(jolted, shocked, by shots of wisdom for which I would not trade a sound night's sleep at any time)—that because I deprived from her my alcoholic lover's first love alcohol, she was determined to deprive me of herself. O what in life is worth the wisdom of the heart? As I stand alone in my New Orleans hotel room at 3:15 A.M., my body subtly shakes, like Baudelaire's. I feel my intuitive powers, feel their end, too, for I am weak now, and the body which warreth against the spirit, does not last long under such treatment.

4/25/48

The homosexual is a higher type of man than other men. Inevitably he partakes less of the physical and the biologic forces for his passions, his intellectual powers. Is his sexual love not entirely within the highest faculty of humans, the imagination? And danger, uncertainty, incompleteness, an imposed and loathed philosophy of transience (with which his ideals are always at war) keeps him stimulated as if by drugs and mortal combat to the greatest effort of his mind and heart. It is this that makes him philosophically and artistically productive. Creative, I should say, not always productive. The homosexual's normal plane is that to which every ordinary artist must attain by chance or effort in order to align experiences for artistic value.

5/8/48

All the world is unreality, as the believers in Christ are the first to aver. Therefore, why do my parents assert that I live unreally? I live more purely, on more pure illusion, on more beautiful dream, than they, who live also on dream. Theirs happens to be the dream of the heterosexual world which lives undisturbed, untormented, buying and living in houses with the persons they love, as I cannot.

MAY 11–30, 1948

What to say of Yaddo? I shall never forget it. A singularly dull bunch, no big names—though Marc Brandel[*] is interesting. Bob White, Clifford Wright,[†] Irene Orgel, Gail Kubik,[‡] Chester Himes,[§] and Vivien K[och] MacLeod, W. S. Graham, a Scots poet, Harold Shapero[¶] & wife, Stan[ley] Levine, painter, Flannery O'Connor.[**] Great desire to drink, after 3 days. The drunkest evening of my life after ten days. At the Maranese Restaurant btw. here & Town, the place we took dinner when the kitchen moved from garage to mansion. None of us ate much. We trooped into the bar & drank as if we had never had cocktails before. Mixing was the order—for a thrill—Marc soon succumbed, with carrot hair in his carrot soup. I exchanged a revealing phrase with C. Wright, the solitary gay person here, which was carried no farther. We both know. So what?

I must have had five martinis or six. Plus two Manhattans. A near blackout at Jimmy's with Bob & Cliff, who had passed out at the Maranese, & had to be carried by three of us into the cab. We propped him on a stool in Jimmy's, whence he fell like an egg. We seated him in the taxi, but when we came out he was gone! The taxi fare $7.50 for Bob & me by the time we finished looking at Bob's drawings in his studio. The driver drinking & looking too. When we refused, we were whisked back to town, passing Cliff on the way, staggering under the dark elms of Union Avenue on his 2-mile trek back home. This night has become legendary as "the Night Clifford Fell in the Lake."

---

* Marc Brandel (1919–1994), a British author and TV producer who wrote several titles in The Three Investigators book series.

† American painter Clifford C. Wright (1919–1999) went on to marry Elsa Gress, a famous feminist Danish writer.

‡ Gail Thompson Kubik (1914–1984), American composer.

§ Chester Himes (1909–1984), Black American crime novelist.

¶ Harold Shapero (1920–2013) was an American composer, his wife the abstract expressionist painter Esther Geller (1921–2015)

** Flannery O'Connor (1925–1964), short story writer and novelist from Savannah, Georgia.

^GChester tried (in his room) to kiss me. Did I mention it already? Doesn't matter.^{GG}

There are six artists here. We are all very different from one another, yet remarkably sociable, I think. What strikes me most forcibly, is our basic similarity, in fact. It occurred to me last night, if any of us saw a white note being slid under the crack of our door—with a sound like thunder in the silent depths of mid-morning—each of us would drop his work and spring for it. With what hope? Perhaps a friend, some sign of personal choice, of a singling out from the rest. And it followed— personal security, ego assurance, a lover. These every artist needs and wants. Even the married artist is constantly attuned to these needs. The mornings. Energy is too abundant at ten. The world is too rich to be eaten. One sits in a whirl at one's desk thinking of drawing, writing, walking in the woods. The overwhelming flood of experience rushing in from all sides. In the morning only do I ever desire a drink to reduce my energy from 115% to 100%.

5/15/48

Please try to notice if every artist isn't ruthless in some way. Even the sweetest of characters have done something, generally because of their creative life, that to the rest of the world is inhuman. Some cases are more obvious, others may be more concealed. I know mine exists, my cruelty. Though where, I cannot precisely say, for I try always to purge myself of evil. Generally it is selfishness in an artist. And because he subjects himself so cheerfully to all kinds of privations for his art, it is difficult for him to see wherein he has been guilty of selfishness. He sees it as selfishness for such an obviously worthy cause, too. Generally, in one form or another, it is a self-preservative selfishness, in regard to his not giving enough of himself to the world or another person.

[NO DATE]

After three weeks at Yaddo. The soul lusts for its own corruption—after only one week. Desperately, through alcohol, it tries to reestablish contact with the rest of humanity. One's eternal and individual loneliness is silhouetted sharply against dark green pine woods where it seems no human figure has ever walked or will ever walk. And too, there is the desire born of loneliness also, to mingle spiritually with all the rest of the world of this year 1948 which is now starving, fighting, writhing in agony of thirst and undressed wounds, whoring, cheating, scheming, develop- ing private, secret fondnesses for the stinking gutter. We want that, for

it is our destiny too, and Yaddo is depriving us. There is the moment
of utter corruption, around eleven or eleven thirty in the morning. One
goes to urinate, washes their hands and looks into the bathroom mirror.
The clock in the workroom grows audible. One realizes the isolation and
imprisonment of the body, one realizes the hell of the body (and not only
here, everywhere and as long as one lives, one longs for another body,
naked and loving, a man or a woman, as it may be). One mixes a drink
of rye and water, sips half of it truculently at a window, looks at the sterile, made bed and contemplates masturbating and turns from it in fear
and scorn. One stalks about the room like a criminal imprisoned, unre-
generate, incorrigible. This is the moment delicious, nihilitive, supreme,
all-answering, the moment of utter corruption.

JUNE 2, 1948

Happiness overwhelms me. Twenty-three days at Yaddo. My life is regular, pleasant, healthful on the obvious plane. (And how often and where
in the past eight years, since I lived with my parents, have I been able
to say this?) On the less obvious plane, it restoreth my dignity, my self-
confidence, it enables me to complete what I have never completed, that
child of my spirit, my novel, and give it birth.

JUNE 17, 1948

This persistent need to be forgiven. Romanticism? Mother complex?
For it is always by a woman, one I must love. But how have I sinned?
Tonight—depressed for the first time at Yaddo, due mainly to cumula-
tive fatigue. Three days after Jeanne. I was with her Sunday afternoon
to Tuesday morning. My book is nearing its close. I am no longer able to
think about it logically or imaginatively, and feel I write like the blind.
My contrary system will buck ferociously in the next days against the finish, but I shall conquer. (Which is I?)

    If I cannot give birth in the supreme hospital of Yaddo, where can I
ever? Here are no sexual or auditory distractions. Yet today so restless—
melancholy—I asked myself whether I had bettered by seeing Jeanne or
not, though she made me so happy. Incredible! Less than one year ago I
hurried to my first anniversary with G[innie]. Now overwhelming fact
and circumstances against my will have forced me to forget her. Yes, at
last forget, the last step to annihilation! And no sooner is this done, than
the emotional system begins to assimilate another, and to make her a
part of it!

JUNE 23, 1948

ᴳAt 6:17 P.M., wrote "Finis" to my book. Feel tired, bored, and not excited. When I'm not tired, I suddenly see all the good spots in my book. Marc is very sweet, and treats me with increasing care. He's leaving Monday. And I'd like him to visit me in Hastings.ᴳᴳ

JUNE 26, 1948

A turning point. Went with Marc to the lake and discussed homosexuality quite a bit. Amazingly tolerant he is. And he convinced me I must abolish guilt for these impulses and feelings. (Can't I remember Gide? Must I always try to "improve" myself?) I returned with quite a different attitude. I think more highly of myself. I have opened myself a little to the world.

6/30/48

A certain calm is essential in order to live, relief from anxiety. I myself can never have this without belief in the power of God which is greater than man and all the power in the universe.

7/2/48

The attraction of bars: one can make of them what one wishes. As one can make of a woman what one wishes. A bar room is a laboratory to the artist, an opium chamber to the escapist, humanity to the lonely man. (And who is not lonely?)

JULY 5, 1948

I cannot uncoil myself—I have been a coiled spring so many weeks. For four days have tried to work leisurely. Now the tension is at the base of my neck in back. Psychosomatic, says Shapero. I long for the moon. Unshakable fatigue. I never want to go to bed. Aimlessly go to town with the crowds here, and long for something which alone will satisfy me, which I know I shall not find these evenings, the kiss of someone I love. Mrs. Ames* has classified me (included me) among the "hard drinkers"— Marc, Bob, Chester, who are leaving. Marc sends me his book, *Rain Before Seven*. And declares again that he loves me. I long to go away with someone for a new life. Maybe N. of New Orleans, as Marc suggests. Yet won't this be further seclusion? Basically what torments me is

---

* Elizabeth Ames, director of Yaddo in 1948.

a basic mistrust of men. Marc is exceedingly tolerant (and very affectionate) saying for instance, he considers me very feminine.

JULY 16, 1948

[Mother's] overconcern with me is our undoing. Tonight, walking to
Hastings to see a movie, we discussed it over beer, and she almost wept.
(Much sentiment intrudes also, beclouding.) I take her appetite & ability
to work she says, through my curtness & lack of encouragement. Yet I
shall not leave, though I offered to, for that would be worse. (Am now at
Hastings since July 10, and shall be perhaps a month.)

JULY 20, 1948

[G]Conditions in Hastings unbearable, and I'm leaving. The most awful
Sunday afternoon, when I reminded her of the anguish of my youth, and
only S[tanley] understands a thing. Mother simply says: "You don't love
me. I've failed." And—I can't bring myself to respond.[GG]

JULY 21, 1948

[G]Will probably work with Ace Magic, where Marty Smith works. Thank
God! Herbert L. called. We had dinner and he spent the night. The best
yet. God—maybe I'll learn to love men.[GG]

JULY 22, 1948

[G]Too many martinis—and another two at Leighton's. Kissed Jeanne like
a lunatic in the car, and was too late getting to Hastings. Jeanne spent
the night here—which I'd promised myself would never happen again.
But I was so drunk—dangerous, like Yaddo.[GG]

JULY 23, 1948

[G][Spent] the evening with Marc before he leaves for Kent, Conn[ecticut].
He spent the night—(three nights, three people!) He held me and was so
sweet. I hold him in very high regard.[GG]

7/28/48

A coolly objective remark: in happiness, the artistic mind tends better
to pare an idea to its essentials. Only the melancholic mind clutters and
complicates. Once more, be damned to the people who think the artist well off when he suffers! Would my parents could read this, but they
never will.

AUGUST 2, 1948

ᴳThese days, I've been speaking with Jeanne about the need for us to separate. Promised Marc I would. She was sad, but understands. Mostly she was jealous, I think. And later with Marc. I asked if he could spend the night with me. Said yes. He was very sweet, but nothing happened, and I was upset again.ᴳᴳ

8/5/48

Persistently, I have the vision of a house in the country with the blond wife whom I adore, with the children whom I adore, on the land and with the trees I adore. I know this will never be, yet will be partially, that tantalizing measure (of a man) which leads me on. My God, and my beloved, it can never be! And yet I love, in flesh and bone and clothed in love, as all mankind. The pulse of love in me beats strongly in the winter as in the spring. Which is to say, I am no animal in season. I am God's man in all moments. Never will my strength fail. At night, alone, I walk the hilly roads of the country and the woods with feet that can if I wish run up hill and down, that balance perfectly, that keep their power in reserve. At night, I lie in moonlight on my pillow. My love is not with me. I am not with my love in flesh. Ah, yet my love is with me, purer than she ever was!

AUGUST 6–9, 1948

ᴳThese are important days, because I'm making the greatest effort with Marc. He wants to go to Louisiana in the spring, with me—to live and to work. Wants to marry me, too, but I prefer to wait. I don't want to hurt him. But I fear I will never love him. So disgusted with him on Saturday—he was drunk, ugly, not at all appealing. I lay there thinking, how beautiful and lovely and pure girls are! And I [was] terribly sad.ᴳᴳ

AUGUST 14, 1948

ᴳI love Jeanne. I'm in love with her. It's because I've grown up, that it now takes on a different form. I'm slower, more serious and not more serious, but truly attentive. And today was hell. (2:30 P.M.) Had a tooth pulled.ᴳᴳ

AUGUST 20, 1948

ᴳJeanne called me at 11:38 P.M. Made me very happy. J. and I were here again. But tomorrow I will seek her like I seek the sun. I want her. I only like women. Marc said last night, I want to spend my life with you, even if I have to sleep with whores, and you with women.[GG]

SEPTEMBER 8, 1948

[G]Saw Rosalind. And each time I see her I feel like she grows a little duller, a little smaller spiritually. Awful to see, to say. But true. I feel as though she envies me because I finished my book. Meanwhile, she's earning her 125 a week, running around with all her "chic ladies," but doesn't have a novel to show. She can't congratulate me, and was so short that she had to call later to say a proper goodbye. I've never felt so "free." It matters so little to me, how much money I have, what I'm doing, for instance, in December. If I have to work, I'll work. "Working!" What nonsense, to fear that! Was I not just working like a Hercules? As Thos. Wolfe said— aren't there a hundred thousand easier ways to earn a living?[GG]

SEPTEMBER 10, 1948

Provincetown.* [G]Marc drunk when I arrived. Ann Smith[†] visited us, I think probably to get a look at me. She interests me—young, pretty, simple, and understanding. We wanted to take a walk (a few days later), and Marc accompanied us. Yes—I feel like I'm in prison. Always has to be like that—with a man.[GG]

SEPTEMBER 26, 1948

[G]Can't stand it any longer. This boredom, loneliness. So I took a walk to the train station to check the bus schedule. I'm leaving tomorrow, I told Marc. And because of that, of course, I have to sleep with him. And the fact that it's the last time is the only thing that gives me the strength to endure it.[GG]

OCTOBER 5, 1948

[G]These days pass quickly. Marc came back, and we ended things while he was drunk. I said it was impossible physically, and he cursed, called

---

* Provincetown on Cape Cod started to attract artists and bohemians around the turn of the twentieth century, especially from New York's Greenwich Village community, for its beautiful setting and light. By the 1940s, it was firmly on the map as a getaaway for artists and the gay community. Pat returned several times over the years.
† The painter, designer, and ex-*Vogue* model Ann Smith was an acquaintance of Marc Brandel's and vacationing nearby.

me a liar, etc. and said the novel is worthless, but I listened to everything and reminded myself: this will help me.[GG]

11/23/48

Opening at Midtown of B.P.'s [Betty Parsons's] gallery. All the ancient acquaintances, friends of my friends of my twenty-first year. Age has sagged a chin line, silvered a golden head, stamped its uniform signature of tiredness on a dozen faces. I think of Proust, re-seeing the Guermantes clan in the last chapter of *A La Recherche du Temps Perdu*. Apart from that, it becomes increasingly difficult as one's age and the complexities of this century's existence increase, to merge two personalities. How hopeless for real friendship, the savage crucible of an art gallery!

NOVEMBER 30, 1948

[G]First visit to psychiatrist: Eva Klein, M.D., recommended by D[avid] Diamond. I like her a lot   asked the most important questions first, and I asked: "You can't squeeze me in?" Need to take a Rorschach test. And of course need to find work to pay for all of this. Only $15 an hour, though. Following her questions, we first discussed the story of Ginnie—(just last Thursday I had one of my strange dreams about her) and that, and my work—that's all that concerns me. I left with a new happiness. What does the cost matter?[GG]

DECEMBER 3, 1948

[G]More dumb work on a hopeless comic. And trying to get work. God, this struggle! But I'm happier than I have been in many months! I'm on my way out. I'm already half in love with Mrs. Klein.[GG]

DECEMBER 4, 1948

[G]Think about my analyst constantly. Back to the book this morning. But couldn't sleep last night, and was dull. Went to Stern's to find work. Too many there. So finally, after some hesitation, Bloomingdale's, where I immediately found work. Monday morning—8:45 God!

Am most tempted to call my parents and tell them to go to hell! I'm almost free of my neurosis—as from a cancerous tumor![GG]

DECEMBER 6, 1948

[G]First day at Bloomingdale's. Training, and then toy department. Very pleased.[GG]

DECEMBER 7, 1948

^GHard work. Selling dolls, how ugly and expensive! And then—at 5:00 P.M., someone stole my meat for dinner! What kind of wolves one works with!^{GG}

DECEMBER 8, 1948

^GWas this the day I saw Mrs. E. R. Senn?* How we looked at each other—this intelligent looking woman! I want to send her a Christmas card, and am planning what I'll write on it.^{GG}

DECEMBER 15, 1948

^GLunch with Mother. Very pleasant, and I told her almost everything I've learned from Dr. Klein. She understands. They were going to transfer me to "Lingerie," but I resigned. Am considering a novel about Bloomingdale's.^{GG}

DECEMBER 17, 1948

^GI am very, very happy. So much happier than last December! And—why should I not be in love with Mrs. Klein? Has she not given me more than a mother?^{GG}

DECEMBER 23, 1948

^GSick. 102° fever. Wrapped presents. An address book and parcel for Marc. Only wanted to see Mrs. Klein! She's the only person in the world who gives me the right answers! Was afraid, because I was so sick, hot, and weak. Hence the fainting spell in the subway. 58–125 St. She asked me what I was thinking about then. "About death," I responded, "and that there's nothing to hold on to in those moments."^{GG}

DECEMBER 25, 1948

^GChristmas. Don't have enough presents for my parents. Or enough strength to open mine. Poor Jeanne—I couldn't sleep last night, so hard for her. Have fever, and so many more chickenpox.^{GG}

---

* After her brief encounter with Kathleen Senn—wife of Mr. E. R. Senn—Pat went straight home and, as if in a fever dream, wrote the plot sketch for *The Price of Salt* in her notebook, titling it "The Bloomingdale Story": "it flowed from my pen as from nowhere—beginning, middle and end" in just two hours.

DECEMBER 26, 1948

[G]The worst day. Had to call the doctor because my throat is unbearable. Fever of 104½ or higher.[GG]

DECEMBER 27, 1948

[G]A little better. My parents called me downstairs, to the fireplace, just to criticize me, to argue with me. Couldn't speak (sore throat) to defend myself. And wished I were alone upstairs again. God, what horrible people! ("You're disgusting, etc."!) Just see what we do for you![GG]

12/31/48

Really how the others live, the quality of their two-dimensional experience is really beyond me.

1949

PAT RETREATS to her parents' house in Hastings-on-Hudson in early January to recover from chickenpox. Rather than medicating her, Pat's mother embraces a Christian Science treatment, which is ineffective. Similarly futile is the psychoanalysis Pat resumes with Dr. Eva Klein upon returning to the city; although unable to help Pat reconcile her intention to marry with her aversion to sleeping with men, Dr. Klein does advise Pat not to rush into anything. In April, however, Pat officially becomes engaged with beau Marc Brandel. Following the news that Harper & Brothers wants to purchase her debut novel *Strangers on a Train*, she goes so far as to set a wedding date during the champagne-fueled celebration.

Between the failed psychoanalysis and ill-advised engagement, Pat's only remaining option is to flee, as fast and far as she can. In an impromptu decision, she buys a ticket on the *Queen Mary* with some of her comic book earnings and sets sail for England on June 4. She has long had many ties to Europe, from high school classmates to Greenwich Village emigrants and other friends who have invited her to visit the other side of the Atlantic.

In London, Pat falls in love with Kathryn Hamill Cohen, an American Ziegfeld girl turned psychiatrist married to Pat's London publisher, Dennis Cohen. Not much happens between them though before Pat leaves for Paris in late June. There, she spends her days sightseeing and touring the Louvre, then whiles away her nights in such haunts as Le Monocle in the Latin Quarter. Despite these diversions, she pines for other lovers. Pat travels next to Marseille, where she visits (and flirts with) the cartoonist Jean "Jeannot" David before continuing on to Cannes; there she encounters her ex-girlfriend, Natica Waterbury, and accompanies her to Saint-Tropez.

After Pat visits Rome, which she hates, she is eventually joined in Naples by Kathryn, with whom correspondence has grown increasingly tempestuous; together they tour the Amalfi Coast, and somewhere between Sicily and Capri, the two become lovers. By the time Kathryn is called back to London, though, Pat is also ready to go home.

Upon returning to New York, where she anxiously awaits word from Kathryn, Pat turns to her most reliable form of distraction: writing. She puts the finishing touches on *Strangers on a Train*, which will be published the following March. Having cashed in half her war bonds, Pat goes Christmas shopping and excitedly plans a trip to New Orleans with her friend Elizabeth Lyne, just like the two heroines of her work-in-progress, the lesbian romance *The Price of Salt*.

JANUARY 6, 1949

G Marc at 9:30 P.M. One of our best evenings. Discussed my book, and he said that several pages made him quite envious, that many were absolutely wonderful. That was maybe the best thing I've heard in weeks. GG

JANUARY 16, 1949

G Mrs. Klein says that I'm far too young for twenty-eight. (Are married people that much happier?) GG

1/19/49

The writer projects, in projecting himself into his characters, his value of himself also. In an era noted for its unmemorable fiction heroes, the psychologists are quite right to diagnose a universal guilt complex.

JANUARY 27, 1949

G Page 195 of my novel. Marc says I'm working too hard. It's true. But I can't change it. [Dr.] Eva Klein—major progress today. GG

1/30/49

If I knew I should die tomorrow, with what eagerness I should visit an ordinary brownstone tenement in my block, look at all the children I have been mildly disapproving on the sidewalks all these years, admire the household's details, and love the expressions on the blunt Irish faces.

FEBRUARY 6, 1949

G Marc gave me an "Authors Guild" membership (as a second birthday gift). Since meeting Marc, I've had so much more to do. Want to improve "Mrs. Afton," (for instance). Marc liked the story a lot. Worked alone this evening, my novel should be done by next week. GG

FEBRUARY 27, 1949

ᴳJeanne at 11 o'clock. [We] went to Nyack with Dione* to see Carson McCullers.† Jeanne bores me. I suddenly feel so free, without hard work, apart from dreaming, planning, etc. Carson was very hospitable, and we stayed about 4 hours. [Her husband] Reeves, her mother [Vera], Margarita Smith, her sister. Carson said repeatedly that I have "a very good figure." We drank Cokes and sherry. Books on the chairs and her and her mother were both wearing pants. I heard Reeves and her were drinking too much in Paris ᴳᴳ

2/28/49

Give me back the sensual pleasure of my aloneness. In these eighteen months, I have done a journey. I have listened to people shouting at me directions to get between rocks, over seas where I did not want to go, where I was tired of going. We shall lead you back to yourself, they cried, but I did not believe them for a moment. I only knew I must go. I knew very well they would lead me back to someone else, and cry triumphantly, "There you are!" but perhaps I should never get acquainted with that other person, and eventually kill us both. But I have back the sensual pleasure of my aloneness, that they will never touch, I know now. Like Ulysses, I am weary (but my wife has been faithful) and sitting about in the evening, I do not always know what to talk about at first. Yet the sea of words, the sea of my aloneness rocks me gently again, and after I rest a while, I shall know once more where to dip, where to drink, where to ignore the green current.

MARCH 3, 1949

24th Visit [with Dr. Eva Klein]. I hate and resent my mother to a very great extent, says Eva. Therefore my guilt drives me to girls, overcompensation. She declares I really hate women & love men, but renounced men, etc. For the first time, by these plain words, the muddled relationship with my mother begins to be clarified. I do not wish to see her now, feel contemptuous, sorry, ashamed of her, toward her. And now—for the past fortnight with Dione, Ann, Jeanne, I am "acting out" that with which my mother served me—the loving and leaving pattern, the basic heartlessness & lack of sympathy.

---

* Dione is a new love interest Pat has just met.
† Carson McCullers's family lived in Nyack, New York, half an hour by car from New York City.

MARCH 4, 1949

There were three girls tonight, whom I might have called and passed the night with. I called one—a bit too late. But the point was, I didn't care which one I might have seen. I cannot work any longer in the evening when I have been working all day. Something different, but then, there is something different in my work lately too—more passion, which pays off even in the comics, even in the photographs in *LIFE* magazine, even in the shmoo.* No doubt Marc was especially annoyed because I was at Rosalind's. Because consciously or unconsciously, he knows she, in general, poisons my mind against him. "I doubt if he is good enough for you," she declares.

3/14/49

One's lover disappoints one, refuses to be seen, to be kind, to forgive, on a certain evening, and momentarily, one feels plunged in melancholy and grief. An hour later, or the next morning, the event seems less important, but this is illusion. Love itself has died in that instant of disappointment. Love always dies behind one's back. Later, weeks later, in the vacuum, one wonders at first what has happened? Why? When? Farther down on the vine, the stem has been broken.

MARCH 16, 1949

Eva minimizes the drinking thing, confident I am always repressed. This is not enough for me. No curse. Am 13 days late, though M. assures me I have no cause for concern.

MARCH 27, 1949

Analyst [Dr. Eva Klein]. Accuses me of being still the "nice" girl with her. Won't let my aggressiveness come out as I must. Pleasant evening cooking for Marc & a movie. He frets about money, has written to four colleges about a teaching job this fall. How wonderful if we could go to Tulane [University], since N.O. offers everything. But I still hesitate, have nightmarish dreams, of marriage.

MARCH 28, 1949

No word this weekend from Marc until now, though nothing was amiss. Oh, the unfairness of this sexual business to women! My sleep is even

---

* A comic figure from the strip *Li'l Abner.*

disturbed by the fear I might be pregnant, whereas Marc doesn't even know how I feel.

MARCH 29, 1949

With trepidation, wrong addresses got my alcohol-steeped specimen of urine to the bureaucratic laboratories of Garfield & Garner, 60 St. this noon. They clipped me $10 the first thing. (Who's going to pay $10 later, for a simple no—or a terrifying yes?) My head does not rest so easily tonight.

MARCH 30, 1949

A miserable morning trying to work. Got some beer for Ann [S.] & me, drank it to celebrate the good news of my negative [pregnancy] test results. Amazing how good the world can look in one moment! Though Marc who called later, said he was a bit disappointed, since we might have married sooner. Ann wants to go to Europe with me this spring. I rather hope she doesn't, for I'd like to be with Rosalind, or alone.

MARCH 31, 1949

Margot reports my alcoholic story needs drastic cutting. This writing game is never ending! Oh to write a story or a book which comes out properly the first time! And the doctors, the doctors! Now the general practitioner, who has to fit me with a diaphragm. The sign of the whore, to me, though I understand whores don't even wear them. I wrote to Rosalind. I eat her Tiptree Scarlet Strawberry Preserves in the mornings, sparingly, and dream of being with her. But now, I meant to do more than dream. Babs & Bill quite absurd last evening with their black & white communist outlook. Marc is so intelligent about such things, can say in a short sentence the fault of their thinking—which is that they do not think for themselves at all: The remaining communists are a lot of fanatics. And actually it seems to me, they serve Russian fascism, by breaking up the real liberals everywhere.

APRIL 4, 1949

Cocktails with Duchess, who has become a tequila addict, apparently. Vulgarity, coarseness, selfishness, materialism rampant—all this most hideous and depressing. The St. Regis waiters bow and scrape. Mentally I cringe with shame. So happy to come home alone and work. First evening free in 10 days.

APRIL 9, 1949

Trouble with Marc because I like to be alone—this evening intentions of seeing Ann or Dione, and decided on Dione. Marc called yesterday evening at 7:30, after Eva, and thank goodness we straightened out this slow warfare about my "time." I do not want to be absurd about it, but I cannot yet—bear to see him 6 nights per week, be dragged around here & there where I do not wish to go.

APRIL 10, 1949

The New Yorker, alas, does not like my alcoholic story. "Too unpleasant a subject—two people who become alcoholics," says Mrs. Richardson Wood. Talk, and puzzle working with Marc. Tonight we decided to be officially "engaged." Marc even wants to get me a ring!

APRIL 12, 1949

Evening with Ann, when I got woefully tight. (Why doesn't she serve canapes anyway?) Disgraced myself once more at the Brittany. Have only been there once sober. Continually reproaching myself about overdrinking. Terrific night with Ann.

APRIL 16, 1949

That I had to work seemed to make little impression on Dione. Marc for dinner tonight. Alas, I am weary from Dione, work, no rest, and he stayed the night. Disgusting business of diaphragm, which I trust eventually I shall get used to. We saw Liam O'Flaherty's *The Puritan* with J.-L. [Jean-Louis] Barrault. And Paul Monash.* When I am tired, as tonight, all becomes distorted, I lose all the ground I have gained. I want to be alone, I hate Marc, Paul, all people. I must discuss with Eva.

4/19/49

Will this longing never cease? Will this striving toward the unattainable never be discouraged? I have prayed and striven, too, for exhaustion, purification by pain, surcease for lack of fuel, but I come to think the fuel is life itself.

---

* The Emmy Award–winning American author, screenwriter, and film producer Paul Monash (1917–2003), a new acquaintance of Pat's.

APRIL 23, 1949

How much I resent about Marc these days—his never doing anything but reading when he is here, while I attempt to play records, fix drinks, watch meat & canapes in the oven, simultaneously fix dinner, wash dishes, do the bed (and disgusting diaphragm) and in the morning, prepare breakfast. He hasn't the particular sensitivity to realize that a person in the bathroom does not wish another person sitting at the table just outside the door. These and a thousand things disturb my digestion, banish the gains made at other times. Eva suggests my illness Thursday morning was resentment.

APRIL 29, 1949

S. & S. [Simon & Schuster] rejected my book, though all have some praise for it, and all, like Margot, say I should have no difficulty finding a publisher. It now goes to Harper, though Knopf is very interested. Have rewritten a few pages. Margot so indifferent whether I put them in before sending it out; I so convinced they may make all the difference in the taste & style of the book.

4/29/49

And anyway, is there any abnormality which is a bizarrer departure from "health" than art is from the normal living of the normal man?

MAY 1, 1949

Up after 4 hours' sleep to breakfast with Ann. Ann never looks more charming, or younger, than in her levis and big jacket. I dream fantastically of living with her, of having, for a time, the Bohemian life I have always been too constrained to take for myself.

5/1/49

Back of it all is a feeling that all this will change. A different life, different setting, something more permanent will evolve in the near future. (Homosexuals live more in the future even than most Americans.)

MAY 7, 1949

Very happy still, filled with expectation of Mme. Lyne's* party tonight. The party a fiasco, because dear Marc thought two boys were making

---

* Elizabeth Lyne, fashion designer and painter from Great Britain who emigrated to the United States and designed collections for Hattie Carnegie.

passes at him. I got my coat and left. Wish I'd stayed on or told him off—one or the other, for I came home in a silent, pent fury.

MAY 8, 1949

In Connecticut with Ann. Very depressed from last night. "You'd better make up your mind whom you love," said Ann, "because you're wasting a hell of a lot of valuable time . . . irrevocable time." I feel she refers to my lack of achievement in my work, my age, etc. and it all overwhelmed me. Moreover, I feel literally deprived of something, now that I cannot fall in love with anyone. However, it takes only a lunch with Dione (or even a good drawing) and laughter, to make me feel, and know I am, happier now, enjoying life more now, than ever before. Such a fact allows me to bear a great deal—even the thought of going away with Marc. Though actually, Saturday night dissuaded me from that. I will not be imprisoned so.

MAY 18, 1949

45th Visit [with Dr. Klein]—After the discussion with [Dr.] Gutheil, who has a shorter, stricter method of dealing with homosexuals. He strongly advises my not changing, of course. But he also prohibits alcoholic, homosexual, dope patients from "indulging" during treatment. Eva—flared up in typically Jewish way after I mentioned seeing Gutheil. In a spirit of honesty & scientific progress- -I mentioned it. Deep analysis, the slow method (she is orthodox Freudian according to Gutheil, though Eva calls herself between Freud & Horney)* is the only one for me, and she suggests I consult with 20 analysts whose names she would provide, and unless they all concur with her my money back (!) We discuss progress in general. She says

1) a basic maladjustment to people
2) a basic maladjustment to sex.

From earliest anal-sadistic years.

MAY 18, 1949

Have a ticket on the *Queen Mary*, June 4th!

MAY 19, 1949

Europe crept up on me slowly, much a matter of friends, pressure, no doubt. Everyone so kind to me, and everyone to see there!

---

* Karen Horney (née Danielsen, 1885–1952) was a German psychoanalyst who practiced in New York from 1932. She is considered the founder of feminist psychology in response to Freud's theory of penis envy.

MAY 20, 1949

A gloomy, uneventful day, until Margot informed me that Harper wants my book! Everything happens at once! After all these months of plodding dullness, the book and Europe. And—so I asked Marc to come over for dinner. He brought champagne. And we decided to marry Christmas Day. Three high points of my life—definitely! And to crown my good fortune—the curse tonight also, for the first time in over four months. I wonder if today is also Rosalind's birthday? It is mine anyway!

MAY 23, 1949

My book's being taken does great things for my ego. No longer ashamed to face people, etc. Mother here, and Marc for a drink. He thinks she is "weird," and can scarcely believe she is my mother. "It may sound trite, but you have an air of breeding that she just hasn't," said Marc, which surprised me indeed.

MAY 24, 1949

47th ᴳvisitᴳᴳ [with Dr. Klein]. Last visit before sailing. I told her of book & menstruation, but she showed little estimation of either. General pep-talk and coaching about not getting emotionally involved with people (I am not so detached as she suggested, she says). And not expecting anything from them, so I shall not be disappointed. (Bloody angry at having to pay this bill before I leave.)

MAY 28, 1949

The fiasco party with Marc. Alas how dull all evenings that should be social, because I cannot adjust to this hetero-social. Rather stay home & play chess with him. On the other hand, I view less dimly lately the idea of being married to him. Whether this is because I have the immediate escape of travel, I don't know.

JUNE 1, 1949

Nervous. Lunch with Joan Kahn* of Harper. All went well, and I believe we like each other. A very fine first novel, etc. and said it may (or may not) catch on extremely well. At luncheon, I decided "The Other" might be a good title, in fact, the best yet.

---

* Harper & Brothers commissioned experienced editor Joan Kahn to supervise the Harper Novel of Suspense imprint. This was a period in which pulp publishers and publishers of "quality" books began to push into the others' respective territory.

JUNE 2, 1949

Red tape. Renting the apartment. What results the *N.Y. Times* gets! People telephoning all day! With Rolf & Marc at Hastings with a load of stuff. Very nice, dull evening. Marc & I talked over beer. How I've got to be better (more affectionate) if we're to be married in Sept. Or December. We talk endlessly, mincing every point fine, then reminiscing!

JUNE 4, 1949

Because of Eva I go tourist instead of first class. Today I loathe her,—rather, am regretful of what I have spent, and do not intend to return. Rosalind, Marc, my mother saw me off. A short farewell, for the cabin is not attractive (D deck!) and the *Queen* sailed promptly. I could not see any of them from the deck. Who is with me most? Ann. I think of her thinking of me today. Everything a madhouse. One gets lost dozens of times a day. The meals are thrown at one, then snatched away. No one attractive in tourist class, and we are very effectively barred from fraternizing with the other two.

JUNE 6, 1949

A mad rush to the movies every night. There is not enough space for all of us anywhere. Especially at tea, where if one does not use a pig's tactic, one doesn't get anything. Began to write comics—very successfully. Six pages for Timely. My cabin is horribly crowded with two Scotswomen (good eggs) and one snobbish woman from Illinois, whom we all dislike.

6/7/49

I am curious as to that part of the mind which psychology (which denies the soul) cannot find, or help, or assuage, much less banish—namely, the soul. I am curious as to the soul's dissatisfactions, that ever unsatisfied portion of man, which would ever be something else, not necessarily better, but something else, not necessarily richer, more comfortable, or even happier, but something else. It is this I want to write about next.

JUNE 9, 1949

Grand pre-preparations for landing at Cherbourg at 3 and Southampton at eleven tonight. Alas, I know the truth—I do not wish to change. I see marriage, babies, cooking, smiling when I don't mean to, don't mean it (and it is not being cheerful that I object to at all, but the falsity of all of it, the absence of love), the trips, the vacations together, the work, the movies, the sleeping together. The last repels me chiefly—

and at times I feel I know it all, have been through it all somehow, and I say, not for me.

JUNE 11, 1949

A delightful first-class carriage ride from Southampton to London, where both Dennis [Cohen]* & [his wife] Kathryn met me at Waterloo Station. Dennis in a Rolls Royce. And a beautiful house to come home to—a Siamese cat, a superb lunch with Riesling. Kathryn is charming!

6/13/49

The warmth of brandy is very like that of mother's love.

JUNE 17, 1949

With Kathryn to Stratford. Poor Kathryn—she unburdens her heart to me, I trust, about Dennis. She has money to play with, but passion—she cannot spend at the moment, and she has a treasure of that. A rushed bite of dinner at the Avon [Hotel], and to *Othello* with Diana Wynyard as Desdemona, John Slater as Iago, Geoffrey Tearle as Othello. What a beautiful performance, and a beautiful town. Visited Diana's dressing room afterwards. Then to her apartment in the Avon Hotel. She is charming, so sweet to us. A grand party also, and a walk home in pitch darkness. I felt well, thanks be to God, in my nice tan suit, which Diana adored.

JUNE 20, 1949

London. Increasingly I must be drugged to be creative. Whether this is a stage, whether it is wrong (it is momentarily wrong) is the great problem. The worst letter from Ann. She writes me almost daily. "Why do you write to me. If you loved me, we should live together & there would be no question. It has been almost a year . . . I cannot keep the light touch much longer." And from Marc, the first letter. Rather cool, otherwise all right. I feel so tenderly toward him. But which is I???? Extremely tired. I grow ever thinner.

6/20/49

There must be violence, to satisfy me, and therefore drama & suspense. These are my principles.

---

* Pat's first encounter with her UK publisher, also a friend of Rosalind's, and his wife, Kathryn.

JUNE 22, 1949

Today at last a grand decision. It is impossible to think of marrying Marc—a sacrilege. I prefer Ann. But as yet, I cannot trust my emotions enough to believe I love her enough. Perhaps that will come—immediately—for her. But I know I would only hurt Marc and myself by marrying him. As Kathryn says, it is not enough.

6/23/49

How far I drift from sensuality. Away and away and away.

JUNE 25, 1949

Last evening. Tickets to the Monte Carlo ballet. And this morning climbed to the top of St. Paul's, a nightmarish venture. The highest thing in London! And this afternoon visited Westminster Abbey, Poet's Corner—where I found myself treading on the tombs of Charles Dickens & William Thackeray! And the beautiful Henry VIII chapel, the Catholic saints' names erased for the new Protestant faith. Kathryn so beautiful in her gray silk foulard and pink kid gloves. We had drinks between the acts, and loved the *Sleepwalker* ballet, both of us. Very new it is. A late supper—much talk afterward.

On saying goodnight to K. in my room, I asked her for a glass of milk. She ran down for it, tired as she was. And put her face up to be kissed. When I embraced her—it was with that sudden release as if we had been waiting long for it. I do not mean to read too much into those short minutes. I mean to read very carefully the small thing that is there. She let me kiss her twice on the lips. "I never thought I'd kiss you good night." "Why not?" she asked. "Because those things never come to be—And now I don't want to let you go." But of course we did let each other go, and there's the pity.

JUNE 26, 1949

Up early to catch the train *Golden Arrow* at Victoria [Station]. And Paris hell tonight. Mme Lyne gone, no message, no friend, no French money. Had to be lent 1500 francs by two women in the Pas de Calais [Hotel]. Made direct from the Gare du Nord to Rosalind's hotel Les Saints-Pères. But it was full. *Alors.* The Pas de Calais. A very small room, without water, without a window! But on the street I met Valerie A., dined with her. And rather pleasantly drunk, back to my dungeon at the top of the Pas de Calais.

[NO DATE]

Paris. Bold, sprawling, dirty, magnificent in a thousand places, indifferent, curious, amused, tragic, silent, laughing, awake, awake, awake
always. The Seine—Breast and blood and dream of Paris, glassy sur-
faced, proud of herself, rippled by coal barges and the darts of fishing
lines held by boys along the sloping rock banks.

[NO DATE]

How I miss the long talks with Kathryn. What things go through my
head. What a charming woman is she. And the pity. The unjustness.
The male form without context: Everywhere. Dennis incapable of loving
her. How alive she still is. How worthy of adoration. What a beautiful
instrument to play on! What songs could she sing! How proud could she
make her lover! I come to Paris thinking of the strange kiss she gave me
the night before I left, the way she held me close and would not let me
go. And why? And why? And why was I not bolder? How many years
since someone had kissed her—a modest kiss, but one with reality—as
I did that night? I should have liked to hold her in my arms all night,
to give her the feeling of being loved and desired, because the feeling is
more important than the deed.

JULY 4, 1949

Five letters from American Express. What a lift for the morale! One from
Marc, Ann, Mother, Margot. The world resumes again, I am attached
again. But most of the time, it is like cotton wool in the head. No pleasant moments of clarity, none.

JULY 11, 1949

Day with Alan Tenysco, Eiffel Tower, Art (Modern) Museum, then
white suit & called for Natica [Waterbury]. I like her instantly
again—more candid, thoughtful, than before. Drinks, then to Nuit de
Saint-Jacques for dinner of Chateaubriands béarnaise. (But I reproach
myself for ordering Vin Rosé d'Anjou.) To the Monocle—dull enough.
Someone sat us down for champagne, but we got out. To the Rive
Droite, Montparnasse, for the Fétiche, which was closed. Some other
place on the Place Pigalle instead. Dancing, a party of girls, one
(whore probably) in black dress, whose neck I kissed. Danced often
with Natica. Out in broad daylight, 5 A.M. & a taxi ride (300 f.) to

Quai Voltaire where we spent the remainder of the night. Natica—
Nike Samothrace* —

JULY 13, 1949

How miserable can one be? The French train was the acme of discomfort—
soot, noise, heat, no water, no food—and I was overtired, dirty, hadn't
even been to the john—In such condition, arrived at Marseille 8 P.M.,
and was met by Jeannot with orchid and mother's cover, framed. He
took me home to very ordinary apt. 19, rue des Minimes. [His mother]
Lily, *charmante*! I had a bath—washed off layers of Paris dirt and Midi
soot! Everything is fascinating—Jeannot much as expected, chubbier,
graying at temples, but real American esprit. We drove to nightclub—
champagne & dancing—La Plage. I think of Natica in Cannes.

7/16/49

How like a child she slept.
The light of the Paris afternoon
Painted a tableau of our bed,
Gilded the hairs of her sprawled brown legs,
Silvered the tumbled white of her slip.
I kissed her naked feet.
How like a child she slept,
And how like a thief I crept
Beneath the tumbled white of her slip,
Between the tumbled golden legs
That clasped me faster and faster
        For N.W. Like the arms of a little bear.

7/17/49

The French are very good for an English and or American writer to live with
for a time. They bring the Anglo-Saxon back to the physical things, the
body, to a certain practicality, obviousness of human relation, which in the
Anglo Saxon is decked in formality and reserve. Curious thought, watching
the first French tender from the deck of the *Queen Mary*, first glimpse, first
hearing of the French: They are like extremely intelligent, extremely shrewd

---

* One of the world's most famous sculptures, the *Nike of Samothrace* is housed by the Louvre. It depicts
the Greek goddess Nike, who is said to bring victory as well as peace.

animals. Like a superiorly sharp intellect concerned with the animal aspects of existence. Somehow a frightening thought, and a fascinating one.

JULY 18, 1949

I wrote to Marc—finally—severing everything, telling him I am sure I cannot be to him what I should.

JULY 20, 1949

Cannes unusually comfortable the first few hours. Met Ruth Yorck in the street. We had coffee—talked. How casual she is about Europe—all Europe like her backyard, or her large old house in the country. She went to Paris at 5 P.M. And I went swimming, miserably, in my new tomato colored bathing suit.

JULY 21, 1949

Prolonged negotiations with Natica, quartered at La Bocca, to get her to come to St. Tropez. At last we took off, 4 P.M. Swimming in St. Raphaël before bus (the last one) left for St. Tropez. Everything ideal—absolutely ideal—A lonely town—LONELY & LOVELY, 8 P.M. Natica on my hands—I simply yelled "Lyne!" and she came down & welcomed us, found us a hotel room, invited us for drinks and dinner in a place filled with ivy & leaves.

JULY 23, 1949

Stayed another day in St. Tropez. And evening—Discovering for the second time (as I did in Paris): There is only once to do everything. And one night that is the best, and that is the first.

7/29/49

Europe for the first time at twenty-eight: it widens one's interests again, makes one diverse as at seventeen. This closing up! I hate it. It grows on one slowly from nineteen onward, as S. [Samuel] Johnson said.

AUGUST 12, 1949

Still in Marseilles. And Thursday, the contract from England* arrived from Margot. I signed it—it looks very good—and sent it on to London. Jeannot much impressed also.

---

*Presumably the contract for *Strangers on a Train* from Dennis Cohen, her British publisher at Cresset Press.

AUGUST 16, 1949

Very sad and rather frightened to set off into Italy. Gave Lily flowers, said a slow goodbye to everyone in the family—Difficult. Jeannot drove me to Nice, just in time for the bus and a brandy before. An Italian bus already. Night in Genoa. As usual painful experience with money, luggage, taxis and hotel. How I hate arriving at night, not knowing the language, being weighted with luggage!

AUGUST 17, 1949

Milan bustling and prosperous. Accosted after dinner tonight near cathedral by an Italian guy. (What forward young men, and old, they are, dear, dear!) He turned out very nice, engineer, blond. Tonio Ganosini, blue eyed. The rather tough but very intelligent & intellectual banker type. He was between the acts at a theater, & invited me to see the rest—a modern anti-communist play. Tonio invited me to lunch tomorrow.

AUGUST 18, 1949

Very much happier with Tonio. We speak French. After lunch, he persuaded me to stay till this evening before going to Venice, so he can accompany me. We took off at 7:30—much fun, really, riding at night, arriving in V. [Venice] at 11:30, without hotel room. We checked everything, & took a taxi boat along Grand Canal to hotel near St. Mark's. Then dinner. Tonio most well behaved, never a pass, good hotel. Venice is spectacularly beautiful.

AUGUST 19, 1949

Venice—the Lido—I didn't want to swim, with all the museums to look at. St. Mark's a mosaical masterpiece. All gold, blue, and Moorish in style. Tonio & I to Bologna at 7:30, where we parted, he back to Milan. He invites me & Kathryn, too, to Sicily, Palermo, when he goes there next—7 Sept. Am very lonely suddenly to find myself on the train to Bologna, alone. I wonder would everybody be as lonely?

AUGUST 20, 1949

To Florence at noon. I do love Florence. Bought a handbag overnight, which will permit me to check stuff at station. Found, also, one of those Italian restaurants people are always talking about and never find— cheap, good, jolly, everybody in the family working, some conception of American needs in the W.C. such as a piece of newspaper.

AUGUST 21, 1949

Wanted to make the 1:30 train (noon) for Roma. My one regret—the fast trip through the Uffizi Gallerie. One astounding room after another, & I looking at my watch! Arrived in Rome 7:00 P.M. Miserable start, and miserable finish. Everything went wrong. Natalia* not at home. Finally in Hotel Bologna, where my acquaintance of the train (who said he would be there) was not. Dined alone. Town full of little alleys—Christ how old! When do they decide an alley gets too old and needs rebuilding? Never, apparently, in Roma. Small boys with the devil in their eyes, suddenly flying a bucket of crap at one's feet after a slow approach. I sat after dinner in a coffee shop—everyone takes coffee at a different place from where they dine, as the French sit on sidewalk cafeterias—My novel is here, all my mail, can hardly wait until tomorrow morning.

AUGUST 22, 1949

Letters from everyone except Marc. A check—$28(!) and $400 from my bank. This leaves a mere $154 in now. + $500 War Bonds. Alas, my ups and downs seem measured not by my own achievements, but by other people's estimation of me. I must learn to make a complete shift in my system of measurements. Wonderful letter also from Ethel Sturtevant, which I shall keep. A real writer's non-writer, is she! (or maybe she is writing something). She congratulates me on the book's publishers, on my new Bloomingdale thing especially,† and the way I feel about it, and thirdly on my breaking off with Marc. Says his book seemed very young for me, advises marriage to an older man less demanding (I'd like to be married to an 80 year old, maybe, very wealthy!) And my book, in Xray box of Kathryn's. Changed my hotel, unfortunately, stupidly. Hotel Roma, near the station, run by a fantastic old gourmand I should never forget. Ball bellied, half drunk, a hole of a room, no service, no hot water & bad light for £800 (lire) the day, an economy of 230 lire, to make me feel like an idiot!‡

AUGUST 23, 1949

Roma—a dirty town. All the men masturbating or something, staring with idiotic fixity at me. Wired K. [Kathryn Cohen] last night & she telephoned at 6 last night. Wants to join me in Naples. Was so happy

---

* The journalist Natalia Danesi Murray, longtime partner of American author Janet Flanner. Her mother worked as an editor and later acquired *Strangers on a Train* for the Italian publisher Bompiani.
† Pat's "Bloomingdale Story" will evolve into her novel *The Price of Salt* (New York, 1952).
‡ One U.S. dollar was worth approximately 600 lire in 1949.

suddenly—a proper date with English speaking friend—and what a person—I bought cognac, wore my sweater from Florence. How lucky I am. Though suffering backache (?) and sore stomach, I feel like a god as I lie alone in my room, too sick, too frightened (physically) of what might happen in Rome, should I fall sick, to move out. Out finally to eat a beef-steak & nothing else. Had had nothing but 2 omelets for 2 days. Forgive food details, dear diary, but they become life details, perhaps. Kathryn will join me Friday. I spin out the days in Rome until then, therefore, hating it.

8/23/49

The emotional problems of men are universal, the negative and positive reactions to women, and the causes thereof. But a Latin man, being superior in his Latin country, can arrange his life, or arrange it so that he can believe, that he is superbly content. In America, the man having failed from the outset as a man, as the dominant sex, cannot do this, and is infinitely more miserable, he takes himself to the psychoanalyst. But they suffer the same malady.

AUGUST 24, 1949

A study in misery. So miserable yesterday, it became funny. Everything *"chiuso"* the only time one gets there. Shall leave having seen very few museums, etc. Took off for Napoli tonight—this P.M. 3. And very happy to be leaving Rome.

AUGUST 26, 1949

I love Naples—clean, orderly, interesting as a port. Thousands of American sailors in town. Spoke with Kathryn last night. She can't come before Tuesday. I was profoundly depressed about this, but shall bear up with the aid of work, I suppose. I have enough to do. Cannot sleep well these nights. No doubt because much on my mind—Kathryn, boat ticket, homesickness, etc., etc. I am up to the hilt in *turismo*, really had enough. Christ, how happy I shall be to get home! I like Italy less than France—I really cannot stand the filth after a while, the sudden sight of a snotty nosed baby (or a baby's rear end, in mother's arms) when dining, which happens at the best of restaurants.

8/27/49

I shall have the best, in the long run. Not a home with children, not even a permanent thing (what is permanent in life or in art? Whatever is permanent except one's own heartbeat?), but the best will always be attracted to me. For this, I do, most sincerely, thank God.

AUGUST 29, 1949

Had meant to visit Pompei, but an abortive phone call from K. [Kathryn] kept me nervously (didn't sleep last night) glued to the phone—which never rang again. Tonight a cablegram, saying she is delayed until next Saturday! More than a whole month! But man's patience is infinitely extensible.

AUGUST 31, 1949

Great joy: Got passage SS *Exeter* 20 Sept. out of Naples! Now I cash checks. My story "The Great Cardhouse"* is coming nicely, I think, I dream—nothing more—of a book of short stories after my novel, of the snail story, the alcoholic, a few others. And this one. Perhaps, I have never been so happy as in these quiet, lonely days in Napoli. It is a profounder—though less exciting—happiness than Yaddo was. For the first time in my life, I like myself. I do not wish anything changed. What philosopher can make a greater statement than this? What poet a happier one?

Of course it is the foreignness all around me, which compresses myself within myself. But this leaves out the reason why I am content with myself. Perhaps it is merely because I am happy, which in the truly good person, is always the best criterion. I am happy. I feel how much longer I shall live. I accept and love the burden of man's responsibility to himself and to humanity during his lifetime. And of love I am sure, too. With these principles I cannot help but love. (And as my master Kierkegaard says, one must love always, whether one is loved in return or not. Thus one must be always, inevitably, truly happy.)

I have never felt so old before, so wise. It is not so. It is merely that I live with myself now, as I might have done, had I not been so confused, so undecided, since I was six years old. I feel for the next five years, I shall look even older than I am. I am in love, in love, in love! While in Marseille, I thought a little of how it would be, of how it would be possible to be Jeannot's wife, as he really seriously proposed. The reason I could contemplate it must have been due to its foreign setting, the external fascinations of the new language, country, relatives,

---

* "The Great Cardhouse" is a story about an art expert who collects forgeries and has his mystique of infallibility.

customs—the beautiful French Riviera. How strange, how superficial am I at times.

SEPTEMBER 3, 1949

At last, the telephone call, and Kathryn downstairs in the lobby. They'd told her I was no longer here. I went down to find her—as she came up—and she approached me from behind—Some poor Italian cognac, much talk in my room before lunch nearby.

SEPTEMBER 5, 1949

How wonderful to walk along the street with K. speaking English, instead of being by myself, wandering, isolated, unhearing and unheard, unnoticed and unwanted. Men stare one out of countenance. This is a country of starers. Reading, writing, working, has blissfully stopped. This is vacation at best, at last I adore my company, and wish only to please Kathryn.

9/7/49

Between the pleasure of a single kiss, and the pleasure of the sexual act, is only a gradation. Between the pleasure of the single, unexpected kiss of two girls, and the sexual act which results in a child, is only a gradation. Therefore the kiss is not to be minimized. It cannot be adjudged by any standard except the subjective. Does a man adjudge his pleasure on the terms of whether his actions produce a child or not? Does he consider them more pleasant, more important, if they do?

SEPTEMBER 8, 1949

I wanted to embrace and kiss Kathryn. Depression—for what? I am not in love with her, only afraid to show the least spontaneity in my emotions. Always afraid? Always afraid—not really of offending—but of being offended by someone else's rejection. With her, I can only think of my bad points, my untidy hair, bad teeth, my untidy shoes, perhaps. We leave tonight for Palermo. The boat is beautiful. Suddenly we both purr like kittens, responding to the cleanliness, the good service, above all the leaving of Naples, the change ahead. K. will stay with me until I go, then return to Rotterdam, finally to London where—everything hellish awaits her—

SEPTEMBER 12, 1949

Rest in bed, not even swimming. My stomach is upset, but am always hungry. I grow thin and ardent on pure feeling, which is too much for flesh to bear, too rich. There is so much, so much too much to digest and to absorb into myself. K. is a little bit in love with me. And I with her, only I know, to less extent. She is a delight. And I am flattered. A honeymoon must be like this. One exists in order to exist like a picture. The waiter where we get our 6 o'clock coffee smiles at us. The weather is kind, and the darkness. Before dinner, we walk along the sea road, palm trees, beach cabins, holding hands. Oh the newness is always so delicious!

SEPTEMBER 15, 1949

The train to Siracusa, and the loveliest day of all. Hotel des Etrangers on the sea front. Engaged a taxi driver to take us to the catacombs—where a demented little friar showed us through the early Xtian [Christian] hiding places, the tombs with bones, the cloister. And K. and I embraced, kissed at every opportunity.

SEPTEMBER 20, 1949

The day I was supposed to sail. We go to Capri on the nine o'clock boat—running. A lovely two-hour trip. K. very excited and silent at the rail. I was too bored, too scared to swim past the urchin laden waters. Disgraceful. My first trip to Capri, my one day, & the water is too much for me! K. terribly sweet & keeps me much company. For we are in love a little these days—and such people always like to be with other people in those first days. The visible—invisible!

SEPTEMBER 21, 1949

To the Grotta Azzurra with K. Very cluttered with rowboats, so certainly 50% of the light was obscured. What a shame. Caught the 4:10 bus back to Napoli. Then the parting. And the rushing. Grapes. And a last dinner with K. I in my white suit, which I'd wanted to wear the first evening with her. We dined—indifferently—at the vine balcony restaurant of our first lunch. K. often holds me, looks earnestly into my face, and kisses me on the lips. What does she wish me to say further? (I have said nothing.) She doesn't wish anything. But mightn't I? Plans—does K. want them? I know it is I who do not want them. That K. could more easily bear than I could say, I shall come to London next year and we shall live together. No, I don't not know what I want. With perfect equanimity, I can contemplate nothing but brief affairs—promiscuous ones—in N.Y. And yet I hope for a jolt (of time, in time) to crystallize my desires. I long to write, and dream of its coming out easily as a spider's web. Now I know why I keep a diary.

I am not at peace until I continue the thread into the present. I am interested in analyzing myself, in trying to discover the reasons why I do such
& such. I cannot do this without dropping dried peas behind me to help
me retrace my course, to point a straight line in the darkness.

9/24/49

Capri. From the Piazza, the piled up black & white domes of the church
resemble one dimensional stage sets. Middle aged women sitting at the
tiny tables, gazing straight before them with a dazed alertness, their
bright, overfed, over-experienced eyes like shining jewels, so terrifying in
their richness that one can scarcely meet them.

SEPTEMBER 24, 1949

Genoa. Morning spent in ascertaining stuff about the *Louisa C.* Departing at 5 P.M. The boat a bit cockroachy—but just a little bit. Much better than *Queen Mary* accommodations tourist class, & altogether a nicer
bunch of people traveling on it. I am happy.

SEPTEMBER 25, 1949

The voyage may take 18 days. And we do not stop in Marseille. Probably
touch Philadelphia first.

OCTOBER 1, 1949

The coast of Spain dry and mountainous, in sight all day yesterday and
today, tho maybe it was islands yesterday. Rewrote & typed the last
chapter of my book, condensing the tunnel explosion & rescue and
results to two & ½ pages. Perhaps I am lazy, perhaps tired of it. Perhaps
I shall decide it does not suffice. I hope not. I dread the first hectic weeks
in N.Y. For this, one needs a wife. (For this, a wife needs a husband,
strangely, just as imperatively.) We pass Gibraltar at 3:00 A.M. The
whole ship will be up.

OCTOBER 2, 1949

Does K. think of me in this long silence? I know she does. We have a
strange psychic communication, we two. I began my novel, *Argument of
Tantalus.** Seven or eight pages that went along with that ease and fluency
(of vocabulary) that generally means, nothing much need be changed later.
Naturally, I am very happy today. The happiest since leaving Kathryn.

---

* Later *The Price of Salt*.

OCTOBER 5, 1949

Page 28 of *Tantalus*. I have no clear detail of what happens once Therese meets Carol. But it goes romping along, much as I do. All is my own reaction, to things—with only at the extremes, some extensions to follow more closely the attitudes of my main character. The sea is rolling rather heavily tonight. Could not sleep until 2:00 A.M.

OCTOBER 9, 1949

Have never felt such outpouring of myself—in all forms of writing. A great gush. I want to get this book out of me in the shortest possible time, not even stopping to earn a bit of money. If I could bring out some short stories as well as *Tantalus* in the next six months! Three books in six months—that would mean something. Only disaster the breaking of the little glass from the Hotel des Etrangers, Siracusa, for which I would gladly have given several fingernails. And Kathryn—Kathryn—I am afraid to write her that I love her, that I should like us to live together in London—all of which I want to say.

10/10/49

Ship's rigging seen against the sky. Geometric complexities, rhomboids, parallels, triangles and intersections of vortices, all in swift and shuttling movement by day. By night, against a dark blue sky on a calm sea, there is nothing more static than the stump of a mast, supported and balanced so perfectly by the slanting ropes. One cannot believe then that the ship is moving. One thinks surely something has gone wrong.

10/11/49

On thinking early in the morning, before getting out of bed: one suddenly knows the why of everything, intuitively.

OCTOBER 15, 1949

Land at Philadelphia. Steaming up the Delaware since dawn. No one to meet me, of course. Very ecstatic to board a train at Phil. and arrive in New York at 7:00 P.M.

OCTOBER 19, 1949

Marc called yesterday, to my surprise. We had drinks and dinner tonight, says he still feels the same, still talks of marriage, "not in two years or even more, but you're still the person I want to spend the rest of my life with." Marc stayed the night, trying to please me, but being too self-effacing even.

10/21/49

On the insane: they are only trying to find a reality. It is very difficult, if not impossible, to find a reality in existence. The greatest philosophers have never found a satisfactory reality, or its explanation. Going under gas, for instance, the world is quite different, more overwhelmingly convincing than the so-called normal world, as to its reality. There is really no reality, perhaps, only writing a system of expedient behavior, action and reaction, by which people have come to live. That is, most people, who live like this for the same reason most peas fall into the center compartment when dropped from a central point above.

OCTOBER 22, 1949

Date with Marc. Went to dinner—bad at Le Moal's—and movie. He stayed. I was excessively tired, and then—(in fact, unless I am drunk) he is so much dead weight in my bed. Oh Christ, I want Kathryn in my bed! I trust her. I like the fact she is older than me. I think she is beautiful and intelligent. I had another letter from her. More affectionate, I would say, more half said, than the other.

10/24/49

In New York the ground is fertile for paradox—and nothing else. I realize the necessity for the tempering effects of common sense and practicality. I realize that these alone would operate in a climate in which I imagine I should be most content—say, a village in England, or a countryside in Italy. And yet, the choice seems really as inconsequential as a diet. One should live, perhaps, entirely on vegetables and cheese, fresh water and bread, yes. But it is not death to drink wine and to eat pâté de foie gras either.

OCTOBER 24, 1949

This day completely yielded to being in love with K. What happiness upon admitting it, believing it, fully. The future suddenly spreads wide, revealing a whole golden-pink horizon. I have not been so happy since Ginnie. Jeanne called in at 9. I kissed her finally, *chez elle*—(why else did she ask me up?) and though she is engaged, to a numbskull, I gather, aged 35, I am quite sure she will be available.

The spirit of reconquest, of ego, (of evil) motivates me tonight and tomorrow.

OCTOBER 28, 1949

Dinner with Jeanne here. She is being very stubborn. So be it. Very little cause for sour grapes. And perhaps she really wants it so. She is very kind, generous, a good friend. I don't want to lose her, and really can't think of anything short of assault and burglary that would.

11/1/49

Aged 28. If I didn't know liquor, nor its social place, nor its usages, nor its ills, I should be utterly fascinated by it. (I should have tried it, as I try a pecan pie in the South.) I should have respected it as that gauge between a man's potentialities and his achievements. For every man has greater potentialities than his achievements. This is his blessing as a child of God, and his burden as a child of the Apes.

NOVEMBER 3, 1949

Last December, I went running to the psychoanalyst, asking to be made over, knowing very well I could not physically survive another debacle like Ginnie. I was not made over, but circumvented the problem by not falling in love any more. I began to feel better, with a gradual lessening of the barrier between myself and all kinds of people. In September this year, rather in October, I began to realize, I could fall in love again, even thought I *was*. Now (at this exact date) in the face of possible defeat, I quickly deny and flee. Should I meet disappointment in the next weeks, I shall, quite aware of it, try to stamp out any little flames in me that might have been said to be the beginnings of love. In short, I must be in the same conditions as last December, so far as courage goes. And yet, can one honestly speak of *courage* in such cases? Why speak of courage! I know what is unbearable. There are some tortures that are unbearable for the human being. There are certainly some tortures—perhaps only this one—that are unbearable to me any longer.

NOVEMBER 5, 1949

Time marches backward. Myron Sanft very amiable *chez lui*. Gore Vidal.* And an indifferent dinner at the Bistro. Party of neurotic people,

---

* Gore Vidal (1925–2012), openly bisexual American novelist. Almost forty years after this encounter, Pat and he will take up a correspondence, mostly on politics.

where, typically, I did not get on swimmingly, being tired. I swear to make more effort next time.

NOVEMBER 6, 1949

Typed almost all my [story] "Instantly and Forever" today. All I can say is, I've seen such things printed. Marc came up with a title this morning. *Strangers on a Train.* I like it very much & hope they do. God bless him. He helps me so much. Am very grateful.

NOVEMBER 9, 1949

I feel vaguely guilty. And vaguely vague, I suppose. Should I write "Love Is a Terrible Thing"* or another horrid commercial story? Or should I go ahead on the novel? I must gather all my energies this winter, or rather now, for the great effort. There is no reason to wait, even one week. I have not the slightest desire for "social life" or for a girlfriend—who would take my time and my little money. And that last item will soon be a problem, too. I do not want to think of spreading the book over a period of time. I must fire it out, like a bullet, at one sitting. The painters come tomorrow AM to varnish the floors and then I'll have done with them. I so want tranquility—of living quarters. It always seems "only another week off." I have, strangely enough, a tranquility of mind (in the face of no income). And I make of Kathryn a religion.

NOVEMBER 11, 1949

Lunch with Harper. Joan Kahn & Mr. Sheehan, an editor, junior, who says he likes my book tremendously, thinks it's wonderful. (Later spoke with Mme Lyne, who said Sheehan dropped in, raved about the book, without knowing she knew me.) Kahn against short-story book, adamant. Will allow me to finish *Tantalus* without showing even a piece of it. And some money can be arranged, too. Wants McCullers, etc. to read *Strangers* and comment for jacket.

NOVEMBER 13, 1949

I finish my story at 6 PM & read it to the family, who pronounce it neurotic, all but degenerate. No sympathy whatever for my mind. Again they attack symptoms: "Pat, why are you preoccupied with such things? Don't

---

* Pat attempted to sell "Love Is a Terrible Thing," about a spurned lover longing for a letter, to *The New Yorker,* but the story ultimately only appeared as "The Birds Poised to Fly" in *Ellery Queen's Mystery Magazine* in 1968 and in her collection of stories *The Snail-Watcher and Other Stories* (New York, 1970).

be." (Just don't be!) The asses! When I told my mother, re Marc, that I had a nearly insuperable block against men: "Hm-m," with a frown. "Now, I wonder why, Pat. What could have brought that on?"(!)

NOVEMBER 14, 1949

Happy day. Bought Levi's. ($5.50 now.) And worked on story. Visited Rosalind at 9:30, Betty Parsons there. Betty and I are kindred souls.

NOVEMBER 15, 1949

Typed on yellow paper 20 pages "Love Is a Terrible Thing." I like it. But grew terribly restless 3 PM. The story is so much K. and myself. And surely my parents must have remarked it, too. This past weekend, I was too open about matters homosexual, in general. Must strike a medium. Why don't they ask me pointblank some time. "How do you feel about women?" my mother asked me. "I trust them much more. But you see, I have never lived with any. I am the remote type—forever."

NOVEMBER 19, 1949

Visited Rolf, who is still very much abed with jaundice. Poor fellow. Marc at seven. I remind him of his brother Aden. "Look like him?" "A little." I shall leave it to his psychoanalyst to tell him that he is attracted to me for homosexual reasons, which I have always known. Resented him so terribly, after this unaffectionate evening, when he asked to stay. When he touches me, anywhere, I cannot bear it.

NOVEMBER 23, 1949

Thanksgiving Morn: 2:45 AM. No letter from Kathryn. She doesn't love me. I had my chance, and I muffed it. (Will that be engraved upon my tombstone?) There is nothing in the world I want so much at this moment as a word from her. A new word. One cannot go on forever rereading the same letter. I am sick, and starving, from living on what one always lives on. Hope. The future that never comes, because one never makes it. That is, I don't. I must tell her that I love her. I want her. I am hers. I want only to be with her. I must ask her, does she want it, too.

11/23/49

Continually I toy with my "if—ifs." For instance, if my experience should be shut off now, sexually, emotionally (not intellectually), but mundanely, practically, I feel I should have enough. I have stretched an

hour into eternity. It is all within me. I have but to draw upon it. I have
not been to sea for many months, but neither have I been immured.
And yet I know as I write this, that in a week, I shall condemn it as sterile, decadent, simply stupid. Thank God, I am not the single person,
not even worshipping the Intellect and the Soul with single mind, like
Melville! For Melville became insane, and I shall not. This afternoon
in Hastings, I raked leaves, in the sun and the air and the smoke. And
I loved my love with all my heart. Therefore, I felt and I knew that I
was not entirely the priggish person I had been half an hour before,
immersed in Melville's *Pierre* and following his vagaries of soul with
the most personally involved fascination. Therefore, I know I shall not
ever go mad. Which is one of the matters for which I give thanks this
Thanksgiving Day.

NOVEMBER 26, 1949

Another letter from Kathryn. The first in two weeks, but well [worth]
waiting for. It transforms everything. She misses me. It was a very intimate letter. I have never been so happy in my life. I must literally rest a
while each day, lest I drop dead with the absurd ailment of Euphoria.
Not that I am excited. I am calm, serene, my concentration is even good.
But I am blessed, and I know it. All these years of repression, sacrifice,
disillusionment, frustration, have come to be of value, for they help me to
measure my extreme happiness now. Rosalind says: "You've always been
happiest when you're alone, haven't you?" "Yes—physically perhaps."
"Or do you consider yourself alone now?" "Yes."

NOVEMBER 26, 1949

Lyne informs me Sheehan of Harper was chiefly fascinated by my book's
[*Strangers on a Train*] "homosexual theme" and presumably subject matter. I was astounded, a little disturbed. Felt wonderful this evening, going
downtown after one martini here, my pinstripe suit. I prefer my hair
straight. Frightfully, dangerously tired when I went to bed at 4 A.M. I
am always afraid of dropping dead, of course.

11/29/49

However passionately one believes, and tries to live, and tries to write,
how many days of passion can one net per week? About one. One's
health must be perfect, and this is not even mentioned in the formula:
food, sleep, exercise. The house must be clean, or passably so. There
must be no social engagements to prey upon the mind. One must be emo-

tionally secure, or have an emotional goal. (One is as hard of attainment as the other.)

DECEMBER 5, 1949

Delivered "Heloise"* [to Margot], & learned the *Companion* & *Today's Woman* rejected "Instantly and Forever." Which of course translated itself only as not seeing K. any ways soon. Gradually yielded to profoundest depression in months—mostly that interlude between projects, stories & the novel, in which I live suddenly, and realize the world around me. My world being most unsatisfactory, financially and emotionally at present.

DECEMBER 8, 1949

I read my notebooks all evening. A real thesaurus! I lay closer plans of *Tantalus.* I believe it will go well. I must not be too loose, that is all! I am happy tonight. And if I don't have a letter from K. tomorrow, the fourteenth day? I shall be disappointed, sorry, but not unhappy. For betrayal of faith and trust is the very theme of *Tantalus*, which tomorrow I hope to begin to write once more.

DECEMBER 10, 1949

Worked. And had a very pleasant date with Jeanne. A bad restaurant, she took me to, and to an English movie. This evening not so marvelous. I feel so detached from her, really, more than usually, due to *Tantalus.* How well it all goes. How grateful I am at last not—as Lil says—to spoil my best thematic material by transposing it to a false male-female relationship! In Europe they would print "Love Is a Terrible Thing" as a story between two women, she says, and it would be excellent— wonderful!—like my "Heroine." But these shit-heels—!" says Lil. Lil is very fond of me. We are like our old selves again. I hope nothing ever happens to change it.

12/12/49

I don't think I trust anyone under the sun farther than the length of my arm. This—for the record—in a period of greater happiness and contentment than in the past three or four years.

---

* "Heloise & Her Shadow": a short story that has not survived.

12/12/49

I wonder if I reject Christianity—for the most part—because it is so obvious that the Christ ideal cannot be attained on earth? There is so much else in my own life that is obviously unattainable—the excellence I should like to see in my work, the straightening out of my emotional life, I mean some resolution of it. Therefore, I must have some religion more possible to attain. The bliss, of course, will always be higher than one can quite reach. That is quite to be desired.

DECEMBER 13, 1949

Mother here for breakfast. I talk quite freely to her about *Tantalus*, but not the love part.

R. [Rosalind] C. making an issue of the party, apparently seizing the opportunity to criticize my selection of guests. But I rebel against R.'s tyranny in the matter. *Tantalus* goes swimmingly.

DECEMBER 14, 1949

Lunch with Margot. She suggests I don't take an advance from Harper, so she can get better terms—but Christ! Today is my first real holiday. And moreover, Lyne & I talk of going to New Orleans together next week.

DECEMBER 15, 1949

Day of the party. I drank nothing. All went well after a sticky beginning. Lyne liked Tex best. R.C. accused Lyne & Lil of being of the same blood— meaning Middle European, which Lil took to mean Jewish. All too silly to recount. Sylvia wants to see me. I got many fine compliments. But I would not wish to see her again. "Totally base," I said. "Not quite," says R. and cites her money! Damn Rosalind for being a snob!

Yes—a wonderful letter from Kathryn this morning, which of course shed its light over the entire day and into the night. She makes me feel like a saint and an angel and a poet. It is no wonder people liked me tonight and that everyone had a good time.

DECEMBER 20, 1949

Took Marc his present yesterday. A little martini mixer. Alas, after New Orleans, I fear I may have to start back on the comics. I hope to be able to invite Lyne to Texas, and to put her up with Dan or Claude. Mother here. I am very excited by the trip. Unavoidably, since Therese does the same thing with Carol.* And I mean to keep my eyes, my heart open. I must feel everything, love everything, hear everything. Read Paul Bowles' *The Sheltering Sky* yesterday. Dreary with Sartre's dreariness.

DECEMBER 22, 1949

Too late a start after big social breakfast, and I am worried we shall not make it to Texas by Xmas. Manassas† campaign grounds, where my grandfather's two brothers were killed. Manassas, which means nothing to Lyne and so much to me.

DECEMBER 23, 1949

Lyne surprised it is already Friday, and I think we shall make progress after this. To Knoxville to sleep tonight. I try to choose the best restaurants—something piquant—and thank God she loves to stop for coffees as well as I—but the South is not always good.

DECEMBER 24, 1949

We drive all night. The nightmarish café in Arkansas. We race for the Texas border. Lyne makes me feel wonderful, i.e. she makes me watch my manners. Always I am attracted to civilizers.

DECEMBER 25, 1949

Dangerously sleepy. Lyne singing songs to keep herself awake. We catnapped twice before getting into Dallas at 10:50 AM. Then to Ft. Worth. Claude & new wife welcomed us. New wife Doreen in a slip— to my great confusion. I dressed in Levi's, according to Dan's instructions. The hell with my tan suit. We met Claude, Ed, Grandma, wives, etc. at the Facette Apts. before trailing them out to Dan's. Much dinner, insufficient drinks, and dull, dull people sitting around. Where do they all come from? Women in glasses, sitting on couches, saying nothing, neither drinking nor smoking, waiting for the grand dinner to be served: turkey, cranberry sauce, potatoes, peas, gravy. Florine† did a heroic job. Dan in typical good form, charmed Lyne, I think, with Texas style table conversation: The disadvantages of a mustache, which gets wet and dirty. All the women screaming in horror & loving it. I had thought the family might speak more to Lyne. I had forgotten they were so self-

---

* Therese and Carol are the protagonists of *Tantalus* or *The Price of Salt*.
† Manassas, Virginia: Two important Civil War battles took place near the city, which were referred to as the First and Second Battles of Manassas, or Bull Run.
‡ Florine Coates, the wife of Pat's cousin Dan.

absorbed. The asses. They really do not care to find out about things European. Whereas, Lyne is fascinated by the things Texan. We got too sleepy to stay for Dan's movies. Played football with Dannie. And rode Butter bareback.

DECEMBER 26, 1949

Luncheon with Lyne chez Grandma's. More turkey, eggnog. My father came over. He wasn't bad, talking to Lyne about Grand Mulet, Zermatt & the Matterhorn. At least he is interested in a few general things. Lyne enjoys everything. She understands. She tells me to take it easy—as yesterday, when I could not sit still before arriving in Ft. Worth. And I know she is independent, that whatever happens cannot bother her in the least.

DECEMBER 27, 1949

These days go by like St. Tropez, proving it is the company, not the scenery.

DECEMBER 29, 1949

We leave Ft. Worth after breakfast with Grandma. Very tired tonight when we got into Houston at 9:30.

DECEMBER 30, 1949

The day very agreeable. We are in perfect coordination like a single thing. We drove to Baton Rouge—a dull town. Lyne spoke with a Cajun café proprietor near Opelousas. I couldn't understand him, but Lyne did very well. She hopes to find French in New Orleans—we speed up as we get there—but I am not too optimistic.

DECEMBER 31, 1949

Good start for N.O. [New Orleans]. We came in about 11:30 A.M. The town a roaring mess, because of the Oklahoma-Tulane football game in the Sugar Bowl* Jan. 2. Lyne looks everywhere with all her eyes. I feel so *en rapport* with her, so much of the time. I got canape stuff for cocktails at 6. Before the Grand New Year's Eve celebrations. The whole town is drunk & I most of all. Too late for dinner at Tujaques, which I realize now (after France) is the only real Frenchy place in New Orleans. We

---

* The Sugar Bowl is an American post-season college football game between top-ranked teams played annually in New Orleans since January 1, 1935.

went to Broussard's. Oysters Rockefeller & *pompano en papillote*. [F]Lyne is charming when she's tipsy.[FF] Got quite drunk, but perfectly under control, says Lyne, as we walked down the street, she holding my hand. She often teases me, or makes leading remarks, when I am drunk, though I never felter.

Falter, alas!

1950

FOLLOWING HER TRIP over the holidays with Elizabeth Lyne, Pat returns to her apartment at 353 East Fifty-Sixth street in Manhattan and the manuscript of her second novel, *The Price of Salt*. Writing the book is an almost physically painful experience that defines the entire year for the author. "What is the life I choose?" is the question Pat asks herself, both in her personal life and in the book.

In the novel, characters Therese and Carol embark upon a trip across the United States to pursue their forbidden love. In an early version of the manuscript, the romance ends quickly and dramatically. Indeed, this is how same-sex love stories *must* end during the McCarthy era, if there is to be any hope of passing the censors and getting published. Until 1958, the U.S. Postal Service had the power to open any magazine or mail they determined to be "obscene, lewd, and/or lascivious." They also had the power to keep lists of people who received such publications. In her second draft, however, Pat allows her protagonists the prospect of a shared future, flouting sociopolitical norms by giving the novel a happy ending.

Regarding publication, Pat is faced with a critical decision: Wouldn't publishing a lesbian love story at this stage in her career risk her standing with her publisher and audience as a writer of psychological thrillers? She follows her agent's suggestion and decides to publish *The Price of Salt* under a pseudonym. There is no way for Pat to anticipate that the American paperback version alone will sell more than one million copies and that she will be inundated with fan mail by readers who, because of her, for the first time dare to hope for their own happy ending. It will be almost forty years before Pat will finally risk a professional coming out in 1990 and rerelease the novel under her real name and a new title: *Carol*. "Prior to this book," Pat writes in the foreword to this new edition, "homosexuals male and female in American novels had had to pay for their deviation by cutting their wrists, drowning themselves in a swimming pool, or by switching to heterosexuality (so it was stated), or by collapsing—alone and miserable and shunned—into a depression equal to hell."

With the subject matter so close to her heart, it is no wonder there are many parallels between Pat's life and her novel. The character of Therese is the author's younger alter ego, and like Pat in 1949, she has a fiancé at the beginning of the story. Carol displays similarities to her current flame Kathryn Hamill Cohen, as well as her past lover Virginia Kent Catherwood. Mrs. E. R. Senn, the woman who inspired the novel, is also still on Pat's mind. To see her once more after their short encounter at Bloomingdale's, at one point, Pat goes so far as to seek out her home in New Jersey.

Although Pat creates the life she would choose for herself in her novel, in real life lasting happiness eludes her. Her relationship with Kathryn currently consists of little more than exchanging letters and doesn't otherwise hold much promise—Kathryn has no intention of leaving her husband and comfortable life behind to start over with the considerably younger writer. Still, Pat plans to visit her as soon as possible in London.

There's very little standing in the way of attaining this dream, at least financially, after *Strangers on a Train* is finally published by Harper & Brothers on March 15. Pat's first novel is an overnight success with readers and reviewers alike, and the film rights sell immediately—to Alfred Hitchcock, no less! Pat calls off the engagement for the umpteenth time with her on-again, off-again fiancé Marc, but on the very same day receives a breakup letter from Kathryn. Hurt and humiliated, Pat moves upstate to Tarrytown, New York, and comes to occupy the world of her second novel. She identifies so closely with her characters that she feels happy for the time being, even without a partner. The love triangle with Marc and Ann S. resumes briefly, which Marc will later fictionalize in his novel *The Choice*. It's only once she finishes *The Price of Salt*, in October that Pat finally breaks up with him for good.

JANUARY 1, 1950

Foul humor this morning. But after breakfast a perfectly lovely day at Audubon Park, which reminded me again that one can never be out of sorts in New Orleans. The animals were very amusing, and we were both euphoric. I am very content to go about with Lyne, trying to find funny bistros. Tonight more cocktails at the St. Charles, and then to Tujaques. Polygamous as I am, I imagine myself in love with her from time to time.

We bought some good wine for our dinner. Lyne very pleased. Then Lafitte's* again. A couple of piano bars. Wasn't drunk this evening.

JANUARY 8, 1950

Tedious trip to N.Y. I am very happy to come home, though it is hideously cold. I had to walk a mile in the cold to fetch gas when we ran out in Jersey. No home-cooked food at Lyne's as she had expected, but she is so hospitable, buzzing around fixing things while I showered, drank martinis, and played our records. Life exceedingly pleasant with her. It is not the luxury I like but the manners that go with it. She even drove me home.

JANUARY 9, 1950

The galleys [of *Strangers on a Train*] are here. The entire book. I did half of them today, but intend to go over the whole thing twice. It will run about 330 pgs. it seems. My money is depressingly low. No letter from Kathryn. Dammit.

1/10/50

Loneliness. Not a mysterious visitation, not a disease. It depends what one has been doing last, what one will do next, whether it comes or not. This has nothing to do with "distraction" either. I mean loneliness has to do with the psyche's rhythm alone. Distraction never keeps loneliness [at bay], of course. I honor loneliness: it is austere, proud, untouchable, except by what it would be touched by. Melancholy on the other hand can quickly be touched by distraction. For it is a more logical thing. (And I can also see myself writing the very opposite of all this one day.)

1/10/50

A note on hearing "America."† From sea to shining sea. The many small towns I have driven through. The many lighted windows on the second floors of small homes, where young girls stand brushing their golden hair. The houses certain people call home. The rooms that are certain people's own rooms, unforgettable. And perhaps the rooms they will have all their lives. And the shaded window with the red cross over the sill, that I passed every morning on the way to high school in Ft. Worth.

---

* Café Lafitte, which opened in the 1940s in a Creole cottage-style building built in 1772, became a popular gay venue in the early 1950s.
† "America the Beautiful," a patriotic song.

The bread they eat, and the boyfriends who call them, the cars they drive to hamburger stands in, the summer evenings when the boys are home from colleges, and the betrothals are made. The children that are born to lead the same simple lives externally. And always, the loneliness, the unsatisfied striving that is below the surface, much or little below. The girl who is unsatisfied, and yet has not the energy or perhaps the courage to escape. She dreams of something better, something different, something that will challenge and use up the aspiration that she feels clamoring within her, that cannot be satisfied by the men she meets, the stores she buys her clothes at, the movies she dreams in, even the food she eats.

JANUARY 12, 1950

FLunch with Joan [Kahn] at Golden Horn. The famous seven martinis. One here, five during lunch. "One thing I must say. I always have fun with you," said Joan. I was almost drunk. Went to Harper's to deliver the galleys, then another drink. Joan is very beautiful.FF

JANUARY 13, 1950

FBad luck. I owe the government $122, which I won't pay. Margot says that I have to continue working for the comics industry for several months at least. Well, then I shall do that. At least I don't have a hangover this morning. Ann [S.] came to see me. She's not going to Europe this summer. Ann is too slim, not as attractive as before. My God, how many women do I want? Well, I don't get anything from Jeanne these days. How cold she is! Not the least bit of tenderness. I'm not a machine!FF

JANUARY 15, 1950

FDamn it, why do I drink so much? Actually I know very well why— that's why I allow myself to do it. I have nothing but my work. And now not even that. What's the point, God?FF

JANUARY 19, 1950

FMy birthday. 29. Work—I thought that the comics might be stimulating now. Unfortunately not. However, the checks will doubtless be. But the stories—! With the family tonight. martinis, good French wine, presents. And a check over $20 for a macintosh. Couldn't sleep tonight. I think of Lyne—who tickles my curiosity, that's all. Isn't that normal after three weeks together? And I was also thinking about my life. I should be writing now. I cannot possibly justify these two months I plan to work on comics. I don't get any younger.[FF]

1/25/50

Education. How we should love those years of formal education, especially in the university. To the reflective person, it is the last time he will remember that the world made sense, the world promised to continue to make sense. It is the only time when all he is filled and concerned with really concerns life. No wonder he is happy! No wonder each day is heroic adventure! No wonder he doesn't want to go to bed at night!

JANUARY 26, 1950

[F]I said goodbye to Marc. He looked very handsome and leaves for Los Angeles tomorrow. He asked: "Did you change your mind, Pat?" He wants to try again when he gets back. And I do, too. Only dead ends where women are concerned. And maybe, deep down, I want to try again with Marc because he complements my ego. And I admire him so much.[FF]

1/26/50

Insanity. When one has glimpses of it, it is not in the form of random irrational thoughts, but as the entire structure of one's information slipping. It is as if the crust of the entire world slips a bit, so that one easily imagines the north pole at the south pole one day.

1/29/50

And never forget (how can I) the energy remaining after frustration. The creative, demonic-angelic, bittersweet, and if the truth be told joyous energy remaining when one cannot leave home at midnight to go and meet her.

FEBRUARY 1, 1950

Thus, I go through life, subsisting on one drug or another.

2/2/50

I do indeed grow tired and depressed by realism in literature—especially à la O'Hara,* or even à la Steinbeck. I want a complete new world. Paint-

---

* Likely reference to John O'Hara (1905–1970), whose short stories began appearing in *The New Yorker* in 1928 and whose successful first novel, *Appointment in Samarra*, was applauded by Ernest Hemingway.

ers are doing it. Why not writers? I do not mean the pixie-like fantasy of Robert Nathan.* I mean a new world that is at once not real, and at once fascinating and full of message, that is art, too, as simply, timelessly, and unrealistically as the best of the cave dwellers' wall paintings.

2/2/50

I shall go and write a poem of silence.
I shall go and write a small black cube
Of silence, dedicated to you.
Through barred windows, I shall write
A poem about the view.
And of music as the deaf hear it.
And of your smile while I made love to you,
As seen reflected twice by mirrors.
For I am twice crazed and twofold mad,
Reflected in a mirror, too, flat, bloodless.
Reflected in a mirror, and twice removed.
And yet as full of life,
My head as bloody with love,
From dashing it into the mirror,
As any lover who ever plunged
With his lover down a cliff to the sea.

FEBRUARY 9, 1950

Margot likes *Tantalus*. What more can I say? I am alive once more. I am in love with Kathryn. I am a writer, as I was on the Italian freighter. I am an angel, a devil, a genius. I must have nothing more to do with Lyne, who will not grant me her bed, as simply and partially as I should take it. (Idiot, she is!) I love Kathryn. My eyes are on the stars and beyond. My spirit wanders in the galaxies, and under the oceans. My breath is in the coming spring winds. My fertility is in the dry, living seeds as yet unplanted. My food is my love itself, better than any feast! The frame of my life is the frame of my work. *Gloria in Excelsis Deo!*

FEBRUARY 15, 1950

FEvening with Marc. He leaves for Plymouth Monday. For two months. Again—he still wants to marry me. He invited me to come to Europe

---

* Robert Nathan (1894–1985), favorite author of both F. Scott Fitzgerald's and Ray Bradbury's. His biggest success was his 1940 fantasy novel *Portrait of Jennie*.

with him in April or May. "I want to go there," I said—"But with me?,"
he asked.[FF]

2/27/50

The entire pattern of my life has been and is: She has rejected me. The
only thing I can say for myself at the age of twenty-nine, that vast age, is
that I can face it. I can meet it head on. I can survive. I can even combat
it. It will not knock me down again, much less knock me out. In fact, I
have learned to reject first. The important thing is to practice this. That
my limping crutches are not trained to do. Ah, how insignificant it all
is! And how significant! To one more love, goodbye. Adieu. But no—
God will not be with you, not you. But fare thee well, all the same. God
knows, I hold thee high.

MARCH 11, 1950

Worked. How hard the comics grow! Especially the dismal love story
ones. I sit here, I stew here, goalless, getting sores on my gums, marking
time in my career, imprisoning myself. A postcard from Natica.(!) She is
with Jane Bowles in Paris, going to N. Africa next summer. Why don't I
hop over, she asks. The Duchess arrived blind drunk at 6:30 at my party,
held forth in praise of me for an embarrassing 3 minutes until her escort
arrived to take her to dinner. I shall ask her to the party, Friday.

MARCH 12, 1950

Frightfully difficult days—chiefly because I have no immediate goal. No
prospect of having enough money to go back to Europe this summer
(consequent guilt, self-reproach for stupidity). Situation with Kathryn
still unclarified. Also due to my lack of money and therefore power. It
shouldn't be, I know with all my heart, but I let it be. Whether I shall be
with Marc—most likely this summer, I shall be. But where? And married
or not? Not too happy a prospect either. My friendship with Rosalind
continues to degenerate. Do I torture myself also by trying continually
to return her coldness with my warmth, her duplicity with my sincerity?
Lyne calls her a snob and a phony. And Christ—how I admire G[raham]
Greene's 19 Stories!

MARCH 17, 1950

The broadcast [of the interview] at 1:15. Very early, I was reading *The
New Yorker* in an effort to be calm. Excellent review by the way of
Strangers, ending up "Highly recommended." And calling Bruno [an]

"oddly ingratiating young man who has about all the complexes you ever heard of." The broadcast in a small cozy room, not at all terrifying.

Helped Walter & Jeanne with the party preparations at Lyne's.* Caviar, all kinds of liquor, almonds, pastry, gigot & *jambon*.

The guests: Marjorie Thompson, Kingsley, Rosalind & Claude, de la Voiseur, Dick Sheehan, Joan Kahn, Babcock of the *Chi. Trib.* [*Chicago Tribune*] (drunk & very nice) Toni Robbins of *Holiday*, gay & very attractive, the Duchess—but not H. Carnegie. Djuna Barnes called me at 9:30 AM. She would have come, but was down with a sprained back. Leo Lerman offended, I think, because I didn't send him an advance copy of my book—didn't come. Everyone considered the party a big success. Jeanne seemed irritable, so I was careful to help clean up. I also thought the butler was a guest—and invited him for a drink.

MARCH 22, 1950

Margot reports a $4,000 movie bid, which she turned down. Local. Hollywood hasn't had time yet. Margot doesn't hope for more than $10,000 unless 2 companies start bidding. But anyway, it will be soon, and it looks as if I can go to Europe this summer, if I please.

MARCH 24, 1950

I don't like this upset state I live in—no inner peace, stability, concentration of thought. I await word from Kathryn & from Harper. Not to mention Hollywood, which will also alter my life somewhat.

MARCH 28, 1950

Lyne told Marc all I need was a man to "make me feel like a woman." Her usual, refreshing tack, and to hell with Freud, and even past history. Pat's not queer, Lyne says. She's got this wrong. Spent night with Marc. I am easier with him, but much rebellion left, I can feel. And if Kathryn writes me favorably? I envisage 2 months now with Marc, when I shall write my book, followed by movie money, Europe, and I hope Kathryn. If I were to do what I feel like doing, it would be Kathryn & Europe, and not these 2 months (so far as pleasure goes) with Marc even. Feel like a woman? He makes me feel like a male pervert, a sailor in the Navy, a naughty little boy at school. He has a knack of not knowing what I want.

---

* A party celebrating the publication of *Strangers on a Train* on March 15, 1950.

4/2/50

A note after rereading all my notebooks—rather glancing through all of them, for who could possibly read them?—(and Kingsley, have some taste, have at least the taste I have in 1950 in weeding out what is already written, and recently written).*

Impressed only by the range of interest, the terrible striving in all directions. Depressed by the monotonous note of depression, and the affinity of melancholy. Impressed very rarely by cleverness, by poetry. But sometimes, I think, by an occasional good insight. A few usable things in literature.

Having made of my diaries exercise books in languages I do not know, the journals overflow with comfortable personal outgushings. I suffer too many hitches and delays, stagnations and frustrations, by self-consciousness, dwelling on melancholy. But this I must say: the sackcloth ashes age has past. The adolescent aloneness (reluctance to join with humanity) has past. So melancholy now, on the lonely gray seas, is tempered with sight of shore. I have my friends. More than that I have Life, and know how to repair to it at all times, under any conditions. Things which once were so bewildering and complex, marriage and sex, for example, are not so now. They have been torn down a bit. Become more lovable in fact.

I must get it all to flow. To let it dam up till it is an insufferable force, that has to be knocked out by liquor and dissipation to tire the body. In short—as I have ivy-towerishly preached since adolescence—I must learn to find life in my work, living there, with its dramas, hardships, pleasures and rewards. For I have yet another long road to go, before I can find in another person those compatible elements, which will enable all this to flow. I have merely learned, so far, to avoid those persons who would stop it.

APRIL 3, 1950

Margot sold my book to Hitchcock for $6000 + $1500 for Hollywood work or not at time of filming—6–9 months hence. Celebrated wildly with Lyne (broke date with Jeanne). Then called Ann at 3:00 AM. & was stupidly inveigled into inviting her here. Dismal, and I feel it's the last time.

---

* For a long time, Pat intended Gloria Kate Kingsley Skattebol to be her literary executor after her death.

APRIL 4, 1950

Very tired when went to Hastings at 6. Big gabfest, first visit in weeks. Family very proud of me & movie sale. I offered to pay off mortgages & interest-demanding debts. My mother refused loquaciously at first, then accepted a bit.

APRIL 7, 1950

Hysterical, because Lyne made me wait an hour for her. I have a cold & fever, but that's small excuse. The point is, the pattern resumes. The point is, I have a chance out of it now (a bit of money), and my imprisoned soul (in such bad shape that an ASPCA* would have guillotined me years ago, had they known, and God himself must be wishing, o profoundly wishing, he hadn't made such a creature or let such a creature be made). How about the insect in the country brook, born to live 30 seconds due to natural enemy living in the proximity? I think such a creature even would be considered happier. At any rate, drunk and sober tonight, I feel myself approaching the end of phoniness. I have lived as a phony too long. The honest money in my pocket is crying out against it. What do I cry? What is the cry of my soul? Kathryn. (Result of waiting for Lyne 45 minutes, plus 102 fever, plus lousy dinner in a nightclub, + 3½ martinis + a crying jag.)

APRIL 10, 1950

Excellent reviews last week sent by Joan Kahn. I copied them & sent them to Dennis, with news of movie sale. Didn't tell Kathryn of Hitchcock yet. Jeanne for dinner here. I took pains—and my pains were rewarded. We both were very, very happy.

APRIL 12, 1950

Am tired and terribly fed up with New York & this rat race I keep leading socially. Visited Lil. She tells me (reminds me) I care so little one way or the other about Marc, I shouldn't even treat him this way, pretend to. Yes, a word from Kathryn, and I should sail away.

APRIL 15, 1950

Rosalind & I went to Italian film at Museum [of] M.A. which we walked out on (we both confessed preferring "brawls" to polite parties) then to party at B. Parsons', and to the Village, where the usual muck was stirring.

---

* American Society for the Prevention of Cruelty to Animals.

APRIL 17, 1950

I have borne heavier crosses than Kathryn. The letter came today (written Thursday April 13) and it is not good, I suppose. She is incredibly burdened with all kinds of things just now. "I have to learn to walk alone," she wrote, "before I'll be of any use to myself or to anyone else." And that she would like to see me whenever possible. Whatever remains but friends? Marc got my negative letter today, too. Thus we both get it in the neck the same day.

APRIL 19, 1950

Where have these five miserable months gone? Down the drain with martinis, late coffees, naps in the daytime, a few comics, and tears.

4/19/50

The one sane way of being successful in love—have the lowest possible aspirations. What a season of vinegar this is!

APRIL 20, 1950

[Port Jefferson.]* One inconvenience after another. No gas. Parents left at noon, and I sat huddled by a fire the rest of the chill, rainy day, reading Greene's *The Man Within*. How brilliant it is. How like Kathryn is Elizabeth. And Andrews like me in my most cowardly, indecisive moments. (My cowardice, if any, lies in indecision alone.) I wept at the end. Real tears, à la *David Copperfield* when I was a child, tears now because I am grown up, and so are these people.

5/3/50

Herodotus says that certain Thracian tribes hold a weeping rite over every newborn babe, for the ills he will have to suffer in life. They bury a man with joyous laughter. This is ritual and nonsense to the modern man, who, however, could well do with a few of his emotional pipes opened up. Modern man goes about in a paralysis of fear, keeping ninety percent of his energies, his scope in general, repressed and hidden, even from himself. A man is unable to wave his arms, to leap with happiness, walking down a public street the first spring day.

Primitive man for all his rituals and his frightfully barbaric-seeming laws and customs, was freer. They lived closer to poetry, orally if they

---

* Pat leaves the city for some weeks, first for a cottage in Port Jefferson on Long Island, then a furnished room in a castle in Tarrytown in upstate New York.

could not read it. Above all, they lived closer to their emotions. Education notwithstanding, a man got more out of himself in primitive ages than modern man. A man realized himself better, therefore was more godlike, more creative. What people am I talking about? I know few were educated, a mere handful, and that multitudes were slaves. I mean, however, the common men who were the farmers, the unbonded soldiers, the craftsmen, the bakers and the shoemakers. They might not have waved their arms, either, and they might have. They might have thought Jupiter sent the rain, and not cold air striking warm, but if they did, so much the better for their emotions, and their emotional happiness. What were their fears? Only of the gods, really, even if they fell ill of a disease. The gods made them better social beings, too.

What are modern man's fears? He doesn't clearly even know. They are: Financial Insecurity—War—the Atom Bomb—his own old age—death (the physical)—cancer—tuberculosis—and the fact that the world, his world, might not exist in ten years—and the fact, a much more real one, that individually he can do nothing about it. For the first time in history, an individual man can do absolutely nothing about saving his own skin! He can't even run off to a desert and hide. The atom bomb will find him out there, too. And he made the atom bomb! What a basis for frustration!

People tell him to read books. His children go to public schools where they are told to read Shakespeare, Lamb, Wordsworth, Tolstoy, and told to keep reading them when they get out of school. That's the last thing they'll do. What should they be, recluses? They've got to mix in the world and add themselves to the inarticulate, paralyzed masses doing nothing about saving themselves or even preserving what they've got.

MAY 3, 1950

Ah, life can be beautiful. Chapter Nine done. P. 111. And the next chapter planned at the moment. Symbolism coming out fine. I've my sloppy shirt-paper notes pinned beside my desk. I might go all day without speaking to anyone here, except perhaps for my mail.

MAY 4, 1950

This is such a painful novel I am doing. I am recording my own birth. My 8-page stint is sometimes agony. So far, generally, I feel happy at night, however, after the pages are done.

5/4/50

To hell with the psychoanalyst's explanations of Dostoyevsky's gambling as sexual release. Dostoyevsky wanted to destroy himself, to experience his own destruction. Purge of the soul! Dostoyevsky knew. Touch bottom before you can thrust to the heights! Touch bottom, indeed, merely for the sake of knowing bottom. I know all this so well, I feel it, I enact it, too.

MAY 5, 1950

A letter from Kathryn. A good one. Very good. She liked my post cards, letters, congratulates me on the movie. "You are neither an irrit[ation] or a distraction, but someone whom I feel very close . . ." Excoriating letter from Marc, telling me I cling to my disgusting, infantile sicknesses like as a little girl clings to a doll, ending "and let's get married."

5/5/50

To own a house is to stop in a way, in a way that I can't as yet.

5/6/50

This won't come again (some things I know, as I knew when I was twenty-three, and twenty-one, that the same sensations cannot be redu-plicated because of the very age element), the sheeplike clouds on a pleas-ant evening in May, with the castle nearby, all black and dark and huge, where I shall work alone. And while my friends are leaving in the car. It is all pleasant, I welcome it, and I am not afraid, and yet love goes with them, the human voice, the touch of the flesh at all, and the possibility of something failing, some little thing, while the group goes out to get into the car, while one or all of us look for a place which sells newspapers after ten o'clock in the evening. No this will not come again, I standing in the dark driveway, lighting a cigarette to comfort me, while the auto-mobile purrs away in the darkness. I staring to a different world and one which I love better. Living life I do mistrust, but friends and lovers one has always. One has always, at least, the remembrance of how the lovers were, which indeed is no different from the way the friends are. For I do project into friends the imaginative virtues, capabilities, which I project into lovers. Both are created. And a man does love by an illusion.

5/7/50

It is freedom, which muddles a man up. I am not advocating totalitari-anism. But a writer must learn how to impose his own totalitarianisms upon himself, himself being sole governor, knowing that he is free to change discipline and routine after due process of altering within himself his legislation.

MAY 8, 1950

Immensely happy tonight. Why shouldn't I be? This will be the finest book I have ever done, finest thing, I believe, better than "The Heroine." O to remove that curse one day!

MAY 10, 1950

This book I am cautious about, no headlong rushes as [in] the first. If I thought the ice had broken Monday, it is not quite so. The condensation and selection required in this book always demands effort. There are as many kinds of writers as people. Perhaps more.

MAY 12, 1950

Very pleasant. Worked, 7 usual pages. And read a bit to the family tonight. First chapters—tedious, full of extraneous matters, the characters weakly drawn. Other chapters—far superior, but I cannot read them to the family, since I balk at telling them T. falls in love with a woman! The family is interested, respectful, due to first book's success, but they cannot have real enthusiasm from this reading!

MAY 14, 1950

I began *Ulysses* but have little taste for fiction. I believe one can keep only one set of fictional characters, one family, in the head at once.

MAY 15, 1950

My happiest days are never spent with people. I wonder do I cherish only a dream of happiness, one day, with the person I love. I wonder do I want it as superficially as I want, sometimes, a house of my own. Oh, I am not willing to give up that dream of a person yet, though. I shall part with it most unwillingly. I am greedy to live so many lives, that is it. I shall be so many different persons before I die. And one has to be alone to be able to change so often. What would anyone make of it!

5/17/50

Writing, of course, is a substitute for the life I cannot live, am unable to live. All life, to me, is a search for the balanced diet, which does not exist. For me. Alas, I am twenty-nine, and I cannot stand more than five days of the life I have invented as the most ideal.

MAY 23, 1950

In a burst of confidence, I showed Ethel [Sturtevant] chapter six, in which Carol appears, picks up Therese. "But this is love!" Ethel exclaimed upon reading half of the first page. I admitted it was something like that but in later discussion, said T. had a schoolgirl crush, wanted back to the womb relationship, which Ethel said was borne out by the milk episode, but not in their meeting. "That's a sexual awakening. Your genius ran away with you here . . . Now this packs a wallop! This is an excellent piece of writing, Pat."

MAY 25, 1950

Decided to abandon the castle, so laboriously moved all my stuff out at noon. Stanley most helpful in taking me to Hastings, but no time to take me to New York. Stanley has to work constantly, and fast. I realize they have just about been making both ends meet the last few years. And they are not getting any younger. Something must happen soon. And now—now that I have $6000—mother says I have had it "too easy"— the old story. In fact, reminds me that most children help their parents, contribute to their upkeep. By George, not if they are both earners. And seldom, indeed, if the child is one afflicted with the fury of the arts. I do resent all this.

5/27/50

The happy fact for me at this date, May 27, 1950, is that the pleasant way of writing, the most entertaining and at the same time the most profound, is also the best writing for me. When I worry and rearrange, I always fail and always write badly.

5/28/50

I have just heard a remarkable popular song called "Let's go to church on Sunday" (we'll meet a friend on the way).* They will meet a friend on the way. Next Saturday night, the young man will hold up a candy store and

---

* In the song Pat refers to, "Let's Go to Church (Next Sunday Morning)" by Margaret Whiting, all that the singer envisages is going to church—and through life—with her love. Pat's dark imagination takes the story in a completely new direction.

the girl will sleep with the man who will necessitate an abortion. These two will marry in less than a year and produce five more Catholics. They will vote in the Catholic senators and boycott the best artists and writers. They will provide sons for the next war and dedicate the next superwar *mondial* to the unknown soldier. They will prevent people from parking on their block and they will turn the stomachs of the rest of us when they appear in bathing suits on public beaches. They will be honored because they carry on the race. But they will not be the people by whom this century will be known.

MAY 30, 1950

Worked well. A sunny day. Lil & Dell for dinner. A holiday today. They brought champagne—and we had a wonderful time. Later, went alone to the village, Pony Stable Inn. $3.00 in my pocket. I feel very self-confident these days, very cheerful, very secure in my book.

MAY 31, 1950

Went to Wanamaker's* on luxurious lady of leisure shopping tour, & picked up maps from RCA for Carol & Therese's trip. I live so completely with them now, I do not even think I can contemplate an amour (I am in love with Carol, too) and cannot read anything except Highsmith in the notebooks. Frightful egomania it must be!

JUNE 1, 1950

Intolerably dull writing today, for the simple reason I was too healthy. My Muse will not come at 9:00 AM after a healthy breakfast.

JUNE 4, 1950

Walked to hospital to see Lil—accompanied by the young man I met last night in the Irish bar, after seeing Marc. (Incidentally, Marc & I agreed to get married at the end of the summer.) Interesting—Sam (who is insufferably dull) said suddenly, "Oh, I was raised in Ridgefield N.J." as we walked in the park. My heart took a jump. "Do you know Murray Avenue?" I asked. I asked if he knew anyone named Senn. (Her name.) He said he'd take me there one afternoon. Alas, should I see her, my book would be spoiled! I should be inhibited!

---

* John Wanamaker Department Stores were one of the first department store chains in the United States.

6/6/50

Today I fell madly in love with my Carol. What finer thing can there be but to fling the sharpest point of my strength into her creation day after day? And at night, be exhausted. I want to spend all my time, all my evenings with her. I want to be faithful to her. How can I be otherwise?

JUNE 11, 1950

The book must come now to a swift and tragic close. Visited Hollis Alpert last week, now an editor of *The New Yorker*. He says they are immensely interested in my stuff. If I can get something short enough, perhaps it will go.

JUNE 12, 1950

I worked well, feeling even too well physically. On an impulse at 5 PM went to Hastings for this reason, I know: to steep myself in that which I hate, in that rejection, which is what I am about to describe in my book. My mother grows increasingly neurotic—my God! She never thinks, only opens her mouth and shouts! I drank too much Imperial, ate little. Told mother, Marc & I would marry. "I'm glad. I want a grandchild." "I haven't the courage." "I'd be ashamed. What's the matter with you?"

6/12/50

Suddenly the writing of novels has become a little game (even as I learn more and more that a single novel can absorb my last strength and tax my entire brain) that the main object is to please and to entertain and condense one's material, that the finished product is but a tiny fragment broken off of the great mass of material, and polished to the highest degree. It will be the same if at fifty I can look at a shelf with fifteen of my books on it.

JUNE 13, 1950

Unable to sleep last night. At 4 AM I thought out the ending—in action—of my book. What joy and relief!

JUNE 14, 1950

7:00 PM. Proposed sleeping with S.—most fluently. "Well, when?— Please." "Could be," says S. Jazzed around the Irish bar here. I am so elated yet tragically sad. I know I have written a good book, how good I don't yet know. And that is it.

JUNE 14, 1950

Carol has said no now. Oh God, how this story emerges from my own bones! The tragedy, the tears, the infinite grief which is unavailing! I saw Marc for a beer. Very detached, unreal feeling tonight.

JUNE 15, 1950

More work, and I draw very near the end, letting it come out—so it seems—in a wonderful natural way. It is all in action, no summing up, no philosophizing, no tying of ends. But I feel exhausted. My sleep is broken every night by stopped-up nose, and in the morning my thrashing brain is a blank until after strong coffee.

6/16/50

(One day before finishing my second novel.)

I have learned the trade of writing rather late. I am later still learning the art of life. I came home and only happened to look into Emily Dickinson, and was reminded afresh of that poor woman's (and rich poet's) fate of loving a man she saw so briefly—and of what she made of it, of what she gave the world and herself in beauty. I said, that's for me. I remembered my journal entries of my eighteenth year. I remembered that those things cannot be changed. Take a woman for what she is worth and no more. This is the art of life, or the most important rule of it.

JUNE 16, 1950

Showed R. [Rosalind] C. the letter of renunciation in my book, also the 4th chapter in which they meet. How odd that R.C. always exerts her dampening influence! And I think, how she would like to have written all that, though, and I know it is incontrollable jealousy. "This bit has your usual suspense . . . I don't think she sounds attractive here . . . The girl's rather dingy, isn't she? . . . It certainly needs a lot of work . . . Such an old cliché, I wouldn't be caught dead making a pass like that." How different from Lil!

I think I have suffered a minor relapse this week. I am profoundly and nervously exhausted, eager for the nepenthe of alcohol of an evening if I have a friend to share it with. Interesting concomitant: cynicism, caused only by nervous exhaustion. It is always so easy for me to see the world upside down.

JUNE 20, 1950

Summer begins. An era closes—this is Kathryn, my book, and many, many ideals.

JUNE 24, 1950

The doctor gave me some seconal. In order to relax enough to sleep. This exhaustion is like a solid thing within me, a disease over which I have no control. Now that I have money—why can't I go to a resort, pick up a girl, have a whirl, and drop her? Thus, one is free emotionally. I am ravenously hungry for a woman—It invades dream and waking hours. Yet so tired and pessimistic.

6/28/50

Thanks be to God. Glory be to God, I have finished another book today. In God is all my strength and my inspiration. In god and Jesus' name is all my courage and fortitude. I happen to have just come from a miserable party on South Fourth Avenue. Given by an impecunious and execrable painter. He said tonight, in his dirty white suit, with his dirty nails, dirty as his guests: "There are no absolutes in this world. If there were the world would stop." But I feel this in the marrow of my bones, and therefore would not readily utter it at a party. I feel a tremendous significance in the cross. Two opposite directions. In the instant of our revelation, the conjunction of the opposites will be manifest, and shown to be the sole and absolute truth.

JUNE 30, 1950

Today, feeling quite odd—like a murderer in a novel, I boarded the train for Ridgewood, New Jersey. It shook me physically, and left me limp. Had she [Mrs. E. R. Senn]* ever taken the same train? (I doubt it. She'd use a car.) Was compelled to drink two ryes before I took the 92 bus, the wrong one, toward Murray Ave. I asked the driver, and suddenly to my dismay and horror, I heard the entire bus shouting "Murray Avenue?"—and giving me directions! Murray Avenue is a comparatively small lane going into thickly wooded land, on one side of Godwin Avenue. There is a building on the left, a big, quiet, fine house on the right, where two cars stood, and women sat on the porch, talking. The number was 345—and I pushed on, seeing 39—on the next house, and thinking the numbers were going the wrong way, for hers is 315. Besides the street was so residential, there were no sidewalks, and I was a conspicuous figure. I dared not go any further up the avenue where the trees grew closer and closer, and hers might have been the only remaining house (I caught no glimpse of it!) and where she just might have been on the lawn or porch,

---

* The real-life inspiration for the Carol character in *The Price of Salt.*

and I might have betrayed myself with halting too abruptly. I walked on the opposite avenue, which was not even called Murray. (And felt safer because it was not hers.) And then as I came back to Godwin a pale aqua automobile was coming out of Murray Avenue, driven by a woman with dark glasses and short blonde hair, alone, and I think in a pale blue or aqua dress with short sleeves. Might she have glanced at me? O time, thou art strange! My heart leapt, but not very high. She had hair that blew wider about her head. O Christ, what can I remember from that encounter of two or three minutes a year-and-a-half ago. Ridgewood is so far away! When shall I ever see her in New York again? Shall I go to a party one evening and find her there? Pray, God, she never troubled to look up my name. (After the Xmas card.)* These things I shall never tell Mr. M.B. [Marc Brandel] of course!

7/1/50

I am interested in the murderer's psychology, and also in the opposing planes, drives of good and evil (constriction and destruction). How by a slight defection one can be made the other, and all the power of a strong mind and body be deflected to murder or destruction! It is simply fascinating!

And to do this primarily, again, as entertainment. How perhaps even love, by having its head persistently bruised, can become hate. For the curious thing yesterday I felt quite close to murder, too, as I went to see the house of the woman who almost made me love her when I saw her a moment in December, 1948. Murder is a kind of making love, a kind of possessing. (Is it not, attention, for a moment, from the object of one's affections?) To arrest her suddenly, my hands up on her throat (which I should really like to kiss) as if I took a photograph, to make her in an instant cool and rigid as a statue. And yesterday, people stared at me curiously wherever I went, in the trains, the bus, on the sidewalk. I thought, does it show in my face? But I felt very calm and composed. And indeed, at a gesture from the woman I sought, I should have cringed and retreated.

JULY 6, 1950

Rosalind resents me thoroughly. Called me eccentric for living alone. R.C. and I shall never be the same again. I left in incontrollable tears. It

---

* Pat wrote Mrs. E. R. Senn a Christmas card following their short encounter in Bloomingdale's in 1948.

is not this morning's outburst from her I hated but all the years past, all the horrible disillusionment—for I cling so to my gods and my loves.

JULY 12, 1950

Chez R.C. at 1:30 AM. I informed her quietly that I couldn't stand it any longer. The snobbery, her resentment against me in every way. With that she cut loose on a long array of insulting accusations, bitter, false observations, too long to recount. But I had shed my last tear. I took this calmly. When I took my leave, R.C. remarked I was surely going to the bar to pick up somebody else. Another whore. I went home and to bed, scarcely shaken by this cataclysmic, horrible end of a ten-year friendship.

7/17/50

Women came before men. Women are thousands of years older than men.

7/21/50

The night. I dream of earthquakes, the earth shaking and tipping out the window, while the house stands still! One half awakens—more than half!—sits up in bed with the dream clinging heavily to the edges of one's brain, tipping the whole brain like a house itself, caught in an earthquake. I call out someone's name, because I don't know what bed I am in, or what house. I see and hear myself doing it, knowing I am both asleep and awake, and the limbo is horrible! I walk into the kitchen, thinking of getting some hot water and milk to drink, but my brain grasps even this simple idea like the clumsy hands of a primitive monster. And the primitive monster is myself. I chew voraciously at a half-eaten chop which I really do not want, and put it down again. The earth shakes, and I doubt even gravity. I am suddenly somebody else, another creature I do not know. (I know, though, that I lived a hundred million years ago.)

7/22/50

Because of a very simple combination of love & hate in myself in regard to my parents, I am absorbed today in the ambiguities throughout nature and philosophy. Out of this, I shall create, discover, invent, prove, and reveal. Thus, life—thus all, all, all of life is a fiction, based on something that might have been otherwise, yet which all is true! These things I shall do and discover, they will all be true, too. (This, I sometimes speculate, will finally drive me mad. I can feel its intimations, sometimes. But then,

I have always known the "insane" were not really insane. And this transcends, my dear philosophers, solipsism and idealism, existentialism, too! I am a walking perpetual example of my contention: as I said brilliantly at the age of twelve, a boy in a girl's body.)

8/11/50

Texas: I shall write about it as it has never been written about before. The Levis, the second-hand cars, the oil millionaires, the jukebox songs of women (redheaded, slatternly, in cotton housedresses) who must be loyal and true (my God, what are they doing?). Always be mine, that we never will part—(the second-hand car) but mostly the clean young dunces, the lean thighs, the blond girls, the fresh food in the refrigerator, the sense of space just beyond the town limits, the rodeo next week, and the absolute certainty that the young men's bodies are in perfect condition, the legs spare and hard, and the spirit, too, clean. The women's voices southern but not dazingly southern, soft without being weak. They are clean like the bodies and minds of the young men. The jukebox songs, though whining and sentimental, are only whining because we have not yet developed our poetry. Texas—with the faith of the people who were born there, living there still. The beautiful, quiet, flat homes, the beautiful girls who inspire the men who drive bombers over Germany, Russia and Korea.

Infinite is the word for Texas. Infinite!

8/13/50

The secret of every art, of good art, is love. It is so pleasant to love, I wonder there are any bad artists. Yet I myself have been so guilty of not loving! O my Cornell!

AUGUST 17, 1950

Jolly good news—the chauffeur story sold for $1150! Margot & I very happy. ᶠSeriously—I must get to work immediately on my book. I dream of titles—"The Sun Gazer." "The Echo—" of some sort.ᶠᶠ I know what causes the apathy—the disillusionment today. It is that the first and second World War were fought in vain so far as the following peace machinery was concerned. Now the United Nations have failed to maintain peace. And it does seem horrible, ridiculous, that no one in South America, or France, or Turkey, no one but England and France, and they only a handful, have sent anything to stop the Reds in Korea.

SEPTEMBER 6, 1950

Subscribed to a British Clipping Service. My book comes out in October.* Marc came over at 8:30. He is bored with his wealthy and very ideal girl, and wants to marry me—incredible dictu!—again, now on flatly companionable basis. Like putting a thin, slack leash on me. He in fact no longer wants a heterosexual marriage. His head is turned all the time, he says. But they all love him, if taken on a lifetime basis. Some sense there. We shall have something like Jane & Paul B. [Bowles]. For I think I may do it. It will not interfere at all with London this winter—which I dream of—or anyone or anything else. Hitchcock telegraphed me in P'town, but I didn't come back to see him. He seems to be going tennis mad over my book,† and apparently is already shooting at Forest Hills.

SEPTEMBER 22, 1950

I am tolerably happy. Yet not living yet, living only on the thought life will be more, more pleasant, more rewarding, more beautiful in the near future. Of course, it is all tied with emotional satisfaction. If Kathryn did not exist, I should contemplate it in New York. But I know now, too, that no one affects me more deeply, no one has roots in me as Kathryn has.

9/22/50

Of my book, in conclusion, two weeks before finishing the rewrite: this is not a picture of the author sweating. The bookstores at this moment happen to be glutted with tracts excusing and apologizing for homosexuality, depicting their very rugged male heroes writhing with heterosexual disgust as they try to throw off the hideous coils that bind them, while in the last scene, their beloved is without reason killed, lest somebody in the Bible Belt despise the fact they may continue living together in a cohabitation he has been hammered into countenancing, but which may sour in his mind a week later. This is the story of a woman weak because of social weaknesses in her society, having nothing to do with perversion. And a girl starved for a mother, in whom the artificial upbringing of an orphanage's home, however scientific, has not sufficed as parental love. It is just a story that might have happened, with no ax to grind.

---

* The first UK edition of *Strangers on a Train* (London, 1950).
† Hitchcock changed the character of Guy Haines in *Strangers on a Train* from an architect to a star tennis player.

SEPTEMBER 26, 1950

Why do I work so hard on a book that will undoubtedly ruin me? Today I was at least concerned with the typewriter for twelve hours, and only with difficulty produced ten rewritten pages.

OCTOBER 12, 1950

In furious mood. Walked furiously up 2nd Avenue. And at 4:00 PM got the curse! First time since end of May or June. Because I finished my book today, too, perhaps. A nice writing streak, with the end in which Therese does not go back with Carol—but refuses her, and is alone at the last. Shall show M.J. both versions, and am sure she will prefer the "lift" ending in which T. & C. go back together. In the course of the evening got horribly blind drunk! Blackouts and everything else. Including spending all the money in my wallet. Lyne eventually poured me into a taxi at 3:00 AM.

OCTOBER 14, 1950

[Arthur] Koestler didn't know about movie sale of my book. "Then why do you need my patronage?" He wants to introduce me to *Partisan Review* crowd. He is tolerably respectful. But he won't be until I manage to hold my liquor a little better.

OCTOBER 16, 1950

Dinner with Koestler tonight. Semon's. He suggests I send novel to a typist immediately, get it back with a "new dignity" about it, and give him a copy to read. I don't really want him to, for he wouldn't like it. I go about vaguely depressed about my book, dreading publication day. Yet optimistic when I discuss it at length with someone. The newspapers are mentioning "my name" thrice weekly, about, so people tell me. Koestler came back here, we tried to go to bed. A miserable, joyless episode. Absurd and blush making to set down—he proposed that we lie together and do nothing, which of course he found impossible. There is a mood of self-torture in me—when it comes to men. Plus remembering the times I have lain in the same bed with women I adored and longed for, whom I loved so much I did not wish to annoy them, or jeopardize the pleasure of merely being with them later. And so hostility, masochism, self-hatred, self-abasement (making myself feel inadequate, out of step with the world, deficient in half myself) all these play their part in these scenes which leave me weeping at four AM and then alone at five.

Koestler, efficient as always, decides to abandon the sexual with me. He did not know homosexuality was so deeply ingrained, he said.

OCTOBER 17, 1950

Day entirely devoted to errands, housecleaning, the doctor, dinners, and cocktails. Three gins in the Mayfair with Lyne, and we—I—told her miserably and weepingly about Koestler, and about my book—my feelings of having wasted my time writing something no one will want to read, etc. Perhaps the fact is, I cannot bear the thought of its appearing in print.

OCTOBER 18, 1950

Walter & I discussed my book. I told him I did not mind shelving it for five years. He suddenly agreed, and said Sheehan told him—"I'm glad Pat tackles a subject like this, because it's something she really knows about, but for her career I think it's very bad." To get a label. And I've already one as a mystery story writer!

OCTOBER 19, 1950

So that is the big news—I shall try to persuade Margot J. that the book should not be published now. And she will doubtless argue otherwise. Everyone will. But it is my career, my life.

10/20/50

Now, now, now, to fall in love with my book—this same day I have decided not to publish it, not for an indefinite length of time. But I shall continue to work on it for some weeks to come, to polish and perfect it. I shall fall in love with it now, in a different way from the way I loved it before. This love is endless, disinterested, unselfish, impersonal even.

OCTOBER 21, 1950

Margot reports [French publisher] Calmann-Lévy bought *Strangers* in Paris. Koestler's publishers, & of course he claims credit, though M.J. said she'd had requests before. $200 and 7% on first 5000, I believe. Shall let the money sit there.

10/23/50

The whole trouble, of course, is caused by my present struggle within myself, whether to follow my own nature, which I feel maimed, or to borrow a few crutches from the world around me, the rest of the people. As an artist, I can and should follow only my own nature. Yet I debate putting the crutches under that, too, and wonder if it is possible. It is for this reason only that I am egocentric at the moment. I should like to look quickly and get the operation over quickly. But the process is not a quick one. It is for this reason only, too, that I "live below my mental level," as Koestler tells me, that I seek out the advice of other people, feeling that because I have let other people control my emotional expression (the lack of it) I must take their domination in my general mental operations also.

OCTOBER 27, 1950

With Lyne. Saw a Forain* exhibit, lunched late. And being tense for some complicated psychological reasons, I drank 3 martinis, in good, calm spirits, at 6 PM and in the course of the evening—later Spivy's—drank too much. I fell apart at 3:00 AM when Lyne left me. Wanted secretly to go home with her—and ended by making a vain call to her, to tell her rather sadly I did not think I should see her again, because since I loved her it was most difficult and hard on me, etc. A taxi home at 3:45. I am ashamed of my self-indulgent and destructive behavior—which I cannot seem to control. I can blame fatigue—but not entirely. Such a deplorable waste of time and money.—And I feel I sink as low morally as any of the Village wastrels of whom I have heard, have known, all my life, without suspecting I could ever be like them. I called Ann Smith at 4:10 AM and she came up. I told her I was blind drunk. Actually, I went to bed rather sober at 5:15—and suffered the minimum of hangover.

OCTOBER 29, 1950

Margot has finished my book. "I'm very pleased, Pat," but not with too much enthusiasm, I thought. "What do you think of getting it published under another name?" she asked. I don't mind. Temporary, partial relief from shame. We must get the opinions of several "independent readers." I was drunk again, not so much from liquor as emotional relief and plain nervous fatigue. But I think seriously these days of therapeutic measures against alcoholism. Something must be done.

---

* Jean-Louis Forain (1852–1931) was a French painter and renowned caricaturist. He was a close friend of the poets Arthur Rimbaud and Paul Verlaine.

OCTOBER 30, 1950

Koestler called. He'd just finished his book. We went to the Turkey Town
House where I stood him drinks. Very pleasant. 4 martinis and more for
me, and I was sober all the evening, because of guilt. Hubris, I told Koestler. He has bought an island in the Delaware River, invites me to come
and work there next week. He is very generous, impulsive, and we enjoy
each other's company, I think. Stayed out until 4:15 with Koestler, who
continued to drink & bore up very well. Had been living on benzedrine
finishing last details of his novel. Wants Jim Putnam [of G. P. Putnam's
Sons, publishers] to read mine. Suspend judgment about homosexuality
label until after he has seen it.

11/2/50

Random thoughts when too tired to work, lying on my couch with a
beer and Koestler's *Dialogue with Death*. Some satisfaction and assuage
of guilt (for laziness this past week, since finishing the second draft of
a novel) in the thought that the short story I am lazily working on is
not bad and may well sell. Outstanding characteristic of these past nine
months for me: a turn away from religion, from my old introspection
with mystical revelations. Not entirely explainable either by more social
life and less solitude, but by world events, and a more personal participation in the world of people and events. This is an age of war & neurosis and conflict within conflict, and of Communism versus Capitalism.

NOVEMBER 14, 1950

These days are on the brink again. The least thing depresses me to the
point of suicide. A completely tangled and stupid relationship with Lyne.
I believe I am dedicated to madness. I know exactly what I should do, to
"lead a happier life, etc." I cannot and will not do it, though the other
way is death—preceded by unhappiness, frustration, depression and
worst of all, inferiority.

11/14/50

In this past year: turning away from the mysticism that sheltered and
glorified my youth, turning also from the Bible—especially in this
period of crisis—as a sort of consolation & source of strength whatever. I am still subject to depression. A setback however small, in the
midst of successes can nevertheless knock me down. Neurotic: the
chief source of depression is emotional reversal or rejection. And—as

a writer, a sense of chaos and decadence pervading my age. The greatest achievements in any age in writing will be made by the students of chaos. Lives fly off in every direction, and where they cross is no point of surety or security. Every man contains his own morals like an envelope, like a little world.

11/14/50

I am afraid there is no rest on earth for me, because I shall forever avoid it. The rope I am given everywhere lies slack around my feet and tangles me up.

DECEMBER 3, 1950

Saw Margot three successive nights. She reiterates most boringly, is very self-centered, but Christ, she has put up with my shortcomings, too, and she is a great girl. B.C. came in Monday—we sat on the sofa until late, drinking too much. Later, a terrific but slowly growing lust in me for Miss Bertha [C.]. I love her body. And quite by delicious & wonderful accident, she came into the dark room after me and joined me in bed. (Margot slept in the living room.) I had almost forgotten,— alas, I had almost forgotten that pleasure beyond all pleasures, that joy beyond all treasures, pleasures, findings, the pleasure of pleasing a woman. I did please Bertha. And her body, her head and hair in the darkness—as she lay by then with her head near the foot of the bed— was suddenly more than Europe, art, Renoir whom she resembled, one of his women. Bertha was mine then, a woman with terrific breasts and a figure like an hourglass, Margot says, but all women, the woman, a woman, woman, and I felt all the extraneous ones drop away from me, all the barriers dissolve. She is mysterious in a Russian-Jewish way, melancholic, devious by nature in her mind, witty as a fairy, however, and unfortunately now on the brink of a serious operation. That night was Tuesday. On Wednesday, she had a hemorrhage—not my fault— and she went to the hospital Saturday. Too bad I am going to Europe, for we can't plan a life.

12/17/50

Total mobilization over the world.* The edges of everything crumble, and the bottom drops out of the plans to spend next year in Europe. A day

---

* Reference to the national state of emergency declared by President Truman on December 16, 1950, following a crushing defeat by Chinese troops in Korea.

off in the midst of work, and a book at that, au contraire to all that the world is coming to today, and in the evening a somewhat broken somewhat engagement. Night falls. The radio plays Debussy's "Children's Corner." One has to have someone to love these days, I think tritely and immediately sound myself to see if I've still the necessary enthusiasm. I telephone my favorite friend—but not my love, who lies, potentially my love, in a hospital—but no one answers. I want to see a movie tonight. I work tomorrow, I am like a million other people, perhaps a little lonelier, a little more wistful, a little more violent, a little more enthusiastic, a little more despondent. O what will she [B.] say in one hour? O where shall I be in a month? And what will become of us? My darling, give me at least a sign to remember. Are all women nothing but images to look at and remember? Will I never get to know you? Never know whether you prefer roses to chrysanthemums? Or even take milk in your tea? Are all women nothing but symbols?

DECEMBER 19, 1950

Cooked steak for Margot last night, and this evening she wanted me to have dinner with her. She always overdrinks, undereats, and we end up sleeping at her apartment.

DECEMBER 20, 1950

Wrote to Marc last week, on his book, and for my $50 dollars. His book *The Choice* has me & him in excruciating funny bedroom scene, all literally me & my apartment. In general, I feel enormously more relaxed than before, like a different person. Less regimented—which of course is the anxious child's effort to build a stable existence around him—and I have that new surge of love for Bertha. How I wish I knew what will happen in advance. Do I really want her enough to go after her & demand her? For I think I could get her.

And how long will I be in Europe? K. [Kathryn] is impossible— alas. She will never give up what she has, or want to. Let's face it. On Europe—Margot wants this book [*The Price of Salt*] definitely to be done anonymously. She said it may sell like hotcakes, however. Harper may accept it. But I believe Margot will wrest it from them and give it to Coward-McCann. In which case, I can then go to Europe & she'll handle the rest—as if I were dead—but not before Jan. 30, probably, can I get away. And of course these days I look for my Carol, Mrs. E. R. Senn, of Ridgewood, New Jersey. I look for her around Bloomingdale's, though I should think it more likely that she shops at Saks oftener.

DECEMBER 21, 1950

The War: We are losing again in Korea. The Chinese Communists
are pouring down on us. The British want appeasement. The United
Nations cannot afford to appease, recognize Communist China. HST
[Harry S. Truman] proclaims state of emergency. Prices are frozen, and
wages. D. D. Eisenhower leaves for Europe to head the European armies.
I shall have to finagle to get to England under such conditions, for there
may be restriction soon.

Everyone expects war immediately, the U.N. to get kicked out of
Korea, and for Russia perhaps to sweep into Germany & France. I call
often to see how Bertha is. I perhaps can visit her tomorrow, when I go
also to pick up my new pale muskrat-lined coat—assembled for me by
Lyne—and to cash in my remaining War Bonds with the dollar at .55 and
going lower! Dennis [Cohen] will publish my book in January, suggested
my being there for the appearance, but I can't. France has sent the contract [for *Strangers on a Train*] with Calmann-Lévy. Two bids from Italy,
one from Denmark. My career—goes luckily, perhaps. But I must write
another book immediately under my own name, I feel. And what shall
I ever tell the family? That it is anonymous, first of all, and I have. And
when it does appear next fall, I suppose I shall ignore it, not tell them.
Say it's postponed. They have bought the trailer & sold the house. For
$15,000. They leave Jan. 22. In time for Jan. 19—to see my 30th birthday
in. I shall be delighted with it.

Yet withal, colossal depressive moments recently—as Sunday night
when I had a date broken by Margot, and I at last could see Bertha in
the evening, at the hospital. And I thought—what will B. want when she
comes out. If she even wants me, what good is it if I go away? And there
is all this so close & heavy in the heart, plus the dismal atmosphere of
war hanging over the whole world, because I had that unexpected and
wonderful night with B. in my arms and my mouth against her breasts,
and she as happy as I. So close—and yet so far—farther than ever. I
feared like a soldier about to die, it might have been our first and our last
night together. I wouldn't bet on it, says Margot cheerfully. Oh, Margot,
thou sweetie! I told her if we did sleep together it would have to be at her
house. I'd admire to let you both sleep there, she says. God bless her.

What shall I write about next, I think here in this diary where I think
aloud. O more definitely than ever this 29th year, this third year and I
always change on the thirds, has seen much metamorphosis. It will come
to me. My love of life grows stronger every month. My powers of recu-

peration are wonderfully swift and elastic. I think of writing a startler, a
real shocker in the psychological thriller line. I could do it adeptly.

DECEMBER 30, 1950

A bit tight after fine evening in the Village with Lyne, I called Marjorie
from here at 3:30 AM and announced in a clear loud voice that I was in
love with Bertha. I don't remember the ensuing conversation. Had meant
to see Kay G. tonight for a moment, because I spent last evening with
her, here, and it was stupendous, beautiful and all that, but I can't anymore. Besides, there is the guilt lest Margot should learn.

DECEMBER 31, 1950

Very tired. 2 PM date chez B.G. on 59th Street then to Margot's in fine
mood, as Bertha was to be there. But got blind drunk. At first, tearful
but excellent confab with B. in Margot's kitchen, telling her Europe
didn't matter, the time I should spend away from her. She said, "Does it
matter to you I'm going to share an apartment with Marjorie? Because it
doesn't to me." Slight blackout delayed my arriving at Lyne's until 9:30
PM. Home at 8 & delighted to see bed. Emotionally—exhausted by B.,
tears, frustration, desperation, and yet hope somehow.

1951–1962

LIVING BETWEEN
THE UNITED STATES
AND EUROPE

1951

SHORTLY AFTER SHE turns thirty, energized by a new love interest and her professional success, Patricia Highsmith departs on her second trip to Europe, which will last for more than two years. Unlike her first tour of the Continent in 1949, this time she has no set itinerary as she visits friends and work contacts. Her current location is reflected in her diary entries, switching to French when she's in France, then featuring long passages in German as soon as she crosses the border to Germany.

The advance from Harper & Brothers for *Strangers on a Train* covers the cost of her flight and allows for this peripatetic existence. Before long, though, her persistent fear of penury returns, and she starts writing travelogues, short stories, and radio dramas to sell to publishers, magazines, and broadcasters. She uses her personal networks in Italy and Germany to find publishers interested in purchasing the rights to her first novel.

The trip begins in Paris in February, where Pat spends much of her time with openly gay *New Yorker* correspondent Janet Flanner ("Genêt") and her lover Natalia Danesi Murray, an editor at the Italian publishing house Mondadori, as well as legendary literary agent Jenny Bradley, who will become Pat's representative in Europe.

From Paris, Pat flies to London. The English edition of *Strangers on a Train* has just been published by Cresset Press, run by Dennis Cohen; Pat has hungered for his wife, Kathryn Hamill, ever since their passionate affair in 1949, but now she is vexed by Kathryn's cool, almost hostile manner. When Pat presents her with the manuscript of her second novel, *The Price of Salt*, which is inspired in part by her, Kathryn acts unimpressed and does not recommend it to her husband for publication.

Pat can't sleep. She revises her novel obsessively and conceives the idea for her next book, aptly titled *The Sleepless Night* (later retitled *The Traffic of Jacob's Ladder*). This story focuses on the close relationship between two men, Gerald and Oscar, one of whom is sent to Korea, presumably to serve in the war that will drag on there until 1953 (one of the rare references to contemporary world events and politics in Pat's work). All but the final pages of this manuscript have been lost; at the end, Oscar kills himself, leaving his entire fortune to Gerald.

Dismayed and mired in self-doubt, Pat makes a hasty departure for Paris, then travels on to Marseille and Rome. For all the trouble her second novel has presented her, Pat's debut continues to enjoy great success: Alfred Hitchcock's adaptation of *Strangers on a Train* premieres in American cinemas in July, and the book itself is nominated for the prestigious Edgar Allan Poe Award for Best First Novel.

Pat passes through Naples, Capri, Florence, and Venice, where she crosses paths with Peggy Guggenheim and Somerset Maugham. In Munich she runs into Jewish writer Wolfgang Hildesheimer, who takes a shine to her. The two spend a great deal of time together on Lake Starnberg, and travel to Mannheim, Frankfurt, and the Odenwald Mountains.

Pat is not surprised when her New York literary agent, Margot Johnson, informs her that Harper & Brothers do not want to publish *The Price of Salt*, after all. Just three weeks later, Coward-McCann—an imprint of G. P. Putnam's Sons—swoops in to save the project.

Pat's old friend Jo P. is also in Munich and puts her in touch with an ex-girlfriend, Ellen Blumenthal Hill, a sociologist six years Pat's senior. Ellen becomes Pat's new love, in a relationship defined by powerful attraction and powerful aversion. And throughout the rest of her travels around Europe, Pat hardly mentions what she must have seen at every turn: destroyed cities, broken people, rationing, and reconstruction. Her diaries and notebooks are focused solely on the battlefields of writing and her own life.

JANUARY 6, 1951

I've been so busy on the book. Even now it must be reread by me, and every 24 hours counts in my getting away to Europe at the end of January. Oh, I write a book with a happy ending, but what happens when I find the right person? When I return from Europe—and I don't think I'll ever want to live there—I want a house with a woman I love.

JANUARY 23, 1951

Margot reports from Harper Joan K. found the book perfectly fascinating. More enthusiastic than usual. Wants to read it again & make editorial comments for minor corrections.

JANUARY 25, 1951

Consultation with Margot, Red, E. Hume over a pseudonym over drinks this afternoon. Claire Morgan, perhaps.* Hence, I was late for Kay, who was waiting *en bas*—Disgraceful. Must cut this with Kay. Not only can it have unpleasant—ghastly—reverberations with Margot after I'm gone, but it is whorish on my part. I don't care for her. Rather for Sheila! Wrote Lyne & told her I shall fly. Air France.

JANUARY 27, 1951

Ann brought my book [the manuscript of *The Price of Salt*] back with enthusiastic praise. So much better than the first. Even minor characters come out, etc. And what a hell of a shame I can't have my name on this one instead of the first! Home alone tonight. Suspenseful: in seven days, I may be gone. Waiting, too, for the creative springs to fill up the well. And where, my God, will that mysterious and yet unknown impetus come from next? That meteor flung out of space that will strike my heart so invisibly and so violently?

FEBRUARY 1, 1951

I gave [Sheila] my oldest Levi's to keep until my return from Europe. Later we called Margot, who'd invited us for a nightcap. There is no more delightful boîte to bring a girl after dinner than chez Margot. We ended by sleeping two floors up in Dickie's apartment. Sheila had said she hadn't a place to sleep that night. An absurdity, but God bless it. Life has no pleasure equal to that of the moment under the shower, singing, with a wonderful girl waiting in her bed in the next room. Joan Kahn at Harper's at 11 AM. She'd like the MS by March, for fall publication. 'Twill be a sweat in London.

FEBRUARY 2, 1951

Lunched with Stanley. Ship's Grill. We talked of human will. And of mother's eccentricities. Tonight B. [Bertha]. Greatest effort on my part— and successful, to give her a decent evening and dinner. B. treats me with the contempt she feels for herself for even noticing me. B.C. is the woman with the past lovers of Great Stature, to which no one in the present can measure up. B. hears Scarlatti and winces—"Oh, that reminds me of

---

* Claire Morgan did indeed end up being the pseudonym under which *The Price of Salt* was first published. Only in 1990 was the novel finally released under Highsmith's own name.

what I was once . . ." She kisses me, with a passionate mockery of that first and one night.

FEBRUARY 4, 1951

Packed suitcase & cleaned house all day. For dinner with Margot at 6 PM. Wanted to see Sheila tonight—the last night—but she was studying. I got too weepingly drunk on gin. Margot put me to bed: fatigue, disappointment. Oh damn—S. was so almost perfect, but who will be there the very moment you need her?

FEBRUARY 5, 1951

Hectic departure. Rosalind brought stockings for me to take to her mother. Ann S., Mother & Stanley, who couldn't drive because of a sore back. My eyes looked awful, due to weeping last night. Plus a slight hangover. My mother her usual inefficient self. My lord, she could no more drive a car, for instance, than she could fly. Margot remarked on her utter and total difference from me. There must be some mistake, Margot said. My mother's mind jumps to five things in two minutes. And there is open antagonism between us. Took off at 12 noon from the International Airport for Paris, non-stop, 19,000 ft. flight—11-hour trip. I arrived in Paris at 5:15 AM. Lyne had expected me at 9 AM.

2/6/51

5:15 A.M. We are coming in slowly over Paris, hovering, almost, in the pitch darkness. I watch just beyond the edge of the gray wing for the first lights down there, but it takes minutes and minutes, until finally two, four, seven, there they are. Suddenly there is a panoply of lights, a long row of them, the runway of Orly field. The plane sits down on the earth more gently than several bumps we have taken in the air, as if it were nothing, sitting down on France. The bus into Paris rattles and bumps, and there are only four of us inside. As we enter the city streets, I see vignettes of lighted café windows left and right. It is six in the morning. A woman wipes a table, a workman stands sipping coffee at the counter. Another bar with gay lights is closing. The atmosphere is so densely Paris, all one ever thought of Paris, that one feels a congestion in the throat. Where else are there lights like these—fuzzy and soft in the black building, peculiarly soft yellow as indivituates a certain painter's yellow. The bus whisks across intersections, over a bridge. A cycling workman turns in from a street beside us. We stop at a great terminal, where only a handful of people are. I go to get a coffee and manage to exchange a Camel for a Gauloise bleu. Then I feel quite at home, reading *Le Matin* at the counter. It's too early to call my friend, but at quarter to seven I can't wait any longer. It isn't the gay welcome I'd anticipated. The plane was four hours early. Arrivals in Paris are never very glamorous.

The Louvre: second day. It is quite chilly, and the glimpse of la Victoire de Samothrace sends another chill from head to foot. There is a very warm air vent in the floor directly in front of the Mona Lisa, but there is also a guide group clustered around the picture and clearly intending to stay there an hour. Europe teaches an American infinite patience. Something is always dirty that he expected to be clean. He trudges [several] blocks to a museum, and finds it closed. He rushes his dinner to be punctual at the theater and discovers the French and the French actors are quite casually half an hour late themselves. One must either blow up or become infinitely patient.

FEBRUARY 7, 1951

Last night I called Kathryn. She & D. [Dennis] were playing canasta—K. winning £2. She sounded wonderful, and I told her so. Spoke nearly *deux mille*'s* worth with K. Last evening, too, cocktails & dinner with Natalia M. [Natalia Danesi Murray] & Janet Flanner, whom L. [Elizabeth Lyne] & I met in the Hotel Continental—a very chilly place somewhat like the Plaza. Lunched at Ruk's—a good restaurant near *Jardin des Modes*,† where the Vogels‡ work. Ruth Yorck is in Germany at the moment.

FEBRUARY 8, 1951

Exhaustion catches up with me. Raining. Had a date with Mme Bradley§ at 6, which I walked to, endless kilometers, it seemed, to the Quai de Béthune. She is very cordial, a bit deaf, gave me Ivory soap & a washrag, two blessings I am extremely grateful for here.

FEBRUARY 10, 1951

Tonight—visited Carolle's with Lyne, phony lesbian night club off Champs-Élysées, which L. tells me was a favorite haunt of Peggy Fears.

---

* One U.S. dollar was worth approximately 400 francs in 1950.
† A monthly women's fashion magazine cofounded by Lucien Vogel.
‡ Lucien Vogel and his wife, Cosette (née Brunhoff), were the founders of *VU*, the first magazine in France that reported on the Nazi concentration camps.
§ Jenny Bradley (1886–1983), an internationally known literary agent who gave financial assistance, as well as a writing table, to the impoverished James Joyce. In the interwar years, she and her husband, novelist William Bradley, were primary liaisons between Parisian and New York authors. Their home on the Île Saint-Louis was a literary salon that hosted the likes of Joyce, Gertrude Stein, F. Scott Fitzgerald, and others.

Saw tail of Balenciaga show. Pretty damsels in fantastic evening clothes. Lyne must buy 350,000 francs' worth of dresses—generally two—for no purpose other than courtesy, and then she gives them away to someone who can wear them in America.

FEBRUARY 12, 1951

Met Mr. Keogh at Deux Magots. He had not known I was his wife's* acquaintance, so had to fetch her. I relayed the reviews of *Double Door* at which she seemed unconcerned, and rightly. 27 and she's written two books & finishing a third. He works at *Paris Vogue*.

FEBRUARY 14, 1951

Yanked around by Lyne to meet last-minute people. Lunch with Germaine† [Beaumont] in St. Cloud. She is still mad as ever and a joy to be with. Lyne rushed madly all afternoon, and rushed me. My God, I really don't see how she stands it at her age, except of course she doesn't drink. I am within hours of seeing Kathryn, after over a year's waiting. Met by two reporters at Northolt.‡ They took a few snaps. About *Strangers*, etc. Then Kensington, where I called Kathryn. K. is thinner, it seems to me, though she says it's only in her face. I can see she is anything but the radiant, smiling woman I waved goodbye to at the airport in Naples. And I foresee that this trip here, from point of view even of cheering her, will probably not be successful. I didn't come to London with an idea of resuming, at least in the house, our relationship: it is the cheerlessness in K. herself that wounds me.

FEBRUARY 16, 1951

The atmosphere [in London] is such a relief after Paris, just as I had anticipated. Only it is raining—raining—raining.

FEBRUARY 18, 1951

This afternoon visited Victoria & Albert Museum with K. [Kathryn] and D. [Dennis]. But fever gave me chills. The grand bed, enough to give any sensitive young scion a psychological impotence—gazing up at his

---

* Theodora Roosevelt Keogh, a ballet dancer, was a granddaughter of Franklin Delano Roosevelt. In 1950, Pat wrote an enthusiastic review of Theodora's sensual debut novel, *Meg*.
† The novelist and critic was the first female recipient of the prestigious prix Renaudot for her debut novel *Piège*, inspired by Colette (her boss at *Le Matin*) and Virginia Woolf (whose diaries she translated).
‡ RAF Northolt, an airport west of London that was used for commercial flights during the construction of Heathrow.

history in heraldic bas relief on the bed's canopy. Home to bed. I am sick now—103° fever.

FEBRUARY 19, 1951

A day in bed. Much needed, and gratefully and rapturously relished. Margot & Kay G. sent me the sentence from D. Kilgallen's column, about the "N.Y. celebrities" worried sick because soon to be mentioned in nom de plume novel by P.H. the thriller writer—and my mother quoted it in full. Stupid and erroneous, says M.J. Doesn't know where it came from.*

André Gide died last night in Paris. Only a few days ago Lyne was saying I should improve my French so I wouldn't sound like an idiot when I met him—how sorry I am.

FEBRUARY 24, 1951

The days go by idly. Idea shaping up for my next novel—born last Friday night when I couldn't sleep. *The Sleepless Night.*† A third decadent novel, perhaps, but I should be really decadent, blind, were I not concerned with these things. I have the thread on which to string all the 20th century characters which interest me, but not yet the electric force to make them move. That will come this time.

FEBRUARY 25, 1951

I grow depressed—for K. has finished my book today and I don't think she likes it. That is, I don't think she likes it enough to recommend it to Dennis as she did the last. She says, I've had too much interference just now, so she'll say nothing more. Didn't comment on the writing. "Well— as a job—no, I don't—" (When I asked her if she liked it as well as the first.) Perhaps the entire subject is distasteful to her. Perhaps she thinks it much ado about nothing. Am eager for D.C.'s opinion but meant to fix it perfectly first. They went out tonight. I confess I am depressed. To have failed with K.—as a person, as a writer, I now feel.

---

* There were rumors that Pat had written a lesbian love novel under a pseudonym. By 1959, when Pat met her future lover Marijane Meaker, the rumor had become an open secret: "She was better known in the outside world as Patricia Highsmith, author of *Strangers on a Train*, which had become an Alfred Hitchcock thriller in 1951. But in L's [a Greenwich Village lesbian bar], Pat was revered for her pseudonymous novel, *The Price of Salt*" (Marijane Meaker, *Highsmith. A Romance of the 1950s* [San Francisco, 2003], p. 1).

† Pat began working on a new novel, *The Sleepless Night*, which she would later call *The Traffic of Jacob's Ladder*. This novel remains unpublished and has mostly been lost.

FEBRUARY 28, 1951

Met Maria* and we dined at Hungarian Czarda finally. We rode the King's Road bus to Piccadilly, stopped in a pub for a last one. Then we phoned B. Belmore, whom we picked up at His Majesty's. She took us to the downstairs drinking club we failed to find the other night. I loved Maria all evening. We dropped B. off in a taxi, Maria invited me for coffee, and of course I stayed the night, which was perfectly delightful. I do think she likes me, a little bit, no more than advisable under the circumstances, which are that she lives here and I over the water.

MARCH 1, 1951

Home at 10:30, and I don't think K. knew I'd been gone overnight, though I don't know. Such are our remote relations now (how much closer I've been sometimes in America, writing her a letter!) that I can't trouble to mind if she knows I've spent the night with Maria or not. Interview by one Hazel Rogers at 11:30 AM here. I in Levi's, discussing Yaddo again. What would I talk about if it weren't for Yaddo? Dullish. But Dennis says he's placed 1500 books with dealers, which is good, and is due to chat in the newspapers. The Cresset printing is 3000 at first. A reprint would have to be another 3000, and would be a risky business financially. The paper shortage here is a serious disadvantage, too.

MARCH 2, 1951

I worked. And dined with Maria. Maria is something to look forward to at 7 PM and I told her so. We had a lovely night—a bath and a hot water bottle, and that happiness to which nothing can compare. "Don't ever leave me," Maria said with her arms about me, before we got undressed. "If I should ever say that to anyone, and I wouldn't, I'd say it to you, don't ever leave me." I don't remember it precisely, and that is life and that is that—that which means more to me than anything I have heard in London. And am I so neurotic for that? We made love in the morning too.

MARCH 4, 1951

I am almost "thru" the book once. Dinner out at the Savoy. Too expensive. I wince at it, & feel guilty. K. seldom smiles, only pleasant on necessary occasions. Harper contract [for *The Price of Salt*] came yesterday & I signed. $750.

---

* Maria was Rosalind Constable's former lover.

MARCH 7, 1951

The days roll by slowly and I am not in the best form for writing, working. Luncheon with Raimund von Hofmannsthal, who always lifts my spirit, and I do mean my spirit. Suggests I live in England. Rather, agrees with me. Charming 2-story house, good martinis & a good dinner with French wine. And a wife, and books, and a Siamese cat. I got pleasantly high, and dreamt of having all this myself.

MARCH 12, 1951

A beautiful day for a change. Took Maria out to the Pheasantry* for dinner. She was tired, wore no coat over her dress, since I suppose she has only the plaid. Maria said I was too young for her, that she'd never live with a woman. I merely asked her how she would feel, if I took a flat in London. Of course, I should like to live with her. But I shouldn't like to pin her down. "I'd come to America with you, but I shouldn't with Rosalind."

The next morning as we lay in bed, after the most delicious moments, I said: "Do you know what you said last night?" "Um-hm," she said, as if she knew precisely what I was talking about, and she did, "I would, too." That is bringing the night into the day. That is bringing paradise into the prosaic. I adored her for that.

MARCH 13, 1951

Immediately one is on the train—this one—the tension disappears. I become nobody, and the imagination swims to all quarters. Everything is delightful. I am alone and nobody and myself. We got to Salisbury at about 5. The cathedral is a short walk from the railroad station, the town being no size. A beautiful and tranquil and virginally clean cloister—or precinct of the cathedral—surrounding the old church, which is green and tan mottled with age beyond reckoning mentally. The 11th century knights' tombs are magnificent sculpture, they lie on their backs, sleeping, noble knights with a mere slab and a slit for forehead and eyes. I was profoundly impressed, admired them with all my heart. The choir boys assembled as I looked over the church, but I did not stay for all their singing. A bit of the ethereal in my ears, emanating from the nave. When I came out it was of course raining, and I made my way generally toward

---

* Humphrey Bogart, Dylan Thomas, and Francis Bacon were among the patrons of this bohemian restaurant and bar, a favorite with actors and artists.

the station. Stopped at a boys' haberdashery and bought a black & white woolen muffler for 11/6. Then hopped toward the station.

MARCH 16, 1951

Had to fly to Paris abruptly at 7:20—Kensington. The French girl with whom I spoke yesterday told me I'd have time to pick up the ticket before 5 today—but no. So I had to leave without saying goodbye to Kathryn. I wonder sometimes, when I am low, how I shall survive this rambling about Europe alone. But this lowness is only tonight—combined with an objectivity that is only age creeping up: after all, my third arrival in Paris. I am used to it.

MARCH 19, 1951

Suddenly peace in the midst of chaos. I feel better, so much better mentally since leaving London. How depressed & repressed I was there.

MARCH 25, 1951

Quiet work. Walked my story by Janet F.'s [Flanner's] hotel—everybody away this weekend. And feel very content, & superior to most of these Americans around here.

MARCH 27, 1951

Letters from Rolf [Tietgens], Kathryn, Natalia (very warm) & Ann S. N.M. welcomes me to Rome, says Bompiani contract is cinched. Letter from Kathryn: "I shall never cease to regret your visit coincided with such unhappiness here. There was a time when this home was a pleasant place to come . . ." It made me sad—It is a terrible blotch—and nothing can ever be done.

MARCH 28, 1951

Walked to Place Pigalle with Louis Stettner*—photographer, boring, aged 28. A bottle of champagne shot down in a gallery. Recreation & exercise, walking there, and nothing means anything to me these days but getting my book off in as good a form as possible.

---

* Louis Stettner (1922–2016), celebrated American photographer known for his portrayal of New York and Paris life.

MARCH 31, 1951

Work again. Very nervous (these *klaxons*!) yesterday. We went to the montagne Sainte-Geneviève this evening. Danced with N. [Natica] & M. [Maria] & we played kissing games with telephone-book pages. Very pleasant and exciting, uselessly. Maria is a charming *ivrogne*.

4/3/51

The agreeableness of foreign countries is very much like the common anodyne of escaping, particularly suited to the alcoholic temperament. Look at E.A. Look at myself, content in a Paris hotel room, where I've been working happily for two weeks. With an income to ensure inner (outer!) security, what better life? Perpetual escape, plus changes of friends, plus the semblance of a productive and even adventurous life, and then the remoteness: whoever never knew us well will never ever really know how really well or ill we are faring. The nomadic element, of course, suffices to placate the natural restlessness and panic of this age.

APRIL 5, 1951

[F]Date with Jeannot, which I canceled because I wanted to be with N. & M. at Sides. After, we (M. & N. & I) went down to the street, where we sang. Finally to Montmartre, to a bistro where Natica invited the prostitutes to eat onion soup. And Jeannot? I'm ashamed.[FF]

APRIL 7, 1951

[F]Practically sick—travel, any kind of travel, always gives me constipation or diarrhea, foot pain, headaches. (My eyes are always swollen.) I am tired. And dirty. And one must always remain polite, which I find difficult.[FF]

APRIL 8, 1951

In the worst possible physical health. Overeating and what can one do? Ah, to run along the rocks and lunch on a pear and a glass of milk! I am not Louis XIV.

APRIL 8, 1951

Lyon—breakfast served by a lovely old lady, most gracious in the fine French manner the tourist never sees. Everything elegant and nothing convenient, with the serviette under the *sous-coupe* [saucer], and nothing but the knees to put it on. I caught the 2:40 train for Marseille. Lily was there to meet me. How sweet she is. Jeannot was not at the station

(I think he's a bit sore). The house overwhelms one with the old odor of *famille*—well-cared-for establishment, but tremendously cute.

APRIL 17, 1951

Two hours' sleep & I catch the 6:05 train from Marseille. Wonderful going through Cannes, Juan-les-Pins, Nice. Rome at 11:30—midnight, & Natalia [Danesi Murray] there to meet me. How nice of her!! We had coffee, etc. Then I bedded down in Mediterraneo near the station.

APRIL 18, 1951

Lunch with Natalia *chez elle*. Splendid morning. Now & again I am able to live expansively, to feel expansive, with nothing & no one to do it for. Then I am happy, or happier than otherwise.

APRIL 19, 1951

Princess Elizabeth & [Prince] Philip back in town, and across the street tonight. Traffic bottlenecked & everyone angry & bewildered. Have in mind to do a few pieces as travel diary for [Fort Worth] *Star-Telegram*, if they wish it. News from America: *Strangers* nominated for the Edgar[*] to be awarded 27th April. Along with 5 other men's books. Visited Keats & Shelley memorial chambers next to Piazza di Spagna. Very touching indeed. Prompted me to write a poem on Keats' death.

APRIL 22, 1951

Up early to be on time for N. [Natalia] Murray. We drove to Naples & caught the 4:30 boat to Capri. The boat is new but how it all reminds me of Kathryn! How much we managed to crowd into those 24 hours! Swimming, martinis in the piazza, the Grotta Azzurra—and all the hundreds of views and scenes that revoke those moments!

APRIL 25, 1951

Returned to Rome. Haven't yet begun that relaxation which I still need. Time to think. I'll plan my itinerary later.

APRIL 28, 1951

Letter from Margot. I didn't win the Edgar, an enclosed letter from the Mystery Writers' secretary informs me. [Thomas Walsh's] *Nightmare in Manhattan* won it. Margot writes Harper still delays the book [*The Price*

---

[*] A reference to the Edgar Allan Poe Award, also known as the Mystery Writers of America Award.

of Salt], which makes me somewhat anxious. Janet [Flanner] left this PM. How like a schmuck I feel in comparison to her—and in accordance with my perverse nature, I am immediately better (more open in every way) as soon as she is gone, while all I should have liked to do was please her, naturally (I don't mean I emotionally cared) when she was here!

4/30/51

Roman streets: the handsome, tall men, two cavalry men strolling along in handsome black boots, fuchsia or purple striped trousers, double striped, riding crops. And the poor, nearly barefoot woman scurrying by with her baby wrapped in a holey shawl. This is a man's country. Roman hotels: the peculiar homo sapiens who latch onto solitary women in hotels, the weepy, semi degenerates from good families. Pudgy handed, soft, his face oval, long and plump, soft brown eyes. A habit of pawing. Will not listen to excuses, when he wants you to come to his house at 1:00 A.M. "Just for half an hour—" of course. And he has another roly-poly bachelor with him. Skim: the lonely, serious, inferiority ridden photographer. Cesare who can efface himself in five seconds in others' company. Small, timid, balding, a prince of a fellow actually, and a good photographer. Rome by night: moonlight on the gray-white side of a church steeple. Luminous, incomparable with anything else. It is itself, a Roman church in the moonlight.

4/30/51

When the intellect is at peace with the heart, then one should get out of bed in the early morning and write (create) with the night's dreams still in one's head like wraiths of smoke, before one has dispelled them all by the first word to another human being.

MAY 2, 1951

Went to Tivoli on my own. Villa d'Este, which I didn't care for so much as Hadrian's Villa. I met a pleasant bachelor, whose ambition is to own a ranch in Texas. He flies to U.S.A. tomorrow for a week, unfortunately. The kind of man I should marry, if I ever do: an ordinary bachelor, aged 45, intelligent technically but not romantically, a real American.

5/4/51

Rome: the shortest distance between two points is never a straight line. One always describes an arc. It is how the streets are made, how the statues are made, in Rome: Is the Roman character. Or rather, the Italian.

MAY 5, 1951

Letter from Mother, telling how she's bursting with pride of me. I can see her down there amid all the clucking Florida hens, showing them the big spread of *Strangers* with my photo and script of the play, which has just come out in [a] movie magazine. She's dumb enough to say: "Take care of yourself—you are not all yours, you know." However, I did write her this evening. And sent her a check—as this damned insurance thing has turned up again.

5/5/51

How many times can the heart renew itself? Six, seven, eight? Twenty? I have been five or six people in thirty years. The process is a mental one, the mind has an age like the body. The mind's life span is about a thousand years. The heart lives on hope and confidence. Melancholy and despair are its death. But one must die completely in the heart to be reborn.

5/5/51

The inflections—every language has a different inflection in its questions. The Italian, the English, the New Yorker, the Texan. I've not heard the Germans in ordinary parlance, but I imagine they question like a statement.

5/6/51

An ephemeral thought in Rome: I have lived a lot in my thirty years. In America, even a month ago, I thought I hadn't. I have been supremely happy and unhappy, and done a fair amount of traveling, and have accomplished a fair amount. All in all, I don't think Fate is holding back.

MAY 6, 1951

Worked, happily, in the sun. Made a date with Sybille Bedford[*] & her smooth-faced friend, Evelyn Keyes, I believe. It might have been pleasant, though Sybille is difficult (veddy English) but Tommy Peter Tompkins[†] came along, and English wife. Only Ed Androvik was a regular guy, turned up by accident. We plan to drive to Florence together Wednesday.

---

[*] Sybille Bedford (1911–2006), German-born English journalist and writer.
[†] Possibly Peter Tompkins (1919–2007), American journalist, best-selling author, and former World War II undercover agent in Italy.

MAY 7, 1951

Natalia's mother Ester Danesi has the Bompiani contract [for *Strangers on a Train*] at last! Finished finishing my story. Christ, I can write, but when I am done, I need an editor! Tonight with Grant & the beautiful Deidre. Margutta Tavern. We drank lots of wine & I gave her my Vallauris necklace. And might have made a pass at her, I know, but I didn't. Instead took Grant home with me. Better than I expected, but in the morning, I am uncomfortable and ashamed & feel unnatural.

MAY 10, 1951

Left for Florence. Arrived in the rain. Berchielli Hotel room—small, no hot water, but I am rather content. I am quite alone in Florence.

MAY 12, 1951

Took the evening train to Venice.

MAY 13, 1951

My room has a delightful view. I made a sketch from it.
    Lui Salm does not answer her bell!

MAY 15, 1951

At last Lui called. Was delighted to see them. Ruth Yorck invited me chez Lui to sleep. She has a cat. How wonderful in Europe to have friends! Lui is an angel, but Ruth bitches [at] me—à la Constable.

5/15/51

It is not age in the sense of an unknown future that is so terrifying. It is the people in the past that we ourselves have been and left behind and do not know any longer.

MAY 17, 1951

The filling I lost en route to Capri has at last sent me to a dentist. My life, my destiny, my hell. Lui & Ruth are sweet & sympathetic, and it isn't bad, having a drink at Harry's Bar and in our sloppy dirty clothes, feeling quite elegant. Cocktails with Peggy Guggenheim,* Somerset Maugham attending. Short, stutters, extremely polite. We did not talk

---

* Peggy Guggenheim moved back to Venice from New York in 1947. From 1951 on, Guggenheim opened her home—the Palazzo Venier dei Leoni—and art collection to the public in summer.

about writing. Evening with Rino, who does not suggest an affair, but only tearfully swears eternal love!

MAY 18, 1951

We leave for Austria in Lui's big service car. Taxi is a gondola to the pier where we load up.

MAY 20, 1951

We are in Dobbiaco, where we say goodbye to Lui. Tyrol Tracht. And the inn very clean & German in atmosphere. Ruth & I caught the train to Innsbruck. We got there about 6 PM. We saw a fair of peasant dancing. And I became ill on Würste [sausages], Bier [beer] & Nürnberger-Lebkuchen [Nuremberg gingerbread].

MAY 21, 1951

Arrived this AM in Munich. I liked it instantly. A big station restaurant where I devoured breakfast at 6 AM. The pension built on three upper floors of remodeled building. Munich shockingly filled with bombed-out buildings. Ruth is very interested because I am buying a car. But she is too unpleasant to be invited—anywhere.

MAY 24, 1951

Called on Jo*—Met Wolf [Wolfgang Hildesheimer] again, who invited me to Ambach [on Starnberger See]. ᴳHe is very hospitable, amusing, makes outstanding coffee. Talked about life—the way I can only talk to people like Cornell, Lil, Rolf.ᴳᴳ

MAY 30, 1951

ᴳStill working, and very well. Another weekend at Wolf's soon. I like him very much. He is generous, smart, funny, and all-around nice. Strange that I like him better than I ever did Marc. Harper still waiting with their decision about the second novel [*The Price of Salt*]—which makes me terribly nervous. Lunch and dinner with Ursula.† Always nice. We have a date planned for tomorrow, too. I change quickly. I grow older, wiser, and so on.ᴳᴳ

---

* Pat's old friend from the early 1940s in New York.
† A German princess and friend of Ruth Yorck's.

JUNE 5, 1951

The day of the alarming letter from Rolf. He sounds on the brink of suicide. I wrote him immediately—as best I could. But this German weltschmerz and negativity is so hard to deal with! I felt very neurotic (something brewing), bought Steinberger [schnapps] & drank a good bit with Ursula.

6/6/51

^GMunich.^{GG} 3:30 A.M. Palest blue-white out the window. I cannot sleep tonight. A woman is airing a white dog, slowly, on a distant corner. Is she up late or early? Is this night or day? The birds are twittering. How long they will have to wait before I share my breakfast with them. For the first time, I examine the pictures on my pension room walls. A silhouette group of man, woman, and pedestal with a rooster on it. Biedermeier period, made of lace bits and black paper. I feel as isolated from my friends sleeping across the street, a few blocks away, as if I or they were dead, removed to another earth. This is Germany. In the silence without languages, it might be Ohio, Southern Virginia, or England.

JUNE 6, 1951

The day of the rejection from Harper. Went to Siegestor actually to see Ruth, & found letters from Margot, Janet W. in Paris, Kathryn in England, Mrs. Webster. Harper reports not enough enthusiasm from the editorial board, that I probably can't do the book because I am too close to the subject, haven't the "mature approach." Margot's comment: she is sure Joan K. [Kahn] wasted 6 weeks telling me this. Is sure Frank MacGregor & Canfield put the ban on it. And has submitted it to Coward-McCann. Her letter was of the 22 May. She keeps writing to Rome! It doesn't depress me in the least as I feel quite refreshed now! Sent off: "Party at Bony's" to Margot this AM. Laid out another story and also the radio piece, jottings. And contemplate buying a car. Also sent for $1000 from my bank. All derring-do. How is that for positive reaction? Because logically I see no reason to be downcast.

JUNE 14, 1951

To the Odenwald—A small train to the wonderful village Wolf knows. Good food. Honeymoon atmosphere. Wolf says he wishes I'd fall in love with him, but is sufficiently wise to know I won't.

JUNE 15, 1951

Sherry and gins. I work on my snail story.

JUNE 23, 1951

After much trudging found thru Happy Glöckner a BMW, which I
bought for 1800 marks. Red seats, 4 passenger, belonged formerly to
Wilfried Seyferth,* the actor.

JUNE 24, 1951

Wolf invited Ursula & me to Ambach this weekend. I came on Friday,
with Alfred Neven DuMont,† the handsome young man, grandson of
Lenbach, whom Wolf knows. He is vague, vaguely conceited. Showed
me his home in Starnberg, very modestly, though his air of success-with-
women is to me not attractive and I don't think to most women. I was
not persuaded to stay overnight, but caught the evening bus to Ambach,
with typewriter.

JUNE 25, 1951

Returned to Munich to the good news Coward-McCann has taken
my book [*The Price of Salt*], with compliments on it. $500 to come on
delivery.

JUNE 30, 1951

Cocktails *chez moi*, Ursula & Jack [Matcha].‡ Was to dine with J.M. but
Ursula wheedled herself into invitation. Got very drunk (she is greedy
where the bottle is concerned) and accompanied us, then walked out of
the Siegestor. Jack and I went on to Haus der Kunst for dancing. And
coffee. I enjoyed this conventional American evening for a change.

JULY 3, 1951

More struggle with ᴳthe police,ᴳᴳ licenses, incredible trudging from
bureau to bureau. I am not "*gemeldet*"—registered. So nothing can be
accomplished. If I were only a U.S.-employed citizen, I could do it all so
easily: But I must get a license thru German driving schools.

---

* In 1951 Wilfried Seyferth headed to Hollywood after a stint at the theater in Munich. In Hollywood,
he was cast in the war movie *Decision Before Dawn*.
† Alfred Franz August Neven DuMont (1927–2015), German publisher, and nephew of the painter Franz
von Lenbach.
‡ An American journalist and writer Pat knew from the United States and chanced to run into in Munich
a few days before.

JULY 4, 1951

Tonight I felt fat, old, I heard my heart and felt mortal as mortal can
be. It startled me so, I had a hard time getting to sleep. I was alone, a
physical body that one day would run down and die and be buried. So
I thought. It was dreadful. And unforgettable. Thirty—what a turning
point. I remember Natalia's saying in Capri: "Thirty? You don't begin to
live until you are 30." Tonight. My movie opened, I believe.

JULY 11, 1951

Up at 9:30, worked until 8—then with typewriter—All over again. Hope
never dies, nor my perseverance, thank God.

JULY 12, 1951

Inquiries in the village re rooms finally netting something. But tonight
in Ambach, I learn I can get a room at Bierbichler's. 2.50 D.M. per day! I
am so happy about it.

JULY 13, 1951

Slept at Jack's. Up and out at 7 with loot of Nescafé, cigarettes, and
liquor, 2 Gordon Gins. An hour late for Wolfratshausen driving school,
and I walked back to Ambach. Typical also of the general hell, physical hardship of this license business. A trudge next to Holzhausen for
another signature, then to Wolfratshausen for another signature, show
them to Führmann the teacher, get something from him, take it to the
police, and at last hand in the paper with the two photographs. Appropriately I am reading a book called *Is Germany Incurable?* by one Brick-
ner. The paranoid complex, the military rigmarole, etc. Collectively they
behave like the individual paranoid. There is something in it. Undoubtedly the Germans have an inexplicable temperament to the rest of the
world. It is not inexplicable to the psychoanalyst.

JULY 14, 1951

Big Sommerfest this evening at Wedekinds,* which I found more boring
than not. Germans are fond of necking, heavy dancing. Since the war,
Wolf says, more promiscuous behavior on the part of husbands and
wives. Home at 3:30.

---

* Probably at the Ambach home of Pamela Wedekind (1906–1986), daughter of writer Frank Wedekind
and actress Tilly Newes, a German actress and singer, as well as the literary translator of Stendhal and
Marcel Pagnol. A childhood friend of Erika and Klaus Mann's, she was engaged to the latter in the
1920s.

7/14/51

I refuse and shall refuse to consider myself lucky, just as in my youth
I refused to consider myself unlucky. (Note after attending a German
party in Bavaria.)

The same American boredom, in me, manifests itself after a while.
The same anguish. The same circumstances, the same misfortune,
which can never be remedied. I stagger home in the dark at three in the
morning. My mother once said, one day your worldly success will turn
to ashes in the mouth. This isn't so, because I shall give it away beforehand. The time is approaching, but I have already offered. Even if it is
not accepted, I shall not have lost. The tides have turned for me, I no
longer float on the rushing tide of youth. I grow older and uglier. The
inward part is being perfected. (It'll never be perfect, at best, and there's
the pity. Because with a woman it could be perfect.) Neither shall I ever
be strong in a tough, financial, practical sense. I have taken my measure.
It is five feet six and one half inches, never to be higher. This year I am at
my most commercial. It strikes some people as shocking, whom I do not
wish to shock. They strike me as shocking in other ways, but mostly—I
envy everyone I meet because he has not only someone to love him but
someone he loves. The forest of no's is springing up again. I shall combat
it with every yes, every gift, every gesture positive, generous, and self-
abandoning that I possess.

7/19/51

The danger of the celibate. The danger of disaster. He lives for himself
alone, must be his own spur, his own inspiration, even his own goal. It's
so difficult, and so inhuman, it's so easy to work for someone one loves.
It's so easy to love.

JULY 22, 1951

Quite suddenly I age: not taking exercise regularly, not writing in any
diary regularly. Accepting responsibility for a car, being hospitable
with nothing, not watching my diet, not counting my money. Being
infinitely patient about fate. Oh, it's all to the good!—And not falling
in love and being patient, patient, patient. And in general optimistic.
That is all to age.

JULY 23, 1951

Should like to call my book "The Giant Step" but Margot says "It
doesn't hit me hard." Oh hell. Soon it'll be over, and I shall be able to

think about the next. The next will be much shorter. Left *Strangers* at Piper Verlag [publishing house] on Georgenstrasse, and then visited Helena [for a] moment. A curious premonition she would fall in my hands if I should make an effort. But I am so tired of rebuttals. And even now, if I should fall in love, it would be such a thoughtful logical process, like walking instead of flying.

7/26/51

Thomas Wolfe often was attracted to Jewish women. I can go down the list of my friends, the Jews are always more generous than the gentile, there is not one gentile to measure up to them. It is a neurotic generosity, perhaps, they do not on any count want to be considered stingy. But it suffices. It is dependable and therefore true. On what other impulse or character trait can we depend so safely in these times as on the neurotic?

7/27/51

I think I should make a serious effort at psychoanalyzing my relationship with my father [Bernard Plangman]. Something certainly tremendous is there. And I have buried it under total neutrality of attitude, under ten feet of cold ashes, dull as a roadbed. Psychoanalyze him, of course, as well.

JULY 27, 1951

Troubled by toothache & fear it may be the crown again. God help me, no. Also—psychologically correlative—troubled about finances. A thousand dollars have melted like butter in the sun here in Germany. I am going over my novel with that fine-toothed comb, retyping whole pages to add a sentence, which generally contributes in an analytical or introspective way. O Christ—what a book for difficulties! So much has to be tortured out of me instead of flowing.

JULY 28, 1951

Very restless. Difficult to keep the social relations I'd like to have. The language etc. Walked, swam with Wolf. He treats me with customary courtesy, no more. And troubled also by amorous desires, naturally, after all this time. (How long since those wonderful mornings with Maria in London! My salutation, my respects to her!) And because, too, this intellectual labor is over. (Soon, I shall plunge into another. Probably no interlude, amorous, between.)

7/28/51

Ginnie—at exactly the same period, in the writing and finishing of a book—I must write again "Ginnie." How little we actually know of each other. Ginnie-and-I—that is two different people from ourselves, not dead but forever unreachable. (How little she knows now, that I sit here in Germany tonight, thinking of her!) The physical desire that so tortured me in 1948 in Texas, when I wrote, has almost vanished, that is the senseless longing. She is an age, a time, a world ^Ggone by.^{GG} She is more than a person, she is a piece of time, which is a piece of life, Ginnie a tremendous piece in my life. Because of when and where she stands in me, she will never have a rival. That is a comforting thought to a lover, time is always presenting us with new lovers that dim the others, and overlap some of their virtues, and this will never happen with Ginnie. Absolute as my youth is she.

AUGUST 1, 1951

I make great progress driving. Worst will be the oral part of the exam.

8/2/51

Alfred [Neven DuMont]'s cousin. Wolf goes to greet her, having seen her through the open window, as she comes into the room. She is tall, smiling, shortish brownish hair. As soon as I see her, I think of Ginnie, and I am lost. The same forehead that sinks in above strong brows. Even the same arched short nose (though Ginnie's was broken), the same clean full lips that I cannot look at without wanting to kiss, passionately, and knowing I cannot, my first reaction, almost, is that I must not see this girl again if I can help it. I should like to leave just after dinner, but rather than be a victim of my self-pity, I stay on till the end, which is after a swim and more Kirschwasser. Has she any inkling how much I should like to make love to her? I think of Fitzgerald, going right up to Zelda, and wish a thousand times that I could. O my Christ, then what am I working for and what have I achieved? Merely to be able to offer such a girl my American cigarettes, my American money in the form of a *Schnaps*. And to be here in Germany and meet her and know she will marry and go to bed someday with a young German who does not consider her particularly different from dozens of other girls, who might have borne him children, and she will bear him children. To me she is so beautiful, Helen of Troy. To others? Merely attractive, perhaps. How many others?

8/3/51

I want to break every "novel" rule in the book. I have only two criteria for a novel: it must have a definite idea behind it, precise and evident; it must be readable, so readable the reader doesn't want to put it down even once. I don't know but that I set the second criterion higher than the first.

AUGUST 5, 1951

Almost no sleep, due to toothache. Christ, two to come out! O God, life sometimes—but even this doesn't even dampen my fantastic good spirits these days. It's the philosophical asset—the shedding of possessions. Tonight tried to finish (and did) "The Laurel on the Siegestor." It will be good.

AUGUST 8, 1951

I had gin at Jack's & with Cecil, Tessa, we finished the bottle. Tessa gazes at me with love in the surface of her eyes, and indeed it was a curious evening. Tessa & all of us pleasantly high. Cecil gaily invited me and Tessa to come to his house in Harlaching to spend the night. His house is a mansion, delicious comfort, and Tessa was happy as a child in the hot bath. By heart-shattering thumps and jumps we came closer & closer, until Cecil said he'd have to billet us two together. And having held hands so pleasantly in the car, it was quite easy to continue. We made love quite passionately—she with no inhibitions whatever, though she says I am the first woman. (No reason for her to lie but I doubt the truth of this.) She likes me because I am ⸢so slim.⸣ She bites my lips, she is full and strong and straight and easily aroused. But we were both a little too tired (or tight) for the climax. Ironic!—that I have consciously been knocking myself out physically lately (I was exhausted) because I've no sex life, and when it comes suddenly, there I am, incapable!

AUGUST 10, 1951

Wrote seven letters—including a long one to Piper [Verlag] with synopses of my second and third novels. Which incidentally inspired me to get the title for the second: *The Price of Salt* which I love and think is it.

AUGUST 10, 1951

Wonderful letter from Lil Picard, completely reconciled after my nice letter from Germany. She tells me interesting news of my movie on Ocean Beach. Dinner with Wolf and too stimulating conversation about everything and about pornographic book we plan to write together. To be published in English in France by Obelisc, Paris.*

AUGUST II, 1951

Ended my book and it is ready to pack. Packed suitcase for Munich & decided to give up German license. Wrote letters. Schnapps. I think of Tessa the whole time, of tomorrow's interesting encounters. Wolf asked me, when I mentioned Munich adventure, didn't I sleep with her and I admitted it. Says it has done me much good, made me gayer, and wishes something "nice" would happen to him! Him with half the beds in Ambach open to him! I have never felt so (dangerously) alive at all pores as in these last days. One cannot live long at such a rate, and yet, I think Fitzgerald & Wolfe lived so all their lives (about 40 years on the average!). I am filled with ideas, ambitions, and feel generally at the top of my powers. As for the emotional life, an artist does not want anything more confining or definite. I may as well face it.

8/15/51

Munich—Walking to Jack's in the evening, five blocks away, I pass a delightful vaguely hexagonal park, Possartplatz,† weeping willows, with the moon caught in them at night, or a streetlamp: like light in a woman's hair, revealing the strands, blond, thin and straight, that beautiful young green. I look up at the round moon sailing behind the bruised blue-black clouds—and my heart is young. I feel all my talents stirring. I am alive! (O this trip!)

AUGUST 17, 1951

Munich cannot be called lucky for me, though I have been so happy here, in Ambach, too. But every undertaking seems doomed to failure, and if Piper rejects—that will really be a blow.

AUGUST 20, 1951

Jo [P.] is very poised, has that inimitable, amiable look of having come through a good love affair (however bad the end) and having learned how to enjoy the sensual things of life, having been happy, and I know she is still happy. My inquisitive (and isn't it rather objective than subjective?)

---

* The common book project of Wolfgang Hildesheimer and Patricia Highsmith was unfortunately never realized.
† Today's Shakespeareplatz, in München-Bogenhausen.

brain turns over—could I really love her? My objectives are different from the insubstantial things I used to love. Shan't I be quite another person and love the simpler, reliable, plainer person? I honestly think I shall be. Jo & I went to the Kasbah. A delightful meal. Jo breathes not a word of Ellen Hill, except "She's not speaking to me, but I'm speaking to her—"

I asked Jo, more or less, to stay with me, which she did, gradually but unhesitatingly. If Jo would talk—for I am curious whether she has someone, or is starved (she could be) or how much she likes me. "You're not ready for me yet," she murmured as I lay in her lap. The old Jo. We had a lovely night. Jo is terrific. Intense like me when I'm in love (cf. Ginnie!) and with wonderful strong, neat, sensuous hands.

AUGUST 22, 1951

Had to move. Went to Jo's with help of her driver. A splendid pension room, hot water, beds, and a lovely day. Looked for work and then met Jo 6:30 at the Casa Italiana, where rather *schmuck* [smart] and discriminating people go. To the theater. Cocteau's *The Typewriter*, with Jo, then a bowl of soup at the Siegesgarten. This is the kind of evening (and life) of which I dreamed in college—and in a very F. Scott Fitzgerald kind of way: Europe, a girl, money, leisure, a car. Now I've had one night of it, after twelve years. Jo is primarily so serious, un-fantasied, we have a hard time talking. But we have the physical thing.

8/25/51

Why writers drink: they must change their identities a million times in their writing. This is tiring, but drinking does it automatically for them. One moment they are a king, the next a murderer, a jaded dilettante, a passionate and forsaken lover; other people actually prefer to stay the same person, stay on the same plane, all the time. (This of all the psychological intricacies of the human species is the hardest for an artist to understand.)

AUGUST 29, 1951

Jo again suggested to me: "Why don't you call up Ellen?" I did. We have a date for Sunday at 10 to drive. Ellen inquired carefully whether I preferred rococo to baroque castles.

8/31/51

As to plot: to what end is individual man tending? What does he want or aim for? To leave his son with a better established business than his father left him? To die wealthy? To enjoy life as soon as possible, and as much as possible? To win the love of a certain woman? To acquire fame as a scientist? A writer? A musical comedy singer? To visit every country in the world? (No, that passes.) To understand the world as a philosopher? Most people in my book have forgotten, gradually and in the abrasive rush of time, the sharp pricking edges, the arresting colors, of their original ambitions. Their ambitions are like old lost loves, pricking them to dull attention in the middle of a drink, of a conversation, with a dulled recognition. "That is mine," they realize suddenly, as they would think on seeing a photograph of the girl they once slept with: "She was mine once!" To make a plot of individual objectives and to see them lost and forgotten, that is logically the plot of *The Sleepless Night*. Carry the reader on as the ambitions carry the characters on for certain periods of time. Then simple life takes over.

SEPTEMBER 2, 1951

Ellen at 10. We drove to Tegernsee, had coffee & wine before lunch— which was the first moment it stopped being sticky. She is small, efficient looking, well-groomed, sharp, rather humorless, very polite. Conclusion: mildly attractive. We stopped at Jack's, who had invited us for a drink. I had changed to slacks, to annoy Jack, & for my own pleasure. Pleasant cocktail hour discussing the occupation, Ellen invited me to come to meet her friend, but I preferred to stay where Tessa was, drinking martinis, & asked Ellen if she could come back, or I join her later. At Ann's, whom Tessa calls "Harmless Herbert." They went out to buy gin—& I tried looking for them when they didn't return for an hour. And meanwhile Ellen had called, and she was coming for me. By that time I was somewhat tight, and lying on Tessa's voluptuous shoulder, after tiring myself out standing on my head and doing flips for her amusement.

SEPTEMBER 4, 1951

Went to Haus der Kunst—after ^Gputting on more makeup^{GG} than ever I've done. Apparently my unconscious knew why. Found Alan & Ellen in a corner of the inner bar where I'd never been before. Alan, a genial middle-aged pansy, couldn't have been nicer. We told funny stories (Ellen's somberness inspires me). Then more drunk than sober, back to Ellen's for something, then on to dinner at Kasbah, which she hated: empty, a spooky oriental 3-piece band, and a peregrinating parrot, who chews my forefinger. Ellen & I argue or misunderstand in all of our conversations. And perhaps I was too tight to know we were falling in love. Anyway we have, we did. We went back to her apartment to listen to poetry & music program which was excellent. I asked her to sit with me on the couch, I held her hands that felt like Ginnie's, and her body, too, and soon she asked me to come to bed. Or would I rather go home? I stayed. Ah, she is much like Ginnie. Tonight was only wonderful sensation—blotting out everyone who's been between Ginnie and her—

SEPTEMBER 5, 1951

Quite to my surprise Ellen did something nice & unexpected. Took off the whole day from the office. Breakfast was fun, she in a sleek robe, and most of the time we lay on the couch, happy and wordless. I felt I had known her at least 6 months and was very much in love. We drove to Tegernsee, lunched, lay on the grass in the sun beside the lake. It was Europe as Europe is supposed to be, and so few individuals find. Besides, I have found a love. We called on her mother, ill in a rest home here, then on to Munich where I made dinner *chez elle*. Champagne. Stories of my past. To bed. "I'm very much in love with you," she said. "We're very different. Do you think that matters?" I said, "I like it." She is that rare combination—passionate when we are alone, and rather icy when she is up and working.

9/8/51

Sensations: for about ten minutes this morning when I woke up, I didn't remember. Suddenly I did, and it was like an electric current discharging itself inside me, holding me for one instant in some realm not of the earth, and I came shuddering down again. I worry that I've said too much about some little matter that may be worrying her now. O the benevolence! O the beautiful world! O the generosity of the heart as I go walking down the street. My head is up and all men are my brothers. (The poet, the philosopher in me shake their wiser heads, but I am alive today, I am vaster.) How could it be? Isn't she like Titania charmed into loving the donkey? I imagine again and again that instant I shall see her, after these two days of separation, and draw her into my arms, imagine that sweet pain-pleasure, that shock of our touch, that miracle. I am not so young that it hasn't happened before—perhaps twice. But I am not so old I cannot wonder as if it had never happened before, why is it, how can it be, what made it, and will anything ever take it away? O not for months, maybe not forever. I don't care for explanations. This is something not of the intellect. Our intellects have so far not begun calling each other by their first names. Perhaps she is a mathematician. Perhaps I am a cobbler. Yet in possessing each other, we possess each other's intellects and wills also. It is no wonder I am for moments as terrified as I am happy. Thor has put into my hands bundles of lightning bolts, my own and hers. It is so difficult to tread both lightly and boldly. I remember her face, is that a bad sign? Her arms are like petals unfolding for me, I am trapped like a bee. I wonder if I am not hypnotizing her somehow by the force of my own will and the contagion of my own pleasure. If I should ever slip, will she not make up? There is much, much more to know in each other's minds. Will hers be a green field with trees? Some curious houses, and a place where once a home burned down, I hope I shall not have too many wastelands and ashes for her. I have many rivers and streams, blue and gray and green. One day we shall be lost for a while in each other's territory. We shall forget which land is whose.

SEPTEMBER 8, 1951

Terribly happy today. Bought candy for Ellen. I think of her all day. I am in love, but terrifically as I thought I could never be again, because I thought it was adolescent. Days ago Ellen asked me to go with her to Venice—or anywhere I'd pick—when her 2-weeks' leave starts Friday. Christ, it's all happened fast. And we trust each other totally, overnight This is why I came to Europe, why I stayed in Munich, why I shall stay in Europe. I can't sleep well and am losing weight. Can sleep best with her, of course.

SEPTEMBER 9, 1951

Wrote Mother yesterday. I do only about once a fortnight now. I am at last growing up. Ellen called at 5 instead of seven—and I am yet emotionally so weak that the unexpected turn of events threw me. I dressed in a mad rush, for she wanted to pick me up in 15 minutes. Eventually we dined at the Italian Cafe, and I drank much too much. A strain. Living is so difficult—reality so much less friendly even (in the face of the one we love!) than on paper.

SEPTEMBER 17, 1951

[Venice.] This noon in Harry's Bar (after morning shopping expeditions). Noisy, but immensely agreeable. Ellen drinks two Americanos, and is pleasantly high for an hour. And she prefers canapes to a real meal anytime. The painted, hard, sophisticated, wrinkled, bright, jaded faces of the Americans in Harry's! How sophisticated Ellen seems in all this, too—only because she knows Venice from a thousand times before, and knows faces and places of these Europeans, and who is a good lover and who is not. I am jealous, frequently, of her past girlfriends, and even men friends. There was, too, a Herbert in her life, the first man she was head over heels about at 21, and whom she did not succeed in marrying. She married the Frenchman Jean instead. Tonight I scarcely remember. Cocktails with Peggy Guggenheim: Sinbad, looking sickish, other guests. Peggy jaded, barely took in fact of my movie.

SEPTEMBER 21, 1951

[Cernobbio, Lake Como.] A passionate morning. And the scarf shop across the court of the Villa d'Este. Bought one for mother. I care nothing about money these days, not that I have any. But it is this hitherto unknown side of me that Ellen finds so attractive: impracticality, generosity, imagination, the poet, the dreamer, the child. And I am too inclined to enact a part, in all of it. This fact is to make the next few weeks difficult.

SEPTEMBER 22, 1951

We drove to Ascona. It's a quiet lake village, full of tourists, however, and attractive Italian and Swiss women in slacks. We adore the Espresso cafés with creme. Lunch at Lugano, my first coffee. I bought the *Companion* (for .65!) which has "Where to, Madame?" as the first story. With the movie, not bad publicity.

9/23/51

Ascona—snake show. Walking down the narrow Capri-like streets, innocent as the streets of a fishing village, I see a lighted doorway, a placard: *Esposizione*. Admission one franc twenty. Glass tanks, lighted, lizards, snakes, a man and woman, oddly ill-assorted, run the place. He is husky, Bavarian like, she is perhaps a lesbian, of about 50, sharp black eyes, graying hair, short cut, a shabby rayon blouse, feminine and meaningless on her sexless body. The man talks to me about snakes. I ask about the shriveled egg I see lying on the sand. The lizards bury themselves. In the tank of African snakes, there is a long slim green one, weaving like a wand though the twigs, climbing, poised like a baton, gliding bright pale green. GG"Yes, of course the little green one has a rather fast metabolism,"GG says the Bavarian man to his audience of five. Two German or Swiss women watch unmoved as another snake, also no more than an inch broad, swallows a live frog head first, choking a bit as the legs disappear, and feet disappear. The green snake I like is from India. Watching him I hear music, I feel the tempo of the slow steady jungle, and I want to go there. In the next cage, a snake is eating its cast-off skin, and the woman intervenes, pulling and pulling.

SEPTEMBER 24, 1951

Another day of doing nothing, scarcely even reading. We drink coffees, look in shops and bookshops, take naps and make love.

SEPTEMBER 27, 1951

We leave for Zurich, as the weather is still overcast. Rain in fact. The St. Gotthard pass most exciting and thrilling to me. As much as the Endless Caverns when I was a child. Zurich is very prim and bourgeois and opulent. Ellen goes insane over the shops here. We stay at Baur au Lac tonight at vast expense. I am a bit sated on luxury.

9/27/51

St. Gotthard pass. A long climb up the highway where rock mountains grow taller and taller, streaked with white frothy rivulets, the pure crystalline water of the Alps. It is raining, perhaps there is more water than usual, and the light makes the grass bright green, shading smoothly as a painter's gouache into darker green, houses bordered by neat brown wooden rail fences. The road begins to twist and turn. Some of the mountains are covered with clouds. The car whines up in second gear, first, second again. The road becomes the hard, well paved gray brick road of the pass. Napoleon marched here, horses, men, caissons. Signs warn of military maneuvers again by the road. The first fortification boxes appear. (The San Gottardo has never been defended, as Switzerland hasn't been in a war since it was fortified. But it's all mined, says my friend, they can blow it up in a second.) The rocks are gray, brownish, the road is long loops, climbing one above the other, steeply as if one were going upstairs. Soon we can hardly speak to each other, our ears are cracking and stopped up. I sit on the edge of the car seat. There is somehow a tremendous excitement—of height, of history, of space, of the cool unconcern of nature here, allowing man to conquer it with roads, to come all the way up and marvel and grow dizzy. We go up and up— when the mileage ends in 32, we shall be at the crest. 2400 meters. We go into a cloud. At the crest is [the] Ospezio, which the monks built in the eighteenth century.* A great lake made by a dam, and in front of it, a war monument to some Italian aviator, 1928, two eagles lifting on a rock and one below over the inscription.† It is cold and raining. We cannot see the mountains all around here, it is as if we were on a peak alone, in thin air, a little frightened, like the cars that cautiously begin to descend the road on the other side. Here the road is unpaved, for some engineering reason, and we must go slower & the rocks are greenish now, the brownish earth and grass speckled with rust-colored moss or grass, a few daisies. Cows with great beautiful buckles on their leather collars are grazing by the side of the road. We pass fifteen cows being herded, walking all at an even pace, and the rhythm of their bells—tin, or copper, or the heavy, beautifully cast, brilliantly ringing bells with engraved designs—sound like Scottish bag-pipes, like dozens of instruments, playing in tempo. Strong wet backed gray and brown cows. A shivering young sheep dog on a leash walks beside his master. Cars creep down through the fog that allows one to see only about ten feet ahead. At several curves the fence is knocked down. Do people simply get panicky here and forget to turn their wheels? It is endlessly down, down, toward Andermatt. Hospental comes before Andermatt; a tiny clean ski resort village. A glimpse from between narrow two houses on either side of the narrow street shows a rectangular bluff of green mountain beyond, a brown roofed house half way up the mountain, a tree, and sky. The arrows point the other way now: to San Gottardo, to St. Gotthard, beckoning the cars up, and the drivers look frightened as they pass us. The fog and rain are terrifying as night. I shall not forget the pillboxes set everywhere in the hills, square fortified doors, ready to open fire.

[Zurich.] Incredibly neat and clean, nothing like it have I seen except perhaps certain prosperous little towns in Connecticut. The lake on the right, as we go into the *Stadtmitte*. The lake narrows into the channel that crosses the city. Bahnhofstrasse is the fanciest street. American cars, beautifully kept streetcars, with everyone on them well dressed, not a shabby article of attire on anyone. Brand new cars that are washed every morning. The main street. Solid looking stones with thickly decorated windows. Spinning wheels displaying woolen materials, model stands

---

* It is unknown when the first chapel was constructed on the top of the pass. The hospice for travelers and pilgrims was enlarged in the fifteenth century, destroyed in 1799, and rebuilt in the nineteenth century by the canton of Ticino.
† A 1928 memorial for the Swiss pilot Adrien Guex, who in 1927 had an accident in the region caused by poor visibility.

with black silk skirts, sweaters, leather goods, shoes, a Cook's Tours the epitome of bourgeois respectability and smugness. No scrap of paper to litter the streets. Trees along the Limmat canal, street cars crossing the frequent plain bridges that are like continuations of the street merely. Yet behind this, cobbled old streets with overhanging widows, like Old England or France, or Germany. Bierstuben [tavern] windows full of flower boxes, and everywhere round stone fountains with a little human statue, spouting water, and bearing some inscription to the glory of Zurich.

We have reserved a hotel room, but for tomorrow, and because the hotel is filled up, the Swiss proprietor is completely unconcerned whether we return tomorrow, or have any other place to go tonight, charges us 20 centimes for making a phone call to another hotel to reserve a room. At the Baur au Lac we are not allowed to leave the car in the court-yard, though several other cars are there. A toothy, horse toothed man behind the desk—big, dark blue suited, the typical Swiss in the typical business—speaks in English to an American guest. The hotel room has electric buttons that release the door lock from the bed. The Select Cafe, on the corner of a little square, white curtained windows, modern archi-tecture. I go in and climb the stairs to the second floor. It is an intellec-tual café, students, the most unwashed of the Swiss populace, drinking coffee, reading newspapers. Men in unpressed trousers. What torch are they carrying these days? What do they believe in besides Harvey's the-ory of the circulation of the blood?*

SEPTEMBER 30, 1951

Packing to leave. I feel most indecisive, useless, vaguely guilty for not attending to social obligations here. I am not really content unless I am pulled at like something on a rubber band. Only with more social graces can I obviate this American habit of having to be doing something. I am about ready to go to Salzburg to stay and work.

OCTOBER 2, 1951

[Munich.] Tonight saw *Strangers* at McGraw Caserne. I am pleased in general, especially with Bruno, who held the movie together as he did the book. I missed the first 5 minutes, as Ellen & I were late. Jack M. was standing there—Ellen had given me strict instructions she

---

* The English physician William Harvey (1578–1657) is credited with discovering the system of blood circulation throughout the whole body.

would not dine anywhere with Jack & Tessa—as they are beneath her socially. There followed the stickiest moments of my life when Jack wanted to accompany us after the movie. I got no backing from Ellen, who accuses me mysteriously of wanting to dine with Jack & Tessa alone, etc. and other things I do not want. At last Jack joined us alone at the Schwarzwälder and all was pleasant. Though the experience had given me nervous indigestion, made me feel sweaty, utterly lost, without a wish in my head. Ellen can be so damned unpleasant, especially her voice—and I am ashamed before Jack, who might be a proletarian, but who is still a real guy. "The minute something goes wrong, you take to the bottle," Ellen accuses me (unjustly—but if anyone ever did drive me to drink, it's she!).

OCTOBER 3, 1951

Jo says, "Ellen was born old. Some day you'll just get awfully fed up and walk out—because it isn't worth it. Everybody does that." I narrated our tours to Jo. And in general left her with the impression, calculated, that Ellen & I shall not be together very much longer. I must get away to work, etc. and cannot work in Munich, or near Ellen. Ellen is pleased enough with this.

10/4/51

Autumns in the heart, and old tragedy, tears, the echo of pain and the hollow echo of a cry aloud in the midst of weeping. I stared at her until I no longer knew her or her name, knew only her form and her bones and the shadows at the sockets of her eyes, and then I began to draw, while the radio played a Chopin étude. Oh how beautifully my pen behaved! The autumn came swiftly, a rising shadow of night, telling me, one day you will no longer be with her, whom you love now, but your hand in drawing, your talent and your desire, your courage, your selflessness, your happiness when you draw, these will always be with you, be you seventy and toothless, poor and alone, but she? She under the light now—I can hear her breathing—she will be gone, and worse, almost forgotten. The tragic chorus chanted in my heart, and I followed the distant play closely, tears coming to my eyes.

OCTOBER 5, 1951

Packed for Salzburg, where we go this afternoon at 4:30. Very very happy. Lunch with Jo. Very nervous. She wants to give a wire-haired dachshund to Ellen, to compensate for Amor.

10/7/51

Salzburg—One looks out the hotel window onto a panorama of grayness at eight in the morning. The autumnal fog from the mountains lies thinly over the town, veiling the black roofs and towers, and making the distant stone castles and palaces pale as ghosts. There are no less than four spired towers in the direct line of vision toward the fortress—one with a clock, one with a gold spire ball and a needle-sharp spire, one the heavy-set Tyrolian style steeple that in the country is developed into an onion dome or a double onion dome. In the distance, the fortress lies atop its hill, long and gray, with small blind windows in a row. Trees spill down from its side into the city. Farther beyond, smoky blue mountains can barely be seen. There is the sound of the hooves of a pair of horses and a moving wagon turns into view in the square below. The fountain with the white marble horse and the elaborate balustrade enclosing the whole basin of water is still dripping audibly. The fruit merchants are opening their carts and arranging their apples, grapes, potatoes, peaches, and the long roots with the unrememberable name that the Austrians put into soup. Now the sun shines momentarily, gleaming first on the gold sphere of the church tower, along the ridge of a black roof, on the delicate green of a piece of forest; and then vanishes again.

OCTOBER 20, 1951

We lay in bed forever this morning. Why should we ever get up? We retire again after breakfast. We are the happiest people on earth. But we aren't on earth, either of us, ever, these days. No, not even Ellen, certainly not me. We talked of character—she can't make all mine out, she says. Perhaps she means, what kind of illogic do I have. She says she wonders how I survive, in the world, all alone. She means, I suppose, I can't remember figures, and I seem to trust everyone. On this, she drank a gin before getting out of bed to dress for dinner. Later, we went to Flora for brandy, for more talking. She said: she'd been worried this past week, because she thought she was a passing thing with me. Now she doesn't think so. How could she? I've never been so in love with anyone, not even, I think, Ginnie. (At last!) She brought mail from Margot: Coward-McCann like my book! I'm so glad! Also the chief salesman likes it, which is important. Occasionally, I think of a paragraph I want inserted. Perhaps I shall manage it. Damn it—the kind of book which keeps growing. Sweden also sends me a $200 check [for *Strangers on a Train*]. My finances, all in all, in better shape at this moment than I had anticipated.

OCTOBER 22, 1951

We have flowers, a radio, books—we have silence and peace, present and most of all future. (And I have the curse.) Breakfasted with Ellen at 7:15 AM. Depressed to see her go. I do enter another world when she leaves. Ellen said last night: "You and I are a marvelous combination. I know it. I've known it all along." (We are precisely the opposite, but extremely. Masculine and feminine, even, in precisely opposite respects also.) She is like a bowl full of magnolia petals, soft and white, shining and dusky, soft and sweet, I drown, yet can breathe, too. I can make her drunk when I make love to her. She says: "You're the best lover I've ever seen—heard of—read about." . . . and: "I didn't know you'd ever say a thing like that. I've thought it." She is so much happier this week. This is the best week.

OCTOBER 25, 1951

Tonight I am more content than I have been in years. I have everything I want. And am at peace with myself. I can honestly say, reckoning up, I've not been really happy, as I am now, for more than six months—adding various times together—in the past. The damn curse continues—the fifth day—stopping all day, coming on like a faucet at 5 PM. Terrifying.

OCTOBER 26, 1951

Ellen's letter. Beautiful, and a great deal on one page. (I remember Rosalind's letter—with a twinge of shame. I had no evaluation then.) " . . . know every hour that I love you and will never change." At all hours. Worked on in my notes [of *Sleepless Night*], a great sheet of yellow paper, with the characters, and general outline of chapters. But there will be no "chapters." There will be no quotation marks, no prose description or background work. Each person will be the style of it, and that will probably take experiment.

She came at 7:15. We are both still nervous but it's considerably better. And absolutely all I want when she is here. We have dinner, read mail—a letter from Ann S. says she has inherited $30,000 from a grandmother. We discuss finances—which are never far from Ellen's mind—and she says, "Don't you know I know what I've got? I'm not that stupid," meaning a non-financing artiste. But more often than I she says, "I love you. I absolutely adore you. You're exactly what I want."

OCTOBER 30, 1951

Began my book *Sleepless* [*Night*] this morning in a leisurely way. Page six. I am happy with it. But can tell little as yet. The style may change.

The difficulty to make it readable, with that appealing, understandable quality natural to me. Pray to God it will go, and with His help it will.

I long for word from Margot. Feel very dependent on her these days. Am most depressed this evening. I wonder why—because the first lines on paper of a new book are inevitably a fall from grace? Every book is perfect until one begins to write it.

NOVEMBER 5, 1951

Tired. Hitchcock is interested in new material, would pay my way to London if I had any new gimmick ideas to tell him.

11/15/51

Living alone, absolutely alone. Boredom doesn't happen. Nor loneliness in the usual sense. Only the tension, the tempo, the rhythm goes out— and that is enough. Life becomes a slack sail. I personally should not be among the best at staving off madness in solitude (if madness is to come in solitude). I'd thought that I would be. Perhaps I give too much thought to details. That is as bad as the love of freedom and the wide-open spaces, for the solitarily confined.

NOVEMBER 27, 1951

Dies Irae. Worked nervously all day. Ellen exhausted this evening, and once more sent me home. I should have loved merely to lie with her a while. So insecure am I, so absurdly hurt when I am not continually pampered. Dangerous discussions this evening about my messiness, my selfishness, etc. Forcing again at the only crack that can ever possibly split us. I quake as at the edge of an abyss, and at the same time always do all I can to darken the view, to crack the crack wider, by proposing action on the idea immediately.

11/30/51

This ferocious strife between people in love, this clash of arms between the placing of a clock upon the bed-table, when the other will not take his best suit out of his trunk and hang it: two people in love stare at each other across an abyss, bewildered as modern armies fighting with each other. (This balderdash! This meticulousness! This unreality, this selfishness, this grimness!) I will not stand it! Rather loneliness to the end of my life than this! I will not stand it, rather boredom and loneliness than this barbarity.

DECEMBER 1, 1951

Curious jealousy I have for the dachshund, because he is in love with Ellen, too, and manifests the same insecurity, need for constant reassurance. He will not eat unless she sits beside him. He insists on his portion of the bed. Tonight when we returned from seeing *The Idiot* he had torn up the room, brought clothes racks down to the floor, tattered a beautiful Xmas package I'd made for Ellen, and crapped on the floor. I was so enraged, I should have throttled the dog if he had torn up my manuscript, I am sure I'd have had his blood. He rather ruined our plans for this evening.

12/4/51

What a leap world literature would take, if everyone who writes a book were able to have ideal working conditions—a quiet room, regularity, freedom from anxiety. The writer's demands are so simple, yet the most difficult thing in the modern world to achieve is privacy, and the most expensive. Perhaps not one book in a thousand is written under ideal conditions, that is to say written at the writer's best. The world is full of writers writing in exhausted spare time in noisy uncomfortable corners of rooms, interrupting themselves to do work for others, etc., etc. and only the ones with burning conviction bring it off. In view of the psychological handicaps of the writers of this age, this ruthless survival of the sternest is not entirely fair, either.

DECEMBER 10, 1951

Ellen left in a foul mood, due to not sleeping & to my being inefficient, about opening a can of milk. (I am always inefficient & Ellen never loses an opportunity to tell me so.)

12/20/51

One attribute of mine is immeasurable—ingratitude. So profound, so sincere, that it militates most against myself. I cannot remember any of my past achievements, cannot take moral strength from any of my virtues or talents. One off day can make me forget not only the one who loves me and whom I love, but also that I have ever written a good line.

DECEMBER 24, 1951

Jack arrived at 12:45. Down with a cold. We celebrated Xmas this evening with champagne—my new white blouse from Salzburg—pâté cut by Ellen. A bit dismal due to Jack's cold, & consequent silence. Ellen's pencil broke its spring—and I on the other hand was overwhelmed with a plethora of presents. I'm not sure Ellen will like the ring well enough to wear it. She says it needs aging. I swear I shall make amends—get her a chain perhaps.

I was very sick after dinner—when Ellen lectured me on the bed about my absent-mindedness, & her feeling I am not with her due to absent answers, etc. She feels I am too much alone, and God knows it is true, & Salzburg has lasted much longer than I intended. 2 months solid on the book, whereas it shouldn't have been more than six weeks. And it is so difficult to defend myself—before Ellen's harangues which I always feel are camouflages for more grave complaints—because I work alone, apparently selfishly, self-centeredly, and for benefit of no one. The climax this evening when I returned at 12:45 from midnight Mass, and awakened her much later going into her bed. (I was hungry, far from sleep, but that's not the point.) She accused me bitterly of doing it every night of our acquaintance, and announced it or us must stop. Finally, that in Munich I must treat her as an ordinary friend, as I am getting much too absorbed in her.

DECEMBER 25, 1951

A most un-Christmas-y day. Ellen up early & left by electric light. I feel dismal; remorseful I did not please her more at Xmas, doubly remorseful that our experiences in bed lately, except for Friday night, have been merely quarrels, apologies, accusations of callous indifference (mine) to her biological needs of sleeping. She says she has steadily lost sleep since Sept. when she met me. Pattern-like, I make my habitual error of letting this throw me, and in a swamp of doubt, inferiority, remorse, disappointment—depression—tell her I fear I can't do any better, even with the best intentions, in Munich, & therefore it's safer for us both if I remain in Salzburg. This was last night. Ellen insists I come.

DECEMBER 26, 1951

The stores again closed. Amused myself today writing nine pages of a short story—about the man impersonating the missing son. But I am frightfully tired of this room, this existence—this solitude. My mind rusts in the conversation department. No doubt that is something of what is the matter. At the moment I am a prime example of the saying: All work & no play . . . Ellen has given me quantities—and qualities—a gray corduroy shirt, a compact, stockings, a pair of drinking glasses in a

leather container, a beautiful white silk blouse like Little Lord Fauntle-
roy's. This town is much less attractive to me than a cemetery when
the stores are closed. I dine alone downstairs, on nothing, and without
interest.

DECEMBER 31, 1951

Indifferent day. I am still unhappy—because of E.'s & my relations,
sleep badly and alone. Never have I had to beg anyone to sleep with me
& I don't intend to start. Doesn't she realize that? Tonight I blew up
& mentioned the drinking remark of last evening. She says first, "I'm
sorry." Then that I am exaggerating. I simply tell her she must be used
to addressing German underlings. She does not give me the dignity of
a dog. We saw *Minna von Barnhelm* [by Gotthold Ephraim Lessing] at
the Kammerspiele, excellent production, Seyferth also. Went in evening
clothes. I was still shaky & near tears. What a hole all this has put in our
relationship, and even patched, it will remain a weak spot. My mother
sends two slips & cold cereal–fruit cake much appreciated by Ellen.
Very attractive homesick-making box. Went to big New Year's Party.
The first New Year's I've spent with someone I cared about, now marred
by mutual repressions, defensiveness, etc. We are both tired, no doubt.
Home at 2:30 AM.

1952

IN MANY REGARDS, 1952 is a trying year for Pat: she cannot find the inner (or outer) calm and focus she needs to work, and the royalties from her books are just barely keeping her afloat. Most trying, however, is the roller coaster of emotions she feels for her lover Ellen Blumenthal Hill. The couple's relationship continues to be a strenuous one, characterized by volleyed accusations, incongruous lifestyles, and fundamentally different needs. Life is generally hectic as the two women rove about Europe, alternating between Munich and France, Italy and Switzerland, rarely spending more than a few weeks anywhere they go.

At the beginning of the year, Pat is still living in a modest hotel near Ellen's in the Schwabing neighborhood of Munich. They make love, then fight, only to make up again, each leaving the other by turns, yet neither able to let go entirely. Ellen's wire-haired dachshund named Henry drives a wedge between them—as does Pat's drinking. In mid-January, the couple drives to Paris in Ellen's tiny Fiat for the launch of the French translation of *Strangers on a Train*, *L'Inconnu du Nord-Express*. Pat is met with countless interview requests, enthusiastic critics, and flattering reviews comparing her to her literary hero, Dostoyevsky. Her French publishing house, Calmann-Lévy Éditeur, will remain a trusted partner for the rest of her life.

In May 1952, *The Price of Salt* is published by Coward-McCann in New York under the name Claire Morgan. Immediately following the hardcover publication, the paperback rights are sold, which provides some financial relief. In her diary, however, the author disparagingly describes the $6,500 she receives as an impressive fee for unimpressive writing.

Meanwhile, under less-than-ideal circumstances, Pat is doing what she can to finish novel number three, *The Sleepless Night*. Both of Pat's American publishers—Coward-McCann and Harper & Brothers—reject the ill-fated manuscript. An entire year's work, all for naught.

To make up for this significant financial setback, Pat starts writing short stories again, but her agent in New York struggles to find any takers. Pat writes travelogues, including a chronicle of a summer road trip she and Ellen took from Paris to the Côte d'Azur and an account of her solo stay at the Bartolini, a dilapidated *pensione* in Florence, in late autumn; these pieces are so laced with situational comedy that the reader could never guess at the author's financial straits and toxic love life. A planned collaboration with *Reader's Digest* falls through, and the ideas she sends Alfred Hitchcock, at his request, similarly founder.

Even so, Pat starts laying the groundwork for her fourth novel, *A Man Provoked* (later renamed *The Blunderer*). The story follows a man who wants to imitate an unsolved murder he reads about in the newspaper. His victim: his wife, whom he despises and who bears an uncanny resemblance to Ellen. Progress on the novel stagnates, however, as Pat lacks inspiration and Ellen can't stand the clack of the typewriter.

Two other pieces colored by her unhappy relationship with Ellen, written in close succession, are the short stories "Man's Best Friend" and "The Returnees." In the former, a man tries to kill himself to escape the scornful gaze of his German shepherd, an animal far superior to its master. The second story depicts the gradual deterioration of a couple's relationship; its setting in Munich and references to the anti-Semitism still common in Germany after the war make "The Returnees" another rare example of a Highsmith story with a contemporary historical-political backdrop.

By late October, Pat cannot stand the psychological warfare any longer and sets out for Florence on her own. Finally alone, she instantly pines for Ellen, curses her own fickleness, misses her mother, and feels homesick for America.

While in Positano, Pat steps onto the balcony of her hotel room one morning and in the distance spies a man in shorts and sandals walking along the beach, towel slung over his shoulder. He appears lost in thought, and there's something enigmatic and captivating about him. She never sees the man again, but those few minutes are all it takes to make him world-famous: he becomes the model for Tom Ripley, the antihero who will finally secure Patricia Highsmith's literary breakthrough. Pat doesn't record this moment in either her diary or any of the notebooks. Readers first learn of it in an essay from 1990 about the creation of the *Ripley* series.

JANUARY 1, 1952

Stayed at Ellen's as [Pension] Biederstein* is not ready. Took a walk with [Ellen's dog] Henry to Englischer Garten & got caught in hail & snowstorm—frightful.

JANUARY 5, 1952

Drove with Ellen this noon to Gmund, etc. to lunch with her mother. We got caught in a snowstorm, and lost control of the car trying to get up a hill. I'd gotten out. I & two other fellows had to hang onto Ellen's car to stop it while she got out. Another car hit the left door—600 DM's worth—and Henry was terrified. We arrived by train & taxi at 6 PM from this terrifying excursion. Even Ellen suggested a stiff drink. We had martinis—then went to bed. Which was very pleasant. And I spent the night as well. Unfortunately Ellen cannot sleep on the narrow bed & must go to the other room.

JANUARY 6, 1952

Jack [Matcha] called—Ellen was here at Biederstein with me. He invited us for this afternoon—to hear records. We did with pleasure, with Henry (carless) via 22 bus. Had a couple of fine martinis—Returned & made Ellen a brandy menthe drink to clear her proletarian stench away. I have more tolerance for such people, because I think they are better than nothing, in Munich where there is nothing.

JANUARY 7, 1952

I am tired & don't know if I shall finish my book [*Sleepless Night*] this month or not. News that Ellen's Italian will be of use, & that IRO† will resume in another form. So concerned is she with getting a new job, I am quite sure if one arose Majorca would go up in smoke. Fortunately one can't arise so soon. Anyway, I committed my usual atrocities in the kitchen: salad-oil spot on the cloth, a smell of burning onions—cooking onions, which 99 out of 100 would like, Ellen abhors. I fed the dog at the table. Neither did she like my lumberjack shirt for Kitzbühel where she evidently intends to dress me like a dummy. I brought her (always) such things as I am able on the German economy—candy, oil, florentines,

---

* A bed-and-breakfast in the direct vicinity of the Englischer Garten, a park in the Schwabing neighborhood.

† The United Nations' International Refugee Organization was founded in the aftermath of World War II and operated until 1952, when it was replaced by the UNHCR (United Nations High Commissioner for Refugees).

what else can I do? I walked out tonight, unable to stay any longer. I was
furious. And very tired.

JANUARY 8, 1952

Wrote E. a note, after cooling off, that I cannot bear such intense &
constant criticism from her. She came up this AM with my suitcase.
Thinks a hug will cure everything. She doesn't know me entirely. All
this resentment—and it will always be so, so until the end—is due not
to it per se as much as to Ellen's magnificent talent for saying the harsh,
the inhuman, the unhumanitarian, hence the cruel, excoriating phrase
at exactly the moments when it hurts. Her sentiment, even sensibility
(except on matters of cold politesse) emerges rarely. She keeps my letters.
Otherwise where she might be sentimental, she is brutal. Totally lacking
in genuine warmth, as manifested in such social circumstances as hospitality, pity for human weakness or stupidity or impulsiveness or trust or
short sightedness or abounding faith—in short, she has no pity for the
mistakes resulting from those spiritual strengths & weaknesses which
make the human human, and make the individual a man. Despite the
harsh scene today Ellen wanted to dine with Jack & me. I wriggled out,
infuriating Ellen. Tho I say Jack & I wish to discuss literature and not to
have her.

JANUARY 13, 1952

Friday evening Jo invited both Ellen & me to drink up some bottles
in her place. Ellen eats her way thru canapes, I drink thru 4 martinis, nearly, with little effect, & listen to music. Ellen wanted to stay, I
thought I should depart. I walked, went to Jack's, found him out, went
to Leopoldstr. & was picked up by one Boris, taken to the Siegesgarten,
where I had coffee & danced. Returned at 12:45 AM stone sober, to
find Ellen nearly weeping in my bed! She was suddenly extremely sweet,
brushing my shoes, saying she thought I was in the [River] Isar.

JANUARY 16, 1952

Much confusion—all hell breaks loose as soon as Ellen has a slight bump
in her professional road. Now Kurt, Clarissa have jobs. Jo P. possibly.
Ellen none at the moment. This being depressing, uncertain, Ellen immediately falls silent, takes it out in bitter, malicious complaints to me, and
if I ask a question about her work, explains impatiently with a "Is that so
difficult for you to understand? I thought you had a high IQ!" O Christ,
if Ellen could only forget hers for a while! How much happier she & I &

everyone connected with her would be. Half her brilliant mind is occupied with assessing her superiority over everyone else she deals with, from her driver to President Truman.

JANUARY 17, 1952

Letter yesterday from Margot. Swedish serial rights to *Strangers* bring only $40.00. Yesterday evening—long talk with Ellen, who wants to know exactly my funds, I didn't tell her, a matter of foolish pride perhaps—& if I wouldn't stay on if I were broke. I'd prefer to go to U.S.A. where I could work. To her this is treason. We have a different way of looking at finances. I am too much aware of the MacDowell writers* living off other people & don't want to be one of them. I know staying on in Europe indefinitely presupposes a greater rate of sales than I have had to date. I am still optimistic. I can see two whole years ahead—but Ellen wants an answer now. Letter from Mother. They have bought a house, shrimp pink, at 56 West Pine St. [in Fort Worth]. Reports big open House at Xmas in Texas. Jack M. called. Reports on my MS: not enough narrative line, or interaction of characters. A darling card from [Jeannot's mother] Lily saying *Strangers* is profound. She read it twice!

JANUARY 18, 1952

Fever & reading my book conceived in fever. 100°. Jack & Ellen, dinner at Schwarzwälder, E. trying hard to be regular & companionable. But not too pleasant. She will not enter into my very simple world of plain friendliness, which is perhaps too simple for her intellect. Always, therefore, trouble is brewing.

JANUARY 19, 1952

Thirty-One years old. As unmemorable as Xmas. Ellen goes to Zurich at midday, leaving me with Henry & a bit shaky on my feet. I tend the store & read my book. Which isn't too bad.

JANUARY 22, 1952

Ellen wants me to see people, yet makes it impossible to see them alone or with her, as she complains about both arrangements. The result is,

---

* An artist's colony in Petersborough, New Hampshire, founded in 1907 by composer Edward MacDowell and his wife, Marian, a pianist. Notable residents include Aaron Copland, Leonard Bernstein, Thornton Wilder, James Baldwin, Willa Cather, DuBose and Dorothy Heyward, Alice Walker, Michael Chabon, Alice Sebold, and Jonathan Franzen.

I feel I cannot possibly make friends now, and it is all I can do to keep those I have!

JANUARY 25, 1952

To movie with Jack. Cocteau. Then martinis & to Faschingsball [Carnival ball] at Haus der Kunst. Ellen invited (J. never fails) & she toyed with the idea, then backed out. *Fasching* virtues—rough good fun, & the abandon the Germans so much need in wild costume. Home late, found Ellen as usual awake & waiting (3 AM!). The only time she is thoroughly sweet is on such occasions when she thinks I have run off perhaps with someone else, or intend to, or have seen, perhaps, someone else I am attracted to.

JANUARY 27, 1952

Writing the last pages of the *Sleepless Night*, & difficulties, bad work, due to resentment & the fact I do not even feel kindly enough to use her living room to work in. Jack said Sat. night over the martinis, "I just hope she doesn't change you too much, Pat. You're a personality." And that E. is not my mother, etc.

JANUARY 29, 1952

Left for Paris. Hungover A.M. with Jack calling at 11 during working hours to bring me a compact. He was very touched, & touching, his affections having grown somewhat in these last days before my departure. Ellen says she has been living with him, is sick of him & his telephone calls & mine to him. Whether all this is pure jealousy—I'm afraid it'll always be so with her & my friends.

JANUARY 31, 1952

At Sézanne, Hôtel de France, a restaurant hotel for Paris men to take their mistresses overnight. We had a pleasant evening in a small restaurant. To bed at 9:10! I have never felt so guilty about not being able to drive before & Ellen does not let me forget for one hour that I am a useless passenger and that she has all the work & responsibility, that I cannot even read a road-map, etc. Christ, how I long for someone cheerful!

FEBRUARY 1, 1952

Paris at 11:30! The city jammed with automobiles. We stop at Hotel St. Honoré. Natica [Waterbury] is in Rome with Maria. I called Janet [Flanner] & made dinner date. She received us in the Continental. Ellen's opinion—a grand old dame, very full of esprit, but with a bad memory & showing signs of senility. Specially criticized her thinking IRO was a U.S. organization instead of U.N. which it is. We dined at Janet's favorite Rive Droite bistro. I invited her. A very nice, lucky first evening. Ellen enjoyed it.

FEBRUARY 2, 1952

Called Lyne at 11 AM. She popped in Café de Flore* in slacks at 12:00 en route to Flea Market. Ellen disappointed in her after my build-up. I can see E. prepares to take a scunner to anyone I am particularly fond of. Lyne has bought an apartment. Now she is a bona fide resident of Paris, much happier, more Bohemian than ever. Ellen thinks her friends are pretty dreadful, classes Lyne in with the Bronx Jews, like Jack Matcha, of whom E. says I know too many. All I know is the evenings are governed by E.'s moods—generally of disapproval & fatigue & horrification. I should like to see Lyne alone & find it impossible to secure Ellen's permission thereto.

FEBRUARY 3, 1952

This trip so long-looked forward to is falling apart because E. says I have "the upper hand" with all my friends here, though she is always invited. Only tonight helped. Our ways of life diametrically opposed every hour of the waking day.

FEBRUARY 3, 1952

Saw Calmann-Lévy (M. Robert) at 5. He showed me 12 (good) reviews, some fairly raving. All favorable. Asked me to dinner, made it later for a drink. At 6 at Esther [Murphy] Arthur's† 5 rue de Lille. A beautiful subleased apartment, palatial. Esther more entertaining than usual. We had a fine cocktail hour, departed with great goodwill. I gave her a pot of red flowers. Ellen & I quarreling—up to the very instant we step into the Alexandre Bar to meet M. Robert & girl. Very agreeable she is, a red-headed damsel who had actually read my book! They dropped me home—after arranging for a press interview tomorrow.

---

* One of the oldest cafés in Paris, famous for its clientele of high-profile philosophers and writers such as Georges Bataille, Robert Desnos, Raymond Queneau, Pablo Picasso, and Eugène Ionesco. Since 1994, the Prix de Flore, inaugurated by Frédéric Beigbeder, is awarded annually at the Café de Flore.
† New York socialite and intellectual Esther Murphy (1897–1962) was, like Pat, a friend of Janet Flanner's.

FEBRUARY 4, 1952

Called [Jenny] Bradley. Saw her this evening at 6. Bradley charming.
Talked of everything, however, but my book. I have seen it: *L'Inconnu du
Nord-Express*,* a fairly nice jacket & excellent translation. A very pleas-
ant evening, us two.

FEBRUARY 7, 1952

Press interview (Opera) at 11. Gave frank answers, to Ellen's horror. I
should have said I adored the country, thought the people's mores were
superb, etc. I said I thought the French impolite, on the traffic situation,
& that I liked Gide because of his religious attitudes. The reporter was
a Catholic, like all the young intellectuals. The hell with it. Ellen professed to be tired, said she might stay in or go to a movie . . . when Lyne
called at 7, I made a date for 8 alone. Then of course, E. throws it down
my throat. Lyne took me to the Dôme, Monique's hangout, full of queer
young people & general Bohemians. Lyne loves that. E. pronounces her
totally unconventional, certainly sleeps with women, & neither Ellen nor
I can explain why Lyne never went to bed with me.

FEBRUARY 8, 1952

Very hungry this AM but our plans for a real breakfast in a bistro before
departing vanish in the humorless flurry & grim business of the trip.
Throughout there is never a smile at some accident of the voyage, never
a break for pure whim or for beauty of the countryside. No digressions!
We make it barely to Lyon, where I run smack into the arms of Germaine
& husband. We dined with them. The dog takes precedence over all
humans. If the dog doesn't get his damned milk, there's hell to pay. Also
I am expected to give him half my beefsteak at dinner, the one meal of
the day for me (unlike Lyne, Ellen doesn't stop for lunch!). No wonder
I resent the dog at times: especially when he enters the bed between us,
with dirt, confusion, & general disorder.

FEBRUARY 9, 1952

Got to Cagnes-[sur]-Mer at 7 exhausted & dirty. Snow-boots & all on
the Riviera. We are both ecstatic at the first sunlight we have seen since
weeks ago in Munich! I have an idea for a travel piece about a couple
who choose to do everything the hard way, seek out dull spots, bad

---

* The French edition of *Strangers on a Train*.

hotels, & travel in an uncomfortable car, with huge hotel-messing dogs.*
We are at the Cagnard, on whose terrace, E. says, the picture of Kathryn
(which I carry in the blue suitcase) was taken. It's like a French Taxco
here.

FEBRUARY 10, 1952

To Nice. It's one long horror. Except for the nights which perversely get
better, & have never been better for either of us with anyone else.

FEBRUARY 16, 1952

To Barcelona. Exhausted. We've had more than enough of travel in
FIAT. Relations worsen daily between us. My most obvious sensation is
resentment. Hers also. I don't do my share. Yet her personality cramps
my style, squelches me. If I am to suggest something, and do, then she
has good reasons against it & we don't do it. She knows a better way of
doing everything. A curious similarity (I think) between our relations &
those of Stanley & mother: his maternal vision of her, due to real youth,
resulting in Oedipus-like resentment of me, as a child, intruder, rival.
And my resentment of the dog for the same reason. Consequently—
potentially a paralyzing, castrating, inertia & dependence might result,
like that which so finally debased Stanley's ego that it destroyed all push
& ambition. Ellen I feel has no respect for me as a writer. But I shall not
let the S. parallel go further, having recognized it. But these days are so
full of psychic battles, like Moby Dicks dashing fathoms below the surface!—that I cannot refrain from writing outright that fraction of them
my physical mind & eye can perceive.

FEBRUARY 17, 1952

Palma [de Mallorca] so cold I got a chill waiting on the docks for the car
to be unloaded. The island is quite beautiful, clean, new, orderly, simple.
I love the Cathedral. I feel rotten, exhausted from battling cold, time,
distance, and reality.

FEBRUARY 18, 1952

I feel unsociable, long for privacy. Too much travel is too much—for a
while. The kaleidoscopic view leads to the kaleidoscopic mind. Also, I
long for mail.

---

* Pat will write a draft and call it "Hell on Wheels."

FEBRUARY 19, 1952

I still feel not so peachy. The hotel fare is abundant & good. The wine oversweet. The populace penniless.

FEBRUARY 20, 1952

Papers still full of king [George]'s death. Great good luck to get an English or American newspaper here. Want of reading material would soon drive us out. I have not the knack yet—necessary to every married person—of working in a hotel room in the presence of someone else. Tonight dined at El Patio—38 pesos. Ellen takes this festive occasion to quarrel in a way that would upset the digestion of a rhinoceros. That I am selfish, lazy, indifferent to her, use her, consider all she is interested in unimportant, and behave like a man married 20 years & very sure he has made & finished a conquest. [The] dog spoils our nights, mornings, dinners, makes traveling uncomfortable & constantly offends me aesthetically. She said only 2 days ago she is still willing to get rid of the dog—in Cagnes or thereabouts—I am not willing to be so selfish as to demand it. (Might it not be like the time my mother got rid of S. & my mood was no better? The roots of resentment are deepest of all roots!) Yet I realize too the happiness just inches away from me, if I were sweeter, kinder, more generous. And I say the dog prevents me from being. Oh the silly games the subconscious plays!

2/25/52

Hotel life—Better be a fireman than answer these calls to meals, there is less anxiety between bells. One meets a few individuals in the bar, the anxiety becomes jagged laughter over the second martini. In three days, one is corrupted as a drunkard, it becomes gleeful to shop all morning, to sit an hour & a half in the sunlight, or hoping for it, in the local square café, even to a flooring dull English lunch, then a demi afternoon of demi ghosts and demi intentions never carried out. Where is my wooden spoon, my grand-father's knife, my books of St. Augustine, my drawing in the evening window after supper, my live idea silver and bright and live as a fish? Where my lean muscles springing me up from bed at six in the morning, to the open window where I may drown if I choose in the cool air that has bathed me all night?

FEBRUARY 26, 1952

To Soller, very disappointing after Alcudia—the only other attractive town on the island. Mail from Margot, Matcha, Kingsley brings the world back again, and to me it is welcome. *Price of Salt* to be published in May.

FEBRUARY 29, 1952

Idle, sunny day, when as usual the chance repeated action from one day to the next simulates routine & pleases me, i.e. my mornings alone in the hotel room, sketching, while E. suns below. My drawing improves. Like Matisse I must draw a thing many times—a face or a scene—to become familiar with the few essential lines that constitute it really.

MARCH 2, 1952

To Yacht club of Palma with the Bissingers,* Winifred getting tight on 2 martinis in the sun. Henry *prohibido*, Ellen angry, insisted on my coming home. I grew impatient, for the dog is spoiled. "I shall never forget this," E. said bitterly to me, meaning my ungentlemanly behavior. If things between us were better, I shouldn't have these lapses into barbarism. We came home, washed & went to bed, for we are in love with each other very much these days.

MARCH 3, 1952

These days are bewildering, for I am not used merely to living. Tear me away from solitude & I no longer get ideas. And I am longing for ideas—though too sated on life & events to have them, perhaps because I no longer need to manufacture the fantastic or the imaginary. All I want is to be rich & famous! Not much, eh? Have just read Graham Greene's *The End of the Affair*. Very disappointing, so beautiful technically, yet written sans love, as if by a crude bastard named Marc Brandel. One cannot write however well & leave out the heart, the accidental. E. had a dry martini at 7, a red-letter day. Then she told me ours was a difficult relationship because our interests had so little in common. She thinks I've no place for the theoretical or abstract, being a feminine (i.e. stupid) intellect, etc. However, my relations with E. definitely are improving. This is her kind of life. I should go mad were it for long. I only hope I'll have enough solitude when we live together, otherwise I cannot function, even in non-writing periods. And I'd so like

---

* Karl and Winifred Bissinger. Karl Bissinger was a photographer for the likes of *Harper's Bazaar* in the 1940s and a political activist. He was Pat's neighbor in midtown Manhattan and organized a drawing class which Pat had attended.

to produce another Hitchcock thriller.* And buy E. a mink jacket. She doesn't even want a coat.

MARCH 12, 1952

Barcelona. E. tripped & sprained her ankle. Had to have a doctor tonight put a gum cast on it. We got to Carmen Amaya somehow. Lasted until ten of one. Very native. Very good. Though E. received it rather coolly.

MARCH 14, 1952

Got to Marseille at 2 & called Lily soon. Wanted to visit the family in the PM. but E. held me to a promise I should not see them before 6. For this I cannot prevent myself resenting her, and this is a bitter emotion indeed. With Lily at the Cintra Bar at 6:30. I was very constrained. We dined—I am sure inadequately in L's eyes—at the Campa. Then dropped L. at Fouquet's Bar. E. went home, & I've joined Lily. Who said: ᶠI think she's a woman who gets her way with everyone . . . when you say yes and she says no, that means no, doesn't it? Yes, it does. Jeannot, M. Potin, and Sylvia arrived at the Fouquet's,ᶠᶠ where they kidded me unmercifully about E.'s domination of me.

MARCH 15, 1952

Off we go from Marseille. Cannes at 5 PM. I cannot feel friendly toward Ellen under these conditions, however much I try, because I know we shall soon be in a house together. God knows, I am far from any desire to sleep with her. The least requisite is that one's partner be friendly!!! Life is grim even when I propose having a café after a movie. For if I cannot find the café, then I am slave-driving her around town!

MARCH 17, 1952

We move to Cagnes this AM. This PM a final discussion. Ellen says I am abnormally related to people, all people, my friends, etc. Tearfully volunteers to go away, now that she has driven me where I wanted to go. The thing came up when I said I would under no condition go to Rome, where I had friends I intended to keep. And there it rests at an impasse. I am not happy.

---

* Pat drafted several ideas for films in 1951 at Hitchcock's request, none of which were ever realized.

MARCH 19, 1952

More hell. I contemplate leaving, and flinch at my cowardice. Longing to write Margot, to find sustenance anywhere, for this is my 23rd Psalm at stake.

MARCH 20, 1952

Wrote a bitter, bitter poem tonight. Your philosophy yields a bitter distillate. Better my simple and unnourishing dew to run the engines of my soul, where hate cannot exist, nor pain, nor you. Four stanzas. All my nature revolts against this. It strikes far deeper than personal pain. What she would have me do is change my relationship to people and the world.

MARCH 21, 1952

Letter from Lyne, your friend's twisted mind. She thinks herself so superior to other people, she cannot enjoy anything. Are you an artist or a petit bourgeois? Ellen quizzed me at length about what was in it.

MARCH 22, 1952

The atmosphere is intolerable. I could not write in such negation. Resumed on the book [*Sleepless Night*], suicide of Oscar, which comes stickily and was not the thing to plunge into. Found a book called *Married Love* by [Mary Carmichael] Stopes, 1918 classic. So absorbing I cannot put it down, nor can Ellen, and very funny. How a man should make love to a sensitive woman. Stop the brutality permeating the world! I put my foot down about what I would stand from her. Wrote a note about ramming Henry down my throat—for she makes a great to-do about sleeping with him and arranging the bastard comfortably in her bed when I do not go there! I said this ramming is spoiling my chest, signed Henry. Had instantaneous good effect. Tonight opening night at Jimmy's Bar. I continued the discussion, no protective attitude on my part—take it or I go—with continued good results. Moral: Beat your wife once a week. They love it. Tonight we slept together, first time in a fortnight.

3/26/52

The alcoholic writer—He drinks when he has to face people and the noisy, blatant, obvious world. He is vigorously sober when he works, in order to see clearly those people and those motivations so much subtler to perceive.

MARCH 27, 1952

Reading [Irwin] Shaw's *The Troubled Air*. Sleek stuff, designed to capture the Wolfe fans, the Fitzgerald fans—ah, but he lacks the poetry.
Man must take flight, not caring where he lands—now and then—to
make literature. I am haunted by Jack [Matcha]'s remark that my 3rd
book is not pulled together. Nothing to do but type through. I like and
do not like to let E. see it. She'd be a good critic. But can I take it?

MARCH 30, 1952

P.84 typed! Not bad. Ellen very restless, wants amusing café to sit in
and there is none here, not one, nor in Nice. I cannot see her enduring
another fortnight in this doldrum atmosphere. We went out and had
drinks. I am very content the last 5 days. It takes crises & the pulling
through to make contentment.

MARCH 31, 1952

Ellen met Peggy [V.] in Nice, brought her here at 2 PM. With her arrived
Price of Salt—outwardly very pleasing, but I fear the insides are horrid,
& I see now what I was too blind to see before: it is not a good book. It
will take a good bit of time to live this down.

APRIL 3, 1952

Good work. But the typing noise drives Ellen mad. Never are we exactly
harmonious. I suppose we both pull each other back from the extreme,
which is good. Essentially my life is too quiet and egocentric for her.
I am content with much less outside diversion. (Which is why the
dog irritates me: why be hypocritical? I shouldn't like a person of the
same nature. His only activity destruction, his only pleasure noise and
movement.)

APRIL 12, 1952

With Denise to Yvette's secret bar in Cagnes. A "big night out" but no
interesting people. We called on an American painter Denise knew.
Varonich, or Vavronich, not too bad, surprisingly neat domicile, a cat
named Hannibal. A bit high on red wine, he narrated a (to me) charming
story of the *tepezcuintle** dog of Mexico. Ellen was bored, & of course
proposed leaving early. Especially as the guy spiced his conversation with

---

* Not a dog but a large rodent, the lowland paca.

such phrases as, & told her to go take a flying fuck at herself. Home at 1, very wicked.

APRIL 14, 1952

To Florence along the seacoast, a flat ugly terrain of shallow beach and water, but covered with summer beach houses, resort cafés, hotels, etc. and I gather immensely popular with the Italians in summer. Ellen revels in the Italian air. Lunch in Pisa. The tower splendid. My first real view.

APRIL 16, 1952

Margot reports Bantam Books paid $6500 for the [paperback] rights to *Price of Salt* already. I get, therefore, about $3000 in a year, and the rest Coward-McCann must put into advertising. Ellen very happy about it. So am I in a very quiet way. The Pocket Books are currently outbidding the general Hollywood buyers, and claiming to reach a hitherto unexploited audience—unexploited is the word—of the middlebrow, who yet wants "realism."

APRIL 19, 1952

Loafing. Saw San Gimignano. Reading Saul Bellow. I like him— enthusiastically. *The Victim.*

APRIL 20, 1952

Blanche Sherwood here. Though no dates with the gang as yet. The American homosexual-neurotic habit of traveling in rolling groups is a mysterious phenomenon to Ellen. To Fiesole.

4/20/52

[*Keime.*]* Murder by mental nagging. Woman nags her husband to suicide, which he does so it looks like he has been murdered. Poison, which he puts in her desk drawer, her fingerprints on it.

APRIL 22, 1952

[Florence.] We debate the 60,000 Strozzino Palace—really exquisitely furnished, but no *pied à terre* at that price! Looks like something the Sitwells† could compose little gems in. No work done, of course, and I tried

---

* Highsmith's German expression for "germ" (of a story idea).
† Poet Edith Sitwell (1887–1964) and her brothers.

in the hotel room, tho this busy life, with bars & café sitting, is just to
Ellen's taste.

APRIL 24, 1952

Signed Stross [house] contract for 2 months, 40,000 Lire. I find it rather
stark, despite swanky street and adjacent tulip estate. Saw Titi Mazier,
old friend of Ellen's here, & ex girl friend of Curzio Malaparte.* She is
charming. Told us the fascinating story of Mrs. Stross & her 76-year-old
husband who, apparently, hung himself with a dog leash from a bathroom ceiling only two months ago. His mistress used to live in our little
house, on the grounds!

5/4/52

No human activity marks the face and molds it into more beautiful and
natural line, than art. The faces of old painters, sculptors, and writers—!
Compare them with the voracious, frightened faces of old American
businessmen!

MAY 4, 1952

We went to the Ponte Vecchio & I bought Ellen the kind of gold bracelet
she has been wanting, a plain chain of small round links. Only 60 bucks.
It made her very happy, thank God.

MAY 6, 1952

Reviews yesterday from Calmann-Lévy [on *Strangers on a Train*]. All
but 2 praise gaudy. Comparisons with Dostoyevsky, etc. which of course
pleases me most, even if it is badly done.

5/7/52

With these serious people, these *bons vivants*, who take so much more
seriously their amusements, their aesthetic surroundings, than any artist
takes his work or his creative process, the creative process begins to atro-
phy in their presence, for the curious reason that their pursuit of pleasure
is so business like. And once they have it—pleasant café-bars, shopping-
centers, an efficient maid, a garden, sunlight, then life, instead of relaxing, becomes shopping, getting repairs done, planning, anxiously, next
summer's vacation: in short, the element of pleasing, of amusement, goes
out of the artist companion, and he can no longer find his proper plane.

---

* Italian diplomat, writer, and filmmaker Curzio Malaparte (1898–1957).

Amusement, entertainment, via writing, disappears in a fantastic world somewhere far away. As is usual, the paradox in this fascinates me.

MAY 8, 1952

More and more often I think back on Joan S., and feel my leaving her for Ginnie was the greatest mistake I ever made, both emotionally, and for my career. There is doubtless something like this in everyone's life. That is why life on earth is not entirely heaven. Nor entirely hell, thanks to these pleasures snatched, even if paid for so dearly.

MAY 11, 1952

To Geneva at 5 PM. Remarkably like Zurich, only bigger, more expensive, more formal.

MAY 12, 1952

I am full of ideas, for stories, etc. Very content alone all day while Ellen flew madly everywhere.

MAY 13, 1952

Letup on Ellen's job hunting. She so flew yesterday, she collapsed at 8 PM. We sat in cafés, handled the car, which is rapidly breaking down at the 28,000 kilometer mark. But I am more bored and restless sitting in cafés than seeing museums. I long to get back to Florence and begin work again, yet feel guilty because Ellen doesn't like the house and is bored there. To feel guilty even about working!

MAY 16, 1952

Went to Portofino this AM. I recognized Gordon Gaskill's boat "*The Huntress*," and hailed him. A 39-year-old, bearded American, adventure novelette writer. He invited us aboard and for lunch, which Ellen, not I wanted to stay for. The man's hairy legs offended me rather, & I'd have preferred not to lunch there! When Ellen was away airing the dog (who promptly chewed nearly through the anchor rope) Gordon asked me if I were free to come with him & could I work on such a boat. He actually wants a sleeping partner, a woman. We went swimming with him at 4:30—then Ellen & I returned, more than ever content with each other, and made love before dinner—A decent dinner finally—there is never anything else to do in the evenings, because Ellen abhors bars, alcoholic ones, and she doesn't even drink café after dinner. Only tonight she did, which apparently made her very amorous, because it was suddenly wonderful in the night, erasing everything, and every problem.

MAY 21, 1952

[Florence.] Inch by inch I try to work. Between quarrels that leave me shaking and wretched, and quite off the creative plane. Much of this work will later have to be done over. Dedicate my book to Ellen? Not ever! She could not be sabotaging it more effectively—unless she burnt the manuscript.

MAY 24, 1952

Day off. To please Ellen. But I am exhausted, too, not from work, but trying against odds to work. Ellen wept last night at Nandina's for "the life I make her lead." Actually, she worries about her not having a job plus her old (God, how old?) brutality complex which she lets off on me.

MAY 25, 1952

I write one page. And try to think, not too well. An atmosphere of mutual resentment poisons even the blossoms on the tree. Lunch, cleaning, and ballet at 4 PM. [Stravinsky's] *Firebird* reminded me much of Joan S. I remember the day I last lunched with her, she had it on the machine and had just played it. The lumbering, somber introduction. Later, during cocktails at the Excelsior, Ellen discourses, monologues, on the wrongness of my accepting mediocrity in the arts when I know better. One of those gambits which do not tempt me to expatiate upon. I should not judge it so, were I writing about it. But I could not create (I said exist) in that negative, sneering mood in which she mostly lives. And I wonder is this continual warfare between us a tolerable state of affairs, a fate, or will we part eventually and inevitably? Never having been quite in such a situation, I leave my "mind open." Always I tend toward the "salubrious" for myself. Whether this hell is eventually so educational, stimulating, and salubrious, I do not know. I only know, hearing the *Firebird* this afternoon, I remembered Joan, and knew I had made the mistake of my life (or of that period) creatively, personally, emotionally, when I let her go. Her child would never have been born. But I should have written *Strangers* at least, for I had the idea then. I wrote two good short stories in the brief time with her. My wagon was hitched to a star then, I should have done God knows what. My wings, whatever they were, would have unfolded in her air, that, my God, I do know.

MAY 26, 1952

Saw Ellen off, getting her raincoat to her, thank God, in time. Ellen very sentimental and affectionate when the train left, I not at all. Doesn't she know our relationship has cracked irreparably? To lunch with Titi, *chez elle*, alone. She astounded me by going right to the problem, without any prompting, saying: "You must not let her trouble your mind so, otherwise you cannot work . . . Nobody likes Ellen. But nobody. She never had friends. Everybody like you, but nobody like her." I almost wept at this overwhelming sympathy & understanding. Titi advises me to be strong. "You are stronger than she is. She is looking for somebody strong to handle her." I went home with a greater sense of life, of love, than I have had since the first days with Ellen. I make a resolution: I shall be myself with Ellen, nothing more nor less. Either she can take it or she can't. But I will not be bossed around any longer. I do not fear walking out on her— except over hurting her. I pity her now, I must no longer pity myself!

MAY 28, 1952

Letter today from Ellen. Very affectionate, how she can't live without me. But I can live without her only too well. Work improves. Two new scenes rewritten today & tomorrow.

MAY 30, 1952

Jack arrived at 8:03. Dined at Nandina's & talked endlessly over coffee. He will go on to Rome to speak to Mike Stern* about a job with Fawcett for when he returns to the states. We taxied to the house—1000 lire!— Jack sleeps in my room. Very happy and cheerful about having a guest.

MAY 31, 1952

Roamed around town with Jack, to Excelsior, many bars, before 13-man luncheon chez Titi Mazier. Eduardo charming, serving martinis— Luzzati,† Mary Foster O., Contessa Arance, etc. & was in good form and had a good time. So did Jack.

JUNE 2, 1952

Ellen greeted me rapturously at the station, said she doubted I'd come at

---

* Adventurer and journalist Mike Stern (1910–2009) went to Italy as a foreign correspondent in 1943, entering Rome a day before the American forces. He stayed for fifty years, writing about the most scandalous and exciting people he encountered in *No Innocence Abroad*.
† Possibly the Genovese artist Emanuele "Lele" Luzzati (1921–2007), who was nominated for an Academy Award twice, in 1965 and 1973, for his animated shorts *La gazza ladra* and *Pulcinella*.

all, and did I love her? And she had decided if I would "take her back" she would be angelic. I am kind, optimistic (terrified by possibility of having to have a major tooth extraction!), but I cannot but doubt this will last more than 24 hours, for it is Ellen's basic character she proposes changing!

JUNE 5, 1952

I have but one scene to do in my book—the last. Even so, I get panicky when Ellen slides into her tyrannic moods—I have sat here so many pitiful hours, trying to gather myself to write, when without quarrels and resentments, it would all have been so easy! And perversely, it is Ellen herself who is so eager to be gone from here, which depends when I finish my work! I'd thought, even hoped, she'd go to Capri. I feel this is disintegration. I cannot imagine we shall still be together at end of summer.

6/6/52

In my scheme of things—life becomes much or little. I should jump off a cliff for someone. (Life is worth much.) Or I should live on, unorthodox manner. (Life is worth little.) For Kathryn, I should have dared much and given much.

JUNE 8, 1952

Finished typing "The End." Loafed.

JUNE 12, 1952

God has blessed me with a new idea.

JUNE 13, 1952

R. Tietgens rang the bell at 6 and stayed for dinner. He is returning soon to the States. Looks extremely well. And has unwittingly stolen Jim Merrill, Bobby I.'s boyfriend, during his sojourn in Rome. We took coffee on the Piazza Maria Novella. He asked me how I got on with Ellen. So, so, I said. "I feel it. She's rather belligerent."

JUNE 16, 1952

Ellen took a Veronal last night, late, being unable to sleep. This AM she irritates me by enacting a drama of suicide—i.e. walking about all morning as if she were half-alive—apparently enjoying the soporific effects of the pill. Then she confessed she'd read my diary yesterday while I was listening to the 9th Symphony. All the parts about Titi's (betrayal) instead of the building resentment, etc. I wanted her to read by way of understanding our present difficulties. Ellen was chiefly annoyed by my talking to other people about her, and by Titi's lies. Utter lies, said Ellen. Ellen is bent on giving Titi a piece of her mind. I pled with her not to—the silliness of a diary! Nevertheless, I have not lost by these revelations—neither of us has. The truth can only make one stronger—or wreck things entirely. Ellen took this surprisingly well.

JUNE 22, 1952

Errands. Morning of work, last work, on the MS [*Sleepless Night*] which is ready to go tomorrow to the States. I saw—suddenly after lunch, looking hopefully into the *Albatross Book of Living Verse*, a title: The Traffic of Jacob's Ladder. From a poem by Francis Thompson*—in which the ladder goes from Charing Cross to heaven. My use of it is, of course, ironic.

JUNE 23, 1952

In good spirits. Mailed the MS. 1 kilo 900 grams. I wrote Margot yesterday to show it to Harper if Coward-McCann didn't like it. I wish now I had held out—and I probably could have—for Coward-McC. to take *Salt*, and give me back the right to show Harper the 3rd novel. What can happen now? The only miracle—that Coward-McC. will not like the book. We left Florence at 3:30 PM for Perugia—a beautiful town full of ancient mellow stone buildings like a Shakespearian stage set. Steps going down to back streets in which cozy trattorias nestle like lights in a forest. We have a beautiful hotel room. I in good spirits but not sexy at all, and indeed not very amicable to Ellen.

JUNE 25, 1952

Rome yesterday at 3:30, where Henry jumped into the fountain in front of the Inghilterra, it was so hot. Our room there is hot, noisy, and unattractive, so Ellen is determined to leave. *Int'l. Theater* had sent me celebrities' names in Rome this week, but I'm too exhausted to attempt it, and sadly enough, it looks like another shoestring year for them—Grant Code† already cutting down the $20 per fortnight check to 5¢ per word. And that depresses me these days, too, having earned no money in so long, and having so little coming in, despite being dead tired from work already.

---

* Francis Thompson (1859–1907), English poet and mystic. His most famous poem is "The Hound of Heaven."
† Grant Hyde Code (1896–1974), an actor, dancer, and writer on theater and dance.

JUNE 26, 1952

Called & visited Bobby Isaacson & Jim Merrill in their apt. in Via
Quattro Novembre—which partakes emphatically of Rolf Tietgens'
decor. Stark, etc. The boys were quite nice. (I shouldn't mind living alone in Rome, either!) Formia to Positano. Positano is larger
than I expected. Ellen knows the proprietor of the largest pension
here—Doio. Heard the incredible news that Jean van Geld, Ellen's
ex-husband, is due here in a few days! Neither of them has been
here in 16 years! We stay at Doio's noisy pension on the beach. Ellen
complains—so we shall undoubtedly move.

JUNE 27, 1952

Reading McCullers' *The Heart Is a L[onely] H[unter]*. Beautiful—
rediscovery. So are her short stories—all under one cover, the 3 novels &
the stories. I am so exhausted, I suspect anemia besides wine saturation,
& decide to cut out wine, or cut down considerably.

JUNE 29, 1952

The maid made a *letto matrimoniale* out of our 2 beds, in order to make
full use of this single mosquito net, and this will improve our relations no
end. Something chemical seems to happen when we are in bed together
and we should always sleep together—for this is one of the strongest
things we have. Days like this, I feel we can go on, and I can go on writing while living with her, and writing my best, too—and other times I
feel strongly the opposite. So actually, even now, I do not know if I am
kidding myself sometimes, and acting the coward.

JULY 1, 1952

Heat wave continues. Dark clouds of mist hang low, almost touching &
obscuring the village. But there is no cool wind to precipitate them. Have
never seen a sky like this.

JULY 3, 1952

Began story about Baldur,* the German shepherd, who is more noble
than his master, who eventually commits suicide to escape him.

---

* In the final version of "Man's Best Friend," a short story published posthumously in *Nothing That
Meets the Eye: The Uncollected Stories of Patricia Highsmith* (New York, 2002), Baldur survives.

JULY 4, 1952

One firecracker heard at 9 PM at a distance. John Steinbeck dined with
Ann Carnahan* & Carlino in the hotel dining room this evening, but I did
not see him, or know of it. I contemplate the fourth novel also—which
will be about the man who murders by imitation.[†] A model of brevity,
with good characters, humor, and tragedy in the hopelessness of his
unhappy marriage, which I shall create from the worst aspects of mine.

JULY 7, 1952

To Salerno and then Paestum—a tiny village, with three Greek Temples
(Doric) standing near the sea on low cliffs. They are bright tan, worn
by water, the ground surrounding them quite flat, and excavations are
going on at present, revealing a whole city like Pompeii, except that no
vertical walls stand. Had the good fortune to pick up a small Greek
head made of red brick tile, some 3½ inches high. And a couple of
small tile bases of things—one of an oil lamp. Ellen sat in the shade of
the huge (3 ft. circumference) pillars, while I went roving around in the
broiling sun, thru the excavations, whose dirt was still moist from the
morning's work. It was the noon hour for the workmen. Shall never forget this excursion, and the first time I stood within a Greek temple.

JULY 9, 1952

Met Walter Stuempfig, painter of N.Y. & Philadelphia, whom I've heard
of, tho can't place his work.[‡] Very amiable & like the Constable set, generally speaking. Ellen talks of going to New York in November possibly
renting Lil Picard's room, then wintering in Santa Fe. But meanwhile,
the job with the Tolstoy Foundation[§] may come through. Either in Paris,
Munich, or Beirut.

JULY 11, 1952

Cocktails with Walter on our terrace, at hotel. We were (I was) rather
high, visited Kurt C., old acquaintance of Ellen's, victim of polio, and
homosexuality. He paints much like Cornell. We played *Kiss Me Kate*
music and *Guys & Dolls* which Ellen thought impossibly rude, as I did

---

* Writer Ann Carnahan, author of *The Vatican: Behind the Scenes in the Holy City* (1949).
† Pat's next novel, *The Blunderer* (New York, 1954).
‡ The American painter Walter Stuempfig's (1914–1970) romantic style was unusual for his era but met
with considerable success, with institutions such as the Whitney Museum and the Museum of Modern
Art among the purchasers of his works.
§ The Tolstoy Foundation was founded in Paris in 1939 by Tolstoy's daughter Alexandra to raise money
for Eastern European emigrants getting settled in their new homes in the United States.

not speak first (very long) with mine host. But then, whatever I enjoy immensely, she attacks. It is my manners, my untidiness, my absent-mindedness, pessimism, lack of enthusiasm—my over-readiness to perform a task, or my laziness—performing a task. Any way you play it—you can't win.

JULY 12, 1952

Reading arrangements are hell, because Ellen retires early, wanting silence & darkness, and is fond of telling me she has not had one night's sleep in the 10 months she has known me. Now I read in the bathroom with the door closed, sweltering.

JULY 15, 1952

Usual pleasant day. Walter, Aldo & Vera (Italian couple) for cocktails at 7. Then later with Walter down to the shore for a coffee. Ellen thinks I have a crush on him, & should try & marry him—ideal—a painter, wealthy, right age, etc. etc.

JULY 18, 1952

Ellen most affectionate and all goes well everywhere if we but sleep together. Then even the minor things iron out, and I can even envisage happy years ahead; the imperfections being but the stamp of reality on us.

JULY 19, 1952

Walter had drinks *chez nous*, dined with us, tries to persuade us not to leave, as he says he wouldn't be here if we weren't. Doubtless an exaggeration. His boys run wild, he needs a wife in the worst way. I indulge in fantasies of being it. I rather like him, though of course not physically. He admires Degas extravagantly, but not van Gogh. Knows all the café society gossip of Rome, etc. Ellen considers him the best-informed American she has ever met. Ellen quizzes me eternally: Do I want to go to Ischia? Venice? Ascona? I want to go to Ischia (mildly) just to see it, and also to speak to W. H. Auden.

JULY 23, 1952

The curse. A lot it matters anymore. We live like a couple of old maids.

7/23/52

You know what they say about lazy people—that they are really the most ambitious, and they don't make an effort for fear of falling short of their high ideals. Well—it is just like that when I am depressed. It is because of all the things I believe in, fine and beautiful, natural and real things—and I am depressed when I see them dim a little, when the false and the ugly, the trivial and the mediocre come in front of them like dark clouds in front of a mountain. It is not that I dwell upon myself at all—au contraire!

JULY 28, 1952

To Ischia by slow boat. Rained at noon & we stayed in hotel room drinking wine. It's great to be moving! Bus to Forio, where I called on W. H. Auden,* barefoot, tended by Italian pansy, young. We talked exclusively of money, or rather Auden tended the conversation to the financial aspect of every topic. When I made the first daringly personal remark about Rolf, he warmed up. We talked of American publishing and movie prices. He at last went off to his tailor in Forio, where he was saving ⅔ by having a tux made. Forio is shockingly primitive but some nice people live there & for a writer it would be very pleasant. I can hardly imagine la vie bohémienne any longer, after living with Ellen nearly a year. When my resentment is at its height I imagine alone I'd accomplish things that with her would never cross my mind. Perhaps this is fatuous. The fact remains, I can never duplicate again that month of Oct. 1951 when I began my 3rd novel with my sights set high, with pride, confidence & optimism, because my love affair was 3 weeks old. We haven't that anymore. A long and choking death.

JULY 29, 1952

To Naples & to Capri this AM simultaneously with Farouk's outing from Egypt† & arrival in Naples. His yacht Farad El Bihar in Capri harbor. Ellen is happy. She wanted to come here. Whatever she wants, she gets.

AUGUST 2, 1952

Toothache & general deathly feeling. Plus atmosphere between us of governess accompanying hopelessly moronic and filthy child. Timidly, I ask if she minds if we wait an extra day for Natalia [Danesi Murray], as her maid says she is arriving tomorrow. We shall.

---

* Wystan Hugh Auden (1907–1973) was an English poet. He moved to the United States in 1939 and became an American citizen, while retaining his British citizenship. He won the Pulitzer Prize for Poetry for his 1947 poem "The Age of Anxiety," which subsequently became a much-cited phrase describing the modern era.

† On July 23, 1952, King Farouk was overthrown in a bloodless coup and forced to abdicate in favor of his infant son Fuad II. He retreated to exile in Italy.

AUGUST 3, 1952

Natalia did not arrive, though we watched anxiously on the Piazza
at 7:30 when the last boats were arriving. Daily around 5 PM I suffer
attacks of fatigue and faintness. Ellen is quite impatient with it, and
when I can avoid it, I do not mention it. Except, she is apt to inform me I
look green.

AUGUST 4, 1952

To Naples, then to Positano before noon, where I found mail. Three letters from Margot, all with good news, and for a time the world looks
brighter! Corgi books of England has bought [paperback rights of]
Strangers for £200. Terese Hayden* is going ahead with screen treatment
of *Salt*. And Margot likes the 3rd novel. "Am impressed. But very. You
have real maturity here. Brilliant characterization." Major objection,
Gerald's murder at the end. I'll change that to his walking into space.
Remains for Goldbeck† to see it.

AUGUST 6, 1952

[Rome.] Saw Sergio Amidei,‡ in bookshop, & we dined with him &
Rudy S. as in the old days in Rome. We all had a good time. Amidei in
the same gentle confusion, getting nothing done on assignments except
endless talk in restaurants. Moreover he paid the check.

AUGUST 9, 1952

To dentist this afternoon. He put a medicament in the empty tooth,
which calms the trigeminal nerve. Thank God. Yesterday in Viareg-
gio, I broke out in a rash like great mosquito bites on legs & arms, was
so terrified I came near fainting—exciting further violent contempt in
Ellen—went to a doctor who said it was due to aspirin, gave me another
tooth-pain killer, which didn't work, so I had a ghastly night. How different from the way Joan would have treated me! I do not wish to be
pampered or waited upon. But there is such a thing as sympathy and a
sense of humor. Tonight freedom from pain for the first time in 10 days.

---

* Theresa Hayden ran the Theatre de Lys on Christopher Street. She wrote a film treatment for *The Price of Salt*, titled *Winter's Journey*, in which Carol became Carl.
† Presumably Cecil Goldbeck, vice president of Coward-McCann, who had already supervised the paperback edition of *The Price of Salt* and would later edit *The Blunderer* and *The Talented Mr. Ripley*.
‡ Sergio Amidei (1904–1981) was a writer and producer who worked with directors such as Roberto Rossellini and Vittorio De Sica. He wrote the script for *Rome, Open City*, for which he received an Academy Award nomination.

AUGUST 14, 1952

Letter from Natalia via Margot that Bompiani offers me the handsome sum of 50,000 lire for serialization of *Strangers* in a woman's magazine of Milan. I wonder will Margot accept but imagine she will have to. Sweden offered only $40. & we took it.

AUGUST 15, 1952

[Ascona.] The great Ferragosto, holiday. Boat ride at night to Locarno with friends to see the lights on the water. Much firecrackers displaying, best I've ever seen. Octopuses in the air, tiger lilies of many colors, explosions and rains of sparks—as under a volcano.

AUGUST 22, 1952

Ellen returns tonight with the job in Paris, Tolstoy Foundation, for at least 6 months. White Russians, whom she does not consider so deserving as D.P.'s [Displaced Persons]. Seems Jo P. was also offered the job & turned it down because of low salary. E. decides to be very nice to me. Excess of good spirits due to job. A total whirl, one I wish to stay out of.

AUGUST 24, 1952

Rainy. I love to be alone & it is a rare pleasure in this small house. I get on famously with Fran, whose feathery brain is a delight to me. We giggle, drink tea, and with her healthy Dutch girl visitors around her, she is a tonic to me—simple, natural, everyday people. She wants me to return in winter to work in the little house alone. I should love it.

8/26/52

The soul—poets, philosophers and theologians spent lifetimes trying to find out precisely what it is, and where. It is a figment of man's imagination. He has imagined it, as one man imagined the ghost ship of the Flying Dutchman. Or what use is it to search for it?

AUGUST 27, 1952

I think of writing to Lyne that I am coming to Paris, but am ashamed to say with Ellen, ashamed that we are still so unhappy together and yet together. So I do not write at all.

SEPTEMBER 2, 1952

[Munich.] Met Mike Stern this AM & lunched with him. Full of information about book market in the States. He has his *No Innocence*

Abroad coming out in Nov. with Random House. Plus $65,000 offer from Hollywood to play in his own picture of his Italian vita. Very stimulating to talk to, & we got on well, and Jack M. is always pleased at the "damn good impression" I make on everyone. Actually, I am so delighted to be with pleasant people for a change. I suppose it shows, and everyone likes to feel his own presence is appreciated.

SEPTEMBER 4, 1952

Ellen frank enough to say she'll give me transportation to Paris, & "you can leave me there if you want to." But if I talk in the same vein, she knuckles down, and placates me. In other words, the trauma of my leaving will be just as bad as the Florence Veronal scene when it happens. To Strasbourg, rather easily. A pleasant twilight, walking through the old city and the Cathedral which has a magnificent & somewhat irregular-looking rose window.

SEPTEMBER 5, 1952

To Paris by 6 PM. I called no one, playing it cautiously this time. Ellen is in good spirits & I pray God it will last, though I know I have but to call or see a friend and it will vanish.

SEPTEMBER 7, 1952

To the Bois [de Boulogne] & I'd have called Lyne, as she loves to go, but E. says "We'll never get rid of her all day!" Of all the unpleasant people in the world—Ellen!—yet she expects me to want to spend 99% of my time with her in Paris, after having had six solid months of it before!

SEPTEMBER 10, 1952

Lyne came by at 6 for a drink. She likes the dog (tho lately he has been attacking me without provocation, except that of general jealousy), and Ellen talks of having him killed or put away. Besides, he has to be concealed when we look for apartments. Hell at 2:30 when Ellen awoke me. I was not angry, but spoke freely and it soon got into a noisy, disgusting brawl, with E. swinging her feeble fists at me, and our voices undoubtedly penetrating to the Americans on either side of us in this hotel. We must have argued an hour—a degrading, useless, inconclusive fight. Caused by Ellen's trying to pin me down as to how many evenings I wished to go out in Paris. Just as Jack told me would happen. Lyne asks me how can I stand it. It's worse than being married.

SEPTEMBER 12, 1952

Retyped dog story & mailed again to Margot. I await Coward-McCann news [on *The Traffic of Jacob's Ladder*] anxiously.

SEPTEMBER 13, 1952

Worked a bit—flying saucer story. Quiet day.

SEPTEMBER 23, 1952

Fine day. Worked. Saw the Keoghs in Montana Bar, both very cordial. I'll put in a word for Theodora for Bradley soon. She has a third novel out, *Street Song*. Got fine reviews in England.

9/23/52

The bad poetry of the first days of being too much in love.

SEPTEMBER 29, 1952

Wrote to Margot Johnson rather hysterical letter asking her did she think it logical or advisable if I stay on in Europe, earning so little money, and apparently getting more out of touch with American editors. (She is to take nearly a month to answer.)

SEPTEMBER 30, 1952

Work. Lunch with Bradley, a great pleasure for me. She likes the book very much. (I think she'd read it by today.) Likes me anyway. Amazing grasp of real importance or unimportance of certain American writers like Capote, Williams, and their circles.

OCTOBER 1, 1952

We moved to 83 rue de l'Université. The big box & all that, and a mad rush all day. Mme Lanbeuf comes in every moment, and so she is to continue to do. Ellen in the [hotel] Montalembert stated she would not live with me if I went out more often than 2x weekly, or did not give her "more consideration."

OCTOBER 6, 1952

News today that Coward-McCann gave *Traffic of J.L.* [*Jacob's Ladder*] a flat rejection, saying it was "old-fashioned . . . 3 heroes who got nowhere, and like something written after World War I." It does not discourage me in the least, in fact, I'm glad. I wrote to Harper, Joan Kahn, saying I'd told M.J. that Harper was my first choice.

OCTOBER 10, 1952

Letter from Margot. Contract with Portugal for *Strangers* and $1300 royalties coming in, including $1000 guarantee for Pocket Book Bantam on *Salt* next spring.

OCTOBER 11, 1952

Worked hard all day and finished up the book this evening, including page of corrections to be made in the States.

OCTOBER 12, 1952

Hellish nightmare day. My Sundays are no longer "days off," with Ellen, in any sense. I cannot relax, draw, loaf, or anything I need. Furthermore, X in afternoon, which I did to keep peace. She thinks, as usual, that is the tie that binds. I don't operate that way. Perhaps maleish, perhaps prostitutish, I don't know.

OCTOBER 15, 1952

Worked on German story, introducing more "story."

OCTOBER 16, 1952

Worked all afternoon on cocktail party. Seven of our friends didn't come—Janet, Esther & K. and the Keoghs. The Rosenthals* were charming, though very shy. I talked with them about translating—she corrects his work, without the book—and they were very nice about trying to find me a place to work near Paris. Mme Bradley was angelic, intelligent, put in good word for my book with Calmann-Lévy, who was also here with his girlfriend Edith Bohy, the Hungarian redhead. Lyne had 2 martinis, and got a bit catty with Ellen on the strength of them. Also Enrico and Pernikoff. But I consider the party half a failure. Dined with Lyne, & Ellen with Enrico.

OCTOBER 18, 1952

Went to Bal Nègre† with Lyne & Monique, which bored finally. Moreover, I cannot sleep enough as Ellen & I regularly fight till 4 or 3 AM & must be up at 8.

---

* Jean Rosenthal was Highsmith's French translator.
† One of the regular dance nights at jazz bar Bal Blomet (33 rue Blomet) that was frequented by countless artists since the late 1920s, the so-called *années folles*: Joséphine Baker, Ernest Hemingway, Kiki de Montparnasse, Man Ray, F. Scott Fitzgerald, Joan Miró, Robert Desnos, Piet Mondrian, Kees van Dongen, Jacques Prévert, Juliette Gréco, Jean-Paul Sartre, Simone de Beauvoir, Francis Picabia, and Elliott Erwitt.

OCTOBER 20, 1952

Working, finished the German story, & wait till tomorrow to re-look at it. A nice documentary which I tried to make as good as a *New Yorker* study. Bradley reports 75,000 franc royalty from *Strangers* even after commissions. Did *Reader's Digest* synopses.

OCTOBER 21, 1952

Went over German story, worked on it all afternoon, last improvements. "The Returnees."*

Ellen burst in this evening, asking for a drink, then point-blank answer whether I want to divorce her or merely to go away and work. I do not want to hurt her, that prevents me from saying emphatically we'd both be happier apart. She gives me 4 days while she is in Munich to make up my mind. "I think you are ambivalent—that's why you must take time to decide." Things further complicated by my mother's writing she'd like to come over & see me, providing she can stay in our Paris apt. I'd love to have her. But would not postpone Italy for it. And Ellen protests she'd not stay here alone in Paris, were I to go away. She'd never counted on that, she says. So everything is up in the air. I toy with the idea of temporary parting—yet know (though she has been angelic for days now, very affectionate, protesting that she will do anything for me) that I have but to express a wish conflicting with hers, or see some friends too often, for the old horror to rise out again. Therefore if I have both intelligence and courage, I shall divorce, regardless of "throwing away" what we have, that modicum.

OCTOBER 22, 1952

Saw Ellen off to Munich. Stayed alone all day reading and planning my suspense novel about the imitator.†

OCTOBER 23, 1952

Worked some more planning. Beyond a certain point it is difficult for me, and I prefer to have the thing "going" on paper, before I think further in the air. This is not wise. Bradley phoned that she liked my short stories very very much, wants to show six of them to French magazines, some of which publish in English. Especially likes "Love Is a Terrible Thing."

---

* Pat's story about a woman escaping her unhappy marriage was published posthumously in *Nothing That Meets the Eye: The Uncollected Stories of Patricia Highsmith* (New York, 2002).
† *The Blunderer.*

Others are "Siegestor," "Man Next Door," "Man's Best Friend," "Flying Saucer" commercial, and I'll send her "The Returnees" which I sent to Margot yesterday. Margot reports a conference with some short story editors would be of value, but not enough to warrant coming home for. Thinks Florence a good idea, and says my relationship with E. has been haywire far too long. But the above encourages me to stay in Europe. Financially advisable, too. Only I am homesick, a little like a plane that has been out too long without fuel and overhauling. Ann S. invites me to stay at her house, with Betty. Nice of her! Went to Harry's Bar with Jeannot. A dreary drunken-American-infested place, with a sloppy piano.

10/24/52

I am rich, I am lucky, I am handsome, attractive, I shall live for years and years! Moreover, I am on the right side! That makes all the rest! Tonight I met a model. She had posed for A.C. [Allela Cornell] when she had the studio—that magnificent studio—on Washington Square South. Rita, the model, is a simple, honest, sophisticated, naive, generous, straight thinking, primitive thinking woman, all that. But the fact that her heart, her taste, her ideals, her truth is on the side of Mozart, Henry Miller, Rimbaud, places her among all those she will ever pose for. She is of them, she understands them, she is like them. Like beautiful music, like the Greek skies she describes so well, she refreshes the artist, she reminds him (if he needs it as I do now) that he is human if he remembers to be. And she took it for granted that I am. Tonight is one of the happiest nights of my life, since I have known Cornell. Homage, greetings, Cornell, from Paris tonight!

OCTOBER 25, 1952

Work again. The curse. Jean Rosenthal & wife came at 7:45. Took me to dinner then to Rose Rouge.* Very fine show, very clever & smooth. Cost them an outrageous sum, I am sure. Jean is extremely serious. His wife very attractive. They must be happy.

10/25/52

Letter to an American friend coming to Europe: You expect to find Europe artistic. (First of all what do you mean by that word? Creative,

---

* Legendary St-Germain-des-Prés nightclub started in 1947 by the charismatic film director Nico Papatakis; André Breton, Jean-Paul Sartre, Jacques Prévert, Boris Vian, and Miles Davis have sat in the audience, and it's where Juliette Gréco started her career.

free, active now in the present? Europe is not. Europe is artistic in her old architecture, a few modern painters, musicians, and is, in the American sense Bohemian, the freedom of her ordinary individuals who for the most everyday part, do as they each please.) But America is filled with young men, slightly eccentric, painters, or writers, who at the age of 22, after college, have the courage to take their young wives into the country, be it Connecticut or Arizona or Maine, and live in levis, and raise healthy children, perhaps in the progressive way, to spend their last dollar on music albums of Mozart, Hindemith and Bartók. And in America you will find a wider and deeper appreciation of music than in Europe, than anywhere in the world, in fact. When you come to Europe, you will find the people—not artistic, and bold, and dashing as you may expect—but afraid, constrained, cynical, and above all, a little tired. In their painting and in their architecture, you will see what they have done, and you will readily admit that America has not yet equaled it. But you will gradually and surely be proud of America, too, for her mediocre painters, the young men in levis, whose hearts are free, and generous, as artists' hearts should be. And the heart of Europe has hemorrhaged. There is no such thing either, as the "new" artist's heart. The artist is an old animal. He is a little like Christ. But he is not like either the European artists, solemnly, cynically, seriously—yet always with a look over his shoulder for the thief—pursuing his work, nor is he like the do-nothing anarchists of St. Germain-des-Prés, whose chief works are acts of senseless rudeness, destruction without recreation. The real artists do not overly concern themselves with their age's social problems. They concern themselves with themselves, working from that germ plasm that has not changed for millions of years in their race, which never will.

OCTOBER 26, 1952

Worked. Then a drink with Esther Arthur at 4 at Deux Magots.* She advises me to go home for a year, if I have the slightest leaning in that direction. Gave me another big push in that direction—dreaming of Texas, Florida, N.Y.—the prodigal's return, all that. Met Ellen—after long waiting—at the Invalides. Very affectionate. All so much better, due to peace of mind this last week, I shall probably stay in Paris. I wrote my

---

* The rival to Café de Flore, Les Deux Magots was frequented by numerous intellectuals during the postwar years, including Jean-Paul Sartre, Simone de Beauvoir, Albert Camus, Ernest Hemingway, James Joyce, Bertolt Brecht, Julia Child, James Baldwin, and Chester Himes. Since 1933, the Deux Magots literary prize has been awarded to a French novel.

mother to cable me if she intends to come at all—ergo, I'd hold onto the apartment. Ellen even promises she'll tolerate a cat!

OCTOBER 27, 1952

Sent letter to TM* postponing indefinitely, due mainly to the *Reader's Digest* highly approving my synopsis of the Italian restaurateur of Naples. Renay called this AM & I saw him this afternoon. Very encouraging. $1200 up to $2000! God—for 12 pages! Wrote my mother also.

10/28/52

The really depressing thing about being depressed is that one's own thoughts and their obvious courses (into all the little cul-de-sacs of impossibility) are so ordinary. To a much stupider man than myself, the same thoughts would occur, one realizes. And worst of all, the same emotions! A human creature, torn apart on the old rack of indecision and ambivalence of desire, is like any dog hesitating between the fleeing squirrel and the terrified, paralyzed rabbit—and losing both!

OCTOBER 29, 1952

Lunch with Bradley—civilization. And I overturned a water glass. She admires all my stories still, including "The Returnees." Wants me to go to the theater with her next week. She has that ineffable understanding of writers and their lives I have not encountered since Sturtevant. We have a new maid—Renée—who is splendid and makes life much easier. I am, in fact, suddenly quite happy. I long for a cat now. Perhaps Sunday we can find one. Mice we still have.

OCTOBER 30, 1952

Mailed the *Digest* pieces to N.Y. and Renay, with good hopes. Reading—Marcel Proust's letters. I await now—news from Margot & Harper. The apartment increasingly comfortable. After all my contortions, public and private, I begin to be reconciled to staying here. But not, I think, to write the book. Ellen is happy with her PX card,† and brings home loads of cans.

---

* Reference unknown.
† The Army & Air Force Exchange Service (AAFES, also referred to as the PX) is the retailer for U.S. Army and Air Force installations worldwide. The card and its benefits are available exclusively to military personnel and their families.

NOVEMBER 4, 1952

Eisenhower is elected—a real surprise to me. A landslide, moreover. The English papers are cool, report the French, though the old *Herald Tribune* reports them congratulatory and happy. The world is a mess now. More and more reasons not to go back. Finished my story well. 13 pages. Lyne telephoned, downstairs, being now forbidden the house because Ellen thinks her rude & insufficiently hospitable to her. We dined at Monique's, thence to L'Escale* with Monique. A jolly old time till 4:30 AM.

NOVEMBER 6, 1952

Good work. Quiet day. American movie tonight, not so good. Then E. quizzed me whom I was trying to telephone (Vali to postpone date one hour, because a hoity-toity friend of Ellen is also coming at 7) the whole thing came out and Ellen is fit to boil. To bed in growling, disgusted, sickened mood—after these lectures on why I should and must observe class distinction so long as I live with her—or else. O bitter! bitter! She tried to get affectionate with me in bed. I struck at her, had to, to ward her off. By Christ, I do believe she is insane. And I still fear for my life when I leave. She asked me why I stay. I said I ask myself the same question. I said for the *R. Digest* & my mother. "Why, so it'll be cheaper for the old lady when she comes to Paris?" Do dogs talk like this. I'd never have my mother here after that remark anyway!

NOVEMBER 7, 1952

Finished story typing. We prepare to go to Geneva. I'd rather stay here. But I too am going insane, doing things I do not want to do, always. Date with Monique & Lyne tonight. L'Escale later. Came home 2 AM & repeated to Ellen I didn't want to go to Geneva with her. Locked my room door, & when I awakened . . .

NOVEMBER 8, 1952

At nine, she was gone, a coffee cup standing on the corner of her dressing table. I made up my mind to leave. I called Jeannot at once. Saw him at 11. The drawback about taking his studio is that he & S. would want it about 5 days a month & I'd have to move to his mother's. So I chose Florence. Also with the help of Mrs. Bradley whom I saw at 12:15. Came

---

* Parisian nightclub since 1945, a favorite venue for lovers of Afro-Cuban and Latin American music.

home & lunched, then went to Les Invalides & called Titi, saying I'd be in Florence Wed. I bought my plane ticket. Saw Jeannot & girl tonight. Dinner *chez moi*. Very good. Then we went to the Monocle—I in my best pants—danced with several girls, & was of course refused by the woman I'd have preferred to dance with. Sylvia wants an affair with me. She isn't appealing & I'm not in the mood.

11/9/52

   To E.H. Hello and good bye.
   I take leave as I met you,
   With a rather stunned voice,
   And a little wonder in my face.
   Though in between was enough definite and concrete,
   God knows, to clarify anything.
   To generate
   Pure hate,
   And calorify
   The coolest lover, which I wasn't.
   Enough concrete to sink a ship,
   If I may make a pun,
   And to crush a character
   A lot stronger than mine.
   Don't you think I held up well?
   But there's no need to ask you.
   You thought you were all right
   And I was all wrong.
   Which is why I am going somewhere else.
   Where I belong.

NOVEMBER 11, 1952

   Ellen did not return until 10:30. We talked sanely for a couple of hours. Then she became hysterical, said she'd kill herself, etc. I tried to comfort her. She wanted to make a date Xmas. I wanted none ahead of me. Shall I make a date to sleep with you Xmas Eve in Venice? I asked. Because she said I was the first and last person she'd want to sleep with.

NOVEMBER 12, 1952

   In the morning, we both looked like hell, of course. We parted miserably at the Gare des Invalides, a handclasp, a touched cheek—Maybe in 3 or

4 weeks you'll change your mind, she said. But en route I felt increasingly freer and better. A man shared his lunch with me from Milan down. The flight over the Alps was spectacular and lovely. Called Titi at 6:20—was enthusiastically welcomed, and asked up for ten. My room is cold. But I am optimistic.

NOVEMBER 13, 1952

I worry lest a terrible telegram arrives from Ellen.

NOVEMBER 17, 1952

No mail. Especially from Ellen. Which drives me insane.

NOVEMBER 19, 1952

Lonely. Very depressed. To point of tears. I have no rock, no salvation, without work.

NOVEMBER 21, 1952

Very upset. Tried to call Ellen at 3, and was unable to get a line thru. At 2 AM suddenly got out of bed and called Paris. Ellen said—"I know you love me. I've written you a long letter. I've tentative reservation on a boat for 25th December. Can you wait that long? I'll do anything you say. We can go to Santa Fe or wherever you like." I'd only asked her how she was. She said "I'm all right"—her voice very precise and English over the phone. I said I'd go home with her. Then I couldn't sleep for a long while. But I am suddenly happy—love is a strange neurosis. Is this love? It is certainly sex. Perhaps I need her nagging discordant personality around me. I lay thinking, so must my hero* feel when he kills his wife in hatred and discovers she was necessary to him.

NOVEMBER 22, 1952

Packed & moved to [Pensione] éolini—haven of D. H. Lawrence and other notables, a maze of dark stone corridors and steps and oubliette toilets, tile stones, and bleak, barren rooms with prison cell blankets. Dreary but perhaps good for mental discipline. And I am in no state of mind to care.

---

* Walter in *The Blunderer*.

NOVEMBER 25, 1952

Cable that Trieste job has been tentatively offered Ellen. Would I like it? I cabled okay, but this evening lapsed into awful depression—that like a disease. I am homesick. I should go. If I can afford it.

NOVEMBER 27, 1952

A turkeyless Thanksgiving for this American. First sunny day in weeks. It has been raining and the Arno is high. Book progresses in thought. It resembles *Strangers* perhaps too much in structure but not in story. Nevertheless this is the structure of my own mind.

11/30/52

"Care of Mrs. Somebody." I am always "Care of Mrs. Somebody." Or "Mr. Somebody." I have never a home. I wander from New York, to Paris, to London, to Venice, Munich, Salzburg, and Rome, without a real address. My letters arrive by the grace of God and Mr. or Mrs. Somebody. Someday, perhaps, I shall have a house built of rock, a house with a name—Hanley-on-the-Lake, Bedford on the River, West Hills, or plain Sunny Vale. Something. So even without my own name on the envelope letters will reach me, because I and only I shall be living there. But that can never make up for these years of standing in line at American Express offices from [Place de l']Opéra [in Paris] to Haymarket [in London], Naples to Munich. Can never make up for the tragic, melancholic, humiliating mornings when one has gone with hope for a letter, and turned away empty handed, empty hearted. There are millions of Americans like me, who have tasted without pay the bitterness of colonial empiring. England's corps had their camaraderie. The French had their wine, The Americans, official colonizers, have their pay checks, perhaps even their wives. But what have the solitary Americans? Often not even a friendship with Mrs. Somebody. Or a good odor with the Pension Sporca in Florence, where they left without tipping the maids. (The fact was, that last bill cleaned them out.) They wander, unattached atoms, over the face of the earth, care of Mrs. Somebody. Until that glorious day they embark from Naples, or Cherbourg, or Genoa, and proudly start giving their new address: So-and-so East Sixty-Third Street, or something-or-other Jane Street. But it's still care of Miss Somebody. And when they get to America, they forget about the house they wanted, made of rock. They sit about, walk about, rush about, dreaming of the Pension Sporca, and of how soon they can get back.

They long for the rocky, blue-watered beaches of Italy, for the soft colors of Florence, for the nocturnal haunts of Paris. And soon (as soon as they can scrape up the money again) they are off. With a new address: care of American Express, Paris. Care of Mme Carpentier, Paris. Care of Mr. & Mrs. So-and-So, Rome. Care of the Yacht Club, Mallorca, Palma de. Wandering atoms, forever in search of alone, forever isolated. For who can match them, who can be their mate? They have an aversion for each other, and are more tourist-hating than any European on the continent, not excepting the Communists. They are shuttlers. Atoms. Wanderers. The homeless, the addressless, the migratory birds of America.

DECEMBER 2, 1952

Telegram suddenly at 3 that Ellen is in Geneva 5 Dec. Wants me to meet her there with all my luggage. Whether we stay or go, is unknown. I cabled yes, I would. Wrote well for the first time here in Florence.

12/3/52

It really is difficult to be the person one should like to be—civilized, always self-possessed, ever receptive to stimuli and receptive at our most sensitive and intellectual and romantic and classic peak, if one has not the money to take a taxi when it is raining or when one is tired, or to go to America, an essential, crying need of the spirit, too. It really is hard.

DECEMBER 5, 1952

I am sorry to leave all the nice people in Florence. Took the train at 10:40—to Milan at 3, in time to miss the 2:45 to Geneva. Bought Ellen a sweater & tried to kill 5 hours constructively. Got to Geneva—cold as hell—at 1:30 A.M to the Hotel de Russie at 2. Ellen in bed, having tried to pick me up at 9:30. XX, etc. very wonderful after all. But I am a cork on her stormy sea, drifting where she goes.

DECEMBER 5, 1952

The Trieste job [for Ellen] is materializing, ruling America out. I am disappointed. And it is easy for Ellen, by way of having her way, to convince me I haven't enough money to go to the States. Plane to Paris at 7:30. I am mentally fatigued at the thought of all that lies ahead. Plus telling my mother, already depressed, that I am not coming over. Mother says, business still dull in Orlando, she'll go to Tampa. How dismal must it be to have set one's heart so low as the commercial form of one's art all one's life, and then to find that that does not provide for one's old age! The heat at 83 feels delicious.

DECEMBER 7, 1952

Day of leisure. Showed Ellen the Avon letter,* which is the best money bet to work on—the gay book. I begin thinking about it, as the suspense novel needs a freer mind than I have at present. XX etc.

DECEMBER 9, 1952

Lunch with Bradley. Discussed briefly advisability of changing agents with Bradley. She says also Margot "no longer uses the usual courses" in submitting stuff. Short cuts, tips, and the higher prices. Margot has made no great effort to hurry Harper. Neither has she sold one story in over a year, as Ellen frequently points out.

DECEMBER 13, 1952

Letter from Lil [Picard]. Sympathizing, calling Ellen a selfish bitch-witch, hard, knowing exactly what she wants and out to get it. Unfortunately at present she wants me.

DECEMBER 14, 1952

Work. First chapter rewrite. To Posnanski's for aperitif. She says Ellen suffered "moral collapse" when I was gone. This embarrasses E.

DECEMBER 15, 1952

Depressed generally about everything. Mainly dissatisfaction at the ocean of (stupid) work ahead of me before any recognition or publication is possible.

DECEMBER 16, 1952

Barely finished 1st chapter rewrite last night & Ellen comments barely enough sex in it for consumption of public.

---

* Avon had started out in 1941 as a mass-market paperback reprint publisher. By the time they asked Pat to write a "queer" book in the early 1950s, they were starting to publish original fiction and to extend their list from mostly mystery to fantasy, science fiction, and romance. In the end, they decided against Pat's novel—working title *The Breakup*—of which she'd already written at least three chapters.

DECEMBER 17, 1952

I note: "the insanity that stalks: isolation and semi-failure." One does turn to religion or rink—in both cases something stronger than one is oneself.

12/17/52

Manès Sperber*—chief reader for Calmann-Lévy. Tells me right off, "I wish I had asked you to come here to tell you something more favorable than I am going to tell you." Proceeds to rip into my book—I have *raté*. What did I mean by the whole thing, anyway. Various frustrations, I say. Frustration is a word almost unknown in France, except in a legal sense. "I can tell you right now—and I know, I have never been wrong— your book would fail in France, would be read by nobody, reviewed by two or three people, and those badly . . . your men are ridiculous, if I may say so, and you know better than I (with a shrewd look) why they are . . . they operate by tics instead of character." The redeeming feature is that he asked me did I take an advance and have to write this book? I told him I'd taken nothing and if any book was written by me because I wanted to, this was it. His house is stark and simply furnished, the house of an intellectual. A modern painting by Vargas on the wall, Japanese mats on the small square end tables. He smokes Gauloises with his tea and does not eat anything. Another gaffe—reminds me that the Café Flore & Deux Magots are not the real Paris! Any attempt I make to say other people have liked the book, M. Sperber counters with the information that these people, in fact, never read books. He knows.

DECEMBER 24, 1952

To Bradley's champagne cocktail party—20 odd serious French people and Mina Kirstein Curtiss,† with whom I discussed M. Johnson as agent. She knows her well, says there is no better in New York. Mina taught Margot English at Smith College. Says she is Margot's last literary conscience. We left 2 valises with Bradley which she very kindly offered to take. Sent New Year's cards the other day—one to A. Koestler in London. Tonight—a small delicately delicious dinner all alone with Ellen

---

* Manès Sperber (1905–1984), renowned Jewish exile writer and longtime editor at Paris publisher Calmann-Lévy. He was particularly successful in Germany, and received the Friedenspreis des Deutschen Buchhandels (Peace Prize of the German Book Fair) in 1983.
† Mina Kirstein Curtiss (1896–1985) taught English at Smith College until 1934 and again in the early 1940s. She also published several biographies and translated Proust.

chez nous. Then present opening, Ellen's sweater I so hopefully bought in Milano is too big!

DECEMBER 25, 1952

Got away at 8 A.M. in the dark still. Xmas Day—all France awake & buying from the *boulangers* & the *laiteries*. With very hard driving we made it to Bâle this evening. Drei Könige Hotel. Ellen wants so to enjoy her *vacances.* I'm doing my best & shall succeed. One must look at longer & longer range. Letter yesterday from my mother of their hard times in Orlando this month & past. Depression set in after the elections & they "waited too long" as usual to get out. S. is slow, my mother does not face unpleasant facts until they are upon her & it is too late. Hence this: They have gone to Miami, that crap town, & she has a small fashion job she already anticipates losing. I can easily foresee them on the rocks at 60, which is not far off. Then what? It is another *Death of a Salesman* saga in commercial artist profession. To me overwhelmingly —terribly tragic. What am I supposed to do? Tit for tat? And what other way can I look at it but that?

1953

IN 1953, PATRICIA HIGHSMITH gradually moved back to the United States and gradually separated from Ellen Blumenthal Hill. She also gradually finds her way back to the genre that suits her best, and which will allow her to survive in the world of literary publishing: the thriller.

Pat is ashamed of her home country, which is in the grips of Senator Joseph McCarthy's reign of terror. But she is even more ashamed of returning to that country penniless, without more to show for herself than a single novel and a handful of short stories. She will keep her pseudonymous second novel, *The Price of Salt*, secret from her family.

Pat's twelfth diary is relatively slim in comparison to Diary 11. Many entries are written after the fact, and she writes in English, at least until early September, when she moves back to Fort Worth and—perhaps out of longing for Europe—begins to write in Italian, a new "secret language."

At the beginning of the year, Ellen and Pat are still planning to stay in their apartment in central Trieste, where Ellen has found new employment. Ellen is a woman of independent means, though, and within four months has resigned from her job. Meanwhile, Pat takes whatever work she can. She applies for a position teaching English to city government employees, composes short stories, and thinks about interesting topics for articles to write. With the prospect of a $5,000 advance, Pat is also working on another "queer book" that she considers more honest, more interesting, and altogether better than her first. At the same time, Pat feels sluggish, uninspired, and hampered by Ellen. In the hope that a change in scenery will help with their relationship issues, the two travel by ship from Genoa to Gibraltar, then explore southern Spain. They cross the Atlantic in May, headed for New York. Pat spends the voyage ruminating on her current psychological thriller, *A Man Provoked* (later renamed *The Blunderer*); she has completed the first draft in late November of 1952 in Florence, but tabled it for lack of inspiration.

While Ellen visits her mother in Santa Fe, Pat rents a room in New York. After two and a half years in Europe, she struggles to regain her footing in the New York publishing world and feels like a failure, broke and beyond hope. She turns to old friends for comfort, including Rolf Tietgens, with whom she unexpectedly spends a night, years after their first fling. When Ellen returns from Santa Fe, she attempts to kill herself in Pat's presence and nearly succeeds. Pat flees the city, running straight into the arms of Lynn Roth, a blond actress with whom she has a brief, intense affair. The new novel Pat has so resolutely revived is dedicated to her.

Ellen returns to Europe and Pat accepts her cousin Millie Alford's invitation to come back to Fort Worth. She feels good there, she frequently goes riding, continues to drink heavily, and hunkers down with her typewriter. In a frenzy, Pat finishes *The Blunderer* by the end of the year. The thirty-something-year-old protagonist Walter Stackhouse, who is nearly the same age as his creator, also shares her disillusion. At first glance, he leads a successful life: he has his own law practice in Manhattan, a house on Long Island, and a wife who earns good money. Still, he feels alienated and falls victim to his own imagination when he uses it to fight the banality of his life.

JANUARY 1, 1953

The Year begins with much XX, I hope it goes on. Last night very wild & divine, taking those words in primitive and profound sense.

JANUARY 3, 1953

Plans of St. Moritz. Ellen is alternately bored, restless, wanting to leave, chiefly because I type all day.

JANUARY 4, 1953

Half working. Finished drastic cutting of first 2 chapters. It will improve. A pity this book wasn't longer digested, but the writing, in haste, is good practice of its kind.

JANUARY 5, 1953

Work at a standstill as Ellen cannot bear the typing. It leaves me with little to do. With an impatience I can bear only philosophically, certainly not logically. No mail at all. Margot, I hope, is having herself a good time.

JANUARY 7, 1953

We were off in hellish darkness at 8 A.M. A tense ride to Lugano, where we left the car & caught the 10 A.M. bus to St. Moritz, arriving at 3:15 after several kilometers of level mountain heights. This district is beautiful! The Sils[-Maria] village, where Nietzsche wrote *Zarathustra*. St. Moritz is a military looking village, towering hotels flying Swiss and English flags, snow covered streets filled with chicer & bigger shops than Kitzbühel. We decided on the Kulm [Hotel]. It is nearly empty here, very formal, very stuffy. I wear my sleeveless dress to dinner and catch a cold. But otherwise the evening very very agreeable.

JANUARY 9, 1953

To Chantanella for picnic lunch in the sun. Full of happy English skiers. The mountain top goal impossible due to wind & snow: Glühwein & Viennese music.

JANUARY 11, 1953

Caught 9:40 A.M. bus from St. Moritz to Lugano. The car fine in Lugano. Very nice to return to. We reached Milan by 4:30. Ellen's mood goes steadily upward now that she is about to go to work again, and possibly to leave me alone for a few days.

JANUARY 12, 1953

At 9:00 A.M. at the consulate to renew my passport, which we learn can be as well done in Venice. So off we go early. Venice is frightfully cold but sunny.

JANUARY 13, 1953

Called Peggy Guggenheim for 6:30 cocktails at Harry's [Bar]. With 3 dogs & a fairy in tow she appeared. James Monroe Moon, Jr.[*] of N. Carolina. Ellen very popular due to her interesting work. I began talking with one Mary Oliver & friend Jody in Harry's—a red headed horror of an international tramp. Jane Bowles' friends types. Both queer, in pants. Peggy nervous but very amiable.

JANUARY 14, 1953

Very sad parting with Ellen at the station. She drove off in a Fiat, which the Porta Roma man had "aestheticized." I came home & worked well

---

* James Monroe Moon Jr. was an American artist (1928–2019).

the rest of the day and evening. Though James M. M. invited me to Harry's for a huge beer. He is very nice about showing me apartments, though there are few here.

JANUARY 15, 1953

At 6:30 met James and went to the house of the 2 boys who are going to Capri to start a bar, Richard Page-Smith and George, a painter. R.P.S. plays the piano, evidently well as he accompanied Bricktop.* The boys knew me as I had been to that party of Maud Basserman's in Capri in 1951. Then the long walk home, dinner alone at my favorite trattoria where a distinguished Italian was reciting poetry. Mostly men. I was offered a glass of good wine by one—the same men eat at the same places every day. Drinking coffee afterward, I met two strangers who invited me for brandy at the Luna Hotel. And there also was Mary Oliver, deep in her 20th cup—of rum. She poured the remainder of the bottle into a coke bottle—insisted we all drink more brandies—and held forth, about how her friend Jody McLean has "subsidized" Paul and Jane Bowles for years, "Jody must have poured a million dollars into those two." They are also going to Trieste tomorrow, which will provide some amusement. Ellen called at 8. Has found an apartment, large & expensive & romantic.

JANUARY 17, 1953

[Trieste.]† Saw two apartments, took the one on 22 Via Stuparich, chez the Luccardis. Too big, 90.000 lire per month with ½-time maid. But we have no choice. The hotel would be more expensive, though Ellen says without me she'd stay in the hotel till spring. I have mail—but none from Margot. Trieste is gloomy, masculine, functional—I imagine a town that grows on one. Should love to know where Joyce has been here.

JANUARY 18, 1953

Tonight, cocktails with Mary Oliver & Jody McLean. Jody paid the huge check. She was also the keeper of Jane Bowles for a while—the same gray-haired spinster with whom Janey went to N. Africa. I hear Janey is now in New York. (I wish I were.)

---

* Born Ada Beatrice Queen Victoria Louise Virginia Smith (1894–1984), Bricktop was an American singer and dancer who owned a nightclub in Paris.
† Trieste, a port city on the Adriatic, officially became a part of Italy in 1954. It was polyglot and divided because it had been liberated by two different countries (the United States and Great Britain). The city was still controlled by British and American forces when Pat and Ellen settled here.

JANUARY 19, 1953

My birthday and who cares? We moved this morning. It is hard to imagine staying here a year, even many months. I am not very happy—am restless, not knowing yet what Harper has said [with regard to *The Traffic of Jacob's Ladder*].

JANUARY 20, 1953

Ellen's birthday. I wasn't even inspired to make a card, alas, though I had one in mind. Can any artistic, warm, outgoing emotion flourish in such atmosphere? No moment is there a tempo like mine! Oh my God—bodily chemistry should be taboo! And for conversation, repeated stories of how someone has praised her brains that day! At least it is more tolerable to me than was Florence, when I was working well, on something good, when $3,000 had just been announced for me, when Ellen had no job & felt inferior. She is far more malicious than I, though I do not deny malice exists everywhere.

JANUARY 22, 1953

Best working day yet. Third chapter done for the book (the queer one for Avon). It is over simple—but maybe what they like. I think better & more interesting than [*The Price of*] *Salt* though not upper upper-class writing. Still there is room for honesty. Else I couldn't continue.

JANUARY 23, 1953

I cannot believe—I shall not go to America this year. Had a most seriously depressed letter from my mother when I got to Trieste. She contemplates a trip to Texas for the "emotional help" it may give. I wrote back a heartening yet still honest letter, in which I reminded her she had a habit of not facing facts until too late. Stanley also wrote, very thoughtful, likes the Italian notebook immensely, worried they wouldn't be able to offer me a home when I come. They shuttle between Miami & Orlando now. Alas I foresee them not bettering things—in spite of Stanley's optimism and assuring Mother that her fears are "grossly exaggerated." Now my poor mother is even ashamed to return to Texas for a visit because she needs a new bag, hasn't a winter coat, & because they are all swimming in money there. This fills me with more tragic emotion than I realize consciously & accounts for much of my depression lately. I should really not be surprised if one of them should commit suicide for the insurance—it would have to be Stanley, I believe. A horrible thought. How much saner is my grandmother, with her far superior brain! My mother now speaks of "possibly falling ill" unless she has some change, even of scene. This is a death wish. And there is no use praying, no use suggesting any bucking up: I am sure they both feel the handicaps of age creeping up, of inferiority to other artists in their line, etc. I answered airmail. I only expect the worse in the next letter. To be perfectly realistic about it.

JANUARY 27, 1953

Work. At last the letter re Harper arrives and to my rather great disappointment, they don't like the book—evidently not at all. "What do you want me to do about it?" Margot asks. They say too much ground covered, not new or newly expressed ideas, the damning worst, with regrets. Joan Kahn writes it is "not worthy of Pat." Apparently, I am wrong—if the whole world is in accord against me. I wrote Margot I shall reread the book & let her know what to do. Meanwhile they want a suspense story [Gerry Rhodes. *Today's Family*, a new magazine]. I shall do the radio suspense story "Innocent Witness."* *Barnard* [*Quarterly*] printing an anthology & ask for my printed short stories. Got my new brown corduroy jacket. Italian cut.

JANUARY 31, 1953

Errands by the dozen. To the opera tonight with Sra. Luccardi. Returned to find a surprise champagne supper on the kitchen table, prepared by Giustina—sausage & cake. Frankie, Yolanda's daughter, came down. We were up late—until Ellen broke it up by the simple expedient of removing the ashtrays and glasses from underneath us.

FEBRUARY 12, 1953

Read 3rd book. Find it inconclusive—perhaps should be cut enormously. I wrote Margot: she may show it again as it is, if she so decides. It is difficult for me to cut from here, and I guess I am willing to believe that not every publisher will feel as Harper did. Sent stories to *Accent*. "Man's Best Friend." And "Love Is a Terrible Thing." It's cold, grim life, I note. Mornings almost never pass without vicious exchanges—so horrible to begin the day. I lie in bed, reading, riding it out until it is over, she is gone, and I can begin my quite different day with some semblance of peace and order. Tonight attended lecture by Prof. Stanislaus Joyce, of Trieste University (Prof. of English) on [his brother's James Joyce's] *The*

---

* A script Pat is writing for a German broadcasting company.

Dubliners. I found him very entertaining, as different from James as night and day. I long to write more and more acquaintances in the States, in hopes of a letter. I am so terribly lonely, lost, stagnant. Wrote [*Fort Worth*] *Star Telegram* asking if they want a piece on D.P. [Displaced Persons] camps, which I visited today. Secretary Mrs. Lipsky took me thru, I saw the mess, the cubicles in which they live.

FEBRUARY 14, 1953

Letter from Margot. Margot "likes the girls in *Breakup* better than in *Salt*." Now being shown to Avon books. But I am in the dumps and feel like a 3rd rate writer. Where are the winged days of 1946? That spring— Christ, what a mistake I made! Starting with Ginnie. This is Valentine's Day. It passed unnoticed.

2/14/53

My Epitaph '53. Here lies one who always muffed his chance.

FEBRUARY 15, 1953

The Bora began last evening. It fairly confines us to the house today. By this evening, a pane of glass in the foyer roof is broken out, 2 shutters destroyed, and our tea guest was even unable to come! The worst wind yet.

2/19/53

I have to start a completely new life; these words are all cousins to: I am going to kill myself.

2/19/53

I have nothing of beauty to be my joy forever now, but my idea of beauty remains; that is my joy forever. Trieste—I am a thirsty tree here. I have many roots, and much need of many kinds of water. I long for sidewalks with a strip of grass beside them, white windowsills, ivory piano keys with the sunshine on them, red brick houses with chimneys, with leaves to be gathered and burnt in October.

FEBRUARY 24, 1953

Am still paralyzingly homesick. I'd love to be in Texas. These are days without letters, without Ellen, without money—and very difficult to live thru. Now Ellen accuses me of "letting her down on Trieste" because I want to go home. As I feel these days, I should not return if I went, for what'd I be returning to?

FEBRUARY 28, 1953

Arose at 4:10 A.M. and caught the 6 A.M. train for Venice, sleepily reading [Samuel] Hoffenstein's *Poems in Praise of P.N.* [*Practically Nothing*] the while. Arrived very dramatically in Venice at 8:30. Saw a most fascinating small boy solemnly waiting for the Diretto at 8:20 at the R.R. station, book-bag in his lap, tiny feet crossed, a somber heavy face, intelligent, and fearsomely thoughtful & wise for his age. A small scar of sore on his temple, showing beside his aviator's helmet. He looked at no one, boarded and debarked at Accademia. I wonder what kind of parents made him so somber? I found Ellen in a dark room at the Luna Hotel, her breakfast tray beside the bed. I embraced her and to my great joy and surprise, she responded. So abruptly are our month long feuds dispersed! The weekend was heavenly—and so unexpected.

MARCH 1, 1953

An idle day. We sunned, & I walked along by the Bridge of Sighs, where they were getting ready for a circus. Giant swings that make complete revolutions, with bottom side ever parallel to the earth. Ellen's reentry permit is held up—due to what we don't know. Association with me, the new law, or an error. Her mother hasn't written in weeks & Ellen is sure she's dead.

MARCH 2, 1953

Job hunting. There is an English elementary teaching job open but I have little teaching experience, so it is dubious. But it would be 45 per week if I got it, which is like riches to me now. Prepared Trieste-Brussels refugee story to send to Margot. I am planning, though only half-heartedly, several things to write. I am in need of many things now—but chiefly encouragement, a pep talk from my agent.

MARCH 3, 1953

Ellen remarkably changed since Sat. Now I suppose my only trouble is earning money—for such strange changes have occurred in me about my work, I don't care sometimes if I write another line, if I gain money or fail thereby or not. In the face of bleak discouragement, one cannot go on forever. It now does appear that Ellen may never be able to get into the States again. Her mother is well. Has been waiting for news from a lawyer. Under the new McCarran Aliens Act,* reentry permits can be renewed for only one year, not seven, as E. has done. She may transfer all to Switzerland soon. Wrote more importunate letter to Margot, asking her what's what about the book. She could spare 15 minutes to tell me (her opinion also) after these 8 months!

MARCH 5, 1953

Went yesterday to AFN [American Forces Network] radio here. They wanted sample of my work, so sent the Munich suspense play.† It is all irons in the fire.

MARCH 7, 1953

To Udine with Ellen. I am rather tense. The marriage relation is no relation at all. Ellen's castration complex is to make the next two weeks hellish. Udine has a beautiful cluttered square of statues, overlarge churches & administration buildings jammed too close together, a painter's delight. But it is cold.

MARCH 11, 1953

P. 39. How little does plot matter, whose it is. The joy and the art is how it is handled. Drove some at noon. But "the impasse holds," I note— Impossible to approach Ellen in bed or really anywhere else. If I want to talk to her, she is too busy, too tired.

MARCH 13, 1953

A nice letter from Ann S. about soothing subjects, the fatal error of most liking one's mate really, and her supreme contentment with Betty. "There's lots of pretty nice girls around," Ann reminds me, as she does not have to.

MARCH 17, 1953

Ellen will not listen, nor understand a fraction of my side. I say: "People do not say such things to each other continually. It isn't done between married people . . . Nor do they sleep with each other only twice a

---

* The Immigration and Nationality Act, also known as the McCarran-Walter Act, is an American federal law from 1952 regulating immigration in the United States.
† Probably a reference to "Innocent Witness," Pat's suspense radio play.

month." (If I am lucky it is that these days, and when she chooses.) The human ego, anybody's, cannot stand up under constant belittling. I tremble, weep, smoke, and make myself a nervous wreck over this— unreasonably, because I need not stay—and God knows, if I were in New York, I should not stick. My tooth worries me, somewhat my finances. I am afraid, a little, to cross the ocean to nothing and start a new life, but this is precisely what I should do. (Why don't you go back to Ginnie? Ellen asks rhetorically & with bitterness, if I ever try to illustrate a point.)

MARCH 19, 1953

A splendid morning of sunshine, a long walk, and feeding the pigeons. Came home and finished Part one well. 90 pages. Then Balalaika, which I enjoyed. Russian D.P. entertainment. Thane & friend Ryder behaved like the heels they are, the latter mixing his own drinks! But he has promised to secure for me an illicit PX card.

MARCH 22, 1953

Rereading (queer) book, which takes comparatively little correcting. O to be on the beam, and to produce reams, for dear old pocketbooks! At times it seems not bad to do, at others, I am disgusted with myself for contemplating it, and therefore jeopardizing the few good years I have to write better stuff. A feeling of renunciation, I note, with hatred running red & hot in the blood.

MARCH 23, 1953

I give up any X future with E., not without bitterness. I scrape thru these remaining days until we go to the States—20 April—

MARCH 26, 1953

The dreamy days. Ellen decides to go over Easter. I, too. Though she still tries to dissuade me, due to my low funds. She cannot understand that it is my home.

MARCH 27, 1953

Big scene last night, I believe—because I said she must know that we are through, that I'd be insane to choose to continue a discordant relation-ship like ours. I said, let's take separate boats if we go. She had drinks, wept, I drank quietly, felt sorry for her. And of course later, ended up with X after Enrico's.

MARCH 31, 1953

Work. P. 80. Very sweet letter from Ann [S.] asking me to stay on Fire
Island with her June 1 onward. And saying her X with Betty has gone
to pot. And A. is having affairs on the side, with little remorse finally. A
thoroughly wonderful letter.

4/5/53

[Ravenna.] San Vitale: 550 A.D. The most beautiful church or cathedral
I have ever seen, and it was a real pleasure to discover a church which in
beauty & proportion, richness of decoration, so definitely takes the palm
from St. Peter's, St. Mark's, St. Paul's. It is small and round. Everywhere
marble, like Rorschach tests, symmetrically set slabs in the pillars that
circle the main dome. Galleries, behind which smaller, further galleries
are to be seen, like the unending chambers full of treasures said to be
awaiting us in Heaven. Over an arched door to an alcove, I saw a most
striking Christ I've ever seen, stark and ugly as Rouault's Christs, though
with more shading around the sad, dark, exhausted, reproachful, indig-
nant, threatening, yet rather weak eyes. Flowing up to him, the disciples,
Laurentius, Paolus, Johannus, Marcus, Ippolitus, Vitalis, etc. And all
this in mosaic, of course.

APRIL 5, 1953

Delighted to get home. The last trip we shall make in the noble little
Topolino,* which has just been sold to an American G.I. for $500. Ellen
does not lack for cash these days.

APRIL 6, 1953

Wanted to go out on the town with Ellen, but of course she refused.
I called Tom, & with Banjo we went to the Balalaika, danced, drank
wine, grappa, coffee, beer, and had a wonderful time. Scrambled eggs at
his house. Of course Ellen awoke, sour, solemn, hurt, shocked at my 2
AM lateness, when I arrived. Alas, I'd just been having too much fun to
suit her.

4/12/53

It is easier to be a poet today than a novelist. The poet can create healthy
prose and simple; the novelist has to write within the framework of a
philosophy, and can any novelist today build one? Can he even write

---

* The Italian word for little mouse is both the name for Mickey Mouse and the Fiat 500.

about himself with respect, mystery, pride, enthusiasm, joy? The psycho-
analysts have torn open his soul, everyone has taken a look, and no one
is any longer interested in the little gemlike gallstones the writer may pull
out of himself and offer, in however a charming setting.

APRIL 14, 1953
Work. Writing FBI story "Blindman's Buff."*

APRIL 18, 1953
Letter from Margot. She says when pocketbook [i.e., *The Breakup*] is
done, I'll have enough money to do anything I wish.

APRIL 19, 1953
Depart Trieste via sleeper to Genoa at 8 P.M. Sad at leaving.

APRIL 20, 1953
Genoa morning. Colombo hotel, a lovely room. I told Ellen she must
think I am insane to continue living with her. She asked: "Do you like
me?" "How can I?" Ergo she would neither sleep nor eat with me, & I
dined alone on a real fish soup in a backstreet of the port. Thus our last
night on real European soil was the epitome of our miserable relationship.

APRIL 24, 1953
[Gibraltar.] The hotel is ½ mile up from town, magnificent view of the
harbor, hills of Africa on the left. (The Rock behind us, said to be the
habitat of several apes.) I like the town very much—one main street,
cluttered with the junk & signs of England and Spain. In the hotel are
a weird couple—Mr. and Mrs. Kent, she the most deformed & hideous wretch I've ever seen—hair-lipped & hunchbacked from birth,
victim then of paralysis of some sort of the legs, deaf to boot, hair of
waved dyed blond, which looks like a wig, aged about 55. I have to
turn my eyes away at table (another table, thank God) to avoid being
sick. Mr. Kent is about 40, reddish complexion not unattractive, attentive to her to such an extent, there must be some guilt somewhere.
They are certainly married as their passports testify. He looks like
a paid gigolo, who has sold his freedom for a lifelong security. One
longs to ask him her story.
     Who would dare?

---

* This short story has been lost.

4/27/53

Lower Spain. From Gibraltar to Algeciras, the paddlewheel ferry is laden with smugglers, the rattiest, most bestial people I have laid eyes on anywhere. Twenty men and fifteen women, they frantically repack their Gibraltar purchases in their filthy canvas bags, pasteboard cartons, in some mysterious system so complicated that they are busy with it the entire trip: bread crusts on top, cigarettes, honey, Peek Frean's, ovaltine, chocolate wafers below. Whom they expect to fool is a mystery also, for their pockets are bulging, their rubber boots are so stuffed they can scarcely walk. One woman ties a packet of cigarettes into a handkerchief, which she ties to the back of a crucifix necklace, and conceals under her dress on her back. They tip the police, I have heard, though I do not see it. The land above Algeciras to Seville, is empty of people, but filled with pigs, chickens, goats, horses of all ages.

MAY 6, 1953

Gibraltar never looked so good as at 4 P.M.—today after Spain, that uncivilized country! And the Rock Hotel with the glorious towels! The tea! The comfort!

MAY 7, 1953

Up at 5 to catch the boat. All very chic & clean & hospitable aboard. We moved to a splendid cabin for 4, as cabin class is almost empty. Cocktail party this evening. E. has champagne, I 3 martinis. Saw *Peter Pan* which I thought only fair. Disney's latest.

MAY 11, 1953

Absolutely nothing happens. I try to think intensely about the suspense novel—#5. It will not jell yet.

MAY 13, 1953

Landed punctually at 1:00—a thrilling entry up the long channel west of Long Island, into Manhattan, which very slowly grew discernible through the fog. Then the sun came out. I peered for Ann S. on the dock, but could not see her. She called at 2:20, and said I'd told her not to come to the dock—Anyway, she came at 5:30 for a drink at the Winslow, Ellen joined us, then Margot, really glad to see me—a lovely 3 drink cocktail hour.

MAY 14, 1953

Shopping—vainly but for ballet type shoes, which now hurt me. On to
Margot's for a gala evening of Margot's best cooking, television, then
going over 2¼-years' work of mine. As usual, the editors all seem to
want to print me, all praise the writing, and even suggest they give me
plots to write up! Am to lunch with [McCann editor] Goldbeck (who
might take the 3rd book on strength of a suspense fifth), Lee Schryver,
and Eleanor Stierham, now the editor of Collier's. Should stay a month,
my time will certainly not be wasted. But the home here is filthy, and
worst of all, so cluttered I have hardly any room. Lil made the minimum effort to get it ready—and certainly it is not capable of containing
two. Ergo, and with the tearful insecurity Ellen feels at being in my old
stomping ground, she is talking of taking off at any moment. She has
asked me to come to Santa Fe, for about a month, then perhaps on to
San Miguel Allende. I have said yes one time and no another.

MAY 16, 1953

We rearranged the room, long & earnest talks with Dell, who agreed to
let me stay 2 months & get out then if I want to. Ellen thinks I'll want
to after Avon book is done. (Then she wants me to go to Santa Fe for a
month.) Signed Dell $150 check for 2 months. Which leaves me about
$750 in each bank! Margot can get me $1150 of the $2300 due this year
from Bantam Pocketbooks for Salt. Perhaps I'll take it. So it looks finally
as if Dell's place will work out. By accident, I learned that I have a piece
in the Neue Zürcher Zeitung. The "Magnet Zurich" (Schweizerische
Heimwehkur) which I wrote in Ascona & Ellen translated. Am terrifically proud of that!

Cooked in very amiably with Dell & Ellen tonight. I resent Ellen's
blithe unconcern about food (except to eat it). But after all—that's a
small thing to resent compared to the colossal half-assedness of most
of America's queer girls. T'would be strange indeed if America sent me
back to the arms of Mrs. Hill. It has become more deeply depressing to
me—to see the scores of vapid minded girls sitting in American bars—
professional homosexuals.

MAY 17, 1953

Loafed, dreamed of writing & read the big Sunday papers. Ellen lunches
with Jim Dobrochek—the painter she lived with in Florence. She would
like to marry him, I think, for the passport. Would mean, however, eter-

nal suspense, as they would neither clear her nor fire her during the ensuing investigations. At least, being British, one is not investigated. Every
page of the paper echoes with McCarthy & this week [Clement] Atlee
lambasted him, & McCarthy demanded apologies & threatened to cur-
tail money. I trust Attlee will continue not to apologize. Ellen becomes
impossibly frantic when I cannot tell precisely how many blocks walking
we have to do. Like a virago, she blames me, & says she will not walk a
step further. Then I hate her.

MAY 19, 1953

Lunch with Rolf here. Very pleasant. Told me he did not try to see me
again in Italy because with Ellen he could never see me alone & that he
was worried over her apparent domination there. Saw Margot in office.
Penthouse. Cocktails with Krim, which led into dinner at Paris-Brest. He
has gained weight. A nice guy. In the Village, I met Dylan Thomas[*] in a
crummy beer house on Hudson St.[†] Pearl Kazin[‡] was pawing over him—
home late & high.

MAY 22, 1953

Spent a quiet, constructive evening, the first alone in weeks, thinking
about the suspense book, which is slowly working itself out as something
that must be written. It shocks me to recall how unplanned *Strangers*
was, except for the central idea, when I began. I really composed as I
went along, which necessitated some rewriting. But the main thing in any
book, for me, is the momentum, the enthusiasm, the narrative rush. That
I have also in the one I am planning.

5/22/53

A lover's prayer: Let us please realize that we have the power to hurt each
other, and therefore do it as little as possible.

---

* Dylan Thomas (1914–1953) was a Welsh author and poet. He would die later that year.
† Presumably the White Horse Tavern on the corner of Hudson and West Eleventh Streets, a writers'
favorite in the Village where Dylan Thomas got heavily drunk on several occasions. Some of the others
who've frequented the bar over the years include Jack Kerouac, James Baldwin, Bob Dylan, and Hunter
S. Thompson.
‡ Pearl Kazin (1922–2011), once the lover of Dylan Thomas, was a writer and editor who worked for
magazines such as *Harper's Bazaar*, *The New Yorker*, and *Partisan Review*.

MAY 23, 1953

Worked second day on short story of man who was a failure.* X before Rolf and after dinner. E. is being angelic. Rolf called for me at 10 & I departed for Locust Valley [on Long Island]. Caffè espresso & crème de menthe at midnight. I wished I could have shared it with Ellen. I long to have a house, with her, to have decent possessions, quiet days of work.

MAY 24, 1953

Fine day, awakened by cows. Tonight steak chez Rolf—nothing but the best for him—and two young friends of his came just at dinner & stayed. Strangely, half seduced Rolf, who later invited me into his bed. I feel with him as if he is another girl, or a singularly innocent man, which he is in these respects. Not quite successful, but still the most successful, and I at least found it pleasant. In my system of morals, I do not feel this in the least unfaithful to Ellen.

MAY 25, 1953

Terribly upset, either by coffee, or by Rolf of last night, which did not improve until X with E. this P.M. Tonight Walter Riemer's good tickets to *Porgy & Bess*. First row. Noisy, but I loved it. Very content tonight. This weekend, Rolf said perhaps we could work it out, he thought. So it goes. I am blown here and there. But I do love her physically and that is heaven, not to be easily thrown away.

MAY 26, 1953

Date Wed. with Avon people re the pocketbook [*The Breakup*]. Goldbeck does not want another gay book, so gave us "a nice release" said Margot. Home to fix Chinese dinner, Ellen's last here. We had planned to go hear a quiet piano somewhere, but we never got that far. I love to be with her these last hours. And that is that. And I weep at the thought of her departing tomorrow, for twice the length of time, at least, that I spent away from her in Florence.

MAY 27, 1953

Ellen left at 12:15 by taxi: for Grand Central, & I wept parting, but not when she was gone.

---

* "Born Failure," published posthumously in *Nothing That Meets the Eye: The Uncollected Stories of Patricia Highsmith* (New York, 2002).

MAY 28, 1953

Ann T. in good humor, but she must have hellish troubles: two years' analysis, and cannot make it to Europe due to being broke. The usual tragic picture of the homosexual, caught in his own trap, emotionally alone.

MAY 29, 1953

Lunch here with Betty Parsons, who was fine. Told me Carson McCullers fell madly for Kathryn [Cohen], lingered 3 mos. in London, asked K. to live with her. I understand K. was fascinated, but there was no affair. B.P. prefers my doodles & abstracts of course. She is of the doodle school.

JUNE 1, 1953

I produced 9 good pages of new Trieste story. I like it, but it is unsellable, probably. I do it only to keep from going mad in my old city where all the business people neglect me as if I were officially boycotted. I ought to be working on the Avon Book & every day that goes by, I fret.

JUNE 2, 1953

Work. Rosalind C. for lunch. A fine pleasant time we had with martinis & hamburger & talked of girlfriends, whom we agree are very similar, Claude & Ellen. Even in looks. Shall certainly see R. again soon. To Margot's to see the coronation on television.* 4:30 & again at 10. Splendid show, the most important thing I have seen on television at all. Margot cooked for me. As usual I stayed up late, but drank little.

JUNE 3, 1953

Lunch with Chas. [Charles] Byrne & Mr. Hanna re the Avon thing. Infinite hedging & double talk. They are concerned about morality changes re this book, and picking at minute flaws in my MS (without volunteering it was exactly what they wanted) and I had the awful feeling they were preparing for a tactful rejection. But Margot still thinks I'll get a contract, & Byrne said "Oh, we definitely want the book!" So there it hangs—my hopes of the last 6 months, and such terribly important hopes for the future with Ellen. Now they want a one-page statement, really important, to show the "publisher" saying I'll do this & that. Margot reminded Byrne I was offered $5,000. All this makes me desperately nervous, tense, makes me oversmoke, & refuse attractive invitations to

---

* The live broadcast of Queen Elizabeth II's coronation.

the country on weekends, because I cannot relax anyway. How I hate to tell Ellen this, instead of that I am $5,000 richer and on my way! The riveting below the window drives me insane 8–4!

JUNE 4, 1953

Did the one-page piece for Avon & took it over to Margot, who said at worst I'd be paid for the work I have already done. So there is that awful possibility already foreseen. Then worked. Not too well. How contagious is success or failure! And these days are the climax of the blackest streak in my career. Actually, ever since I met Ellen nothing good has happened. But I do not connect Ellen at all with this. (She has not that pervading optimism of Joan S., but I enjoy Ellen. She has taught me much else. I no longer dream these days. I doubt I'd change girls if I could.)

JUNE 6, 1953

Ellen writes that she loves Santa Fe, thinks I would, & is trying to get a job there. So –She is madly eager to hear about the Avon thing, which she will today.

JUNE 8, 1953

Tired. But did 1½ pages of the novel [*The Blunderer*], the start, for the sheer joy of it, & that security that comes to me when I start on a long work. I am sorry & ashamed not to have more money now.

JUNE 10, 1953

I got much too little sleep due to Ann's coming back with me. Meaningless, & I shall not repeat it.

JUNE 12, 1953

Good work, though very nervous. God, writing is not a healthful pastime! Destroys sleep, health, nerves. R. [Rosalind] does not like "The Returnees" but will show "Blindman's Buff" to the *Reporter*. Calls it sticking my neck out. Though I do not think the action impossible in the U.S. these days.

JUNE 13, 1953

Tired. Walked to Library for law book, benefit of Walter [Stackhouse] in my book. It rains. A real gloomy day which I try to spend as constructively as possible. The second character in my novel, who torments the innocent Walter, is as unformed in my mind as Bruno was at the beginning & I hope will emerge with the same success. Saw Jack [Matcha], drinks here & dinner in Village. Jack same as ever. I cannot ask him anywhere because of his appearance. Interesting item: that it is common knowledge among reporters that Kay Summersby, 25-year-old WAC captain, was Ike's mistress in Europe, & Matcha thinks McCarthy may be holding this over Ike.

JUNE 14, 1953

Worked on my book—(suspense). I am on the brink of a depression quite as serious as the 1948–49 winter one. It is Margot (her not working for me), Ellen—my doubt of her & the troubling nomadic element in our dwelling—anywhere. Nothing is ever permanent.

JUNE 15, 1953

Ah, it is awful to sit working on a Monday morning & to feel that I have not the right. I am beginning to be paralyzed by a fear of having no money again. I have the feeling I should take a job. But I should hate this even more than being broke. The circles of my dismal mind these days—I am acquiring a defeatist complex, and even when I cannot sleep o' nights, I take it calmly, as part of a generally lousy destiny, that's all.

JUNE 16, 1953

The Rosenbergs about to be electrocuted for A-bomb espionage & the whole nation is protesting, some for humanitarian reasons, some because it would endanger our international prestige. Though how it could sink much lower with the present book-burning of the Amerika Häuser I don't see. D. Hammett's *Thin Man*, Howard Fast, Langston Hughes, were among those which were removed from the libraries.*

JUNE 17, 1953

At 5 invited Kingsley very pleasantly, talked about writing. Her half-sister is the famous Dorothy Kingsley of the movies.† To Jim Merrill's cocktail party at 28 W. 10 St. where Jane Bowles was. She looks plumper, older, and is otherwise much the same—moderately friendly. Jim looked

---

* Under McCarthy, scores of books were removed from American overseas libraries—e. g., Berlin's Amerika Haus libraries. Dashiell Hammett and Herman Melville were among those on the index, as well as the poems of Langston Hughes and Howard Fast's *Citizen Tom Paine*. Protesters of this act of censorship spoke of "book burning," thus linking it to the book burning in Nazi Germany exactly twenty years before.
† Dorothy Kingsley (1909–1997) wrote the scripts to movies such as *Pal Joey*; *Kiss Me, Kate*; and *Seven Brides for Seven Brothers*, which got her an Academy Award nomination.

sweet in a lavender shirt of subtle hue. Also Oliver Smith, Johnny Myers, Harry Ford & wife, etc. Tietgens is not invited. Joined Jean P. & two fellows at Theatre de Lys, now under management of Terese Hayden, the one who did the (apparently) unsuccessful screen treatment of *The Price of Salt*. She & I ate dinner instead of going. Amusing mutual attraction that will probably come to naught. She has an 11-year old cat, & a charming studio for $13.75 per month on Washington Street.

6/18/53

A curious dream on a nearly sleepless night: I was with Kathryn [Cohen] and a naked girl in a closed room. Our intention was to burn the girl alive. We sat her in a tiny wooden bathtub, in which also was placed a tiny wooden effigy of my grandmother with arms outstretched. I had to pick the whole bathtub up and ignite the papers under it before it caught. K. began to weep on my shoulder, and I reminded her, "Don't forget, the girl asked us to do it to her!" But at that instant, I saw the naked girl's lips moving, her head turning miserably as she tried to avoid the heat of the flames. A horror went through me at her suffering. A moment later, the naked girl simply stood up, stopped her crying, and stepped out of the bathtub unhurt except for singes: the fire had gone out. I felt guilty at the thought the girl would report what we had done, though her face was expressionless, had no hatred in it as she looked at us. Then I awakened. I subsequently had the feeling the girl in the tub might have represented myself, because she looked a little like me in the dream, at the end. In that case I had two identities: the victim and the murderer. A horrid, vivid dream.

JUNE 23, 1953

Party chez somebody on Riverside Drive in honor of Betty Parsons' departure for Greece. Rosalind & I bored stiff, so I made a date to pick J. P. up at 12:30 A.M. & she spent evening *chez moi*. "It won't last," says Rosalind, meaning Jean is not my type.

JUNE 24, 1953

Lunch Cecil Goldbeck—whom I so much like—better than any editor to date. Offered me 1000 sight unseen on my suspense novel.

JUNE 25, 1953

Telegram this A.M. that Ellen arrives tonight by plane. Ellen looks tanned, nervous, and not at all sweet to me in the later discussions tonight.

JUNE 27, 1953

Fire Island. I'd arranged it with Betty—to accept with Ellen her standing invitation to come to Natalia Murray's home. We arrived at 2 and met Jean P. at 5. Jean wonderfully poised throughout. But tonight, Ellen ripped my French shirt off me on the porch, trying to hold me back from a late party at Chris D.'s which I wanted to go to. I spent major part of night chez Jean.

JUNE 29, 1953

Work. I argue with Ellen that I do want to leave her, which simply does not penetrate.

JULY 1, 1953

Home at noon, eating raisins en route. Hot as a furnace, & the miserable pneumatic drills go on. Ellen & I argue ourselves black in the face, getting nowhere. Talk in private with Goldbeck, who still assures me Margot is the best agent I could have. Sees no major disadvantage to her. The others are like factories & you produce or are thrown out. Back to Ellen at 5. Violent argument until 7:30 when I threw a glass down on the floor to emphasize I *did* mean it when I said I wanted to separate. She has tried everything from sex to liquor to tears, to wild promises of giving me my way in everything. She threatened veronal [sleeping pills], & insisted on having 2 martinis along with me, which she tossed down like water. I said go ahead with the veronal. She was poking 8 pills in her mouth as I left the house. "I love you very much" were the last words I heard as I closed the door. She was sitting naked on the bed. Had just written her will giving me all her money, & saying to give Jo $5000 when I got around it. And called me the nicest person in the world for having stayed with her as long as I did this evening. Visited Kingsley & Lars [Skattebol] *chez eux*, having previously canceled Ellen's date with Jim Dobrochek for her in the Five Bros. Tavern. They ripped me mercilessly (& stupidly) re my third novel:[*] a purgative, and I'd never write another decent novel having spat out such negativism. K. hardly said a word; one can't, with Lars. I did not get home until 2 A.M. & found Ellen in a coma—out, anyway, beyond coffee & cold towels. Called Jean, then Freund. A Dr. Pierich (?) arrived & pumped her stomach to no avail. Had to have the

---

[*] The lost novel *Sleepless Night*, or *The Traffic of Jacob's Ladder*, which Pat wrote in 1951–52.

police, then Bellevue [hospital], where I delivered her at 4:30 A.M. There was a note on the typewriter which the cops took: "Dear Pat: I should have done this 20 years ago. This is no reflection on you or anyone—" Went to Jean's in a sprinkling rain. Slept till 8:30—and went at once to the hospital. She showed no change.

JULY 2, 1953

Stayed an hour or so with doctor, answering questions re her health. It is excellent. Dr. gives her an even chance. Drove to hospital to see Ellen 11 P.M. No change. I am exhausted. Her mother arrives from Santa Fe by plane at 9 A.M.

JULY 3, 1953

Met Jim at 9 at hospital. He had been walking streets all night. Told me over A.M. coffee Ellen mistreated him on his arrival here (when she was living with Jo), buttonholed him at the pier & said. "Don't ever tell a soul that I am Jewish!" I had not known before she was totally Jewish, from that tight, sophisticated, brittle German Jewish intellectual set of pre-Hitler Berlin. Went at noon to F.I. [Fire Island] in Ellen's car with Jean P. Ideal weather & connection & it's heaven to be out here. I am escaping from hell.

JULY 4, 1953

Forced myself to work, half believing Ellen dead at this point. Called Jim [Dobrochek] at 6 from Duffy's & heard she came to yesterday—early this morning. The strain is over—and I picked a fight with some late girl callers this evening at 9:30—and was sadly beaten, saved by Jean P. Much drinking, naturally.

JULY 7, 1953

Moved to 25th St. with cats, & am very content. But these days torturous lest Ellen resent me & not want me to see her. The old ambiguous pull— toward safety, toward destruction.

JULY 9, 1953

Lunch with Goldbeck at Yale Club—and told him my marital troubles, & that I am starting a new life. The kind of man one can confide in, more than my parents.

JULY 15, 1953

Errands. Dates. Enough to exhaust Mrs. Roosevelt. This evening I met Lynn Roth—267½ W. 11 St. Ex-girlfriend of Ann S.—& roommate Doris.—

JULY 16, 1953

Moving, packing in studio. Ellen called—nearly wept—I offered to come. She accepted and I flew. Never under-estimate—I held her in my arms for 45 minutes. She doesn't know how she feels. Passive, sentimental, and of course weak at this period.

JULY 22, 1953

Roman Holiday preview. I wept throughout. Every beautiful place in Rome (and in the world) reminds me of Ellen. Walked home barefoot, pained by Trieste shoes in more ways than one.

JULY 27, 1953

Saw Ellen. She has an apartment, One University Place [in Greenwich Village].

JULY 30, 1953

Saw Ellen *chez elle* 3 P.M. Helped all I could with her apartment, which can be charming & is certainly chic. I want to give her all I can—Mallorca, & Trieste watercolor of course, framed.

8/3/53

There should be gold rings, watches, beautiful necklaces, beautiful books and also paintings, which are given away after a time to a friend who admires them, and who in turn will give them on to somebody else. Gifts are food for the heart, to give and to be given. These should take the place of religious idols, for they symbolize human love in the name of a charitable God.

AUGUST 4, 1953

Furniture shopping, bored to tears, & over-expensive. Ellen convinced we can "arrange something—," our lives together. She wants me back. It's simple.

AUGUST 5, 1953

Have ambiguous feelings about Ellen, which hopelessly thwart me: to take her for what I enjoy about her—leisure, *her*, the civilization. Or to be strong & fend for myself?

AUGUST 7, 1953

Work. Better. I am very unhappy—because of sheer indecision. I am not happy with Jean. Not decided about Ellen. If decided, I should make a move. I cannot. So I drink. Like any American.

AUGUST 8, 1953

Occasional visits from Lynn [Roth]. Whom I find very attractive.

AUGUST 13, 1953

Cocktail party chez Bill Hanna, who did not invite Jean. Sneaked out & called Ellen. Met her at 59 St. apartment of a stranger & drove down to One Univ. where I spent first night, unbeknownst to Jean. This afternoon—a visit from Lynn. Makes me very nervous.

AUGUST 14, 1953

The suicide & Ellen's character in the book [*The Blunderer*] I find very disturbing & too personal, of course. Slows the beginning. Perhaps hopelessly.

AUGUST 18, 1953

Lynn called at 12. She always will drink a martini & so will I. We visited Ellen's where I have the key. Lay on the bed. And that was all. Nescafé & beans & 3 hours of it.

8/18/53

It is curious that in the most interesting periods of one's life, one never writes one's diary. There are some things that even a writer cannot put down in words (at the time). He shrinks from putting them down. And what a loss! Like a lot of outrageous, apparently senseless losses in nature, due to an assumed superabundance in nature. Even experience is superabundant, but it is at times more difficult to ferret out—that is, in dull times—than in more dramatic times. But the value of diaries is their dramatic periods, when one has "perhaps" shrunk from setting down the weakness, the vagaries, the changes of mind, the cowardices, the shameful hatreds, the little lies carried out or not, which form one's true character.

8/18/53

I have never for a minute thought that life was easy. Perhaps that was a mistake. I have no reserve of humor, no happy go lucky period to look back on. It is all one stretch. And now the screw turns tighter every day. To use another figure, I live like a soldier for whom the battle goes harder every day, yet my facial expression, like a good soldier's, doesn't change, and nothing, no reversal, no further disappointment, could possibly surprise me. A good soldier is incapable of surprise, in any department, good or bad.

AUGUST 19, 1953

Millie* arrived. Failed to get her in Ellen's due to foul switchboard woman. Called Lynn who had a date with Doris. Many martinis, dinner & we bounced Millie impolitely & went to Lenny's in a taxi. Where Lynn got the key—so easily from Sara H. I know it was planned: clean sheets on the bed & a perfectly heavenly night with Lynn & all night. 266 W. 11 Street—five flights up. I adore Lynn—

AUGUST 21, 1953

Ellen called this noon from P'town [Provincetown]. I'd sent her a letter which arrived Monday, saying I'd "spoken" to Jean P. re putting this thing on a platonic basis. Jean agreed but was much broken up. [Ellen] sounded wonderful from P'town. She loves me, is confident "we can arrange our lives."

AUGUST 22, 1953

Better work. And suddenly great success with Lynn at 4 P.M. Or rather tonight at Sara's. I painfully finagled the keys from Sara while we & Mel & Jean were at the Bagatelle, shot out of there as if fired from a gun & went to 266 W. 11 St. Had called Lynn—who has to get away from Doris on pretext of "taking a walk." I told Lynn she didn't want to make love to me—didn't have to—her mind was on getting home. Clairvoyant, she remarked. & that she had a wonderful time—

AUGUST 23, 1953

Unfortunately, Doris found Sara's keys, which Lynn had deposited in her mailbox, & threw them all over the garden. Sara couldn't get in when she returned at 3 P.M. Sunday. Keys spotted Monday by Lynn who saw the cat playing with them in the sun! *Quels Jours!* Today worked fine—4

---

* Millie Alford was a third cousin of Pat's.

pages—visited Lynn at 35 Street, where they just moved in. Lynn alone, of course, polishing floors, drinking gins, & we made love on the floor. Got drunk, & played records. Then taxied to 11 Street, & to bed for 20 minutes, while Sara & someone else was actually in the living room. Such is Lynn—a gay Italian spirit has she, God bless her.

AUGUST 24, 1953

Dinner chez Ellen. Legitimate date. She returned from Provincetown. All tanned & beautiful. But I'd seen Lynn for a wonderful if exhausting afternoon & could do very little tonight. Lynn for me is so complete & completing.

AUGUST 28, 1953

To P'town. How beautiful & madly attractive with Ellen. We found the same house she had—upper end of Commercial Street. This is the height of Ellen's possessiveness toward me: she adores me, is affectionate & admiring & couldn't wait for my letters, nor me. Bought a card "We were so Right Together" for Lynn—Ellen blew up, made me promise not to send it.

AUGUST 31, 1953

Searching for crabs & mussels, neither of which E. eats. X every day & very fine. Ah, habit! And how easily one can forget the one supposedly loved—because in this it is so hard (and so impermanent when achieved), to make any fixed arrangements. I do not forget Lynn, yet am content, temporarily, with Ellen.

9/3/53

An artist will always drink, even when he is happy (that is when he is working well and with a woman he loves) because he will always think of the woman he saw last week, or the woman who is a hundred or three thousand miles away, with whom he might have been happier, or just as happy. If he did not think of this, he would not be an artist, suffering with imagination.

9/4/53

What it is to know Europe: it is to sit in a restaurant of one's neighborhood in America, compliment the food to the waiter, and have him nod absently or take no notice at all, because you will probably not come back, and if you do, what does he care? That is to evoke Europe more strongly than the smell of fish at Santa Lucia in Naples! Ah, I remember the docile young blond waitress in Camillo's in Florence! And across the Arno, the bustling, willing, balding waiter in Nandino's, always terribly concerned that I got the kind of bread I like with my *insalata*. They will remember me in two years, or when I go back! Or in five, or more. I remember Florence's dreary rains that never quenched the joy of life, however, as the rains do in Paris. Paris goes sullen and grim for the winter, and bursts forth as if from a gray cocoon in spring. But Florence is always there—elegant, proud, full of fortitude, on the Via Tornabuoni, proud also, hard-working, hopeful, faces uplifted at the other end of the Via Maggio and all her little side streets. The waiters may not remember me in Germany. They are too preoccupied with muddled personal destinies to enjoy a contented customer. But I am aware of Germany's dark green forests, the patient streetcar drivers to whom being on time—even their battered antiquated streetcars deserved to be brought to their stops on time—is a matter of personal honor, a measure of their stature.

SEPTEMBER 15, 1953

ITI was with Lynn all day—We saw Jiynx and Ann M. The very two people we shouldn't see, at Doris' house, who shouldn't know we spent the week together. Then Showspot—I'm very happy and think that Ellen can go to hell. I'm in love with Lynn. There's no doubt.ITIT

SEPTEMBER 17, 1953

ITI signed the contract with Coward McCann for *Salt* and a new suspense novel, without a title. Lynn's at 4 to drink the champagne I bought last night. I don't like it much but Lynn does.ITIT

SEPTEMBER 21, 1953

ITNervous. Rushed. Lynn called at 1:30—she came at 2:30 to go with us to Newark airport. Alone with her for only half an hour—I said I love you—she said it too, but I don't believe it. Tired, pensive—at Ft. Worth at 10:30—I'm disturbed—the Claude hotel*—comfortable and horrible, like everything in Ft. Worth.ITIT

---

* Her uncle Claude Coates's guesthouse.

SEPTEMBER 22, 1953

ᴵᵀLittle breakfast with the family. Returned to work after a beer in Huder's Cafe. Lynn called, I told her "how wonderful to hear your voice in this room!" I wanted to know if you were safe, she said. Very serious about getting back to work.ᴵᵀᴵᵀ

SEPTEMBER 23, 1953

ᴵᵀAt Millie's for the night, first time.ᴵᵀᴵᵀ

9/24/53

The only solution for me, is perhaps to take each affair lightly, enjoying in memory what I *had*, instead of what I haven't and shan't have. Without some of this, I feel I shall be a suicide before forty-five. Actually, stupider people than I have always practiced this attitude, very naturally however, like a natural self-preservative measure. Hence the awful changes of partners, infidelities, new loves today, and gone tomorrow—most of the N.Y. professionals are like that.

SEPTEMBER 28, 1953

ᴵᵀClaude over for lunch at noon. He says that the room would cost me $110—the one he showed me yesterday. I'd thought my uncle would give me a good price—but no! I'm very disappointed in my entire family! Meeting with the *Star Telegram* reporter in the afternoon. A photograph taken—Lynn called again, she said that she left Doris—I'll believe it when I see it. She wants me to come to New Hope.ᴵᵀᴵᵀ

9/28/53

[Allela] Cornell—Why does the artist commit suicide? Because he sees and longs for more intensely than other people what he cannot have— the happy home, the children, the piano, the sunlight on the lawn, the years of satisfying work ahead, each year like the other. The artist cannot make up his mind. The artist is half homosexual. The artist is torn between the partner who challenges and the partner who complies. I am thinking of Cornell, and the Grecian freshness of the world in her childhood, and the successive, warping, educational blights of her adolescence. She loved too much and loved too many, but above all she loved too much. She was wide open, and life, like a tangle of bayonets, guns at cross purposes, loves at cross purposes, hit her right in the heart. She became physically tired with the strain, to the point of delirium and insanity. She came to realize, at thirty, that to be able to paint a beautiful picture did not compensate for the husband or the lover and the children and the domestic, very ordinary peace that was not there. In a moment of exhaustion, when like a suffering Hindu she thought she glimpsed the truth, she drank the nitric acid. It is a beautiful story, really, the first three quarters. Even the last is beautiful in its psychological inevitability. It should be about 250 pages.

SEPTEMBER 30, 1953
ᴵᵀMillie here for the night.ᴵᵀᴵᵀ

OCTOBER 2, 1953
ᴵᵀAlmost every day I get a letter from someone regarding *The Price of Salt.*ᴵᵀᴵᵀ

10/3/53
LR [Lynn Roth] I can never forget her eyes, looking at me on the sofa that day in New York. The color of wrens' eggs, dark lashed, and her young faun's face, smiling at me. I'd kill the guy who hurt her. And if she were killed, I'd search the earth for her murderer and beat him up bare-handed. Under the right circumstances, the avenging of a dead love can be the most dramatic story in the world.

10/7/53
The Saddle Cafe—Ft. Worth's North Side Stock Yards' finest & most popular coffee & eats joint for the drunken cowboy after 11 P.M. About twenty or thirty dusty, generally crummy looking cowboys, five women, slatternly, or the good time Charley I'll-take-care-of-my (married) man type. An old boy named Red McBride, who rode in the first rodeo in New York at the Yankee Stadium, tells me what a calf fry is. "It's calves' notsies," he whispers slyly. When I start to play the jukebox, a sly young man in clean spanet trousers slips a quarter in and asks me to play what I want. The general level is low—and rather depressing after one has idealized the golden West. The truck driver next to me makes lewd propositions for the night. The other cowboys, too drunk to handle their eyeballs, nevertheless attempt a leer. One man of 40 in a handsome pair of blue dress cowboy pants, has to be threatened with a blackjack before he will get out of the place—though

I understood he was protesting only that his car had been stolen. A lanky, Mexican looking cowboy in black Stetson and levis is draped over a stool at the counter. Sooner or later all the men have managed the come-on look: I am there with a woman.

10/7/53

Western hillbilly: the errant self-assurance of these braying voices, the conviction that they are entertaining to listen to and that they have an important message to deliver—that is what fascinates and astounds me! "Hang up that telephone." It is significant of the brutality and materiality of our age that cars, TV, telephones, refrigerators and washing machines figure so often in these songs—happy or sad. Seldom if ever do they refer to weather, the fields of Texas, or any beautiful or tragic things in nature. Radio commercials: "Don't throw your radio or TV set out the window when they start acting up. Just call Fortune 5–888, the universal radio & TV repair, 800 S. Jennings." "I said, Grand Prize Beer. I said Gra-a-and Prize."

OCTOBER 9, 1953

ᴵᵀEllen leaves for Europe.ᴵᵀᴵᵀ

OCTOBER 10, 1953

ᴵᵀFirst letter from Lynn—says that she loves me, but that this couldn't be worse now—why? I wanted Millie to come over tonight, but Dan arrived—from Houston. Letter from Ellen. Says she's thinking of me always, and when I'll be ready, she'd be, too—in Europe, or no matter where and how—Good work—as always when I feel loved.ᴵᵀᴵᵀ

10/12/53

Texas—So distracting, surface-dwelling, sensory, I have to go to bed and pretend to be trying to fall asleep in order to think about the book I am writing.

OCTOBER 18, 1953

ᴵᵀMillie tells me she loves me a lot and that I wouldn't be happy for a long time with Lynn. All true. I wonder if I should stay in Texas, because I see little, always less for me in New York and Lynn. Lynn I'd only have for one week in New Hope.ᴵᵀᴵᵀ

NOVEMBER 7, 1953

^(IT)I finished the first draft! At 3:30 PM. I'm sad, exhausted, and thinking of Lynn.^(ITIT)

NOVEMBER 9, 1953

^(IT)I read ¾ of the book. I keep asking myself if it's not as good as *Strangers* because I wasn't able to work on it in the same calm way. I named it *The Blunderer* instead of *A Deadly Innocence*. I found it in my dictionary: "C'est plus qu'un crime, c'est une faute."* Walter is truly a Blunderer!^(ITIT)

NOVEMBER 11, 1953

^(IT)Difficult to work—and in the evenings there's always music, TV. We eat with the TV turned on! Horrible and unbelievable!^(ITIT)

NOVEMBER 20, 1953

^(IT)Mother more and more serious, I feel.^(ITIT)

NOVEMBER 26, 1953

Thanksgiving. ^(IT)Enough martinis here before leaving for Dan's house, where there were 16 of the family, even Ed Coates from Houston! Amused myself well with Danny and the Appaloosa of which Dan is still afraid.^(ITIT)

NOVEMBER 29, 1953

^(IT)I think—I try to think. This year—I was never alone, and this didn't help me. I want to go to Salzburg perhaps, or a small Italian city, near a library, and be alone, to come up with a new story for a suspense novel. It wouldn't matter if Ellen was in Rome, because I probably wouldn't have the money to live in Rome. Ellen. Jean. Lynn. Millie— and in Salzburg there won't be anyone. I'll be too alone, but—^(ITIT)

DECEMBER 18, 1953

^(IT)Tired. The dentist again at 2. I lost consciousness from the horror and fear^(ITIT)—Scraping a tooth root—etc.

---

* It's worse than a crime, it's a blunder.

DECEMBER 19, 1953

ᴵᵀI drank too much—wonderful company here—½ a bottle of gin for me.ᴵᵀᴵᵀ

DECEMBER 20, 1953

ᴵᵀA day without work. With Millie—golf—then in Dallas to eat lunch just the two of us, in a restaurant where they have an all you can eat menu for $3.00, including wine—all fried food, too. Very Texas! And the waiter was rushed—nothing here is aesthetic! We need to find moments to be together, sometimes we're forced to tell a lie. Millie always suggests that I stay in Texas, where I work better, etc. She's right, but the politics here, and the treatment of Negroes, disgust me.ᴵᵀᴵᵀ

12/20/53

And I have heard girls singing in the shower, before they come into bed with me.

DECEMBER 23, 1953

ᴵᵀI finished the novel [*The Blunderer*] Ten days ago, I completely immersed myself in order to finish strong. Today, I wrote page 312—a very good ending. Now I'm free to buy presents, for which I have no money.ᴵᵀᴵᵀ

DECEMBER 24, 1953

ᴵᵀAt 5 we opened our presents—together. Also some from Ellen from Ascona. Also a telegram: All my love, darling, which arrived from Locarno at 5:30 P.M. With the family tonight.ᴵᵀᴵᵀ

1954

PATRICIA HIGHSMITH rekindles her relationship with Lynn Roth in early 1954, and for a short while the two even live together in the Village. When Lynn decides to go back to her ex after all, Pat starts drafting *A Month of Sundays*, which will bear several provisional titles (*Pursuit of Evil, The Thrill Boys, Business Is My Pleasure*) before emerging as *The Talented Mr. Ripley*. Pat revels in the pleasure writing this story gives her, and she describes the sentences going "down on the paper like nails." Within six months the draft is complete.

Pat withdraws from the world around her this year. In mid-May, she leaves the dynamic, artistically fertile landscape of Manhattan for self-imposed solitude in the Berkshires, relocating to idyllic Lenox, Massachusetts, where she focuses entirely on her new book. Given her budget, she finds a small, cheap room, then moves to a rental cottage belonging to the local undertaker. This period also coincides with an extended pause in her intensive journaling. She has long recorded every last detail of life, love, and loss in her diaries, complemented in her notebooks by philosophical observations and sweeping insights into her writing process. Her jubilant entry regarding *The Talented Mr. Ripley* on May 12, 1954, however, marks the final page of Diary Number 12, and Pat will not return to the practice for seven years. We therefore have to draw from the entries in her notebooks—previously only used for work projects—to derive information about what happens in Pat's life.

She doesn't give much of an explanation as to why she no longer keeps a diary, only the one: that Ellen is back in her life, and Pat yet again discovers her snooping. In September, the two travel to Santa Fe together. Living under the same roof, they fall into their old quarrelsome habits. Pat will retrospectively classify the time in New Mexico as "*l'enfer*" (hell) after reviewing the notebook's contents.

Before Pat has even unpacked her bags, she dives back into the book, which is initially inspired by the Henry James novel *The Ambassadors*. Pat will later describe her (anti) hero as her alter ego; Tom Ripley is a charming, unassuming, yet potentially psychopathic young American in Europe. To make Tom the character he is, Pat reflects extensively in her notebooks on what it means to be American and, more specifically, what it means to be an American expat in Europe. She comes to recognize that above all, it's the mentally ill and criminally minded who fascinate her most and inspire her best characters. "No book was easier for me to write," Pat will recall in her primer on writing thrillers, *Plotting and Writing Suspense Fiction* (1966), "and I often had the feeling Ripley was writing it and I was merely typing."

That fall, alongside potential plotlines for *The Talented Mr. Ripley*, Pat's notebooks feature initial thoughts on a new novel, *Dog in the Manger* (later retitled *Deep Water*). The story explores sexual attraction, rejection, and reconciliation. The characters Victor and Melinda have a complex, modern marriage, in which mutual obsession leads inexorably to mutual destruction.

In December, Pat, Ellen, and Ellen's new French poodle Tina head for Acapulco by way of El Paso. Before leaving, Pat sends her grandmother Willie Mae a copy of the completed Tom Ripley manuscript. The book is published a year later, in December 1955, by Coward-McCann in New York.

JANUARY 1, 1954
ITThe last days. A visit to my parents. I think it's also the last time I'll see my grandma*—dearest. I'll leave on January 4th.ITIT

JANUARY 3, 1954
ITTonight I sent a telegram to Lynn in New York, telling her I'd arrive Monday morning, but not to come to the airport if she didn't want to. Changed at two to go to the airport. Couldn't say anything to Millie, who was tired, but very sincere, serious and easy-going—sweet—all that is Millie.ITIT

JANUARY 4, 1954
ITGot a message from Lynn to come to her's after landing at La Guardia. First Jean's, then to drink a martini, then Lynn's to go to bed at 4—with

---

* This is indeed the last time Pat will see her grandmother. Willie Mae Coates will die a year later, on February 5, 1955, while Pat is on her second trip to Mexico.

a bottle of gin. Dinner with Ann S. this evening. I drank 7 martinis, two glasses of wine.^{ITIT}

JANUARY 5—7, 1954

^{IT}Slept 8 hours. I feel very well this morning. There is not enough space at Jean's.^{ITIT}

JANUARY 9, 1954

^{IT}With Millie all day. Art exhibit. Betty Parsons, Rosenberg, etc. Very pleasant. To Margot's at 7. I called Millie to come there for dinner. Love at first sight! From Margot's side—they were dancing all evening.^{ITIT}

JANUARY 13, 1954

^{IT}Yesterday—or the day before—I took my suitcase and my typewriter to Lynn's. Now I live with her in 36th Street.^{ITIT}

JANUARY 16, 1954

^{IT}Work. *Blunderer* editing even on Sunday. So tired, Jean gave me a deximill.^{*ITIT}

JANUARY 18, 1954

^{IT}And today I'm at Lynn's again. Doris has gone to Gert's[†] in Snedens Landing[‡] for 3 weeks. Lynn told her she would rather stay home alone. What a joke! Lynn can't be alone, not even for an hour. I'm very happy!^{ITIT}

JANUARY 20, 1954

^{IT}Lunch at Ann S.'s. Very pleasant, and like Europe, these afternoons when it seems like there's nothing to do and that we're blessed poets and artists. Ann very optimistic about Lynn and me.^{ITIT}

JANUARY 22, 1954

^{IT}Lunch at noon with Margot and Goldbeck at Michel's. Until 6 PM! The whole book, all the small edits. After—I went back to 111th Street for a moment, to find a few things to bring to Lynn's.^{ITIT}

---

* Dexamyl, the brand name for a drug combining an amphetamine and a barbiturate, depressing appetites and lifting moods.
† Gertrude Macy (1904–1983), Broadway producer and head of the American National Theater. She was also actress and writer Katherine Cornell's lover.
‡ Snedens Landing is in Palisades, upstate New York.

JANUARY 25, 1954

ᴵᵀDoris and Lynn talk every day. Generally L. calls D. in the office. Tonight conference of D., L., and Gert at Lynn's. Came home at 8:30 to prepare dinner. Doris is staying at Gert's.ᴵᵀᴵᵀ

FEBRUARY 2, 1954

ᴵᵀCocktails at Jean's. Ann S. has begun to paint my picture. Peaceful days, those.ᴵᵀᴵᵀ

2/2/54

Homosexuality—The mutual mistrust from the start: don't deny it's there, it *is*. Except perhaps at the very start, when one is eighteen. But after 30 or so, it is there. Love can never take a straight, hard, fast course, running to the other, growing stronger day by day. One's relationship in bed improves, we are easier around the house together, but even in this greater ease lies the danger that she is "getting on her feet" now, and may no longer need me in ten days. That is because we suspect that such relationships are based only on need, selfishness, anyway. And now we are only 30 days old, in this new relationship of admitting we love each other.

Types interest me. I loathe the virago-mother type. It partially includes E.H. [Ellen Hill] though she is indeed more sui generis. It includes Doris S. and J.A.* both of whom show the same unwarranted jealousies, the same method of fighting, wounding, shaming the partner, as things begin to crack up. Of course, such people choose particular partners, too, the younger girls, who for a time endure the domination: the mother child relationship. How difficult it is for the younger to break away from it and assume an adult partnership with anyone later.

FEBRUARY 5, 1954

ᴵᵀI'm moving to 11th Street.ᴵᵀᴵᵀ

FEBRUARY 6, 1954

ᴵᵀHome with Millie this evening. (Lynn was with Ann S.) We all had dinner together at Old Homestead Restaurant. Later to Show Spot, where Lynn was sweet to me, and Ann and Millie got along so well they left together!ᴵᵀᴵᵀ

---

* Judith A., former lover of Ann's.

FEBRUARY 9, 1954

ᴵᵀI think, always, still, about Claire Morgan's new novel.ᴵᵀᴵᵀ

2/26/54

The knock on the door at night. Utter silence. A triple knock at first, then too short a pause before another knock comes, cautious and yet insane because there is a horrible effort to be polite in this knock, a horrible persistence at the same time, and utter madness directing it. And one suddenly remembers, the door is unlatched . . .

MARCH 16, 1954

ᴵᵀLast yearᴵᵀᴵᵀ—nothing made sense. My attitude was, "Have another drink." Nothing makes sense now either but as long as one has decided to live, one must try always to do "the right thing." I did not try last year. I spent my money like a drunken sailor. And the worst was, I knew what I was doing. It serves me jolly well right if I am broke, or if I land in debtor's prison, even. It does not matter that I have worked pretty hard, harder than many people I know. I have been imprudent, irreverent, false to myself, in fact.

3/28/54

A character like Chas. [Charles] Redcliff in Positano (or somewhat like David in Palma).* A young American, half homosexual, an indifferent painter, with some money from home through an income, but not too much. He is the ideal, harmless looking, unimportant looking, numerous enough, kind of individual a smuggling gang would make use of to handle their contacts, hot goods (I can see him casually carrying off a hundred German cameras in an Italian orange crate, while the Italians think he is "moving again" with all his bad paintings). He gets into deeper water, this careless, carefree young man (who is able to have affairs with both men & women) and after adventures in the Simplon Tunnel, protecting the girl he is interested in, then himself, turns out to be more of a hero than a coward.

He is partly an ass, partly intelligent, eminently self-preservative basically. With a gentlemanly attitude that keeps him from sliding over the border to opportunism and rattiness. At first, a harmless attractive-to-some, repellent-to-others kind of young man, he becomes a murderer, a killer for pleasure. The organized crime of the group with which he

---

* Pat's first note on what will become her best-known work: *The Talented Mr. Ripley* (New York, 1955).

finds himself becomes a means of inflicting punishment on others (cf. political parties, etc.). He could, in the course of the story, effect a purge of himself, becoming actually heroic and even altruistic at the end. He has the analytical capacity to understand all this while it is going on. He cannot do anything about it until he is faced with a choice, which enables him to show what he is made of (good & bad choices) and to turn his back, by choice, on what he has done before. (Much research on current smuggling conditions is necessary for my own purposes.) Like Bruno, he must never be quite queer—merely capable of playing the part if need be to get information or to help himself out in an emergency. Ah, I can see him, amusing himself in shorts at the Terraza in Palma de Majorca, smiling in the sun. His name should be Clifford, or David, or Matthew.

3/31/54

People forget or do not even know, the violence that Europe has known. Europe is not only a museum, it is the habitat of people who have known more violence, more life than we have.

4/2/54

There is no moral to my life—I have none—except: "Stand up and take it." The rest is sentiment.

4/4/54

The weekend after. She [Lynn Roth] is gone, and the house is haunted with her. I have done a modicum of "constructive" things this morning, but by noon I have no desire to do any more. Whom am I doing them for? I should like to be able to write a poem, to get it out of my system (my unhappiness, disappointment, not her, because the disappointment is temporary and she is still here and will be). Perhaps the poem will come later. I have no desire to see anyone. Who can share my grief? And I do not care to escape it. (What a word, escape!) I embark on an orgy of reading. Political science is a particular delight. One can become insane, getting over enthusiastic about political science, when all alone, brooding about a girl. I long to work—my best opiate, really my only one—but I won't even do that today, because by taking a day off (Sunday) I am more fit to work the rest of the week, I wonder if many people of the many who have killed themselves on a Sunday, were idle for the same reason? Some days are just difficult to get through. Mostly Sundays.

4/7/54

Lynn—She should know that life—real life as it is generally lived in Europe—has extremes of gentleness and violence; that it takes a tremendous effort to live in the dullish, middle-of-the-way manner, in order to live at all and to get on with other people. She knows violence from plays only. Such American children are unaware that the dignified woman with whom they may be having tea has been, if she is a European, perhaps raped many times by Russian soldiers, that she has managed to "digest" this in her experience and to carry on from there—unresentfully, the richer for it, in fact.

4/10/54

As long as beautiful women exist, who can be really depressed? By beautiful, I also mean (tonight in very thoughtful mood) that they must also possess a modicum of virtue.

4/16/54

L.P. [Lil Picard] on murder. That no one murders who has a satisfactory sexual outlet. This I apparently unconsciously did in Bruno and Kimmel.*

4/22/54

Despair. Something takes over. It is miraculous. So strong and sure and optimistic (even when one is physically too exhausted even to smile) that it crosses my mind I am actually insane. Which I prove to be not so, by following attentively and with interest a news broadcast on the radio. (I was more insane in Texas, suffering, and even more personally somehow, under the many injustices that did not directly concern me: the Negro prejudice, the lack of music, the biased newspapers that were my only sources of information, and the ignorance and banality with which I was surrounded.) At this moment I am homeless, miserable where I am, my possessions—scattered, my love gone and yet worse, not entirely gone: she tantalizes me. My jaw is swollen with an infected tooth, and the many, many other bodily ailments that remind of Death, the final conqueror. Yet the amazing thing is the steadiness inside. This time I do not think of God.

---

* Bruno and Kimmel are characters in *Strangers on a Train* and *The Blunderer*, respectively.

4/22/54

Whatever pity I have for the human race is a pity for the mentally deranged, and for the criminals. (That is why they will always be the best characters in whatever I write.) For normality and mediocrity? They do not need help. They bore me.

4/22/54

I was told today that the manic-depressive affliction is one of the few psychoses that are innate. Therefore, nearly impossible to cure.

5/2/54

The three women I have loved most intensely in my life have been the only ones of all my amours who were definitely "bad for me." J.S., G.C., F.H., and now L.R.

5/5/54

The neurotic: he is happiest when several people are in love with him, or love him. The more the better; it is like money in the bank. The ultimate confusion of all this, the necessity of a choice finally, does not trouble him in the least. It never crosses his mind.

5/8/54

O glorious spring of 1954! Love is rewarded with indifference, and hard work with bad health. I am becoming a little odd, personally. Nothing in the world makes sense to me. There is too much disappointment, illogic, pain and ugliness. The one I love is a voluntary prisoner, a couple of miles away. She loves me too. O glorious, noble spring of 1954!

MAY 12, 1954

I am happy—after all this. Very happy working on my new book, *A Month of Sundays*.* I have never felt so sure—except perhaps for much of my third book which was never published. The sentences of this book go down on the paper like nails. It is a wonderful feeling. If a word is wrong, ever, I know it at once and fix it. The whole reads very strong at present. (p. 44.)

---

* *A Month of Sundays* was the first of many working titles for *The Talented Mr. Ripley* (New York, 1955).

5/26/54

Alcoholism for the writer: He carries around his wonderful gift. It is the only sure thing, and it is stronger than any bank. He can sit down any time, and with a modicum of peace of mind, write more beautifully than 999,999,999 people out of 1,000,000,000. So he drinks away the afternoons. The gift is there. It will not go. No, only something else will come: death.

5/28/54

Deliberately avoiding that tranquility without which I can do nothing . . .

6/1/54

Among heterosexuals, the marriage is difficult, the divorce fairly easy. Among homosexuals, the marriage presents no difficulties at all, but the divorce is torturous, lingering. It can last for years.

6/13/54

Stockbridge,* Mass. Even the oldest homes are all undersized, like the people's souls. Poor Mrs. Murphy lives in a narrow two-story with a bitch of a driveway in the back and a one-car garage. (In a room of the garage, her son fixed himself up a room, for the sole purpose of having a smoke when he came home from school weekends; his father most severely objected to his smoking.) Mrs. Murphy takes in roomers at the rate of $15 per week including breakfast (abundant: orange & grapefruit juice very much watered down, a bowl of stewed fruit, a dab of oatmeal, a boiled egg, toast, and the worst coffee in the entire town).

Almost fearfully, Mrs. Murphy announces one's bill at the end of a sojourn. "Will that be all right with you?" So genteel is she, she cannot refrain from bemoaning the price of her arthritis, shots, or something, as she tremblingly deposits one's money in her handbag. Her bony, New England face is narrow, raw looking despite its pallor, her blue eyes pale, I am told she is desperate for people to stay in her house, but she makes them so uncomfortable, through pity, they soon leave. Her husband is a kindly man with a game knee, who courteously carries up people's suit-cases to their rooms. The rooms are grim and clean, all small, as if the

---

* Pat leaves town for the summer. Like many other American authors, she retreats to (in her words) the "bucolic Berkshires" in western Massachusetts. She initially lives in a tiny, inexpensive room rented out by a friendly elderly lady in Stockbridge, near Lenox.

original inhabitants of the house spent very little time in their individual rooms. Surely for the average person, a cramped bedroom, one's own room, produces a narrowness of spirit and of movement finally, too. I presume it was the cold winters that made small rooms necessary.

6/14/54

Some women will always complain about the very things they like in the people they love, or half love. It is a compulsion.

6/27/54

It is the artist's dream to dream of being personally happy and also to create at his best during that time, too. The unfortunate truth is that art sometimes thrives on unhappiness. It is one thing to realize this dimly at seventeen, and another to experience it, tragically and ecstatically, at thirty.

6/28/54

What nation hasn't something atrocious in its history to be ashamed of? Namely, inhumanity. The Spaniards to the Indians of the New World. America to its Red Indians and now still the Negroes. France—had colonies once. Russia. Germany. Only individuals can hold their heads up with pride and say, I should not have done this. Individuals of all nations. I am speaking of the lack of equality, the overwhelming existence of inequality. And the final result, inevitable, which is world citizenship, without nationality. No individual can be proud of belonging to any nation in 1954. No, not even to the youngest! Israel. A nation, like a child, can be born into the world without sin and white as snow. It has only to live a year, a week, and it will have sinned through greed and selfishness. There should be an altogether freer movement among peoples, so that they might choose their government country (until the world state comes into being) with greater facility. There would be a flocking to Switzerland, Russia and England. America: I shall soon leave it. It is not my nature to ally myself with the top dog, certainly not with a Second Roman Empire. The unholy American Empire.

7/1/54

My emotional life—it is as blind, unending, direct and hopeless, as a plant thrusting its head toward the light—which is reflected in a mirror anyway, and won't do it any good.

7/3/54

I am always in love—with the worthy and the unworthy (of anybody's love, not necessarily mine)—and I wonder now is it a giving or a taking? Before, it was obviously a taking, because I needed merely the emotion, if nothing else. Now that I have grown up a bit, it is both: what I take, or what I get, is nothing but an internal sensation. At present I am given nothing, less really than I should have from any well-functioning friendship. So I conclude, with thanks to God, that giving has also become a part of this, I cling to it now only because I can give. Substantiating me, I think, are such cases in the past when I was not only unable to take anything, but unable to give, either. E.g. A.K.* which lingered morbidly, and produced nothing out of those melancholic depths but the idea for *Strangers on a Train.*

7/3/54

I keep myself going with various kinds of dope: books, written and read, dreams, hopes, crossword puzzles, the sentimentality of friendships, and real friendships, and simply routine. If I were to relax and become human, I should not be able to bear my life. Still, there are many things I could have done with my life, and I have chosen to do this (to take a house in Massachusetts for the summer, to be lonely, and within tantalizing distance of the girl I should like to live with and never shall). There are many other things I could have done with my life this summer.

7/7/54

If I were to say what has impressed me most in my thirty-three years—it is not even the appalling fortune of a torturous sex life, far from it. It is the unavailingness of good in my generation (though it has been on its way, visible, since about 1900). I mean, of course, in international politics, and other intra-social examples of man's inhumanity, and moreover, the inhumane inevitably conquering. I am not talking about the nice lady next door who does volunteer work at the hospital. Neither am I minimizing her. I am simply talking of something much bigger! Eventually, in my modest way, I shall depict the "good" side of my books as utterly

---

* There are several people with these initials Pat could be referring to. She also mentions "A." in an undated entry roughly outlining the novel's plot in Diary 8: "Think of how A. lived before—her life— and their togetherness, their separateness."It seems likely she means Anne K., a woman she had a short but intense crush on toward the end of 1945: In early 1946, while in the early stages of writing her novel, she twice mentions—sadly without going into any detail—an "Anne K. story" in Diary 7 that "embarrasses me so much because I get off so badly."

futile, and consequently, by passivity, then activity, actually bad. The good can so easily become bad in 1954 and in future.

7/9/54

The greatest and most honest book about homosexuals will be written about people who are horribly unsuited and who yet stay together.

7/11/54

Lately in America, I hear everywhere: "Politics don't interest me." "It's always the same story. What can I do about it, anyway?" or, "Turn the radio off! It's depressing—news broadcasts!" Which is the mental attitude the powers in America would love to promote, and do, in subtle ways. The Guatemalan "uprising" would be far more interesting if social conditions there had been given a good airing to the American public, and if the United Fruit Company's tactics had been thoroughly exposed. There should be discussion clubs set up all over America to show the forces behind things that are happening. Trade needs, for example, in the allies' pleading for recognition of Red China. As it is now, we have dialogue without scenery and without character. But anyone attempting to start such clubs would be quashed as a Communist—perhaps by the very first person he attempted to enroll. Sleep on, America. The missing sun will come—out of the East. When a Russian statement is quoted on the radio, I find myself adopting the general attitude (after fourteen months in this country) of "this isn't going to be true, it's going to be something outrageous, ludicrous, so why listen at all?" If I am already this way, what about the 155,000,000 others here, already victims of thought control? Yet it so happened that from 1936 to 1939 the Russians were the only people giving a correct interpretation of the Spanish civil war, giving the reasons for the behavior of each country. There was no explanation but theirs which made sense. The allies made only feeble attempts to offer any.*

7/20/54

Taking life seriously—taking life lightly—those are just phrases. They don't imply any eventual course of action. Personally, I couldn't take life at all, if I didn't take it seriously. It contributes to my happiness as well as

---

* "EDITH'S DIARY" is written in the margin next to this entry. This is one of many examples that illustrates how Pat reread her notebooks even decades later to find inspiration for new works. Her novel *Edith's Diary* appeared in 1977.

to my unhappiness. If I didn't take life seriously, I'd have been a suicide long ago, strange as it may seem.

7/27/54

It is better to be depressed than confused.

7/30/54

Unless even the ordinary hardships of life are met with more than ordinary energy, they are overwhelming. Weakness distorts the proportion. Think of the many semi-invalids and invalids (of the spirit) who suffer severely and are never heard of, because they did not fight back. And think of the few heroes, invalids, who did fight back and managed to be happy and to give something to others. Mozart, Helen Keller, Schubert, Dostoyevsky, and Homer. These are some of the truly great of all mankind. I am thinking of L.R. [Lynn Roth] tonight, who has given me, temporarily, such a spiritual setback. She is the epitome of all failure and disappointment in my personal relationships, which have and always will be, probably, beset with disappointment. She has the distinction of being a failure before we begin. And it is as if I cling to her, exploring, feeling to the utmost, in order to learn, through pain, all that I saw. Well, perhaps I have learned something, through the painful, masterful, destructive means of chaos of the mind, the inability to concentrate, the daily waste of my daily powers. I have learned to love more dearly what she cannot give me. Tranquility of spirit, the ground on which I stand when I work. She has shown me how to love and give, when I know I am not loved in return, and shall be given nothing in return. She has shown me the magnificent and horrible vision of loveliness of spirit and of body. For such a little girl, she has shown me a great deal.

9/9/54

Santa Fe—the West. It breaks like a new land at Texola, like crossing from one country into another. The billboards and the cafés and the gas stations disappear. The land widens, empty as the day it was created. Broad, flat, green-blue plains, and in the distances a careless hill, and a long low mesa with a top more level and straight than the horizon. The sunset here makes all other sunsets small and insignificant by comparison. A streak of pink cloud hundreds of miles long hangs in the sky. A gigantic blueness is rising below it. The West was made by a generous hand. Looking ahead of me, I feel I see half of the world, and the wonder is that it is empty, and that it is so beautiful, so huge, I cannot think of a thing to say to my companion* to express what I feel about it. An *arroyo* on my right is cut like a miniature Grand Canyon, yet it is big enough for a skyscraper to lie in it. The edges are rounded with erosion, yet the cut itself looks violent and rugged, as if it had sunken suddenly one day long ago. Yellow tufts of grass, tan earth, red earth, a struggling patch of green. The colors are both subdued and garish. The land seems to say "Look! Look! Here I am. Here I was. Here I shall be." Gigantic and arrogant and slightly defiant. Here it is the land itself and not the perishable trees that is so beautiful.

9/13/54

Philosophers never come to a decision. Philosophy never comes to a conclusion. This is almost a definitive description of the science of philosophy. It is the most disquieting of sciences. Its only virtue is the moral strength it gives, merely because it grapples continuously and honestly with the unsolvable problems that torment the human being from the time he begins to think until he dies. The majority of people close their eyes to such problems. Philosophy is a game, like solitaire with one card removed from the deck so that one never can get rid of all the cards and "win."

9/14/54

The homosexual relationship is so bound up with the imaginary anyway (what might be, what I shall pretend is) that it is impossible for them to make as clean a break when an affair is over, as for a heterosexual to do so. The homosexual continues for months to play his game of pretending, and in the face of what he knows to be the truth, and the truth about what the future would have been (because in truth, he knows his own character & that of his lover's) he continues to say, but for this little this and that, I know we could have lived happily ever after. Therefore, he pretends in torturous daydreams that everything will someday be all right between them again. No wonder the melancholia drags on! There was so much fantasy from the start! The horrible fact is that the homosexuals are philosophically and poetically and idealistically right. Only psychiatrists can treat human beings as if they were chemical formulas, predictable. Many, many times the human being behaves not according to prediction or Hoyle.† In which cases, the homosexuals are borne out,

---

* Ellen Hill has come back from Europe, and Pat and she are traveling together.
† Sir Fred Hoyle (1915–2001), British mathematician.

with all their fantasy and wishful thinking. The reason being that their subject matter is as neurotic as they are.

9/21/54

Oh, the imaginative, the too imaginative men, who are always in love, but never requited, only noticed, boasted, their flowers and dedications received! Like Beethoven, Gide perhaps, Goethe, all the impulsive ones, who instinctively want to hitch the tail of their rocket onto something that remains on earth, before they take off into pure space. Such people cannot live without being constantly in love. Requited or not doesn't matter. It is a sine qua non of their creativity, their happiness of course, and their existence.

I lay with her looking at the stars. I am extremely conscious of the stars, the fact that the Great Dipper, perceived by the Chinese, is flying apart at a fantastic rate, and still, at the time of my death, will be seen to be no further scattered than it is today. Well, with her, it didn't matter, I knew that she, and I, would be dead, or near it, in another thirty years or less. It didn't matter, because I had discovered something with her that I had never known before. It was like a secret, a secret of living. It was peace. It was something at the core, beyond life and death, living and dying. It was something happy, because it was true and eternal, even more eternal than those stars. I hope I can be excused for saying more eternal, since we human beings cannot entirely understand the word eternal, anyway. With her, I was suffused with more beauty than I could discover on any trips to Greece or to the Louvre. With her, I knew more pleasure (which is happiness) than I should ever know with Plato, Sappho, Aristotle, or Alfred Whitehead. (Plato! All you say I should have. I had!) Her body between my hands! Her lips accessible turned to me. And that sadness waiting, Ovid, when we were done.

9/24/54

"Well, is it too much to ask, just to be friendly?"

"That's not all you're asking."

"It is. It's the basis of everything!"

"You want me to love all your friends—"

"I don't. Just give them a chance. It doesn't cost anything to smile—"

"You sound like a popular song."

"Darling, I love you so much—I don't expect you to like everybody or even to want them to see them again. But I want everybody to like you."

"I don't. You shouldn't either."

"You still don't understand. You're my wife. I want everybody to
think you're charming, friendly, affectionate, gracious, and everything I
love and admire in a woman."

"Why should I be affectionate to everybody?"

"You pick on that one word."

(Impossible interviews, Number One.)

10/1/54

Happiness, for me, is a matter of imagination—at the happiest moments,
lying in bed with a cup of coffee and the Sunday papers, perhaps, I can
think myself into gloom and despair in a matter of seconds. The corollary of this is what I really wanted to note: that existence is a matter
of the unconscious elimination of negative and pessimistic thinking. I
mean, to survive at all. And this applies to everyone. We are all suicides
under the skin, and under the surface of our lives.

10/1/54

What I predicted I would once do, I am doing already in this very book
(Tom Ripley), that is, showing the unequivocal triumph of evil over
good, and rejoicing in it. I shall make my readers rejoice in it, too.
Thus the subconscious always precedes the conscious, or reality, as in
dreams.

10/16/54

On the grudgingness of my chosen partners, and my consequent low
estimation of myself, I believe this self-depreciation partly due to my
evil thoughts, of murder of my stepfather, for example, when I was eight
or less. Also the realized taboo of homosexuality, my realization, even
at six, and at eight, that I dared not speak my love, and of course this
persisted with its adult ramifications of social life, guilt. Unfortunate
that this is so buried, for consciously I am not in the least ashamed of
homosexuality, and if I were normal, and equally imaginative, I should
probably consider it very interesting to be homosexual, and wish I'd had
the experience. Attitude toward money (and in the twenties, on my own)
and recent one of overspending & carelessness. Also toward food during
these years. Saving part of anything, living like a rat. Self-depreciation.
Lack of food intake in adolescence, to get attention of parents, also to
punish myself, for sex reasons, etc.

10/30/54

When one falls asleep, one also surrenders one's ego. In that, it is akin to sex. And in fact, uncorrupted children have erections in the morning, simply because of the sensuality of their sweet, warm, solitary bed.

11/2/54

If the world does not make much sense to you, it does make slightly more sense, literally more sense, after one drink or two drinks. (I do not recommend even three drinks.) This is perhaps unfortunate, but indisputable. It is unfortunate from the moral and even aesthetic viewpoints, also the religious, but it is not unfortunate from the philosophic. Bless the philosophers! In their quiet, sober way, they have always known there was something wrong with the world, therefore they wrestled with it. The wrongness of the world is not a phrase to be used carelessly. It must mean something. The wrongness of the world can generally be defined simply as greed, or base objectives of individuals and groups—which leads to the pain and detriment of innocent people. It is the little innocent people who drink, O God the Father, and pity them if you have any pity really in you, O mighty Jehovah!

11/19/54

If I shall ever pay tribute to Ellen Hill in words, the most important thing I shall say is that with her, I often had fascinating and valuable conversations between the breaking of a dinner plate and the bathing of a dog. I don't mean that the breaking of the dinner plate was an act of violence. Merely a household accident. Waiting in a dentist's office with an aching tooth (mine) we have discussed the fate of America if its present tendencies continue. Of no other woman can I say this. She could also do it with an aching tooth, by the way. It was her challenging mind often irritating, her point not always justified, that inspired the conversations generally, however.

11/19/54

After a year and a half, finally, I am appreciative of my new nomadic, improvident habits. I haven't cared a hang about money, or keeping it, for a year and a half. Either the government or my dentists will get what I earn. No use feeling resentful, and I don't. I feel happy and free and alive! If my rich friend won't buy a bottle of wine for his dinner party, because the wine is too expensive, I'll buy it for him (even if I don't go to the party). There are ways and ways of shedding a little shower of happiness in this world.

12/14/54

If all the digital power that it takes to type up a book could be gathered into one blow, it would probably knock a hole through the Empire State Building.

12/27/54

Ciudad Juarez—After a day of desert emptiness, a day of passing through crossroads of towns, we come to El Paso—a glorified Texas city that reminds one of those inconsequential and vaguely maddening Hollywood trailers of movies like *The Egyptian*, *The Colossus of Colossi*, etc. They route you through an artificially cut gap in a couple of little hills, so that you see El Paso like a mirage, dust-laden, two skyscrapers strategically placed, hotel signs against the sky, and on the extreme right a few tall smoking smokestacks as if put there by a commercial artist who intended that his picture of the city should clearly be that of a commercial city. The approach is through a hideous margin of motels—("The Westerner"—a goonish neon cowboy beckons you in to TV, air-conditioning, and other horrors, unknown to ranchos or true westerners).

The border: one comes abruptly upon a drawbridge-like structure, an imposing U.S. Guard Station out of which a uniformed guard leans towards one's car window demanding twelve cents. Is that all? It can't be. But it is. You are now in Mexico, folks. The stream of cars is dividing between the bridge (for habitual travelers who already have their passes), and newcomers like us, who must get their tourist cards stamped with some new unimportant classification. The clerk takes my friend's tourist card (which is in quite a different category from mine) and mine, together making the operations twice as long and mixing them up, too, giving her the ownership of my car. Which in the next office has to be rectified. A short, mustached Mexican with more than a smattering of English, disappears with my registration card, reappears, perfunctorily checks my luggage, and then informs me, if I want to give him something, because he is not working for the government . . . We drive off. Into the chaos of Juarez, which combines the baser features of Gibraltar, Algeciras, and Laredo. Booze, *cambios*, cafés, cabarets (but very few hotels) all burst at you in neon. The traffic is the worst I have seen since Paris. Undernourished horses pull wagons nearly empty, sandal footed Mexicans—the old shocking poverty, the new Mexico, the moderately rich here, and the terribly poor. We install ourselves finally at the Hotel San Antonio—42 pesos a day for two, with bath, and smuggled dog, which the clerks and even the manager have decided to ignore after several belligerent phone calls—the room is small, the bathroom also small, with a shower. But it is clean, and that is luxury, even if the fixtures are 1925.

DECEMBER 27, 1954

From Juarez to Hidalgo del Parral. Another incredibly straight road—sometimes from horizon in front to horizon in back. I have never seen anything like it, even between California and Colorado. We have awakened, anyway, to find Juarez covered with snow, three inches for all practical purposes, and probably six inches as reported by the weather department. It must be rather a phenomenon, because all the Mexicans are huddled in blankets, and walk along with their faces and ears covered with handkerchiefs.

I stop at the darkestly written town—Villa Ahumada, and buy four oranges and three bananas, no prize specimens, for two pesos—sixteen cents. Chihuahua is spectacularly elegant compared to anything we have seen. A real little Pittsburgh with smoking stacks of mining industries, a swank hotel called the Victoria, which will not take dogs and does not know of any hotel in Mexico, D.F. that will either. Two cups of American coffee with a bit of milk are two peso here, but with white table-cloths and real napkins.

I am quite taken with Hidalgo del Parral, where we arrive at 4:30 P.M. (having left Juarez at 8). A winding road—and then a pretty town—as Mexican towns go—sheltered by rising hills all around, and with a stream running through it, within a deep trough through the town and leaving the backsides of people's houses rather bare: it looks like Florence. One pinkish, much weathered cathedral. Inside it is rather blank and empty, the only decor being the real gilt-molding of the panels. Beside the cathedral is the square—the plaza, with a lighted bandstand, quite empty, benches all around its edges. (Benches around the cathedral, too, dedicated and presented by people who have lost loved ones.) I bought a bottle of tequila for 5 pesos 50—less than fifty cents, and a full quart.

DECEMBER 29, 1954

Mexico City—The city has grown out all along the Paseo, and Madero is now a cheap shopping district, packed to the gills with traffic and people at all hours of the night and day. There are no more siesta closings of shops and stores. Sanborns does a rush business from nine to seven, and the service is slow and indifferent. The Majestic is the only hotel we can find by telephone, in one half hour, that will accept a dog.

DECEMBER 31, 1954

The bellboys are drunk at 8 P.M. and we have an absurd conversation re the placing of the car in front of the hotel, until it dawns on our Anglo Saxon minds that the bellboy *is* drunk and on duty, and nevertheless demanding that we give him the keys of the car so that he can put it into a garage for us. To get an idea of the dining time, we asked by telephone what time the hotel was serving. An astonished voice replied: "Dinner is seventy-five pesos, Madame," as if to say, you couldn't be so stupid as to pay that much for your dinner, could you?

1955–1956

ONE CAN largely reconstruct the major phases of Patricia Highsmith's personal life from her diaries and notebooks until early 1954. From 1954 on, there are fewer entries, as Pat limits herself mostly to her notebooks—her focus there on writing—to protect against her lover Ellen Hill's prying eyes. The couple will finally break up in 1955, but Pat won't take her diary back up until 1961.

Many of Pat's notebook entries in the summer of 1955 are descriptions of travel destinations in Mexico and the people she encounters there. In March, she starts brainstorming her "Mexico novel," with the working title *The Dog in a Manger*. The male protagonist seems a likable criminal at first, a house-husband *avant la lettre* who declines sex and instead observes the mating rituals of his pet snails. Retitled *Deep Water* and published two years later, this is the second marriage thriller (after *The Blunderer*) in which Pat fictionalizes aspects of her romance with Ellen Hill. Their hostile relationship is now in definite decline. When the couple finally separates, Pat returns to her apartment on East Fifty-Sixth Street, where she completes the first draft.

In December 1955, *The Talented Mr. Ripley* is published by Coward-McCann. The book is well received and nominated the following year for an Edgar Allan Poe Award by the Mystery Writers of America. Despite being back on the road to success, Patricia Highsmith finds herself in a dark place in the new year. At age thirty-five, she suddenly feels old, burned out, unmoored—with the only semblance of stability coming from self-discipline and work. The accolades pouring in from American literary critics for *The Talented Mr. Ripley* do little to bolster her self-esteem. Well into spring, Pat's notebook entries revolve around ideas of impermanence, religion, and alcohol.

In early February, a teenage gang breaks into Pat's apartment from the fire escape, a deeply disturbing violation that clearly moves her to write "The Barbarians." In this story, one of the young burglars is collared by the fictional robbery victim and beaten to death with a rock. After this incident, Highsmith is all the happier to leave the city behind and move upstate into the home of her new love, copywriter Doris S., two cats and pet snails in tow.

Safely settled in the exurban hamlet of Snedens Landing (now Palisades), New York, an enclave for artists and celebrities, Pat starts singing in the local Presbyterian church choir and gets back to work. She begins sketching out plotlines and characters for a philosophical whodunit, *A Game for the Living,* largely inspired by her reading of Søren Kierkegaard. There's little mention of *Deep Water,* as yet unfinished, in her notebook. Work on *A Game for the Living* soon falters, and in November, Pat starts a third big project, a political satire "à la Voltaire," as she would later reveal in an interview with author and critic Francis Wyndham. In this book, a young man is sent by order of the crown to eulogize his imperial homeland around the globe. *The Straightforward Lie,* as Pat planned to call it, was never published.

2/1/55

I think to every man, the sensitivity of his youth is his secret chalice. Those days of twenty-two and even twenty-five, when (too arrogant really to dare to assess his own worth and his own opinion of it) he escorted ugly women home late at night, grew justifiably angry and proud at a breach of morals in someone he loved, when he saw for the first time England and France, when Shakespeare's most idealistic pentameters were fresh and strong in his brain—those were the days which make the fabled perfection of Heaven effete and stagnant by comparison. Few men today could hold their heads up so high unless they remembered the Shining Knighthood of their youth, and could know, that that was they, too, the same flesh and mind that they are today. But it is not true. I wish I didn't believe this, but the past mind is no more the present individual (except for certain violent emotional memories) than the cells of the body are the same after longer than seven years. The ideals, the models of behavior, the credos, which, however feebly, governed our important decisions then, these have all been swept utterly away by time also. Of morals, all that remain will be those instilled by extreme fear in early youth. Few of us have been threatened by or know such extreme fear. Others, more courageous, will have broken utterly from the childhood patterns, by strength of intellect and of real moral fiber. These latter will run the risk of being called immoral, soulless, dogs.

2/3/55

Cats are the least primitive and the most sensitive of any animals except men. Is it any wonder they are the favorite animals of so many people who appreciate these particular things?

2/13/55

It is assumed that it is easier to love an individual than "everybody"— mankind. This isn't true—unfortunately for one's individual personal happiness—it is just the other way around.

2/14/55

The main reason I write is quite clear to me. My own life, however interesting I try to make it by traveling and so forth, is always boring to me, periodically. Whenever I become intolerably bored, I produce another story, in my head. My story can move fast, as I can't, it can have a reasonable and perhaps perfect solution, as mine can't. A solution that is somehow satisfying, as my personal solution never can be. It is not an infatuation with words. It is absolute daydreaming, for daydreaming's sake.

3/5/55

If people are really emotionally bound together, they often can't be funny, or witty, or light. It takes the stranger, and a passing affair.

3/21/55

Atmosphere is the thing in this book.* An atmosphere of hatred, of comic petulance among all the characters, which, however, occasionally rises to the heroic and tragic. Such can Holy Matrimony become! Sniping, sniping, ambushing, the ballet of the wearing of the nerves. Naps are snatched the way boxers snatch respite, leaning against the ropes and relaxing while their opponents are down for a count, but a count of only nine, they know.

3/27/55

Jealousy. One of those negative, useless emotions like hatred. Jealousy never inspired a poet to write a good poem, or a painter to paint a good picture. I feel myself strangely free of it. I progress rapidly from suspicion (if confirmed) to hatred, whereupon I drop the subject. It is only when

---

* Pat is referring to her new book in progress, *Deep Water* (New York, 1957).

the subject, the situation, involves someone one loves, that it lingers. But then it does not linger, at least in me, as jealousy, but as a hopeless, self-torturing passion for someone I cannot possess.

3/30/55

The making of a book, from the germinating idea. You look ahead, two, four or five hours a day, and progress what seems like one inch on the plot. The brain refuses to advance into thin air, consciously, just as one would refuse consciously to walk off the edge of a precipice above Niagara Falls. Then in the other more relaxed and unaware hours of the day, one does advance. One steps off the precipice. A new stretch is gained. The plot advances. The characters solidify. And one can always depend upon it, the subconscious. The book will grow, as long as one concentrates those two or four hours, as long as one is, oneself, alive and living.

4/6/55

I preach against the debasement of the flesh and of the spirit by sexual abstinence! I want to explore the diseases produced by sexual repression. Men without women and women without men are equally bad and equally sick (though between the two, women often appear to be faring better; such women are at best only half human beings and so don't matter). From this unnatural abstinence evil things arise, like peculiar vermin in a stagnant well: fantasies and hatreds, and the accursed tendency to attribute evil motivations to charitable and friendly acts.

4/7/55

Waiting for you—a terrible, amazing sense of calm. Where is the tempest I'm not looking at? Somewhere on me. I have been reading a particularly tempestuous section of Dostoyevsky tonight. Perhaps that's why. Turbulent things calm me. Like you. You are so wild, you make me tame, and slow, patient and, in fact, understanding. The mind is raging fit for King Lear, and the surge of it is like the tires of a car stopping on the gravel. The swaying of the gate sounds like someone opening and closing it, yet because of you, I can carry on a long train of thought, while expecting you to open the door at any moment. And this goes on from 12:30 A.M. to 3. And that doesn't bother me either. There is another, far more important reason, philosophically, why I am so happy these days. I am no longer pervious to disappointment. I have said this before, but I should like to say it again in red letters, if one is disappointed often enough, or if one really anticipates it often enough, then it loses its sting and its power to hurt. Disappointment, to me, has lost its original meaning. If it has any meaning to me, it is that of a slight surprise. By my logical friends, I shall be asked if I don't mean that the subject in question has no import on me. On the contrary, I do not dismiss "disappointment" unless its antecedent has the greatest import.

4/7/55

After ten years (since the war) the American newspapers are still talking about the Germans' opiate of work. Unfortunately, it is true, of course. They have never learned how to enjoy life and never will. Such people are dangerous, and the rest of the world realizes it without having to analyze it. Personally, I regret this, I deplore it, but why deplore nature? The Germans are here, like the crows and the poisonous spiders, working out their destiny like the more harmless species on the earth. It would be against all my philosophy to deplore them too much.

4/27/55

Acapulco—A light-rimmed bay. That memory of my youth, the old-fashioned hotel with the veranda and steps, near the long thin wooden pier, is now so overgrown with first class bamboo restaurants as to be almost unrecognizable, even by a Proust. The lights at night: mostly like horizontally lying stars, punctuated by brilliant vermilion reds. Red and green lie on the water, bright but gentle, subdued yet iridescent, and rather oily on the water's surface. There is a huge building not yet completed, which one can look through, like an egg boxframe seen sideways. Is this going to be another great hotel, or a lot of cabañas for voyeurs? But there are so few voyeurs, really. The atmosphere is sexy, yet with a Latin frankness that removes all psychopathy. Who was thinking of psychopathy in the first place? I wasn't. In April, 1955, there are no more than five or six huge hotels, about ten smallish ones, eight of which cater to the Mexican middle class, and two to the American not-so-rich. You must put your car in low to get up most of these hills. The roads are not cobbled, but are full of the most impossible and incredible holes, twelve inches deep, sunk like blister burstings, for no apparent reason, all over the roads. La Quebrada—a sloppy yet sophisticated hotel on the hill. A rambling bar with soft radio phonograph, piano music. Vines growing, a swimming pool in the background. Run by a semi-pansy Mexican. I have heard there are 28,000 living here now. The market is bigger and more organized (not according to the ideas of an American housewife) but the same flies are still playing around it. Acapulco has acquired already the horrible, inhuman loneliness of the big city. On the roads—which are constantly in repair—whole gangs of men attack with pick axes a cement road or sidewalk, the side of a dry rocky hill.

4/30/55

The irking dissatisfaction of living with someone whom one is not thoroughly in love with, does not love thoroughly and unquestioningly. Ah, that nagging inner question, that defiant exclamation: "Surely I am not fated to live with her the rest of my life! I can't believe I am fated to live this!" What irks the honest man and the honest artist (a redundant term!) is that inevitably, if he is human and kind, the world—for him will be seen through the eyes of the person whom he does not entirely trust, and whose imperfections (nothing but dishonesties) he has already tried hundreds of times to correct and explain away, without success. To be bound to a warped and dishonest person, to be emotionally bound, is like being compelled to wear distorting glasses the rest of one's life. An unbearable fate for an artist! The world is difficult enough to bring into perspective, even seen purely!

5/4/55

Acapulco birds—early morning, off and on until late at night. They must have a siesta somewhere, like the people here.

"Pretty-girl—pretty-girl-pretty-girl!" says one.

"Here-we-go, here-we-go, here-we-go!"

"A rich chick! A rich chick! A rich chick!"

"Per-pe-trate, per-pe-trate, per-pe-trate!"

Most of their calls are in three-note arrangements. If one catches sight of any of these birds—and it is difficult to see them under the palm and coconut banana leaves, they are skinny, crested, alert and nervous, bright orange, or bright blue and red, or yellow. The other noisiest noisemaker is the gecko, who sits on one's ceiling from dusk onward. "Keck-keck-keck!" he says, perhaps calling to a lady friend. It sounds like the clucking a driver gives to a horse to make him start. Or like a rather harsh, reprimanding "Tsch-tsch-tsch!" It is remarkably loud considering the seven or six-inch length of the lizard (including tail). Geckos are the color of tea with milk in it, their eyes jet-black round dots in their heads. Their suctional finger-and-toe-tips look like round protuberances at the end of each finger and toe. Their tails taper down to a point. They never are close together, and don't seem to mind sitting for hours in an isolated corner. The birds say "Queer pee-pul! Queer pee-pul! Queer pee-pul!" It is the same bird, with a variety of things to tell his girlfriend, to arouse her interest or her curiosity enough for her to come to him.

5/6/55

I do believe in luck. I am superstitious. Not about opening umbrellas in houses, or anything so primitive. I am superstitious about the influence of mental attitudes, even when the agents, or people, or the factors one is dealing with cannot actually see or know the mental attitude (of success or failure). Therefore I am superstitious about the objects and people with which I surround myself which in turn create my mental attitude. It is, if one acts upon it, a really strong superstition that I am afflicted with.

5/10/55

The dotting of the i. There is much more to be said for it than merely to label it as conscientiousness, punctiliousness, duty observed. It is found in odd places, among odd people. It is found among bohemian atheists; and among scholars and petty bourgeois, the omission is found. Shall there be tattooed in the palm of my hand, when I die: "Bourgeois"? because I dotted my i's punctiliously, whereas I never bothered crossing my t's when they preceded an "h"? My i dots come exactly over the i's. God's in his heaven, Mr. Browning reposes where he should, on rather dusty library shelves. I am alone and lonely as usual (though worse now, in bad company) so all's right with the world. The girl I love wants me, too, as I want her. That is the main thing, not the physical proximity.

5/19/55

Conversation with a servant; Acapulco: At 11 o'clock I asked what time the mail came, and was told around twelve. At one I came in, found no mail, and said, to make sure: No mail has come today?

No, señorita, the mail comes around four.

Oh, it comes twice a day?

No. Once a day.

You told me it came around twelve.

Yes, but it comes around four.

You mean, it comes at four, not at twelve?

No, señorita, it comes at four.

Always?

No, señorita. The mail comes today around four. (He begins to smile.)

You mean today is a special day?

No, señorita, not a special day.

Then—how do you know it comes at four?

Because.

5/19/55

We are so unhappy up to the age of thirty-five, because we put the phys-ical first: how much money am I making (and why can't I make more, if I try a little harder, but mostly one can't); and how to arrange one's love life: surely she will marry me if I wait a little longer, if I try once again to win her, or, Sheila isn't the wife for me; how did I get myself into this? I must get out of it. At thirty-five, two things begin to be obvious: 1) you haven't the courage to make a move in regard to your love life, or you make the move and fail, either because the girl you want won't marry you, or if she does, she isn't the right one either; and 2) you can't, or don't make more money, and give it up as a useless effort. In middle age, early middle age, the happy man decides to put his values on intellectual pursuits, and leading the noble life, with all the human virtues. This is at least more attainable (though due to the need for money, imperfectly attainable). Happiest of all is the old man, who is able to smirk at the vanities and the impossibilities of both types of endeavor.

5/26/55

Problem—to create a moderately sized state such as Athens was in the Peri-clean age, to institute the same form of government, and instill, through similar education, a similar sense of responsibility for the public welfare—and see if, per capita, the same number of "great men" would arise.

5/27/55

One crime I consider so despicable, I should never write about it, and that is robbery.* To me, it is worse than murder, and for this irrational opinion I have a rational explanation: robbery is passionless and motive-less, except for the motive of greed. The epitome of a robbery, the ideal set-up, is a passed out drunk in a jail cell, whose family ring, for exam-ple, is stolen by his degenerate cell companions. The ring has little value in money, but a great deal perhaps, sentimentally, to the passed out man. Murder on the other hand (provided it is not incidental to robbery!) has at least some color. It is done for emotional or logical reasons, however

---

* Despite such vehemence, in 1956 Pat will write about this very topic in "The Barbarians," a vaguely autobiographical short story (*The Snail-Watcher and Other Stories*, New York, 1970).

indefensible they may be in a court of justice. Murder is a manlike act. Robbery is for dogs and wolves.

6/9/55

People who despise writing letters are 1) those who are so immature or cowardly or simply lazy, who cannot bring themselves to formulate in a few words what they are really thinking or feeling, and 2) those whose literary pretensions keep them from dashing off a letter which may not be the equal of Madame de Sévigné's.* Between the two, obviously, most people fall into the former category.

6/12/55

Diaries: it occurs to me that honest diaries help to keep one on the right moral track. Who wants to put down his self-indulgences in black and white, even if he is the only person who's going to read it? I speak from experience. I stopped writing my diary nearly a year ago—but for the very good reason that I knew somebody was reading it (E.B.H. alas). A second disadvantage of not writing diaries is that it takes away the purging effects of putting down things in words. It takes away the analysis—which however slight, always emerges when something is put into words.

6/12/55

Taxco, the cathedral bells. They are not sonorous, not gloomy, just deep enough to have dignity, just accurate enough to be cheerful, just fuzzy enough to be unshocking, gentle, melting into the soft landscape of Taxco's unchanging houses. They are never accurate, the Santa Prisca bells. At a few minutes before seven and again at about a quarter to eight in the evening they burst out in a whanging abandon, for nothing in particular, as if the bell ringer were simply having fun, or wanted to remind the townspeople of Santa Prisca's existence. Nobody ever pays any attention in the Plaza. The bells are superb—two large ones, one in either tower, two smaller ones above. I believe they use only the smaller ones, as I have never seen the big ones move. Last night was a great night for donkey braying. I wondered if some donkey was giving birth? But it couldn't have lasted so long. It starts out with a honking, squeaking sound, like a bucket being hauled up by a rusty crank, progresses to

---

* The letters of the Marquise de Sévigné (1626–1696), of which more than a thousand have survived, are considered French literary classics.

the agonized "E-E-E-aw—E-E-E-aw!" which winds down to a very melancholy, sobbing line of "onck–onck-onck—" as if that donkey's world had come to an end.

6/13/55

Typical day dream—that a total stranger comes to me when I am alone, criticizes me, points out the ideals to which I have not remained loyal, or have failed to meet; leaving me in tears, completely broken in spirit, leaving me with the idea my life is worthless and I had better not have been born.

6/26/55

Nagging. The rag-tail end of a man's life, the frayed edges of his dreams. The voice that frays, that unravels the substance of a man's life, is the voice of the woman he once loved. The tune and the instrument once sounded in a sweet, secret song of triumph. Now it is chaos, and the constant, maddening drumbeat of hell.

7/3/55

Maturity descends like a slowly collapsing cake, enveloping the individual, pinning his arms, pinning his legs, making walking difficult. Maturity makes one look at a new landscape and say, "well, it's not bad, it's not good—but I wouldn't know what changes to make in it." Maturity makes you make allowances for everything, makes you forgive the wrong things (because other mature persons do), makes you much too sensible to attempt the difficult. Makes you stop trying practically everything, because you have had time to see something like it done better somewhere else. Worst of all, maturity destroys the self, and makes you like everybody else. Unless, of course, you have the wisdom to become an eccentric. Maturity on the other hand makes you see so many sides and reasons for everything (a form of truth, to be sure) that the direct response becomes impossible—even to things worth responding directly to.

7/3/55

In the moon garden, tremble the fat tropical leaves, oily with joy. The warm sea invades the air. I am no longer human, breathing with lungs, I breathe with gills and through my pores. The mind speaks in soft guttural sounds, the sounds of ecstasy. Shaken in orgasm, a mango drops. Plop! And the waves curl over and laugh, laughing, splashing up the beach. And the sweet little sand grains tumble and roll. And the crazy patrol of the night seabirds comes squawking along the line of sea and beach: "Awrk! Awrk! Tweet! Is there anything amiss tonight?" A mango has fallen (a bird has found it) and the leaves are oily with delight, but there's nothing amiss on the beach tonight. The path of the moon is alive and well, shimmering, rolling, grinding and sliding. The path of the moon is well. In gigantic silence the bird flies up, outspread wings and open mouth, crying, "Awrk! Awrk! It's a night like any other! Awrk! Awrk! Does anybody know the time?" "Awrk! Awrk! There's a dying starfish down on the sand!" The air is sweet with gardenias and mango blossoms. "Awrk! Awrk! Who sees a fish for me?"

7/7/55

Puebla—on the clean side. Pink, balconied houses down the neat streets, and occasionally a beautiful, dusty, weathered facade of a church or of a private house, with twisting columns of stone, clusters of stone grapes, a gray-and-black weathered crest. The cathedral, touted to be the best in the Americas, is not remarkable, only big. How disappointing these Catholic cathedrals are on the inside, when one has first seen the outside! Just as in Europe. Inside is all gold leaf, enormous and mediocre paintings of St. Christopher or of the miracle of the holy water descending (whatever that is). The almsboxes have padlocks, and a rebozoed woman approaches, telling me to cover my head. (Madam, I may not cover my head, but neither would I steal from your almsboxes.) An abundance of confession chairs, take your pick. Most are open in front where the priest sits, some have white napkins pinned over the grill as well as the customary folding screen which the priest maneuvers. Ah, the dreary little stairways winding to the dreary little rostrums where such dreary words are spoken! In a back pew a young man and woman are discussing something earnestly together. The Fort Guadalupe where the famous Cinco de Mayo (1862) battle was won against the French. No admission, and the dog goes romping around in its pictures of Maximilian, Zaragoza, and the arrogant words of the French Comte de Lorencez* that he has the cowardly Mexicans well in hand.

---

* Charles Ferdinand Latrille Lorencez (1814–1892) was a general of the French Army. During the French intervention in Mexico, even though his troops by far outnumbered those led by his opponent, General Ignacio Zaragoza, he suffered a crushing defeat at the battle of Puebla.

7/8/55

Oaxaca—The housing is short for Americans. Apartment, untenable, and the town so attractive! Social life centers around the Del Valle Hotel café on the Zocalo, which much resembles a Parisian sidewalk café. Bearded young men drinking endless beers, a middle-aged couple from a border-town in Texas, very much au courant in Oaxaca, who play bridge in the evenings. A retired 50-year-old American man, shabby, over-friendly, who buys his own groceries and lives in some furnished apartment, one of the few.

35 miles east of Oaxaca. A good road till you get to the village of Mitla. There a bridge is out, due to the rains which have not been equaled in nearly 200 years. Finally a puddle six feet in diameter and God knows how many feet deep, daunts us, and we ask the villagers for an alternative road. There is no alternative road but there is a circum-vallation, equally bumpy, pairs of oxen mysteriously going home alone and dragging their whiffle trees, cocks, geese, single women in rebozos and long Oaxacan skirts, small boys, always outnumbering the small girls. Eight feet tall cactuses are used as fences along the road, bounding the barren front yards of the houses. Mitla, the ruins, resemble those of Monte Alban, are less spread out, and the designs are more distinguish-able in the sunlight along the friezes. Zig-zag, swastika-like, repetitions conventionalized floral patterns. A couple of roofless oblong courts, twenty feet by six. Tombs half underground, approachable by tunnel, on hands & knees through the low doorway. Mitla sits on a few hills, is comprised of scattered "temples" in pyramidal form, boasts the ruins of a fortress half a mile away on a great hill. The catholic church has superimposed itself upon the site of a Zapotec temple, now gone except for the long horizontal rows of tan bricks that formed its base.

[NO DATE]

Cuernavaca—Hotel Quinta Las Flores. Hard to get to, off the road to Acapulco at one end of the town. Even the thin tall letters of its name are hard to read once one stands in front of it. It used to be a private house, this pleasantly spacious, pleasantly small hotel with its lawns & swim-ming pool. The servants are only five or six, the watchman acts as bell-hop when it is necessary to carry a suitcase, but most people who come here stay a few weeks. The prices are moderate 60–70 pesos daily with food, but the hotel is empty, simply because nobody has ever heard of it. Nobody but a few middle aged American couples of the upper middle-class variety—all quite nice, the kind you wouldn't mind sharing your cocktail hour with. The Hotel Administrator, Carmen, a Spanish refugee, Communist no doubt, adamant hater of Franco, unmarried, fairly tall, gray hair, attractive, pleasant personality, about 50. She makes the atmosphere very pleasant here; consistently friendly, catering to everybody's whims. On her name day, everyone gave her a little present and she gave a cocktail party in the main dining room.

7/11/55

If not for its social approval, religion, like any other kind of baseless belief, might lead to insanity. Paranoia is such a belief, though unsupported by the rest of society (yet in some primitive south sea societies, paranoia is the rule and those not displaying it are ostracized). Thus we arrive at a useful deduction: organized pretensions. To pretend, to hope for something unattainable, know it is unattainable, yet hope because it is beneficial to hope—that should be the new religion. How blissful that instant of deciding to hope! Thus the artist, Lucullus, deprived of Lesbia, can write great poetry by thinking, if I write beautifully enough, she will love me and come back to me. I cannot fail. Therefore, he doesn't fail, at least in writing good poetry.

7/12/55

The idea of killing his victims comes as a surprising discovery, and all the repression of years is unleashed. The moral of the story [in *Deep Water*]—what repressed emotions can become: schizophrenia. Plus showing the devotion-through-habit of married people.

8/21/55

I revert more and more to the projected novel of my parents and myself. The *Death of a Salesman* theme in another profession, another period— and to me far more tragic because the aspirations were higher. In this book my parents will be writers, becoming increasingly hack, and I shall become a painter. The pure, wordless line, the word—which lives only by its color and character. Taken from the time I am six.

8/22/55

A real live writer, in captivity! And the world is so full of so many things worth more than you. Europe and tilting Italian towers, drunken laughing nights, and nights in bed with other people. I would not exchange my filthy soul for your shining sterility for all the money in the world!

I would not exchange the evil distorting lens of my eyes. I would not exchange the things that I laugh at for the things you laugh at, nor the things that I cry over for the things to which you are indifferent. I had rather be schizophrenic, schizoing madly up and down my typewriter all day, and keep my own gods, than to be taught by you.

8/22/55

Well, that's America. Nothing but the newest, the finest, the brightest, the two-tonedest, the fastest, with the mostest! Yassuh!

9/28/55

Her chaste kisses cannot hold me.
Oh! Oh! Oh! Oh!
Nor the way her arms enfold me.
Oh! Oh! Oh! Oh!
Though I know that she has told me
She would love me all my life,
She would always be my wife.
Oh! Oh! Oh! Oh!
I want stronger arms around me,
Insane arms and devils' kisses,
Teeth that bite my lips and wound me,
Girls whose love will never last.
Oh! Oh! Oh! Oh!
I am as mad as they, and seek
A vixen's face that stays a week
That fine torture that one day kills.

11/9/55

[New York.] The Eighth Labor of Hercules. Or If you Can Afford a Cold Water Flat, You Can Afford Sutton Place. My rent is forty dollars per month, a modest sum certainly. That was my idea, to take a place for little money, which I could leave, locked, snug, when I traveled. I hadn't much money to lay out, that September when I began. I figured that a hundred and fifty dollars would do it—a friend was giving me a practically new bed, I had to buy a bookcase, a couple of chairs, curtains, an inexpensive carpet or two, and that would be that. But I discovered I had no refrigerator and wasn't getting any. My landlord is a mercenary bastard. He is an Italian, who shall be nameless, and since I am fond of Italy and the Italians, I'd like to say he's a fine fellow, but I can't. Joe is a stocky, flashily dressed young man of thirty-two who looks forty-two with a cigar eternally in his mouth—a short, soggy, unlighted, thoroughly disgusting cigar, and his crude wide mouth resembles a scarcely healed gash in his pasty, unhealthy bluish face. You can never catch him in his office. When I was looking—rather waiting—for this apartment, I called him ten times to get him in once, came to see him a dozen times, by appointment, to find him out, and the tiny Second Avenue office locked tight as a drum. Once, he called me: "Got an apartment for yuh. Come down Monday morning round eleven." I was there, but Joe was talking to two young men who stood in his office with very dejected even expressions on their faces.

"Nah—well, I already got it rented," Joe was saying to them.

"But you promised it to us—"

"Not only that," the other interrupted, "we're the tenants! We were just in the place."

"You ain't got no lease," Joe reminded them coldly, shoving his hat back on his forehead. Joe never removes his hat. The telephone was perched on his shoulder. He was also carrying on a desultory conversation with someone on the other end of the telephone. This is typical of the atmosphere in Joe's office: you can never get his undivided attention. When he is addressing you and nobody else, he is a master of the ambiguous answer. "Yeah. Well, I'll see what I can do. I got my own lock and my own key to that place now." ("But is anybody ahead of me?" you demand anxiously.) "We'll see. Nah, nobody's ahead of you," Joe replies smiling superiorly. You wouldn't know if anybody were ahead of you or not from that answer and that smile. But one thing dawns on you very soon: Joe doesn't keep a list, nothing so orderly or so fair; he gives an apartment to people whose looks he likes, i.e. to people who he thinks will not go running to the Housing Administration to report that he is charging too much for his rents. The apartment which I took for $40 per month is worth $28, the previous tenants having paid $23. For some reason, which God only knows, cold water flats are at a premium. Everybody wants one—every artist and writer whose incomes are uncertain, every aspiring junior executive, whose income is not uncertain, but who wants to spend his income on more important things, like clothes, restaurants, entertaining, the theater. Nearly every young man of twenty-eight, whatever his profession, wants a cold water flat. He'll fix it up, he says—and he does, breaking his back, his ribs, his bank account very likely, before he is done.

11/15/55

N.W. [Natica Waterbury]. She will make some desperate marriage at 38, perhaps, which won't last, but if it lasts two years may give her (or her age will) that poise and confidence in her own special personality, which she so badly needs. She is so far superior to most in an intellectual and idealistic sense. She thinks and questions, and most of us do not, most of us live nearer to the animal level. It is this inquiring and this doubt (with consequent indecision) which I most admire in her and which will always make me love her. It is the big sine qua non of civilization, of the emergence of the human race from the more bestial organisms on earth. She can never be ignoble, whatever happens to her, however the buffetings of life force her to behave. She has that which Shakespeare meant when he compared men to angels.

12/14/55

On A—(I shall always refer to her in these notebooks as A)*— trying to decide why we couldn't and can never get on. I decided, in a conversation about it with a friend, that it is because we have the same types of pessimism, almost the same degree and in the same places. In every other respect we are complementary and congenial. But I cannot imagine myself allying myself with another pessimist. In a lover, I shall always look for an optimist, an out-goer. This in the profoundest sense complements me.

12/15/55

The excesses of February to April of this year have taken their natural sequence from September to December. That hubris (on finishing a fairly good book, on having used a human being) is followed by humility— which it takes quite a while to discover and identify—a vague depression, which however doesn't much interface with anything. I continue to surround myself with mediocrity, rolling out my reddest carpet to bores, drunks, the feeble-minded, the unaspiring, the contemptible. "I wasn't myself from February to April," I thought in late April—and even realized while it was going on. I am not myself now, I often think. Am I destined to live like this? In a cold water flat, chilly most of the time, half ashamed to invite my more formal friends here (but not my best friends). Neither is quite true. No use looking for one's "self" in a static condition, surrounded by the things, attitudes, people one thinks of abstractly

---

* "A" is Pat's new code name for Ellen Hill.

as ideal. The living self is always in flux. We can say only what we consider "typical" for one person or another. It is never achieved, never all at once. Comforting to analyze.

1/3/56

To find a justification for one's sins, one's errors, one's weaknesses—that is what one seeks in the depths of the night, when one wishes to be alone. One searches in many books (and one doesn't find the specific remedy or justification). One finds, finally, a human thought, one of those splendid endeavors at categorizing, comparing, synthesizing, which is the justification of the whole human race. And then alone, unconsoled, one rejoices suddenly at being able to take part in that purely human sport of thinking. One is at least a member of the human race, in the only way one can be. To think, thinking, is the only passport.

1/4/56

"I dedicate this [note]book to alcohol, in all its charming guises, its delightful forms, to its lifting of the heart, to its rending of the dark, close curtain of reality that enables man to behold the depth and breadth of his imagination, to its power to relieve pain, to its power to give courage to those who are in need of it. To alcohol, hermaphrodite, seductive and gentle as a maiden in love, vigorous and bold as a giant who champions a friend with a strong right arm."

1/5/56

What is more delicious than to slip back into old vices? What pleasure more sublime than to savor the whiskey once given up forever? What joy more divine than to return to the woman once condemned as bad for us, to sink into her arms, to yield completely to whatever evil she has in store? There is such pleasure in self-destruction! There is such overwhelming truth in it that man feels a profound affinity! O Siva! O Pluto! O Saturn! O Hecate!

1/6/56

Is Christmas really turning into something happy? Money helps, of course, which makes it automatically so much easier for Americans. At first, the shopping is a nuisance, for the presents one has to send away, one has to buy for close friends. Then the "Christmas Spirit" sneaks up on you—around December 20th. What is the Xmas spirit? Behind it all, the half mythical faking that we are being kinder, happier, more generous than we are all the rest of the year—more generous than our real selves, in fact. It is a form of acting, in a way. We also know it won't last. We think: let's give ourselves a better reputation than the next guy this Xmas by being outrageously cheerful, generous, kind, decent, upright (lend a helping hand in the subway, give up that seat!). Invitations are accepted, invitations extended. One becomes a whirlwind of hospitality, making drinks, washing glasses, cooking and shopping, until one feels like a dishwasher, cook, and Elsa Maxwell* all in one. Hangovers are soon forgotten, drowned in another deluge of alcohol, beginning at noon. The knowledge that the whole city has gone mad keeps even the most disciplined from working, finally. Finally, the Xmas spirit— of wanton giving, getting, drinking—seeps into one's own room. The pleasantness in America is largely derived from the sense of abundance of everything, not from a seriously moral or religious experience, unfortunately, which is the case in much of Europe. The bleak Protestant churches with their gold ornaments—a very few—fir branches, candles, are a plain symbol of the abundance in every home, of packages heaped under trees, of tables with more varieties of food than any one person can ever sample. Christmas is reaching its final wearing before extinction—the apotheosis of American commercial prosperity. In later generations, when history has all but died out, Christmas may be taken to have been a collective celebration of American stores and department stores, nothing more. It is their big holiday, their great joy, let's face it.

1/10/56

I am within a few days of being thirty-five, and while I sincerely rejoice in the sensations of being a human being, a person, I am just as aware of the dogging footsteps of death coming after me—which, in a curious way, I relish also. So, feeling both these things, maturity and mortality, I shout "Hooplah!"

1/13/56

The hell of depression is that it brings with it a paralysis, a meaninglessness. At home, alone, one does not want to read anything, knows to

---

* Elsa Maxwell (1883–1963), writer and gossip columnist famous for her professionally organized parties for an A-list clientele.

drink is bad (conscience speaks), does emphatically not want to go to a movie. The telephone may ring. But here's the awful point, too, there is no one of our acquaintance whom we want to see. Our best friends—we are ashamed, we wouldn't inflict this on them. Our lesser friends—how boring they seem! One wants to die, simply. Not to die, but not to exist, simply, until this is over.

1/28/56

Depression. I wish there were a more terrible and explicit word. My life, my activities seem to have no meaning, no goal, at least no attainable goal. I can learn Italian, but shall I ever master it? If I conceive a short story tonight, begin to write it, can I ever sell it? My goals these days are inevitably and horribly tied up with money. I can feel my grip loosening on myself. It is like strength failing in the hand that holds me above an abyss. This is after a quarrel with E. [Ellen] when if I were to believe her words, which I don't, I should be utterly alone. I have my friends, however, a marvelous consolation, a source of real pride. But it so happens they are busy this Saturday night when I do not want to be alone. It is the purposelessness that will finally be my downfall—*could* be. I know one important counteragent, to do things for other people, large or small. But that, alas, will not root it out of myself. I do not deserve this depression, I feel, and yet my intellect tells me that one gets nothing but what one deserves, what one makes for oneself. It is a comfort to know that there are psychiatrists to help people such as me, and that they are so familiar with so many worse cases!

1/29/56

Q.* Do you believe in God?

A. No, but I often pretend that I do, because it makes me happier. But this never lasts long, the pretense or the happiness.

Q. What is the difference between pretending to believe in God and in believing in God?

A. A very slight one, fortunately. When pressed, how many people would say that they really believe, because they are sure it is a fact, that God exists and controls the universe and their lives? Very few, and those so unthinking, undoubting, that they would not be able to substantiate themselves in words. It would be more honest of the majority of

---

* An extended version of this dialogue will find its way into the next novel Pat is starting to gather ideas for, *A Game for the Living* (New York, 1958).

people to admit that they have found it expedient to pretend to believe in God, and that this little hiatus between pretending to believe and believing has long ago been leapt by their minds, and can no longer trouble them. By accident I have used Kierkegaard's own verb, to leap. Faith is a leap, into the abyss or whatever, and believe and trust and never doubt, that is, never subject belief in a divinity to any logical, material criteria of proof, what is really the difference between this and pretense of belief? One decides to pretend, that is all.

3/20/56

The hardest truth that one ever has to learn is that truth is a compromise.

3/20/56

And to say "It's very bad luck to say my work is going well," is the same as saying, "I have a low opinion of myself. I am afraid, but more ashamed of blowing my own horn, or I am ashamed of living at all, ashamed to admit I may be handsome or attractive to many people with whom I come in contact."

3/25/56

The humanistic morale versus Freud. It shows best in pre-Freudian Joseph Conrad. At the end of *The Outcast of the Island*, the old man's speech against the young outcast is devastating: "I don't consider you an evil soul in an evil body. You are merely a mistake of mine, my shame." He says also, that he doesn't know where the young man came from—though as it happens since he picked him up at the age of twelve, abandoned and afraid, he knows that there has been some deprivation in his childhood. Freud would point to this as an excuse for the young man's self-indulgent, amoral behavior. Conrad simply condemns him, finally, after he has failed test after test, chance after chance. The Freudian hypothesis means:

1) He cannot help himself
2) Somebody else is to blame.
3) By understanding this, he can be helped to overcome his weaknesses—by analysis.

The trouble is, the average case stops before step three is half completed. Conrad morality says:

1) A man who selfishly seeks his own pleasure and welfare at the expense of others is a wicked man and deserves to be punished.

2) But whatever the background, there is hope for an individual if he but clings to his high principles inherent in him because he is a man. (So does Dostoyevsky imply this, whatever the background: there is always redemption through confession, through trying again.)

3) It is the duty of every man to live his life fully and honorably, to shrink back from no experience that fate puts in his way.

It is easy to see that the Freudian conception makes for weaker human beings, baser, more timid, and essentially more selfish. If, however, Freud's "working through" effected cures in all cases, it would be a different story. Then one would see Freud's ideal come to be: psychologically healthy individuals, trustworthy, happy, courageous.

The old-fashioned pre-Freudian morality is in many ways harder for the individual to comply with. It is the rod and parental and public opinion against the seemingly insuperable demons and weaknesses within. It is an appeal to a human dignity which may never have been awakened in the individual. It implies a social background with a conscience, a moral education, almost, a back corner of the memory where some person or persons once stood for the superego. Perhaps these things can never be appealed to.

The old fashioned, human morality is far more appealing to the writer, freeing him for one thing of the clutter of psychoanalytical jargon, or that whole process of analysis and working through, which he knows so well. The old-fashioned morality appeals to the heroic, which every writer knows, almost as an axiom, to be present in every character, however villainous, that he writes about.

The Greeks believed that the Moral Order was an objective fact in the world. Hubris was punished inevitably by Dike.* Good was good and to be desired because it produced a well-being in humanity. Theirs was the cleanest, loftiest vision of all. A sinner was merely unwise, inviting punishment, unfair to himself. How seldom did they say anything resembling "His soul is bad"!

3/28/56

I plunge into my particular *mêlée*, that habitual tangle of related and unrelated facts, which never will become resolved, and which is as much me as the smell of my own room. A stimulating book does it, a couple of

---

* In Greek mythology, Dike is the goddess of justice.

drinks alone, a sticky love affair. It is composed of my undefined, unrec-
onciled self.

4/13/56

What a strenuous thing it is to be in love.* What a difficult thing it is to
realize completely the existence of the person you are in love with. Is
this a weight that the mind or the heart cannot bear? It is too sweet, too
miraculous. It shakes one, like an electrical charge. And the memory
of the first embrace whenever and wherever and every time we meet—
merely the memory is charged with all the force of reality. The same
nerves are struck again with that ecstatic impact. It is too much. The
nerves become bruised. One becomes sick, surfeited with simply too
much happiness.

5/7/56

(D.S.)

This is love overshadowed by nightmare,
Intimations of immortality
(And you say yourself it may last until we die and after)
Overshadowed by the nightmare terror
Of your scorn and of my death.
My fear of Death has many forms!
This is the forest of Oberon, Oberon,
Pulsing with deep and hollow bassoon notes,
Infused with silken rays of light
Among the leaves— and there are your lips
Parting under mine. The silent music
Trembles in my blood, I am drunk,
And mad with fear.
Are you also afraid?
(Perhaps we really share so little!)
I await the falling rock, the bridge
That breaks under me.
I await the Guillotine of your displeasure.
Why must you spend more time judging than loving?
Questioning than tasting?
What are these defenses defending?
But the nights are silent,

---

* There is a new love in Pat's life, advertising writer Doris S.

Nuits blanches pleines de cauchemars, *
And who can hear my cries,
Which are silent as the music in our veins?

5/29/56

My dear God, who is nothing but Truth and Honesty, teach me for-
bearance, patience, courage in the face of pain and disappointment.
Teach me hard, because I am stubborn and desperate, and one day I
shall take you by the throat and tear the windpipe and the arteries out,
though I go to hell for it. I have known heaven. Have you the courage
to show me hell?

6/8/56

The trust in the eyes of a girl who loves you. It is the most beautiful
thing in the world. It is stronger than steel, stronger than oaths, stronger
than fear and terror, more powerful than Death. It can make the coward
brave. It is his shield against all his enemies. It is the source of his energies and of his courage. In the face of ugliness, lies, disappointments,
it is what he will remember, and it will suddenly—suddenly—He will
be born again, renewed, and he will hold the world in his hands, and
Heaven, too.

6/10/56

Satire on America [*The Straightforward Lie*], forty years hence, after
one war with Russia, which ended in stalemate (one atom bomb was
dropped by each nation, destroying respectively Archangel and Boston).
America is going to lose the coming war, now, and the reason will be
her failure of faith. Russia and its great allies, China and India, have
unconsciously, subtly, broken down prejudice and the old unthinking
hostility by their plain good will, their easygoing New Look (new in
1956 even) and by the infectious, joyous enthusiasm of their people.
Moreover, the U.S.S.R. now has a standard of living comparable to that
of America—in some respects higher! She is spreading that standard to
all her satellites. In America, satirical writers have been debunking the
advertising-television-high production and salesmanship philosophy for
several decades. It is they—not the communist agents—who have struck
the fatal crack in the Americans' morale.

---

* Sleepless nights full of nightmares.

6/25/56

Mountains, how do you do?
I shall die in you.
Clouds, be my shrouds!
Alpine lakes, however cold,
Thou shalt be my graving mold!
Girls of Florence,
Girls of Rome,
Thou shalt be
My final home.
Australia,
Audacious! Keep thyself.
I haven't time this life.
I haven't time
I haven't time!
No time even to commit a crime,
Or to tell the smallest lie.
All day today I wanted to die,
I wanted to cry,
And did.
I am in New York.
Where are you? Does it matter?
Don't take the time to answer that question.
I haven't time, have you?
I haven't time to be dishonest.
I haven't time to finish this.
This is my life.
I'll never finish that either.
I hope! I hope! I hope!

7/5/56

Modern television. The need of the ordinary person to be reassured that everything will turn out all right. Fred Allen* so interesting on the subject in *Treadmill to Oblivion*.

He remarks that radio's sound effects enabled everyone, according to his imaginative powers, to experience any scene the performer wished to evoke. And that the advertising hogs saw in TV a quicker, easier (ergo

---

* Fred Allen (born John Florence Sullivan, 1894–1956), was an American actor, comedian, and popular radio host.

more popular) medium, which would enable them to sell more crap.
Allen: Television has taken away one of the last human attributes of the
common man: his imagination.

7/13/56

Life—existence—getting along with people—or even getting along
totally with oneself—is a matter of compromise. A platitude. But the
wisdom (or the stupidity) depends on the things one compromises with,
and also one's sense of humor, or detachment, or earnestness, in compromising. It is the most important and the most difficult art in the
world. But it is for people who have chosen happiness, alone. It is not
really for artists, though they have to compromise, too (e.g. when they
greet their cranky landladies; or do they always? No). One must either
know instinctively when and how much to compromise, or one must
have an intellectual system worked out about it. One must compromise
the whole way, with a sense of humor and an absolute, beautiful conviction that one is not compromising oneself in doing so; or else one must
be grim and equally well defined, saying basically I shall not compromise any more than is necessary for me to keep myself out of jail. But
there are times when one should go to jail, prefers to go to jail. This is
really the Endless Circle, the rat-race of Twentieth Century America.

7/13/56

I know why Byron said sleep is the sister of death—and many other poets
said it too. Not so much romantic as physiologic. Have you ever seen the
girl you loved asleep? Not just dropped off, but by herself gone to sleep,
when you were reading a book? It is as frightening as death.

7/31/56

The danger of living with somebody, for me, is the danger of living
without one's normal diet of passion. Things are so readily equalized,
soothed, forgotten with a laugh, with perspective. I don't really want
perspective, except my own. The latter after four months of it. This
problem did not arise with A., because she kept me so furiously angry
and resentful much of the time, it was really all the passion and mine-
own-perspective I could handle. At this moment I am extremely tired
of material acquisitiveness, whether it takes the form of a check, a new
piece of furniture, a new appliance to "save time and effort" or a new pet
in the household.

8/13/56

Feeling lousy? Depressed? Like a failure? As if what you're doing at the moment is futile? Just decide you're going to feel happy. Enjoy feeling sweaty and dirty in levis that should go to the laundry. Forget your bank account—and your lack of income. Possibly make a martini. But only one. Enjoy that cigarette. And that cup of coffee. Be a perfectionist. Get a real lift from meticulously correcting a spelling mistake in a manuscript that isn't going to sell. Smile—*inside*!

10/20/56

It would be ironic indeed if the U.S.S.R were the country that would abolish war—I mean big world wars. The U.S.S.R is a "peace loving" country (even more than the U.S.) in the sense that it realizes the expense of war and knows that it cannot afford wars. Peace, propaganda, the conversion of men's minds—those are the weapons of the Soviet. So much more effective than bullets! So much cheaper! The effects so much longer lasting! We in the West still bombast about the military armaments, and we threaten military reprisals, while the Soviet quietly sits on one country after the other, and continues its work of proselytizing, conversion, spreading hatred against the West. It will take a generation to undo the work of the Soviet on the minds of young people in East Germany. Perhaps it will never be undone, anyway. Perhaps that step into a country of Western Europe is the beginning of the propaganda march which will never go backward and which will cover the earth!

10/21/56

My continuing troubles about my work. My writing, the themes I write on, do not permit me to express love, and it is necessary for me to express love. I can do this only in drawing, it seems. One of my friends suggested I see an analyst about it. What's the use? There is no solution except to write and draw as well, as I have been doing. Occasionally, I get an idea for a story or a book which I *have* to put on paper. It is because of its novelty or sensation, however, not because of a message, or affection, which I have to externalize and share. And when all's said and done, the final comment will be (from me at least) so what? I'll live with my neuroses. I'll try to develop patience, temperance, try to give as much love as I can with my handicapped personality. But I prefer to live with my neuroses and try to make the best of them.

10/30/56

I have an idea to go to Rome and Paris, live for a year, and write a novel
(authentic to the last minutia) of young writers, painters, dilettantes
there, in relation to the rest of the world. Of such ideas novels are not
made. This would not be a novel in that sense, but would be partly documentary, in the impassioned [Curzio] Malaparte style. In it there is room
for hope as well as despair. Not every life is the only life, or the only
possible life. There are as many lives as there are people to live them,
and each person himself has the choice of many! Thus I refute Freud and
Marx, and pay homage to Kierkegaard and Jaspers.

11/14/56

Wretched, on the edge of a hatchet,
I salute you, heroes and heroines of eternity!
Glory be to us, who loved life!
Glory be to us, who were not too much concerned with
What our fellow political men thought of us.
Tonight I celebrate the useless beauty of the Villa d'Este,
And certain high tors* I attained which are purely personal.
It would be selfish and even redundant to enumerate them,
Because others, I am not the worst, have reached them too.
I have learned to love, perhaps that is the highest tor.
There is no insurance, no parachute.
But there is the merging with the insect, the bird, the flower
Which dies at end of summer.
There is the death without regret before the death actual.
And actual is factual, actually, and factually actual,
And who cares for that?
In the midst of ugliness, I have seen beauty,
And to my credit, I have called nobody's attention to it,
In an era when nobody wanted to be tarried by it.
Evviva Amore! Evviva bellezza!

11/23/56

FA dream. I was making a bed with two sheets on two sofas. I was told
I didn't have to sleep there. I was relieved. I found myself in bed next
to my mother and my step-father. My mother said to me: "I have news

---

* "Tor" is a word for a hill or mount in the UK's Devon dialect.

for you. I'm throwing you out." I was surprised, but began to get up.
My mother said emphatically, "You see, I *love* Stanley." I answered,
despairingly, "But mother, I have no doubt you love Stanley!" and
wanted to cry. She made it seem as if I was interfering in their relationship. I left the room and entered another, where I found several candles
burning under the bed, burning the bottom of the bed. I screamed,
"My God! If there are more accidents around here, what on earth will
happen to the house?" I snuffed out the candles. In a corner of the room
I saw small plants (like mine, but prettier) and a dreadful fight: a small,
twelve-centimeter-tall gorilla that was pummeling a tiny, defenseless
tortoise. Disgusted, I slapped them and separated them, and I saw that
the tortoise had a second head coming out of its shoulder, which was
looking around awkwardly and fearfully. I woke up. (Last evening, I
heard an incredible story about a young girl of twenty who had under-
gone surgery for back pain. They discovered that she had a small child
inside herself, a boy, they said—the young girl must have been one of
two twins.)

The scene with my mother is reminiscent of the evening I spent at E.'s
[Ellen's] this week. She accepted me, but then rejected me—she didn't
want to be lovers again—we did not discuss it, but it wasn't necessary.
(N.B. Upon waking, I touched D—and was very happy to have her
there.)FF

11/27/56

My loafing. Not merely to recover physically (the dentist now) but to has-
ten the process of becoming the roughly bored with day-to-day, under-
my-nose existence, which is what prompts me to write (work) at all.

11/27/56

E.B.H. She & people like her, they chew it up and spit it out—
philosophy, history, politics, sociology, psychology—in the form of
reportorial papers, or grim, fast conversation. If they ever have an idea,
however tiny and it usually is for they lack the breadth, the generosity of
mind to conceive a system themselves, they nurture it and show it to their
friends as a proud mother shows a tiny, red-faced baby. They produce
nothing, I do not envy them. They never know free flight into the imagination. They are like fishermen going over and over their nets to see how
they are made, without ever capturing or being interested in capturing
a fish. Their pitiable reward for their diligence is in feeling superior to

everybody who does not happen to know (from a textbook) what they know. Their faces become finally the sterile, frightened, cold images of what they are within, unable to smile with tenderness as their hearts are unable to open. They bestow a smile, or a present, upon another human being, only after much analysis to see if the person is deserving and if they can afford to give that much.

1957–1958

PATRICIA HIGHSMITH TAKES ANOTHER trip to Mexico, this time with Doris S., in early 1957. Together they visit locations that will be featured in her sixth novel, *A Game for the Living*—Mexico City, Veracruz, and Acapulco, sites Pat not only details at length in her notebook, but also records visually in sketches and vibrant watercolors. There's otherwise little color in Pat's life, beyond her imagination, and she entertains romantic flights of fancy, both personal and professional. At this point Pat's notebook reads like a diary.

In March 1957, when her crime story "The Perfect Alibi" appears in *Ellery Queen's Mystery Magazine*—now her primary publisher for short stories—Pat returns home to Sneden's Landing with Doris, the mood subdued after their Mexican vacation. In an attempt to hold her world together and endure the endless cycle of conflict and reconciliation with Doris, Pat turns toward faith, joining the choir at a small Presbyterian church in Palisades.

In July, Pat informs her editor Joan Kahn that she's twelve pages shy of completing the first draft of *A Game for the Living*. Kahn, however, is critical of the manuscript and demands extensive revisions, including a new ending—and thus, a new murderer. Between four revisions of her novel—work that extends into the spring of 1958—Pat teams up with Doris to write a children's book, *Miranda the Panda Is on the Veranda*. Rather than patching up their relationship, this collaboration accelerates its demise. Pat becomes increasingly withdrawn, escaping the cramped confines of the converted barn in which they live and work by exploring her own imagination.

Pat falls hopelessly in love with commercial graphic designer Mary Ronin in the summer of 1958, but Mary is in a committed relationship with another woman. She becomes a source of inspiration for Pat's next book, the story of chemist David Kelsey, whose true love is married to another man. David is convinced he can fix "the situation" and that he will win Annabelle over, whatever it takes.

Between mid-June and mid-September, Pat lays out individual scenes for the new novel—titled *This Sweet Sickness*—then essentially assembles them before the reader's eyes. Pat makes no further mention of the manuscript from October 1958 onward, which might be attributed to the fact that she and Doris move to Sparkill, New York, in September. The couple end their relationship in early December, and Pat moves into a furnished studio at 75 Irving Place in Gramercy Park, adjacent to Pete's Tavern. At this point, the love affair with Mary, so long fantasized, appears to have become reality.

1/15/57

In view of the fact that I surround myself with numbskulls now, I shall die among numbskulls, and on my deathbed shall be surrounded by numbskulls who will not understand what I am saying. A curious thing to be disturbed by at thirty-five, perhaps—Numbskulls have a way of being very disturbing in all departments of life at this particular time, in the first month of the second Eisenhower administration. Whom am I sleeping with these days? Franz Kafka.

1/18/57

My growing problem since 1951: (in Riesman's terms) from inner-directed (ambitious, idealistic, self-driving, diary-keeping) I have become somewhat other-directed;* and this is against my nature, or at least my nature until the age of thirty. Among its manifestations (which irritate the inner-directed side of me) are carelessness about money, looseness of morals in sex and drinking, smoking, abandonment of daily exercises (physical), abandonment of diary keeping, perhaps over tolerance of the mediocre in people and in art (this has its good side and is hard to make a judgment about), laziness (sporadic) about my own work, and a general lowering of sights in my themes. Time something was done about it. Something in between inner and outer, if possible.

---

* David Riesman (1909–2002), American sociologist. In his best-selling landmark study *The Lonely Crowd: A Study of the Changing American Character* (1950) he differentiates between three types of people: tradition-directed, inner-directed, and outer-directed.

1/18/57

A dream. A large, mixed party, given by my parents & me, in a large house. Joan K. [Kahn] is there, also Jeva C., who alternately say "Come here, Pat," and call me into a bathroom or closet and kiss me on the lips. Extremely pleasant, and I cannot make up any mind which I want. (D. not present.) I so seldom have sexual dreams, I must have a strong censor. D. reports she has some, always involving men, though her daily life (non-sexual) situations always have women characters.

2/16/57

Love, being so different from marriage, permits of one's really being "in it" forever. It is destructive, interrupting, and of no importance except to the artist. To be in love is to fly as high as anyone ever will be. The important thing is never to let one's sexual or bedroom passions guide one's life. Ironic that to be in love is only of importance to the artist, and to him only is it important to be alone. The artist, moreover, can face death alone, as he has faced life. Life has prepared him ten times over. It is a winking out, an instant forgotten, as was the instant of birth. And so is the nightly experience of falling asleep. A pox on my peers! Goodbye, my brothers! Some things, such as painting, a poem, a novel, a love affair, a prayer, must be done alone. Let me alone. *Noli me tangere.*

2/20/57

Order in my life. It has to be an internal order, of course. To make a sketch of a view from my Acapulco terrace conquers the muddled scene in front of me. When I get up from writing and drive through these casual, disorderly streets, a veil is before my eyes. And yet I really see them for the first time. The veil comes between me and the person I am supposed to love, also. This I do not like but cannot help. It will be so with any individual with whom I am in love or with whom I live. The particular individual does not matter.

3/3/57

It is the instinctive hankering after the lie which creates human credulity.

3/6/57

Sit in a well-lighted cell with no window save one at the top open to the sky (which, however, no bird crosses). Then paint. Paint what you remember of people, flowers, houses, water, ships and landscapes. It is not necessary to see a beautiful image, a scene, to paint it. I am sick of real images. Perhaps I have lived too long, imagining the person with whom I should like to live forever. Having the person, I am confused and feel actually frustrated! To visit Vera Cruz, four days ago, was a pleasure in my old style: to glimpse but for three hours or so (and two of them in frothing anger with an avaricious petty official) was to call upon all the resources of my imagination. I should like to write about this town: thus I would possess it, preserve it, enjoy it to the depths.

3/7/57

And haven't you noticed how much more attractive a non-fiction book of anything, anything, is than a fiction story? A lousy book on tourism— "then we packed the baby away, sent the dog to a kennel—." Who the hell wants to remember that Lawrence, jr. was the third cousin of Mabel Lawrence, who had married Philip, second (and occasionally rumored illegitimate) son of Alexander. Anything, even the Olympic records, is preferable to immersing oneself, imagining oneself, in that never-never land of current fiction!

3/7/57

Vera Cruz. Never, since perhaps Jalapa when I was 22, has a town so captured my affection. From my short observation, my imaginings go on—I can set stories here. I can make it better than it is. What more is fiction? I saw it the first day of Mardi Gras—for Carnavale. Gay boys, unmasked, so that their very faintly made up features could be seen. One in drag, black short dress, pink cheeks, and a bawdy "I dare you" impudent stare, pursed mouth, and then the tongue stuck out. It has had a most bloody history, sacking by pirates, burning, starvation. (With apparently no succor from nearby towns.) In 1825 it was the last point held by the Spaniards, the Isle of San Juan de Ulúa, and having cannons there, the Spaniards shelled the city until it was reduced to powder. They have had a more blandly, isolated and courageous his-tory than even the thirteen Colonies of America. And it is heartening to think that many of the families living there are descendants of these brave "first families" who stopped at nothing, and who now do not live as any of the rest of Mexico lives. La Parroquiá is a tile-lined, half-black long café, with excellent espresso for one peso, white tables, some with table cloths, ice cream chairs, sidewalk. Tables under a loggia— mostly men, talking business, at the top of their lungs. On Carnavale evening, however, there are several women. Opposite is the church, La

Parroquiá, gray and plain, buttressed, however. Next door, across the street, another café at which sits an odd rabble: a thin emaciated man who suggests Jean Cocteau. Expensive clothes, a painful scar from corner of lip to under jaw & neck. Everyone fawns on him. Photographers press around, telling people to stand back. He is with a pretty, fortyish woman who is some celebrity herself. She goes into a bar wearing a black mask (else not in costume), which for some reason brings down the house. Along the street, no end of gay boys, Mexican, one an especially accomplished female impersonator, pink cheeked, wearing a 20's hat, high heeled, lanky in a black dress, ogles the crowd & sticks his tongue out lewdly. Others merely sit at tables, well dressed in casual sports clothes, and wearing no masks, the better to see the pickings.

3/29/57

Series of bird drawings. Cartoons in color: The Hammer-headed Rumrunner. The Tripletailed Floozie. The Grossbeaked Parson. The Nimblefooted Clad. The Monowing Organgrinder. The Gliding Octave. The Gravel-throated Triller. The Common Nutstuffer. The Eggsucking Wrangler. The Tousled Towhead. The Clinging Bidawee.

3/30/57

What it comes down to is that I admire the common virtues of the Europeans more than I admire the common virtues of the Americans (generosity, openmindedness, etc.) and obviously, since I act upon all of my loves and preferences, I shall eventually act upon this.

4/26/57

The English crossword puzzle as a surrogate for alcohol. Both are escapes. Both obliterate the present scene and present another. Both cut the ties and send the spirit (the mind) adrift to find what pleasant shores it may. The crossword puzzle is quicker, more delightful to the intellect, and gives no unpleasant hangover. An article extolling the joys, the minor triumphs, the laughter, the desperate brain-cudgeling, of English crossword puzzles. Keep one on your desk, writers, admen, creative people of all kinds. Take a mental shower in forty-five seconds! Solve a five-letter word problem and get a lift!

5/19/57

Question of a Congressman to Arthur Miller: "Why do you write so morbidly, so sadly? Why don't you use that magnificent talent of yours

in the cause of anti-communism?" (Feb. 1957)[*] An artist writes of truth.
There is therefore truth in Communism. Axiomatic, of course, ideal,
Communism. The time is ripe for a new Communism of the purer sort.
The world is at present sullied by the Hungarian uprising, and its putting
down; and by the regrettable circumstance, everywhere, that the vicious
upper-class of 1917 and of the years that followed had to be thrown out
or killed outright. It is conceivable that mankind, with the guidance of a
dominant faith in God, can work a system out for their own good, which
will be closer to Communism and the word of Jesus Christ than any
form of government yet seen on earth. I do not intend to sound so vague
as F. Dostoyevsky, but alas I do.

5/20/57

I walk along a tightrope, several tightropes.

5/24/57

Yes, there can be an ideal Communist state. But not as long as part of the
world remains poor, not as long as the people who consider themselves
brighter, can tread on the faces of the others. Another way of saying
what Jesus said, of course. Perhaps subconsciously the more privileged
(monetarily) of the twentieth century realize this, when they grasp for
material benefits, even when they grasp illegally. Perhaps Christ even
would have granted this. They wish the best. If there's a hell, God grant
them this.

7/15/57

Thought on the Soul. What is it? A combined working of conscience,
ambition, degree of sensitivity mental and physical, aroused and
unaroused ideals (I am purposely choosing non-psychoanalytical terms)
which create collectively a force and an untouchable essence of oneself—
untouchable that is by psychoanalysis. I have heard some analysts speak
of a "final untouchable, unreachable part of the mind." This is the soul.

8/27/57

Discussion (one sided) with D. tonight on X and the impossibility of
attaining perfection in it. She agrees, agrees it is pretty bad to call some-

---

[*] Because of the obvious allusions to McCarthyism in his 1953 play *The Crucible*, Pulitzer Prize–winning
author Arthur Miller (1915–2005) faced questioning by the House Un-American Activities Committee in
1956. On refusing to give names of pro-communist friends and colleagues, he was fined and sentenced to
prison on May 31, 1957. The conviction was overturned in 1958.

one a "sinner" who is doing his best and is doing quite well. And yet, she made no further comment. I wasn't advanced in my thinking. I have the depressing feeling that I could live to be eighty and still not be advanced by myself or other people. Not that I wouldn't get fragmentary ideas here and there—

8/29/57

On hearing some bad music of the nineteenth century. What is wrong with it is the same thing that is wrong with any inferior painting or book or poem, etc., the self-consciousness of the author, and his obvious use of his brain. When something is done consciously, as one fills out an income tax form, it should be destroyed and not permitted to take up room on the earth.

9/15/57

Most impressed by a filmed show on TV—one half hour of Picasso at work and of his paintings and drawings. Judging from the drawings of nudes at the age of seven, he was where most artists are at 20, or 30. No, it cannot even be compared. His sketches of his parents at 15 show more. The life-size (larger) statue of man and sheep, now in the M. of M. Art, was done in one day. For his murals, many of them, he never makes a preliminary sketch on the wall. A great artist indeed, who plays as artists should. A pity novels cannot be done with this joie de vivre, which I worship especially when connected with creativity. But for the writer, alas, never shall it be.

9/29/57

On concentrating. (For *The Writer** possibly). A small matter, concentrating. But how many young writers can do it? It is not a new typewriter, a cushion in the chair, even necessarily stimulating or tranquilizing music playing. For most people, it is a guarantee of privacy. One cannot tell someone how to write a novel, the ingredients. One can only tell if they are not there. Privacy. An expensive thing in the modern world. How many young writers give themselves a chance? It is considered eccentric to like to be alone. Yet for such a short time, either a stay at a country cottage, or absolute quiet for six hours a day produce far

---

* Even though this particular paragraph did not ultimately make it into *Plotting and Writing Suspense Fiction*, this is the first mention of the autobiographical workshop report Pat will put together for the magazine *The Writer*. It was later also published in book form by the same publisher in 1966.

more than the trouble costs. Take yourself seriously. Set a routine. Once you are alone, relax and behave as you will. Stand still for a moment and relish the novel sensation of knowing that you are utterly alone and will not be disturbed by a ringing telephone, a baby's cry, an order from a boss, a groan or a whine from a spouse. Privacy is expensive. Perhaps it costs somebody *else* something. Relish it. But don't feel guilty about having it. Take it as your due. Indulge yourself in everything that can possibly contribute to your writing. For instance, in the height of composition, which may last a week, a month, three months, you may not feel like writing personal letters. Don't write them. Personal letters take something out of you, something of creative energy. It may be also that you cannot read other people's fiction, however inspiring, or however much you may admire the author and wish to emulate him or her. To read a novel over a period of days means that you carry around in your head an emotionally charged atmosphere, a whole stage full of characters. While you are writing a book, you must carry around your own stage full of characters with their emotional charges. You have no room for another stage.

The suggestions I make here as facts I do not mean to say are facts for everyone. These are my experiences. The only one I am sure of is that concerning the reading of fiction while writing fiction. It would take a mental giant, or mental freak, to sustain his own fictional world, and create it, while sustaining that of someone else. The real work of a writer is done away from the typewriter. In a fictional way the mind must not be cluttered. Non-fictional reading may well be a recreation and refreshment, history and biography. It is because the business of fiction is so tenuous, hard to pin down, that one must, as I do, write around it with a host of petty details, suggestions, ideas of approach, which of course will not apply to everyone.

The Writer magazine, I know, is read by many aspiring and young writers whose work may not yet have seen the light of print. All of us who write here to you can say only, "Take what you can of what we tell you, and use it if you can. The only requirements are genius, talent, fortitude, perseverance, and a respect for craft, an insane perseverance, in fact, which can fly in the face of discouragement, poverty, criticism, frustration." In this article I am trying to tell young writers how to eliminate the more obvious causes of frustration. Many may not know what is wrong with their writing. Many simply have never been blessed with such a plain everyday thing as privacy. Because it is not plain and every-

day. A novel pertaining to our times may be concerned with the lack
of belief at thirty, the casual but philosophically systematic smashing
of ideals, that which Russia does not tolerate. Man needs: ideals, and
though theirs are materialistic, they have the virtue of being philanthropic. They raise mankind. We have lifted mankind, and weakened
the Church, La Patria, and patriotism, until the latter is something to be
hastily summoned in time of war. This eventually will not work. Better
to abolish Christ and set up a machine God at Detroit. Better to face the
ugly facts of our civilization. (Not better for me, of course, but for the
American 20th century civilization if it wants to preserve itself.)

9/30/57

Colin Wilson's *The Outsider.* A delight to read, because I feel that
in its subject matter lies all I know or need to know—certainly the
enigma of consciousness, of self, of destiny, which has fascinated me,
specifically since seventeen, when I asked myself no longer why but
how I was different from other people. The book stirs my mind to
the murky depths (emotional depths) in which I lived my adolescence
like van Gogh and T. E. Lawrence trying "to gain control" by fasting,
exercise, routines for doing everything. This afternoon I awakened
from a nap, thought suddenly of the German atrocities against the
Jewish people, and had a strange feeling that it hadn't happened, that
it was impossible—and then—knowing it had happened—that it was
more horrible, more bestial than the most eloquent describer has yet
said. Also—imagining imaginary people. The attractiveness of other
people's lives, whose complexities, uncertainties, defenses, etc. I do
not know, only their polite, friendly exteriors. I am in a state of cowed
abeyance, like someone who has been whipped—or laid low after
pride. How I thought I had reached it in Sept. 1955! This is worse—
accentuated by the presence of the pretty girl I wanted and got, who
loves me still. I have lost, in this year of reverses, the power almost to
love, having lost the right. This is absurd, I know. But the emotions
do not always bow to logic.

10/2/57

There'll come a time, when you have to say to hell with you to everybody
on earth. When you have tried your best, and destroyed yourself, to live
with somebody, simply because that is what the rest of the world does,
then say goodbye.

10/12/57

This age is paralyzed by the great that have gone before, Eschylus, Shakespeare, Keats, Tolstoy, Dostoyevsky, even Hemingway. Only the poets seem to break through it, like Dylan Thomas. The people who don't give a hang, the people who go on their own.

10/12/57

Who is not revolted by self-slavery?
Yes, let us look at it objectively,
The way we look at specimens embalmed.
That's you there, though, wriggling on a pin.
Where is your youth that they make fun of?
Where is your manhood and womanhood?
All concentrated in the sexual organs?
Then you are no better than an animal.
You know you have emancipated yourself from this
Il y a longtemps. Mais—[*]
Let's have a cup of vichyssoise, *une autre boisson*[†]
Lets forget, until the mortician arrives.
Lord my God, groveling in the subway muck
Between the subway tracks, babbling and drooling
Before it's too late: "I have loved life.
I have loved women and written poems to them.
Now I'm begging you for my life! I'm begging
You to acknowledge that I've been alive at all.
Oh, I remember so many things, walks by
The East River, climbing stones, finding stones,
Running down dangerous hills at full speed,
And that dazed and dazzled, smiling, gaga look
At anything new—a new friend or a new corpse
In the river. In short, all the things it takes
To be a human being. Lord God, I babble,
I was once. *Ein Mensch.*[‡]
Capable of friendship and the enthusiasm for friendship
Susceptible to idolatry,
And with some ability to choose.

---

[*] It's been a long time. But—.
[†] Another drink.
[‡] A human being.

Lord God, save my soul!
I no longer believe even in hell!
Lord God, save that small core of right what I believed in!"

10/22/57

Why non-fiction writers almost invariably write a bad novel, if they
attempt to write a novel: they are far, far too used to working with their
conscious minds. A novel is not primarily written with the conscious
mind. It is two thirds emotional and non-intellectual, only about one
third conscious and intellectual.

10/31/57

Why while reading sometimes, do old scenes appear, childhood memories of no specific emotional content, and untraceable in the prose one
is reading? It is most mysterious to me. Many times I have looked back
through the prose and tried to find the word or phrase that has evoked it.
Always in vain.

11/15/57

The horrors of analogy. Reading Herbert Lüthy* on the passing of the
European order. He compares colonization with the hellenization of
Europe in 300 B.C. One gets the feeling there is a limited number of
moments, actions in the world. Finally perhaps only one! (This has
impressed me before in regard to the atom's resemblance to the solar system.) This is frightening (why I don't know; a primitive fright) because
it approaches the core of things, death, life, the soul. God is excluded.
I will not go running to him and dump into his lap the residue I can no
further explain. It is this residue that holds the secret. Let us keep it and
cherish it. One day we shall divide it into its components, as we have the
atom. And, when I wrote in *Strangers on a Train* at twenty-seven that
perhaps God and the Devil dance hand in hand around every atom, that
was also getting at the truth, the same truth. Man simply drags in his
metaphysics and attaches them to his profound discoveries with no more
logical motivation, no more intelligence than an simple minded explorer
shows when he plunges his country's flag onto a newfound slot of earth
which really belongs to no one and everyone.

---

* Renowned Swiss historian and journalist Herbert Lüthy (1918–2002) regularly wrote for various
international newspapers and published several books.

12/10/57

The peculiar arrogance, the sad "to hell with the rest of the herd" attitude that one finds in American intellectuals and men of distinction. Most apparent in F. L. Wright and in Robert Frost, kindly as the latter is by nature. They have fought a long hard battle alone, they seem to say, against the tide, and if now they are honored and adulated, it's no more than what they deserve. In fact, they'll take a little more of it, thank you, and maintain a rocklike, austere dignity in every one of their personal appearances. This is not apparent at all in Igor Stravinsky, though he has been an American citizen for some time. In Europe (witness Cocteau) the intellectual has more of a feeling of participating, working with his contemporaries, however few, throughout his artistic career.

12/31/57

What a delightful thing is a dream! And how many people have said it before me! A universal pleasure. Last night, I dreamt I was a student in an art school, though I was about as old as I am now, doing very nicely, and prolifically, and the one curious departure from the usual mood of my dreams was that I was cheerful because I was well liked by everyone. Many people called my name, greeting me, chatting, as I left the building. I went back to see if Doris was still there, as she studied there, too. I don't think I could find her. I awakened happy and refreshed, as if for a period of weeks I had really been living such a pleasant, congenial kind of life, the life I so often dreamed (that is thought) of leading when I was much younger.

1/3/58

The astonishing and horrible things that cross my mind once I spend a few months (nearly two years) out of my old adolescent-adult status quo. And just what that status quo is, I have only a slim idea, but I do know that I spent much time alone. I do know that I went from elation to depression and that eventually out of this I got the best writing I have done to date, possibly because it was the only writing I have or had done to that date, March 1956. If my new book, *A Game for the Living*, is well received, my mind will be set at rest insofar as worldly opinion goes, but not so far as my own mind goes. I have not made so many notes in this *cahier* in a time comparable to the notes of other *cahiers*, for the simple reason that I have spent less time alone. Thus a most profoundly important matter to myself reduces itself to a simple physical fact. My present house is not big enough for two people, especially if one is a writer. (Or even two.) No, the interesting problem is why I endure it. Is it not a further and more serious dissipation under the guise of the bourgeois, the healthy, conventional, comfortable and orderly? It is no guise to me, I have always consciously hated it. Perhaps what it comes down to is that I have had about enough, perhaps spoiled my last book effort. I am trying to save myself. Like Gide, I can exist, and of course grow, only by change, a challenge to which I have to make an adjustment, an upsetting, of course, which in the end is beneficial, though in the course of it I may lose an eye or a leg. What profiteth it a man, however, tranquility and orderliness, if thereby he lose his own soul?*

JANUARY 5, 1958

ᶠI'm playing a game with myself. The more I disgust myself, the more I want to escape from myself. The question of what I am escaping from—myself, or the prison of other people—is not at all important. I confuse them. This is my prison. I am disgusted by the fact that I am comfortable with the knowledge that tomorrow will be just like today, and that this is the life I now have. I'm playing games with someone who thinks differently from me. I would prefer to be surprised by the unexpected, by a robber, a liar, a new situation. And after such an experience, I would like to be alone and calm, work, write, and feel at home once again. I'm playing a game to discover how much I can disgust myself with a disgusting life. I have only one fear: that I will become too angry and grow violent before I leave. I would like to always remain calm and self-possessed. I hate violence.ᶠᶠ

1/16/58

Dogs. They have an immediate appeal, but not a lasting one. Cats are nearer to nature, with all its obvious, despicable selfishness. A cat will not let you down finally, because you know very well in advance how it will behave. The dog tempts you to trust in its heroism, as we do in

---

* Pat's take on either Mark 8:36 ("For what shall it profit a man, if he shall gain the whole world, and lose his own soul?") or Matthew 16:26 ("And what do you benefit if you gain the whole world but lose your own soul?").

friends, who sometimes let us down. When a dog does it, we don't mention it. Man wants to believe the best of dogs, only because the dog loves them so.

1/20/58

A time of abeyance for me, I have had small ones before, but none so long or profound as this. A caesura in my life. Knowing that only out of leisure can come art and real inspiration, and trusting in the restlessness of my temperament. I am content to wait for the finger of God. Nature is an inspiration. And also is the shortness of my life.

1/24/58

The trouble with the country (rural)—practically none, except that one cannot often ask one's friends to drop by. It becomes such an issue. And at night, we cannot burst out of the house for those harmless walks to the corner Riker's for a coffee or to Joe's for a beer, for that wonderful change that comes from looking at a few ugly or attractive strangers one will never see again.

1/24/58

Two notes on marriage. This is really such an art, unknown to all who embark upon it. Among the facts not often mentioned, I think, is that the more insult one gets, the more one learns to take. And that knowing one's partner has offended other partners by being unfaithful, one is more often apt to give him (or her) the same treatment back. A corollary, if one's partner is virtuous, serious, and trustworthy, one is much less likely to be unfaithful. One is more apt to discuss and to make a clean breast of things, in case of a desire or a decision to be adulterous. (A propos of nothing, I consider nothing more intolerable than the continued cohabitation of two people who know each other to be unfaithful to the other.)

1/28/58

Sneden's Landing. A splendid fireplace in our house. Five feet wide, and the back of it, I am told by experts, at just the right slant to give heat. Wet wood now, but after an affectionate struggle of two hours, it goes, and makes charming noises as if a nest of young birds in the center of the flames have just been brought a lot of worms by their mother. I am home alone this morning, thinking out details for a short story

(aniline*) and wondering what J.K. [Joan Kahn] at Harper thinks of
A Game for the Living.† And wondering, idly, what I'll ever do about
a real journal, which would have personal matters like this down in it
as well as the mostly impersonal things this one contains? I'd also like
to have drawings in it now and then. Why is it I go on doing nothing
about this? Because I want this kind of *cahier* to contain my best. I
cannot imagine a diary of nothing but personal items. That is just not
worth writing. So there I am. With nothing but this, and a most beautiful book upstairs, waiting for drawings, waiting really for a trip.

1/28/58

The moment of dying, which everybody (almost) fears. Perhaps it is not
a fear of being confronted by God or any kind of judge, or of a pain, or
of any unknown and formless terror, or even of entering upon a different
and possibly uncomfortable mental state. It is the instant of revelation,
like that of an epileptic the instant he is seized, when we shall realize that
such and such is so, and this and that is not so, dashing all our conclusions so long worked for, or so long neglected in our lifetimes. Perhaps
all we fear is the possibility of truth.

2/2/58

On the similarity of religion and drugs. Much has been written on the
subject. But from the approach of "human nature," I feel more strongly:
it is human nature to long for a faith beyond the reach of intellectual
proof, and without this man is not complete. So he clings to drugs, too,
including alcohol. Alcohol is an experience, not a means to obliterate
experience. Therefore, without the warning from the Church to abjure
alcohol, we should have more alcoholic visionaries. (When I speak of
the powers of alcohol, I never mean its powers to the point of stupefac-
tion.) I am talking of the emotional affinity. It is not a heightening of
consciousness (which is often said) so much as a change of consciousness,
that experience everyone has a right to, and a longing for, which can be
achieved also by traveling to a foreign country, or by falling in love again.

---

* Aniline, or benzenamine, is an organic compound used mainly in the production of synthetic materials.
It has a distinct odor of rotten fish.
† On February 5, Pat will receive a five-page letter from her editor, Joan Kahn, outlining why she feels
A Game for the Living is not yet ready for publication. Pat will have to revise the novel four times. In
Plotting and Writing Suspense Fiction, she will acknowledge that it is one of her lesser works, concluding
that the whodunit genre is not her forte.

2/11/58

Edith Wharton's *The House of Mirth*. Marvelous evocative power in her love scenes! Equal to [her] *Ethan Frome*, so vastly superior to Hemingway's rutting for sheer sexual emotion!

3/13/58

L.L. tells me that during the last war it was found that the more imaginative men made the best fighter pilots after all, because on the ground they had already imagined the worst that could happen to them.

3/13/58

Surely to a musician, music is a world within a world. I feel this must be more so than that a writer's world is apart. A writer cannot afford to be apart for long. I am probably quite wrong in this (about the musician). It is that I envy them the beauty they live with and hear, even in silence. For the moment, I am forgetting the work involved. In the order of happy making professions, I'd put music first, painting next, dancing next—my own last. I suppose everyone would put his own last. Egocentric human nature.

3/15/58

Jean Dutourd's *Five A.M.* A delightful book, for the usual reason a book is delightful; I agree with it. It appeals to my (current) view of life that all "serious" things are really—a futile game. His own phrase. It is not only current, it will last. It would be my very attitude even without the atom bomb's existence, but I must say the atom bomb corroborates it. To think of Shakespeare, Plato, da Vinci, even Einstein, being utterly, tracelessly effaced from the globe. What are we all working so hard for? Let's enjoy life a little more, while we can, and in an Epicurean manner, too. No need to get drunk and become as mad as the men who will finally bring about the bomb firing.

3/19/58

As someone said in the *Brothers Karamazov*, what good if I am saved, if the rest of mankind cannot be? Or, where is God, if one innocent child suffers and dies? Where indeed. Old and wise as I may grow, I'll always ask these questions, too.

3/22/58

An intellectual friendship: "Theirs was a cerebral kind of palsiness."

5/1/58

I'd rather live with a human cow. Than with a shrew, as I do now.

5/8/58

Well, yes, I must be leaving you. But if I can leave some idea with you of what life is—and is all about—

5/10/58

I have this evening been accused of hopeless, incorrigible jealousy. Manifesting itself in the destruction of a dog, several friends,* and a cat beloved by the accuser. This I cannot bear, perhaps for its possible truth. It is quite likely psychologically, that I'm guilty of the vice I most abhor. By the same token impossible to face.

   *mere coolness; nothing specific. And with many notable exceptions in which I especially like the friends.

5/17/58

Whether I am more than most people more easily "hurt." Behind this simple word lies a multitude of shadows. Pride comes to my mind first. In the English language it has ambiguous connotations. I do not care to turn loose of mine; therefore I have an excess, or have pride to a fault. I have it perhaps too much on some scores and not enough on others. I will not "take" some things, make some compromises (of the sort I am told is necessary for marriage), and I'll add that at the age of thirty-seven I know that I'll never have cause, to regret this peculiar and possibly excessive presence of pride.

6/3/58

Marriage: Or the Art of Taking Guff. It is not the quarrels that I dread, it is the reconciliations. It is the rehashing of old arguments (yesterday's), "I said that you said, etc." The nagging disgusting impulse in oneself that makes one want to go on clarifying, mitigating, explaining oneself after all interest, and objective has really gone. The dreariness of not even being able to escape to another room! Give me my fantasies any day! Fantasies of making love to an attractive friend who is unavailable; expectations, more certain, of books and stories to come. These at least are delightful, harmless because they take up little time, and silent because one never puts them into words to anybody else.

6/13/58

D's idea.* A man, for a certain purpose, creates a second character, another man whose life he leads at certain times. Later, having a reason to do away with him, he does, in an ideological fashion. Circumstances point to the man's being murdered, and our hero is trapped because his fingerprints are found on the scene of the "crime."

7/8/58

I'll always feel so painfully the difference between what I possess and what I look at. An attractive window in a dark house in the country, a pointed top to it, tall and narrow, a yellowish curtain which makes such a warm color: my first thought is, I don't live there, my second, that I never shall. This sadly applies to people, landscapes, experiences. It is a form of inferiority merely. My poverty has become a disease, unfortunately one of the mind. O waters, rains, loves—though for the time I am in abeyance, I am your humble obedient servant!

7/23/58

It's inconceivable to me to "fight" for one's lover or for someone one loves. Either people come to you, and stay, or not. I do not believe people can be held onto by machinations, stolen from another—or any of that. This eliminates many, many romantic plots for me, as I could not even imagine it well enough to write about it.

7/30/58

Since time began, the essential ingredient in the recipe for romantic passion has been separation. Hurrah for Eros! Hurrah for glands and memories and reflexes! Hurrah for sweet telepathy, which serves me as well as a bed. Curiously, I am even averse to going to bed with her. I'd like to be with her, alone with her, for a day and a night—simply because this is the first step, the first condition, and I can't have it. For my namesake,† for her sake, I feel young today as if I were seventeen. The world has put on that thin but dazzling veil, my mind leaps like a young deer. I dream of pressing my lips into her palm. It is like the knight who fights in armor wearing the image of his beloved over his steel heart like a further protection. Last night I kissed her neck, her hair, her lips and her body was

---

* Pat's lover D. provides her with the premise for her new novel, *This Sweet Sickness* (New York, 1960). On May 27, she also records notes "of possible consequence" for a "historic murder novel" that never comes to fruition.
† Pat's given name was Mary. This is the first hint of her new love interest, Mary Ronin.

against mine. It could be that it will never happen again. "It'll be just a dream," I said, "something I hope for and can't ever do." "I live on dreams," she replied. And she knew everything about this, without my telling her. "I know," she said. "I know!" And: "It's just the way I imagined it. It's like a dream come true."

7/30/58

She makes me happy, when I am alone with my thoughts. We share the moon with 3,000,000,000 people. But I know she thinks of me when I look at it, and that my thoughts are the same as those of a Chinese peasant, who perhaps cannot yet write what he thinks and feels. What I would like to say and believe is that she is the last woman I shall ever love. Love is an idea, and one person can as well embody it as another. *Buona sera*, Maria.

[NO DATE]

(And though you smile, I'll have no remorse,
When this sweet sickness has run its course,
And left me dead and dry.)

7/31/58

This sweet sickness runs its rapid course. I should like to chart it for the pleasure of charting it, not to look back—unless, like a good poem, it can revive in me the joy of these emotions in years to come. This sweet sickness—I lie on my bed at noon between sleeping and waking, tortured and delighted at once, and unable to make a move in this world until I attempt to feel a little more intensely what I feel, because I must learn a little more. I know she is writing paragraphs like these, too. Crueler than separation is that we cannot even exchange a letter!

8/4/58

How many thoughts, that I'd like to tell her, I've let escape! They might have made her smile—or made her a little happier. Let us be foolishly happy for as long as it can possibly last, and with our pessimism, perhaps it will last. At any rate, time will not be my betrayer and perhaps not hers. Neither will familiarity, I'd like to write her twenty pages, very solid pages, and hand it to her, somewhere, some time when we're alone, but when will that be? I remember her voice and her laugh. It isn't like anyone else's, not the overlapping similarity to ten other voices. There isn't any other like hers. She is patient, too. What a virtue!

8/12/58

This solitary love affair, with nothing of the physical in it! It is like the love affair I shall have with my next book—*This Sweet Sickness*. I shall be alone with my love, my book.

8/14/58

The best way for a homosexual relationship to work is on an affair basis, preferably with separation more than togetherness. Love is an idea, a dream. Those are cherished, made more beautiful by dreaming and by imagination. They are kept free of strife, embarrassment, guilt, and that merging of personalities which can go only so far before it becomes oversaturated and crystallizes into something else. There is not enough difference between people of the same sex for them to maintain that healthful tension and misunderstanding that a man and a woman do. Yet homosexuals will always start out hopefully, because they do not yet know all those big things and those details, in their cases so soon learned, which make for the continuing interest—and even "health." By forty or before, one finally prays, "Oh God, let this girl be the last!"

8/16/58

What a love is this!
At any hour of the day
You turn me, with iron hands,
Toward your lips.
And this sweet bondage,
This iron cage, by its intensity,
Will keep me from you!
Which of us could survive contact?
Yet what I say is of the mind, in solitude,
Our flesh would be kinder,
And resolve all tumult.
The silly brook would rush into the sea.

8/29/58

I love friends. They are to me the most delightful and the most precious of gifts that existence offers. So delightful to me is the breaking through of barriers—of which I have and had a few more than most people, I am sure.

9/29/58

A vision of a strangely glassy photograph with intense three dimensions: a man in circus tights sits on a floor in classically regal pose, surrounded by wicker furniture, a leaning battle shield, a brass chain. It is glassy, like the surface of clean, still water. Where does reality end and photography begin? A sense that some secret truth is to be found in this picture, if I am only able to hold it long enough to analyze it. Yet as in other such self-induced images, the mystery lies not so much in the picture as in the question why one happened to think of a picture like this. Why a circus performer, why wicker furniture? And why the glassiness.

10/8/58

What a pleasure is reading the dictionary! The only book I know that is true and honest.

10/29/58

To a New Love, Wishing She Were the Last
Now you—who have so metamorphosed my days
By nothing more than a glance and a stolen kiss,
For four months now, sweetening the summer
And gilding the autumn as if for a coronation,
For months now, making me a little better than I am.
O Christ, preserve yourself tomorrow when we meet alone
Through longer kisses, while your hand
(So much dreamt of) moves across my eyes,
Enchanting too strongly with your perfume and your flesh
My inward vision of perfection.
O Christ, come not too close nor change,
By deadliest familiarity, my self-created miracle
Of hair and eyes and hands and feet
Too beautiful for walking.
(Nor tell me, tragic muse of lyric poetry,
That love is not the time for you,
But that you must be called on only when love's gone.
There is a time also for writing of withered grapes.)

11/5/58

Yesterday she called me darling twice, for the first time, in a manner of speaking, in three months. Election day. I have been elected to darling status. Was it Thursday that did it—five days old now. Or was it my two letters? We both have unusual sensations of each other's presences. E.S.P. messages. How I should love to loaf and invite my soul these days! My book [*This Sweet Sickness*] is half done, physically, in 5 and ½ weeks! Without her, it would have been quite a different book.

11/5/58

To be tired while writing a book. For me there is always a natural caesura, and I don't have to think when to take off for a few days, nature does it all. But how terrible one's own personality then. It's as if a facade is torn off and the ugly, jagged edges and background are all that I can see and feel, all that I am. The show is not on now, only the dusty, filthy stage machinery is apparent. Not nearly so familiar as that, not familiar at all. I am frightened by this abyss in the middle of myself, dark and deep, and lying useless, waiting for an innocent victim to fall in. I cannot help thinking isn't this my soul, my innermost being (I know damned well it is) all that I try to make contact with by my conscious mind? Then the stones I have seen in graveyards lose their terror and ability to evoke reverence. It is a horrible thing to see one's insides and to find them like the cold side of the moon, but when one realizes and admits it is truth and not a poetic image—then one can face death a little better.

11/9/58

A diary in sketches. A word and a thought or thoughts for each day. Only those who can understand the painter's work can understand what he says. Yellow days and black days. Days of complexity and simple days. Days of love and days of happiness. A truly private diary. Those able to read it could not be prurient prowlers, anyway.

11/9/58

I know she thinks I exaggerate. Who but a fool would put his soul in a stranger's hand? She doesn't know yet and it's just as well. Intensity, after a certain point, is not becoming and may frighten and repel. Curiously enough, she is as romantic and insane as I. How love thrives on separation! It is like good soil, water and sunlight to a plant.

11/9/58

Forsaking all others.

11/9/58 (at 4:30 A.M.)
Allegro Con Moto
    Race, fire!
    Catch my love!
    Brand me with her.
    This is for always.

11/9/58
    Why does death come so close,
    Showing his face beside yours?
    I have never seen him before.
    I have never loved before you.

11/27/58
    By the age of forty, one has amassed so many associations with music,
    colors, sounds, tastes, words, that it is possible to foresee life becoming
    unbearable. Every Beethoven sonata drags a nightmare in its wake. Every
    scent that women wear brings tears and trembling.

12/7/58
    Mental peace. Who wants "happiness"? A requited love, a check from
    the publishers, those lead me to contentment. They stave off anxieties,
    real and imagined, just a while longer. I am like a ship continually in
    danger of springing new leaks, and I rush around trying to plug them up.
    Contentment, therefore, is the absence of things I don't want rather than
    getting anything.

12/21/58
    After a month in the city. What impresses me most, what comforts me,
    is to find that everybody else has the same anxieties, frets, troubles, dif-
    ficulties, dreads, as I have. Many of them are specifically concerned with
    city life. But the underlying horror of them is not. It is universal.

12/29/58
    Women—sensitive and intelligent women—have a patience that I find
    irresistible. By their very silence and reserve, they call attention to them-
    selves. Whenever I meet it, I succumb completely; not always displayed
    in action but in inner attitudes. Perhaps it is that patience is the virtue I
    most love in women. Next to it, repose. They overlap.

12/30/58

M. [Mary Ronin] My darling. A most curious combination of naiveté
and wisdom, [and] practicality or common sense. I have never seen anything like it. It charms and pleases me. She is not old enough to be so
wise. But probably she has always been observant and she remembers.
I have been observant of physical details, less so of people. Just here, I
speak of people. She is as impulsive as a sixteen-year-old and perhaps
more generous and open hearted. She lacks the fear, timidity, selfishness
of sixteen-year-olds (and of many adults). She is naively romantic. How
can one have preserved this through all the disillusionments? Or has she
had so few? Perhaps she did not repeat mistakes over and over, as I did.

12/30/58

No use asking if a crime writer has anything of the criminal in him.
He perpetuates little hoaxes, lies and crimes every time he writes a
book. It is all a grand masquerade, a shameful deception in the guise of
entertainment.

12/31/58

Why is the Second Piano Concerto of Saint-Saëns so brilliant in comparison to all the rest of his work? Probably because he had just started an
affair with his cook or his maid.

1959–1960

READING PATRICIA HIGHSMITH'S notebook entries from these two years would be accompanied by a healthy dose of head-scratching, were it not for outside sources of information on her personal and professional life. The pages are littered with Marys—Mary Ronin, mother Mary, and yet another M. starting in 1960, Marijane Meaker. All the while, Pat juggles a variety of projects.

As is so often the case at the turn of the year, Pat sinks into depression in early 1959. She turns thirty-eight and feels the end is near. Utterly exhausted, she submits the second draft of *This Sweet Sickness* to her editor Joan Kahn in February. Although impressed, Joan Kahn calls for extensive revisions (as she did with Pat's previous book), thus delaying publication of the American first edition until spring 1960.

Margot Johnson is no longer handling Pat's contracts, after Pat terminated their professional relationship in late 1958 because of poorly negotiated advances. Pat's new agent is Patricia Schartle (or Schartle Myrer, following her marriage in 1970), whose services Pat will retain for the next twenty years. Pat fails to record this significant event in her notebook, nor does she mention her European agent Jenny Bradley's coup in selling the film rights for *The Talented Mr. Ripley*, which is released as *Plein Soleil* (*Purple Noon*), starring Alain Delon as Tom Ripley.

In March, Pat ends her relationship with Mary Ronin, who never left her partner in the first place. That summer, Pat visits her parents in Texas and presumably takes a jaunt across the border to Mexico. The evening she returns to New York, she meets author Marijane Meaker in a bar. Marijane is six years younger and pens crime and lesbian romance novels for the pulps under various pseudonyms. She and Pat have a late summer fling, a detail Pat ignores in her notebook.

In late September, Pat leaves for a European book tour with her mother, Mary, who is recovering from a serious bout of depression. Once Mary leaves, Pat travels on to Athens by way of Salzburg with her ex-lover Doris. During her book tour and all through 1960, Pat writes a lot of love poetry, partly in remembrance of Mary Ronin, but soon also on her rekindled relationship with Marijane Meaker after her return to New York in February 1960. In late August, the couple take their six cats and move to a farmhouse outside New Hope in Bucks County, Pennsylvania, an area known as a haven for well-heeled homosexuals and for bohemians like Dorothy Parker and Arthur Koestler. The house, located on a sprawling property dotted with apple trees, is big enough for Pat and Marijane each to have their own office.

As we learn from Marijane's reminiscence in *Highsmith: A Romance of the 1950s* (2003), work soon stagnates for both. Pat struggles mightily with her tragicomic novel *The Two Faces of January*. She doesn't finish the book until 1964—only to have it become the most rejected manuscript of her career.

1/1/59

My river, flow into me.
Bring red sand and pebbles
To hold me down.
Flow over me clearly,
With sunlight on your surface.
And down below let me drown smiling.

1/1/59

Living alone. One has the same terrors and anxieties living with someone, essentially the same fears of insanity, even of not being loved or
wanted. To live alone only heightens them a little bit. Perhaps even better
for an artist. Life is too short anyway, and the craft so long to learn.

1/3/59

The peculiar loneliness and tragedy of the person who loves, and is having an affair with, someone who lives with someone else. However we
rationalize it and explain and excuse, it is never right. The affection and
attention and even great measure of love are never enough. (I saw it, of
course, in C. & in Santa Fe.* Now I am in the same position myself.) Out
of this sadness, however, which is so hard to deal with because we can-

---

* This reference is unclear.

not pinpoint it or really suggest a remedy, out of this sadness for me will come, as usual, the truth. Therefore I do not, objectively, mind it.

1/13/59

On this happiest of all our days together, I foresee the choking death of me at our separation. I shall crumple by a bare wall, in a black coat, blend my tears into my fist, and you will watch from a distance with somebody else. You will bring your fist up to your mouth, too, and you will have tears, but they will be under control. You will know that I am dying and yet—very likely—that my body will go on living. So you won't come to me. You will only wish you had later, just for a moment perhaps.

1/19/59

Is it not violence, of one sort or another, that ends all homosexual relationships?

1/28/1959

My life is absolutely desperate. There is no use in getting sufficient sleep, keeping a smug set of hours, producing a "satisfying" portion of work per day, and feeling complacent in the evening. My life is desperate. It hangs by a thread. I do not wish to veil this fact by a routine, as army men veil the fact that they cannot stand on their own feet, despite their privilege of taking human life. At the moment I am involved in two crucial things: a love affair apparently hopeless and which (due to psychological factors rather than the girl's worth, which I do not completely know as yet) may last all my life; and a caesura in my work, which is essential that I make. I have just become 38, and no doubt this is a factor. I am coming closer and closer to the end, and therefore must make as much as possible of what is left.

1/31/59

Above—when I say "my life" hangs by a thread, I mean my morale hangs thereby. But life and morale with me are practically synonymous.

1/31/59

Living alone. There are times when I am happy for long minutes simply with my own consciousness. This is seldom possible if one lives with someone. (Never.)

2/5/59

The deaf-mute girl. She is 22, very pretty in a French, brunette, pale-complexioned way. She has two children, both boys, one's picture in her wallet, looks very much like her. A great vitality and sparkle in her black eyes. Her face is most expressive, compared to the immobile faces of people who can speak. And her secret is that she communicates with her exaggerated facial expressions. These take the place of many words. She is 5'6", wears slacks nicely, though is not particularly slender or boyish in her figure. She is comfortable only with pencil and paper within reach, and she writes more rapidly and more clearly than anyone I have ever seen in my life. She is willing: when I came into a bar, on second acquaintance, she wrapped her arm about me and wanted to introduce me to her friends there (deadpans all). Her name's Jan D. 68 Charles. No phone, she writes me. She lived with one man for four years, never married. He fathered her two sons, evidently. (I didn't ask specifically.) To make love to her would be a pleasure. When a page is used up, or even before, she seizes it, wads it up, tosses it into an ash tray and dusts her hands. All this very quickly.

2/7/59

Writers' friendships. Is it the times that make us so belligerent? There is a reason why writers always have so few friends that are writers. Their special egotism and self-centeredness do not blend. They clash. My emotions are as good as yours are, they seem to say to each other, like small boys, flexing their muscles, or boasting about their fathers. In particular recently J.G.V. whom I liked better on first acquaintance than anyone I have ever met. Having just lost a lover, he can talk of nothing else, at the same time exuding his smiling optimism and confidence about acquiring another. I don't mind such frankness, even appreciate it and respect it, in moderation. With him, it is as if he continually shoved one of his poems under people's noses and said "Read it! Appreciate my vitality! My love of life!"

2/7/59

It is very, very difficult for me to know what to forgive among people's vices (mine, too). Where to take a stand and say, finally, this is wrong, and therefore this person or that no longer deserves my love or friendship or anyone else's. Europeans are better off than Americans in being brought up from infancy with clear ideas on morality—at least compared to Americans. Believing as I do that only out of personal chaos and failure and humiliation can truth and real character come, it is twice as hard for me. When should one's patience give out? When should one stop believing in the core of goodness in everyone? In this is the whole art of life. And because it is an art, not a science, no one will ever lay down the laws. It is for this reason only that people are different, one from another. It is because of its flexibility that it torments me.

2/10/59

In the presence of the wrong person (emotionally speaking) I drink too much, and have that impulse to take the two too many that make me silly and unadmirable, I have long realized this, but didn't know it was such an ironclad law. How very delightful to realize it has an obverse!

2/11/59

Discipline, solitude and the ascetic life are not difficult for me, but I do not like the feeling of being virtuous that comes when I lead such a life even for two days. I resent feeling virtuous, just as I resent "virtue" and consider it stupid. Small use—at this point in my life—to remind myself that I am being virtuous in order better to practice an art that is by no means dedicated to virtue.

2/15/59

Manic. There are not enough girls for me, not enough gin, not enough hours in the day to dissipate. I have just finished a book [*This Sweet Sickness*], almost. After a period of near impotence (frigidity?—get some more ice out) I now want to make love ten times a day. And it is surprising how the girls come!

2/18/59

For the time, fatigued by my book. What a pity to feel jaded over something so essentially emotional. I have been looking at it and concentrating on it too long without a break. I am not in the least worried about its eventually successful (satisfying) outcome, but I do not want to pause just now, and yet I must. The brain (any brain) finally balks after being applied to one theme, one idea, for so long. It takes quite as much will power to take a respite as to work in the most difficult and unhappy days. I am exhausted in every way and what is even worse have had my faith shaken in the girl who inspired the book. She did nothing. It is my fault, my fickleness alone that has caused the weak link between us. I am testing her now as well as myself, a condition that life and time imposes. It has nothing to do with my book, and just happens to work against it.

2/18/59

Astonishing how fate puts the right books in one's hands at the right time. I have just read a delightful biography of Dostoyevsky by [Marc] Slonim. *Three Loves of Dostoyevsky.* No bowdlerized journals of his wife and daughter. He was far more highly sexed than I had dreamt, even until his sixtieth year when he died! But what interested me most in Fyodor and St. Beuve* is their unfortunate tendency to fall in love with a woman whom their best friend loves or is married to, their willingness— even great desire—to be a true friend of the other man. To be a true friend is impossible, however one rationalizes it, and I'm not here concerned with the word "true." It is the flirtation with the possibility that fascinates me, this tempting of the devil, tempting of the axe that will cut in two one's honor, and that in the eyes of the whole world as well as in one's own self. Dostoyevsky wanted to be personally degraded, cursed, spat upon, for his finest emotions. So do I.

2/23/59

To be in love with two people at the same time. What depressing immaturity! To be so in love with love.

3/8/59

The Beatniks†—nothing but a terrible, urgent need for communication. Communication is the sister of love. It is necessary for happiness. People who communicate, like Jesus Christ or anybody else with a message, do not need the love of a human being, singular.

3/18/59

These days I laugh too much. It is because life and real seriousness is upon me. I cannot be serious or silly here. I do not regret my laughter, or look down on it—a comic idea in itself—to look down on laughter.

---

* Charles-Augustin Sainte-Beuve (1804–1869) was one of the most important French literary critics of his time. He was very close with Victor Hugo and his wife, Adèle Foucher, with whom Sainte-Beuve was rumored to have had an affair.
† Beatnik subculture began to emerge in the late 1940s, following the example set by Jack Kerouac and other members of the "Beat Generation." Characteristics of the movement were a liberal stance on sex and drug use, a love of jazz, (pseudo-)intellectualism, and anti-materialism.

There is empty laughter, regretted a week later, if one remembers it at all. Tonight I laugh at myself, and with Shakespeare who said all the world's a stage. One is never more sad, more real, in a very large sense, than when one laughs. When an artist is serious, he is busy manufacturing a tiny pearl and not the whole of himself.

4/5/59

The lovers next door. He is twenty-five, she twenty-two, and they are going to be married in a week. He talks almost constantly in a loud, self-confident voice and she giggles and coos appreciatively. Inspired by this he begins cooing, too, in a deeper tone. I am struck by their resemblance to the pigeons that *roucoucoule* in my tiny courtyard. "Roucoucoule," they say, "cou-cou-coule" over and over, with the wordless expression of their undying affection. One more example of the similarity of human beings to the beast and the fowls of the earth.

4/14/59

Even the best of painters can strike me now and then as overly decorative. So are writers decorative, but to much less extent. A writer can seldom if ever get that overall view of his work, however short, and stick to it, achieving that "desired effect." Self-forgetting will show somewhere. But a painter can constantly judge in a trice and maintain this conscious goal until it is achieved.

4/23/59

Praise be to little flowers
That give me such pleasure,
That teach me patience,
That live in their gentleness,
And present their calm faces
When I enter my room with a bruised heart.

4/27/59

It's the mistakes, the blurtings, that touch the heart in a love affair and that make people different from others. On their good, orthodox behavior, all people are alike. I always listen and remember when she is a bit high, and angry with me or not. Terrifying phrases, incredible ideas, and often words of tenderness that bring tears to my eyes when I hear them, and tears later when I remember them.

5/8/59

After doing a little painting in oil: I realize the fascinating interaction between art and craft, accident and intention, in a way I am no longer able to realize it when writing. Both are essential. The world is full of mediocre artists who have too much of one or the other, and perhaps will never be able to combine them in the right proportion. To do this is to be a great artist. It is in the art and the accidents that the mind must function. The craft is only in the hand.

5/8/59

John Wain[*] reading his poetry before an American audience. On the radio for me. I was impressed and very moved by his Song about Major Eatherly, the soldier who dropped the atom bombs on two cities of Japan.[†] Later, he had nightmares and cried out: "Release them!," much to the disturbance of his wife. The government pensioned him at $270 per month. He refused to cash the checks and took to petty thievery. He was then imprisoned in Fort Worth penitentiary. Wain's last stanzas are powerful. They did not imprison him for his nightmares, but for his petty thefts. Give his pension to the shopkeepers, and tell them it comes from the consciences of us all. And to the major, give a folded paper, lay it beside him as he sleeps, nothing official, only a few words in pencil: "Eatherley, we have your message." It brought tears to my eyes, and the audience (I could not see their faces) applauded loud and long. I would like to write a book against the waging of war. But one cannot begin with such a premise to write a work of fiction. I feel a void in the public mind, a vagueness, like a cloud of indecision that waits to be blown by the strongest wind toward a particular point on the compass. This will be toward war (with a sigh, a reluctance, a curse or two, to be sure, but the enthusiasts, the mindless youths, will always be in the majority), or toward peace and an invincible determination not to fight. And the latter course takes the most courage. At first a very few will have to suffer the scorn of their friends and fellowmen, and perhaps jail. But to increase their heroic number! This is a goal worthy of an honest writer. The world has need now of honest writers.

---

[*] John Barrington Wain (1925–1994), English novelist, poet, journalist, and critic.
[†] While pilot Claude Eatherly did not actually fly either of the planes carrying the bombs to Hiroshima and Nagasaki—his part in the mission was scouting the weather—he did struggle with guilt after the war.

5/24/59

Palladium dance hall. $2.50 admission, male or female, taken by a grumpy man in a cheap tuxedo. It is a dance hall, bar on the left, a small section, fenced off, of tables, $2.00 minimum per person, for the aged and disabled and well-heeled. The exhibition dancing comes on at 11:00 P.M. Afterwards, wild entertainment: three half naked girls in scarlet, slit sheathes; a pansy male solo dancer, dressed in black tight trousers, fly laced with heavy tan cord, a leotard top. My Paris friend remarks that he looks like a man who moves furniture. The bulk of the audience—couples averaging 28 years of age; a few gray-haired businessmen, not drunk but of the sort who enjoy dancing, with cheap blonde pickups. A tall girl with a very short man. St. Germain des Prés types, with ordinary or tough American men. My French friend very attracted to a blank faced brunette in gray too short dress, dark stockings, straight black hair cut in windblown style. Thought the man with her dull by comparison. Minute gin and scotch drinks. Drinking is of no importance here. There is a real frenzy, a real bacchanalian joy in the dancing. Seeing the solo items, when the couples separate after their entry numbers, one can believe a new classic (though of 1959) ballet is being born.

5/29/59

Anxiety has become habitual, a normal state. I now have, for a few days, the two cats I know so well, and soon shall have the black one as long as he lives.* Yet whenever I look at them, I experience a small twinge of apprehension: I imagine seeing them struck by a car, falling out of a window, swallowing a bone that will strangle them. All unnecessary. Rather, all quite possible, and part of life. It could happen to me. Someday, something like this will happen to me. But why anticipate? Perhaps because my anxiety is projected onto the cats from something quite else. I worry, subconsciously, about the responsibility of M. and myself, and my guilt feelings in regard to R.† Have just had dinner with BA. In her quiet way, she remarks that R. may be (is!) happy to be free of M. and why should I care about R.'s feelings? Because I doubt my reliability. And why that? It is an endless chain, going back into the unconscious, the little shames best left buried.

---

* Her black cat Spider, to whom Highsmith will dedicate her tenth novel, *The Glass Cell* (1964).
† R. is the ex-girlfriend Mary R. left (temporarily) for Pat.

6/1/59

Easy to see why writers drink. There is nothing rational about writing
either.

6/2/59

A peculiar period for me, creatively speaking. No idea for a short story
possesses me, and so I do not attempt any, knowing they will be failures
without inspiration. I wonder often if it is the fact I have achieved this
much with M.? The uncertainty of the situation—the possibility of disappointment if M. at last tells me she has not the courage to leave R. and
live with me, should be good for creativity. Am I really too happy now?
Am I psychically exhausted after writing *This Sweet Sickness*? Am I only
waiting to see if the magazines will buy it, if Harper really has no more
corrections? Guilt has not yet taken hold, and I hope it doesn't. Why not
a long, quiet interlude between books? God knows, it is futile to want to
write another book immediately, to strive for a theme. (I have several,
just not the fiction, or story, to go with them.)

6/2/59

Sometime I wish I had kept a diary of this. Its little (so far unimportant) rises and falls; the moments of faint doubt; the near quarrels—as
the time when she misunderstood me and assumed I was asking her to
choose—to act at once to leave R. or I should go with B. then immediately (this was an afternoon in early March). M. crumpled, was defeated,
and looked fifteen years older. She said not a word, sat staring at the
floor, and would not let me even touch her hand. At last I said, "You
must know I prefer you." She proposed a trip, gloomily. I gave her the
wallet from Mark Cross. Looking into her bag a moment later, just to
see again if I thought it thin enough for her liking, I saw she had replaced
the snapshot of herself she had just given me. I took it out again and
reproached her about it when she came in from the bathroom. Now,
2 months and more after R. has gone to Utah, she says often that she
loves me, says it with fervor. And Sunday evening, when a man friend of
hers with whom we had dined out returned to pick up something at her
apartment, she amused me by inventing a reason for me to stay—(I was
bustling about as if to leave also.) "I'm going to put you to work Pat. I've
got to get that rubber cement off that bunch of illustrations." Delivered
so seriously, with such conviction, I almost burst out laughing. She is a
genius for the quick little falsehood that saves the situation, that soothes

and banishes all suspicion. She produces them with lightning speed, rather the speed of veracity.

6/8/59

All my life I have striven more or less consciously for love and money— sufficient money to relieve me of anxiety. Now I have them both, though with a rather unresolved situation in the love part. There is nothing now irking, nothing left to strive for but to write a better book, a different book. But now I am a prisoner, strangely enough, of my conscious mind; whereas before I had thought my conscious strivings interfered with my subconscious and creative side. Now I have not an idea in my head that I consider important enough to write about. Ergo, I don't write.

6/11/59

Is this weariness and anxiety I feel every morning in her apartment an unconscious knowledge that we shall never really be together? Lately, awful, fatal (they could be) premonitions of defeat. R. has asked her to come out to Utah as soon as her book is finished. M. says she can't wait to get to Las Vegas to gamble. Such is the mood she is in. Escape. Not take chances—perhaps. I fear that it will be easy for R. to exact a promise from her, once they are out there together. And will forewarning M. of this be enough to ward it off? Difficult for me also the procedure I should follow at the moment. M. is getting quite used to me—that is, the fire of love dies down, after eight months, four months privacy more or less. I have not made plans with her, and feel perhaps I should so she will have something to stand on in Utah. We must at least talk about it. Merely to have her tell me she wants to live with me, and that so do I— what to tell R. would be sufficient.

6/16/59

On returning to Astoria, Long Island.* I arrive at the vacant lot, and find a well-dressed man of apparently Italian descent regarding the same scene, the vacant lot of my games twenty-five years ago. I wonder was he one of my playmates? Why else is he here, but that he has been acquainted with this plot of ground? Or is he possibly thinking of buying it? The ground has tin cans on it—but is mostly tall green grass, grooved

* Pat and her family lived in Astoria, Queens, from 1930 to 1933, first at 1919 Twenty-First Road, near the East River, before moving to Twenty-Eighth Street.

still with the trenches ten-year old hands have dug. Trenches and tunnels. Sweat, fears, dreams—and all related, they must be, to my life as an
adult. The gas tanks. The tennis court. The oil-covered road. The backdrop of well brought up Italian youths, male and female. Do not forget a
single grass blade. All here is association.

6/21/59

Comparative zoology can reduce the praise of nature to nonsense. We
like the rainy days, the sun, the ocean, the changing of the seasons,
because we are animals who have survived under these conditions, with
these phenomena. Other species who may not have "liked" them have
now died out.

7/6/59

People in love, or who really love someone, are no longer the masters of
themselves. This may be no news to anyone but me. It is strange to me
to be pushed and pulled, made to cry, made to feel utterly crushed, by a
word, an imagined happening.

9/28/59

Absolutely frightening to me to see the resemblance between my mother
now, at 64, and my grandmother, at an older age. The absentminded-
ness, the repetition, the ludicrous, shameless boasting! My mother seems
already to have entered senility. It's inevitable, too, to think that there go
I in another twenty-five years. Why does the ego set itself to fall to such
dismal disappointment? I wonder if my ego is already too high without
my awareness? Finally, these people start eulogizing their own mediocre
apple pies. The ego has at last turned loose of impossible professional
achievements.

9/28/59

Dream last night, my first night in Paris in seven years. I was a man,
coughing blood of a pale lavender color into a white napkin. A doctor
looking over my shoulder said, "That's a lethal color, you know." I
took him seriously and was frightened, but tried to make an excuse for
the color, insisting it wasn't fatal. My recent associations with lavender: the cornflowers I bought for K. [Kathryn Cohen] in London, the
color of her eyes sometimes, and the color (purple) of a printed dress
she wore.

10/16/59

The Pas de Calais Hotel.* Downstairs from me, down the curving, red carpeted stairs, stand two pairs of shoes outside the door. A man's and a woman's shoes. The door is small and narrow, the room must not be much better, and they came in quarreling at night, probably sleep in a double bed, and in the morning when I go out at 9, the shoes are there, side by side, a little shabby, shamelessly waiting to be shined, male and female, ready for another day soon, and another evening of quarreling.

10/16/59

Insanity as a form of fainting. Especially cyclic types like the manic-depressive. Nature's way of protecting the mind and nerves from a too painful reality. From what I observe of my mother, she is far more rational, though pitiable, when in the depressed state. The "high" period is definitely off, arrogant, repetitive, with much need of ordering people about, asserting self, etc. With this a ludicrous self-confidence.

10/21/59

After seeing my mother on a plane to Rome, goodbye for God knows how many years. I am happy to be alone, glad to be free. Even M. who promised she would come join me in Greece: she is not coming, and the old adventure and loneliness calls again to me. There remains at this date only to take off really alone, the small lonely hotel room, the view of some river at night, the lights of some restaurant where there is no one to dine with me. Out of these things come my stories, books, and my sense of life.

10/26/59

Most of the zest and the sense of adventure and danger in a love affair—what to a great extent gives it life, in other words—is the precarious state of one's ego while in it. Will I make out? Will he or she accept me? Love me? If so, how much? For how long? Always? A lot of it is a despicable betting on (or against in the neurotic) the ego.

---

* Pat is on a book tour through Europe, which first takes her to Paris. Her mother, who is recovering from a serious depression, accompanies her.

11/5/59

In Barbizon,* I found a little blue horse
In the gutter.
I said, "Maybe we'll bring each other luck.
Will you bring me luck?
Bring me a letter from Mary in Paris,
And you can go live with her."
I named him Lucky.
But there wasn't any letter in Paris.
I said, "You're a rotten horse
And I've a mind to throw you away."
But I also thought, let's be unlucky together.
But finally there came a good letter
And I wondered, was that Lucky or not?
I said, "You can go to Mary."
Was that lucky?
Is that lucky?

11/19/59

All the misery on the earth is caused by the indifference of the better off toward those with less. Not only in economics, but in personal
misfortunes—so much easier to bear, if there are friends or strangers
who show that they care what happens. With this, there is no bitterness,
no cursing against God, no resentful attacks against one's fellowman.
No revolutions.

11/20/59

It has been a long time since I have been so disturbed by anything as I
was by my mother's presence in Europe the first month of my trip. As
that, it is nothing. As personality types, intellectual opposites, old underground warfare—and include the men of the family—that would be
something else. The passive, feminine woman who schemes viciously,
behaves always selfishly, without even knowing it. Her unconscious is
more intelligent than her conscious. Always her conduct is justified by
the prevailing filthy, narrow-minded, essentially sick, complaisant morals

---

* A hamlet in the Fontainebleau forest south of Paris famous for its mid–nineteenth century back-to-nature
school of painting. A few years later, Pat (and her alter ego Tom Ripley) will live close by. At this stage of
her European book tour, Pat pines for her ex-lover Mary Ronin, whom she hopes to meet up with later in
Greece.

of the time and of her milieu. Perversely, these people enjoy real tragedy
and a sense of being persecuted, singled out by God for ill-luck when
everything goes against them.

11/29/59

It's quite obvious that when I return to New York, in January 1960, I
must either cut out my emotional life or resolve something from it. I
can't go on leading an undecided, undefined, not to mention unsatisfactory emotional life, as I have been doing for the last five months. Going
to Europe, seeing my life in perspective—this has netted me, if nothing
else. The older I grow, the less I know. Is it supposed to hit me between
the eyes? Then I would mistrust it. Is it supposed to grow slowly and
surely? Then I would mistrust it, loving the quick. I think I'm destined to
be what they call sick, what I call well. And what the hell? Anyone who
loves me can find me. And all the others I should put behind me. I might
add that those who love me already I do not love (already—that goes
without saying). And I say this redundantly, profundantly.
Let a girl not love me, who's mildly attractive,
And I'm quite active
Old age will find me its favorite butt
If I were not a hopelessly serious nut.

12/7–8/59

These days of secret misery I now go through in Paris will stand me
in good stead, for such misery is universal (I do not mean perpetual!).
How one clutches at the merest lift of hope and energy—which is no
more than the lifting of a dead leaf would be on the sidewalk. (Emotionally speaking, there is nothing worse than not knowing, not being told
the facts by someone one is in love with. I do not mean—weeks from
now—for this paragraph to be misread by me because of my present
unhappiness.)

12/8/59

Mental and emotional hardships become harder, in one sense, to bear,
when one is older—or over thirty. Then one knows something of unhappiness, it's always a matter of pride to think how much one has been
through successfully and that one can still operate—but if something
harder than all before occurs—then one knows also, unfortunately, the
perils of the pit of despair, and all the horrors there.

12/15/59

Without a design in one's living, there can be no design in one's drawings or paintings.

12/26/59

Dream in several parts. 1) M.'s apartment. 11:30 P.M. 2) no time transition—to meeting with R.—passionate words. I sneak across room in pajamas (at RR station) and walk home ashamed of pajamas, accompanied by a girl who says M. has such a crush on you. I know it is K. (M. has been out to theater with K. until 11:30.) 3) M. is too quiet re my cat she has been keeping. "I threw away his pan today," with a grimace. I conclude she is disgusted with him, doesn't want to ask me outright to take him away. They have two large white cats and one small black in a gray turtleneck sweater. I return to the house when M. is not there to take my black cat away. To my horror, I hear the bell, then the key in the lock: M. & R. are returning home, and I am there, not even fully dressed. I hurry to dress—then retreat to the last corner as they come in. 4) Rolf Tietgens called from restaurant table to help at a fire. He saves a woman's life, pulls her up through a window. She is very grateful, exhausted. He returns rather a hero, in Levis, sits down to eat.

12/30/59

Athens. A motley, yellow, dusty place, short buildings, and even the big official buildings look flimsy, as if they were only facades. Streets are cluttered with traffic and people at all hours of the day. Only one million inhabitants, I read, and they all seem to be on the sidewalks at once. Endless balloon sellers, peddlers of cheap billfolds, jewelry of dubious value, machine made clothing. First impressions, that people here are less civilized than those of Mexico. In public places—e.g. the railroad ticket selling agency, D.* was twice shoved aside by women in the crowd of some 12 or 15 (who showed no tendency to form a line). The third time, the two clerks behind the desk, plus a couple of men in the crowd, protested on her behalf. Above all, an atmosphere of poorness, if not poverty.

---

* Pat has asked Doris S. to accompany her on her travels to Salzburg, Athens, and Crete.

1/1/60

At present, the dominant theme to me is the difficulty of merely living
as I stated before. Not living in conformity with the world or society,
but living at all, moving at all, doing anything at all. This can be argued
tediously, as I of course don't want to do, or quite casually and lightly—
because it is a desperately serious problem, which most people hurdle
rather than face. It is the Gorgon Medusa: nobody can look it in the face.

1/17/60

Flight from Athens to Corfu. Over land most of the time, mountains and
sea. For scenery, the best flight I've ever made. Snow frosted mountain-
tops, blending with pine and scrub trees into dark green and brown hills
and foothills. Muddy shallow streams coming from nowhere in the hills,
and emptying themselves, delta-less, into the blue water; they leave deposits the color of tea, resembling empty silk stockings, far out into the Adriatic. From a height, the neat but jumbled formed patches are pale green,
pale brown, looking like the crosshatch work in a sketch. The plane was
a two-engine, not properly pressurized. My ears began to ache—worse
on the coming down, with sharp pains in forehead and cheek. The luggage of the Greeks, made of cardboard and artificial leather, falls apart
under the handling. Handles come off. Many have to be tied with rope.
In Rome the same evening, I see a handle come off for the second time.
Goodbye to Greece, until I can come here with someone with whom I can
be happy under any circumstances. I found this experience essentially
humorless and depressing. Not to mention obscenely expensive. Every
contact with a public servant or hotel personnel was a minor nightmare.
Taxis, porters, small wars between Greeks and Americans.

2/11/60

"That fell upon mine like an unslaked summer." Then goodbye, Doris,
and welcome to all my sicknesses that bring tears of enthusiasm to my
eyes, and those dark birds that plumb my depths. I cannot figure out how
I must live.

2/12/60

If only you had moved that day I kissed you,
Stirred your lips as other women do when I kiss them,
I should not love you as I do.
But you were so still I might have thought you had stopped breathing.
A statue, a picture, death, life, sleeping and the core of myself.

And all my soul desired that quietness.
Our last kiss, and you knew so well
How to bind me with no effort.
Darling, what sweet memories can become horror.
As the trail in time behind you
Grows longer, thinner, a spider's web
Recall that last kiss and its trickery,
Or recall it—recall it—
Our lips murmuring together
Our useless, "I love you."

2/24/60

The abolition of Latin in Oxford, soon, they say, to be followed by Cambridge. All well and good to spare 20th century students the memorizing of subjunctives, the necessity of a reading knowledge. But it would take no more than a month to acquire a basic vocabulary in both Greek and Latin—a feat of memory, after all, that should be refreshed after six months and a year. Without this, they cannot appreciate the best writers in their own language, English. One month is a small thing compared to six and seven years of each language. This from one who refused to take French or German (at the age of ten) until Latin had at least been begun, because that was the English and therefore correct thing to do by way of becoming educated.

2/24/60

The potential alcoholic who cannot be made an alcoholic. Look what liquor does to varnish! cries a friend. Look what salt does to a snail, he replies. But I love salt and it's also a necessity.

2/26/60

—What a bloody bore this income tax season is—and the necessity of keeping records at all. The only time I am interested in money is when I don't have it.

2/29/60

Playwrights seem to me to use the cart before the horse method of creation. They fall in love with the theme rather than a person or even a dramatic incident or nucleus of people. Perhaps it is the right approach to plays. It is not mine to books.

3/1/60

Mary Ronin is another world to me. That is why I love her. This may
be unnecessary to say to many of my friends, but it is not them that (or
who) matter. I love her, because she changes my thoughts completely. She
changes my world. She changes everything but my past.

3/8/60

People dancing around the fringes of the law, living purely by skulldug-
gery, are my delight!

3/9/60

And somehow, make love to her as they might, this fickle and jealous
mistress Art does not come—for the people who have scorned and
neglected her in their youth, and who court her in middle age.

3/18/60

What a person thinks of himself—that is all that life and mental health is
all about.

3/19/60

And then liquor came along in my life, when I was twenty. I often wonder if it really changed anything, if I would not have abandoned my
youthful serious dreams anyway. Would I without liquor, have a piano
now in my apartment, would I know how to knit very well, would I have
read all the books I vowed to read at 20? Well, the point is, I didn't, I
haven't done any of these things, and the person I am now is the person I have to live with. Go a bit farther, and say without liquor I would
have married a dull clod, Roger, and had what is called a normal life. A
normal life is also so often boredom or violence, divorce, unhappiness,
unhappiness for the children I never had.

5/3/60

America is subjected to more reality than any other country I happen
to know: everyone, nearly everyone, has to work for a living, hands in
dishwater in the home, washing machines, pregnancies of unmarried
high school girls, violence in the streets from people and in places least
expected, and moral cynicism rampant. Yet we as a nation are the least
likely to permit a realistic motion picture to be seen or such a book to
be read.

5/17/60

> Aged thirty-nine. A peculiar failure of dedication. Consequently, life is harder instead of easier. This after two evenings solitary *chez moi*. An unusual thing since March-April 1959. Oh, I'll be a better person for it! Onward and upward! For the past solid year (thank God, no more, it seems like more), I have been avoiding being alone. The sad part of this story is that I ingratiate myself with, consolidate myself better with—no one. People take a pleasure in pointing out my short-comings and con-genital, psychological deficiencies, and in lecturing me on them. "You'll never improve, never change. Face it," they tell me with a smile. Since I have so few years to live, perhaps it's back to the anchorage, the garret for me.

5/31/60

> I am more and more interested in the "older woman" heroine for this book.* I can't fit Therese into this—unless I have Carol playing around. Ergo—very likely brand-new characters. To explore the magic attrac-tion, the underlying tragedy of youth and of being enamored of it. This would fascinate me. The cruelty of youth and also its vulnerability. Its selfishness and its unbelievable dedication sometimes.

6/7/60

> There probably are a few true things in the Bible, such as that the people who already have more than enough will be given still more.

6/8/60

> Happiness. Merely a state of mind and the difference between life and death. Merely a floating, fluffy daisy seed. Now you have it, now you haven't, now you have. No, it's gone.

6/10/60

> Pushing a little too hard at the walls themselves. I need to stand back and contemplate their strength and the best ways of jumping or scaling them. It is the latter attitude that makes poetry.

---

* For some time, Pat considers writing a second, semi-autobiographical queer novel, reviving the characters from *The Price of Salt*, or *Carol*, for this "Girls' Book," which she leaves off after fifty-nine pages.

7/3/60

I like a country in which there is an acknowledged peasant class, such as Italy, Mexico. The peasantness that is in the foundation of every aristocrat equals character also in a country. The absence of an avowed peasant class in America is what makes its people so extraordinarily dull, similar, and characterless. We are all semi-peasants, all striving, all restless, all discontent. America is beautiful only geographically.

7/5/60

Woodland dream in Manhattan bed:
My girl, my woman, my wife in the country.
Beating my eggs and arranging my bed,
Arranging my hair—just as she likes it.
Fresh flowers on the table and behind her ears,
In her hair. Wood fires and twigs,
Apples and figs, and thwacking
Footsteps across a wooden floor, on Monday morning.
And also on Tuesday.
No telephone, no guests, only our ego-system
Of work, love making, and who will cook today?
All our striving will be who shall please
The other the most or the more.

7/11/60

P. 104 on a book.* Worrying is fatal, thinking of the things I might and should have put in is useless and stagnating—and anyway luckily can be done later. All this stewing in non-working hours is a counter-current. Go on, for Christ sake, in a big rush!

7/13/60

With a modicum (a modest modicum) of physical health, there is no depression that can't be remedied by a book, by writing a letter, by some thought we've already thought and once believed and can believe again. Why can't I remember all this at the times I really need it? I must have written this same thing twenty times before this, yet I'm always forgetting. The world is often new to me, but it is often newly black, too.

---

* Pat is working on final revisions of *The Two Faces of Janus* (later renamed *The Two Faces of January*). The book will be rejected by both her agent, Ann Carson, and her editor, Joan Kahn at Harper & Row, before eventually getting published by Doubleday in 1964.

7/14/60

Honesty, for me, is usually the worst policy imaginable.

7/24/60

Who cares if a writer lives or dies,
Until he wins the Nobel Prize?

8/19/60

There is no depression for the artist, except a return to the Self. The
Self is that shy, vainglorious, egocentric, conscious, magnifying glass
which should never be looked at. The sight of it happens in midstream
sometimes, when it is a real horror, and between books, and on vacations. Such a depression consists in (besides tears) the vain questions,
the exclamation, how badly have I fallen short of the aspirations and the
promise of my youth! And the even worse discovery (which should have
been remarked long ago) I cannot even depend on the one who is supposed to love me! I mustn't show myself in this moment of weakness. It
will be thrown at me at some later date, like an old bloody bandage that
should have been burnt—tonight. Let the memory of the black nights
live only in me.

Do people who can really talk to each other, without fear of reprisals, have the best marriages? Where has kindness, forgiveness, gone
in the world? And friends.—In the moment of the real grappling with
the enemy death, the potential suicide calls upon them. (One by one,
they are apt to be not at home.) The telephone doesn't answer. Or if it is
answered, one is too shy, too proud to break into tears. (Besides, it may
not be quite the friend we wanted, not one of the three closest friends.)
But the last effort to make contact with life: This is the bit of floating
wood, the splinter in the hand of the drowning person. How pitiable,
how human, how noble—for what is more godlike than communication?
The suicide knows that it has magical powers. (This whole blast tonight
set off by looking into my diary of 1944 when I was twenty-three, a most
immature, retarded, self-centered twenty-three. All my diaries should be
thrown into a furnace.)

8/19/60

Mrs. Anne C. How sad she is without her handsome husband. Arrives at
my cocktail party apparently having had a few, though actually it takes
only two to set her off. Sits immediately beside R.T. [Rolf Tietgens] who
is the most virile looking man in the room, and soon asks him to come

next door to her place. (After an hour of this increasingly drunken conversation, he simply has to get up.) At 10 P.M. a nonentity from upstairs arrives, grinning, has three quick Scotches. She tells someone she is having an affair with him. Later asks me my opinion of him. Tells someone he has said she is the sexiest dame he has ever met. She has wrinkles and bags under her eyes. It is all so sad—the woman who should be married! She works part time as a secretary at Bellevue Hospital.

8/23/60

(One important lesson for me: it is possible for me to write a book with no great definiteness of plot in mind, but it is not possible to continue without a definite idea of my intention. I suppose, a first law of any artistic creation.)

10/11/60

Vivaldi's "Summer." Something threatening, angry and unhappy in this music—which is so unlike the heavy-fulfillment-of-nature atmosphere found in other compositions on the same theme. It is as if Nature says: I am not satisfied with my lot and with this climax which is supposed to bring completion. There wasn't enough rain. Something choked my roots, and then a vine nearly strangled me—me, the handsomest giant of the forest. My seeds I scattered—but they did not find a growing place. Is this what Life is all about?

10/14/60

There isn't any constant personality for the writer, the face, with which he meets his old friends or strangers. He is always part of his characters, or he is simply in a good or bad mood, one day and another.

10/14/60

Once more a comparatively small hitch in a book, and I forget all the larger, more depressing ones I have had in the past. I go into my new room, excellent for writing, and I think again—fortunately I can remember this—four years from now, I'll say how wonderful, how ideal were the conditions and the atmosphere for writing here.

10/21/60

Novel about the peculiar defeatism in America now—and all over the Western World. It is in every country which is not in an emergent or revolutionary state. It is a peculiar, weird atmosphere—as if psychologically—rather literally—speaking, a great axe is about to fall and cut off all our heads at once.

Partly, it is because we feel we deserve this. We are well off, much due to exploitation of others, and most of the world's peoples are poorer, and will never, for instance, in our lifetime, know the joys of using their own washing machine. As to what is needed to remedy all this, I am not so much concerned. One would have to see a definite abolition of all military goods and expenditures, arms, ships, planes—all of it. One would have to know and see that the entire entire entire world rejoices over this. But I am only interested in the growth of this defeatism in the individual and in its manifestation today throughout the entire nation. Naturally, it would show up first in America, and be most interestingly incongruous, because of the wealth and comfort and the pioneering ideals on which this nation was founded.

11/7/60

Lots of writers, especially young writers, think they will put down "everything" in one book. They mean human consciousness (that mystery!), emotions, atmosphere, the whole gamut of existence. When they begin writing their book, they realize how much must be left out, how painfully specialized a work of art has to be to be any good at all. They'll tell only a fraction of what they want to in each book.

11/7/60

There is no meaning and no objective
Beyond the beauty of the day,
The kindness given.

11/10/60

It does not take two to argue, and a soft answer does not turn away wrath. It is more likely, that music hath power to charm the savage beast.

11/19/60

It's regrettable that I have to pretend to be immensely pleased with myself to have any mental peace and equilibrium at all. Actually, I am not at all pleased with myself in any way.

11/26/60

How great I am on Sunday mornings,
How much I shall be, ah, the many things I shall do,

The pages I shall write!
Great prose will flow, I shall love every face
And understand—of course, understand without effort.
I shall be great, esteemed, rewarded by the affections of men.
How great until Monday, when my hand
Writes the first clumsy, essaying word.

12/16/60

Claire Morgan.* Possibly each story told from older and younger point of
view. Complete new beginning & end of each.

1) The Ellen Story, Santa Fe episode. (+ she as opportunist,
   ambisexual)
2) The M.R.-R.B.† situation.
3) Helen M. & myself. On how incredibly badly the young can play
   their cards.
4) The M.J.-M.L.L. situation.
5) The transients—MAM and her etceteras.
6) The R.C. Half assed forever we stand! With something substantial in the background, if one is lucky.
7) The virginal quarrelers, the meshing of neuroses, R.S. and H.M.
8) The advantageous meeting in mid or late thirties, something
   which might last.

(But these are general. Had wished to do specifically, the older-younger,
with the older being constant.)

12/18/60

The muse doesn't come when you beckon. She comes when you've tried
all day to get something right, and you're tired and about to go to bed—
and then you stay up. She comes when you've lost your love. She touches
you, she touches your shoulder, and then you know you're not alone
after all.

12/31/60

The neuroticism, that is the unreasonableness, that springs up unexpectedly, like a jack in the box, in the most reasonable appearing women.
What can be done? It takes more than a diplomat. It takes a magician, an

---

* In a new approach to her "Girls' Book" Pat intends to publish under her pseudonym, Claire Morgan.
Rather than incorporating the characters from *The Price of Salt*, she considers creating new characters—
based on real-life ex-lovers and acquaintances.
† Mary Ronin and her other lover.

alchemist. Silence is fatal, a conciliatory word disastrous. Nothing can be done. It's a big rock in the sea. The boat has a hole in it. Peculiarly, these boats keep floating afterward. The party who was unable to speak, or who spoke in vain, remembers the injury. ᶠIt is that horrible cross, that horrible truth it takes so long for me to learn, that people thrive on quarrels, that quarrels are natural.ᶠᶠ As I write this, I know they are not. It is as if I am being brainwashed by experience, life, which I am supposed to believe is truth, the only truth. Yet I can never believe, unless I'm under the influence of drugs, that quarrels are a natural concomitant of the state of being in love or of loving. The resolution of all this ought to be quite simple. Some people are accustomed since childhood to saying anything they please and of never being held to account for it. They themselves don't remember it. So far, so good. But curiously, many people do remember, and do not regret, do not apologize, explain, or try to set things right again. It is not that they do not know that they have wounded, but that they (because they are post-developed lesbians, perhaps) think that their partners ought to go on as before with that wound which they made still open. "There is my power," they seem to say, "behold it, for all time, or for as long as you care to believe, care to love me—care to believe that you love me."

12/31/60

The statements are unbelievably harsh. It isn't a marriage at all. There's no attempt to understand, just a bristling offense-attack, as if they were each other's lifelong and natural enemies. This is a horrible concomitant of homosexual affairs. Ah and alas—was there not a marriage, with—all those phrases—in sickness and in health. Oh, God, where is the light touch on my forehead when I am low with fever? (Alas—I remember Trieste: "There's no reason why you should feel this bad.")

1961–1962

PATRICIA HIGHSMITH turns forty in 1961 and another separation is looming, this time from lover Marijane Meaker. Pat takes refuge in her work, but the place by her side doesn't remain vacant for long. She first finds comfort in the young Daisy Winston in New Hope, but in July 1962, during another trip to Europe, she meets and falls head over heels in love with Caroline—the love of her life.

At the beginning of 1961, notebook entries detail increasingly frequent domestic disputes—primarily fueled by Pat's drinking and Marijane's jealousy and nagging—as well as reflections on the topic of homosexuality. The pair finally separate in April. Pat stays in New Hope, where within ten months, and without a single direct mention in her notebook, she writes *The Cry of the Owl*, one of her most celebrated titles. In it, Pat portrays Marijane Meaker as a jealous, failed painter with multiple pseudonyms who is stabbed to death. (Marijane wreaks her own vengeance on Pat in her 1962 book *Intimate Victims*, by killing a character who shares Pat's birth name, Plangman. Like Pat, Harvey Plangman is a compulsive list-maker who peppers his sentences with German words.)

Soon after separating from Marijane, Pat begins a new relationship with Daisy Winston, a thirty-eight-year-old waitress in New Hope. During this time, Pat reviews books for the local newspaper, *Bucks County Life*, and writes several stories for *Ellery Queen's Mystery Magazine*, including "The Terrapin," in which a little boy murders his mother for cooking his favorite pet turtle. Although their romance lasts only a year, Pat and Daisy will remain lifelong friends, and Pat dedicates *The Cry of the Owl* to her.

Pat heads back to Europe in 1962, arriving in Paris in mid-May to promote *The Two Faces of January*, which has just been published by Calmann-Lévy. She then travels on to Sardinia, Capri, and finally Positano, where she and her ex-lover Ellen Hill rent a house and immediately fall back into their quarrelsome old dynamic. Although they visit Rome together, Pat sets off on her own to Venice, where her 1967 novel *Those Who Walk Away* will be based. She seems unable to keep still, though, and by the end of July she's in London, where she meets and falls desperately in love with Canadian expat Caroline Besterman. Caroline is married with a child.

Pat goes home to New Hope, and in September begins work on her next novel. Progress is hampered by her infatuation with Caroline. A few months earlier, in June, her American publisher Harper & Row rejected *The Two Faces of January* for the second time. In the void following a novel considered a flop, the author begins grasping at straws in her search for material. She comes up with a protagonist suspected of a murder he did not commit, although he had a motive for the killing. The story is inspired in part by letters Pat exchanges with an incarcerated convict; she also visits a nearby prison, accompanied by a criminal attorney, to conduct research.

In September, Pat returns to Paris, this time with Caroline, whom she decides she can no longer live without. In November, Pat packs up her cat, Spider, and takes a leap across the Atlantic to be closer to Caroline.

1/10/61

We shall never know much if anything more about "life" than we know already. The eternal, unanswerable questions, the efforts to solve the mystery and the intent repeat themselves through the centuries among philosophers and artists and writers. For the writer—he is always absorbed in these questions, deeply involved with them, and inspired by a genuine and undoubting hope of advancing what we already know about consciousness and life and its meaning. But all he can definitely do is describe life as it is, and try, aim, for the rest. To tell a story, about other people. We learn from others. Psychology and psychiatry, the new sciences, are peculiar in that dealing with the mind, with aspirations incidentally also, they have not brought us closer to the solving of this mystery, which every man and every artist feels. Will it be one short statement at death, heard with the inner ear? Will it be that all is quite purposeless, like a daisy in the field? A daisy is beautiful or a weed, depending on how one looks at it.

1/23/61

Painting. To simplify and simplify interests me now. In the Matisse manner, though Matisse as a painter is by no means my favorite. I am absorbed in the element of drawing in painting—and in principle too much just now, I realize. I dislike the building up of forms in daubs of color, and prefer the line elements.

3/3/61

The ultra-neurotic, which is myself. The Underground Man. To hell with reader identification in the usual sense, or a sympathetic character.

3/10/61

The homosexuals are more than heterosexuals tempted and flattered by an announcement of love. "I love you and I want you." When has this failed to capture a homosexual? It's a pity their egos are so weak, that their heads and hearts are so easily turned.

3/14/61

O, the ghastly slough of grief, unhappiness. There is no one word for this. Except—incapacity, but that Latin monster is so inaccurate. My hands are tied, the ear is closed to me, the eye is blind. A sense of futility, hopelessness, is the worst. I am this evening not hopeless, but the way is so slow. Yet how much better than last evening! The last words on the phone today were kind, even if the tone was not. What do the poets say about the power of love? I need it now. I believe in it. (I believe when the two people love, not when only one does.) I reread my first sixteen pages and found them better than I had dared hope.* Almost but not quite as heartening as her [Marijane's] softening words today. How much longer will it take? Curse that idiot of last Thursday night who convinced her I would harm her! That has done all the current damage. What I am looking for is the missing link. Why does she so obviously attempt to slander me and to punish me? What is the real relationship between her weak and oversensitive ego and her blind spots and her cruelty? I shall try and try to grope it out—then one day, like any other idea, it will be suddenly clear to me, and then in future, I hope I'll be able to handle it wisely— that is with long tongs.

3/16/61

Tonight neither the ear nor the door closed for reconciliation. I knew within thirty seconds of when she came in the door. She was smiling,

---

* It is unclear which project Pat means. It could be the autobiographical book she began in January (and abandoned after sixty-nine pages), with the working title *Girls' Book* or *First Person Novel*, or her next novel, *The Cry of the Owl*.

shyly, she asked me to repark her car. Then I settled down to read her letter (6 pages) while we both had drinks. (I after asking her [for permission], as I've been more or less on the wagon.) "We're celebrating"—was more or less the idea. Her long letter advocated more privacy for us (by commenting on sensation seekers of New Hope who have been observing us) plus an idea of two houses for us. A four-page letter it is, full of reserve. "I love you, but—" She does not want me to discuss her with my friends (she is justified; but my discussions have been mostly complimentary to her; I have always told my friends I love her—friends being now the Lewises, whom I do not consider close friends, and only Peggy [Lewis] at that). She cites Janet [Flanner] and Natalia [Danesi Murray]'s relationship. Well, I'll keep the letter always. Rereading it, I find it cool, but basically hopeful. More goes into all this, is behind it, than we can state or have stated. It is also ego—more fear on her part for hers than mine, I think. She is "afraid" of my drinking. I am terrified of her temper. At any rate, a good evening of love making tonight, after dinner at the Cartwheel, and Friday morning. She was tipsy enough to tell me she had read my diaries of Ellen etc. (and to mix chronology most maddeningly!) She said in essence: "It's clear you loved Ellen and wanted her, you were human in your diary. I loved you there. So why talk against Ellen?" What she may not realize is that circumstances change in a relationship.

3/19/61

I still cannot have a conversation with M. on a point that is bothering me. Her own abrupt arrangements of all this have caused me to be in the position of having to move [out and] to a larger house more or less soon. All the more reason why she does not want to discuss it—would not even listen to my words saying I was quite with her in opinion, I had to move, was going to, and to hell with the way it "looked." I said, "I also want to conform to the ways of the community. I don't want to look like an irresponsible oddball, though that is perhaps the way I look now. I can't help it."

3/21/61

What my pessimistic, flaw-seeking nature fears in this change is the beginning of the end. The only real bulwark we have against it is the extreme unlikeliness of "some other girl" really entering either of our lives or hearts—or plain bed. But I already see her highhandedness (Sunday P.M.) because in a sense she has won a victory, done with me as she wished, and yet still has me, too. It's perhaps my unfamiliarity with such an arrangement as this. Plus my ideal, to live with the person I love. Yet I know now we have too many sources of friction within a household for safety. And I am content and won't fret if this works out—that is, if we keep our tempers, and simply skirt, if possible, all the sources of discord which other people might be able to overcome, but which would wreck us. These days I regret so much that she can not reply to me quietly when I want to discuss a problem. She turns on me with claws, like a crotchety cat that has been disturbed from a nap. But these days also I want to see the good side of all this, the promise. She wants to see me every evening now. Even this mustn't go too far. We both need privacy. This time, I don't want it to be her again who turns on me and says, "I've had enough of you! I banish you for the second time!"

3/22/61

These days swim all one into the other. Today at 12 noon she called me, sorry she had shouted, but within seconds, shouting that she had been right to shout, that I had shown my (two) drinks at the dinner table. At 4 she called in quite a different mood: she had bought a puppy in Doylestown and she accepted my invitation to come to my place for dinner with the Ferres.* When they left, I broached the matter of mutual apologies to M.J. and our need to declare a truce on any further insults to each other, which could only lead to real disaster. M.J. ran. She ran up the stairs, saying "You're drunk, I don't want another fight, Pat." We slept in separate rooms. The morning was the worst. The worst of any verbal conflict to date. M.J. keeps me on the defensive, by wild attacks. E.g. accusing me the night before of having whined, of having said that I have the worst of it, in regard to housing. This was the least of my problems! This morning: "You're such a cheapskate, you won't get yourself a decent place. You'll be there all summer." And: "You're trying to defend yourself with what's left of your logical mind, because gin has got it. You can't make it with Marijane Meaker. I threw you out, Pat, because you're a common drunk." I said, hang onto it. It's all you've got.

3/23/61

This morning her lies reached psychopathic proportions for the first time. She denied having asked me, when I was replacing a hammer in the rack last night, "Do you want to hit me, Pat?" I said, "Of course not,"

---

* Betty and Al Ferres, a couple of friends in New Hope where Pat was always welcome.

and hung the hammer, and: She accused me of running out on the phone
bill, whereas I had volunteered to pay it. All this of importance, because,
heartened by my work. I, for the first time ever, said that I would no
longer accept her lies and exaggerations. This shook her, indisputably.
I denied what she would have put in my mouth this morning. The letter
she got this noon was neither insulting nor pleading. It was a straightforward statement that a) I should cut down drinking, on general principles,
and b) that she had to watch her temper on the same principles as there
would be girls after me. The essence this evening: the insults from her
have gone beyond bounds. I have swallowed a lot, and thought there was
no limit to what I could swallow. But I'm afraid there is. Without a real
apology from her, a promise about the future, I can't go on. When I ask
for this—she says: "Resentment burns in you like a bright torch."

4/3/61

The pattern of quarrels and reconciliations in the very first days of a relationship (however minor the quarrels then) is the pattern that will prevail
throughout, grow bigger perhaps, become insufferable, perhaps. The
story of M.J. and myself. Off to a crippled start. The brain washing. The
rivalry between two in the same profession. The desperate efforts of one
to best the other; and the other's efforts to preserve the relationship, at
any cost. And at the same time saying, "Why am I in this? I'm intelligent
enough to see I must get out." But what is there "out"? The same sort of
relationship with someone else? Better to stick it out and to try, say all
the marriage counselors, all the psychologists—in regard to heterosexual
relationships.

4/3/61

Each day a conscious struggle to maintain sanity, to appear calm when
one is not, an effort to make the smile seem spontaneous—though occasionally it's genuine. The struggle to appear like everyone else—never
anxious, never rushing, never doubting, never feeling melancholic.

5/14/61

Homosexuals prefer one another's company not so much because of a
common sexual deviance from what is socially accepted, but because
they know that they have all been through the same hell, the same trials,
the same depressions—and those who meet have survived. Those not
present have killed themselves, or have managed, or decided, or were
able to conform. Homosexuals' friendships or acquaintanceships may

appear to be superficial, may be superficial in fact, but that underlying bond remains: and they are blood brothers and sisters, because of what they have suffered: This unites the high and low, the intelligent and the stupid.

5/29/61

What is life all about? It is the futility, and the hopelessness that obsesses and overwhelms the philosophers. If I am lucky, when the darkness closes in, and the senses dropout one by one, there will be a couple of friends standing by, who knew me. This is what life is all about. It's no different if one has children and passes on the race or the family. Life is about nothing but hopes of contacts. Friendships are the most durable, and really the most profound contacts, though people are often deceived into thinking that the sexual is the most profound. It is pleasurable and it appears to rearrange the emotional structure, but it does not.

6/1/61

Spent two hours reading old diaries of mine, sixteen years back. My life is a chronicle of unbelievable mistakes. Things I should have done, etc. and vice versa. It is not pleasant to face, especially not pleasant to realize I am still doing the same thing, and now moreover doing it even while trying to put to use the lessons of the past. What is the solution? Avoid sadists. Don't show how much emotion you have when you have it. Play everything cautiously, with a view of saving yourself. All useless for me. I avoid nothing, I show everything I feel, even without speaking. I play nothing cautiously, and least of all will I ever save myself in an emotional situation.

6/1/61

[Heitor] Villa Lobos' music. In it I hear the green depths of the Amazonian forest, wildly colored birds, the beauty and the tragedy of love and life and death. It is music without boundaries, like a picture without boundaries, without a frame, yet beautiful in its vermilion red center. It has the range, the joy of freedom, also the knowledge of death. And the notes that have never been sung before by the voice of a passionate woman in love.

6/16/61

[Positano.] The Gay Book Part One: the Rejection by the girl I love. N.W. type. C.S. type, R.C. type, idealistically. Part two. The Torturers, the M.J.M. type, tempered even by the M.R. type, available yet not. Part three: the J.S. type who loves me and whom I cannot accept. This would create a trilogy. Untrue to my life as it was lived chronologically, however.

6/18/61

Measles (German).* The spots break out in a matter of minutes. Preceding symptoms are nervousness, and for a day before that, flinching from light. Stomach and back and upper arms are the worst. Fever by evening, though not severe. Dark glasses an essential and a great comfort. It is no comfort to visit a brusque doctor who gives no medicaments and little advice, except to stay away from women three months' pregnant. It may have dire effects on the child, not the mother. Liquids; guard against chill, spread corn starch on the skin to cut down the itching. Nights are unpleasant, one hour of sleep followed by 2 hours of scratching and lying awake. As usual, I have found the fever beneficial to the imagination, and found an ending on my book [*The Two Faces of January*]. The face becomes merely roseate, no spots individual. Painful glands in the neck. The ears and nose are sore and seem swollen. It is said to last three days. I am writing this at the end of the first thirty-six hours, wishing I were more than half through with it. Next day, evening. The spots have almost all disappeared. The arms' spots last of all (somewhat confused in my case with poison oak!). Recurrence of fever at sundown, but this soon left, and I felt quite energetic, due to two days' more or less rest.

6/20/61

The world remains the same. It is only you who change. *Sic transit* all depressions! Would that it were so!

6/21/61

Drinking requires an audience of one, or of many, but of one at least. Sometimes, there is not even the audience of one. Then drinking has no interest.

6/22/61

When my existence is beset with hellish, dancing, fiendish demons, when my mind is exhausted with coping, when I wonder what's the use of

---

* As with her second novel, *The Price of Salt*, which profited from her chickenpox fever, Pat considers her illness as conducive to her writing.

anything—how I welcome the insane sanity of an English crossword puzzle. There the world for all its crazy puns, is logical and even fair again.

7/3/61

What's the crucial question? Can we make each other happier, even for a brief time?

JULY 7, 1961

New Hope. Is misery a little bit different when set down on paper? Yes. Or on canvas, or in musical notes. It is not merely externalized, it is also changed, made more clear, dominated, in a sense. Above all, changed. Tonight I am not miserable, anyway. Only the character I am writing about in my book is. Tonight I have called a friend who was in mild distress. What is mental health? Actions like this, regularity of actions—but above all kindness to others, at all times, without exception. At times, I must be physically tired, very tired, to achieve a peace of mind. Yet even then, without a kindness done by me that I can think of, there is no contentment. And sleep is the sweetest balm of all, restoring vision again, restoring perspective, restoring truth, giving not only life back, but optimism and hope, without which life is unbearable. I am working in the middle of my book now, having finished a first draft of 263 pages last Sunday—

JULY 8, 1961

The same again. Friday. Lots of good work. Drinks with Peggy Lewis and an invitation to dinner which I did not accept. Is there any use of putting down a few lines every day? Yes. Nothing keeps me, or possibly anybody else, going, except routine.

Spider caught a half-grown rabbit. Little Daisy* eats like a horse.

7/7/61

Casual observation. A gay girl who has since the age of twelve or earlier identified herself with the masculine sex will take no trouble to remain slender and agile when middle age overtakes her, with the spreading hips and the tripled bosom. And this is because she takes no pleasure in being a mature woman, takes no pride in being at all one of the feminine gender.

---

* One of Pat's cats.

JULY 9, 1961

I spent the day pottering, writing letters, thinking about my book in the unconscious way which is necessary now. It has to have more of the tragic-neurotic, which to me is the only truth. I am troubled this night by external influences, plus the overhaul on my book which I understand and can do—perhaps by the end of July.

8/8/61

And every word a drop of blood,
Every line a thrust of pain
(Thus I give you pain and pleasure),
Molten gold your body in my brain,
Your form seared in my flesh,
Little golden amulet!
By the black fire in your laughing eyes,
I swear,
I pledge myself to joy.
I swear to protect you,
  To D.W. [Daisy Winston]* "Little jewel of black and gold."

8/31/61

Good books write themselves.

10/27/61

To try to be content, to learn how to be content, to be content—this is of the greatest importance to me. The potential danger of smugness is far offset by the fact that one produces more and produces better, that one gives a little happiness to others also.

11/3/61

The world is so full of a number of girls, I think we should all be as happy as squirrels.

11/26/61

For a Weekend
  L.R. [Lynn Roth]
What was purple last week

---

* This is the first mention in the journals of Pat's new love interest, Daisy Winston, who then worked as a waitress in New Hope.

Has become red.
The sky is wider.
The brook out my window,
With the little waterfall—
Does its water change,
Or is it the same water
Arrested, forever tumbling
Its pretty length downward?
I wish the landscape out my window,
The barren, beautiful trees,
The functional train that passed,
When you and I stood watching,
Would arrest themselves forever,
Forever, forever.
Your hand, your eye have captured—
I want no spring,
I want for nothing.

12/12/61

There is a fate, there is a desire—downward. Nothing and no one and no philosophy and no body of doctors can save the person whose destiny is to destroy himself, but in destroying, [to] discover.

12/12/61

It must be strange to enter a house and begin living there, and fix it up, knowing it is the last house you will ever live in and fix up, and that you will die there.*

1/1/62

There is a little secret of mental health. Something for the simple minded. That is, to see progress in whatever we do. If the progress does not exist, see it anyway. This was the great attitude of my grand-mother, who indeed made progress, it was no fallacy, but who saw and

---

* By now Pat must have moved out of the house she shared with Marijane Meaker and into a temporary stay in the same village.

thought about only the progress, not the setbacks, not the disappointments, not the plain failures. It is the privilege, the duty, of a man to
contemplate objectively. Whether we are happy or not depends on what
we choose to see.

2/3/62

Art—working—does the same thing as alcohol. It changes the world
until it is tolerable. If a writer or a painter is working well, there is no
need to drink or to take any other form of narcotic, which alters reality. This is also why the true artist will drink or take narcotics when not
happily or successfully at work, or when not at work at all.

2/3/62

A most important fact in my character is that I did not begin, as a child
and an adolescent, open, free, naive, gullible and so forth. Naive I was,
no doubt of that, but I was closed up and reserved. I did not begin to live
until I was thirty. I developed via friendships after I was an adult. It is
still going on—the opening, the accepting, the tolerance, therefore the
feeling and the caring for other people. Until around thirty I was essentially like a glacier or like stone. I suppose I was "protecting" myself.
It was certainly tied up with the fact I had to conceal the most important emotional drives of myself completely. This is the tragedy of the
conscience-stricken young homosexual, that he not only conceals his sex
objectives, but conceals his humanity and natural warmth of heart as
well. But as about every other fault I am strapped with—I cannot say I
deplore or regret it. And that's because—what good would it do to wish
things had been otherwise? Water dammed up will one day burst forth in
a torrent.

5/3/62

Ishi by Theodora Kroeber. Why do I prefer the factual to the invented
fiction? I long for facts, and the terrible truths of this Indian's story make
me ashamed, angry, frustrated, and make me weep. I remember when
I was eight years old at the Sixth's Ward Grade School in Fort Worth.
Once a week we had a library hour. I was reading about Indians in their
teepees, Indians making bows and arrows and Pemmican. I carried it in
my head for a week and could hardly wait to plop down on my backless
stool—a dark, docile lump—to reopen the book where I had left and go
on, finding out about the people who had lived on the land where I was
born, long before I was born.

MAY 15, 1962

Paris. The streets seem darker at night. The people are nervous, Renée*
says, men having been known to kill each other over a minor collision of
their two cars. The peculiar boredom of Paris. I am not content when I
am not working, and actually become stupid not working. It's the util-
itarian American in me; which I don't like. I cannot simply exist. I like
the consciousness of simply existing, but I cannot enjoy it for more than
one minute at a time. It will be interesting to see if I can improve on this
regrettable condition during this trip, when I am free of the anxieties
which formerly (I thought) made me so nervous and shy. I.e. teeth and
money troubles.

MAY 21, 1962

Doris quizzes me on Daisy [Winston]. I told Doris I prefer to live alone in
New Hope.

5/23/62

Today in an interview with Mademoiselle de la Villain of *France Soir*, I
showed her the book and told her of my pleasure in reading about animals. She asked why. I said, in a time of anxiety and the constant threat
of war, I like to read about animals who remain always the same, loyal to
their nature, therefore beautiful and pure.

MAY 24, 1962

Bought my ticket to Cagliari for 381 NF [Nouveau Francs] at Les Invalides. Then a long and pleasant lunch with Doris S., a brandy & coffee at
Deux Magots. We parted at 4 P.M. Dinner at 7 with Janet Flanner. 2½
martinis in the Continental Bar. She looks well, and I found her much
warmer than ever before.

MAY 26, 1962

Bought the reservation for the boat on the 31 to Naples. E. [Ellen Hill]
is full of interesting anecdotes about the primitivity of the natives here.
Their habits of thinking & acting. All traditional, & the result of centuries of oppression. We drove to a beach where we could not swim.

---

* Renée Rosenthal was the wife of Jean Rosenthal, together the couple translated many of Pat's novels
for the French publishing houses Calmann-Lévy and Laffont.

MAY 31, 1962

At last the boat sailed at 5. We have a second class cabin out of which a woman moved—luckily for us. A three-course mediocre dinner. I did not bring anything to read, which left me alone with my own thoughts. My love of ships never grows old.

JUNE 1, 1962

A very crowded car for the drive to Positano. Ellen's house is charming, on two levels, accessible from top or bottom. Ellen harks back to my "ill-treatment and neglect" of her after meeting Daisy. Only an emotionally involved person would say that. My unfairness in general. I mentioned finally hers in regard to Santa Fe: Mexico: *Deep Water*: suicide threats, which of course she wished to turn aside, ᶠI did not mention her reading my diary in '54, causing me to stop keeping one, after 19 years of keeping one—until now, I suppose.ᶠᶠ I think people involved emotionally over such a long period of time will be hit and will strike back. Tit for tat, so it goes. I would invite her to put into the scales our blows against each other, our good deeds toward each other. I think they would come out very even.

JUNE 3, 1962

[Positano.] I made two drawings. E. prefers my black & white. Went to dinner at Edna's* tonight. Edna's house is full of interesting paintings and furniture.

6/5/62

Every gun should be broken. We live in the twentieth century.

JUNE 7, 1962

Edna wants my (3rd) Positano drawing in black & white, & can probably sell it—10 or 17,000 lire. I did another today. The old difficulties in regard to the typewriter. E. cannot stand the noise. It reminds me of Taxco when I was trying to write *Deep Water*. Since it is her typewriter, she wants really to hoard it.

6/8/62

Decision of today, not to live (share a house) with anyone again. The impetus to this given by my discomfort at being told what to do and

---

* Edna Lewis was Peggy Lewis's mother-in-law and ran an art school in Positano.

when to do it. I have a real knack for finding people who do this. Apart from this, my past associations have left me either emotionally or financially bankrupt, and the prospect of another such abyss and of hauling myself out of it utterly dismays me. I am too old to have that kind of courage anymore.

6/26/62

Rome. To an American, the inconveniences of Europe and European hotels in particular seem not so much examples of behind-the-times mentality as products of sadistic, misanthropic minds. Who but a vicious schemer could have designed or constructed clothes hangers with necks fourteen inches long and shoulder spans of ten inches, causing even a jacket to trail the closet floor and to sag as if it hung on a scarecrow? The bathroom's water tank in such hotels is apt to be over the front half of the tub, so projecting that one can hardly reach the taps under it. The toilet is designed with no knee space between it and the tub. The paper roll is directly behind it, or out of reach on an opposite wall, and there is no paper in it. Doors that have to be operated by three keys turning simultaneously in three locks. Was eighteenth-century man three-handed?

7/6/62

To see a virtue in "movement"—i.e. in doing the everyday things of life and doing them energetically—is all I need to defeat the most obvious signs (and handicaps) of my neurosis. I should say one of my many neuroses. Shyness plus a rather Buddhistic disbelief in and contempt for movement and action is what generally paralyzes me. This is most notable to me on vacations, when to me the most (the only) useful objectives are removed: work and taking care of my house. It is a painful effort for me to pick up an airplane ticket.

JULY 7, 1962

William Faulkner died yesterday in Oxford, Mississippi of heart failure. A strike of Italian newspapers and I read of it only in the *Daily Telegraph*.

7/7/62

The experience of traveling forces me to live, which I do not want to do. I do not like the interruption of my unconscious thoughts by the consciousness of: "Now I am living, struggling, if only mentally, to maintain my place in a line of people, which has been usurped by a plump woman from the Abruzzi." I stand there letting her take my place, and thinking what I should have done. On the other hand, I enjoy visual impressions to the full. The pink and yellow lights on certain Venetian buildings. To put it most simply, I do not like crowds of people. This is more and more apparent to me. I think much of it comes because I never had siblings.

7/8/62

Truest love, greatest love is that given to those most in need of love. Those most in need can give nothing in return.

7/12/62

[Paris.] Père Lachaise Cimetière. The only name which interested me on the map presented by a caretaker was Oscar Wilde's. There are also Georges Bizet, Balzac, Alfred de Musset buried here. It is a tremendous place in the east of Paris (direction Porte des Lilas), with real roads through it. Oscar Wilde's grave is in section 89e, in the north central part, and I reached it after nearly a mile of walking. Among darkened (with time) rectangular vaults, mostly with triangular headstones, I came upon Oscar's—a large nearly square rectangle of granite with a large Egyptian figure in headdress, flying horizontally. Only his name on the front in large letters. On the back those great and most fitting lines:
And alien tears shall fill for him
Pity's long broken urn.
For his mourners shall be outcast men,
And outcasts always mourn.

JULY 20, 1962

[London.] At 10 to Billingsgate to see the Coal Exchange, the City and Guild School art exhibit, and the Sir John Soane museum collection. Then to meet Camilla Butterfield. Was with her until 7, then the Bestermans came after dinner for a drink. Caroline Besterman is quite charming, animated—pink in her face after her drink in the manner of the English, but she is French Canadian. Very friendly to me indeed, and we'll probably go to Lord's to see a cricket match Monday. Camilla alas goes for a week tomorrow to the country to visit her first friend Diana. She is in much the same boat as I with her present friend Maggie in L.A. Wants to make a break and knows not how without hurting.

7/23/62

    "At the Picadilly end of the Burlington Arcade,"
she said, "I'll meet you, I'll meet you.
At ten thirty in the morning.
Can't make it at ten, unless I get there in my dressing gown."
"All right, I'll look for you in your porter's jacket,
Looking as if you—"
"As if I'm about to port something."
"At Piccadilly end of the Burlington Arcade."
"Bye bye." "Bye bye."
She's free tonight. We're both free tonight.
Ah, tactics!

7/26/62

    And a necklace of verses
I will make you. One by one,
Strung on a brief time,
A thread of time to remember,
To remember these few days,
To keep these few days forever.

AUGUST 1, 1962

    Hampton Court—then 4:30 P.M. Caroline's for dinner with her husband
and son—Tennis in the dawn and the first falling leaves.

8/1/62

    To do you grace,
I should paint for you,
That evening. That evening
When I should either have stood up,
Or fallen. I loved you the moment,
The moment I saw you.

8/4/62

    Was my life the least bit better when I walked at twenty-four up Third
Avenue, past my old high school at Sixty-eighth, browsing and sometimes buying in the antique shops? It was better because of a misplaced
hope. It was misguided, untrue—but it was good because it sufficed.
Better I wouldn't say it was. It was an illusion. They were the days when

I thought every piece of information could be put to some use, and consequently ought to be stored. The days when I thought every love was the last. Now they seem halcyon. Then they seemed turbulent and dangerous. I'd have thought such a life as I am leading now the last word in conservatism, quietude, the absence of risk. Now is when the risks begin, the danger, the anxiety. Now I am face to face with the iron mask, the sharpened blade that life is. It is now in security that my back is really to the wall, and the knife of fate at my throat. Now I have few illusions, and I know that illusions are like ballast or excess baggage in an imperiled boat: throw them overboard. My excess baggage—no pun—I'm in no mood for joking—is the eternal love I cannot turn loose of. I say eternal somewhat mockingly. The love changes, but the need of it is eternal, or as eternal as I am. Let someone else bear the torch when I am gone! There will be enough people!

8/25/62

London—the sound is Big Ben, slow and solemn. (I will gladly die for the Queen.) Londinium, Cockney and Oxford accents. In that depth. In that grayness. In that fog and that weather. And Caroline is a sparrow I once saw and thought I once knew, because it sat twice upon the same brown fence out my window. Saw twice and once knew, once upon a time. Her wrists are somewhat plump, and she wears a narrow dark band a little more above the wrist than usual. The color comes and goes in her cheeks. Her brown eyes look at me directly. And brown is absolutely the last color I would think of in attempting to describe her. Cream, pink, even white—and what is the color of warmth? A very pale beige sweater, a tweed skirt. A hat of gray, like bird feathers, though I am sure it wasn't. I remember her laughter. And on the boat from Greenwich, finally, "I'm cold." And of course, nothing could properly be done about it, and we were both very proper.

SEPTEMBER 3, 1962

Today a good day as I had hours' sleep plus a nap. Majority of my time was spent plotting a story which I hope Maurice Evans* may like. Oh, well, the main thing is that it happened at all. It happened last night. Sometimes one can see the end of the beginning, that short stretch of

---

* Maurice Evans (1901–1989) was an English actor and film producer. He gained fame on the stage and even won over American TV audiences with his performances of Shakespeare. He also appeared in such popular films as *Planet of the Apes*. Pat wrote a synopsis for Evans, *The Suicide on the Bridge*, but the piece was never produced.

life called maturity, life, the end, the goal, happiness, of what life is all about, and this last can as well be a promise or fulfillment. The important thing is to see it at all. And of course I never suspect or hope or dream or think that she sees it in my dejected or beaten up face. That I would leap over the side of the ship if she asked me to. Who cares, really?

SEPTEMBER 4, 1962

Caroline's letter made me happy all day, and started me out properly. She wrote—after three casual pages, "Please write soon as I feel rather as if the oxygen system had been cut off—" since she hadn't heard from me in a week. I do love her and I often think of the first moment I ever saw her, walking in white—and I was immediately smitten and smashed. How long will it be till I see her again, I wonder? And how much work must I do? But the work will be happy. I am happy with things as they are. But it is distressing not to be able to write her as often—or Christ write her what—I wish to.

SEPTEMBER 5, 1962

After infinite debate, I telephoned this evening at 5:05 A M, 10:05 AM London time. Caroline was perfectly charming, and I hope she enjoyed it as much as I did. Not only was I constrained in this exceptional call, but I am now just as unable to write her as I should like to. This is really time for the *fou rire*. But I adored every second of our conversation. There was nothing missing but Big Ben. I said finally, "Have a good day." "I will—now—"

SEPTEMBER 6, 1962

Slept till noon and felt wonderfully euphoric all day long, remembering Caroline. She said last evening: "This is the most delightful extravagance." I do love her, and it was lovely to think of London in the 10 AM sunlight, and to hear Caroline chatting away as casually as if I lived in the next block. I told her I had just sold an ancient story* to *Story* magazine, hence my celebration.

9/6/62

I live my life backwards. In childhood I was lugubrious and very grown up, in adolescence middle aged, now in middle age adolescent, and even my hair has changed from black to brown and is becoming lighter.

---

* The short story "The Great Cardhouse," which Pat wrote in 1949.

SEPTEMBER 8, 1962

No letter from Caroline. Went to Odette's tonight, where I had only
vichyssoise, but it was delicious. I was drunk, however. We later went to
Instant London's for a drink. I was quite gay and happy, I must say.

9/10/62

Address to younger writers, who think older writers like me are so
famous and so different. We are no different at all, we are just the same
as other writers, only we work harder.

SEPTEMBER 12, 1962

I wrote a long and rather messy letter to C. mostly about my "not" being
able to write now. A double meaning. I trust she will understand. Have
you any suggestions, I asked, meaning a friend to whom I might write
her. I am afraid she hasn't. How could she explain this to anyone? Yet
from her matriarchal background, I suspect she has had emotional relationships with women friends before. If not actual affairs. I simply don't
know.

SEPTEMBER 13, 1962

And today, to my surprise and joy, another letter from C. written
Monday—when she got the curse a week early, it was raining—and she
writes: "I have this urge for constant communication with you." And—
"when I drink too much gin on an empty stomach—it prompts me to
want to say all sorts of things like, when are we ever going to meet again,
which, considering the fact that you've hardly left, is scarcely constructive—" My love to you—Caroline—that crazy C! C comme ça. I am
anxious all day, because of future obligations, but things are better. At
least five letters or "pieces of mail" get done each day, chores, but nothing is ever quite finished.

9/16/62

I carefully cultivate the art of being cheerful—art indeed, as it is so artificial to me now. It is like a very sick plant that I have to water drop by
drop lest I bruise it. I tiptoe into the room where it is. And on it my own
life hangs. One question I must not ask myself—though I do—is how am
I to live and work during these next many, many, how many, weeks? I am
absolutely sick for her, and I must summon up every bit of courage and
determination that I possess in order to carry on alone. And I must try

to remember, by way of giving myself courage, that out of these terrible dark valleys and abysses sometimes come things of great beauty. I have been here before, yes, but never has the valley been this long, so dark, and so deep.*

SEPTEMBER 19, 1962

Camilla counsels me to go slow, to find somebody within a 50-mile radius of New Hope. I replied that her advice was good and that I would do my best to be sensible. I wrote a book review of [Rachel Carson's] *Silent Spring* for the B.C. [*Bucks County*] *Life*. I approach the TV script with trepidation, but I shall try my best. Yesterday a letter from Connie Smith in regard to $6,000 for hour-long scripts for CBS for "established mystery suspense writer." I do hope to have a letter from C. tomorrow. The boring husband leaves tomorrow.

SEPTEMBER 22, 1962

The most startling letter of all from Caroline. "Why were there no signs in the sky in July 62," she writes, "no statues weeping—to warn me of the thunderbolt that fell—I love thunderbolts—they fall so seldom." She longs for an excuse to make her presence in Canada vital—(just as I scheme for Paris) and if this is not a love letter, I don't know what is. All this is dangerously shaking to me, and I must arrive at longer, steadier working hours, or else. Well, I am not merely in love, I am smashed and smitten.

SEPTEMBER 24, 1962

A good day. Worked better. 14 pages at least on the TV script, which now interests me. Camilla says—"I have no doubt C. is strongly attracted toward you and would have no (squeamishness?) about lesbianism—but I wonder just how far she would go if the situation became any more realistic?"

9/25/62

I want to stumble
And fall into your arms.

---

* When Pat later rereads and annotates her journals, she comments below this entry: "I must say still, the above was and is rather true" (8/30/69); "Alas—still true, nearly exactly twelve years later" (7/14/74).

9/26/62

With my heart spilling out of my eyes,
And your heart out of yours,
I salute you, stumbling and stammering again.
I greet you badly, you who would forgive
All my *bêtises* et mes *gaffes*.
I perish for your embrace.

SEPTEMBER 29, 1962

Today C. writes, "Have you thought of Invisible Ink?" What a question!
Has she not thought of, in all London, a place where I might write her?
It is quite hard to conceive that she has not. Yet she has quite effectively
censored me and tied my pen by not providing a place!!!

SEPTEMBER 30, 1962

C. is going to Paris in November for a week and could be staying with
friends. She seemed pleased with the idea I would come over. Talked perhaps 15 minutes. I told her I'd have a letter at the Haymarket for her by
Thursday. She keeps my letters. [Her husband] reads most of them. Alas.

OCTOBER 6, 1962

Went with Kips [Rachel Kipness] to Maurice Evans' for dinner. They had
read the script last night. It needs work, tightening and improving—all
that—but they were most helpful in their suggestions. Most interesting,
"*Piège*"* came up again, & when I said I was going over, Morse was glad
to suggest I be his unofficial spokesman. The rights are free. He wants to
do it on the stage in N.Y. and in London. So I have an assignment—not
to mention the fact Robert Thomas & I may finally collaborate. This is
marvelous in regard to the situation with C. It gives me a reason to go.

OCTOBER 7, 1962

Two wonderful letters from Caroline. "My dear, my dear, you are a miracle. I have lost my heart and everything else to you already." [Her hus-
band], alas, is spiteful—C's word—so all is a bit perilous. But the good
news is that she'll be able to come over to Paris November 12 and will
not have to stay with S. until the 15th—How wonderful that will be—

---

* Presumably *Piège pour un homme seul*, a 1960 play by French writer and director Robert Thomas.
A tremendous success from its opening night in Paris, it was soon performed on stages around the
world. Hitchcock secured himself the film rights. Pat might have been interested in collaborating on the
English-language version.

"we can therefore be alone at least for these few days without anyone knowing."

OCTOBER 10, 1962

Bad news from France. I am out the $8,000 I was expecting this year, as they are not necessarily shooting an English language version.* But I wrote to Caroline, that my plans were unchanged in regard to Paris.

OCTOBER 12, 1962

At last a letter from Camilla—very cool, almost sarcastic about the situation with C. "Go over to Paris—get it out of your system . . ."

OCTOBER 14, 1962

C. is too romantic for me, perhaps.

OCTOBER 17, 1962

These days so tangled with beautiful letters from Caroline—I live in an exotic jungle. Exotic except that it is the English language.

OCTOBER 19, 1962

Work. Not too well. Letter from C. They could not be better. "Do you really mean it when you say you think you have never been so much in love? I hope you mean it. Because neither have I." How can I deplore my small bit of professional bad luck when fortune has brought me this?

OCTOBER 23, 1962

Two letters from C. Astounding phrases in regard to [her husband]. "He has a creepy mind . . . Very slimy." In another letter, "an Alice-sit-by-the-fire." In another, "He sticks like glue—" Always—the derogatory word or phrase. Today I wrote her mentioning this. *Nous verrons*. Possibility that [he] is masochistic—Well, possibility?! I am very curious to know if they sleep in the same bed.† How could a man stand it? "Heavens how I love you. It is frightening," writes C. "Don't speak of kisses or bed or I shall go mad."

---

* Probably a reference to the movie adaptation of *The Blunderer*, which was made into the French movie *Le meurtrier* in 1963.
† Here Pat later added between the lines: "They do."

OCTOBER 24, 1962

Speculation—uncertainties—especially today—Russia is bringing arms to Cuba and there seems to be a real danger of war. There is also the possibility [C.'s husband] may decide to come to Paris, too. I'd have to cancel my trip. I've written C. this. Meanwhile we live on this tightrope—or whatever—something may still go wrong.

OCTOBER 29, 1962

Was shattered by the letter from C. today as she is troubled by New Hope's apparently being full of Lesbians. I put the best of my energy this PM into explaining a) that there are no Lesbians in New Hope, b) Peggy [Lewis] is certainly not one, c) there are no cliques here d) she is in no danger of losing me. The latter because of her sentence, "I am terrified of losing you." I have never read—much less received—a more passionate letter. "I don't want a sentimental pining relationship à la Swinburne* either. I want you in the flesh."

OCTOBER 31, 1962

I waited for the mail. Two nice letters from C. Later over 2 drinks, I told Pat [Schartle]† the situation in London. Pat was kind enough to say it was a wonder I could work at all. Things cannot go on as they are, that is evident. I promised Pat (and myself) to do all I could to clear them up.

NOVEMBER 1, 1962

Home in New Hope by 9:30 PM—still missed ½ the Hitchcock show, as I couldn't find Duffy's. Hitchcock did a rather good job of *This Sweet Sickness*, according to Pat.‡ But quite some exaggerating.

NOVEMBER 4, 1962

Bad sleep last night. But a good day of chores, last of all some more definite thoughts in regard to *The Prison*,§ which gave me a new lease on life

---

* In his then-deemed scandalous early works, Victorian writer Algernon Charles Swinburne (1837–1909) wrote about such topics as sadomasochism, the desire for death, lesbian fantasies, and anti-Christian attitudes.

† Pat's new agent, Patricia Schartle, was editor-in-chief at Appleton-Century-Crofts Publishing in New York, before joining the Constance Smith Associates literary agency. Following Constance Smith Associates' merger with McIntosh & Otis, Schartle was named president of the new agency. In addition to Patricia Highsmith, Schartle represented writers such as Mary Higgins Clark and Noah Gordon.

‡ Pat's novel *This Sweet Sickness* (New York, 1960) was adapted for a 1962 episode of *The Alfred Hitchcock Hour* called "Annabel."

§ This is the first mention of Pat's new book project, *The Glass Cell* (New York, 1964).

today; I should say made me feel alive for the first time since April, 1962, when I finished [*The Two Faces of*] *January.*

NOVEMBER 8, 1962

Got more Travelers Checks, so now I'll be going with $1040. No letter from C. but she said she wouldn't write again. (I do not believe her.) She described Aldeburgh* in her last letter. Interesting people, bloody windy in winter. I hope we'll have a house there. So much depends on how well we get on in these 17 days! So much! "I'll kiss you on the red sofa Nov. 26—why not?" she writes. It is indeed either/or, for us. I love her letter: "I shall probably feel quite shy. Which is rather nice." Yes, it is. And she need not worry.

NOVEMBER 12, 1962

[Paris.] A rather enchanted day during which I did nothing but slowly shop for gin and oranges, some—cornflowers. Went to the Gare du Nord at 5:10—had a coffee—and Caroline's train was exactly on time, 5:50 PM.—Voie 19. She was among the last, walking very slowly, and saw me before I saw her. She took my hand and fairly collapsed against me. I felt rather stiff. Trouble getting a taxi—and then she took my hand, and it was a bit better. She is absolutely divine in every way! Dinner at Raffatin [et Honorine]'s, a mistake, as it was too expensive, but a lovely walk home along St. Germain—"can I kiss you in some doorway?" "Never mind the doorway." We were holding hands, and—I lost an earring. *Fine*† at Deux Magots—or was it the Flore?—and a wonderful night in which we hardly slept at all.

NOVEMBER 14, 1962

Again late starting, as C. likes to take a 45-minute bath, at least. We bought tickets for Victor after a wonderful lunch at L'Escargot Doré, which C. knew. Bottle of Pouilly Fumé—then a fire—and we are talking a bit better. As C. said, for people who're so voluble on paper, we are awfully quiet when we're together. To bed at 7, with some intention, which went by the board, of getting up at 9 for a movie. We did not even go out to dinner, but slept and made love all night—more or less. I adore

---

* Aldeburgh is a village in Suffolk, about ninety miles northeast of London, where Caroline and her husband seem to have a weekend house. Pat will move there in 1963, residing first at 27 King Street before purchasing Bridge Cottage in Earl Soham, Suffolk, where Caroline can visit her on the weekends.
† French for brandy.

her. And this morning she said: "I've never loved anyone the way I love you. I shouldn't say a thing like that, but I will anyway."

NOVEMBER 16, 1962

She is quite aware of her charms and & melts into my arms as if she were smelted by Vulcan expressly for that purpose. I can make love happily to her all night long, as I am never satisfied myself. When we wake up early, I make love to her again, twice. She was—and is—divine all night. Perhaps shy about me, because I am getting over the curse. We will see. (N.B. later: My fault. I was consistently shyer than she.) Then I came back to the Pas de Calais [hotel] and changed, to Laffont*—J. [Jean] Rosenthal. I spoke with Laffont—things are not impossible there, and it may—would be—a lot better than going to Gallimard, where I'd be swallowed up in a series. Robert Laffont, he says, did not want to take me away from a publisher who was doing well for me, but I hastened to assure him that my droits [royalty] statement was ludicrously small.

NOVEMBER 22, 1962

C. said she was "back in the old black pit" of herself again. I said, please wait, and don't worry. I said, "You mean you don't like me anymore?" Which she did not deny. She said she had lost contact with me. It was quite dreadful, as I thought it would last. "I have lost touch," she kept saying. I was frightened that it was all over, as C. said this always happened. She went off to lunch alone with [her friend] S. while I got some Diorissimo perfume for her and fixed my air ticket for 1 PM Sunday to London. When I came back to the hotel to meet C. between 1:30–2, I was so anxious I called Doris. C. did not arrive until 3:15—looking quite radiant and like herself again. She'd had two gins & a bottle of wine. And a discussion with S. which was all important, relieving her guilt.

NOVEMBER 23, 1962

How she gives herself! "Oh, darling, I love you," she says, & this morning under the sheet with the light on, my eyes filled with tears. Hers did at the Gare du Nord at 12:21 PM when the train was about to pull out. "*A lundi*,"† she said. We hastily took two pictures which may not come

---

* At this point, Pat considers changing publishers in France, either to Robert Laffont or Gallimard, her French translator Jean Rosenthal acting as her counsel.
† French for "See you Monday."

out. I have her film to take to America. Now—we have something quite
strong together. I am sure of it & so is she.

NOVEMBER 25, 1962

I got to my hotel by 2:45 London time. Quite adequate, a bit Victorian—
a letter from Caroline and what a marvelous one, written on begged
paper on the boat. [Her husband's] suspicions are rampant again, & C.
puzzles and confuses me by her desire to tell him to relieve the vague
melancholy, etc. that is bothering him now. I told her to wait, please, for
several days. Alas, he may litigate, or maybe he would litigate, if he knew
about C. and me. This is the very real difficulty and question for C. [Her
husband] is about to accept the fraction [he] has been offered, but he is
not pleased with it. Within a couple of days, he'll get the estimate of costs
for litigation & must come to a decision.

NOVEMBER 27, 1962

C. called at 9:05—I was there by 10:45 I think. Feeling and looking
awful, I'd done my packing and put my bag in the lobby. Then C. said,
somehow, in the bedroom, "Let's lie down on the bed." And the next
thing we knew we were in bed, C. in a most wonderful mood. She
smiled—"I feel like laughing!" she said. It was her mother's bed. Very
pretty posts, head and foot. We were there till the last possible moment
before we had to go to the air terminus.

DECEMBER 2, 1962

Up at 9, the latest since Europe. I got the MS of [*The Two Faces of*] *January* from Peggy's at 10. and made a beginning (79 pages) of reading
January with corrections. "Whenever I think of you (which is always),"
she writes, she feels a great joy, a great thankfulness. I pray to God as
she does that nothing happens to this. And to be honest, nothing could
happen, except that I betray her trust—but not even a catastrophe due to
Camilla could destroy us, I know. Only another girl could, on my part,
but that is impossible, and far from my thoughts—or abilities. I am reading about prisons—four books. I do miss her kisses—though I have had I
am sure more than a thousand, I want still more.

DECEMBER 3, 1962

Two letters from C. She was sick Thursday. So she excused her despon-
dency & her thoughts of telling [her husband] (which however still nag)
her difficulties with leading a "double life" on the grounds that she was

physically sick. Of course true, but the situation remains the same: I know she wants to tell him. Now—we must brace him, she writes, at least a month in advance about Positano. I wrote her on my feelings about a home plus possessions, & the fact that a reliable emotional relationship was of more importance to me than possessions and a home. How sordid & topsy-turvy were those years 1952–56, Ellen, Lynn, Jean P. and Doris—I told C. the essentials.

12/5/62

Beauty, perfection, completion—all achieved and seen. Death is the next territory, one step to the left. I don't want to see any more, to feel or experience any more. Anything else would be a lowering, would put me into the vegetable category. I have known beauty, dear boys, more than I—or if the truth be told, anyone else—would ever expect or extort by worldly ransom for worldly good behavior. Pleasure has already killed me, transformed and translated me. And in fact belonging to you, I have no right and no power to take my own life. I am the drunken bee wandered into your household. You may with courage eject me through the window; or by accident step on me. Be assured, I'll feel no pain. I have felt your fine red brown hair across my eyes, over my face as I lay half asleep, and I have felt your warm breath on my lips. In those moments I lived and died, was born and knew in anticipation death, and knew there was nothing more I need fear on this earth or anywhere else. In the wake of a ship, in the blue nothingness out the door of an airplane—I shall have no fear, my darling. I christen you my darling, my forever, my only love. To your kisses, your lips, I pledge my life.

DECEMBER 6, 1962

I got the photographs (Paris-London). One of C. on her front steps I am having enlarged. The one of her in Paris looks so happy! That one I should enlarge also. Today I almost loved cameras. Today a check for $471—checks are coming in this season.

DECEMBER 7, 1962

I have reread her four letters since Paris (3 since I saw her) and such passionate outpourings—not like mine, always conscious and careful, lest I make an ass of myself or frighten her. She does not worry about that. "All, all my love darling, past, present and future." "Such a perfect eleven days, such a perfect beginning—for our future" (she probably says it better). I cannot go on like this, I shall simply clear my complicated decks as best I can, & go over again to be with her. I'd like to do a short story & make a beginning on paper of the prison novel. But there is no use in making any further effort to live without her. I cannot. And in all my 41 years, I have never said or written this about anyone else before. It is (perhaps the not too distant future will show it) regrettable that I, [her husband] and Caroline are for our various reasons at that time in life when happiness will be no longer denied. I believe in mine. I shall not be selfish or pugnacious when the crisis (if there is one) comes. But neither will I be noble and disappear. We are all, dramatically speaking, in fighting mood, this may be bad, but at least it is sincere.

DECEMBER 9, 1962

I cannot do anything smoothly today. And I must return to my grim schoolgirl rituals, ½ hour or one hour of Italian now, 6 days a week of 5 hours' writing, plus some piano. Otherwise I shall go insane. I must envisage a life without Caroline, and this I cannot do. She says it more emphatically and certainly more often than I: "This is an admission: I cannot live without you." For the first time in my life, I really believe that someone loves me.

DECEMBER 11, 1962

Today I gave notice to my landlady, who said she was sorry to lose me as a tenant. I've not heard from Ellen H. C. makes me sick with desire and with love.

DECEMBER 12, 1962

I write her now these apparently perilous notes, folded within Carlton Hill letters. [Her husband] is at the boiling point, as I mentioned to her three days ago. She'll get today, Tuesday, 4 or five pieces of mail at the Haymarket, including the photographs. I said within six months I felt something would have to be said to [him]. Meanwhile let it go. It is ironic, silly—and so false, that the pretense for strictly social reasons must be kept up, while the emotions on which the social structure was originally built must be kept hidden. (Social mores being originally built on loyalty.)

DECEMBER 12, 1962

A marvelous day. I wrote business letters—to begin with. Germany bought *Deep Water*, France wants "Camera Finish" for television.* Slowly I begin to realize, to dare to believe what C. said to me in Paris: "I belong to you." And so forth. That I dare to write it, even, is unusual for me. I have learned to be cautious. But I wrote to her today, "You are the last person I'll ever love. I have never said this to anyone before."

DECEMBER 14, 1962

I felt very well today—mostly due to eating well, I am sure. I retyped the story 15 pages, finished except for the title. Today letters from Rolf, Ellen Hill, who advises me not to give up this house, therefore I got permission from my landlady, rather to my surprise, to sublet it. The prison book shapes up emotionally, which is better or as good as its shaping up in a plot way.

DECEMBER 16, 1962

Such unhappiness and loneliness as I felt today must be counteracted by work, or I shall go mad. 10:45 PM I have just written C. on this subject, asking how she feels about "convention"—which I didn't put in quotes. A more important letter I have never written to her, a more important question she will never have answered to me. I reminded her of the Paris episode, and of its implications, & of the form it took which was cutting me off, but that it came out as: "I have lost touch. This always happens." I said I did not want this to happen again, in the future, & I also said I was not at all bored or impatient with her domestic situation, but only wanted to know from her what form (outward) of life she thought she needed to make her happy. She may not get the letter before Thursday— ah, these delays! But how I shall await her answer! Such a day this has been! Gloomy, I can change my mood, with effort, as a ship's course is changed by a resetting of the sails. In one day, to have felt, as I did, my joy and richness in C.'s love, and to have felt the gloom of its possible loss, of her present absence (what a phrase!), that is a day to exhaust a stronger person than I. I derive much consolation, however, from being able to put it all down here.

---

* According to Pat's notes, this thriller short story was published as "Camera Finish" in the U.S. *Cosmopolitan* in 1960 and rereleased as "Camera Fiend" in *Ellery Queen's Mystery Magazine* in 1972.

DECEMBER 19, 1962

To Doylestown* by 10 AM: A large, Sing-Sing like place, with gun turrets, but clean and modern inside. I was not allowed in the long corridor. The prisoners were walking about freely in the corridor, their cells not locked.

DECEMBER 23, 1962

Yesterday a small package with two presents from mother & Stanley. They sent me a basket of fruit from Keith's and also a fruit cake. I retyped "Love Is a Terrible Thing" after alterations also. 13 pages with a carbon. My [Christmas] tree is quite pretty. But I long for Caroline after all. What else matters? The rest is a tedious form that I have to go through.

DECEMBER 28, 1962

And what on earth did I do today? No letter from C., anyway. I hauled out [the short story] "The Car" and went over it.

12/28/62

In depressed moments, remember—everything that you want can be obtained. Work, a vacation, a new coat, etc. That is what makes this the best of all possible worlds. Of course, the minute I write this, I think of C—And yet somehow I believe it, too.

DECEMBER 30, 1962

A storm, plus snow. Zero tonight & the worst yet in Bucks [County] for me. I finished typing "The Car," vacuumed the house, did the silver, & was otherwise virtuous without stirring out even to buy a newspaper, which would've been the *Inquirer* or the *Bulletin*, impossible after the *Times*. I hope so for a letter tomorrow. London Airport is closed today, as they have worse gales and snow. 10 below everywhere in these parts. I look forward to tomorrow and the Eve alone. 40 below in White River!

DECEMBER 31, 1962

3 letters from C. She is happy, tired (from Xmas) & tells of being trailed about London by the two bloodhounds—and reassures me that she would put her foot down "very firmly" if [her husband] ever objected to her seeing me frequently. Wants me to come to London in July for the Bolshoi Ballet at Covent Garden.

---

* The prison site that Pat visits to research her novel-in-progress, *The Glass Cell*.

1963–1966

ENGLAND, OR THE ATTEMPT TO SETTLE DOWN

1963–1964

A BUOYANT Patricia Highsmith spends the early part of 1963 packing up her house in New Hope and preparing for her move to Europe. Pat's perennial pecuniary concerns are no match for the thrill she feels having fallen in love again, this time with Caroline Besterman. A period of emotional upheaval lies in wait.

In mid-February, Pat's boat docks in Lisbon. From there, she continues on to the house she and Ellen Hill rented for a year in Positano, where she enrolls in art classes and spends much of her time drawing. Mentally prepared to live alone until Caroline ventures to join her, Pat immerses herself in work on her "prison book," *The Glass Cell*. A cry for help reaches her from London in early March: Caroline, torn between family obligations and her love for Pat, has suffered a nervous breakdown. The two lovers are granted a month in Italy following this episode, but ultimately Caroline must return to her family; by this point, her husband is aware of their affair. For the first and only time in her life, Pat seriously considers suicide.

This painful relationship, perhaps best characterized as one spent "together, but apart," will continue for four years. Some details find their way into *The Glass Cell* in the character of Hazel Carter, a wife and mother with conflicting love interests. The dramatic climax of the book, at least, is followed by something of a happy ending. In late summer, Pat and Caroline vacation together in Aldeburgh, a town on the North Sea in the county of Suffolk.

In early October, Pat sends the first draft of her prison novel to New York. Editor Joan Kahn rejects *The Glass Cell*, as she did Pat's prior novel, *The Two Faces of January*, and Pat finds herself without an American publisher. Moreover, she hasn't written—let alone sold—a short story in more than twelve months. In December, she retreats from Rome to a rented house in Aldeburgh.

A glimmer of hope emerges on New Year's Eve, when Pat learns that the American publishing house Doubleday has acquired *The Two Faces of January*. Her good fortune continues into the new year: the London-based publisher William Heinemann releases *The Two Faces of January*, which receives the Silver Dagger Award for best foreign crime novel by the Crime Writers' Association of England.

In the spring of 1964, Pat buys an eighteenth-century cottage in Earl Soham, a thirty-minute drive from Aldeburgh. For the most part, Pat lives like a recluse with her pet cats and snails (which she smuggles through customs between Britain and France many times by hiding them in her bra), with Caroline coming over to visit on the weekends. Pat also makes a number of friends in her new home, including writers Ronald Blythe and James Hamilton-Paterson. In early May, she begins the remarkably brief four-week planning period for her eleventh novel, with the cheery working title *A Lark at Dawn*. Incipient plotlines and other ideas can, however, be traced back to notebook entries from May 1963. Pat finishes the first draft by September, when she takes a trip back to the United States to pack up and ship her remaining belongings to England. She also meets with Larry Ashmead, her editor at Doubleday. He considers the new manuscript "very promising." Pat's English publisher, William Heinemann, is also impressed and releases the book—now called *A Suspension of Mercy*—in early 1965.

※

1/4/63

> And off a certain boat at Greenwich
> You took my hand descending,
> Slicing, swift, gentle, fatal,
> I was in love with you.
> One strong grip of four fingers—
> For the time it took me to gasp, in silence,
> And it was done.

1/19/63

> —What a pleasant thought, that I shall never go mad. I have always imagined worse. No reality could exceed what I have imagined, or surprise me. And what am I boasting about? A lucky set of genes, a good first three years. All yet to be proven, perhaps, but I am confident. Up, pipers! I am in love with a most wonderful woman. I am saved. Look me up in ten or twenty years, and see.

2/22/63

Lisbon. A vaguely messy and sprawled port. I walked inland some three blocks, then turned right for the "center." Little girls of about ten begging, barefoot and bare legged and in rags. Their lower legs are traced with pink veins—the onset of varicose? Or is it from the cold of this winter? I picked some *genêt*, broom, from the iron fence beside the pavement and stuck it in the buttonhole of my raincoat. It began to rain, then stopped and the sun came out, then it rained again. It was 4 P.M. I took a tram to the Rua de Oura. Jewelry shops, delicatessen, cafés, bought a gold chain for $30.00 American express Checks. Then a rather delicious espresso in a stand up and stool counter café. Saw *A Game for the Living* in a newspaper kiosk. A very serious and nice little boy passing out pink paper circulars about a folklore show at a night club tonight. He was in knickers, white stockings over his knees, a red vest. The railway terminus is Byzantine with an arched doorway, old statues of kings and heroes on the outside, modern inside. It resembles Spain more than anything else to me. The taxis are all Mercedes-Benz. Mostly the people look well off. The streets curve, leading to a monument. A man on horseback, a column.

Down by the port Joseph I in greening copper—or bronze—on horseback. A parking lot all around.

2/23/63

—In mood of schizophrenia, remember that there must exist the society which you are making fun of.

MARCH 1, 1963

[Positano.] Is this any better or not? I suppose it is. The third day of arranging the house and I am nearly done, having at last put my typewriter onto one of the two sagging desks that I had at first thought too weak to bear its weight. I wrote 12 lines (at 8 PM) of a short story, after a trip to Dr. Rispoli's for my cold and cough, now back in full force. He gave me Vitamin C intravenously. The lights went out just as I was sitting down to dinner. It is cold enough to snow tonight and I am sleeping downstairs. I am glad to be alone and in silence.

3/1/63

C. and I talk and talk, by means of letters. We want to let each other know what we are doing and thinking at nearly every minute of the day. That is really caring, love, communication, a desire to be one.

MARCH 2, 1963

At 2:30 P.M. the glass door blew in on the Via Monte. The *tramontana* today. I was too uncomfortable to write, and furthermore the doctor says my throat is red. Night cap chez Mimi with Beatniks. Most frightening. They burn cigarettes and have no discernible pride—unlike any young people I have ever really known. A letter from C. today. I love with all my soul. Whenever I think she cannot surpass herself, she does. How I love her—dangerously—with all my life.

3/3/63

The art of being content is the only necessary art. The rest is quite unnecessary. Purely ornamental. This may sound paradoxical. What-ever artist was content? I speak for and about myself. Without a certain degree of what I call contentment (within a life which the majority of people would call unsatisfactory and lacking in every possibility for con-tentment) I cannot even create anything. I cannot even think about it. Distractions and obligations put me on a different plane, a plane that has nothing to do with creativity or the artistic drive.

MARCH 7, 1963

Letters from [C.'s husband] and from C—very reassuring on [her hus-band's] part, not any better on C.'s. At 6:30 a telegram from both of them asking me to call, which I did at 8 P.M. The upshot is I go Sunday to London. I spoke with [her husband]—C—[her husband]—collect. She has had a psychiatrist since Tuesday. Consensus is I can cheer her up, therefore I shall go.

MARCH 8, 1963

Great news from Pat Schartle that Heinemann will publish *The Two Faces of January*. Interesting that I received [both] the rejection and acceptance in 15 Via Monte.

MARCH 9, 1963

A day of endless chores. This evening I prepared the house, liver for Spider, spoke with Signora Rispoli about feeding Spider [in my absence]. It seems I'll never have the tranquility or the time to work again. The prison book is in my head, but how ever to get it on paper?

MARCH 10, 1963

The flight to London was only 2 hrs. 10 minutes and quite beautiful. I was on time and called Caroline at 6 PM. All is well (reasonably) tonight. We love each other (I thought she might have forgotten) but she needs to get out, to take her thoughts from herself. She has laid enough bare in these last days to herself, psychiatrist & [her husband]. I am in the extra room upstairs.

MARCH 11, 1962

C. very melancholic & barely got out of bed. She moves very slowly. Last night's effort (the very nice dinner) was really too much for her. I slept badly. Had another sweat in the night & awakened freezing.

MARCH 12, 1963

C. had a great change for the better. I learned yesterday through C's real efforts to tell me, that her *crise*, her "nervous breakdown," is due to her first "real marriage, real emotional attachment," which is to me. She had somehow to be reassured by my coming here, so it was indeed important that I did. Today she said, "Why don't we go to bed. I think it might be good for you." So we did and no housework got done, but housework never made history. She is wonderful in bed and only astounds me by her appetite—I fear something may be wrong, that it may go as easily as it is so quickly formed again. I have never known a woman like her. She is quite to my taste.

I do think this will last. This fact also I have not assimilated yet. C. has to square it with her marriage, I with my solitude & my work. As I said to C. we must accept the facts as they are, that we shall continue to love each other, but that we cannot see each other, probably, more than three months out of the year. I read over *January* and made almost no changes.

MARCH 15, 1963

Day of departure. Trouble getting a taxi—at 9:40 AM. C. very tense at the take-off (Caravelle) but after 45 minutes on the airplane she looked out the window (and after a gin & tonic). I was sitting by the window. I'm so pleased, happy, even ecstatic to be with her and to help her get over some of her fears. Today really great progress, as she rode up in the elevator in the [Grand Hotel] Santa Lucia. The view of Naples was beautiful from our hotel room—the bay.

MARCH 22, 1963

Learned from MWA [Mystery Writers of America] that "The Terrapin" will win some award April 19th at the Astor dinner. I told Pat S. & asked if she could go for me. Failing that, Joan Kahn.

APRIL 7, 1963

We left by taxi at 10:30 for Naples after a boiled egg and sufficiently leisurely breakfast. C. was worried about the *gallerie*—but there were no real *crises*. It does help if she has something to do, such as having a meal. We arrived in Rome at fourish, went to the Hotel Condotti, where the room and bath was adequate, but not luxurious. Cocktails with Ellen at 7. Ellen as usual talked constantly, much to my annoyance and embarrassment.

APRIL 11, 1963

This morning we were very happy and I was very awake. We packed with the aid of a couple of gins. There was no time for lunch before she had to be at the Air Terminal at 1:00, but she could get lunch on the plane, which took off at 2:25 PM. I saw her plane take off, and then I went back on the bus to Rome. Two good things: She left in a good and true mood, and she wants me to come to Aldeburgh in July, in fact stay at the house,* which I said might be one straw too many. We shall see.

APRIL 17, 1963

Looked over the prison book material. It must well up once again. It is a thing I must write, and these last months of moving about plus the difficulty of the subject, have not been conducive to the welling up.

4/19/63

The continuation of McCarthy. Strong men shaking: they are afraid of losing their reputation and of losing their jobs. They are afraid, therefore they do not fight back. Analogy with the Hitler situation. Men who were afraid of losing their lives—not only their jobs and standing. The point was, nobody fought back until it was too late. This has very nearly been happening in America. These are two forms of fear, nothing more. Is every nation capable of such fear? Hitler had the Jews to hate, America the Communists. Hatred, so artificially created in both cases, is like an

---

* Caroline and her husband's weekend retreat in Aldeburgh.

injection of cancer virus in the population. We had and have this virus still, just as the Germans still have theirs.

4/21/63

What did I live on, how did I live before this? Other loves I have known, but none like this, where I am met completely—in words and in actions—and to be without her is so difficult to understand and therefore to endure. It is now taking all I have in the way of patience, in the way of effort. It is senseless not to be with her. And the difficulty is to render myself totally senseless also so that I can accept the fact I am not with her. It is so senseless, it is even difficult to compose a logical sentence about it.

APRIL 22, 1963

Today far happier, because I worked better. My book looks better today—much grim work ahead, but it is alive and that is what matters. I had simply thought it was dead. I had another evening alone, which slowly revives me. I am happy and confident in my love—and that is everything. So great is she that my own life no longer belongs to me, to preserve or to destroy. I shall do with it what she wishes.

4/24/63

—My present life (very quiet) in Positano. Quite the opposite of going through life with every nerve exposed. To be able to feel happiness, or at least contentment, for days or weeks at a time only—that's a necessity for me, because "life" as an entity has never presented a picture of calm contentment, even in my imagination or my boldest dreams.

4/25/63

—Every day around 1:10, I manufacture a crisis in regard to the post. The post is due at 1:20 approximately. I cannot work after 1:10, and sew on a button or straighten my room to pass the time. Finally, I start fixing lunch, though I cannot eat before the post, and turn it off at ten to 2. The post is always late in Italy. The post is like an incurable disease that one must learn to live with.

4/25/63

—God, like nature, is completely indifferent to our problems and sufferings here below. God is completely indifferent as to whether I behave well or badly.

APRIL 27, 1963

I am at a time in my life when the themes I wish to write about are greater than I myself have been heretofore. Lest this sound pompous, I merely mean that I must now work at a speed more in keeping with these themes & with the complex thoughts & emotions I wish to express. This is only difficult for me, because on the surface it seems that I'll have to work more slowly. Not necessarily true. At any rate I am really happy and more happy I think than I have yet realized. I am happy because of C.'s love for me, which I believe (because she says so) is something that will endure. If she will, I certainly will. As for the prison book, I have yet to strike the vein—in the French sense. The prison part is difficult—but by no means beyond me. On the contrary, I am only confused by the great many things I have to say.

MAY 1, 1963

To p. 88. Today a holiday. I worked pretty well & am very happy. A truly horrible and frightening depression came over me, produced by many things: I think even of killing myself, if anything goes wrong between me and Caroline (what could probably hold me back is the knowledge of how upsetting it would be for her). My bronchitis is no better, a bad pain in the chest when I cough. My book is not yet going under its own steam, the repair of these 104 pages is like all repair work tedious & uninspiring. And of course middle age is now quite upon me, and at night my eyes show signs of deterioration. All this—plus the utter hopelessness of ever living with C. for more than the briefest stretches.

5/1/63

This is the end of my life. That can have a disastrous as well as a happy meaning. And yet, even if it be disastrous, it happily and heroically is. I am happy as I have never been, nor is much on the surface happy as underneath, where she has churned me up, made me myself again, and opened depths in myself which I will explore as much as I shall try to learn about hers. To each other we have given each other—like two rocks splitting after having collided. I do not want anything else in life.

MAY 2, 1963

Also letter from Tex, who has not been receiving mine. She has been using my car all this time (2½ months) which I am a bit annoyed about, as I did not give her leave. Told her the Pa. [Pennsylvania] State Police are looking for it. I won only second prize in the MWA [Mystery Writers of America] awards. A raven scroll. First went to a *Cosmo* story.

5/4/63

It is not one woman, but the idea of a woman that I love. It is for this rea-son that I appear to be (or am sometimes) fickle. But what I set out to do, love and be loved in return, is very difficult to achieve over any length of time for a variety of reasons, therefore I do not, cannot honestly say I am fickle. One I want, for all time.

5/9/63

On happy nights, everything seems perfect, excellent, or at least on the way to being excellent. On other nights, everything seems unfinished, a mess, a bore all—not as good as it should be. I like to work "hard" with my nose rather close to the grindstone, assessing every day's work severely. Only then can I feel happy and satisfied with myself. I would never tell this to anyone else. It sounds smug.

5/9/63

—Are the great books of the mid–twentieth century only those that tell what is wrong with our civilization and our time? They are the most interesting to the majority just now. Due to Freud, or American self-doubt? I don't believe at all such books are or ever will be the greatest. Art is not made by griping or by grinding an axe.

MAY 15, 1963

I continue to live mostly on spaghetti with meat sauce! I am at p. 170 of my novel as of yesterday. Ph. [Philip Carter]* is just getting out of prison. I feel "stuck" as (I thought) the remainder of the book is not precisely worked out. Actually, this is not it: it is the mental state of Ph. [Philip] that is not worked out. However, I stewed over the plot all afternoon.

MAY 16, 1963

Raining like yesterday. I wrote to Ethel Sturtevant about my life—my difficulties with the bank and with car & house! A real jeremiad! It is difficult to keep my spirits up—unless I am plunged into work. I wish

---

* The hero of her new novel-in-progress, *The Glass Cell.*

Lil Picard were here. We would talk and laugh. I am working on a small painting of a man opening a door for a huge Siamese cat.

MAY 22, 1963

I am a bit hungover today, did seven pages. I must collect myself before going further. The mediocre reviews from London on the [*Cry of the*] *Owl* are not doing me any good. It is time I had a break—and yet it will be a week before Ellen or Lil arrive. There is not enough distraction here of the kind I need—a good movie, a good friend, music. I have been rather too intense of late—and cannot keep it up longer than a month, and it has been. But a most beautiful woman is in love with me. All will take care of itself. I have nothing, nothing to worry about in the world!

5/24/63

—When writing a book—how often do I forget that I ever worried about other books! Now on P. 207—I worry—a terrible four days of abeyance and self-doubt here. It is caused by two other things: too intense work for the past five weeks, followed by a loss of vision of the theme of the book. I am only undecided whether to put it aside for two weeks, or to use the brain, which I seldom do, to put myself on the track again. Shall try the latter today, at any rate.

MAY 29, 1963

Lil Picard arrived at 1:30 PM. I met her at the bus. Lil is at the Buca [di Bacco hotel], as my steps are too much for her blood pressure. She will be here for a month, & has $900 for this, and 2 weeks in Paris. So she wants to work tomorrow, needs my typewriter, which she is most welcome to. ᴳIn the mornings.ᴳᴳ Thus my holiday with her will not be a holiday. Just as well. I must get back to my routine work, sunning, & the French dictionary. I am only happy, after all, working hard, expecting & receiving letters from C. This is my whole life, & it is a good one.

JUNE 3, 1963

Good news from C. The *New Statesman* has a good piece about me in the current issue, which C. is sending. Also Hachette Livre de Poche* will take *Le Meurtrier* [*The Blunderer*], *Eaux Profondes* [*Deep Water*], and

---

* In 1953, Henri Filipacchi and Guy Schoeller introduced an adapted version of American publisher Simon & Schuster's "Pocket Books" for the French market. They were an overnight success.

M. Ripley. $600 each. More dough for Margot J. [Johnson] alas.* Still this cheered me considerably. I was in no condition to work today. The Pope [John XXIII] died around 6 PM. I have no comment on this.

JUNE 4, 1963

I stewed all day over Pascal's *Pensées* and my own plot, getting nowhere until 11:45 this PM when I thought that—Ph. [Philip Carter] should go a bit more berserk, which is quite within his character. Am at a spot in which anything can happen from now on. These inevitable days. Lil wants to go to Capri & to Paestum—I only to Paestum, still I must be agreeable and take some days off for her. I so want to have a first draft done before going to England.

JUNE 8, 1963

I "thought" a bit more on my novel, but cannot get a word out. The presence of Ellen and Lil (to whom I owe more hospitality than I have been showing) does not help, but mostly I am "afraid" of going too fast. In two weeks in June, if I still have them, I can finish the first draft. *The New Statesman* arrived with the excellent piece on me by Francis Wyndham,† the best general review I have had. Two columns also—*Un jeu pour les Vivants* [*A Game for the Living*] of Calmann-Lévy is in a tan hardcover with a cheap looking jacket.

6/18/63

In an English review of a book of Gide—some comments on his persistent interest in violence and that this was "undoubtedly" tied up with his homosexuality. Is it? It is easy to think of other homosexual artists who have not this interest in violence (in Gide, violence as a "Necessity" to man). I can only think at this point that homosexuality—or rather society—enforces a strict and painful repression on all homosexuals, and this is bottled up energy. It is maddening to see some clot of a man fondling a girl whom you would like to touch yourself.

JUNE 19, 1963

Lil says my "blood is all alcohol" and went from insult to worse insult to get an effect.

---

* Pat's former agent Margot Johnson negotiated the contracts and was therefore entitled a percentage of the royalties.
† Francis Guy Percy Wyndham (1924–2017) was a British author and journalist.

JUNE 20, 1963

I did 7 pages to 305—A letter from Pat Schartle saying [her literary agency] C.S. [Constance Smith] Associates have merged with McIntosh & Otis, Inc. of 18 E. 41 St. Pat sounds very happy about it. She has bought out Connie's share & will be a director "& all that jazz." Pat reports an English movie interest in the [*Cry of the*] *Owl*, by no means definite. Would be a $22,500 thing, or $15,500 should it go through.

JUNE 21, 1963

Plopped, sad, and self-absorbed, as always at the end of a book. P. 312 today. Shall finish Monday.

JUNE 27, 1963

Finished my book at 4:30—341 pages. I did nothing to celebrate—but I feel quite happy—elderly, wise, somewhat virtuous.

7/1/63

There is something naked about poetry, such an awful sticking-the-neck-out—well, in every art. Today I am supposed to take my own three drawings to an art gallery to leave them there for sale. How I dread it. Yet without this ᶠannoyingᶠᶠ kind of enterprise, nothing happens. I do the same thing when I send a manuscript to a publisher. But it is nearly as painful as looking for a new house and moving.

JULY 3, 1963

No sleep. Quite wonderful to come to London—on schedule—and C. in her dressing gown to open the door! I had a gin & she coffee at the dining room table then a nap—then a lunch of lamb chops. We took a car with all the cats to Aldeburgh. Quite like a dream come true. A letter from Ellen Hill—Tex returned my car to Meyer after the registered letter. I have written Ellen that I want my things stored.

7/14/63

Aldeburgh. Full of the atmosphere and domestic decor which I call 1910 or Edwardian, for want of a more precise period name. Actually, I do not know what it is—non-U furnishings of pseudo-Jacobean, bad oriental rugs, and too much clutter in the rooms. After Italy what strikes one is the lack of greenery and flowers. The sea front is bleak with trim houses, each with its straight front walk between chest-high cement or brick walls. Up a few steps and into a foyer with prints of maps of Suffolk or à la Turner landscapes. The stairs are carpeted. All is quite clean. A young mother airs her diapered child in a pram or on a blanket on the front walk. The beach is too windy & chill even in mid-July and underfoot there is shale—rather pointed stones of which flints make up a good many. Rows of upended logs called groins go at right angles to the shore into the sea, disappearing, and at their highest are five feet, most being about three feet high. The sea is a gray, gray green. On the horizon are oil tankers, mostly going toward London, southward. The main street, the High Street, is lined with shops. At least three butchers, a chemist's, the Post Office and bank, several Greengrocers', the Louvre—a clothing store for men, women & children, where I bought a sheepskin rug for 65. The Aldeburgh Jubilee Hall, very small, is the theater for the annual June music festival presided over by Benjamin Britten. In summer, residents rent out their houses and flats for goodly sums. The roads around go immediately into moist green countryside, the road bordered by six feet high grasses, two-lane. The trees look like Fragonard sketches, lower branches wrapping about the trunk. Only one tobacconist sells Philip Morris [cigarettes].

JULY 23, 1963

C. feels that I have grown distant and sad—not really true. Pre-curse, perhaps—so I begin drawing again, because she says I haven't been. She is most sensitive in these matters. Actually, I think of the flying days and of the tedious days of work ahead when I'll have to be sustained by work alone, not by kisses, food, and the sight of her face and figure everywhere around me.

JULY 28, 1963

Have decided Rome is the best choice of a place to winter—so long as I have not enough money in hand to contemplate buying a house. Money—I have decided to produce one short story per month besides my book work. Plots are my best asset & I must exploit it. Have discussed all this with C. who is most patient. She will visit me in Rome if I have an apartment there.

AUGUST 5, 1963

[Positano.] Read 50 pages of *The Prisoner* and liked it better than I had thought. By before Aug. 31, I should have it polished for typing up.

8/8/63

Women have not evolved in the same sense as men have. Women are
still not only conservative but primitive. They are inclined to give
food and assistance only to those to whom they are personally related.
This attitude is fatal to the progress of civilization. They are even now
staunch backers of such primitive sports as wrestling and boxing. They
are currently making the male sex baffled as to what they really want.
They really (first things first) want a husband and children. They act
upon this wish very early, and acquire them. Why all this complaining
afterward? It is for women themselves to make jobs for themselves, to
see where they fit into the economic world, or if they fit in at all. It is
not for them to gripe about in circumstances which at twenty-one, and
with a college education, they might have foreseen. Let them go back to
school for advanced degrees, if they wish, but shut up about it. There
would be jobs for women, if women would give, and if they could be
depended upon to give, the major part of their time and energy to them
that is what jobs today demand. If a woman asks time off in summer
(a long time) to spend with her children on vacation, then she will be
given a respectively unimportant job. She has no right to ask for better. Women have not yet come to terms with the fact that they cannot fully combine a home and family with a really demanding job or
career outside the home—unless they are able to have servants, as few
women are. And it is only the exceptional woman, that is one able to
concentrate well in a short span of time, who is able to be a good writer
or painter or anything else within the home, while taking care of children and cooking and caring for a husband. Women are, alas, showing
themselves more infantile and incapable than ever in whining about
their lot in 1963.

AUGUST 13, 1963

Much noise & disturbance, the noisier of the two days of Ferragosto.*
Spider is marvelous & catches lizards during the worst gunfire.

8/18/63

If I had known at the age of twenty,
Seeing a picture of you at the age of sixteen,
"This girl will be mine,

---

* On August 15, predominantly Catholic Italy celebrates the Assumption of Mary and most companies,
shops, and industries close until mid-September for their summer break.

This the one destined forever,"
How I would have stopped my adolescent tears,
Stunned with a miracle a little greater
Than any I ever read about in the Bible.
I wonder how I would have waited
(Believing, of course, unshakably in you)
For fate to throw us together in twenty-one years?
Half a lifetime, a whole lifetime at twenty!
I would have thought, "Fantastic wait!"
Your picture with flowing dark hair,
Young, calmly arrogant eyes,
Lips of disciplined curiosity
And of promises unrevealed, unknown even to you.
Could I have waited without seeking you out?
Such metaphysical predictions never happen.
I fumbled on through my youth,
In fact, I never saw your picture at sixteen,
Until the twenty-one years had passed.
Now with the courage of my years,
So different from the courage of a twenty-one year-old.

AUGUST 21, 1963

After some more stewing, I decided I must begin typing up the prison
book, so I did. Shall try to cut as I go, as it is about 320 at present. Can-
tani will make me a "proposition" of heat, maid service, midday meal
chez moi, for the winter. She needs a tenant. She has not quoted a price. I
wrote to Ellen about this. I am on the fence, because C. might visit me in
Rome, if I had an apartment, in Nov. or Feb. On the other hand, it might
be better if we saved our money for a house. I have written her about
these alternatives.

8/21/63

For men, war provides pain and possibly death. It is this they are after,
this that is the male counterpart of women's masochism in childbirth.
Etc. Masochism (and sadism) are quite equally divided between men
and women. I am interested very much in this because it is part of the
causes of war. War is a psychological sickness of man. We should always
have been interested in curing it, but only now (rather late) that the more
destructive bombs have been invented, have we decided to become more
worried, about this psychosis.

AUGUST 21, 1963

Found an apartment via Ellen & the Domus Agency at 38 Via dei Vecchiarelli—near Castel Sant' Angelo [in Rome]. One room with balcony.

9/21/63

—The mind of a drunk wanders, to himself. The drinker drinks for his own audience. Therefore the person who asks (or who apes) the challenging question, "Do you drink alone?" does not at all understand the drinker.

OCTOBER 18, 1963

A month of slow wearing down due to lack of sleep. The Circolo Vecchia Roma and Circolo della Caccia here keep the big doors banging until 3 AM and sometimes later. I finished typing my MS & called it "The Glass Cell," posted 188 pages airmail to Pat [Schartle] Oct. 3, and should hear any day from Harper. Wrote a short story called "The Suicide on the Bridge" and also 3-page synopsis for Maurice Evans ("Vengeance") which he asked for—wanting a low budget idea for a movie. No incoming money save $25 from E.Q. [Ellery Queen] for the reprint of "The Terrapin" included in E.Q. Mystery Mix published Sept. 1963. I have touched the depths in the last days, being worn down by constantly interrupted sleep. I have put an ad today in the Messaggero to rent this place—not easy if I am honest and say it is 4 AM before one can sleep, then at 7 traffic. Last night at 5 AM a delivery of bricks next door. For one hour. How deeply I regret having left my dear Positano, where life was so tranquil and cheap also.

OCTOBER 23, 1963

Wed. Packed some cartons. I hope to leave for London Oct. 31 or Nov. 1. Slept and feel much better. Monday Oct. 21 from Harper (Joan K.) a letter saying my 188 pages are very slow, characters unidentifiable with, & they must see the rest before they give me a contract. This is a disappointment, but an emotional relief. I am optimistic. Life goes on. I spend more than I earn, that seems to be life. $1400 due soon from France, where Strangers has recently sold 40,000 [copies] in pocketbooks.

OCTOBER 26, 1963

My gloom doesn't lift. Everything has gone wrong this year, financially, with the sole exception of Heinemann's buying January. I have not sold anything I have done in the last 15 months. Is there any wonder I am discouraged? Hope springs eternal, but physical energy sometimes does not.

DECEMBER 1, 1963

A bad, hectic November just over. Harper rejected *The Glass Cell* out of hand, Enders may not pick up the *Price of Salt* option—and all in all, my financial precariousness is doing as much as I ever could by "bad behavior" (which I've not yet been guilty of) to shake C. & me. I bought a white Volkswagen Nov. 9—insuring it at £42,10. Was busy with Heinemann proofs of *The Two Faces of January*. I saw B. [Brian] Glanville & family for tea mid-November. He is doing well just now with U.S. magazine sales, *Mlle.* [*Mademoiselle*] & *Holiday*. Meanwhile I have not sold anything written in the last 16 months, so my ego is at its lowest. Harper says the prison book is full of self-pity, that Carter does not come through. These are days when I do not think the writing of a diary is silly. It is a big crisis in my life. These anxious days (when C. says I am so different from the July days when I was on holiday) have exposed to her & me the tremendous differences in our characters, weltanschauung, ideals & goals. We have admitted them. I have said to her, they can either be a strength for us, or we can let them tear us apart. At least my lease here [in Aldeburgh] goes only till Easter, with an escape clause Jan. 7.

12/3/63

—Aldeburgh. Paper-bags move crazily, like frightened cats and dogs in front of the headlights of my car. The sound of the wind becomes confused with that of the sea by night, and unfortunately it is an enemy, the wind, because it is always interfering with something I am trying to do— to open or close a door, to round a corner, to hang onto my parcels while pulling the scarf away from my face so I can see. One evening the waves were ten feet high, pounding on the beach, and the wind came from the NE: I am told the NW wind is worse, "Piling up the water," also raising the carpets mysteriously. It is hard to imagine anyone wintering here by choice.

DECEMBER 14, 1963

Letter from Jack Matcha saying he likes the snail story ["The Snail-Watcher"] very much and will publish it in Feb. Good! In *Gamma*. Today it went to 32°—and I spent much of the day stopping holes & cracks—front & kitchen door. 20 things assault me as soon as I get out of bed. All the dull mechanical things of life—even duller here setting them down. I hope that in my curious way these arduous but lovely days are preparatory to another bash at the *Glass Cell*. I have *not* as yet any revolutionary ideas as to how to revise it.

12/18/63

The taste of death is sometimes in my mouth, these solitary evenings.
Each day I live means one day less to live.
That's evident!
Before I die, I'd spend some time with her,
Just living.
Mornings are frantic, like all mornings,
The too fresh mind incapable
Of the maniacal decisions that produce art.
Exhausted by afternoon, I have completed my chores,
And am faced with myself and my hot-self again.
Then I work. I work like a worm in the earth,
I work like a termite fashioning a tunnel, a bridge.
I work for a future I can no longer see.
That's my life.
Will I in five years, two years, one,
Gnash my teeth again (teeth long ago gnashed to bits)
And curse what I hesitate to call my fate, my pattern?
Or should I call it my stupidity?
Who but an imbecile would have chosen such a hard way?
Or shall I in five years or one,
Grow like an oak dressed in evergreen.
Happiness having swollen in me, become me,
Because of the devotion which she swears?
This I argue with myself on paper.
That is what I feel like sometimes,
Paper.
Thin, perishable, burnable, tearable.
Matterless.

DECEMBER 30, 1963

A day of chores & letter writing. A letter from Pat Schartle just before Xmas—Doubleday will take *January* if I cut 32 pages. And *EQMM* bought "Who Is Crazy?" thus breaking my 17-month jinx—since meeting C.

1/2/64
> A quiet room in the country.
> A candle burns by the bedside.
> A warm yellow light is on our pillows.
> In this scene that Vuillard would have loved, too,
> Lie all my expectations
> Of beauty, all over the world,
> Strange rivers, cities, woods,
> And avenues—like the one in Paris
> Where we first kissed in public.
> My love, let us not disparage
> The magic lantern of our country room
> Where a candle burns by our bed.

JANUARY 3, 1964
> A good day's work—on what might have been finished three years ago—
> *January.* Cutting & so forth. Telegram from Daisy Winston in Amster-
> dam that she arrives tomorrow. I am delighted that Daisy got the Stewart
> family papers.*

3/15/64
> *To Spider*
> To my dear cat I address these lines
> Your yellow eyes will never read.
> By the trust implicit in your love for me,
> You have outdone me, demonstrating
> That life consists in a delicate webbing
> Of spider-thin threads flung out into space—
> And on them we walk, the brave and living ones
> Like us, before we know if they will hold our weight.
> You and I would walk anyway.
> I went away from you, on a thin strand,
> And having no other love, you were more loyal
> And abandoned.

---

* Pat's maternal grandmother's family papers, which Daisy Winston presumably gathered up in Pat's
New Hope home.

MARCH 22, 1964

I go to Paris 28th March, after much tax consulting. *P. of S.* [*The Price of Salt*] money hanging fire and this is of influence in my buying Bridge Cottage, Earl Soham, which C. so much likes also. Today an insane blast of 29 pages longhand from my mother, dredging up all the sludge of ancient time, like a bitter old woman with nothing else to do. It upset me despite myself, though I ought to be used to it.

MARCH 25, 1964

I am calming down somewhat after 36 hours after my mother's letter, I regret it bothers me this much, but it is never pleasant to be called a liar. As I mentioned to C. this is her way of "erasing" the truth she will not face. It all stems from this, plus a strange sexual jealousy—as if I were male. She craves my attention, devotion, etc. hence is so jealous of the women in my life. I walk more along the beach, the weather is so much nicer! It is good to feel free, if temporarily, of my bank.

4/1/64

Paris. Easter Time. I am in the Rue Jacob, [Hôtel] des Marronniers. A view of the spire of St.-Germain-des-Prés out my fifth-floor window. The clock there strikes three times at 7 PM. And apparently at every hour. Tall recently clipped chestnut trees in the yard below. A typical view of skylights, gray, slanting tin roofs, a wretched triangle, gable window with a flowerpot on the sill, a window that would be charming in a house, but I know some person lives there with all worldly effects in one room. My room is clean and new, but walls are paper-thin. I am next to a much-frequented WC. What were you going to tell me about San Francisco? Such a masculine voice, very accented, as he enters a girl's room.

6/2/64

Life, pursuing, thread
Through the extraneous.
I gasp for breath,
Forced to live too long
In the atmosphere of the airless.
My love walks here and breathes freely.
She is a bird and I am a fish,
Or perhaps she is a fish, I'm a bird,

At any rate, we breathe different nourishments.
Even gravity is against me
As I typewrite on the floor.
Is the house upside down? Yes.
All my whites are black here,
And vice versa.
I am big and strong enough to laugh at it.
It is a part of the mockery, the great vest,
Life itself. Only an idiot like me
Takes it seriously.

JULY 1, 1964

After 2 months, ten days in Bridge Cottage, I am working away on the
Suffolk-set book.* P. 151.—C. may come up this week, she wants to, but
in London it is one obligation after another—Succubi I call them, visiting
firemen. She jumps out of a frying pan into a fire, if she can find one. In
London cat sitting June 3 15, I typed the Stewart family papers and am
now proofreading them.

8/1/64

My love, don't falter,
Or I will, too.

SEPTEMBER 3, 1964

Some tumultuous weeks, during which I discovered I have to be alone in
the house to work. I do not think the difficulty is due to anything in C.,
just in me. Today, alone since six days (before C. was here for 10) I had
the first decent day's work, and feel I am master of the book and not vice
versa. Polishing up the 256 pages—much of which was sloppy due to my
lithe plowing on.

SEPTEMBER 4, 1964

Splendid day, did 15 pages—to new P. 250. May finish tomorrow. Psychologically—(how else is anything?) something is coming to a *crise.* I am
resentful of not having her when I want her—and of having her so rarely,
really, that I am not used to working with her. It should be an everyday

---

* Pat's novel *A Lark at Dawn* (working title) will be published the following year in the United States as
The Story-Teller (New York, 1965) and the UK as *A Suspension of Mercy* (London, 1965).

occurrence working and being with her—not such strange and heady wine. Now she believes simply I cannot work with her, period. It is not so simple. I am vaguely depressed tonight, my only joy from the fact the book is nearly done—simple, but entertaining, I hope.

9/4/64

Her most powerful (i.e. exciting also) memories are of childhood experiences and atmospheres. The atmosphere was one of security. The result is a retreat from active participation in life. The theater she likes is the traditional sort, for the most part. Mozart and Strauss seen again and again, Callas doing old favorites. Books she discusses are childhood books—*Winnie the Pooh*—and England's familiarity with it was what swung her from France to England as a place to live. (Not the French language which she mastered at a later date than Winnie.) Even such retreat could lead to great inner strength, yet her strength is shaken by any change in circumstances, routine—almost the manner of making a bed. Airplane trips terrify her, and murmured, frantically murmured prayers give no strength either. Doubt of my love shook her recently (doubt that I loved her) and this came about because my love was shaken first by her visible ᶠlack of courageᶠᶠ—about airplane trips, about life in general, about any sort of risk to her status quo. This at a time when I have risked and changed so much to be with her struck me as abhorrently selfish, stupid—and of course unloving on her part. She loves me, but she loves security better. Since I have long believed and felt that courage is the essence of womanhood (and gentleness of manhood) this was like seeing my image of her blasted before my face. I could not put all this into words and watch her crumble further. I like simplicity, devotion, even the clinging to routine that is characteristic of women— but what am I to do about this depressing absence of courage? Were I to be in the balance against the weight of "security," I know which she would choose. A fox in a cage in a zoo has security, but this is not life for the fox.

SEPTEMBER 8, 1964

Failed for the second time the driving test. This time "stewing" as they do not like a hand or fingers on the spoke. Also gears—which I did well; and know not how to improve. I am sure it looks good on their record to fail the average candidate three times, in view of the accident rate, which is due to dangerous roads rather than drivers.

SEPTEMBER 10, 1964

Snails all wizened but two which moved today. Tomorrow the driving test. I have tried to memorize the Highway Code, as they are such sticklers. I think Germany would not have been so tough.*

SEPTEMBER 10, 1964

I do not look forward, emotionally speaking, to this weekend. [C.'s husband] is fighting his battle also, and with such quiet, insinuating methods, simply [by] being present as a wedge between us.

11/8/64

England. The disciplinary aspects still impress me most, after a year here. America is lax, a child's paradise by comparison. The liquor and cigarette prices, quite out of ratio to the average wage, proclaim that they are disciplinary measures also. Do you really need this liquor and that pack of cigarettes? No, you are a depraved, self-indulgent, unhealthy slob, and the exorbitant price is your just punishment for being addicted. Your penalty for wanting a beer after the theater is missing the last bus; it'll cost you seven shilling now to get home; the fares go up at night. (The barman, too, has announced it is almost closing time when you have ordered the beer.) In New York, one can eat or drink at any hour of the day or night. The subways never close, though they may be a bit slower. One can buy any kind of food on Sundays at delicatessens in every neighborhood. The British restraint makes for resentment in me at least. It is militant, juvenile.

12/15/64

My self-esteem has a duration of not more than twenty-four hours.

12/16/64

For the Notes on Suspense (*The Writer*).†

Suspense writers, present and future: Remember you are in good company. Dostoyevsky, Wilkie Collins, Henry James, Edgar Allan Poe . . . there are hacks in every kind of literary field. There are hack journalists, and journalists with genius. Aim at being a genius. It is,

---

* Pat took driving lessons in Munich in 1951, but abandoned the pursuit shortly before she could pass her driver's test.
† Pat is starting to prepare her piece on *Plotting and Writing Suspense Fiction* for the magazine *The Writer* (1966).

after all, ninety percent effort, ninety percent the standards one sets for oneself, whether one is a genius or not. The other ten percent is the unknown, the unteachable, the untouchable, the indestructible thing called talent. Without talent—which is an eye for the dramatic, a zest in fixing it on paper for the delectation of others—hard work will not put one at the top, and may not get one even published. Have you talent? Do you enjoy telling stories and seeing your audience spellbound? Good. You should do this for your friends every weekend for practice, and then—if you are so inclined—start putting it down on paper. Talent is of course something magical, but no more than storytelling is magical. Can you make your audience hang on your words? Or if you are too shy even to tell a story to a group of friends, can you tell it well in a letter? Who can say how this is done? It is magical and unteachable. But its essence is the entertainment the narrator derives from the writing or the telling.

12/19/64

—The love that is madness will last forever; it's the only kind of love that does.

12/26/64

By your love for me
(And mine for you,
A shattering experience!)
You lay me open like a rock.
I am full of fissures, holes,
Lumps, hollows, knots,
Even abysses. Small wonder
Sometimes I look at you
And feel myself a monster,
And proceed to act like one.
Small wonder I would both kiss your feet
And imagine beating you cruelly.
I would make you laugh and cry
To show myself my power
For your power over me
Is embarrassingly great.
This is not the right analysis,
But it is half right.
You are the other half,

Which remains a mystery,
That other half in the scales
Which makes them balance,
So there is neither foot-kissing nor beating.
But you who believe in wonders
Should not wonder in these wonders.

12/28/64

Sometimes I remind myself of a small, rather intelligent mouse trying to dig its way out from the center of a mountain of sand which has fallen upon it. The mountain of sand is my brain, and the mouse is me, whatever it is.

1965–1966

PATRICIA HIGHSMITH'S once euphoric relationship with Caroline Bester-man nears its somber end. For three years, Pat has tried and failed to convince Caroline to commit; so Pat begins to travel more frequently, hectically, writing wherever she goes, and Caroline rarely visits her at Bridge Cottage in Suffolk, the little house that gets deathly cold in winter.

To combat the chill in early 1965, Pat chops wood, builds bookshelves and small tables, and works. She writes *Plotting and Writing Suspense Fiction*, a handbook for aspiring writers that will be published the following January, and offers considerable autobiographical insight. Pat also ruminates on a range of topics—from Jesus Christ and suicide to religion and unrequited love—that will appear in her forthcoming novel, *Those Who Walk Away*, a thriller without a corpse set in Venice.

In early May, Mary Highsmith comes to visit. The visit is a disaster, and is followed by the steady deterioration and ultimate collapse of the mother-daughter relationship. During Mary's visit, Pat is approached by the BBC to write the screenplay for *The Cellar*, a made-for-TV thriller that airs in September. This collaboration leads to other screenwriting projects, including a religious TV drama called *Derwatt Resurrected*; although the show is never produced, it contains the plotline for Pat's second Ripley novel. The story is inspired by painter Allela Cornell, the ex-girlfriend Pat revered during her freewheeling twenties in New York, and who died from complications following a suicide attempt.

After Mary's departure, Pat and Caroline travel to Venice, but it isn't the relaxing getaway hoped for. In response to Pat's attempts at intimacy, Caroline distances herself. To compensate, Pat draws, researches the setting for *Those Who Walk Away* on location, and then travels around Europe by herself, seeking out the comfort of old friends.

After finishing *Those Who Walk Away*, Pat vacations in Hammamet, Tunisia, with her old friend from New York, painter and fashion designer Elizabeth Lyne. Pat records her at times derogatory impressions of North

Africa in a travelogue for the *New Statesman* and in her next novel, *The Tremor of Forgery.*

In September, Pat's peregrinations take her to the south of France. She meets with film director Raoul Lévy, who hopes to enlist her help on his screenplay for *Deep Water.*

After Pat's final attempt to patch up her relationship with Caroline in Paris, their erstwhile city of love, and after Caroline's rejection of Pat's proposition to live together in London, the pair break up in October, leaving Pat so devastated that words fail her completely for the rest of the year.

2/1/65

There is seldom enough strength left to scream when dying, otherwise I think more people would.

2/10/65

Winter in England
    Once more I balk, my mind
    Unutterably bored and depressed
    By sameness. Therefore, I will not
    Utter—anything. Shut up.
    Then I am wretched.
    Oh, God, a potted plant can stop growing
    In winter, a snail hibernate,
    A tree shed its beauty and stand still,
    But what can I do in this hyperborean realm
    That would enforce its sameness on me,
    Incapable of tolerating sameness?
    Human beings cannot stand still.
    I imitate the climate in my clothes.
    The warmest clothing, day after day,
    Therefore the same clothing
    Day after day. It is encroaching
    On my dreams and stilling them, too,
    And because of this I rage.
    Monotony and gloom has stilled my love and will,
    Preventing me from varying these days

Even with nursery—pleasures—
Soap bubble blowing and finger painting.
But I am an inventor and now,
Like a rat trapped in a cave
Into which a gray sea advances,
England,
I will invent, invent
Away to save myself.

3/23/65

On TV I saw a documentary on old people in Florida. Room in a nursing home, people in the last stages of senility. Mumbling to themselves like children, fingering the last drops of tea out of their cups. A young nurse spoke—straight-forward, simple, strong and kind herself. She said they never hurt each other, but do damage to themselves, pull their own hair out, pull their nails out. Some have to be fed. Their staring eyes do not see anymore. One stood beside the nurse and the reporter as the interview went on, and the nurse patted her hand which rested on the barrier. It was frightening.

4/9/65

Vaguely apropos: the question of some children's existence; some children (like me) are accidents, and certainly not begotten to carry on any father's business or kingship. The child must make values (often in a Puritanical sense, especially if he is not born into money) in order not to be a weak shrimp. He must invent his own values. The values can as well be pleasures, indulgences, without which he is not complete. Again, no moral judgement implied.

4/23/65

The coal fire suits the English character, as one must pay for this bit of warmth and comfort by enduring a vaguely sooty room, and by the task of cleaning the grate each day, which means getting on one's knees, soiling the hands, and a trip to the dustbin with the clinkers. Nothing lavish here, keep it miserly. It's no more than you deserve.

5/17/65

Venice—I arrived at 3 AM at Marco Polo, had to take the fast, large motorboat to San Marco. A boatload of silent English, and rather stunned Scandinavians en route to the Holy Land. The boat is as fast as a motorboat and occasionally plays jazz music.

5/18/65

A cloudy day, extremely light and pleasant rain by 5 P.M., very brief. Then tonight, at twenty minute intervals, it comes down very hard, and the waves make a little roar. I took a walk from Zattere across Accademia bridge, through Campo Morosini, Parochio S. Stefano, to the Rialto, quite dark at 9 PM. And the streets beyond it dark. The Hotel Rialto, my first here, looks as if it has come up in the world. Walked in the Merceria to San Marco's whence it becomes impossible to walk along the quay toward Accademia because of the hotel backs which possess riparian rights. Back through S. Maurizio to the bridge once more, after a toast (150) and a glass of white wine (40) at a small empty bar. Pensione Seguso: the shutters are green and fold once after they open. Windows tall, French windows. A pregnant ash gray cat sleeps on the landing of first floor. I am moved at 11 (rather, I move myself in the fact, that I carry my own suitcase, etc.) from 21 to 28 today, which has no view. I was told I could have 45 by 2 PM at least, but at 2:30, it appeared the man in 45 was sick and not moving. At last by 5 he had moved, and by dint of many telephone calls, I ascertained that the room was ready. I again moved myself, as the only boy was glued to TV in the lobby. No ashtrays, only one glass, insufficient (8) hangers. The doors all have fingerprints on them. There are no pictures on the walls. All the beds seem to be twin. But there is a view from 45, the same one I had on a lower floor in '62, two weeks before I met C. who is joining me tomorrow. I have bought a little key for her bracelet, of gold. Also postcards and oranges.

5/23/65

Torcello. The boat from the Fondamente Nove, 120 lire, which touches at Burano, Murano, finally Torcello through narrows bordered by stakes. No coffee. Waiters in clean white jackets. Afterwards a walk into the church (L.100) of mosaics, a dog running loose, dragging his leash. A beautiful tall Virgin with small head in an oval niche of gold mosaic. We were later annoyed by a four-man band of hoodlums who came along the path, interrupting my drawing, touching my friend, but I feel this is her precinct and not mine, as I have shot of them, and never knew at all how to handle them, gentlemanly or not. The cat has had her kittens, perhaps three, in a wooden box in the back lavatory of the Pensione Seguso. The old porter showed them to us.

5/26/65

"O-o-ol" or "Ha-ool—" the cry of the *gondoliere* coming round a corner. A gondola from Seguso canal, with small white light on the prow, can be across the canal (Giudecca) in two minutes. Freighters, American and English, come through the canal every thirty minutes. The lion of Venice is shown on the smokestacks. Gold against blue. San Giorgio—

6/16/65

In adolescence the world is like a forest full of trees. There is a bewilderment of interests. At fourteen, thirteen, I was mad about the sea. I almost ran away—How did I ever sort things out? Well, I haven't.

6/23/65

Religion: mainly a tremendous outlet for guilt; more for this than for taking in anything. It therefore should be of great significance to the human race that with education and philanthropic assistance, man need no longer feel that he is dominated, even only at times, by evil emotions. Evil emotions are inevitable, especially in youth, but they can be seen to be minor and never dominant.

8/2/65

Love, the state of being in love, the one thing that cannot be explained logically in people's relationships. In case of a snag in a story, the inexplicable, if we are told he or she or they were in love, we think, "Oh! That explains everything." The apparent incongruity—that foreign element.

8/5/65

The affair with the married woman. One may say or think for a while that one is satisfied with the small amount of time together—and maybe that's true. But one is not satisfied with taking second place emotionally or even sharing equally, or even being preferred emotionally to the other person of whom she says: "My services to him I discharge like a duty." The fact remains that duty creates habit, and habit becomes emotionally charged. It is a rare human being that can serve another's breakfast with care every morning and not concern himself with that person's moods.

Therefore with the best rationalizations, it is jealousy, and resentment that wrecks this boat. And furthermore it is often a case of "Only duty? Prove it!" when the living is easier, lazier, more secure with the spouse. Cowardice and laziness are horrible strikes against the person one loves. (*So are gluttony and vanity.*)

8/5/65

Art—all of it, whoever is doing it—is a most courageous attempt at the impossible. The failure is either total or partial. It is the selfless courage that matters. One of the very few things that distinguishes man from the animals, perhaps the greatest, because the products have no use, come from nowhere, spun out of nothing—and remain nothing unless received by a like mind. This is sufficient metaphysics. The joy of creation and of reception cannot be surpassed by any other joy.

8/9/65

With the new acquaintance: that moment in the conversation when I realize he has a different morality, weltanschauung from mine, like a sudden canyon between us. We can change direction and find some bridge across somewhere else. But the knowledge lurks. It will turn up again years from now to part us, in every way, though we remain friends.

8/11/65

Naples—Da Umberto. In a narrow street near the Piazza dei Martiri. A bus ride down from the Capodimonte Museo—where over solicitous guards wanted to show me the fayence especially. At Umberto's *vongole*, *mollusc* [clams, mussels], full of garlic and butter and bread-crumbs, 400 lire. Rather modern decor—a picture 7' x 3' of outdoor restaurant back grounded by faintly smoking Vesuvius. A fish display in center of room. Umberto's did not look so grand as I remembered from 1949.

8/19/65

A dream, Lynn [Roth] was in my arms, her slender, firm body. I said, "God, how good it is to hold you, " and I woke up with my own words. I met her twelve years ago. I am in love in the best and realist sense of the word, quite irrationally. I suppose she thinks me too serious, or too heavyweight, a disgusting phrase sometimes attributed to me. How beautiful when she came for her birthday November 23, 1961, invited herself for two nights (of joy for me), and on the third—by gentle persuasion. It snowed that morning. Nature shed pristine blessing! I hoped we were housebound forever. She is so tender, incapable, unprotected. Nervous and doomed. I love her. Girl of magic! My—heart? My heart is yours, of course. I collapse and grow strong at the mere sight of you.

8/27/65

Prostitutes at least admit what they are, and don't go through with the farce of wedlock, as do so many women who are no more in love with their husbands than they are with their chars—and perhaps less so sometimes.

9/1/65

It is a mistake for people to think they have finished striving or arrived at anything—like retirement or a house. This is when discontent sets in. Man is never finished. No house, no place should be his last in his mind. Man lives and is happy only by projects alone.

9/2/65

It is presumably necessary to be among people now and then to find one's real level—not a real, final one, but a crude rule of thumb one. I think mine becomes rather low when I live alone, which I do much of the time.

9/7/65

First class cabin overnight on the *Valencia* from Palma to Barcelona. We take off at 10 PM, considerable vibration once we are under way. Impossible to order a coffee or a pernod at the bar. An English person would go mad from claustrophobia and warmth, but fortunately I am not English, and I have been here before. My cabin is D43. There is a jiggling motion, not like a ship's. Faulty engines, not due to rough seas.

9/12/65

Deya, Majorca. In the Restaurant Jaime I saw Robert Graves[*] in sloppy jeans, a studiedly tied red kerchief around his neck. His current mistress is the Black Goddess, a Mexican-American girl with perhaps some fire but little beauty. He takes her along with his wife to the beach. He

---

[*] Robert von Ranke Graves (1895–1985), author and poet who lived in Majorca since 1929. His mother was German, his father the Irish poet Alfred Perceval Graves.

has an air of self-esteem and smugness. I would much prefer to meet Alan Sillitoe.*

11/16/65

If Christ had only had one Negro disciple!

12/5/65

I enjoy work best around 4:30 PM when I am becoming tired, and when I know I have three more pages to go to complete my daily stint. The world may fall around me—it has a few times—but work remains, untouchable by others, pure if it is hard and honest.

12/14/65

The forces of love and of hate in the individual have more or less the same intensity at all times. The only thing that changes is the object. It seems everyone needs a few things (or people, or a race) to hate. It is important what this is. Love is less harmful, unless it (the object) is socially disapproved.

12/23/65

I dreamt I sat beside Lynn who was pregnant five months. Her lover had pinched something inside her, releasing water. The curious thing was she was unconcerned about the pregnancy and had been unaware of it until her boyfriend informed her. I said, "I'm so sorry, because I wanted it to be ours—I wanted us to have one." She only smiled.

No use going on with this, it is so obvious I long for someone to love and to love me, as I have at least in New York found at times. (In the dream, the skyline of New York was recognizable not far away.) These dreams after shattering criticism lately and no personal understanding whatsoever. I have reached (again) a point of preferring to forget that the person I am supposed to love exists. And to think that if she now wishes me to "miss" her in these long weeks when I have not seen her, then this is only a rather cruel wish.

---

* Alan Sillitoe (1928–2010), English writer best known for his novel *The Loneliness of the Long-Distance Runner.* He is commonly grouped with the so-called "angry young men," a group of British writers of the 1950s.

⚘

1/4/66

Going to bed in the English countryside. This gives enormous pleasure to the majority of people I know, and all of them sleep alone. They talk about going to bed with anticipation hours before they do, and the next day tell you how nice it was, with hot water bottles, books—and one wonders with what else?

1/13/66

The reward of virtue
Is loneliness.
The reward of hard work
Is higher taxation.
If virtue is its own reward
It is physical and mental ill-health.

1/15/66

Actually, the world itself is so much more interesting than all the people we are always striving for. If these people were books, they wouldn't get printed.

2/5/66

At the end of a love affair, one person becomes a religion in reverse. The one who seeks to break finds faults or imagines them everywhere in the other person, and believes them in the face of fact; just as the religious person believes what he wants to believe, in the face of fact. Or the lover, too, of course.

2/5/66

Love (amorous or romantic love) is nothing but a form or various forms of Ego. The thing to do is to direct one's Ego to other recipients of love. It is important that the objects be nothing but what I have said—the recipients. Love is outgoing, a gift that should not be expected to be returned.

2/13/66

Cruelty is mainly a lack of imagination. There is also the element of hitting back at something, or someone, but this is not so important as the former.

3/1/66

The essence of life is to welcome a challenge, even though not being quite sure how to meet it.

4/20/66

America—the good things about it are so very good, the bad things so very bad. At this point, I cannot live there, as I am too personally ashamed of the bad things. I think sometimes of living in Santa Fe. The climate suits me perfectly. However, America is still all around, and cannot be shut out. New Orleans is another possibility on the American map. But one would have to live like a recluse, enjoying the old New Orleans, and mainly in imagination at that.

5/26/66

In any creative work, if one pauses to consider its value or the time it involves, all joy goes out of the work.

5/27/66

The constant falling a little short is the only thing that takes the terror out of the strange act of creation.

6/24/66

Africa—a long low horizon of one- and two-story buildings, an occasional smokestack. The port is shallow. We come in on green water, evil-smelling. Dark men sit fishing with hand lines. Some wear red fezzes. Djellabas among the people waiting on the dock for the tourist passengers. Jostling on the lines for passport stamping, and in fact no lines. Queuing unknown. Endless papers to fill out about the car. Because my friend [Elizabeth Lyne] makes a row about stolen cushions (she has been informed her insurance covers only the car, not what is inside; there are also two dents outside) we are not given the last piece of paper which enables us to leave the port, but have to drive back to the waterside for it. In Tunis, some cars stop for a red light, some do not. The people are mainly Arab, a little French, only rarely a Negro.

6/30/66

Hammamet—61 Kms [kilometers]. From Tunis SE and on the water. A real Arab village, two restaurants, a pharmacy, a "youth center" that was a former Catholic church, and which now looks like a coffeehouse (as many coffeehouses look like town halls, or bingo parlors, with small tables). We walked in the native quarter. Casbah-like tunnels, white arches, dirt street, but all more than reasonably clean. Many of the women pregnant. No women in the restaurant where we were.

7/7/66

Hammamet—of five people of whom we expected slight help—all have let us down here. They take names and telephone numbers, make promises, and do not follow through. It must be a curious god they have.

7/13/66

Africa—[F]A splendid place for thinking. One feels naked, standing alone against a white wall. Problems become simplified, one's directions clear. Is this because the land is so different from Europe, the people so different from one's own? I know that I'll never try to make a home here, never try to use the land, and that the land stretches for more than a thousand miles south and west of me. Africa does not even turn over in her sleep by way of entertaining tourists. It is like a great, fat, half asleep woman in a comfortable bed—naked herself, indifferent to any approach. At night, a few half-hearted but raucous locusts start up; tied dogs bark in the distance, a windmill creaks, voices are loud in the empty hotel halls.[FF]

7/19/66

African mornings in the Parc Plage Hotel, Hammamet. Breakfast ordered for 9:30, does not arrive until 10:20, because the few adolescent Arab boys are overworked. In the morning besides struggling with breakfast—without coffee one cannot wake up in this heat—one must at once look for the plumber, as on the preceding evening a pipe burst under the new cement of the kitchen. The plumber replied that he had not the ring to connect two pipes, but had hoped that they would stay connected. There was a small geyser beside the pipe going down from the sink. If the plumber is side-tracked by another, he will attend to them before us. So we gave him 200 millimes for his bad job yesterday, 100 for today. At 11:30 the cleaning boy actually turns up to do his job, but incidentally has been trained only for swabbing floors, not for making beds, washing dishes, emptying ashtrays. At noon, I could be a nervous wreck if I were self-indulgent. (A beetle just fell from the ceiling onto my notebook.) The post is due at 11, but another authority says at 1 P.M. The post is supposed to be delivered at 11—or—"There can be at most a 12-hour delay" for a 300-yard distance.

7/24/66

The article for the *Statesman*. Arrival at Tunis docks—the heat, closed doors of the bureau where they examine passports . . . First glimpse of Tunis—dust, heat, confusion, the bell-hop's order to remove everything from car pockets, subsequent disappearance of Tunisian Michelin map, unobtainable in Tunis . . . The Café de Paris. Eternal jasmine. Sidi Bou Said—the masses of young men who sit in cafés all day and are finished working by 11 A.M. The young sheikh who wants to rent us a house at Paris prices—80 d—$160—per month, & has to be found in a café. Parc Plage—the lazy French manager—Mokta—the ever ready, meaningless smile. The first up, last to bed. Vendetta at night in front of the Brise de Hammamet.[F]A man in shorts shoves a dark figure near the doorway,[FF] then sits down on a bench outside the café. The dark figure lingers ominously, a bit drunk. Two men come and try to persuade him to leave. He goes toward the sea and the Arab village by the fortress, but lingers, still visible, for fifteen minutes or so. The chief of tourism is present this weekend, and no one wants him to see a drunk. It is only the third drunk I have seen in Tunisia in a month.

8/3/66

Utter demoralization today. No post. An African kitten sits on my chest now, fascinated by my pen, and I dare say she has seen few in her seven weeks of life, but my old favorite has been lost or stolen here, a month ago. It is, every morning, like trying to push a mountain with one's bare hands. The mountain will not budge, but there are certain duties which one must try to perform—or else slip into madness. Nothing wrong with that, really, except that I am afraid of it, not interested (on the contrary I am very interested in madness) but I am convinced that I, at least, cannot achieve anything in writing or drawing, without an orderly life. Here— the appalling sleepiness of everything, the climate—the unbuttoned shirts—the undone tasks everywhere. Where does it begin? Once here, walking on these sands, in this heat, one knows defeat is ahead. It is foolish to fight an entire continent.

9/15/66

Wrote a "ghost" story ("The Yuma Baby") which was supposed to be depressing to the protagonists and readers, but I found I was depressed.* In some curious way, the writing had effected its desired results on me, but the effects were not enough apparent in the prose. This was the creator as audience or reader. I made the story more explicit, was no longer depressed by it, though not as jolly and laughing as I usually am after writing something, which, sometimes to my surprise, frightens readers.

11/3/66

In the most terrible and terrifying moments of my life (ten, perhaps, in a lifetime) Mozart, not a sedative, is the hope—though not the healing power. There is no healing power. But Mozart knew all that. I, or we, suffer here and now, and he often wrote his music during the worst. It is this that I admire, and only this spirit that gives me courage to go on also. It is (apparently!) impossible for me to convey the joy I felt one miserable Saturday morning, listening to the 24th piano concerto on a transistor radio in the bathroom. I had been wretched a moment before. But with Mozart's courage, I could face lions. Bach for minor crises. Mozart for major ones.

11/20/66

The action of abortion is entirely the women's business, not the Church's. It is firstly the women's business, and secondly but only secondly the business of the future supporter of the child—because sometimes the woman can do this for herself. Where the anti-abortion church makes itself most obnoxious and noxious to the public weal is in compelling a birth and then disclaiming all or nearly all responsibility for the mother's welfare and for the child's upbringing. It is one of the ironies of humanity, or of sociology, that the women of such anti-abortion churches are their stronger supporters—stronger than the men.

11/21/66

Strychnined lipstick.

12/11/66

[Copenhagen.] Arrival at 6 PM in the dark. A very spread out town, with lots of blue lights. Prim, unmoneyed private houses between air-

---

* "The Yuma Baby" was a ghost story Pat wrote at Caroline Besterman's suggestion. Pat found the story so depressing that she later rewrote it; this second, funnier version, called "The Empty Birdhouse," was published in the January 1969 issue of *Ellery Queen's Mystery Magazine*. It was also included in the collection of short stories *The Snail-Watcher and Other Stories* (New York, 1970).

port and city, a little more "Dutch" than British counterparts. Mr. Birger Schmith*—bearded, forty-eightish, with modest blond wife—meets me at airport, and we drive to Imperial, a businesslike, decent, almost swank hotel, in business section. Dinner there. The people look cleaner, blonder, more attractive than the English. Smoked salmon or salmon with various sauces, is insisted upon to commence a meal. Afterwards, a nightcap in hotel bar. The copper towers of churches, etc. are all pale green. The general scene confused with tram wires, tracks, gigantic advertisement & shop signs.

12/27/66

I respect madmen, and am becoming mad enough myself to benefit from listening to soothing or good music. This I write in a moment of self-flattery.

12/27/66

The lost cause appeals to the artistic temperament, and to the handful of non-English who choose to live in England. It is a losing battle with the moisture in the house, possibly with one's health also. It is like the painting or the book which is never as good as what one had in mind before beginning.

---

* Her Danish publisher from Grafisk Ferlag.

1967–1980

RETURN TO FRANCE

1967–1969

PATRICIA HIGHSMITH'S breakup with Caroline Besterman leaves her disoriented and adrift. In response to the pain, she buries herself in work and unearths Diary 15, abandoned three years earlier. Since she had only moved to England for Caroline, there is little keeping her there now; in early 1967, she tries to escape her emotional misery geographically, if by no other means. When invited to judge short films at an international film festival in Montbazon, near Tours, France, Pat takes her friend Elizabeth Lyne's advice and rents a house nearby after the festival concludes. In September, the two women buy a house together in Samois-sur-Seine, an ultimately catastrophic idea, as consequently their twenty-year friendship ends in court, and Pat hits rock bottom.

Professionally speaking, Pat would have reason for optimism at this time: her agent is negotiating a lucrative film deal for *Those Who Walk Away* (although the film will never be made), and for the first time, Pat is entering a prolonged period of financial security. In the German-speaking market, she moves from the mass-market paperback imprint of her Hamburg-based publishing house Rowohlt to Zurich-based Diogenes Verlag, which will publish her books in hardcover and successfully market them as literary fiction. Moreover, the critically celebrated publication of *The Tremor of Forgery*—a book she also declares her own favorite—finally elevates Pat's status in the United States from mere genre writer to recognized literary talent.

Alone and lonely in the countryside, however, Pat feels increasingly disconnected from her French surroundings—a feeling that will intensify when she relocates to the tiny farming village of Montmachoux in mid-1968. When she gets to know twenty-six-year-old English journalist Madeleine Harmsworth, Pat latches on to her for support, however temporary, and flies to London to be close to her. After Madeleine ends their relationship, Pat stops journaling, a practice she'd only just revived in January 1968.

When Pat returns to Paris on May 6, student demonstrations are under way. Amid street protests and general strikes, Pat feels even more alienated in her self-imposed exile. Perhaps it's this sense of isolation that compels her to set her new novel, *Ripley Under Ground*, in France, situating her fictional alter ego Tom Ripley in a villa near her own home. She provides him with a wife who bears a resemblance to her latest crush, Jacqui, and a tenuous existence as the head of an international art forgery ring.

In February 1969, Pat's agent sells Doubleday on the idea of a book of short stories, a long-held dream of Pat's. The eleven selected pieces published in *The Snail-Watcher and Other Stories* (1970) are literary, not suspense fiction; some are even humorous, and many were written before Pat's debut novel, as the young author was still honing her craft.

Pat, who in the wake of her many amorous disillusions grows steadily more bitter, critical, and acerbic in her comments now, allows herself a brief moment of happiness in August, upon reading the polished final draft of *Ripley Under Ground*. In her diary, she admits to how much she likes the book. It's dedicated to her neighbors Agnès and Georges Barylski, a Polish farming couple, among the few people whose company she truly enjoys in France.

1/2/67

I heard today that Raoul J. Lévy* shot himself New Year's Eve in St. Tropez. Alas I never liked him, and obviously he did not like himself. His last film *The Defector* was not well received. His terrible unhappiness showed in his inability or unwillingness to communicate with the people who were working on the project which presumably engaged him at the last—I was one of them.

1/15/67

Since I no longer keep a diary, I think I should write a few things here before they go out of my head. The years are beginning to swim into each other, one being like the other, since I moved into this house. By April-May 1967, I shall have been in Bridge Cottage three years. In May 1965, I went to Venice for ten days, my first vacation in nineteen months, and this beclouded by a BBC deadline (*The Cellar*—or *The Prowler*) for which they had foisted on me a portable typewriter. C. [Caroline] was

---

* Raoul J. Lévy (1922–1966), Franco-Belgian writer, film director, and producer, is best remembered for his films starring Brigitte Bardot. Lévy wanted to collaborate with Highsmith on the film script of *Deep Water*. The project was abandoned after his suicide.

reasonably cheerful and nice to me. I was cheerful enough to do a lot of drawings, several pretty good. (And Peggy Guggenheim was cool—not knowing me? —by telephone, not inviting me for a drink, nor accepting my invitation to Harry's [Bar].) Later—C. would to say, "Venice could have been better." But how? Why? She is never explicit. She is the mental, [the] hypochondriac, always imagining moods, withdrawing into mysterious distances in her own mind, and expecting others to puzzle out what is eating her.

From October '65 to March '66 I wrote *Those Who Walk Away*, set in Venice. During the entire first draft I barely saw C. once, certainly did not sleep with her. Some of the blackest days—I passed then. As she was continually harping on my drinking, I took my first drink at 6 P.M. and went to Dr. Auld for phenobarbs. Without C.'s odd treatment, I shouldn't have needed either sedation nor a glass too many.

In Feb., C. fell down the kitchen stairs on her head! Ha! Ha!—just for a change in this lugubrious text, a little laughter, please! Not fully recovered (not that that is much better) she had lunch with me Feb. 25 or 26th 1966 in London, when I asked her if she'd be willing to sell the house, if I took a flat in London, or if she preferred to rent it with me, or buy it? I received not an answer, but a harangue about the instability of my character! This in a loud voice which had the waiters staring, while she polished off every morsel on her plate. I was delighted to chat with the Italian Consulate office by telephone that afternoon (a cheerful voice!) and even happier to get back home—alone.

On March 7, 1966, I went to Paris, as they were bringing out the *Glass Cell* there. Good to see [Elizabeth] Lyne. I then wrote "[The Quest for] Blank Claveringi,"* and a children's snail story for Australia, which was later rejected. In June, I went to Paris to join Lyne and we went to Tunisia. During this time I wrote C. some letters in which I said I loved her, but would stand no more of this nonsense. C. joined me in Paris Aug. 5— 1966—but in one of her "withdrawn" moods, for the first few days. We were there five days, she leaving a day ahead. On my return to London, I came to her house by arrangement, and she drove me up to the cottage, where a mountain of post awaited me, which took me thirteen days to get through.

In essence—C. would prolong forever her sadistic relationship with me. It is not a relationship—it has no flow, no joy. As the reader will see—she would not have broken it off, ever, I think. But I did in October 1966.

---

* Story collected in *The Snail-Watcher and Other Stories* (1970).

1/16/67

I wrote a "ghost story" called "The Yuma Baby," put up a heavy kitchen shelf, made two small tables—and early September [1966] received a telegram from [Jenny] Bradley that Raoul Lévy wanted me to collaborate on the film script of *Deep Water*. This resulted in my going to Nice Sept. 22—where he wanted to set it: St. Tropez, Vence. I was accompanied by Isabelle Ponsa, also a director. After five days there, I saw Ann D. [Duveen] Caldwell and met the two Barbaras—Ker-Seymer and Roett.*
I was still tired from Tunisia, where I did not get enough sleep, where the heat was exhausting, and I hadn't even the lift of having done any decent painting. For one thing, Lyne and I met for lunch; and we were in the same large room for several weeks, and I cannot work well unless alone. It took me three agonizing weeks to get out of Monsieur Lévy exactly what he wanted, once I got home. I had every neurotic symptom: fear of failure; painful exhaustion, combined with inability to sleep or eat properly. When I got proper orders Oct. 20, I had the script finished by November 14, on which date Monsieur Lévy went to New York for a month. He never signed the contract nor paid me anything, and all I know is he was very pleased with the first 44 pages. He shot himself Dec. 31. in St. Tropez. Madame Bradley is fighting my case now, but she should have obtained his signature, and some money, in all the time she had.

On November 17, by telegram, the news I was to do a condensation of *Those Who Walk Away* for *Cosmopolitan* for $4,500—(after agent). A pre-Christmas deadline. This I did by Dec. 14. On Dec. 6–8 I went to Denmark, where I was guest of Grafisk Ferlag—(*The Glass Cell*, *Two Faces of Jan[uary]*.) and met Birger Schmith and Gudrun Rasch— the press conference went well—not so well the speech, I think, which plunged me further into gloom. On October 14 (when I had to make a speech in Stowmarket [Suffolk]) C. and I had our last and most typical maladjustments: I came up to bed five or ten minutes after her, she left the bed, I assumed in her usual silent huff, and I handed her bag into the next room. She did not return, and slept—I saw later—with one pink blanket in the twin bedroom. I told her in the morning I had had enough huffs, and was finished, and she left at 4 PM.

On November 23, I had the sebaceous cyst of my left cheek removed. I'd had it about ten years. So this autumn—and to the present—has

---

* Barbara Ker-Seymer (1905–1993), British portrait photographer. A fixture in London's bohemian scene, she was closely associated with many members of 1920s and '30s café society. Barbara Roett was her life partner. Pat met the "two Barbaras" in her friend Anne Duveen Caldwell's house in Cagnes-sur-Mer, near Nice.

been grueling work, typing, public appearance strain—and all alone, emotionally speaking. The very worst time of my entire life, as I have never had to end a four-year affair before: yet it was no longer an affair. Three months could intervene between the times we made love. I never rejected her—or showed myself in a huff to her advances. Daisy Winston visited Dec. 15–29. A godsend. She cheered me—but I cannot love her in a physical sense. Possibly the best friend I have now. My mother, for six months, has been writing hateful and upsetting letters—just to add one more nail.

1/23/67

Paris—Hôtel de la Paix—225 Boulevard Raspail. No. 11. *Voile* white polka-dot curtains, with the tall windows I know from Marseille. 2 AM. Someone above turns his (or her) basin on, and I lie on my bed now with this typical view, window (on warehouse-like structures) bordered by red and white curtains. My friend L. [Lyne] and I have been discussing this evening the importance of doing something important now, or not at all. This in regard to our current abeyance of creative activity, which perhaps cannot be entirely blamed on January and the absence of vitamin D. My agent [Jenny] Bradley I have learned this evening has had a heart attack. I knew she was in Antibes since Saturday.

1/25/67

Tours-Montbazon-en-Touraine.* From Paris farmlands, simple houses with kitchen gardens, and lots of canals, mills, irrigation gulleys, moss-covered, through the pine woods that surround these farmhouses. Black and white cows. I miss the "greeters" in Tours, so have to wait 25 minutes for the suburban train to Montbazon. Another wait while the train man does his job of flagging shunting trains, then I ring the hotel, and am taken.

1/28/67

Latest comment by my American agent [Pat Schartle] on why I don't sell to paperbacks in America: they report "too subtle," or "no one likable in the book." Perhaps it is because I don't like anyone. My last books may be about animals. I understand the American situation and have

---

* Pat was invited to sit on the jury for an international film festival in Montbazon, in the Touraine region of France.

no regrets. One can't have everything. If America liked me, France and England wouldn't, nor would Scandinavia.

2/4/67

For *The Writer* article.

About being stuck—at various ages, perhaps. Mine—one wants at 46 or thereabouts, to do something better than one has ever done before. One doesn't want to repeat oneself. With this comes a temporary paralysis, with all kinds of rationalizations. I am resting because I need it. I am gathering my forces. It would be silly to dissipate energy. The destructiveness of public appearances and speeches. A sad discovery, because since writing is a form of communication, writers love to communicate—therefore, why not an opening of the mind and soul in speeches? Well, the reality is not always as exhilarating as the successful rehearsal to oneself in the bathtub. Any shyness is fatal. And the television interviews. And the easier interviews across a café table over a glass of beer or a coffee? What is it that they remove? Is it that a writer destroys himself when he speaks so freely, gladly, happily—so willing to assist the interviewer in his possibly difficult job?

I don't know—but something is smashed, distorted, damaged. An inner mirror of oneself? I don't know. I only know that it takes weeks to recover, as if one had been in a car accident, suffered shock or broken ribs or a concussion. Dylan Thomas was destroyed by that appallingly arduous schedule of speeches on his two trips to America. Of course, it is much simpler to say he was destroyed by drink and cigarettes—drink being the immediate physical cause. But he was a man uneasy in crowds of people, or so say some who knew him well. He drank to feel more at ease. But it is not even so simple as this. Writers and poets should not give away so much of themselves in public—and Thomas did, for instance, when he read his poems that he had created in private. And any writer, in an interview, gives away his writing habits and methods, if any, because he is asked them, and he wants to be generous.

The result is as ravaging to his creativity, brain, as some disease of the brain. In my opinion, J. D. Salinger is correct in granting no interviews, making no speeches.

2/24/67

The big majority of my dreams do restorative work. They repair. What a blessing! They also prepare for anxieties, giving me a worse picture than what the reality is going to be.

3/12/67

Getting ready to sell a house [Bridge Cottage]—a house for which I'd had considerable hope. It is a negative thing—perhaps like an abortion—and the negativity can drag one down (with me, it's always feeling tired as well as depressed) until one realizes exactly what it is and starts to correct it—always an artificial process, like taking aspirin for a headache. Morale can be maintained by affecting or assuming a certain dignity, or sense of it, even when alone. Go slow. Don't get flustered. Look ahead and be optimistic. I know while doing this, and getting some benefit from it, that it is not real life, not really living. To live is to accept the sorrow with arms just as open as they are presumably for happiness.

3/24/67

Laws for survival:

1) Think stuffy. That is, be formal, polite, serious, and if possible holier than thou. Outdo snobs.
2) Believe that you are constantly improving.
3) Let other people do as many of the chores as possible.
4) Believe that you have chosen the best possible place to live. Be content.
5) Always get a bit more rest than you need. I.e. quit before you are exhausted.
6) Eat as much as possible at every opportunity. Also take advantage of all sunshine.
7) Believe that you have already accomplished wonders, given your time and energy.
8) Have a cheerful, polite riposte ready for any detractor.
9) Cultivate strain followed by relaxation, in the manner of an athlete.
10) Causes of angst:
    1) Guilt.
    2) A sense of having made a wrong decision about one's life, personal or in business.
    3) Fatigue—which leads to angst because one can look back and see how one could have saved energy. With me, this is always in household chores, never in work.
    4) Envy could be, but there is no one at the moment whom I envy.

3/24/67

It is I who goes ahead and my watch that follows.

3/26/67

Morlaix [Brittany, France]—A delightful town with a Reine Anne house,[*] (closed) of half-timbered 16th century facade. A museum of Bronze Age tools, Egyptian sarcophagi, a mélange of modern painting— Claude Monet, a portrait of Proust, 28. Teashops of crêpes—*fromage ou jambon*. The people are intelligent and friendly—more than one can say of Rennes. Roscoff—27 kilometers away on the sea. Opposite island of Batz. Best meal we have had for 15 NF each, five courses. Chardon Bleu. Blond Bretagne faces. Some tourist spots, but mainly genuine. As usual, the *pâtisseries* look like museums of (very fresh) art.

3/26/67

Society for the Union of Oxford Graduates—should at once be organized. Oxford graduates deserve each other, and I am sure if they are both men, they will know what to do with each other. Graduates of Oxford are well equipped to sit in an armchair and read a newspaper. Their all-round helplessness should not be inflicted upon a non-Oxford mate, male or female.

3/31/67

Oslo. A messy town of neons, much like Copenhagen. The main street includes the Parliament buildings, the King's Palace (a yellow cream Buckingham). Windows are large everywhere. Heating overabundant. Important meal is eaten at 4 or 5 PM, though something is taken at noon or one. Possibly a supper at 9, as this evening I was invited at 8 to a private house. The faces craggy. Good for sculpture. The people say the Norwegians, Swedes, Danish should have been one nation. A man with a masculine puppet—Arild Feldborg.[†] Very amusing. He made the speech at Gyldendal [publishing house]. Went to dinner also. A great drinker. The taxi driver knew him from his television programs. Satire.

Gordon Hølmebakk[‡]—somewhat like Fredric March.[§] 38. Extremely bookish, knows that Thomas Mann's wife was a kleptomaniac. He would rather discuss Ford Madox Ford than take care of the business at hand. Married, like all of the under forties I have met at Gyldendal.

---

[*] The house in question is the Maison dite de la duchesse Anne in Morlaix, where Anne de Bretagne is believed to have lived in the sixteenth century.

[†] Arild Feldborg (1912–1987), Norwegian writer, humorist, and TV host.

[‡] Gordon Hølmebakk (1928–2018), Norwegian essayist, novelist, and editor for foreign literature at Norwegian publishing house Gylendal Norske Forlag.

[§] Fredric March (1897–1975), Oscar-winning American actor and one of Hollywood's biggest stars in the 1930s and '40s.

Snow on the ground at my host's. Some difficulty walking. They have an eight-month old Irish setter, red, which they tie up. She is charming, subject of much conversation tonight, as I do not approve of tying up [dogs], nor does Feldborg.

4/13/67

A lovely dream during one hour's nap in the P.M. I was lying on a downward sloping grassy sward, with a girl—and the girl is somehow always Lynn [Roth]. I had a newspaper—out of the top of the newspaper grew fresh, real honey-suckle blossoms. I told Lynn how to find the honey in them. A view of a room with at least six young men, all in good mood. One on a chaise longue was tattooed in black where a swimsuit might have fitted him, and besides that had pink roses, a headdress tattooed. A charming dream, a good sleep, a good day's work. I so often think of Lynn, the joy of my life, and for a time I was the joy of hers.

4/24/67

The improved communication of our era has brought a more pessimistic view of mankind. The hope, naive as it may have been, of a better life for everyone, has now been proved to have been silly. This is the real tragedy of this age—1920—to the present—and beyond.

4/26/67

Forty-eight hours with a gumboil, which I thought was an abscess over a sensitive tooth. It deflated by 90% overnight and gave no pain. My first thought was to sacrifice my cat [Sammy,], my most treasured live possession. Primitive religion. On second night of painless terror, but much dread, I thought I heard burglars downstairs, put on my robe, and went down. How brave one is, when one thinks there is neither health nor life to lose anymore. No doubt Mann says something of this in *The Magic Mountain*. It is part of the courage of criminals, convicts in submitting to possibly fatal experiments. It is not here, however, that men have lost their hope of life—often they are not condemned to death. They have lost long ago their self-respect, which is morale, which is, finally, what some woman thinks or could think of them.

4/28/67

Ipswich, Suffolk. A town of fabulous, Dickensian houses. I love to look at single houses here, those with short windows in the first story, bespeaking cramped—and in the winter cold—bedrooms. The crochety, crochety ornaments on the houses cannot be weakened, in their emotional effect, by the ghastly opticians' signs that sometimes adorn the same facade. But the overall picture of the town is depressing. There simply has to be a supermarket everywhere, a Co-op this and that, a Sainsbury, Woolworth, Boots, because there simply has to be too many people. I wonder always what really animates their lives, what gives them cheer? The young secretaries (girls) and the men riding home on bicycles at 5 PM, getting out of the way of nobody and of no car: the cars must wait. It is perhaps the old answer, the family life, a love affair, plain sex, that keeps people going, and keeps them happy. I tend to think "What is your work? What is your aspiration?" when I see people walking along the pavements in such cities as Ipswich. If they had aspiration, perhaps they'd not be there? Yet it is quite possible to be a scholar in Ipswich—if scholars still exist, and to be writing a great book on any subject.

4/29/67

The strongest of all emotions is the sense of injustice. A baby can feel it. Unlike the desires of hunger and sex and sleep, the sense of injustice rankles, cannot be appeased and forgotten so quickly. It remains alive— may be one of the many human, advanced, intellectual emotions that the human baby is capable of experiencing. One can see a difference when the human baby is six months old. The demands are different from those of a puppy or a kitten.

Injustice is abstract.

5/7/67

Melancholic, negative days before departure. I cannot get anything to move for the past fortnight, neither the rental agents, the French consulate, the removal men, the car insurance, and yesterday someone gave my fender a dent. Mainly I am depressed because not actively working (writing) much less drawing. I hope it is a better life I go to. One must have plans, arduous ones, difficult ones, in order to be happy.

(Ah, sweet optimist! And what a dupe you were! 1/6/69)

5/21/67

Reader's Digest snail piece. Something New in Pets and Snails.*
    1) The unusual pleasure of keeping snails—their silence, their modest food demands, their decorative virtue, their strange mating—

---

* An as-yet-unpublished text of Pat's.

2) —hence my having them at all . . . the production of babies. Inability to mature in America—vs. England.

3) Their cry (of an owl?) as they climb the glass of the tank.

4) Remarkable stimulus to the imagination. Short stories.

5) Ability to travel with ease. Though people may think me a bit cracked to ask for half a leaf of lettuce in French hotels, lettuce without dressing, please.

6) Jealousy of my jealous cat.

7) The snail in literature—Bartlett—leading to conclusion, that it is a most admirably adapted creature, able to withstand hardship, hold off enemies, reproducing in abundance, unchanging for millions of years, whereas man has changed strikingly. Essentially of factual value in the reproductive descriptions. Fact, please, loyalty to mate. Can go over razorblade edges—and glide over their own children—to whom they are indifferent—without harming them.

7/21/67

If one has enough innate guilt, one does not need Christianity—which chiefly supplies guilt to quite innocent and pagan-like and natural people who had not thought of guilt before, and who would be happier without it. This is like saying, all of us are alike. Atheists and religious people. It is saying that everyone needs a certain amount of guilt feelings. This is the price one pays for intelligence. Man is more intelligent than the gods and knows it unconsciously, so feels guilty about his superiority, so denies it.

7/26/67

My oldest snail died today, or maybe yesterday as Camus would say. Born around late September 1964, died July 25, 1967. She traveled from England to America and back, went to Paris five or six times, to Majorca and Tunisia. She produced some 500 eggs, though she herself was from a deformed batch of eggs, the soil having been too wet. I saved six of a batch of eighty. Her shell was also deformed, crusty, like a diseased fingernail. The oldest snail I ever had.

8/28/67

Curious when "plotting" that money has the same value as love—as a motive, as a force that becomes almost real; as real as desire, ambition, zest. How and when did the person acquire the money? Was it in his family? All this is almost as boring and depressing as the themes of Jane

Austen. Yet her novels are anything but boring. Money, position—they ought to be as unimportant as the color of a character's hair, yet with her, they place and motivate. All a matter of morals, of course. I am more interested in the morals of a person stripped naked of the conventions. Man and his conscience alone—without even his neighbors to guide or influence him.

10/24/67

Amazing how many world "leaders" show paranoid tendencies— and manage to implant similar fears in those around them. From the old Romans to Stalin. One can see it in some households (viva at the Coates'). Paranoids are also inclined to be bossy. Bossy people acquire followers, partly due to the fact most people would rather be told what to do than to act on their own; partly because most people would rather avoid a quarrel, therefore are obedient to the tyrant or bully.

11/1/67

Why don't the Americans drop some bombs on the Vatican? Look at all the human misery and poverty they are causing by their dilly-dallying over birth control. But no, the bombs are being dropped on innocent farmers. I propose a toast to the Pope.* "I wish you eternal pregnancy! Breach deliveries every time, preferably sextuplets! May your vagina be torn to pieces! May your teeth fall out! May you be bed-ridden with ane-mia! But may you continue to bear, into eternity! Do you not think these birth pangs wonderful? They will go on forever and ever. God is Eternal Life!" Twenty-five years ago, Rolf Tietgens said, when I could not too well understand it, being twenty-one and hopeful, that we are living in the Middle Ages now.

11/11/67

Doing little things in a regular, vaguely constructive way, is so essential in order to get through life at all. It also gives a certain contentment, even pleasure. Then along comes someone—I seem to know so many—who says "You are doing it the wrong way! You are wasting time! You are not efficient at all!" Then I say "Oh, sorry!" (for no particular reason), try perhaps to change, and am miserable. (It's a severe and very unhappy-

---

* In 1968, Pope Paul VI (1897–1978) will reaffirm the traditional position of the Catholic Church regarding contraception in his encyclical *Humanae vitae* (*Of Human Life*).

making fault in me that I never stand up for myself at the moment I should. I collect tyrants as plush material collects dust. You yield once to a tyrant—it is like yielding once to a blackmailer.)

12/5/67

I don't understand life. Are objectives and pleasures the same thing? What should one be concerned with? How should one spend one's time?

12/11/67

The strain under which we all live now should be no greater than in past times, but is made greater (real) by fairly good information services today. We know what is happening—more or less what is happening really—on the opposite side of the earth. How can any honest and intelligent man bear it?

12/12/67

[Samois-sur-Seine.] 20 Rue de Courbuisson. Never in any house have I felt so mentally uncomfortable, and now (due to coldness and various continuing inconveniences) so physically uncomfortable as in this house. L. [Lyne] made me feel it was not half mine, that my possessions were sordid, that I was hopelessly disorganized—by nature. This must have been her objective and indeed she succeeded. I dislike the garden and feel no love for it. I am uneasy using any "communal" room such as the living room and the kitchen. It will be interesting to put into a book or a short story someday, because one's feelings about a house are of some importance—especially to someone who does his work there. Especially to someone who owns the land and the house, even half of it.

12/14/67

To opt out is the only thing to do now—unless, preferably from a social point of view, one attempts to form a "third" or independent party. Depressing for Americans to attempt this, because it seems the majority are brainwashed to vote in the accustomed channels, so frequently against their interests. But perhaps the cause isn't lost—and in fifteen years, after ridicule and failure, the Flower People will win. Nothing makes any impression except the economic boycott. The only thing to stop wars, the only thing to effect social justice.

DECEMBER 14, 1967

^FFrom the frying pan into the fire. The script of *The Tremor of Forgery*[*] is done, and now I polish and retype certain pages, arriving at the end of January to send it to the USA and England.^{FF} I await Daisy W. [Winston] for Christmas, arriving the 18th I think. For the record, I am still in love with Lynn and always will be.

※

JANUARY 2, 1968

Anxious about Lyne's arrival, with her furniture. I dread her arrogance and unfriendliness—but in fact don't know what to expect. She may be friendly—who knows? I am pleased with *The Tremor of Forgery* and tomorrow will begin typing it up. But tonight at 11 PM, I wrote to Rosalind Constable of my trepidations here. The temperature is about 59°F due to my inability to close off the living-room fireplace or to get the ceiling insulated. Prices seem to get higher daily, and in fact did today, milk and other items in the supermarkets. I've had to stop patronizing a couple of shops here because they overcharge me in particular—i.e. when other people are not in the store to be witness to my anguished queries about prices! I dreamt a couple of nights ago about Lynn. I wrote yesterday to Ann [S.]—saying among other things that Lynn was the love of my life, and what a pity that the love (on my part) is all wasted. I wonder if anything will ever come of it? And yet, my attitude is not one of hoping, which would be rather absurd, but of resignation to fate and to fact, and to appreciating what I had, what I have. Do many people have even one great love? Or are they too early attached to one person, by marriage, so that they come to know a certain "contentment," much more, with children, yet which is not the magical thing of being in love, groundless as that may be.

Tonight, I searched in vain for the 1953 diary (April? March? I think May) when I met Lynn. But I did find a poem (September, I think) which I liked very much. I was as usual appalled by the abundance of my diary prose in the past. But these particular winter days in November [1967] to January 1968 in Samois-sur-Seine are distinguished by a more than usual

---

* In a small Tunisian village near the Mediterranean, an American tourist writes a screenplay about a love triangle and longs for news from his lover. One dark night, a visitor intrudes and the writer hurls his typewriter at him. Soon his life and his moral foundations begin to blur.

amount of frustrations of the "adult" or "businessman" variety, having
nothing to do with love affairs. My house and company in England are
not yet settled, tying up $18,000, on which I've presumably lost 14%.
Lyne is in one of her now familiar moods of "I couldn't care less," and
I've been paying our bills since October—and have not had a Christmas
greeting from her over these days—though she has written from Paris
that she awaits her furniture (from USA), and will presumably come here
with it as soon as the weather permits. I don't know who will ever read
these lines, or who should bother. But these are the shakiest days—or
some of the shakiest—I've ever tried to live through.

Life here is perilously expensive, the household potentially hostile and
untenable as soon as Lyne returns (she has made me quite uncomfortable in the kitchen, and it's rather necessary to eat) and the frustration of
being unable to get any action out of workmen is something quite new to
me. The only thing going well in my life now is my new book,* in which I
have great confidence and expectations.

JANUARY 6, 1968

Good news from Eugene Walter of Rome. Muriel Spark has [my cat]
Spider and he is apparently doing well after 13 days with Muriel. So one
of my five problems is lifted. Dear Spider made the trip Positano-Rome
by bus alone.† I wish I could do more for him than dedicate a book [*The
Glass Cell*] to him. I've told Eugene in case he falls ill—I'm here, and can
not only take him on here but pay for him and see that he is comfortable.

Lyne arrived yesterday 2 PM. A trifle contrite, because she'd "left me
alone all winter" though she knows that's what I want.

JANUARY 11, 1968

Tonight (now 2 AM) rather disturbed by finding out October 20 (or so)
1950 in my diaries. I was seeing Koestler, and a great deal of Lyne. She
and I went to Hastings that day, and dined in Chinatown, and I had
lunched with A.K. and Louis Fischer in the Village. It's good to keep a
diary—at least for me, as I need a sense of continuity—but what a lot of
rubbish one should not bother writing!

A good letter from my mother yesterday. Stanley began his retirement
just before Christmas. All the chores—according to my mother—fall

---

* The future *Ripley Under Ground*.
† On moving to Suffolk, Pat had to leave her cat Spider behind in Rome, where he was later taken in by
fellow writer Muriel Spark.

upon her, and S. is in pajamas by 6 PM. She does the gardening, his
present-giving, card-writing, etc.

JANUARY 18, 1968

I was enormously cheered yesterday by a letter from Rosalind—always
so sane and happy, it is a treat. She thinks I "bury myself in the country."

JANUARY 23, 1968

Pat Schartle sold "Love Is a Terrible Thing" (now called "The Birds
Poised to Fly")* to *Ellery Queen's Mystery Magazine*, which now seems
the last resort when the slicks reject my stories. She sold also—"The
Yuma Baby" to *EQMM*—neither yet paid. I live on Columbia Pictures
[London] money ($26,000) since June 1967 and bought the house here in
Samois-sur-Seine with it. My English accountants sent me what money
remains—so I often feel one of the few people on earth who a) answer
letters promptly and b) work Saturdays and Sundays. Last evening, I
wrote a short letter to Lynn Roth, to which I dare not expect an answer.
She is eternally living with someone. But I asked how she was, told her
how I was doing, & asked if she might like to come to France for a visit
this year.

1/26/68

Am within four days of finishing the typing up of *The Tremor of Forgery*
and I fear its themes are not great enough, that it is not as "great" a book
as I had wished.

2/8/68

Democracy and Christianity. In moments of depression, they seem to
have suffered from a similar catastrophe—an influx of the inferior and
the commonplace, the crude and the vulgar. What has happened to
America? Is it merely a gigantic and dangerous illustration showing what
a class system ought to be, given so many and so heterogeneous a people?
The living standard (high) is by no means impossible, but some people
will always exploit others. As a current French magazine says, America's
real problem is a deep-seated racialism. Given the mediocrity of education, the pockets of ignorance everywhere in the country, there is simply
no end in sight for this racism.

---

* This story was first written in 1949. It appeared in book form in *Nothing That Meets the Eye: The
Uncollected Stories of Patricia Highsmith* (New York, 2002).

FEBRUARY 9, 1968

I alternately think of inviting more people to the house, and of detesting it, and preferring to remain alone—when I am positive I can accomplish something (but would it be better if I saw people?) and I know I can be sufficiently content. Emotionally speaking, I am now conditioned to rejection, which is an absurdity.

I now even toy with the idea of spending a year in New York—for two reasons at least (obvious ones) to become knowledgeable about America again, to change my scene, to see some girls. I am afraid I could not face Texas.* 48 hours are the most I can bear. It is merely depressing to me. I am always interested in the innovations there, but much can be seen of this in N.Y. too. Just now—for comic relief—a garbagemen's strike of 8 days is happening in NY, snow and rain and rats. Where is Ginnie— without whom *The Price of Salt* would never have been written?

2/10/68

On looking through *The Price of Salt* for an hour tonight. Great sense of the teeming New York scene— to me now, after nearly 12 years of coun- try life. A certain quickness—which I wish I had now, which I fear is missing from *The Tremor of Forgery*—which is only partly youth (I was 28 when I began the book) and partly city life. The liveliness (if I may say so) is certainly an asset. It was starting June 1956 that I began "The Country Life" with D. [Doris] S. in Snedens Landing. Though that was less isolated than New Hope. That was followed by Positano (1963) and then Earl Soham (1964–1966). Perhaps I have overdone it. Perhaps the cure is more trips to Paris, more social life. I am lazy about these coun- try to city trips. I am physically lazy, I may as well admit it. I can always think of books I prefer to the city cinema, etc. I shall have to prod myself.

FEBRUARY 23, 1968

Much relieved to hear at 4 PM today that *The Tremor of Forgery* was well received by Doubleday. In fact, Pat. S. has asked for $3,000 instead of the usual $1,500—and it will not go into the Crime Club series, but will be published as a rather straight novel. It looks as if I have about 4 days' work on it. I informed [Jenny] Bradley and Rosalind C. (to whom I wish to dedicate the book).

---

* Not only do Pat's uncle and cousins reside in Texas, her parents have now moved back as well.

2/23/68

It takes two mirrors for the correct image of oneself.

2/27/68

If I had been blind, I could have got married, I am pretty sure.

FEBRUARY 28, 1968

A splendid, happy day. I do have one now and then. I'll see Nathalie Sarraute* Friday, it seems. Via Calmann[-Lévy]—Madame Bradley likes my book (characters in particular and she is right) and I'll see her after Calmann Friday. I feel marvelous. Perhaps I've T.B.? My cat is splendid. My house is sold. (Alas, no.) My book is accepted. Three problems solved out of five that I've had over my head for some six months. Why should I not be happy?

3/17/68

My nervousness and anxiety which gives me such trouble from time to time, is caused by a failure of faith in doing things slowly and steadily as I usually do them. I have always been able to accomplish something if I do it regularly, work at it in peace. I cannot at once grasp the tempo at which someone else is working and quite unnecessarily sometimes assume that it is faster. This presents as unattractive a picture as would a pair of dancers moving to a different tempo. The energy wasted is enormous. How to correct this? Self-confidence would be a help. Why shouldn't other people worry about my tempo—which in fact I am not trying to impose on them? And perhaps they are not trying to impose theirs on me.

MARCH 17, 1968

A fortnight has gone by since Madeleine Harmsworth's[†] visit. She has been on my mind ever since. She will do a piece for *Queen*[‡] on me, and a bit in a collective piece for the *Guardian*. She arrived Saturday, March 2 at 12:33 on a day when my car refused to start, so she had to take a taxi. Lunch on the plaza. The questions went on. We went to bed together

---

* Nathalie Sarraute (born Natalja Tcherniak, 1900–1999), French actress and novelist with Russian roots.
† The young British journalist Pat will have a year-long affair with.
‡ *Queen* magazine, a favorite among London's young jet set as of the late 1950s, was sold to *Harper's Bazaar UK* in 1968.

that night. Serious, idealistic, practical, too. Admires me absurdly—
which, with some Scotch—was perhaps why I had the courage to try. I
succeeded. She is not used to women, but perhaps makes an exception
for me. Since then, she and I have written increasingly warm letters.
Meanwhile in the past fortnight I have had more interviews—maybe
seven—in Paris and here. My "timing" is all out of whack because of
these interviews. One must slow up, which is tough when people ask or
demand ever more productivity.

3/26/68

A day that has already seemed endless to me. No letter from Madeleine
Harmsworth since Friday morning. I simply wanted to state that to love
a girl like her, to make love to her, is like conquering, or at least pleasing,
a continent. It is somehow so important, so important.

6/5/68

The French General Strike.* One doesn't mind it for five days—though
the worst is the absence of post. Then the absence of petrol creeps up.
One starts walking in Paris. One goes to Paris, because at least there are
telephones there. In Paris, chez Jacky [Jacqui], the telephone is either
ringing, or someone is talking on it. Young people in the house, absorbing the bottle of whiskey which I buy daily, yakking, never stopping. If
[Prime Minister Georges] Pompidou or [President Charles] de Gaulle
makes a speech,† there is so much talking in the room, that one must read
the newspaper the next day (I must) in order to know what he said.

   I went to Paris also to escape Lyne. She has now appropriated the
living-room and the garden. If I throw in an abscessed tooth, ten days
ago, I can convey my misery—perhaps. She has refused, via her lawyer,
to pay me my half—so I've withdrawn by telex $20,000 from the States,
yet to be confirmed in Paris.

   Seven days ago—or so—two evenings a First Aid station was set up
on the Ile Saint-Louis. Bloody heads, one gas case I saw. Jacky insisted
upon going out on the street at 10:30 P.M. and did not return till 1:30
AM., gassed by chloral, she said, making quite a to-do about it. Nothing
serious. I regret to say she is worthless. I am utterly sick of the French

---

* As in the United States and Germany, France experienced a period of widespread civil unrest in 1968.
Student protests were followed by a week-long general strike during what is known as May 68.
† Georges Pompidou (1911–1974) was French prime minister under Charles de Gaulle (1890–1970) and
followed him as president from 1969 until his death in 1974.

yakking. The best people I have met are Mme Yvonne A. of Samois, and Basile R. and his family here. Also Jean-Noël of 55 Rue Saint-Louis-en-Ile, where Jacky rents him a room. He is about 23, blonde, queer, attractive, a painter, generous, polite, not very tall. He too warned me against Jacky. She has borrowed 500 NF from me. I doubt if I'll see it, I owe her about 100 for telephone calls.

My new house in Montmachoux* is five kilometers from Agnès [Barylski]'s† father's house. I do not look forward to having a telephone, if people who do not pay bills are going to be on it all day. Meanwhile Lyne here [in Samois-sur-Seine] keeps up her incredible fury, ready—on the brink—to throw something at me at the mere sight of me in the kitchen. She prances into my side of the house at 9:30 this morning, making good her threat to take a bath *chez moi*. It is a nightmare. Incredible.

Today I wrote the first eight pages of my play. The first work in over a month. This month, as I wrote to Madeleine this evening, has been lost, worthless, exhausting. I was able to get out five letters. One to my mother, also to Madeleine (from whom I haven't had a letter since I saw her May 6th!!!) and to [the A.M.] Heath [Agency] and to Pat Schartle, telling her the difficulties here. To make this world complete, Robert Kennedy was shot twice in the brain early today in California, where he had just won the primaries. The assassin is called Sirhan Sirhan— Jordanian Arab. Kennedy will lose the use of his legs—possibly his sight—if he survives.‡ Los Angeles—I write this at 1 AM June 6th—his life is still in the balance and political campaigning has ceased in the U.S.A. The assassin was 23. The world seems a bit mad. One's friends are not even one's friends. I hate the dog-eat-dog of the atmosphere here. What can one do? Do a favor or a kindness—or give a small gift to someone worthy—like Madame A. or Basile R.

JUNE 15, 1968

Things do not actually improve. Back (from a 4-day stay in Paris) yesterday, with 20,000 N.F. cash, 70,000 as a check. Sent contracts for 3 books (paperback) to Pat Schartle, airmail. Dear Sammy will spend her first real day in the new house alone. She is very English—loves the rain.

---

* In order to escape the stalemate situation with Lyne, Pat searches for a new house nearby and finds one in Montmachoux, but still lives in Samois for the time being.
† Agnès and Georges Barylski were farmhands and Pat's next-door neighbors in Montmachoux, where they lived in a nearby trailer.
‡ The assassination of Robert Kennedy occurs at 12:15 a.m. on June 5, 1968. In fact, Robert Kennedy will die the next day.

I hope she will understand my departure—I'll try to explain I'll be gone just a few hours.

6/18/68

At this late date it occurs to me that Lyne had this in mind all the time: to secure a rather good-sized house while paying for only half of it. In November, in America, she brought back enough furniture, to take over the living room, while knowing I needed to share that room for my lamps, a rug, chairs, etc. At present my beds, rugs, which she used for a few months (six) are unceremoniously and without any word of thanks, of course, dumped on my side of the house.

JUNE 24, 1968

[Montmachoux.] Tuesday. No telephone. No fridge. Carpenter due Thursday. Electrician Friday. No outlets here. Every room needs paint-ing. The toilets run. I wrote Madeleine 2 days ago, I was loaded with francs—8,700 extra. Since then I've been relieved of 6,000 by the *notaire*.* However today a commencement of sanity because I'll not have to have the house in apple-pie order before starting to work.

JUNE 27, 1968

This AM—tired, discouraged—I thought of finding another house with less work to do in it. I even canceled the carpenter, electrician—then after an hour laid them on again. Extremely cool letter (June 25) from Madeleine, who it appears did not get my Samois telegram of last Wed. saying "Moving tomorrow." And plainly M. doesn't know Montma-choux 77 is the only address I have. Samois was death compared to this life. I wrote my mother, Jacky, Eugene Walter. Spider is living in a palace with a four-hundred-yard square ballroom and he and Muriel Spark play "Magic Carpet Dance" games in which she pulls him about on a small Persian carpet! My eyes, alas, are rapidly worsening for reading—as my handwriting lately shows.

JULY 14, 1968

I feel disorganized and for perhaps the third time in 2 years must muster what organizational powers I have. Little by little. Is there ever any other motto for me? My clothes need overhauling, the house needs plumbing, a heating system, a whole painting. And I waste time here writing about it,

---

* Pat buys the house in Montmachoux and needs a notary to seal the deal.

simply because I am a writer. An invitation to go to Zurich for Diogenes Verlag October 12 for a "ball" for writers, critics, press.*

7/17/68

I seem to suffer involuntarily, like an animal, from a sense of overcrowding, or the fact of overcrowding. A sudden jam of four cars in a usually quiet country road is irksome to me. (So is the increasing amount of papers we all must attend to and carry about—surely due to the abundance of people and the need to see that every man gets his just due.) The other source of discomfort is intellectual: one cannot forget the fact that people are increasing in number, that something will happen finally—a brainless, furious internecine war, started by sheer irritation. I have no confidence at all in present Western birth control methods. I write all this, because my feelings have determined where I live—in a tiny town of 160 inhabitants—with attendant inconveniences such as the absence of garbage disposal, a library, a butcher. Company in the evenings. But it is worth it to me to have a sense of elbow room.

7/29/68

I have been fond of church music since sixteen without realizing why, as I am not a believer. It is the fatalism, the resignation that appeals to me. In all good church music—Mozart's "Requiem" and so on to the unsung (mostly) composers, there is the note of true reconciliation to man's fate. The hope of an after-life is perhaps a dream, but a beautiful one. How can any man find confidence in having a family, knowing his children's lives will be the same as his own has been? I realize the drive of nature in producing a family, the happiness and pleasure in having children. But philosophically I do not understand it.

8/7/68

It is quite obvious, that my falling in love is not love, but a necessity of attaching myself to someone. In the past, I have been able to do this without any physical relationship—just to prove my point here. Perhaps a great source of shipwreck in the past has been to expect a physical relationship. I forgot too much the quite idealistic and helpful attitude or relationship which I had with R.C. [Rosalind Constable] from 1941 to 1943—more or less.

---

* At this ball, Pat will meet authors such as Eric Ambler and Friedrich Dürrenmatt, as well as Italian filmmaker Federico Fellini.

AUGUST 31, 1968

Worked hard Aug. 22–August 31 without a break on *When the Sleep Ends** as I now call the play. [Martin] Tickner† is pleased enough. I had to enlarge it by 24 or 30 pages, which was quite a sweat. Rolf T. sounds as usual on the brink of suicide. I've asked him to visit—he may in February. Tonight my first evening of reading in months—which accounts for this entry here—which no one may ever read. I am quite off my tracks, with unfinished houses for 15 or 16 months now. August was lost, legally, with the Samois affair—Earl Soham is said to be sold, but no money as yet.

12/12/68

To live alone, to feel occasional depression. Much of the difficulty is from not having another person around for whom one puts on a slight show—dressing nicely, presenting a pleasant expression. The trick, the sometimes difficult trick is to maintain one's morale without the other person, the mirror. I am in a very small French village where there is not only no English speaking person, but no one "like me," all are farmworkers, masons, housewives. I have been unfairly treated—my own fault for being overpolite—and have tied up four-fifths of the money I came to France with. It is a situation ripe for rankling. For bitterness. I cannot afford to indulge this, because it is fatal to creative work, and I am on p. 121 of a new novel [the future *Ripley Under Ground*], in my third week of it. Extremely few people in the world, I think, live as "lonely" a life as this. A Frenchwoman, Jacqui, on whom I pinned quite some hopes as friend, for moral support, has broken seven dates with me, and I endure the dark winter alone.

12/16/68

Jacqueline Kennedy—the Americans are offended because she is actually in bed with Onassis. The moral turpitude is in the background—but it forms a rather solid background. Jacqueline is consistent. Kennedy had money also. She has a taste for power and money. I suppose one should look at the brighter side—dim though it be. Men and women of America hoped for an idealism in Jacqueline, imagining an ideal because her first husband was an ideal. But women will sleep with anything which has to

---

* There is no trace of this play in her archives.

† Martin Tickner (1941–1992), English theatrical manager.

do with power, social status, and money. It would not be half so bad if they slept with it for pleasure, but to marry it is pretty low.

12/19/68

What do Sammy and I want for Christmas? For me to be sick in bed for at least five days, with someone to wait on me. I would read and sleep, eat and make notes, Sammy would purr, sleep, and eat from my plate. She is now learning to like scrambled eggs from my plate, though she doesn't in principle like eggs.

12/28/68

In November (early) 1962, when I began to take pleasure in existence for existence's sake—it was the beginning of the end for me.

1/1/69

Nervous breakdown, or *crise de nerfs*, which might not exist without an audience. Jumpiness, loss of appetite, but mainly a loss of routine—and it is important whether this loss is due to individual or external conditions. Finally, due to grasping for sleep at any cost, the day may as well become night and vice versa. Above all, unfortunately for the poet, it is a physical phenomenon, which can be corrected by pills or forced feeding. Above all, unfortunately, it is unproductive, artistically, like this charming pen I write with now, which I have to hold backwards in order to get ink to flow out of it. For God's sake! What we all want is fluidity! Is it only sperm these days? We want also ink, water for the dry fields everywhere.

1/2/69

Madeleine Harmsworth has a curious lack of enthusiasm—about anything. Of course I understand this, in her, knowing quite a bit about her blood and experience. But I find it curious—just abstractly—to meet in someone twenty-seven. I will be happy if she is concealing a hidden fire.

1/6/69
(J.V. [Jacqui])
Togetherness
Why not take pleasure in these nights without sleep?

It's little enough time I have to spend with you,
Even in imagination, such as this. And leisure
Such as sleeplessness comes not often
In a lifetime of trying for leisure.
Leisure doesn't exist. It's a hope, an illusion,
Like love. A word I don't need. Enough of words.
This is the age of the telephone without a real message,
Of the letter, which though promised, does not arrive.
Like the friend who promised to come, and doesn't
Though desperately needed. These disappointments do not quite kill
The person who waits.
And since this is the age of false promises,
Why not have a completely false love,
Made of imagination? What's the difference?
What sustains all the other people on the streets,
The people who appear so sustained,
Walking about, talking, smiling?
What keeps them going? The same phoniness?

1/7/69

Will it ever be possible to enjoy existing every day? To take a joy in being
conscious—which means to take a pleasure, somehow pride in the everyday things of life, to believe that a certain corner in one's house is beautiful, even satisfying, not only to oneself, but perhaps to a stranger. All
this means a slowing up, a radical change for me, if it were an everyday
occurrence, something unceasing. It's happiness and I am afraid of it. It's
like stepping out of a capsule into thin air.

2/12/69

So what? She [Mother] inspires me to write poetry. How many women
do? I do realize I am captive of past experiences with my mother. Betrayal.
Neglect. One continues to seek this. It's destiny. It can be corrected artificially, but this is not emotionally satisfying. It is like wearing a brace all
the time for a crooked back. The brace is so heavy and tedious, boring
and ugly, it is almost better to walk with the crooked back and suffer a little pain now and then. At least one leaves one's flesh open to the pure air.

2/15/69

In love, for illogical reasons, one struggles against all logic to make of
the other person what he or she is not. This is unconsciously deliberate,

of course, giving one a chance to hit back at the parent who has caused it all, by rejecting the beloved, or at least the temporary object. One small one-upmanship for psychiatry: once one understands this, one may not repeat it. And if one repeats it, one is at least forewarned and forearmed by psychology. I don't think it ever destroys the whole pattern—unless someone comes along to whom one can tell all this, and who is in fact quite different from the pattern one has been using perhaps for many previous years.

2/23/69

Two brief notes tonight: my affinity for the amoral, or the positively criminal or—in that splendid phrase of Doris' (Jungian) analyst re Lynn Roth: "She has not the stuff of which character is made." Neither has Jacqui V. She didn't start early enough in childhood. Perhaps it was never there. Honesty, diligence—that difficult trait which I and all good peasants possess, the ability to work for hours without necessarily seeing a result of the work, and certainly receiving no word of praise, no penny of recompense immediately. It is too late for people like Jacqui. But I love her because I understand her, and there are few if any women I understand in this world.

Second note: Re the sense of inferiority, or perhaps simply anxiety, which comes after the age of forty. A feeling one ought to do better work; that one is judged by the brilliance or originality of one's earlier work. An absurd, unfortunate handicap—because over forty-one has something different to offer. Better "art." In truth—more imagination.

5/1/69

London—20 Chesham Hotel. A cruddy batch of newspapers sticks out of the post slot of the door across the hall from me. I am room #67 on the seventh floor, the newspapers have been there for several days, worn at the edges, and judging from the bad service in this SWI hotel, one might assume that no one occupies the room. I pulled the newspapers— five days' worth—out of the slot late one afternoon, and hardly thirty seconds later there was a knock on my door. A frowsy, kinky American woman of about 60 or 55 stood there, saying, "How dare you remove my newspapers, they are four months old, you have no right." "Indeed I haven't," I replied, and handed them to her. They were dated March 5th 1969. I asked the Italian housekeeper what went on there. "She puts them out in the morning, and takes them in in the evening." They were gone 5–8 PM, but as I write this at midnight, the papers are back again. "Don't you dare do that again!" she told me.

5/4/69

Brighton—Dolphins doing tricks in the aquarium. Barbra Streisand filming in the [Royal] Pavilion. Daisy W. & I played push-penny machines on Prince's Pier, losing finally, of course, but we had a good time.

5/27/69

My gambling, my vice, my lure, my evil, is a woman who is not exactly honest. It is quite obvious, I cannot stay away from it. At home, I curse, preach to myself (but never swear oaths to stay away), I analyze it and her, and yet I go back. It is the same thing with my writing, an attraction for the evil. Not, by any means, that I consider myself the "good" side of this picture. I am cautious, stingy, easily offended. And yet, Daisy, Rosalind—my good friends who know me best—have pointed out that I am gullible and have a deplorable bad judgment of character.

6/2/69

Today I realized that I have enough carbon paper to last me the rest of my life—three boxes of it. This was the most depressing thought I have had in years. I was tempted to throw away one box, so I would not quite have enough carbon paper to last me the rest of my life . . .

6/5/69

I have an unfortunate habit of not taking comfort or cheer from what I have already done—or achieved. How many times and in how many ways have I said this in these notebooks! This, tonight, 3 AM, P. 197 of 2nd Ripley—Brainfog. A more complex book than I thought.

6/9/69

Voulx,[*] 77—the single butcher shop dislikes me, because I seldom buy meat for myself, only spleen for my cat, and liver for her. Amazing to me that they remember me at all—since I go there only once every ten days or so. And they remember me unkindly because I do not spend enough money there.

---

[*] Voulx is a neighboring village located about three miles from Montmachoux.

6/14/69

Enough of hope, the future. I have always lived on it. It serves one well in my society, because it implies work, achievement, for the future, which is or soon becomes the present. In 1958, I thought I had a caesura. This one now 1969 is more important and I cannot face it. A reassessment. A bewilderment of riches confronts me. I would say this if I were poor in health and in money. I mean a richness of life—How can I say it? The beautiful green horizon, the blue sky, they are in my future. I love them. I look forward.

6/18/69

How many months has it been now? Slogging. Maybe twenty months. Disappointments, hurts, tears, even loneliness, something a bit new, and something else quite new, a sense of being surrounded by enemies. I hate this. All this has led to depression and lack of concentration such as I have never known before. The pull-out, alas, will be slow. I try. I wish I could leap out. But it is like climbing out of a ditch where I am in mud up to my thighs. I hope it's only to my knees now. I write this as my father (I heard today) is seriously ill. Four things hang fire—including my novel-in-progress. And the shoddy people I chose as my friends cannot even send (return) a cutting, or two or three books. Rudeness, dishonesty, untrustworthiness, disappointments—that has been my lot for two solid years in France.

I do *not* want to look back. I want to look forward. I don't even want to look at the present.

6/23/69

Looking—in fact just glancing—back five years: the moral is, stay alone. Any idea of any close relationship should be imaginary, like any story I am writing.

7/14/69

One can hide being in love, but one cannot fake it.

7/16/69

If I shed a few tears at 3:AM, while reading the dictionary—tears, because of personal matters—I know where I am now. Nothing is out of order. The tears in fact are a good idea. It is not like being twenty-eight years old, perhaps full of self-pity without admitting it, above all being inexperienced.

7/18/69

Salzburg. The plane is called "Johann Strauss" whose portrait is in the cabin.* 70-minute flight. The terminus bus forgot to charge me 10 shillings for the trip to town. Taxi at the bus stop to Getreidegasse 265. Getreidegasse [a] one-way [street], full of tourists & beatniks. #20 room at Goldener Hirsch, no bath, but charming dressing room through a low door—2 cupboards, mirror & dressing table, a window, & room to stand up in. Lanz of Salzburg has very shabby & boring window display, but still boasts of "originals." (It is hot here—no purpose for Ripley in this.)† Café Tomaselli—green & white awning & sidewalk tables. Many of the native women wear the [dirndl] bodice of green with the white blouse, etc. of the Austrians.

7/19/69

Bürgerspitalplatz—goes to G'stättentor—to Eigler (Café). A walk to Mirabellschloss. Beautiful view of Feste Hohensalzburg, seen past the directly straight gardens. Red flowers (little box hedges in winter?) monogram-like design. Marionettentheater, *Die Zauberflöte*. I go tonight.

7/20/69

The moonship continues on course. I expect to watch it tomorrow evening (20 July) with Arthur [Koestler]. I think the only man who can grasp this is Wernher von Braun.‡ The astronauts are merely well-trained pilots.

7/20/69

I have seen people who have no souls by any stretch of the imagination. If one calls "soul" something hopeful, higher than the animal. It is possible to say some people have corrupted souls, perhaps, corrupted minds, wills set to evil purposes. I do not believe in the divine spark in the case of a person born by accident, unwanted, hated, trained in a childhood of corruption, theft, dishonesty. The divine spark, like any spark, can be put out by stepping on it.

---

* It is unclear whether Pat means Johann Strauss I or II. Both father (1804–1849) and son (1825–1899) are among the most famous Austrian composers.
† Pat is as usual combining pleasure with work, visiting with old friend Arthur Koestler in Alpbach and researching for her second Ripley novel, in part set in Salzburg.
‡ The first manned moon landing on July 20, 1969, was the greatest accomplishment of German engineer Wernher von Braun (1912–1977), an American citizen since 1955.

7/29/69

I can easily bear cold, loneliness, hunger and toothache, but I cannot bear noise, heat, interruptions, or other people.

8/21/69

Game with chickens next door. I toss a couple of pieces of white fat from a heart for my cat. Thirty or forty chickens swarm, and one gets a piece and runs like a football player with six in pursuit, fat is snatched by a smaller chicken, who is bounced off, by a larger—never has a chicken the tranquility to stop and take a peck of it. After ten minutes— the game is like life—the biggest guy has it, running, running, with no peace to enjoy it.

9/16/69

Today—the hunting season having been open forty-eight hours—hunters shot Agnès [Barylski]'s two pigeons—mother and father of two orphans now. Agnès had had the mother nine years, and she used to come into the house to eat, and sit on Agnès' shoulder while she washed clothes at the brook.

9/17/69

The French woman when angry must displace something. Not usually the furniture. Usually a person. If one is comfortably in bed, then she says you must move to another room and another bed. If one does it, to prevent further screaming, this gives her a sense of power.

If she is a guest and becomes angry, she can scarcely displace the hostess, so she displaces herself, inquiring, "When is the next train to Paris?" and is annoyed when one calmly looks it up and puts her on it.

10/16/69

Third snail story.* The atom bombs have fallen, and all life is destroyed except for snails, which have been able to retreat into their shells, survive for months without food or water. Some snails' shells (therefore the snails) have been destroyed by the foul atmosphere, but enough survive. Laboriously they dig beneath the corrupted surface to find a safe place for their eggs. They seek the fresh wind. It takes time. They are clever

---

* The "third snail story" follows "The Snail-Watcher" (written in 1948) and "The Quest for X Claveringi" (written in 1965–1966 and first published as "The Snails" in the June 17, 1967, issue of the *Saturday Evening Post*).

about finding food, grass, in the remotest spots where it commences to grow, thanks to blown seeds, the wind accidents which remove the foul dust. The radioactive forces delay reproduction, but on the other hand, the snails have no enemies now. They are numerous in a short time. Some have two heads, others two shells. Some are giants, others never grow. Some are cannibals, eating one another. Others are unusually intelligent—leaders by example rather than by communication or domination of their fellows. They know where to go for food. In a hundred years, snails have encircled and populated the earth. They feed on the toughest vegetable life—no bird or fish life existing any longer.

11/9/69

A bad day. Paris. And my car stolen from the parking lot in Montreau between 1 PM and 8 PM. Lawyer presenting me with 2,000 NF bill, saying I am really a charity case and he makes it so low because I am a friend (client) of Madame Bradley's. He even harked back to the Raoul Lévy fiasco, saying he had lowered the price of *Deep Water* rights, when it was a plain matter of time expiration. Paranoia? Not quite. I admire my car thieves, because that shows courage—to pinch a car conspicuous for its right-hand drive, English plates—and moreover they got a bonus of the pocketbook, gift-wrapped, which I bought for my mother today, for Christmas.

Long live the French, their Catholic Church, their charity, honesty, and above all their chauvinism. There is indeed no other country on earth with such self-esteem, with so little reason for it.

11/10/69

Life in France. It's like a prison, with the difference that things here can change—and become worse, whereas in prison the unpleasant situation usually doesn't change, or become increasingly frustrating, unless of course one is trying, and failing, to gain reprieve and so forth.

11/11/69

Being ostracized. At 14 in New York it began for the usual racial religious reasons. Now at 48 in France I feel it for the same reasons, oddly. Here as in New York, I am neither Latin, Catholic, Jewish. I have actually fierce economic objectives—yes—I'd like to earn money and put it aside, save it. But the French attitude is quick and thoughtless: grab it, don't question origin. If it is offered—like a leaping fish—seize it like a hungry seal. I feel very much alone. It was the same in my adolescence.

No mate for me. If I was in love, I had to hide it. I fail to find beauty, honor in France. I find no openness, happiness or generosity. People live as if they expected to be cheated tomorrow. In such a country there is no real love—because love wishes to stand unprotected by any kind of shield.

11/17/69

The few things of beauty in life are like flights—light things with white wings. They do not change with one's age, but remain the same as they were when one was seven—as when one is forty-seven and so on. (Not to mention the fact I was then not burdened with the world's opinion of my emotions, not so much. It was not so dusty, sordid, then, not so limp from having been shoved back into a drawer so many times as now.)

12/30/69

Actually I write this January 5, 1970, but for two weeks I was paralyzed by the shock of Sammy's death December 11–12. The most recent of a lot of shocks since 1967. The kind of grief that cannot be shared by well-meaning friends—and maybe no grief can be. Sammy like all cats was unpossessable, yet I was the only person in her life and certainly she was my only companion. In a countryside of pigs and people unattractive to look at, I appreciated her beauty especially. Her demands I adored. Sometimes she chose to sleep in my bed, sometimes not, and it did not depend on the weather.

I don't know what killed her. She was found at 10 AM Friday Dec. 12 not yet stiff with death, and she had seemed normal and happy the night before. Happy? I'll never know. I was gone in London 27 days. Only I really knew Sammy and her moods. It's a final blow in this kind and hospitable country, and I shall not be sorry to go. Only sorry that my Sammy lies here. She deserves to be buried in England.

12/30/69

There is no official funeral,
Just a shock, and an absence.
Solitude, death become suddenly real.
Walking around the house,
That flexible and warm Egyptian work of art,
Arrogant, demanding of my coffee cream,
Or simply of attention.
That extra arrogance when I came home from a short voyage

And you wouldn't look at me for hours.
The only thing beautiful in my sight,
The only thing to remind me
That there is a land more civilized and gentler
Than this France, and to remind me
That the mourning for the unpossessed and unpossessable
Cannot be shared. It isn't public
Like a family funeral.
I regret you are buried in this alien soil.

1970–1972

FOLLOWING THE DEATH of her cat Sammy, Patricia Highsmith is consumed with grief around the holidays of 1969 and into the new year. Unhappy as she has already been in Montmachoux, the added devastation prompts her to consider a permanent return to the United States, a plan she abandons after a trip back that spring, partly because of her dissatisfaction with the Nixon administration. In late 1970, she relocates to a house on the Canal du Loing in Montcourt, just a few miles away from Montmachoux. Although she feels better in her new home, the underlying current of depression persists, albeit punctuated by manic phases.

Years later, Pat will wax nostalgic about her time in Montcourt. Her notebooks, however, tell a different story: her entries are acerbic and reveal a deep loneliness and disorientation, as well as harsh prejudices. She lashes out against Catholics, Jews, America, her neighbors, French people in general, and French bureaucracy in particular. By contrast, her diaries have little to offer: Pat barely writes a thing in Diary 16, half-heartedly begun in 1969. There are just two pages for 1970 and 1971, respectively, and no written entries at all in 1972, much of that diary filled with drawings. In between, there are long periods of silence.

Pat's relationship with her mother reaches an all-time low after her trip to Texas in 1970: "My doctors say if you had stayed 3 more days I would be dead," Mary Highsmith writes to her daughter. Pat responds in rambling letters to her stepfather about "her buck-passing, evasions, arrogance, her stupidity." Stanley Highsmith dies in November 1970. In the period that follows, Pat and Mary keep exchanging hateful letters, despite having decided—and not for the first time—to cut off contact completely.

The 1972 publication of Pat's novel *A Dog's Ransom* adds fuel to the fire, as it's dedicated to her biological father Jay Bernard Plangman. Pat began work on the book about a dognapping in June 1970, after completing final revisions to *Ripley Under Ground*, which appeared later that year. Within a month of starting *A Dog's Ransom*, she had more than 250 pages typed; her college friend Kate Kingsley Skattebol provided critical research, including details on the everyday workings of the New York Police Department.

Pat's progress on *A Dog's Ransom* is delayed as renovations to the Montcourt house and preparations for the move take priority. When she finally leaves Montmachoux, she feels relieved and cautiously optimistic. Her new neighbors, journalists Desmond and Mary Ryan, are friends of hers. "In this way, I hope to pull myself out of this eremitic existence," she writes to her friend Ronald Blythe in Suffolk.

As Pat types up the final manuscript for *A Dog's Ransom* in August 1971, the idea for a new Ripley novel has already taken shape in her mind. She starts writing *Ripley's Game* in February 1972 and completes 140 pages in just two weeks. Around the same time, Pat begins to plan *The Animal Lover's Book of Beastly Murder*, a second collection of short stories following *The Snail-Watcher* (New York, 1970, published in the UK under the title *Eleven* the same year with a foreword by Graham Greene). Animals are unquestionably superior life-forms in Pat's estimation, and in gratitude, she gives them the upper hand in each of these stories.

1/5/70

I swing these days between resentment (a sense of being badly treated by other people) and aggressive hatred. This way lies madness and paranoia. I have problems unsolved here, problems that have to do with other people—some slow, some dishonest. Perhaps all other people have the same problems as I? I don't know. I do know I rejoice when I can say the problem is solved, obliterated. But I dislike the adrenaline in my veins.

These are "man of the house" problems, for I do think if it concerned a married couple, the husband would worry more than the wife, as he would be expected to deal with them. No wonder men die a bit earlier than their wives. It's 3:30 AM. I lie in bed reading in this first hideous month without my cat, wishing I could find some consolation somewhere. It is to be found neither in friends nor in success in work, I think, because I have both, and declined an invitation to dinner for tomorrow. I keep trying to grasp within myself (actually by working) the solace and security I need. To look outside—just to have the company of other people—seems escape—though I write an absurd amount of letters. Obviously I am self-absorbed. But what writer isn't? My besetting sin— lately—is that I reproach myself too much. I am constantly telling myself

I don't accomplish enough, I don't work fast enough, I could do better. (This perhaps is not even the opinion of people who know me.) Alas, it is so difficult for me to know when to flog myself, when to say "Thank God (or luck) that I have done as well as I have"—or am doing as well. What is this terrible drive? It makes me miserable. The only consolation (one must find one) is that there are other tormented ones who scribble such things in the early hours of the morning.

1/12/70

I learned to live with a grievous and murderous hatred very early on. And learned to stifle also my more positive emotions. In adolescence therefore I was oddly in command of myself, more so than most people—judging from case histories of more average or ordinary (whatever that is) people that I read about. It is strange. Some adolescents explode at nineteen or twenty and get into trouble. Others—well—

JANUARY 17, 1970

Returned Dec. 13–14 to find that my Sammy had died for no known reason Dec. 11–12. Nothing else civilized being in my neighborhood, I have had a hard time since. With effort I recommenced work Dec. 24, and now have signed USA and Calmann-Lévy contracts. My life is changed, I shall go to USA Feb. 3 to stay at the Chelsea Hotel* till 15 February when I shall go to Santa Fe with Rosalind Constable—there to remain for a month with typewriter. I fight three battles now, here, in France, too tedious to describe. Am reading Christopher Isherwood's *Down There on a Visit* just now. Delightful reading. In effect, I am lost now, depressed, defeated—yet oddly I keep earning quite suffi-cient money, the absence of which is the source of unhappiness for the majority of people. On the contrary, I am now cynical, fairly rich (at least far from worried financially), lonely, depressed, and totally pes-simistic about any future emotional entanglement, love affair. I do not wish any. I should love to meet, however, Anne Meacham,† an actress

---

* The Chelsea Hotel at 222 West Twenty-Third Street is the stuff of legends. It was there that Andy Warhol and Paul Morrissey filmed their experimental movie *The Chelsea Girls*, featuring Nico, in 1966, that Robert Mapplethorpe and Patti Smith shared a room, and William Burroughs wrote *Naked Lunch*. It was from the Chelsea that Dylan Thomas "sailed out to die," and there that Leonard Cohen had the affair with Janis Joplin he sings about in "Chelsea Hotel No. 2." Arthur Miller moved into the Chelsea after his divorce from Marilyn Monroe, stayed for six years, and described it as knowing "no vacuum cleaners, no rules and shame."

† Pat discovered Anne Meacham's photograph in a magazine and asked to be introduced to Meacham by her friend Alex Szogyi (1929–2007), American professor of French literature, Chekhov translator, gourmet critic, astrologist, and film actor. Meacham and Pat never did meet.

of New York. Alex Szogyi knows someone who knows her—same house. And why write all this? Because it is comforting. Because it is too utterly boring and too much for anyone to plow through after I am dead. Graham Greene has written a 500-word introduction to my short story collection *The Snail Watcher* which will appear in London and New York in the summer. The death of my cat remains the most important event—I am not recovering, and shall rid myself of this house as soon as I can.

1/24/70

It is possible to fall in love with someone poor in spirit, or rich in money. These things don't matter. The above both can be equally disastrous. I think of this because of odd questions put to me by interviewers. They always put their questions as if a writer were calculating. I don't calculate about themes. It's embarrassing for me to write this. Corroborated once more today in *Guardian* of London. From Dostoyevsky to Melville, Bellow to Koestler to Highsmith, the victim is bound up with his murderer. Not a bad company am I in, and I am pleased.

1/25/70

My current bureaucratic difficulties are mainly a form of masochism on my part. Very soothing to put this on paper at 3 AM Monday Jan. 26, 1970.

1/26/70

Late middle age: how political idealism vanishes! At twenty and thirty, boycotting stinking countries (like Spain then, like Greece now) had a point. Now I find R. C. [Rosalind Constable] and myself contemplating a summer cruise 1971 in Greece.

1/30/70

Especially delicious pleasure to look back three and four years ago, to 'remember my peaceful garden in England—to believe that I was happy and calm then. A photograph of that period seems almost shocking. In the last two years eight months—too long a period by far—life has been little else but struggle, difficulties, unfairnesses. I find not one compensation for being here in France, that's the real rub. I don't even like the food. However, I began this entry to remark on pleasure. Yes, idle pleasure of the aging. But a pleasure—yes. I have to find some pleasures—now—or I shall go mad before I can possibly extricate myself.

1/30/70

To Franz Kafka today I lift my hat in respect. I fall on my knees. I cry briefly on my bed. I have spent the day fighting bureaucracy and have failed. Furthermore, they have billed me as usual. Money is the least of it. It is the time wasted, and the depressing sight of 30- and 40-year-old men delighted with their paper-pushing jobs, their dishonest profession, their power over honest people. It is the power of paper, of someone always above them to whom they say they are answerable. God fuck them when they die. Their God is ready to pay for a lay, anyway, so they can make a bit more money.

2/10/70

If you open the cupboard door, five people fall out. New York. Togetherness. Solitude. Beauty. People are beautiful until you have too many of them.

3/8/70

Near-panic is over. In Texas I was hardly able to work, afraid always that the telephone would ring, that my mother would come in. I have a deadline of 31 March to repair *Ripley*[*]—a most intellectual repair. I fear I am slighting it. No further incident takes place, only closer questioning. Texas was a nightmare. The taunts, the stupid and shabby taunts of my mother I'll never forget. She is growing hard of hearing and will not admit it. I think she will outlive my stepfather, and what then? She will make foolish purchases, and her money will not last forever. I shudder to think of having to take care of her, because I could not bear to live under the same roof.

3/9/70

[Santa Fe.] Cafés on the street said to be open are not open. The people and cars are slow and polite. Here lives Mary Louise Aswell, who bought "The Heroine" for *Harper's Bazaar* when I was twenty-three. She lives with Agnes Sims[†] in a very pretty house with some Ibizan dogs. Happy Krebs, Alison still here. It is a car town, a supermarket pay-by-check town. A satellite town—squatters, hippies, product of population explosion—is soon to appear near Santa Fe. The word is UGH!

---

* *Ripley Under Ground* was published in 1970 by Heinemann (London).
† Agnes C. Sims (1910–1990), painter and sculptor who drew her inspiration from prehistoric artifacts in New Mexico.

3/9/70

Texas. I met alas a lot of elderly people. All coasting on mysterious or inherited money. All like cars going on two cylinders, but in fact how many cylinders have they by nature? They all watch lousy TV and are familiar with the most forgettable performers I have ever seen—or heard of. Voices of women in the drugstores and supermarkets sound uncannily alike not merely as to accents but as to pitch. All the women over fifty wear yellow or green "slacks" and scarves on their heads, funny jackets, carry straw handbags, wear horn-rimmed glasses—and talk alike. Many people live in utterly sloppy houses, dirty and full of old newspapers. Others are so neat, their homes look like a series of hotel rooms. I saw nothing in between. The efficient working are neat. The retired are a mess.

3/23/70

My mother is manic-depressive, my stepfather has Parkinson's Disease & should not even be driving. While my portrait—me much glorified by my mother—hangs over the living room fireplace and she praises me to her friends behind my back, she attacks me to my face. Even once physically, when I tried to pass a doorway she was blocking. She seems to want to label me stupid before my stepfather, but not before her friends so much. She would not assist me by telling me which of two telephone listings was most likely to find [cousin] Dan at 3 PM, but asserted before Stanley that I was unable to find Dan's name at all. Another such occasion when I pointed out that the garage light had been on all night, there were three switches in the kitchen, & she ordered me to "figure out" which one worked the garage, as if this were an I.Q. test. I found it quiet on the Negro question—the various people I met. The TV mutters constantly chez mother & stepfather, & my mother mutters over it. My stepfather needs rest, regular meals, a neat house, and has none of these. He weighs 135 lbs. should weigh 170—but thank God spends Sat-Sun with his stepfather who insists upon his presence. The house is in shambles— closets, drawers, kitchen shelves, fridge, unsorted, one cannot find anything. I react badly, drift about the house trying to do "projects" to tidy up the place, my efforts usually resisted by my mother. She wishes ever to expand into new, uncluttered territory, so that she can mess it up. They've bought a $6,000 property in Arkansas, now being paid off on mortgage, & now she wants to buy land in Arizona, which Stanley is against. But if he dies in two years? Who will have control over what she does with their money?

3/27/70

Palisades, New York. P. [Polly] Cameron's* house a pointed 3-story dark red, with balcony, in the woods near Gert's. I saw three of four houses for rent. $275 to $300 per month empty. Two in Piermont, which at least has a tidal estuary with ducks. The barn where I used to live was burnt down at a time when no one was living in it. What a pity. Only the chimney stands. Two years ago. But what prices—for the nearness to New York. Today, all day on the West Side, I am depressed by the vulgar looking, vulgar speaking proletariat and wonder if I could stand it all again.

3/27/70

Awaiting a bus in 40th St. Manhattan Terminal. I saw a 19-year-old girl who resembled very much J. [Joan] S. as I knew her in 1947. It could have been her daughter—same hair & eyes, large Germanic hands, a narrower face. A slight shock. It could have been a boy. One can go on from there.

4/30/70

The tragic irritation given by a mentally sick person. I mean, if the person is backbiting, combative, resentful, falsely accusing, it is damnably difficult for family & friends to continue to have patience. The sick person so full of nasty energy, so spoiling for a fight, and has more energy in fact than those around who are probably supporting the sick person. (R.T. [Rolf Tietgens])†

5/15/70

My emotions, passions in childhood and adolescence were strong as murderous impulses and had to be repressed just as much.

5/15/70

America now hesitating about employing a black woman professor who is an avowed Communist. It should be interesting & stimulating to have a Communist professor, providing she lets her polemical ideas filter through now and then. No one balks at Christian professors. Christ

---

* Polly Cameron is Pat's American friend in Palisades, New York, who designed a few of the book jackets of Pat's novels for Harper & Row.
† The thirty-year friendship between Rolf Tietgens and Pat ends in New York in 1970, after a heated argument.

was essentially a communist. No one fears that Americans will begin to practice what Jesus preached. Why fear the preaching of Communists or communists? When it comes to sharing the wealth, American workers have a tight fist on their paychecks, and their eyes on the glory to come— retirement with a pension, not the Kingdom of Heaven.

5/15/70

I can imagine committing suicide if I had severe pain. Mental pain, however, bad as it may be, is so far bearable, furthermore interesting, as physical pain is not.

5/22/70

If I cannot see the end of a short story or a novel, no use beginning.

5/22/70

It is easy to see why a novelist turns to fables in his old age —the short, simplified form of what he has been trying to do all his life. The virtues of youth are energy and detail, the latter usually amusing. Thought comes later. Witness Dickens.

5/23/70

Comforting to base happiness & satisfaction in life on one's children; not so comforting to realize they are going to make the same mistakes.

6/1/70

The misery of middle-age is caused by the ability to see things in proportion. I mean mainly work, the value of it. At twenty, one can spend a disproportionate amount of energy—become exhausted perhaps—but one has produced a flower to give to someone.

8/7/70

Bloody flies. Three solid weeks of them. Today the first rain in ten days and the flies are worse. "God fuck it!" I say as they bomb my hair, perhaps laying eggs as they zoom. Why else this suicidal descent into foliage—which doesn't even stink since I wash my hair every two days to discourage flies? A fly is now dying, half dead from "Néocide" bomb, in my wastebasket. A formidable French farmer here eats flies with his soup, being too tired of scraping them off the edge. Every morning, fourteen or so to be gathered with a bit of paper from sink & drain board.

Revolting? So are the cow stables here revolting. The situation could be improved. The *hortus* [garden] situation here could be improved if the whole village at once made an attack on nettles. Hitler could have been stopped in 1940 if the whole nation at once had made a consistent, courageous counterattack.

8/10/70

To find in your death joy,
To find some reason why you died not old
And in beautiful health,
To imagine without resentment
The worms making play and food of you,
And your pointed white teeth
The last of all to go,
And surely there in the earth as I write this—
That perhaps is wisdom.

AUGUST 16–17, 1970

A dream that my cat Spider (now with Muriel Spark) was hit by a car and nearly cut in two at the stomach. He went running about, not in pain, and I saw that he had a collar around his waist. It was bloody. I said, "I'm going to remove the collar." Then he fell in two.

8/17/70

Revising first 258 pages. It is painful to live through the development of a book*—because I have not thought this one out completely before I began. All my books are like this to some extent. At least now I know it will be a book, whereas I was in some doubt in the past month.

9/9/70

Religion is an illusion, a very sustaining one for some people. But everyone needs an illusion of some kind to endure life with the necessary fortitude. It is strange that the human animal is like this—to depend utterly upon an illusion and at the same time to be able to realize that it is an illusion. My illusion is that I make progress. It is also an illusion, the

---

* Writing *A Dog's Ransom*, her novel about a "poison pen letter" demanding ransom for a kidnapped dog, Pat spends several months wavering between different scenarios. It will take her until December to decide how the novel should end, and what will be the fate of the culprit.

value of work for work's sake. This is the illusion that sustains the brainless ant also.

11/2/70

Zurich—the seagulls glide over the city all day. How do they see their way home? Do they sleep in the same nest every night? Or do they out of breeding season find a different nook every night?

12/20/70

My mother is the type who fires a shotgun and then wonders why some of the birds are killed, others wounded and the rest scared. "Why don't the birds come back?" I came back several times to suffer always the same shocks.

12/20/70

USA. The hardhats (American peasant stock) having affiliated themselves with the self-made millionaires, if not the USA Eastern seaboard intellectual casually moneyed   the hardhats and hardworking proletarians cannot be got at by the left. The carrot is too close to their eyes for them to see anything else, or any distance beyond three inches.

🐦

1/2/71

Death. The telegram about S.H. [Stanley Highsmith] said "S. died November etc." and it had to be true, but even after a couple of family letters which were concerned with it, the fact does not seem true. This despite the fact that the death was not a great surprise to me, because S. had been looking very bad in April, seven months before.

1/15/71

A dream in which I murdered two people (the first Maggie E. [Tex], second unidentifiable) and managed to hide their bodies on a large garbage dump, unburied. The realization I had killed two people gave me a shocking, very real sense of shame, guilt, and insanity. I talked to myself briefly in public, and thought that if a persistent police official quizzed me, he could break me down. The murders were irrevocable & unforgivable acts, changing my life forever. It is the first time I have ever had a dream about murder. Plainly an extreme attempt of the unconscious to throw guilt and anxiety on my head.

2/10/71

One of the depressing things a mature woman has to look back on is the insipid grin that she wore as the men's advances continued—even into bed—until perhaps unpleasant sensations, or a bad smell, wiped it off. The bland assumption of men and young men that what pleases them pleases all women is one of the wonders of the world.

2/11/71

American togetherness or any other kind of togetherness gives to some people a sense of being alive. Just because the doorbell or the telephone is ringing, or there is some awful noise from somewhere, a certain type of person feels more alive. There is one way of killing off these people: put them in comfortable solitary confinement with desk, writing and reading material, and they would go mad.

2/20/71

Hero (or heroine) meets a stranger one or two days after hero, etc. has developed a headache (which may be a tumor) or has been given bad news by his doctor. The stranger is not death, but the hero believes he is. Therefore, his attitude is fearful, respectful, contemptuous.

2/27/71

Above idea has somehow influenced the 3rd Ripley* I began today. Implanting the idea of impending death in the mind of a man who is not really going to die. The idea of associating a real person with "Death" is a different idea.

3/19/71

One reason to admire the automobile: it demolishes more people than wars do.

APRIL 16, 1971

Returned April 3 from London, must go again April 20–23 for my accountants, & will stay chez the Barbaras.

---

* In *Ripley's Game* (1974), Tom Ripley tries to manipulate someone into committing a murder by starting the rumor that the man, Jonathan, has only months left to live.

Have not quite finished my novel [*A Dog's Ransom*], because (mainly) of lack of technical information from N.Y. Police Dept. which—thanks to G.K.K.S. [Kingsley] came in March 15—I hope the last I'll need.

My cat is Tinker—born August 15, now 8 months, intelligent & affectionate.

For further information: I live next to Mary & Desmond Ryan and am considerably happier than when I was in Montmachoux—18 kilometers from here.

4/16/71

To have respect for God equals having respect for electricity for example. One (mankind) has given a name to a power. That of electricity is more tangible. It is wrong to put either on a pedestal. But people in the past have worshipped rain, or the cat.

APRIL 17, 1971

Temporary triumph: a day of chore accomplishment, so I feel almost normal again. Gardening & repair of two items broken by guests. I hope to have no guests and no vacation till Sept, when I may go to Wien Tink does well with her new cat door. Letter from Tristram Powell* of BBC London. Would I like to script a documentary on a French château-robbing gang. I hope to see him in London.

4/27/71

Because the animals require land to raise the food that they eat (not, God knows, if He looks down, for them to gambol on and nibble from), their food will be increasingly grown in laboratories a hundred stories tall. More and more food must be grown, because more and more animals must be raised to feed more and more people. Thus, in a way animals and people are eating each other. Animals eat man's spiritual heritage—the land—and man eats the flesh of his cousins, the animals. But both man and animal are imprisoned in the twentieth century.

This is not only a story of over-population but of philosophy of life—that life itself is somehow "worth" the hemming in. That there is some virtue in numbers. The more the merrier reversed. Or cannibalism rampant. Now, animals live in layers, never putting a foot to the

---

* Tristram Powell (1940–), English film and theater director, producer, and screenwriter. In 1968, he made *Contrasts*, a film about Japanese writer Yukio Mishima.

ground. Soon people will have to do the same, will be born and will die on the 500th story, and the Earth will present a bristling appearance to extra-terrestrial observers, because of the prevalence of skyscrapers— the true Living Machines. This is the *Tier* [animal] Age. Next will come the Pier Age. Piers will be built out into the ocean for as many miles as man dares. But this Pier Age is for another story—the extra-spatial snail story.

5/6/71

Some news, for today: self-confidence is everything. Everything? Yes, everything.

5/14/71

I could be so much happier if I could learn to take a little pride, satis- faction in something I have done—especially now around the house (a new house where I've been six months). But the guestroom doesn't look quite attractive enough, or finished—or inviting. The garden is still 30% a mess. Some light bulbs are still naked. So be the mess. My style of life. Partly my dissatisfaction comes because I'm having a hell of a time put- ting an end on my book in progress. There is no way out but my old doc- trine: work daily for work's sake. Never pause to look at the result. The result will come by itself.

5/17/71

I think it is true that very young people, falling in love, are in love with themselves—fascinated by what they are feeling. A person much older does not "fall" in love but is still capable of curiosity (despite all he or she may have experienced) and is enchanted perhaps also by what he has come to regard as beauty, in a face, by no means dependent upon youth. There is the real joy now, even need, to make another person happier, possibly, by declaring one's love. Such a thought rarely crosses the mind of a young person. There is of course also the feeling that it is one of the last opportunities to know a close- ness with someone.

6/5/71

As a novelist, I can say—or I'd like to make a statement here anyway—the dictionary is the most entertaining book I have ever read.

6/5/71

In regard to concentration, so important when writing a novel or doing
any other work of art, there is also a concentration on the past of mankind, perhaps stretching back to 4,000 BC—but certainly it ought to go
back to Chaucer: an ever-present framework in which to live, by which
to measure what one is doing at the present time. A happy thought. It is
what is meant by education, perhaps. I wish everyone felt this way. How
absurd of me. Yet how easy and pleasant a way it is, simply a consciousness of history, a seeing of things in proportion.

There was always fighting, in the sense of competition, among merchants and intellectuals, even. Now in the age (of all ages!) of radar and
long-range guns, we have street-fighting—among illiterates—in an age of
the education of the masses. God, how the masses resist!

7/15/71

Living out of one's native land. That a certain degree of "feeling lost" in
a foreign country is not unreasonable and not undesirable. It may take
me till I am seventy, if I live that long, to return to Oaxaca, where I shall
never thoroughly understand the traditions and the family habits of these
hospitable and peaceable people. The important thing is mutual good will
and rapport, or the effort toward it. Where else? Austria is beautiful, but
I'm told the country people are not basically friendly (by A.K. [Arthur
Koestler]) but rather suspicious or cool. Italy? A village—but that's boring.
The diminishing of the church in 20 years would do much to improve the
climate.

7/20/71

In a hundred years one will read about millions being killed in India,
or South America without batting an eye, or sending one dollar to help
them. (A hundred years? Thirty.)

8/15/71

One situation—maybe one alone—could drive me to murder: family life;
togetherness. I'd strike a blow in anger, and kill, probably, a child aged
from two to eight. Those over eight would take two blows to kill. From
what I observe, the adults who get along in a household with children
have essentially joined the children, that is, the house is a finger-printy
mess, interruptions reign supreme. What a pleasure it must be for the
man of the house to go off to work and escape.

8/18/71

On hearing that the *Reader's Digest* may print a condensed version of *Strangers on a Train*—presumably the size of a bouillon cube: maybe science will one day create edible books, so much easier on the brain than reading anything. Then we can see astronauts popping a cube into their mouths before donning space suits for some planet. "That was *Anna Karenina* they just swallowed. Good psychological bolstering for the day's work."

9/11/71

Dreams have become a substitute for reality. Mine are at least more entertaining.

9/12/71

What troubles the small and the great is the difficulty of reconciling their personal dramas with such things as the moon in its course, the strength of the sea, the inevitability of death. Everyone feels so small, yet his problems shake him with the force of hurricanes. It does not make sense.

10/17/71

The peculiar, extra, awful fatigue after being with people—now after only thirty-two hours with them. Is it because of the phoniness? I wasn't particularly phony. It's my own inward tension.

10/20/71

L.P. [Lil Picard] writes me about her depression with the "art world" of New York. I'm sure she'd be the first to call it normal. For at least 12 years she has been mocking art herself. Curiously art is a word like God, with more ramifications than anyone cares to admit. Curiously art is just as pure as God. Curiously neither can be defined, to suit everyone. But everyone who cares about truth and beauty, and who cares about decency is somehow saddened when one or the other is mocked.

10/20/71

Vienna—At first a sprawling looking town with black, gray or grimy buildings. The main color is dark gray, even in daytime. They are now working on a subway which I am told will take them 10 years. The Germans offered to do it in three years, the Americans in two, but the

Austrians prefer higher employment for ten years. The people over thirty-five are for the most part overweight. The younger people are slender and fair, with delicate Donatello noses, chins, eyes, which must be of short duration, because surely, the sturdy people about are their parents. They push a bit much on the trams, worse than the French, I think.

I stay with T.G. [Trudi Gill]* and husband at 4 Johann Strauss Gasse. T. paints in an exuberant manner, bringing off free washes of human figures. As for the paintings, I do not find them united (or see as yet that they develop) in a certain direction. She herself (I have known her since 1961, but have seen her almost not at all) is extremely nervous with the maid. It is a waste of energy, her nervousness; a drive without direction. I am guilty of the above fault also: misdirected nervous energy. Very bad for the health, and unattractive to see.

T. would like to reform the world, without becoming Marxist, yet she is extremely concerned that the dollar just went down from 25 to 24 for the schilling—in regard to her USA income. I shall sound her out about the crux of the matter: would you give up all the money you have (save what you need for a simple existence) and use your artistic talents mainly and consciously to fight for the welfare of the less better off people of the world?

Shall I say here, in context, that I wouldn't. It is not merely because that at age fifty I have less energy and that I think I have a right to enjoy some of the leisure and pleasure which my own work and talents have brought me. But it is also that I become impatient with lack of endeavor in other people, and peoples, their stupid resistance to outside help in the form of advice—not to mention help in the form of money, policing, efforts at birth control.

I should perhaps have been more privileged at birth, then I would have chucked the whole thing aged 21 out of a sense of guilt and also a real desire to help people.

10/24/71

Tour 2 from the Opera at 2:30 PM this warm Sunday. Some 22 people on an Austrobus, shepherded by a tall dark young man, student at the University of Vienna, who spoke in German and English. Several

---

* Pat's friend Trudi Gill is a painter who studied in New York under George Grosz and Max Beckmann, among others. She is originally from Vienna and married to a diplomat.

times over the Donau [Danube], also the canal, "a natural arm of the Donau," and another "lake" where the Viennese go sailing and swimming. Heiligenstadt, where Beethoven was in 1802, and where he wrote his "Testament" and realized that he was deaf, or becoming deaf, it seems. It is a charming two-story house of buff color with skimpy upper windows, and a peaked roof. Ivy growing on it. A thirty-five-minute stop at top of Karlsberg, where to my delight I was able to buy cigarettes and matches (short since yesterday noon) and I drank two glasses of Heuriger white wine. Hectic—no, busy waiters and waitresses carrying bills in their teeth and trays of sausages or beer in bottles in both hands. Everyone sturdy looking and taking on a pair of sausages like afternoon tea. Grinzing—sloping hills on the left, wine fields. Charming houses all at least 300 years old, wine-serving inns— all very close to Vienna on the 38 Bus.

The flavor of Vienna—old-fashioned, and more than a hint of Latin-Italian temperament—oddly in people speaking German. Rococo and Baroque state buildings—in state—amid the barren squareness of 20th century office buildings and municipal housing. One of the latter I saw today was of reddish stone, four or five stories high, a continuous building of a kilometer length, arches, and apparently one could walk all through it in its 3-sided form. A long stop at the Augustinerkirche today, on the tour—so boring and Catholic-depressing inside that I went outside to smoke.

[NO DATE]

The "happenings" of the 1960's are shown to have no real context, import—or place in the continuity of art. It does not impress anyone to break something—in the name of creativity. The trouble with the modern New York art scene is that the artists are too much together, too jealous, too much worried about what the next fellow is doing. Each artist should follow his own path (dim as it may be) and what if he can't find it in the forest and he dies of loneliness—that's his fate.

To be concrete: for an artist to paint on the model instead of painting the model is a verbal joke, leading nowhere. A temporary insult to his vocation. It will lead to laughter, then depression—like as does drinking too much. Surely artists do not impress themselves by such jokes—and what can such jokes do to the public? What's the matter with Vincent [van Gogh] who painted so terribly alone? He had his brother to talk to, in letters, a brother not an artist, but sympathetic. That's all one needs, one person: a wife, a lover, a friend.

10/24/71

My mother told me she saw my [biological] father first in a photograph in a Fort Worth photographer's window and—sought (somehow) his acquaintance. It occurred to me I have preferred people who sought me out, essentially, rather than those I had to make an effort for. I mean my emotional fascination lingered (or lingers) longer for those who made the first advances to me.

11/2/71

Post office clerk at Grez/Loing. Little pudgy is delighted when something goes wrong for the public and he can assert his "laws," the rules of the game are on his side. Such people do not even inspire a revolution against them. They might serve as protection in a shoot-out—like a straight chair one pulls in front of oneself as a shield against a foot in the stomach.

11/29/71

The idea of helping "undeveloped" countries, giving abundant refugee aid and so forth is such a good idea, so in keeping with democratic and humane principles. But it is the number of the people which dismays, the seemingly incontrollable and increasing numbers. Now it is the Bengali refugees, numbering six or seven million. The human mind boggles, then becomes numb. The problem is taken over by governments, who give money in figures that also stymy the imagination. Finally, the human part of the mind (the emotional part, the kindly part) rejects or ceases to think. Individual moral charity disappears.

12/16/71

One's face in the looking-glass comes to look more handsome, just because we're used to it—reversed. Photographs are a shock. This sounds healthy (assuming that I do it, as I do, and that most people do, which I'm not sure of) because it means that one is trying to take the best view, the most cheerful attitude about the face one is stuck with.

1/13/72

The greatest disservice the Catholic Church has rendered its followers is to have deprived them of their conscience. It's a human right to have a conscience. Everyone is born with one, but it can be taken away.

4/4/72

Work is the only thing of importance or joy in life. Trouble begins when one pauses to consider what one has done.

7/14–15/72

I was leading an ordinary life in the present, but someone referred to a murder I did in 1945. Didn't it bother me? In my dream I had committed murder—but of whom I don't know. Actually 1945 was a hard working, recuperative year for me, during which nothing of much emotional importance happened to me. This is the second murder dream I have had, the first being early 1969 or late 1968. Interesting (or not) that this disturbing dream occurred in a period in which I was especially active, happy, working well.

8/5/72

Diary writers—at least they aren't ashamed of their activities, if they set them down honestly. Some diary writers may be merely obsessed by themselves, of course. Some people do not, and never intend to, look back—in the diary. But there must be a certain core of self-respect in a person who continuously keeps a diary. Maybe he doesn't intend to look back, but someone else might, even if the diary is in code.

8/12–13/72

Mood Diary—Somewhat manic, wrote 9-page story (good). Big appetite. Energy & up early.

8/16/72

Same, nervous, good for working, imagination. Half-moon. Cool weather, for August.

8/17/72

Every country, in one way or another, is a trap. Whether it be England, America, which is rapidly becoming tantamount to Australia, or France, each has its firmly bolted doors. The individual finally lives like a mole, and willy-nilly a rebel. The only people free of this are the young-married, absorbed in ever producing children, a blind end itself, somehow, to them.

8/20/72

Slow decline in past few days till today Sunday I felt quite faint at 7:30 PM when I tried to resume work after a nap. Probably caused by nearly

3 hours of gardening. Still irritation on finger of left hand. Very much colder since yesterday.

8/22/72

Extra tired—but willing. Full moon. P. 239 [of *Ripley's Game*] and in the middle of two murders.

8/23/71

Socialism means there is no more place for the merit system. Quite apart from trust-boosting, socialization of utilities, etc. which is all to the good. Maybe the trouble is, some people like a high degree of luxury, and comfort, and if they feel they have earned enough by their talents to pay for it—why not have it?

8/29/72

Very tired, a bit discouraged & depressed. No energy—but I hope a night's sleep will cure it. 13 days since the manic period. Gave a dinner party last evening. Did not even attempt to write today which is unusual for me. I must now wind up my book, and do it superbly well also.

8/31/72

My French house is like my life and body. The garden represents work, very hard work, never perfect, never finished, and I find there is hardly one day a year when I can say, "It all looks nice."

9/4/72

On 30 Aug. Monday and on following Friday received a letter from my mother, in frothing rage because *A Dog's Ransom* was reviewed in Texas, with dedication to my [biological] father. Depression caused by these insane & hopeless letters sets in on me two or three days after I receive them. Am still suffering 4th Sept. and recover by the usual means: work, laughing, music.

9/7/72

Interesting that art & architectural schools demand that students copy the old masters, i.e. draw their works. This shows how much of the hand itself is in the art of painting, sculpture, or architecture (even). The same copying of old masters is not demanded of students of writing—if there is such a thing, and there is. It would not be a bad idea to ask students to copy out an entire chapter of Henry James, or the Bible. Influences sink in imperceptibly, subtly. It is what the Romans of the year zero meant when they simply exposed boys to the poetry of Horace and Virgil.

9/7/72

I wish I could go to the grocer's and buy jokes in tins. They're just as sustaining as soup.

9/17/72

Seventeenth September and just pulling out of a worse "depression" than the above. Cats mating (two depressing trips to Paris), second letter from my mother telling me to ignore her birthday (she once forgot mine but she never forgets her own), four days' blasting of the house by good-natured plumber Gauthier; hang-ups in carpentry, closet, finishing by Robbe, blast from Barnard Alumnae calling me a racist, which I replied to today. Above all a sense that I cannot cope with all I have to cope with, in the house, and actually I have abandoned my writing for the past two weeks, if not three.

9/30/72

Absolutely wretched for days. Millie (and Flint) visit 24–28. I feel over-tired, unsmooth, nervous. But tonight went to guitar concert at Grez church. Alexandre Lagoya*—not even very good—and this changed my thoughts. Letter from RC asking me why I live here, a question I can't answer—in a few words. The decision must be: to try to make a go of it here (various efforts to be cheerful) or to move somewhere else. RC thinks me too lonely. Yet happiness is always within. I obviously need some other opinions.

10/19/72

It is very tiring to be in love. Just thinking about it is tiring.

11/25/72

There is flame, you just can't see it for the light.

11/27/72

American greed: There wouldn't be so much greed if there were more socialism in America. No one wants to become a pauper at sixty, because he has developed tuberculosis or cancer at fifty-five. But this is what hap-

---

* Alexandre Lagoya (1929–1999), classical guitarist.

pens now in America. Because many Americans really have worked hard
to get where they are, they are unwilling to share any of it with people
who apparently have not worked as hard.

12/6/72

No shame attached to Dostoyevsky these days, but I am ashamed to tell
my accountants I could use some more money, because I would have to
explain I have lent ⅓ my salary to three people from whom I cannot as
yet collect. However, if life were not ironic, I would have to adjust to a
new kind of reality.

12/6/72

Recurrent dream: being pulled off balance by something heavy that I
carry in my hands, and I fall into an abyss.

12/15/72

Taking a drink should not be inspired by self-pity, but by a desire to feel
more respectful of oneself. If everyone thought this—there wouldn't be
any shambles of people due to booze.

12/15/72

—I live on thin air
And thin ice.
Nothing tangible.
Thin ice is tangible,
But not for long.
It's all in the head.
So my wings
Or my earth
Will endure as long as I do.
Nothing to pass on
To anyone else.
Anyway, I wouldn't advise it.

1973–1976

EVEN AFTER six years of living in France, Patricia Highsmith does not feel at home. She has her garden and her cats in Montcourt, but contentment remains elusive. She's still in love with her ex-girlfriend Caroline Besterman, however unhappily; she isn't sure what to write next; and despite their many differences, she is worried about her mother's failing health.

Pat types up a clean draft of *Ripley's Game* in early 1973, and without a new book in the works, she then finds herself in unfamiliar territory: leisure. Workaholic that she is, Pat is troubled by these unstructured days and unable to relax. She distracts herself with gardening, painting, and woodworking. As usual, her calendar fills up with interviews and other professional commitments, many of them abroad. During those years, Pat travels repeatedly to London as well as Germany, Switzerland, Scandinavia, and the United States.

In spring 1973, Pat digs out her *Little Tales of Misogyny*, a collection she began in 1969. Each story features a female protagonist who meets an unfortunate, but deserved, end. As in earlier notebook entries, the way Pat writes about women in her notes for this book suggests that she does not identify as a woman herself.

This year and the next she also composes more stories for *The Animal-Lover's Book of Beastly Murder*. Starting in the 1970s, Pat's publishers begin reserving space on their lists for her short stories, which she had been writing since high school but which so far had largely been relegated to magazines. In the case of *Little Tales of Misogyny*, the collection will first be published in German translation by Diogenes Verlag in 1975, two years before the same book is released in English.

After Caroline Besterman's husband dies in 1973, Pat sees an opportunity. The women meet up in London and Montcourt several times before Pat is forced to abandon any hope of reconciliation. In late 1974, Marion Aboudaram enters her life instead, and the two begin a relationship that will last for four years. Marion had been determined to meet Pat and even lied to her, pretending she'd been hired to interview her for the French edition of *Cosmopolitan*. Pat dedicates her next novel, *Edith's Diary*, to Marion. It's the story of a woman who escapes into a fantasy world by means of her diary, thus gradually losing touch with reality. The novel demonstrates Pat's disdain for the life of an average suburban American housewife, without freedom or possibility. Pat draws on notebooks from years past for many of Edith's more extreme political views.

In the fall of 1974, Pat visits Mary Highsmith in Texas. She's shocked by what she finds: her mother in serious decline, the house in disrepair. Barely a year later, Mary accidentally sets the house on fire with a lit cigarette and has to be transferred to a nursing facility—just a few months after the death of Pat's biological father, Jay Bernard Plangman.

2/19/73

Thoughts after flu. That nearly all people who die in bed die in the same manner and in the same mood—unless they are doped on drugs. A slow failure of energy, a hopelessness. One hears seldom of a fear of death expressed, or any kind of "struggle" against it. There isn't that much energy left. The more intelligent person perhaps has a few more intelligent thoughts than the average in these last moments, although it takes energy even to think and I doubt if much important thinking goes on. The intellectual dies essentially like the simple peasant.

5/14/73

Marriage is the easiest way of avoiding sleeping with a man.

6/7/73

Women—they believe they manipulate other people. Actually, they are still puppets, never alone, never content to be alone, always seeking a master, a partner, someone really to give them orders or direction.

6/7/73

Music establishes the fact that life is not real. The joy, the fortitude to live comes from the realization that life is not composed of realities—and also that one doesn't even have to worry about this fact.

6/27/73

Cheerful, dismal, cheerful—all in the same day. I am afraid to put my allegiance where I would like to. C. free,* if reverting to type, with the absence of discrimination perhaps characteristic of C's adolescence: that was a snobbism insecure. Mainly confused because of no definite program of work at the moment. Between books, as they say, *Ripley's Game* being put to bed chez three publishers.† And I go to Hamburg in a fortnight.

6/28/73

The notaire. The one in Nemours,‡ the well-fed, stuffed shirt usurer, who cows the humble peasants who must go to him, to have papers signed. The peasants in rusty Sunday best may be stingy as hell, but they are comparably more honest. Get this bastard, some day in a short story. Say—a Frenchman, desperate—desperately hating, for nothing can be done against papers in France—wants to kill him, and fate does it first.

7/1/73

Leisure. What a difficult thing to handle. Even for me, and I've been at it since 12, or 8. One has certain projects, yes, but they don't give satisfaction. What gives satisfaction? Curiously it is aiming at what is impossible, day by day. It is possible to say "What a good day's work!" to go to bed tired and to sleep, and to realize that the final objective is always impossible to achieve.

7/2/73

R.C. reports N.W. [Natica Waterbury] broke her neck Jan. in California—drunken driving—and recovered. Car and mower broken down. And why do I write this, as I'll have no desire in future to read it? A stupid effort at organization—the inadequate kind.

7/6/73

I clear out my 3 files—some stories written 25 years ago. C. [Caroline] phoned yesterday. Cat Luke was runover. 1 PM and killed in front of the house. C. having delayed reaction to all of this; eczema on hands, etc. as had her mother, she says, after C's father's death. Humility. A

---

* Caroline's husband has died.
† These three publishers are Heinemann (UK), Doubleday (United States), and Diogenes (Switzerland, for the German-language market).
‡ A town near Montcourt.

personality at war. Habitually she is sure to the point of arrogance and mercilessness. Now she is faced with death, loneliness, eczema. I write sympathetic letters which I mean to the core. I have never minded exposing my own emotions—which I do not do now, yet merely by kindness, in a sense, I am doing that.

7/11/73

What a war between the deadline and the creative brain. The latter won't budge. I am caught in the middle and become exhausted in 24 hours. I beseech either side, both sides at once. An iron wall divides them! I cannot penetrate. And I don't know what to tell the outside world.

7/14/73

To Reeperbahn this PM to buy blue & white shirt worn by fishermen and butchers. Hamburg is surrounded by swank residential sections Altona, Blankenese—well established pine trees, lawns, substantial houses. The Reeperbahn is a mile-long stretch of crummy striptease, crack bars, porn bookshops, sexual gadgetry. Near the docks, some of which are (the warehouses of red brick) intact after the bombing.

7/16/73

Evening party chez A.U.* Canapes, punch with floating strawberries. Eight or nine people, all sitting in erect beach chairs on the heated terrace. All speaking German. No one can move with ease, we confront each other in a circle. No one talks much at first. Two married men who talk excessively and want to be "leaders," the brightest intellects of the assembly. One sees the same type in France occasionally.

7/19/73

[Berlin.] C. still in a state of coming to terms with everything. Death of L. 3rd July did (or did not, conventionally) help toward the inevitable jagging. Doctor says lose weight. So this will give her something to do, self-directed, egocentric. It is perhaps good that she seeks every chink through which to attack and criticize me at the moment. However, I believe more in the reversion to adolescent values and habits, in her case gregariousness and balls chasing; meaning marriage after the discreet interval of about a year.

---

* Pat is on a book tour in Germany to promote *A Dog's Ransom*, and while in Hamburg, she stays with her longtime translator Anne Uhde. She and Uhde enjoy a close working relationship.

7/19/73

Berlin: Ku'damm a blaze of neon shop signs, advertisements, snack bars. Toward the Kaiser-Wilhelm-Gedächtnis-Kirche—the shops became more elegant. A confusion of letters, signs, so that it is difficult to see the buildings or street names. I've been here since yesterday 5 PM—suffering from trots—today went to zoo, and in PM took a 15 DM tour to East Berlin.

Much examination of passports, recording of numbers, and "How much DM are you carrying?" This to avoid black market on other side. At Checkpoint Charlie, a delay of at least 25 minutes, while the gray-green Polizei do God knows what.

The Wall is in sight, looking like gray cement about 11 feet high. Dreary little cement huts about, all containing officials. We lumber off between rather dismal flat dwellings today bedecked with flags for some kind of Welcoming of Youth festival to take place tomorrow. Flag of Ost-Berlin is of course the German flag on which has been superimposed a circle of wheat plus hammer and compass—representing the obvious. Unter den Linden described by the East German woman guide as "once the most beautiful street in Germany." Many palaces, embassies of England and Switzerland, have been transformed into "Ministries for People's Culture," "Workmen's Organization" for Health and Recreation. I think the [East German] passersby stared at our bus now and then. The less bright clothing, the less new cars, really is evident. We visit Pergamon Museum—Abyssinian ruins, all authentic and not reconstructed in imitation of the original. Eastern Ancient Museum, also Islamic, is here also. I don't know what to do at night—as I am not interested in going to a film, for instance. I'll perhaps take a bus tonight. One must explore. But I think I'll go to France Saturday 22, a day earlier than I had expected to.

At the zoo—slothful, stupid looking orang-utangs, fringy red hair that looks in need of combing. They sit in a fat heap ten feet up on a girder, and gaze at the public, arms hanging. All the monkeys seem to be approaching breeding season. The orang-utangs lazily chew oranges. The Siamese-catlike Puma showed irritated interest in small running child beyond its wire cage, and I feel sure would have jumped out and drawn blood with an insolent slap—blood which it would have disdained to drink.

7/20/73

Berlin—Quite a beautiful [castle] Schloss Charlottenburg. Really from the front it manages to look like a palace as well as home. The interior

full of oil paintings, portraits of the royal family, chiefly obese, genre
paintings by [Antoine] Watteau*—excellent and famous, and [Jean-
Louis] David's† *Napoleon Crossing the Saint-Bernard*, a miracle of
craftsmanship, and he has signed David many times on the bridle. The
successful completion of this picture must have boosted David's spirits
for months.

7/23/73

It is perhaps better never to mention again to C. anything. She did not
clearly answer, not at all, my question early this month, "Were you consciously or unconsciously trying to end it for a year and a half?" I said. I
broke abruptly to stop this cutting of the dog's tail off by inches.

7/27/73

When the animals reverse things in the zoo—their captors are captive,
forced to defecate and make love in the presence of spectators who laugh,
point, and stare. Alternative is not making love at all. The lights are on,
the park open, all night.

7/30/73

My deathbed words should be: "It was all so predictable." The same
thing goes for the history of the human race from prehistoric time
onward.

7/30/73

In the last five years I've noticed I don't like to travel alone. Mainly the
thing gone is the indiscriminate curiosity of youth that used to send me
prowling strange and foreign streets, just because they were new to me,
even if they were in mediocre towns. But the main burden of age is the
increasing complexity of one's affairs—the ownership of a house, banking problems, agents, commitments.

8/5/73

Courage has to be measured by the ability to imagine disaster. If someone does not think at all, and dashes ahead into danger, he is called fool-
hardy (especially if he fails). The greatest courage is that of a person who
imagines fully the consequences and still goes ahead.

---

* Antoine Watteau (1684–1721), French rococo painter.
† Jean-Louis David (1748–1825), French neoclassical painter best known for his history paintings.

8/14/73

At least my mother will die with the firm conviction she was right. To few is this satisfaction given.

8/16/73

Appalling fatigue caused by writing an 8-page synopsis for a one-hour drama for BBC. Almost like post-flu fatigue, and what B. [Brigid] Brophy* calls, the cool hand of death on one's shoulder. Are you coming soon?

9/9/73

Conrad Aiken† recently died saying "Perhaps there are no answers—and nothing has any meaning." I am impressed by this, even believe it, yet life, experiences, are all we have to deal with. It is putting "no value" on them to say that they are meaningless. Unfortunately, there is nothing else to deal with or to give meaning to.

10/20/73

Leisure creeps up slowly, five days after having been in London five days: the knowledge that one can be happy (and happier) alone. I always come back to chores, post to be answered, all of which I do conscientiously. From 4–6 AM awake, thinking of C. and trying to analyze, indeed find, her motives. She will never admit them, anyway, so it is a personal exercise. C. is now without buffer state. I would be a fool not to be patient for another year, in view of the fact I've sunk eleven years into this. But I am haunted by the remark of Ernest Hauser in Paris—also Koestler's: "She's nothing but a little housewife." Who—to continue—knows where her bread is buttered and who will butter it and who just because he is male will look presentable to society.

11/16/73

Little Crimes for Little Tots. Things around the house—which small children can do, such as:

    1) tying string across top of stairs, so adults will trip.
    2) replacing roller skate on stairs, once mother has removed it.
    3) setting careful fires, so that someone else will get the blame if possible.

---

* Writer and activist Brigid Brophy (1929–1995) was an admirer of Pat's and later became a friend.
† Conrad Potter Aiken (1889–1973), American novelist and poet.

4) rearranging pills in medicine cabinet; sleeping pills into aspirin bottle. Pink laxative pills into antibiotic bottle which is kept in fridge.

5) Rat powder, or flea powder into flour jar in kitchen.

6) saw through supports of attic trap door, so that anyone walking on closed trap will fall through to stairs, or worse onto ladder below.

7) In summer: fix magnifying glass to focus on dry leaves, or preferably oily rags somewhere. Fire may be attributed to spontaneous combustion.

8) Investigate anti-mildew products in gardening shed. Colorless poison can be added to gin bottle.

11/16/73

Zurich—Four-day stay for Diogenes 7–11 November at Hotel Europe, 4 Dufourstrasse. Very proper, clean & comfortable. Gerd Haffmans[*] and Lili-Ann Bork[†] at the airport with a bottle of whiskey to bestow on me (from Dani)[‡] as the hotel is dry. Other writers staying here are Walter Richartz[§] and wife Mari—charming—and I think Loriot.[¶] Hotel room: double bed, saucer of fruit, excellent bouquet of artificial flowers which appear to be growing from a pot. Overnight clothes press resembling instrument of medieval torture: you put trousers in it, close it, turn electric switch hot as desired. Many lunches and dinners at the Kronenhalle, Rämistrasse—big restaurant, à la carte, where James Joyce used to eat. His waitress Emma now on part time duty. Miró, Braque paintings. Now it is expensive (used to be cheap) and service is slow, but the food excellent. Sherbet with Kirsch. Dani entertains 30 people at a time, at two big tables.

Swiss TV—most painful 9 November. Preceding evening: readings began at 8 PM in Zunfthaus zur Meisen. I read in German & English from "The Snail-Watcher"[**] (all of it). Then free for all among the 1,000 people, TV, red & white wine, autographing lots of books. Up until

---

* Gerd Haffmans, editor-in-chief at Diogenes at the time.
† Lili-Ann Bork, chief press officer at Diogenes at the time.
‡ Daniel Keel, Diogenes founder.
§ Walter E. Richartz (1927–1980), German author with a doctorate in chemistry. He also translated English-language literature, including works by F. Scott Fitzgerald and Thoreau, as well as Patricia Highsmith's *Little Tales of Misogyny*.
¶ Loriot, the stage name for Vicco von Bülow (1923–2011), was one of Germany's most famous humorists.
** The title story of Pat's eponymous collection *The Snail-Watcher and Other Stories* (New York, 1970).

nearly 4 AM, as Dani invited us to his house, then I asked Zimnik* (artist) & the Richartz to my room for drinks. Returned home Sunday Nov.
11 rather up in the air, consequently nauseous in evening, ill at night &
morning diarrhea and cramps. It takes me three or four days to quiet
down and rest enough. Am also rattled because of awaiting an appointment for medical check-up in London any day now. Lunch in Zurich
with Elizabeth E. Gilbert (whose husband [Robert Gilbert] wrote the
lyrics for *Weißes Rössl*).† She is charming, very polite, reminds me of
Madame Bradley in her contempt for writers who are not genuine artists.
She is translating Yeats still.

11/25/73

The Great American Novel—will deal with the betrayal of the American hope. The great thing about America to this day is that its idealism
is still there. We have opened the country to all kinds of people, of all
races—and they all had or have a hope, still. America is growing up,
becoming more cynical. Yet it is not basically cynical. America needs
always an idealistic leader—even if he runs the risk of being naive—
such as George Washington (called shy by Gore Vidal), Woodrow Wilson, J. F. Kennedy—F.D.R.—cagey but idealistic in his way. This is a
sine qua non for America. And one can see Nixon is so precisely the
opposite, the USA is suffering a prolonged attack of acid stomach, an
irrepressible urge to throw up.

11/25/73

Sadism is alive and doing well, alas, flourishing. It has other names: vengeance, my pound of flesh, getting one's own back. The perpetrators do
not stop there. They have tasted blood. It is my experience that women
are the more vindictive, firing their shots verbally, playing with people
who desperately try still to love them—because they need to love. The
vindictive ones—curiously they do not need to love, I think. Is this true?
They need to have power over someone, to be loved, or to be needed.

12/2/73

[London.] Wimpole Street heart specialist. A banker-like office. He takes
my age & family history (the latter good). A heart exam, with stetho-

---

* Reiner Zimnik (1930–), Bavarian poet, illustrator, painter, and children's book author.
† *Weißes Rössl*, light opera with a dance interlude written in 1930 by Ralph Benatzky.

scope, then six small rubber suction cylinders, with tubes attached to each. Result okay. Femoral artery pulses. Palpitated; okay. I ought to stop smoking entirely if I wish to correct muscular pain in calves after brisk walking.

12/3/73

Is not all writing born out of some kind of resentment? Not so much writing comes from an overflow of joy.

12/12/73

Try to bear in mind the purposelessness of life. All depression, therefore defeat, comes from trying to see purpose and failing to achieve it (or even see it clearly).

12/17/73

What is the ideal vacation? To do absolutely nothing, not even sightsee, in a completely new place. Quite an art to achieve this state of mind.

12/17/73

Ten days after visit from C., I was utterly depressed, exhausted, for three days after she left. I asked once again hadn't she had a campaign against me 1966—with specific questions sometimes. "I don't remember," she said, like Nixon. I remember now I stopped spending the night at London house, hoping she would withdraw her troops from Earl Soham. The mischief began early, in February 1963, when she wanted to (and did) spill the beans to her husband. She wanted (only?) one big happy family. Did she give me credit for having more leisure than I had? Alas I had to work flat out in 1964–65. Not to mention that other people (over the age of 5) could separate us in a house. She said 10 December mine was a love-hate relationship with her. True. She gave back her nightdress (taken to Rome whence she'd come) saying she wanted to be rid of it. Adamant. She says, "You killed my love," without at all acknowledging that she wrongly accused me of two or three serious acts, or matters: the venereal disease bit, which in the first place was not a disease of "sexual intercourse"—of [her son] and me laughing at her behind her back. The matter of [her son] playing his own cards, perhaps, saying he liked carpentry & drawing (quite false!), because he could then, aged 14, pretend I'd become a father figure. What fun! Fortunate in a way I write this tonight when I'm feeling

"better." My right hand becomes so tired, I switch to left. A death of
sorts, I felt the day & the days after she left, because there is nothing
so impossible to swallow as her absolute refusal to face the facts, the
history, the incidents, which most surely she remembers. I feel it is cowardice and evasion. The mystery, as ever, is why she apparently likes
to keep me on her social list. I at least did not wish to be on it six days
ago. I was equally fatigued and depressed as when in October 1966 I
broke it off with her.

12/22–23/73

To Toulouse. [Caroline's husband] wasted the best (meaning the only
ones left) years of his life, putting a spoke in the works. Aldeburgh, Earl
Soham, weekend after weekend, doing nothing but waiting for the next
meal, and separating me from Caroline. He never finished his book, or
progressed beyond the first chapter, apart from [an] outline. Am I worth
a man's lifework? I do not consider it a compliment. I deplore it. Mission
achieved, but what a worthless, negative mission.

1/20/74

Lot*—Rolling terrain with unexpected gentle valley, even gorges. Dry
looking land in December, broom, yellow-white stone out of which most
of the houses are constructed. Near Cahors, an interesting spring on the
wrong side of the city for watering purposes. A small waterfall, a "pond"
about twenty feet, thirty square. Cahors has sophisticated shops along
a tree bordered avenue. Perfume shops, an excellent delicatessen, also
hardware shop. The supermarket has pop music booming out, a café just
inside (bar combined) and many more international goodies than Fontainebleau. Much empty land, uncultivable. Stony. Sloping meadows.
Pigs who look for truffles. Families (Roques) who speak the dialect to
animals, for example. Town names, Carnac-Rouffiac. Sauzet. Luzach.
(Languedoc.)

---

* Pat spent Christmas 1973 and the first weeks of 1974 in the Lot region of southwest France with her
close friend Charles Latimer, who had previously worked for her British publisher Heinemann, and his
longtime partner, renowned pianist Michel Block.

1/26/74

Polyclinique, Fontainebleau. I am to get there 9–9:30 AM 18 Jan. for
extraction of teeth at 4:30 PM. I am there at 9, fistful of papers including information as to whether I pee at night. I have no handicaps
whatsoever. Rehabilitation room is not reposeful after 10 AM, because
a pair of Spanish mothers with two tots are awaiting something in
adjacent room. Yakking. Impossible to get another room (I inquire)
just to snooze in, I'm short of sleep, and—forbidden to eat, drink even
water, smoke. Hell, as I sneak fags, and nip from my flask. Awfully
nice to see familiar face of Dr. Aupicon in operating theater. Anesthe-
tist gives needle left arm. I am strapped down. Overhead a circular
light composed of concentric fluorescent. Second needle goes in and in
30 seconds—blank. I awaken an hour later in strange room, unable to
take enough air into my lungs. I gasp with the sounds of a whooping
cough victim, ring bell, then get to my feet and stagger to door which
I open crying "Help! *Au secours!*" Two nurses arrive, thank God, at
once, ignore my cries for "*Oxygène!*" and tell me to relax. They hold
me down by the wrists, and of course I half believe them, because
they *are* nurses, and maybe 25% enough air is coming in. All this lasts
about a minute.

2/28/74

I do live within my income. I only wish my friends would.

3/4/74

A bad mood just now. A sense of being rushed. Do I need a vacation?
Yes, perhaps, but one must prepare for that, not just drop everything. It
is leisure which I constantly pursue, as if she were a nymph I half imagined in a forest.

4/1/74

If it were not for the ambiguity of Christ, he would be nowhere.

4/30/74

Note written around April 9, re Mary Sullivan, who died April 19 in
New York. Why did you let the Catholic religion ruin your health and
your brain? What has the Catholic church given you in return? Do you
not remember when I wrote that self-torture and an inbuilt, ready-made
sense of guilt is the stranglehold of the Christian (including Protestant)

religion? Mary, arriving with R.M.* around 25 March, had begun drinking (after 7 mos. abstinence) the day they flew from N.Y. Rose & I had to hide the bottles here, and even so, it wasn't enough. Little bottles of cognac in Mary's handbag. She'd been sufficiently warned in NY, as she had a bad bout with cirrhosis of liver. A deliberate suicide, at 73. Here, she kept mentioning church, never actually getting there—[to] Grez or Nemours. At 6 AM, she'd go downstairs to find something to drink, and by 10 AM I would find her asleep on the living room sofa. When I suggested they go to Paris for a few days, Mary turned bitter, as if I were throwing them out of the house. R.M. and I—extremely nervous, & we'd talk & laugh & have a nightcap in kitchen at 2 AM. to preserve our sanity. Final days in Paris, while I was at home. R.M. reported M. was cutting down, doing better. 25 April I received telegram from RM saying M.S. had died. Learned later that sister Polly returned from a walk & found M. dead in the apartment.

5/4/74

Angus Wilson†—with such a different background from him, I am also concerned with the facade everyone has to put up to exist. As Wilson says, true facades. Without them—people would collapse. This is why a person living alone with a minimum of social life and no reason for facade in regard to earning his living perhaps comes closest (can) to being simply himself.

5/12/74

The entire human race (the intelligent part of it) is too nervous. Therefore, there is a movement backwards toward the simpler, less mechanic. Or hippie. There remain two problems: too many people to deal with; and the absurd aspiration toward luxury and—and—not even leisure, because hardly anyone knows what to do with it. An interesting revolution; the intellectual versus the multitudinous peasant. Yet they both are at variance in a comical way. The intellectual wants the simple, the peasant wants the machines, the luxury.

---

* Rose M., then partner of Pat's old friend Mary Sullivan, with whom she had a short affair in 1941.
† Sir Angus Wilson (1913–1991), British novelist, short story writer, and biographer who, like Pat, lived in Suffolk.

6/2–13/74

How many ends to this thing? How many duplications of the same sense of resentment, of being victim of double-thing? On my 2nd trip within a month to London, Caroline retreated on three fronts. One front, the absurd "show for the public" has fairly collapsed in the last decade. I scored by mentioning the time her husband wasted trying to bollix us by his mere presence. "Marriage has nothing to do with a love affair," C. says. Ergo, why doesn't the spouse keep out of the love affair & treat it with the contempt it deserves? C.'s "All's fair in love & war" doesn't hold, if she puts love & marriage on two different planes as she does.

6/18/74

These emotional misfortunes, the ones that hang on, are really dead ends. I would shake them off if I could. And yet, are they not a part of the character, the personality? One would not be the same, not oneself, without them. There is finally a part of the brain that cannot be tampered with—not even by a psychiatrist whose words would go in one ear and out the other. It is necessary to come to terms with an emotion like this, to admit that it is not to be changed—otherwise one is torn apart by a struggle against it. What do all the other people have except a faute de mieux to keep them company? Don't the majority of people dream? Alas, the majority doesn't.

6/23/74

Idiotic discussion last evening on radio about man's "direction" and what is it? Philosophers have failed to find, or successfully label any for nearly three thousand years. The true direction of man is toward play, discovery, invention. No morality can be easily attached. The drive toward play and invention is intimately bound to health and zest. If those two primitive things are missing, life really has no more value or significance than has a pebble on a beach. In fact, less.

6/26/74

The rankling continues. In a way, it is a waste of time. My thoughts are sad, resentful, sometimes angry. Yet I've come to the conclusion it (being in love) is an emotion that I must simply live with, and face that fact. Of course, all these ranklings become more intense now, because I have not been working (writing) for about a month.

6/28/74

Visit from Wim Wenders[*] (producer, German, living in München) and
Peter Handke,[†] Austrian writer. Both about 30, I think, 6 ft. tall. Wim
silent, brooding at first. Red lips, low blood pressure, he says. No coffee after dinner, little drink. He spoke finally concretely about *Ripley's
Game* saying that it became Jonathan's story, because of impending
death, and of simply taking up more action in the book.

Peter has the soft face of a girl. His body could be more feminine,
however, than it is. He liked the tequila. He has separated from his wife,
and has custody of daughter Amina, aged 5, in Paris. He works 2 months
of the year. Says Germany has no tradition of literary agents, that writers are "apart" from society. True; also in USA. Such a weak face, in my
opinion, he has. We dined at le Chaland Qui Passe. *Chez moi* raspber-
ries, snapshots. Wim said he knew a cartoonist who killed himself, and
Wim attributes it to the man's being dissatisfied with himself as artist
because he was merely a cartoonist.

Peter said: "When I start any of your books, I have the feeling that you
love life, that you want to live." (That's very nice!) They brought me an
ingenious ball on [a] pedestal—ball about 2 inches in diameter, black and
clear, a present from Jeanne Moreau.[‡] Peter has no agent. Germany is
anti-agent, he said. "My publisher acts as my agent," I was amazed to say
the least!

7/1/74

Hans Christian Andersen always carried a rope when traveling (to
hotels). A question: what could he tie it to? Round a servant girl, perhaps,
whom he dragged toward a nearly closed window? But—presumably a
bed leg was always handy.

7/3/74

Rankling continues, though less, & I make notes for short story "Something You [Have Got to] Live With"[§] which may better things. 31 days of

---

* Wilhelm Ernst ("Wim") Wenders (1945–) is a German film director and photographer who rose to
prominence in the 1980s with his films *Paris, Texas* and *Wings of Desire*, among others.
† Peter Handke (1942–) cemented Pat's status as a literary heavyweight in the German-speaking world
with a piece for *Der Spiegel* magazine on January 1, 1975, "*Die privaten Weltkriege der Patricia
Highsmith*" ("Patricia Highsmith's Private World Wars"). He was awarded the Nobel Prize for Literature
in 2019.
‡ Pat has recently become friends with Jeanne Moreau (1928–2017), celebrated film star of the French
New Wave.
§ This story appeared in the March 1976 issue of *Ellery Queen's Mystery Magazine* and was published
in book form in *Slowly, Slowly in the Wind* (London, 1979).

"vacation" & am in a good trim due to heavy gardening. I try watercolors & have carpentry projects. Much cheered yesterday & today by London & Zurich news that publishers adore the animal stories and want to publish them—London before "misogyny."*

JULY 4, 1974

Just when I'd spent part of the day writing "Pros" and "Cons" re CB and coming to no great conclusion about them, she rang at 9:15 PM and spoke for about 20 minutes. "I care about being liked, not loved." As for myself, the conversation picked me up a good deal. C: "I like people who make me laugh." A bit of the old style.

Thirty-two days of "vacation." My mind, and body, are full of creative ideas, and they are inevitably bound up with C. to whom I said tonight, "You must know I love you—after all these years." In less than a fortnight, it will be twelve years. How many twelves does one live?

7/4/74

For *The Writer.* Article on potential scope, on not specializing in western, crime, or even sex. Let your imagination wander. Daydream. And for a change, treat yourself to a busman's holiday and "waste" a few hours writing something you don't expect to sell. Write it simply because it's fun to write it. E.g. the Misogyny—and the cockroach story†—which led to the main idea of a whole book about animals.

We live in an over-specialized age. A man is an electrician, a stockbroker, or a lawyer, and nothing else. The writer in his imagination can be, has to be, sailor, housewife, an adolescent, a barkeeper. Do the same in the kind of thing you write. For daydreaming: It is necessary (I find) to be doing something else, something mentally untaxing such as gardening, knitting (if simple!), polishing silver, ironing. Don't try to think: concentration and imagination don't go together. Fairy tales, fantasy, the supernatural, all these are fields where the seed may grow. Leading to subject of discipline. Has too much been said about plugging away, writing daily, and even if you don't feel like writing, force yourself? What about forcing yourself to daydream instead, and if you daydream successfully for even two minutes, consider this a successful working day? Let

---

* *Little Tales of Misogyny* was first published in Walter E. Richartz's German translation, with illustrations by Roland Topor, by Diogenes (Zurich, 1975). The book was only published in its English original by Heinemann (London) in 1977.
† "Notes from a Respectable Cockroach" was first published in *The Animal Lover's Book of Beastly Murder* (London, 1975).

your mind alone for a change. Stop the flagellation. Remember the classic the Reverend Charles Dodson created, mainly while drifting down a stream in a rowboat.*

7/7/74

For the Suicide—that W.W. [Wim Wenders] remarked someone he knew killed himself because he thought his art was "inferior" (to a fine artist). There could be the thought: everything funny is really bitter. So one's mind passes over that borderline, middle zone, and all life becomes tragic and bitter. Alvarez[†] offers so many reasons for suicide (all except the old obvious one of trying to call attention, trying to impress someone else—those attempts that often fail). Desire to join dead father (Sylvia Plath); a statement of power & independence (which I do not fully understand); a fitting grand finale to a life—drama, dignity. I don't completely understand this either. Even the noble Romans had a provocation. They didn't kill themselves in the best of physical or political health.

7/16/74

Loneliness. Maybe only once a year I feel "lonely." It is a matter of needing adjustment, which a two-minute conversation (best with a friend) can do. In this sense, people are necessary. They restore proper proportion.

7/21/74

The whole world of art is fantasy. Today I have the alarming feeling that fantasy alone keeps me going—that is some pleasure and satisfaction in what I am doing (not what I have done in the past). Doubtless I am saying nothing new. It is 12 years & one day since I met C. What has kept me going these past seven years?

7/22/74

On seven weeks (five) of leisure: Nothing is ever what we think it is. Leisure doesn't settle the nagging problems. Therefore, the Christian Scientists, even, have something to stand on. It is all mental. Inward. The outward tidiness doesn't count for much, just helps a little. And activity is a cover-up.

---

* Charles Dodson (1832–1898), better known as Lewis Carroll, author of *Alice in Wonderland*.
† Al Alvarez (1929–2019), English poet, author, and critic. *The Savage God*, his renowned study of suicide, gained added attention because of his friendship with Sylvia Plath, who famously took her own life.

8/5/74

When the chips are down, death is an informal matter.

9/30/74

Fort Worth, shopping centers all along the road between the city and
Weatherford. The latter has a slightly New England flavor. My cousin
[Dan Coates] knows everyone on the street.

No music, no pictures (by artists) on the wall at my cousin's. But it's
a happy, healthy life. No talk of politics, no thinking—to get life into
proportion.

Rather shattering first visit to my mother's house. TV set (I think)
muttering as usual. I had to crawl in via a window into bedroom, and
let Dan in. 8–10 inches deep in newspapers on the floor, two wigs, telephone books, letters, cigarette stubs, ashtray. "A fire hazard," says Dan.
We depart, return a bit later (after telling the person next door we'd be
back). My mother doesn't want me to tackle the filthy heap of dishes in
the sink, but I insist, and Dan takes her out for coffee, the usual hostile
atmosphere.

It is hopeless. I cannot get her consent for me to throw away any newspapers. It'd take two weeks to clean the place. Excess of crummy dishes,
cutlery in the kitchen, and no place to put the few I have washed. An
interesting sink, by the way, green, foul-smelling slime at the bottom—
all hopelessly stained. What terrifies me is the insanity, the knowledge
that it will only get worse. She doesn't eat properly. Food is rotting in the
fridge, countless items wrapped in wax paper, bacon liquefying with rot.
One dog has the mange. My cousin has the best attitude—real concern,
but with the ability to laugh. We visit a lawyer, get a power of attorney
form, but lawyer remarks the best thing may be to let her alone. I worry
that she may run out of money—she signs checks twice, does not always
post them.

10/23/74

New York. *Chez Rose.* Doorman, black, is called Randy. Wears vizored
cap, cigar in mouth. On from 4 PM to midnight. One must have a key
for the big front door. At 10:30 AM one morning as I went out, I let in
a fat woman, returned 4 minutes later to find the lift awash with urine,
which remained there till 5 PM getting ever muddier. No furniture in
lobby, as a sofa was slashed; table stolen . . . by kids off the street. People use the buses now, not so much the subway. SoHo is the art center,
below Houston Street, big lofts, colored canvases, galleries, dwellings.

Bob Gottlieb:* about 38, balding, blue denim western shirt. He doesn't
smoke; never lunches out, as they'd ruin his health, he says. 21st floor
of Random House building Fifth Avenue & 59 Street. Spacious offices,
but stale, uncirculating air. B.G. says if they paid $16,000 per year more,
they could buy one hour more of air 6–7 PM. The cleaning women, then,
work in stale air. Lots of employees work till 7. Presumably at 11:30 AM
I was breathing fresh air.

Jane Street quite lovely west of 8th–9th Avenue. People make an effort
at greenery in front of their houses. Variety—no doubt, in New York.
One is flung from the best in the arts, to the worst of humanity. The
town is full of nervous stimulation, which forms the most part of all
the stimulation. Has anything changed in 40 years? Yes. Eighth Street
viewed from 6th Avenue (now determinedly labeled & called Avenue of
the Americas) looks like a dump and a slum. What a shame! I remember
it aglow with pretty shops. What of the people who ruined it, the slobs,
thieves, prostitutes, shoplifters, vandals? Well, why should they care?
The only answer is around the clock doormen and guards. What an
unproductive use of human labor!

12/1/74

Erich Fromm states boldly that if a person cannot get from another the
love he desires, the person resorts to sadism. This was plainly illustrated
by MJM [Marijane Meaker] in 1960, also by [Elizabeth Lyne] in 1969.
Curious also how these tried to hold on (by direct or devious means) to
their victim.

1/31/75

Drink to me only with thine eyes, and hand me a glass of gin.

2/4/75

Millet the barber narrated the story of my twice-time gardener, who lives
in rather nice yellow house on the corner. I knew his wife was ill, back
from hospital, that he had to tend her. It seems they had an only child,

---

* Robert Gottlieb (1931–), American writer, editor, and publisher. He was editor-in-chief at Simon &
Schuster, Alfred A. Knopf, and *The New Yorker*. He became Pat's editor when, after publishing five
titles with Simon & Schuster, she moved to Knopf.

daughter aged 22, scholastically brilliant, overweight, dieting with pills, in love with Polish chap in the village. The love affair went askew, the girl set the car on fire on road to Dervault near here on a Monday, was taken to hospital, died on a Wednesday, with plastic in her lungs due to the car's interior.

3/12/75

With greater universal education, there is paradoxically greater stupidity. One gets further from the land and nature, instead of being in harmony with it, as were our less educated forebears. We now read about pills and take them—and are afraid to give an honest belch.

3/12/75

Eskimo sculpture: fat, roly-poly figurines—made mainly to be touched. A sense of warmth and of abundant human flesh.

3/31/75

By the circles made by raindrops
On the pond outside my window
I shall remember you
And be troubled by my death to come.
(for M.A.)*

4/15/75

It is necessary sometimes to have a wrestling with oneself. Thus, I torture myself with a novel. A friend has literally nightmares. It is finally a proof of strength.

　　It is a postponement before satisfaction.

6/6/75

The profound indignity of being interviewed. Funny the way it eats at you, slowly. I have now had nearly a month of it, including television, which of course I did not watch. Seven interviews, perhaps. After every break, it is like going back to the dentist chair. I do realize that the interviewer must sometimes be as bored and miserable as I am. I now feel shattered and exhausted and cannot even get down to a proper short-story—a simple one! I have promised to do it. Why should life be so ghastly? So wretched? Such a torture?

---

* First hint of Pat's new girlfriend, Marion Aboudaram.

6/10/75

At dawn, after my death
The night before,
The sunlight spreads at seven A.M.
On those trees which I knew.
Greenness bursts, dark green shadows yield
To the cruel, benign sun.
O Egypt! Sicily! Mexico!
Stand the trees in my own garden
Unweeping for me,
On the morning after my death.
Their roots athirst as ever,
The trees rest in breezeless dawn,
Blind and uncaring,
Trees that I knew,
That I tended.*

7/18/75

Ascona [Ticino]—White, creamy facades of new boutiques. The only
thing that remains is the red cobbled street—here and there. Blue jeans,
open-fronted bar-restaurants, people speaking German (sometimes), and
the Italian dialect mostly. EBH [Ellen Blumenthal Hill] lives in Cavigli-
one 7 kilometers from Locarno. This is a tiny village [on the] edge of [a]
ravine, much wooded, Italian-speaking, and all doors must be locked.
Seven miles from the Italian border. Robbers.

I bought a travel-clock and wristwatch today in Ascona. Maybe 380–
400 Swiss Francs in all. Money means nothing to anyone any longer.
Maybe everyone is nervous? EBH is worried about squatters invading her
house by next October. They have already stolen her [Max] Pechstein
[painting]. I shouldn't care to live where I had to lock upstairs, downstairs of a house—in a village.

8/6/75

A day to remember—perhaps. On 6 August, my mother accidentally set
her Texas house on fire—with a left cigarette. The place is gutted. My
mother is now in the Fireside Lodge (White Settlement Road) thanks
to Dan's work. He wrote his letter to me 9 August. She was already

---

* This poem appears in Pat's next novel, *Edith's Diary*, and was printed on the handout distributed at
her memorial service in March 1995.

installed. I fear a shock reaction (I write this 17 August) a week or so later. All her clothes are gone, piano, drawings & paintings, my college diploma, and maybe the watch & chain I wanted. Danny* and wife Judy are going over it all with a fine toothed comb, according to Dan—and will try to salvage something for a sale. I predict my mother will need sedatives—and doctors, in the next months.

9/21/75

Leuenberg (Hölstein). A youth hostel in the mountains. Conference of Swiss Association of Teachers of English. Perhaps a hundred and twenty here. Michael Frayn† joins us from London. He is tall, slender, smiling, thinning blond hair. Very modern design, two Bibles in each room. Beer and wine buyable, but nothing else. Herr Wagner is proprietor, in a way, ever practicing Swiss democratic procedure, which means raising of hands to vote on every smallest issue. Pedagogy—greater or less— appears in nearly everyone.

Stanley Middleton,‡ Yorkshire (I think) is the third writer, tall, slight paunch, ruddy cheeks, a peasant homespun manner. His book *Holiday* won the Booker Prize jointly. We are (after enormous discussion) divided into three groups. First day Monday quite strenuous. I talk about the *Glass Cell*, its origins and difficulties. One morning session (sticky) with twenty people at least, two in the afternoon. They discuss the culpability (moral) of [the book's hero] Carter after killing Sullivan. Everyone speaks quite a high level of English and mostly sticks to it, even when talking to colleagues. Otherwise it is dialect, little High German.

10/2/75

The mutual embarrassment of two honest people who meet for the first time.

10/31/75

Dreams—Marion and I arranging things in the house I live in. M. tells me "two suitcases are too close together." To look nice. I have idea for 3 typewriters with fewer keys, each to produce from letter of rejection, acceptance or say the matter is under consideration, must be discussed. Water. Big pond grows in middle of living room floor. Two creatures like

---

* Danny Coates, the son of Pat's cousin Dan.
† Michael Frayn (1933–), British reporter, columnist, playwright, and novelist.
‡ British novelist Stanley Middleton (1919–2009) won the 1974 Booker Prize along with Nadine Gordimer.

muskrats live in it, heads down to get as much water as possible. It takes me a few seconds to realize they love it. I increase the water for them and they gambol and leap with delight. I say to M. "We have a swimming pool right in the house!" I am repairing wall of deep gorge, water and rocks below. M. tells me to hurry up so I can tell her my idea about type-writers. I have to climb up, debate asking M. to pull me over top, reflect that if she slipped, I'd be badly injured, & so decide to get myself up. I wake up talking—"if you slipped."

11/11/75

Result of five days in Switzerland and meeting 75 people or so—less shyness on my part. Maybe a realization that other people can suffer as much. At least that's something gained. And to me quite important. It really makes me happier.

11/22/75

The word normal ought to mean according to some "rule." It should have nothing to do with what the majority does.

⚸

1/3/76

Cities, and life. The shyness, the aging of everyone, the fear of failure, perhaps in the most minor of human tasks—taking a short railway journey somewhere. The reality, the awareness (as one grows older) of the vulnerability of one's friends. Faces, expressions that we know well become charged with a new meaning. One *should* become kinder, more tolerant of people's efforts—assuming they are making efforts! But most people do. In Paris, any city, people often go about with pained expressions, like me, as if their shoes hurt, but my shoes seldom hurt. And we walk amid architecture disfigured by electric wiring, work in offices, once grand private houses, with electric cords sneaking around paneled doorjambs, plugs bulging near the wainscoting.

1/22/76

A curious, terrible mixture
Of tenderness and fear,
A desire to protect,

A need to protect myself.

Does everybody feel the same?

3/10/76

Why is the church—most churches—so anti-sex? Because they realize that sex is stronger than religion. That is why they spit on sex, give it shame if they can, make the mother of Jesus a virgin—and her mother before her! Another crashing, disastrous mistake of the Christian church. They should realize that sex and religion are both allied, both mystical, each able to contribute to the other, in fact, and thereby gain strength. As usual with misguided zealots, the churchmen (Rome) have made things more sordid and of this world than ever (surely not their intention) by ordaining that intercourse is for procreation only.

3/13/76

M.C.H. My mother. Since August 7 or 8, 1975, in the Fireside Lodge, Fort Worth, for elderly & invalided. For all intents & purposes, she is insane. Latest from Dan says she cannot carry on a telephone conversation (bad hearing?) and the place confines her in an adult high chair (for how long? just at meals?) otherwise she would wander about switching people's false teeth, or drinking out of all the orange juice glasses. How ever, she is a source of entertainment to the home. Sometimes she recognizes Dan and [his wife] Florine, sometimes not, sometimes thinks she is in Paris, and asks how they all got there? The place costs more than $400 per month, but Dan has put $16,000 on deposit for her, and this earns that much—or anyway if she has to dip into capital, she has a long way to go. Every 20 days, she gets a shot to thin the blood, so it can better reach her brain. I hesitate, even to write the word brain in regard to my mother, as I believe she has only a ganglion (of nerves) there. As I have said elsewhere in this *cahier*, she will die believing she was always right and other people wrong. She talks now frequently of her own mother, says she has made a marvelous meal, etc., talks about a baby in the house. Apparently never talks of me or Stanley. [Jeva] Cralick writes her from New York, gets no replies. It seems the shock of burning her house down 6 or 8 August 1975, has sent her retreating into near total fantasy. That way the facts hurt less, and cease to exist if she does not admit them. I hope never to see her again, & hope I'll have the strength to wriggle out of going to the funeral. Everything is now exaggerated: the flippancy, arrogance, cursing people one day, meek as a lamb the next. Millie Alford asks me to "forgive" her, and I have explained to Millie it is not necessary to forgive someone insane. In the past she was not insane, merely appallingly selfish, self-indulgent, merciless in regard to the feelings of other people—my father, me, Stanley. I said to Millie, I now prefer to keep my distance, because since 1958 I have been consciously afraid of her, when, for instance, she wrote me insulting and upsetting letters. The real mental trouble was very apparent in 1959–60—when I thought it was manic-depressive. Can it all be merely an arterial thing? Not enough oxygen to the brain? Or do many old people have to have blood-thinning shots?

6/3/76

Catholic funeral [of Desmond Ryan], Fromonville church. Some thirty people. Eldest son takes widow into church first, followed by nearest of kin. The corpse is in purple robe-covered casket, feet toward us. The priest in white robe, purple cross, makes us sit and stand four times, then bow heads, as he reads in French about death being a pathway to making acquaintance with God. Organ plays, and thin, awful soprano sings in French and maybe some Latin. Pall-bearers in shiny gray suits (4) with long leather straps over shoulders—but before they come up the aisle, each of the congregation (after priest, eldest son, etc.) must shake the baton-like dispenser or whatever—pass it to the next person, who shakes the water in gesture of sign of the X over head of casket. By my turn there is no more water. 4 pall-bearers carry coffin out into church-yard, where grave has been dug, then lower it out of sight. Family tosses in flowers & small bouquets. Two lean, un-French-looking gravediggers watch on the sidelines, reminding me of Shakespeare. One has a lean, weathered face—he could play Starbuck. The priest speaks briefly. Eldest son Sebastian at edge of grave reads from Samuel Beckett's *End Game*—a passage that ends with a firm "Happiness!" Mary [Ryan] invites us all home for food and drink. We laugh about the soprano.

6/19/76

The essence of existence is a question. "What do you think of yourself?," or its answer. It can be called self-esteem. It is the difference between happiness and unhappiness—even something worse, a hesitation, lack of decision, inability to estimate oneself. The latter is semi-misery.

7/4/76

France. New youth style for adolescents is "the interesting silence." In 1968 they were gassy, spouting the latest revolutionary undigested jargon to impress the opposite sex. Now the meditative young male sits about, naked to the waist in the heat contemplating his destiny, responsibility, masculinity.

8/9/76

Love is a desperation,
A necessity.
Do I even know you?
Not completely.
But I need you completely.

9/1/76

First note on 4th Ripley.

9/21/76

Berlin. A week of Festival. One month 2 Sept. till Oct.* Multi-gravitational Aerodance Group, New York. In English. Big theater. People on bleacher seats of wood. The futility of life is the theme. *Raucher* [smokers]: a room to the left (or right). Pretty blond girls. I am told Berlin is an artificial city, which houses a lot of elderly people, living on pensions. Berlin makes light bulbs with heavy coils in them, as in the old days. Second evening. Night club disco called Romy Haag†—Transvestite entertainment at 1:35 AM (scheduled for 1 AM). Before that a hypnotic hour watching gilded ball, which revolves—like the world or some gambling device over the heads of the dancers as the music booms. Mainly young people in blue jeans, but some older couples—respectable and married. "Berliner Luft—Luft—Luft—Duft—Duft—Duft."‡

   It is after 3AM when I go to bed—tired too from L..P.[Lil Picard]'s increasing "anger." She is now "left wing." I must not call the Communists bastards—suddenly. She calls me racist, fascist. I refuse to fight with L.P., tell her she is always right. (And something is wrong, because my heart beats as if I were fighting, & I detest it.) Her own blood pressure is high and who could wonder! It is all the art world, the

* Pat went to the "Berliner Festwochen" for a week. Other attendants of the month-long festival included William Burroughs, Susan Sontag, Allen Ginsberg, and Trisha Brown.
† Former circus artist and legendary transvestite Romy Haag (1948–) opened her nightclub, Chez Romy Haag, in Berlin Schöneberg in 1974, attracting famous guests such as Udo Lindenberg, Zizi Jeanmaire, Bryan Ferry, Freddy Mercury, Lou Reed, Mick Jagger, and onetime lover David Bowie, who moved to Berlin for Romy.
‡ "Das ist die Berliner Luft" ("This is the Berlin Air"), a 1904 song from an operetta.

art world—much of it full of crap as usual, but Lil seems to love it all indiscriminately.

Restaurant: Old ladies at adjacent table talking of old age and their mothers whom the doctors will not let die. Money, money. After L.P. returns to hotel at 6 PM (after long day of dictating) she starts *again* and I refuse, politely, to spend another evening with her like the last. I long in fact to join Anne Uhde in the Schwarzwald instead of this! E.g. I mentioned to L.P. that I was annoyed that Tom Ripley was made a hoodlum in Wenders' film* script—or at least a little more common. Lil apparently objected to the word "hoodlum." I asked, "Perhaps you think they don't exist?" She replied, "They don't exist. They are made hoodlums by society."

9/22/76

East Berlin via S-Bahn at Charlottenburg, to Friedrichstraße. All train overland. Disagreeable (or bored) officials in police-soldier gray green uniforms. We present passports, wait 5 minutes, no smoking, have been given white cards to fill out, our 7-digit number is called & we go to reclaim passports from two blonde women. Next we must buy with 6.50 DM equivalent in East German money—of which I could finally spend nothing but return S-Bahn fare, because shops were closed for lunch. I walked along Friedrichstraße and back and was glad to depart. The clothing looks better than it did 3 years ago. Workers' Schnellimbiss are little stands in the wall, rapidly serving beer, frankfurters, sauerkraut, potatoes. Dreary leather shops. But perhaps I didn't go to the best street. Long rows of dark gray residential houses right & left, not all with flowerboxes. Physically, it seemed to me, the people looked coarser, heavier, more working class. Fare: 80 Pfennig. Typically my pen ruptured in pocket of red raincoat. Arriving people, mainly W[est] Berliners, are laden with food baskets, suitcases. Careful check of amount of DM coming in, in wallet, & this is written on white card, but not checked upon leaving.

9/22/76

Allen Ginsberg reading "Vortrag, Lesung, Film." He reads well, with pauses, and loudly.

Introduction an old-fashioned explanation of 1945 as time of tolerance

---

* *The American Friend*, Wim Wenders's 1977 neo-noir adaptation of *Ripley's Game*.

of homosexuals—thus placing Ginsberg 2,400 years behind the times of Greece. Anti-capitalist but also anti-Communist. What side is he on?

9/23/76

Cars drive around [the Berlin] Olympic Stadium, on which teams of 14-year-olds were practicing relay racing for future Games. Hitler built this, & it has not much changed. Kilometer distant is Teufelsberg,* made a rubble heap, now used as a toboggan hill. Paths, car paths, kids flying glider model planes by radio control. Woods all around, suitable for hiding overnight. Longer drive to Glienicker Brücke, where the water is divided exactly down the middle between East-Berlin & West-Berlin. A sign on both sides of West-Berlin end of bridge: Those who gave it the name "Bridge of Unity" also built the wall, drew barbed wire, created death strips and thus prevented unity. This bridge is sometimes a spy exchange, spies being handcuffed to guards, who meet in the middle. 4,000 spies in Berlin, or one for every 1,000 people.

Illogics: Berlin has to dispose of sewage in East-Berlin, & pay Russians for use of disposal plants originally built by Berlin. Telephone calls from East to West cost more, as if to a different country; though not the other way. Russians benefit from Common Market, despite their different country attitude. Treaties: both Germanies write "can" effect something (expedite to best of ability) instead of using more binding language, such as Congress shall make no laws to prevent freedom of speech. Beautiful woods, pine and oak, and many black & white birches.

9/23/76

Susan Sontag, longish introductory speech, in which she stated that she personally did not belong to any group of writers nor would care to. Then Israeli film, banned by Jews & Palestinians. She read a short story about a trip to China before she had gone—30 pages perhaps, reinforced by interesting childhood activities & facts about parents.

11/22/76

Confidence, flitting away sideways, like a bird, out of sight now, hard even to remember its image, reminding me that even physical strength is a mental attitude. The causes? Dull question. Several projects, and not concentrating on one at a time. Vagueness in three departments of life at

---

* One of several hills created from rubble in bombed-out postwar Berlin.

present. It is no longer even gambling, but a kind of darkness full of dark and empty shadows.

11/28/76

The very fact that god does not interfere in present day religious conflicts should prove to mankind that it is dealing with self-made illusion.

12/1/76

And to have patience? It is to erase all pride, satisfaction in a day's work. Very hard for me.

12/24/76

France. Atmosphere best described as hateful. Unhappy young people without jobs. Tax investigators invading people's houses by surprise (and carrying guns) at 4:00 AM. A woman accused of owing 45,000 francs committed suicide. Yet if everyone paid up, properly, there would be no need of VAT. All this because of a "spend it, buy this and buy that" attitude. The young in USA haven't the money to buy discs, clothes, motorcycles—so they mug the elderly. The French smuggle all they can out to Switzerland. Are they afraid of devaluation, taxes, or what? (Taxes are much assessed by outward appearances, style of life.)

It is all dreary, everywhere, not merely in France, but in the West, especially this Christmas Eve purporting to worship Christ! Quarries, lorries already break the tranquility of Montcourt. Double taxation due by 1978.

There are moments of silence. That is the only pleasure.

1977–1980

EDITH'S DIARY IS PUBLISHED in 1977. For her next book, Patricia Highsmith returns to her favorite character, Tom Ripley, for the fourth installment of her "Ripliad." She considers setting parts of the story in divided Berlin and travels there for research. During one of her trips, she meets twenty-five-year-old actress and costume designer Tabea Blumenschein. When Pat is invited to be a jury member for the Berlin Film Festival in February 1978, this provides her with a welcome opportunity to see Blumenschein again. Although Pat and Marion Aboudaram are still an item, once Tabea introduces Pat to West Berlin's gay subculture, Pat falls head over heels for the avant-garde film star. The two enjoy a successful reunion in London in April—but Tabea is unable to travel to France as planned. In August, she writes to Pat in Montcourt, declaring that she never falls in love with anyone for longer than four weeks. Pat is shattered and turns to a new French acquaintance, Monique Buffet, for comfort. She and Monique, a young English teacher, become romantically involved at the end of the summer in what will be Pat's last relationship.

Monique has a positive influence on Pat and her writing, and Pat is finally able to wrap up work on *The Boy Who Followed Ripley*, which was delayed by the emotional tumult of recent months. She completes the rough draft in November, delivers the final manuscript in April 1979, and dedicates the book to Monique. Before the new Ripley novel comes out, however, Pat's fourth collection of short stories, *Slowly, Slowly in the Wind*, is published in 1979, featuring pieces from 1969 to 1976.

By 1979, Pat is considering the idea of purchasing a house in Switzerland and spending most of her time outside France, in order to evade the country's higher income tax rates. She is outraged when the French fiscal authority raids her house in Montcourt in March 1980. Before she can leave the country, however, she must deal with a series of health scares; having already been hospitalized in Nemours for severe nosebleeds in January, in May Pat has to undergo bypass surgery in London to restore circulation to her right leg—for years, she has suffered chronic pain in her calf, due to constricted blood vessels caused by smoking. Still, it becomes increasingly clear: once she's back on her feet, Pat's time in France is drawing to a close.

⚐

1/31/77

If one's entire life is work, preparation, diligence, eternally aiming toward something as a student aims toward a diploma, it is bewildering to reach the goal—or even 90% of it. What does one do then? And why? Was the objective money? No. Leisure? No. Fame? Again no. Just an abstract excellence really. One can have the same feeling at seventeen or nineteen, having written a short-story word perfect, or nearly so.

2/15/77

Vienna begins at the airport on arrival—not a very big airport and not one that looks like a half-dozen others you have seen so that you have to think for a moment whether you are in Paris or London. Furthermore, the Viennese are handing out roses! It is Valentine's Day and a couple of girls in stewardess uniforms are distributing wax-paper wrapped bouquets—each containing five long-stemmed roses—to men and women alike. France earlier this morning was not even selling roses. The ubiquitous hypochondriac taxi driver is here in Vienna too, and I listen to him expecting a little more eccentricity, a little more whimsy perhaps than I would find in the French. No smoking please. With the explanation that it is his stomach. From what I can gather he has two open wounds in his stomach. Ulcers? He is hiding them even from his doctor, he says. Doesn't want any operations. My friend T. [Trudi Gill] is waiting in the hotel to meet me with a further Viennese welcome of a box of chocolates and Russian vodka. The Hotel Bristol (since 1900 and possibly earlier) has the comforting storm doors, the plush carpets, the brass probe and rails of the old school. Dusty-pink cloth on the panels of my room, the same pink as the drapes at the window, chaise longue of generous proportions, a fireplace and mantel.

2/15/77

Graben. Formerly a moat. In 1679 a place of burial after the pestilence, monument extremely busy erected to Leopold I with an angel holding his crown, all some 3.5 ft. high, one figure after another, standing on bulbous stone resembling footstool mushrooms on a tree trunk. Baroque c. 1710. "*Deo Filio Redemptori.*" One holds a lute in dreamy mood, while adjacent figure is about to throw a spear, and the viewer's mind wobbles. Pride of Tracht.* Little headgears for men. Café Rabe near Michaelerplatz. Unpromising modern sign, red arrow, then an opening two doors, second the old semi-circular, one is in 19th century, with newspapers on sticks, marble topped tables, quiet businessmen having a Monday coffee, reading. But table of three women, another two tables one woman each, shows I have walked into a coffee break of local whorehouse. They are talking about rudeness of local policeman re: parking offenses. One single woman with dyed blond hair seems to be in a huff & does not join in. Circular coat trees. Loden Plankl best [shop] in town. Michaelerplatz. Old scrolly sign outside. Busy windows of green Tracht jackets, one 2300 ATS. A masterpiece of green with green leather collar, horn buttons, silver chain to link the jacket in front, pleated skirt. I like the pride implied in this national costume. If one remarks (in course of complicated conversation re chauvinism or anti-German attitude) that Hitler was Austrian, the reply comes, "But Hitler could have done what he did only in Germany, because the Austrians are not at all military."

While everyone seems at least a little bit snobbish, people take great pains to point out how snobbish certain other people are, and how free they themselves are from this vice. Many are the stories recounted! One of the Diplomatic Corps—and my Crétin Distingué translation of C.D.† brings gratifying roars—is reported to have said, "Don't sit at that table, he's only a Second Secretary! We have an Ambassador at our table."

Vienna. It seems to go on forever, after a kilometer of torn up streets and dull modern edifices, one will come upon a beautiful church such as the Piaristenkirche, all clean and smut free, lovely big court in front, elegant column in mid court dividing the scene, column topped with golden horns. Next to this is the Piaristenkeller, which seems the real thing. Cither music, old vaguely dusty atmosphere of a cellar, which it is, as it used to be part of the church. The white napkins have a limp look as if they might have been used once before, but they haven't, they are merely homey, like the rest of the place.

---

* "Tracht" and "Loden" describe the traditional Austrian costume.
† In Pat's joke, the C.D. abbreviation stands for "Distinguished Cretins," whereas the actual meaning is, of course, Corps Diplomatique.

2/16/77

Underground excavations: 6 PM—3 men working in a hole about 18
ft. deep, 12 wide, 16 long, sound of ordinary hammer at work which
attracts attention of one passerby and of me too. At Karlsplatz, the
works are vast, and this will be the largest of the underground stations.
They were about to take the root protective covering off a tree when
I went past, a lovely, hope-filled sight to see, the root ball of the tree
being 8 feet in diameter, and four or five men discussing the situation,
apparently—the depth for the tree already there, and heaps of freshly
dug up earth all about in what will one day—1982 maybe—be a lovely
square. The eloquence of the buildings, the ebullience of the statues
reminds one of human speech, of the desire—and the ability—to communicate. Vienna still communicates, even though old Europeans (from
elsewhere) are apt to call the city "half-dead."

8/17/77

USA boy on train to Paris & Zurich. Aged 19–20, tall & slender. Blue
jeans, talks with everyone in intense manner, and with Irish accent
whose song never varied and which I thought phony. Passport man
(French) informed him his card of identity was not "valable." I asked
to see it. The boy was an American private, "working" (so he said) in
Stuttgart.

"Oh, he's just a fellow from a dinky little town!" boy says to me re the
Swiss inspector! He had earlier said, "I work for one of the world's biggest employers. Oh, aye!"

The employer was the U.S. Government. I felt he was putting on an
act. Why? He looked—or acted—stupid through & through. In the
army, perhaps he is the company clown? Is that a role that makes army
life easier for him? He said, "I'm working now in defense of Germany
against the Russians—the border. New guns." The thought of his hand
on any trigger is terrifying. [A man from] Zurich shakes his head with
a smile as he overhears boy saying one has to have 5,000 DM to get into
the casino at Baden-Baden, and 1,000 is to tip the doorman! "Oh, aye!"
People listen to his nonstop drivel with amazement. This boy could later
become a murderer.

10/28/77

The human race has become so revolting anyway, by their number and
their stupidity, why not drink and smoke to escape the facts? To shut out
the truth for a while?

10/29/77

The ground under Las Vegas is sinking, due to use of water for plumbing, etc. A fine end, if the whole corrupt city, with its prostitutes and bars and casinos sank into the desert sands, moistened however with their own excrement, which cannot be flushed farther away, because the pipes now slant down ward, due to the land's sinking.

11/17/77

To Remember Ulrike, Tabea, Walter, Berlin Nov. 17 1977
     Hotel Franke—5:30 AM!
[extra special] indeed! And a glance through a lift window. And a black lighter left on the table in my hotel room and the lighter returned late February to T.*

12/12/77

Tomorrow I must busy myself looking up a bailiff, as the mason has abandoned his work on my land, his wife having run out of his house. Next door is an alcoholic adulterer, now pilfering firewood bought by me to give to the poor. The locals avoid income tax by receiving—nay, insisting upon, their payment in liquid [cash], thus putting an increasing burden upon tax-payers. It's a Merry, merry Christmas—and though many may go to church on the eve, I feel glad that Christ is *not* here, *not* within their hearts or spirits—and I know why. And so does Jesus.

⚶

2/1/78

Since morale means "how one rates one's self," it becomes hard to maintain when confronted with problems one cannot really handle: income tax, household chores. I realize it is all absurd. I pay the accountant his usual fee of $65 and $75 per hour. Why after two years (almost) is my legal residence not yet determined? And the masons—too busy to work for you, no matter how much you pay them. Why do I drop my own work even for two weeks because of this rubbish? Because I am badly

---

* Pat penned this entry on the label of a bottle of Bell's Old Scotch Whiskey of the "extra special" variety as a reminder of just such a night she spent in Berlin with German avant-garde filmmaker Ulrike Ottinger (1942–), a person named Walter, and actress Tabea Blumenschein, with whom she will soon begin an affair. She put the label in Notebook 34 for safekeeping.

organized, and realizing this, my morale drops even lower! However, many insane people have an insanely high opinion of themselves, so perhaps all is not lost for me.

3/13/78
   —*First anniversary.*
   For Tabea. One week. Berlin.
   Her favorite)
(The aquarium. Three beers—
In my room. Hazelnuts and—
A blood orange on a towel.
Good-bye, good-bye,
In our room.
To walk with you as if you were
The Parthenon, down a corridor,
To find the lift,
To descend, with the Parthenon,
Strikes me as funny.
Laughter is protective.
When I saw you walk to the left,
Outside, gone from me,
Then poetry began, and memory,
All your words to me,
And what else?

3/22/78
Berlin. Element of disguise and humor in the bars. People carry two changes of clothing for the evening. I mean, one besides the clothing they are wearing. I think this is a reflection of the unreality of the city itself. The nervousness and liveliness comes from the fact or the realization that the city is artificially maintained, and in danger of being abandoned. It is like the end of the world (not a world), the end of an individual also. Perversely, this may make for preservation, or health, in the individual, in his behavior and attitude toward himself or herself. The rest is mockery of what they, the Berliners, see with their eyes. The Ax Bax. 12 Leibnitzstraße off Kantstraße open till all hours, but sometimes closed without warning. Excellent Pilsener Urquell. Lots to eat. Gay Kellner [waiter]. I shall never forget it, nor forget how it saved my heart from the boring bourgeois I was otherwise surrounded by. [F]Tabea has bowled me

over, knocked me mentally on the floor! To laugh and have a beer with her—that seems all I want in life right now.[FF]

A pity I didn't keep a diary all those thirteen days. Yet it would just be to tell if I went to the Ax Bax on Monday or Wednesday. I think I went at least three times, and the real dates do not matter. At Pour Elle* a sturdy macho girl poked me in the ribs, said I was not too soft at all—meaning I was okay—then threw my vodka (which she had bought me) onto the floor! Her girlfriend sat quietly on adjacent stool. I shall remember the zoo, with its crocodiles, and Tabea leaning on a rail, on the left, gazing down into their heated pond. She remarked that they had wounded each other (one another) by their biting. True. The blood was visible. I was spinning for fourteen days after Berlin, not helped by a letter from Tabea which came eight days after my arrival back home. Not helped either by a nostalgic record of Berlin songs, which I play compulsively. Not helped by the blue and white bathmat from Hotel Palace, dated 1973, from my room.

4/3/78

It is a rather frightening fact that absurdity, or the risible is truth and reality. This is why so many of us walk on the thin edge. The thin edge of what? Anyway, we are bared by seriousness, which does not give us all the answers.

4/4/78

London. Christopher Petit, journalist about 28, *Time Out*, one of very few journalists I've ever liked! He was going to Berlin next day, so I gave him T.'s *Wörterbuch* [dictionary] to deliver. He said, "Visiting East-Berlin is less of a cultural shock." Whereupon I said that was the funniest remark I'd heard in a week. The people in London streets *do* look scruffy, shabby, unwashed even. There is only a vestige of chic left around Piccadilly. Simpson's. Even Regent Street begins to look like Oxford Street.

APRIL 4, 1978

SHEILA "HELL" FROM HARPER'S RANG. SHE WISHES TO HAVE YOUR COMMENTS ON THE PSYCHOLOGY OF THE MAN WHO HAS JUST KNIFED THE POUSSIN IN THE NATIONAL GALLERY

---

* Berlin's oldest lesbian bar, located in Schöneberg.

KINDLY RING 892 96 36 (AND TELL HER SHE CAN "STUFF IT")*

APRIL 9, 1978

Poem for T., Written Not on Horseback
I fell in love not with flesh and blood,
But with a picture: the sailor cap,
Perched on the girl-sailor's right shoulder,
And the puzzled and somewhat serious eyes.
What were you thinking of then?
There is a pop song called "Living Doll."
Can't do better than that?
Your image changes, and so do my emotions.
It is a voyage more strange than that of Madame X.†
I don't know where I'm going to be tomorrow,
Because certainly I've never been here before,
Never on these seas! No!
I try to imagine you asleep.
I have seen you awake—and walking!
I can't believe it.
This is why I shut my eyes when I see you.
If I would touch you, maybe you would shatter
Or dissolve, like a dream one tries too hard to remember.
I don't want to destroy you.
I want to keep you in my eyes.

APRIL 11, 1978

Strange impulse or desire,
Twice in a week, last week,
To throw myself into the nearest
Body of deep water,
And drown.
I am not trying to prove
Anything to anybody.

---

* A message written by the friend at whose house Pat was staying in London and that she kept in her notebook, with the typed addendum: "Note from Barbara Ker-Seymer, London, 4 April 1978, re interviewer." *The Adoration of the Golden Calf* by Baroque painter Nicolas Poussin had just been slashed with a knife by a man who managed to escape.
† The pirate film *Madame X—An Absolute Ruler* (1978) by Ulrike Ottinger (1942–) with Tabea Blumenschein in the lead role is considered a milestone in queer film history.

This isn't blackmail.
I'd do it with a smile.

APRIL 26, 1978
For the Sailor Box for T.
  Some more *seemännisch** stuff,
  Which I always want to give you.
  A box for nothing, *für Träumerei,*†
  Or maybe hairpins.
  It is for *Die Blauen Matrosen.*
  But I think *die Betörung*‡
  Is of Pat.
    BERLIN 30 APRIL   LONDON 29 APRIL

4/28/78
  With sex: it is availability or the forbiddenness which influences the emotions, I for one have had it too long forbidden. I don't speak of morals
  here, I speak of an individual's emotions.

4/29/78
  The majority of people cannot handle the brains they have been given.

4/30/78
  The world is full of people who can't master it, or cope. Aren't they perhaps the most idealistic of all? The rest, perhaps, is the physical stamina.
  One must never say to one's self, "I can't make it." One must never ring
  up an SOS on the telephone. One must take care of one's problems at
  home.

[NO DATE]
  Your kisses fill me with terror—
  And we laugh in the Cockney Pride.§
  How awful that I hurt your feelings
  That Tuesday night, our third evening.

---

* Sailorly.
† For reverie.
‡ *Die Betörung [infatuation] der blauen Matrosen [The Blue Mariners]* (1975), another film by Ulrike
Ottinger with queer artist Rosa von Praunheim and Tabea Blumenschein, the latter in the roles of siren,
Hawaiian girl, and young bird.
§ Pub near Piccadilly Circus, London.

I shall never forget you, standing in your raincoat,
In the living room, looking at the floor.
You said, "It was not easy for me to come here."
I had asked if you played with people.
You don't. You exist.
That same Tuesday night
You said "Yes" six times.
Thank you very much, as you would say.
My enthusiasm is as great as yours.
But I am not quite released yet.
It's the terror.

5/31/78

The ebb and the rise—high tide?—of energy, when one is in love, is frightening. A piece of news, information can suddenly relieve a tension that has lasted for days—the result is sudden sleepiness and sleep. It is even absurdly physical and down to earth. T. and I in London, asleep on the sofa one half hour (or less) after getting to the flat, after the meeting at the airport. Asleep for at least half an hour, both of us! I at least had been in tension for days before, in France, alleviated only slightly forty-eight hours before, by the confirming—that she would make it. Then the next tension set in. I suppose I am really amazed that she experienced the same thing. It is I who care very much more than she does.

JUNE 2, 1978

I realize that any sorrow I may know
Will come from "wanting,"
Desiring what I cannot have.
I know its unwisdom.
But it is so difficult
For an artist, creature of passion,
Not to desire,
So difficult, if I want to be happy—
Not to hope,
So difficult to deny myself
This strictly mental and even idealistic
Pleasure.
What code of ethics, what philosophy
Would prohibit
Something of thin air?

6/3/78

    Sleep, blonde, sleep,
    Was never so beautiful as with you.
    The calmness incredible
    After tension.
    I can't believe it!
    But I remember waking up
    At the same time as you.
    With, at last, no one else around us.
    After a year—how long?—
    Of never touching hands,
    We fell asleep on a London sofa
    As soon as we met!
    I like it because it's funny.
    I like it because it's real.
    You and I, asleep.

JUNE 4, 1978

    Why should I doubt? Why should I torture myself with doubt?

6/17/78

    Girls are never anything but an idea. As Goethe said, *"Das ewig Weibliche."** But it is only ideas that influence mankind.

6/20/78

    Today is so much better than yesterday.
    And the day before yesterday so much worse than—
    The day before that!
    What kind of calendar marks dare I make,
    When my whole goddam morale is at stake?

6/22/78

    This business of "having fun"—I am not sure I know how to do it, even for two or three days, much less six weeks. That period of time frightens me. One evening, yes.

---

* *"Das Ewig-Weibliche zieht uns hinan"* ("The eternal feminine draws us onward"), the final words of Goethe's drama *Faust II*.

7/15/78

Families are nice to visit, but I wouldn't want to live with one.

11/29/78

Jeremy Thorpe case just broke, Scott shedding tears of virtue.* Somehow this public display, populace hanging on it, is more amusing than [Menachem] Begin of Israel.† I read him backward for the truth and call him the End. In both stories, it is the pot calling the kettle black, which has always comic value. I note with equal pleasure that in this week's news, the prostitutes of England are going to demand to know their clients' names, and the ladies will be joined by others of their profession in other countries in asking the same question.

🕊

1/2/79

Do the Jews in Israel realize that they do not want peace, or are they fooling themselves? (Later: only part of them just now are fooling themselves. Alas, the majority.)

1/9/79

The French become female when behind steering wheels, or when panic-buying. It would be easier to endure if they were prettier to look at.

2/11/79

How to be miserable: compare yourself to other people—who may not exist—who might have done it all better and more quickly. How to be happy: tell yourself you are doing well, when you aren't, that you are cheerful and efficient, when you aren't.

4/9/79

It is never reality which counts, only your opinion of reality.

---

* British politician with whom an acquaintance, Norman Scott, claimed to have had a sexual relationship—at a time when homosexual encounters were still illegal in the UK. Scott was later threatened with a gun by an acquaintance of Thorpe's and his dog was shot. The affair started in 1976, but the trial took place in 1979. It is unclear what Highsmith is referring to here.
† Pat is appalled when the divisive and controversial politician Menachem Begin becomes prime minster of Israel in 1977—to such an extent that she forbids any further publication of her books there.

6/17/79

Everyone lives (or not, meaning suicide) within a framework, given by one's parents, or society, or a framework made by oneself. The people who make their own patterns may be the stranger, but they have to be very strong. Lately I have seen a lot of failures.

JUNE 12–18, 1979

Munich. Hotel Biederstein, 18 Keferstraße, Schwabing. Countess Harrach, proprietress.

One walks out from the hotel into an atmosphere of trees, Chelsea-like boutiques, English-style lampposts. It did not take me long to find a very small *Kneipe* [pub], that would be crowded with 12 men in it—as it was. Jukebox. Dumpy woman in white serving behind the bar. T[abea] B. came two days later. T. erect, brisk as usual. She has even gained a little weight (in past 13 mos. since I saw her) despite travails of past six weeks. Friday, at 4 PM. to *"Die Gläserne Zelle"** which T. had already seen. Computer recording used in it to blackmail Carter (Philip) into either confessing murder of David, or killing Gawill. Brigitte Fossey left me cold. David was played by a hairy type, not at all the smooth gentleman.

T. cool and calm. I was disappointed, maybe my eyes opened a bit. T. is not only careless of other people's feelings (which I attributed to youth) but also perhaps tough! But—I trust—I did the right thing and things.

I was polite—maybe more so than usual!—and Sunday afternoon I said, "Why not spend it alone with your Munich friends?" I slept in hotel, thinking, dreaming. T. and I had four nights, and she was cooler to me the second two, the opposite of London. T. spoke often of the Berlin discos, the one-night-stands. T.'s Budapest job was postponed from 18 June to August, so, "I came to see you," said T. I was pleased to pay hotel bill, & to buy her a wristwatch: black face with no numerals. T. liked the strap! Marienplatz. 495 DM.

Annetti[†] offered to pay a steady monthly rent to T. and said I could stay when I was in Berlin. NO comment from T.—or from me, then. I never thought T. wished me in Berlin. I can't see myself at discos! Till 6 AM. T. is another world now. When I say I have loved her for 18 months now—no comment, not even a faint smile of amusement. Blank. T. is

---

* This refers to the 1978 film adaptation of Highsmith's *The Glass Cell* by Hans W. Geißendörfer that was nominated for an Oscar in the category of Best Foreign Language Film.
† A friend and apparently patron of Tabea's in Munich.

out for herself. (Ambition is okay with me. I wonder if U.O. got tired of her one night stands, her different hours?) "Do you make love now in the loos too?" (I meant the bar loos.) "Any place," she replied. How well I remember her Aug. 10, 1978 letter to me: "I am so constructed that I can be in love with someone only 4 weeks." (or maybe "relationship.")

Maybe my illness is over. I flew back from Munich in puzzled state of mind, knowing I had to readjust, to see T. in a different light. Today is 21 June, appropriately the longest day of the year.

9/15/79

By an act of will it is possible to achieve all the states of mind that drugs and alcohol and opium and so on—are supposed to put us into. Simplest illustration of this is certain music—which can be remembered accurately, effecting the same response as if we had heard it.

11/24/79

Preparatory: a course early on in all schools, when the child is about ten, on life's problems, the objective being to learn to give them a name. This is in the direction of analyzing the problem, which means facing it. Jealousy, wounded ego, et cetera—so many heart-breaking and disturbing situations which start appearing at twelve even. So many adults can't or are afraid to label their own problems. I think such a course, one hour a week even, would be very popular among the children. It would prevent many suicides. Stories told should be fictitious. The children will identify soon enough.

12/8/79

Certain kindnesses and goodwill are now thwarted in so many people. We are aware more than ever of the need, and it is apparently hopeless to do anything (or very much) about it. This causes the ill-at-ease feeling, defensiveness, bitterness, cynicism as protection. It's all contrary to nature. TV for example expands pity, also blood lust, but quickly cuts both emotions off. These emotions are contradictory. It is like arithmetic equaling zero at last. TV gives the state-desired effect of impotence.

12/16/79

For a short time in youth, men are sex objects for women also. What is the fuss about? That women wish to be sex objects for a longer time? It is so easy for both sexes to use the boycott.

12/21/79

What a writer is in love with, and why, cannot be put into words by the writer, any more than he could explain why he is in love with a woman his friends consider worthless. This mystery the writer also does not wish to explain. It is a lovely and precious gift. And I am not afraid of sentimentality.

12/21/79

Two rules for dealing with girls. And women, neither of which works, and together they don't work either:

1) find out what the woman wants. This may take a minute, or months.
2) Yield at once.

1/2/80

Income Tax; French fisc: "Where were you physically when you wrote the book?" Reply: "I take the Catholic Church's attitude toward creation. And surely you do too? Life begins at the instant of conception, and as for this book, I was on the Mozart Express between Paris and Vienna when the entire plot came to me. I wrote it in France and Germany, even America. But surely you cannot deny that its conception is its life. To deny that is a sin, an abortion."

1/15/80

Nemours Hospital. I'm admitted at 2 AM for streaming nosebleed which turns into periodic gush every two hours or so for next five days. No chance of sleep or eating. It was interesting to let the mind go blank, deliberately to think of "nothing" and see what happened. It was a steady movement neither fast nor slow, like looking down from an airplane when one is still nearly two miles high. For a few seconds I saw sentences coming out on the typewriter. I thought quite a bit of T., maybe because her life is so merry compared to my warm bright rushes of blood, which are my life pouring out into kidney-shaped basins. I thought of the start of a plot for a Dracula film, forced myself to create a middle and end for it, which I did in three minutes. I had a sensation of endless diversion, of floating over a patchwork quilt whose patterns were all the fascinating things I could think about if I just kept on and on. When I was feeling better and able to sleep, I had a dream of walking down steps [toward a] square like Trafalgar. Water was running in all the gutters, and people would cry out, "There's an otter! Look!" It was a dark night, around midnight. I had left my small suitcase under a streetlamp near a taxi stand. I saw someone steal it before I could get down to where it was. In it was a manuscript and my current notebook. I was shocked and pained and said something to a woman on the street. I was walking toward the place where it was stolen. Then I woke up and said aloud, "Maybe it was all a dream! It was all a dream!"

Death. An irritating possibility for two days and nights. I was losing more than I was gaining. I thought of the scrap paper in my typewriter at home with income 1979 USA in the roller, and thought how appropriate—to be bleeding in two places. To be bled to death, to be so tormented mentally that the pulse will not quieten, as the nurses wish, but keeps pumping more and more blood out. Down my throat the nurse have poked—with aid of stiffish plastic tube down nose—a thread that bears a tampon of cotton that hangs. Thread is taped to right cheek. This is nauseating, blocks air to some extent and I have to breathe entirely by mouth for five days. Every three hours I have to press the bell for a nurse to bring me another. "Oooh-la-la!" they say and "—*énormément*" when they are reporting to the doctor. I wonder if they think I may die.

Third or fourth day I was afraid of dying and asked for door of my room to be left open. The nurse would not do it, because children are very frightened by blood. Too bad! This made me angry, also ashamed of my fear of dying alone, since I've always known death is an individual act anyway. I swear to myself next time I'll be better prepared. With morphine it's easy, like an anesthetic or a sleeping pill. Maybe it's a sign of vitality or brotherliness to want to speak to someone at the last and say, "Stay with me a minute, please—I'm going."

Final item: "Look. Blood's coming out of her eyes now! Did you see that?"

2/3/80

It's easier to die in a silly way,
More or less suddenly with no background music,
No memories of the Engadin at Christmas,
Or of Bach's St. Matthew,
No memory of four years' pleasure and pain

Of a love that was great but ended sadly.
Better the quick-flick of one-night stands
That flash by like lights along a highway,
All more or less fun, and none involving pain,
Or even leaving a clear recollection.
Gone the chocolate cake of yesterday,
Unfinished. The excellent stereo at home,
The promise of next summer's vacation
In the Algarve, and the face
Of the girl who tends the bar,
And who promised a date next Saturday.
As I wrote the above, I think of Sakharov in Russia, a 58-year-old man
prepared for death, a brave man, who thinks of millions of other peo-
ple who know about Him. He has the courage to value these millions
more important than himself, though he risks torture before death by his
statements.[*]

2/24/80

Vague depression lately, for a reason I might have expected. Lately I have
to live on a plane of reality. It never does for me. I feel happy and secure
of myself only when I am daydreaming and creating a story or a book.
Unfortunately, it would be dangerous and unwise to get off this plane of
reality now.

4/5/80

Switch off TV and the whole family with it.

5/9/80

It is impossible for me to live from day to day without putting myself to
a judgement—of some kind. How well have I done? What did I mean to
accomplish today? Also troublesome is what do other people think of
me? This is why interviews are so abhorrent, and also boring. It is not
necessary that I should be subject to the question, what do other people
think of me. It is therefore destructive for me to think about this. Inner
contentment is another matter. A great or proud objective isn't the point.
Something constructive during the day, however little, is the point. Idle-

---

[*] Andrei Dmitrievich Sakharov (1921–1989), Russian nuclear physicist, human rights advocate, and the
first Soviet citizen to receive the Nobel Peace Prize in 1975. He was arrested in January 1980 following his
protests against the Soviet intervention in Afghanistan in 1979, and was pardoned by Gorbachev in 1986.

ness and daydreaming—they give pleasure, and suffice for what I am talking about. It's not really the Protestant work ethic.

5/9/80

Morale—How do various people maintain theirs? And how about people who never give it a thought and get along? People who never give morale a thought never give anything a thought.

5/29/80

Fitzroy-Nuffield Nursing Trust Bryanston square, where I was 21 May till 1 June. Bypass of iliac artery, right groin, with removal of vein from right thigh as bypass. Now on 29 May when I walk about & climb stairs comfortably, I can understand why a certain type of person with little else to do becomes obsessed with operations, having them.

6/29/80

It isn't women or girls; it is yourself to learn about, and to blame.

7/7/80

The curious thing about sex is that it is of great importance, and also of no importance at all.

7/10/80

Nervous Breakdown Number Two. "How can you lead a healthy life if it is dominated by an emotion of hatred and resentment?" Abandon all but the lifebelt. But that's a late thought in the whole picture. First and slowly comes the abandonment of the only thing that counts, work. This is the hell, the only potential cause of breakdown. Nervous breakdown is the same as flying a white flag of defeat.

8/24/80

To be in love: the mixing of what one knows to be fantasy, idealization, with reality (there is no doubt the loved one exists, because the body is tangible), causes a mental state akin to drunkenness. This in turn creates "the lover being in love with himself" state. It seems truly best to be in love with someone we cannot touch and do not profoundly know. One is always in love with an idea or an ideal. All this has nothing to do with the sexual drive. In a way, it is amazing that an attraction to, or admiration of someone, has anything to do with a desire to make love to that person.

9/13/80
Love is sharing—ideas? Love is courage? Both. Love is daring to risk being hurt. Love is to stand naked and honest, concealing nothing. To love really is to be hurt again and again, and still to try again. Maybe love is, above all, courage and also generosity.

NOVEMBER 1980
An artist tells his life story
In the mosaic pieces
Of his creations,
Set any old way.
When he dies, a self-portrait,
That he had no idea of at the beginning,
Is finished and fixed.

1981–1995
TWILIGHT YEARS IN SWITZERLAND

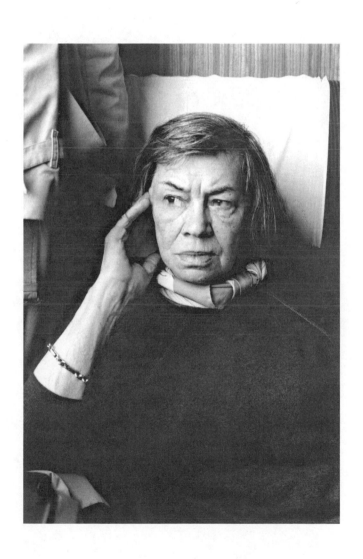

1981–1985

In an effort to avoid the double taxation she is subject to as an American citizen living in France, Patricia Highsmith decides to move to Switzerland in 1981. Her literary home has been in Zurich since 1967, when she joined Diogenes Verlag under the helm of its founder Daniel Keel, who by now also acts as her international agent. At a recommendation from Ellen Hill, Pat buys a house in a small village in the Vallemaggia district of Ticino, and begins a gradual relocation, dividing her time for the next few years between Montcourt and her new village of Aurigeno. Her purchase was a mistake: the house is dark and uncomfortable, especially in winter. And, spending more and more time away from Montcourt, Pat has to give up her relation ship with Monique Buffet.

These details are mentioned only in passing in Pat's notes. In 1981 she starts her final diary, number 17, which will last her the next ten years. Her entries have become brief, sometimes containing no more than key words, and between 1982 and 1986 they once again cease entirely. She continues to write in her notebooks, but mainly uses this space to develop story ideas, not chronicle her personal life. Although Pat is busy as ever with work-related travel, she remains unforgiving in her expectations for her own productivity.

The idea for a novel about Christian fundamentalists in the United States came to Pat after a weeks-long trip to Indiana (much of which was spent watching religious TV shows), Fort Worth, and Los Angeles in January 1981. *People Who Knock on the Door* is set in the fictional town of Chalmerston, based on Bloomington, Indiana, where her good friend Charles Latimer lives. The novel is published in Europe in 1983, at which point Pat is already busy with three new projects: two collections of short stories as well as her next novel, *Found in the Street* (1986). In this story, men and women alike become infatuated with Elsie, the protagonist; it is the first time Pat openly integrates gay characters into the fabric of one of her thrillers, having so far kept the two worlds separate.

Like most of Pat's stories and novels, despite her having lived in Europe for the past two decades, this one is set in the United States. And yet it is her home country of all places where she still struggles time and again to get her work published. When *People Who Knock on the Door* gets turned down by her American editor at Doubleday, Larry Ashmead, Otto Penzler offers to publish the novel at short notice, and it comes out in 1985; Otto Penzler Books already published *Slowly, Slowly in the Wind* in 1979 and will later also release four further collections of her short stories.

After *Mermaids on the Golf Course* (London, 1983), Pat publishes *Tales of Natural and Unnatural Catastrophes* (1985), her seventh collection of stories, all written in the early 1980s, an era dominated by such societal concerns as the Cold War, nuclear threat, and environmental destruction. Pat's personal unhappiness and the bleak mood of that decade define the character of this collection.

JANUARY 9, 1980

[New York.] Lunch with Larry Ashmead, after meeting Jeff Ross. Trouble over 4 Ripleys, rights of *Talented Mr. Ripley*? Penguin— Bloomingdale's to buy pajamas & T shirts.

1/10/81

New York. Bus to "subway" from J.F.K. Airport $4.00. Policeman in subway (express) waiting room very friendly and helpful. This new subway makes amazing and convenient stops, such as Canal Street, West Fourth & Washington Square. 42nd & Sixth, my stop, into a grimy old ordinary subway station, three flights of filthy stairs, into freezing cold of 16°.

New York has a patina now. Something old-fashioned about it. Now even—a shade on window of my bathroom in Hotel Royalton with a cord and thread-wrapped ring to pull it by.

Manufacturers Hanover [Trust]* teller balks at cashing $250 USA Traveler's Check & I've to go to 7th floor to get it authorized. They seem to know me upstairs.

---

* One of the largest banks in the United States, part of JPMorgan Chase today.

1/14/81

Lunch Joan Daves,* agent of Diogenes, at Gay Nineties, East 54th Street. Very pleasant. Berlinerin. Brooks Bros. morning where I bought white poplin trews $19.50. Drink Wed. PM with Alex Szogyi [at the] Algonquin. Then home to sleep for early departure to Indianapolis—where I was by 4 PM—Charles Latimer.

1/16/81

Bloomington, Indiana. A flat, low-built city, 40,000 students, etc. and 20,000 population. TV religious program: affable 40-year-old carefully groomed woman at left, MMC middle, "guest" on right: moustache, plump, a psychiatrist, he says. He came near dying 3 times in hospital, but called upon Jesus X who answered. He says "laying," for "lying," which makes some of his statements doubly funny. Organ music trembles. One shot of audience (in color of course) clapping in unison. Phone number with area code constantly displayed on screen.

I am reminded of sensation I had in NY when watching TV at midnight: these people are all insane, smiling, saying words they surely don't believe, in order to advertise some product. Have they sold their souls, or had they ever any souls? They have thrown away any intelligence that they may once have had.

1/17/81

TV Indianapolis. Concentration on New Testament; send contributions to our new church. God is walking by your side. Radio program: saving the one lost sheep.

1/19/81

Corner shoe repair. Cheap, quick, good, says C.L. [Charles Latimer]. Also a sale on. I bought a pair of black anti-snow boots, regrettably not of leather, for $5.95, reduced from $17.50. Atmosphere of 1930 in this small, square establishment. The deep boredom of all this! The lack of variety! A hard price to pay for security, physical comfort, room. I take comfort in the fact that my life in Europe is "interesting and varied," even though it is tough, more expensive, more lonely—though it really isn't—than this middle-west city.

---

* Joan Daves (born Liselotte Davidson, 1919–1997) was an influential literary agent, representing Nobel Prize–winning clients such as Elias Canetti, Hermann Hesse, and Nelly Sachs.

1/24/81

Texas in January. The same flat dry looking prairies, now full of two-
and four-lane highways. Temperature 70° tomorrow, and still a lot of
heat coming out of every private and public radiator or vent in the walls.
There is no general remark about the USA economy, much less the
world's. Great attention paid to certain details, for instance whether a
facade was on a building ten years ago or not.

3/18/81

Journalists: I prefer prostitutes, who sell only their bodies, not their
minds.

4/8/81

Indecision, that great source of misery that afflicts the human animal
more than any other animal, is also the source of misery in big and little
love affairs. The pain derives from being undecided in what attitude to
take, but alas the victim doesn't even realize that the pain could, almost,
be totally assuaged by deciding on an attitude!

6/25/81

Liszt's Hungarian Rhapsody 2 especially fitted for dialogue:
    "And then I kicked him *down* the stairs, and then he kicked me *up* the
stairs! I didn't know what I should do, and furthermore I'd lost a shoe."
    And *finally*—I'd lost my *tem*—per. I told them if they didn't *scram*,
I'd get the cops and then KA—*BAM*! "Whoops! La"! I tell you "Whoops
La!" I've never seen the like of all those flying heels and swine! It's Hoop-
la I'm doing *fine*, dear."
    New York apartment life.

7/30/81

Punks. Unfortunately, the world needs more of what they are protesting
against, or mocking: tradition, ceremony, loyalty, and the doing of the
right thing socially speaking. Is it any achievement to have made a pigsty
of Washington Square, New York?

8/12/81

The British Royal family. They remind us (at the wedding)* that good
behavior, morals, are all thin air, but—they can be visible also. The vir-

---

* The wedding of Prince Charles and Lady Diana Spencer on July 29, 1981.

tues the Royal Family tries to symbolize are intangible, yet all people have a need for them; even a hunger, as for vitamins when they are missing. This is why rich and poor loved this short display of the best.

8/20/81

Any person who wants to stay sane has to end up praying, in one form or another. Praying can be merely ritual, a way of doing everyday tasks or work. It is still ritual, and it is about the only thing one can hang onto. One has to inject meaning and value into it.

9/26/81

It is best to learn at a very early age, say ten, that the world and the people in it are 80% phony. This may avoid a crack-up later. However, most people do not realize the phoniness, but begin conforming at an early age. Most people need only an ego-satisfaction, whatever that may be: a successful marriage, career, love life, sufficient money. Mainly it is the failure of one of these that causes a breakdown. One has to be rather intelligent to realize the phoniness.

10/16/81

Death of Marge.* Breast cancer which spread to lymph. Aged 64. Plump, soft, thin-haired. She had had chemotherapy and X-rays which caused hair loss, upset digestion. I met her in Jan. '81. She died 14/15 October while I am [again] in Bloomington. Story from C.L.'s point of view, with houseguest. C. & M. [Charles and Michel] are almost her only friends, save for Dennis, a homosexual whose new boyfriend Marge didn't like, so she dropped Dennis.

Last Sunday evening C. and I went over to Marge's for a drink, and she was dressed, proud of her three inch hair which was "her own stuff." She had booked an air ticket to California.

C. & M. went over Tuesday evening to see how she was. We had hardly persuaded her to stay home from her university cafeteria manager job on Monday! Wed. afternoon, C. telephoned, then took consommé and applesauce over to her. She was still on the sofa, he had to hold her head up for her to drink a bit. C. returned after 45 minutes. He rang the hospital, and ambulance came in very few minutes.

"Who are you?"

---

* Highsmith's character Norma Keer in *People Who Knock on the Door* (London, 1983) was based on Charles Latimer's neighbor Marge.

"I'm just a neighbor," C. said, later reproaching himself for not having said "a friend."

Doctor impossible to find, because her doctor was physician of the football team and was usually at the university gym! Thursday noon C. rings hospital and learns Marge died at 9:15 Wednesday evening. She was Irish. Six months short of getting her pension at 65, always talking about going to Ireland.

11/24/81

French Christmas cards—the Virgin looks like a dummy. Joseph at least looks like what has happened to him has really happened.

12/8/81

The "Mystery" of women is because of what people, mainly men, read into women, and because in most societies, old and new, women are sex-objects, human spittoons. I just heard of a primitive contemporary Society, in which husbands and wives live apart. After marriage, the husband spends weeks learning phrases, charms, to "protect" himself from his wife.

12/15/81

Poland. It is so difficult to live, when the framework of society is false and rotten. Today, Wednesday, is a day of sadness when Solidarity is for the moment apparently defeated.* Maybe the most sad is that President [Ronald] Reagan does not speak out.

1/24/82

The computer is now being used for "birth control." A battery-operated gadget tells the woman's temperature, every morning. And this, it is said, meets with papal approval. Strange that the present age has to drag humanity from the moral laws of the past!

1/26/82

Kafka. A major subject for him was dramatization of the life in which I spend my days also. It must have been a relief for him to write in the eve-

---

* Between December 13, 1981, and July 22, 1983, the government of Poland instated martial law in reaction to the rising influence of the Solidarność movement.

nings and on weekends. Unfortunately for me my present theme in writing has nothing to do with the bureaucracy. Maybe my salvation also will be to invent a story based on present torments. I do know—there's no solace, or life-saving except in the imagination, in the creation of another world. This present world for me is hell, and like a prison, even though at the moment the house happens to be well-cleaned.

3/31/82

Is a society effete to have a bottle of milk and a newspaper delivered at the door every morning and not to have it stolen?

5/20/82

Jewish attitudes in this year of 1982. Not even the Germans present such a picture of the individual behaving as does the race. Anti-semitism. They profess to dislike it and to fight against it, whereas they really need it and are consciously or unconsciously aware of that need. Where would they be, in 1982, without it? Thanks to Hitler, they can appeal to every one's sympathy and charity, and far more important, menace their critics with the "anti-Semitic" epithet. There's no greater anti-Semite of our times than Menachem Begin, no greater enemy of the Jewish people. Where else in past history has a country (America) guaranteed financially and military another young country whose people are not even a majority, by race, of the sponsoring country? When else has one seen the using of this favor to wage war for more land, to practice a racialism from which they themselves have so recently been rescued?

5/20/82

Swiss—or rather expatriates who live here: it seems to me that they pay extraordinary attention to social slights, or what they imagine are slights. Others are certainly more outspoken, really laying EBH [Ellen Blumenthal Hill] out the evening about her heckling me.

Gisela Andersch—Prussian-type, speaks mainly German only. Crisp and sharp to others, upon death of her son early this year, which followed death of Alfred* pretty closely. But such behavior from bourgeoisie could not be found in England—or I'm sure in Anne Uhde of Hamburg. Everybody knows details of others, as if it were a small town.

---

* Alfred Andersch (1914–1980) is considered one of the most influential authors of German postwar literature. He and his wife, Gisela Andersch, lived in Berzona, Ticino, as of 1958.

7/2/82

The Lovers and the Calculators. The lovers fall in love, and do love. The calculators play a game. The latter are usually very pretty or handsome, or at least they think so which is half their battle won, because self-assurance creates the effect they want.

10/11/82

On writing with women as heroines. It seems to me that women are not often themselves, but rather creatures made by environment and society. Even if a man is such, he has usually ambitions, objectives, and tries to carry them out, thus making himself a more active creature at any rate.

11/25/82

A game, "Havoc." Any number can play. Single card is dealt to each and player becomes China, UK, USA, France, etc. Next card deals Nuclear Strength, then conventional Army, Airforce, Navy. (Better if countries have invented names, as power is associated with population.) Next cards give power for nuclear or conventional land attack. There must be a map of world in center of table different from real world. Players can hold back nuclear first strike power, and pass. Winner can blast all at last moment and maybe win—unless an opponent has a "direct hit" card on a vital base of his opponent. Ships, men, bombs, could be real miniature objects on the board in center of table. Napalm swoops. Vegetation kill-ers. A few cards maybe saying "one month elapses"—starvation in Agent Orange areas.

12/7/82

To all peoples of the world whose daily bread, if they have any, has the bitter taste of injustice.

☙

1/1/83

The big-name writers in America, such as Stanley Elkin, Vonnegut (best-sellers) now go into fantasy in their novels, words like fuck used often. It is as if they have given up faith in human nature (the positive and opti-mistic part of it) and chosen to rely on shocking the reader, making him laugh, or taking him into another world, which may be past or future.

One would think that the present world presents more than in the past a choice of lifestyles, many interesting, most "socially acceptable" or at least tolerated. To turn so much to fantasy (Doris Lessing, outer space) shows a lack of interest or a hopelessness about human existence in 1980–2000, it seems to me. It would seem that one hero—or twenty—is no longer of interest to these writers to pit against what is left of mores and social structure.

1/9/83

Love. To come to terms with it. To say, I'll ask for nothing. Love is enough (in my breast) even if miles separate us. Is this satisfactory, even genuine? At any rate, this attitude can give one the feeling of being happy for moments at a time. It will be interesting to see how long it will or can last, proving whether it is an illusion or not. Since love is said to be an illusion itself—perhaps the above attitude is apt. The above also is an attempt to avoid suffering.

T.'s [Tabea's] words: "But for me it is not so stupid because it gives me courage to live." Does this mean that she hoped for or expected something in the future, or that the state itself was enough?

1/9/83

Further to above. Morale and courage is attitude, and part of this is even phony, at best experimental (if one thinks about it and decides upon it). In youth, one runs on the forward energy of the body—and mind. Later one has to find the attitude that will enable one to keep going forward.

1/10/83

I was at the rail of a large ocean liner—black ship, dark sea. I was alone. I was held (from falling into the sea) only by a rounded silver-colored thick outside rail, which held me at the waist. If I ventured to move sideways where I might have climbed up to the deck, I risked falling through, as my feet rested on nothing. I woke up. Anxiety dream number—what?

1/14/83

Ambitious men have to fall in love frequently, and do. The reality of the girl doesn't matter, it's what the man puts into her. Therefore it doesn't really matter if they ever get into bed, much less if he ever gets to know what she's like, as both can be a disappointment. As Arthur Rubinstein said, "If you meet a pretty blond with nothing in her head—marry her! Live a little!"

3/1/83

Dostoyevsky. *Letters from the Underworld*. Very revealing about the author's attitude to women. In fact, it's about nothing else. The sexes are different to Fyodor, and indeed they are. F.D. seems first conditioned to rate a female by her social level. Then—to dominate or to be dominated? In real life, he was in love with a Polish actress whom he never married. (This is easiest for me to imagine!) Then he settled for the quieter type, Anna, the practical, and married. In this F.D. seems like every man. Why the sadism, the domineering? In a flash, he can switch to the opposite, and be a slave of a woman. Did he, like a lot of men, prefer to believe that he could not understand women; thereby keeping for himself his belief in their mysterious power?

3/9/83

[*Keime*.] The Pocket Watch—or The Gentleman's Pocket Watch.

Being the story of the biscuit watch I bought from my grandfather when I was 12, for $12, for cutting the lawn 24 times at 50¢ a mowing. The two lawns, divided by a straight cement walk, and the two big walnut trees, one on each side of the lawn. The watch, Hamilton, with a scrolled gold back that opened on a hinge. Inside this could be seen pawnbrokers' numbers galore, scratched lightly and minutely, some legible, some not without a magnifying glass. The three initials on the handsome gold back I have forgotten. It was a stem-winder with grooves in the stem, and had a white face with the hours in Roman numerals. It kept excellent time. Since a girl of 12 could not carry such a watch with any safety, I gave it to my stepfather when I was 13. (Curious, as at that time I had reason to dislike him.) Then—he used it and loved it, when I was 21, and earning $19 a week, I bought a French watch chain of gold for the watch, costing $30, I recall, from a small jewelry store at 59th Street and Second Avenue. This wiped out my current savings in December of 1942. My stepfather used the watch, mostly without the chain, I remember, but the chain was carefully kept in the house. I had moved away in June 1942, after graduating from college, and had my own apartment.

The years—a lifetime nearly—went by, and I saw the watch in 1970 in Texas, where my family had finally moved to. I did not see the chain, then, and it did not occur to me to ask to see it. When my stepfather died in November 1970, I asked my mother if I might have the Hamilton watch. As I was receiving absolutely nothing else from him, neither money nor keepsake, I thought this a not unreasonable request. My mother first said, "Of course," and then the watch never arrived. I was living in France. An idea to send it to NY to be brought to me by a friend en route to France came to nought. In Texas in 1974—Well, in the intervening years, my mother, growing ever more daft, wrote to me that she had decided that she had "inherited" it, as my stepfather's widow. Then she would alter her judgment and write that I could have the watch. In 1974 when I visited her briefly (1 hour with cousin Dan) I asked my mother if I could have the watch—and she could not find it, or said she couldn't. This was when the house was in total disorder.

There was a long cat-and-mouse game about the watch between '70 and '74. My mother used the watch as bait to keep me writing to her—about *something*. However I must check this, as in 1971, I wrote my stepfather the 3 long letters of which I've 2 carbons, explaining why I did not wish to write or to be written to by my mother. This watch story illustrates perfectly my mother's jealousy, malice, ambiguity, vacillation, mixture of feelings toward me.

6/1/83

Life in Switzerland (after a year and a half). It seems to me that people could be much influenced by the lack of sunlight. This makes of winter self-sufficiency in the valleys. The prevailing religion (Protestant) admires personal achievement and upright character. This can lead to paranoia, unfriendliness, in individuals, consequently seriousness to the point of depression. I personally like the touches of "democracy," such as—it's a sin to litter the landscape, because (it's not the law or a fine) one's fellowman does not enjoy looking at sandwich papers and untidy garbage. Above all, the seriousness of the people strikes me.

Here a year ago, I knew some of the blackest moments of my life, when for fifteen minutes at a time, I would feel that I'd got myself into a trap, and an unhappy one. In those moments, I remembered Montcourt and its sunlight which I shall never forget. Then I also remembered the *douane* invasion of 10 March 1980, and I knew that I would not want to live in a country which assumes everyone is a slight crook, or would be one, if he could get away with it.

I happen to like calmness, because I am nervous inside. Didn't Nietzsche like Switzerland after all? He did spend some time here.

8/11/83

I envy people with the energy left over to dance!

8/14/83

Women's shoes. They're supposed to look—as if you can't do anything in them, even walk correctly. It's the next thing to Japanese or Chinese foot binding. All this is to excite the sex drive. Women want to be swept off their feet.

9/18/83

Barcelona. A beautiful view from the airplane coming in: The town looks tan and flat, bordered by the blue sea (it is a sunny day in Sept.) and like an old-fashioned surface map. One thinks of Columbus setting sail. We are met by Jorge Herralde* and his friend Lali: Anagrama— a publishing house. They accompany us to San Sebastián in a plane with two propellers, which flies low; view on the window dry looking dark green and gray mountains for miles, evidently not used for farm- ing. What a waste of land! Villages very few and far between. I've been warned [San Sebastián] is a spa or tourist place. But it is much bigger than I had thought, with old section on the water, streets too small for cars. Rather expensive restaurants. People have secondary residences here. Well-dressed. It is hot. Second day I notice Julian Symons† in the lobby! I'd forgotten he was invited. Surprise "press conference" at what is supposed to be drinks parties. Very stupid questions by TV people: "Why did I decide to write gumshoe fiction?" Only one young Span- iard in a red sweater in San Sebastián asked brilliant TV questions. The Prado: I was able to go twice. The first time, I walked to second floor to meet the Director, who greeted me warmly, and asked me to sign the big guest book in his office. His woman secretary then accompanied me (also Marianne)‡ to the Velasquez§ rooms. The people are happy with the greater openness of the Socialist government, but fear a military coup.

[NO DATE]

Madrid: the thesis writer. We made a date for 4 one afternoon, I was late, of course, because a lunch with 10 doesn't start till 2:30, but I got

---

* Jorge Herralde Grau (1936–) founded Editorial Anagrama, Highsmith's Spanish publisher, in 1969.
† Highsmith had already met the British crime writer and literary critic Julian Symons (1912–1994) in 1964, when he was a member of the jury for the British Crime Writers' Association.
‡ Marianne Liggenstorfer-Fritzsch was the director of foreign rights at Diogenes and accompanied Highsmith on two press tours of Spain, here to the San Sebastián film festival, where Pat was invited as a guest of honor to view René Clément's *Plein Soleil/Purple Noon* (1960), a filmic homage to *The Talented Mr. Ripley*.
§ *Las Meninas* is one of the most well-known works at the Museo del Prado by the Spanish Baroque painter Diego Rodríguez de Silva Velázquez (1599–1660).

a message to the hotel. These thesis students try to make an organized discipline or science out of my writing, and I feel they are disappointed when I tell them my ideas, therefore my thoughts and processes come out of nowhere. I signed a book for her, praised her pen, which she insisted on giving to me. I'm writing with it now, red and yellow thing, clown like. Julian Symons: had a well prepared comment on Dashiell Hammett's* objectives, in San Sebastián. 13 men, and I, including Sam Fuller,† garrulous, cigar-smoking, playing the old left-wing codger. German leftwing wife, 39, with him. I was given a wooden plaque with map of Basque country on it in metal—as my books sold the most at latest book fair.

10/31/83

Halloween Eve, and I thought of exactly fifty years ago, when I was 12 in Ft. Worth, too "young" to be invited to a party by my 14-year-old classmates. I was living at my grandparents', and had nothing to do, no way to celebrate; so I took a walk late at night and removed one cap from the tire of a car parked on a dark street. I felt very furtive. I did not let the air out of the tire, though I knew how to do it.

Ah, 12–13, the most miserable year of my life.

11/30/83

Lunch with GKK [Kingsley]. Westside—very good "pub" called The State. Then a bus ride, downtown Ninth Ave.(?) the "unchanged" sloppy west side. Old stone fronts with dwellings above them, shabby fruit & veg. shops. A walk eastward at 44, 43. Unbelievable dusty old shop, selling old film posters, narrow, sign saying where to push the bell. Who buys such stuff? VACANCY sign in dingy window of near brownstone house, even a hotel like this. Good place for a crook to hide out. A pair of black women. One tosses an unfinished paper cup on pavement—splat!—the pale tan of weak American coffee, the cup rolls into the gutter.

12/20/83

Courage is a dream. It follows that one must make it last, and not wake up.

---

* Samuel Dashiell Hammett (1894–1961), famous American mystery writer of the early twentieth century.
† Samuel Fuller (1912–1997), American actor, screenwriter, novelist, and director.

2/1/84

Amazing how many times before my N.Y. trip (25 Nov.–12 Dec.) I imagined collapsing on the streets of Manhattan, unable to keep a date because of failed physical strength. I was ill before departure. But in N.Y. my strength held up quite normally.

3/4/84

Dreams— My mother in Lady Macbeth murderous mood, cut the head off T[abea] B. and said to me, "You will have to help me get rid of the body." I was shocked, paralyzed, and said nothing. My mother coated the head with transparent wax, thoroughly. I do not know what happened to head and body.

3/16/84

O my cats! O my barometers!

3/16/84

My worst and most frequent depressions are caused by a too severe judgment on myself. I could have done better, I have not been efficient and so on. Of course, the very worst melancholy comes when for some reason I am not able to work for several days, due to outside facts. Reality is the real boredom.

3/24/84

Alcohol versus cocaine, the latter said to be a stimulant comparable to a couple of double espressi. It will be interesting to see what good writers come from the cocaine takers. The alcohol lovers are famous, Poe, Scott Fitzgerald, Faulkner, Steinbeck. Do the writers prefer to dream in near-sleep? Instead of being stimulated and turned toward the external?

4/30/84

Elderly Swiss (or anywhere) reach that point of keeping themselves alive as long as possible. Their minds are on it. They eat the right things. They grimly try to enjoy what's left of life.

9/30/84

[Mozart's] ^GFantasia in D minor^{GG}—K.397, the piano piece I heard frequently from the flat above at one Bank Street, when I was 13–17.

OCTOBER 5, 1984

Istanbul. Taxi-ride from the airport about 30 kilometers. Dry half empty land, then the glimpse of sea on the right—a broad curve of the mainland, fascinating.

3/12/85

Vietnam War. Maybe for the first time in American history, young American soldiers saw that war was a business: fight because you are told to; fight against an unseen enemy; fight when America is not using its "full strength." And along with this an unaccustomed contempt for the life-worth of the enemy had to exist, otherwise the soldier could not have gone on fighting.

4/18/85

London—Electroencephalogram. About 45 minutes. 10–20 electrodes? attached to scalp, forehead, cheeks, plus one to each wrist. Open and close the eyes, please. Then breathe deeply for 3 minutes, mouth open. Electrodes attached to circular disk on pedestal near patient's shoulder. Wires of black, red, green, etc. Patient has scalp marked—after measuring—then glue is applied, then a jelly in certain spots to facilitate electric current. Result—comes out on a long paper 16 inches broad, which feeds into basket, where it folds itself. The paper looks like a musical score. CB [Caroline]'s face was rosy red (cheeks) from beginning to end, even before wires were attached, though the same noon, she had been pale.

5/8/85

The only thing that makes one feel happy and alive is trying for something that one cannot get.

5/28/85

Re MCH [Mary Coates Highsmith]—the insane elements in the brain take over from the sane, because the subject cannot face the reality that she is a failure in profession, marital life, and in the job of bringing up a child. Retreat into the fortress of femininity and female helplessness follows. She used S.H. till his death; now uses D[an] and me financially, though she is too far gone mentally to realize all this. Anyway, she is safe in her insanity, safe in being on home ground, Texas; safe in having a nephew, one of the family, dancing attendance. Safe and comfortable in her insanity of TV, dreams. I hear of her occasionally lashing out at nurses or fellow-inmates. That is what she did all her life to her best friends. The sane part of the brain retreats, the wounded Ego retreats to protect itself. Perhaps a phony insanity emerges, grows ever larger, if the surrounding family is sympathetic and indulgent (S.H.), until it takes over. My mother would not have become semi-insane, if I had not existed.

8/23/85

Troubles in the farmlands of America. Farms and all the implements up for auction. In the newspaper, a woman said, "When I saw the old shovel go—" Ah yes, and if I ever saw my Suffolk fork (modest size, suitable for women) [go] due to penury, I wouldn't know what to do. The shovel is a symbol of self-respect, not just a tool. When that is gone, life is gone, all connection with progress and happiness is gone.

1986–1988

IN APRIL 1986, Patricia Highsmith's doctors in London detect a tumor on her lung and she is rushed into surgery to have it removed. After a few weeks' convalescence in London, Pat returns to Switzerland in early May. At her follow-up exam in July, she receives the all-clear: the operation was a success, her overall test results promising. Finally, Pat decides it's time to leave the dark old house in Aurigeno, which has never felt like home. She toys with the idea of returning to France and even visits Montcourt in August to shop around for a house, without luck. She had sold her old property there just two months earlier, in June, and immediately regretted it.

Pat ultimately opts to stay in Ticino, but move to a new place. Friends tell her about land for sale in Tegna in the Centovalli area; she views the plot in late 1986, purchases it the following April, and hires an architect to design and build a "strong house" there, la Casa Highsmith. Between the construction project, extensive travel plans, and her continued health concerns, writing is the last thing on Pat's mind. Though she does develop ideas for another Ripley, for the first time in her life, Pat eases off the pressure to be productive. Whereas she has typically released a new book—and often more—every two years since 1951, there are now long periods between publications.

The move to Switzerland has not had the desired pecuniary results, and in her continued effort to escape double taxation, Pat considers applying for Swiss citizenship. However, she still follows the social and political developments in the country of her birth with great interest, and keeps her criticism coming; Pat has for some time been particularly rankled by American policy regarding Israel, and even dedicates *People Who Knock on the Door* to "the courage of the Palestinian leaders and their people in the struggle to regain a part of their homeland." After the First Intifada in 1987, Pat begins to follow the conflict in the Middle East even more closely. Fittingly, her most political book yet, *Tales of Natural and Unnatural Catastrophes*, is published the same year by Bloomsbury in London. Pat turned her back on Heinemann, which had published all UK editions of her books for the last twenty years, most recently *Found in the Street* (1986), as she was no longer happy with how Heinemann was marketing her work.

Pat remains highly sought-after and continues to make frequent public appearances. Her diary—which she starts keeping again in 1987—is full of references to award ceremonies, speeches, book fairs, and interviews. Among other destinations, Pat travels to Berlin, Paris, London, and Spain, despite the toll on her health. A private trip in August 1988 takes her to Tangier, Morocco, to see her old friend Buffie Johnson and Buffie's neighbor Paul Bowles, another old acquaintance from New York. Many of the experiences and impressions gathered during this time she will incorporate into her fifth and final novel about Tom Ripley, *Ripley Under Water.*

✎

3/15/86

Cousin Dan reports my mother for the past year lies in bed, sits up sometimes, does not recognize him, does not hold a conversation. NO will to live or to die. Nurses simply keep poking trays of food onto her lap. And I presume she needs bedpans. What kind of end is this? Since 1974 autumn, she has been there! What goes on in her head? Foggy dreams, cleared memories? Plain sleepiness (pleasant sensation for most of us)? How is it to live with no will at all? Merely to "exist" passively—indeed with no thought of the morrow, or who's paying for all the services.

6/21/86

[*Keime.*] Famous writer has illness, recovers, but is puzzled by outbreak of sales, anthologies, radio, TV series of book and story serializations. As if the world expected him dead. By now very pleasant. Better than reading an obituary, as did Hemingway.*

8/3/86

What can one ever pray for except patience?

8/30/86

5 April 1986. My doctor is John Batten, Harley Street, secured by CB on short notice Tues. 1 April, after my phone call Easter Monday 31 March.

---

* Hemingway twice had the opportunity to read his own obituary. He survived two plane crashes in Africa with his fourth wife, Mary, in the 1950s.

Ingeborg Mölich* drove me all the way to Zurich airport Wednesday for appointment Thursday with Batten, X-ray (again) and entrance into Brompton [Hospital] Friday for biopsy. Batten rushes up, as I am leaving (after overnight stay), asks me to "sit down," glancing away for an instant, "We think it should be taken out and we hope you'll agree."

This sounds like a death sentence to me, taken out or not, as I've never heard of anyone surviving such, or anyway, not for long. Of course, I agree, and then am taken into a room with five men, one of whom is Mr. Matias Paveth, who operated on Princess Margaret for (nearly) same thing. Paveth sinks strong finger ends into base of my neck, as I lie, clothed as I recall but it doesn't matter, on a high table at 3:20. Meanwhile Roland Gant† has come to fetch me and been told the bad news. We go out to his car and drink boilermakers. He tells me of Dwye Ewans‡ recovering well from same, alive this day ten years afterward. Surely, this is cheering. We drive to [Caroline's] house. She takes it with such calm, I later suspected hospital had rung her up, but now I don't think so.

After all, from December 1985 onward I'd been feeling awful. Terrible cold at Xmas, & despite anti-flu shot I had intestinal flu all January, was much weakened. I then had to go to London on business. No sooner back from London than I got bronchitis, due to shoveling snow off my car, clad in levis without heavy underwear. [To] Dr. P.D.N. for antibiotics, and when I returned a week later, as he asked, he suggested an X-ray "because you smoke." This X-ray late Feb. revealed a spot in upper right lung lobe (there are 3 lobes in rt. lung). So—more X-ray, long waits, in Locarno hospital, finally needle suction for biopsy, and before results could be obtained—I had to go to France for 6 days for *Found in the Street* for Calmann-Lévy. I said nothing of my troubles and angst to business colleagues or to friends while in France. EBH said, "Don't waste time with Locarno; go to London." I then rang C.B. on 2 April. So by 10 April—the operation—and by 17 April I was released. A scar 14 inches long at least, along 5th rib, ending under right breast. Returned home 1 May. 31 days in London. CB was cool as a cucumber, no doubt the wisest manner to assume. Vivien de Bernardi§ was a gem, and in the Angst-

---

* Pat's neighbor in Aurigeno, a former opera singer.
† Roland Gant was editor-in-chief of Pat's British publisher, William Heinemann.
‡ Dwye Evans was the former chairman of William Heinemann.
§ American pedagogue Vivien De Bernardi worked with Down syndrome children. Pat had gotten in touch with her through her friend Ellen Hill and consulted her on the short story "The Button." Later, Pat would name Vivien an executor of her estate, along with Frieda Sommer and Daniel Keel.

filled days of late March when all was inconclusive" and I was unable to sleep well or to work, she had said, "you know there's a guest unit in my house—so just come, you don't even have to telephone." She sent flowers to hospital, as did Daniel Keel, Heinemann too, plus luxury food basket; plus champagne from Kingsley! To me—pretty slow time in recovering strength. Dr. Batten said to rest one hour after lunch. Very good idea!

The mental fear needs a thousand words to describe. It is as though death is right there—suddenly—and yet one feels no pain, one is talking in a calm voice to friends & doctors.

12 July. Mr Paveth and Dr. Batten X-ray at 10:30 AM Brompton. One X-ray. They keep me waiting in the little booth for more than 10 minutes, during which time I nearly finish the little glass flask I've brought in my handbag. I dress on top, come out, can find CB in waiting room, and we cross street to Foulis Terrace, where Paveth has his consulting rooms. X-ray by now is hanging high on the wall with light behind it (I think). Paveth says, "Perfect," in a calm voice, a word I never expected to hear. It is like a reprieve from death.

11/15/86

The Eternal Pep-Talk. At twenty, the pep-talk is not seen as such. One is young and successful (in school and with sexual partners and with beginnings of art or whatever). This goes on till forty, when there is the mildest blip on the happy screen. People, light-years later, start saying "no" in one form or another. At sixty, one must constantly and consciously keep up (or start) the pep-talk to oneself, otherwise depression can set in. I think of the millions who tried their luck in Manhattan (but the USA has other merciless marketplaces too). Many are no longer there, as they had to look for cheaper rents or merely a job. Many hang by their fingernails, and these people interest me, as do their pep-talks to themselves.

11/23/86

Artists in any kind of personal difficulty will make that difficulty worse. Just as there is an element of exaggeration or cartoon in every work of art.

JANUARY 16, 1987

Again to 11 Foulis Terrace and "excellent" from Mr Paneth and Dr Batten, the latter having received an honor this New Year's. He is Queen's physician. This time I had more confidence than on 11 July 1986 re-examination (X-ray preceding).

APRIL 15, 1987

Monday. I have bought the Tegna plot, 2,100 sq.m. of which I have 1,400 officially. Mortgage. Letter today from Tabea B. to my surprise, after 4 years nearly of silence. She has not been in best of health (?) and had to give up Erdmannstraße apartment, alas. Now staying with "Wolf" in Kurfürstenstraße, Berlin. [In] photo she sent looks thinner.

4/23/87

On the Morality of Artificial Life-Preserving.* What is the difference between an iron lung and the spooning of food into a mouth and the emptying of the diaper? One is a machine, one is a human performing a service. The difference is the age, or the condition, the person requiring the iron lung may have no future. The baby has a future with spooned food, and diapers. The aged person with spooned food and diapers has no future except more of the same. Is the spooned food, etc. "artificial means of life sustainment" if the person in bed is unable to reach (or see, even) the food placed nearby?

7/24/87

Long period now of not being able to endure Beethoven Symphonies, any of them, though the 6th fares best. I prefer string quartets, Scriabin, Dvořák, Smetana.

8/1/87
Drugs
      Lovely word. Enchantment,
      Another world, a happier place
      To be,
      Some think of crack,
      Others of Mozart.
      I think of a few phrases of Scriabin
      Thrown away casually
      In the manner of an artist.
      Drugs. In New York, it's

---

* A topic clearly related to her mother's health, which Pat explored in the story "No End in Sight," published in *Tales of Natural and Unnatural Catastrophes* (1987).

Oh, Christ, not again! From
The public Police Sirens,
Crazed teen-agers looking
At you, as if they could kill you
For ten bucks, which they will do,
If you're handy and nobody's looking
And in Stock Island, Key West,
The cops look, behold, and do nothing.
Law-abiding citizens behold
Sex for $10 from 13-year-old,
And up. Ten buys a rock of crack,
Sold and bought before the cops' eyes,
And the shocked, law-abiding citizen
Thinks: are the cops after the *big* dealers?
Maybe, but why not these, meantime?
These kids, missing school, love, and beauty,
The starvelings, hurry through
A stranger's orgasm, and push
The tenner into another stranger's hand.
The slightly intimidated law-abiding citizen
Beholds, thinking: "Am I missing something?"
Can it be as simple as all this?
Drugs, for some the atmospheric smoke of a cigarette
The familiar warmth and taste of scotch
(Or gin) on the tongue, at the back of the throat.
Primitive, enhancing, dangerous and civilized,
All at once. We grew up with these drugs.
We don't steal to get them, nor prostitute ourselves.
What's the matter with other people?
Am I old and intolerant, to be asking
Such a question?
Put the Scarlatti cassette on,
And let's forget about crack, and theft,
Shocked householders with their finest books
Gone, owners of cars who took pride in their car's stereo—
Well, it's only self-pitying to cry over spilled milk.
Isn't it?
Listen to Scarlatti and Stravinsky,
While the machine's still here to play it.

With the drug of music, forget for a while
That you're outnumbered.

8/24/87

My cat Charlotte, 3 yrs. 3 mos., shows pointer talent. She points in
silence at unaccustomed presence of man 4 meters from me in garden
above; also at window, small and shuttered, which shouldn't be open but
is, in my downstairs porch. She has many (useful) doglike qualities. And
she has a strong sense of fairness vs. unfairness.

SEPTEMBER 13, 1987

[Berlin.] My reading was 8 July at the Hebbel Theater, a nice old famous
place with two balconies. Wim Wenders was to have introduced me (for
reading of "The Mysterious Cemetery")* but his father was ill in W. Germany, had to have spleen operation—or gall bladder, so W.W. turned up
briefly at my Hotel Steigenberger and was very polite, downstairs. Saw
Christa Maerker,† also Tabea B. at least twice. T. is evasive about what
has happened to cause her to lose furniture, apartment, & apparently
jobs(!) She calls one "Freddy" her mate; 23 and dealer in drugs says T.B.,
I was appalled! She wore black punkish suit, male shoes, black ribbons
behind each ear.

SEPTEMBER 15, 1987

Must have the cleaning woman more frequently! Yesterday she found my
gold ring on carpet in room where I sleep. I thought I'd left it in Deauville
by telephone in my room. A pleasant relief—ring E.B.H. gave me 1/19/53
in Trieste.

   And I think of becoming a Swiss citizen. S. H. Okoshken's‡ balls-up of
Tomes Inc. has pushed me in this direction too. Nobel§ says I must stay
in same house one year after applying for citizenship. Pity if I have to stay
in Aurigeno that long, but I can get by by owning it, no doubt. And in
summer, it is mercifully cool!

---

* A short story begun in 1983 under the title "Cancer," and collected in *Tales of Natural and Unnatural Catastrophes.*
† Christa Maerker, a journalist, novelist, and film critic. She had already interviewed Highsmith in 1977 for German TV.
‡ Samuel Okoshken, Pat's tax attorney and accountant in Paris in the 1970s and 1980s.
§ Professor Peter Nobel, Zurich attorney.

OCTOBER 1, 1987

Life ever better as I slowly get used to having some free days—rehearsed my "reading" for perhaps 4th time. Rudi Bettschart* comes tomorrow at 11 to discuss finances. I am ready to become Swiss citizen to escape the time-consuming & meaningless USA tax. I expect never to go back to live. The very thought of the news reports—now called "bites," depresses me. Now it's as if I throw $155 (approx.) out the window 7 days a week, part tax, part my mother. The tax is the worst.

OCTOBER 12, 1987

First snow appears on mountain tops, thin & powdery. It has rained for 5 days and nights.

OCTOBER 18, 1987

Off to Toronto. Reading on 20th at Harborfront Reading Theatre. Canadians are v. friendly & helpful. I read from (well-rehearsed) *Found in the Street*, 4–8 pages. Two other fellows on same evening as I. Well filled.

OCTOBER 21, 1987

Off to Niagara-on-the-Lake at 10 AM. Wm Trevor[†] said hello to me, so we become acquainted on this tour. I sat next to his wife Jane in back seat of big car. Pleasant lunch at Prince of Wales Hotel (Edw. VII) then the Falls—by funicular, then small boat, *The Maid in the Mist*. Blue macs for all. 3 days in Canada, I think. Met Margaret Atwood,[‡] who rang at my hotel & invited me for tea. Also lunch with Sheila Waengler at Royal Ontario Museum (National History) & a drive around the city. Then Friday 23 Oct. flight to New York where I was met by driver laid on by Atlantic Monthly Press.[§]

OCTOBER 23, 1987

N.Y. Betty M. & Margot Tomes v amiable. Nice old apartments with cats, Brumaire & Frick drifting back & forth. On Wed. Margot T.

---

* Rudolf C. Bettschart (1930–2015), Daniel Keel's business partner and co-publisher of Diogenes until his demise in 2015.
† William Trevor (William Trevor Cox, 1928–2016), Irish novelist, short story writer, and playwright.
‡ Margaret Atwood (1939–), Canadian writer and poet made famous by her novel *The Handmaid's Tale* (1985), which Pat reviewed for *Le Monde*. Atwood received the Booker Prize in 2000 for *The Blind Assassin*.
§ After Otto Penzler published five of Pat's books between 1985 and 1988 in his imprint Mysterious Press, Pat moved to Atlantic Monthly Press.

turned up at Endicott Bookshop, W. Side, so did G[ary] Fisketjon,* Anne
Elisabeth Suter.† It went well, lots of books brought by the public for me
to sign afterwards. One "Mario" from the Philippines had a good many!
Then supper with Suter. She has offices W. Side of Union Square & is
quite proud of them. Design firm shares office space.

NOVEMBER 1987

Then to London 29 October, the usual frustrating taxi ride from Heathrow with a driver who doesn't know how to get to NW8 but pretends he
does. £21 on the meter and CB says one can get it for £15.

   1 Nov. etc. About 3 interviews per day for Bloomsbury. All in offices.
Except for TV one afternoon at BBC studios. This was "Cover to Cover"
for *Tales of Natural & Unnatural Catastrophes.* Then there was a drinks
party with Jonathan Kent‡ chez CB.

NOVEMBER 1987

Then! There is 8 November and home, after weekend (day & ½ at
CB.'s). I have terrible cold & slight bronchitis, and GKK [Kingsley] is due
15 Nov. in Zurich.

NOVEMBER 15, 1987

GKK arrives well. We went over bank, stocks, in superficial way & I
hope she has an idea where to find papers in my desk and room.

NOVEMBER 1987

Christmas here quiet indeed, loads of cards here on 2 strings across the
livingroom. CB reports that she is being v social as usual. I wrote 12½
page article for *New York Times* magazine on Green-Wood Cemetery,§
which I called "[Green-Wood]—Listening to the Talking Dead"—in
which I rather contrasted the flamboyant tombs with the reticent urns in
the crematory. In the columbarium. Truly a remarkable cemetery!

---

* Gary Fisketjon was Pat's new American editor, editor-in-chief of Atlantic Monthly Press from 1986 to
1990. In 1990, Pat moved with him to Knopf, where he was editor and vice president from 1990 to 2019.
† Anne Elisabeth Suter, head of foreign rights at Diogenes before moving to New York in the early 1980s
in order to open a literary agency, Gotham Art and Literary Agency, which represented Diogenes in the
United States from the mid-1980s onward.
‡ Jonathan Kent (1949–), British actor and director and Pat's favorite Ripley since Alain Delon.
§ The researcher the *New York Times* sent along to accompany her was Phyllis Nagy, who soon became
a friend and went on to write the screenplay for *Carol,* filmed by Todd Haynes in 2015, starring Cate
Blanchett and Rooney Mara.

12/25/87

How to get rid of the body—in France. Unattended packages at Orly
Airport are destroyed after 20 minutes. Taken away at best. Destroyed
how? Immersed in water? Must find out.

A corpse could be cut into four or five pieces, wrapped and put into
duffel bags.

JANUARY 15, 1988

My free days this month are blighted by having to deal with instructions,
advice from lawyer Nobel re tax-and-will. He assumes too much that I
wish to become Swiss, not necessarily true. But it is depressingly time
consuming.

2/8/88

I think of T[abea] who occupied my thoughts 78–82, but not much
any longer. Was she too "mighty," as one friend put it? Preposterous?
Demanding too much money for clothes designing, not coming through
with promises? Anyway, she now lives on Government assistance, out of
a suitcase. I wonder what goes on in her head? She reads, makes sketches
of bizarrely made-up female faces and torsos. Watches TV. Has no plans.
At 36 she seems washed up, a failure. Very few social contacts in Berlin,
I gather.

In desperation, the extremism interests me. She was once 100% sure
of herself. It suggests the image of the crazy moth zooming, hovering
around an electric bulb—said to have a chemical attraction for some
insects—at her best, doing this! At 28, she was given an award for clothes
designing by Min. of Interior, Germany West. What a splendid beginning! And then what? Arrogance? She was doing all right, alone in Berlin
flat, from '79 till autumn '83 (I think). I find it unusual to have a career
tragedy so young. There are certain resemblances to Truman Capote,
though his came in late '50's (his 50's) after *The Answered Prayers* slan-
dered his adulators.[*]

---

[*] Truman Capote's *Answered Prayers: The Unfinished Novel*, a thinly veiled portrait of the high (and
low) society of the era, appeared posthumously in 1986. Several chapters were first serialized in *Esquire* to
the shock of many of Capote's friends, acquaintances, and patrons, who were quite candidly portrayed.

FEBRUARY 28, 1988

Saw the Tegna house yesterday with Ingeborg. I foresee that I'll use "dining room" as second work-room with 2 tables, bookcase for files. The rooms do not appear large. Roof supposed to go on next week—cement any way. Taking some days off (again?!) to straighten out papers, tidy cellar, cut kindling. I must pull out of stagnant (mental) feeling, due to having external obligations. 1) to deliver introduction to Gudrun Müller* art show 31 March, Ascona, in German. 2) to go to Paris mid-April for a prize award-giving to Calmann-Lévy contest winner.† Alain O[ulman] is not happy with entries! Then the uprising in Gaza strip & West Bank, now in 9th week, is increasingly upsetting to me, and I spend a lot of time composing letters I think may be useful to peace and stopping the deaths. 72 Palestinians so far dead.

Right thumb is getting arthritic, much to my annoyance. Nice to know I've a good left hand.

2/29/88

EBH—as perpetual tester of love. I opened briefly my diary of Jan '53 (Trieste) and found it heart rending—if I wished to be self pitying, which I don't. I mentioned the total absence of "feminine sympathy, tenderness" at a time when I was broke, homesick for friends, worried about fate of last book, which must have been *The Price of Salt*—of all things to worry about! I slept on the living-room sofa, and was ashamed of "tear-redded eyes" the next day. EBH is doing the same thing '88—testing her friends till they break—and depart.

MARCH 10, 1988

My war against paper continues. All possible to be thrown out! Sheer bliss, however, to read some fiction in my "spare time" when I'm not working. My Simenon piece in *Libération*, Paris is out,‡ & wanted by *El País* and *Tintenfass*.§ Nice to be so popular. Big Vitra photo is out in *Der Spiegel* now, was in *Neue Zürcher Zeitung* last week.¶ People like it. Seated, and in Brooks Brothers red vest, photo black & white. My house

---

* Gudrun-Müller-Pöschmann (1924–2007), one of Pat's friends in Ticino, was a painter and graphic artist with an art school in Ascona.
† Calmann-Lévy created a writing contest for first-time authors and asked Highsmith to be on the jury.
‡ Highsmith's review of Patrick Marnham's Simenon biography, *The Man Who Wasn't Maigret* (London, 1988).
§ A periodical by Pat's Swiss publisher, Diogenes.
¶ Pat was one of a few celebrities photographed for Swiss design company Vitra's fiftieth anniversary. She was portrayed sitting on an Eames chair.

to be in Tegna: Red brick walls all up. [Tobias] Ammann* thinks it may be done by end June. The proportion is good. 1,400 square m.

MARCH 27, 1988

Wretched over last week with French TV final day, & Tues./Wed. interview all day with Joan Dupont of *New York Times*. She stayed at La Pineda pension-pizzeria on highway, where the people are very nice.

Dr. Nobel advises me to become Swiss as soon as possible. It would seem I should give away as much as possible now—then put some into foundation. I'm trying to protect some for Yaddo, and a tough job it is!!! My Tegna house has the roof on, begins to look nice. Red brick at present. It is not too big. I was there Sat. with Ingeborg & Silvia. Much exercise this Sunday as I got the dahlias in. Early. Must try to get such exercise daily or almost.

3/27/88

AFN news, which I often switch on at 8:30 AM if I awaken: "Do you know that kids are inhaling blue, benzine, that they put into paper bags, plastic bags and sniff? Our kids are dying from this—while they try to get kicks. Tell your kids!"

MAY 11, 1988

I was in Paris 16–20 April. Dinner chez A. Oulman & wife. Cees Nooteboom[†] one evening, Dutch novelist. Jo Savigneau[‡] both evenings but I did not spend much time talking with her, & should have. She is fond of me & my work. "It's a passion," says Alain. Still not working, and I feel I need the leisure still. I tidy up papers, & there's more to be done. I sent 20,000 [NF] to Nemours hospital where I had the nose bleed; and $1,100 to Yaddo—had a nice letter in return from them, too. *Catastrophes* (French) is #5 on bestseller list. It sold 13 to 15,000 in German-speaking within first two months. Paris: Salon du Livre. I was at (18 Apr. PM) *Télérama* [magazine] stand to announce the winner, *Baby Bone* (novel), and the runner-up—not one I'd expected. First prize gets printed by Calmann-Lévy, 2nd serialized in *Télérama*. This is called Highsmith Prix du Suspense, though all the manuscripts I read were

---

* Tobias Ammann (1944–), Swiss architect.

† Cees Nooteboom (1933–), an award-winning Dutch novelist.

‡ Josyane Savigneau (1951–), French author and journalist, editor-in-chief of *Le Monde des livres* at *Le Monde* from 1991 to 2005. In the previous year, Savigneau had asked Highsmith for a review of Margaret Atwood's *The Handmaid's Tale*.

mysteries. I was tired for 2 days once I got home. Now I don't have to travel till 22 September to Hamburg and have declined at least 2 invitations recently.

JULY 17, 1988

London was late June. Interesting Open-End [*After Dark*] TV program 11:30 and 2:30 AM on a Saturday night. [About] aftercare for families in which there has been a murder.

15 July about, I sent off [to] *Nouvel Observateur* short story "A Long Walk from Hell."* And dined 11 July with Mario Adorf† & Wolf Bauer,‡ Terri Winders, who want to buy *The Blunderer*. Still, I opted for John Hardy§ 3 days later, & D. Keel agreed.

JULY 27, 1988

Wrote to Dan III as I am worried because I've not heard from him. Letter from Buffie Johnson who goes to Tanger 14 Aug. for 2–3 weeks. It seems she has made a mistake with her lawyer re 77 Street town-house, possibly 102 Greene Street also, as business does not interest her. May go to Tangier, as Buffie wishes me to.

AUGUST 3, 1988

At last bought my ticket for Tangier for 17 Aug., open end. There is good news, that King Hussein [of Jordan] has given West Bank leadership into hands of PLO. The Jews will again "refuse" to deal, etc., but the world will see. The timing is good. The Pres. Candidates should state their attitudes—& may not out of fear of "money withdrawn."

8/17/88

Gibraltar a low mountain on the right, dark gray. Pity there is a haze at 6 pm on landing at Tangier. Prongs of the city stick out. The plane flies over creased greenish countryside. The city looks like little whitish boxes scattered up a slope; or at least this is a part of the city. The plane taxies for ten minutes after landing. Long hot wait at passport. I change 100 SF

---

* "A Long Walk from Hell," a noir homage to her new home in Ticino, was first published in French as "La longue marche de Luigi le damné" in the "Les séries noires de l'été" of *Le Nouvel Observateur* (July 29–August 4).
† Mario Adorf (1930–), German theater, film, and TV actor, novelist, and audiobook reader.
‡ Wolf Bauer (1950–), German film and TV producer.
§ An American film producer. *The Blunderer* had already been adapted for film in 1963 as the French production *Le meurtrier*. It would take almost thirty years until an American adaptation—*A Kind of Murder*—was released in 2016.

for 541.80 dirams, get a taxi, to the city. My friend B.J. not at home to
my surprise. I go to "Paul's," the apartment above: Paul B[owles]* is eating in bed from a tray, but very cordially makes me welcome. He says B
doesn't always remember dates.

The apartment building—5 stories or 4, Paul on uppermost. Functional, not 100% clean "since the French left," a phrase I am to hear
over and over. Then Buffie arrives—from Yoga class. Her flat is much
lighter than P's and has freshly painted white walls. The fresh breeze is
a pleasure!

8/18/88

Librarie des Colonnes [& éditions]†—run by Rachel Moyal,‡ who was
born in Tangier, is Jewish, about 45, very warm and friendly, invites B.
and me to Minister of Culture's dinner same evening in Asilah. But earlier in the day, two beers finally at the bar of Hotel Minzah, with pool
adjacent, very handsome pool with lush trees and flowering plants at the
edges, tables and chairs also. One Patrick Martin approaches me, I auto-
graph his copy of *Catastrophes* in French. He invites us to drinks at 6 pm
following day.

B. has not paid rent for 8 months, deliberately, as landlord is trying
to augment the rent. B. inherited it from Maurice Grosser,§ in whose
name the telephone still is. The view of the Medina, or Old City from
my breezy window would be a joy for Braque—and it looks already like
a horizontal Klee composition—chalky-white squares of houses of varying sizes with tiny dark squares of windows in them, the scene topped by
what looks like a water tower. So little greenery, I can count the trees or
clumps of them: twelve. One a giant fir, another a huge palm. Only the
children and adolescents seem lively. The others adjust to a slow pace to
get themselves through the heat. The party begins in someone's court,
drinks, wine or scotch, etc. With few exceptions, the men are informally

---

* Pat will write an article about her stay in Tangier, "Tengis—Tingis—Tangier—Tanjah; A Week Among
the Residents," which *Le Monde* will publish under the title "Un croquis de Bowles à Tanger." According
to Pat, she and Paul had not seen each other since their New York days.
† The Librairie des Colonnes was a cultural hotspot where Jean Genet, Paul Bowles, Mohamed Choukri,
Marguerite Yourcenar, Jack Kerouac, and Samuel Beckett were regulars. Until Morocco's independence
from France, the bookshop was affiliated with Parisian publisher Gallimard. Later, it was for some time
run by Pierre Bergé, the partner of Yves Saint Laurent and a former bookseller himself.
‡ Rachel Moyal (1933–2020) was the first Moroccan Jew to receive the French order Chevalier des Arts
et des Lettres in 1996.
§ Presumably Maurice Grosser (1903–1986), American painter, art critic, and longtime partner to
composer Virgil Thompson.

dressed, short sleeved shirts of all colors, blue jeans. It's a party for painters and journalists however.

8/19/88

Alain C. and house of Barbara Hutton*—built in the 30's. We drive toward Bay of Tangier (with Patrick Martin at the wheel), get out & walk to parapet overlooking the bay & the sea. Spain is visible, Algeciras, west of Gibraltar (where many Tangier people have small apartments). One of the two horns of the Bay curves beautifully in our view, a white ship, which looks like a luxury liner, is anchored, and there are sail boats anchored—not many.

The Hutton house: Palatial Arab style, wandering atria and rooms off, the downstairs devoted to welcoming guests. Blue and white predominates. The "walls" are composed of squares of white stone, about 6x6 inches, hand-carved with filigree, all identical. It is said that 1,000 workmen worked here at the same time. A.C. shows B. & me around, also upstairs, the bedrooms whose furniture looks suddenly American. Each bedroom has a private terrace. A few steps higher in the garden (high three steps for the "service" bearing trays of food, M. Chevalier remarks) is the swimming pool with blue initials B.H.on its tiled bottom, visible through the water. The house was built around an old tree, which has branches that stick out like elbows, one of which touches the house. Hutton house is in the Medina. Alas, just five meters from its front door, there is a noisy café, where men sit drinking tea & soft drinks. On other side is a mosque, huge pale green dome, with 4 loud calls per day, first starting at 3.30 or 4 am. I am somewhat bothered by dogs barking at night. Beyond Medina the arm (arc) of land ends with a lighthouse.

8/20/88

At 13:15, Rachel, Yacht Club lunch on the Bay. Spain and more vaguely Gibraltar in the distance. Lovely here off the water, people lunching in bathing suits. To the Kasbah (fortress) again, near Hutton house. York Castle, now owned by two men, one a clothes designer.† A Paris car is

---

* Barbara Woolworth Hutton (1912–1979), American department store heiress. She married five times. After divorcing her third husband, Cary Grant, she moved to Tangier.

† Built by the Portuguese in the sixteenth century, York Castle, with its crenellated rampart walls, was situated above the beach on the edge of Tangier. In 1951, Yves Vidal became its president and transformed it into a contemporary sumptuous abode.

parked in front. This was once a fortress. It overlooks the harbor of
Tangier.

8/21/88

It takes three days to feel the proper tempo here, become used to it. It is
easy & unstressful. First 2 days may be annoying, with the slowness and
disorder.

8/29/88

Home notes: La Haffa, the Hole, on the ocean, a tea-café, arcades, where
one can smoke kiff, recline on mats, be semi-private. Stone steps downward, and mind how you go. Bar Rubi RUBI and Grill. At least I can get
a beer here. Wine or beer. T-shirts—Off the Wall; Alive with Pleasure
(sleepy male wearing this).

SEPTEMBER 22–24, 1988

In Hamburg, where Christa Maerker came, also Gudrun Müller, &
Anne Uhde on 23rd for my reading with Angela Winkler* in Die Fabrik.
The reading: I in English, A. Winkler in German & different stories.
[*Little Tales of*] *Misogyny*, then 4 pages from [*Plotting and Writing*] *Sus-
pense* [*Fiction*].

Paul Bowles is getting much publicity!! Germany reissuing three books
by him. *L'Espresso* [magazine] September has long & excellent article
with photos. He looks good. My 4 photos of him (Cap Spartel) also—I'm
pleased with.

NOVEMBER 1988

Paul wrote me twice by October 4, says Buffie's bronchitis came back, &
that she wrote from N.Y. that she has but $500 in the bank, & doesn't
know how she's going to make it. I can't believe this, as B. owns 2 buildings in Manhattan.†

11/9/88

[*Keime.*] Short story. A man's cat begins to shun him when he is in last
days of dying. This enables him to die more easily. The dog may linger.
Even at the grave.

---

* Angela Winkler (1944–), German stage and film actress famous for her lead roles in *The Lost Honor of
Katharina Blum* (1975) and *Edith's Diary* (1983).
† In 1943 Buffie bought a building at 235 East Fifty-Eighth Street. She lived there herself and also leased
the first floor of the house to Tennessee Williams and Frank Merlo for some years.

1989–1993

PATRICIA HIGHSMITH spends the last years of her life in Tegna, Switzerland, in her fortress-like home, designed in the shape of a horseshoe with stunning views of the mountains. She reveals little about herself during this time: her diaries and notebooks are patchy and stingy on personal details. Increasingly, she only records events months after the fact. In September 1992, in her early seventies, she finishes Diary 17 and doesn't start a new one. Most of her writing energies now flow directly into her work.

In May 1989 Pat begins *Ripley Under Water*, the fifth and final installment in the "Ripliad." In the novel, Tom Ripley, seemingly untouchable for so long, comes within an inch of losing everything. Pat completes the first draft a year later, almost to the day. Before Ripley returns, however, first Diogenes, then Bloomsbury reissue her lesbian love story *The Price of Salt*, retitled *Carol*. Initially reluctant, Pat finally agrees to publish it under her own name for the first time. This moment amounts to a literary coming out.

Mary Coates Highsmith dies in March 1991, just shy of her ninety-fifth birthday. The last time Pat saw her mother was presumably in 1989, when she went to visit her cousin Dan in Texas. She makes no direct mention of it in her notes. The following December, however, she starts working on an idea for "The Tube," a sequel to her 1987 story "No End in Sight." It doesn't take much imagination to read the piece as a satirical depiction of her mother, who has grown increasingly senile living in a nursing home for the past fifteen years. Pat does not attend her funeral. Instead, she puts the final touches on *Ripley Under Water*, which is released simultaneously in English and German in the fall of 1991.

Reviews for the final Ripley are mixed, but do acknowledge Pat's talent beyond crime writing. Both in the United States and in Europe, literary critics have applauded her work since *Edith's Diary*. In 1990 she is made an Officier de l'Ordre des Arts et des Lettres in France, and her name is even suggested for the 1991 Nobel Prize in Literature.

In March 1992, Pat begins work on what is to be her last novel, *Small g: A Summer Idyll*, published posthumously in 1995. The book is part thriller, part love story, set in a Zurich dive bar with a largely gay clientele. One last time, Pat takes everyone by surprise—the last word of the book is happy.

Her health, however, is worsening fast, which leads her to delegate extensive on-location research for the book to her friend Frieda Sommer, but does not stop her from traveling repeatedly to London, Paris, and Germany; in the fall of 1992, she also visits Canada and the United States for the last time. Pat completes the first draft of *Small g* in March 1993, then spends much of the remaining year in treatment. Pat does not share these details herself.

After more than five decades of keeping diaries and notebooks, Pat writes her final entry—one of just two recorded that year—in October. She states that she would rather death came as a surprise: "In this, death's more like life, unpredictable."

᪄

JANUARY 30, 1989

I moved to Tegna 13 Dec [1988]. Much help from Peter Huber.* Much to put away—still! I wrote 500 words for *Die Welt* on subject of moving.† Ingeborg [Moelich] was wonderful as usual, sewing up curtains (yellow) for my living room. I think about 5th Ripley book. Shan't be happy till I get down to another book.

2/15–17/89

[Milan.] I am at Hotel Manin, beside the Public gardens. Very busy district, grayish, bustling, trams working on Piazza Cavour, newspaper kiosk, bookstand. I was driven from my house—Italian chauffeur, with woman from Bompiani [Editore]. Four Interviews per day, but in the salon of hotel, near bar where one can order café or a beer. Newspapers, magazines—only one photographer first day, & I wore my "Palestine PLO check" sweater for this.‡ I was able in perhaps 4 out of 12 interviews, to express genuine USA opinion on Israeli atrocities in Gaza & West Bank.

---

* Peter Huber is Highsmith's friend and neighbor in Tegna.
† "Moving House," published as "Und der Siam-Kater heult dazu. Auch ein Thriller-Star muss manchmal umziehen," in *Die Welt*, January 7, 1989.
‡ Pat will dedicate the book she is currently hatching, *Ripley Under Water*, to "the dead and the dying among the Intifada and the Kurds, to those who fight oppression in whatever land, and stand up not only to be counted but to be shot."

3/4/89

"Old Books." Perfume-name. Smell guaranteed to attract & hold the intellectual type of man.

MAY 7, 1989

Green grass now, all bushes doing well, Semmy [cat Semyon] still has up & down days & I don't want to think of him on terrace (up) here, where he has never been yet. I've written 2 more articles for *Die Welt*, preface for [*The Price of*] *Salt*—Diogenes edition [as *Carol*]. Still not enough work done to please me. Another visit from Frieda,* who is most helpful with my bookshelves, in organizing.

5/12/89

Rachmaninov's 3rd piano Concerto. Exuberantly beautiful and strong. Not so sad as #2. Tom [Ripley] would like the 3rd.

MAY 28, 1989

I began Ripley book & have 4 pages (at 5 PM). Sunflowers staked. Only 6, about 8 inches high.

AUGUST 6, 1989

I was twice in London in June, first time for a few minutes on Wim Wenders for Paul Joyce, second for Vamp Productions, the 12-story affair.† Cardiff one night after Paris one night. Anthony Perkins‡ introduces & concludes. Dominique Bourgeois is excellent. She had to go with Perkins to court the one morning we had Monday; he was let off with £200 fine for having 2 cannabis cigarettes, according to him sent to himself to the Angel Hotel, received & reported by another Perkins there. By taxi to CB on that Monday.

SEPTEMBER 18, 1989

I go to NY 21 Sept. on a 14-day trip. Would love to go to Texas & see Dan & Florine, but no word from them or answer to my letter of 2 weeks ago. I can't stand any more strain from Tegna house, talks with [archi-

---

* Frieda is Pat's Zurich friend, whom she met—along with her Tegna neighbor Peter Huber—at a teachers' conference in Hölstein near Basel in 1975.

† Twelve of Pat's short stories (including "Under a Dark Angel's Eye," "The Day of Reckoning," "A Curious Suicide," and "What the Cat Dragged In") are turned into TV dramas, co-produced by Vamp/Paris, Crossbow, and HTV/UK.

‡ Anthony Perkins (1932–1992), American actor most famous for starring as murderer Norman Bates in Alfred Hitchcock's *Psycho*.

tect Tobias] Ammann and bank. The land itself is tough to deal with, all sandy & stony. Requiring much digging, humus, grass, I would think. C.B. rang 2 days ago to say that cat Omen had died—a Sat. AM. with lung tumor, shortness of breath. Aged 15. So is Semyon. He is slender, but I try to keep his strength up with vitamins.

I would like to get back to work, 4 hours a day at least, but till now it cannot be done. When Ammann is done, if the char [cleaning lady] maybe comes an hour more per week, it will be possible. Else I'll be ill. This is not a normal life for me, to keep postponing work. It is wretched & false. I'll take Menninger's *Man vs. Himself* with me on airplane. I may've read it before, but he is always new and reassuring. Something like Christian Science: his attitude toward what makes mental health. I return from USA 7 Oct. before noon.

NOVEMBER 17, 1989

Successful 15-day trip. All pleasant. P. Huber was at Murray Hill East Hotel, and eventually I moved there. The Rainbow Room for his birthday (his idea) with Annebeth Suter, very pleasant dancing & music. Texas even better. I invited myself for 5 days & the time flew. J. W. Stoker* lives some 2 miles away or less & seems to be closest friend & neighbor: very self-absorbed, training Hot Diggety still, 3 other young horses to go, unshod yet. It was interesting to see the life of Dan III & his good wife Florine. I work when I can & try to keep up morale. Dan, my cousin, was having a bad time, as he thought he was due for an operation on hernia that developed from stabbing suffering one year ago. The surgeon made 4-inch vertical incision above navel to clean the wound & Dan did not wear plastic cummerbund which would've helped the incision to heal properly. It now sticks out alarmingly like small football.

DECEMBER 24, 1989

We at last had 15 inches of rain in past fortnight. I try to get back to the Ripley book, now have 59 pages. I am unsure of the plot, & it must come by itself. Inge brought me lovely Stollen [cake] today. She had to bake some 12 by hand (yeast) for all Aurigeno. Ammann came by with good cookies, & I gave him a bottle of wine from Diogenes batch. I must put

---

* J. W. Stoker (1927–), international trick rider, roper, and rodeo performer. He doubled Clint Eastwood in the 1980 western romance *Bronco Billy* and was inducted into the Pro Rodeo Hall of Fame in 2010. Pat's cousin Dan was also a rodeo performer.

more variation into my life, such as drawing & carpentering. The big news in last days: Overthrow of Ceausescu in Romania,* causing possibly 12,000 deaths of civilians. Tank murders and soldiers shooting the unarmed. Panama: USA invades some 6 days ago.†

※

FEBRUARY 17, 1990

Semmy had to be put to sleep 15 February, Thursday, because of kidney failure. He had been eating poorly before, nearly nothing toward the end. Gudrun Müller was able to go with me to the young Vet in Locarno. The end was peaceful with 2 injections, & Semmy did not even twitch. I try this Saturday to get back to work on Ripley novel. My friends do not ring me PMs, on my suggestion, a real break for me. I must go to Paris 4 March for 5th do, being given Ordre of Officier of Arts & Lettres. Jack Lang.‡ Must stay till 8 March, Paris—because of the 12 short stories for TV now. Then I hope to go to London.

4/21/90

Oscar Wilde: biography by Richard Ellmann. Surely reading Oscar's story over and over is one of the pleasures and solaces and catharses of the twentieth century. Here we see the small-mindedness, the vindictiveness of hoi polloi, the sadistic pleasure in watching a sensitive person suffer, watching him brought low. His story reminds me of that of Christ, a man of good will, with no maliciousness, with a vision of expanding consciousness, of increasing the joy of life. Both were misunderstood by their contemporaries. Both suffered from a jealousy, deeply buried in the breasts of those who wished Christ and Oscar dead, and who mocked them while they were alive.

5/20/90

Oscar and Bosie.§ When together, Oscar worked well, with surprising concentration. He wrote *The Importance of Being Earnest* and another

---

* Dictator Nicolae Ceaușescu (1918–1989) and his wife, Elena, were executed as a result of the Romanian Revolution on December 25.
† The United States invaded Panama on December 20, 1989.
‡ Jack Lang, French minister of culture under President François Mitterrand.
§ Lord Alfred Bruce Douglas (1870–1945), British writer and translator, notorious for being Oscar Wilde's lover until Wilde's arrest in 1895.

play, while Bosie was interrupting, running up bills, but also livening Oscar's existence. Later in Paris, alone Oscar could muster some ideas, but not the same kind of pep and enthusiasm. It reminds one of Proust's—"nothing is more pleasant than falling back into the arms of (someone) who is bad for us."

Art is not always healthy, and why should it be?

SEPTEMBER 6, 1990

Alain Oulman died in his sleep 28–29 March. His partner Jean-Etienne Cohen-Séat* rang to tell me on 29. I sent a good bunch of flowers. Funeral was following Monday, in Père Lachaise [cemetery], family plot, with rabbi. I'd thought the Jews wished to be buried on same day. Yorgo is a bit lost, went to Portugal, where the 2 sons were. Meanwhile, I had interviews for *Carol* (*Price of Salt*) now 4th on German bestseller list.

On May 27, I finished first draft of *Ripley Under Water*. I'd begun it 28 May last year and had interruptions enough! Xmas and Easter this year were excellent for work, however.

OCTOBER 27, 1990

I went to London late June, after finishing first draft Ripley. Caroline really pounced (I was at her house) re [my] appetite,† of course. I think she was also annoyed by the *Carol* publicity, though my 2 interviews, 2 photo sessions were not in her house. Unpleasant atmosphere. My energy level was so low I did not even get to Simpson's,‡ which is saying something.

OCTOBER 28, 1990

Raining all day. Re London, I met Dr. Stewart Clarke, who took over after Dr John Batten. He is tall & lanky type, rather casual about cholesterol. Pronounces me in good shape. (!) I had to ask for chest x-ray to be on safe side. I heard in September that G. [Graham] Greene has been very ill since Xmas & lives between blood transfusions. He may be in Vevey [Switzerland] with daughter, but I've no address for them.

---

* Jean-Etienne Cohen-Séat, publisher of Calmann-Lévy as of 1985.
† Many friends and visitors of Pat's remarked on her lack of passion for food—toward the end of her life, she seems to have subsisted mainly on peanut butter.
‡ Simpson's-in-the-Strand, one of London's oldest and best-known restaurants.

OCTOBER 31, 1990

Hallowe'en—And quiet here! The kids have a week off for "Festival of the Dead."

NOVEMBER 25, 1990

I discovered A. L. [Andrew Lloyd] Webber's wonderful music for *The Phantom of the Opera*. Spellbound was I. Now, Shostakovich as I finish washing the dishes.

DECEMBER 10, 1990

Heaviest snowfall in 100 years in Ticino over the weekend—Ingeborg Moelich snowed in today. Here I fare better with 10° higher temp. The Machine came yesterday & today to clear the lane between Speck Haus and mine. I must write to CB to explain as best I can my feeling of déjà vu in June. Surely the same feeling of being shoved aside prevailed in England in May '65 till I broke it off in Oct. '66—when C. was "getting her own back" as she put it. Now I've a house & cat to return to while in '66 I had nothing. And "friendship" does not hurt quite as much as a love relationship into which one has put everything.

From London: Bloomsbury likes *Ripley Under Water* including the title. Liz Calder* rang me up. I also sent her (for fun) the *Über Patricia Highsmith*[†] book of Diogenes, though she doesn't read German. Now—a break, vacation at home. Efforts at getting things in order as usual.

12/13/90

Further to "No End in Sight," the reason why my mother does not die is that she is already dead and has been for about eleven years. (Brain dead. No pleasure in sound, music, reading, watching TV, conversing with visitors. How dead can you get?) It is an insult to the individual—not a favor—to maintain a person's life under such conditions. It is a burden on the state which pays 45%, and on me who pays 55%—for years now and with no end in sight.

---

* Pat's publisher at Bloomsbury.
† *Über Patricia Highsmith* [*About Patricia Highsmith*], a 1980 Diogenes book with "testimonials from Graham Greene to Peter Handke."

JANUARY 14, 1991

The pleasant break continues, but tonight is eve of the deadline set by
Bush for Saddam Hussein to quit Kuwait.* Saddam vows he'll fight to the
death. America has nearly ½ million men, ships, planes, Germany &
Eng. not so much. Much hypocrisy and macho bombast from Bush. PLO
has sided with Saddam, and who could blame them? (Jews, of course.)
Paul B. writes that there'll be a general strike in Morocco tomorrow, and
that things will be worse if the Israelis come in.

JANUARY 15, 1991

Wrote to Bettina Berch[†] who writes me enchanting letters about Belize
and what she can grow there in coral-derived soil.

JANUARY 21, 1991

War broke out Wed-Thur 16–17 Jan. when USA and allies began bombing Iraq airfields. Now it goes on, escalating daily. Saddam Hussein has
been able to hit Israel with Scud missiles, the whole world worries that
Israel may come in—thus causing Egypt & Syria to desert the alliance,
though they had promised not to desert.

   Saw *The Sheltering Sky*[‡] on 20 Jan. evening, & thought it came off
very well. True setting & in Niger & Algeria. Beautiful camels. [Mari-
jane] Meaker rang from L.I. [Long Island] last evening to tell me Polly
wrote via USA, because she thinks I'm "very famous"!

JANUARY 23, 1991

Birthday Sat. 19th—Phones & flowers. Telegrams. I still write thank-you
notes. Flowers from Theo Sontrop, Arbeiderspers,[§] Amsterdam. From
the Keels a lovely box of oil paints, chosen by Anna who wrote me a nice
note. I intend today to take some [painting] lessons from Gudrun M.-P.

2/1/91

Salt arrived yesterday from Naiad Press[¶] under my name but with old

---

* Under the leadership of Saddam Hussein, Iraq had invaded Kuwait on August 2, 1990. On January 16,
1991, following a UN resolution, the United States and its allies embarked on a military intervention.
† American scholar, book critic, and biographer Bettina Berch (1950–) visited Pat for the first time in June
1983 to write a feature article about her. The two became friends and kept up a regular correspondence
following this.
‡ A 1990 film directed by Bernardo Bertolucci and based on Paul Bowles's 1949 book of the same name.
§ Theo Sontrop (1931–2017), Dutch author and head of De Arbeiderspers from 1972 to 1991.
¶ After many years, publisher Daniel Keel convinced Highsmith to republish her second novel under her
own name. Newly titled *Carol*, the novel was a worldwide success and was turned into a film in 2015 by
Todd Haynes, starring Cate Blanchett and Rooney Mara.

preface! I wrote to them and today rang Marianne L. who was just as shocked as we sent them the new in good time.

2/9/91

Some painting. Am of course not content. Cold and snowy.

FEBRUARY 12, 1991

Juliette rang at 7 PM to say that Mary [Ryan] had been found dead in the garden Saturday 9th. (I suppose by the Knets.)* She'd taken a sleeping pill, plus "a drink" said Juliette. Funeral Sat. next at the church between Nemours & Montcourt where D[esmond] R[yan] is buried. I rang B. Skelton,† who had also just heard. I rang B.S. a 2nd time to say I thought I'd not go. People are worried re bombs at airports—I not so much, but I debated should I out of decency? I'll send flowers & write to Juliette and Knets. (I wonder will Sebastian turn up?!) Barbara S. is sure the death was on purpose. It was (is) very cold. She fell asleep and froze. At my house in August last, she illustrated same by twice "falling" and deliberately.

FEBRUARY 12, 1991

Saddam today apparently rejects Russia's (Gorby's) proposal to pull out of Kuwait and also hold Palest.-Israel talks later. So the ground war is about to begin.

MARCH 2, 1991

GKK says she may be able to visit early April. I think of going to Rome. GKK sagacious re CB's despotism—1st cousin to sadism in my books.

MARCH 8, 1991

Heard from Ernst Hauser that he's in Rome just till 10 April. How's that for luck? I so informed GKK. Rain for 3 days, more for tomorrow. I've a cold—most unusual. I take aspirins & naps, and fancy they do wonders. Sent Anne Uhde my 3½-page review of *Hothouse by the East-River* by Muriel Spark.‡

---

* Neighbors to Pat and the Ryans in Montcourt.
† Barbara Skelton (1916–1996), English novelist and socialite. After being King Farouk's mistress, she first married critic Cyrill Connolly, then publisher George Weidenfeld, and went on to live in the Île-de-France, where she became Pat's neighbor.
‡ For Anne to translate it for publication in German paper *Die Welt*.

MARCH 17, 1991

Dan rang 3:30 AM 13/3 to tell me my mother had just died—8:30 PM his
time. Just faded away, I gather. I said I was not coming to funeral, as I'd
said before. Just the Coates, I assume, as she'd outlived all her friends &
would've been 95 this Sept.

APRIL 12, 1991

Last week rough, with G[raham] Greene dying on Wednesday and Max
Frisch* on Thurs. *Die Weltwoche* [Zurich] rang me Wednesday asking for 500 words on G.G. which I managed to do! The Jews today say
they'll continue building houses in West Bank & Gaza Strip, regardless
of what USA says. Bush goes fishing. The whole world collects money to
feed the deprived that USA has created in Israel (West Bank, etc.), Iraq—
the Swiss chip in too, a big TV donation program.

6/5/91

Man praying to God is man talking to himself. Why does man make
things so complicated, when they are simple?

MAY 11, 1991

Charlotte is 7. Mother's Day. 2 Bayreuth tickets came via [Victor von]
Bülow & today I try for a 3rd for Ingeborg Moelich. Charles Latimer
very pleased about his ticket. Yesterday I.M. & I went to Locarno to
buy—2 black, pleated skirts; mine definitely for Bayreuth!

JUNE 13, 1991

Marianne's [Marianne Fritzsch-Liggentorfer's] boy came 13 May—
Frederick Samuel. She had a hard 2 hours, she said. I'm v. happy for her,
that she stays home now for at least 2 yrs. [and] works from home. By
2 June I persuaded Moelich to accept my Bayreuth invitation. V. Bülow
now has 3 rooms for us in Goldener Anker Hotel, Opernstraße I. Moelich will take a chance on a ticket, once we're there. I expect my new VW
Golf next week: white. I try painting, with terrible shyness—till yesterday. I want to have 2 things to show G. Müller before I ask for another
2-hour lesson.

---

* Max Frisch (1911–1991) was considered, next to Friedrich Dürrenmatt, the most significant Swiss
author and playwright of the twentieth century.

6/19/91

Unhappiness is due to personal judgment of a situation.

JUNE 26, 1991

Today Gudrun Müller came at 10 AM to give me "a lesson." She refused any money—even 30 out of 60! Liked best my father pointing at the train wreck.

7/6/91

The Puzzlement of Summer. A busy person can't come to terms with free time. The world seems askew. This leads to terrifying examination of existence, consciousness, the meaning of going on living—if there *is* a meaning. Does one just go on, because other people do? It is worse than a nightmare, the confrontation of leisure.

8/1/91

Bayreuth. Tea with Wolfgang Wagner* and wife in a room near box office, on afternoon of *Die Walküre* during 1st intermission. W.W. very jolly, wife speaks English better than he. I inquired about tickets for I[ngeborg] M, We still can't explain this, but I was given 2 more tickets for *Siegfried* & *Die Götterdämmerung*, for I.M. & not allowed to pay for them! (180 DM each.) The town: Bourgeois, the food confined to Bratwurst, Sauerkraut, beer, and very expensive Franken wine—6.00 a Viertel Glass (or less) in restaurants & Kneipe [pub]. It is not worth looking for dinner, as nothing else is to be found.

The performances. Modern dress & scenes, as if after a hard war. The Walkure comes up a white metal scaffold, peering into fog to see if all are arriving safely. Everything finally seems slow & long, because this is an uncut version. Much back and forth argument, apparently. And in this show, people are always flinging themselves to the floor, or singing on their knees, crawling on knees. Very sexy performance of Siegfried drawing the sword Nothung from tree, and staying the night with Brünnhilde. People drink and sleep but do not eat.[†]

---

[*] Wolfgang Wagner (1919–2010), German opera director and nephew of Richard Wagner, was first co-director of the Bayreuth Festival with his brother, Wieland Wagner, then became sole director after Wieland's death in 1966.

[†] The Bavarian town of Bayreuth is famous for being since 1876 the venue of an annual, much-noticed music festival of Richard Wagner operas, most famously *The Ring of the Nibelung* that Pat describes here.

NOVEMBER 15, 1991

Late Sept. One week of heavy work in London for Bloomsbury re *Ripley Under Water*, 3 signings in bookshops. I was in Frith Street in Hazlitt's Hotel. Very old-fashioned & convenient between Bloomsbury and the Groucho Club where most of the interviews took place. Bloomsbury paid my airfare, plus hotel, but certainly worked me for it, including morning of departure, when I finally finished signing the "luxury" edition, selling for £32 (London Ltd editions). Hardly time to recover, 9 days before I had to take off for Germany. GKK met me in Frankfurt. (In London I did not ring CB, but wrote her after the trip.) 2 days Frankfurt, 2 in Hamburg, 2 in Berlin.

NOVEMBER 23, 1991

Had meant to invite GKK but D. Keel very kindly paid. Hotels and airfare. Hamburg was the prettiest. We had a boat-ride from Streekbrücke to the Jungfernstieg. Dinner in Berlin chez A. Morneweg & Claus K. with Christina Reutter,* GKK and Walther Busch.

20 Nov. after working weekend with [GKK], went to Zurich with Frieda Sommer & met Dr. B.G. [lawyer]. She suggests my giving away Tegna as "Foundation" for writers, artists, from everywhere. This may work to let me off 48% estate tax hook on death; not yet sure. I wrote to SHO [S. H. Okoshken], asking would it let me off USA hook too?

JANUARY 9, 1992

I had wished to finish these "pages" by December 31. But no. Dreary thought in a way as a couple of days ago, I felt I should (ought to) burn all my diaries before my death.[†] I read that Brett Weston, son of Edward, burnt all his negatives the other day, in the presence of a few friends, saying that no one would ever use his negatives with his skill & intention. My purpose would be to thwart idle curiosity. 13 December I gave a party—some 9 or 10 people, Gudrun Müller who brought Pauline Kraay English painter living in Ascona. Vivien De Bernardi also, who considered the evening a success. I. Lüscher, I. Moelich also.

---

* Christina Reutter, then head of publicity at Diogenes.
† Pat decided against this step in the end and instead listed her journals expressly as part of her work when she appointed Diogenes Verlag the holder of her world rights in 1993.

1/12/92

A boring thought with which to begin this year: I am sick of thinking
about myself and about my own problems (and especially sick of having
made little progress in the latter in the past year). Not enough people
around me. I must do better about this! Christmas quiet. 3 books from
Marijane Meaker. Cards galore & I had a batch to send also. I rang (&
wrote) London & arranged to go 14 January for appointment 15 January with Geo. Hamilton, for blocked left artery. I don't know what to
expect, & hope not a bypass.

2/8/92

The saga of London Jan. 14 to 23 Jan. My first meeting with [Dr.] Hamilton whom I liked at once. He looks under 40, Scots accent. Against
surgery; he said after visual exam, and it might be better to learn to live
with the pain. This was depressing, as the pain was much worse past 2
months, turning up after I walked a block & a half. Departure at 11:45
AM for Hayward Gallery, Toulouse-Lautrec, & I met Geraldine Cooke*
there. The steps involved, to climb to tower, made my left leg ache pretty
badly. Geraldine was a dear. We had 2 delicious lagers before the expo—
marred a bit by loud Indian music (2 or 3 players) who were supposed to
provide entertainment. The Lautrec show was large. There were round
or square stamps on the prints (often on inferior or tracing paper), stating
ownership of the drawing-watercolor-oil-pastel (all combined!) so that
no thief could steal it—as destroying the stamp would mar the work.
Heather gave a tea party 19 Jan. 4 pm, Sunday. Jonathan Kent there—
now manager of the Almeida Theatre. Linda [Ladurner]—seven others;
egg salad sandwiches. Rupert also. Liz Calder picked me up at 6:30 for
supper at her house, I think in Hampstead. She has a parrot called Jon-
Jon—maybe 38, light green.

   Monday I was on the table 2 hours, operation took about 35 minutes.
Mr Platts performed it, holding something in his rt. hand which looked
like a chopstick, and was perhaps a funnel to get the cord in. Through
the right groin pulse across to left, then downward halfway down thigh
to knee direction. "More pictures, please!" Mr Platts said three times.
Heat under buttocks then, as the dye went in. The only "discomfort"
was near the end, when my left calf felt as if it were being squeezed hard.
Mr. Hamilton reported expansion from 1 millimeter to 6 in left femo-

---

* Geraldine Cooke was the rights administrator for Headline and Penguin publishing and has since
worked as a literary agent.

ral artery. For me—most impressive. Instant improvement. "Well, you were lucky," said Mr. H.H. the following Friday when I came for final checkup.

MAY 7, 1992

Marlene Dietrich died 2 days ago (Paris) at 90. And Francis Bacon 2 days before that at 82. 27 April I went (was driven) to Peter Ustinov's at Rolle, near Geneva. He was informal & friendly, wife Hélène more formally dressed—but just as friendly. This for German *Vogue*. Living-room a mess of stacked magazines, letters. Nice oil paintings which I'll never forget. P.U. by his mother when he was 7. One of his father by her also. P.U. & I would've had no trouble in conversation topics, but the presence of 2 others. Then P.U.'s Portuguese servant drove me to Geneva (Hotel de la Cigogne) & I had dinner date with Marilyn Scowden.*

MAY 22, 1992

Have 92 pages of new book & am not satisfied. Slow, unfocused.

MAY 23, 1992

Another non-work day (2nd) as I rethink my book *Small g*. It's an interesting plot. The same ever-current problem, 3 legal things—my will, my house—have to be arranged, lest I die in my sleep with the unfinished matters still unfinished. I tell myself I do ever better keeping the questions, the unresolved, at bay, while I summon the creative part of my brain. Would it were so. My dry gorge (filled on my portion) now looks great with royal blue cornflowers, lots of blooming poppies, yellow something else. Birdweed that one has to watch out for.

JUNE 20, 1992

2nd day reading of Phyllis Nagy's gay-bashing play in London & I'm interested in reception! The Court. Today got the 31-page treatment of "An Exchange of Glances" ready for Ph. N. & shall send it Monday. She has agreed to try it as a play: to do the rest. Christina Reutter has upped our expectations as to money. Today rang Betty M. who informed me that Lynn Roth died 3 or 4 weeks ago. Emphysema. She was in a home— and still with that S.!—after 36 years! And how many affairs on the side?!

---

* Marilyn Scowden, Pat's bookkeeper, friend, and the last person to see her alive.

SEPTEMBER 2, 1992

To end this little book. A hot summer here. Hurricane a week ago in
Miami. Bush is sliding, Clinton & Dole rising. Jeanne Moreau visited
17–19 Aug. A great pleasure! Peter Huber came down to cook dinner for us, stayed 2 nights. Am trying to buy a Fax, Jeanne also says I
should have one. My *Garbo* (and *Green-Wood Cemetery*) piece bought
by FAZ [*Frankfurter Allgemeine Zeitung*], who will photograph the
watercolor from the Garbo collection for the article. I go to USA NYC
1–9 Oct. and see Daisy W. the 9th. Then Texas, 6 days, then Toronto,
& ½ hr. reading, & 8-day stay. Knopf and Annebeth Suter pleased
with good notices in *Kirkus Reviews* & *Publishers Weekly* for *Ripley
Under Water*.

SEPTEMBER 3, 1992

The 2 Goethe Poems books (Diogenes) are a joy. So attractive! Must get
them for Jeanne too. She said she could "almost" speak German. Sent
D.W. a check for $5,000-odd—better recipient than my mother or Dan,
who doesn't so much need it.

10/10/92–10/13/92

[Texas.] At the Box Canyon, now my only family-connected house in
Texas. Nothing changed, except that the dictionary under the sofa is
at other end of the sofa. I had to get on hands & knees and back up.
Saddest is Dan 3, who has Parkinson's & will not take his pills, as
they give him nausea; a well-known fact, but the sufferer is advised to
compromise—which would spare other people: e.g. he can't cut his own
fingernails now, and I cut the 3rd finger I attempted which made me
lose my nerve to continue—so violent is his trembling. Also he will not
experiment to find a proper hearing aid. And with one eye, he should not
drive, but does, in the neighborhood. This is really dumping his problems in the lap of wife Florine.

Politics: all (Dan 4 & [Florine]) conservative & pro-Bush. I listened
to all political debates I could in Canada and Texas too, while D. & F.
would walk out on [Ross] Perot, not in contempt, but because sleep was
more important.

11/27/92

On visiting Texas—something is missing: it's Europe, it's the world
missing.

11/23/92

I was very impressed by (no doubt) second reading of [F. Scott Fitzgerald's] *This Side of Paradise* which I picked up in New York last month. Such moralizing for a young man of 23—I suppose, as it was published when he was 24. And a lot of poetry—bad but fluent, influenced by Tennyson. I wonder if Princeton threw him out because he could not master comic sections, or did he quit? After 3 years. Unfortunately, he took not much strength from his education—considered Hemingway his superior! What a pity! His prose has some wonderful flights of poetry, especially in regard to being in love—so much better than what he puts into verse form.

12/1/92

Aids. Rampant now in India. I heard today, oddly, by killing off millions, AIDS will prolong the life of humans on earth by a few centuries! By sexual intercourse without birth control, the human race is breeding itself into a condition of starvation, death and extinction. Before that, soldiers in "developed" countries will have become quite used to bombing & machine-gunning invading hordes at their borders.

12/31/92

A final note on CB. She is afraid of flying, of dying, because she believes in an afterworld. And she is intelligent enough to know that she is not merely "not a nice person" as she put it to me when I last saw her, but also a phony who has taken boyfriends, husband, son, me for a ride— while keeping up such a nice facade for the public. No wonder she crosses herself before take-off and landing. No wonder she is terrified by slightly weak moments (heart beating too fast, tachycardia) and has to ring up a neighbor to come be with her—in case it's the moment of death.

6/26/93

Why can't I solve the riddle of art vs. drugs? My idea is that the arts are drugs for those who love them—from the classic to the popular. Therefore who needs opium, etc? I try to solve it by thinking of the desire for immersion, losing oneself—physical participation. This doesn't satisfy me. Art does not mean that one passes out. The basic premise—even fact—is that all humans want to be taken out of themselves—by religion, music, good paintings. Also some drugs achieve this taking out-of-self. But what I mean is not destructive, just the opposite. Maybe the clue lies in the true participation, appreciation & worship of the arts. This is not passive but active. To be knocked out by drugs is passive, easy, and has little to do with learning further about oneself, the human race, or consciousness.

10/6/93

Some monks—the Carthusians?—slept in their coffins, apparently preparing themselves for death, pondering it frequently by night and day. I prefer the surprise element! One goes about life as usual, then death arrives maybe suddenly, maybe via a two-week illness. In this, death's more like life, unpredictable.

1993–1995

PATRICIA HIGHSMITH's October 1993 note was her last coherent entry. Although she started both a new notebook and diary, the former—hand-titled "Book Thirty-Eight Tegna" on the cover—is empty, and even the diary, number 18, contains just a few key words about her last-ever trip in November 1994 to Paris. She jotted down appointments with Mary Kling, a French subagent for Diogenes Verlag, and Patrice Hoffmann, her new editor at Calmann-Lévy. She also noted details about giving a few interviews and seeing old friends such as Jeanne Moreau. This marks the end of Patricia Highsmith's chronicle of her life.

She has now added her notebooks and diaries to her formidable legacy comprising twenty-two novels and numerous short story collections. Her books have inspired dozens of film adaptations, most famously *The Talented Mr. Ripley*. While she was most popular in Europe during her lifetime, in recent years interest in the United States rekindled many movie adaptations, most prominently Anthony Minghella's adaptation of *The Talented Mr. Ripley* (starring Matt Damon, Jude Law, Gwyneth Paltrow, and Cate Blanchett), Todd Haynes's *Carol*, based on her friend Phyllis Nagy's screenplay of *The Price of Salt* (starring Cate Blanchett and Rooney Mara), and Adrian Lyne's *Deep Water*, after her eponymous novel (with Ben Affleck and Ana de Armas).

Graham Greene called her "the poet of apprehension"; Peter Handke felt "protected by a truly great writer." What we can add here is that she anticipated many of the cultural and sexual themes that pervade our lives today and that we are slowly catching up with some of the ways Pat saw things. She is both feared and admired for her skill in blurring the boundaries between good and evil, innocence and guilt, sympathy and hatred, confronting readers with their own deepest and darkest abysses. Brilliantly refuting along the way with her both popular and critical success the prejudice that suspense, a genre long treated with disdain, should not be considered literature.

In 1993 Diogenes Verlag acquired the world rights to Highsmith's collected works; Pat also personally entrusted Diogenes publisher Daniel Keel with the hand-over of her literary estate to the Swiss Literary Archives in Bern (where the Patricia Highsmith papers are among the most consulted), and appointed him her literary executor. In 1994, she made a number of sizable financial gifts to Yaddo, and even left her assets and royalties from book and film rights to the artists' colony. After all, it was there that she completed her debut novel, *Strangers on a Train*, in the early days of her career.

When Pat started to require in-home care, Daniel Keel stepped in; she also relied on driving services to shuttle her to and from doctor appointments. Keel eventually arranged for Bruno Sager, a recently unemployed music agent, to move in with Pat in 1994 and serve as her right-hand man for six months. In early February 1995, Pat asked some friends to bring her to the hospital in Locarno. She died from lung cancer and anemia on February 4.

Following Pat's death, Daniel Keel and editor Anna von Planta found folders of unpublished stories as well as Pat's diaries and notebooks hidden in a linen closet at her home in Tegna. In Notebook 34, they discovered a poem that would be shared at Pat's memorial ceremony on March 11 in Tegna, where her friends and publishers traveled from across Europe to take leave of her:

> A toast to optimism and to courage!
> A glass to daring!
> And a laurel to the one who leaps!
>
> (NOTEBOOK 34, "A Toast," 1979)

AFTERWORD

PAT HIGHSMITH'S
AFTER-SCHOOL EDUCATION:
THE INTERNATIONAL
DAISY CHAIN

by Joan Schenkar

✥

How Patricia Highsmith got herself from West Texas Cow Country to the "pot of gold" at the end of her American Dream had a great deal to do with a sophisticated international society of gifted, prominent, willful women who were making their lives with other women. In the 1940s and beyond, their tendrils of influence curled around every corner of Pat's life and work.

And Pat was ready to meet them: an attractive, intermittently forward, highly talented college junior with brains, a photographic memory for women's telephone numbers, and two fixed directions for success: Uptown and Europe. Until she could be famous, however, Pat was settling for seductive friendships. And many people were interested.

The prelude to Pat's initial Summer of Social Success began when she coolly dropped her first relationship with an older woman, a woman she'd met in a bar the month before: the "interesting" Irish émigré Mary Sullivan, who ran the bookshop in the Waldorf Astoria Hotel. It was Mary Sullivan who took Pat to gay parties in the Village, where Pat, precocious as ever, was already a young guest at the regular gatherings of (mostly) women hosted by the great American photographer (and inventor) Berenice Abbott (1898–1991) and her lover, the art critic and historian Elizabeth McCausland

(1899–1965), in their two flats and a hallway on the fourth floor of 50 Commerce Street.

It was at one of Abbott's parties with Mary Sullivan that Pat first spotted the expatriate German photographer Ruth Bernhard (1905–2006).* Ruth emigrated to New York in 1927, and her career as a commercial photographer was already detouring into the kind of high art that would lead Berenice Abbott to describe her as "the best photographer of the female nude." Ruth developed an intense friendship with Pat, an *amitié amoureuse*, which, like so many of Pat's friendships, briefly broke into something like love before Pat triangulated it with another of her fascinations, the gay male German photographer Rolf Tietgens (1911–1984). Ruth knew very well that Pat "had a lot of connections," a lot of "love affairs." "Pat," she said, "was a very attractive person, a wonderful-looking woman, and people were drawn to her." Ruth made a classically aspirational photographic portrait of Pat in 1948—a "thoughtful," dignified, enduring image of the twenty-seven-year-old writer facing her future. And she was certain she'd photographed Pat in the nude.

Fifteen years older than Pat, Ruth Bernhard continued to meet Pat for coffee and conversation and mutual comfort: They went to gallery openings together, they took subways to Harlem, and they were equally enthralled by the female flamenco performer and singer Carmen Amaya, who dressed as a man and took the "male" part in legendary flamenco performances with her sister.[†]

Three years before her death, Pat telescoped her unlikely social successes as a twenty-year-old in Manhattan "trying her luck"—a phrase she used repeatedly—by attaching it to the string of high-style coincidences that began with her introduction to Janet Flanner (1892–1978) in the summer of 1941 and to some "20 [other] interesting people all in a fortnight, many of whom I still know . . ."[‡]

This necklace of sinuously linked introductions ushered in an after-school education for Pat the year before she graduated, jobless and embarrassed about it, from Barnard College in 1942; an education that was a direct result of the war-driven exodus from Europe to New York of a phalanx of older, accomplished, expatriate mostly lesbian women: a great international

---

* Ruth Bernard was the daughter of Lucian Bernhard (birth name Emil Kahn), Germany's most inventive graphic designer and typographer.
† Pat was sufficiently taken by Amaya to send Gregory Bullick, the artistic teenage boy who spies upon and enters the life of another, far wealthier boy in her first unpublished novel, *The Click of the Shutting*, to a Carmen Amaya performance at Carnegie Hall.
‡ Pat in a letter to Bettina Berch, December 22, 1991.

daisy chain of intelligence, professional success, abundant talent, wealth, and/or privilege and freedom.

Among these women, recently arrived to New York from Paris, were Janet Flanner (*The New Yorker* magazine's Paris correspondent since 1925) and the painter Buffie Johnson (who had been studying painting with Francisco Pissaro in Paris and living in the famous soprano Mary Garden's Paris house). Like their much-traveled women friends, they had been guests (and Flanner was a regular guest) at Natalie Clifford Barney's (1876–1972) fabled salon* of late Friday afternoon literary readings, theatrical performances, and amuse-bouches at 20 rue Jacob and at Gertrude Stein's (1874–1946) curated displays of modernist art, literature, and temperament on Saturday nights at 27 rue de Fleurus.

✄

Pat took many of these older women to heart, and she took some of them to bed. And in her cramped and costive handwriting she also took relentless notes on what they said and did.

Janet Flanner, the incomparable purveyor of Paris's *air du temps* to *New Yorker* readers in the United States for five decades, filed nearly seven hundred witty and incisive "Letters from Paris" under her nom de plume of Genêt. Over the years, Flanner and her principal lover, the editor and broadcaster Natalia Danesi Murray (1901–1994), invited Pat to their summerhouse in Cherry Grove, admired her writing in letters to each other, touted her work, and were generous with introductions, translations, and help with book contracts in Italy and France. It was likely through Flanner in Paris that Pat met the critic and novelist Germaine Beaumont (1890–1983), Colette's protégée (and more) and, like Flanner herself, a regular at Natalie Barney's salon. Beaumont was one of the first (and most intelligent) French critics to write favorably about Pat's work. And Janet Flanner was probably Pat's Paris introduction to the flamboyant, wealthy Cuban-American poet and memoirist Mercedes de Acosta (1892–1968), another frequenter of

---

* The Barney salon, during its sixty years in Paris as the twentieth century's most subversive literary gathering (despite its *haut bourgeois* trappings and genteel mise-en-scène), entertained not only all the great male modernist writers, but also recruited, attracted, and showcased all the female subverters of the modernist style. Among them: Natalie Clifford Barney; Renée Vivien; Colette; Élisabeth de Gramont, duchesse de Clermont-Tonnerre; Romaine Brooks; Isadora Duncan; Ida Rubenstein; Gertrude Stein, Alice B. Toklas; Lucie Delarue-Mardrus; Mercedes de Acosta; Janet Scudder; Sybille Bedford; Esther Murphy; Radclyffe Hall; Una, Lady Troubridge; Bettina Bergery; Djuna Barnes; Marie Laurencin; Mina Loy; Marguerite Yourcenar; Janet Flanner; Elisabeth Eyre de Lanux; and Dorothy Ierne Wilde.

the Barney salon, who accommodated Pat with social introductions, dinner invitations, and her flat on the Quai Voltaire in Paris.*

But it was the well-connected, generous, and very social artist Buffie Johnson† (1912–2006) who was responsible for introducing Pat to her most intense and enduring "useful" friendship—and to the decades-long cascade of professional, artistic, and emotional consequences that followed. Buffie, who met Pat at a party in 1941, found her (as everyone did that year) "terrifically attractive and sparkly and energetic." Pat, Buffie said, was "bold in her approach," "far from sweet," but "sure of what she wanted," and they quickly became lovers. Buffie, who knew everyone and went everywhere, offered Pat the use of her town house on East Fifty-Eighth Street and continued to provide her with introductions to New Yorkers like the cult lyricist and wit John La Touche (Pat was more interested in La Touche's wife, a lesbian from a prominent banking and investment family), the painter Franz Léger ("Simply wonderful," Pat enthused), the architect Frederick Kiesler, the heiress, art philanthropist, and gallerist Peggy Guggenheim (who exhibited Buffie's work and introduced Pat to Somerset Maugham),‡ and many other pivotal people to whom Buffie had access and to whom Pat, still just a junior at Barnard College but circulating socially with astounding assurance, did not.

And then, two weeks after she met Pat, Buffie was invited to the party of a friend whose husband was the editor-in-chief of *Fortune* magazine. Knowing this occasion might prove "fortuitous" for her new college girl lover, Buffie took Pat with her—and Pat, said Buffie, immediately occupied herself among the partygoers. In Buffie's version of the evening's events, Buffie looked up from a deep conversation with her friend, the room had emptied, and Pat—"without even saying goodnight"—had left the party with a group of Henry Luce's magazine editors.§

---

* De Acosta's chief claim to fame, was, as Alice B. Toklas put it, that she'd "slept with three of the most important women in the 20th Century." Marlene Dietrich and Greta Garbo were two of them; Eva Le Gallienne and Isadora Duncan were candidates for the third.

† Buffie Johnson was the painter of the largest abstract expressionist mural ever commissioned in New York, for the old Astor Theatre; also the close friend of Carl Jung, Tennessee Williams, et al. A world traveler, and a proponent of feminist goddess history. She had just come from Paris, where, irritated by being consigned to a corner with Miss Toklas and the "wives" in Gertrude Stein's salon (while Stein spoke of important matters with the husbands), Buffie reached over and pinched Stein's bottom on her way out. It had, said Buffie, "the consistency of a solid block of mahogany."

‡ In 1943, Guggenheim included Buffie Johnson in the notorious 31 Women show at her just-opened avant-garde gallery Art of This Century on West Fifty-Seventh Street. Djuna Barnes, Elisabeth Eyre De Lanux, Elsa von Freytag-Loringhoven, Gypsy Rose Lee, Dorothea Tanning, Leonor Fini, Frida Kahlo, Meret Oppenheim, and Louise Nevelson were among the other exhibitors. The painting Buffie contributed, entitled *Déjeuner sur Mer*, was a seascape with two women clinging to a wrecked ship.

§ Pat had a different memory of the evening. She describes a party at which only four people were present, with no mention of an early departure by her or anyone else.

Among that group was Rosalind Constable (1907–1995), the sophisticated English arts journalist who would haunt Pat's diaries, notebooks, and
emotional life for the next ten years. Rosalind had light blond hair, light
cold eyes, a serious intellectual background, and a pronounced ability to
spot trends in all the arts. Long employed at *Fortune*, she was greatly influential in the magazine publishing world that Pat was finding so attractive.
Sybille Bedford (1911–2006), who met Pat late in the 1940s in Rome "when
she was a little bit wild" (Bedford was as much a part of the international
daisy chain as Rosalind), knew Constable very well. In her beautifully etched
memoir *Quicksands*, Bedford wrote that Constable was "a bright light of
the *Life/Time* establishment, hard-working, hard-playing." Rosalind was
hard-drinking, too, and fourteen years older than Pat. She edited the Luce
Corporation's in-house newsletter, *Rosie's Bugle*, whose sole purpose was
to alert all the other Luce editors to the cultural subjects about which they
should be writing.

Pat telephoned Rosalind the day after they met and, vigorously pursued
by Pat and affectionately indulged by Rosalind, a long, complex friendship
was launched. Done with sleeping on the current Highsmith living room
couch, Pat spent nights in Rosalind's guest bedroom. (Pat was always spending nights in her older women friends' guest rooms—and then sometimes
ending up in their beds—or, in the case of her longtime, hardworking agent
Margot Johnson, in bed with their lovers.) And Rosalind, who brought Pat
everywhere, was certainly responsible for Pat's introduction to Mary Louise
Aswell (1902–1984), the literary editor at *Harper's Bazaar*, who, along with
Rosalind, recommended Pat to the art colony Yaddo in 1948 and published
her superb story "The Heroine" (rejected by the Barnard College literary
magazine as "too upsetting") in *Harper's.*[*] Rosalind and Pat's relationship
continued to be alimented by long hand-holding walks and long alcoholic
lunches, with Pat sometimes ending up in Rosalind's lap. It was the kind of
courtly love story Pat preferred when she was young: the sensual pursuit of
an older woman lightly masked by an artistic and professional mentoring.
This one had all the intoxications of a love affair that would never be physically consummated.

Rosalind introduced Pat to her own influential lover, the painter and revolutionary gallerist Betty Parsons[†] (1900–1982), and Pat took to spending

---

[*] And when Mrs. Aswell retired to New Mexico with her lover Agnes Sims, she and Pat would keep up
with each other through lesbian circles far and wide.
[†] Betty Parsons's eponymous gallery, opened in 1946 at 15 East Fifty-Seventh Street as a locus for
abstract expressionism, was the only gallery willing to represent artists like Jackson Pollock after Peggy
Guggenheim closed Art of This Century in 1947. Parsons ran her gallery until her death in 1982.

time in the Wakefield Gallery where Parsons held sway. Parsons requested a copy of Pat's essay "Will the Lesbian's Soul Rest in Peace?"—Pat seemed to think hers might not—and Pat invited Parsons to dinner to look at her drawings. Betty Parsons (as Rosalind Constable's lover) gave Pat yet another opportunity to be the third arm of a triangle.

And it was through Rosalind that Pat met the Ziegfeld Follies performer turned influential Broadway producer Peggy Fears (1903–1994), a close friend of Louise Brooks's, and whose three marriages to the wealthy producer A. C. Blumenthal never interfered with her relationships with women. She built the first yacht-club-cum-hotel on Fire island, and Pat, "looking for adventure," began visiting her every day, and then dropping in on her late at night, making Rosalind jealous.

Like Buffie Johnson, Rosalind Constable was responsible for Pat's introduction to both "quality" and opportunity in her life in art. So it is fitting that it was at one of Rosalind's parties in 1944 that Pat first met Virginia Kent Catherwood (1915–1966), the beautiful, witty Main Line Philadelphia socialite and heiress who would become Pat's Muse for Life, and her lover for a turbulent year in 1946—in not just one, but two triangular love affairs with two other women,* and then in an unusually long and focused relationship: the four-year union in which Pat Highsmith siphoned, as directly as a blood donation, the life history and styles of speech of Ginnie Catherwood[†] (as well as the very best version of her love affair with Ginnie) into a novel unlike any other she would ever write again.

This was the novel Pat released in 1952 as *The Price of Salt*. She published it under a pseudonym, dedicated it to three people whose names she made up, left the United States before the book was released, and refused to acknowledge her authorship for nearly forty years. But the extended metaphors through which Pat associates *The Price of Salt*'s two accomplished women and their life-changing love affair with an ice-cold world of violence and danger and harm is the true language of Highsmith Country.

And the high-powered, communally driven engine of the group of

---

* Natica Waterbury, another daughter of the American Patriciate, who flew her own plane and assisted Sylvia Beach at Shakespeare and Co. in Paris, was Ginnie's lover when she got together with Pat—who then fell in love with Ginnie. Sheila Ward, an heiress from the West Coast (guano was the unlikely source of her fortune) was the photographer who eventually lived with Ginnie in the Southwest, but not before she and Pat got together briefly while Pat and Ginnie were still involved. The triangle was always Pat's favorite geometry in love.

† Ginnie Catherwood's alcoholism was advanced enough to make Pat's own youthful capacity for alcohol look almost reasonable. It was very far from reasonable, but in the 1940s, when everyone drank in quantity, it would have taken a keener eye than the casually admiring (or coldly curious) ones turned toward Pat during all her Manhattan nights to see that her seductive behavior, heavy imbibing, rapid advances, and acute withdrawals were signals through the flames burning in her psyche.

women friends and lovers Pat met in New York in the 1940s continued to turn its wheels of influence in every hidden corner of *The Price of Salt*'s creation. The steady hum of their exits from their marriages, their love affairs, their families, and their other social martyrdoms idles in the background of Pat's least characteristic (and most true-to-self) novel like the getaway car at a bank robbery.

ACKNOWLEDGMENTS

I WAS LUCKY enough to have known Patricia Highsmith personally. Though her prickly facade featured more prominently, I was familiar with her softer side as well. Pat was a fascinating, complicated person and author who left us with eight thousand handwritten pages of diaries and notebooks that reveal things about her personal and creative development that she shared with only a chosen few during her lifetime—and even then, she never told the whole story.

This collection should not be read as an autobiography. By necessity, autobiographies are written retrospectively, often carefully edited to present events in a certain light, whereas Pat's diaries and notebooks provide a running account of a life in progress. They are, however, like two mirrors reflecting the interplay of her life and work from different vantage points.

How does one approach a body of work eight thousand pages in length and condense it to a single volume? During the coronavirus pandemic, no less, when work-from-home routines became the norm?

One certainly doesn't go it alone—to wit, this project represents the yearslong work of an truly exceptional team.

Thanks to Ina Lannert and Barbara Rohrer for their exacting transcriptions of Pat's handwritten diaries and notebooks, respectively. Gloria Kate Kingsley Skattebol, Pat's closest college friend, compared these transcripts against the originals, making corrections as needed, and annotated them extensively. As a lifelong confidante and contemporary of Pat's, Gloria Kate Kingsley Skattebol approached these annotations with unmatched insight and sensitivity.

"It takes two mirrors for the correct image of oneself" (Notebook 29, 2/23/68): Neither the diaries nor the notebooks could have been published as stand-alone works. I am most thankful to Daniel Keel, executor of the

Highsmith estate, for his support in finding a suitable way to merge these two mirrors of Pat's being; and to his son and successor at the Diogenes helm, Philipp Keel, who not only trusted me but provided me with the time and means to complete this project. Corinne Chaponnière, Gerd Hallenberger, and Paul Ingendaay played central roles in the process as well: Corinne Chaponnière and I conducted the initial experiment of connecting diary and notebook, which gave way to a structural model I developed further with Gerd Hallenberger that took the characteristics of both into account while presenting Pat's life, loves, and work and the worlds in which they evolved. Paul Ingendaay and I compiled the thirty-volume collected works, one of my first exercises in looking back and reassessing the "work behind the works."

Philippa Burton, Lucienne Schwery, Stéphanie Cudré-Mauroux, Ulrich Weber, and Lukas Dettwiler at the Swiss Literary Archives provided expert guidance in navigating the Patricia Highsmith papers housed there. Ina Lannert's detailed time line of Pat's personal life and literary output, complete with quotations from the diaries and notebooks, was an indispensable resource, a map that allowed us to explore the Highsmith cosmos with a sense of direction.

For a long time, we hesitated at the idea of including Pat's early diaries in this edition, written as they are largely in foreign languages. Credit and thanks to Elisabeth Lauffer (German), Sophie Duvernoy (German, French), Noah Harley (Spanish), and Hope Campbell Gustafson (Italian) for their superb translations of these entries back into Pat's mother tongue—without them, the early diary years of Patricia Highsmith would have remained largely obscure. My colleagues Claudia Reinert and Silvia Zanovello thankfully rendered standardized versions of the Spanish and Italian—Pat's weakest languages—to better allow Noah Harley and Hope Campbell Gustafson to translate the passages into English.

Kati Hertzsch, Friederike Kohl, Marie Hesse, and Marion Hertle, my co-editors, were a dream team, astute, passionate, relentless, and giving their all. They followed the structural template we had established in compiling and condensing more than fifty years of Patricia Highsmith's diaries and notebooks. The introductory texts preceding each chapter were written by myself (1941 through 1969) and Friederike Kohl (1970 through 1993) and translated by Elisabeth Lauffer. The annotations, beyond those provided by Gloria Kate Kingsley Skattebol, were written by myself and Friederike Kohl, and translated by Elisabeth Lauffer and Sophie Duvernoy, who also translated the texts in the appendix. Peter Theml created the index. For the final sprint, Friederike Kohl was my most trusted co-driver.

Many thanks to Susanne Bauknecht, Claudia Reinert, Andrej Ruesch, and Karin Spielmann at Diogenes Verlag for ensuring clear communication with our publishing partners around the globe. Publisher Philipp Keel and designers Kobi Benezri and Carsten Schwab were the minds behind the book layout, format, and typography. Thanks to Charlotte Lamping for extensive preparatory work on this project. Susanne Bauknecht and Susanne von Ledebur advised on legal matters. Special thanks to Bettina Wagner, Diogenes Verlag's publishing representative in Austria, who conducted last-minute research on the ground, retracing Pat's steps through Vienna—all in the midst of coronavirus restrictions.

Last but not least, this book would not have been possible without editors Robert Weil and Gina Iaquinta at Liveright in New York, as well as copy editor Dave Cole, who masterfully edited the English version.

My sincere thanks to all,
Anna von Planta

A TIME LINE
OF HIGHSMITH'S LIFE AND WORKS

❧

1921 January 19: Mary Patricia Plangman is born in Fort Worth, Texas, to Jay Bernard Plangman and Mary Coates, who have recently divorced. Both parents are freelance graphic artists.

1924 Mary Coates marries Stanley Highsmith, another graphic artist, who becomes Patricia's stepfather.

1927 The family moves to New York, where Patricia attends school under the name Highsmith; however, her stepfather officially adopts her only in 1946. Pat spends her childhood alternately in New York and Fort Worth, largely in the care of her grandparents.

1934–1937 Pat attends Julia Richman High School in New York. She publishes her first short stories in *Bluebird*, the high school newspaper.

1938–1942 Pat attends Barnard College of Columbia University in New York and majors in English literature (with ancient Greek and zoology as secondary fields). Receives a bachelor of arts degree.

1942 onward Pat makes a living producing comic book scripts and writes in her spare time. She travels frequently, first to Mexico, later to Europe.

1948–1949 A stay at the Yaddo artist colony in Saratoga Springs, New York, allows Pat to finish her novel *Strangers on a Train*. She begins psychoanalysis to "cure" herself of her homosexuality, and agrees to get engaged to Marc Brandel, a colleague at Yaddo, but later breaks things off again.

1950 *Strangers on a Train*, Pat's first novel, is published. Alfred Hitchcock's film adaptation—the first of many film versions of her books by prominent directors such as René Clément (*Plein Soleil*, 1959), Claude Autant-Lara (*Enough Rope*, 1963), Anthony Minghella (*The Talented Mr. Ripley*, 1999), and Todd Haynes (*Carol*, 2015)—propels Pat to overnight fame.

1951–1953 Pat takes off on a two-year-long voyage across Europe (England, Italy, France, Spain, Switzerland, Germany, Austria). In 1952, her second book, *The Price of Salt* (later renamed *Carol*) is published under the pen name Claire

Morgan. Since a lesbian love story with a happy end is a rare phenomenon at the time, it becomes an iconic book in the lesbian scene.

1955 *The Talented Mr. Ripley* is published. From now on, Highsmith will publish a new novel every two to three years, including four further *Ripley* novels. She must constantly find new publishers and is often forced to make significant revisions. In addition, many of her short stories are published, first in magazines and later in anthologies.

1964 After several longer stays in Europe, Pat moves to England to be near her lover Caroline. She lives in Earl Soham, Suffolk, in England, where she buys a house.

1967–1968 Pat moves to France, via Fontainebleau and Samois-sur-Seine to Montmachoux in the Île-de-France region, approximately fifty miles southeast of Paris.

1969 Highsmith's thirteenth novel *The Tremor of Forgery*, which draws upon a trip to Tunisia, is published. Graham Greene and literary critics praise it as her best work yet.

1970 Pat moves to Montcourt, near Montmachoux.

1980 Several surgeries due to blood circulation problems.

1982 After several run-ins with the French tax authorities, Highsmith moves to Aurigeno in Ticino, Switzerland.

1986 Lung cancer operation. Pat briefly gives up smoking.

1988 Pat moves into a house in Tegna, Ticino, which the architect Tobias Ammann designed according to her own specifications.

1995 February 4: Patricia Highsmith dies in the Locarno hospital, of cancer and a blood disease. She leaves her estate to the artist colony Yaddo, which had enabled her to complete her first novel, *Strangers on a Train*. The Swiss Literary Archives in Bern acquire her literary estate in 1996.

A SAMPLE OF HIGHSMITH'S
FOREIGN-LANGUAGE NOTES

"Exercise books in languages I do not know."

❈

Pat's original diary entries are written in English, French, German, Spanish, and Italian—and sometimes a mixture of all of them at once. She bends all of those languages grammatically, idiomatically, and syntactically toward her mother tongue, sometimes with unintentionally amusing results. Often, Pat jumps from one language to another even within a single sentence.

> *Habe Flohen. Tengo Pulges. I have many fleas, und eine purpurrote Bespreklung auf meinen Beinen. Ich bin elend!*
> (JANUARY 10, 1944)

Her foreign-language notes are intelligible—provided the reader has decent command of both English and the respective foreign language; after a quick mental translation back to English, most of it makes sense. That's because she usually simply translates her English word-for-word. "To phone" thus becomes *phoner* in French, a word that does simply not exist, and *phonieren* in German, where it does exist but does not mean "to phone" but "to phonate." In the same way, a turtleneck sweater becomes a *Schildkrötenhalssweater* in German, where this kind of pullover is much less graphically just described as having a "rolled-up collar." Wherever a term has various possible equivalents in her target language, Pat displays a bit of a knack for choosing the wrong one.

FRENCH

Of her foreign languages, French makes the most regular appearance in Pat's early diaries. Interestingly enough, she scarcely uses it during her years living in France, from 1967 to 1981. In the 1940s, it is often her language of choice when writing about romance, her frequent use of several "false friends" rendering her entries involuntarily amusing: Much like mid-century usage of "gay," for instance, the French word *gai* means "cheery or tipsy," but does not signify sexual orientation. The verb *baiser* means "to fuck," and not "to kiss," as Pat intends; on a related note, *dormir* means simply "to sleep," and not "to sleep with someone," which would instead be *coucher.*

Va. [Virginia] m'a phone à 7.30.h. Je l'ai rencontré chez Rocco-Restaurant à 9h. avec Jack un gai garçon—et Curtis et Jean—deux gaies filles. Sommes allés au Jumble Shop, etc. Des Bièrs et martinis et je suis ivre maintenant. Mais Va m'a baisé!! Je l'ai baisé—deux—trois—quatre—cinq fois dans le salon des femmes au Jumble—et aussi même sur le trottoir!! Le trottoir! Jack est très doux, et Va. voudrait dormir avec lui—mais d'abords elle voudrait faire un voyage avec moi quelque fin de semaine. Elle m'aime. Elle m'aimera toujours. Elle mè l'a dit, et ses actions le confirment.

(JANUARY 11, 1941)

GERMAN

Pat's "father tongue" is the second most common foreign language in her diaries. What she lacks in vocabulary, she makes up for in creativity, like when when she describes herself as *ein Ohnegeschlecht* ("one without sex, gender"); based on the context of the entry, what Pat presumably means is *ungeschlechtlich,* or "asexual." Again, she uses English syntax and translates idioms literally, at times calling attention to them. *Als wir in Englisch sagen, das Spiel ist nicht der Kerze würdig.*—"As we say in English, the game is not worth the candle" (December 30 1944).

Her German sounds especially odd in those regular instances when she borrows from antiquated sources such as Johann Wolfgang von Goethe, Friedrich Schiller, and Johann Sebastian Bach's chorales. For instance, Pat's *Seelenschafe* ("sheep of the soul," a coinage of hers) graze upon the *Seelenweide* ("meadow of the soul") of Bach's eponymous cantata BWV 497.

Ich bin ganz verrückt mit diesen Abenden ohne Ruhe, ohne Einsamkeit, worauf meine Seelenschafe weiden. Mein Herz ist so voll, es bricht in zwei, und die schöne Kleinodien und Phantasien sind wie Giftung in meinen Adern.

(OCTOBER 28, 1942)

SPANISH

Pat picks up some Spanish in anticipation of her 1944 trip to neighboring Mexico, her first time abroad, but her vocabulary remains paltry. While in Mexico, she evidently continues to learn by ear, because she has no grasp of the orthography, mixes in Hispanicized French words, and uses all three past tenses as well as the subjunctive, seemingly at random—or at least led by unreliable instinct. *Incapable*, for instance, is a false cognate that actually means "impossible to castrate," and *yo quite las cadenas* ("I remove the chains") is not a common metaphor in Spanish.

> *He trabajado muy duro, esta mañana, tarde, y hablabamos de mi novella esta noche. Goldberg dice que yo soy incapable de amar, que yo soy enamorido de mi misma. Es falsa. Mi grande problema es de escribir esta novella, así que yo quite las cadenas que me lian.*
> (MARCH 11, 1944)

ITALIAN

Pat writes in simple, though flawed, Italian that's easy enough to follow. English, French, and Spanish terms find their way into these entries as well. There's a peculiar coupling of Pat's basic Italian vocabulary with her use of *passato remoto*, the literary past tense, which elevates the overall feel. *Passato remoto* is, however, sometimes used colloquially in southern Italy. Pat exhibits her old habit of translating common expressions directly into whatever language she happens to be using at the time—in this case, Italian. For instance, a French expression for "go to hell" (which in English would translate to "go to the devil") becomes *puo andare al diablo*. Similarly, the French phrase for "without any doubt" is translated into Italian as *senza alcuna duta.*

> *Restai con Lynn tutto il giorno—Vedemmo Jiynx con Ann M. Precisamente le due che noi non devremmo avere veduto, a casa di Doris, qui non devrebbe sapere che noi abbiamo passato questa settimana insieme. Dopo Showspot—Sono molto felice e penso che Ellen puo andare al diablo. Sono inamorata di Lynn. Senza alcuna duta.*
> (SEPTEMBER 15, 1953)

NOTES ON THE JOURNALS'
COMPOSITION

Pat's thirty-eight notebooks all looked alike: Starting her freshman year at Barnard College in 1938, and for the rest of her life, Pat exclusively used Columbia University spiral notebooks (*cahiers*) for her notes. From Europe, she frequently asked her friend Gloria Kate Kingsley Skattebol to send her more: "The point is I need three more cahiers, these spiral notebooks— which measure 7 inches by 8¼—have faintly greenish paper, emblazoned with Columbia on the front cover . . ." (PH to GKKS, July 9, 1973); "You know what a stickler I am for uniformity" (PH to GKKS, May 12, 1944). Pat's diaries, meanwhile, were uniform in format, but varied in thickness and provenance. Unlike several of her manuscripts, not a single diary or notebook was ever lost during a move or one of her many trips. She regularly returned to them, revising and building upon entries, dating her edits and thus engaging in a decades-long conversation with herself. She later copied diary-like notes written in high school (1935–1938) into her ninth notebook. On every trip, Pat took her current notebook and diary with her, while she entrusted the rest of the collection to close friends in her absence.

In her first notebook, which marks the beginning of her life as a writer, eighteen-year-old college freshman Pat still lacked the experience to know she should record dates and times. Meanwhile, the care with which she compiled this first notebook—creating various categories and consistently adding entries to each—already appears quite professional.

On the front cover of her notebooks, Pat usually wrote her current home address(es) and travel destinations in the designated address field. In the field provided for one's graduation year ("Class of"), she might record a self-assessment or her general state of mind during the period contained in that notebook; on the cover of Notebook 24, for instance, which spans 1955–1958, she wrote, "Greater outer and inner mediocrity." From Notebook 17 onward, she listed the people, topics, and works occupying her mind. On that very cover, she wrote: "1. Cornell" (in reference to artist Allela Cornell), "2. Notes on an ever-present subject" (N.O.E.P.S., her sexual orientation), and "3. Notes on Novel" (meaning novels in general as well as a "second novel," which in 1948 still lacked any clear form). On the inside back covers, Pat jotted down quotations by other authors as well as possible titles for her own projects.

Over the years, the structure of the notebooks became more systematic: personal details; travel writing; broad commentaries with an aphoristic bent; remarks on literary and political topics; generalized observations of personal situations; insights into art, writing, and painting; personal biographical comments and notes (even more so during periods in which she didn't keep a diary); scenes tied to the novel or short story collection she was currently working on; famous quotations; and, later, figures of speech and dreams as separate categories. Pat took her notebooks very seriously and habitually consulted them for creative direction, praising some entries while scrapping others entirely. They represented a literary reservoir that the author tapped into when the time came to flesh out the details of a novel. Each of the notebooks, except the very last, spans about two years. The amounts of time her diaries covered, on the contrary, varied greatly.

Over both formats, Pat's notes between the ages of twenty and thirty are more extensive than all she wrote over the rest of her life, or a good forty-five years. The entries dedicated to *The Price of Salt* and its predecessor, *Strangers on a Train*, comprise a total of more than twelve hundred handwritten pages. The notebook entries are more fluid and detailed, the diary the place "where I think aloud" (Diary 10, December 21, 1950).

Pat initially attempted to distinguish strictly between the two. In December 1987, she stated: "These are not diaries, but contain ideas for short stories and novels, some poems, notes on countries and cities I have visited, people I have met. At the very back of these *cahiers*, quotations I copied out from other writers, etc." Each format was originally intended to serve a different purpose, one for private personal matters, the other for work, but there were phases in her life when the lines blurred. Art and life couldn't always be filed away into separate drawers. A veritable osmosis between the diary and notebook set in while Pat wrote *The Price of Salt*, because the experience entailed so much more than the act of writing: "How well it all goes. How grateful I am at last not . . . to spoil my best thematic material by transposing it to a false male-female relationship!" Many key entries were not written in Pat's notebook, but in her diary. Barely a day went by without some mention, every date written out: "I live so completely with [the characters in the novel] now, I do not even think I can contemplate an amour. (I am in love with Carol, too) . . ." (Diary 10, May 31, 1950). *The Price of Salt* represented the blueprint of an undisguised existence Pat wished to embrace, but didn't (yet) dare. She must have identified intensely with her protagonists, as she herself swung between wedding plans with various men and same-sex love affairs: "Oh God, how this story emerges from my own bones! The tragedy, the tears, the infinite grief which is unavailing!" (Diary 10, June 14, 1950).

Following that brief, intoxicating osmosis of life and art, diary and note-book, Pat soberly reverted to the old divisions.

Diaries 11 and 12 outline Pat's experiences during her second major trip to Europe. Ellen Hill's curiosity allegedly compelled Pat to abandon journaling altogether. Private thoughts were reduced and recorded in her notebook instead, her categories became more porous, her dates jumbled. Personal passages in the notebooks, along with sporadic diary entries, revealed moments of reflection, but no longer provided insight into the whole picture.

Whatever the reason, Diary 12 cuts off on February 9, 1954, on page 136. The next diary doesn't begin until July 1961, following Pat's breakup with Marijane Meaker, who also read Pat's notebook behind her back.[*]

Another diary, this one labeled "Travel Diary," follows in 1962 and details Pat and Ellen's two-month sojourn in Italy as well as Pat's next serious love interest, Caroline Besterman. Starting in 1963 and throughout her four-year relationship with the married woman, Pat returned to regular journaling and continued through 1971 (Diaries 15 and 16), well after the relationship had crumbled. Then followed a decade-long pause until Pat started Diary 17 in 1981, only to leave right off again, not to continue until 1987, when she again took back up writing until 1992. The very last diary, Diary 18 (1984), only contains a few words regarding her last trip to Paris.

---

[*] See Marijane Meaker, *Highsmith: A Romance of the 1950s.*

commit suicide together, unbeknownst to the
others. But the man intends to kill the girl himself, and claim whatever proceeds may be. The
quiet boy falls in love with the girl, and the man
manipulates them so the young man will be
angry. Then to his surprise the young man murders the girl, and he is found at the unusual moment standing near the corpse. (i.e. her husband.) Who has done it? And it might be the girl
killed herself to blame it on the husband, knowing his schemes against her.

The husband would of course claim the girl
first killed herself, would confess their plot.
Oddly, it would be true. Meanwhile, the boy
flees, and the police are after him, for it looks
like murder.

Texas: I shall write about it as it has never
been written about before. The ferns, the second
hand cars, the oil millionaires, the jukebox
songs of moment (redheaded, slatternly, in
cotton housedresses) who must be loyal and
true (my God, what are they doing?)
"Always be mine, that we never will part—"
(the second hand cars) but mostly the clean
young unicotined lungs, the clean thighs

the blend fields, the fresh food in the grain elevator, the sense of space just beyond the
town limits, the nudes next week, and the absolute
certain of that the young men's bodies are in
perfect condition, the legs spare and hard,
and the spirit, too, clean. The women's voices
southern but not deeply southern, soft
without being weak. They are clean like the bodies
and minds of the young men. The juke box songs,
though whining and sentimental, are only whining
because we haven't yet developed our poetry.

Texas — Green fields, millions miles without thought, insolent still as they were in a brown
schoolroom, in a brown desk. Texas — with the
faith of the people who were born there, living there
still. The beautiful, quiet, flat homes, the beautiful girls who inspire the men who drive
bombers over Germany, Russia and Korea.
Infinite is the word for Texas. Infinite!

Diaries

Diary 1	1940-12-31/1941-12-31	French, English, German
Diary 2	1942-01-01/1942-08-07	English, Spanish, French, German
Diary 3	1942-08-08/1943-01-11	English, French, German
Diary 4	1943-03-30/1943-09-26	French, German, English
Diary 5 ("Mexico Diary")	1943-12-14/1944-05-13	German, English, French, Spanish
Diary 6	1944-11-14/1946-01-23	German, English
Diary 7	1946-02-03/1947-05-06	German, English
Diary 8	1947-05-07/1948-03-17	English, German
Diary 9	1948-03-26/1949-10-30	German, English, French
Diary 10	1949-01-01/1951-01-28	English, French
Diary 11	1951-02-22/1952-11-21	English, German, French
Diary 12	1952-11-22/1954-02-09	English, Italian, French
Diary 13	1958-01-05/1963-02-06	English
Diary 14	1962-05-15/1962-07-20 & 1963	English
Diary 15	1963-03-01/1964-09-10 & 1967-12-14/1968-09-06	English
Diary 16	1969-01-27/1971-04-18	English
Diary 17	1981-01-04/1981-01-28 & 1987-01-16/1992-09-04	English
Diary 18	1994-10-05/1994-10-09	English

Notebooks ("Cahiers")

Notebook One	1938 until 1939	1938–1939
Notebook Two	November 1939 until July 1940	1939–1940
Notebook Three	August 1940 to November 1940	1940
Notebook Four	October 1940 to June 1941	1940–1941
Notebook Five	June 1941 to December 1941	1941
Notebook Six	December 1941 to May 1942	1941–1942
Notebook Seven	May 1942 to July 1942	1942
Notebook Eight	August 1942 to November 1942	1942
Notebook Nine	October 1942 to January 1943	1942–1943
Notebook Ten	January 1943 to November 1943	1943
Notebook Eleven	November 1943 to October 1944	1943–1944
Notebook Twelve	October 1944 to August 1945	1944–1945
Notebook Thirteen	July 1945 to June 1946	1945–1946
Notebook Fourteen	June 1946 to December 1946	1946
Notebook Fifteen	January 1947 to July 1947	1947
Notebook Sixteen	July 1947 to January 1948	1947–1948
Notebook Seventeen	January 1948 to July 1948	1948
Notebook Eightteen	September 1948 to October 1949	1948–1949
Notebook Nineteen	November 1949 to September 1950	1949–1950
Notebook Twenty	October 1950 to October 1951	1950–1951
Notebook Twenty-One	November 1951 to December 1952	1951–1952
Notebook Twenty-Two	December 1952 to February 1954	1952–1954
Notebook Twenty-Three	February 1954 to September 1955	1954–1955
Notebook Twenty-Four	December 1955 to February 1958	1955–1958
Notebook Twenty-Five	March 1958 to May 1960	1958–1960
Notebook Twenty-Six	June 1960 to September 1962	1960–1962
Notebook Twenty-Seven	August 1962 to December 1964	1962–1964
Notebook Twenty-Eight	December 1964 to January 1967	1964–1967
Notebook Twenty-Nine	January 1967 to July 1968	1967–1968
Notebook Thirty	August 1968 to January 1970	1968–1971
Notebook Thirty-One	December 1969 to November 1971	1969–1971
Notebook Thirty-Two	October 1971 to November 1973	1971–1973
Notebook Thirty-Three	December 1973 to August 1976	1973–1976
Notebook Thirty-Four	September 1976 to October 1979	1976–1979
Notebook Thirty-Five	November 1979 to July 1983	1979–1983
Notebook Thirty-Six	August 1983 to August 1988	1983–1988
Notebook Thirty-Seven	September 1988 to December 1992	1988–1992
Notebook Thirty-Eight	Empty	1993–

BIBLIOGRAPHY

N

Primary Sources

A complete bibliography of Patricia Highsmith's work is beyond the scope of this book. The website for the Patricia Highsmith Papers at the Swiss Literary Archives in Bern, Switzerland (http://ead.nb.admin.ch/html/highsmith.html), will guide interested readers beyond the current Highsmith canon.

For the German-language *Werkausgabe der Romane und Stories*, the complete edition of Highsmith's novels and short stories, edited by Paul Ingendaay and myself (Zurich: Diogenes, 2002–2006), I had consulted not only her eighteen diaries (1940/41–1994) and her thirty-eight notebooks (1937–1994), but also many manuscripts of her unpublished works, among them more than a hundred hitherto-unknown short stories and essays (many of which had been published in various women's magazines and, later, in *Ellery Queen's Mystery Magazine*), and of course her letters to her friends and editors; all this material now could be brought to fruition again.

The following works are among the primary sources for this edition. They are listed here along with the details of their first publication in the United States.

NOVELS

Strangers on a Train (New York: Harper & Brothers, 1950).
The Price of Salt (as Claire Morgan; New York: Coward-McCann, 1952).
The Blunderer (New York: Coward-McCann, 1954).
The Talented Mr. Ripley (New York: Coward-McCann, 1955).
Deep Water (New York: Harper & Brothers, 1957).
A Game for the Living (New York: Harper & Brothers, 1958).
This Sweet Sickness (New York: Harper & Brothers, 1960).
The Cry of the Owl (New York: Harper & Row, 1962).
The Two Faces of January (New York: Doubleday, 1964).
The Glass Cell (New York: Doubleday, 1964).
The Story-Teller (UK title: *A Suspension of Mercy*; New York: Doubleday, 1965).
Those Who Walk Away (New York: Doubleday, 1967).

The Tremor of Forgery (New York: Doubleday, 1969).
Ripley Under Ground (New York: Doubleday, 1970).
A Dog's Ransom (New York: Knopf, 1972).
Ripley's Game (New York: Knopf, 1974).
Edith's Diary (New York: Simon & Schuster, 1977).
The Boy Who Followed Ripley (New York: Lippincott & Crowell, 1980).
People Who Knock on the Door (New York: Otto Penzler Books, 1985).
Found in the Street (New York: Atlantic Monthly Press, 1987).
Ripley Under Water (New York: Knopf, 1992).
Small g: A Summer Idyll (New York: W. W. Norton & Company, 2004).

SHORT STORY COLLECTIONS

The Snail-Watcher and Other Stories (UK title: *Eleven*; New York: Doubleday, 1970)
   [The Snail-Watcher—The Birds Poised to Fly—The Terrapin—When the
   Fleet Was In at Mobile—The Quest for Blank Claveringi—The Cries of
   Love—Mrs. Afton, Thy Green Braes—The Heroine—Another Bridge to
   Cross—The Barbarians—The Empty Birdhouse]

The Animal-Lover's Book of Beastly Murder (New York: Otto Penzler Books, 1986)
   [Chorus Girl's Absolutely Final Performance—Djemal's Revenge—There
   I Was, Stuck with Busby—Ming's Biggest Prey—In the Dead of the
   Truffle Season—The Bravest Rat in Venice—Engine Horse—The Day
   of Reckoning—Notes from a Respectable Cockroach—Eddie and the
   Monkey Robberies—Hamsters vs. Websters—Harry: A Ferret—Goat
   Ride]

Little Tales of Misogyny (New York: Otto Penzler Books, 1986)
   [The Hand—Oona, the Jolly Cave Woman—The Coquette—The Female
   Novelist—The Dancer—The Invalid, or, the Bedridden—The Artist—The
   Middle-Class Housewife—The Fully Licensed Whore, or, the Wife—
   The Breeder—The Mobile Bed-Object—The Perfect Little Lady—The
   Silent Mother-in-Law—The Prude—The Victim—The Evangelist—The
   Perfectionist]

Slowly, Slowly in the Wind (New York: Otto Penzler Books, 1979)
   [The Man Who Wrote Books in His Head—The Network—The Pond—
   Something You Have to Live With—Slowly, Slowly in the Wind—Those
   Awful Dawns—Woodrow Wilson's Necktie—One for the Islands—A
   Curious Suicide—The Baby Spoon—Broken Glass—Please Don't Shoot
   the Trees]

The Black House (New York: Otto Penzler Books, 1988)
[Something the Cat Dragged In—Not One of Us—The Terrors of Basket-Weaving—Under a Dark Angel's Eye—I Despise Your Life—The Dream of the Emma C—Old Folks at Home—The Adventuress (also as When in Rome)—Blow It—The Kite—The Black House]

Mermaids on the Golf Course (New York: Otto Penzler Books, 1988)
[Mermaids on the Golf Course—The Button—Where the Action Is—Chris' Last Party—A Shot from Nowhere—A Clock Ticks at Christmas—The Stuff of Madness—Not in This Life, Maybe the Next—I Am Not as Efficient as Other People—The Cruelest Month]

Tales of Natural and Unnatural Catastrophes (New York: Atlantic Monthly Press, 1987)
[The Mysterious Cemetery—Moby Dick II; or The Missile Whale—Operation Balsam; or Touch-Me-Not—Nabuti: Warm Welcome to a UN Committee—Sweet Freedom! And a Picnic on the White House Lawn—Trouble on the Jade Towers—Rent-a-Womb vs. the Mighty Right—No End in Sight—Sixtus VI, Pope of the Red Slipper—President Buck Jones Rallies and Waves the Flag]

The Selected Stories of Patricia Highsmith (New York: W. W. Norton & Company, 2001)
[contains all the short stories published in in the following volumes: *The Animal-Lover's Book of Beastly Murder—Little Tales of Misogyny—Slowly, Slowly in the Wind—The Black House—Mermaids on the Golf Course*]

Nothing That Meets the Eye: The Uncollected Stories of Patricia Highsmith (New York: W. W. Norton & Company, 2002)
[The Mightiest Mornings—Uncertain Treasure—Magic Casements—Miss Juste and the Green Rompers—Where the Door Is Always Open and the Welcome Mat Is Out—In the Plaza—The Hollow Oracle—The Great Cardhouse—The Car—The Still Point of the Turning World—The Pianos of the Steinachs—A Mighty Nice Man—Quiet Night—Doorbell for Louisa—A Bird in Hand—Music to Die By—Man's Best Friend—Born Failure—A Dangerous Hobby—The Returnees—Nothing That Meets the Eye—Two Disagreeable Pigeons—Variations on a Game—A Girl like Phyl—It's a Deal—Things Had Gone Badly—The Trouble with Mrs. Blynn, the Trouble with the World—The Second Cigarette. Afterword by Paul Ingendaay—Notes on the Stories by Anna von Planta]

NONFICTION

Plotting and Writing Suspense Fiction (Boston: The Writer, 1966).

CHILDREN'S LITERATURE

Miranda the Panda Is on the Veranda (Doris Sanders, illustrations by Patricia Highsmith; New York: Coward-McCann, 1958).

Secondary Sources

REFERENCES AND FURTHER READING

All books are dated according to the edition used, not the date of first publication.

Abbott, Berenice. *Aperture Masters of Photography*. Introduction and commentary by Julia Van Haaften. New York: Aperture Foundation, 2015.

Baldwin, Nell. *Henry Ford and the Jews: The Mass Production of Hate*. New York: Public Affairs, 2003.

Barnes, Djuna. *Nightwood*. London: Faber and Faber (Faber Modern Classics), 2015.

Bedford, Sybille. *A Visit to Don Otavio: A Mexican Journey*. New York: New York Review of Books Classics, 2016.

Berg, A. Scott. *Lindbergh*. New York: G. P. Putnam's Sons, 1998.

Bérubé, Allan, *Coming Out Under Fire: The History of Gay Men and Women in World War II*. Chapel Hill: University of North Carolina Press, 2010.

Bradbury, Malcolm (ed.). *The Atlas of Literature*. London: De Agostini Editions,1996.

Brandel, Marc. *The Choice*. London: Eyre & Spottiswoode, 1952.

Broyard, Anatole. *Kafka Was the Rage. A Greenwich Village Memoir*. New York: Vintage, 1997.

Cavigelli, Franz, Fritz Senn, and Anna von Planta. *Patricia Highsmith: Leben und Werk*. Zurich: Diogenes, 1996.

Chabon, Michael. *The Amazing Adventures of Kavalier & Klay*. London: HarperCollins, New English Edition, 2008.

Dictionnaire des cultures Gays et Lesbiennes. Sous la direction de Didier Eribon. Paris: Larousse, 2003.

Dillon, Millicent. *A Little Original Sin: The Life & Work of Jane Bowles*. New York: Holt, Rinehart & Winston, 1981.

Dostoyevsky, Fyodor. *Crime and Punishment*. Translated and edited by Michael R. Katz. New York: W. W. Norton, 2019.

————. *Notes from Underground*. Translated and edited by Michael R. Katz. New York: W. W. Norton, 2000.

Faderman, Lillian. *The Gay Revolution: The Story of the Struggle*. New York: Simon & Schuster, 2015.

————. *Odd Girls and Twilight Lovers: A History of Lesbian Life in 20th-Century America*. New York: Columbia University Press, 1991.

Flanner, Janet. *Darlinghissima: Letters to a Friend*. Edited by Natalia Danesi Murray. New York: Random House, 1985.

Gide, André. *The Counterfeiters*. Translated by Dorothy Bussy. Penguin Books (Twentieth Century Classics), 1990.

Gronowicz, Antoni. *Garbo. Her Story*. London: Penguin Books, 1990.

Guggenheim, Peggy. *Out of This Century. Confessions of an Art Addict*. New York: André Deutsch, 2005.

Hall, Lee. *Betty Parsons. Artist, Dealer, Collector*. New York: Harry N. Abrams, 1991.

Harrison, Russell. *Patricia Highsmith* (United States Author Series). New York: Twayne, 1997.

Hughes, Dorothy B. *In a Lonely Place*. New York: Feminist Press, 2003.

James, Henry. *The Ambassadors*. Edited and with an introduction by Adrian Poole. London: Penguin (Penguin Classics), 2008.

Jones, Gerard. *Men of Tomorrow: Geeks, Gangsters, and the Birth of the Comic Book*. New York: Arrow, 2006.

Kafka, Franz. *In the Penal Colony*. Translation by Ian Johnston. https://www.kafka-online.info/in-the-penal-colony.html.

————. *The Metamorphosis*. Translated by Susan Bernofsky. New York: W. W. Norton, 2014.

Katz, Jonathan Ned. *The Invention of Heterosexuality*. Chicago: University of Chicago Press, 2007.

Köhn, Eckhardt. *Rolf Tietgens—Poet with a Camera*. Zell-Unterentersbach: Die Graue Edition, 2011.

Koestler, Arthur. *Darkness at Noon*. London: Vintage Classics, 1994.

Lerman, Leo. *The Grand Surprise: The Journals of Leo Lerman*. Edited by Stephen Pascal. New York: Alfred A. Knopf, 2007.

Maclaren-Ross, Julian. *Memoirs of the Forties*. London: Abacus, 1991.

Marcus, Eric. *Making History: The Struggle for Gay and Lesbian Equal Rights 1945–1990. An Oral History*. New York: HarperPerennial 1992.

Kaiser, Charles. *The Gay Metropolis. The Landmark History of Gay Life in America*. New York: Grove Press, 1997, 2019.

Meaker, Marijane. *Highsmith. A Romance of the 1950s*. San Francisco: Cleis, 2003.

Menninger, Karl. *The Human Mind*. New York, London: Alfred A. Knopf, 1930.

Newton, Esther. *Cherry Grove, Fire Island: Sixty Years in America's First Gay and Lesbian Town.* Durham, NC: Duke University Press, 2014.

Packer, Vin [Marijane Meaker]. *Intimate Victims.* New York: Manor Books, 1963.

Palmen, Connie. *Die Sünde der Frau: Über Marilyn Monroe, Marguerite Duras, Jane Bowles und Patricia Highsmith.* Zurich: Diogenes, 2018.

Plimpton, George. *Truman Capote: In Which Various Friends, Enemies, Acquaintances, and Detractors Recall His Turbulent Career.* New York: Nan A. Talese, 1997.

Poe, Edgar Allan. *Complete Stories and Poems.* New York: Viking, 2011.

Powell, Dawn. *The Locusts Have No King.* South Royalton, VT: Steerforth Press, 1998.

Schenkar, Joan M. *The Talented Miss Highsmith.* New York: St. Martin's Press / Picador, 2009.

Schulman, Robert. *Romany Marie, the Queen of Greenwich Village.* Louisville, KY: Butler Books, 2006.

Spark, Muriel. *A Far Cry from Kensington.* New York: New Directions, 1988.

Van Haaften, Julia. *Berenice Abbott. A Life in Photography.* New York: W. W. Norton, 2018.

Wetzsteon, Ross. *Republic of Dreams. Greenwich Village: The American Bohemia, 1910–1960.* New York: Simon & Schuster, 2002.

Wineapple, Brenda. *Genêt: A Biography of Janet Flanner.* Lincoln: University of Nebraska Press, 1992.

Wilson, Andrew. *Beautiful Shadow.* London: Bloomsbury, 2003.

Wolff, Charlotte, M.D. *Love Between Women.* London: Duckworth, 1971.

Yronwode, Catherine, and Trina Robbins. *Women and the Comics.* Forestville, CA: Eclipse Books, 1985.

FILMOGRAPHY

- *Strangers on a Train*, Alfred Hitchcock, 1951
- *A Plein Soleil* (*Purple Noon*, after *The Talented Mr. Ripley*), René Clément, 1960
- *Le meurtrier* (*Enough Rope*, after *The Blunderer*), Claude Autant-Lara, 1963
- *Once You Kiss a Stranger* (*Strangers on a Train*), Robert Sparr, 1969
- *Der amerikanische Freund* (*The American Friend*, after *Ripley's Game*), Wim Wenders, 1977
- *Dites-lui que je l'aime* (This Sweet Sickness), Claude Miller, 1977
- *Die gläserne Zelle* (*The Glass Cell*), Hans Geissendörfer, 1978
- *Armchair Thriller* (TV Series based on *A Dog's Ransom*, 6 episodes), 1978
- *Eaux profondes* (*Deep Water*), Michel Deville, 1981
- *Ediths Tagebuch* (*Edith's Diary*), Hans Werner Geissendörfer, 1983
- *Tiefe Wasser* (*Deep Water*), Franz Peter Wirth, 1983
- *Die zwei Gesichter des Januars* (*The Two Faces of January*), Wolfgang Storch, 1986
- *Le Cri du hibou* (*The Cry of the Owl*), Claude Chabrol, 1987
- *Húkanie sovy* (*The Cry of the Owl*), Vido Hornák 1988
- *Something You Have to Live With*, John Berry, 1989
- *La ferme du malheur* (*The Day of Reckoning*), Samuel Fuller, 1989
- *Der Geschichtenerzähler* (after *A Suspension of Mercy*), Rainer Boldt, 1989
- *Les Cadavres exquis de Patricia Highsmith* (*Chillers*, TV series)
  - *Pour le restant de leurs jours* ("Old Folks at Home"), Peter Kassovitz, 1990
  - *L'Épouvantail* ("Slowly, Slowly in the Wind"), Maroun Bagdadi, 1990
  - *Puzzle* ("Blow It"), Maurice Dugowson, 1990
  - *La ferme du Malheur* ("The Day of Reckoning"), Samuel Fuller, 1990
  - *A Curious Suicide*, Robert Bierman, 1990
  - *L'Amateur de Frissons* ("The Thrill Seeker"), Roger Andrieux, Mai Zetterling, 1990
  - *Légitime defense* ("Something You Have to Live With"), John Berry, 1990
  - *Époux en froid* ("Sauce for the Goose"), Clare Peploe, 1991

- *La Proie du chat ("Something the Cat Dragged In"), Nessa Hyams, 1992*
- *Sincères condoléances ("Under a Dark Angel's Eye"), Nick Lewin, 1992*
- *Passions partagées ("A Bird Poised to Fly"), Damian Harris, 1992*
- *Le Jardin des disparus (after "The Stuff of Madness"), Mai Zetterling, 1992*

- *Trip nach Tunis* (after *The Tremor of Forgery*), Peter Goedel, 1993
- *Petits contes misògins* (*Little Tales of Misogyny*), Pere Sagristà, 1995
- *Once You Meet a Stranger* (after *Strangers on a Train*), Tommy Lee Wallace, 1996
- *La rançon du chien* (*A Dog's Ransom*), Peter Kassovitz, 1996
- *The Talented Mr. Ripley*, Anthony Minghella, 1999
- *The Terrapin*, Regis Trigano, 2001
- *Ripley's Game*, Liliana Cavani, 2002
- *Ripley Under Ground*, Roger Spottiswoode, 2005
- *The Cry of the Owl*, Jamie Thraves, 2009
- *A Mighty Nice Man*, Jonathan Dee, 2014
- *The Two Faces of January*, Hossein Amini, 2014
- *Carol* (*The Price of Salt*), Todd Haynes, 2015
- *Kind of Murder* (after *The Blunderer*), Andy Goddard, 2016

ILLUSTRATION CREDITS

INDEX OF NAMES AND WORKS